W9-DAS-172

Also by Walter Isaacson

Steve Jobs

American Sketches

Einstein: His Life and Universe

A Benjamin Franklin Reader

Benjamin Franklin: An American Life

Kissinger: A Biography

Pro and Con

Also by Evan Thomas

The War Lovers: Roosevelt, Lodge, Hearst
and the Rush to Empire, 1898

Sea of Thunder: The Last Great Naval Campaign 1941–1945

John Paul Jones: Sailor, Hero, Father of the American Navy

Robert Kennedy: His Life

The Very Best Men: Four Who Dared:
The Early Years of the C.I.A.

The Man to See: Edward Bennett Williams

THE
WISE
MEN

SIX FRIENDS
AND THE WORLD
THEY MADE

WALTER ISAACSON
AND
EVAN THOMAS

Simon & Schuster

New York   London   Toronto   Sydney   New Delhi

To Cathy and Oscie, and to the memory of Betsy Isaacson

SIMON & SCHUSTER
1230 Avenue of the Americas
New York, NY 10020

Copyright © 1986 by Walter Isaacson and Evan Thomas

Introduction copyright © 2012 by Walter Isaacson and Evan Thomas

This Simon & Schuster hardcover edition May 2012

SIMON & SCHUSTER and colophon are registered
trademarks of Simon & Schuster, Inc.

For information about special discounts for bulk purchases,
please contact Simon & Schuster Special Sales at
1-866-506-1949 or business@simonandschuster.com.

The Simon & Schuster Speakers Bureau can bring authors to
your live event. For more information or to book an event,
contact the Simon & Schuster Speakers Bureau at
1-866-248-3049 or visit our website at www.simonspeakers.com.

Designed by Levavi & Levavi

Manufactured in the United States of America

10   9   8   7   6   5   4   3   2   1

Library of Congress Cataloging-in-Publication Data

Isaacson, Walter.
    The wise men : six friends and the world they made : Acheson, Bohlen, Harriman, Ken-
nan, Lovett, McCloy / by Walter Isaacson and Evan Thomas.
    Bibliograpy; p.   Includes index.
    1. Statesmen—United States—Biography. 2. United
States—Foreign relations—20th century.   I. Thomas,
Evan.   II. Title.
E747.I77   1986   327.2'092'0   86-11860

ISBN: 978-1-4516-8322-6
ISBN: 978-1-4391-2653-0 (ebook)

CONTENTS

Two CREATION 251

Three WISE MEN 587

INTRODUCTION

I n their time, they operated largely behind the scenes, little known by the public. But they achieved great things: the shaping of a world order; the creation of international institutions; the forging of a lasting peace in a perilous time. They were private men who avoided publicity but were comfortable with public power, not as an end in itself but as a force for prosperity, security, and freedom. Those who called on their services used the term "Wise Men" half tongue in cheek, but presidents from FDR to Richard Nixon counted on their wisdom.

In the twenty-five years since *The Wise Men* was published in 1986, we have often been asked, "Who are the Wise Men today?" We have groped for some semi-plausible names, but in truth, it's harder now to be a Wise Man than it was in 1945.

A half century or more ago, as America was assuming its place as the world's greatest power, government was much smaller and more intimate. High policy is no longer made over cocktails, as it was in 1947, when President Truman's undersecretary of state Robert Lovett went over to the apartment of the chairman of the Senate Foreign Relations Committee, Republican Arthur Vandenberg, to share some top-secret cables in order to win support for the Marshall Plan. When the Wise Men were creating the Western Alliance in 1948, the White House had no national security staff—just presidential aide Clark Clifford meeting or having lunch at the F Street Club with, say, Averell Harriman. National security policy-making may be a more orderly or democratic process these days, but it is also far more cumbersome, if not sclerotic.

The social elite that spawned the Wise Men is a vestige of the past. The meritocracy has long since replaced what columnist Joseph Alsop labeled the Wasp Ascendancy. The Ivy League still staffs many of the top jobs in any administration, but not with the sort of free-spirited preppies who came to Washington during the 1940s. The great Cold War secretary of state, Dean Acheson, last in his class at Groton, wouldn't have gotten into the twenty-first-century Yale; Russian expert and diplomat extraordinaire Chip Bohlen, kicked out of St. Paul's, wouldn't have gotten into Harvard. The think tanks and committee staffs of Washington are filled with overachieving men and women with impressive résumés and SAT scores, but they often come across as more careerist than creative.

Government service, sadly, has lost its luster. At Princeton, alma mater of foreign policy visionary George Kennan, a wealthy graduate endowed the Woodrow Wilson School of Public and International Affairs expressly to train Foreign Service officers. But by the late 1990s, very few Woodrow Wilson School students were taking the Foreign Service exam. Many more were looking instead for Wall Street jobs.

During and immediately after World War II, investment bankers like Lovett and Harriman and lawyers like John McCloy and Acheson could, without too much fuss, go back and forth between their private sector jobs and government service. Today, they must divest themselves of any assets that might conceivably pose a conflict of interest and hire lawyers to get past the erratic, seemingly endless Senate confirmation process. Not surprisingly, quite a few able men and women are unwilling to make the sacrifice.

The ones who do go into government don't seem to have quite as much fun as the Lovetts and McCloys of the old days. When these two young Wall Streeters went to work for Secretary of War Henry Stimson in 1941, they were able to wield their considerable power with élan. Today's government servants must run a gauntlet of reporters and congressional committee investigators—important and sometimes essential checks on the abuse of power, but often vexing nonetheless. Foreign policy-making was relatively free of partisan politics in the early days of the Cold War; today, nothing is.

The Wise Men had the exhilarating sensation of being, as Acheson put it in the title of his zesty memoir, "Present at the Creation." The American Century, in the 1941 phrase of Time-Life founder Henry Luce, was just beginning. Today the talk (alarmist and unfounded, we believe) is of American decline. No wonder the esprit of government service has declined as well.

It is, of course, easy to mythologize the Wise Men and overstate their significance and worth. Indeed, one could write a cautionary lesson about the Myth of the Wise Man. Presidents can be badly served by former statesmen who pretend to know all but don't—whose prejudices have hardened but whose real-time intelligence is lacking. Dean Acheson gave John F. Kennedy dangerously hawkish advice during the 1961 Berlin and 1962 Cuban missile crises. He and Bob Lovett also unwisely encouraged Lyndon Johnson to show backbone by escalating the war in Vietnam in 1965. On the other hand it was Acheson, along with several other Wise Men, who forced LBJ to confront the bad news coming out of Vietnam after the Tet Offensive in 1968.

"Speak truth to power" is a cliché notable for its rarity in modern-day Washington. Robert Strauss, a kind of latter-day Wise Man who counseled Democratic presidents from LBJ to Bill Clinton, enjoyed describing what it was like to bring visitors to offer advice to the president. On the way over to the White House, the visitors would work themselves up, practicing brave speeches (Strauss would imitate them: "I'm gonna tell that S.O.B. in the Oval Office a thing or two!"). But once actually inside, their courage would wilt; they would become supplicants and sycophants. Strauss would mock their prating: "Oh, Mr. President, you're doing such a wonderful job!"

Presidents need men and women who are confident enough— independent enough—to level with them. No one would argue that the president's top advisers should be chosen from an elitist club of Anglo-Saxon white males who graduated from certain schools (the parody version of the Wise Men; also the reality). But it would serve the country to have public figures with the confidence to rise above party or the search for celebrity. The self-confidence of the Wise Men was liberating—it gave them the freedom to be creative and bold.

The Wise Men fashioned not just the ideas but also the institutions that ran the postwar world. Those institutions are still largely in place— long after the world has changed. Are the World Bank and International Monetary Fund the right institutions to manage the new global economy? Radio Free Europe and Voice of America worked brilliantly to spread the word of freedom to the Communist bloc. But what is the right sort of agency to fight cyber terror or Islamic fanaticism? Is NATO the best military structure for resolving messy insurgencies or civil wars in countries like Afghanistan and Libya? These Cold War–era institutions creak and labor along, but a new generation needs to create whole new structures and systems for the world as it is or will be. This task will require the same kind of inspiration and energy that seized Acheson as he sought to create a Pax Americana to replace Pax Britannica and Kennan to imagine the containment doctrine. The Wise Men, whose story we tell in this book, are gone forever. But their spirit should live on.

—Walter Isaacson & Evan Thomas, May 2012

ARCHITECTS OF THE
AMERICAN CENTURY

I t was not a lavish party. Despite his enormous wealth, Ambassador Averell Harriman was uncomfortable with social frivolity, particularly when there was a war going on. The guests who gathered at his Moscow residence on the night of April 12, 1945, had to make do with dance music from Harriman's Victrola and snacks from the embassy's kitchen. Many had already headed home by 1 A.M. when the telephone rang with the news from Warm Springs. With his daughter and a few close aides, Harriman went upstairs and sat by the fireplace in his bedroom. There, warming himself against the Russian night, the financier-turned-statesman ruminated about the death of the only President he had ever served and speculated about the man who had become the only President in his lifetime he had never met.

Harriman had grown increasingly dubious about Franklin Roosevelt's hopes that the U.S. and the U.S.S.R. could be allies in peace as they had been in war, and he had been hectoring Washington for permission to return home and present his case in person. With an inexperienced new President suddenly in power, one whose only trip overseas had been as a soldier during World War I, Harriman bluntly cabled his "intention" to come back for consultations. When the State Department finally relented, Harriman left Moscow aboard his own private plane at 5 one morning and arrived in Washington just over forty-nine hours later, easily setting a new record for such a journey.

As embassy counselor, George Kennan had helped harden Harriman's views about the Soviets and drafted some of his sharpest cables. Harriman's departure left the introverted young diplomat in charge and gave free rein to his tendency to send long telegrams describing the inherent conflicts between America and the Soviet Union. Roosevelt had pursued his own foreign policy with little heed to the Cassandras in the State Department. Harry Truman, on the other hand, stayed up late his first evening in office poring over recent reports. When Kennan's messages began to flow, he found a receptive reader in the White House for a change. As Truman noted after one particularly downbeat missive from Kennan about the Soviets: "I realized only too well the implications in this message."

John McCloy, Assistant Secretary of War, was a man more suited to action than reflection. After an aide rushed into his Paris hotel room and awakened him with the news, McCloy jotted in his diary that Roosevelt would probably be remembered as a great President, "but the press of current and impending events leaves no time to speculate on his position in history." McCloy's inspection tour of Europe had heightened his conviction that the U.S. must not retreat into isolation after this war the way it had after the last. A ravaged Continent would have to be rebuilt. America would have to assume its rightful position of leadership in a shaken world. Cutting short his trip, he rushed back to Washington, stopping briefly in London to attend the memorial service for Roosevelt in bomb-scarred St. Paul's. He found it fitting that the boys' choir sang "The Battle Hymn of the Republic," though he noted that "they sang it too slowly."

Robert Lovett, McCloy's "Heavenly Twin" as an Assistant Secretary of War and Harriman's former Wall Street partner, was preparing to depart for Europe and Asia to oversee the redeployment of the air force he had built. Convinced that strategic bombing had softened Germany for the kill, he was anxious to do the same to Japan. Yet in the back of his mind, he later recalled, there were thoughts about a revolutionary weapon he barely understood and which the new President knew almost nothing about. Lovett decided to delay his trip while President Truman pondered the best way to pursue the war against Japan.

Dean Acheson, who as Assistant Secretary of State had worked with Harriman on Lend-Lease negotiations with the Kremlin, was having his portrait done by photographer Yousuf Karsh when he heard the news. Most of his friends had never met Truman and were dismayed by the prospect of a failed haberdasher from Missouri becoming President at such a critical time. But Acheson sensed that Truman had good instincts and would depend on the right people. "I think he will learn fast and inspire confidence," Acheson wrote to his son.

Only hours after he was handed the news flash, Charles Bohlen began preparing a background paper for the new President. As the State Department's liaison to the White House, Bohlen met Truman for the first time the next afternoon when he delivered the report. The Soviets were ignoring the pledges made at Yalta two months earlier, it declared, and they had been "consistently sabotaging Ambassador Harriman's efforts" to reach an agreement over Poland. Upon Harriman's arrival in Washington, Bohlen set up a meeting with Acheson and others at the State Department, where the ambassador stressed the "basic and irreconcilable differences of objective between the Soviet Union and the United States." Then Bohlen walked with Harriman to the White House, where the education of Harry Truman— on the Soviets, on the need for America to help rebuild Europe, on the bomb—began in earnest.

• • •

Six friends. Their lives had intertwined from childhood and school-days, from their early careers on Wall Street and in government. Now they were destined to be at the forefront of a remarkable transformation of American policy. As World War II drew to a close, most of their fellow citizens wanted nothing more than to turn inward and, in Harriman's words, "go to the movies and drink Coke." But by breeding and training, this handful of men and a few of their close colleagues knew that America would have to assume the burden of a global role. Out of duty and desire, they heeded the call to public service. They were the original brightest and best, men whose outsized personalities and forceful actions brought order to the postwar chaos and left a legacy that dominates American policy to this day.

Working together in an atmosphere of trust that in today's Washington would seem almost quaint, they shaped a new world order that committed a once-reticent nation to defending freedom wherever it sought to flourish. During the late 1940s, they authored a doctrine of containment and forged an array of alliances that, for better or worse, have been the foundation of American policy ever since. Later, when much of what they stood for appeared to be sinking in the mire of Vietnam, they were summoned for their steady counsel and dubbed "the Wise Men."

WILLIAM AVERELL HARRIMAN'S first visit to Russia was in 1899, when Nicholas II was czar. His last was in 1983, at the invitation of Yuri Andropov. In between, he negotiated his own private Soviet mineral concessions with Trotsky, spent more time with Stalin than any other American, and worked out a limited test-ban treaty with Khrushchev. Yet throughout most of his career, his attitude toward the Soviets was that of a tough businessman toward a competitor, firm yet pragmatic. The son of E. H. Harriman, the steely entrepreneur who built the Union Pacific Railroad, Harriman often seemed a sovereign in his own realm. After graduating from Groton and Yale, he formed his own shipping line and merchant bank, then entered government as one of the progressive businessmen who supported the New Deal. As Roosevelt's "special envoy" to Churchill and Stalin, he began a career as a freewheeling diplomat that continued through the Vietnam era. Plodding yet at times strikingly bold, detached yet also intense, he earned the nickname "the Crocodile" by affecting a drowsy manner that would suddenly give way to a snap of action.

ROBERT ABERCROMBIE LOVETT spent much of his childhood playing games at the Harriman estate. His father was E. H. Harriman's trusted right hand at the Union Pacific and later its chairman. The two sons became fellow members of Skull and Bones at Yale, directors of the railroad, and partners on Wall Street. At the outset of the Depression, they helped merge Harriman's banking interests with those of Brown Brothers, where Lovett had become a partner. When he came to Washington as Assistant Secretary of War, Lovett operated as he had on Wall Street, discreetly backstage. With his patrician demeanor and charm, he was a masterful administrator who did more than any other man to bring the U.S. into the age of strategic air power. As Under Secretary of State, he was the chief operating officer of the department during the early showdowns of the Cold War; later, he went on to become Secretary of Defense. When John Kennedy became President, he reached out to the man he considered the living embodiment of a noble tradition and offered him a choice of three top Cabinet posts, State, Defense, or Treasury; Lovett, devoid of personal ambition, spurned them all but suggested the three men who ended up in those jobs.

DEAN GOODERHAM ACHESON, son of
the Episcopal bishop of Connecticut, was
at Groton and Yale with Harriman, who
taught the somewhat cheeky younger boy
to row crew. Even then Acheson was
known for his flashy wit, but it was not
until he studied under Felix Frankfurter
at Harvard Law School that his mental
agility was honed into the intellectual intensity that was to mark his
tenure as Truman's Secretary of State. He entitled his memoirs *Present
at the Creation*, and though he was rarely accused of excess modesty,
the phrase actually understates his role. Indeed, he was the architect
of the creation he describes, a man who was more responsible for the
Truman Doctrine than President Truman and more responsible for
the Marshall Plan than General Marshall. In and out of power, Acheson and Harriman maintained a gentlemanly rapport that overcame
their occasional rivalries; it was a relationship that culminated more
than three decades after they entered government service when Harriman helped Acheson fathom the dark realities of the Vietnam quagmire with the same care he had used in initiating him to the intricacies
of rowing a shell.

JOHN JAY MCCLOY, JR., like Acheson, experienced an intellectual awakening at Harvard Law School. But for the poor boy from Philadelphia, the experience did even more. It provided an entrée into an American Establishment that he came to revere—and to epitomize. As a Wall Street lawyer, he learned to win the confidence of the nation's most powerful men. He and Lovett were recruited by the venerable Henry Stimson to help run the War Department, and McCloy went on to become president of the World Bank and High Commissioner for Germany. With his distaste for ideological battles, McCloy illustrated how those who administer a policy often have more impact than those who conceive it. Later he served as chairman of the Chase bank and the Council on Foreign Relations. He may hold the record for the number of Cabinet posts rejected by one man, preferring to spend most of his life as one of the nation's most influential private citizens.

GEORGE FROST KENNAN, an insecure boy from Milwaukee, came to Princeton as an outsider and resolutely cast himself in that role even after he became the intellectual darling of the Washington elite. His long career in the Foreign Service was an anguished one: he seemed to relish being unappreciated and mis-understood. Yet for a brief period at the onset of the Cold War, his ideas about the Soviets helped coalesce a nebulous attitude among policy makers in Washington. First through the famous Long Telegram, which warned of the Kremlin's expansionist ambitions, and then through a scholarly article written anonymously as "X," Kennan formulated a containment theory that was embraced in Washington with an enthusiasm that soon caused him to squirm. As Henry Kissinger has noted, "Kennan came as close to authoring the diplomatic doctrine of his era as any diplomat in our history."

CHARLES EUSTIS BOHLEN was in many ways the opposite of Kennan; he was born with the social graces that allowed him to be an amiable insider amid circles of power. Yet the two men became best of friends and close intellectual partners as they rose within the Foreign Service to be the nation's foremost Soviet experts at the outset of the Cold War. Together they helped open the first U.S. mission to the Soviet Union following American recognition in 1933, and for the next two decades they served alternately at the State Department and as diplomats in the Moscow embassy, both culminating their careers by becoming ambassador there. While not as creative as Kennan, Bohlen had a subtler yet almost as important role. Far more adroit at dealing with others in power, he gently paved the way for the official acceptance of the view of Soviet behavior that he and Kennan shared.

Harriman, Lovett, Acheson, McCloy, Kennan, Bohlen: two bankers, two lawyers, two diplomats. Besides being major players in their own right, they represent a cross section of the postwar policy Establishment. The values they embodied were nurtured in prep schools, at college clubs, in the boardrooms of Wall Street, and at dinner parties in Washington. They shared a vision of public service as a lofty calling and an aversion to the pressures of partisan politics. They had a pragmatic and businesslike preference for realpolitik over ideology. As internationalists who respected the manners and traditions of Europe, they waged a common struggle against the pervasive isolationism of their time. Their world view was shaped by a fascination with the emergence of the Soviet Union as a world power and an unabashed belief in America's sacred destiny (and their own) to take the lead in protecting freedom around the globe and create what Henry Luce in a 1941 *Life* magazine article envisioned as "The American Century."

There were, of course, other men from the same tradition who could also be included in a biographical narrative of America's emergence as a global superpower. Several, in fact, play important roles in the story that follows. James Forrestal, though he became more intensely ideological than the others, brought from Princeton and Wall Street much of the same outlook as his close friend Lovett and their colleagues; had he not committed suicide at the height of his career, he might have come to be considered a personification of the Wise Men tradition. Paul Nitze—who was Bohlen's clubmate at Harvard, Forrestal's partner on Wall Street, and Kennan's successor as chief planner at the State Department—was not in a position of influence during the initial showdowns of the Cold War in 1945 and 1946, but he soon became an important member of the crowd.

Nor are the six men profiled in this book wholly compatible. Kennan, for example, hardly fit into the clubby comradery that helped unite the crowd (he even quit his eating club at Princeton, a matter that still seemed to cause some anguish as he recalled it decades later in the elegant drawing room of Manhattan's Century Association). McCloy was likewise not to the manner born, although he early on adopted it with relish. Lovett and Bohlen, the most socially secure of the lot, arguably had less direct influence on the making of policy than many of their contemporaries. Harriman, for his part, had serious bouts of political ambition that caused Acheson and the others to regard him with raised eyebrows.

Yet when considered together, these half-dozen friends fit together in a complementary way, epitomizing a style and outlook that played a dominant role in modern American policy making. Regarding service as an honor and imbued with a sense of noblesse oblige, they glided easily between private and public careers. As individuals, and even more so as a group, they embody what has been called (by those who venerate them as well as those who malign them) the American Establishment.

•   •   •

The field that has been ostentatiously labeled, by both self-serious scholars and those who satirize them, "Establishment studies" is a tricky one. On both the left and the right, there is a tendency to treat "the Establishment" as a gigantic conspiracy that needs to be exposed, as if it were a mysterious Masonic cabal. Wide-eyed right wingers distribute leaflets filled with exclamation points and arrows that purport to show the insidious reach of the Council on Foreign Relations and the Trilateral Commission. Zealots on the left use the same ominous tones in revealing the influence of the power structure, disagreeing with the right only on whether it is a conspiracy of capitalist imperialists or Communist one-worlders.

Those with greater insight can also be sharply critical. John Kenneth Galbraith, no stranger to its hallowed precincts, takes great joy in unleashing his irreverent wit on "the Establishment." In a celebrated 1966 speech to the Americans for Democratic Action, the acerbic professor blamed the deepening Vietnam entanglement on "the foreign policy syndicate of New York—the Dulles-Lovett-McCloy commun-ion, with which I am sure Secretary Rusk would wish to be associated and of which Dean Acheson is a latter-day associate."

On the other hand, there are those insiders who speak with reverence of the bygone elite. "For the entire postwar period," writes Henry Kissinger, "foreign policy had been ennobled by a group of distin-guished men who, having established their eminence in other fields, devoted themselves to public service." Citing McCloy, Acheson, Har-riman, and Lovett among others, he goes on to call them "an aris-tocracy dedicated to the service of this nation on behalf of principles beyond partisanship." Paul Nitze mentions the same names when speaking of the "golden age of the Establishment," noting: "I have never seen such a panoply of first-class people, who never thought of putting their interests before the nation's."

The English journalist Henry Fairlie first popularized the phrase "the Establishment" in a 1955 article describing the circle of powerful men who dominated Britain. Six years later, in a mock-serious parody called "Notes on the Establishment in America," Richard Rovere deftly poked at those who took the notion seriously while, with the other edge of his pen, executing a delightful drypoint of the subject at hand. Recounting a purported conversation with Galbraith, who "had for some time been surreptitiously at work in Establishment studies," Rovere described his discovery of the chairman emeritus of the Es-tablishment. "Suddenly the name sprang to my lips. John J. McCloy."

It is a notion that rankles McCloy. "Oh, no, not me," he protested years later. "I was not really a part of the Establishment. I was from the wrong side of the tracks." As Rovere dryly noted in his essay: "Naturally, Establishment leaders pooh-pooh the whole idea; they deny the existence of the Establishment, disclaim any connection of their own with it." For McCloy, it is the latter reaction. "Yes, of course," he says when asked if there was ever such a group. "They were Skull and Bones, Groton, that sort of thing. That was the elite.

Lovett, Harvey Bundy, Acheson, they called on a tradition, a high tradition. They ran with the swift. I always had in mind, even to this day, that I was not really a part of that."

In fact, however, one of the salient features of the tradition McCloy invokes is that it has not been a closed circle admissible only by birthright. In many ways it is meritocratic, at least for those eager to accept its style. The two men Rovere cites as putative Establishment chairmen, McCloy and Dean Rusk, were both from poor backgrounds. The cultivation process was a mutual one: Just as they sought admission to what they considered a special elite, the group sought to groom them and others for inclusion in its tradition of high-minded service.

Among those who most vehemently disparage the idea that there is an Establishment is McGeorge Bundy. (Clearly it would be futile for him to disclaim any connection if it did perchance exist: his father, Harvey Bundy, was a longtime aide to Secretary of War Stimson; McGeorge Bundy coauthored Stimson's memoirs; he edited a collection of Acheson's speeches; his brother Bill married one of Acheson's daughters; he served as Kennedy's and Johnson's National Security Adviser; and he was president of the Ford Foundation.) The notion is far too nebulous to be of any use, Bundy contends, and the differences among those usually included under the Establishment rubric are far greater than the similarities. And yet, it turns out, it was Bundy who wrote a memo for Lyndon Johnson entitled "Backing from the Establishment," which set the stage for the formation of the group that became known as the Wise Men. "The key to these people," Bundy advised, "is McCloy."

When Bundy was seeking Lovett's advice during the Cuban missile crisis, the elder statesman nodded toward a photograph near Bundy's desk and intoned that "the best service we can perform for the President is to try to approach this as Colonel Stimson would." That, in fact, might be the truest touchstone of Establishment credentials: reverence for the tradition exemplified by Henry Lewis Stimson, the consummate American statesman and Wall Street lawyer who served as Secretary of War under both William Howard Taft and Franklin Roosevelt and as Secretary of State under Herbert Hoover.

In its twentieth-century incarnation, the tradition began with the group of internationalists who acted as an informal brain trust for Woodrow Wilson at Versailles and returned home to found the Council on Foreign Relations. The founding father of the line was Elihu Root, who served as William McKinley's Secretary of War and Theodore Roosevelt's Secretary of State. Root was revered as a mentor by

Stimson, just as Stimson became the mentor for such men as McCloy and Lovett.

These men helped establish a distinguished network connecting Wall Street, Washington, worthy foundations, and proper clubs. "The New York financial and legal community," former JFK aide Arthur Schlesinger, Jr., wrote in 1965, "was the heart of the American Establishment. Its household deities were Henry L. Stimson and Elihu Root; its present leaders, Robert A. Lovett and John J. McCloy; its front organizations, the Rockefeller, Ford and Carnegie foundations and the Council on Foreign Relations."

Opposing this tradition is a populist strand that has run through American history since Jonathan Edwards led the Great Awakening against the sophistication that was blossoming in the eighteenth century and Andrew Jackson spearheaded a popular revolt against John Quincy Adams. In fact, the division between populists and the Establishment has been a more fundamental one in U.S. politics than that between left and right, liberal and conservative. Both Jimmy Carter and Ronald Reagan, like many of their predecessors, rode to the White House in large part by tapping an anti-Establishment vein in the populace.

This populist resentment of the Establishment—shared by the Old Left, New Left, Old Right, and New Right—accounts for much of the hostility faced by Acheson, McCloy, and their colleagues. For it is another defining characteristic of their group that they were decidedly nonpopulist, serving in the executive branch while remaining proudly aloof from the pressures of public opinion and its expression in Congress.

These men did not adhere to a single ideology, nor was ideology a driving force in their lives—except insofar as an instinct for the center can be called an ideology. They were equally opposed to the yahoos of the right and the softies of the left. Ideological fervor was frowned upon; pragmatism, realpolitik, moderation, and consensus were prized. Nonpartisanship was more than a principle, it was an art form: the only public jobs held by John McCloy or Robert Lovett, both mainstream Republicans, were in Democratic Administrations. "Damn it, I always forget," FDR muttered when McCloy once reminded him that he was not a Democrat.

There were, however, some basic tenets these men shared, foremost among them an opposition to isolationism. They were internationalists, and more specifically Atlanticists, an outlook that resulted in a certain willingness to make sweeping American commitments. They viewed America's leadership role, and their own, as part of a moral destiny. Godfrey Hodgson, an insightful British journalist, notes in an essay on the American Establishment that it was "characteristic of these men to take on the burdens of world power with a certain avidity." It reflected, he said, a "grim but grand duty" that was a "legacy from half-buried layers of New England Puritanism." Louis Auchincloss captured these Puritan underpinnings in his 1985 novel *Honorable Men*. Its hero, Chip Benedict, at one point declares to his wife: "What about our national honor? What about our commitment to world freedom?"

Their other basic tenet was the doctrine of containment. The notion that the primary goal of U.S. policy should be to limit the spread of Soviet Communism by force and diplomacy was their paramount contribution, one formulated jointly by Kennan, Acheson, Harriman, Bohlen, McCloy, Lovett, and Nitze. It became the core, indeed the creed, of a foreign policy consensus that prevailed for almost a generation; despite the destructive involvement in Vietnam that was its bastard legacy, the idea of containment remains, in a form strikingly similar to the way these men first conceived it, a fundamental precept of American policy.

In addition, they believed in a certain noble style of leadership, both for their country and for themselves. Galbraith likes to call it "the Groton ethic," the notion of duty and honor that Endicott Peabody tried to instill in his pupils. Lovett and McCloy were gentlemen, far different in manner from the ambitious power players who hold similar positions today. It was a tradition that they bequeathed to such men as David Bruce, Clark Clifford, Douglas Dillon, William and McGeorge Bundy, Dean Rusk, Cyrus Vance, and many others.

The Establishment label can therefore be a useful one. However hazy its outlines, the men who fall under the rubric shared many assumptions, and being part of a close-knit coterie added to whatever influence they had as mere individuals. Yet to treat the Establishment as a monolith, as many historians do, is less than enlightening. Stimson may have considered McCloy and Lovett "twins," but the fact that they came from decidedly different backgrounds is crucial to a full understanding of the style that both came to exemplify. The same is true of Kennan and Bohlen. Even Acheson and Harriman, whose shared experiences began at the Groton boathouse and lasted through the final meeting of the Wise Men more than sixty years later, illustrate the intriguing diversity within what is often regarded as an undifferentiated group.

This, then, is primarily a story about six influential men: their friendship, their power, their world, and their creation. However one defines the Establishment, these men were at its core, both because of who they were and how they were regarded. But by regarding them as individuals, the group becomes slightly less mysterious, and a lot more interesting.

•   •   •

Looking at the lives of these men, at their experiences and feelings, helps provide a personal perspective on the postwar period. Even the most careful scholars (in fact, particularly the most careful ones) sometimes seem to forget that at the midst of the momentous forces that shaped the modern world were flesh-and-blood individuals acting on imperfect information and half-formed beliefs. Like most human beings, these men were influenced by a mixture of principles and prejudices, noble goals and personal conceits. Their ideas sometimes reflected their lofty visions, at other times their momentary indignations, and occasionally their personal moods.

Choosing a group of close colleagues also made it possible to explore an important facet of why people act as they do: the influence exerted by friends, the desire for peer approval, and the pressures to conform. In forming their attitudes about the Soviets, for example, Kennan and Bohlen helped shape each other's ideas in the 1930s, then had an impact on Harriman's thinking during World War II, and he in turn helped sway McCloy, Acheson, and many others in Washington as the war drew to a close.

The debate over the extent that great individuals affect the flow of history is destined to remain unresolved. But one thing is certain: The men in this book deeply believed that what they thought and did could be a contributing factor, that persons and personalities could play a role on history's stage. They were, at least to an extent greater than noted in many histories, correct. When Harriman flew from Moscow to tutor Truman on the nature of the Soviet threat, when Kennan sent his Long Telegram that helped focus what had been a somewhat amorphous attitude in Washington, when Acheson took over a meeting about aid to Greece and Turkey and spoke of "rotten apples" in a barrel, events unfolded in a way that might have been different if others had been in their positions.

One reason the personal angle is missing from many of the otherwise penetrating studies of the Cold War is that the subjects of this book, important as they were to their times, were very private men. Unlike the more ambitious mandarins who pervade today's professional policy elite, these men did not seek to purvey their influence in the public realm. Later, of course, some wrote memoirs, but none wallowed in the self-serving revelations so popular today. They abhorred publicity; neither at the time nor in retrospect did they seek to enhance their role for popular consumption. Partly as a result, there are no full biographies of any of these six pivotal players (although some are in the works), and most histories treat them as two-dimensional characters.

The story is told mainly from the perspective of the men involved, exploring what they saw and felt at the time. Judging their role of course requires factoring in knowledge available only in retrospect, which we freely do; but it also requires regarding their actions in context, neither embellished by misty memory nor diminished by hindsight. To this end, we have relied primarily on the papers of the men involved, the letters they wrote and the interviews they gave at the time, their personal memos and their occasional private journal jottings. These proved to be an abundant and largely untapped resource. Particularly useful were reams of papers of Harriman, McCloy, and Lovett, and the family letters of Kennan that have not yet been made public, as well as the letters of Dean Acheson deposited at Yale in 1983. In addition, we interviewed scores of relatives and old colleagues, many of whom gave us access to papers and memorabilia.

• • •

In embarking on this project, we had no ideological ax to grind, no theses to prove. Nor was it our goal to apportion responsibility for the Cold War. Instead, we sought to understand why a group of important players came to act as they did. The main characters in this book, we came to believe, made mistakes and wrought some unintended consequences. But they were not guided by sinister or selfish motives in shepherding American policy.

They were staunch capitalists for whom liberal free trade was a creed; some had extensive financial holdings that would today be considered conflicts of interest; they believed in using economic policies as levers of diplomatic power. Yet they were not primarily motivated by imperialist impulses or fears of an impending capitalist crisis. Although their belief in the ideals of democracy was not always evenly applied, they were sincerely repulsed by the tyrannical tactics of the Kremlin and understandably anxious to keep them from spreading.

In their minds there was a link between free trade, free markets, and free men. The fact that the U.S. would be the prime beneficiary of a system of open global markets was clear to the protagonists of this book, but that did not make the goal any less sincere. Much of what they advocated was in fact largely selfless: the notion that Europe should be protected from Soviet domination had less to do with a desire for lucrative markets than with an affinity for the traditions and aspirations of Europeans.

The creed of Soviet containment that they formulated reflected their instinct for the pragmatic center. On one side were the liberal visionaries who believed that the Grand Alliance that had won the war could work together to preserve the peace if only Washington would make concessions to Stalin's legitimate security needs. On the other side were the fanatic anti-Communists who viewed the coming East-West showdown as a holy war.

Having seen firsthand the reality of the Soviet system, Harriman and Kennan and Bohlen came to believe that it was dangerous to put much faith in postwar cooperation, and they soon persuaded Acheson, McCloy, and others. Yet as pragmatic men, they were not primarily worried about Marxism or Communist ideology; far from being McCarthyites, they became some of the prime targets of the Red-baiting scares. What they sought to contain was the spread of Russian domination. They would likely have reacted much the same way if the xenophobic and expansionist empire at issue was still czarist rather than Bolshevik.

Their primary reason for resisting the spread of Soviet power was the same as the one that has motivated most Americans ever since: an abhorrence of the imposition of totalitarian systems on people yearning to live freely. They were tacitly willing to cede the Soviets some sphere of interest, but in return they saw no reason for Moscow to crush all freedoms in that realm. This outlook involved, of course, an implicit assumption that the rest of the world naturally desired the system of democratic capitalism, liberal values, and economic trade enjoyed by those in the West.

They viewed the Soviets in the way a businessman might regard a competitor: concessions and appeasement would not serve to buy goodwill, but it was possible to achieve a realistic modus vivendi that included cooperation on matters of mutual interest. They favored, for example, a postwar loan to the Soviets and efforts to work out a system of joint control for the atom bomb. Yet Acheson and others consciously overstated the threat they perceived in order to sell their vision of America's role in the postwar world. Eventually, they began to internalize their own rhetoric. Even more importantly, people less comfortable with the subtleties of the businessman's approach turned the competition with the Soviets into a life-and-death confrontation.

• • •

Most historians date the onset of the Cold War to the cold winter of 1947 or even later. In the minds of the men in this story, however, it began much earlier—and thus in fact it did. At the time, they were reacting to specific events while grappling for a strategic doctrine that would order their thoughts. They would have been appalled (as indeed they later were) at the prospect that the struggle they foresaw would result in a world dangerously divided for decades to come and locked in a frightening arms race.

History will bestow a mixed judgment on what they bequeathed. The world role that they carved for the U.S. left a costly legacy for successors who were neither as pragmatic nor as flexible when it came to balancing commitments with resources. The unchecked interventionist spirit resulted in unwise political and military involvements that the nation, by the end of the Vietnam War, was neither willing nor able to keep. Their policies also did nothing to alleviate, and perhaps even exacerbated, the evil they were designed to combat: Moscow's paranoia, expansionism, and unwillingness to cooperate in a liberal world order. Their reaction to the Soviet threat, Walter Lippmann has charged, "furnished the Soviet Union with reasons, with pretexts, for an iron rule behind the iron curtain, and with the ground for believing what Russians are conditioned to believe: that a coalition is being organized to destroy them."

Yet it is hardly fair to blame such men as Acheson and Harriman and Kennan for Stalin's intransigence or for the inability of others to adapt the policy of containment to changing situations. Reacting prudently to the threats they perceived at the time, they were able to create a bipartisan consensus about the goals of American policy that worked well for two decades. They countered what was, in fact, the very real threat that the power vacuum existing at the end of a devastating war would result in all of Europe and the Middle East coming under Soviet domination. "It is to the lasting credit of that generation of Americans," Kissinger has written, "that they assumed these responsibilities with energy, imagination and skill. By helping Europe rebuild, encouraging European unity, shaping institutions of economic cooperation, and extending the protection of our alliances, they saved the possibilities of freedom. This burst of creativity is one of the glorious moments of American history."

Whatever the final verdict on America's postwar policies, any assessment requires knowing and understanding why certain integral players acted the way they did. Their story is ultimately a human one, a drama of courage and conceits, wisdom and folly. It is, as Acheson has written, "a tale of large conceptions, great achievements, and some failures, the product of enormous will and effort." And it begins with boys rowing at a New England prep school and riding horses in the snow on a sprawling ranch in Idaho.

PART ONE

GATHERING

I am sure you will catch on,
and go on and on
and be something and somebody.

—E. H. HARRIMAN TO HIS SON
AVERELL

CHAPTER 1

Harriman, standing fifth from left, on the Groton crew

WORLD OF
THEIR OWN

To the manner born

As he stood on the dock of the brown-shingled boathouse, Averell Harriman paid little notice to the spindly boy rowing in seat seven of the shell hacking up the languid Nashua River. Dean Acheson was more than a year younger and two forms behind him, and at Groton there was little fraternizing between boys of different ages. In addition, with his air of stoic detachment, Harriman seemed aloof even to students his own age. He had been taught to row by a private tutor on his family's own private lake, and the other boys came to regard him as more of a coach than a schoolmate as he helped organize the underclass crews. Acheson, on the other hand, had quickly earned a reputation of being too cheeky for his own good. He went out for rowing only because the school required that each boy play some sport. Yet Harriman soon came to believe, as he later recalled, that the boy with toothpick legs and an impish demeanor showed some promise, at least on the water. He began to

offer unsolicited tips, a bit of encouragement. Eventually he would
bestow the pronouncement that Acheson "was a good oar."

In the years to come, Harriman would continue to fancy himself
a tutor to the fresh schoolmate he had helped with the intricacies of
stroking an oar. He would lecture Acheson about the postwar Soviet
threat and, much later, gently prod him about the futility of the
Vietnam War. Acheson, for his part, would later confess to being
bemused by Harriman's plodding and sovereign style, though he would
find him ever a reliable ally when it counted. And when it was all
over, just weeks before he died in 1971, Acheson would recall the
relationship fondly in a letter to his old friend:

> Sometimes it amuses me to confuse the young by pointing out what
> really elder statesmen we are by telling them that our friendship began—
> though perhaps neither of us knew it at the time—sixty-six years ago this
> month. Then I came as a new boy to the school at which you were a
> little, though not much, my senior. In most of those years that have
> passed, we have joined in activities that sometimes have been pretty stren-
> uous, first of all on the water, where we rowed, and later in government,
> where we struggled.

•　•　•

Harriman's sense of sovereignty and detachment was hardly surprising: he was the eldest son of one of America's richest men, a
domineering railway tycoon whose family more closely resembled a
medieval duchy than an American household. Edward Henry Harriman's personal fortune surpassed $70 million at a time when there
was no inheritance tax, the average hourly wage was twenty-two cents,
and a dollar could buy an imported linen dress shirt or a hundred
eggs. His money was entirely self-made. "My capital when I began
was a pencil and this," he would say, tapping his head.

The first American Harriman was a London stationer who had
migrated to New Haven in 1795 and made a comfortable fortune
chartering vessels for trade in the West Indies. But E. H. Harriman's
father had been an itinerant Episcopal clergyman who wandered
through California preaching in prospecting camps before returning
east as the rector of a small wooden church in Jersey City. At age
fourteen, E. H. dropped out of school to become a five-dollar-a-week
messenger boy at a brokerage house on Wall Street. "I have become
convinced that there is something else in life for me besides school
and books," he told his disapproving father. "I am going to work."

A compact dynamo, he plunged with relish into the cutthroat market of the Robber Baron era. With three thousand dollars borrowed from a wealthy uncle, he bought himself a seat on the Stock Exchange and captured Commodore Cornelius Vanderbilt and Jay Gould as his mentors and clients. By twenty-six, E. H. had parlayed his own first fortune of $150,000 by selling short in coal-mine stocks when he guessed that a speculator's attempt to corner the market would fail.

Marriage to Mary Williamson Averell in 1879 brought Harriman his first link to railroads. Her father, William Averell, the president of a small upstate New York rail company, provided a special train for the couple's honeymoon with "E. H. Harriman" painted on the locomotive. It was the first of many destined to be so emblazoned.

Harriman's railway holdings were built with both paper and steel: he became an adroit and notorious speculator in railway stock options and an energetic builder of the lines he thus came to control. The empire that he eventually accumulated as chairman of the Union Pacific and Southern Pacific stretched twenty-three thousand miles and was capitalized at $1.5 billion. In the process he made some daunting enemies, including J. P. Morgan and the President of the United States. After a feud that began over a political appointment, Theodore Roosevelt took to calling him an "enemy of the Republic" and a "malefactor of great wealth."

The railway madness of that era was noted for its untrammeled excess, epitomized by the brutal take-over battles between E. H. Harriman and James J. Hill. Theirs was an exalted realm. "When the master of one of the great Western lines travels toward the Pacific in his palace car," wrote the awed British observer Lord Bryce, "his journey is like a royal progress. Governors of States and Territories bow before him; legislatures receive him in solemn session; cities seek to propitiate him."

•   •   •

William Averell Harriman, born on November 15, 1891, bore many of his father's traits. To his childhood friends, who called him Bill, Averell was noted for his curious combination of tenacity and detachment. Unlike his small and tightly wound father, Averell was somewhat plodding, almost to the point of seeming dull; but both were blunt and unvarnished—proudly so. No jokes or small talk crept into their conversations, no easy laughter or self-deprecating tales. Although his older sister Mary and younger brother Roland abounded in gregarious charm, Averell displayed little of the frivolity of youth. He affected an imperious demeanor that was accented by his quiet manner.

Even when he was young, Averell looked somewhat haggard and sallow, but appearances were deceiving: he was tough, physically and mentally, and relished putting his abilities on the line. Recreations were challenges to be mastered, and Harriman invariably did: polo, rowing, skiing, bowling, croquet, and even backgammon. "He went into any game lock, stock, and barrel," Robert Lovett later recalled. "He would get whatever he needed—the best horses, coaches, equipment, his own bowling alley or croquet lawn—and work like the devil to win."

"I like the kind of play that is as strenuous as work," the young Averell told an interviewer. "I like to go into each, in its turn, as hard as I know how." It was an approach he learned from his parents. "Father," Averell once recalled, "could not imagine doing anything just for fun." His mother used to carry a rule book while she played croquet, citing it often to insist that the finer points be followed.

E. H. Harriman, short and stern, was hardly a doting father, but he took a great interest in his children, taking them on his far-flung excursions and playing childhood games with them in his study after dinner. He insisted they look him straight in the eye during all conversations and rewarded them with pennies for performing self-improvement chores such as keeping a daily diary. "In everything he did he took command, no matter what was going on," Averell later recalled. "Even if we went for a walk, he'd tell us where he wanted to go. He knew what he wanted to do."

On one of the cross-country tours E. H. took with his older son, their private train started swaying out of control as it sped along a stretch of rough track. After almost derailing, it screeched to a halt. The Union Pacific president, Horace G. Burt, explained to Harriman that a construction crew had been working on the roadbed and failed to send a flagman out to signal oncoming trains. "Fire everyone on that gang," said Harriman as Averell listened in awe. "That's really rather cruel on these people," Burt replied. Said Harriman: "It may be cruel, but it will probably save a lot of lives. That sort of thing won't happen again."

The elder Harriman imparted his wisdom through oft-repeated adages. "A good workman can work with poor tools," he would tell his children. "Whatever you have anything to do with, your first thought should be to improve it." And his favorite maxim: "Great wealth is an obligation and responsibility. Money must work for the country."

His children took these sayings to heart. When his daughter Mary made her debut in 1901, she balked at the expenses that were being lavished on the extravaganzas of her friends. Even though she was a vivacious partygoer, she felt that such displays were unnecessary. So she put part of the money to better use and helped found the Junior League. Its first project, even before it was formally an organization, was bringing the flowers from lavish parties to local hospitals and seeing that they were properly distributed. This sense of social obligation, of noblesse oblige, was something she often urged on her brother, who respected her enormously.

Averell's reserve resembled that of his mother. "Her rather formal pattern of living provided, in a sense, a shield against intrusion," her biographer wrote. Some people, because of their style and grand bearing, tacitly command attention simply by entering a room. Mary Averell Harriman had such an air, and so too at times did her older son. She managed her households, which included up to a hundred servants and retainers, with the same authority and attention to detail her husband brought to running the railways. Her diaries, studded with biblical sayings and meticulous financial accounts, reveal a shrewd outlook which was only rarely apparent in public.

During Averell's childhood, the Harrimans owned a series of elegant town houses on Fifth Avenue in Manhattan. The grandest was a cavernous Georgian pile of marble that overlooked the site where the St. Regis Hotel was being built. Averell would stare from its windows for hours, fascinated by the horse-drawn trucks and steam-powered pulleys and the marvel of human construction they were slowly creating. E. H. Harriman kept a string of trotters in the city to pull his sons through Central Park and later was driven about by one of the country's first automobiles, one he had imported from Germany.

Averell dutifully attended Miss Dodson's dancing school and other such Social Register rites of passage, but he stonily avoided the young social set whenever possible. He was more in his element at Arden, the Harrimans' baronial estate fifty miles up the Hudson where the family spent spring and summer.

Begun as a modest wooden cottage on the shore of a lake, Arden was gradually expanded by the Harrimans into a rambling three-story mansion with squash courts, billiard room, and separate guest quarters. For E. H. Harriman, even his home was a potential industry: iron mines on the property were reopened, dairy cows were raised to sell milk to the military academy at West Point, and electricity plants were built at Arden and neighboring Turners Village (now Harriman, New York) to sell power throughout the area.

The Harriman household formed a world unto itself, self-contained and self-sufficient. When it came time for Averell and Roland to learn how to row, their father hired the Syracuse University crew coach, Jim Ten Eyck, to provide private lessons on a course set up on their 150-acre lake. An island in its midst was outfitted with special wood-floor tents for camping trips. As his boys would swim or canoe to their little island, old man Harriman would sit in a camp chair on the dock, watching and thinking.

When Averell was ten, he spent many mornings riding with his father, while the rest of the family followed in carts pulled by trotters, surveying their property for the perfect place to build a new mansion. The search was somewhat moot: Mrs. Harriman had decided early on that it should be built on the summit of Mount Orama, the highest point between New York and the Catskills. It was a desire that required the full might of the Union Pacific to fulfill: the top of the mountain was sliced off to provide a level foundation and a funicular railway was stretched up one slope to haul material.

The "new" Arden was the grandest of palaces, but a distinctly American one. Other wealthy barons of the time were building imported castles, shipping them stone by stone from Europe. But E. H. Harriman, with no less ostentation, told his architect, Thomas Hastings, that he wanted everything in the house, from the granite to the art, to be American. Six hundred workmen labored three years on the mansion, which was completed just six months before Harriman died in 1909.

Arden, which remained in the Harriman family until Averell donated it to Columbia University in 1951, had more than a hundred full rooms, including forty bedrooms and a hotel-size kitchen. There were a tennis court, a croquet lawn, forty miles of bridle paths, and later a set of bowling alleys. A private polo ground was built, and there the Harriman children and their friends would challenge the cadets from West Point.

Arden's voluminous hall was dominated by an organ, for which Mrs. Harriman retained a full-time musician. When he was not performing, the children would work the majestic instrument by attaching player rolls and pulling on the various stops. Mrs. Harriman dedicated herself to collecting the finest of American art, tapestries, and furnishings. The only imported items in the house were the linens; they came from Ireland because she could find no domestic ones that suited her standards. The servants were ordered to keep every room ready for occupancy, bedizened with fresh flowers, to encourage the children to invite friends to their isolated castle. On some summer weekends the table would include as many as twenty guests.

The community of retainers and servants at Arden provided Averell with his steadiest playmates. At one of Mrs. Harriman's annual staff Christmas parties, there were 65 men, 25 women, and 188 children. Averell and his siblings worked with their mother's secretary to choose small gifts for every child, such as skates and mittens, and distribute them at the party. At the end of the party one year, Averell remarked on the absence of a young boy who lived with his drunken father in a shack about four miles from the main house. It turned out that the child had been mistakenly left off the list. Averell and his father rode out into the night and found the forgotten boy, presenting him with a sturdy new sled.

In 1899, when Averell was not quite eight, his father was advised by his physicians to take a restful vacation. "His idea of a rest was to charter a steamship out of Seattle and take a group of distinguished scientists on a three-month jaunt along the Alaskan shore," Roland recalled. The party included sixty-five crew members, twenty-five scientists, eleven woodsmen, three artists, two photographers, and a cow to produce milk for Averell and Roland.

E. H. Harriman's primary ambition on the trip was to shoot a Kodiak bear, and he did: a huge seven-footer whose skin thereafter graced his parlor floor. When both the captain and pilot balked at exploring an uncharted inlet, the brazen industrialist personally took the helm. As a result, the fiord and glacier they found were named Harriman. In addition, the scientists discovered thirteen new genera and six hundred new species of flora and fauna, took five thousand photographs, and published thirteen illustrated volumes and eleven monographs in conjunction with the Smithsonian Institution.

Among those aboard was the renowned conservationist John Muir. One evening, the scientists on the forecastle were praising Harriman for the benevolence of his wealth. "I don't think Mr. Harriman is very rich," Muir interjected. "He has not as much money as I have. I have all I want, and Mr. Harriman has not." Harriman heard about the remark and raised the matter at dinner. "I have never cared for money except as a power to put to work," he said. "What I enjoy most is the power of creation, getting into partnership with nature and doing good, helping to feed man and beast, and making everybody and everything a little better and happier."

That self-appraisal, although hardly a precise one of the railway baron's career, deeply impressed Averell. The expedition came just as he was beginning to comprehend his family's enormous wealth and power, and the burdens as well as benefits it brought. As an awkward socializer, Averell had already become uncomfortable with the frivolous society life of many of his friends; his father's belief that money was a tool rather than a goal burned a lasting impression.

The trip also gave Averell his first glimpse of a country that would figure prominently throughout his life. His mother insisted that the voyage not end at the Seal Islands, as scheduled, but instead cross the Bering Sea to the coast of Russia. "Very well," replied Mr. Harriman, "we will go to Siberia." Upon landing at Plover Bay, the family spent the day buying artifacts from the natives, taking photographs, and picking the unusual wild flowers. For the next nine decades, Averell was to return to Russia at regular intervals, his last visit coming in 1983. During World War II he was able to tell Stalin that on his first trip to Russia he had entered without a passport. "Well," Stalin replied, "you could not do that now."

With the acquisition of the Pacific Mail Steamship Company, E. H. Harriman began to have visions of completing an around-the-world transportation system. So with his family in tow, he headed for the Orient in the summer of 1905. Japan had just wrested control of the South Manchuria Railway from Russia, and Harriman wanted to add it to his empire. A preliminary agreement for a lease was reached with the Japanese government, but it was scuttled a few weeks later amid the anti-Americanism that erupted in Japan after President Theodore Roosevelt mediated the peace terms for the Russo-Japanese War. All Harriman got from the Japanese were some cases of captured Napoleon brandy, a supply ample enough that Averell, then thirteen, would savor it years later.

The Harriman family then proceeded by chartered steamer to Port Arthur, on the Manchurian coast. Averell, however, was unable to accompany them. Although Averell's father had moved mountains, he was unable to move Endicott Peabody, the immutable rector of Groton School. The rail baron had cabled from Japan an urgent request that Averell be excused from the first two weeks of classes so that he could tour the Asian mainland. Any student, Peabody replied, absent from the first day of term would be "fired" from the school. In order to extend Averell's stay by three more days, Harriman rerouted a Pacific Mail liner.

•   •   •

"The experience released me from the Groton rigidities and perhaps contributed to my becoming something of a nonconformist," Harriman later said about the Rector's refusal to let him tour Manchuria. Although the school was just twenty-one years old, those rigidities were already firmly entrenched. Modeled after an English public school, Groton was New England's new Eton. It was Episcopalian (one founder was Phillips Brooks) and amply endowed (another was J. P. Morgan). "Ninety-five percent of the boys came from what they considered the aristocracy of America," wrote George Biddle, a 1904 graduate. "Their fathers belonged to the Somerset, the Knickerbocker, the Philadelphia or the Baltimore Clubs. Among them was a goodly slice of the wealth of the nation."

The school's purpose, according to its first brochure, was to develop "manly, Christian character." Life was strictly regimented and ascetic. Students lived in six-by-nine-foot bare wood cubicles in which no ornamentation, except family pictures, was allowed. They arose at 6:55 A.M., attended chapel seven days a week (twice on Sunday), and were allotted twenty-five cents a week as spending money (a nickel of which was for the Sunday collection plate). Yet there were some amenities: They did not have to make their beds or wait on tables, and their shoes were polished overnight by servants. At dinner, the required dress was stiff collar, black tie, and patent-leather pumps.

Groton's driving force was Endicott Peabody, who ruled the school for its first sixty years. Educated in England at Cheltenham and at Trinity College, Cambridge, the Rector was a perfect Victorian. Tall and muscular, regarding his body as a temple, he always dressed in highly polished black shoes, blue suit, and white starched bow tie. As a thirteen-year-old Averell Harriman described him in a letter home: "You know he would be an awful bully if he wasn't such a terrible Christian."

Peabody cared more about sportsmanship than scholarship. "I'm not sure I like boys who think too much," he once said. "A lot of people think a lot of things we could do without." He personally taught two subjects: football and sacred studies. "The way of the non-athlete at Groton was not so much hard as inconsequential," wrote the school historian. "Football was the King of the Games. Theoretically, a boy does not have to play the game, but moral suasion on the part of the faculty and students makes it almost impossible to avoid doing so."

The rest of Groton's curriculum included large doses of Latin and Greek, ancient history, and European studies with a particular emphasis on England. American history was generally snubbed: Roland

Harriman noted that history teachers "made us learn all the names and dates of the French and English kings while neglecting to tell us that one hundred years before the Pilgrim fathers landed in Massachusetts, the Spaniards were in California." The students were graded weekly, and each month their performance was ranked by Peabody, who sent stern and unvarnished reports home to their parents.

Although Peabody was thoroughly intimidating, most of the students also revered him. He remained a loyal and powerful force to most of them throughout their lives, marrying them off, christening their children, and even on occasion visiting them in jail. (When one of his old prefects, New York Stock Exchange president Richard Whitney, was convicted of embezzlement, Peabody visited him at Sing Sing. He brought Whitney a first baseman's mitt so he could play on the prison team.) Franklin Roosevelt cited him as "the biggest influence in my life."

Peabody was dedicated to the ideal of public service and to instilling a sense of Christian and patrician obligation among his charges. "*Cui Servire Est Regnare*" is the motto of the school. Literally translated, it means "to serve Him is to rule." Peabody, drawing on the Book of Common Prayer, gave it a more ethereal translation: "Whose service is perfect freedom." He meant not only service to God, but also to country. "If some Groton boys do not enter public life and do something for our land," he said, "it will not be because they have not been urged." At the school's twentieth anniversary celebration, the President of the United States, Theodore Roosevelt, summed up that message for the students by paraphrasing the gospel of Luke: "Much has been given you. Therefore we have a right to expect much from you."

Groton did produce more than its share of public servants. The school history notes that Groton's first thousand graduates included a President, two Secretaries of State, two governors, three senators, and nine ambassadors, grandly extrapolating that if the rest of the U.S. population had produced leaders at the same rate, "there would have been 37,000 Presidents, 350,000 ambassadors, 110,000 Senators..." With some exceptions, most notably Franklin Roosevelt, Groton's graduates avoided politics and tended to prefer the more discreet branches of government, particularly the OSS and the CIA. Few entered the ministry, and virtually none pursued the arts. Service to God and Country was overshadowed by service to Mammon. The largest single category of career choice in the school history is "finances, stocks, bonds, etc."

To most twelve-year-olds entering Groton's Second Form (eighth grade) in 1904, Groton would seem a severe institution run by a formidable man. Yet the Harrimans were, as John Kennedy described Averell many years later, a "separate sovereignty." As an institution unto themselves, they tended to be less intimidated by presidents, premiers, and rectors. Throughout his life, Harriman would remain an unusual blend of loyal public servant, dutifully undertaking tasks requested by various presidents, and an unfettered diplomat, eschewing detailed instructions and dealing with foreign powers as he saw fit.

The rectitude Averell found in the Rector was similar to that of his father: both Peabody and E. H. Harriman stressed the virtue of work, the burdens of privilege, and the obligation to repay society. The senior Harriman even became involved in guiding the school. Upset that there was neither a full-time athletic director nor a tutor to provide remedial instruction to struggling scholars, he made arrangements to fund these positions. Students were required to write home every Sunday; Harriman's parents demanded that he also send a postcard every night.

Averell started off shakily at Groton; in his first year, he was in the bottom third of his class. Peabody noted on a February report card: "Poor in English; capable of better work all around." This resulted in a rather stern intercession from E. H. Harriman, one that provoked the desired effect. The next report from Peabody read: "Has been working rather harder since your visit." By Harriman's Sixth Form (senior) year, he was in the middle of his class and, more importantly, rowing on the varsity crew. Wrote Peabody: "Fair in his studies. In other ways he has been gaining steadily."

This was still not enough for his father. "Can you not 'jack up' on the English?" he wrote from San Antonio, where he was supervising the construction of a new railway to Mexico. "I know you can as well as some other subjects. It is encouraging to have you so improved, and I am sure you will catch on, and go on and on and be something and somebody."

That phrase, "be something and somebody," stayed with Harriman always; he was still invoking it as a legacy from his father at age ninety-two. "Groton gave me a great sense of obligation," he said. "But so did my father."

Harriman's streak of independence came through in his letters home. When his father, worried about Roland's performance, asked Averell to "do something to wake him up," Averell replied: "It seems to me that the whole Groton organization needs an awakening, the masters one and all, as well as the scholars like Roland." Yet he was still a loyal Grottie. When Peabody, in his usual fashion, sent a letter to Harriman on his birthday the year after he had graduated, Harriman responded dutifully that the Rector's greetings "come as a reminder of what Groton has done for us, and what Groton stands for, and what Groton expects of us."

• • •

On the day that Dean Acheson was born—April 11, 1893—some friends came to call on his family accompanied by their teen-aged son. The Reverend Edward Acheson, impressed by the visiting boy's bearing, asked where he went to school. After hearing an enthusiastic description of Groton, then only nine years old, Acheson decided that his newborn son should be placed on the admissions list for twelve years thence.

Groton at the turn of the century was a curious melting pot of money and status. The explosion of industrial wealth had blurred class lines; Groton, like the other High Church prep schools in New England, became an arbiter of its own, not just a measure but a maker of social distinction. It brought together the children of Boston Brahmins and Mrs. Astor's "400" with the offspring of commercial magnates, some of whose money was still a bit crisp. There was, in addition, a special place at the school for another group that the Rector believed should be part of the backbone of America's establishment. If he was willing to accommodate new money, he was just as anxious to make room for the sons of the Episcopal clergy, some of whom were quite threadbare.

Acheson's family was perfectly comfortable. Yet next to the Harrimans they were church mice. The descendant of a Scotch-Irish clan that was fiercely loyal to the House of Stuart, Edward Campion Acheson had been born in 1857 in southern England, where his father, a professional soldier and Crimean War veteran, was garrisoned. On the eve of his thirteenth birthday, Edward bought himself a present: a prayer book that he put under his pillow so it would be there on his birthday. The following year he ran away to London, and two years later immigrated alone to Canada. There he worked his way through the University of Toronto, fought with the Queen's Own Rifles in Saskatchewan, won a gold medal during an 1885 Indian uprising at Cut Knife Creek, and subsequently began training for the ministry.

While attending All Saints' Church, Edward Acheson had met Eleanor Gooderham, the daughter of a prominent Toronto whiskey distiller and bank president. Their first son, christened Dean Gooderham Acheson, was born in the rectory of the Holy Trinity Episcopal Church in Middletown, Connecticut, where his father had taken a job.

Over the years, nothing could do more to soften Dean Acheson's sometimes acerbic demeanor than misty memories of his days under the arched elms of Middletown. It was a carefree Huck-and-Tom childhood of smoking corn silk and playing ball that grew rosier with each retelling.

The golden age of childhood can be quite accurately fixed in time and place [he wrote in Morning and Noon, a volume of early reminiscences]. It reached its apex in the last decade of the nineteenth century and the first few years of the twentieth, before the plunge into a motor age and city life swept away the freedom of children and dogs, put them both on leashes and made them the organized prisoners of an adult world. . . . No one was run over. No one was kidnapped. No one had teeth straightened. No one worried about children, except occasionally my mother, when she saw us riding on the back step of the ice wagon and believed, fleetingly, that one of the great blocks of Pamecha Pond ice would fall on us. But none ever did.

Dean had a pony (with a "grand design of how to live in idleness"), a dog named Bob (purchased for five dollars), and a ready supply of playmates. Unlike Harriman, the mischievous young Acheson was never considered excessively mature for his age. On the three-acre field between the church and rectory, he and his friends would re-create battles of the Boer War and Teddy Roosevelt's charge up San Juan Hill, little deterred by counterattacks from irate neighbors whose laundry lines and gardens became bunkers and battlegrounds.

Each evening Dean would walk to the firehouse to watch the men drill and then run to the wharf in time for the arrival of the boat from Hartford. "To me, it seemed that the ladies and gentlemen promenading the deck of that ship were the most fortunate people on earth," he later recalled, "and watching them night after night, I imagined myself plowing across the open sea, some nights to Europe, some nights to China, some nights to darkest Africa."

Acheson's lifelong Anglophilia was instilled as a child. He and his two younger siblings were the only U.S. citizens in the household, which included his parents (who were loyal subjects of Queen Victoria), two Irish servants, and a Canadian governess. Celebration of the Queen's birthday in May ranked with St. Patrick's Day and July 4: a Union Jack would wave, and after dinner the children were given a glass of diluted claret so they could join their father in toasting Her Majesty.

Edward Acheson often took Dean and his friends to cottages on Long Island Sound or campsites in the woods of Maine. With utmost patience, he taught them how to fly-fish and build fires. But he was generally a stern father, tall and intimidating, remembered most for his Olympian detachment. His most severe punishment was an icy stare and banishment from the house, such as occurred when he caught Dean pitching pennies during church while he was serving as an acolyte. His son learned to view morality, and also punishment, as natural rather than spiritual phenomena. "The penalty for falling out of a tree was to get hurt," he said of his childhood. "The penalty for falling out with my father was apt to be the same thing. Result followed cause in a rational, and hence predictable, way but left no spiritual wound."

Yet Edward Acheson had a jovial sense of humor and talent as a mimic. "He could have made a fortune in vaudeville with his Irish brogue," his son recalled. He loved to read stories aloud, particularly Kipling, doing the different voices with great gusto. In the evenings he would carry on discourses with his pet parrot, until one day the bird bit him on the finger. Acheson refused to speak to the bird for weeks, despite numerous squawked "hellos." Finally he relented and solemnly fed the bird a cracker.

He also had a grand sense of style and drama. His choir, clad in scarlet cassocks, would open the church service with a great drum roll leading into Gounod's "St. Cecilia Mass," and then the rector would bellow the creed, "I believe in one God!" Because he knew everyone in town, his walks with his son Dean would last for hours as he stopped for chats with policemen, the blacksmith (where Dean learned to curse), the garbage collector, and the millowners. All revered him. One Jewish shopkeeper, Isaac Wrubel, brought his boys to Acheson to be taught religion. He did not care what religion was taught, Wrubel said, as long as Acheson was the teacher. "Well, then," said Acheson, "I'll teach them your religion. The Old Testament is good enough for me."

As a man who believed that theology could not be kept separate from worldly action, Acheson frequently sermonized on the need for such reforms as workmen's compensation, often to the consternation of his conservative congregation. "You know that forty people in the drop-forge plant are going to lose their hands or smash their fingers before the end of the year," he preached. Unlike the fire and brimstone that came from many pulpits at the time, Acheson's sermons were commonsense lectures on hope, charity, and good works.

Mrs. Acheson made her home a center of hospitality for the town, but was far more concerned than her husband with social status. "She was in many ways the social arbiter of Middletown, and was inclined to be an aristocrat," remembered Ray Baldwin, who later became a U.S. senator from Connecticut. She wore tailor-made clothes, affected an English accent, and carried herself with a regal air that struck many as somewhat presumptuous.

Until he was nine, Dean was educated by his governess and at a small local private school. When his mother fell ill, and Dean and his sister, Margot, became more quarrelsome, he was sent off to a boarding school called Hamlet Lodge in Pomfret, Connecticut. It was near enough to Middletown to permit weekend visits from his father. One Saturday, Joe Lawton made the trip with the Reverend Dr. Acheson. As they walked up the path to the school, they met a young man marching back and forth. "I'm being punished," he explained. The stern minister, who was soon to be elected bishop of Connecticut, reprimanded the boy and then asked if he knew where to find his son Dean. "That's him walking over there," said the boy, pointing. "He did the same thing."

Dean developed a cocksure style, a sense of fun and a streak of independence. "He did everything that came into his head," recalled his friend Lawton. "He was a good mixer, but very, very independent." Lawton, a Catholic boy who went to parochial school, remembers most of all that Dean, when young, took no note of the social and class differences among his playmates.

From his father Dean inherited a devotion to valor and duty, from his mother a sense of fortitude and grace. He also had a keen intellect that, once awakened, was at times all too aware of its own brilliance. As he grew older, his wit and elegant charm made him a convivial companion to friends who pierced his intimidating haughtiness. His reverence for the protocols of power (which sometimes failed to conceal a touch of arrogance) inspired a forceful loyalty among those he served as well as those who served him. The lessons he learned as a child developed into a dedication both to high principles and tough pragmatism. Although he occasionally found himself caught between the two, he seldom seemed paralyzed by doubt. He had the calm assurance of a man who had grown up believing that problems were meant to be solved and challenges were made to be met.

· · ·

When the time came for him to enter Groton, Dean had no desire to abandon Middletown. But his father had gotten to know Peabody, and was more convinced than ever that the decision made twelve years earlier was the right one. So in the fall of 1905, the Achesons rode up to northern Massachusetts to enroll him in the school's First Form.

Groton's rigid environment was, for Acheson even more than Harriman, a cold dousing after the warm days of childhood. In *Morning and Noon*, Acheson never mentions the school by name. "The transition from the wild freedom of my boyhood to the organized discipline of adolescence at boarding school was not a change for the happier," he wrote. "At first, through surprise, ignorance and awkwardness, later on and increasingly through willfulness, I bucked the Establishment and the system. One who does this fights the odds. The result was predictable, painful and clear."

Groton graduates may seem to outsiders all cut from comparable cloth. But in 1905, as in later years, there were deep social distinctions among the students. Acheson came from a far different milieu than Harriman, and he had none of the social ties that could ease the transition through the initial hazing that was endemic to the school.

Acheson was slight and hardly a practiced athlete; worse yet, he was independent, even cheeky. To such people, Groton could be terribly cruel. Oliver La Farge, who later won the Pulitzer Prize for his novel *Laughing Boy*, would wake up all through his life having nightmares that he was still a Third Former at Groton. Cass Canfield, who became a distinguished publisher, was greeted upon his arrival by an older student who said, "So you're the new kid," and proceeded to punch him in the face. George Biddle, later an accomplished painter, bitterly recalls the punishment known as "pumping" meted out to young boys thought too fresh. With the Rector's tacit acquiescence, the offender would be dragged from study hall by older boys and thrust headfirst into a lavatory sink, where he was "held upside down while water was sprayed on his face until he was jerked to his feet, coughing, choking, retching."

Acheson was subjected to "pumping" as well as to a crueler torture. Spindly and puckish, he was forced to stand like a Maypole while a circle of mocking students danced around calling him a "fairy." Nor did Peabody take kindly to him. "I find him a very unexpected sort of person," the Rector wrote on one of his first report cards. "Irresponsible, forgets books, doesn't remember lessons, makes excuses." In May, Peabody simply wrote, "Immature." Three years later, Acheson had become more rebellious. Wrote Peabody: "He is described by some of his masters as by no means a pleasant boy to teach." Even in Acheson's final year, Peabody's judgment was harsh: "Needs open-mindedness. He is full of immature prejudices."

At the end of Dean's first year, Peabody dolefully informed the Achesons that the school was unable to make a "Groton boy" of their son. Mrs. Acheson was determined to keep him in the school, fearing that otherwise he would forever carry the scars of dismissal. Showing some cheek of her own, she told Peabody that she did not want the school to make a Groton boy out of Dean, but simply to educate him. Peabody, who preferred to save souls rather than lose them, relented.

Academically, Acheson stayed mired near the bottom of his class. On his final report card, he finished with a 68 average, the very lowest among the twenty-four in his form. In athletics, he showed his disdain for the intensity of the team loyalties, so alien to the pickup games in Middletown, and made the first crew but only in his final term. "At Groton I didn't happen to feel like conforming," he later said. "And to my surprise and astonishment, I discovered not only that an independent judgment might be the right one, but that a man was actually alive and breathing once he had made it."

Despite his discomfort at Groton, it instilled in Acheson a desire to seem tough, a resistance to being considered a pushover. His mannerisms, cultivated from his childhood home and his boarding school, were thoroughly British, even dandyish—but never effete. Having braved the Maypole taunts and the pumping with a stiff upper lip, the bullying tactics of Senator Joseph McCarthy and others would seem pale in comparison.

Although Acheson mocked Peabody's pieties, a bit of the Rector's sense of duty stayed with him. "Under Peabody, the idea of service, so strong with Dean, was first instilled," his classmate Joseph Walker III later recalled. Five years after his graduation, when he first began to consider seriously his role in life, Acheson wrote Peabody to apologize for not revisiting the school. The reason, he said, "was entirely one of shrinking from a place where I knew I had been a failure and where I felt that the masters and the boys who knew me had an opinion of me far less charitable than the present one of the world at large." When his son, David, came of age, Acheson sent him to Groton.

The Grotonian for Acheson's senior year includes an essay he wrote called "The Snob in America." It was fashionable then, as it has often been, to take a hard stand against snobbery in a way that suggests that by avoiding snobbery one is exercising forbearance. Acheson did precisely that in his flowery and contorted prose. He was already wrestling with a conflict that would be evident throughout his life: an intellectual attachment to democratic values pitted against a personal elitism that caused him to view with condescension "the vulgar mass of humanity." Both the style and the content of the four-page essay are revealing:

The institution of snobbery is in a foreign land when it alights on the shores of America. Not that it will not meet many compatriots; far from it. It will almost feel at home in the crowd of friends. But soon there is that in the atmosphere which makes it old, shriveled and spiteful... Snobbishness is not mere conceit. Conceit is the glorification of oneself, snobbishness is the abasement of others. A conceited man says "I"; a snob says "we." Conceit may give a man self-confidence, unfounded perhaps, but conducive to effort. Snobbishness produces nothing but the sneer... In America the antipathy to the snob goes deeper than the scramble for gold. For the essence of democracy is belief in the common people, and the essence of snobbery is contempt of them... It is wonderful, this spirit of democracy and, whenever we hear it raved against as being too strong, or too radical, or too popular, let us remember that in it lies the ever virile power which keeps us from being a nation of snobs. D.G.A.

•   •   •

Echoing his father, Acheson in his essay took issue with those who thought that laborers were showing ingratitude by trying to organize unions. His fellow students, he felt, should become more sensitive to the plight of the working class. Upon graduating in 1911, he took his own advice: through family connections he got a summer job with a work crew on the Grand Trunk Pacific Railway being pushed across northern Canada.

On his way to the railroad camp in the wilds near Hudson Bay, Acheson boarded a freight car filled with itinerant workers only to discover that even among railwaymen there was a rigid class system, one that he had violated. "Residency types, even axemen, did not travel with common laborers," he recalled. "I had let down the barrier of caste, albeit through ignorance, and with it our side—a minute group, as I learned later, for whom prestige was a major factor in handling large numbers of illiterate laborers."

The initiation rites on the railroad were similar in some ways to those of Groton: as a neophyte he was taken for a ride in a handcar that the other workers tipped over at a prearranged signal, sending Acheson sprawling. "My own merriment was somewhat forced," Acheson recalled. But he reveled in "the intoxication of knowing that this was 'life.'" As he traveled from camp to camp through the wilderness, he derived a sense of security from the gruff hospitality, the shared soup and hardtack, that greeted each new visitor.

At his final workplace, an outpost known as Residency 25, Acheson fell comfortably into the close-knit crew. There was the chief engineer who "lived alone, as a captain should. Exuding authority, he commanded almost without words." Then too there was the hearty instrument man and the French-Canadian cook, Lorin, a Falstaffian man of great gusto prone to ribald soliloquy and song. "Months later, when I had gotten to college, Lorin's recitations and stories put me in the novel role of ribald wag."

"These men," Acheson later wrote, "had given me new eagerness for experience. The simple, extroverted pattern of their lives had revived a sense of freedom amidst uncoerced order. They had restored to me a priceless possession, joy in life. Never again was I to lose it or doubt it."

• • •

St. Paul's School in Concord, New Hampshire, in many ways mirrored Groton. Opened in 1856, it was ardently Anglophile and Anglican. Like the other Episcopal schools of New England, it broke with the academy model of American private education (as exemplified at Andover and Exeter) and consciously imitated Eton and Harrow. For years baseball was forbidden; the boys played cricket instead.

The formidable and pious headmaster of St. Paul's, Dr. Samuel Drury, could match Endicott Peabody starched collar for starched collar. "The school might make one condition for its diploma: the ability to recite the Sermon on the Mount," he proclaimed. But whereas Peabody was hale, Drury was dour. According to the school history, he was "reserved, cheerless and solemn" and regarded American boys by nature to be "slovenly, dilatory, inconsiderate and slack." He inveighed against the use of banners in student rooms because he considered them "an offense against art and hygiene."

St. Paul's was larger than Groton (four hundred boys instead of two hundred) and drew more from the New York–Philadelphia Main Line axis than Boston's Brahmin families. In 1923, 199 students were from

New York and only 26 from Massachusetts. Among them was a boy whose family had lived in both states, Charles Eustis Bohlen, known at St. Paul's and for the rest of his life as "Chip."

St. Paul's and Groton, along with a few other High Church boarding schools in New England, offered those born into America's new industrial wealth, such as Harriman, an induction into the nation's aristocratic old boys' network. They also helped provide a proper place in this circle for the sons of the right sort of Episcopal clergymen, such as Acheson. But no less importantly, they permitted the sons of the old-line social gentry to retain their connection to the country's Establishment. The Bohlens were very much a part of this slightly frayed American upper class, a family of social distinction but somewhat less wealth. *

Chip Bohlen was born on August 30, 1904, at his family's home on Grindstone Island, in the St. Lawrence River near Clayton, New York. His father, also named Charles, had a modest but comfortable inheritance that allowed him to live graciously as a hunter, rider, sportsman, and "gentleman of leisure." He prided himself as a suave and gracious bon vivant—fond of strong drink, spirited horses, and the opera—and though his children often found his style a bit embarrassing, it rubbed off on each of them. Once during a trip to Paris with Chip, he caught the bouquet of violets tossed by Raquel Meller after her "La Violetera" solo, kissed them, and with a dramatic flair threw them back onstage.

Celestine Eustis Bohlen, Chip's mother, was eccentric, domineering, and charming. A member of one of the most distinguished families of New Orleans, she was raised in perhaps the grandest home in that city's Garden District. Her grandfather, a Massachusetts lawyer who migrated south in 1822, was chief justice of the Louisiana Supreme Court. Her father, James Biddle Eustis, was a Civil War hero and U.S. senator. When he was appointed in 1892 to be American envoy in Paris, a job that then held only the rank of minister, Eustis said he would accept only if it were upgraded. Thus he became the first American ambassador to France.

Because he was by then widowed, James Eustis took his daughter Celestine, known as "Tina," to serve as his official hostess in Paris. Her service in the embassy, combined with her Creole heritage, in-

---

*The Bohlens were descendants of John Bohlen, who migrated from Germany to Philadelphia with his brother Henry in 1790. Henry, who returned to Germany, had a grandson who married Germany's richest heiress, Bertha Krupp. Their son, Alfried Krupp von Bohlen und Halbach, was tried as a war criminal after World War II.

stilled in her an abiding love, bordering on infatuation, for France. She took her children there almost every year; Chip Bohlen remembered her pointing from the window of a Cherbourg–Paris train at a field of cows and saying: "You must admit that they are prettier than cows in America."

The Bohlens kept a winter residence in Aiken, South Carolina, a resort favored by wealthy northern families of the day. When Chip was twelve, they moved their main residence from Clayton to Ipswich, Massachusetts, north of Boston. At the Ipswich home, a rambling farmhouse surrounded by woods and streams, Mrs. Bohlen re-created the congenial hospitality of her childhood. Her husband became a gentlemanly fixture at the Myopia Hunt Club. Between their mother's natural grace and their father's relaxed outlook on life, the three Bohlen children developed a social ease that could charm both friends and elders.

Such qualities were to play an important role in making Chip Bohlen a consummate Foreign Service officer. By nature and breeding he was neither an incisive strategist nor a forceful advocate. His flair came from his easygoing and charismatic personality; his success came from his ability to gently guide the shifting framework of American policy as a respected member of the State Department's inner circle. With unbroken service as a Soviet expert to six administrations over forty years, he would come to embody the bipartisan consensus that dominated the postwar period.

At St. Paul's, Chip was overshadowed by his brother, Henry Morgan Bohlen, known as Buffy. Chip, a year younger, was by school custom designated as "Bohlen II." During his final year, Buffy won the school prize for "Greatest Distinction Jointly in Scholarship and Athletics." Chip that year played third-string club football and joined the radio club. His academic record was respectable but modest; he showed little interest in history, but did slightly better in science and math. In his Sixth Form, Chip finally made the football team; "from a rather mediocre player, he developed into a most useful and hardworking guard" was the limp praise of the school paper.

Despite Buffy's schoolboy success, he was in fact a quietly tormented boy who took to drink at college and killed himself shortly after graduation. Chip, for all his failings at St. Paul's, found early in life an inner balance. Instead of competing with Buffy, Chip dedicated himself to having fun, honing a devil-may-care attitude, and rebelling against Dr. Drury's pieties.

In the eyes of his masters, Bohlen II suffered from that most grievous

of schoolboy maladies, "bad attitude." Two months before graduation
it caught up with him. Bohlen and some friends were seen using an
inflated condom as a soccer ball, kicking it about the Upper School
courtyard. One of the masters identified Bohlen as the culprit. Off to
Dr. Drury he went. Drury, who sometimes knelt and prayed with
students who were being expelled, did not waste his prayers on Bohlen
before sending him packing.

It might seem curious that Acheson, Harriman, and Bohlen were
less than total successes as schoolboys. Acheson, in particular, was
thought of in later life as the epitome of a Grottie, regardless of how
Peabody felt at the time. But then, Churchill was a disaster at Harrow.
Those who became senior prefects at Groton and St. Paul's—solid,
stolid boys, square-shouldered fullbacks, reliable, unquestioning, and
loyal—quite often grew up to be respectable bankers and to pass the
plate on Sundays. It is not all that surprising that imaginative boys
with visions of broader vistas often did not take well to the rigid
conformities of life at high-toned church schools.

Expulsion from St. Paul's did not greatly disturb young Bohlen,
because Drury had refrained from exacting the ultimate punishment—
withdrawing his college recommendation. Bohlen was still free to go
to college, and for boys from Groton or St. Paul's in that era, college
meant Harvard, Yale, or Princeton. From 1906 to 1932, for example,
405 Groton boys applied to Harvard. Three were rejected. St. Paul's
had a similar track record. Bohlen, like his father and uncle and
brother, chose Harvard.

•   •   •

The first snow came early that fall to the ranch in Idaho, clinging
to the branches of the jack pines and falling on the young boys as
they cantered past. Like many of the games played at the Harriman
household, the horseback jousting could get rough. The object was
to grab the handkerchief looped around another boy's shoulders and
yank him out of his saddle. What most struck skinny Bob Lovett, he
later recounted, was that the older Harriman boy, on vacation from
Groton, wore neither jacket nor tarpaulin. Protected by only a large
V-necked sweater, Averell appeared not to notice as the wet snow hit
him in the neck and melted down his chest.

To Lovett, Harriman's ascetic qualities would seem, in later years,
to suggest a somewhat oblivious attitude, perhaps partly feigned, about
the world around him. While working together as partners on Wall
Street or helping to shape America's world role in the difficult early

days of the Cold War, the conscientious Lovett would learn to laugh at the headstrong Harriman's ability to seem more like a sovereign than a subject to the Presidents he served. But on that day at the Idaho ranch, as Lovett watched from afar, he recalls that he merely marveled at Harriman's casual hardiness and envied his cool indifference.

Lovett's first introduction to the Harriman family was a grandly befitting one: at a small way station in Texas in 1903, his father's private railway car was coupled onto E. H. Harriman's private train. The new boss of the Southern Pacific was making a tour of his realm, and he sought the counsel of the most respected railway lawyer in Texas. Judge Robert Scott Lovett, a successful and dignified attorney who had earned his honorific by a short stint on the Texas bench, was hired to handle Harriman's interests. Within three years he would move to New York as Harriman's chief counsel.

As the two men discussed business, young Bob, then eight, explored Harriman's elaborate private car with the magnate's younger son, Roland. Spying a parallel bar in the exercise cubicle, Bob began to show off his acrobatic skills, chinning himself a couple of times and ending with a whirl of giant swings. E. H. Harriman came in and watched. Turning to the somewhat pudgy Roland, he demanded: "Why can't you do that?"

Like Averell's father, young Bob's was a self-taught man. To support his family, R.S. Lovett had quit school at fifteen and taken a job as a station agent in Huntsville, Texas, on one of the lines that was eventually incorporated into the Southern Pacific. Most of his education came from visiting the rectory of a local Catholic church where he was informally tutored by a kindly priest. Later he read law in a Houston firm, served briefly as a state court judge, and at twenty-six became a member of the famous Houston firm of Baker and Botts.

Judge Lovett married a member of Huntsville's aristocracy, Lavinia Chilton Abercrombie, a daughter of a Confederate Army officer originally from Alabama. After attending Randolph-Macon College in Virginia, she became a teacher at the Peabody Normal School in Huntsville and was in the vanguard of the town's effort, not altogether successful, to become known as the "Athens of the South."

Their only child was born on September 14, 1895. Although the family moved to Houston shortly after his birth, Robert Abercrombie Lovett would later affect the style of a small-town Texan, even on occasion writing Huntsville as his residence in guest books and hotel registers. His mother, anxious that he respect the codes of chivalry of the old South, plied young Bob with romantic novels and histories of the Civil War. He learned from her an aversion to conflict and a respect for civility. Disputes were matters that ought to be hastily resolved. Other people, including his parents, should be addressed as "sir" or "madam."

The elder Lovett cultivated in his boy an attention to detail, observation, and factual organization. After they moved to New York in 1906, Bob bicycled between their home on Central Park West and the Hamilton Military Institute where he attended grammar school. His father would ride to work along the same route and question Bob each evening about the sights along the way. "How many horses were pulling the cart?" he would ask about a midtown construction project. "How many girders were in the cart?" "How were the horses hitched to the cart?" Bob was rewarded or penalized a quarter depending on the accuracy of his answers.

Rigorous intellectual discipline was also demanded by the Hamilton Institute, where the curriculum included drilling by a military master who had served with the Queen's Guards. In spite of, or perhaps because of, his rigid training, Lovett developed a wry sense of humor. His enigmatic but warm half smile, when combined with his quiet courtliness, endeared him both to his contemporaries and their parents, and provided the foundation for what was to be his greatest strength in later life: a winning ability to defuse personal tensions.

Tall and slender, with hooded dark eyes and a full, almost feminine mouth, Lovett was strikingly handsome. He possessed an inner security, a genial warmth that made him comfortable with himself and with others. It allowed him to enjoy being off on his own; when he traveled with his father on long excursions he often dropped off in Wyoming or Colorado to enjoy a week of solitary fishing. Yet he also formed easy boyhood bonds with friends in both Manhattan and near Woodfold, his parents' country estate in Locust Valley, Long Island. Along with the Harriman boys and other young men from fashionable families, he was an avid member of the Knickerbocker Greys, a kind of upper-crust Boy Scout troop replete with military ranks and uniforms.

Like E. H. Harriman, Judge Lovett used to take his young son on inspection tours of the railways. On one such trip, a man flagged down their car and pleaded for help. His baby, he said, was suffering from seizures in a shack near the tracks. As the older men pondered the child's plight, Bob diagnosed the problem and insisted on administering an enema. The cure worked. Lovett thus gained a lifelong reputation of being a frustrated doctor: from then on he eagerly diagnosed ailments and prescribed cures for reluctant friends from the bottles of medicine he invariably carried on his travels. He was, himself, a confirmed hypochondriac, a condition partly vindicated by a recurring array of actual health problems throughout his life.

Bob often traveled with the Harrimans to their fishing camp at Klamath Lake in Oregon or to the Railroad Ranch the Lovetts and Harrimans had bought in Idaho. He was also a frequent weekend visitor to Arden. To him the rambling estate was a wondrous oasis, filled with such friends as the Harriman boys, Norman Reed, and Charles "Pat" Rumsey (who later married Mary Harriman). A particular favorite was Mrs. Harriman, whom Lovett later called "the epitome of charm and beauty." Together the polite young man and the formidable grand dame would play backgammon in the parlor at Arden. In Manhattan Bob would call on her after school even when her children were away.

After E. H. Harriman died in 1909, Judge Lovett not only took over the chairmanship of the Union Pacific, he also handled Mrs. Harriman's legal affairs and helped groom Averell to take over the railroads. During the summers Mrs. Harriman would move her whole household out to the Idaho ranch. She and Bob once took a cross-country train trip together, sitting up late every night talking and playing two-handed bridge. Along the way she bought a memento for him, a large piece of petrified wood that she had sawed in half to make matching paperweights for the two of them. In later years, while he was Under Secretary of State and later Secretary of Defense, it was accorded a prominent place on his desk.

As a boy, Bob Lovett tended to view Averell Harriman, who was four years older, from a respectful distance. In any game they played, Harriman was not only naturally better, but was also more determined to be better. Lovett, on the other hand, was far more studious. He seemed to have an inner security and confident outlook that allowed him to genuinely enjoy his schooling, to excel without either embarrassment or grinding effort. Nor did his parents see any reason to send him to one of the rigidly disciplined and potentially stultifying church schools in New England. Instead they chose The Hill School, near Philadelphia, which was more distinguished academically than it was socially.

The Hill's headmaster, John Meigs, shared the piety of Peabody and Drury, but he was not a minister; his field was modern languages and his training was as a teacher. Nor was he burdened by the stiff style of most New England headmasters. The school history notes that he had "exuberance, infectious humor, and an often stinging wit." One of Lovett's classmates wrote a school newspaper editorial that would have been considered heresy at Groton: "Last week the seeds of iconoclasm were sown at the YMCA meeting. The time was ripe for it. Bible classes were assailed for their sluggishness and enough argument was instilled to make it spirited instead of dry."

Lovett, who for a time picked up the nickname "Jake," was the outstanding boy of his class. "Born for success he seemed," said his senior yearbook. He was head of his form academically from his first year until his last. Those with top marks were excused from midyear exams, and Lovett regularly used the exemption to travel with his father inspecting the Union Pacific system.

His other activities included being yearbook business manager, a cheerleader, and a skinny but accomplished tumbler on the gym team. As an avid thespian, Lovett co-founded the school's Shakespeare Club (for which his father endowed a theater) and performed in *The Merchant of Venice*, *Twelfth Night*, and *A Midsummer Night's Dream*. Of the eighty-six boys who graduated from The Hill in 1914, more than half went to Yale, among them Lovett.

CHAPTER 2

Lovett, seated left, in Skull and Bones

TAP DAYS

"To run with the swift"

Anna May Snader McCloy, the strong-willed daughter of a proud but poor Pennsylvania Dutch family, had one major goal in her life: making sure that her sole surviving son became part of the world of wealth and power that she admired from her vantage as a hairdresser. Her husband had died of heart failure at age thirty-nine, shortly before the boy's sixth birthday. Her other son had died of diphtheria five months later. From that day on, she devoted her considerable energies to the two tasks that her acute social instincts told her would ensure her son's advancement: getting him a good education and seeing that he met the right people.

Few mothers have ever been more successful. John McCloy eventually came to be considered the leading embodiment of the East Coast's inner circle, a "Chairman of the Board of the American Establishment." Throughout his life, he would rankle at the notion that he was an Establishment archetype, noting time and again that he had been "born on the wrong side of the tracks." In fact, however, he was one of the best examples of that most salient feature of America's social structure: that its upper echelon admits not only those born into it, but also those with talent who are eager to accept its cultivating process.

The Philadelphia neighborhood where McCloy was born on March 31, 1895, was actually north of Market Street, and thus on the "right" side of the city's tracks. But back then, North 19th Street was a drab working-class area with few social pretensions. He was baptized John Snader McCloy, his name taken from a brother of his mother. McCloy liked neither the uncle nor the name; years later, as he was about to embark on his career, he would adopt the name John Jay McCloy, Jr., in honor of his father.

The senior John McCloy, a staunch Presbyterian of Scotch-Irish descent, left behind little money and no insurance when he died, even though he had worked for nineteen years as a claims officer for the Penn Mutual Life Insurance Company. When an official of that company years later mailed him a picture of his father as a young man, McCloy replied that "it all gave me a very strange feeling, inasmuch as I knew so little about him." The company also sent McCloy a copy of a letter his father had written about a person who had been refused life insurance because of a heart murmur. "My mother tells me that he himself had endeavored to get insurance with the company, but his own heart condition stood in the way," McCloy replied. "When he talks about the soft and low murmurs surging through a laboring heart, I am quite sure he was thinking a little about himself and so spoke sympathetically of the turned down applicant."

To avoid the drab fate that usually befell penniless widows and their children at that time, Anna McCloy learned home nursing and massage techniques, visiting neighbors and friends to conduct her trade. She also built up her hairdressing business, "doing heads," as McCloy liked to put it, at fifty cents apiece. She often took her son along to meet her rich clients, who included the town's foremost lawyers and their wives. To save money, Anna set up house with her two maiden sisters, Sadie, who earned money as a milliner, and young Lena, who did the housework, looked after Jack, and saved her nickels to take him on trips to the circus and the zoo.

Above all, Anna McCloy was a proud woman. One wealthy businessman whose family she worked for was particularly impressed by her beauty and strength. When his wife died, he proposed marriage and offered to adopt John as his son and heir. There was one condition: John would have to change his last name. Anna said she would prefer to keep "doing heads."

The streets of Philadelphia offered carefree joys not all that different from those Acheson found in Middletown. In a speech to the Pennsylvania Club in 1948, McCloy recalled:

Life for small boys was most intriguing. There was the reservoir, down whose very steep approaches you could sled on snowy days if only you had the nerve to accept the awful chance of hitting a horse and buggy or ice wagon on Corinthian Avenue. Brewery town, in whose stables were the brewers' big horses, was not far away. Only a relatively short way out Fairmont Avenue was the park itself, with the trolley, the zoo, the views of the destruction of Pompeii left from the Centennial Exposition, and railroad tracks with standing freight cars and other attractive nuisances to deal with. We were chased from time to time by what we called railroad dicks, always more exciting to run from than mere cops.

The summer jobs that Anna chose for her son were designed to expand his contacts as well as help pay family expenses. Through her wealthy Philadelphia clients, she was able to get work for him as a chore boy at the fashionable resorts and camps of the Adirondacks. He did everything from delivering dairy products to cleaning bathrooms. By toting milk and ice with a shoulder yoke and wagon, he developed into a strapping boy. Soon he had taken responsibility for maintaining the tennis courts at many of the camps and serving as a volleying partner for the better players.

Having learned his mother's lessons well, Jack began lining up work tutoring the children of the families he met and coaching them in tennis. The powerful lawyers and judges in Philadelphia (George Wharton Pepper, Matthew Stanley Quay, Boies Penrose, Samuel Pennypacker) became his heroes and the subject of dinner-table discussions; McCloy would spend as much time as possible with them during the summers, quietly yet persistently grilling them about their work.

Even more important to Anna was her son's education. The senior McCloy had dropped out of high school but had taught himself to read Latin and worked with a friend on a translation of Vergil's *Aeneid*. His greatest regret was not knowing other languages. On his deathbed he told Anna: "Have John learn Greek." His other wish was that his son become a lawyer.

Fearful that continuing at public school while living home with his aunts would not provide a sufficiently manly challenge, she saved enough money to send him to an inexpensive but rigorous Quaker school called Maplewood, then to The Peddie School in New Jersey, near Princeton. When McCloy enrolled in 1907, Peddie still catered to boys of moderate means and retained many of its traditional ties to the Baptist Church. But the atmosphere was far freer than at Maplewood. Recalls McCloy: "I found you could raise your voice and talk out loud in the world."

McCloy got excellent grades, was noted for his forceful writing style, and became fascinated by the glory of ancient Greece. For the rest of his life, he viewed the ultimate goal of public service to be re-creating a "Periclean Age." In his final year he captured the school's Hiram Deats Greek Prize (the award: five dollars). He also became a favorite of the athletic coach, a man named John Plant, who taught the stocky yet quick young man to excel in football and tennis. Plant's exhortation, "Run with the swift," became one of McCloy's favorite phrases. "Being at Peddie taught me how important it was to run with the swift," he later said, "to work with people who were better than I."

Throughout his life, he retained this genuinely humble awe about those he called the swift, the people he worked with who somehow seemed "better." In his own mind, at least, there was always a bit of the chore boy in his nature. He became known as a man who could get things done, who never caused a stir, who could handle inordinate amounts of work, who could edge people toward a consensus without making them feel manipulated. Whether as a top official at the War Department, High Commissioner for Germany, or president of the World Bank, he was most comfortable when keeping a low profile. His immense influence came not because he had an outspoken ideology or an overt political agenda; rather, it grew out of his ability to make the people he dealt with think each idea was their own. Because he was an expert at avoiding trouble for others, the word "trusted" always seemed attached to his name. Because he was a good listener, one who could guide decisions without noisy infighting, Jack McCloy was considered the consummate wise man.

• • •

On the strength of both his academic and athletic record at Peddie, McCloy won a scholarship to Amherst, where he matriculated in 1912. While there he began his unusual lifelong habit of staging "reading debates" for himself: he would choose books on a certain topic but with different viewpoints and read them concurrently. Philosophy and history were his greatest academic interests. He was a dogged student, not naturally brilliant but endowed with a stolid, reliable intellect. Friends compared his academic approach to his style on the tennis court, where he was a hard-driving though hardly graceful player always eager to rush the net. Although he was graduated cum laude, to his deep disappointment (and that of his mother) he just missed making Phi Beta Kappa.

His best friend was Lewis Williams Douglas, the raffish son of "Rawhide Jim" Douglas, a man who had made a fortune as a miner in Arizona. Lew Douglas went on to become a congressman, Franklin Roosevelt's budget director, and Harry Truman's ambassador to the Court of St. James's. The two were oddly matched: Douglas had an engaging diffidence; McCloy, an intense desire to conform. McCloy's favorite recreation was to take long hikes, often alone, through the Holyoke mountains; Douglas, on the other hand, preferred chasing the girls of Smith College, which he did with notable success. Using a colloquial term for womanizing, the 1916 yearbook noted: "Jack McCloy and Lew Douglas hold the two ends of the fussing record."

Two of the women who used to visit Douglas from Smith were the Zinsser sisters, Peggy (whom Douglas soon married) and Ellen (whom McCloy married years later). Neither of the young women, however, remembered meeting McCloy at Amherst. Douglas joined the high-toned Alpha Delta Phi fraternity; McCloy, by waiting on tables, was able to afford only Beta Theta Pi, which was then far less opulent. Yet the two young men became close and fast friends at college, and as brothers-in-law remained fly-fishing buddies and professional associates until Douglas's death in 1974.

While Jack was at Amherst, Anna McCloy decided that the best way to broaden her son's circle was for him to spend vacations in the affluent resort communities along the coast of Maine. At her insistence, McCloy knocked on doors of the great estates, as he had done in the Adirondacks, to arrange jobs teaching history, sailing, and tennis to the young boys there. "Part of my mother's genius was to get me a good summer," he said years later. "I remember very well the day she made me work up the nerve to ring the doorbell at Seal Harbor, where the Rockefeller estate was, and try to get a tutoring job with their children. I got turned down, but I did teach them a little sailing." In his later career as a Wall Street lawyer, he handled the personal affairs of the Rockefeller family.

With the war in Europe under way, the Amherst campus split into the "pacifists" and the "militarists." McCloy and Douglas were firmly in the latter camp, steadfastly defending in late-night bull sessions the need for American preparedness. They were among the first to enlist in the Plattsburg movement, the fledgling reserve officers' training camp set up in Plattsburg, New York, and eventually around the country. "It seemed to me that all the right people went," McCloy later recalled. While there, he distinguished himself as a marksman, winning top honors at the camp during the summer of 1915 and tying with Douglas (each scoring 448 out of a possible 450) in 1916.

· · ·

Harvard Law School represented the pinnacle of Anna McCloy's dreams, and hence those of her son. It was indisputably the foremost law school of the time, and its dean, Roscoe Pound, the nation's greatest legal scholar. Teaching was largely done through the Socratic method, in which professors prodded their students with questions and dialogue, and courses were built around case studies, in which legal theory was explored through concrete examples of important cases. Most important, from McCloy's standpoint, the institution was a meritocracy; grades, not social standing, counted. For a poor boy struggling to succeed, it was the perfect ticket to the top.

McCloy was elated when he was admitted to the school, and he enrolled in the fall of 1916 after leaving Plattsburg with a commission of second lieutenant in the Army reserve. America's entry into the war, however, presented him with a dilemma. His mother strongly felt that he should do everything possible to finish his studies before joining active service. But because he had argued so strongly in favor of the cause, he felt uncomfortable not enlisting. So at the end of his first year, he left Harvard to become a second lieutenant in the regular Army at Fort Ethan Allen in Vermont.

His commanding officer was General Guy Preston, a salty caval-ryman who had fought at the Battle of Wounded Knee, where the Sioux Indians made their final stand in 1890. Still lean and flagpole straight, Preston had organized an artillery regiment, noting that he had no trouble making the transition from the cavalry because "I learned what a trajectory was while pissing against the schoolhouse wall." McCloy's meager agility as a horseman indirectly led him to be plucked from the ranks and made a staff aide to the general. "One day at Fort Ethan Allen, I walked behind you after you had been riding and I could see blood all over your pants," Preston later recalled to McCloy, with whom he corresponded until his death in the 1950s. "I said to myself that any son of a bitch who could keep riding with that much pain must be a damn good officer."

Preston and his field artillery regiment, with McCloy as the chief operations officer, arrived on the western front in France shortly before the armistice. Positioned on the Moselle River, they spent a few weeks in isolated skirmishes with enemy artillery and were preparing for an assault on the town of Metz when the war ended.

Upon their return in August of 1919, Preston tried to convince McCloy to take a permanent commission. But McCloy was already back to reading his lawbooks. "One evening McCloy came to eat with me at my camp table in the mess hall," Preston recalled years later. "I saw he was preoccupied. Finally he exclaimed, 'General, that abstract law is beautiful stuff!' I glanced at him and saw his face was radiant as an angel's. I said at once, 'Mac, I'll never again ask you to stay in this man's army. Your destiny is too manifest.'" At age twenty-four, McCloy returned to Cambridge for his final two years at Harvard Law.

"The courses were wonderful, and I got caught up in the flavor, the excitement of the law school when I returned," McCloy later recalled. Professor Joseph Beale, known for his textbooks on civil damages and federal taxation, gave him particular encouragement. The clarity of his thought was excellent, the professor noted, although his writing style lacked elegance. He was able to stay near the top of his class, but to his chagrin he barely missed making *Law Review*. "I had to run as fast as I could to keep up," McCloy remembers. "I worked as hard as I knew how to work."

His mother was still an ever-present force in his life; she even moved to Cambridge so that she could share an apartment with him while he completed law school.* Her savings and earnings as a hairdresser helped supplement McCloy's scholarship, and he earned extra money teaching handball and squash. The financial burden seemed especially difficult after a heady year commanding troops. He felt older, more experienced, than the other students, and certainly not inclined to be distracted by social frivolities.

The prospect of returning to Philadelphia, where few jobs were waiting, also seemed unexciting. Upon graduation, he instead headed for Wall Street. "I knew the pace would be thrilling there," he remembers. "I knew that was where I would have a chance to run with the swift."

· · ·

---

*Franklin Roosevelt, Woodrow Wilson, and Douglas MacArthur also had mothers who followed them to college to help take care of them. Anna McCloy lived to be ninety-three, later moved in with her son in Georgetown, and often traveled with him on his trips throughout the world after he became successful.

He was a shy boy of moderate means from a family of modest social stature. Yet despite his background, or perhaps because of it, George Kennan became entranced with F. Scott Fitzgerald's romantic portrayal of a young Midwestern boy caught in the Gothic and glamorous swirl of Old Nassau in the early part of the century. "From the first he loved Princeton," Fitzgerald wrote of his hero, Amory Blaine, in *This Side of Paradise*, "its lazy beauty, its half-grasped significance, the wild moonlight revel of the rushes, the handsome, prosperous big-game crowds, and under it all the air of struggle that pervaded his class." During his senior year at military school, Kennan read the novel avidly. Even though no other boy from his school was going east for college, Kennan resolved that he too would break into the world of power and prominence by enrolling in Princeton.

As America entered a new competitive era, the right college education became as important as birth or prep schools in determining a person's social status. The top colleges, and in particular Harvard, Yale, and Princeton, began to be regarded (and regard themselves) as great national institutions, important rungs on the American ladder. Young men who attended them, particularly those tapped for the right clubs, felt graced, as if they had been singled out in the quickening race. College spirit flourished, and the school ties that bound Old Blues or Princetonians were at least as strong as those formed by survival at Groton or St. Paul's.

Like McCloy, Kennan had a lifelong fascination with what he considered the American elite. And though Princeton would turn out to be, as he noted in his memoirs, "not exactly the sort of experience reflected in *This Side of Paradise*," it served to pluck Kennan from the obscurity of his background and set him on his way to becoming the most celebrated product of America's Foreign Service and the designated intellectual within the postwar policy Establishment.

Yet unlike McCloy, Kennan had tortuously conflicted feelings about being tapped to be part of the American elite. Whenever he seemed about to meld comfortably into the American Establishment, be it at Princeton or in Washington, he would resolutely cast himself as an outsider, deriving an almost perverse pleasure from the stings and slights that can befall those who neither fully accept nor reject its embrace. Deeply insecure, he would alternate between yearning for acceptance and acting diffident. He claimed to relish the role of outsider, but it was important for him to be an outsider from within, a person who liked to think that he was continually miscast. "To the extent that I was accepted among those in the Establishment, it was in the role they decided to cast for me, rather than because of who I really was," he reflected at age eighty from one of the leather armchairs of the Century Association clubhouse in Manhattan. "I like to think, too, that this was my own choice."

Even as a child, George Frost Kennan had felt a sense of isolation. He was born in Milwaukee on February 16, 1904, the only son of Kossuth Kent Kennan and Florence James Kennan. Two months later, his mother suddenly died. His father, then fifty-two, had little talent for providing youthful love or companionship. His work as a tax lawyer (he formulated Wisconsin's state income tax, the first in the nation, and wrote two books on the subject) generally kept him secluded in the dark study of the rambling Kennan home. "He had a way of churning his teeth together so you could see the muscle, sort of suppressing things," George recalled many years later. He perceived his father as a "shy, lonely and not very happy person," and was able to communicate with him mainly by "bashful sidelong glances."

Nor did George receive much parental love from his stepmother, Louise Wheeler, a teacher from Ripon College whom his father married when George was five. "I don't think she was capable of deep affection," Kennan later recalled. One of his earliest memories is of her severely punishing him when, after watching some other little boys urinating in a lavatory, he cut a slit in his own trousers because they had no fly. From then on, as he was growing up, he felt acutely uncomfortable about his stepmother seeing him even partly undressed. Despite his interest in music, his stepmother forbade him to play the family piano. Yet she pampered her own son, Kent Wheeler Kennan (who later became an accomplished musician), with private lessons.

Although later prone to the ailments that accompany a dolorous disposition, Kennan was a strapping young boy. Yet he was not aggressive, and in fact he was often accused of being a sissy. Once when he got into an argument with another boy, the two were taken to a yard to fight it out. Kennan and his similarly timid antagonist revolved around each other for so long without throwing any punches that the other boys finally called off the fight.

When Kennan was eight, his father took the family on a six-month trip to Germany. They lived in Kassel, where the elder Kennan worked on a tax book. With an apparently natural facility for language, George was speaking German quite respectably by the time he left. In a letter to his father, who had returned home a few weeks earlier than the rest of the family, George revealed his first career interest. "May I join the Navy when I grow up?" he asked.

For the most part, Kennan was raised by his three older sisters, Jeannette, Frances, and Constance. As he said in his intensely confessional *Memoirs*: "I lived, particularly in childhood but with lessening intensity right on to middle age, in a world that was peculiarly and intimately my own, scarcely to be shared with others or even made plausible to them."

It was a childhood far removed from the secure world of a Harriman or a Lovett, one that seemed to engender emotional extremes. "My behavior knew only two moods: awkward aloofness and bubbling enthusiasm," Kennan noted in his *Memoirs*. Actually, there were many more moods, many more conflicts. His character contained a curious blend of arrogance and insecurity, haughtiness and self-pity, sensitivity and coldness, assertiveness and shyness. He would grow into a tormented romantic who liked to view himself as a cold intellectual pragmatist, one who felt, as he later wrote, "a guest of one's time and not a member of its household."

• • •

Kennan attributed much of his conflicted personality to his ancestry. In an unsent letter to his two daughters in 1942, written to be delivered in case of his death, Kennan described his mother's side of the family as "utterly lacking in sentimentality" and his father's side as having "an ugly tendency toward it." Both sides were "extremists" in their own way, he said, with a "tendency to shyness and introversion." He took a great interest in exploring his own genealogy, and in 1961 wrote his children a fifteen-page letter detailing his findings. "That heredity does play a part second to none in making us what we are, no one would deny," he told them. "I find it a source of strength to picture myself as part of a continuity."

The Kennans had come to New England from Scotland by way of Ireland in the early 1700s. James McKennan, the first direct ancestor to arrive, settled in the Massachusetts Bay colony, shortened his name, and had ten children. Most of his descendants were farmers or Presbyterian ministers. As George Kennan later wrote to his daughters: "None took the easy path of picturing themselves as downtrodden. None threw themselves on the charity of others. It is this middle ground they managed to preserve—between the humiliation of selling one's labor to others and the moral discomfort of having others in one's employ—to which I often felt indebted when I grappled with the problems of Marxism."

Thomas Lathrop Kennan, George's grandfather, moved west to buy a farm in Wisconsin and eventually became a lawyer in Milwaukee. (He was a descendant of Elder Brewster, of the Mayflower Company, but George Kennan cautioned his children against false pride: "For every *Mayflower* ancestor we could probably find a hundred ne'er-do-wells in the family tree.") As a tax and estate lawyer who dabbled in real estate, Thomas became the first Kennan to make money. He built an ornate stone house on Prospect Street and settled into a life of Victorian pretension.

Kennan's father was named after the famous Hungarian freedom fighter Lajos Kossuth, who visited Milwaukee during a tour of the U.S. in 1851. Kossuth Kent Kennan, known generally as Kent, worked his way through Ripon College, studied law while working for the Wisconsin Central Railway, and traveled through Europe recruiting laborers for the railroad. While there, he learned to speak German, French, and Dutch. He became an ardent admirer of German music and theater, which he helped support in Milwaukee, and collected a fine library from which he spent long evenings reading aloud to his family.

After a childless first marriage, Kossuth married Florence James. Her father, Alfred James, had run away at age thirteen and shipped out on a whaler for New Bedford. He spent several years before the mast, rounding the Horn of Africa twice before returning to Illinois. He left to his grandchildren a privately printed leather-bound account of his adventures. George, who read it many times as a child, attributed to his grandfather his own love of the sea and "the rebellious pride which seems to crop up in us from time to time."

One of the most influential relatives in Kennan's life was a man he met only once. As a young schoolboy, he traveled with his father to Medina, New York, to visit a cousin of George's grandfather, a man also named George Kennan. Born in Ohio in 1845, the elder George Kennan had at age twenty explored Alaska and Siberia for a telegraph company and written a popular book called *Tent Life in Siberia*. After becoming famous as a journalist and lecturer, he set out in 1885 to visit Siberian prisons and the czarist camps. The resulting articles appeared in *Century Magazine* and were subsequently published as a two-volume book, *Siberia and the Exile System*. By exposing the cruelties of the Russian autocracy, the pieces made the elder George Kennan the first bearer of that name to be declared persona non grata in Russia. Shortly before his death, in 1923, he completed a laudatory two-volume biography of E. H. Harriman.

During his stay with his distinguished relative, the younger George Kennan became fascinated by Russia. He enviously eyed the various artifacts in the home. But the visit was not without tension. Young George was somewhat sulky and petulant, especially toward the elder George Kennan's wife. She and her husband were childless; their only son, who had also been named George Kennan, died in infancy. She resented the young usurper of the name, and worried that her husband might bequeath him some of his treasures. After two days, there was an argument, and the Kennans from Wisconsin were asked to leave.

Kennan never saw his distant cousin again, but he noted in his memoirs "the feeling that we are connected in some curious way by bonds deeper than just our rather distant kinship." The two George Kennans were, each in his own way, loners and skeptics, men who came to their own highly personal conclusions about the Russian people and their rulers. "There was in both Kennans," says Harrison Salisbury, "a cranky, against-the-grain quality."

• • •

Fearful of the feminine influence in his household, Kennan's father sent him to St. John's Military Academy, a small, rigorous school twenty-four miles west of Milwaukee. Kennan was deeply unhappy there, writing forlorn letters to his sisters about the discipline, the loneliness, and the spartan life. "I learned then that I was not cut out for the military," he later recalled. His chief distinction at the school was as "class poet" in his final year. The yearbook's assessment of his character was, certainly in retrospect, remarkably insightful. It notes: "Disposition—vacillating" and "Pet peeve—the universe." Kennan was an avid reader (he spent vacations at home in a small room in the attic poring through shelves of old books) and averaged about 90 percent in his English studies. His math and science grades, however, often dipped below 60 percent.

Kennan nevertheless decided, spurred by his headmaster and F. Scott Fitzgerald, that he was destined for Princeton. After flunking two of his college entrance exams, in Latin and math, he was drilled by Jeannette in preparation for retaking the tests. He passed them only after he arrived in Princeton, and was the last boy to matriculate in the fall of 1921.

Because he had enrolled late, Kennan had to settle for a room far from the campus. In addition, he was afflicted, as he wrote in his memoirs, by "being the slowest and last to learn the ropes in any complicated organizational structure. Too shy to ask, I never found out."

After an orientation lecture during the first week at Princeton, Kennan turned to another boy and asked the time. Taking a drag of his cigarette, the student blew the smoke in Kennan's face and walked away. "This little touch, it just seared me," Kennan recalled more than fifty years later.

Unwilling to ask his father for the money to return home for Christmas, he took a job his first year as a mail carrier in Trenton. There he caught scarlet fever. It was in the days before penicillin, and his frightened father banished George's sisters from the house while George was recuperating. When he returned to Princeton later in the spring, friendships and social groups had already formed; the shy and naïve Midwesterner had his propensity for being a loner involuntarily reinforced.

At Princeton, clubs totally dominated undergraduate life. Social status was rigidly determined by the ranking of one's eating club. At the top of the hierarchy was Ivy, "breathlessly aristocratic" in Fitzgerald's breathless description; when Ivy took in only eleven men in a year, a bitter sophomore complained, "Even Jesus Christ took twelve." At the bottom of the heap were the clubs that had to scrape to fill their sections. Non-club members were virtual lepers.

During bicker week of Kennan's sophomore year, he avoided campus "in a veritable transport of false pride" lest he be invited into a club. When he was finally asked by an acquaintance to join one that had not yet been able to fill its quota, the now-defunct Key and Seal, Kennan cried and accepted. In his memoirs he writes of having "pangs of conscience about the decision," and he says that he resigned shortly afterward. In fact, his letters of the time reveal that the pangs were more pecuniary. "Am enclosing the receipt for the check you just sent," he wrote his father in May of his sophomore year. "I hope I can make it go for the rest of the term. I certainly let myself into something when I joined this club—but it's the social thing."

Kennan worried that if he quit his club he would embarrass his roommate and cousin from Milwaukee, Charles James. After meticulously itemizing his expenses (among them: tuition, $175; books, $20; laundry, $25; trips, $15; club, $40), Kennan admitted to his father that he could drop the club, but fretted: "I would hate to do that, though, as it might throw a sort of social stigma on Charles, to be rooming with a non-club man." For a while Kennan was "assistant manager" of the club, which meant that he worked in the office in return for a reduction in his bills. Finally, when his money ran out, he was forced to quit and eat "among the non-club pariahs" in a gloomy refectory known as Upperclass Commons.

College, especially as a non-club member, was a lonely and scarring experience for Kennan, one that heightened his sense of alienation. He had few acquaintances other than Charles (Andover, varsity soccer team, Quadrangle Club) and his friends, who were two years younger. Still smitten by the romantic vision of Fitzgerald, Kennan read *The Great Gatsby* while in college and wept at the epilogue's description of the Midwesterner's reaction to the fashionable East.

One of the few friends Kennan made on his own was a boy named Constantine Messolonghitis, an Ohio waif who tried for one year to work his way through Princeton after transferring from Kenyon. He convinced a nervous Kennan to spend a summer scrounging through Europe. In London, Kennan (who at that time was dreaming of becoming a lawyer) spent his time hanging around the Royal Courts of Justice at Temple Bar; in Italy, he developed dysentery and had to ask sister Frances to wire him money to come home.

Kennan was particularly ill at ease with women. At St. John's, he had worried about adolescent homosexual stirrings. From afar he had admired an older boy on the basketball team whom he thought "terribly good-looking, physically attractive." He later recalled: "Had I remained in an all-male environment any longer, I like all of us would have developed homosexual tendencies simply because of the lack of other objects." At college, although attracted to women, he found it impossible to overcome his painful awkwardness; he was envious of the sexual success his acquaintances bragged about.

His sister Frances, who had become a struggling actress, was living a bohemian life with a group of young women in Greenwich Village. Kennan used to enjoy going to visit them and sleeping on their couch. One night Frances brought home a friend with the unlikely name of Puritan, "thinking that I ought to have a girl." Far less happened than was hoped. "I wasn't prepared to go to these lengths yet," Kennan later recalled in an interview. "I just idealized women so, you know." Afterward he wrote Puritan a passionate love letter. Her response was cool.

Despite his later reputation as a prescient analyst, Kennan did not have a great innate intellect. Even those who would come to respect his reports and judgment often privately noted that he showed little native brilliance and in fact sometimes seemed surprisingly obtuse. At Princeton, his grades bordered on the abysmal. The academic marks there ranged from 1 ("very high") to 5 ("very low"). At the end of his first year, he got 5s in physics and history, a 4 in English, and 3s in Latin and French.

Partly this was due to his freshman illness and the limpness of his St. John's preparation. He was also far from adept at charming his professors. "You will probably get a flunk notice saying that my standing in Economics 302 is now below standard, but don't be worried about it," he wrote home. "My instructor is notoriously about the worst in college and I can't help arguing with him sometimes." Yet Kennan continued to get 4s, even in a senior-year history course. "You had better wait until I have found out whether I passed my exams before sending the money," he wrote his father at the beginning of his final year. "They have no compunctions about dropping people here."

Not until his senior year did he achieve a couple of 1s, in politics and economics. That year he did a short (and poorly written) paper for an international law class that he sent home with the proud comment that it had scored highly. It analyzed the laws designating legal domiciles, and it seemed to reflect his own growing unsureness about where he could call home. He described the class to his father: "Most of the students believe the only ultimate international law is force, while Prof. Brown claims that the law we study is definitely sanctioned by what he calls the 'anticipated advantages of sovereignty.'"

The 1925 Princeton class book has a poll with forty-seven categories, such as "best-looking" and "most studious." It lists anyone who got as few as three votes in any of the categories, which in some cases amounts to thirty or more names. Kennan is unmentioned in any of the groups. "I may have been the most undistinguished student Princeton ever had," he recalled years later after he had returned there to work at the Institute for Advanced Study and serve on the university's board. "I was certainly the least memorable." Princeton, however, left its mark on him. As he would later note, "Sometimes it is the moody, unadjusted student, struggling to forge his own standards in a callous collegiate society, who develops within himself the thoughtfulness to comprehend a foreign environment."

Kennan's early letters home expressed a desire to follow in his father's footsteps as a lawyer, but he came to realize that he had neither the money nor the grades to enroll in law school. He toyed with the idea of trying to find outdoor work, having enjoyed the invigoration and solitude of crewing on a cargo boat one summer. Another option he considered was joining a corporation such as General Electric.

The class book notes little next to Kennan's name except that his intended occupation was "unknown."

• • •

The unabashed elitism that pervaded East Coast campuses in the years before World War I was particularly prevalent at Yale, where Harriman and Acheson headed after graduating from Groton and Lovett went after finishing at The Hill School. College was a business for the true Yale man. One did not simply attend; one had a "career" there, with a ladder to be climbed and immense prestige for those who reached the top. Students were measured by what they did "for Yale" in student organizations, publications—and especially on the playing fields.

"For a brief time at the beginning of this century," wrote one historian, "the close-knit, intimate world of the American gentry fixed in the drama of intercollegiate athletics, particularly those of Yale, Harvard and Princeton, all the limited but quite genuine idealism of their romantic culture." As Yale football coach T. A. D. Jones told his charges: "Gentlemen, today you play Harvard. Never again will you do anything so important."

Scholarship was a lesser measure. "Now you've got to do a certain amount of studying here," an upperclassman warns Dick Stover in Owen Johnson's 1911 novel *Stover at Yale*. "Better do it in the first year and get in with the faculty."

In some ways, the pressure at Yale to conform and perform was as great as that exerted by Peabody. Yale spirit was referred to as "sand." Placed under the wheels of a locomotive, it made the train go. "Sand" was grit, determination, persistence, reliability.

Although Yale boasted of its democracy, the Class of 1913 was still virtually all-white, conservative, and well-off. Prep schools supplied 61 percent of the class (until the 1960s, a majority of Yale undergraduates came from private boarding schools), and some 20 percent were the sons of Yale men. A class poll done during the election of 1912 showed 111 students for Republican Taft, 74 for Democrat Wilson, and 34 for Progressive Roosevelt.

As a way to get ahead, and as a means of self-defense, Yale men joined organizations, scores of them. There were clubs for singers (such as the legendary Whiffenpoofs and its half-dozen farm teams), clubs for scholars, clubs for mandolin players, clubs for wits, clubs for drinkers, clubs for believers, clubs for achievers. Stephen Vincent

Benet, '19, wrote a ditty with the refrain: "Do you want to be successful?/Form a club!/Are your chances quite distressful?/Form a club!"

Membership in a senior society was the capstone of a successful Yale career. The oldest and greatest, indeed the most legendary of all college clubs, was Skull and Bones. To be tapped by Bones in that era was akin to canonization, and its prestige was enhanced by its secrecy. Members—fifteen seniors, typically two or three of the major sports captains, the editor of the *Lit*, the chairman of the *News*, and other such Big Men—did not even mention the society's name in public. When nonmembers dared to breathe the words, self-serious Bonesmen would leave the room. Underclassmen were afraid to be caught even looking at Bones's "tomb," the windowless Egyptian-style mausoleum on High Street guarded by a massive oak door with oversized padlocks.

Skull and Bones had a wealth of hocus-pocus ritual, but it was hardly a frivolous fraternity; no liquor was consumed inside the building, and the clocks were set five minutes fast to symbolize that Bonesmen started life a leg up. In the inner sanctum, known as "322," members would gather two nights a week to explore the character and being of their fellow Bonesmen. With the room dimly lit, a member would sit and talk about himself—his fears, his sexual experiences, his ambitions, his inner self. Other members would press him closely, forcing self-criticism and revelation. (One reason secret societies endured at Yale through the turbulent 1960s was because they were, as one undergraduate of the era put it, "therapy-groups with million-dollar buildings.") The purpose was to develop members for later life, to strip them down and make them whole again with the inner strength necessary to lead. It was assumed that Bonesmen would be leaders, and the assumption was not unfounded: Henry Stimson, William Howard Taft, Henry Luce, Justice Potter Stewart, William and McGeorge Bundy were among the many prominent citizens who as undergraduates revealed themselves in the sanctum.

Tap Day was a momentous event on the college calendar, described in the 1915 yearbook as "that annual revelation of the generosity and essential manhood of recurring Yale classes." On a Thursday afternoon in mid-May, the junior class and hundreds of onlookers would gather on Old Campus to await the verdict. As the chapel bell struck five, the roar would go up: "First man!" Grim as death's hand, dressed in black with a gold Bones pin, a member would suddenly appear and head straight for some trembling junior. Grabbing him by the shoulder, he would wheel him around and slap him hard on the back, crying, "Skull and Bones! Go to your room." Legs shaking, the Chosen would stumble off through the parting crowd.

It was in a driving downpour on May 16, 1912, that Averell Harriman became the first man tapped his year for Skull and Bones. The honor perfectly suited the sense of obligation felt by the aloof, strikingly handsome, enormously wealthy young man. "It gave me purpose," he recounted more than seventy years later. "I scoffed at Harvard's Porcellian Club. It was too smug. But to get into Bones, you had to do something for Yale."

Harriman regularly went back to the tomb on High Street, once even lamenting that his duties as chief negotiator at the Paris Peace Talks on the Vietnam War prevented him from attending a reunion. So complete was his trust in Bones's code of secrecy that in conversations at annual dinners he spoke openly about national security affairs. He refused, however, to tell his family anything about Bones. Soon after she became Harriman's third wife in 1971, Pamela Churchill Harriman received an odd letter addressing her by a name spelled in hieroglyphics. "Oh, that's Bones," Harriman said. "I must tell you about that sometime. Uh, I mean I can't tell you about that." When Harriman carried secret dispatches between London and Moscow during World War II, he chose as the combination on his diplomatic case the numerals 322, the society's secret number.

Harriman's Yale career did not mark him as an obvious candidate for Skull and Bones. He participated in a variety of organizations, but only in such positions as assistant manager of the hockey team and as a member of the Wigwam Wrangler debating club, posts that usually do not cut it on Tap Day. Academically, he was at the bottom of the top third of his class, performing slightly better than a gentleman's C. Nevertheless, he was enormously respected. In the yearbook, he is on the top-ten list for "Most Admired," "Most Thorough Gentleman," "Handsomest," and "Most Likely to Succeed."

Coming from a wealthy family and Groton helped: he slipped easily into the most prestigious underclass fraternity, Fence Club, a breeding ground for Bonesmen. During each of his four years at Yale, he roomed with fellow Grotonians, and his friends tended to be upperclassmen, mostly Bonesmen. As a freshman, he and Walter Camp, son of the legendary coach, made a reputation by trumping their elders at bridge.

Harriman's greatest interest at Yale was the crew. Rowing was a serious business at Yale, so much so that Cole Porter, a student at the time, mocked it in a song: "I want to row on the crew, mama!/ That's the thing I want to do, mama!/To be known throughout Yale when I walk about it/Get a boil on my tail and then talk about it." As a six-foot-one-inch, 150-pound freshman, Harriman was a bit too light to make a good oarsman. By his sophomore year he had gained eighteen pounds, but his doctors discovered a slight heart murmur and advised him against competitive rowing. So at his request he was made the coach of the freshman crew and was granted permission to spend six weeks at Oxford studying the English rowing technique.

The combination of Harriman's reserve with that of the British made his reception in Oxford somewhat chilly. The blue-boat captain crunched up Harriman's letter of introduction and, leaving him standing in the drizzle, said: "We're going up the river in half an hour. Take the towpath and you can watch." Harriman did, riding the bank on horseback and making careful notes about the long reach and slow layback of the tricky English stroke. Finally, one Saturday when the crew took a break from training for a champagne dinner, the captain issued a formal invitation to the American who had been dining alone in a corner each evening. "Mr. Harriman, would you care to join us?" he asked. Harriman thus became an accepted member of the coterie, and their famed coach, Harcourt Gold, invited him to watch the training from his launch.

Harriman was tempted to extend his leave for a few days so as not to miss the Oxford-Cambridge race, but fortunately he thought better of it; had he stayed, he would have sailed the following week on the doomed voyage of the *Titanic*. He subsequently spent six hours a day in the New Haven harbor teaching the techniques he had learned to his freshmen crew, which ended up beating the Yale varsity.

Even though the freshmen lost their race to Harvard, Harriman was asked to coach the varsity the following year, only the second time an undergraduate was so honored. Once again he traveled to Oxford, and he spent the summer commuting from Manhattan to conduct afternoon training sessions. But the varsity oarsmen did not adapt as well to the new style; they were soundly thrashed by Harvard yet again, and Harriman was relieved of his coaching duties.

What struck his classmates most about Harriman was that he displayed a cool, almost remote, detachment from the youthful frivolity. He was no snob, nor did he affect regal airs, yet he exuded an aura of maturity and gravity. He had always been somewhat aloof as a boy, but at Yale he seemed more than ever to be sovereign to a world of his own. Above all else he was not a Yalie, not a Grottie, but a Harriman.

This sense of his station in life was understandable. A few days before he enrolled in September of 1909, his father had died (bequeathing his $70 million fortune to his wife in a one-hundred-word will). As a freshman, Averell was appointed to the board of the Boys' Club, an organization his father had founded. As a sophomore, he took the train down from Yale to make the public presentation of ten thousand of Arden's acres and $1 million to the state of New York for a park. In his senior year, he was elected to the board of directors of the Union Pacific, arriving at his first meeting armed with a textbook on psychology.

Like most of his friends at college, Harriman strongly believed that the U.S. must prepare itself for entry into the European war, and he supported the Navy League's drive for increased naval appropriations. Yet when America finally entered the conflict, he was not eager to enlist for active service. In 1915, two years after his graduation, he had married Kitty Lanier Lawrence, the daughter of a New York banker, after rescuing her from a runaway horse that was dragging her along a Manhattan street. By the time President Wilson declared war in April of 1917, they had a three-month-old daughter, Mary; their second child, Kathleen, would be born that December.

Harriman realized that the war would open up opportunities for him to serve his country without disrupting his personal or professional life. British orders for new vessels were inundating American shipyards, and Wilson was pressing for an increase in U.S. naval and shipping capacity. Within days of the President's decision to break diplomatic relations with Germany, Harriman bought the Chester Shipbuilding Company near Philadelphia and set about expanding its output. After winning a government contract for the construction of forty steel cargo ships, Harriman formed the Merchant Shipbuilding Corporation and built a major new yard on the Delaware River north of Philadelphia in what became known as Harriman, Pennsylvania. The government paid out $92 million for the work, yet by Armistice Day not one of the ships had been delivered. (Eventually, they were.) In a brutal report on the operations, a government auditor wrote in 1918: "The Merchant Shipbuilding Corporation is absolutely without a leader who can inspire their men to work and build ships."

In later years Harriman would confess a slight unease about his decision not to enlist in the military. In his book *Special Envoy*, written almost sixty years later, he noted that he "had long regretted the family and business circumstances that had kept him out of action." At the time, however, he contended that his work getting ships built was the greatest service he could render. As he told *Forbes* magazine in 1920: "I felt that in no other way could I contribute half as much to the urgent needs of the nation in the supreme emergency that had arisen."

• • •

When Acheson entered Yale in 1911, he was no longer the scrawny, cheeky boy who had been so miserable at Groton. His summer in the Canadian woods had filled him out, made him more self-possessed, honed his skills as a raconteur, and given him a start on the mustache that he would grow on and off until, years later, he was able to perfect the dapper style of a British Guardsman.

There was a solid niche at Yale for charm and wit. Cole Porter, for instance, was a runty nobody from the Midwest, but he was enormously clever. Discovered by Gerald Murphy (the one who with his wife, Sara, learned that "living well is the best revenge"), Porter became the focal point of a popular "smart set" at Yale. Acheson fell right in with the Cole Porter circle, which also included Archibald MacLeish, the poet and playwright who during World War II worked with Acheson in the State Department.

Together they joined a variety of clubs dedicated to songs and spirits, such as the Grill Room Grizzlies, the Turtles, the Hogans, and the Mohicans. Acheson was also a member of DKE, the Fence Club's rival for the most popular men. "What I remember best about Dean was his ebullience, his bright subtle wit," said Joseph Walker III, Acheson's roommate and closest friend. "He was the wittiest one in our group. I don't remember seeing Dean study, although he must have. He was always ready for a good time, for a new experience." MacLeish later recalled: "He was the typical son of an Episcopal bishop—gay, graceful, gallant. He was also socially snobby with qualities of arrogance and superciliousness. Dean led a charming social existence at Yale."

Upon his arrival, Acheson had been recruited by Harriman to row in seat four of the freshman crew. Although he had picked up the techniques well at Groton, Acheson was still not quite powerful enough to make the varsity. So the following year Harriman bequeathed to his old schoolmate the job of coaching the freshman crew. When Harriman was sacked as varsity coach, Acheson lost his job too. "I have been fired since then," Acheson later recalled, "but never in better company."

For the young boy who once wistfully watched the ferry depart from Middletown, there was a vast world to be explored, and cohorts to accompany him. When Harriman visited Henley for the second time, Acheson and some of his rowing friends tagged along. But while Harriman studiously watched the training sessions, Acheson's crowd spent most of its time drinking champagne and eating strawberries at the lawn parties. Acheson had been to London once before, with his father; on his trip with the crew team, however, he discovered that the Episcopal preacher had left many pleasures still to be experienced. During the summers, Acheson and his friends went to a cabin in Maine for a week of beer drinking and poker playing. Thomas Denegre, captain of the crew, took a group during one Christmas vacation down to New Orleans, where, Walker recalled, "we hardly ever went to bed."

There was, for Acheson, little time or cause for academic application. Only two teachers there stimulated his interest: Chauncey Brewster Tinker and William Lyon Phelps, both noted English professors. Because of their influence, he briefly considered becoming a writer and spent time perfecting his literary style. Otherwise, most of his studies were "meaningless," he later recalled. "You memorized more facts about subjects you had already memorized at school."

Acheson's career at Yale was capped, as was Cole Porter's, by being tapped for Scroll and Key, second only to Bones in prestige among the secret senior societies. While Bones was deadly serious, Keys was unabashedly congenial and convivial. Liquor was allowed in its fanciful Byzantine tomb, and it flowed abundantly. Yet membership was extremely esteemed; for Acheson it was the culmination of his journey from miserable Groton outcast to worldly and popular college blade.

Acheson kept in close touch with his friends from Middletown. He would often drive up on Sundays in his roadster, a trimmed-down Knox car, to visit his family and spend time with Joe Lawton and other childhood companions. On one such weekend, his sister, Margot, had brought home her college roommate from Wellesley, Alice Stanley, as a date for Lawton. The daughter of a lawyer for the Grand Trunk Railroad in Michigan, Alice was tall and lovely and respectably liberal. Lawton ended up with Dean's original date. Acheson ended up eventually marrying the girl he stole away.

In his senior year, Acheson was voted as among the "wittiest" in his class and, having spent far more than he could afford on dapper dress, was also selected one of the "sportiest." Yet he had little idea of what he would do with his life. The class historian, Charles Merz (who became an editor of *The New York Times*), satirizing the bon vivant reputation of the Episcopal bishop's son, wrote in his list of graduation-day predictions: "Dean Acheson leaves next week to do mission work in British East Guatemala." In fact, Acheson had decided, almost by default, to go to Harvard Law School. Before settling down to the rigors that would entail, he embarked on a farewell fling with his friends, traveling to San Francisco for the world's fair and then on to Japan for the geisha girls.

• • •

Acheson's roommates at Harvard Law School were not exactly conducive to study. He rented an apartment in Cambridge with Cole Porter, who had transferred from the law school to the music school, and among the rotating visitors and boarders were other Yale blades, including Archibald MacLeish. Law school threatened to become, for Acheson, an annex to the DKE House. Instead, it became a time of intellectual transformation: the intricacies of the law and the rigor of the law school stimulated the careless young man into becoming a serious scholar. "This was a tremendous discovery: the discovery of the power of thought," Acheson later recalled. "Not only did I become aware of this wonderful mechanism, the brain, but I became aware of an unlimited mass of material that was lying about the world waiting to be stuffed into the brain."

It was at Harvard Law that Acheson realized that "excellence counted—a sloppy try wasn't enough." He began comparing his mind to a welder's torch, waiting to be focused. His sense of security firmly re-established after the grueling trial of Groton, Acheson began to push himself intellectually, to take great pride in the sharpness of his mind. At Groton and in Middletown, intellectual ambition was considered socially suspect. But at Harvard Law School, Acheson found it prized as a path to social distinction.

The type of intelligence that Acheson developed through immersion in the law was a logical and analytic one, "learning that you need not make up your mind in advance, that there is no set solution to a problem, and that decisions are the result of analyzing the facts, of tussling and grappling with them." But the law held even more for Acheson: he saw its evolution as a mirror of the economic and philosophic forces that ordered a community; when those forces changed, he came to believe, so too should the laws.

Harvard had already developed its reputation as a laboratory of reform and an incubator of social activism. "It is the crowning glory of this Law School that it has kindled in many a heart an inextinguishable fire," said Oliver Wendell Holmes, who urged his students to be involved in the "actions and passions" of their time.

The most influential professor, at least from Acheson's point of view, was a young Jewish refugee who had arrived at Ellis Island from Vienna in 1894 at the age of twelve. Felix Frankfurter was the spirited embodiment of the school's intellectual meritocracy. "I have a quasi-religious feeling about Harvard Law School," Frankfurter once said. "I regard it as the most democratic institution I know anything about."

After graduating from the law school, Frankfurter had served as an assistant U.S. attorney in New York under Henry Stimson. While working on the antitrust cases against E. H. Harriman, Frankfurter had developed a strong distaste for the role of corporate lawyers, taking particular offense at the way Judge Lovett was forced to act as Harriman's lackey. So in 1914, he accepted an invitation to return to Harvard as a professor. There he joined the vanguard of scholars who felt that the law must be an impetus rather than an obstacle to social change. In a memo to himself weighing whether he should accept the job at Harvard, Frankfurter spoke of his desire for "jurisprudence to meet the social and industrial needs of the time." In 1915, the year Acheson enrolled at the law school, Frankfurter told the American Bar Association: "We must show young people the law as an instrument, and not an end of organized humanity."

Frankfurter's teaching style was highly personal. Francis Plimpton, later a distinguished New York lawyer, parodied his course on public utilities: "There is no law in Public U/That is its fascination/But Felix gives a point of view/And pleasant conversation." An aspiring Brahmin by instinct if not by birth, Frankfurter would seek for his favored coterie not only the brightest students but also the cleverest, wittiest, and most socially adept. Dean Acheson was a standout in all these regards; he became Frankfurter's most ardent protégé and later one of his most intimate friends. In fact, his transformation into a serious scholar can be dated to the beginning of his second year when he took his first course from Frankfurter.

Years later, John McCloy would joke about Frankfurter's select circle at the law school. During his first year there, McCloy would recall, he would audit Frankfurter's lectures from the back row and envy those such as Acheson, a year ahead, who sat up front and were invited to the professor's house for tea afterward. After McCloy entered government, Frankfurter brought him under his wing and became a close friend. But at the law school, the struggling scholarship student from Amherst could only admire from afar the ease with which people like Acheson were tapped for such attention.

Under Frankfurter, Acheson became fascinated by the relations between legal problems and socioeconomic ones. He even developed a curiosity about the works of Karl Marx, albeit a detached one; although he scarcely read any of Marx on his own, he avidly sought out those who could discuss Marxism. He was selected for the board of the *Harvard Law Review*, and the following year he graduated fifth in his class.

Upon leaving Harvard, Acheson enlisted in the Navy, where he served as an ensign at the Brooklyn Navy Yard. But before he saw active service, the armistice was signed, and Acheson returned to Cambridge with the vague goal of pursuing an academic career.

Under the supervision of Pound and Frankfurter, Acheson wrote a short book on labor law that was intended as part of the Harvard Studies in Jurisprudence series. But Harvard never got around to printing it, and it was later declined by the Yale University Press. The manuscript, 140 typewritten pages, explored the legal concepts developed by the War Labor Board to regulate disputes between unions and management. "Because it recognizes with the Board that such things as trade unions exist, some idiots will call it radical," he wrote to his friend George Day, who was president of the Yale University Press. He explained that his piece merely tried to show how labor law could play a role in balancing the conflicting interests of individuals and society. "These principles would seem to me to be as valid for Russia as for the United States," he told Day.

Acheson's ties to the Democratic Party were formed during this period. He even considered pursuing a legal career within the labor movement, and sought contacts within the AFL and the plumbers' union. He also discussed with some of his colleagues the possibility of becoming a law professor. In a letter to his friend John Vincent, who had been a classmate at Yale and Harvard Law School, Acheson joked that some at Harvard were cautious about making him a teacher and wanted to find out "whether my book was to be published in Moscow."

His immediate course was settled, however, when Frankfurter got a letter from Louis Brandeis seeking a bright law student. Brandeis, a Supreme Court justice, had begun the practice of hiring graduates to act as his clerks. Acheson was excited, but worried that a clerkship might not help his career. "I cannot afford even the unusual association with a great man if after a year it leaves me as comparatively unfit for what I want to do as I am now," he wrote Frankfurter. "You do not know how a letter from you would help to clear away the confusion of my thoughts." Frankfurter did clear away those confusions, and Dean and Alice Acheson soon left New England for a new life in Washington.

•   •   •

Lovett, who entered Yale in 1914, was a far more serious student than either Harriman or Acheson. He was elected to Phi Beta Kappa and voted by his classmates as among the "most scholarly," "most brilliant," and "hardest working." When his freshman Latin instructor became ill at Christmas, Lovett took over and taught the class for the remainder of the year.

Having sworn off athletics (for life), Lovett found other activities to round out his Yale career. He sang second tenor in the freshman glee club, was floor manager of the prom committee and assistant manager of the drama society. As qualification for admission to the Elizabethan Club, Yale's gracious literary bastion of watercress sandwiches and afternoon tea, he wrote a paper about a line from Shakespeare's *Hamlet*: "The play, I remember, pleased not the million; 'twas caviar to the general." Lovett suggested that the line referred to Shakespeare's own *Troilus and Cressida*, which many authorities thought had been completed after Hamlet.*

Mildly bored by the studies and social life at Yale, Lovett and his friends became increasingly interested in the European war that America was about to enter. Together with a dozen of his friends, he formed the Yale Unit of the Naval Reserve Flying Corps during his junior year, leaving New Haven behind to fight, as one of them put it, "for God, for country and for Yale."

The formation of the Yale Unit was inspired by Lovett's friend F. Trubee Davison, who had left Yale in 1915 to become an ambulance driver in France and returned with tales of duty and glory. "I picked out Bob Lovett and poured it into his ear," Davison recalled. "We made a sort of compact that if war came we should go into aviation." A year later, while Davison was on a training trip as a manager of the Yale crew, he sent a telegram to Lovett to come discuss forming a flying unit.

Lovett quickly embraced the idea and lined up a floating hangar

---

*The exact date when Shakespeare completed *Troilus and Cressida*, sometime around 1600, was and still is in doubt.

near his home in Locust Valley, Long Island. Other of their Yale friends were recruited, among them: Artemus "Di" Gates, captain-elect of the football team who later became Assistant Secretary of the Navy for air; John Vorys, later an isolationist Republican congressman from Ohio; David Ingalls, who became Assistant Secretary of War for air (a post Lovett eventually held); and Kenneth MacLeish, Archie's younger brother.

Training for the Yale Flying Unit was not exactly boot camp. Davison's father, Henry, a partner at J. P. Morgan & Company, helped finance them royally, and newspapers of the day dubbed them "the millionaires' unit." They cut rakish figures, and knew it; though some dismissed them as dilettantes, the hearts of young Long Island belles fluttered at the sight of the dashing amateur aviators.

When a seaplane being flown by Lovett and Davison conked out over the East River, they made an emergency landing under the 59th Street bridge. Ever cool, the young pilots went off and had lunch on Davison's yacht, which happened to be moored nearby. On a trip to Pensacola, the unit made a detour to Palm Beach, where they ostentatiously pursued a relaxed style. "They were rolled about in wheel chairs by African slaves amid tropical gardens and coconut palms," wrote the unit's historian, tongue in cheek. "For light exercise, they learned to glance at their new wristwatches with an air of easy nonchalance."

At the center of both the frivolity and intense training was Lovett, who became the group's most respected pilot, sharpest wit, and de facto leader. "Lovett learned very quickly," Davison recalled. He was made chief of the unit's private club, the Wags, whose members started their sentences, "Being a Wag and therefore a superman..." He was also the group's strategist. "Observation—Reflection—Deduction," their historian wrote. "Lovett was insatiable in pursuing information to its lair and a master hand at making use of it."

Despite the snide comments of those who dismissed them as frivolous rich boys, Lovett's unit proved to be daring and imaginative warriors when they were dispatched for active duty in 1917 with Britain's Royal Naval Air Service. Lovett noted that 85 percent of German submarines tended to be at dock at any one time. Hunting them at sea, he figured, was a far less efficient way of destroying them than attacking the bases. He meticulously plotted the costs and benefits of different methods of destroying submarines from the air and wrote a long memo to the Navy Department that prompted the formation of the Northern Bombing Group. Its thesis: The only way to penetrate the German air defense system was by incessant and unremitting night attacks focused on one base at a time. The U.S., using British fields in France, was the only country with the resources to do this.

Lovett led the assaults with true bravery. Using British-made Handley-Page bombers, the studious and well-bred young man perfected the techniques of glide-bombing and dive-bombing. As he put it in a report: "With our full load of bombs we were unable to climb more than 7000 or 8000 feet. This necessitated our bombing from a glide, making us some 5000 or 6000 feet over the objective. At this altitude we were frequently hit by shrapnel and high-explosive fragments; never, however, in a vital spot."

He would later admit he was scared to death to look out of his cockpit. His official report of three days and nights assaulting the German facilities at Bruges is harrowing.

> Its defenses far exceed anything one could imagine. On the first night an extremely intense barrage was put up, consisting of "flaming onions"— a series of green luminous balls attached to one another somewhat in the manner of a chain shot—of shrapnel shells and high explosives. The barrage is almost box-like with layers of high explosive and shrapnel and an over-generous supply of green balls. Due to the small size of the objective . . . the enemy is able to obtain a terrific concentration of his anti-aircraft defenses.

Having lived to tell the tale, Lieutenant Lovett, who became a squadron commander and then the acting wing commander of the Northern Bombing Group, was awarded the Navy Cross. From the experience he developed definite ideas about the use of air power, ones he would carry through World War II and even Vietnam. Intermittent or random bombing did nothing to lessen enemy morale; if anything, attacks that were not sustained heightened the will to resist. "Keep it incessant" was his war cry. Enemy production facilities could be destroyed through concentrated efforts, but it was ineffective to try to weaken them randomly. Future wars would be won by long-range bombers with large payloads that could deliver a powerful offensive punch.

One who did not survive was Kenneth MacLeish, Lovett's beloved companion and Yale Unit colleague. Lovett was neither a hell-bent military man nor one whose sensitivity had been sapped by war; he cried when he heard of Ken's death, and cried again a week later when he wrote Ken's brother. In his "Dear Arch" letter, Lovett reported that Ken had been killed because he rejected a promotion to squadron commander in order to remain on the front lines.

> I fairly crammed the squadron down his throat, when any other man in the whole service would have sold his last package of chocolates to win the job. Then the answer came back, only a few lines, but I'll never forget them. It began, "Bob—There's no use trying to make a commanding officer out of me if I can't fight and fly all I want when I want. Some people were born to paint, some to write, some to lead, and some to just plain go out and do-it-all-by-yourself." I believe he was the best we had in the line of a pilot, and I don't want a finer pal than a man who can give up everything for his ideal of service and honor.

Lovett never completed his final year and a half of college; his diploma was awarded in wartime absentia. He was tapped for Skull and Bones not on the Old Campus but at a naval station in West Palm Beach; his initiation, instead of being conducted in the "tomb" on High Street, occurred at the headquarters of the Navy's Nothern Bombing Group between Dunkirk and Calais.

The wartime experience was maturing and sobering, and when it was over, Lovett had no desire to return to classes. At his father's insistence, however, he agreed to give Harvard Law School a try. Unlike McCloy or Acheson, he soon found himself bored by both the law and the law school. Joseph Beale, McCloy's favorite professor, struck him as imperious and out of touch with the real world, he later recalled. Frankfurter seemed to him a self-important social crusader. In his second year, Lovett transferred, briefly, to Harvard Business School. A few months later, he fled to join Harriman and most of his friends from Yale who were already making good in the real world of Wall Street.

· · ·

For most students in the 1920s, Harvard College meant freedom. Its students, then and now, were largely left alone. Charles Eliot, whose forty-year tenure as president ended in 1909, described his legacy as "to allow each man to think and do as he pleases." Individualism was prized; even in that most boola-boola of college eras, Harvard indifference was preserved. "Our undisciplinables are our proudest product," said the resident philosopher William James. "Heresy has always been a Harvard institution," wrote John Reed, chronicler of the Russian Revolution (*Ten Days That Shook the World*) and the only Harvard graduate (or American) to be buried in the Kremlin.

When Chip Bohlen enrolled in 1923, after his graduation from St. Paul's, about half of the student body was from private preparatory schools and also about half was from New England. Seven out of ten came from Republican homes. They were, however, hardly all reactionary: in a detailed survey of the attitudes of the Class of 1926 shortly after their graduation, 32 percent said that they were "strongly sympathetic" or "mildly sympathetic" to the Soviet Union. (When these same alumni were polled again after World War II, only 4 percent expressed any degree of sympathy with the Soviet Union.)

For Bohlen, like most graduates of Groton or St. Paul's, Harvard meant no more required chapel, no black marks, no rector. The prankish humor and irreverence that were frowned upon at St. Paul's merely made Bohlen popular at Harvard. Like most of his prep-school chums, he lived on Harvard's "Gold Coast," the row of boardinghouses just south of Harvard Yard. He and eleven other friends from St. Paul's and St. Mark's moved into a thirteen-room yellow frame house at 9 Bow Street operated by a lovable landlady named Mrs. Mullin. The rat-pack atmosphere perfectly suited Bohlen's congenial personality, and his housemates were destined to become lifelong friends. Among them were Cecil Lyon, who became a diplomat and served as minister under Bohlen in Paris, and J. Randolph "Ducky" Harrison, who until Bohlen's dying day (literally) engaged him in ferocious political arguments.

Clubs did not play the same role at Harvard as they did at Yale and Princeton. They existed mainly for boys who attended the church schools; those not from "St. Grottlesex," such as Walter Lippmann and John Reed, though they felt some envy, found they could succeed quite well without them. But for the boys of the Gold Coast, the club hierarchy was the essence of Harvard life. "Every one of us in the Bow Street house of course joined a final club," recalled Lyon. "It would have been unthinkable for one of us to do otherwise."

The eligible were sifted through a series of testing grounds. First there was election to the Hasty Pudding, a song-and-drink society that produced musical comedies on the side. Next came a "waiting club," such as the Sphinx-Kalumet chosen by Bohlen and his friends. The process culminated with election to a "final club." It was a man's final club that really counted, and none counted more than the Porcellian.

Founded in 1791, the Porcellian was deemed so important to young Brahmins that disconsolate sophomores were known to drop out of Harvard upon rejection, there being nothing more to look forward to in college life. When Theodore Roosevelt informed Kaiser Wilhelm of the engagement of his daughter Alice to future House Speaker Nicholas Longworth, he noted: "Nick and I are both in the Porc, you know." More than a half century after his election, and after he had won the Pulitzer Prize for fiction, Owen Wister said that membership in the PC was his greatest success. The man the Porcellian is best known for snubbing, Franklin Roosevelt, did not drop out of college, but he later admitted that his rejection was the worst blow of his life.

Unlike Skull and Bones, the Porcellian made no pretense of rewarding achievement; blood and congeniality were the criteria, in that order. Chip Bohlen's father, uncle, and brother had been members, and his charm was already becoming legendary, so he was a natural choice despite his undistinguished career in academics and college activities. "The club prided itself on not being based on merit in any way," recalled Paul Nitze, who was a class behind Bohlen at the PC and would later work closely with him shaping America's postwar policies toward Russia.

The Porcellian clubhouse, located above a clothing store across Massachusetts Avenue from Harvard Yard, is anything but ostentatious. Inside are the requisite battered leather chairs and a wide assortment of pig figurines and stuffed boars' heads. In Bohlen's day, there was no card playing or gambling, no billiards or pool or any sport other than quiet games of chess. Undergraduates were not even served regular meals other than breakfast. Bohlen and his friends had to go to the Hasty Pudding or the SK Club for their rowdy poker games or dinners.

The main activity at the Porcellian was drinking. This was done seriously and at all hours, even during Prohibition. (Prohibition only made hangovers worse. The favored drink of Bohlen and his friends was ginger ale with bathtub gin, most of which was made and supplied by the steward of the SK Club, who later bought a boat and sailed off to Jamaica with his profits.) Members would compete in a ritual known as "The Day of the Book." It began shortly after dawn with shots of gin, moved on to champagne with breakfast, a martini every hour for the rest of the day, switching to Scotch after dinner. The goal, rarely achieved, was to be standing at midnight. Bohlen's poor brother, Buffy, was among those who tried and failed. Chip, while never a serious contestant, was able at the PC to develop a skill that would be invaluable for a diplomat in Russia: he could down great quantities of alcohol while barely showing it.

Bohlen made a halfhearted stab at continuing his career as a football player, playing third-string tackle on the freshman team, which beat Yale that year 59–0. But he never made the varsity. As an upperclassman, he tended to confine himself to the more gentlemanly sports of squash, golf, and shooting. Nor were his academic interests profound; despite being a voracious reader and having a highly retentive mind, he compiled an undistinguished record as a modern European history major.

What Bohlen excelled at was making friends, and occasionally enemies, sometimes one and the same. He loved to talk and argue, doing so a good part of the day and much of the night. Silence unnerved him. When conversation lagged at 9 Bow Street, he would pull out a book and read it aloud to his friends.

He also had an eye for women, and they for him. Though sloppy in his manner and dress, he had shed his boarding-school pudginess. With his handsome face, warm smile, easy charm, and charismatic glow, Boston's debutantes seemed to find him quite irresistible.

Bohlen's late-night discussions at Harvard increasingly revolved around Russia. Though neither especially liberal nor political by nature, he avidly read *Ten Days That Shook the World*, and became fascinated with John Reed, who had died in Moscow, at age thirty-two, three years before Bohlen entered Harvard. Reed's romantic Marxism appealed to the spirited, well-born young man with limited resources and unclear ambitions. He sang Russian songs, read Russian literature, and even had a Russian girl. "This is the correct way to learn Russian," he joked to his friend Paul Nitze.

Excited by the passion and energy of the Bolshevik experiment, Bohlen gamely tried to defend it to his skeptical clubmates. These debates over Marxism with Ducky Harrison and others would rage late into the night in the incongruous setting of the Porcellian's paneled sanctum, fueled by adequate amounts of bathtub gin. Finally spent, Bohlen would stumble into bed fully clothed, his hat crumpled on the pillow.

Toward the end of their senior year, the clubmates found their discussions at the Porcellian revolving around a more practical matter: careers. Bohlen would proclaim that he was far too irreverent to become a lawyer. Following the rest of the herd to State Street or Wall Street as a financier, on the other hand, struck Bohlen as "an unsuitable form of bondage." At a loss for alternatives, he and Harrison signed up as twenty-seven-dollar-a-month crewmen on a U.S. Steel cargo ship headed through the Panama Canal to Manila, Manchuria, and beyond.

Bohlen dropped off in China and spent a few months working his way to Calcutta. When he finally rejoined the ship for the voyage home, he was bursting with stories of exotic adventures and reports of the revolution that was stirring in China. Upon his return, a relative arranged for him to meet William Castle, an Assistant Secretary of State. It was this discussion, Bohlen recalled, that "finally fixed me in my decision to become a diplomat."

CHAPTER 3

JOINT VENTURES

Harriman and Lovett
on Wall Street

With the end of the War to End All Wars, America quenched its yearning for a return to normalcy by retreating into isolationism. Woodrow Wilson's dream of U.S. participation in a stable world order was shattered by the Senate's rejection of the League of Nations in 1919 and the election of Warren Harding in 1920. Main Street turned inward, became more insular.

Wall Street, on the other hand, did nothing of the sort. Europe was industrially devastated and mired in debt; America was throbbing with revitalized factories and in need of new markets. The situation was ripe for financiers interested in foreign investment and trade, internationalists such as Harriman and Lovett who understood America's historic ties to Europe and felt comfortable with her growing involvement in global affairs.

Through his wartime contracts with the government's Emergency Fleet Corporation, Harriman was already a shipbuilder. Imbued with his father's infectious vision of a worldwide transportation empire, he began in 1919 to put together a network to operate and underwrite ships of his own. He formed the Independent Steamship Company and bought into the American-Hawaiian Steamship Company, Coastwise Transportation Company, and the American Ship and Commerce Corporation. In 1920, he consolidated these holdings (which included ownership of sixty-three ships) into one company, United American Lines, forming the largest commercial fleet yet assembled under the American flag.

To finance marine securities, Harriman founded the investment banking house of W. A. Harriman & Company in November of 1919. "I am profoundly convinced that the necessity for developing American shipping is upon us," he told the magazine publisher B. C. Forbes in 1920, "and I regard as embodying a fundamental truth the axiom that 'what becomes a necessity always becomes an eventuality.'" That had been one of his father's axioms.

Although he collaborated with his brother, Roland, and other partners in the shipping and finance business, Harriman remained very much a loner. He delegated authority and shared responsibility well, but he was never one for collegial operations. He viewed himself as a man of action, a doer. Focusing on each task at hand, he seemed to wear blinders against peripheral distractions.

Harriman's approach was, above all, pragmatic; the goal of businessmen, unlike stiped-pants statesmen, was to cut through abstract posturing in order to reach a deal. Even after he became a diplomat himself, Harriman would harbor the belief that foes could be bargained with as easily as friends. Thus he had no qualms about entering into a shipping agreement with Germany, even though the final armistice had not been signed, and a mining concession in the Soviet Union, even though the United States had spurned diplomatic relations with that country.

During a visit to Germany in 1920, Harriman began secret talks with officials of the once-powerful Hamburg-American Steamship Company, whose vessels had been confiscated at the end of the war. They quickly arranged a deal: The Harriman interests would supply the company with ships if it would act as the German agent for Harriman's own lines. "The arrangement gives us the benefit of some of the best brains in the shipping world," Harriman said, "men who before the war demonstrated their ability to develop a shipping business second to none."

The nativist sentiment that caused some American towns to ban sauerkraut and forbid the teaching of German in high schools had not yet subsided. Harriman was pilloried. "Do you find yourself at all tempted to slacken your efforts because of the criticism and condemnation now being heaped upon you from various quarters?" a journalist asked. "No," Harriman replied. "Fortunately I am blessed with a sense of humor and also a big bump of patience." (Neither of which was exactly the case.) As the criticism mounted, Harriman reluctantly took his case public, releasing the details of his project to New York newspapers and telling reporters: "We regard the whole undertaking as a brilliant American opportunity."

It was, however, less than a brilliant financial opportunity. Interest rates were rising, prices falling, and exports declining. New restrictions on immigration cut the flow of steerage-class passengers, and Prohibition precluded the sale of alcohol on ships of American registry. Harriman embarked on a campaign for lower tariffs and increased subsidies for the shipping industry, casting his crusade in terms of the country's need for a strong merchant marine. The Democrats, he found, were far more receptive than the isolationist-dominated Republican Party then in power.

Even though Western nations had imposed a strict blockade on trade with the Soviets, and even though the U.S. was in the throes of a virulent Red scare, Harriman and officials of the Hamburg-American Company began talks with Moscow in 1922 about establishing a jointly owned shipping firm, the Deutsch-Russiche Transport Company. It began its meager operations in November of that year. "I know what prejudice there is against us in the U.S.," the director of the Soviet Trade Ministry told a *New York Times* reporter in 1922, "but one must believe that Mr. Harriman does not share it, since he is associated with the Hamburg-American line in placing half the capital in a steamship company in which the Soviets will hold the other half."

Indeed, Harriman shared few of his countrymen's ideological suspicions about the Soviets. Through the Berlin office of W. A. Harriman & Company, he joined with a German bank to buy at a discount Russian notes from firms that had taken them as payment for exports. He was impressed when the Soviets made good on the notes; they appeared to Harriman serious about keeping their financial commitments.

Harriman also reached a tentative agreement with a German export group in 1926 to offer $42 million of bonds in the U.S. to finance long-term credits for the Soviet Union. When officials at the State Department heard of the arrangement through press reports, they were furious. Harriman, in Berlin working on the deal, was summoned to see American Ambassador Jacob Gould Schurman, who protested that providing credit to Moscow was contrary to U.S. policy. Harriman argued that the deal would benefit American business by allowing the Russian market to absorb German exports that might otherwise be dumped in the U.S. He also contended (as he would in later years) that economic isolation of the Soviet Union was impractical and would make it harder to bring the country into the world community. Trade and credit, he told the skeptical ambassador, could be used as levers in gaining concessions from Soviet leaders.

Harriman sailed back to Washington to present the same arguments there, but the State Department had already secured opposition to the plan from the full Cabinet. He was accorded only an unproductive meeting with an Assistant Secretary and subsequently decided to drop the credit plan.

The most ambitious deal that Harriman made with the Soviets went forward despite Washington's qualms. The Kremlin had come to view Western technology as critical to its industrial plans, but it had no foreign currency to purchase it. So Lenin announced that concessions to develop certain industries, similar to those granted by the czars, would be available to foreign investors. In 1924, Harriman began secret discussions with Soviet commercial agents in New York about obtaining a twenty-year concession to operate the manganese mines in the Caucasus Mountains of Georgia.

Before the revolution, these mines had been the world's largest supplier of the element, an essential alloy for steel. But the facilities were archaic. The Soviets drove a hard bargain: Harriman agreed to supply new machinery, return production to postwar levels, and upgrade the port—an investment that could ultimately reach $25 million. The Soviets would get up to four dollars per ton of manganese extracted, and Harriman decided on his own to pay a royalty of one dollar per ton to the former Russian owners from whom the mines had been expropriated.

The concession could turn a profit only if manganese prices rose substantially. Instead, they fell. New deposits were found in Africa, and the Soviets expanded production in the Ukraine. In addition, railway and port improvements cost several times what Harriman had estimated, especially after new laws were passed requiring additional benefits for workers. Consequently, Harriman went to Moscow in December of 1926 to renegotiate his concession.

Stalin, the Secretary of the Communist Party, was at the time maneuvering for total power. He had succeeded in having Trotsky demoted from Defense Commissar to chairman of the Concessions

Committee. Grasping the internal struggle, Harriman pressed to see Stalin, but was told he was out of town. Instead, he met with Trotsky for four hours, going over the contract paragraph by paragraph.

Trotsky's mind impressed the American businessman; he understood points rapidly but betrayed no emotion. His silence, as Harriman realized, was out of fear for his own tenuous position. Trotsky later explained to Maxim Litvinov (the future Foreign Minister) that he suspected Stalin of appointing him to the concessions post in order to compromise him in the eyes of young Communists. "It's already being said that I'm on Averell Harriman's payroll," he complained. Six months would elapse before the Soviets approved a modest change in the concession, decreasing Soviet royalties and releasing Harriman from responsibility for upgrading the railway.

On this, his second visit to Russia (the first being to Siberia with his father in 1899), Harriman found the artistic life in Moscow and Leningrad to be flourishing. He met with many painters, writers, musicians, and actors, and took a special trip to see the collection of works by Matisse and Gauguin in Leningrad. For ordinary citizens, however, conditions were grim. Although normally somewhat oblivious to the people around him, Harriman was deeply shocked by the *bezprizornye*, the starving Civil War orphans who roamed the streets during winter like wild animals.

Harriman was not inclined to tailor his life-style for the Bolsheviks, nor did he think they would respect him more if he did. So for his 1,500-mile trip from Moscow to his mines in Georgia, he recalled, "I decided to behave like a capitalist and asked for a private car on the train." The czarist-vintage car was the most ornate he had ever seen, lavishly decorated with gilt scrollwork and wood inlay. At every station there were the ubiquitous hordes of wandering Russian peasants, weighted down with household goods and straw suitcases.

After four days, Harriman reached Tiflis, where local officials feted him at a party in the bulging cellars of Grand Duke Nicholas, renamed the "state wine library." The caviar-laden feast (featuring a Rhine wine of the 1860s, a 1906 Bordeaux, a Napoleon brandy, and a number of local vintages) introduced Harriman to the prolonged drinking sessions that would later be a working hazard for himself and other diplomats. He recalled: "By the time we emerged from the cellar we knew no pain."

The engineers at the manganese mines stressed their difficulties in dealing with the Soviet bureaucracy. Harriman, who had traveled to Russia with high hopes, would later claim that the trip produced a lasting skepticism about the Soviet Union. "I became convinced that the Bolshevik Revolution was in fact a reactionary revolution and that it was not 'the wave of the future,'" he said in a 1970 lecture at Lehigh University. "It denied the basic beliefs that we value so deeply—the rights and dignity of the individual, the idea that government should express the will of the people."

Those recollections, however, were embellished by hindsight. At the time, his disapproval was mixed with respect for the stability of the revolution. In a letter he wrote to his Yale class yearbook upon his return, Harriman reported that there was no chance of a counter-revolution. Even though the new economic order required sacrifice, he noted, the peasants were as well off financially as they had been under the czars, and they had more freedom. Any change "will come as a development of ideas from within the Communist Party," he said. As for Stalin, "He is not a dictator in any sense of the word, as has been expressed, but he is a political boss in the sense of Charles Murphy of Tammany Hall."

Throughout his life, no matter how important he became himself, Harriman relished meeting famous and powerful leaders. This was partly because he valued discourse with them as an antidote to the triviality he found in other conversations. Yet it was also largely due to Harriman's lifelong boyish fascination with collecting important acquaintanceships almost in the way that others collect stamps. (His friends would joke in later years that whenever Hitler's name came up, Harriman would remark almost wistfully that he had never met the man, conveying the air of a big-game hunter who had been eluded by one valuable trophy.)

On his way home from Russia, Harriman netted a pair of big names. At the urging of a group of Milan bankers who wanted him to sell bonds in the U.S., he visited Rome to meet Mussolini. In the enormous room used as an office by the dictator, the American financier argued that he would be unable to sell Italian bonds unless the plan to revalue the lira was dropped. "Mr. Harriman, you don't understand," Mussolini fervently responded. "I must restore the pride of the Italian nation."

His advice shunned, Harriman asked for some guidance of his own. Should he invest in the Soviet Union? Mussolini counseled that, even though he strongly opposed Communism, he found a moderate amount of trade with the Russians to be profitable. In Cannes, Harriman put the same question to the British Chancellor of the Exchequer, Winston Churchill. Get out of any business deals with the Soviets, said the future Prime Minister. In later years Churchill would boast that he saved Harriman millions of dollars with that advice.

Harriman in fact had already resolved to back out of the manganese concession, despite the renegotiated terms. In a 1928 settlement, the Soviets agreed to buy out Harriman's investment for $3.5 million, to be paid in fifteen-year bonds bearing 7 percent interest. In return, Harriman had to agree to lend the Soviets an additional $1 million. *The New York Times*, like most of the press, had long been dubious about the entire enterprise. The stately paper indulged in uncharacteristic flippancy on its business pages: "It would seem certain that Harriman Manganese has passed away after several months' illness, aged 3-½ years. Though its birth was accompanied by prodigious hopes, it never was a healthy child..."

The Soviets proclaimed that the settlement constituted the first U.S. loan to Moscow and proved their good credit. They eventually made good on the bonds, causing Harriman to conclude that they were tough bargainers but lived up to their commitments. He later claimed to have made a small profit on the deal, although a State Department attaché at the time estimated that he lost about thirteen cents on each dollar invested. Certainly, he fared better than those who tried to hang on to their concessions longer. Not only did this keep him from becoming embittered toward Russia, it also allowed him to boast in the future that he knew better than others how to bargain with Moscow.

•   •   •

Although E. H. Harriman's contributions to party coffers had tapered off after Teddy Roosevelt's personal attacks, his family remained nominally Republican. Averell, however, soon began to waver. As a businessman he had shown little interest in politics, but his international dealings and his support for Woodrow Wilson's vision of a League of Nations convinced him of one thing: "Republican isolationism," he told a journalist, "was disastrous." The problems faced by the shipping industry, he felt, stemmed partly from the Republicans' failure to reduce tariffs. In addition, he increasingly worried that stock market speculation was going "haywire," and he blamed the Republicans for refusing to restrain it.

There were also personal ties tugging him toward the Democrats. His activist sister Mary had become a close friend of Eleanor Roosevelt, who taught calisthenics at one of the Junior League settlement houses Mary had founded. At Groton, Averell was a classmate of Eleanor's brother, Hall; orphaned as a schoolboy, Hall had moved into Eleanor and Franklin's New York City town house, where Averell became a frequent guest. Through his service on the Palisades Interstate Park Commission, Harriman also became friendly with Governor Al Smith.

When Smith ran for President in 1928, Mary Harriman announced, through Eleanor Roosevelt, that she would vote for him. It was not hard for her brother to follow suit: the Democratic Party chairman was General Motors Vice-President John Raskob, a successful financier who had bolted from the GOP and declared his intention to make the Democrats the party of business. Harriman's switch in party loyalty was reinforced when the stock market crashed the following year, confirming his doubts about the Republicans' ability to manage the economy. From then on, he was a loyal Democrat.

At the time, however, polo rather than politics provided his primary diversion from the business world. Harriman would often leave Wall Street at 4 P.M. for a quick game at the Meadowbrook Club, on Long Island, before dinner. He bought a house at Sands Point, near the club, and acquired a string of ponies, frequently paying up to ten thousand dollars for a mount.

It was the perfect sport for an intense and driven (and rich) young man, made even more so because Harriman approached it the way he did business. "I like recreation that calls for just as much energy as work calls for," he said upon taking up the sport in 1920. "When you're playing polo you have to keep your eye on the ball every minute and you haven't time or inclination to think of anything else." Hardly a graceful player, he practiced with typical discipline to achieve an eight-goal handicap (ten being the best) and in 1928 scored four of the seven goals for the U.S. in the international championships against Argentina. That victory, wrote one newspaper, "amounted to a personal triumph for W. Averell Harriman, the American No. 1, who played startlingly beautiful polo."

Harriman also took up croquet at Sands Point, and became, along with his neighbor Herbert Bayard Swope, editor of the New York *World*, one of the country's masters of the game. A meticulous strategist, Harriman would take up to twenty minutes scrutinizing the lay of the court and individual blades of grass before making a shot. His deliberateness so infuriated friends that whenever any other dawdler took too much time he was addressed as "Averell." Harriman's playing style gave a clue to the oblivious manner he often affected in business and social life: he would sometimes seem to forget which ball was his, act as if he had lost track of the order of the game, and then proceed to execute a carefully plotted strategy. Asked by a novice for the secret to his prowess, he replied: "I just kept at it. Persistence is the key." (At age ninety, he would lament to an interviewer that he had difficulty finding suitable opponents. "There aren't a whole lot of good croquet players still around," he said. "Very subtle game.")

Kitty Harriman had accompanied her husband on his trip to the Soviet manganese mines, and for a while they seemed to enjoy an active social life together. But both were quiet and inward in different ways, and they soon drifted apart. Although he was not the sort to expend much energy chasing other women, Harriman gained the reputation as a man with a wandering eye. He and Kitty were divorced in 1929, and the following year he married Marie Norton Whitney, herself recently divorced from Cornelius Vanderbilt ("Sonny") Whitney.

Whereas Kitty had been shy and retiring, Marie was witty and outspoken, brash to the point of abrasiveness. "Oh, come off it, Ave!" she would snort in her husky voice whenever he became too ponderous. They shared an interest in Impressionist and Post-impressionist art, and on their honeymoon in Europe collected dozens of masterpieces by Van Gogh, Degas, Cézanne, Picasso, and Renoir. Gertrude Stein, whose salon they visited in Paris, was in need of money to publish the Plain Edition of her works, and she sold the Harrimans her treasured Picasso, *Girl with a Fan*. The paintings the Harrimans collected became the nucleus of a gallery Marie opened on East 57th Street.

Marie also introduced Averell to café society. Although he remained a wallflower even at his own parties, Harriman found his new artistic acquaintances an amusing diversion from the bankers he dealt with by day. The group orbited around Alexander Woollcott, *The New Yorker* magazine and Algonquin Round Table humorist (who later was to remark upon arriving in London during World War II, "There'll always be an England, now that Averell's here"). Woollcott and Marie came up with the idea of filling all the rooms at Arden with guests at Thanksgiving, which soon became an annual tradition. The Harrimans delegated to Woollcott the task of making the guest list for these five-day extravaganzas. Among the celebrants: Harpo Marx, Helen Hayes and Charles MacArthur, Ernest Hemingway, Heywood Broun, Herbert Bayard Swope, George S. Kaufman, Robert Sherwood, William Paley, Moss Hart, Ben Hecht, and Harold Ross.

The frivolity was manic. The cavernous entrance hall with its great organ would be turned into a badminton court. Woollcott and Swope presided over the intensely serious croquet matches on the lawn, while

Broun was the master of the indoor bowling alley. The favorite party game was "Murder," in which each guest had to devise a plausible alibi for an imaginary homicide; Broun, who was involved in forming the American Newspaper Guild and other union activities, once won by claiming that he was in the kitchen organizing the Harriman help. Marie seemed to have only the vaguest idea where the kitchen was. After one early-morning bowling tournament, she led an expedition to raid the icebox. After boldly venturing through a maze of subterranean passages, she happened upon one of the large service pantries. One woman opened a walk-in closet and found it filled with priceless silver trays, goblets, flatware, vases, and other loot. "Well, what do you know!" Marie exclaimed. "I never realized all this stuff was here."

Harriman's new social circle often had trouble knowing what to make of the somewhat aloof financier. Despite his general popularity, there was always a shell around him, a wall that separated him from fraternal comradery. They sometimes wondered whether he had any truly close friends. He was affable enough, even quite interesting when engaged in a discussion of foreign affairs or finance; but in a sharp and witty crowd, Harriman was resolutely neither. His mind would often seem to wander into some distant world. When there was speculation, even back in the 1930s, that Averell might be having trouble with his hearing, friends would use Dorothy Parker's comment when told of Coolidge's death: "How can you tell?"

Harriman's parsimony also became the butt of many barbs. Even though his family foundation was noted for its philanthropy, prying a contribution out of him was next to impossible. Harriman picking up a lunch tab or taxi fare was unheard of. In fact, legend had it that Harriman rarely carried cash. Even in money matters, he operated in a realm of his own.

His was a cheapness, of course, peculiar to the very rich. Even though his most daring international ventures were somewhat less than resounding successes, Harriman prospered in business with shrewd investments in such booming fields as radio stations and commercial airlines. He even weathered the collapse of the stock market in 1929 better than most of his colleagues. Yet by then, with the domestic economy and the prospects for world trade collapsing, Harriman was ready to pull back from his more venturesome financial dealings. His childhood and college ties provided a ready-made opportunity to consolidate his activities.

•   •   •

When he returned to New York after the war, there was no doubt that Robert Lovett was destined for a Wall Street career. Law school was unable to hold his interest. At his parents' homes in Manhattan and Locust Valley, he encountered a much headier atmosphere. His father, then chairman of the Union Pacific, had served on the War Industries Board and become a leader of the economic establishment. Among those who came to his dinner parties were others who had been on the War Industries Board, such as Bernard Baruch, the financier and self-styled sage of Wall Street. Bob listened to discussions about industrial mobilization and offered his own ideas on the importance of airplanes to the nation's transportation and defense.

He even embarked on a dogged crusade to convince his father that the Union Pacific should establish an airline. While driving his father to work in his snappy new roadster one day, young Lovett wore his father down and convinced him to order a study of the idea. A few hours later the phone rang. "Have you seen the morning paper?" Judge Lovett asked. "Look at page one." There was a picture of an airplane that had crashed into the house of an ex-governor of New Jersey, its tail sticking from the roof.

"Well, that might happen once in a thousand times," said Bob.

"Once is enough," his father replied.

The idea was killed, and by the time Bob became a Union Pacific board member, federal legislation had been passed barring railroads from the air transport business.

Along with the Harriman brothers and other Yale chums, Lovett was a regular at the weekend parties given at the home of James Brown in Oyster Bay, not far from Locust Valley. Lovett had met Adèle, the youngest of Brown's three daughters, before he went off to war. "When he first came over, I thought he wanted to see one of my sisters," she recalls. "But when he kept coming over, I found out he had wanted to see me." Adèle was impressed by Lovett's lanky and angular good looks, his wry smile and humor. Bob was taken by the striking beauty of the girl whose debut had provoked more than the usual fawning in the glossies of the time. They were married in 1919, taking their honeymoon across country by train, stopping at the Harriman hunting lodge on the way.

Judge Lovett, ever eager to hone his son's mind, gave him four volumes of Immanuel Kant to read on his honeymoon. Young Lovett, who prided himself on an agile mind unclouded by dogma, was particularly struck by the section of the *Critique of Pure Reason* called the Antinomies, in which the German philosopher places pairs of contradictory propositions side by side and proceeds to offer airtight "proofs" of each.

James Brown, pleased by both the marriage and the prospect of treating Lovett as the son he never had, secured for Lovett an apprenticeship at the National Bank of Commerce, where he worked the overnight shift checking out the balances of each day's transactions. He joined Brown Brothers in the autumn of 1921, starting as a "runner" carrying messages and transactions. He quickly became interested in European transactions; during his training he worked both in London and New York for Brown Shipley & Company, a Liverpool-based merchant bank founded by the Browns in 1839. He was made a full partner of Brown Brothers in 1926, the same year that he joined the board and executive committee of the Union Pacific.

The Great War finally had dissolved many of the social barriers between the new money of industry (such as the elder Lovett and Harriman), the patricians of old society, and the gay café life of artists and writers. Robert and Adèle Lovett settled easily at the confluence of a new cosmopolitan life-style marked by wealth, cleverness, and social grace. They built a town house on East 83rd Street, with a living room adorned by a cathedral ceiling and a panoramic view of the East River. Their home in Locust Valley, next to the elder Lovetts', was decorated in what Dorothy Parker, the Algonquin Round Table wit, called "lovely soap-bubble tints" and murals painted by friends.

Lovett's closest companions were those he had met at Yale, such as Davison and Gates. But he and his wife soon became part of a social set dominated by writers and artists. Archibald MacLeish, the poet, was the older brother of Kenneth, the fallen hero of the Yale Unit. The playwright Philip Barry, author of such social comedies as *The Animal Kingdom* and *Here Come the Clowns*, was also a friend from Yale, and his wife, Ellen, was a schoolgirl chum of Adèle's. Others in the circle included Robert Benchley, Robert Sherwood, Lillian Hellman, and Dorothy Parker, many of whom had also become friends of Averell and Marie Harriman.

Lovett's favorite relaxations were jazz music, mystery novels, and movies. After a few early forays on the golf course at the Links Club, he developed a lasting disdain for both exercise and the outdoors, pleading a series of ailments that were partly real and partly well-honed hypochondria. On some afternoons he would sneak away from work to take flying lessons on Long Island or, on occasion, spend a flirtatious afternoon on the beach of the Piping Rock Club with a woman he knew. Adèle likewise enjoyed her own social dalliances, including a noted friendship with Benchley. For a while, the Lovetts drifted apart; their marriage survived, however, and lasted happily until Adèle's death in 1986.

At one dinner party in Locust Valley, Lovett was called from the table to the telephone. "Yes, yes, why yes!" his guests heard him shout. "Let Austria have eight million dollars." When he returned to dinner, Benchley and others dubbed him "Give Austria Eight Million Dollars Lovett" and spent the evening asking if he had a few more dollars to spare. The next day he received a telegram sent anonymously by one of his guests: "You have made me the happiest little country in the world—Austria."

Lovett retained some of the traditions of the old style, wearing stiff collars with his dinner jackets rather than following the fashion for soft shirts. In a crowd of heavy drinkers, he was considered quite moderate, limiting himself to a couple of martinis or Bourbon mists before dinner and a brandy afterward. But in general he enjoyed the loose and relaxed attitudes of his New York circle. With his rubber face and wry humor, he was a great mimic, entertaining dinner parties with his imitations of great statesmen and parodies of the Chinese and the Russians. He could also do a wicked version of Averell Harriman, with a thick, plodding voice and glazed, deadpan eyes.

•   •   •

According to company lore, the talks began in a parlor car of the New Haven Railway in the spring of 1930 as the classmates returned from a Yale reunion. Actually, the idea of merging the century-old private banking house of Brown Brothers & Company with the aggressive new Harriman brothers' firms had been discussed years before. Roland Harriman had mentioned the possibility in the mid-1920s to Ellery James, his close friend from Groton and Yale who had joined Brown Brothers in 1919. Averell and Roland also brought it up with Lovett, who became a firm advocate of the proposal.

From a personal standpoint the merger made great sense. The Harrimans and their two top partners, Prescott Bush* (vice-president of their investment firm, W. A. Harriman & Company) and Knight Wooley (managing partner of their private banking house, Harriman Brothers & Company), had been Bonesmen at Yale with four of the younger partners at Brown Brothers: Lovett, Ellery James, Laurence

---

*Prescott Bush was later a U.S. senator from Connecticut; Vice-President George Bush is his son.

Tighe, and Charles Dickey. Their friendships had flourished in New York, where they shared each other's apartments and attended many of the same social events, in particular the weekend tennis parties given by James Brown.

The merger was also logical from a financial standpoint. Brown Brothers, with a venerable reputation built on four generations of wise stewardship of other people's fortunes, was faced with the imminent retirement of five of its senior partners, who wished to withdraw their accrued profits. Both of the Harriman brothers had large personal fortunes—about $80 million between them at the time—and an aggressive style of raising and investing cash. "Old-timers in Wall Street have seldom seen a more potent blend of conservative experience and aggressive practice," one financial expert said of the merger.

Thus on the evening of December 11, 1930, a select group of partners was summoned to the home of Thatcher Brown, a tall, scholarly-looking senior partner of Brown Brothers. He was not well known even to the financial press, but reporters were familiar with the man standing next to him in the library of his Park Avenue residence: Averell Harriman, now a bit slouched at age thirty-nine, a chain smoker with a somewhat haggard air, yet still trim, athletic, and imposing. When Brown finished reading his statement, reporters peppered him and Harriman with tough questions about whether the merger indicated any financial difficulties. But the stories that appeared the next day were universally adulatory, even celebratory. It was a welcome piece of good news amid the 1930 gloom. Indeed, the front-page *New York Times* story on the merger ran next to a report of the closing of the Bank of the United States, a commercial bank with sixty offices in New York City. (The New York *World* front page that day also contained stories on the suicides of two bankers.)

The new Brown Brothers Harriman firm established its headquarters in offices at 59 Wall Street where the Brown family's businesses had been located since 1843. Shortly before the stock market crash and the merger with the Harriman interests, Brown Brothers had built a thirty-six-story addition to its imposing marble building on the corner of Hanover Street. The dominant feature of the new building was the Partners' Room, an ornate sanctum with deep maroon carpeting and dark wood paneling, which had been transferred from the old building along with an imposing painting of four of the original Brown brothers. There the partners worked alongside one another at rows of bulky rolltop desks while British floor attendants, silent and correct, served as clerks.

While the rest of the country slept in deep isolationism, a close-knit clique of Wall Street bankers and lawyers, most of whom had traveled through Europe as children, met in the clubs of London and Paris and Berlin as friendly competitors putting together suitable investments for their firms. In a private and profit-seeking capacity, they were rebuilding a war-ravaged Europe in a manner as grandiose as many of these same men would employ a world war later with the Marshall Plan. In 1927, for example, three years before their merger, Brown Brothers and Harriman Brothers shared in a $250,000 line of credit to finance the export activities of a Berlin metals firm. An advertisement for Brown Brothers Harriman in 1934 boasted of investments in forty-five different countries.

The firm financed much of America's imports of metals, raw materials, and foodstuffs, and it pioneered a system of letters of credit and bankers' acceptances that eventually involved more than five thousand correspondents around the world. Responsibility for these transactions naturally fell to Lovett, who was nimble with complex calculations and enjoyed going on long inspection tours to observe how other companies operated. After the Brown Brothers Harriman merger, Lovett took over the international currency and lending operations of the new firm. On his twice-a-year trips, he would drive through Belgium, France, and Germany for six weeks at a time, inspecting industries and analyzing their finances. He particularly loved their organization charts, management systems, and details about the flow of products and profits.

Lovett's work was mainly that of an operating officer; Harriman was still the entrepreneurial force behind many of the firm's more venturesome international deals. They each seemed to represent a different stereotype of the Wall Street banker. By nature and breeding, Lovett was tactful, suave, and smooth; he excelled at bringing people together, calming controversies with his congenial wit, resolving problems in a collegial way. Harriman was imperious, or at least gave that appearance. People were able to work under him more easily than they could work with him. He believed in maxims and standards, many of them inherited from his rigid father, and was prone to impose them on situations. Lovett had doubts about Harriman's intelligence, though not his tenacity. Harriman, for his part, thought Lovett too cautious and unimaginative and tended to treat him as a subordinate.

Nonetheless the two men worked together well, Lovett remaining the more deferential, Harriman always a bit more magisterial. Whenever they were apart, they would write each other once or twice a day, special delivery letters speeding back and forth from Lovett on Wall Street to Harriman in his suite at the Mayflower Hotel in Washington or ski lodge in the Rockies.

"I very much hope that your discussion with Vincent Astor will not necessarily develop into an argument," Lovett wrote, with typical conciliatory style, in a "Dear Averell... Yours as Ever, Bob L" letter in 1934. The issue at hand was the weekly magazine *Today*, a pallid publication that Harriman, Astor, and others had founded to support both the New Deal and the interests of business. (In 1937, it was merged into another Astor venture to become *Newsweek*.) Lovett convinced Harriman that *Today*'s editor, the once and future FDR brain truster Raymond Moley, was turning the publication into "a personal journal dealing very largely with whom the editor hates or loves as the case may be." Lovett bitingly told Harriman that "the present magazine's slogan, 'A Personal Journal of Public Affairs,' should be changed to 'A Public Journal of Personal Affairs.'"

But when it came time to confront Astor, Lovett, as usual, fretted about Harriman's lack of tact.

> I do want to emphasize what appears to me to be the strategic advantage of making your criticisms broad while at same time being prepared to produce specific examples only if challenged [Lovett wrote]. Unless challenged, I don't think that specific examples do a great deal of good since they most frequently start bickerings about interpretations of language rather than getting the sense of the entire criticisms over... There is no point in unnecessarily making an enemy.

• • •

Ever since Harriman and Lovett had graduated from college, Judge Lovett had been grooming his son and that of his former boss to help run the Union Pacific railway empire. Averell had been elected to the railroad's board in 1913, while still a senior at Yale, and upon graduation began work in the railroad's operational headquarters in Omaha. "Judge Lovett was anxious for me to get training," recalls Harriman. Although he arrived in Omaha in his own private railway car, Averell had begun work as a lowly "trackwalker," and his fellow inspectors referred to him as "Bill." Within two years, Judge Lovett had made him vice-president in charge of all purchasing for the Union Pacific.

Harriman had quickly displayed his no-nonsense approach. The Union Pacific had been buying locomotives from the nation's two major suppliers, Baldwin and American. Baldwin invariably bid lower on contracts for freight engines, and American always submitted the best bid for passenger engines. The twenty-three-year-old Harriman figured that they were privately dividing the market. "A locomotive costs so much a pound, no matter what its details," he noted. So he calculated a reasonable price per pound for each locomotive and summoned to his Omaha office the sales executive of Baldwin. The company could have all or nothing at that price, he said. "Well, wait a minute. I can't give you an answer until I talk with my president," said the worried man. Harriman handed him the phone. "He says we'll take the business," the salesman reported after a quick conversation. American was upset, but Harriman saved the Union Pacific hundreds of thousands of dollars.

While he was engaged in his own shipping and investment ventures during the 1920s, Harriman had let his involvement with the Union Pacific lapse. But after he settled into Brown Brothers Harriman, he once again became active in railroading. The Illinois Central, which was still controlled by the Union Pacific, was in danger of collapse in 1931, and Judge Lovett gave Harriman the task of rescuing it. His remedy was drastic: He cut maintenance, stopped buying rails, reduced service, and laid off employees. "It was rather ruthless or else the company could not have survived," he later recalled. But the cuts pained him. He decided to be more creative and constructive in his approach to the Union Pacific when Judge Lovett died in 1932 and was succeeded as chairman by the son of the man he himself had succeeded twenty-three years earlier.

Bob Lovett was also actively involved with the Union Pacific by then, having been elected to its executive committee in 1926. It was an inauspicious time to be running the railroad: gross revenues had reached a record high in 1929 only to plunge 50 percent by 1932, a year that produced the company's first net deficit in more than thirty years. Harriman and Lovett, along with Roland Harriman, decided that the answer was to upgrade rather than cut back on passenger service.

When Lovett met him at an airplane one day, Harriman pointed to a stewardess and said: "We need those." So female passenger attendants were added to Union Pacific trains. Harriman also came up with the idea of having good, inexpensive meals for all passengers. Lovett, as might be expected, objected; according to his calculations it would be cheaper to pay every passenger the then-grand sum of two dollars to refrain from using the service. But he was overruled. To expand the tourist trade, Harriman decided to build a ski resort in Sun Valley, Idaho. Even Marie Harriman got involved, insisting that the unattractive green plush seats and curtains be redecorated in red and other bright colors. "But we've always used dark green," one of the officers told her. "Precisely," she replied. Passenger revenues rose 21 percent in 1935 and 35 percent the following year.

Their most important innovation was developing a radical new "streamlined" train with diesel power and sleek aluminum coaches. When a three-car demonstration model was ready for display, Harriman envisioned a major unveiling: a well-publicized Chicago-to-Washington run ending with an inspection by President Franklin Roosevelt. As usual, Lovett was more cautious. He phoned Harriman in Washington to dissuade him and followed up with a letter later the same day. "Assume that, after all this hullabaloo, it jumps a switch point and gets cracked up, or some bad engineering bug develops in it and makes the affair a fiasco," he wrote. "The safer and more reasonable procedure would be to get it safely into Washington, shine it up and polish it within an inch of its life, and then make the announcement."

Even the following week, after the train had reached an astonishing 75 mph during a test in Michigan, Lovett was dubious. "I am still scared to death of an exhibition run," he wrote. "While it would undoubtedly be grand publicity, I still wonder whether the game is worth the candle. If any slight thing should go wrong, it would be magnified and receive a degree of publicity which might retard the advance of speed trains for years. I feel better having got that off my chest and I won't bother you about it any more."

Harriman had no such qualms. On February 15, 1934, the *City of Salina* streamliner arrived in Washington, where Harriman proudly posed with FDR on the steps of one of its gleaming cars. Three more trains were ordered for transcontinental service. The first made its inaugural cross-country run in October in less than fifty-seven hours, shattering the previous record.*

---

*The old record had been set when E. H. Harriman returned in 1905 from his trip to the Far East, having sent Averell home early so he would not miss the beginning of Groton's term. Alice Roosevelt, TR's older daughter, happened to be a passenger on E. H. Harriman's private train, which reached such speeds as it crossed the U.S. that it became a matter of newspaper comment. "Please take care of the safety of my daughter on your train," President Roosevelt wired in what was to be one of the last friendly exchanges between the two men. Replied Harriman: "You run the country. I'll run the railroads."

• • •

Harriman had supported Franklin Roosevelt's candidacy in 1932, paying a well-publicized social call at Hyde Park shortly after Roosevelt was nominated. The following year, his sister Mary had become the chairman of the NRA's Consumers Advisory Committee. At the urging of Herbert Bayard Swope, Harriman also accepted a volunteer position with the NRA, as New York State chairman of the Emergency Re-employment Campaign. The group's work climaxed with a Blue Eagle procession down Fifth Avenue in September of 1933 in which 250,000 marchers and more than a million spectators made up the largest crowd that had ever gathered for a parade in the city. The heady emotionalism of it all helped make politics, a realm of power Harriman had hitherto left unexplored, a new source of fascination for him. Although he was not yet ready to join the government, Harriman decided he was willing to serve part time as one of the tame businessmen Roosevelt was recruiting to Washington.

In November of 1934, Harriman became the Chief Administrative Officer of the NRA, moving from Wall Street down to his suite at the Mayflower until the Supreme Court abolished the agency six months later. In an article he wrote for *Today*, he defended the New Deal against businessmen who were attacking Washington's right to regulate labor conditions. "The man who can hold his place in the competitive system only by working women and children for long hours at low wages has no right to survive." Partly as a reward for his NRA work, Harriman was chosen as vice-president and later chairman of the Business Advisory Council, a group of corporate leaders, such as Thomas Watson of IBM and Robert Wood of Sears, who advised the Commerce Department and sought both to defend and moderate New Deal programs. The positions allowed him to continue his work on Wall Street while remaining involved in the world of Washington.

Lovett's economic outlook, on the other hand, was traditionally conservative, and he heartily disapproved of what he regarded as Harriman's unholy alliance with the Democrats. In 1933, Lovett joined with the banker J. P. Warburg to issue a public warning that New Deal policies threatened to cast the country into an inflationary spiral. Four years later, he wrote an article for *The Saturday Evening Post* called "Gilt Edged Insecurity" cautioning that what seemed to be blue-chip investments could prove to be less than secure. Keynesian economics he haughtily dismissed.

Scattered blasts at the New Deal's "reign of terror" against business began to crop up in Lovett's regular notes and letters to his partner.

"The young hot dogs have taken the first step toward breaking down the channels of private capital," Lovett wrote Harriman in one missive, referring to Felix Frankfurter's protégés. "The Administration should not permit this situation to continue and should no more be intimidated by the Brain Trust than by business interests or the Stock Exchange." But their friendship far transcended politics. As Lovett remarked at the end of a particularly scathing three-page note about Roosevelt's policies: "Don't judge from the heat of this missive that I hold you personally responsible for it."

Indeed, most of their correspondence involving Harriman's government work was of a very practical nature. Like many other financiers of the time, Harriman and Lovett tended to blur the boundaries between their public and private affairs.* Whenever Harriman was down in Washington, Lovett tended to write about economic matters that he thought should be "of vital interest to the Administration."

Some letters were quite specific, involving what today would be seen as clear conflicts of interest. "We have been swamped with cable inquiries from abroad as to whether or not we would buy gold," Lovett wrote in 1934, noting that Brown Brothers Harriman could purchase one million French francs ($63,000) and reap a $2,800 profit if they could be exchanged for gold that the U.S. Treasury would buy. The problem, which Lovett asked Harriman to explain to his colleagues in government, was that the Gold Revaluation Act released the Treasury of the legal obligation to buy private gold offered to it. "This, of course, has thrown the exchanges into a state of great uncertainty," wrote Lovett, "and it is really a darn shame that someone familiar with the market did not forewarn the Treasury as to what would happen." Unable to resolve all the uncertainties, Lovett wrote the following day that the firm had decided on "marking time" before making a move.

Despite Harriman's dalliances on the periphery of the New Deal, he and Lovett had been mainly concerned with private business affairs during their two decades on Wall Street. Foreign developments tended to be viewed from a financial perspective, with Lovett cautiously guiding the international business of Brown Brothers Harriman while Harriman slowly withdrew from his most venturesome endeavors to become a pillar of the financial establishment.

---

*Harriman, for example, continued to be involved with his business interests and to hold his Soviet securities throughout World War II. Unlike Lovett, who resigned from Brown Brothers Harriman upon entering government in 1940, Harriman remained an active partner during his wartime government service.

But by 1939, events were unfolding that would inexorably thrust to the fore those whose visions extended beyond the nation's borders. The portents were confusing. Germany and Russia, briefly joined in a cynical alliance, carved up Poland between them, plunging Europe into a war that seemed at once both menacing and phony. Congress resisted Roosevelt's appeals for revisions in the neutrality legislation; the American people seemed surprisingly sympathetic to Charles Lindbergh's pronouncements that "we must not be misguided by this foreign propaganda that our frontiers lie in Europe." Perhaps most baffling was a discovery that few in America knew anything about: Niels Bohr, at a meeting of the American Physical Society in Washington that year, reported that his colleagues in Copenhagen had produced 200 million volts of electricity by splitting an atom of uranium.

"How do you feel about Europe and everything else?" inquired Harriman in a one-sentence telegram he sent to Lovett from Sun Valley in March of 1939. The tone seemed jovial, even flip. But Lovett knew Harriman well enough to realize that he was not simply making idle telegraphic chatter. The question demanded a serious answer. "Consider Czechoslovakian moves logical result of Munich Pact," Lovett replied that same day. "In north danger seems to be quick thrust on Holland in which event believe British would fight ... Foreign news overshadows all factors affecting market here... Good faith of domestic appeasement program again being questioned ... Best regards, Bob."

CHAPTER 4

WORLD COURTS
McCloy and Acheson
before the bar

The Cravath firm on Wall Street was a sweatshop, and John McCloy relished it. Told that a complete reshuffling of the Denver & Rio Grande Railroad was due to be signed the next morning and that he and another associate would have to spend the night drawing up the reams of contracts, he literally rubbed his hands in glee. Nothing pleased McCloy more than having important people counting on him. Donald Swatland, his fellow associate, ordered out for two steak dinners. McCloy called the restaurant back and asked to have a dozen fat cigars included. Deftly flicking ashes into the corner wastebasket, they polished off the documents before dawn. After showering and changing into fresh shirts, they arrived precisely at the appointed hour for the signing ceremony.

The rush by American bankers and businessmen to invest in Europe after World War I set off a scramble by major Wall Street law firms vying for foreign business. The legal world, like the financial one, had always been part of the backbone of the American Establishment. After the Great War, it offered bright and ambitious young men, such as McCloy and Acheson, entrée into that world and more: it gave them the chance to handle international cases, to avoid the insularity infecting the rest of the country, and to become part of the coterie that would eventually spearhead America's wider involvement in world affairs.

At the forefront of this international work was the firm of Cravath, Henderson & de Gersdorff (now Cravath, Swaine & Moore), which John McCloy joined as an associate in 1925 after a brief period doing railway work at another Wall Street firm. The shop, whose roots stretched back to 1819, was being transformed by Paul Cravath into the first of the modern Wall Street law firms. He recruited as associates the brightest law graduates from Harvard, Yale, and Columbia, carefully trained them, and after six or seven years of grueling work invited the best of them into the partnership. This produced what is now common at major Wall Street firms: a sweatshop atmosphere in which associates worked eye-blurring hours scrambling to make partner. It also created a meritocracy, where the tenacity of a young man like McCloy was valued more than family status.

Through his work at Cravath, McCloy became friends with Lovett and Harriman. In the ten years after he joined the Cravath firm, McCloy helped paper more than $77 million worth of bond issues for the Union Pacific. Later he joined Lovett and Harriman on the railroad's board of directors. McCloy even became the paper president of a railroad, albeit briefly. In 1926, he and Swatland worked on a purchase plan for the Chicago, Milwaukee and St. Paul Railroad. For technical reasons, they had to organize a temporary holding company in Delaware. McCloy was designated the president. The next day, just as the holding company was being dissolved, the newspapers published his youthful, shock-haired photograph as America's youngest railway president.

More importantly, McCloy dealt with Lovett and Harriman through Cravath's international work. In 1925, for example, the firm collaborated with Brown Brothers & Company on the issuance of $30 million of bonds for the kingdom of Norway. That year the firm also dealt with some of the mineral concessions being offered by the Soviet Union; McCloy worked closely with Harriman, who was considering an investment in a British firm that had acquired some Soviet mining rights. "The friendships and associations I made, and the work habits I developed, were of lasting value," McCloy recalled later. "I knew I could hold my own with anyone. I knew I could accomplish any task, that I could be the type of person others depended on, rather than the type who had to depend on others."

When he first moved to New York, McCloy took a room with a family in Forest Hills so that he could frequent the West Side Tennis Club. In the winter, he was a regular at the indoor tennis courts of the Heights Casino in Brooklyn, where he once won a set from the legendary Bill Tilden. As a fisherman, he was equally tenacious. On his summer excursions with Lew Douglas, McCloy would wander off alone for miles upstream, sometimes searching all day for the perfect fly-casting spot. Once, when a friend gave him a new casting rod, McCloy was so anxious to try it out that he took it to the roof of his apartment building and began casting onto the street below. When the line became tangled on a pedestrian, McCloy and the friend quickly cut the line and ducked behind the cornice.

Although he led a relatively frugal bachelor's life, McCloy gradually began to blossom socially. Opera became a genuine love, and he enjoyed dressing in full white tie and tails for a date at the Met followed by chowder at the Oyster Bar in Grand Central Station. Eventually, he was invited to join the University, Grolier, Anglers, and Broad Street clubs, which—though not quite as tony as some of those frequented by the Brown Brothers Harriman crowd—gave him access to the elite world he had long admired. He also became a regular at the Long Island and Westchester County house parties frequented by Harriman, Lovett, and their friends.

Lovett, whose father was the Long Island neighbor of Paul Cravath, soon became a close friend. What impressed McCloy most was Lovett's studious yet easygoing manner and social grace. Harriman he considered to be far less clever and a bit too ambitious. "Most of the people who worked with Averell on Wall Street felt he did not pull his weight, and that he was not too bright," McCloy later recalled. "He used to subsidize politicians and people like Harry Hopkins so that he would have a line into power. But he was very tight in other ways with his personal money, particularly when it came to charity. He was good-looking, affluent, and very aloof back then, which made him quite a lady's man. I once attended one of those lavish polo parties and felt out of my milieu. He had an air about him, one that Lovett never sought to affect."

McCloy's early years at Cravath came during a period of rapid growth for the firm. When he joined in 1925, it had forty-one lawyers; when he became a partner in 1929, there were fifty-nine. Much of the expansion came from international business. Before World War I, investment capital tended to flow into the U.S. from Europe. The Cravath firm had handled much of this business ever since founding partner Richard Blatchford was retained as counsel for the Bank of England in 1826. After the armistice, when capital started to flow in the other direction, American bankers, with encouragement from Washington, eagerly sought foreign investments that would help finance the rebuilding of Europe. Paul Cravath, an early bankroller of the Council on Foreign Relations, assured that his firm handled much of this legal work.

Soon after McCloy joined Cravath, the firm participated with J. P. Morgan in a mammoth $110 million loan to the German government. In the ensuing years, McCloy spent much of his time traveling in Europe. For almost a full year he lived in Italy, where the Cravath firm was advising the government. "What took place after World War I was the forerunner of the Marshall Plan," McCloy later said. "But back then the rehabilitation of Europe was done in a private capacity. Practically every merchant bank and Wall Street firm, from J. P. Morgan and Brown Brothers on down, was over there picking up loans. We were all very European in our outlook, and our goal was to see it rebuilt."

As would happen to other leaders of the American Establishment, McCloy became entranced by Jean Monnet, the brilliant French brandy heir, economist, and statesman who later became the éminence grise to the Wise Men of American foreign policy. Monnet was then an international financier with Blair & Company in New York and Paris, and McCloy became his lawyer. Together they worked on issuing securities for European municipalities and the merger of Blair into Transamerica Corporation. Long nights were spent discussing the irrepressible Frenchman's evolving vision of a unified European economy.

One day in 1929, McCloy was in Arizona on business. When he boarded the train for the return home, he unexpectedly ran into his old friend and classmate Lew Douglas, by then an Arizona congressman, and his wife, Peggy. They rode together all the way to New York, where Peggy's sister, Ellen, the one who used to accompany Peggy on visits to Amherst, met them at Pennsylvania Station. The daughters of Frederick Zinsser and Emma Scharman Zinsser, Peggy and Ellen had been raised in a household where German was the first language. The Zinssers were a large family, both in the U.S. and in Germany (one cousin married Konrad Adenauer), and had been involved in various chemical businesses in the U.S. since before the Civil War. In 1897, Frederick Zinsser founded his own company in Hastings-on-Hudson, where he eventually moved his family.

Ellen had what was known in her family as *Fingerspitzengefühl*, a sensitive touch for dealing with people and situations. She knew how to handle the stolid yet driven young lawyer; for McCloy's part, he decided she was exactly what he wanted in a wife. He called her within a week, and courted her for more than a year. Yet he approached marriage in a typically judicious manner, discussing its pros and cons, and the effect it would have on his career, until it became something of a joke among his friends. Finally his hand was forced by his firm: he was chosen to head Cravath's Paris office and was ordered to set sail on April 25, 1930. That morning he married Ellen and they sailed together.

Soon after he arrived in Paris, McCloy got a call from his New York office that would change the course of his career. He was told to travel to The Hague, where one of the firm's clients, Bethlehem Steel, was party to a complex case before the Mixed Claims Commission. It involved a mysterious explosion in July of 1916 at a munitions depot on a small spit of land near Jersey City known as "Black Tom." Bethlehem Steel, which had manufactured the munitions (scheduled for shipment to Russia), and the other plaintiffs sought to prove that the Germans had arranged the sabotage and to collect damages from German funds held in the U.S. McCloy sat in on the hearings and reported back to the firm that the suit would be lost because of lack of evidence. When his prediction proved true, he asked to be assigned to the case to begin work on getting a rehearing.

It turned out to be a ten-year assignment, replete with spooky midnight meetings and evidence worthy of a pulp thriller. One clue came in the form of a message written in invisible ink (actually lemon juice) on the pages of a 1917 issue of *Blue Book* magazine. The message was in the form of numbers that referred to pages in the magazine where pinpricks in the text spelled out words. They seemed to show that Fred Herrmann, a known German saboteur, had arranged the explosion with Paul Hilken, an American acting as a German agent. McCloy tracked down Hilken to a rooming house in Baltimore. He had disappeared, but an old suitcase in the attic contained check stubs showing his connection to German agents.

The Claims Commission again rejected the case in 1932, but McCloy refused to give up. He helped push through a law in Congress giving the U.S. attorneys power to subpoena witnesses. Along with Ellen, he crisscrossed Europe searching for more evidence. In Ireland they met with the fiery labor leader James Larkin, who had worked with German agents during the war. In Germany McCloy tracked down a furtive Russian agent named Alexander Nelidoff, who claimed to have incriminating documents. At one point McCloy reached for Nelidoff's pen, only to have the Russian grab it back and explain it was actually a canister of poison gas. McCloy followed Nelidoff to Berlin, where he got the documents, but research by British intelligence showed them to be frauds, probably planted by German agents seeking to discredit the American case. McCloy also met with Hermann Goering, Rudolf Hess, and other top Nazi leaders (who invited him to their box at the 1936 Olympic Games) to see if a settlement could be negotiated. But the potential agreement fell through when neither the claimants nor the Germans showed a willingness to honor it.

By 1935, McCloy had moved to Washington as the de facto commander of the large battery of lawyers and officials handling the case for the various plaintiffs. He showed an enormous ability for getting people to put aside their own rivalries, brusquely assigning tasks and coordinating the assemblage of mountains of evidence. An important break came when one of the lawyers discovered a handwritten postscript on a letter from an official of a German shipping company that linked German agents to the explosion.

After three more years on the case, McCloy retreated to the Ausable Club, a private community in the Adirondacks where he was a member, to dictate new briefs. When they were presented in 1939, the German representative on the Claims Commission walked out. Nevertheless, the commission rendered a judgment: it awarded approximately $21 million plus interest to the American claimants. After two more years of legal wrangling, Bethlehem Steel and the other companies received their checks.

Such perseverance was typical of McCloy, who was by then becoming a legend on Wall Street. In addition, the case established him as a deft coordinator, one who could get people to accomplish a task with a minimum of problems. Prominent lawyers at the time, unlike some of their counterparts today, made it a top priority to keep their cases and clients out of court, to settle issues rather than resort to confrontation and litigation. McCloy was a master at seeking accommodation and negotiating agreements; rarely did he or his clients appear in court.

All of this was done in a manner that avoided making McCloy any enemies; indeed, the history of the Cravath firm notes that "no Cravath partner has had greater personal popularity in the firm than McCloy." He showed an ability to delegate (knowing that oral arguments were not his forte, he hired former Attorney General William Mitchell for the job) and also to shoulder great burdens when necessary (he worked virtually around the clock in the summer of 1938 drafting the major briefs).

Particularly impressed was a man who had been peripherally involved in the case and who had a cabin near McCloy's at the Ausable Club: Henry Lewis Stimson. The once and future Secretary of War knew that the day was fast approaching when men with a knowledge of German espionage, and men who could be trusted to get things done, would be in great demand.

• • •

Like McCloy, Dean Acheson spent the two decades after leaving Harvard Law School making a national and international reputation as a worldly lawyer. But though Acheson forged many Wall Street connections, he decided from the start that Washington was the place to be.

On a golden March day in 1921, he and a small group of friends stood in front of a house on S Street in Northwest Washington and watched as a crippled, depleted man was helped through the door. Most of the town had flocked to see the inaugural parade of Warren Harding, featuring the world's largest broom topped by an American flag. But Acheson was more interested in paying his respects to a bowed and weary Woodrow Wilson, visionary of new freedom and international order.

Acheson, through his father's sermons and Frankfurter's teachings, had become a conscientious liberal, albeit one who would have felt slightly more at home in nineteenth-century England (with Lord Shaftesbury and the Factory Acts) than in twentieth-century America. There was still within him that tension between elitism and democratic romanticism exhibited in his Groton essay on American snobbery; even as he defended the struggles of the workingman, he chafed at the vulgarity of the masses. In addition, although he supported the League of Nations and labor unions, he disdained the utopian panaceas and socialist visions promulgated by the more woolly-minded reformers within the liberal movement.

In short, Acheson was a suitable protégé of the consummate liberal whom Felix Frankfurter sent him to serve: Supreme Court Justice Louis Brandeis, that imposing admixture of proper Bostonian, courtly Kentuckian, and Anglicized Jew. "I don't think the Justice puts the slightest faith in mass salvation through universal Plumb Plans," Acheson wrote in 1920, responding to Frankfurter's request for his opinion

of Brandeis's philosophy. "People haven't the intelligence for that sort
of thing. They have only the intelligence to operate in small personal
groups which deal with the things with which they are intimately
acquainted." Brandeis's creed combined liberalism with individualism, Acheson later wrote, and was concerned not with "the Holy
Grail" of a utopian society but with removing the obstacles placed by
cumbersome institutions "in the way of the individual search for ful-
fillment." In future years, Acheson would denigrate grandiose schemes
such as the United Nations by using Brandeis's derogatory phrase,
"Plumb Plans."

Acheson's duties included helping host the Brandeis "at homes"
attended by the great thinkers and socialites of Washington, such as
the aging progressive Senator Robert La Follette and the crusading
social critic Norman Hapgood, and serving as confidant during late-
night talks at the justice's office while Mrs. Brandeis was recuperating
from a nervous breakdown. "What is the latest dirt?" Brandeis would
ask conspiratorially as the Harding Administration scandals unfolded.
Acheson recorded Brandeis's pronouncements in his journal. "Isn't
there any way out?" a worried Acheson asked during the bitter coal
strike in 1919. "Yes," replied the patient Brandeis, "and the men will
find it, if only their money holds out and the west freezes for a couple
of weeks."

More importantly, Acheson helped write Brandeis's opinions, the
two of them swapping notes back and forth as Acheson worked at his
typewriter and the justice wrote in longhand. Brandeis was a stern
taskmaster. "Please remember that your function is to correct my
errors, not to introduce errors of your own," he thundered after discovering two faulty citations in the draft of an opinion rejecting an
argument by Elihu Root, who was challenging the nation's Prohibition
laws. As Acheson noted in *Morning and Noon*: "Justice Brandeis's
standard for our work was perfection as a norm, to be better on special
occasions."

Acheson became a meticulous craftsman, approaching both the law
and logic with the same precision as his master. Brandeis taught him
to be both a pragmatist and an empiricist, to be guided above all by
the facts of a situation. Yet he also learned that the law could not be
divorced from the ideals of social justice. In a draft for what turned
out to be an unpublished opinion supporting the United Mine Workers
in a case against the Coronado Coal Company, Acheson began: "The
facts present a picture of a primitive struggle clothed in the forms of

industry." Brandeis approved of the sentiments, but revised the draft to make the point just as powerfully with what Acheson later called "unadorned, uncolored statement of fact."

At the core of Brandeis's rigorous analytical approach was the avoidance of a mushy moral relativism. Like Acheson, the justice believed that laws necessarily had to reflect the shifting attitudes of society. Yet both men believed, with a firmness that sometimes produced a conflict with their pragmatic instincts, that certain transcendent moral principles remained immutable. Acheson once took Professor Manley Hudson of Harvard to see Brandeis. Hudson asserted that moral principles were simply generalizations to be made from the prevailing mores of a time. "The eruption was even more spectacular than I anticipated," Acheson later wrote. "The Justice wrapped the mantle of Isaiah around himself, dropped his voice a full octave, jutted his eyebrows forward in a most menacing way, and began to prophesy. Morality was truth; and truth had been revealed to man in an unbroken, continuous, and consistent flow by the great prophets and poets of all time."

Neither Brandeis nor his own mentor on the court, Oliver Wendell Holmes, wore the nobility of their principles lightly; theirs was a weighty code borne with stoic grandeur. Acheson, likewise, came to believe that a personal code of conduct and the courage of one's convictions provided a person's life with its ultimate purpose. It was a worthy ideal, although it took men of great bearing to pull it off without appearing haughty. In addition, Holmes and Brandeis reinforced Acheson's undue pride in not suffering fools lightly. As Frankfurter later noted: "Holmes possessed a caustic intellectual stringency which when passed on to younger people was not always admirable."

Yet there were worthy lessons to be learned from Holmes's and Brandeis's fealty to their convictions, ones that would serve Acheson well when his own code was assailed in later years. When the Red-hunting fury fomented in 1920 by Attorney General A. Mitchell Palmer was in full force, Holmes and Brandeis stood in lonely dissent to the majority opinions being handed down by a conservative court. One case involved the harsh prison sentence meted out to a Brooklyn man who had distributed Marxist leaflets from his tenement. The other justices pressured Brandeis and Holmes to join in a unanimous opinion upholding the verdict. Acheson's classmate Stanley Morrison, who was clerking for Holmes, described to him how the other justices even enlisted Mrs. Holmes when they came to make their case. Yet neither

Holmes nor Brandeis would budge. "The best test of truth," Holmes wrote in his ringing dissent, "is the power of the thought to get itself accepted in the competition of the market."

Acheson's ambition and pragmatism did make him somewhat cautious in the face of Palmerism, despite his deep revulsion toward it. One evening during the 1919 coal strike, he was invited to the Georgetown house of a friend, the liberal journalist William Hard. There he met three union officials from West Virginia who spoke of the miners' plight. The West Virginia government, they said, was rigged against them, and they wished to secede from the state. Acheson's liberal sympathies did not extend this far, nor did he want to risk being snared in one of Palmer's crusades. Clearly the meeting was no place for a Supreme Court clerk, he decided. He pointed out that the plan was doomed to failure, and perhaps a bloody showdown. "While they digested this somber prediction, I said that I must be off, and left feeling far from a hero, but less like a conspirator," he recalled.

"Nevertheless," he added, "the essential role of labor unions in the scheme of our times was to me no longer a purely intellectual conclusion. I had passed the first test of a liberal; it was a conviction." Like both his father and Brandeis, Acheson had a sympathy for the working class that was bestowed from a consciously upper-class vantage, an outlook that edged him toward allegiance to the Democratic Party. Years later, after the International Ladies Garment Workers Union had become one of his clients, its flamboyant president, David Dubinsky, introduced Acheson to his union convention as "not only brilliant as a lawyer, well known as a progressive, but one who could understand the heart of our labor movement."

His pro-union sentiments, however, never took precedence over his concern for social stability. A breakdown of order, he felt, was an irrational abandonment of common interests, and there was nothing Acheson valued more than rationality. In a letter to Frankfurter in 1921, Acheson discussed the question of whether unions should be "free to organize and strike and picket and throw bricks and generally bust up the other fellow's business." His conclusion: "It may be that the best way is just to bust the other fellow; but when your method would apply to busting any order which possibly could be conceived you must expect to run afoul of the legal tradition."

Brandeis took the unusual step of asking Acheson to stay on as his clerk for a second year, noting sardonically that it would be improper to unloose him on the legal world with his shocking state of ignorance. When it finally came time to foray into less exalted realms, Acheson became one of nine lawyers in the fledgling Washington firm of Covington & Burling, soon to become Covington, Burling & Rublee.

J. Harry Covington was a prominent Wilsonian Democrat who served as a Maryland congressman and as Chief Justice of the District of Columbia Supreme Court. Edward "Ned" Burling, a poor boy from Iowa who had gone on to Harvard College and then the law school, had been the general counsel of the Shipping Board, handling contracts with young Averell Harriman among others. George Rublee, who was to become one of Acheson's closest friends, was in the first class to graduate from Groton, and his athletic and academic prowess, chiseled on the walls of the school, was still legendary when Acheson and Harriman were there. After Harvard College and law school, Rublee alternated between being a professional success and an international social dilettante. He joined Brandeis in the crusade to establish the Federal Trade Commission; with Jean Monnet, he worked on the Allied Maritime Transport Council during World War I.

The firm they formed in Washington was designed to take advantage of the international commerce that boomed at the end of World War I. Just as Wall Street was then discovering the new world of opportunity, the concurrent expansion of American trade and federal regulation in the 1920s transformed the sleepy swamp of Washington into a center of international legal work. By far the firm's biggest case was the one that Acheson was hired to work on: representing the Norwegian government in its $16 million claim against the U.S. for Norwegian property (mainly ships on order) seized during the war. The case was to be heard by the Permanent Court of Arbitration sitting at the Peace Palace in The Hague.

Acheson was fascinated both by the grand stage on which he found himself and by the notion that international order could be based on abstract principles of law. Yet his training with Brandeis taught him that the facts, and not the theory, should sway the case. Returning to the stacks of the Library of Congress, where he had researched his drafts for Brandeis, Acheson compiled an impressive array of precedents showing the U.S. to be liable for the full value of the contracts it had expropriated.

Faced with the impressive brief of the case for Norway, lawyers representing the U.S. countered by challenging the legitimacy of the contracts, arguing that they had been "tainted" because most were "purely speculative" agreements negotiated by a shady Norwegian, Christoffer Hannevig. Acheson and Burling sailed to The Hague in the summer of 1922 to argue the case. Although it seemed to be going well, the "taint of Hannevig" argument was muddying the issue. The challenge faced by Acheson, Burling, and the other lawyers for Norway was to force the U.S. hand, to get the U.S. to admit that the claims were valid and that only their value was in dispute. Acheson was delegated to make the argument.

As he climbed the elevated pulpit in the Peace Palace, the young lawyer decided to gamble by attacking head on the American suggestion that the claims were made in bad faith. "Some very severe things were said about these claims," he noted, "things which look to us as though they related to the validity of the claims and the good faith of the purchasers, and, perhaps, in some cases they tended to reflect somewhat on the Kingdom of Norway in presenting these claims." He challenged the U.S. agents to clear up this implication: "We felt that some statement was due us. We felt that some statement was due the Kingdom of Norway."

In effect, he was demanding that his own government apologize, a demand that the presiding judge noted with surprise and which Acheson confirmed. If the U.S. side decided to respond by vigorously pursuing its contention that the contracts were invalid, the whole case might be lost. Burling scribbled a note and handed it up to Acheson at the lectern. "SHUT UP," it said in a large, emphatic scrawl. But the gamble had been made, and it paid off. The U.S. side was unwilling to hinge its case on the make-or-break argument that the claims were not legitimate. The contracts were valid, conceded the U.S. lawyer, only their value was in question. With that, the Hannevig issue was put into perspective. The court ended up awarding the claimants $12 million.

Upon his return, Acheson settled down to the life of a prosperous corporate lawyer. Years later, Jean Monnet talked of the role played by lawyers in foreign policy. Expressing his surprise at how the law was such an important training ground for statesmanship in the U.S., he speculated that it was because attorneys were trained to deal with complex situations by finding both precedents and innovative pragmatic approaches for dealing with them. Indeed, two of Monnet's closest friends, Acheson and McCloy, came from such a tradition.

Kennan was of a contrary view; he often complained that legalistic captains of foreign policy were continually drafting complex treaties that were never invoked and bore little resemblance to the realities of power. Lovett was also of the school that legal training produced a cadre of bickering wordsmiths who were inept at getting things done. As for Acheson, he occasionally cast a jaundiced eye on lawyers in government, admitting that they were better suited to taking directions from clients than making policy decisions of their own (he attributed Cordell Hull's maddening fecklessness to his years as a judicious attorney); yet Acheson also felt that the best statesmen were those who had the attributes of great lawyers, in particular an ability to remain emotionally detached from a case and appreciate the facts on both sides.

One case that brought Acheson into contact with Harriman and Lovett involved Richard Whitney, a Groton-Porcellian man who became president of the New York Stock Exchange and was later convicted of securities fraud. Harriman was among those who innocently lent Whitney money (fifty thousand dollars in Harriman's case) when he was secretly trying to cover the funds he had embezzled and lost. Acheson represented the interests of the Stock Exchange in the case. He also took on a case at the behest of his friend Lew Douglas, the Arizona congressman and in-law of McCloy, in which he opposed the building of the Boulder Dam. His argument that the Colorado River was not navigable, and thus could not be altered with federal funds, was dismissed by the Supreme Court on the grounds that a handful of adventurers had in fact navigated its course. Brandeis sent down from the bench a consolation note to his protégé: "Felicitations on an excellent argument."

Acheson, in fact, lost every one of the first fifteen cases that he argued before the Supreme Court. Yet much to the envy of the other young members of his firm, who resented his talent for self-aggrandizement and impressing his powerful elders, Acheson's reputation as a brilliant legal conceptualizer tended to rise with each loss. Even senior partner George Rublee took to describing the younger Grotonian, in words William James applied to George Santayana, as "the shiniest fish that ever came out of the sea."

"He always maintained a cool detachment," one associate later remembered. "Some lawyers get so steamed up they think their client is the Lord God Almighty fifteen minutes after he has stepped into the office. Acheson always saw the client as representing a soluble problem, and nothing more." He once wrote a complex brief that prompted an impressed client to accost him at the Oak Bar of the Plaza in New York. "Your brief is a work of art, a masterpiece of legal thinking," said the client, pumping Acheson's hand. With the bemused tolerance he bestowed upon the overly enthusiastic, Acheson replied: "Not a bad brief. It almost convinced me." As another colleague put it: "Dean always had a haughty attitude about clients, as he did about most everything, which was evident whenever he would arch his eyebrows or twitch his mustache."

The mustache. Throughout his life, when friends endeavored to describe him, the subject of Acheson's reddish-gray bushy mustache would come up, as if it were a reflection of what lay behind it. While he was a young lawyer, it was somewhat untamed and overgrown, seeming to mask a remnant of schoolboy insecurity, a touch of defiance. It was tailored not by wax but by Acheson's rough tugging while he thought, making it bristle upward. As he matured, so did the mustache. It came to symbolize his urbane elegance. "Though it once seemed about to climb his cheeks, like a vine seeking sunlight, it now is comparatively self-controlled and at peace with itself, quietly aware of its responsibilities," wrote *The New Yorker* magazine in a 1949 profile. "While still giving off gay hints of the unpredictable, it is the adornment of a man who has conquered not only himself but his mustache."

Acheson took justifiable pride in his ability to cut through a morass of complexities and facts to reach the kernel of a problem. Yet he had neither Harriman's probing curiosity nor Kennan's philosophical depth. "Dean took pleasure in finding the answer to riddles," said a former law partner. "The nature of the riddles did not concern him. He was not a man to wander into the penumbra of thought."

Acheson's success at Covington & Burling (of which he was made a partner in 1926) allowed him to live in the manner he fancied. He and Alice bought, for thirteen thousand dollars, a red brick house on P Street in Georgetown, built in 1843, to which they steadily added rooms over the years. Also during the 1920s, he bought a rambling 1795-vintage farmhouse called Harewood, seventeen miles away in Sandy Spring, Maryland. There he and Alice tended to the horses (including Brandeis's aging horse, named Sir Gareth), gardening, and the raising of their three children.

Perhaps it was his abundance of charm, his polished manner and wit, his agile mind and charming conversational abilities that caused Acheson to shine in the somewhat provincial backwater of Washington. Whatever the reason, he was one of those men who seem larger than life, who exude a compelling aura. Even as a young lawyer, he became the focal point for a wide variety of friends and admirers. Despite all of the social pretenses and latent anti-Semitism that pervaded his social class, Acheson's two greatest personal influences, Frankfurter and Brandeis, were both Jewish, and his friends ranged from Norman Hapgood to Sinclair Lewis, James Warburg to Archibald

MacLeish. He was at the center of a wide variety of clubs: the Penguin, a self-serious liberal discussion group; the Royal Bengal Bicycle, a vivacious social organization; the Alfalfa, named after the grass whose roots go deepest in search of drink. The small dinner parties that he and Alice hosted were known for their sparkle. When his Yale class celebrated its tenth reunion, the increasingly famous young lawyer was the one chosen as speaker.

Acheson, like most of his friends, was very much a Europhile as well as an Anglophile. He considered it madness to accompany loans to Europe with chauvinistic trade policies and harsh tariffs that made the debts difficult to repay. This belief in the orderly international flow of capital and of liberal reciprocal trade agreements was the most important factor in Acheson's disdain for the Republican Party.

Shortly before the 1928 election, he registered as a Democrat, persuaded not only by his anti-tariff and pro-union sentiments but also by the vibrancy offered by Al Smith. "For almost eight years the country, in a trance, seemed to have been following a hearse," he wrote. "Now at the touch of this prince in a brown derby, with his East Side accent, gay humanity and common sense, came an awakening." Yet his party affiliation was hardly firm: at the urging of Rublee, Acheson went up to New Jersey for a few weeks in 1930 to work in the Senate campaign of Republican Dwight Morrow. One great contribution made by Acheson, a confirmed drinker of martinis and Scotch, was convincing the candidate to make the repeal of Prohibition a key pledge of his campaign.

With Frank Page and Heywood Broun, Acheson journeyed to Chicago for the 1932 Democratic Convention that nominated Franklin Roosevelt. He found the conclave a "mad and not a little degrading spectacle," but he enjoyed being invited into the inner sanctum, flowing with strong drink, that the sergeant at arms ran for his cronies in the party. Upon his return to Maryland, Acheson helped run the local Democratic campaign, where his distaste for glad-handing and electoral politicking was confirmed. Most of his time was spent writing pamphlets and position papers. To his great delight, he was asked to the White House shortly after FDR's inauguration to help draft a proposed legislative program, drawing him closer to the flypaper of government service.

The post Acheson wanted from his fellow Grotonian was that of Solicitor General, which Frankfurter had declined in order to teach for a year at Oxford. But when FDR suggested Acheson to the new Attorney General, Homer Cummings of Connecticut, the reaction was violently negative. Acheson later surmised it was because his father, Bishop Acheson, had refused to bless a marriage sought by the divorced Cummings. Friends of Cummings said the rejection was due more to Acheson's hauteur.

A dejected Acheson subsequently embarked on a motor trip to Canada with Alice. When he returned, two old friends who had been top Treasury officials under Hoover and were helping with the transition asked him to lunch with the new Secretary, William Woodin. "I was hardly back in my office before the operator announced Secretary Woodin calling," Acheson later wrote. "Would I become Under Secretary?"

The Baltimore *Sun*, a fan of Acheson's, listed among his qualifications, "aloofness from contaminating contact with the subject matter of his new post." Some of the critics, however, thought him too contaminated by virtue of his Establishment connections. "Mr. Acheson and Mr. Woodin are going to be just as much the agents of the Morgan house as anybody we could possibly put in the Treasury," railed Michigan Senator James Couzens, an anti–Wall Street Republican, in the course of the hearings.

Acheson did not last long. Roosevelt's more liberal economists, led by Henry Morgenthau, Jr., then head of the Farm Credit Administration, persuaded the President that the Depression could be alleviated by raising prices. That meant devaluing the dollar, which in turn meant allowing the price of gold to rise above the price ($20.67 an ounce) that Congress had set by law. A more conservative faction, some of whom saw the unpegging of the dollar from gold as "the end of Western civilization," was led by Acheson's close friends Budget Director Lew Douglas and Wall Street financier James Warburg. For Acheson, who was Acting Secretary because of Woodin's illness, the question was less an ideological one than a legal one. He drafted an opinion telling Roosevelt what the law forbade him to do; Roosevelt responded, to Acheson's annoyance, that a lawyer's job was to find ways to circumvent such laws.

When Roosevelt decided to order a legal opinion from Attorney General Cummings saying that the Reconstruction Finance Corporation could buy gold at higher than the fixed price, Acheson paid a call on Brandeis to solicit his advice. "If I wanted a legal opinion, I would prefer to get it from you than Homer Cummings" was the justice's Delphic pronouncement. To Acheson, that meant he should stand his ground. He did. When Roosevelt summoned him to the

Oval Office, Acheson said that he was being asked to do something "contrary to the law." Asked FDR: "Don't you take my word for it that it will be all right?" Acheson lost his temper, replying that he was being asked to sign illegal documents. "That will do!" thundered Roosevelt.

Acheson wrote a short and graceful letter of resignation, thanking the President for his "many marks of kindness." Roosevelt did not respond, and Acheson learned from journalists that the President had accepted his resignation and chosen Morgenthau as his replacement. Nor was Acheson invited to Morgenthau's induction ceremony in the Oval Office, but he went anyway. Roosevelt, barely acknowledging Acheson's presence, gave a speech to the small gathering in praise of loyalty. There was a silence when he finished. Seeking to dispel the tension, Acheson walked up to the President, offered his hand, and thanked him for the opportunity to be of service. Roosevelt pulled him closer. "I've been awfully angry with you," he whispered, "but you are a real sportsman." Years later, when another official submitted a bristling letter of resignation, Roosevelt gave it to an assistant and said: "Return it to him and tell him to ask Dean Acheson how a gentleman resigns."

Acheson's friend Harriman would never have gone to the mat over a matter of principle with a President; he would likely have merely sidled away from the conflict to work on problems that he would be left to solve on his own. Lovett would probably have worked out some compromise, making any mountainous dispute seem suddenly like a small bump. So too would have John McCloy, the loyal workhorse; like Bohlen, he would have been willing to go along. Kennan would no doubt have agonized about resignation only to become lost in philosophical broodings. But Dean Acheson had a code, a fledgling one perhaps, but one he was stubbornly proud of.

In a peculiar way, Acheson seemed to have relished the fight. It was a chance to affirm his honor. Yet the stance he took was hardly typical: he was, at heart, a man of action, one who believed in the use of presidential power to accomplish social goals. Like most liberals, he objected to the legal obstacles that the Supreme Court was putting in front of the New Deal. In a 1936 speech to the Maryland Bar Association, he criticized the obstructionism of the court and defended the Administration's right to take forceful action to remedy the Depression. A few years later, in a similar situation, Acheson worked with Harriman and McCloy to devise a legal maneuver to circumvent

Congress's Neutrality Act and arrange for Britain to use mothballed American ships. When he served Harry Truman, he came to understand better the need for loyalty and deference. "I did not have enough consideration for the problems of the President," he later conceded of the gold-standard crisis.

Part of Acheson's problem was with Roosevelt personally. "I respected his ability to rule, but I did not like him," he later told a seminar at Princeton. The patronizing informality with which FDR treated other officials, using nicknames and summoning them to early-morning bedside meetings, rankled the proper Acheson. "He condescended," Acheson wrote of FDR in *Morning and Noon*. "To accord the President the greatest deference and respect should be a gratification to any citizen. It is not gratifying to receive the easy greeting which milord might give a promising stable boy and pull one's forelock in return."

An avid reader of English biography and history, particularly of the Victorian era, Acheson glorified that period as one when the Royal Navy and London merchant banks had enforced a Pax Britannica by ruling the high seas and extending capital for development around the world. The Great War had started, he believed, because a breakdown in that order led to the rise of dictators who responded to economic limitations with expansionist policies; it could happen again if America did not step into the vacuum left by Britain's decline. In the midst of the battle over the value of gold, Acheson led another unsuccessful effort to persuade FDR to loosen the terms for the repayment of the British war debt.

The League of Nations, he came to feel, was one of those "universal Plumb Plans" of which Brandeis had been so leery. The foundation for world order, Acheson was convinced, depended upon a free flow of American capital and a pragmatic military outlook. As he wrote in a letter to his son, David, at Groton: "The important thing in thinking about international affairs is not to make moral judgments or apportion blame but to understand the nature of the forces at work as the foundation for thinking about what, if anything, can be done."

Regarding the Soviet Union, Acheson was similarly pragmatic. Although they had no love for the Bolshevik system, Acheson and Frankfurter were strong proponents of recognition, often engaging in long arguments with others on the subject. "Refusing to recognize a situation makes it a difficult one to work with," Acheson noted to a friend.

Upon returning to Covington & Burling after his short stint in government, Acheson appeared to some as a potential leader of the Democratic conservative opposition to the New Deal. Among his major clients was a utility company seeking to enjoin the Public Works Administration from proceeding with rural electrification. He was considered a "sound" man, and was selected as a trustee of the Brookings Institution (then quite conservative) and of the Yale Corporation (edging out Senator Robert Taft for the honor). Yet, as he noted later, "not all my efforts were devoted to representing the forces of reaction in opposition to the children of light." He served as a forceful advocate for the International Ladies Garment Workers Union in its battles to organize factories and defend minimum wage laws. "I understand your difficulty in classifying me as a pro– or anti–New Dealer," he wrote a friend. "I couldn't classify myself. It is much more satisfying to me to consider specific proposals from the point of view of whether they are practicable methods of dealing with immediate problems."

When Lew Douglas and James Warburg, his allies in the gold fight, approached him about joining a Democrats for Landon movement in 1936, Acheson replied that nothing could be so foolish. In fact, he decided to go public with his support for Roosevelt's re-election in a letter to the Baltimore *Sun* (whose editors were so surprised to receive it that they called him for verification). What bothered him the most about the Republican campaign were the Red-scare tactics being used. "It seems to me utterly fantastic to suggest that Communism is in any manner involved in this campaign," he wrote. "It serves only to arouse a spirit of bigotry which we have experienced before and which always results in violation of constitutional guarantees of liberty and makes impossible sane consideration of public questions."

Years later Acheson would find himself the subject of Red-scare rhetoric. In 1939, it was his friend Frankfurter who was on the hot seat. The professor had been appointed by FDR to the Supreme Court and retained Acheson as a counselor for the confirmation hearings featuring Senator Patrick McCarran. Frankfurter refused to be intimidated by the Nevada senator or to be drawn into a discussion of Marxism. "Senator," Frankfurter replied at one point, "I do not believe you are more attached to the theories and practices of Americanism than I am. I rest my answer on that statement."

The room began to stir. Senator Matthew Neely of West Virginia motioned Acheson for a private word. Frankfurter, the senator warned, was falling into a trap. He would have to make some accommodation; he would have to answer a question on Communism directly. Acheson the pragmatist agreed. He returned to the witness table to beseech Frankfurter to be sensible.

When Neely asked his friendly question—"Are you a Communist, or have you ever been one?"—Frankfurter played the game.

"I have never been and I am not now," replied Frankfurter.

"By that do you mean that you have never been enrolled as a member of the Communist Party?" the senator added.

"I mean much more than that," said Frankfurter. "I mean that I have never been enrolled, and have never been qualified to be enrolled, because that does not represent my view of life nor my view of government."

As the crowd erupted in cheers, Acheson breathed a sigh of relief. The Red-baiters in Congress had been staved off. Principles and pragmatism had come to a suitable balance. In order to make sure that the newsreel cameras recorded the scene properly, Acheson had Neely and Frankfurter repeat it a few more times for their benefit.

"Let's see the President before going home," a jubilant Frankfurter suggested afterward. Acheson demurred, but Frankfurter persisted. They were waved past the White House gates and ushered through a back door of the President's office, where Roosevelt greeted Acheson as he would an old friend. Several weeks later, the President called Acheson at home on a Sunday afternoon. "Hello, Judge!" the President proclaimed.

"I'm afraid there's some mistake," he replied. "This is Dean Acheson."

"Not at all," FDR said. "Judge Acheson of the Court of Appeals for the District of Columbia. Your nomination goes to the Senate in the morning."

"But I don't want to be a judge," protested Acheson. "Would you?"

"No," said Roosevelt, "but I'm not going to be one and you are. That's the great difference."

Acheson eventually convinced FDR that he was too young to be sentenced to sedentary confinement on a court bench. "I would rather talk to damn fools than listen to them," Acheson argued. He also dissuaded the President from making him an Assistant Attorney General for civil rights, despite the obvious appeal of that farsighted new notion.

Yet Acheson was growing bored with his legal work; he yearned for a return to the great stage of power. "The heady experience of being in on big political decisions was like getting used to French cuisine,"

Frankfurter noted. "Once Dean had dined on such rare meat, it was painful to return to the hardtack of the law." As Europe edged closer to war, and his beloved England and his dreams of a world order seemed threatened, that yearning to be back in the thick of the struggle began to grow ever greater.

CHAPTER 5

Bohlen, left, with Johnny Herwarth at the dacha

A PRETTY
GOOD CLUB

Kennan and Bohlen
in the Foreign Service

Having decided that law school was too expensive, George Kennan headed for Washington in the autumn of 1925 to apply for a job with the Foreign Service. There he enrolled in a cram course run by a hard-drinking Scotsman from Virginia named Angus Crawford which prepared students for the entrance tests that the State Department had recently instituted. Still moody, still insecure, he was hardly ready to commit himself to the new career. "I haven't much hope of passing these exams," he wrote his father, "and when I've found out for sure that I have failed, I won't stay here any longer."

Although the vigor and solitude of a summer job on a cargo ship had temporarily restored Kennan's erratic health, he literally worried himself sick as he studied. "I hope you will not be alarmed at the heading of this letter," he scrawled on the stationery of a Washington hospital. "I am generally run-down." He continued to live frugally, work intensely, and spurn those who (either out of pity or because he could sometimes be charming despite himself) sought to engage him socially. "By refusing four invitations for Christmas dinner," he wrote in another letter, "I did manage to get a little studying done."

Despite his worries, Kennan was among the 16 students out of 110 to pass the written exam, though he barely made the 80 percent cutoff. His best subjects were international law and German; his worst, arithmetic (which he failed to finish) and modern history. At the oral exam, his voice broke into a squeaky falsetto when Under Secretary Joseph Grew asked the first question, yet he managed to pass that too. "I should be fairly satisfied had I not been forced to reveal an inexcusable ignorance about west central Africa, getting Nigeria and the Gold Coast all tangled up," he reported home. His only failure came on the physical. (In addition to his stomach woes, he had his tonsils removed that winter.) After a few days' scurrying around, he managed to persuade government doctors that he was fit.

With his breezy immunity to the anxieties that afflicted Kennan, Chip Bohlen thoroughly enjoyed his time spent preparing for the Foreign Service exams. Crawford—fond of Bourbon, shapely women, and the Democratic Party—was a character after Bohlen's heart. The day after Herbert Hoover carried Virginia in his 1928 election triumph, Bohlen recalled, "Crawford came to class drunk, delivered an impassioned lecture on the 'black shame of the Dominion of Virginia,' then disappeared for a week." As for the Washington social life, a relative of Bohlen's notes that perhaps the single greatest understatement in his autobiography is the comment that "as a bachelor in a city with many single girls, I enjoyed those charming days."

Although he never had Kennan's analytic depth, Bohlen had a more nimble mind. He found the written tests to be simple, a mere recollection of facts, and scored well above 90 percent. Nor did he get overwrought about the orals; with the help of some bootleg gin, he arrived at the inquisition noticeably relaxed. He muffed a question on the percentage of the U.S. population then living on farms (the correct answer, 25 percent; his answer, 40 percent), but otherwise performed with flawless grace.

One panelist, however, smelled the gin on Bohlen's breath and argued that he should be disqualified for his breach of decorum and of the nation's Prohibition laws. To his rescue came William Castle, the Assistant Secretary who had convinced Bohlen to join the Foreign

Service. A member of the examining board, Castle persuaded the others to overlook the indiscretion.

The Foreign Service that Kennan and Bohlen joined was slowly being transformed into a professional outfit. During the nineteenth century, while America indulged in a self-satisfied isolation from the intrigues of Europe, the diplomatic corps was dominated by upper-class easterners who thought it might be nice, after a career in industry and finance, to dally in the royal courts of the Old World. Ministerial appointments were political plums, and junior secretaries tended to be young dilettantes chosen for their family connections and prowess on the polo field. Most red-blooded Americans disparaged them as effete "cookie pushers" and "boys in striped pants."

The pressures for reform came mainly from the same en-lightened elite of upper-class progressives who were attempting to root out patronage from the rest of government. At the forefront were men like Joseph Grew (Boston's Back Bay, Groton, Harvard). They advocated a professional and dedicated Foreign Service, one that would represent to the world the best of their nation's heritage, culture, and breeding.

The reforms, however, were not exactly an attempt to democ-ratize the diplomatic corps; Grew, after all, took price in wearing his full regalia, including gold sword and fore-and-aft hat, when he presented himself to his Russian counterparts while serving in St. Petersburg in 1908. Of the new embassy secretaries recruited between 1914, and 1922, no less than 75 percent were from eastern prep schools, mainly Groton or St. Paul's. "They possessed a common background, common experience, and a common liking for old wines, proper English and Savile Row clothing," wrote Grew's biographer. The Foreign Service became, in the proud words of diplomat Hugh Wilson (of The Hill School and Yale), "a pretty good club."

The Rogers Act of 1924 carried the crusade for a professional For-eign Service one step further, a bit too far in fact for the likes of Grew and his coterie. The law merged the diplomatic and consular corps, provided for moderate salaries, and instituted standard tests for those seeking membership. After the law passed despite his qualms, Grew made sure that selection would depend heavily on an oral examination by elders in the State Department. It was important, he felt, that the new recruits, whatever their background, be the type who would adopt the values of the old club.

They generally did. Loy Henderson, one of the service's most successful products, recalls: "We accepted the baggage that distinguished the most elite of our members, and in fact did so eagerly. We liked the cloth they were cut from, and did not hesitate to tailor ourselves in their image." Many tried to be, in Felix Frankfurter's words, "more Grotty than the men who actually went to Groton in the State Department." Along with careers in international law and finance, service in the diplomatic corps offered young men a chance to become part of the country's foreign policy elite.

Bohlen instinctively knew the value of having the right connections, and he carefully cultivated the patronage of men like William Castle. For Kennan the discovery came slowly, and it intrigued him. Indeed, the social outcast from Princeton found the idea of being part of an exclusive society quite enticing. As his fellow students discussed whom they knew in the State Department, it belatedly dawned on him that college provided not just an education, but a network of professional and social contacts. When the president of his Princeton class, a celebrated athlete who had never spoken to Kennan as an undergraduate, ran into him on the street and invited him to dinner, Kennan wrote home excitedly: "I'm beginning to appreciate more than ever the value of a Princeton diploma; it's helped me out about ten times just since I've been in Washington."

The candidate in Kennan's class with perhaps the most pull was John M. Cabot, a member of the prominent Boston family and a relative of Grew's. That spring Cabot's mother came down to Washington, rented a big house, and set about putting those connections to work. Just before the oral exams, which Grew was conducting, Mrs. Cabot hosted a dinner in honor of the Under Secretary. To his astonishment, Kennan was one of five students she invited. "I was amazed to be asked, because I had never met her, hadn't called on her or anything," Kennan recalled. He spent sixty-four dollars on a new suit (blue pinstripes, as per a friend's advice) and made an impression as the serious scholar among that year's crop of hopefuls. "I always thought I got in the service because of being invited to the party," he later said.

•   •   •

Upon completing his training, Bohlen was posted to Prague, where he found that the Foreign Service reforms still had a way to go. One member of the mission had suffered a nervous breakdown, locked himself in his hotel room, and lived on raw beef and beer. "When he got word that the consul was coming to take him into custody,"

Bohlen recalled, "he jumped into a taxicab and headed for Carlsbad, scattering hunks of beef on the way, presumably to divert his pursuers." Bohlen's tasks were often less than lofty. Once, in an attempt to protect the dignity of the American flag, Bohlen sought to persuade a clothing manufacturer to quit displaying it on his products. "But I only use the Stars and Stripes," the businessman replied, "on our top-grade brassieres."

Bohlen lived well in Prague, fully indulging his taste for brandy and the theater. But he also impressed his superiors with his diligent interest in Russia and its language. "He appears to have a well-ordered intellect, which, if properly controlled and developed, seems to promise a career of exceptional usefulness," wrote A. C. Frost, the consul general, in an evaluation sent to Washington. Bohlen was a serious student, Frost said, but not pedantic. His greatest weakness: English composition. Bohlen hated to write. His penmanship was so poor he had trouble reading it himself, and he never learned how to type. Nor was he good at organizing his thoughts on paper.

Kennan, on the other hand, took a tremendous pride in his own prose style. Twice a week he wrote long letters home, carefully crafting them in a flowing hand or on his typewriter. When his father casually noted that the family found his discursive missives "interesting," Kennan wrote back that he was considering becoming a writer.

Most of his letters were florid travelogues that displayed his habit of typecasting people. From Germany, where he traveled after his Foreign Service exams, Kennan reported: "The German goes to a resort with the intention of lying around on the sand, of promenading on the boardwalk, of dressing up in white flannels and taking motor boat excursions (which I detest) in company with all the relatives and friends from *Grosspapa* down to the Dachshund, of sitting on terrace restaurants and drinking coffee while the municipal band plays, and finally spending five or six hours a night in the stuffy dining room of a hotel, drinking and making occasional solemn maneuvers which he thinks are dancing." There were, however, also frequent insights: "The students here have no faith whatsoever in representative government as an enduring institution for Germany. They expect that in time Germany will be forced again to submit to a dictator."

As part of his training, Kennan was briefly assigned to the Division of Eastern European Affairs. Loy Henderson, who was also there, recalls that even then he showed signs of intellectual arrogance. His opinions, says Henderson, were highly subjective, and when asked to back them with facts he would argue that they were intuitively obvious.

This did not impress the division's legendary chief and stern taskmaster, Robert Francis Kelley, who insisted on academic rigor and adherence to concrete facts. "He evidently credits me with abysmal ignorance, since all that he has thus far given me to do has been to study various text-books on Soviet Russia," Kennan complained.

Nevertheless, the experience confirmed his interest in the country his distant cousin and namesake had once explored. "I have strong hopes of learning enough Russian during the first part of my service to present the Department with a fait accompli when Russia is finally recognized," he told his father. "That would be more or less in the family tradition—to go to Russia."

But first Kennan had to work his way through the consular ranks, starting with an assignment in Hamburg. Unlike Bohlen, he did not find the manic gaiety of Europe in the twenties all that appealing, but he did enjoy the security provided by the well-defined structures of diplomatic life. "In this new role as a representative (however lowly) of a government rather than of just myself, the more painful personal idiosyncrasies and neuroses tended to leave me," he wrote. "I welcomed with surprised relief the opportunity to assume a new personality behind which the old introverted one could retire." As he stood in his new formal tails playing host at a July 4 reception, Kennan came to a comforting realization: "I no longer had to relate myself to others as a species of naked intruder on the human scene. I had a role to play, a useful, necessary, legitimate role, helpful to others, requiring no justification or apology."

For twenty-five years, until his involuntary retirement in 1953, Kennan found security in the role of diplomat and observer. On at least eight occasions, three of them in his first seven years of service, Kennan would tell colleagues that he had decided to resign; each time he would be comforted, consoled—and dissuaded.

His first decision to resign came while in Hamburg. Although in his memoirs he ascribed it to a desire to continue his education, Kennan's motives were actually financial and romantic. He was engaged at the time to a Washington girl named Eleanor Hard. Her father, the prominent and hard-drinking journalist William Hard, was dead set against her marrying a poorly paid government underling. The only solution, Kennan wrote his family after brooding over the matter, was "to come home and attempt to get a real start on a road that leads somewhere financially...I imagine I will start at rock-bottom in some large business concern."

As he sailed home on his twenty-fourth birthday, Kennan reconsidered his choice. "The things I most love involve a freedom from haste which will give a man time for his own thoughts and his own development," he wrote his father. "These are all things which are clearly incompatible with the present requirements of business life. My only way out of this impasse will be, much to everyone's disgust, to enter such a field as journalism or teaching."

Fortunately for the Foreign Service, and perhaps too for journalism, Kennan was brutally rebuffed by the Hard family upon his arrival in Washington. Eleanor broke off the engagement; when Kennan asked her to return the ring, which had been his mother's, she said she had lost it. "Go back to your teacups and fancy pants and safe obscurity," said Mr. Hard, "and let's hear no more of this." Kennan's superiors at the State Department, on the other hand, could not have been more supportive. They offered to help him become part of a new program to train Soviet specialists, which included study at a European university at government expense.

The driving force behind the program was Kennan's old boss in the Eastern European Division, Robert Kelley. A tall, taciturn bachelor who had been educated at Harvard and the Sorbonne, Kelley spoke Russian fluently and cherished a love for the czarist-era culture of that country. But he was deeply distrustful of the Bolsheviks, or "Boles" as he called them, and adamantly opposed American recognition of the new Moscow regime.

Kelley's Russian training program virtually guaranteed a certain product. It included up to three years of study at a European university followed by a posting in Riga, Latvia, or in one of the other Baltic country capitals that served as U.S. listening posts on the Soviet Union. His purpose, explained Kennan, was to replicate the training "of a well-educated Russian of the old, pre-revolutionary school."

Kelley's anti-Bolshevik outlook and rigorous academic approach were to have an enormous influence on those who became part of his Soviet specialist program. To one degree or another, most came to subscribe to what Daniel Yergin has labeled "the Riga Axioms." These included Kelley's fervent love of czarist culture and his disdain for the ideology and tactics of the new Kremlin regime. Among the first eight officers chosen for his program were Bohlen and Kennan.

•   •   •

Bohlen, not surprisingly, chose to pursue his Soviet studies in Paris, at the École Nationale. The emphasis there was on language, history, and culture. Facts about the Soviet government or its Communist

ideology, Bohlen recalled, "came from books, almost all anti-communist, that we were supposed to read on our own time." With little
apparent effort, he consistently ranked at the top of his class.

With the depressed French currency, life in Paris was easy at first.
Bohlen and his Harvard friend Edward Page (later a member of the
Moscow embassy staff) lived in a luxurious apartment on the Rue de
Lille, ate in the finest restaurants, and "enjoyed all that Paris offers
young bachelors." Just before Christmas in 1932, Bohlen made enough
money beating his friends at poker to afford an impromptu ski vacation
in St. Anton.

In 1933, however, State Department salaries were cut and the dollar
was sharply devalued, forcing Bohlen to give up his apartment and
scale down his choice of restaurants. "Naturally, the drop in the dollar
coming right after the 15 percent cut in salary socked us right in the
chin," he wrote his parents. They too were facing financial problems.
Bohlen had offered to send part of his salary home when he heard
that they were finding it difficult to keep the Ipswich home. "I know
it is hard," he consoled when it finally proved necessary to sell the
house, "but what is over can't be changed, so try to let it go."

Bohlen developed a fervent interest, indeed an infatuation, with all
things Russian, absorbing minute facts with a passion and retaining
them in his cluttered memory. In Left Bank cafés, he and his friends
spent long evenings arguing their theories about Russia and its rulers
and discussing each piece of trivia that could be gleaned about the
enigmatic nation none of them had seen.

For all his fascination with Russia, however, Bohlen was strikingly
nonjudgmental and unreflective about Bolshevism and its aims. Standing in the Place de la Concorde one night and the Rue de Rivoli the
next, he watched as first the right and then the left led protests that
turned into riots. He was curious, even bemused, by such displays of
commitment. But he shared none of the dark forebodings that Kennan
felt upon seeing his first Communist demonstration in Hamburg. After
watching the "ranks of shabby people with tense, troubled faces,"
Kennan wrote that he was "suddenly moved to tears by the realization
of their great earnestness."

Kennan chose to enroll at the Oriental Seminary of the University
of Berlin, founded by Bismarck and infused with the realpolitik vision
that later became part of Kennan's own outlook. Suffering again from
fever, the grippe, and general exhaustion, he checked into a sanitarium
upon his arrival, where he leisurely read Tolstoy's *War and Peace*.

Kennan's professors were mainly specialists in the czarist era, and his private tutors, with whom he spent hours reading aloud from the Russian classics, were highly cultured émigrés. He considered these Russians of the old school to be blessed with an exuberant romanticism. His closest Russian friends were an aspiring writer, his piano-playing sister, and their mother, a penniless refugee. "All were wildly impractical and helpless," Kennan recalled. "I was embarrassed by the reckless spontaneity of their devotion: enthusiastic visits at unexpected hours, elaborate gifts they couldn't possibly afford... Sharing their woes and crises, I felt like a Russian myself."

It was not until a year after his arrival in Berlin that Kennan first met a real Soviet official, a member of a visiting trade delegation. His skepticism about the Soviets was already so deeply ingrained that he discounted much of what the official said. "I expect to read any day of his being brought back to Moscow and shot at sunrise for being seen riding up to the headquarters of the Trade Delegation in a very bourgeois and capitalistic automobile," Kennan said in a letter home. He also described a female Soviet government minister he met later that week: "Very brilliant but very hard-boiled; looked very old and tired, the way a lot of the Soviet people look: as though they had been under a tremendous strain for years—which they have."

Despite his meager contacts with Soviets, Kennan's hard-line attitude was pretty well set by the end of 1930. When the stately editor of *The Nation* magazine, Oswald Garrison Villard, visited Berlin in December, the budding Soviet specialist went to his hotel to argue about recognition. American liberals should be the last to want relations with the Kremlin, Kennan insisted, because it had made a mockery of progressive social doctrines. Although he had not actually read Villard's book about his travels through Russia, Kennan contemptuously called it "a view from a car window." With considerable intellectual arrogance, he told a friend: "When I heard him talk about Russia, I began to suspect that I knew more about it, or understood more about it, than he did."

It would be pointless to argue with Villard, Kennan decided. "I couldn't put across to him in so many words that which I felt about communism and which he had not felt," wrote the twenty-six-year-old Foreign Service officer who had never been to the U.S.S.R. "If I could put it across, it would only disturb him, puzzle him. Better let him go back home as he is, in the comforting belief which I cannot share."

Although historians would ascribe the early Cold War anti-Sovietism of Kennan and other Foreign Service officers to their disillusionment while serving in Moscow, it is clear that for most of them (especially Kennan and to a lesser extent Bohlen) this attitude took root while studying Russia from afar. Kennan would later argue that Marxism was mainly a "fig leaf" designed to justify the repressive tactics of Soviet leaders and Russia's historic expansionism. Eventually he would become an advocate of realism and détente. But in the early 1930s—and as an undercurrent thereafter—he placed great emphasis on the irreconcilable differences between the Soviet and American systems. He had "one firm and complete conviction," he wrote a friend in January of 1931:

> The present system of Soviet Russia is unalterably opposed to our traditional system, that there can be no possible middle ground or compromise between the two, that any attempts to find such a middle ground, by the resumption of diplomatic relations or otherwise, are bound to be unsuccessful, that the two systems cannot even exist together in the same world unless an economic cordon is put around one or the other of them, and that within twenty or thirty years either Russia will be capitalist or we shall be communist.

Kennan was particularly offended by an English-language newspaper edited in Moscow by an American Soviet sympathizer, Anna Louise Strong. "It seems incredible," he wrote home, "that people who identify themselves with the Soviet Government to such an extent as this editress are allowed to keep passports, since they are far more de-Americanized than the most Anglophile and bespatted diplomat." In his first official report, prepared in 1931, Kennan advocated withdrawing the benefits of U.S. citizenship from expatriates who spread anti-American propaganda. He attached a list of three dozen Americans in the U.S.S.R. he considered "communist sympathizers."

In another paper, which analyzed trade between Germany and the Soviet Union, Kennan took issue with businessmen who advocated American recognition of Russia for economic reasons. Communist principles were, he said, "so completely antagonistic to those prevailing in the rest of the world that it is still widely questioned whether mutually profitable commercial relations can exist over a long period of time between Soviet Russia and a country which recognizes the rights of private economic initiative."

After two years in Berlin, Kennan was anxious to return to the field. A letter from the minister in Riga hinted that he might want Kennan to take charge of the Russian division there. "I think that's a fantastic idea," Kennan told his father, adding his anxiety that the "Kennan bubble" would inevitably burst. Indeed it soon did: Kelley decided to send him to Riga, but much to Kennan's annoyance his job there was to be merely a "third secretary" in the consulate.

Before his transfer, however, Kennan had one piece of personal business. In his letters home, he had made only passing reference to "a Norwegian girl" who was working in Berlin. "Having once kept you all in expectancy for the better part of a year with false alarms about getting married," he explained, "I decided that the next time anything of that sort was impending I would hold my peace until a date were actually set." Annelise Sorensen, twenty-one, was the daughter of a prominent merchant from Kristiansand, on Norway's southern tip. As Kennan described her to his father: "She has the true Scandinavian simplicity and doesn't waste many words. She has the rare capacity for keeping silent gracefully. I have never seen her disposition ruffled by anything resembling a mood, and even I don't make her nervous."

Telling his family not to bother to come to the ceremony, Kennan set sail for Norway with a friend from the Berlin consulate to serve as best man. The wedding was a simple ceremony at the town's sixteenth-century stone church. Annelise, her new husband reported, was "nearly on the verge of tears, as I understand brides generally are at this stage of the procedure." At a formal dinner that followed, dozens of telegrams were read and even more toasts were drunk. "How the bridegroom remained sober will never be known, but he did, thereby upholding the honor of the American nation," Kennan boasted to his father. Well after midnight the somewhat dazed couple left by ferry for Denmark, casting the wedding corsage into the Kiel Canal.

•   •   •

The greatest handicap faced by the Russian specialists was that they could not go to Russia. Instead, their windows on that country were the medieval port cities of Riga and Tallinn, the capitals of Latvia and Estonia. Both had been settled in about 1200, conquered by Peter the Great five centuries later, and ruled by the Russians until after World War I, when the Baltic states temporarily won their independence.

For Bohlen and Kennan, the two cities offered a glimpse of life in imperial Russia, replete with the gay night life and cultural trappings of the czarist era. More importantly, the émigrés who befriended them were White Russians who had fled after the Bolshevik Revolution.

Their attitudes toward the new rulers in the Kremlin rubbed off on the impressionable young Americans who studied with them and stayed in their homes.

In Tallinn, which he persisted in calling by its old name of Revel, Bohlen lived at the home of a man who had been a wealthy timber merchant in Russia before the revolution. "The family was," he recalled, "full of the curiosity which characterized the pre-Revolution Russian intelligentsia, and obsessed with deep and unworkable philosophical concepts." Bohlen's greatest complaint: Tallinn's only available liquor was vodka, beer, and local brandy. "It means that I do much less drinking than if I could get the good stuff," he told his mother. Soon, however, he honed his taste for vodka. "Russians are terribly kind-hearted and hospitable, maybe in the long run a little overwhelming but so far fine," he wrote in another letter. "Whoopee can be made, as there are plenty of cabarets and vodka."

Bohlen passed most of his summers in Narva Joesuu, an Estonian beach town that had once been the chief summer resort for St. Petersburg's elite. Its citizens took great pride in their history of battles with Russian occupiers stretching from Ivan the Terrible in 1558 to the Red Army in 1919. The pension where Bohlen lived was run by a pair of émigré sisters, who were "strongly anti-Bolshevik and lived in the hope that someday the nightmare would pass away and they would return to old Russia, complete with Czar and aristocracy."

In his letters home, Bohlen painted an idyllic picture of life in Narva Joesuu, where days were spent foraging in the forest for mushrooms and evenings were filled with brandy and animated conversation. "All talk at the top of their lungs," he reported, "with exclamations of My God, Jesus, and Have Mercy, without which Russians cannot say five words." One night spent around a samovar of tea discussing philosophy and reciting poetry, he said, "was so like one of Chekhov's plays you would have died."

Bohlen got his first glimpse of Russia when a friend from Harvard came for a visit. The two of them took an expedition to the border, walking along a dusty road until they could see the Soviet sentries in their guard tower. After taking some photographs, Bohlen peered silently into the vast expanse until his friend finally dragged him away.

As might be expected, Bohlen's intellectual curiosity about Russia in no way overwhelmed his desire to have a good time. The young bachelor's favorite spot was the nude beach. "I could never get over the novelty of being greeted by a bevy of naked Estonian beauties," he said. "The Estonian people are a singularly handsome race of Scandinavian origin—tall, blond, and well built in comparison with Russians."

Even though Bohlen shared the same contempt for the revolution that imbued the other young Soviet specialists, he developed an easy knack for getting along with the Russian people. Unlike most of the other students, he learned to talk like a native Russian, drink like one, and at times even think like one. Part of his allure was his ability to express blunt opinions with a disarming smile. His capacity to charm the Russians he met was matched only by his capacity to be charmed by them.

Kennan, who was assigned to Tallinn and Riga both before and after his study in Berlin, did not share Bohlen's easy grace. In his own ingenuous way, he could be wistfully charming, but more often he was merely melancholy. When he first sailed into Riga in the summer of 1928, the sight of the squat steeples gleaming in the sun immediately struck him as a reflection of the lost glories of czarist Russia. "This is a place which, although it is not Russia now, was at least Russia ten years ago," he wrote his father. What struck Bohlen as gaiety was seen by Kennan as "a nostalgic, despairing, shoot-the-works sentimentality."

Like a character out of Dostoevsky, Kennan enjoyed the alienation that came from being a detached observer. "My usual companions were landscapes rather than people," he wrote later. His best friend was his cocker spaniel. On the one occasion when the local U.S. consul invited him to visit his weekend cottage, Kennan recalled, "I reverted to the worst reactions of my neurotic student youth, behaved with an atrocious lack of sociability, and merited the general ostracism I received thenceforth in the little diplomatic-consular community." He spent that Christmas as a "seeker of retreat" at a monastery near the Soviet border. Alone, he hiked through the snow to the barbed-wire fence at the border and took a snapshot of the distant guard tower with its hammer-and-sickle emblem. "This is the first quarter-mile of the 5,000-mile expanse," he wrote his father.

While in Riga, Kennan and two other American bachelors shared an apartment of eight large rooms, which came with two servants, shelves of American canned goods, and a wine cellar with two hundred bottles ranging from champagne to rum that helped fuel late-night arguments about Communism. Kennan's view of the world reflected a burgeoning realpolitik outlook: He argued that for all of the phlegmatic independence of the Baltic states, they were as much a part of Russia's sphere as New Jersey was part of America's, and they would inevitably once again provide Russia's warm-water ports on the Baltic.

But Kennan was hardly a regular at the political bull sessions. Suffering from a recurring case of shingles, he preferred spending most evenings alone, occasionally venturing out by himself to the Russian-language theaters. In the summer he rented a tiny dacha on the coast, but instead of seeking out naked sunbathers as Bohlen did, Kennan derived sensual pleasure from "bathing in the sea by day, bathing then later, in the nocturnal hours, in the magic and, to me, commandingly erotic twilight."

Kennan utterly lacked Bohlen's easy grace as a diplomat. One week, when he had been left in charge of the office in Riga, Kennan discovered that the diplomatic mail pouch had been slit open and ransacked. He became quite agitated and spent the entire day cataloging the bag's contents, launching an investigation, and sending coded messages to Washington. In his excitement, he forgot that he was supposed to represent the U.S. at the annual dinner given by the French minister, a haughty man who did not treat such lapses lightly.

When Kennan called to apologize the next morning, the Frenchman refused to receive him. "By that time," Kennan wrote home, "my Scotch blood was beginning to boil with fury at the Latin races in general." The incident became the talk of the diplomatic community. "I scarcely dare to venture forth any more in society," Kennan said. Once again he considered quitting. "As a diplomat, I can neither be honest with myself nor with other people, and I'll be better off out of it," he wrote his cousin.

Kennan's gloomy view of Riga became even darker when he returned there after completing his studies in Berlin. Homesick and forlorn, he attributed his failure to be named head of the Russian section to "petty jealousies." The presence of Annelise only made matters worse. "The illusion of glamor that had hung over the life of the place when seen through the eyes of an unattached bachelor... fell suddenly away as one set about to introduce a young wife into its midst," he later wrote. "One realized at a stroke how pathetically thin and barren of meaning were those habits of casual good fellowship that normally lubricated the official and social encounters of the day."

At first the Kennans were able to afford a cook and butler for their rambling house. But the cut in Foreign Service pay soon made money a worry, and they moved to a smaller apartment. On their first Christmas together, Kennan justified a trip to Norway only because he calculated that it would be cheaper than buying food and a Christmas tree in Riga. When their first child, Grace, was born, Kennan celebrated by polishing off a bottle of whiskey. But he soon decided it was best to send her to live with her grandparents in Norway because the apartment in Riga was too cramped. "As far as my personal life is concerned," he wrote his father, "I might as well be in Siberia."

As Kennan's academic expertise grew, so did his intellectual arrogance, particularly about his intuitive judgments. When the legation's counselor asked him about the sources for one of his reports, Kennan replied: "But I'm the source." It was an attitude that would later cause Eugene Rostow to disparage Kennan as "an impressionist, a poet, not an earthling."

Chekhov remained his primary passion. Hoping to write a biography of the great nineteenth-century writer, Kennan read all thirty volumes of his works and six volumes of his "inimitable" letters. "There could, as it happened, have been no finer grounding in the atmosphere of prerevolutionary Russia," he later noted. He sent unsolicited to the *Yale Review* an article titled "Anton Chekhov and the Bolsheviks." Said the State Department officer charged with clearing the essay: "If Yale can stand it, I can." Yale apparently could not.

Citing his desire to study the Chekhov archives, Kennan applied for permission to visit Moscow in the summer of 1932. The State Department denied the request, declaring that the young Russian specialists should visit that country only when they could do so in an official capacity. "I am homesick and disgusted with Uncle Sam's foreign service," Kennan wrote home on hearing the news. "So if you hear of a good job as prosperity returns let me know."

•   •   •

The foremost question confronting the Soviet experts was whether the U.S. should re-establish relations with Russia. Woodrow Wilson had not only withheld recognition of the new Bolshevik regime in 1917, he had ordered a limited U.S. military intervention the following year to protect American interests. Economic relations, including major investments by Harriman and others, had nevertheless flourished. By 1930, the Soviet Union was importing more from the U.S. than from any other country. Although trade tapered off in the early 1930s, the prospect of expanded markets remained one of the primary pressures in favor of recognition. As the Cleveland *Plain Dealer* editorialized: "America greatly needs the vast Russian market and Russia needs manufactured goods America has for sale. It is a natural process for the two to get together."

In two studies for the State Department in 1932 and 1933, Kennan predicted that recognition would not increase prospects for trade, thus beginning what would become a long career of tugging anxiously at the sleeves of his political overlords. In 1933 he also wrote a long report warning that the Soviets felt free to break treaties whenever it suited their purposes. Yet ignoring the logical inconsistency, he went on to argue that existing treaties between Western nations and Moscow were not worded carefully enough. Because Marxism divided the world into classes rather than nations, for example, pacts guaranteeing the rights of foreigners in Russia had to be phrased carefully.

When the American minister at Riga gathered his Russian experts in August of 1933 to solicit their formal opinions on recognition, Kennan spoke first. "We should have no relationship at all with them," he said, citing Soviet pledges to spread Communist revolution. "There is no sound basis for believing they have changed their minds in any way." He was even more blunt in his letters. "Recognition continues to hang over our head like a sword of Damocles," he wrote home that month.

Kennan's views were shared by most of the State Department Soviet specialists, from Kelley and Henderson on down. "The communist leaders in Russia are unwilling to abandon their revolutionary aims with respect to the U.S.," Kelley warned the new Secretary of State, Cordell Hull. In his voluminous unpublished memoirs, Henderson wrote: "The members of the Eastern European Division believed that regardless of such commitments as the emissaries of the Soviet government might make, the rulers of the Soviet Union would continue their efforts to bring about the overthrow—if necessary, by force—of the government of the U.S."

Nevertheless, Franklin Roosevelt began to pursue diplomatic relations soon after taking office. By then, the idea had wide public support. FDR sent a secret message to the Kremlin saying that he would welcome an envoy with whom he could begin talks, and in November of 1933, Maxim Litvinov, the Soviet Commissar for Foreign Affairs, arrived.

Not by chance, both Kennan and Bohlen happened to be in Washington when the talks got under way. Bohlen had wangled a leave from his studies in Paris and headed straight home to be where the action was. Kennan had a bit more trouble; the State Department kept postponing his scheduled vacation. Finally he had his chief in Riga send a telegram explaining that his father was in precarious health and anxious to see his new grandchild. But when his boat arrived in New York in October, Kennan promptly headed straight for Washington rather than Milwaukee. From there he sent his apologies home: "With Comrade Litvinov on the way over here, there is surely going to be a lot of work for the drones of the Eastern European Division."

There was, but the late nights that Bohlen and Kennan spent preparing reports were peripheral to the political considerations that drove the talks. Roosevelt wanted to recognize Russia, and within eight days he and Litvinov had reached an agreement.

Bohlen was overjoyed. It seemed clear to him that the time had passed when the two emerging world powers could maintain an official silence. A particularly important consideration, he felt, was the need to counter the rise of fascism in Europe and Japanese militarism in the Far East.

Kennan, on the other hand, was torn. Though he could not help feeling some excitement, he was upset that his warnings about the need to secure precise guarantees protecting the rights of Americans in the Soviet Union were ignored. In his memoirs, he wondered whether Roosevelt was even aware of the report he had done on this issue. (In fact, a memo quoting Kennan's study was given to the President, but when Litvinov balked at including the suggested guarantees, FDR backed down.) Kennan regarded Roosevelt's action as purely political. This was "the first of many lessons," he said, on the influence of "those echelons of American opinion, Congressional opinion first and foremost, to which the respective statesmen are anxious to appeal."

More importantly, Kennan did not share Bohlen's belief that recognition made sense in strategic terms. "Never—neither then nor at any later date—did I consider the Soviet Union a fit ally or associate, actual or potential, for this country," he declared in his memoirs.

Roosevelt appointed as his new ambassador William Bullitt, who had helped negotiate with Litvinov. As a member of the U.S. delegation in Versailles at the end of World War I, Bullitt had journeyed to see Lenin in Moscow and worked out a truce between the U.S. and the Bolsheviks—only to have his work publicly disavowed by Wilson. Regarding his appointment in 1933 as a chance to vindicate his earlier dreams, Bullitt set out to recruit the brightest Soviet scholars for his mission to Moscow.

Among the first he chose was Bohlen. "You are not a typical Foreign

Service officer," Bullitt said. "That's why I want you." The new ambassador went on to complain that most veteran diplomats seemed to be in a "straightjacket." They had lost their dash and imagination. Bohlen laughed and promised that he would never let that happen to him.

Later that day, Bohlen's exuberance was tempered by an encounter with Kennan in the State Department corridors. Although they were no more than casual acquaintances at the time, Kennan proceeded to unload all of his dark forebodings about recognition and confide that he had once again decided to resign from the Foreign Service. Bohlen tried to cheer up his highly strung colleague. New vistas were opening, he said, and they were among the lucky handful of young men destined to be at the fore. They spent the evening together, talking and drinking. Once again, Kennan decided not to resign. And so began a lifelong odd-couple comradery. As Kennan would later declare of his relationship with Bohlen: "No friendship has meant more to me."

Bohlen and Henderson, who wanted to make sure that Kennan was chosen for the new Moscow embassy staff, took him to meet Bullitt the next afternoon. The new ambassador peppered him with questions about Russia and its economy. Kennan was impressed by Bullitt's engaging curiosity, and he by Kennan's thoughtful answers.

"Do you know Russian?" Bullitt asked. "Yes," replied Kennan. "I'm leaving on Monday for Moscow," said Bullitt. "Could you be ready in time to come along?"

The room, Kennan recalled, seemed to rock around him. For five years he had been preparing to go to Russia, and the offer, he noted in his journal, "came as a thunderstroke of good luck." His qualms about recognition dissipated in a rush of excitement. Less than a week later, without ever having a chance to get to Milwaukee, he and his family were sailing back across the Atlantic. On the way, he received a telegram from William Phillips informing him that his father had died.

• • •

Aboard the S.S. *President Harding*, the U.S. delegation was infected with the exhilaration that was to mark their early years in Moscow. The irrepressible Bullitt—"young, handsome, urbane, full of charm and enthusiasm," according to Kennan—enlivened the evenings by teaching the ship's orchestra new songs. *New York Times* correspondent Walter Duranty, his cynicism tempered by the excitement, held conversational court fueled by the boat's best brandy. Hovering at the edges, scribbling in his journal, was Kennan.

When their train stopped at a tiny station in Poland, Litvinov, who was traveling with the Americans, reminisced about his childhood in a village nearby and confided that he had once only wished to become a librarian. "We suddenly realized, or at least I did, that these people we were dealing with were human beings like ourselves," Kennan noted, "that they had been born somewhere, that they had their childhood ambitions as we had. It seemed for a brief moment we could break through and embrace these people."

On December 10, 1933, the Americans reached the Soviet border near Minsk. Kennan translated the speech given by the representative of the Soviet Foreign Office, a nervous man whose eyes sparkled with the importance of the occasion. Then there was a banquet in the station restaurant, the first of countless occasions when Soviet cooks would produce lavish meals brimming with caviar and vodka only to watch sadly as American appetites proved unequal to the challenge.

The old Russian sleeping cars that carried the Americans from the border to Moscow had icicles hanging from their eaves. Kennan, too excited to sleep, watched as Russian workers pumped hot water into the compartments at each switching station. "Russia, Russia—unwashed, backward appealing Russia, so ashamed of your own backwardness, so orientally determined to conceal it from us by clever deceit," he wrote in his journal. "I shall always remember you—slyly, touchingly, but with great shouting and confusion—pumping hot water into our sleeping car in the frosty darkness of a December morning in order that we might not know, in order that we might never realize, to how primitive a land we had come."

When Bullitt and Kennan arrived at the National Hotel in Moscow, they had the special privilege of being met in the lobby by Marx— Harpo Marx. The comedian, who was visiting Russia at the time, enlivened one of the welcoming banquets by magically producing forks from Litvinov's pockets. President Kalinin—"old Daddy" as the Americans came to call him—pulled Kennan aside. As young radical students, Kalinin confided, he and his comrades used to read the elder George Kennan's reports on Siberia. The books, he said to Kennan's astonishment, were the bible of the early Bolsheviks.

Harpo and Kennan shared an interest in Chekhov, and they took a group to see a performance of *The Cherry Orchard* at the Moscow

Art Theater. Harpo erupted in "solitary, unrestrained gales of laughter" throughout the play; Kennan got to meet with Chekhov's widow, Knipper-Chekova, and discussed his plans for a biography.

In a grand ceremony in the Kremlin, Bullitt presented his credentials to the Soviet government, becoming the first official U.S. envoy in Moscow since DeWitt Clinton Poole departed in 1919. He also selected the sites for the American mission: Spaso House, a cavernous stucco mansion built by a sugar tycoon in 1914, was chosen to be the ambassador's residence; a seven-story office building under construction on Mokhovaya Street, across from the Kremlin, was to become the new chancery. After eleven days in Moscow, Bullitt headed home to recruit the rest of his delegation, leaving Kennan behind to organize the new mission.

Kennan set up shop in a room of the National Hotel, next to the proposed chancery. While Annelise prepared meals on a whiskey crate and hot plate in the corner, her husband met with his skeletal staff and fenced with Moscow's bureaucracy. The Soviets did try to be helpful. When no mantelpiece could be found to fit a fireplace in Spaso House, the government ripped one out of the Foreign Office. But the problems were legion. Various Russians who had mysteriously established residence in Spaso House, ranging from a Vice-Commissar of Foreign Affairs to squatters of obscure origin, had to be evicted. Writing leases, exchanging currency, and finding furniture all presented tangled challenges; the more minor they seemed, the harder they were to resolve.

Fortunately for Kennan, soon after his arrival he met at the hotel bar "a young American with ruffled hair, a strong Philadelphia-society drawl, and, as conversation soon revealed, a highly developed sense of humor." This was Charles Thayer, a man who would become both a respected diplomat as well as the court jester of the Foreign Service.

Thayer was born to a Main Line family in Villanova, Pennsylvania, attended St. Paul's one year behind Bohlen, and went on to West Point, where his high academic record was matched by an even higher number of demerits for carefree deportment. Realizing that he was hardly destined for a military career, Thayer had sought to resign his commission and study Russian in the hope of joining the Foreign Service. The only resistance came from an eccentric cavalry officer. "The Army's just finished educating you and now you want to quit— to become a damned cookie-pushing diplomat—and in Russia of all places," roared Colonel George Patton. "Are you a Bolshevik?" Eventually, however, Thayer persuaded Patton and others that he would be better off out of uniform, and he embarked on his own to Moscow to await American recognition.

Before Bullitt returned to the U.S. to fill out his delegation, Thayer managed to wangle a job. Kennan immediately put him to work helping organize the embassy, a haphazard exercise at best. By the time Bullitt and his staff returned at the end of February 1934, only a shipment of wall clocks had been installed. But slowly, despite Kennan's anxieties and Thayer's eccentricities, the embassy and its offices began to take shape.

Bohlen joined Bullitt's entourage when the ambassador passed through Paris on his return to Moscow. At the Russian border, while they waited to change trains, Bohlen was struck by a smell that Kennan and Thayer had already come to love and hate. "The odor of wet sheepskin coats, of sawdust spread on the floors to absorb moisture, of disinfectant, of pink soap, of human sweat, and of the cheap Russian tobacco known as Makhorka—still remains for me the smell of the Soviet Union," he later recalled.

When Bohlen and Bullitt pulled into Moscow, Kennan and Thayer were waiting at the station to greet them. Noting a band on the platform, the American delegation prepared for a grand welcoming ceremony. The musicians, however, turned out to be for the delegates to a Women's Day celebration. For Bullitt there was only a handshake from the Soviet chief of protocol, the first of many dashed expectations Bullitt was destined to encounter.

Bohlen plunged right in with the work of organizing the embassy. At breakfast their first morning in Spaso House, Bullitt's French cook burst in and announced: "There is nothing in the house! Nothing! I assure you." Thayer looked at Kennan and growled under his breath. For weeks they had been struggling to make the mansion habitable. The kitchen had no spices, the cook continued, and the bedrooms no coat hangers. So Thayer commandeered a Harley-Davidson with a sidecar from the boy friend of his landlady's daughter and, with the earflaps of his fur cap flying, careened through the muddy streets of Moscow in search of provisions. Spices were hard to come by, but Bohlen was able to figure out the Russian word for coat hangers (*veselka*) and find a few wooden ones for the embassy.

"There were evenings," noted Kennan in his journal, "when we subordinate officers—assembled in my hotel room, gloomily sipping our highballs and watching the mice play hide-and-seek along the base-boards—felt that we were defeated, that we were too weak to bridge even those preliminary contradictions between communism and capitalism, and that we would soon have to give it up and sneak shame-facedly away, the laughing-stock of Europe." By July, however, the mission was finally able to move into the Mokhovaya offices and begin work. On the day of the move, a grizzled career officer who was serving as the embassy counselor stood amid the near-empty rooms and announced to a startled Kennan: "You know, George, I think it's high time we got off a dispatch on the Baltic nonaggression pacts."

Yet the demand from Washington for reporting on obscure non-aggression pacts was minimal, leaving the young officers in Moscow much time for play. Bullitt encouraged them to travel as much as possible, a mandate that Kennan pursued with an intensity his colleagues found amusing. He forayed alone by train to sketch medieval churches and search for Chekhov memorabilia. Bohlen and Thayer, much to the consternation of their secret-police escorts, took the opportunity to hunt wild boar near Baku in the Caucasus Mountains.

Bullitt also emphasized the need for close ties with the people. "As a bachelor," Bohlen recalled, "I eagerly carried out his instructions." After Bohlen arranged a film screening for the corps of the Moscow ballet, ballerinas became frequent guests at embassy lunches and, he noted, "many temporary liaisons were formed." He and Kennan were asked to become consultants to a local production of Charles MacArthur and Ben Hecht's *The Front Page*. The young Soviet actors had their own conceptions of American society. The city editor, for example, wore a top hat and tailcoat because the director assumed this was the normal style for bosses in a capitalist society.

The Russians seemed keen on nurturing the friendship. When Bohlen, at Bullitt's direction, offered to teach them baseball in a local park, a group dutifully turned out. Their mild interest, however, declined even further after one of them was beaned by a fastball. "Apparently," Bohlen later wrote, "they had been ordered to play."

Once, when Thayer was translating at a banquet for the Soviet Defense Commissar, he surreptitiously introduced the subject of polo. Said Bullitt in English: "Ask the Commissar where the best summer resorts are." Said Thayer in Russian: "The ambassador wants to know [pause] why you don't play polo in the Soviet Union." Before Bullitt caught on to what was happening, Thayer had arranged for embassy staffers to teach the game to the Russians. Bullitt, more amused than angry, agreed to serve as referee for what turned out to be a set of wild exhibitions.

The distaste that Bohlen and Kennan shared for the Soviet system was temporarily thawed by the warmth they encountered that first year. Moscow's intellectuals, in particular, seemed anxious to befriend their new American allies, and their wives were intrigued by Paris fashion and American cosmetics. There were signs of a more liberal approach to the outside world. "I bear that pleasant winter in memory," Kennan wistfully notes, "as an example of what Soviet-American relations might, in other circumstances, have been."

Bohlen harbored an even greater optimism; freedom and democracy, he felt, were inherent features of true Marxism, and he saw signs that they might be allowed to emerge. "The young Russians are just like novices in a new faith," he wrote his mother. "I think the people of Moscow don't look very beaten and crushed." He developed a deep love for the Russians as people. "I know of no one who has been in Russia, whatever his attitude toward the regime, who has felt anything but affection for the Russian people as a whole," he later wrote. "Henderson, Kennan and I realized that we had arrived in Moscow at an opportune time, for 1934 may be seen as the most optimistic year in Soviet history."

The culmination of the year of good feeling came at the 1934 Christmas party at Spaso House. To enliven the affair, Thayer and his companions produced three trained seals from the Moscow Circus. At the appointed moment, they appeared through a chute into the cavernous three-story ballroom of Spaso House balancing a Christmas tree and trays of champagne on their noses. The performance climaxed with the seals playing a Christmas carol on harmonicas.

At that point, however, their trainer, who had been enjoying the festivities all too well, passed out on the ballroom floor. "There are several versions of what happened during the next fifteen minutes," Thayer wrote. One of the seals bolted for the kitchen, where a German cook tried to subdue it with a frying pan. Another performed a series of unrehearsed acts amid the startled guests in the ballroom. Wielding brooms and dead fish, the Americans were finally able to herd all three seals back into their truck and, after one last break for freedom on the way, they were returned safely to the circus.

• • •

In order to escape these and less amusing trials of Moscow life, the younger members of the embassy rented a dacha about twenty miles from town. The regulars included Bohlen, Thayer, Kennan, Loy Henderson, Elbridge Durbrow, and Eddie Page. The two-story cottage had only four bedrooms, but soon it became the social center for much of the Western diplomatic corps. It offered skiing in the winter, mint for juleps in the spring, a field for baseball in the summer, and three tired brown horses for riding the year around. Thayer dubbed it a *kolkhoz*, or collective farm, so that Soviet authorities would sell them subsidized oats for the horses. The animals, alas, seemed not to prosper under the arrangement, perhaps because their old Russian groom, a bowlegged former czarist cavalry officer, made money on the side by reselling the feed for his own profit.

In this atmosphere even Kennan seemed to shed his somber demeanor, or at least to make a valiant stab at it. "I learned how to ride a horse," he recalled, "and became an enthusiastic, though hardly distinguished, skater, skier, tennis player and bridge partner." Durbrow's home movies show him lying on the makeshift baseball diamond in his three-piece suit and playing Russian folk songs on his guitar. Annelise was even more social, abandoning her aloof demeanor at the gay parties on the weekends while her husband cornered one or another of his colleagues for intense discussions of Soviet life.

Kennan would occasionally strive to entertain his companions by reading aloud, as his father had once done, from Gibbon's *The History of the Decline and Fall of the Roman Empire* and Chekhov's plays. Annelise, after a few drinks, would have to remind him somewhat forcefully that not everyone was interested in hearing these recitations. Indeed, despite Kennan's efforts to be sociable, his manner still tended to grate on his colleagues' nerves. When he began affecting a pipe, the others laughed at his professorial pretenses; when he churned out long memos and cables, they would roll their eyes. Later, much of his reputation would derive from precisely this penchant for writing long telegrams.

"Almost everyone got annoyed with Kennan after they first got to know him," Henderson later said. "He was so engrossed in his own ideas that he never learned how to go along or get along. After half a year in Moscow, Bullitt had little use for George personally. He did, however, develop a great respect for George's mind. None of us took George's ideas as seriously as George did, but we knew that someday people would have to."

Bohlen, understandably, was far more popular. "He had a pleasing personality, a keen sense of humor, a gift for amusing conversation, and a certain amount of spontaneous joyousness," said Henderson. In almost every way, Bohlen was the opposite of Kennan. "Chip was friendly," Henderson recalled. "He drank and socialized well, and he never seemed like a snob. Above all, he had a kind manner that made people open up to him. He was a very good Foreign Service officer in the sense that he always tried to please those in power. He never questioned policy, except in private where I think he tried to make everyone think he agreed with them."

Despite their dissimilarities, or perhaps because of them, Bohlen was one of the few in Moscow who could genuinely get along with Kennan. They frequently attended lectures and concerts together, and Bohlen, after a night on the party circuit, often dropped by Kennan's room and sat on his bed for midnight chats. He would chide his friend for being too gloomy, both personally and professionally, and for getting so wrapped up in criticizing policy that he found himself unable to execute it in a professional way. Kennan had "a good streak of American morality," Bohlen once said, and found it hard to "divorce his visceral feelings from his knowledge and fact."

For Kennan, the relationship he formed with Bohlen in Moscow was "the beginning of a lifelong intellectual intimacy which, for me at least, was unique in its scope and intensity." At times it could be stormy. "In numberless verbal encounters, then and over ensuing decades, our agreements and differences would be sternly and ruthlessly talked out, sometimes with a heat so white that casual bystanders would conclude we had broken for life." These "painful yet pleasant" arguments, however, seldom involved ideological differences. "Where we disagreed was on how ideas should be translated into policy," Kennan recalled some fifty years later. "Chip tended to be very loyal to the U.S. policy of the moment, even when it was Roosevelt's optimism, which he disagreed with. He did not like to fight the prevailing trends. I used to call him 'the partisan of the moment.'"

•   •   •

The high hopes of that first year in Moscow were dashed by a murder and its grisly aftermath. In December 1934, Sergei Kirov, the party boss in Leningrad, was shot. Although it later became apparent that Stalin had ordered the assassination himself, he used the incident to embark on a series of show trials and purges that terrorized the Russian populace. From then until the outbreak of World War II, while Bohlen and Kennan alternated working in Moscow and on the Soviet desk at the State Department, the horror of the purges would dominate their dealings with the Soviet Union. As Kennan noted in his private journal: "Russia, which had begun to reach out a hand to the West, had once more failed to find the ultimate self-confidence to complete the gesture."

A few days after Kirov's murder, Kennan was struck by one of his periodic intestinal illnesses. As the other officials and their Soviet guests (and the seals) joined in Christmas festivities, Kennan lay suffering in bed. When colleagues came to his bedside to describe the rising fear and xenophobia pervading Moscow, Kennan's alienation came rushing to the surface. "I felt the same sort of slightly snobbish detachment which I am sure respectable ghosts must feel toward those who are still caught in the meshes of earthly existence," he wrote.

One friend unearthed and brought to Kennan some old volumes of correspondence from the pre-revolutionary American mission in St. Petersburg. "These people are obsessed," one minister had written a century earlier, "with a strange superstition that they are destined to conquer the world." For Kennan, the old dispatches reinforced his belief that Russia's plight was indigenous to its culture and not merely a product of Communist ideology. "Most of what was written there was as true in 1934 as it has been a century before," he noted.

Kennan gathered the old letters into a cable for the State Department, which Bullitt agreed to send after appending the explanation that they were a century old. "They were a wonderful support to our own feeling that Russia had to be looked at from a long-range point of view," Kennan wrote in his journal, "that Bolshevism, with all its hullabaloo about revolution, was not a turning point in history, but only another name, another milepost along the road of Russia's wasteful, painful progress from an obscure origin to an obscure destiny."

Part of Kennan's growing disdain for Communism grew out of his rather prissy elitism. On a solitary sojourn to Sochi, a resort on the Black Sea, he was repulsed by the "bored, homesick proletarians" at the hotel. "Had the fathers of the Revolution really imagined that, once the upper and middle classes had been kicked out of these watering-places, the members of the proletariat would move in and proceed to amuse themselves gracefully and with taste?" he mused in his journal. "Did they really fail to foresee that such simple people would make pig-sties of these hotels and villas, would have no appreciation for sky and air and mountain scenery?"

Bohlen, on the other hand, found himself more confused than outraged. "A really accurate picture is impossible as the most incredible contradictions run side by side," he wrote in a letter home. "Whatever has been written about the methods of the state police is true. I know personally of horrible things that have happened. On the other hand, I think they are pulling it off, and hope for the future and a real glorification of work are the two factors that distinguish this country.

This spirit of optimism goes hand in hand with complete repression of individual liberty as we understand it."

What upset Bohlen most were the concrete disappointments. He ran into problems arranging with Litvinov a lease on a riverside parcel of land that Stalin had promised for a new U.S. Embassy. At first Litvinov said the site was unavailable. After Bullitt and Bohlen pressured him, Litvinov relented. But insurmountable obstacles soon arose: Permits would be necessary for each tree that would be cut down, building materials would have to be bought at unrealistic exchange rates, housing would not be available for American workmen. Soon the project had to be dropped. "The Soviets are the worst people to do business with I have ever met," Bohlen wrote home. "They'll try to take the gold out of your teeth."

Bohlen attributed the Soviet disdain for compromise to the fact that they had never been a trading nation. "Russians have concentrated on the acquisition of land, seizing and holding territory," he later wrote. "Such a relationship does not produce the spirit of compromise." This cultural tendency, he speculated, was reinforced by "the arbitrary and intolerant nature of Bolshevist thought" and a sense that compromise was "equivalent to surrender or betrayal." To Bohlen, the consummate diplomat, the ability to compromise was considered a paramount virtue.

Bohlen, who relished the carefree exercise of his personal freedom more than most men, was also resentful of the omnipresent Soviet state police. One evening in June, he and Bullitt decided to go rowing on the Moscow River past the embankments where young Muscovites bathed nude. They were delighted to discover that the agents trailing them did not know how to row. The gumshoes yelled anxiously into their radios. Finally, just as the two Americans were getting out of sight, a police boat arrived to continue the surveillance.

The anti-Soviet attitude of Kennan and Bohlen was partly responsible for Bullitt's dramatic conversion in 1935. "Bohlen and I were increasingly dismayed by the Soviet system and we helped move Bullitt away from his optimistic views," Kennan recalled later in an interview. "It did not take too much work. The Soviet government itself did the most to turn Bullitt off and dispel his ill-placed hopes."

Bohlen was temporarily transferred back to Washington in the spring of 1935 to work in the Eastern European Division. As he crossed the border out of Russia, his elation was perhaps even greater than that he felt on arrival. "It was like coming out into the fresh spring air from a room where the oxygen content was sufficient to sustain life but insufficient to produce any mental or spiritual animation."

Traveling with him was Charlie Thayer. The two men, unpressed and irrepressible, had been roommates in Moscow, where Thayer's sister Avis had paid them a visit. Years before, Bohlen had spent a vacation in Villanova with George Thayer, his classmate at St. Paul's. Avis was only nine back then, and Bohlen scarcely noticed her. But when she visited Moscow in 1934, Bohlen found himself entranced by her fresh beauty and gentle wit. On his way back to Washington, Bohlen stopped in Villanova to make Avis his wife and Charlie his brother-in-law.

Bohlen's reports at the Eastern European Division were sharply anti-Soviet. One of them, on the Kremlin's use of terror, noted that the Bolsheviks had forsworn the tactic when they were not in power, but once in office had come to regard it "as a perfectly legitimate instrument of class warfare." Back in Moscow, Kennan's outpourings were even more harsh, and certainly more prolific. It was the start of a long career producing voluminous reports that were destined to go largely unread and even longer personal memos that would languish in his own files.

The most striking of these was a 1936 paper titled "Some Fundamentals of Russian-American Relations." In it Kennan propounded a deterministic view of history that he was to hold throughout his life. Relations between nations, he argued, "are always governed in the long run by certain relatively permanent fundamental factors arising out of geographical and historic conditions." Because of this, he concluded, there was "little future for Russian-American relations other than a long series of misunderstandings, disappointments and recriminations on both sides."

Kennan's first official dispatch was a report on the Karl Radek purge trial in January 1937. It displayed the somewhat obscure analysis that would later infuriate officials seeking clear-cut answers from him. "Even if all the facts of the case were available, which they certainly are not and never will be, it is doubtful whether the western mind could ever fathom the question of guilt or innocence, of truth or fiction," he wrote. "The Russian mind, as Dostoyevski has shown, knows no moderation; and it sometimes carries both truth and falsehood to such infinite extremes that they eventually meet in space, like parallel lines, and it is no longer possible to distinguish between them."

• • •

Convinced of the bright prospects for friendly relations with Russia, Roosevelt replaced the disillusioned Bullitt with Joseph Davies, a Democratic politico and childhood friend whose support for the Soviet experiment was unwavering. Kennan was flabbergasted. In his view FDR had committed the unpardonable sin of viewing the Moscow post as "only another political plum." At a late-night meeting in Loy Henderson's rooms, where the disgruntled junior officers vented their dismay, Kennan once again talked of resigning.

Soon after Davies arrived, his ebullient trust in the Soviets clashed with the hard-edged suspicions of Kennan and his colleagues. There was, for example, the case of the mysterious microphone. It began when Kennan and Thayer discovered some hidden wires in the Spaso House billiard room. Because the bug had not yet been fully connected, a plan was hatched to snare the perpetrators. Along with Durbrow, they took shifts hiding in the attic with a gun (unloaded) and a flashlight. After a few cold and fruitless nights, the stakeout was abandoned in favor of a jerry-built trap of silk threads connected to an alarm bell. Unfortunately, the alarm depended on the regular house current; while the three guards slept, someone shut off the main switch to the house. In the morning it was discovered that the microphone had been removed.

Davies was annoyed by the suspicions of his subordinates. In the movie of his book *Mission to Moscow*, he is shown chastising a junior officer for suggesting that the Soviets might be engaged in eavesdropping. In one of his books about the period, *Bears in the Caviar*, Thayer pointedly notes: "A photograph of the mike is on file in the State Department in case anyone in Hollywood is interested."

Unbeknownst to Kennan, Davies decided to recommend that he be transferred. In a letter to the State Department, the ambassador praised Kennan's work but added that he had been in Moscow "too long for his own good" and that it would be "a very humane thing" to move him because of his poor health. In the summer of 1937, after an aborted decision to assign him to Jerusalem, Kennan was called to replace Bohlen as a Russian expert in Washington.

Kennan's transfer came just as the department was going through a radical shake-up. Roosevelt's determination to nurture friendly relations with Russia had resulted in the destruction of the Eastern European Division, where Bohlen was working. It was reduced to two desks in a new Division of European Affairs.

Although the reorganization was partly an attempt to streamline the bureaucracy, Bohlen and Kennan believed (with some justification) that it was designed to dissipate the hard-line clique of Soviet specialists whom Kelley had cultivated. "The Russians themselves," Bohlen said, "took part in the campaign against Kelley." They both darkly suspected that Eleanor Roosevelt bore some of the blame. "There was indeed the smell of Soviet influence, or strongly pro-Soviet influence, some-where in the higher reaches of the government," concluded Kennan.

But as was his wont, Bohlen could also see the President's point that "a fresh view was needed in the State Department," and he agreed to man the new Russian desk until Kennan's return. What bothered Bohlen most about the "hoary bureaucratic solution" was the decision to disperse the old division's valuable research collection, which ranged from early editions of *Pravda* to files on revolutionaries in the U.S. So he surreptitiously wrapped the most important material in brown paper and hid it in the cavernous attic of the old State Department building. "The preservation of this invaluable collection of revolu-tionary documents was my first concern."

When Kennan reached Washington in September he was horrified. "It was like one of the Russian purges," he recalls, overstating the situation somewhat. "A beautiful library was being destroyed by people in the White House who objected to our realistic attitude toward the Soviet Union." One evening before Bohlen left to go back to Moscow, the two friends had a few drinks together in the half-cubicle that Bohlen was vacating. Then they climbed into the attic to rescue the hidden books and documents. Kennan kept the most important ones squirreled away near his new desk. The rest Bohlen arranged to have stored in a special section of the Library of Congress. "We agreed," Kennan recalled, "that it was our duty to keep alive the flame of those who believed in objective analysis of the Soviet system."

During his year on the Russian desk, Kennan spent much of his time working with American businessmen, including Harriman, who were interested in increased trade with the Soviet Union. His prickly Puritan streak made him more sensitive about conflicts of interest than many of the Wall Streeters in government at the time. When a Mil-waukee machine manufacturer asked him to use his influence to help win a Soviet contract, Kennan replied that it was not the role of the U.S. government "to push individual deals."

Kennan's only summons to see Secretary of State Cordell Hull concerned a case of some American Communists who had mysteri-ously disappeared in Moscow. Still distressed about the loose wording of treaties guaranteeing the rights of foreigners in the U.S.S.R., the young analyst gave a characteristically tortured analysis of the situation.

"At the end of the brief interview he thought, I suspected, that I was as unbalanced as the Russians whose behavior I had tried to make intelligible," Kennan noted.

In a paper on "The Position of the American Ambassador in Moscow," Kennan provided a detailed indictment of the Soviet attitude to foreigners and the hassles faced by members of the Moscow embassy. To protest "the general atmosphere of suspicion and lack of cooperation," wrote Kennan in a subsequent flurry of memos, Washington should postpone appointing a replacement for Davies when his assignment was over. Like many of his hard-line suggestions, the advice was ignored.

Although his colleagues would often smile wearily at Kennan's unsolicited outpourings, he was slowly carving a role for himself in the foreign policy Establishment as a resident philosophizer; he began to be considered, and most certainly considered himself, an abstract and intuitive thinker able to fathom the complexities of Soviet conduct. The geographic and historic determinism that was nascent in his memos for Bullitt gradually evolved into a coherent philosophy, one that would form the basis for his momentous cables and essays defining the doctrine of containment after World War II.

Its earliest clear expression came in a lecture titled "Russia" that Kennan gave at the Foreign Service School in May of 1938. In it he downplayed the role of Marxist ideology in guiding Kremlin conduct and placed greater importance on the "permanent characteristics" of the Russian national character. Citing his discovery a few years earlier of the dispatches from American ambassadors at the time of Czar Nicholas I, Kennan argued that, both before and after its revolution, Russia had a "definite personality" that included "the constant fear of foreign invasion, the hysterical suspicion of other nations."

This deep-dyed national personality, Kennan theorized, resulted in part from the geography of Russia, a vast and cold continental mass that encouraged "extremism" rather than a sense of limits and whose insecure borders prevented inhabitants from thinking in terms of a "limited well-defined territory." History also played a role: Centuries of invasion by "Asiatic hordes" had produced a system of "Oriental despotism" and xenophobia. In addition, there was the influence of the Byzantine Church, characterized by "its intolerance, its intriguing and despotic political systems."

Kennan's conclusion was almost Freudian in its determinism: "Nations, like individuals, are largely the product of their environment; and many of their characteristics, their fears and their neuroses, as well as their abilities, are conditioned by the impressions of what we may call their early childhood." It was a gloomy picture, one that offered little hope for future friendship between Russia and the West.

Kennan's elitism had already made him scornful of the proletarian pretenses of Marxism. Back home in the U.S., he squirmed at the bitter midterm elections of 1938 with their ill-informed foreign policy rhetoric. His elitism flared anew, and this time its target was democracy. When Bohlen introduced him to the newspaper columnist Joseph Alsop, Kennan proclaimed: "The trouble with this country is that we are a democracy and instead should be ruled by aristocrats." Recalled Alsop: "I was very nearly sick."

The Founding Fathers, Kennan believed, had not meant to establish a true democracy. In a note to a friend as early as 1930, he had posed the question: "If they disapproved of democracy for a population predominantly white, Protestant and British, faced with relatively simple problems, would they not turn over in their graves at the mere thought of the democratic principle being applied to a population containing over ten million Negroes and many more millions of southern Europeans to whom the democratic principle is completely strange?"

While in Austria recuperating from an intestinal illness in 1935, Kennan had been impressed at the way the "distinctively authoritarian" regime in Vienna handled social problems. "There was no demagoguery, no public wrangling and debate by laymen, no appeal to the emotions and greed of the public," he wrote in a private journal he completed in 1939. "Benevolent despotism," he concluded, "had greater possibilities for good" than did democracy. "During the years to come— the uneasy years from 1936 to 1939, when our country rang with shrill debate about the issue of dictatorship vs. democracy—I was never able to forget these impressions. I could not get excited by this fancied issue. I could not follow the fanatical separating of the authoritarian goats from the democratic sheep."

In 1938, Kennan began drafting a bizarre book that advocated an authoritarian state run by America's elite. He completed only two chapters, did not submit them for publication, and never mentioned the proposed book in his memoirs or elsewhere—which was no doubt fortunate for his reputation. In this work, Kennan proposes that the U.S. travel "along the road which leads through constitutional change to the authoritarian state."

The first chapter, titled "The Prerequisites," was written in a messy scrawl that betrayed more emotion than Kennan's usual disciplined hand. Drawing from his perceptions of Austria, he argued that there were no moral distinctions between democracy and authoritarianism. The U.S., he proposed, should be governed by an "enlightened elite." He left "unanswered" the question of how this group would be chosen except to say that members should be "selected on the basis of individual fitness for authority."

Even more startling were the proposals in Kennan's second chapter for "the very extensive restriction of suffrage in national affairs." He explained: "There are millions of people in this country who haven't the faintest conception of the rights and wrongs of the complicated questions which the federal government faces." Those who would be denied the vote under his scheme: women, whom Kennan called frivolous; blacks, whom he considered wards of the state; and immigrants, who were exercising more political power than "real" Americans.

The book draft was littered with intuitive slurs on various groups. Among them: "Newer" Americans (mainly Catholic immigrants) could not understand American principles and would be "happier as passive citizens"; women in the U.S. tended to be more "high-strung, unsatisfied, flat-chested and flat-voiced" than those in other countries and would lead more meaningful lives if they returned to "family picnics, children's parties and the church social"; and blacks would be better off if they were "openly dependent" on the "kindness" of society. "The lack of the franchise could make the negro little more defenseless than he is," Kennan argued.

Buried in the papers of even the most enlightened men are, no doubt, some rather wild notions. The question is whether such idle fancies reflect their true character or a momentary excess. Kennan's book draft was somewhat extreme, even for him, yet it did reflect a dark side of his character. He and Bohlen shared many intellectual notions; yet Bohlen's secure self-perception produced a more optimistic outlook, whereas Kennan's brooding discomfort with the world bred a bleak view of mankind.

Throughout his public career, Kennan bristled at politicians catering to public pressures. He criticized the "political pressures" for helping Jewish refugees before and after World War II and invariably despaired of the ability of a democracy to conduct a coherent foreign policy. "Our actions in the field of foreign affairs are the convulsive reactions of politicians to an internal political life dominated by vocal minorities," he wrote in his diary in 1944. Even late in his life, Kennan nurtured his notions of an elite meritocracy. "We ought to create a panel or pool of outstanding people that would comprise perhaps five hundred to one thousand souls," he told an interviewer. "Appointment to it would be by some detached and austere authority such as the Supreme Court." From this group, he argued, the nation's leaders should be chosen.

• • •

When Bohlen, who had traded jobs with Kennan, arrived back in Moscow in January of 1938, he was again struck by the smell. "There was the same pervasive odor," he wrote. The only difference, as his wife, Avis, pointed out, was the addition of a ghastly cheap perfume Russian women had started wearing and which foreigners dubbed "Stalin's breath." Nor had the oppressive grip of the Soviet police state eased: Authorities refused to allow Bohlen to bring in forty-one of the books he was carrying, some of them from the old Eastern European Division library that he and Kennan had rescued. It was the first time that the personal items of an American Foreign Service officer had been banned.

Bohlen soon found himself at odds with Davies's rosy outlook on the Soviet system. Two weeks after his return, Bohlen visited the Supreme Soviet to watch it adopt reforms that were supposed to separate the policy-making functions of the Communist Party's Politburo from the administrative duties of various state agencies. What Bohlen reported, correctly, was that both party and state were embodied in one man, Stalin. "Judged by the accepted connotations of the word democracy and by the usual procedure of legislative bodies," Bohlen cabled, "the entire proceedings in the Supreme Soviet were a farce." He did note, however, that a pudgy man with a big grin named Nikita Khrushchev was "less obviously boot-licking."

Bohlen's initial reaction to the wave of purges was, typically, a practical one. Like Manhattan apartment seekers who read the obituary columns, he went to the Soviet Foreign Office after the arrests of two Russians who lived in the Mokhovaya building and negotiated to take over the lease of their rooms. "I felt like a vulture," he recalled, "but we needed the space."

Bohlen was assigned to report on the last of the great show trials, that of Nikolai Bukharin, one of the original Bolsheviks. Whereas Kennan had lapsed into convoluted discourses about the contradictions inherent in the Russian mind when he was faced with disagreeing with Ambassador Davies's hopelessly naïve view of the purge trials, Bohlen reacted in a way that was indicative of his own limitations.

The "bloodthirsty" prosecutor, Andrei Vishinsky, repulsed Bohlen,

and he found the evidence and confessions to be "fantastic" and unbelievable (which indeed they were). The judge, "who looked like a
sadistic pig," read the sentences with relish: "To be shot, to be shot,
to be shot." Bohlen recalls: "I felt that the top of my head was coming
off. I could not go to sleep easily for almost a month." He privately
ridiculed the naïveté of Davies. "He had an unfortunate tendency to
take what was presented at the trial as the honest and gospel truth,"
wrote Bohlen. "I still blush when I think of some of the telegrams he
sent."

Yet Bohlen found himself unable to write his analysis of the case,
the only assignment in his forty-year career that he failed to complete.
"I could not separate fact from fiction at the trial," he recalled. "I
knew the trial was a phony, but I could not prove it; I could only
intimate that it had no relevance to reality. Try as I did, and I tried
for over a month, I was unable to present a convincing case."

Loy Henderson, who had assigned him the task, was harsh in his
assessment of Bohlen's motives. "He said he would rather not write
it," Henderson recalled years later. "He knew the Soviets would somehow get hold of it and that he might make them permanent enemies
of his. He also knew that Roosevelt and Davies did not want to see
negative reporting on the Soviets. He was so anxious to please everyone. He would never say anything that might get him in trouble."

Bohlen's and Kennan's hostility toward Stalin and his system might
seem quite unremarkable in retrospect, but at the time it was a stark
departure from official U.S. thinking. Both Davies and his military
attaché were ardent apostles of Soviet-American friendship. So too,
though in a more restrained way, were President Roosevelt, Harry
Hopkins, and Secretary of State Hull. Even the American public,
despite deep currents of anti-Communist sentiment, was fascinated
by press accounts portraying Russia as a potential trading partner and
ally.

While Kennan was wrestling with his abstract theories, Bohlen was
developing a more straightforward view of Soviet conduct. He agreed
with Kennan that Russians had historically been expansionist. In addition, Bohlen felt, their new ideology of international class struggle
prompted them to interfere in other countries. But the primary determinant of Soviet foreign policy, he came to believe, was the desire
of Kremlin leaders to consolidate their own control at home and protect
their national security. Their belief in the hostility of the capitalist
world served to justify their own ironclad rule. In discussions during

the 1930s, Bohlen bounced these ideas off of Kennan, who later became their most eloquent exponent.

What Bohlen concluded from his analysis was that it was foolish to base a policy toward the Soviets on anything other than an appeal to their self-interest. Any alliances the Kremlin made would be temporary and cynical, forged solely on the basis of transitory needs rather than true understandings. As he said in a 1938 cable: "The Kremlin does not envisage cordial relations with the capitalist governments on any permanent basis but rather as a temporary expedient."

Bohlen's insights prepared him to sense a stunning turnabout: that Stalin might abandon efforts at collective security with Britain and France and sign a nonaggression pact with Hitler's Germany. His reporting on this critical event was aided as well by his remarkable ease in establishing diplomatic contacts and his charmed luck.

What first caught Bohlen's eye was a speech Litvinov made in June of 1938. "If the countries with which it was heretofore contented to cooperate do not pursue policies in accordance with the desire of the Soviet government," said the Foreign Minister, "even this slight cooperation might be withdrawn." Bohlen's wariness increased after Neville Chamberlain's attempt at appeasement in Munich, for he knew such a move would raise Soviet fears of "capitalist encirclement." Yet still he was characteristically cautious: "For the moment at least the Kremlin is inclined to await the course of further developments."

Indeed, Bohlen remained reluctant—perhaps too reluctant—to go out on a limb even after Stalin proclaimed in March of 1939 that Russia would not go to war "to pull somebody else's chestnuts out of the fire." When Litvinov was replaced by Molotov, Bohlen stated (correctly) that the personnel change "might be a step away from the principle of collective security and toward the establishment of relations with Germany," but then he added that it might be only a ploy to pressure Britain. Even Bullitt, who telephoned from Paris, where he was now stationed, to discuss how Litvinov's removal would affect France, had trouble eliciting a bolder prediction from his former staffer. Talking in baseball slang to confuse eavesdroppers, Bullitt wondered whether his "friends" might face a "shutout." Bohlen cautiously responded that he found it difficult to predict what a "pinch hitter" would do.

Unlike Kennan, however, Bohlen's reporting skills were greater than his confidence in his own insights. At the American dacha near Moscow, one of the frequent guests was a personable young staffer in the

German Embassy, Johnny Herwarth, who was secretly dismayed by Hitler's tyranny. In May of 1939, the day after he returned from a trip with his ambassador, Herwarth went riding with Bohlen on the spavined nags at the dacha. He told his friend that the ambassador had been summoned back to Berlin and that "something was up." Bohlen immediately cabled the information to Washington, saying it came "in the strictest confidence."

To Bohlen's surprise, Herwarth seemed willing to keep him abreast of subsequent developments. Later in the week, the two went back to the dacha, where Herwarth spilled the details of what had happened in Berlin. In a long and explicit cable, Bohlen reported that the German ambassador had been told "to convey very discreetly to the Soviet government the impression that Germany entertained no animosity toward it."

Bohlen's talks with Herwarth continued, sometimes at the German Embassy, more often at the dacha. Bohlen became convinced that Herwarth was acting out of friendship rather than sinister motives. With his phenomenal recall, Bohlen could remember all the details of what Herwarth said without taking notes. Then, because he could not type and feared that any dictation would be picked up by bugs, he would scrawl his reports in longhand upon returning to the embassy. After stenographers had wrestled with his illegible writing, the messages were coded and cabled.

The big break came in mid-August at a formal ball at the German Embassy. When Bohlen walked in, Herwarth told him that the ambassador was at that moment in the Kremlin talking to Molotov. He promised to fill in Bohlen as soon as he learned what had transpired. Bohlen, anxious to keep a clear head, was careful to drink only moderately. Half an hour later, the ambassador appeared at the party. Recalled Bohlen: "He was the urbane, smiling host and gave no indication that he had just pulled off one of the greatest coups in modern diplomatic history." As they sat in the corner sipping champagne, Herwarth gave Bohlen the details.

Bohlen's cable was greeted with skepticism at the State Department. "This doubt was a sign, I think, of too great a belief in the fidelity of the Soviet leaders to their anti-Fascist views and not enough realization that they put the preservation of the Soviet system high above every other consideration," he later wrote. Nevertheless, Secretary Hull summoned the British and French envoys in Washington to pass along the information. Years later, Anthony Eden, who had been the British Foreign Minister, told Bohlen that because of a Communist traitor

working in the Foreign Office code room, the message was not delivered to British leaders until after the announcement was public.

The final agreement was sealed and announced the following week
when German Foreign Minister Joachim von Ribbentrop flew to
Moscow to meet with Molotov and Stalin. Herwarth called Bohlen
and asked him to visit the German chancery. While Ribbentrop slept
upstairs, Herwarth filled in Bohlen on the secret protocol attached to
the pact, which agreed that Russia and Germany would carve up
Poland for themselves. Both men realized that the upshot would be
a Nazi attack on Poland and perhaps an all-out war. Herwarth, still
a nationalist, returned to Germany to join his old army regiment.
(After the war, he became West Germany's first ambassador to England.) Bohlen, meanwhile, was able to develop a new contact in the
German Embassy who helped him monitor the collaboration between
the two dictatorships.

Early in 1940, Bohlen decided to take Avis, who was pregnant, to
Paris so that she could fly home and have their baby in the U.S.
While in Berlin, he got a chance to spend a long evening with Kennan,
who had been reassigned there. Kennan was in a gloomier mood than
usual, alarmed by the preparations the Nazis were making for their
assault on France. He also told Bohlen that he doubted, incorrectly
as it turned out, that the Nazis would do anything to dissolve their
unholy alliance with the Soviets.

When Bohlen passed through Berlin again later that year, Kennan
had just taken a long trip through the Nazi-occupied countries, resulting in yet another voluminous report for the State Department
files. The tour had strengthened his conviction, Kennan said, that
Russia was a greater threat to most European countries than Nazi
Germany. Particularly in Scandinavia and Eastern Europe, Moscow
inspired more fear. The Germans, Kennan added, were enjoying high
morale. To show Bohlen the pervasive spirit, he took him to a German
music hall where the patrons cheered and banged their beer mugs to
the strains of "Wir fahren nach England."

Kennan's attitude did not arise out of sympathy for the Nazis or for
their aggressive policies. Indeed, he wrote a report in 1940 arguing
that the only way to prevent German domination of Europe was to
destroy the Nazi regime. Yet he thought that Hitler was "acting in
the best tradition of German nationalism" and that feckless Western
liberalism had encouraged this sentiment.

What was most distinctive, and disturbing, about Kennan's reporting from Prague and Berlin in 1939 and 1940 was his callousness to

the plight of those subjected to Nazi terror. One Jewish acquaintance, who had worked for years with the Americans, appeared at Kennan's home in Prague when the Nazis took over. Despairing over the fact that Kennan could not help him escape, the man contemplated suicide. "Annelise pleaded with him at intervals throughout the coming hours not to choose this way out," Kennan wrote, "not because she or I had any great optimism with respect to his chances for future happiness but partly on general Anglo-Saxon principles and partly to preserve our home from this sort of unpleasantness."

After being transferred to Berlin, Kennan complained about the work load, which was partly caused by having to deal with the desperate situation of German Jews. "The heavy attendant pressures brought to bear upon us to effect their release and removal to the United States added to the burden," he wrote. "These pressures tended often to be generated by powerful congressional circles at home."

As Europe edged closer to war, Soviet studies took a back seat to more pressing U.S. concerns. Bohlen was transferred to Tokyo at the request of Joseph Grew, the U.S. ambassador there. Kennan was kept in Berlin. It was not until the war was well under way, and attention slowly turned to questions about what kind of world would rise from the ashes, that the two friends would again be assigned to deal with the country that fascinated and infuriated them both.

CHAPTER 6

ON ACTIVE
SERVICE
Enlisting in a noble cause

A merican attitudes toward the world, Dean Acheson once wrote, have been dominated by "two contrary and equally unrealistic ideas." On one side stands the legacy of George Washington's Farewell Address, which warned Americans to steer clear of entanglement in European controversies. Its twentieth-century expression included a deep nativist streak of isolationism and an advocacy of "America First." On the other side stands the utopian dream of a world order based on international law. It found its expression in Wilsonian idealism, the League of Nations, and, at its furthest extreme, a sort of fuzzy-headed one-worldism.

Situated somewhere between these two poles there has stood, through most of the twentieth century, a group of hard-nosed internationalists. They tend to come from Wall Street and State Street, and thus understand well the importance of a prosperous and open global economy and America's role in such a world. For them, the ideal international order was that achieved between the Civil War and World War I, when trade flourished and the Royal Navy imposed a worldwide Pax Britannica. Priding themselves as statesmen rather than politicians, they have nourished a nonpartisan foreign policy tradition based on the belief that political bickering should end at the water's edge.

The archetype of such statesmen was Elihu Root, a preeminent Wall Street lawyer, William McKinley's Secretary of War, Theodore Roosevelt's Secretary of War and later Secretary of State, Woodrow Wilson's special ambassador to Russia, U.S. senator, the first honorary chairman of the Council on Foreign Relations, and winner of the 1912 Nobel Peace Prize. A man of great wit and charm, he disdained the role of public opinion in foreign policy.

Root worked to secure America's sphere of influence in the Western Hemisphere and championed an Open Door policy of trade and investment. Collective security and other universalist schemes he considered hopelessly dreamy, maintaining instead that world order was best guaranteed through pragmatic bilateral alliances, spheres of interest, and a strong military deterrent. During the debate over the League of Nations, he was neither an isolationist nor an idealist; he was among those known as "reservationists" who helped scuttle the Versailles Treaty by proposing modifications that were designed to protect America's unilateral interests.

Heir to Root's legacy and the most distinguished of his protégés was Henry Lewis Stimson, the son of a well-connected surgeon and professor at Cornell Medical School. A graduate of Andover, Yale (Skull and Bones), and Harvard Law School, Stimson became a partner in Root's Wall Street law firm in 1897; throughout his career he kept his mentor's portrait and collected writings behind his desk.

While riding a horse through Washington's Rock Creek Park in 1903, Stimson was hailed from a distance by Root, who was riding with Theodore Roosevelt: "Stimson! The President of the United States, through his Secretary of War, directs you to report at once." Maneuvering his horse directly through the swollen and icy stream, Stimson arrived at their side. Delighted by what he proclaimed a "bully" gesture, TR took a liking to the young lawyer, and on Root's advice made him U.S. Attorney for the Southern District of New York in 1906.

Stimson's one foray into elective politics, a 1910 run for governor of New York with Roosevelt's strong backing, ended in a crushing defeat. His advisers kept urging him to take on the Democratic bosses of Tammany Hall, particularly their leader, Charlie Murphy. But on the stump, the starch-collared Stimson would only go so far as to say that he "begged to take issue with Mr. Murphy." For Stimson's trouble, President Taft the following year appointed him Secretary of War. In

1917, Stimson, joined the Army and rose to the rank of colonel, commanding a field artillery battalion in France. Under Calvin Coolidge, he served as special envoy to Nicaragua, calling in the marines to supervise an election he had ordered, and also served as governor general of the Philippines. In 1929, Herbert Hoover appointed him Secretary of State, and he made a reputation as a hard-nosed internationalist. Strongly dedicated to the bipartisan tradition in international affairs, Stimson became a friend and croquet partner of his replacement, Cordell Hull, after Franklin Roosevelt's election, and he often sent letters to the *Times* taking his fellow Republicans to task for criticizing the new Administration's foreign policies.

A member of one of New York's most illustrious families, Stimson did not wear his nobility lightly: a *New Yorker* profile in 1930 noted that "he is rather well off and makes no effort to disguise it." His Washington home, Woodley, was a sprawling estate near Rock Creek Park that he purchased in the 1920s for $800,000; generally considered "Washington's greatest manor," it had served as the summer White House of four Presidents. His weekends, which stretched from Friday morning until Tuesday, were spent at his Long Island home, Highhold.

Of stately bearing and dignified countenance, Stimson was highly conscious of honor in himself and others. "Gentlemen do not read other people's mail," he declared in 1929 when a proposal was made to fund a State Department code-breaking outfit. The guiding maxim of his life was that "the only way you can make a man trustworthy is to trust him." It was a lesson, he often said, that he learned as a member of Skull and Bones.

In times of world crises, internationalists from the Root-Stimson tradition have naturally stepped forward. With a somewhat feigned reluctance, they assumed the mantle of power out of a sense of national duty. As fascism triumphed in Europe and Asia, many of these men, with Stimson as their elder statesman, urged a program of rearmament. "There has been no excuse except faulty reasoning for the wave of ostrich-like isolationsim which has swept over us," Stimson proclaimed in a letter to *The New York Times* in October of 1937.

Stimson and Root helped lead the fight for a military draft, which formed the subject of Stimson's commencement address at Yale in June of 1940. In the speech, he also called for an end to America's pretense of neutrality. The following night, in a radio speech, he declared: "I believe we should find our people ready to take their proper part in this threatened world and to carry through to victory, freedom, and reconstruction."

At his law office the next day, Stimson received a phone call from Franklin Roosevelt. Felix Frankfurter, who saw it as part of his mission in life to bring together people he admired, had helped plan a Cabinet shake-up. The President asked Stimson if he would once again step forward and serve as Secretary of War. The situation, Stimson replied, called for a truly bipartisan effort. Roosevelt agreed, saying that he planned to appoint as Navy Secretary the Republican newspaper publisher Frank Knox, who had been Alf Landon's 1936 running mate. A former member of the Rough Riders at San Juan Hill, Knox had once been sent to Stimson by Teddy Roosevelt with a letter of introduction that simply stated, "He's just our type!"

Stimson liked the idea, but he noted that he was nearing his seventy-third birthday. Roosevelt said he was aware of that; Stimson would have free rein in choosing his subordinates. Part of his mandate would be to groom a group of younger men in his tradition.

• • •

Stimson first met John McCloy when, as Secretary of State, he tried to persuade him to drop the Bethlehem Steel suit arising out of the alleged German sabotage of the munitions depot at Black Tom. "You've had your day in court, Mr. McCloy, and the other claimants would say that you shouldn't continue this thing," Stimson argued after one of the early rulings. "Mr. Secretary," he replied, "I can prove this case if you'll let me." Years later, in the autumn of 1939, McCloy and his wife were walking near their cabin at the Ausable Club in New York's Adirondacks. "Jack McCloy," a voice boomed at him, "I'm Harry Stimson." The erect gentleman, who had a cabin nearby, needed no introduction. McCloy had long admired him from afar. Their talk turned to McCloy's triumph in the Black Tom case. "As a lawyer," Stimson said, "I know how tough it is to win a case when your own government is against you."

Late the following year, after Stimson had been named Secretary of War, he summoned McCloy to Washington as a special consultant on German espionage. After six months on the job, McCloy had worked his way up to become an Assistant Secretary, with responsibility for political and military affairs. "His energy was enormous, and his optimism almost unquenchable," Stimson later wrote. McCloy learned the ropes of Washington so well that the Secretary often wondered whether anyone in town ever acted without "having a word with McCloy."

• • •

The last of Robert Lovett's European tours for Brown Brothers Harriman took place in May of 1940, just as the Germans were aiming their panzer divisions at France. While having a drink at his hotel bar in Milan, he fell into conversation with some German airmen. Hitler planned, they claimed, "to give England a taste of frightfulness which will make what has gone before look like a light workout." The airmen also boasted of the scope of Germany's armament efforts compared to those of the U.S. Lovett knew how unprepared America was; his Yale Unit colleagues Trubee Davison and David Ingalls had been Assistant Secretaries for air in the War Department during the 1920s. Returning to New York on a crowded refugee ship with another friend, the publisher Cass Canfield, Lovett resolved to join the effort to advocate American rearmament.

Upon his arrival in June, Lovett got a phone call from Averell Harriman in Washington. Mixing private and government business, they discussed how the U.S. Treasury and Brown Brothers Harriman might go about dealing with France's foreign assets. Lovett recounted some rumors he had heard that Britain might try to come to terms with Hitler. The prospect was horrifying, Lovett said, and hard to believe. But just in case, he had checked the firm's English accounts to make sure there was enough cash to cover unbacked credits.

Then the conversation turned to a personal matter: Frank Knox and others were trying to recruit Lovett to come work in Washington. Ever worried about his health, Lovett told Harriman he was unsure his doctors would let him.* But more importantly, Lovett had a philosophical reservation. Knox and Stimson had both made bold proclamations, which went further than the President's own official position, about America's willingness to help Britain. To the cautious Lovett such rhetoric was foolishly premature. "We should keep our mouths shut and tread softly until we have gained the strength to back up our statements," he wrote Harriman that afternoon in a letter expanding

---

*Throughout his life, whenever he was offered a government job, Lovett would spend days fretting about some real or imagined internal ailments and consulting with a platoon of doctors. His friends often joked that it was necessary to pin him down quick or he would soon have a letter from a dozen specialists saying that he should not undertake any given task. As it turned out, he lived until the spring of 1986, when he died at age 90.

on their conversation. "The public utterances of Colonel Knox and
Mr. Stimson seem to me to be an invitation to war. We need time
and loads of it.

"I am ready and anxious to do everything I can to be helpful in
getting this country armed, equipped and mentally prepared for war,"
Lovett continued. Yet he added that he "could not give undeviating
loyalty" to the Stimson-Knox line, at least not immediately. In typical
fashion, he decided instead that the best contribution he could make
was to prepare a careful accounting of the capabilities of America's
aircraft factories. So he combined an inspection tour for the Union
Pacific with his own private visits to airplane contractors on both coasts.

Upset by what he saw, Lovett wrote a detailed report on the organization of the industry and the poor direction it was getting from the
War Department. "It is my impression that the government will not
get the plane production being talked about from present or planned
plants," he concluded. Manufacturers had concentrated on custom-
ized products; the automobile industry should be brought into the
process to teach assembly-line techniques. "This is a quantitative war,"
he observed. "The airplane industry has, so far, been qualitative."

Lovett showed his report to one of his close friends and neighbors
on Long Island. James Vincent Forrestal was among the Wall Streeters
who had heeded the call to government service as the international
crisis mounted. Born to a family of prosperous Irish immigrants in
New York's Hudson Valley, Forrestal had fervently clambered into
the WASP establishment. As an undergraduate at Princeton, he was
chairman of *The Princetonian*, a member of the Cottage Club, and
was voted overwhelmingly "most likely to succeed." On Wall Street
he rose from a bond salesman at Dillon, Read to the presidency of
that investment house in 1937. Three years later he was appointed
Under Secretary of the Navy, and would be promoted to Secretary
upon Frank Knox's death in 1944.

Unlike most of the others who came from the financial world into
government service, Forrestal did not possess or affect an easy self-
assurance. He did not come across as a pragmatic moderate, like
Lovett, but rather as an ideologue whose ideas were often overdrawn.
Despite his successes, he carried a slight chip of social insecurity.
Within him as well were darker torments, ones that were ultimately
destructive.

A driven man, Forrestal had many acquaintances, all of whom he
insisted on calling by their first names, but few close friends. He was,

however, close to his neighbor Lovett. Their boys used to charge money to rake the lawns of Locust Valley's sprawling mansions and then sell the rose petals they collected for twenty-five cents a bag. Lovett was perceptive enough to see in Forrestal a deep sense of duty and honesty. Forrestal, in turn, admired Lovett's selflessness and envied his internal calm.

When Forrestal read Lovett's report, he immediately arranged to have it shown to Stimson, who was then battling the commercial airline industry's stubborn efforts not to divert resources from civilian contracts. Stimson decided to hire him on the spot. This time Lovett did not demur. His cross-country tour had made him anxious to enlist in the cause. He reported for duty in December, and shortly thereafter was made Assistant Secretary of War for air. "The more I see of him," Stimson recorded in his diary the day Lovett began work, "the more I like him."

•   •   •

Dean Acheson was among the most eloquent advocates in the campaign against isolationism. He was active in the Committee to Defend America by Aiding the Allies, headed by Emporia *Gazette* editor William Allen White, and in the Century Group, which included the most ardent interventionists among New York's business elite. In November of 1939, seven months before Stimson's speech at Yale, Acheson had preceded him to their alma mater to deliver a plea for rearmament. After mourning the decline of the Pax Britannica world order, he urged his listeners to help "make ourselves strong to meet a future which is dark and obscure."

The following June, addressing a convention of the International Ladies Garment Workers Union, Acheson goaded his listeners. Pointing to a banner proclaiming "Dictatorship dooms labor, Labor dooms dictatorship," he issued a sharp challenge: "If you mean it at all, you mean it as a proclamation of your fighting faith. For if it is not a fighting faith, it has no meaning. It is only words, painted on cotton, hanging from a balcony."

Although Roosevelt wanted to help Britain by providing her with fifty aged American destroyers then in mothballs, he worried about the inevitable uproar that would come from Congress. (Only after the 1940 election did he propose the Lend-Lease program.) Acheson, taking a far different attitude than he had during the 1933 gold crisis, decided to help circumvent Capitol Hill. Working with Roosevelt's legal adviser Benjamin Cohen, the restless private lawyer helped draft a legal opinion declaring that the President had the authority to exchange the destroyers for the rights to certain British naval bases.

Along with his law partner George Rublee, Acheson enlisted two other prominent attorneys to sign the opinion. He then called Charles Merz, a Yale classmate who was the editorial director of *The New York Times*, and got it published in full on the editorial page. The opinion attracted tremendous attention; the destroyer deal was approved shortly afterward by the Attorney General and concluded by the President.

Acheson sent a copy of the opinion to McCloy, who was just about to be enlisted into Stimson's service. "I cannot believe," McCloy responded from his Manhattan law office, "that we cannot risk ourselves to move effectively and expeditiously in our own vital defense." McCloy went on to denounce both candidates in the 1940 campaign, criticizing Wendell Willkie for opposing the destroyer deal and "this man Roosevelt" for catering to the labor unions. "People take for granted that such things must be the democratic process," he concluded, touching the elitist streak he knew he shared with Acheson. "If they are, I say a plague on it—let's invent something different."

In late October, with Frankfurter once again acting as a matchmaker, Roosevelt asked Acheson to join some political advisers at the White House for a discussion of the final weeks of the campaign. In his upstairs study, with a tray of cocktails perched on his desk, FDR was bombarded by what Acheson called "an unrelieved tale of woe." Willkie seemed to be catching on, said the pessimistic politicos, by portraying himself as the man who could best keep the country out of war.

Looking for relief from the worried assessments, FDR turned to Acheson, who had been unusually quiet. After pleading "shyness in disagreeing with such impressive political experts," Acheson (never known for his shyness in disagreeing with experts) added a bit less disingenuously that he would appreciate "the courage to be expected from another cocktail." Thus fortified, he argued that the President's only danger lay in seeming to be on the defensive. The great freedoms secured by the New Deal must be linked to the threat to freedom arising from fascism. The President, Acheson proclaimed, must give a rousing speech tying America's ideals at home to the survival of those ideals around the globe. Roosevelt was delighted and asked for a proposed draft. Acheson worked through the night and delivered it to Harry Hopkins the next morning. "We who believe in democracy," it concluded, "have only begun to fight." It was a refrain that Roosevelt adopted, with much success.

A few weeks after the election, Roosevelt invited Acheson to join the Administration. Secretary of State Hull made the formal job offer: Assistant Secretary of State for Economic Affairs. After working around the fringes of government for so long, Hull said, it was now time to take the plunge. Acheson asked for time to consider. But there was no doubt about what he would do. He had long been anxious to return to the fray. The oath was administered in February 1941 by Justice Brandeis at his apartment; among the witnesses were Frankfurter and MacLeish.

• • •

Harriman had gone to Washington in May of 1940 while Lovett was on his trip to Europe. As one of Harry Hopkins's "tame businessmen," he was given a dollar-a-year job as transportation adviser to the new National Defense Advisory Commission. Although still on the board of the Union Pacific, Harriman's first crusade was to get the government to help increase the nation's rail freight capability. As usual, there was little worry in Harriman's mind that what would be good for him and his interests might conflict with what was best for his country.

As the other executives dithered rather helplessly in the cluttered room that served as the commission's office, Harriman threw himself into his work with his usual intensity. He was soon itching to become more involved. In January of 1941, within an hour of Roosevelt's announcement that he was sending Harry Hopkins on a personal mission to see Churchill, Harriman was on the phone from his ski lodge in Sun Valley. "Let me carry your bag, Harry," he pleaded. "I've met Churchill several times and I know London intimately."

Hopkins and Harriman had been friends ever since a chance meeting in a railway club car in 1933. They subsequently became regulars on Herbert Bayard Swope's croquet lawn in Sands Point, Long Island. Hopkins, who was fond of dividing the world into "talkers" and "doers," placed himself and Harriman squarely in the latter category. Although he declined Harriman's offer of traveling companionship, he said he wanted to see him on his return. The President, Hopkins confided, might have a bigger job for him.

Harriman suspected it might have something to do with the Lend-Lease program, which Roosevelt had announced in December. When Hopkins returned, an eager Harriman was waiting at La Guardia

Airport. Back at Hopkins's suite at the Roosevelt Hotel, they discussed Britain's desperate needs. Hopkins, however, said nothing about a job for Harriman.

Part of FDR's reluctance was due to Harriman's ill-concealed ambition. Notoriously tight about picking up restaurant tabs or donating to charity, he was nevertheless quite loose with contributions that could put him in proximity to power. In a conversation after the 1940 election, Roosevelt playfully remarked to Willkie, "Confidentially, Wendell, Averell contributed twenty-five thousand dollars to my campaign." Replied the Republican: "Confidentially, Franklin, he contributed twenty-five thousand to mine." (Harriman later said he had given Willkie only one thousand dollars, and it was for his nomination battle rather than the general election.)

Like Acheson and Stimson, Harriman was vigorously engaged in the struggle against isolationism. At the Yale Club of New York in February of 1941, he tried to inspire his audience by reading a list of fellow alumni—Dean Acheson, Robert Lovett, Henry Stimson, Archibald MacLeish—who "had put aside their private occupations to enter the government because they cared deeply whether Britain or Hitler's Germany would win the war." Later that month, Roosevelt finally offered him a chance to join their ranks. "I want you to go over to London," the President said, "and recommend everything that we can do, short of war, to keep the British Isles afloat."

It was a perfect job for Harriman: a broad mission with wide-ranging authority, personal access to top leaders, and few bureaucratic strings. He would deal directly with Churchill and his production ministers, providing the President with a personal conduit to Downing Street that bypassed Cordell Hull and the State Department channels Roosevelt found so cumbersome. "I suppose you will ask all about his title, so I thought I would invent one," the President told the press in announcing Harriman's appointment. "We decided it was a pretty good idea to call him an 'Expediter.'"

Harriman prepared for his mission methodically. Among those he consulted was his schoolmate Acheson, who confessed to being baffled by the disorganization of Hull's decision-making process. With Lovett he discussed the military's reluctance to part with matériel it might later want for itself. Stimson, over lunch at Woodley, his Georgian mansion on Rock Creek Park, reaffirmed what was a basic tenet of the Wall Street Establishment: Despite the inevitable objections of the reconstructed America Firsters, who were beginning to advocate an "Asia First" strategy, America must concentrate initially, Stimson said, on winning the war in Europe. Harriman agreed.

• • •

On Sunday, December 7, 1941, Averell Harriman was with Winston Churchill at the latter's country home, Chequers. After dinner, the butler brought in a radio that Harry Hopkins had given the Prime Minister for listening to BBC broadcasts. "The news has just been given," the announcer said, "that Japanese aircraft have raided Pearl Harbor, the American naval base in Hawaii." A startled Harriman simply repeated the words, "the Japanese have raided Pearl Harbor." Churchill slammed the top of the radio, jumped from his chair, and put in a call to Roosevelt. "Mr. President, what's this about Japan?" Replied Roosevelt: "It's quite true. We are all in the same boat now." The inevitable, Harriman thought, had finally happened.

Dean and Alice Acheson were having a picnic that Sunday at Harewood, their Maryland farm, with Archibald MacLeish and his wife, Ada. A few minutes after leaving to drive back to Washington, MacLeish roared back into the driveway and came running down the lawn. "The Japanese have attacked Pearl Harbor," he yelled. "Turn on your radio." Acheson drove to the State Department, where small groups were gathered in the hall exchanging information.

John McCloy was at his desk in the War Department, even though he usually worked only half a day on Sunday. He had been reading "Magic," the Japanese cable intercepts, and felt something was brewing, though he was not prepared for the boldness of Japan's stroke. An aide rushed into his office. "There's a report around that they're attacking Pearl Harbor," he said. "Don't kid me," McCloy replied. "Perhaps they're attacking someplace farther west, like Singapore, but they wouldn't dare attack Pearl Harbor."

When the news was finally confirmed, McCloy's first reaction was to assure that the President was protected. He went to see Navy Secretary Knox, taking with him Ulysses Grant III, who was in charge of guarding Washington, and Sherman Miles, a nephew of William Tecumseh Sherman and son of Civil War hero Nelson Miles, who was in charge of Army counterintelligence. "Here's the whole goddam Union Army," proclaimed Knox. Together they ordered a cordon of marines to be placed around the White House. That evening McCloy drove to Stimson's house to read the cables describing the devastation. When he finally got home at 3 A.M., he went to the nursery of his baby daughter. Lifting her out of bed, McCloy smiled for the first time that day, the strain momentarily draining from his face.

Robert and Adèle Lovett were at a movie house watching *Ninotchka*. They had already seen the film, but they made a habit of going to the same theater every Sunday, no matter what was playing. Besides, Lovett remembers, he very much wanted to see Garbo smile again. When they came out, everyone in the street was talking about the news. "Nonsense," Lovett told his wife. "Who would want to do a damn fool thing like bomb Pearl Harbor?" But as they drove past the Japanese Embassy, the staff was in the yard burning papers. Lovett dropped his wife at home and headed for the War Department. By the time he got there, the staff was setting up cots and blankets in the offices preparing for the long hours ahead.

George Kennan, in his apartment in Berlin, heard the news on the faint signal of a shortwave broadcast. He telephoned as many members of the U.S. mission as he could, and they met at the embassy to consider their situation. Over the next few days, their communication lines with the rest of the world ceased to function. On Tuesday night, they decided to burn their codes and secret papers. After a week, with the U.S. and Germany now officially at war, the Gestapo escorted Kennan and his colleagues out of the embassy to be confined indefinitely in a building on the outskirts of Bad Nauheim, near Frankfurt.

Charles Bohlen was riding with another officer from their apartment to the U.S. Embassy in Tokyo. The chauffeur said he had heard reports of British and Japanese fighting in the Pacific. "Probably not true," he added. "Only on Tokyo radio." As they neared their destination, they bought a paper from one of the newsboys ringing bells. The extra reported that British, American, and Japanese ships were battling. In the embassy courtyard, the Americans were busily burning papers. With Japanese escorts guarding him, Bohlen rounded up the rest of the U.S. personnel and brought them to the compound for the internment that lay ahead.

CHAPTER 7

HEAVENLY TWINS

McCloy and Lovett
at the War Department

He called them the best staff he ever had. They called him "Colonel," which is what he had been in the previous world war. At seventy-three, Henry Stimson had been slowed by age, but he was a master at instilling loyalty and dedication among those who served under him. After a lifetime of active service, Stimson had learned to concentrate on one or two large issues at a time, while delegating details to four trusted assistants.

To procure equipment for the Army he hired Robert Patterson, a lawyer and former federal judge who wore the belt of a German soldier he had killed during World War I as a constant reminder of the critical nature of his work. As his personal assistant and aide de camp, Stimson chose Harvey Bundy, a Boston lawyer of uncommon brilliance, modesty, and discretion. A product of Yale (Skull and Bones) and Harvard Law School, Bundy had served Stimson as Assistant Secretary of State in the early 1930s. He married Katharine Lawrence Putnam, of Boston's Putnam and Lowell families, and had three sons. Two of them, William and McGeorge, in their own time would become heirs to the Stimsonian tradition.

But the real dynamos on his staff were the two men Stimson called the "Heavenly Twins," or, in his occasional fits of temper, the "Imps of Satan"—Jack McCloy and Bob Lovett. "McCloy was the man who handled everything that no one else happened to be handling," Stimson said in his memoirs, *On Active Service in Peace and War* (written in collaboration with McGeorge Bundy). Recalled McCloy: "My job was to be at all the points of the organizational chart where the lines did not quite intersect." Lovett's responsibility was "all matters affecting the Air Forces." Stimson's ability to delegate was illustrated by the mandate he gave Lovett one day when someone questioned Lovett's prerogatives. "The next time anybody asks you what your authority is," Stimson said, "you tell them that whatever authority the Secretary of War has, you have."

Their work in the War Department from 1940 to 1945 would earn McCloy and Lovett, who were by then in their late forties, a central place in the nation's national security Establishment. They would first make their names as protégés of Henry Stimson, then as powerful decision makers in their own rights. More importantly, the attitudes they formed and the style of operation they adopted would help set the bipartisan tone for the postwar period, when they and many of their friends who had entered government at the outset of the war assumed responsibility for shaping the peace.

McCloy and Lovett shared an asset that was rare in Washington: they had risen in private life by being able to tackle complicated tasks on their own, rather than relying on others to do their work. "You may think this is a small thing," Lovett said later, "but you'd be appalled at the number of people Jack and I met in Washington during the war who had never learned to handle anything by themselves."

Stimson came to treat his Heavenly Twins like sons. Along with their wives, they spent many evenings out at Woodley, gossiping with the Colonel and joking with Mrs. Stimson about her husband's ferocious temper. McCloy was a frequent deck-tennis partner. Lovett, who had sworn off physical exercise, once relented and came out to Woodley for a game of lawn bowls; he was sore for a week after, and told Stimson that playing sports was the only assignment he would henceforth decline.

In the office, Stimson would summon Lovett and McCloy by using an electronic squawk box. Always confounded by mechanical gadgets, Stimson would start to talk and lean back in his chair, releasing the button. The Twins would then rush down the corridor to his office to see what he was saying. "There were a lot of bone-crushing collisions in the hall as a result," Lovett recalled.

On one occasion when they burst in, Stimson, in one of his foul humors, insisted he had not called them. "Get back to work!" he bellowed. On the way out, they stopped off in the next-door office of Army Chief of Staff George Marshall. A moment later Stimson strode in and berated them for not having gotten back to work. It was the first time, Lovett would later joke, that anyone had been kicked out of two offices a minute after they had been summoned. On another occasion, Lovett wandered into Stimson's office while Stimson was deep in thought and caught the full force of the Colonel's fury. Backing out into the hall, he ran into his fellow Imp of Satan. "Stimson wants to see you right away," he told McCloy.

To outsiders, Lovett and McCloy must have seemed a little boy scoutish, the teacher's twin pets. Yet anyone wishing to get anything done in the War Department soon came to realize this pair of amiable interlopers from Wall Street controlled much of what went on. What made the two men influential insiders was not so much their jobs but the informal social networks they formed. McCloy's small study in Georgetown became a nexus for the exchange of indispensable gossip. James Forrestal, who was having trouble getting inside information from his own navy brass, was among many who came to depend on McCloy, calling him daily to arrange lunch or tennis dates (McCloy invariably won) or just to check in. Felix Frankfurter, as if to make up for ignoring him at Harvard, adopted McCloy as a member of his unofficial war cabinet, which already included Acheson and Lovett. When Acheson's daughter Mary married Harvey Bundy's son Bill, it was Jack and Ellen McCloy who hosted the wedding breakfast.

The Lovetts gave intimate dinner parties on their balcony overlooking Rock Creek Park to which the Bohlens, McCloys, and Harrimans were often invited. More importantly, Lovett learned to cultivate the press. Eugene Meyer, owner of the Washington *Post*, gave a series of parties to introduce the Lovetts to Washington. Among Lovett's closest friends were such Yale chums as Charles Merz, the editorial director of *The New York Times*, and Henry Luce of *Time*.

Lovett did not hesitate to pull on such strings. When *Newsweek* raised questions about the efficiency of the daylight bombing of Germany, Lovett wrote to Harriman in London asking that something be done. Harriman, who had invested in the magazine at the behest of his friend Vincent Astor, laid down an editorial line for his brother,

Roland, to impose. "Tell Roland that I am in dead earnest and will brook no compromise," Harriman wrote Lovett in April of 1943. "I have not supported *Newsweek* for ten years through its grave difficulties to allow our hired men to use the magazine to express their narrow, uninformed or insidious ideas... Roland has my full authority to use any strong arm measures he considers necessary... The other directors can be asked to resign if they do not go along."

Lovett was once asked to pick the greatest negotiator he ever met. Without hesitation, he named McCloy. Indeed, McCloy seemed to have a magic ability to conjure a consensus out of chaos. Blessed with stamina and patience, he could gather a contentious group in his office, outlast their arguments, and gently but persistently prod them toward areas of agreement. He had a sensitive appreciation of how far each could be pushed. One tactic, which he called "yellow padding," consisted of carefully preparing on a legal pad the outcome he hoped to achieve at a meeting; after edging the players toward that consensus, he would pull out his draft of "what everyone seems to be saying."

Lovett did not share McCloy's bottomless energy, but he was incisive and persuasive. He managed at once to seem shy yet commanding, polished yet never condescending. His humor and warmth, sprinkled with light profanity, could be disarming, but he had a demanding and forceful intellect. "There's not a more respected man and certainly not a better liked man in Washington," said an official of the War Production Board. General "Hap" Arnold, chief of the Army Air Forces, defined Lovett's strengths as "his business background and his aviation background, plus plenty of good horse sense."

Bureaucratic runarounds infuriated Lovett. When he asked subordinates about problems and got the stock response that "everything possible is being done," Lovett would unfurl his lanky body from its usual languid slouch, raise his hooded eyelids, and demand reams of statistics and factual evidence. Then he would pore over the figures, challenge them in detail, commit them to memory, and use them as ammunition later.

Unlike McCloy, Lovett did not relish the art of consultation and consensus building; he was, instead, a doer, someone who was a master at accomplishing a task and administering an activity. "To hell with the cheese," he would declare when enmeshed in a tangled problem. "Let's just get out of this trap." When faced with disagreements, he tried to downplay ideological differences. The resolution, he insisted, would come from weighing the facts and figures. As General Marshall put it: "Lovett has the finest facility in the world for handling unpleasant problems without making anyone mad: he solves them."

Both Lovett and McCloy, who had given up lucrative careers for their ten-thousand-dollar-a-year jobs, were nominally Republicans (as were Stimson and Bundy), but neither was politically active or ambitious. "I haven't any political career—don't know anything about politics and never have," Lovett bragged to a reporter. "My business was banking, now it's airplanes. I'm just a regular government employee, working on salary." Once, when McCloy was visiting the White House, Roosevelt took a phone call and started talking unguardedly about campaign strategies. "Mr. President, remember I'm a Republican," McCloy interjected with some embarrassment. "Damn it," said Roosevelt, "I always forget."

Despite their disdain for partisanship, both men were adroit at dealing with Congress. McCloy was instrumental in the fight for Lend-Lease and even helped contribute its key slogan. In a conversation with Frankfurter, he used the phrase "arsenal of democracy," which he had picked up from Jean Monnet. "Don't use those words for a few weeks," said Frankfurter, who then went to the White House and told Robert Sherwood to use the phrase in an address he was writing for Roosevelt. During the Senate debate on the bill, McCloy sat on the floor amid the page boys so that he could help manage the fight and funnel arguments to the Democratic leader, Jimmy Byrnes.

Lovett often rankled at the endless appropriation hearings he had to face while Assistant Secretary, but he made a practice of disarming questioners with surprisingly candid responses and reams of factual material. Although he called congressional oversight one of the "pitfalls of the Pentagon," after the war Lovett told the story of asking Albert Speer why Germany had failed to produce more Messerschmitts. "The Fuehrer told us to take the jet and make a fighter-bomber out of it," said Speer. To Lovett this showed that dictatorships, free from democratic constraints, are prone to pigheadedness.

The former bombardier and the former artillery officer particularly enjoyed inspection tours to the front. During the air attacks on Italy's Mediterranean islands, Lovett went to North Africa to act as a cheerleader for his beloved bomber forces. Flying in a B-17 over the Atlas Mountains, he sat with the crew listening to a BBC broadcast of swing music. When they were stumped by one song, Lovett, for whom swing music was a passion, identified it correctly as an Erskine Hawkins number ("Tuxedo Junction"). "The Secretary is pretty hep, if you ask me," said the radio operator later. "Yeah," replied a gunner, "that bald-headed ol' bird is the first guy out of Washington I ever met who knew anything about anything."

At the front in Germany near the end of the war, McCloy discovered that the ninth-century city of Rothenburg was about to be shelled. McCloy's mother had once visited the town and brought back etchings; he knew it was an ancient center of German culture. "This is one of Europe's last great walled cities," he told the American commander. Perhaps, McCloy suggested, it could be induced to surrender peacefully. It was, and after the war the city voted him an honorary burgher.

Stimson often dispatched McCloy to handle troublesome commanders, among them George Patton, who was publicly grumbling on the eve of D-Day about what he considered his insufficient role. McCloy told him to keep quiet. Drawing himself to his full height and wearing his ivory-handled pistols, Patton declared: "You're taking a good deal of responsibility to come here on eve of battle and destroy a man's confidence." Replied McCloy: "Listen, George, if I thought I could destroy your confidence by anything I might say, I would ask General Eisenhower to remove you." Patton unpuffed and relented.

• • •

McCloy would later refer to the decision as "regrettable in the clear light of perfect hindsight." To Eric Sevareid in 1975 he conceded "they weren't adequately compensated." Yet both at the time and in the years that followed, McCloy found it difficult to wrestle with the moral complexities surrounding one of his most significant actions during the war: overseeing the forced relocation of some 110,000 Japanese-Americans, most of them U.S. citizens, from the West Coast to detention camps farther inland.

"We moved them under the President's order," McCloy recalled. "He was very agitated about what happened at Pearl Harbor and that our first line of defense was gone. He was the only one who could sign an order to move these people. As an assistant secretary, I could not even move a soldier, let alone a civilian." In addition, McCloy argues, the relocated families were not treated all that horribly; they were given adequate stipends, and many were allowed to live and work outside the internment camps as long as they stayed away from sensitive areas.

Much of McCloy's recollection is justified. The Japanese-Americans suffered far less than many other Americans who fought the war.

But the role Stimson's prized chore boy played in the matter was far greater than merely following orders.

During the ten weeks between the December 1941 bombing of Pearl Harbor and the order to relocate the Japanese-Americans, there was a rising public concern, particularly in California, about the prospect of an enemy within. The Los Angeles *Times*, which the day after the attack editorialized "Let's Not Get Rattled," declared in January that "the rigors of war demand proper detention of Japanese and their immediate removal from danger spots." California Congressman Leland Ford insisted that "all Japanese, whether citizens or not, be placed in inland concentration camps." By early February, even respected columnist Walter Lippmann was deploring "the unwillingness of Washington to adopt a policy of mass evacuation and mass internment of all those who are technically enemy aliens."

Much of the fear was understandable, at least in those jittery times. The West Coast was preparing for possible raids, Japanese submarines had been detected off California, and there were reports that Japanese residents using headlights and radios were signaling ships offshore. Until the "miracle at Midway" six months later, the American Navy seemed hard pressed to protect the Pacific.

The FBI began systematically arresting hundreds of Japanese aliens considered a potential threat. But the demand grew for a blanket evacuation that would include not only resident aliens but also the second-generation immigrants, known as Nisei, who were legal U.S. citizens. Leading the crusade were General John De Witt of the Western Command along with the Army's top military police officials. Resisting sweeping measures were Edward Ennis of the Immigration and Naturalization Service and, at least for a while, Attorney General Francis Biddle.

In late December, John McCloy was called on to find a consensus between the two factions. He quickly worked out an agreement to give De Witt broad powers to register aliens—but not citizens—and expel them from certain designated zones. Soon, however, De Witt began to bow to pressure in the military to take action against all Japanese-Americans. The American-born Nisei, argued the Army's provost marshal, were actually more dangerous than the nonnaturalized immigrants, who tended to be older.

McCloy arranged a series of meetings in early February to break the impasse, beginning with a heated Sunday session at Biddle's home and ending with one in Stimson's office. After carefully listing in his diary the arguments on both sides, Stimson concluded that a wholesale evacuation was unjustifiable. "We cannot discriminate," he said, "among our citizens on the ground of racial origin."

In passing along Stimson's decision to General De Witt, McCloy offered a compromise suggestion: "Perhaps the best solution is to limit the withdrawal to certain prohibited areas." De Witt, however, began increasing the pressure for a wholesale evacuation. As he told McCloy: "A Jap is a Jap to these people now."

In the meantime, Biddle's resistance had begun to weaken. After a typically inconclusive lunch with the President, the Attorney General solicited an outside legal opinion from three Roosevelt intimates, Benjamin Cohen, Oscar Cox, and Joseph Rauh. "In time of national peril, any reasonable doubt," they wrote, "must be resolved in favor of action to protect the national security." Anxious to wash his hands of the troublesome matter, Biddle wrote Stimson that any action "should in my opinion be taken by the War Department and not the Department of Justice."

Stimson himself began to waver from his decision not to permit a wholesale evacuation. After McCloy relayed the increasing fervor of De Witt's demands, Stimson telephoned the White House to pose the question to the President. Roosevelt, still remaining vague, told his Secretary of War to do whatever he "thought best."

Once again, Stimson turned the matter over to McCloy to coordinate. Instead of wrestling with the objections of the Justice Department, however, McCloy immediately telephoned De Witt in California. The way McCloy interpreted the President's nondecision tended to guarantee that the final outcome would be a major evacuation. "We have carte blanche to do what we want as far as the President is concerned," he told the general. As usual, McCloy saw his role as that of a coordinator rather than a policy maker. But with everyone seeking to avoid responsibility for making the policy, the decision evolved through the way it was coordinated.

De Witt and his military advisers began preparing a detailed recommendation for an evacuation. "The Japanese race is an enemy race," they wrote, "and while many second and third generation Japanese born on U.S. soil, possessed of U.S. citizenship, have become 'Americanized,' the racial strains are undiluted."

Only after the military men completed their recommendation, which amounted to a full-scale internment, did McCloy take it over to Biddle's home for another meeting with Justice Department officials.

Ennis again denounced the idea, but this time Biddle undercut him. They should get to work, he said, polishing up the plan. After Stimson approved the internment order, the President signed it on February 19. Legislation enacting the program promptly passed both the Senate and the House with only one dissenting vote, that of Ohio isolationist Robert Taft.

During the war, McCloy took a personal interest in improving conditions for the internees, visiting them often and occasionally helping those who passed loyalty tests find jobs or enroll in college in the east. He also helped form the 442nd Infantry Regiment, a volunteer unit composed solely of Nisei, which fought for the U.S. bravely, suffered massive casualties in Italy, and became the most decorated unit in American military history. Formation of the regiment, McCloy later said, was one thing he wanted to be sure was carved on his tombstone.

The moral dilemmas surrounding the program were still unsettled in 1981, when a commission appointed by President Carter examined the matter. The eighty-six-year-old McCloy, bitter at what he considered the panel's bias, became quite prickly when finally called to testify. What occurred "was a relocation program and not an internment," he claimed, causing the audience to hiss. With one Japanese-American commissioner, McCloy uncharacteristically lost his temper and referred to the program as being "in the way of retribution for the attack that was made on Pearl Harbor." The panel's final verdict was that the relocation was the result of "race prejudice, war hysteria and a failure of political leadership."

"McCloy, I think, more than anyone believed in this," Biddle recalled in a 1968 interview. "I never excuse him for doing this." Others were more charitable. "McCloy was distracted and distraught with a number of problems and was essentially motivated, I think, to try to protect his boss, Henry Stimson," James Rowe, an aide to Biddle and Roosevelt, told historian Peter Irons. Shortly before he died, Rowe said in another interview: "I think McCloy's main motives were to try to please the generals and make things easy for Stimson."

Rowe's assessments are probably closest to the mark. In acting as a pragmatic coordinator of the consensus he felt was forming around him, McCloy failed to consider the moral questions involved. But raising moral considerations was not necessarily McCloy's job, and certainly not his style. "There was no real debate about it at the time," McCloy now says. "All of us agreed that this was a prudent step given the nefarious nature of the attack and the dangers we faced. Only in comfortable hindsight can people ignore the practicalities of the situation then."

· · ·

The Japanese relocation was not the only time during his tenure at the War Department that McCloy was involved in defending a consensus based on practical considerations against challenges made from a moral viewpoint. In June of 1944, when accounts from the first escapees of the Nazi prison camps began to reveal the full horror of the Holocaust, Jewish leaders in England and America begged the Allies to bomb the gas chambers and crematoria at Auschwitz in the hope that this would slow the grisly genocide. They pressed their case on presidential advisers Samuel Rosenman and Harry Hopkins and on members of the War Refugee Board. They in turn asked McCloy to find out whether such bombing was militarily feasible.

McCloy showed little sympathy. He had already helped nix a January 1944 WRB plan to have the Army assist in rescuing victims of Nazi repression. "I am very chary of getting the Army involved in this while the war is going on," he scribbled on the proposal. When the request came in to consider bombing the rail lines to Auschwitz, McCloy sought the advice of the War Department's Operations Division. A memo was subsequently prepared by two members of the Army's General Staff, who came to the same conclusions that their British counterparts had reached after a similar inquiry from Churchill. Attacks on Auschwitz would be of "doubtful efficacy," they said, and would divert forces from attacking important industrial targets.

At the time, the military was understandably anxious to focus all available air power in Normandy as the Allies struggled to break from the beaches in the aftermath of D-Day. McCloy reported this back to the White House. According to his recollection, Hopkins and Rosenman made no objection. "What they mainly wanted was for me to get their boss off the hook, for me to write the letters," he recalled.

McCloy subsequently signed a series of replies to those pleading for attacks on Auschwitz. Using phrases from the memos of the Operations Division and the General Staff, he argued that the suggested bombings would be impractical and "might provoke even more vindictive acts by the Germans" (a possibility that is hard to imagine). One of McCloy's letters is on display at the Auschwitz museum.

McCloy's last response on the matter was to John Pehle of the WRB in November of 1944. "Use of heavy bombers from United Kingdom bases would necessitate a round trip flight unescorted of approximately 2,000 miles," he said. "It would be a diversion from our strategic bombing effort, and the results obtained would not justify the high losses likely to result." In fact, there were at the time American warplanes based in southern Italy, six hundred miles from Auschwitz, which were making heavy bombing raids on oil refineries only thirteen miles from the concentration camp, according to historian David Wyman and journalist Morton Mintz. McCloy says he does not remember why it was not considered possible to use planes from there, rather than Britain, to attack Auschwitz.

The decision, McCloy insists, was not based on his personal feelings but on practical military considerations. "If Roosevelt had wanted to divert the planes, we would have," he says. "There is no reason to believe it would have done much good. The best way to help those people was to win the war as quickly as possible." After the war, McCloy in fact worked hard to help displaced Jews and was instrumental in persuading Konrad Adenauer to increase German reparations paid to Israel.

●   ●   ●

Most of McCloy's activities were far less controversial. One pet project, as an old artilleryman, was getting light planes for use as spotters for gun batteries. He was strongly supported by Eisenhower, but Air Corps General Hap Arnold felt it would be hard to spare the pilots. Lovett suggested that McCloy learn to fly as a way to show Arnold that regular soldiers, rather than trained air corps pilots, could handle the spotter planes. McCloy did just that. When he presented the plan to Arnold, the general replied: "Not that! I'll let you have the planes. Just don't make me go up with you."

McCloy was also responsible for the construction of the Pentagon, which became known as "McCloy's folly." One of his greatest difficulties was getting the plans approved by Roosevelt, who fancied himself an amateur architect. He finally resorted to extortion. The President had gotten himself in a bind involving an old Harvard classmate, Putzi Hanfstaengl, a German refugee who had returned to his native country and acted for a while as a court jester for Hitler. Thinking he could pump useful information out of Hanfstaengl, Roosevelt had him sent to the U.S. from England, where he was being held prisoner. Hanfstaengl, however, turned out to be a fool, and Roosevelt wanted to get rid of him. McCloy told a White House staffer he would find a safe sinecure for Hanfstaengl at an army base in Texas if FDR would approve the Pentagon blueprints. It worked. At a Cabinet meeting the following week, Roosevelt turned to McCloy and growled, "You black-mailer!"

As Stimson's personal envoy to foreign leaders, McCloy visited London in 1943 to press for establishment of a second front through a cross-Channel invasion, as the Allies had promised the Soviets. Churchill, who was insisting on pursuing the North African campaign instead, took McCloy on a tour of the devastated city, ending up at midnight in the bomb-gutted Houses of Parliament. "When I look across the well of this house," the Prime Minister said, "I see the faces that should be here. I'm just a sport because most of my contemporaries are dead. They're dead at the Passchendaele or the Somme. And we can't endure the decimation of another British generation."

When Eisenhower became mired in a political quagmire in North Africa after forming, on Stimson's advice, a strange-bedfellow alliance with the Vichy French leader Jean Darlan, McCloy was sent over to coordinate the civilian administration. Upon his return, he and Stimson urged Roosevelt to put aside his personal distaste for Charles de Gaulle and recognize him as the leader of Free France. A White House Cabinet Room pad from the period shows Harry Hopkins's doodles with a notation at the bottom: "One more crack from McCloy to the Boss about de Gaulle and McCloy is out of here."

By the end of the war, McCloy's reputation as an adroit fixer was made. The gnomelike Assistant Secretary seemed able to tread sensitive turf without leaving footprints or enemies in his trail. An aura of wisdom and competence surrounded him; above all, he was trusted.

One day, as American forces pushed into Germany, Roosevelt called McCloy into his office. *"Heil hoch Kommissar für Deutschland!"* he announced. McCloy was baffled. "I'm making you High Commissioner for Germany," Roosevelt explained. "Don't you think that's premature?" McCloy asked. "We haven't won the war yet. You ought to have a military governor." He suggested Lucius Clay. Not only could he command troops, McCloy argued, but he was an engineer who knew how to handle logistical problems. "Oh, McCloy, I'm too tired to argue with you," Roosevelt replied. It was March of 1945, and McCloy was suddenly struck by how weary the President indeed looked.

•   •   •

While McCloy was juggling a mélange of tasks, Lovett was concentrating on a single big one: building up America's air power. In

1938, the Army Air Corps had 1,773 planes and trained 500 pilots. In 1942, it built 47,000 new planes and trained 30,000 pilots. By the following year, planes were being churned out at a rate of 8,000 a month.

To accomplish the goal, Lovett carefully cultivated the White House. In February of 1941, just after taking office, he called on Harry Hopkins, FDR's powerful adviser, taking along McCloy for support. Lovett's modest goal: To get the President to double the production of planes. "While I don't go so far as to claim that air power alone will win the war," he wrote in his memo to Hopkins, "I do claim the war will not be won without it."

Hopkins was impressed. Deal maker that he was, however, he raised another matter once Lovett had concluded. During his recent visit to England, Hopkins related, Churchill mentioned that he was having problems diverting pilots from combat in order to ferry American-supplied planes across the Atlantic. Was there anything that could be done? Lovett went to work on Juan Trippe, president of Pan Am and a friend from Yale, who offered to supply civilian pilots for the ferry work. Hopkins subsequently agreed to press the issue of air power on the President.

Fearing the erratic style of both the President and the former social worker who was his closest aide, Lovett kept up his pressure. "Since the period of gestation of our airplane is unfortunately about twice that of a human," he wrote Hopkins, "we have to make up our minds very soon if we are to have any benefits from added capacity by the end of 1942." The President was persuaded. He sent word to Lovett to draw up a presidential directive vastly increasing the production of bombers and other planes.

Lovett's private inspection tour in 1940 had convinced him that, in order to get these new planes produced, assembly-line techniques must be imposed on the industry. Lovett understood the need for constant design improvements. "What's the use of flying kiddie cars?" he noted. But to streamline the process he designated only a few factories to experiment with new models; others were ordered to churn out standard planes as quickly as possible. "The airplane manufacturers were like a lot of custom tailors, and our job was to turn them into Hart Schaffner and Marxes overnight," he told a reporter in 1943.

Lovett also used more daring methods. "One way I got production moving was telling the companies to go ahead even before the contracts had been written or the money appropriated," he recalled. "I'd give them a letter of intent. If it weren't for the fact that a war was going on, I'd have ended up in Leavenworth." It worked. One factory, in fact, delivered eighty-five completed engines on the day that the government signed the contract for their construction.

Forrestal, working closely with Lovett, was doing the same thing as Under Secretary of the Navy. It helped that Di Gates, Lovett's colleague in the Yale Unit and former roommate in New York, served as his counterpart, the Assistant Secretary of the Navy for air. By March of 1941, six months after Forrestal had taken office, the Navy had approximately $4 billion worth of letters of intent outstanding.

When Forrestal and Lovett wanted to build bases in South America as way stations for U.S. planes flying to Africa, the State Department said it could not be done. Forrestal decided to take the problem to their mutual friend at Pan Am. Trippe agreed that his airline would build the bases using money paid from a secret contingency fund controlled by the President. "You know, Jim, you're taking a big risk," said James Rowe, the President's man at the Justice Department. "If America doesn't enter the war, you could go to jail." Forrestal replied: "I'm so sure we'll get into the war and need these bases that I'll take my chances."

• • •

Administering the phenomenal burst of warplane production was only the most tangible of Lovett's accomplishments. Equally important was his role in changing the military mind-set and bringing America into a new age of air power. When he took office, Lovett said, there were officers who "continued to regard the airplane as a rather dangerous contraption from which a bolt might drop and scare the daylights out of [their horses]." Certainly there was little understanding that air power might be more than an adjunct to ground fighting, that it could do more than merely provide support for infantry and artillery attacks. The notion of "strategic bombing," the use of planes to conduct long-range offensive campaigns, was generally dismissed.

After World War I, the air chief of Allied forces had reported that the "most important and far reaching" contribution of airplanes was their use for observation; the Army's official textbook in 1920 taught that "strategical bombing is a luxury." Waging a lonely struggle against this mind-set was a handful of disciples of the legendary General Billy Mitchell, an ardent air-power advocate who was court-martialed in 1925 for his attacks on the army high command. They formed a small clique at Maxwell Air Force Base dedicated to the idea that strategic bombing could change the course of modern warfare.

In Lovett they finally found an advocate with clout. Through his personal experience with the Yale Unit in Bruges during World War I, the Assistant Secretary had seen what relentless strategic bombing could do. The success that the Nazis were having in adopting this tactic further strengthened his beliefs.

Lovett was among the first American policy makers to envision that effective use of bombers might someday make the trench obsolete. He helped move America into an age in which long-range bombers, freed from the task of providing support for ground troops, could launch offensive campaigns as effectively as army units or navy ships. "Such was the cast of the military mind that the full potential of air power as an independent, offensive weapon had not penetrated the domain of artillery and battleships," Jonathan Fanton, now president of the New School in New York, has written. "It fell to Lovett to weave into the collective conscience a theory of air power as modern as the technology itself." The specifics of Lovett's concept—and in particular his conviction that sustained bombing could destroy the morale of an enemy—may not have been fully justified; but his faith in strategic bombing was destined to change the way America would wage war at least through the Vietnam era.

His first task in breaking what he called the "trench-mind mentality" was convincing Stimson that air power was more than just another weapon to be put at the disposal of ground troops. Soon after being sworn in, Lovett set up a tutorial for the Secretary in which he argued that air power represented a brand-new form of warfare and should be given organizational autonomy as the British had done with the Royal Air Force. "At irregular intervals in history," Lovett told the old artillery colonel, "some new development has altered the art of war and changed the fate of peoples and the world."

The structure of the Army's air forces, Lovett said, "resembled nothing in the world so much as a bowl of spaghetti." The production of planes and the training of personnel was the duty of the Air Corps. The actual use of planes was handled by the General Headquarters of the Air Force. In order to release the potential of air power, he argued, these tasks should be unified under a command of their own.

Stimson was persuaded, but he noted in his diary, "I fear Marshall and his deputies are very much wedded to the theory that it is merely an auxiliary force." So the Secretary asked Lovett to give his seminar to Marshall. "At present, our air force is operating under an organization, the command and control of which is designed primarily to insure direct support of the ground forces and not the entire field of operations open to air warfare," Lovett argued. "The weapon must be controlled and utilized within a tight-knit, flexible organization as modern as the instrument itself."

Marshall proposed a deal: He would support greater autonomy for the Army Air Corps if Lovett would resist pressures from Congress and elsewhere to set up an independent U.S. Air Force as a separate branch of the military. Lovett approved. "Even those... who favor the ultimate creation of an independent Air Force agree that the air forces must learn to walk before they can run," Lovett wrote in a memo for Congress. "Regardless of the merits of the idea in theory, it is subject to the generally accepted rule that a good idea executed at the wrong time becomes a bad idea."

In seeking funds for new warplanes, Lovett placed special emphasis on the heavy-bomber program: the B-17 Flying Fortresses and B-24 Liberators that he hoped would prove the value of long-range strategic attacks. He also worked with Hap Arnold and others to incorporate the role of heavy bombing into AWPD-1, the war plan Roosevelt requested in mid-1941. It advocated six months of concentrated strategic bombing to soften up Germany for a 1943 invasion. Lovett estimated that four thousand heavy bombers could destroy 154 critical facilities in Nazi territory, such as power stations, oil depots, and rail links.

But strategic bombing, Lovett felt, had an even more important role. German civilians must personally feel the pain of war, which had not happened in World War I; only bombing could properly punish them and sap their morale. In the process of destroying their war-making capacity, Lovett told an audience at the University Club in New York, "the German people can be given their first searing lesson in the heart of their hitherto untouched homeland that crime does not pay. This should reduce their will to fight."

In early 1942, Lovett received a captured German document that emphasized heavy bombing of Allied facilities. It prompted him to put on paper his specific ideas about strategic bombing. The most important thing, as he learned from his own sorties during World War I, was that the air attacks must be concentrated and incessant. There was little value in dispersing air power on many fronts. "The success of the use of this weapon depends on its employment en masse, continuously and aggressively," he wrote. "Our main job is to carry the war to the country of the people who are fighting us—to make their working conditions as intolerable as possible, to destroy their plants, their sources of electric power, their communications systems."

When Lovett learned that plans for a cross-Channel invasion had been postponed until 1944, he was upset that this meant the shift of many Allied air units engaged in bombarding Europe. He asked Stimson to resist Eisenhower's request that planes be diverted for use over North Africa. To buttress his case Lovett enlisted friends in the press, particularly at *Life* magazine, to publish articles showing the damage that bombs were inflicting on Germany. The reports gave Congress and the public, frustrated over the slow progress of the Allies, an outlet for their anger. Nevertheless, most of the Eighth Air Force was redeployed to North Africa.

On the eve of the January 1943 Casablanca Conference, Lovett went to the White House to press his views on the President. He also gave his longtime partner Harriman a crash course in the theory of saturation bombing and persuaded him to act as an advocate in Casablanca. There the tactic of bombing Germany relentlessly by day and by night was formally adopted by Roosevelt and Churchill. Its code name: POINTBLANK. Harriman wrote Lovett a long letter hailing the development. "It is recognized that the bombing is an essential prelude to our occupation of the continent," he said. "If there are a few people down the line who have not yet learned the gospel, don't let it worry you."

As the war ended, Lovett hoped to document the critical importance of air power through the U.S. Strategic Bombing Survey, which he organized. It was a mammoth undertaking in which more than fifteen hundred experts tried to quantify the damage bombers had inflicted on German industry, transportation, oil supplies, cities, and general morale. The nominal head was Franklin D'Olier, an amiable former commander of the American Legion and chairman of Prudential Insurance Company. But the main driving force was Chicago lawyer George Ball; he had independently come up with the same idea of conducting a full-scale bombing survey while he was a member of the Air Force Evaluation Board in London and had presented it to Stimson and Lovett. Ball recruited two of his friends: Paul Nitze and economist John Kenneth Galbraith. The three of them led teams of staffers into liberated Germany, interviewed scores of military experts and civilians, and conducted the first full-scale interrogation of Hitler's Production Minister, Albert Speer.

What they found did not exactly confirm Lovett's expectations. Galbraith discovered that the bombing had scarcely disrupted the manufacture of tanks and other panzer weaponry. Average monthly production of 1942 was 516 vehicles; after the 1943 bombing began in earnest, monthly output increased to 1,005, and it went up to 1,583 the following year. The February 1944 concentrated Allied raids on Germany's airframe plants had been similarly ineffective. More fighters and bombers were produced in the month after the attacks than the month before them. Speer also told Ball that some of the urban bombing had actually freed up laborers from destroyed shops to work in outlying munitions factories. All in all, German production in 1944 was three times what it was at the beginning of the war. Especially fruitless had been the attempt to destroy German morale by the bombings; there were no signs that this occurred.

On the other hand there was evidence that attacks on rail lines and oil depots had greatly slowed German troop movements and curtailed training. By keeping German planes in the air, the bombing also helped deplete the Nazis' air force. The massive fire-storm raids on Hamburg did diminish morale there, at least for a while, but the fact that they were not followed up diminished their impact. The bombing of the Ruhr had perhaps the greatest effect, bringing industry to a standstill by destroying the transportation systems.

The final summary report of the survey, compiled after much dispute among the members, was predictably a mixed bag. But the skeptical personal conclusions reached by Ball, Galbraith, and Nitze stayed with them over the years. "History and future policy would have been served by a more dramatic finding of failure," Galbraith later noted of the survey's final report, "for this would have better prepared us for the costly ineffectiveness of the bombers in Korea and Vietnam." When Lyndon Johnson was considering a resumption of the Vietnam bombing in January 1966, Ball was opposed. "I recalled my experience on the Strategic Bombing Survey," he says, "pointing out that in both Europe and Japan the Survey found that 'one does not break the will of the population of a police state by heavy bombing.'"

Lovett disagreed. He felt that some of the findings added credence to his faith in strategic bombing, and he was unhappy with the heavily qualified conclusions. The effects of the bombing were hard to quantify, and Lovett was uncomfortable with things that could not be quantified. He traveled to Germany on his own to talk to Goering, Messerschmitt, and Speer. The production of planes had been hampered, Messerschmitt told him, by the lack of materials. Everywhere he went he saw evidence that German industry had been brutalized by the Allied bombing. What he heard was what he wanted to hear, and he came back convinced that the survey had underplayed the importance of America's long-range bombing.

Upon his return, Lovett set up a task force to produce detailed reports on the status of all Air Force personnel and weaponry. Calculating machines were borrowed from the Prudential Insurance Company and government statistic bureaus. "I wanted to know every morning precisely and exactly how our Air Force was," he recalls.

One of Lovett's most trusted young analysts on the project, who shared his passion for facts and statistics, was Robert McNamara, a Harvard Business School graduate who had been assessing bomb targets for the Air Corps. After the war, when Lovett was at his winter home in Hobe Sound, Florida, his neighbor Henry Ford II mentioned that he needed new talent for the postwar expansion. Chief among the "Whiz Kids" Lovett recommended was McNamara.

CHAPTER 8

Bohlen, Harriman, and Stalin at Yalta

MISSIONS
TO MOSCOW

Harriman, Acheson, Bohlen and Kennan
wrestle with a biting bear

Harriman was the type of busy man who took pride in always being busy. Yet on a hot August weekend in 1941, he found himself idly playing croquet at his Sands Point, Long Island, home and fretting about being left out of things.

As "expediter" of aid to Britain, he had flown to North Africa to inspect the supply routes and then on to Washington to report his findings. After convincing Lovett and others that the U.S., though still not at war, should assume the burden of operating some of the supply lines, Harriman decided to delay his return to London. Churchill was sailing across the Atlantic for his first meeting with Roosevelt, and Harriman hoped to be there.

The President, however, had grumbled about too many people and too little space when his envoy asked for an invitation. Harriman could imagine very little worse then to watch from the shores of Sands Point as the presidential yacht sailed north without him. So he persisted in his pleas through Harry Hopkins and others. Finally the President, quite bemused by Harriman's gyrations, relented. He told their fellow Grotonian Sumner Welles, the Under Secretary of State, to pick Harriman up at Sands Point and join the presidential party en route to Newfoundland.

While McCloy and Lovett helped run the U.S. military effort, their colleagues were making their marks in a variety of diplomatic posts. Harriman, as the London-based coordinator of Lend-Lease shipments, and Acheson, as Assistant Secretary of State for Economic Affairs, were both initially concerned with providing aid to the Allied effort. Kennan, after five months of internment in Germany, was posted to Portugal and then sent to dabble briefly in postwar planning with the European Advisory Commission in London. Bohlen, whose internment lasted six months, was brought back to Washington as assistant chief of the Russian section of the State Department. Eventually, as the war progressed and the peace loomed, all of them would become increasingly concerned with the same issue, one that would have a direct bearing on their postwar outlook: America's stormy relationship with her Soviet allies.

The meeting between Churchill and Roosevelt produced the Atlantic Charter, an idealistic proclamation that envisioned a Wilsonian world of free trade and free people. Nations should have the right of self-determination, it declared, and military force should not be used to dictate territorial changes or spheres of influence. In public at least, Roosevelt would henceforth proclaim that the Atlantic Charter—in particular its opposition to spheres of influence—was the foundation of U.S. foreign policy. Partly it was a matter of political necessity: Americans were more likely to support a war fought for idealistic principles than one designed to divvy up hapless nations like Poland into power blocs. In addition, Roosevelt the idealist believed in these principles. Yet Roosevelt the pragmatist would turn out to be far more willing, quietly and privately, to make the realistic concessions necessary to preserve the wartime alliance with the Soviets. Eventually, conflicts would arise between the principles that Roosevelt proclaimed (even to his closest advisers) and the tacit concessions that Stalin, who had little use for the liberal capitalist idealism of the Atlantic Charter, came to believe that Roosevelt had made.

For Harriman, the Atlantic Conference had a more immediate

significance: he was chosen to accompany Lord Beaverbrook, the irascible newspaper publisher who was Churchill's Minister of Supply, on a mission to Moscow to offer aid to Hitler's newest enemy. The Soviet Union, failing to heed Allied warnings that Germany was preparing to abrogate the 1939 nonaggression pact, had been staggered by a massive assault that began on the same date as Napoleon's invasion 129 years earlier.

Within hours of their arrival in London to prepare for their Moscow mission, Harriman and Max Beaverbrook had a showdown that foreshadowed the passing mantle of Western leadership. At a meeting of their combined delegations in the underground conference room of the War Cabinet, Beaverbrook pressed Harriman to declare the total amount of aid the U.S. would be willing to supply, implying that the British would decide how it should be allocated between them and the Soviets.

In an animated clash, Harriman insisted instead that the two delegations determine jointly who should get what. Although not yet at war, America was no longer willing to take a back seat to the British in European affairs. Churchill supported Harriman. "I know how difficult he can be," the Prime Minister said of his Supply Minister. The following evening Harriman laid down the ground rules to Beaverbrook. "Dinner tonight was in rather sharp contrast to last night with the P.M.," young Kathleen Harriman, his daughter, wrote to her sister. "One's a gentleman and the other is a ruffian. Ave, luckily, can talk both languages."

On the flight from Archangel, Beaverbrook ordered the pilot to break the Soviet practice of flying at treetop level. Consequently, they were met near Moscow by Soviet antiaircraft fire until their plane swooped down and revealed its markings. In a speech to the members of his delegation, Harriman made clear the purpose of the trip: "To give and give and give, with no expectation of any return, with no thought of a quid pro quo."

Late on the night they arrived, Harriman and Beaverbrook were summoned to the Kremlin and ushered into the conference room deep inside. It was Harriman's first visit to that inner sanctum, with its long conference table and huge portraits of Marx, Lenin, and Engels. In ensuing years, the room was to become, in a peculiar way, a source of renewed energy for Harriman. Whenever his influence waned at home, he would find a way to return there, to be invited back to meet with whoever was holding court at the table, and the power in the room would help recharge his own.

Stalin, shorter and bulkier than Harriman had imagined, was candid and friendly that first evening. The situation was near critical, he admitted, but the Soviets could and would hold Moscow. Although they desperately needed American weapons, he promised to avoid "asking for astronomical quantities."

The next night, however, the Soviet dictator, pacing and chain-smoking, was in a different temper. "He questioned our good faith," Harriman recalled. "He seemed to suggest that we wanted to see the Soviet regime destroyed by Hitler." The Allied offerings were not nearly sufficient, Stalin insisted. "Why is it the U.S. can give me only 1,000 tons a month of armor-plate steel for tanks—a country with a production of over 50 million tons?" Harriman corrected him. The U.S. could produce 60 million tons a month. But the demand in the U.S. was great, and the Soviets were requesting a special type of steel. Stalin could be blunt, but then so could Harriman.

Beaverbrook was dismayed by the confrontation, but Harriman counseled patience. Reviewing the list of seventy items the Soviets had requested, they made a few modifications in their own offer. The next night they found Stalin more serene, puffing on a pipe and seemingly satisfied that he had gotten the best deal possible; he doodled on a pad, drawing wolves and coloring the background bright red. When they finally worked out the details of the Lend-Lease plan, the steely dictator actually smiled. "Now we shall win the war!" exulted Litvinov.

Harriman felt that he had learned a lesson about the violent mood swings of Soviet leaders, who could appear gracious one minute, enraged the next, and grandly effusive once convinced that they had accomplished all they could. Exceeding his instructions, he accepted Stalin's request that they put their agreement in writing as a formal protocol.

Harriman had pointedly excluded from the negotiations the U.S. ambassador, Laurence Steinhardt, who had become quite embittered during his tenure in Moscow. Such disillusionment was an occupational hazard for American envoys. In a "half-jocular" discussion, Stalin and Harriman each expressed concern about the other country's ambassadors; Harriman passed on the sentiment to Roosevelt, and both men were soon replaced.

When Hopkins offered him the job of ambassador, Harriman insisted he could be more useful remaining a special envoy. The confined life of a diplomat in Moscow, he noted, "appears an intolerable existence for anyone with an active mind." The post went instead to

Admiral William Standley, former Chief of Naval Operations and a strong proponent of aid to the Soviets.

At the time, the standards of financial disclosure and conflict of interest were less rigid than they later became. During his wartime dealings in London and Moscow, Harriman remained an active partner at Brown Brothers Harriman (unlike Lovett), retained his private business interests, and even quietly held on to his Russian investments. In July of 1941 these included, among other things, $560,000 worth of Soviet government notes from the 1928 liquidation of his manganese contracts. Harriman inquired on the status of various Russian holdings in a "confidential" 1943 letter to an assistant, J. D. Powell. Among them, he was told, were $142,000 worth of Imperial Russian Government Certificates plus 52,500 shares of the Russo-Asiatic Consolidated Company acquired during the 1920s. On his mission to Moscow with Beaverbrook, Harriman took along Allen Wardwell, who was officially representing the American Red Cross. A prominent Wall Street lawyer, Wardwell had helped Harriman negotiate with the Soviets over the manganese concessions.

Harriman knew that the $1 billion worth of commitments he had made in Moscow, which included such things as the delivery of five hundred tanks per month, would be difficult to sell to an American public wary of the Bolshevik regime and still vaguely hopeful that the U.S. could remain aloof from the European war. So he took it upon himself to purchase, with his own money, time on CBS radio to explain the government's case. "I am not concerned with the social and economic beliefs of those who are fighting Hitler," he told his audience. "What does concern me is that the bitter experience of others and our own enlightened self-interest clearly dictate a course of action."

•   •   •

Harriman's job as Lend-Lease expediter was broadly defined, and—being better at carving out authority than following it—he made the assignment even broader when he returned to London. In addition to coordinating aid to Britain, he took on the task of keeping Moscow happy with its new suppliers. Crossing the Atlantic was difficult enough; he was bumped from his Pan Am clipper to make room for some mail sacks, and it took a phone call to Juan Trippe to get him back on. For good measure, a vexed Harriman also called Lovett to insist that a regular military service be set up to cross the Atlantic. The problems with the Soviets that awaited him, however, were far more difficult to solve.

As soon as the U.S. entered the war, Stalin began pressing for an Anglo-American invasion across the English Channel that would draw German units from their assault on the Soviets. Roosevelt, backed by Stimson and Marshall, made soothing promises. But Churchill was opposed. He gave Harriman the same late-night tour of the empty seats in Parliament that he had given McCloy, emphasizing that he could not justify sending another generation of British boys to the trenches until it was absolutely necessary.

Stalin's ire over the absence of a second front made him less than a gracious recipient of Lend-Lease aid. Despite its sincere efforts, the U.S. had trouble delivering the material Harriman had promised to the Soviets. The American procurement bureaucracy was snarled, and the military establishment, with McCloy and Lovett and Forrestal at the fore, was understandably anxious to build up its own strength. An even greater obstacle was the terrible difficulty Allied convoys had surviving German attacks on their way around the northern tip of Norway through the Arctic Ocean to Archangel.

The Soviets were reluctant to promote alternative convoy routes, such as through Iran or Siberia, because these would require greater internal transportation costs. Instead, suspicious of Allied motives, they complained about the timidity of British vessels and the insincerity of Western efforts. "We are turning the town upside down to get supplies for Russia," Hopkins wrote an anxious Harriman in May of 1942. But deliveries lagged behind schedule, and the summer months brought long daylight hours and heavier tolls along the convoy routes to northern Russia. One-quarter of all Allied ships on that run were destroyed by German U-boats in March, April, and May.

With Harriman in tow, Churchill flew to Washington in June to inform Roosevelt that he planned to suspend the convoys until the longer nights of autumn could provide greater safety. In addition, the Prime Minister insisted, there could be no cross-Channel invasion in 1942.

Shortly after they had returned to England, Harriman drove out to Chartwell, Churchill's country home, for a private dinner. The Prime Minister said he had decided to go to Moscow to tell Stalin of the decision to suspend the convoys and postpone the second front. The Soviet leader would be enraged, but perhaps a personal explanation could soften the blow and assure him of the sincerity of his allies.

That weekend, after Churchill left for Moscow, Harriman decided it would make sense for an American to go along. Partly he wanted to make sure Stalin understood that Churchill was not acting alone; partly, of course, he was anxious to be personally involved. But when he cabled for permission, Roosevelt refused. So Harriman appealed to Churchill, who was making a stopover in Cairo. The Prime Minister was only too happy to intervene on Harriman's behalf. "Would you be able to let Averell come with me?" he wired the President. "I have a somewhat raw job." Roosevelt relented. "Have wire from Former Naval Person," he wired his eager envoy, "saying he thinks you would be helpful." The British delayed for Harriman a military flight leaving that night for Cairo, much to the annoyance of the plane's other passenger, a haughty Free French leader named Charles de Gaulle.

At his meetings with Churchill and Harriman, Stalin repeated his pattern of violent mood swings. On the first night he seemed to accept Churchill's plan for a probe into the Nazis' "soft underbelly" on the Mediterranean as an alternative to an immediate cross-Channel invasion. "The Prime Minister drew a picture of a crocodile and pointed out that it was as well to strike the belly as the snout," Harriman reported to Roosevelt. Late the next night, however, they faced the delayed fury of the Soviet leader, who curtly read a scathing message about English military cowardice and broken American supply promises.

Churchill, distraught and depressed, kept Harriman up talking almost until dawn, despite Harriman's assurances that things would go better at their third session. "The technique used by Stalin last night resembled closely that used with Beaverbrook and myself," he wired to Roosevelt. Indeed, the trip ended amicably. "The Moscow visit, which could so easily have turned into a disaster for the alliance, had raised the wartime relationship with Russia to a new plane of understanding," Harriman later noted.

•   •   •

Poland had been the proximate cause of Britain's entry into the war. In April of 1943 came the first ominous signs that debates about its postwar fate would chill any future peace. The German Army announced with great fanfare the discovery of a mass grave in the Katyn Forest, an area that had been swallowed by the Red Army after the 1939 Nazi-Soviet Pact. The Germans charged that ten thousand Polish officers had been executed point-blank by the Russians. Moscow, naturally, claimed that the Nazis had conducted the slaughter after capturing the territory in 1941. Harriman did not know who was right, nor care much at the time.* What upset him was that the dispute suddenly threatened the hope that the Grand Alliance could emerge from the war with a shared vision of how liberated Europe would be governed after the war.

The exiled government of Poland, residing in London, promptly asked the Red Cross to investigate the German allegations. On the surface, the move seemed understandable, even mild. For the prospects of the exiled leadership's postwar relations with Russia, however, it was devastating. Harriman called on the Polish Prime Minister in London and bluntly took him to task. Whether the German accusations turned out to be true or false, Harriman said, the Polish statement was bound to enrage Moscow. Indeed it did. The Kremlin immediately broke off relations with the exiled government and formed its own rump leadership in Moscow called the Union of Polish Patriots. Efforts to repair the breach and save some semblance of Polish sovereignty would consume Harriman—and poison East-West relations—for more than two years.

Churchill sailed on the *Queen Mary* that May for another visit to Washington, taking both Harriman and Beaverbrook with him. During the voyage, Beaverbrook supported Stalin's bitter reaction to the exiled Polish government. Harriman sharply disagreed with what he labeled an "appeasement policy." To Churchill he argued: "I feel strongly that we must be friendly and frank but firm when they behave in a manner which is incompatible with our ideas. Otherwise we are storing up trouble for the future."

The discussion aboard the *Queen Mary* revealed a significant change in Harriman's thinking about Russia. In light of the "ominous rift over Poland," as he called it, and the Kremlin's orneriness over Lend-Lease, he had begun to abandon his belief that the U.S. should "give and give and give . . . with no thought of a quid pro quo." When he met with Roosevelt upon his arrival in Washington, Harriman began pushing what he called a "friendly but firm" approach, one that took a flinty view of bargaining with Moscow that was befitting a pragmatic

*In 1952, a congressional committee reported, after nine months of investigation, that "beyond any question of reasonable doubt" the Katyn Forest murders had been conducted by the Soviet secret police, and subsequent research by historians conclusively supports this finding. When asked about it years later, Harriman said: "My guess is that the Russians did it."

entrepreneur. Partly because of the persistent way he pressed his views, the change in Harriman's attitude would have an enormous influence on American policy.

Ambassador Standley, once a staunch supporter of unconditional aid to the Soviets, had undergone a similar transformation. A gregarious man, he had hoped to make friends with the Russians through such kindnesses as the exchange of intelligence information and the distribution of Walt Disney films. But once in Moscow, he began to bridle, just as Bullitt and Steinhardt had, under the continuous "personal discomforts" and "isolation" imposed by Soviet authorities. Increasingly he argued that any American aid should be given on a "bargaining basis," warning Roosevelt that gifts without strings seemed to "arouse suspicions of our motives in the Oriental mind rather than to build confidence."

When Standley kicked up a storm by telling American correspondents in Moscow that the Soviets were ungrateful for U.S. aid, Harriman supported him. "The feeling is growing here that we will build trouble for the future if we allow ourselves to be kicked around by the Russians," Harriman wired Hopkins from London. To Edward Stettinius, then the administrator of Lend-Lease, he urged: "My experience is that the Russians are brutally and bluntly frank with us and we can well afford to be equally so."

When he arrived back in Washington in May of 1943, Harriman learned that Standley had submitted his resignation. Once again, Roosevelt and Hopkins offered him the post, and once again he expressed a reluctance to abandon his unfettered status. After much discussion, Harriman returned to London at the end of June still undecided. "As you know, I am a confirmed optimist in our relations with Russia because of my conviction that Stalin wants, if obtainable, a firm understanding with you and America," he wrote Roosevelt in July. "Real accomplishment by an ambassador in Moscow is a gamble, with the odds against success, but the stakes are great."

The matter was not settled until August, when Harriman traveled to Canada for the first Roosevelt-Churchill Quebec Conference. Fishing on a lake there with Hopkins, he weighed the possibilities, finally concluding that as ambassador he could help overcome Soviet suspicions. Yet he was worried that some of Roosevelt's ideas were naïve. Over a lunch back at the White House, the President confidently predicted he could explain to Stalin, whom he had never met, the adverse reaction that would result if there were no free elections in

Poland or the Balkan countries after the war. "He did not seem to realize that once the Russians occupied a territory the plebiscite would almost certainly go their way," Harriman later noted.

Yet Harriman also harbored hopes, ones that were perhaps no more realistic than Roosevelt's. The disheartened Admiral Standley happened to be staying at the Mayflower Hotel, which Harriman used as his Washington base. Harriman invited his predecessor to a private dinner in his suite. After discussing Russia until midnight, Standley rose to leave. "I don't envy you, Averell," he said. "It's a tough assignment."

"Thank you, Admiral," said Harriman, forcing a smile. "I know it will be difficult, but they're only human, those Russians. Stalin can be handled."

Standley walked down the hall shaking his head. He had thought much the same thing eighteen months earlier. Harriman later admitted: "A large number of people in the West had the idea that they knew how to get along with Stalin. I confess that I was not entirely immune to that infectious idea."

•   •   •

Harriman and Acheson, like most of their pragmatic friends, did not put undue faith in "universal Plumb Plans." But both agreed with Roosevelt's goal of providing postwar loans to the Soviets and the rest of Europe. To Harriman, this was a way to gain some bargaining leverage with the Kremlin. In addition, both he and Acheson saw the value of helping develop stable economies once the war was over. The first tentative steps toward this goal were proposals for a United Nations Relief and Rehabilitation Administration (UNRRA) that were made to the U.S., in differing forms, by Britain and Russia.

Acheson was designated as the U.S. delegate on a four-member UNRRA committee that began meeting in Washington in January of 1943. Representing the Soviets was Maxim Litvinov, the plump and voluble westernized Bolshevik who as Foreign Secretary had negotiated the 1933 recognition agreements.

During the committee's six months of work, Russian attitudes that would soon become familiar first emerged: the major countries must have a veto power over all decisions, Litvinov insisted, and any programs inside Russia must be supervised solely by the Kremlin. The Soviets seemed concerned, above all, with preventing any penetration of their insular system, even by international organizations offering aid. "Relief, we said with righteous fervor, must be kept free from politics," Acheson later recalled. "The idea amused Litvinov." Nothing in the U.S.S.R. was free from politics, and any aid sent to the country must be fully controlled by the Kremlin. "We were present, so to speak, at the creation of the pattern," Acheson noted.

By June an agreement had been reached. But Acheson faced another touchy obstacle. Senator Arthur Vandenberg, in Acheson's words, "was just emerging from his isolationist chrysalis and had not yet learned to manage his new wings." Flapping with indignation, the Michigan Republican protested that the Senate had not been consulted and that the scheme "pledged our total resources to whatever illimitable scheme for relief and rehabilitation all around the world our New Deal crystal gazers might desire to pursue."

Perhaps because he was similarly susceptible, Acheson recognized Vandenberg's weak point: vanity. Remaining patient through days of questioning (unlike Secretary Hull who had stormed out), Acheson revised the UNRRA text to accommodate congressional concerns. Mostly, however, he simply stroked Vandenberg, explaining to him the importance of a relief organization and the historic role he could play in establishing it.

Despite his "suspicions," Vandenberg decided to declare victory and and hail "the triumph of constitutional procedure." It was the beginning, Acheson later said, of Vandenberg's "long day's journey into our times," one that culminated with his dramatic January 1945 "confession" on the Senate floor of the errors of isolationism and his realization that "our oceans have ceased to be moats which automatically protect our ramparts."

Roosevelt signed the UNRRA agreement in November 1943, and the first session of what was the precursor of the United Nations promptly convened in Atlantic City's Claridge Hotel. Acheson was elected chairman. Although the meetings went smoothly, one incident foreshadowed the troubles ahead. As the conference ended, the Russians asked to show a film of the fighting on the eastern front. Acheson acquiesced. To his horror, he discovered that it was a propaganda piece. The Polish people were shown joyfully embracing their Soviet liberators and, according to the Russian narrator, the Communist doctrines they brought with them. Afterward, Acheson found himself faced with a bitter protest from the ambassador of the exiled Polish government.

•   •   •

"We have found you a very tough man to deal with," said Molotov when the new ambassador paid his formal courtesy call in October of 1943.

"I have come as a friend," Harriman responded.

"Oh, I know that," Molotov said. "I intended my remarks to be complimentary."

Harriman understood that the Soviets did not necessarily consider pliable negotiators to be friends, nor did they regard tough negotiators as enemies. That night he recorded in his notebook that he told Molotov there were many things they disagreed on, but that these could be solved "with a frank personal relationship."

Harriman and his daughter Kathleen, who served as his hostess while Marie Harriman stayed back in New York, found the atmosphere in Moscow during their first few months somewhat less chilly than they had feared. During his tenure as Lend-Lease expediter, the Soviet state-run media had touted Harriman as a symbol of Allied cooperation. With his distinguished bearing, he proved immensely popular with the Russian people, who tended to be far more fascinated than frightened by titans of capitalism. Indeed, he became quite a celebrity in the country and an object of curiosity wherever he ventured.

Kathleen, too, captured the eye of the citizenry, especially with her skiing prowess. She was even invited to race in the Russian women's slalom competition, finishing third and winning a mention in the Moscow papers. With packs of her father's Chesterfields and snacks from the embassy kitchen, she was able to make friends with younger Russians, or at least those less wary of the watchful eye of the secret police.

Harriman occasionally joined her on Sundays on the snowy slopes of the Lenin Hills, somewhat to the chagrin of his secret-police shadows. On his first foray, Harriman went to the top of Sparrow Hill, from which Napoleon had watched Moscow burn, and raced straight down the slope. His NKVD escort made a valiant attempt to follow, only to crash into a snowbank halfway down. "Unfortunately for him," the deadpan ambassador wrote his wife, Marie, back in New York, "he is not too skillful." From then on, whenever Harriman went skiing, a former member of the Russian ski team was added to his NKVD detail.

The Harrimans were permitted contact with a limited circle of Moscow personalities, mainly from the arts. A few months after his arrival, Harriman sent Bohlen a note asking him to get "my newest tail coat and trousers" from Marie and send them along. For the grand parties that the mission held at Spaso House, to celebrate such occasions as Christmas or Harriman's birthday, the new ambassador (salary: $17,500) dug into his own pocket to import such items as turkeys and cases of Bourbon.

He warned his staff and the American journalists to be wary of the Soviet practice of ganging up on one foreigner at each party and toasting him under the table. Harriman could usually hold his own. His only failure came on Red Army Day in early 1944, when Molotov and a bevy of generals cornered him at a reception. Kathleen tried to rescue her father only to be waved off with an "I'm aw right." Finally he had to be carried home. *Time* magazine reported: "As the evening wore on, the Union Pacific's headlights grew dimmer and dimmer."

The Harrimans' closest Soviet friend was the playwright Alexei Tolstoy, a cousin of the famous Leo Tolstoy. Kathleen found him "a very loveable sort." Tolstoy once invited the Harrimans to his dacha for a grand dinner that (apparently with government help) made a mockery of the meager rations available to most of the Russian population and that of the rest of wartime Europe. He expounded on various subjects relatively freely, once even intimating that terror in the Kremlin was not simply a function of Stalin or Communism. "To understand the Kremlin today," he said to Harriman in words that would have pleased Kennan, "you must understand the Kremlin of Ivan the Terrible and Peter the Great."

Spaso House was spacious (thirteen bedrooms) yet bleak. "Ave's bathroom is about the size of my apartment in New York," Kathleen wrote her sister. "His bedroom has the only fireplace. Bullitt apparently had a hand in the interior decorating and for that I'm going to resent him for the rest of my life." Harriman, who generally worked sixteen hours a day, turned the space by his bedroom fireplace into a cozy conference area. There he would meet with aides and reporters early each morning, wearing one of his dark silk dressing gowns and red Moroccan slippers. For exercise he took to chopping the sickly shrubs in the back garden and shoveling the snow off the walk, much to the bafflement of the Russian staffers who could not understand why anyone so rich and powerful would do such things for recreation.

Harriman had traveled to Moscow with Secretary Hull, who was attending the first Foreign Ministers Conference there. Hull confided that he did not want to go, but he feared Roosevelt would replace him with Sumner Welles if he balked. The Secretary spent most of his time securing a four-power Declaration of General Security, a grandiloquent document of dubious value, which the idealistic Hull pronounced would produce a world in which "there will be no need for spheres of influence."

Harriman found himself more concerned with issues that Hull found peripheral, most notably working out an agreement about Poland so that Moscow would not impose a puppet government there. "They gave us no indication during the conference that they were interested in the extension of the Soviet system," Harriman wrote Roosevelt at the conclusion of the conference. "I take this with some reservation."

There would be many other issues on which the U.S. and the Soviets were destined to disagree before the conclusion of the war. But Poland, in Harriman's words, "was to become the touchstone of Soviet behavior in the postwar world, the first test of Stalin's attitude toward his less powerful neighbors." It represented the inevitable clash between the differing visions that the two sides brought into the war: the Anglo-American idealism, enunciated in the Atlantic Charter, of fighting for freedom and self-determination, versus Stalin's harshly realistic view that the Soviet Union needed a ring of "friendly" states along its border, ones that would never again form an antagonistic "cordon sanitaire" or a corridor for invasions from the west.

Postponing the Polish issue until after the Red Army captured the country, Harriman felt, would make a negotiated arrangement next to impossible. So he hoped Roosevelt would raise the matter at Teheran in November of 1943, when the wartime leaders finally got together for their first tripartite summit. The President, however, was more interested in military plans, proposals for the postwar treatment of Germany, and setting forth his vision of a United Nations organization. By making implicit concessions to Stalin on certain border issues and by deferring the question of how to guarantee Poland's sovereignty after the war, Roosevelt (at least in Harriman's view) allowed Stalin to assume that the Atlantic Charter's idealistic proclamations against spheres of influence were mainly for domestic political consumption and would not be used to prevent the Soviets from imposing "friendly" regimes along their periphery.

Harriman did not think that the Kremlin would attempt to swallow up Poland, for its ethnically diverse empire was already showing signs of indigestion. Nor did he feel that Moscow wanted to impose a Communist system on Poland, he told American reporters in Moscow in January 1944. Its goal, as he saw it, was to make sure that postwar Poland was friendly to Russia, something that the independent Polish government in London, composed mainly of aristocratic émigrés, was not. Thus Harriman concluded that tough bargaining could bring about a compromise in which the moderate members of the Polish group in London would join with pro-Soviet Poles in creating a tame but free government after the war. He was worried, however, that in the absence of any compromise, Stalin would find Poland tough to control and would eventually feel the need to impose a rigid Red Army–backed regime in Warsaw.

As Soviet troops were "liberating" Poland in mid-1944, Harriman warned that unless the exiled Polish government reconstituted itself the Soviets would set up their own "Committee of Liberation." Roosevelt, however, was still unwilling to face the issue. So his independent-minded ambassador went on his own to Stalin in February to see what could be done to improve Soviet relations with the London Poles. Stalin hinted at a solution: Their leader, Stanislaw Mikolajczyk, might be acceptable to the Soviet government, but most of the other London Poles, who were hard-line anti-Communists, would have to step aside.

"Again the Poles," Stalin growled when Harriman came back the following month. "The émigré government," as the Soviet leader called it, was making impossible demands. The Polish population, he insisted, would welcome the Red Army as liberators. Harriman doubted it. He thought, but did not say, that the Soviets would be considered just another set of invaders and would be forced to impose police-state controls.

When Harriman brought up the problem of public opinion in the U.S., a fact that Roosevelt often used to no avail, Stalin countered with his concern "about public opinion in the Soviet Union."

"You know how to handle your public opinion," said Harriman.

"There have been three revolutions in a generation," answered Stalin.

At the time, Harriman felt that the problem could be negotiated amicably. "Stalin is convinced that there is no hope for a friendly neighbor in Poland under the leadership of the controlling group in London, and he is unwilling to have the Red Army re-establish them in power," he wrote in a March memo. "I believe he is basically right. In spite of the conjectures to the contrary, there is no evidence that he is unwilling to allow an independent Poland to emerge." Harriman would soon be convinced otherwise.

•   •   •

Late in June of 1944 an event occurred in Moscow that was to have as much effect on hardening Harriman's line than almost anything the Soviets could do on their own: George Kennan arrived at the embassy as counselor.

Harriman, desperately seeking a professional Soviet expert to be his second-in-command, had first requested Chip Bohlen. As part of his duties in the Soviet Section at the State Department after his six-month internment in Tokyo, Bohlen had served as a translator and adviser at the conferences in Moscow and Teheran in late 1943. Bohlen had taken a more pessimistic view than Harriman of what transpired in Teheran, noting in a memo to the ambassador that the Soviets seemed intent on reducing the rest of Europe to impotent vassals. "I knew something of the true nature of the Soviet Union," he recalled of his attitude at that time, "that its leaders were animated by a philosophy not only alien but also definitely hostile to everything democratic governments stood for."

Even so, Harriman was impressed with Bohlen's knowledge of Russia and its language. More importantly, the somewhat stiff Harriman warmed to Bohlen's genial personality, which he found appealing and comforting, even magical. In asking that Bohlen be assigned to him, Harriman wrote the State Department that "we have worked together and come to a clear understanding as to policies."

Unfortunately for Harriman, Harry Hopkins had also come to know and like Bohlen. They met somewhat inauspiciously at a Washington dinner party in late 1942. Hopkins asked—"rudely" as Bohlen remembered it—if he was part of the anti-Soviet clique at the State Department. Bohlen was, in fact, a supporter of the "realistic" approach shared by his boss, Loy Henderson, and most of the others who had served in Moscow during the 1930s. "The Soviet Section was still wary of the Russians," Bohlen later wrote. "From Henderson on down, the specialists shared the view that the Soviet Union, even though now an ally, had to be closely watched because its ultimate aims clashed with those of the U.S."

But despite his love for the occasional good argument among friends, it was not Bohlen's style to challenge (at least with any fervor) Washington's prevailing pro-Soviet attitude nor to tangle with the exemplar of that attitude, Hopkins. He replied that he knew of no such anti-Soviet cabal in the State Department. Hopkins then launched into a discourse about how great the Russians were acting in the war. Yes, Bohlen agreed, that is perfectly true, but there were other aspects of

the Soviet Union that should not be forgotten, especially their opposition to freedom.

Bohlen and Hopkins resumed their conversation while in Cairo
together before the Teheran Conference. What struck Hopkins was
not Bohlen's view of the Soviets, nor even the careful manner in
which he defended it, but rather his amenable style of getting along
with people. Hopkins and Roosevelt agreed that the young diplomat
was the type of man they needed at the State Department. The official
reason they gave Harriman for not sending Bohlen to Moscow was
that he was only a Class IV officer and an appointment as counselor
would require promoting him two grades. In fact, Harriman had sent
a cable saying he would take Bohlen even without the official promotion and leave the post of counselor vacant.

In early 1944, Bohlen was made chief of the Soviet Section at the
State Department. He initiated a series of informal Saturday gatherings
at one of Washington's waterfront seafood restaurants, where officials
from various departments met to discuss Soviet policy. (The sessions
were soon dubbed "fish and Chip.") By the end of the year his leap
into the inner circle of power was formalized when he was appointed
the department's official liaison with the White House.

Harriman, meanwhile, was still seeking a second-in-command.
Hopkins agreed to see if he could get him the services of Kennan.

After his release from internment in Germany, Kennan had been
assigned to Lisbon, where, in October of 1943, he was ordered to
secure U.S. military rights to Portuguese naval bases in the Azores.
The whole episode had become a grand diplomatic snafu involving
crossed wires and unread cables from Kennan explaining to an un-
receptive State Department the need to offer U.S. guarantees of the
sovereignty of Portuguese colonies before making any requests. At the
Pentagon's insistence, Kennan was recalled to Washington for consultations. He ended up sitting in the corner of a top-level meeting
in the office of Henry Stimson, who, at the end of Kennan's explanation of the situation, inquired: "Who is this young man?" When
told that Kennan was chargé d'affaires in Lisbon because the ambassador there had died, Stimson solemnly noted that it was "high time
we had a full-fledged ambassador." Stung by his treatment and upset
with the callous way official Washington proposed to treat Portugal,
Kennan decided to take the matter directly to the President. To his
great surprise, Kennan had no trouble getting an audience with Roosevelt, who helped clear up the matter by writing a personal letter to
Portuguese Prime Minister Antonio Salazar.

When a new ambassador finally arrived in Portugal at the end of 1943, Hopkins succeeded in getting Roosevelt's approval to have Kennan, then thirty-nine, sent to Moscow as the number-two man at the embassy. But Hopkins, suffering from cancer, had a severe relapse at the time, and he forgot to pass the word to the State Department. Nor did Kennan know of the proposed move. Instead he was dispatched by the department to serve on the new European Advisory Commission, which was holding vague discussions in London about the future of liberated areas.

Harriman was desperate. He offered to trade two of his people, Llewellyn ("Tommy") Thompson and Maxwell Hamilton, in return for Kennan. Just as a deal was about to be struck, Kennan (who was totally oblivious to all the maneuvering) proceeded to complicate the arrangements by being hospitalized in London with an ulcer. A despairing Harriman was duly informed.

Upon his recovery, Kennan became embroiled in a dispute within the EAC over the proposed border for the Soviet zone of occupation in Germany. Dismayed (yet again) by his orders from Washington, he flew home and requested another meeting with the President. Roosevelt, amused by Kennan's gumption, quickly cleared things up to the anxious diplomat's satisfaction.

When he returned to Washington in May of 1944, wrote Kennan in his *Memoirs*, "the department, I think, had no clear idea what to do with me." In fact, that was far from the case. Harriman had resumed his struggle to get him assigned to Moscow, and the ambassador just happened to be visiting Washington while Kennan was wandering the city at loose ends.

Bohlen and Harriman took matters into their own hands. Bohlen took Kennan to the Mayflower Hotel, introduced him to the ambassador, and the three had dinner together in Harriman's suite. Kennan recalls that he "took pains to emphasize that my views on policy toward the Soviet Union were not exactly those of the Administration." Harriman did not care. His views, in fact, were also no longer exactly in line. They agreed that Kennan would report for duty at the end of June.

Before his departure, Kennan had one of his periodic arguments with his closest friend over Soviet policy. Over a long dinner at Bohlen's house, they readily agreed about all the faults of the Soviet system. But to Kennan the conclusion was that it was futile even to deal with the Kremlin. Roosevelt's policy of seeking a Grand Alliance was hopelessly naïve, he said. Where the U.S. could force the Soviets to abide by its wishes it should; in areas where the U.S. was powerless, it should simply wash its hands of the matter. Poland fell into the latter category.

Emboldened by not a few drinks, Bohlen lit into his colleague. Although he was not the type to make waves within the councils of government, Bohlen always relished rousing arguments with friends. He accused Kennan of knowing nothing about the realities of power and politics, of having his head in a gloomy cloud of abstract notions that prevented him from dealing with the world as it was. What began for Bohlen as a collegiate sort of joust evolved into a bitter personal argument. He went up to bed angered and drunk. Kennan, far more sensitive to attacks from the man he had come to admire, walked home through the dark streets of Washington in tears.

• • •

Harriman and Kennan had distinctly different personalities and styles. Whereas Harriman was thick-skinned, businesslike, and nearly oblivious to matters he felt unworthy of his focus, Kennan indulged himself as an anguished and sensitive intellectual, tormented by slights and disappointments both real and imagined.

Harriman enjoyed exercising power and being close to it. He sought to comprehend great events by getting to know the great men who determined them. Kennan, on the other hand, felt that he could come to understand the Soviets through detached observation, academic study, and intuitive personal rumination. He became deeply engrossed in the writings of his namesake and distant cousin. Yet Harriman, to his surprise, never mentioned the remarkable coincidence that the elder George Kennan had written the two-volume authorized biography of Harriman's father.

Years later, Chip Bohlen wrote a letter in which he attempted to describe Harriman's style as a boss. "One thing he does not like is too much contradiction," wrote Bohlen, "although he enjoys a good discussion. Above all don't make any smart cracks or anything that smacks of freshness in regard to anything he says or does . . . I think the best way to describe Averell's attitude towards juniors who work for him is 'feudal.' He will give them complete loyalty if they give him in return their complete loyalty."

To Kennan, Harriman's unreflective and cold personality was perplexing. "He had that curious contempt for elegance that only the wealthy can afford," Kennan later wrote. "I often think: what a trial I must have been to him, running around with my head in the usual cloud of philosophic speculation, full of interests other than my work

... bombarding him with bundles of purple prose on matters which, as I am sure he thought, it was the business of the President to think about, not mine."

Such insecurities were legitimate: Harriman did get annoyed at Kennan. He called his deputy's discourses "batting out flies" and considered many of them pointless. "Small wonder that he was often peremptory," Kennan later wrote of Harriman. "He didn't shout you down, for he never shouted; but he had a way of running roughshod over unsolicited suggestions. A hundred times I came away from our common labors asking myself, without finding an answer: 'Why do I still like this man?'"

One answer was that Harriman, for all of his annoyance, genuinely respected Kennan's mind and found himself influenced by his outlook. "I used him on every occasion that I possibly could," the ambassador later recalled, "and I consulted him on every subject. He had good instincts. He is a man who understood Russia but didn't understand the United States."

The gruff entrepreneur and the sensitive analyst would sit up late at night by Harriman's fireplace while Kennan railed against Soviet slights and conduct. As Kennan later noted: "He soon showed, by his own official acts, that he had not been obtuse to the same evidences of misunderstanding that caused me such concern."

•   •   •

Shortly after Kennan arrived in Moscow, the Polish situation came to a head. With the help of Roosevelt and Harriman, Mikolajczyk and some of his colleagues in the exiled Polish government wangled an invitation to see Stalin. As they were on their way from London, the Kremlin announced the recognition of the Polish Committee of National Liberation, a pro-Soviet government that had established itself in liberated Lublin. When Mikolajczyk and his men appeared at the Kremlin, Stalin told them they must henceforth deal with the Lublin Poles.

Harriman asked Kennan for his views on the prospects for the London Poles. Unsurprisingly, Kennan was pessimistic. The Soviets, he said, "will be confident they can arrange the affairs of eastern Europe to their own liking without any great difficulty, and they will not be inclined to go far out of their way either for the Poles or us."

Kennan thought it best not to mention to Harriman a darker suspicion: One major reason that Stalin wanted a puppet group in Poland, Kennan felt, was to prevent the truth about the Katyn Forest massacre

from being discovered. The Soviets had made a great show of summoning reporters to the Katyn Forest once they had retaken it to
produce "proof" that the Nazis had done the killing. Among those
who went with the press corps was Kathleen Harriman, a former
reporter herself. Some of the Soviet evidence seemed persuasive on
the surface, yet there were clear indications that a lot of it had been
faked. Kathleen confessed to be somewhat confused about the truth,
but Kennan had no such doubts. The Red Army had committed the
mass murders as a way to crush any future Polish resistance to Soviet
domination, he thought.* The Kremlin would thus never permit a
government in Poland that might expose this fact.

Kennan found it awkward even to look at the hapless London Poles
who haunted the American Embassy. "They were, in my eyes, the
doomed representatives of a doomed regime," he recalled. When one
of them asked what he thought their chances of regaining their homeland were, Kennan gave a gloomy assessment. "But I warned him that
I usually leaned to the pessimistic side, and advised him to take this
into account."

A paper on the issue that Kennan drafted for his files began, typically
enough, with nineteenth-century quotes about Russia's historic treatment of Poland. "The jealous and intolerant eye of the Kremlin can
distinguish, in the end, only vassals and enemies, and the neighbors
of Russia, if they do not wish to be the one, must reconcile themselves
to being the other," he concluded. So much for Harriman's hopes of
bargaining for an independent Polish government that Moscow would
consider friendly enough. It was "frivolous," Kennan felt, for the U.S.
to make any efforts on the matter. Americans ought merely have "the
good taste and judgment to bow our heads in silence."

In the midst of Mikolajczyk's visit came the doomed Warsaw uprising. On August 1, 1944, as the Red Army neared the Nazi-occupied
city, Polish underground fighters, encouraged by a clandestine broadcast from Moscow, rose up in revolt. At that moment the Red Army
halted its advance, refusing to come to the aid of the resistance. The
Soviets insisted this was mainly because they did not yet have the
supplies to fight their way across the Vistula River. But there was
another reason, one that Stalin himself as much as conceded: the
Warsaw uprising was led by fighters more loyal to London than Lublin-

*Although historians agree that the Soviets were responsible, it is still unclear whether
the massacre was ordered by the Kremlin as a way to insure Soviet control over the
region after the war or whether it was merely an isolated atrocity committed by commanders in the field.

Moscow. It was in the Kremlin's interest to let both the Nazis and the Polish patriots batter themselves to death in the bloody fighting, thus freeing the Soviets from future resistance from either side.

Harriman sent the Kremlin a note requesting landing rights in Russia for American and British planes so they could come to the aid of the Polish resistance. Deputy Foreign Minister Vishinsky, in response, called the uprising "a purely adventuristic affair to which the Soviet government could not lend its hand." Harriman demanded an audience at the Kremlin. "It was the toughest talk I ever had with a Soviet official," he later recounted. Vishinsky again refused to give the necessary landing rights. "I am for the first time since coming to Moscow gravely concerned about the attitude of the Soviet government," the generally stoic ambassador cabled Roosevelt that night. "Its refusal is based on ruthless political considerations."

As German divisions moved into Warsaw and the prolonged revolt became even bloodier, Harriman insisted on seeing Molotov, Vishinsky's boss. Reasoning with Molotov, Harriman discovered, was "futile." He was only carrying out instructions. Kennan recalls that Harriman returned to Spaso House "in the wee hours of the night, shattered by the experience." Kathleen wrote her sister that he was "beginning to show the strain."

Harriman's anger was reflected in his telegrams to Washington. "I feel strongly that the Russians should be made to realize our dissatisfaction with their behavior," he wired on August 21. Four days later he wrote a harsher message that he decided not to send. "Under these circumstances," it said, "it is difficult for me to see how a peaceful or acceptable solution can be found to the Polish problem."

Finally, in early September, Stalin reversed himself. The Soviets and their Western allies began to aid the uprising, although the Red Army still did not move in to join the battle against the Nazis. Stalin conceded to Harriman that he had misjudged the motives of the resistance leaders and pledged to give whatever aid he could to the uprising. But it was all too little and too late. Warsaw was by then in ruins, blanketed by bodies. One-quarter of its population was dead.

In retrospect, Harriman gave Stalin some benefit of the doubt. At an off-the-record discussion of the origins of the Cold War organized in 1967 by historian Arthur Schlesinger, Jr., Harriman said that the uprising "was the London Poles thinking they could put it over on the Russians by seizing Warsaw." The failure of the Red Army to move in, Harriman said in hindsight, was not part of a ruthless political plot (as he had reported at the time), but was dictated by military realities. "In spite of my very strong emotions at the time," he noted in an oral history in 1970, "my guess is that the military facts" were what prevented Stalin from coming to the aid of the Warsaw rebels. By that period in his life, Harriman had become aligned with the more liberal wing of the Democratic Party and had mellowed in his view of the Soviets. At the time of the Warsaw uprising, however, the event deeply disillusioned him. "Our relations with the Soviets have taken a startling turn evident during the last two months," he wrote in a personal letter to Hopkins.

Kennan, as might be expected, was even harsher in his judgment about what was, in truth, an example of Stalin's ruthless nature. "It has been my opinion, ever since, that this was the moment when, if ever, there should have been a full-fledged and realistic showdown with the Soviet leaders," he wrote in his *Memoirs*. The U.S., he told Harriman, should consider cutting off all of its military aid and support for the Soviets. Harriman quietly demurred, but Kennan began to barrage him with memos on the matter.

Harriman had already come to the conclusion, during the first half of 1944, that military aid to Moscow could no longer be given, as he had once proclaimed, "with no thought of any return." In January he had written Churchill that "the Russian bear is demanding much yet biting the hand that feeds it." General John Deane, the embassy's military attaché, had stumbled across the discovery that at a time when the Soviets were requesting fifty more American diesel boat engines, they had yet installed only three of the ninety delivered the previous year. Many of the engines, which the Allies could have desperately used in the D-Day invasion, were rusting on the docks.

Deane and Harriman began to urge Washington to force the Soviets to justify any future requests. "They are tough, and they expect us to be tough," Harriman argued. A firmer attitude would cause the Soviets to "respect us more," he wired Hopkins. "To get a trading atmosphere into our negotiations over mutual assistance in the war is, as you know, most distasteful to me," the former financier explained to the former social worker, "but trading seems to be the language the Soviets understand."

• • •

Despite his hardening line, Harriman still supported providing the Soviets with loans for their postwar reconstruction. He saw such credits as offering many advantages: they would help open a vast Russian market for U.S. goods at a time when there was reason to fear the resurgence of the prewar depression; they would give Moscow a stake in preserving the peacetime economic order; above all, they would provide leverage and bargaining chips that the U.S. could use to influence Kremlin conduct.

Soviet Trade Minister Anastas Mikoyan first made a concrete proposal to Harriman for a postwar loan in February of 1944, suggesting a $1 billion credit at 1.5 percent interest. Harriman countered with his own unofficial suggestion, to both Washington and Moscow, that a $500 million credit at prevailing interest rates was more reasonable. The ambassador cabled Secretary of State Hull that a loan offered "one of the most effective weapons at our disposal to influence European political events in the direction we desire and to avoid the development of a sphere of influence of the Soviet Union over Eastern Europe and the Balkans."

At the time, the Johnson Act forbade any nonmilitary loans to the U.S.S.R., and the matter of outright postwar aid was not seriously considered for a year. But those who favored providing American credits for Russian reconstruction came up with a clever temporary scheme in early 1944: Under a section of the Lend-Lease Act known as 3(c), equipment could be shipped on credit after the end of the war until mid-1947. Designated to negotiate with the Russians for extended credits under the plan was Dean Acheson, who had just finished representing the State Department at the Bretton Woods Conference that established the International Monetary Fund.

Fearful of having no hand in such a critical matter, Harriman convinced a reluctant State Department to allow him to fly to Washington in May to consult with his old school chum. They met in Acheson's office and quickly hammered out a memo for the President. As an opening gambit, they said, the U.S. should offer to "wipe the slate clean" of all Soviet debts at the end of the war and accept liberal terms for aid used by the Soviets for their reconstruction.

Edward Stettinius, who as Lend-Lease administrator in Washington had tangled with Harriman and who continued to do so after becoming Under Secretary of State, was disturbed at the ambassador's presumption. He told Acheson's assistant Eugene Rostow that the Harriman-Acheson plan was "superficial," adding sharply: "It is not something for an ambassador to run to daddy with." Harriman, however, did go to Roosevelt with the plan, and a slightly modified version was presented to the Soviets by Acheson.

Acheson met with the Soviets over the loan plan almost daily beginning in July of 1944. Acheson remembers "the almost unbearable heat" of the old State Department building; but as repercussions from the Warsaw uprising dispute reached Washington, "even the heat of our room could not warm the chill between allies." The two sides disagreed over interest rates and other details. Any attempt by Acheson to find signs of flexibility "brought only the same stolid and verbose replies from the Russians."

Acheson was guided by a lesson from his former crew coach. Vishinsky had once told Harriman, at the intermission of a ballet during his 1941 mission with Beaverbrook, that he should never be upset by the inflexibility of Russian negotiators, who could never make concessions until they had received specific instructions from the Kremlin. Consequently, Harriman advised Acheson, there was little use in trying to argue with or convince a Soviet negotiator. The only way to assure that they reported back to Moscow for new instructions was to present what at least appeared to be a revised proposal and call a recess. "This will enable them to call Moscow and get instructions," Harriman said. Acheson tried the tactic a few times in August, but to little avail.

By that point Harriman's line toward the Soviets had sufficiently toughened. "I hope as a matter of principle no further concessions will be made," he cabled. Acheson had reached the same conclusion on his own. In mid-September he presented his final offer and told his Soviet counterpart to return home to consult with his superiors if he felt he could not sign it. The meeting adjourned and the Russians never returned.

• • •

When the issue first came to a head in the fall of 1944, it was not cast in East-West terms. Instead it was considered a straightforward question of what would be best for the peace and prosperity of all the Allies: should Germany be allowed to rebuild or should it be denuded of its industrial base?

The leading American advocates of a revived Germany were Wall Streeters, men firmly committed to Europe, internationalism, and free trade. Their private careers had been spent making foreign deals, and a multilateral system of commerce was integral to their philosophy of world order. This ideal was as old as John Hay's "Open Door" and had found its twentieth-century expression as the third of Woodrow Wilson's Fourteen Points: "the removal, so far as possible, of all economic barriers." Trade restrictions, it was believed, would lead to gluts in domestic markets, unemployment, and possibly the rise of totalitarian sentiments. A throbbing world economy, on the other hand, would promote prosperity, peace, and democracy.

Cordell Hull, Roosevelt's first Secretary of State, was the most fervent apostle of the cause. Freer world trade, he said, would end "the economic dissatisfaction that breeds war." Henry Stimson agreed. "The essential basis of enduring peace must be economic," he proclaimed.

The rejection of these ideas by mainstream Republicans helped persuade Acheson and Harriman to become Democrats. Harriman had voted for Al Smith in 1928 primarily because of his belief in the need to lower tariffs. Acheson, whose affinity for the Democrats likewise was rooted in the free-trade issue, blamed the collapse of the nineteenth-century Pax Britannica economic order for the rise of "totalitarian military states."

In considering how to treat a defeated Germany, those with an internationalist economic outlook—most notably Stimson, McCloy, Lovett, Harriman, and Acheson—felt that destroying that nation's industry would remove the "spark plug" (to use the metaphor popular at the time) of the European economy. With its capacity to export manufactured goods and import raw materials, Germany could play a critical role in a system of world trade. Part of Germany's production, of course, should be exacted as reparations; but a full-scale looting of its industrial base would lead only to a stagnant world economy and the need for greater American subsidies for the rest of Europe.

McCloy became involved in the issue when he began drafting a directive, known as JCS 1067, to provide military commanders with guidelines for administering occupied territories. In the course of his consultations, he and Stimson invited Treasury Secretary Henry Morgenthau to lunch at the War Department in August of 1944. Despite reams of studies from State Department planning groups, no decision had been made about how to manage occupied Germany. Nor was there any real indication at the time that the issue would divide both the Roosevelt Administration and the wartime alliance with Moscow.

Morgenthau, the son of a successful and politically active Manhattan property developer, had begun his career as a farmer in upstate New York. There he made friends with his neighbor Franklin Roosevelt, whose political career he actively embraced. As Treasury Secretary he had developed a good working relation with the War Department; a prominent Jewish leader, he had defended McCloy against accusations that his hard line on Auschwitz and refugee issues made him "an oppressor of the Jews."

Morgenthau had just returned from Europe, and over lunch he broached to Stimson and McCloy his plan for "removing all industry from Germany and simply reducing them to an agricultural population." Neither of his hosts had given much thought to the long-term treatment of Germany, and Stimson wrote in his diary that "it was a very satisfactory talk." But a few days later, after thinking the matter through, Stimson noted that Morgenthau reflected "a very bitter atmosphere of personal resentment against the entire German people without regard to individual guilt and I am very afraid that it will result in our taking mass vengeance."

Stimson pressed his case on the President. "The need for the recuperative benefits of productivity is more evident now than ever before," he wrote. "Speed of reconstruction is of great importance if we hope to avoid dangerous convulsions in Europe." Morgenthau, however, was more ardent in pressing his case on the President, and soon Roosevelt was proclaiming his willingness to "pastoralize" Germany's industrial areas and let its people survive on "soup kitchens."

McCloy, as usual, was trying to play mediator. His main concern was to give the military enough leeway to act as it saw fit, and he led Morgenthau to believe that their ideas "were fairly close together." The Treasury Secretary noted in his diary that McCloy claimed to have advised Stimson to "modify" his position. At the same time, however, McCloy was warning Stimson against Morgenthau's efforts.

In fact, behind the Treasury Secretary's back, McCloy embarked on a merciless campaign to discredit what had become known as the "Morgenthau Plan." Each afternoon he and Lovett would get together and think up absurd methods for pastoralizing Germany and gleefully spread their satiric barbs through the Washington bureaucracy. The personal parries broke out into the open when the Heavenly Twins came up with a way to ridicule Morgenthau's practice of tape-recording all of his meetings. One day McCloy brought a tiny spy camera into a meeting in Morgenthau's office and began snapping away as soon as the tape recorder was turned on. When Morgenthau interrupted the meeting to ask what was going on, McCloy responded, "Well, since you've been recording everything without our permission, I thought you wouldn't mind if I did too." While the rest of those in the room laughed, Morgenthau fumed.

As an alternative to the Morgenthau Plan, Stimson toyed with the notion of putting Germany's industrialized Ruhr and Saar areas under international control. He and McCloy discussed the idea over lunch with Wall Street's favorite Frenchman, the financier Jean Monnet. Both Stimson and Monnet agreed that the plan would be a fair and safe way to help meet the needs of Britain, Russia, and the rest of Europe. But for the first time, McCloy raised a concern that had not yet entered the calculations about the treatment of Germany. As Stimson reported in his diary: "McCloy, much to my surprise, was alarmed at giving this addition to Russia's power."

As the dispute with Morgenthau became public in the fall of 1944, McCloy and Stimson began to line up support from their friends. Frankfurter came by for dinner, and Stimson noted: "Although a Jew like Morgenthau, he approached the subject with perfect detachment and great helpfulness." On a weekend trip to New York with Stimson, McCloy went to see many of his former colleagues on Wall Street to enlist them in the cause.

Morgenthau, however, was doing them one better. He had been invited to Quebec for the Roosevelt-Churchill summit. There the two leaders initialed an agreement that called for "converting Germany into a country primarily agricultural and pastoral in its character." When Stimson and McCloy discovered what had happened, they were incensed. They blamed the influence of Morgenthau and Churchill's science adviser, Lord Cherwell (Dr. F. A. Lindemann, known as "the Prof"); Stimson called it "Semitism gone wild for vengeance."

The details of the agreement quickly leaked, producing an unexpected public uproar. McCloy drafted for Stimson a memo citing the aims proclaimed at the Atlantic Charter Conference three years earlier. "Under the Atlantic Charter," McCloy argued, "victors and vanquished alike are entitled to freedom from economic want." Roosevelt, as he was prone to do, immediately began fudging his intentions. "No one wants to make Germany a wholly agricultural nation again," the President announced at the end of September. The following month he postponed any further discussion. "In view of the fact that we have not occupied Germany yet," he said somewhat illogically, "I cannot agree at this moment as to what kind of Germany we want in every detail."

McCloy then proceeded to do what he did best: hammer out a vague compromise policy that suited his objectives. Working with the Treasury and State departments, he began revising JCS 1067. The directive, intended as an "interim" guide for military occupiers, said there should be "no steps looking toward the economic rehabilitation of Germany," but it also contained a broad loophole that called for "the production or maintenance of goods and services" necessary to prevent epidemics or serious civil unrest.

The debate over how harsh to be in exacting reparations from Germany was left unsettled for the time being, and it would come back to bedevil the wartime alliance. But once again, in the absence of a clear policy decision, the way the issue was coordinated and administered by men such as McCloy proved to be as important as the way it was finally decided. When Lucius Clay got around to implementing the directive, "he did precisely what the War Department expected him to do," McCloy later noted. "He whittled away the unworkable clauses of JCS 1067 empirically and piecemeal." Two years later, while visiting Churchill at his country home, McCloy brought up the Morgenthau Plan. "He hastily repudiated it," McCloy wrote in his journal. "Damned Morgenthau and the Prof—said they were Shylocks."

•   •   •

Until the fall of 1944, before the Kremlin's brutal response to the Warsaw uprising and before it became clear that Germany would soon be defeated, Harriman viewed the U.S.S.R. as a somewhat schizophrenic ally, one that was prone to erratic lurches from friendship to paranoid fury yet was nonetheless still a partner in the cause of peace. The problem of Poland and the prodding of Kennan, however, had begun to force a dramatic change in Harriman's outlook. The Soviet Union, he came to feel, was more than just a difficult partner: it was a nation with aims and motives that fundamentally clashed with those of the West.

In a letter to Hopkins in September, Harriman explained that the Soviets seemed determined to impose their will on weaker nations rather than join in a collective peace. "Unless we take issue with the present policy," he wrote, "there is every indication the Soviet Union will become a world bully." America's generous attitude was seen in Moscow as a sign of weakness, he argued, and should be replaced by "a firm but friendly quid pro quo approach."

When Hull asked the Moscow embassy to provide an analysis of Soviet attitudes, Harriman told Kennan to prepare a draft. "I slept on the questions we were talking about last night," Kennan said, handing Harriman his notes the next day, "and these are the results." As they worked on the response, Kennan had his first real chance to shape Harriman's philosophy. Although signed by the ambassador, most of the ideas in the two cables they sent were pure Kennan.

The U.S., unaware of the Soviet tendency to use words differently, had underestimated what Stalin meant by his desire for "friendly governments" on his borders, the cables reported. Recent events indicated the Kremlin's secret war goal: a sphere of influence in Eastern Europe firmly under Moscow's control. A year later the idea of a divided Europe half dominated by Moscow would not seem so surprising; in September of 1944, the vision was a shocking one. "I believe that it is their intention to have a positive sphere of influence over their western neighbors," said Harriman's report.

Kennan had been arguing that yes, of course this was true, but the U.S. neither could nor should care about preventing Soviet domination of Eastern Europe. This was the only major point on which Harriman and Kennan disagreed. In the telegrams, Harriman raised Kennan's view only to debunk it. "It can be argued that American interests need not be concerned," Harriman said. "What frightens me, however, is that when a country begins to extend its influence by strong-arm methods under the guise of security, it is difficult to see how a line can be drawn. If the policy is accepted that the Soviet Union has the right to penetrate her immediate neighbors for security, penetration of the next immediate neighbors becomes at a certain time equally logical."

In his rejected draft, Kennan explained his arguments for conceding the Soviets a sphere of influence. If the Kremlin continued "to reserve moral judgment" on American actions in the Western Hemisphere, they would certainly expect to act freely in the Eastern European security belt they had won so dearly. Advocating free elections in Poland, Kennan said, would be foolish and futile. The important thing was to "determine in conjunction with the British the line beyond which we cannot afford to permit the Russians to exercise unchallenged power." The Soviets had probably not yet decided how far to push their sphere and may be waiting "to see how we would react to their efforts toward expansion." America and Britain must be "friendly but firm" in making clear where the line lay. Kennan called these ideas "realistic." In a later incarnation, they would be known as containment.

• • •

The berating he had received from Bohlen before heading for Moscow had caused Kennan to question his deep aversion to the Soviet system. Perhaps things had changed, he thought. He was, he recalled, "prepared to reserve judgment until I could see for myself." What he saw, however, only hardened his attitude. The isolation of foreigners had gotten worse, and Kennan found U.S. diplomats "treated as though we were the bearers of some species of the plague." He even expressed sympathy for the German prisoners who were marched through Red Square by the Soviet Army.

In late September he put his thoughts into a thirty-five-page private essay, "Russia—Seven Years Later," which expanded on the arguments he had been making to Harriman. "In it I poured forth, as in nothing else I ever wrote, the essence of what I knew about Russia," Kennan said in his *Memoirs*. "It was a better paper, broader, more balanced, and more specific than the so-called X–Article written two and a half years later, which went in part over the same ground."

Soviet pledges about collective security, Kennan wrote, were cynical ploys designed to further their ultimate aim, the domination of Eastern Europe. This drive had little to do with Marxist ideology. "Russian efforts in this area are directed to only one goal: power," he wrote. "It is a matter of indifference to Moscow whether a given area is 'communistic' or not. All things being equal, Moscow might prefer to see it communized, although even that is debatable. But the main thing is that it should be amenable to Moscow's influence." Kennan would later come to think that ideology played a role in Soviet foreign policy, but at this point he saw Stalin (probably correctly) as just another in a long line of Russian nationalists pursuing expansionist policies to enhance their personal power and protect the empire from a hostile outside world.

With a combination of self-pity and conceit, Kennan concluded that Russia, riddled with contradictions, would always remain an enigma to Americans. "There will be much talk about the necessity for 'understanding Russia'; but there will be no place for the American who is really willing to undertake this disturbing task," he wrote. "The best he can look forward to is the lonely pleasure of one who stands at long last on a chilly and inhospitable mountaintop where few have been before, where few can follow, and where few will consent to believe he has been."

Kennan gave his essay to Harriman with the notation that he "might want to glance at it" on his trip back to Washington in October. In his *Memoirs*, Kennan says he never found out whether the ambassador read it. In fact, he did. "Bob, I definitely want to read this on my way home," he scrawled to his personal assistant, Robert Meiklejohn. Harriman then gave it to Harry Hopkins, urging him to read it. At

Kennan's request, Meiklejohn also passed along a copy to Bohlen, who after all had helped to provoke it.

• • •

One great believer in a "realistic" policy of spheres of influence, as opposed to a Wilsonian "idealism" about self-determination, was Winston Churchill. The British Prime Minister had been quietly working with the Soviets in dividing responsibility for Greece, Rumania, and the rest of the Balkans. Without consulting the State Department, Roosevelt tentatively agreed to such an arrangement. But he remained uneasy. Any deal, Roosevelt insisted, should apply only to short-term military matters; above all, it should not lay the groundwork for postwar spheres of influence.

Despite all his caveats, Roosevelt's tacit acceptance of military spheres in the Balkans allowed Stalin to believe that the Atlantic Charter was largely window dressing. Roosevelt's advisers thought no such thing, which heightened the conflicts that would occur after his death. But whatever Roosevelt's real intentions were, Churchill took it upon himself in October of 1944 to visit Moscow and work out even more specific arrangements for spheres of action.

The big question was whether the U.S. would be a party to any such deal, and Churchill raised the issue by asking Roosevelt if Harriman could come along. "Averell's assistance would of course be welcomed by us," Churchill cabled. The President, hoping to fudge the issue, sent a lukewarm reply agreeing to let Harriman sit in. On the eve of Churchill's departure, Roosevelt wrote an ambiguous message that merely wished Churchill "good luck."

"Chip, get the hell over here in a hurry," Hopkins barked to Bohlen on the telephone. Hopkins had intercepted the President's blithe "good luck" cable, and he was worried that it implied Washington was washing its hands of the affairs of Europe. Bohlen, no less alarmed, agreed that Roosevelt's wire left the impression that the U.S. would stand aside and let Churchill and Stalin make any deals they wanted regarding the fate of postwar Europe.

Bohlen quickly drafted two cables, one to Churchill, the other to Stalin. Both emphasized that there was "literally no question, military or political," that might arise during the talks in which the U.S. would not have a vital interest. Harriman could serve as an observer, but he could not commit the U.S. to any agreements. Roosevelt sent the wires along with a personal letter to Harriman hammering the point home. Harriman later recalled being "quite unhappy with the President's attitude." He had hoped that Stalin and Churchill, with American approval, would be allowed to work out some hard deals, at least relating to Poland.

Churchill in fact had much more in mind, but Harriman did not discover this until three days after a startling deal had been struck. The secret arrangement came at a late-night meeting between Churchill and Stalin in the Kremlin. (Churchill incorrectly recounts in his memoirs that Harriman was present.) After arranging to have Mikolajczyk invited to Moscow for a new round of talks on Poland, Churchill suggested "let us settle our affairs in the Balkans." Blatantly carving out spheres, the no-nonsense Prime Minister wrote on a scrap of paper the amount of influence London and Moscow would have in each country: 90 percent predominance in Rumania for Russia, 90 percent in Greece for Britain, 75 percent in Bulgaria for Russia, and a 50–50 split in Yugoslavia and Hungary.

Stalin took the paper, paused for a moment, made a large check on it with a blue pencil, and passed it back to Churchill. "Might it not be thought rather cynical if it seemed we had disposed of these issues, so fateful to millions of people, in such an offhand manner?" Churchill asked. "Let us burn the paper."

"No, you keep it," Stalin replied.

Harriman got some inkling of what was up when he had lunch with the two leaders the next day. In a wire to Roosevelt that evening he warned that Churchill "will try to work out some sort of spheres of influence with the Russians." But it was not until two days later that the American discovered what had happened. Churchill was dictating memos in his bed that morning when Harriman walked in. The Prime Minister read a draft of a letter for Stalin outlining their agreement. The President, a startled Harriman replied, would repudiate it. When British Foreign Secretary Anthony Eden came into the room, Churchill told him, "Averell doesn't think we should send this letter." Churchill then agreed that it was "wiser to let well alone."

Eden nevertheless continued to work with Molotov in polishing up the percentage agreement, making a few numerical concessions to suit the Soviets. Despite Churchill's later denials, both the British and the Soviets were aware that the implications of the deal went beyond merely determining temporary military spheres. Would Stalin assume that the U.S., by default, was acquiescing to the idea of dividing the liberated countries into political spheres? Harriman was worried. "Churchill has been using the unpopular term 'spheres of influence,'" he wired Roosevelt. What the British were seeking, he explained, was a "practical arrangement" on responsibility for problems in the Balkans, and "they have explained to Stalin and Molotov that they have no authority to commit us." Harriman went on to emphasize that the plan should not be seen as a precedent for carving Eastern Europe into spheres. "They put Poland in an entirely different category as the Polish question requires a specific solution involving all of us."

Bohlen was among those infuriated when Harriman cabled Washington with news of Churchill's deal. "Aside from its cynicism, the arrangement was unrealistic," Bohlen later wrote. It was ludicrous to trust the Russians to abide by any power-sharing formula. "A non-Communist Premier with Communist ministers would be like a woman trying to stay half pregnant."

Kennan, on the other hand, told Harriman that the U.S. should wash its hands of the Balkans. Since America had "no effective means of influencing" what happened there, it should assume no "moral responsibility" for the situation. Americans, Kennan added, "have been allowed to hope that the Soviet government would enter into an international security organization. We are now faced with the prospect of having our people disabused of this illusion."

Churchill's visit to Moscow prompted the usual outward displays of Allied friendship. Stalin gratefully accepted a bust of Roosevelt from Harriman and fussed about his grand office deciding how it should be displayed. During one of the celebrations, Harriman danced with Madame Litvinov, who candidly confided that "the U.S. should always remember to be firm and not try to ingratiate itself in its international dealings." Her husband, the former Foreign Minister and wily survivor, later asked an American whether it was true that Harriman had a fortune of $100 million. Added the old Bolshevik: "How can a man with $100 million look so sad?"

•   •   •

Harriman, of course, generally sported a somewhat blank hangdog expression. But in October of 1944, he seemed especially forlorn. He had decided it was time to return home to convince Washington that the outlook for Soviet-American cooperation was bleak at best. Even James Forrestal, later one of the most agitated of hard liners, still harbored hopes that Harriman considered dangerously naïve. "There is a great admiration here for the Russians and, I think, an honest desire, even on the part of the so-called 'capitalist quarters,' to find an accommodation with them," the Navy Secretary wrote his friend.

When Harriman arrived in Washington, he was careful not to inflame public opinion on the eve of the election between Roosevelt and Thomas Dewey. With his own money the ambassador bought radio time to speak on FDR's behalf. "Never in the history of the world," he said, "has a nation had so great an opportunity to play such a vital role in affecting the course of history." At an off-the-record press briefing, he studiously downplayed the dire nature of the Polish situation. Russia's concern with having "friendly" countries along her border was "realistic," he said, adding that he was "hopeful" that talks in Moscow would lead to "an independent Poland as we understand it, selecting her own government."

To the President, with whom he had five long talks, Harriman was more candid about his concerns. The problem, as he saw it, was not Communism but Stalinist-style systems. "I have tried to impress the President that our principal interest in Eastern Europe is to see that the Soviets do not set up puppet governments under the Soviet system supported by the secret police," he wrote in his notes of the visit. Roosevelt seemed unconcerned. Noted Harriman: "I do not believe that I have convinced the President of the importance of a vigilant, firm policy."

One person who was shaken by Harriman's tales was Stimson, a man of deep faith in the possibility of postwar cooperation. The ambassador stopped by the War Secretary's office one Monday morning and described how the Soviets were establishing secret-police forces to dominate the countries they were ostensibly liberating. Stimson, who cherished above all the ideal of individual liberty, began what was to be a long and naïve crusade, one that would affect his attitude on the control of atomic weapons. "The foundation of our success" in dealing with the Soviets, he told Harriman, was convincing them to abandon repressive police-state practices. Harriman replied that he considered this impossible in the Soviet Union itself, but perhaps the Kremlin could be prevented from introducing the system in countries they occupied.

That afternoon, Stimson called McCloy into his office to discuss the issue. Paraphrasing his mentor, Elihu Root, Stimson said that the use of secret police "is the most abhorrent way" that governments can destroy individual freedom. The next night, at a dinner the McCloys hosted for the Stimsons and the Harrimans, the ambassador was grilled about the details of Soviet secret-police methods. "Freedom cannot exist in countries where the government uses a secret police to dominate its citizens," Stimson noted in his diary, "and there is nothing to choose from between the Gestapo which the Germans have used and the OGPU which the Russians have historically used."

• • •

Because the Red Army was already occupying most of Eastern Europe, Harriman felt that the only way to prevent Moscow from imposing its system was for the U.S. to have some form of leverage. Thus he continued to support a loan to the Soviets for postwar reconstruction. In January of 1945, soon after he returned to Moscow, Harriman was summoned to the Kremlin by Molotov and was presented with an extraordinary offer: the Soviets would be willing to help the U.S. avoid a postwar recession by accepting a $6 billion loan. "As a banker I've had many requests for loans," Harriman recalled, "but Molotov's was the strangest."

Nonetheless, Harriman thought it opened up possibilities. "I feel we should entirely disregard the unconventional nature of the document," he cabled Washington, "and chalk it up to ignorance of normal business procedures." It should be made clear to the Russians, he added, that U.S. aid would depend on responsible Soviet behavior in Poland and elsewhere.

When the three wartime leaders met at their second summit in the Crimean resort city of Yalta in early February, it soon became clear that the enticement of a loan was not enough to make the Soviets concede on Poland. After the first night's discussion ended in a stalemate, the President asked Bohlen to draft a letter for Stalin pointing out the dire consequences if, just as their armies were converging, the Allied leaders could not agree on which Polish government to recognize.

Instead of being resolved, the differences were papered over. "The Provisional Government which is now functioning in Poland should be reorganized on a broader democratic basis with the inclusion of democratic leaders from Poland itself and from Poles abroad," read the final communiqué. The new government, it added, "shall be pledged to the holding of free and unfettered elections as soon as possible."

The words sounded reassuring, but ahead lay tough negotiations to put them into effect. Perhaps one hint of the eventual problem came when Churchill told Stalin that the first Polish election would have to be pure and above reproach, "like Caesar's wife." Replied Stalin: "They said that about her, but in fact she had her sins." Harriman was designated, along with Molotov and Britain's Archibald Clark

Kerr (later Lord Inverchapel), to go back to Moscow and undertake the difficult task of putting the agreement into effect.

Bohlen and Harriman strongly suspected that the Polish talks would ultimately fail. "There was an expression we used at the embassy at the time—that trading with the Russians you had to buy the same horse twice," Harriman later wrote. "I had that feeling about the Polish agreement and said as much to Bohlen." They both still believed that spheres of influence could be avoided. During a break in the conference, Bohlen told Vishinsky that the American people would never permit the rights of small nations to be denied. Americans should learn to follow their leaders, the Russian caustically responded. "You should come to the U.S. and try telling that to the people," Bohlen countered.

Kennan had nothing but contempt for the idealistic "Declaration on Liberated Europe" that Bohlen helped to write at Yalta and for Roosevelt's Grand Design of a postwar alliance between Russia and the West. The accord on Poland seemed to him "the shabbiest sort of equivocation," and in comments he wrote for himself when the text of the Yalta agreement reached him in Moscow, Kennan wondered whether a "compromise peace" with Germany might be preferable.

Above all, Kennan was distressed at Bohlen's happy-go-lucky tendency to act as "a partisan of the moment," to go along with the prevailing policy rather than stick up for his principles. Back on speaking terms, but still anguished over their argument a few months earlier, Kennan unloaded his feelings in a gloomy letter he typed and sent to his friend in Yalta.

"Why could we not make a decent and definitive compromise with it—divide Europe frankly into spheres of influence—keep ourselves out of the Russian sphere and keep the Russians out of ours?" he asked. He tied this proposal to a strategy of Soviet containment. "We have refused to name any limit for Russian expansion and Russian responsibilities."

Bohlen, in an almost illegible scrawl, dashed off an angry response. "The 'constructive' suggestions that you make are frankly naïve to a degree," he wrote. "They may well be optimum from an abstract point of view. But as practical suggestions they are utterly impossible. Foreign policies of that kind cannot be made in a democracy. Only totalitarian states can make and carry out such policies." He argued that trying to force further assurances out of the Russians would be useless. "Either our pals intend to limit themselves or they don't," he wrote. "I submit, as the British say, that the answer is not yet clear. But what is clear is that the Soyuz [Soviet Union] is here to stay, as one of the major factors in the world. Quarreling with them would be so easy, but we could always come to that." Bohlen, loyal to Roosevelt's optimistic outlook, did not yet believe such a quarrel would be necessary.

• • •

As the talks in Moscow over Poland sputtered along during the weeks after Yalta, Harriman's pessimism grew. "We are going through the usual Russian tactics of trying to wear us down," he informed Washington. The Soviets stretched the vague accord to its limits by insisting that the Lublin leadership could veto the selection of other Poles for inclusion in the talks. As Kennan translated ("with boredom and disgust") the many hours of wangling, it became clear to Harriman that the Soviets and their Lublin clients would permit Mikolajczyk and his London colleagues only token positions at best. "We began to realize that Stalin's language was somewhat different from ours," he later recalled. "'Friendly neighbors' had an entirely different connotation to him than to us."

Harriman's cables back to Washington became increasingly bitter. "I am outraged," he told Roosevelt after one session with Molotov in March. Unless the U.S. was prepared to be firm, he wired on April 2, "the Soviet Government will become convinced that they can force us to accept any of their decisions on all matters and it will be increasingly difficult to stop their aggressive policy." The next day he reported that the Polish talks had reached the "breaking point," and he asked permission to return home.

Stettinius, who had taken over from Cordell Hull as Secretary of State, refused to embrace Harriman's hard-line prognosis. The ambassador was told to stay in Moscow and try to salvage the relationship. But Harriman's cables were beginning to have an impact in Washington. Discussion of them dominated the State-War-Navy meetings that McCloy chaired, and Navy Secretary Forrestal devoted thirty pages of his diary in April to copies of Harriman's official dispatches.

Even more bitter were the cables Harriman wrote but chose not to send. "I feel that the time has come for us to reorient our whole attitude and our method of dealing with the Soviet government," he said in a March 21 message that he decided to hold until he could deliver it to Washington personally. "Unless we wish to accept the 20th century barbarian invasion of Europe, with repercussions extending further and in the East as well, we must find ways to arrest the Soviet domineering policy." At the end of the eight-page memo he concluded: "If we don't face these issues squarely now, history will record the period of the next generation as the Soviet Age."

On the back of some embassy stationery, Harriman wrote on April 10 another cable that he decided not to send. "Our relations have come to such a pass that no halfway measures will do," it said. "I recommend in the strongest terms I can express that I be given some concrete means of showing Soviet officials that their outrageous actions against us are affecting their vital interests. The longer we wait, the more difficult it will be and the more drastic the action on our part will have to be."

As a way to strengthen the West's hand against Soviet encroachment, Harriman was developing a new strategy, one that would grow in acceptance and finally burst forth two years later in the Marshall Plan. He first sketched it out in his unsent March 21 message. "I therefore urge every consideration be given to assisting the welfare of the civilian population" in Western Europe, Harriman wrote. "This policy can be justified as a war measure, but from the standpoint of winning the peace there can be no doubt of its importance. All reasonable efforts should be made to strengthen France, Belgium, Holland, Greece and even Italy."

Harriman took pains to deny that this plan would result in an Anglo-American sphere or the division of Europe, though that indeed was its logical consequence. "I am not proposing the concept of spheres of influence, but a forceful policy of supporting those people that have the same general outlook towards and concepts of life that we do," he wrote in the unsent telegram. "Stalin himself told me once that communist revolution finds fertile seed in capitalist economic breakdowns. When once communist dictatorship, backed by secret police, gets hold, personal liberties and democracy as we understand the word end. There is no turning back."

Two weeks later, Harriman finally did send his thoughts on the rebuilding of Western Europe to Washington. "Unless we are willing to live in a world dominated largely by Soviet influence," he cabled, "we must use our economic power to assist those countries that are naturally friendly to our concepts in so far as we can possibly do so. The only hope of stopping Soviet penetration is the development of sound economic conditions in these countries." American policy should be one of "taking care of our Western allies and other areas under our responsibility first, allocating to Russia what may be left." The reason he gave for embarking on this plan was unabashedly hard line: "We must clearly realize that the Soviet program is the establishment of totalitarianism, ending personal liberty and democracy as we know it."

When *New York Times* correspondent C. L. Sulzberger visited Moscow in early April, he found Harriman deeply disturbed. He looked haggard and had a tic, like a wink, in his right eye. The impasse over Poland seemed unbreakable, and Harriman was beginning to express some of Kennan's ideas about containment. "Averell says we must notify the Russians just where we will not permit them to go," Sulzberger wrote in his diary. "Otherwise, there will be trouble."

There were signs that Roosevelt was moving toward Harriman's position during his last two months in office. He became enraged by Stalin's surliness at being excluded from U.S. Army discussions in Berne of a German peace feeler. In late March, he was handed a Harriman cable as he was leaving a lunch at Warm Springs. Anna Hoffman, who was there, recalls that the President banged his fists on his wheelchair and proclaimed: "Averell is right. We can't do business with Stalin." As Harriman later recalled: "I think he was thoroughly alive to the fact that they hadn't kept their agreements and he was quite bitter about it. I felt his Dutch jaw was out and he wasn't going to be pushed around by Stalin anymore."

Yet just before he died, Roosevelt was still wavering, still harboring hopes that the Grand Alliance that had just about won the war could conquer the problems of peace. In the President's final cable to Harriman, from Warm Springs on April 12, he rejected Harriman's advice that he toughen his cable to Stalin regarding the Berne negotiations. "It is my desire to consider the Berne incident a minor misunderstanding," he said.

Harriman's attitudes toward the Russians at the time were no easier to pigeonhole than the President's. The ambassador's cries of despair, unlike Kennan's, came not because he felt it was useless to deal with Moscow. Indeed, it was almost the opposite: Harriman, the shrewd and practical businessman, deeply believed in the desirability of achieving a workable arrangement. He urged a tough policy not because he felt it inevitable that Soviet-American cooperation would fail, but because he thought such a strategy had the best chance of succeeding. "In spite of recent developments," he wired the State Department in a long report on April 6, "I am still satisfied that if we deal with the Soviets on a realistic basis, we can in time attain a workable basis for our relations."

Although his outlook on the Kremlin had shifted dramatically during the final year of the war, there was still a constant refrain in Harriman's advice: America's attitude must be "firm but friendly." Give him the right bargaining chips, the Wall Street entrepreneur thought, and he could reach suitable accords. That is why he continued to support a postwar loan to the Soviets, "although we should at all times make it plain that our cooperation is dependent upon a reciprocal cooperative attitude of the Soviet Government in other matters."

This was the balancing act he so anxiously wanted to discuss with Roosevelt personally. But FDR would never get a chance to reply to Harriman's telegram about the Soviet loan or summon him home for consultation. He died the day after it was sent.

Roosevelt's death would finally give Harriman a chance to return to Washington and firm up the nebulous consensus on how to handle the Russian bear. That task was both easier and far more important now that Roosevelt, who harbored the conceit that he could conduct foreign policy out of his hip pocket, had been succeeded by a man whose only trip overseas had been as an artillery officer during World War I.

E.H. Harriman, flanked by his sons Roland and Averell, in 1907: *Their home, "Arden," had 40 bedrooms, a polo field, an organ with full-time musician, and a private lake with a rowing coach.* Acheson, in striped bow tie on the far left, with the Groton class of 1910: *"I find him an unexpected sort of person,"* wrote the Rector; *his classmates, who considered him cheeky, subjected him to "pumping" and other taunts.* **Dean at age four with his father, the Rev. Edward Acheson:** *He toasted the Queen with fine claret and delivered sermons on workers' compensation.*

1

2

3

4

6

5

8

Robert Lovett with his mother Lavinia Abercrombie Lovett: *She led the effort, not altogether successful, to have Huntsville, Texas, become known as the Athens of the South.* **Chip Bohlen as a chubby tackle at St. Paul's and lolling on a French Riviera beach in the 1920s:** *Thrown out of school for playing football with a condom, he had an easygoing charm and boyish good looks that made him popular with his colleagues and irresistible to women.* **George Kennan as a solemn Princetonian:** *"I certainly let myself into something when I joined this club,"* he wrote his father before being forced to quit, *"but it's the social thing."* **Acheson as a dapper groom with his wife Alice in 1917:** *After learning from Justice Brandeis to be both a progressive and a pragmatist, he made his name and fortune as an international lawyer in Washington.*

9

10

Lovett with the Yale Unit, above far right, and on the beach: *His initiation into Skull and Bones came at an air base near Dunkirk.* John McCloy, below far right, at the Plattsburg, N.Y., training camp: *"It seemed to me that all the right people went."* Harriman as a polo champion: *"I like recreation that calls for just as much energy as work."* Lovett and Harriman as Wall Street partners in 1935: *Their letters mixed public and private business.* Harriman with his streamlined Union Pacific train: *"I am still scared to death of an exhibition run,"* Lovett wrote.

11

12

13

14

20

21

Stimson commissions McCloy and Lovett: *"I felt a direct current running from Root through Stimson to me,"* McCloy recalled. Frankfurter during his confirmation hearings: *A mentor at Harvard Law School, he became one of Acheson's closest friends.* Bohlen with Harry Hopkins: *The young Soviet expert tailored his views to fit prevailing policies.* Harriman with Churchill and Stalin at the Kremlin in 1942: *He collected famous friends the way others collect stamps.* Lovett on an inspection tour with General Hap Arnold: *He had "plenty of good horse sense,"* Arnold said. McCloy flanked by Patton and Stimson in Berlin in 1945: *They realized that Europe must be rebuilt.* Lovett dining with General Marshall: *Their way of handling tough problems was to solve them.* Bohlen whispering to Stalin at Potsdam: *The differences became immense.*

22

23

24

25

Berlin Airlift: *U.S. planes, one every three minutes, brought supplies and hope to the people of Berlin during the Soviet blockade.* **Lovett laughs with Bohlen and unwinds with watercolors during the long hot summer of 1948:** *Keeping a sense of humor and balance as the cables poured into the darkened code room at State bringing rumors of war.* **Three at the Creation:** *Lovett's tormented friend,* Defense Secretary **James Forrestal** *(top), warned incessantly of America's lack of military preparedness. In 1949, he jumped to his death from a hospital window, the first fatality of the Cold War.* **Clark Clifford,** *Truman's politically savvy counsel, helped sell the need to rebuild Europe and face up to the soviets.* **Paul Nitze** *(bottom) wrote NSC 68, the Cold War blueprint designed to "bludgeon the mass mind of top government."*

27

26

28

Secretary of State Acheson and High Commissioner McCloy arrive in Germany in 1949: *The adoring crowds treated them like national saviors and made visceral their commitment to standing fast in Berlin.* Acheson and Truman: *They were one of history's odd couples, the Grotonian dandy and the plain haberdasher, but they shared a sense of history, irreverence, moral courage, and impatience with waffling. "I have a constituency of one,"* Acheson *liked to say.* McCloy with wife Ellen and children in Germany and kicking off for the High Commissioner's touch football team, the HICOGGERS: *He had the power of a Roman proconsul, but he was careful to try to restore the Germans' sense self-worth and he helped launch their economic miracle.*

31

32

33

Secretary of State Acheson, NATO Commander Eisenhower, Defense Secretary Lovett and Mutual Security Administrator Harriman: *In the early 50s, they switched the emphasis from rebuilding Europe to rearming the Western alliance.* Acheson testifies about his role in firing Korea Commander General MacArthur for insubordination in 1951: *After nine days of grilling, the Secretary vowed to test the human capacity for absorbing alcohol.* Ambassador to Moscow Kennan arrives in Berlin in 1952: *At an airport press conference, he compared Stalin to Hitler and was declared persona non grata by the Soviet Union.* Secretary of State John Foster Dulles and President Eisenhower discuss Bohlen's confirmation to become Ambassador to Moscow in 1953: *Scared of the Republican Right, Dulles told Bohlen to travel to Russia with his wife, lest anyone suspect he was homosexual.* The Bohlens arrive in Moscow: *In later years, Bohlen would regret that he had not done more to make Washington try to thaw the chill between the two superpowers.*

34

35

36

37

38

39

40

41

42

43

Lovett back in the partners' room at Brown Brothers Harriman and with Adele in the 1950s: *As an advisor to the President on foreign intelligence, he warned against "King Making" by the C.I.A.* **Candidate Harriman with New York pols in 1954:** *Old friends like Acheson and Lovett raised their eyebrows at his new calling.* **Harriman celebrates the Nuclear Test Ban Treaty with Khrushchev in 1963:** *The Soviet leader liked the old capitalist diplomat so much he offered him a job.* **Bohlen with President Kennedy in West Palm Beach in 1963:** *The President enjoyed Bohlen's charm, valued his advice, and made him Ambassador to Paris. Bohlen had to quit smoking after he nearly went blind in the mid-'60s; he began chewing golf tees instead.* **McCloy and Lovett as Wise Men advising President Johnson in 1966:** *Lovett sent this photo to his "Heavenly Twin" with the inscription, "Bored of Advisers."*

44

45

Harriman gets his negotiating instructions for the Paris Peace Talks from LBJ at Camp David in 1968: *His last chance to play the Russian card. Bill Bundy is at far right, Clifford at far left.* **With co-negotiator Cyrus Vance:** *As the talks went nowhere, Harriman became angrier at the South Vietnamese than the North.* **Acheson at Harewood:** *Lamenting an age of mediocrity.* **Kennan at Princeton:** *"I'm afraid the cards are stacked for a dreadful, final war."*

46

47

48

PART TWO

CREATION

The enormity of the task before all of
them, after the wars in Europe and
Asia ended in 1945, only slowly
revealed itself. As it did so, it began
to appear as just a bit less formidable
than that described in the first
chapter of Genesis. That was to
create a world out of chaos; ours, to
create half a world, a free half, out of
the same material without blowing
the whole to bits in the process.

—DEAN ACHESON,
Present at the Creation

CHAPTER 9

WORDS OF
ONE SYLLABLE
The education
of Harry Truman

Harry Truman knew all too well that, other than presiding over the Senate, there was little honest labor expected of a Vice-President under Franklin Roosevelt. Besides, the veteran of the Kansas City courthouse steps actually liked the Senate; he certainly felt more at home there than on his infrequent visits to the White House. And so it was that on the afternoon of April 12, 1945, the former haberdasher, wearing a double-breasted suit and white polka-dot bow tie, sat dwarfed by the chamber's Levanto marble pillars as he presided over a water treaty debate. "Dear Mama & Mary," he scrawled as the speakers droned on. "Turn on your radio tomorrow night at 9:30 your time, and you'll hear Harry make a Jefferson Day address to the nation." In those days letters were still delivered overnight.

Truman was primed for what, in his mind, would be a perfect evening. First he would stop by Sam Rayburn's hideaway on the House side of the Capitol, where the Speaker presided over his regular "board of education" meetings. Lewis Deschler, the Parliamentarian, was already putting out the whiskey and ice. Later there would be a poker game in the hotel room of an old friend from Truman's World War I field artillery battery who was visiting town. There was little official business to worry about; in fact, he had not even spoken to Roosevelt since his departure two weeks earlier for Warm Springs.

"Mr. Speaker," said Deschler as Truman poured himself a drink and settled onto the arm of a black leather chair, "wasn't the Vice-President supposed to call the White House?" Oh, yes, Rayburn remembered. Roosevelt's press secretary, Steve Early, had been trying to reach him.

When Truman got through, Early's voice seemed strained. "Please come right over," he said. The Vice-President turned pale. "Jesus Christ and General Jackson!" he said as he hung up. "Boys, this is in the room. Something must have happened."

As Truman's driver weaved through rush-hour traffic, news dealers were busily hawking the final edition of the *Evening Star.* "9TH ARMY CROSSES ELBE," the headlines blared. Truman had been Vice-President only eighty-three days. He had not been invited to Yalta. He had not been briefed about the problems in Poland or about the ominous rift with the Soviets that the President had concealed from the public. He had not been told about the atom bomb. Thus the news that Eleanor Roosevelt gave him understandably fell "like a load of hay" on his shoulders. "Is there anything I can do for you?" he asked after a long pause. "Is there anything we can do for you?" she replied. "For you are the one in trouble now."

Assuming power at such a time would have been difficult enough. But Truman bore the added burden of succeeding a man who had become synonymous with the Presidency. David Brinkley, the twenty-four-year-old deskman at a Washington radio station, ripped off the first bulletin ("FLASH—WASHN—FDR DEAD") and raced into the studio. Soon people were stopping strangers on the street, jumping on buses, bursting into bars and offices with the question: Have you heard the bulletins on the radio? "For what do I need a radio?" one Bronx housewife replied. "It's on everybody's face."

At his State Department office, where he was being photographed by Yousuf Karsh of Ottawa, Dean Acheson looked out and saw the vast crowds gathering in front of the White House. "They merely stood in a lost sort of way," he noted. At the Groton School, students were told just before supper of the death of a member of the Class of 1900; leaving their meals untouched, they headed for the chapel to pray.

In Paris, where John McCloy had gone to assess the war damage, an aide burst into his hotel room and woke him with the news. "It is absolutely impossible to think of its implications," McCloy scrawled in his diary. At Third Army headquarters in Germany, General George Patton was about to get into bed when he noticed his watch had stopped. When he turned on the BBC to get the time, he heard the bulletin. A precise man, Patton waited two more minutes until the announcer gave the correct time before going to awaken his superiors, Generals Eisenhower and Bradley. In a Berlin bunker not too far away, Joseph Goebbels babbled: "My Führer! I congratulate you! Roosevelt is dead!" Exulted Hitler: "Here we have the miracle I always predicted. Who was right? The war isn't lost!"

In Belgium, a young GI ran through a schoolhouse where troops were billeted. "Roosevelt is dead!" he shouted. "Hey, Wallace is President now," said another. "No," said an older soldier, one of the few who could remember a time when Roosevelt was not the President. "Senator Truman is." His companions looked at him incredulously.

Others were similarly amazed by that prospect. Everyone liked the unpretentious dirt farmer from Independence, but he seemed, well, so unpresidential. Only a handful of men realized his potential. Just before Roosevelt died, Acheson happened to have a long meeting with Truman on legislative issues. He liked what he saw. "He is straightforward, decisive, simple, entirely honest," Acheson wrote to his son. "I think he will learn fast and will inspire confidence." On the evening that Truman was being sworn in, the Achesons were sitting in their Georgetown garden with Admiral Alan Kirk and his wife, Lydia. The thought of a haberdasher replacing Roosevelt, Lydia complained, was distressing. Acheson disagreed. "Truman's a great little guy," he insisted, with no intended condescension.

What Acheson instinctively understood was that Truman, even more than Roosevelt, had a deep respect for the office of the Presidency and would insist that others show the same. Truman did not seem bothered when he entered the memorial service at the White House and no one thought of standing for him, although that honor was of course accorded to Eleanor Roosevelt. But gradually the World War I artillery captain began to assert his new authority. When he informed Jesse Jones about the choice of a new chairman for a federal agency, the former Commerce Secretary asked, "Did the President make the appointment before he died?" Replied Truman: "No, the President made it just now."

Truman may have been the least prepared man in American history to assume the Presidency. Never had he been inside the Map Room, that critical nerve center in the West Wing where Roosevelt went

each day to monitor military and diplomatic messages. Never in his
life had he spoken with a Russian citizen; not since his service in the
trenches of France during World War I had he traveled to Europe.
"I knew the President had a great many meetings with Churchill and
Stalin," Truman wrote in his diary for April 12. "I was not familiar
with any of these things and it was really something to think about."

Truman's philosophy of foreign affairs was, at best, nebulous. Just
after Hitler had invaded the Soviet Union, Senator Truman had casually commented to a *New York Times* reporter: "If we see that Germany is winning we ought to help Russia and if Russia is winning we
ought to help Germany and that way let them kill as many as possible."
Shortly after becoming President, he noted in his diary, "I've no faith
in any totalitarian state, be it Russian, German, Spanish, Argentinian,
Dago or Japanese. They all start with a wrong premise—that lies are
justified and that the old, disproven Jesuit formula, the ends justify
the means, is right."

Despite such outbursts, Truman essentially subscribed to Roosevelt's
Grand Alliance strategy. He had lobbied to extend Soviet and British
Lend-Lease aid and cast the tie-breaking vote in its favor after becoming Vice-President. He came into office strongly committed to carrying
out Roosevelt's policy of working with the Russians to win the war
and secure the peace.

The difference between Truman and Roosevelt was mainly in matters of style. The wily Roosevelt could be manipulative and conniving
with both people and public opinion. Truman was forthright to the
point of bluntness. Whereas Roosevelt had affected a haughty air of
detachment, his earthy successor was far more susceptible to righteous
indignation.

In addition, Roosevelt tended to put off major decisions, allowing
a creative tension to build within his inner circle as he toyed with
men and ideas. Truman was far tidier: Weary Roosevelt holdovers
soon came to rejoice as Truman would listen to their advice, express
hearty approval, and announce his decisions in a zesty, even brusque,
manner. "You could go into his office with a question," Harriman
marveled, "and come out with a decision from him more swiftly than
from any man I have ever known."

But perhaps the most significant difference was that Roosevelt handled foreign policy out of his own pocket. He could respect a man
like Harriman while at the same time maintaining a bemused distance
from some of his advice. He could indulge or ignore a Kennan, or a
Bohlen, or even an Acheson. Be it at Teheran or Yalta or in the

White House Map Room, Roosevelt relied on no State Department briefing books or even a Secretary of State; Edward Stettinius had even less influence than his dreamy predecessor in the post, Cordell Hull. With Hopkins as his arms and legs, Roosevelt personally handled the making of policy.

Truman had no desire to do the same. "I may not have much in the way of brains," he told one Cabinet member shortly after taking over, "but I do have enough brains to get hold of people who are able and give them a chance to carry out responsibility."

Such help would certainly be necessary during his first thirty days in office, for he would find himself faced with a sequence of events that would have overwhelmed even the most experienced statesman:

• Molotov would arrive from Moscow with a demand that the U.S. recognize the puppet Communist government the Soviets had established in Warsaw.

• The rift between the Soviet Union and Western Allies would break into public view at the first meeting of the United Nations in San Francisco.

• A twenty-two-pound shipment of enriched uranium would be secretly shipped from Oak Ridge, Tennessee, to Los Alamos, New Mexico, and placed inside a whale-shaped shell, while scientists and military commanders awaited a decision that only a President could make.

• The most devastating war in Europe's history would come to an end, forcing immediate questions about treatment of the conquered enemy and continuation of aid to the shattered Allies.

• The U.S. would have to decide whether Soviet participation in the war against Japan was still desirable, and, if so, at what price.

In short, that month would mark one of the great watersheds in modern history: the end of an international system defined by European alliances and the rise of a global system dominated by a struggle between two new superpowers. As Truman took office, Soviet and American troops were culminating the greatest feat of military cooperation in history. By the middle of May, an alliance unified by war would dissolve into one polarized by peace, a cold and complex peace that would require unfamiliar new commitments by a traditionally reticent nation.

To cope with this thirty-day barrage of events and crises, Harry Truman summoned the handful of advisers who, at least in his mind, could help him carry out the policies prescribed by Franklin Roosevelt. The small group of men, with their public and private experience in helping shape America's international involvement, were willing, even anxious, to answer the call. With their backgrounds in business or in the Soviet school of the Foreign Service, they brought a certain hard and realistic outlook on international affairs. It would be up to them to tutor the new President and shape America's new role as protector of a postwar balance. As Acheson later wrote, they were present at the creation.

·   ·   ·

The party that Averell Harriman and his daughter Kathleen hosted at Spaso House on the night of April 12 was an informal affair. A close-knit group had gathered to toast a departing embassy staffer. George Kennan, as was his wont, left early, but there was still a respectable crowd at 1 A.M. when the duty officer at the consulate called.

After answering the phone in an adjoining room, Kathleen sent for her father. "Soon the Ambassador came out looking very somber," his aide Robert Meiklejohn recalled. "Everybody ganged up on me to turn off the Victrola and get everybody home." Harriman made no announcement, but he asked a few of his closest aides, those he called the Spaso House regulars, to join him in his bedroom to discuss the death of Franklin Roosevelt and the ascension of a new President they knew almost nothing about.

The Kremlin, as Harriman well knew, kept late hours. Having often been summoned there well after midnight, he did not hesitate to call Molotov immediately with the grave news. It was 3 A.M., but the Foreign Minister, who had never before shown any sign of softness in his dealings with the U.S., insisted upon coming right over to express his condolences. Wringing Harriman's hand, he spoke at length of the role Roosevelt had played in winning the war and planning for the peace. Truman would carry out the late President's policies, Harriman assured him. The Soviet government was confident of that, Molotov replied, because Roosevelt had picked him personally. "I have never heard Molotov talk so earnestly," Harriman cabled Washington.

For the third time in three weeks, Harriman requested permission to return home. In fact, more anxious than ever, he virtually announced his impending return. "It is my intention to leave Moscow Monday morning," he cabled Secretary Stettinius, "to talk to you and the President unless you instruct me otherwise." For the third time in three weeks, Stettinius said no. "Now of all times it is essential that we have you in Moscow" came the reply.

How could he brief the inexperienced new President on the Soviet threat if Roosevelt's stubborn Secretary of State insisted on keeping him half a world away? Harriman, not one to be left on the sidelines, hit on a plan. Roosevelt had been anxious to have Molotov attend the grand opening of the United Nations, scheduled for San Francisco at the end of the month. If Harriman could convince Stalin to reverse his refusal to send the Foreign Minister, it would be a potent gesture of Soviet goodwill. As a by-product, a trip by Molotov to America would provide a perfect opening for Harriman to return home himself.

When Harriman was ushered into the Kremlin's inner sanctum the following night, Stalin grasped his hand in silence for almost a minute before asking him to sit down. He seemed deeply distressed. How had Roosevelt died? Harriman described the circumstances as best he knew them. There would be no change of policy, Stalin said. It was more an assertion than a question, and Harriman added his agreement. Truman was the type of man Stalin would like, "a man of action and not of words," as Harriman put it. "Roosevelt has died but his cause must live on," Stalin interjected. "We will support President Truman with all our forces and all our will."

"I am going to make a suggestion," Harriman boldly ventured. The most effective way for the Soviets to show their good intentions, he said, would be to send Molotov to the opening of the U.N. He might even stop in Washington before heading on to San Francisco. The plane Roosevelt used to travel to Yalta could be made available.

It was an unlikely situation for humor, this meeting between the sad-faced diplomat and the steely dictator, but Harriman made an atypical attempt. If Stalin so desired, he joked, the U.S. would paint a red star on the plane. A green one would be preferable, Stalin responded. The entire plane, Harriman quickly added, could be painted green.

Molotov, worried about missing the upcoming meeting of the Supreme Soviet, was not amused. "Time, time, time," he muttered as he hovered in the background. Stalin, however, was persuaded. After a few brusque words with his Foreign Minister, the marshal announced that the trip would be arranged.

At his first press conference, five days after taking office, Truman made clear that he would insist on a proper degree of respect from the visiting commissar. "Do you expect to see Mr. Molotov before he goes to San Francisco?" a reporter asked. "Yes. He is going to stop by and pay his respects to the President of the United States," Truman said firmly. "He should." Reported *Time* magazine: "It had been a long time since White House reporters had cheered a President's answer, but they clapped and laughed and cheered for a full minute."

Even as Truman spoke, Harriman was hurrying back to Washington. "Stalin's reversal of decision," Stettinius had finally cabled, "naturally alters the considerations which led to our disapproving your return home at this time." Molotov insisted on flying the long way around, eastward over Soviet territory and across the Bering Straits. Harriman was anxious to beat him to Washington in order to have a day or so to tutor the new President prior to the critical confrontation. Using his private B-24 plane, *Becky*, he left Moscow at 5 A.M. on April 17. After quick refueling stops at Casablanca, the Azores, and Prince Edward Island, he reached Washington's National Airport at 11:30 P.M. local time the following night. At forty-nine hours and eighteen minutes, it was by many hours the fastest time yet for any such journey.

•   •   •

As the State Department's liaison with the White House, Charles Bohlen had worked closely with Roosevelt and Harry Hopkins, indeed even more closely than Secretary Stettinius had. When he was handed the wire-service news flash by an aide, Bohlen immediately took on the task of phoning his mentor at the Mayo Clinic, where he was being treated for cancer. There was a long silence at the end of the line. "I guess I better be going to Washington," Hopkins finally replied.

From the bed of his Georgetown home, Hopkins, his cadaverous face now deathly pale, spent the next few days consulting with friends, including Bohlen and Harriman. When the hallowed Roosevelt was alive, Hopkins told one visitor, things had been easy. "Whatever we thought was the matter with the world, whatever we felt ought to be done about it, we could take our ideas to him," he said. "Well—he isn't here now, and we've got to find a way to do things by ourselves."

The adaptable Bohlen was able to get along well with Roosevelt, but had never found him truly likable. "Among those who worked with him," Bohlen recalled, "there was real affection for him, but not the kind of human feeling that springs from personal love." FDR's lack of precision, particularly when dealing with Soviet leaders, rankled Bohlen. "I do not think Roosevelt had any real comprehension of the great gulf that separated the thinking of a Bolshevik from a non-

Bolshevik, and particularly from an American," he wrote. "He felt that Stalin viewed the world somewhat in the same light as he did."

Before Roosevelt's death, Bohlen had never met Truman and regarded him as "an obscure Vice-President." Soon, however, he would become an important adviser. In fact, the morning after he took office, Truman asked Stettinius for a background report outlining the principal foreign problems facing the U.S. Preparing such a brief was Bohlen's job. That afternoon, he and Stettinius were ushered into the Oval Room (as the office was then called), finished product in hand.

The State Department, an institutional Cassandra whose warnings Roosevelt had blithely ignored, was anxious to grab the new President and shake him. In ticking off the world's trouble spots, Bohlen's report was stark. Poland merited particular attention. The Soviets had been ignoring their pledges made at Yalta to establish a government of national unity and hold free elections. In addition, the report added, they had been "consistently sabotaging Ambassador Harriman's efforts" to work out a solution.

"The three of us plunged into the harassing question of Poland," Truman later wrote, "and the difficulties we were having with the Soviet leaders because of it." He was already familiar with some of the problems, having read that morning the recent cables from Moscow. The Kremlin's insulting and belligerent attitude affronted his sense of decency. More than that, it got his old-fashioned American dander up.

To Truman, the moral issue was clear. The West wanted to see a government established in Poland that was representative of all the people, he told Bohlen, while Moscow was insisting on recognizing its "puppet regime." Hearing such a forthright appraisal was a welcome relief to Bohlen after dealing for so long with Roosevelt's equivocations.

•　•　•

Washington was set for a showdown. Certainly Truman was ready. Having read the cables that had been sent since Yalta, he had come to the conclusion that diplomatic niceties were actually not all that nice. Harriman was likewise ready. The second half of his "firm but friendly" formula had not worked well, and by his way of thinking the first half had hardly been tried. Perhaps most importantly, in the spring of 1945 the situation was ripe: there were deep rifts within the alliance, and with the war almost won, there was less need to paper them over. Neither the blustery President nor the taciturn ambassador, both blunt men, had Roosevelt's agility at evading such problems.

Harriman arrived in Washington on April 18, the anniversary of Paul Revere's ride. The need for firmness, he emphasized to Forrestal over dinner the next night, was greater than ever. The Soviets were determined to set up puppet states along their borders and perhaps beyond. "He said the outward thrust of Communism was not dead," the Navy Secretary recorded, "and that we might well have to face an ideological warfare just as vigorous and dangerous as Fascism or Nazism." It was a warning that Forrestal found compelling. Forebodings about Marxism had been rumbling through his mind, waiting to be reinforced; he had been reading books on the subject with a vengeance.

The next day Bohlen and Under Secretary of State Joseph Grew set up what was, in effect, a seminar for top State Department officials, ranging from Dean Acheson to Nelson Rockefeller. Those cables that Harriman had written but not sent in March were now delivered personally in his stolid monotone. "We have always dealt directly and fairly and with full candor." Harriman told his rapt audience. "This the Russians, accustomed to an atmosphere of suspicion and intrigue, do not understand. Furthermore, they have undoubtedly viewed our attitude as a sign of weakness."

Underlying the tension, Harriman explained, was a "basic and irreconcilable difference of objective between the Soviet Union and the United States." He had come to believe that Stalin's demand for "friendly" governments in neighboring countries could mean only one thing: regimes that were completely under Moscow's control. The Soviet urge for security was driving the Kremlin to extend its system as far as possible. With the expansion came "secret police and other terroristic and undemocratic methods."

Would it make sense, as Stimson and others were suggesting, to concede the Soviets a limited sphere of influence to assuage their security concerns? Harriman, who along with many of his colleagues had taken to heart the lessons of Munich, had come to feel that any sort of appeasement of the Soviet Union's expansionist desires would only whet the Kremlin's appetite for domination of other areas. "The Soviet Union, once it had control of bordering areas, would attempt to penetrate the next adjacent countries," he told the group at the State Department. "The issue ought to be fought out insofar as we can with the Soviet Union in the present bordering areas."*

---

*American statesmen had begun to develop a series of metaphors for Communist expansionism. Harriman used the analogy of an onion, in which one spoiled layer soon

When the discussion concluded, Harriman walked across the street, accompanied by Bohlen and Grew, to meet for the first time his most important pupil. Truman was eager to learn. When Molotov arrived, the President asked, what tack should he take? Harriman was direct. America had nothing to lose by standing firm on important issues. It no longer needed Red Army help to defeat the staggering Reich, but Russia desperately desired postwar reconstruction aid. Truman broke in to assure Harriman he was uncowed by the obdurate ally. "The Russians," he affirmed, "need us more than we need them."

At the heart of Harriman's dark message was a phrase from one of the telegrams he had written but not sent the month before: the world, he told Truman, was faced with a "barbarian invasion of Europe." Harriman was not the originator of this stark description. William Bullitt, the first in the long parade of disillusioned ambassadors, had developed the theme in a *Life* magazine series months earlier, one that among other things signaled a sharp change in the world according to Luce. But now the notion was being uttered by the formidable envoy who embodied, at least to Truman, Roosevelt's wartime efforts to build a Grand Alliance.

Harriman, whose rush back to Washington was partly motivated by his desire to remain an insider, was flattered that Truman was familiar with his cables. With great relief that he "would not have to educate a greenhorn," Harriman pulled the President aside after the meeting and offered some self-serving praise. "I am greatly relieved to discover that you have read them all and that we see eye to eye," he said. Not everyone was as pleased with Harriman's presumption. "I am burned up with the way in which Harriman has been acting," Secretary Stettinius grumbled a few days later. "He went to see the President without any of us knowing about it and has not reported to anyone yet what took place."

Despite his charged words, Harriman was still very much a pragmatic man, not the type to be swept up by the ideological anti-Bolshevist hysteria that was building among some who shared his qualms about Soviet conduct. The entrepreneur and diplomat, who had survived two decades of dealings within the Kremlin walls, told Truman that he was "not pessimistic" about arriving at a "workable

---

infected the next. Acheson two years later spoke of rotten apples in a barrel. The journalist Joseph Alsop popularized the domino theory, which Eisenhower used in justifying aid to South Vietnam in 1954: "You have a row of dominoes set up," he told a press conference. "You knock over the first one and what will happen to the last one is that it will go over very quickly."

basis" for dealing with the Russians—as long as idealistic illusions were abandoned. But the new President latched on to the dire aspects of Harriman's warnings. Of course, he said, the U.S. should not expect to get 100 percent from the Soviets. But on important matters it should get 85 percent. The Polish question must be settled along the lines worked out at Yalta, Truman added. "I intend to tell Molotov that in words of one syllable."

The confrontation that ensued upon Molotov's arrival marked the first major milestone of the Cold War.* Into the open burst the irreconcilable conflict exemplified by Poland: the weak nations bordering the Soviet Union could not be, as the conferees at Yalta had hoped, both "friendly" and "free." Given their political freedom, at least as that concept was understood in the West, their people were likely to form governments that were hostile to Kremlin control. Since the Soviets had no intention of letting this occur, Great Power unity could be achieved only at the expense of the ideals of freedom and self-determination enshrined in the Atlantic Charter.

With the exception of George Kennan, still a gloomy voice in the wilderness, Americans were not yet ready to conceive of a Europe divided into hostile blocs, East and West. Indeed, those few in Washington who entertained the idea of conceding the Soviets a limited sphere of influence in Eastern Europe did so for precisely the opposite reason: whereas Kennan had long abandoned all hope of cooperating with Russia or influencing its actions in the areas it controlled, Stimson believed that respect for mutual spheres could lead to a system of international cooperation. "Our respective orbits do not clash geographically," Stimson wrote in his diary the day before Harriman left Moscow, "and I think that on the whole we can probably keep out of clashes in the future."

To Harriman this was hogwash. Conceding the Soviets a "limited" sphere in neighboring states, one based only on security interests, would inevitably lead to total Russian domination of those countries. Moscow might not attempt to "Communize" its neighbors, Harriman felt, but its security concerns were so deeply ingrained that it would insist on a system of secret state police and total control of the politics and commerce of its new vassals. Having accomplished that, the

---

*The publicist Herbert Bayard Swope used the phrase "Cold War" in a little talk he gave at this time. He would later include it in a speech written for Bernard Baruch, and it would be picked up and popularized by Walter Lippmann.

Soviets would inevitably seek another layer of "friendly" states, thrusting their totalitarian system ever farther into a weak and prostrate Europe. If Poland and its neighbors fell into the Soviet orbit, he said, could the next row of countries be far behind?

Later events would show that the Soviets, although resolute in fulfilling their long-standing demand for a security belt along their European border, would be somewhat more tentative in their probes beyond that zone. This realization would eventually become the foundation for a policy of Soviet containment. At the time, however, neither Harriman nor most of the others tutoring the new President were willing to count on Polish concessions to sate the Soviet appetite for security.

In addition, of course, there were moral reasons for not abandoning Poland. Just as the Soviets had gone to war to prevent a hostile cordon sanitaire along their border that could serve as a corridor for western invasions, Britain had gone to war to protect the independence of Poland. Aside from the very real pressures from six million Polish-American voters, U.S. leaders, like their British counterparts, deeply believed that forsaking the Polish people to foreign domination was, quite simply, wrong.

•   •   •

They converged at the White House on the afternoon of Monday, April 23, five days after Harriman's return. The purpose of the session was to help the President prepare for his meeting with Molotov; what in fact occurred, however, set the fundamental tone of the new Administration's Soviet policy. From the State Department, in addition to Harriman, came Bohlen and Stettinius, bearing news that Molotov had not budged in his insistence that the Soviet-backed regime in Warsaw would have a veto over any other Poles who sought to be included in the Cabinet. From the Navy Department came Forrestal, fired up from his talks with Harriman. Representing the War Department was Stimson, worried about an awesome weapon he had not yet explained to the President, and General George Marshall, the Army Chief of Staff, who was anxious to secure Soviet involvement in the war against Japan.

Truman had stayed up late over the weekend reading the Yalta accords and was surprised at how vague the language was. Yet Harriman's cables from Moscow had convinced him, he told his advisers, that agreements had "so far been a one-way street." This could not continue. If the Soviets did not want to cooperate in San Francisco, he added, "they could go to hell." Having thus set the tone, he went around the table seeking advice.

Stimson spoke first. The Kremlin's use of secret police and repressive tactics appalled him, and he had often urged a firmer policy. But it was unlikely, he said, that the Soviets would yield on a matter so crucial to their security as Poland. Consequently he urged caution. The U.S., he counseled, might be "heading into very dangerous water" by forcing a showdown on Poland, which in fact was once part of Russia's empire. "The Russians," he added, "perhaps were being more realistic about their own security than we were."

General Marshall supported the view of his civilian chief. The possibility of a break was "very serious" because it might foreclose Soviet support in the struggle against Japan. Forrestal, on the other hand, fully embraced the emerging hard-line consensus. If the Russians were going to be rigid in their attitude about taking control of Eastern Europe, he said, "we had better have a showdown with them now than later."

When it came turn for Harriman to speak, he addressed a question Stimson had asked about Soviet motives. The Kremlin, explained the ambassador, had concluded that free Polish elections would lead to a rejection of its "hand-picked group." The issue now was whether the U.S. "should be a party to a program of Soviet domination of Poland."

There was little doubt which advice Truman would take. Indeed, Stimson noted that his words of caution seemed to disappoint the President. After the meeting, Stimson and the military advisers were dismissed. Harriman, Bohlen, and Stettinius were asked to wait around for Molotov's arrival.

Truman went straight to the point, telling Molotov that he was sorry to learn that the Yalta agreement had not been carried out. The Soviet Foreign Minister interjected that he was sorry too. In order to achieve a solution, Truman continued, all of the democratic elements in Poland must be brought together to form a government of national unity.

Again Molotov protested. The Soviets wished to cooperate. It was a matter of honor, and they were convinced all difficulties could be overcome. Truman said he accepted that, otherwise he would not be carrying on this conversation. At issue was the Soviet willingness to carry out the Yalta agreement. All that remained, the President insisted with a mule farmer's firmness, was "for Marshal Stalin to carry it out in accordance with his word."

Molotov, Bohlen recalled, "turned a little ashy" and tried to steer the conversation to the Japanese war. Truman cut him off. "That will be all, Mr. Molotov. I would appreciate it if you would transmit my views to Marshal Stalin."

"I've never been talked to like that in my life," protested Molotov, who had long labored under Stalin and thus surely had been.

"Carry out your agreements," Truman barked back, "and you won't get talked to like that."

"How I enjoyed translating those words," Bohlen later recalled. "They were probably the first sharp words uttered during the war by an American President to a high Soviet official." Bohlen thought Truman was merely doing what Roosevelt would have done if he had been alive. "Roosevelt's technique would have been different," Bohlen later wrote, "his approach would have possibly been more diplomatic and somewhat smoother, but he was in no mood the last time I saw him, only days before he died, to take further violations of the Yalta accord lying down."

As for Harriman, he remembers being "a little taken aback" by Truman's "vigorous" attack. Not that Harriman disagreed with the sentiments. He only worried that it would give Molotov an excuse to tell Stalin that Roosevelt's policies had been reversed.

Had FDR's approach in fact been abandoned? In one sense it had. While insisting that democratic ideals be given lip service, Roosevelt nevertheless refrained from asserting a direct U.S. "interest" in Poland. When Stalin had told him at Yalta that Poland was, for the Russians, "not only a question of honor but of security," the wily Roosevelt understood, in a way that his righteous successor never would, that realpolitik concessions would have to be made to achieve postwar cooperation. Implicitly, though certainly not publicly, FDR had recognized certain Soviet prerogatives in Poland based on proximity and security. But his pragmatism about power politics was of course incompatible with his public pronouncements of Wilsonian idealism. At the end of his life, even the dexterous Roosevelt was having problems juggling these contradictions.

Unwilling and unable to finesse the issue, the new President sought advice from experts such as Harriman and Bohlen on how to achieve Roosevelt's true goals. "Truman had to rely on State Department advisers, who were much less sympathetic to cooperation with the

Soviets than Roosevelt had been," writes Truman's biographer, Robert Donovan. "What he sought was a settlement on terms consistent with the American interpretation of Yalta as expounded to him by Roosevelt's chief advisers."

One thing is certain: Roosevelt's tone had been abandoned. But even if FDR could have sidestepped such a harsh exchange with Molotov, he could hardly have kept the clash between America's ideals and Russia's security interests under wraps for very long. "The choice between soft words and blunt words," Donovan writes, "was not likely to have made a fundamental difference in resolving the conflict of objectives."

Word quickly spread of the triumph of firmness over friendliness. "This is the best news in months," crowed Vandenberg. "FDR's appeasement of Russia is over." Wrote Churchill to Eden: "My appreciation is that the new President is not to be bullied by the Soviets."

To ordinary Americans, the revelation of such a basic breach was somewhat surprising. Most were still caught in the jubilation surrounding the success of America and her "gallant ally." Indeed, even as Molotov left Washington, reporters and cameramen were reporting on the climactic symbol of Soviet-American cooperation: On a twisted and battered metal bridge spanning the Elbe River near the German town of Torgau, a scout from General Courtney Hodge's First Army and one from Marshal Ivan Konev's First Ukrainian Front met, hugged, beat on each other's shoulders, and waved their tired arms toward the springtime sky. Elsewhere along the Elbe, patrols from East and West were cavorting into the water, cracking open bottles of wine, and dancing to the coming triumph over the common enemy.

•   •   •

The high hopes for postwar friendship, however appealing they might be, were in Harriman's mind unrealistic, even dangerous. With the President now in agreement, warning the press and the public was Harriman's next mission. Thus he flew to San Francisco to outline his concerns for the American delegation to the U.N. Conference and, more importantly, to hold a series of background briefings for key newspaper editors and commentators. "I was there," he said, "to make everyone understand that the Soviets had already given every indication that they were not going to live up to their postwar agreements, and I was trying to explain to everybody what we were going to be up against."

With Bohlen at his side and McCloy listening intently, Harriman told the American delegates that Russia was building a tier of friendly states in Eastern Europe. "Our task is to make it difficult for her to do so, since to build one tier of states implies the possibility of further tiers, layer on layer." When Vandenberg, himself a supporter of the burgeoning hard line, mentioned that premature public statements about Soviet perfidy might provoke an unnecessary reaction of popular sentiment, Harriman cut him off. "I would like nothing better than to have the people rise up in protest."

San Francisco was swarming with journalists, an astounding sixteen hundred of them duly accredited. Society columnist Elsa Maxwell was there, writing about how the Russians were "a bunch of magnificent he-men." So was Earl Wilson, another gossip columnist, who provoked Molotov to stalk out of a press conference by asking the correct pronunciation of the word "vodka." Some of the more serious members of the press contingent were invited by Harriman to his sprawling penthouse suite atop the Fairmont Hotel. There he continued to spread the sobering word about the Soviets. "We must recognize our objectives and the Kremlin's objectives are irreconcilable," he told them. It was "a small planet," he added, and the U.S. must be friendly as well as firm, but it must always keep up its guard.

The briefings caused quite a flurry, much of it directed against Harriman. Editorial opinion at the time, like public opinion in general, was still sympathetic toward the Soviets. Columnist Walter Lippmann and a radio commentator Raymond Gram Swing stalked out of one of the briefings. Lippmann went to his room in the Palace Hotel and wrote a column denouncing those "who, to say it flatly, are thinking of the international organization as a way of policing the Soviet Union." Swing stated in a radio commentary that policy makers who no longer believed in diplomacy with Moscow should step aside.

In the mind of much of the public, America's role at the U.N. was to serve as a mediator between the two powers bent on dominating Europe: imperialist Britain and expansionist Russia. There was no need, they believed, for the U.S. to become entangled in European power politics. "While Roosevelt was alive," I. F. Stone wrote, "the U.S. was kind of a middle man between Britain and Russia. But since his death, the British have been able to . . . play us off against the Soviets." C. L. Sulzberger, of *The New York Times*, worried about "the impression of an Anglo-American front against Moscow," and Lippmann reported that "here in San Francisco the mediator position of the U.S. has been lost temporarily." Such concerns prompted a group of congressmen to publish an open letter criticizing Washington for taking sides in the dispute between Churchill and Stalin.

Harriman was among those who did not share in this resistance to an alliance with Britain. In fact, he heartily endorsed it. He and most of his friends were naturally (and quite understandably) sympathetic to England, the cradle of the enlightened values they so deeply cherished. Partly it was cultural heritage: An Anglophile attitude permeated their lives from boarding school to the furnishings in their homes. More importantly, it was a philosophical outlook: Fundamental moral and political principles were ingrained in the Anglo-Saxon code that the two countries shared.

It was an outlook that the rest of the U.S. was beginning to adopt. In February of 1945, most Americans polled said that they foresaw postwar problems with Britain as being more serious than those with Russia. By May of 1945, that situation had reversed.

•   •   •

Harry Truman used to brag that he could fall asleep as soon as his head hit the pillow. Even so, it was surprising that he slept soundly on the night of May 7. It was the first night he had spent in the White House; twenty trucks that day had helped Eleanor Roosevelt move out her belongings and one truck had helped the Trumans move in theirs. It was the night before his sixty-first birthday. But most important, the surrender documents ending the war in Europe had finally been signed, and he was scheduled to make the formal announcement—simultaneously with Churchill and Stalin—at nine o'clock the next morning. "Isn't that some birthday present?" he wrote his ninety-two-year-old mother.

Churchill had tried to persuade the President to order American troops to push as far east as possible, disregarding the zones of occupation that had been established with the Soviets and keeping as much territory as possible out of Red Army hands. On General Eisenhower's advice, Truman refused. Then Churchill had tried to convince him to ignore the agreement with Stalin and make the V-E announcement earlier than scheduled. Again Truman refused. Churchill, the President told his mother, "was mad as a wet hen."

At the agreed-upon time, Truman's clear and subdued voice came across millions of radios. "This is a solemn but glorious hour...." It was as if a lever had been pulled releasing a rain of ticker tape and emotion across the country. Despite the continued fighting in the Far East, the nation allowed itself an enormous sigh of relief. Men and women danced and kissed in Times Square, on the Boston Common, in Chicago's Loop, on the Washington Mall, and anywhere else where there was room to celebrate. Thoughts turned to bringing Americans home from a smoldering Continent, home to a land soon to be filled with long-restricted consumer goods. "Yes, they're back," read the signs on cigarette counters, referring both to the boys and the butts.

Yet mingled with the relief was a vague solemnity. Churches filled up early that day, even though it was a Tuesday. The President's message ended with talk of the future, a peace rooted in justice and law. "We can build such a peace only by hard, toilsome, painstaking work," he said, "by understanding and working with our Allies in peace as we have in war."

Americans were hardly in the mood for hard, toilsome, painstaking work. Acheson, whose responsibilities as an Assistant Secretary of State now included congressional relations, found himself faced with a rising political clamor to bring the boys home. Yet the men whose duty it was to lead America into the postwar world were already well aware of the awesome challenges their nation would face.

Even as the headlines describing V-E Day were being hawked on the morning of May 9, Stimson was explaining to a new advisory panel, as best he could, a weapon whose scientific underpinnings and historic ramifications he could barely grasp. Harriman was in San Francisco that day working on a way to wind down Lend-Lease shipments to Russia now that the war against Hitler was over. McCloy, also in San Francisco, was putting the final touches on the order establishing American occupation policies in Germany. Lovett, for the moment happily insulated from the diplomatic turmoil in his lair at the Pentagon, was preparing to leave for Europe to determine what air force units could be redeployed against Japan. All of these issues— the bomb, the Soviets, the future treatment of Germany, the Japanese war—meant that victory in Europe would not end America's involvement in the world beyond her shores.

·   ·   ·

Despite his refusal to jump the gun in proclaiming Germany's surrender, Truman ended up scooping Stalin by more than a day. George Kennan, holding down the shop at the Moscow embassy in Harriman's absence, cabled his speculation that the ever-wary Russian rulers were withholding the news from their people lest it turn out to be a capitalist trick allowing the Germans to continue resisting in the east.

It was not until dawn on May 10 that the word filtered out, loudspeakers on the streets began playing the "Internationale" and "The Star-Spangled Banner," and joyous Muscovites surged forth to celebrate. Spotting the American flag waving from the balcony of the U.S. Embassy, the crowds gathered in a spontaneous demonstration of friendship. "Long live Truman!" they shouted. "Long live Roosevelt's memory!" Americans who ventured forth to join the celebrating were, in Kennan's words, "tossed enthusiastically into the air and passed on friendly hands over the heads of the crowd, to be lost, eventually, in a confused orgy of good feeling."

The feeling in fact was so orgiastic that even Kennan got caught up in it, sending a staffer across the embassy roof and into the National Hotel next door to procure a Soviet flag. Renewed roars of approval greeted its appearance on the balcony next to the Stars and Stripes. Ignoring for once the exhortations of police and party functionaries, the crowd surged past the barricades and up to the front of the building.

Feeling the (somewhat surprising) desire to address the demonstration, Kennan emerged from the building and climbed atop the pedestal of one of the chancery's enormous pillars. "Congratulations on the day of victory," he shouted in Russian. "All honor to the Soviet allies!" Erupting in shouts of approval, the crowd hoisted onto the pedestal a Soviet soldier, who kissed a startled American sergeant and tossed him into the friendly arms below. Kennan escaped back inside the building.

Nevertheless, as one might expect, Kennan found cause to temper his joy with melancholy. "Isn't this wonderful?" a pro-Soviet English journalist asked him as they watched the prolonged demonstration from a second-floor window. Kennan, feeling once again his incurable detachment, replied that indeed it was, but that it also made him sad. The world was filled with problems. Peace could not be what these people dreamed it to be. The journalist later reported, and Kennan denied, that the forlorn American diplomat concluded by saying: "They think the war has ended. But it is really only beginning."

As chargé d'affaires, Kennan was free to transmit thoughts that heretofore had languished as unsolicited memos for the ambassador's files. His flurry of missives erupted immediately upon Harriman's departure in mid-April.

Mainly he anguished about Poland. To some extent, his attitude was inconsistent. As one of the first advocates of a division of the world into realistic spheres, Kennan felt, at least in theory, that Washington should wash its hands of the problems posed by Soviet meddling in Eastern Europe. But as a true believer in taking a firm line with the Kremlin, and as a descendant of a long line of Presbyterian moralists, he could scarcely resist the desire to challenge Soviet behavior in Poland.

The first cable he received from Washington was Truman's message to Stalin insisting that the puppet government in Poland be reorganized. On his own, Kennan decided to delay delivery of the message, suggesting in a return cable that Washington might wish to beef it up in light of a new military pact Moscow had signed with the Warsaw regime. It is "of utmost urgency," the State Department shot back, that the cable be delivered promptly.

The next day Kennan passed along Deputy Foreign Minister Vishinsky's response to American questions about the Red Army's transfer of portions of eastern Germany to the Polish regime. He could not refrain from appending his own comments. "I wish to point out that none of these points can be substantiated," he began, launching into a refutation five times as long as Vishinsky's own explanations.

The department simply ignored Kennan's analysis and sent a reply for him to deliver that "welcomed" the Soviet assurances. Kennan was dismayed. In a personal message to his old colleague Elbridge Durbrow, then on the Russian desk, Kennan protested that "this instruction is one which it would cause me considerable anguish to carry out." The U.S. should protest. Even though such a gesture was not likely to change anything, Kennan conceded, it would "teach the Russians an overdue lesson."

Under Secretary Grew finally gave Kennan the go-ahead. He should ignore the earlier instruction and tell Vishinsky that the U.S. was "unable to reconcile" Soviet explanations with the facts of the case. Vishinsky, Kennan seemed happy to report, was "clearly disconcerted by this communication." The Soviets, however, did not alter their course.

Kennan had been left on his own before, and it was not the first time he had confessed to feeling "considerable anguish." Yet suddenly there was a President who actually read the cables from Moscow and did not have a jaundiced eye about State Department suggestions. After studying one of Kennan's telegrams about Soviet motives, Truman noted somberly: "I realized only too well the implications in this message."

• • •

"I think it is very important I have a talk with you as soon as possible on a highly secret matter." Truman knew what the note from his

Secretary of War meant. Roosevelt had briefly mentioned the atom bomb during a photo session shortly before he died, and Stimson had cornered Truman shortly after he was sworn in as President and circumspectly alluded to "a new explosive of almost unbelievable destructive power." The next day Jimmy Byrnes, the South Carolina politician and former director of the Office of War Mobilization whom Truman had privately decided to make Secretary of State, filled him in on a few more details. So did Vannevar Bush, his science adviser, though at the time salty Admiral Leahy had snorted: "The bomb will never go off, and I speak as an expert on explosives."

In fact, Truman's familiarity with the atomic-bomb project (or his lack of it) stretched back to March of 1944 when his Senate committee on military production began poking around at some mysterious plants that seemed to be consuming a lot of money and producing very little. "I cannot tell you what it is," Stimson told Senator Truman then, "but it is the greatest project in the history of the world." Truman in his memoirs recalls telling Stimson: "I'll take your word." In his own diary Stimson recorded a less cordial account. "He threatened me with dire consequences," the War Secretary wrote at the time. "I told him I had to accept responsibility for those consequences. Truman is a nuisance and a petty, unworthy man. He talks smoothly and acts meanly."

When Stimson arrived at noon on April 25, two days after Truman's showdown with Molotov, he brought with him a paper on the far-reaching implications of this "most terrible weapon ever known in human history." Byrnes had already told Truman that the bomb might allow the U.S. to dictate its own terms at the end of the war. But Stimson was more interested in the historic ramifications than the military ones. "The world in its present state of moral achievement," he said, "would be eventually at the mercy of such a weapon. In other words, modern civilization might be completely destroyed."

As a way of meeting this "moral responsibility," Stimson proposed, and Truman approved, the creation of a special group, known as the Interim Committee, to explore the implications of the new weapon. In addition to Stimson, Byrnes, and Bush, the group and its scientific staff included such people as Harvard President James Bryant Conant, MIT President Karl Compton, and the bomb's master scientist, J. Robert Oppenheimer.

The Interim Committee quickly began work on its broad task. But the imminence of such an awesome new force raised certain immediate diplomatic questions that were outside the committee's expertise and purview. To what extent did the new weapon make it less important to secure Soviet entry into the war against Japan? Should the development of this incalculably powerful weapon, due to be tested in mid-July, affect the timing of the proposed meeting of Truman, Churchill, and Stalin?

Stimson, who had not been fully swayed by Harriman's dire pronouncements, believed that a Soviet-American confrontation could be avoided by allowing Moscow a "limited" security sphere in Eastern Europe. Despite his abstract faith in free people and free trade, the old-school statesman felt that the Great Powers were perfectly justified in imposing their security interests within their own regions. The U.S. had forged such a system in the Western Hemisphere under the Monroe Doctrine. It was only logical that the Soviets should be allowed the same prerogatives in Eastern Europe. Such an arrangement might eventually lead to a liberalized Soviet society that could come only through prosperity and security.

With Stimson's approval, McCloy had gone to San Francisco primarily to make sure that the new United Nations did not usurp Washington's security prerogatives in its hemisphere. Stimson and McCloy were both straightforward and genuine, perhaps even a bit simplistic, when it came to formulating a world view. Neither was given to ideological agonizing or geopolitical posturing. "Some Americans are anxious to hang on to exaggerated views of the Monroe Doctrine and at the same time butt into every question that comes up in Central Europe," Stimson told McCloy before he departed. The respective U.S. and Soviet spheres, he added, can coexist "without too much friction."

McCloy seemed somewhat surprised by "the growing sense of Russia vs. the U.S." that he found in San Francisco. But like Stimson he felt that any disputes could be worked out on the basis of a "businesslike" respect for each other's interests. "Here are two vast nations of obviously the greatest political and military force," he wrote in his journal. "It is little wonder that as they emerge . . . as the two greatest powers, they should walk stiff-legged around the ring a bit." The challenge would be to transcend petty Soviet rudeness and work out disputes intelligently. "It is a natural human process which is going on," he concluded. "There is no good in being alarmed about it."

On the phone from San Francisco, McCloy outlined what he called a "have our cake and eat it too" strategy: the U.N. should allow the U.S. to keep its regional arrangements for the protection of the Western Hemisphere while also permitting it to become involved in Europe. "It's not asking too much," Stimson agreed. Yet Russia likewise must be permitted certain spheres. Just before McCloy boarded a plane to return to Washington on the evening of May 9, Stimson explained to him over the phone: "The thing should be pared out so that we are not immersed in what I used to call the local troubles of Europe." When McCloy said he agreed, Stimson added: "Well you don't think Russia is going to give up her right to act unilaterally in those nations around her which she thinks so darned useful?" No, McCloy replied, she will not.

Also heading home from San Francisco that night, in a separate plane, were Harriman and Bohlen. On the way they discussed the ominous decline in Soviet-American relations. Even though he had done much to create the current atmosphere, Harriman had begun to worry that his policy of firmness may have been embraced too enthusiastically. In Moscow, he and Kennan had been pushing against a pendulum that seemed to have swung too far toward accommodating the Soviets, no matter how large their demands or outrageous their conduct. With the new President's penchant for bluntness, Harriman now saw the pendulum swinging the other way, perhaps a bit ominously. It was a perception that Kennan would come to share, though not for at least two years.

The best way to restore working relations, Harriman told Bohlen, was to schedule an early summit. His intent was not to provoke a confrontation. Indeed it was just the contrary. As a businessman and diplomat, Harriman believed that firmness, friendliness, and leverage were all part of a mix that had as its ultimate goal the reaching of mutually satisfactory agreements, not the precluding of them. Crucial to that process, at least in the mind of the man who made it his business to deal only at the top, was personal diplomacy, face-to-face meetings among those who could settle disputes.

Bohlen's views fell somewhere between Stimson's and Harriman's. Although deeply skeptical about Soviet motives and tactics, he had accepted the Roosevelt line that some concessions must be made to Moscow's legitimate security interests in Eastern Europe. Bohlen had sharply rebuked his friend Kennan for advocating that the U.S. abandon any hope of cooperation and resign itself to the creation of hostile East and West blocs in Europe. Yet he was inclined to favor tacit acceptance of limited spheres; later he would call them "open spheres," ones that somehow accommodated both Soviet security needs and America's desire to promote political and economic freedom.

The man who most embodied Roosevelt's approach was ailing Harry

Hopkins. In lieu of an early summit, Bohlen thought, a mission to Moscow by Hopkins might be the best way to restore some balance to Soviet-American relations. Bohlen was hesitant to broach the idea with the man next to him on the plane. Harriman, who had led the inside crusade against Roosevelt's conciliatory policies and who was supposed to represent the U.S. in Moscow, might be offended. Yet when Bohlen tentatively made his suggestion, Harriman "jumped at the idea."

Unbeknownst to Bohlen and Harriman, Truman had been toying with the notion himself and had raised it with Hopkins shortly after the President's funeral. But Hopkins apparently was reluctant, at least at the time, and Truman was himself unsure of the idea. It remained for Bohlen and Harriman to put the plan into motion and secure Secretary Stettinius's approval.

● ● ●

The day that they arrived back from San Francisco, Harriman and McCloy had lunch together with Secretary Stimson at the Pentagon. "Very confidentially," Stimson filled the ambassador in about the atom bomb. This new force, Stimson argued, made the Soviet actions in Eastern Europe less threatening. There was thus little urgency, he tried to convince Harriman, about scheduling a summit until after the bomb had been tested and America's diplomatic ace was in hand.

Stimson, however, did not share Byrnes's view that the bomb could become an instrument of blackmail in a showdown with the Soviets. On the contrary, he felt that offering them a role in developing and controlling the atom might induce them to cooperate on other matters. It could, he thought, be an important bargaining chip to entice Moscow into the community of civilized nations. The only way to earn someone's trust, went the maxim he had learned at Skull and Bones, was to trust him.

Leaving aside (as he did) whether the Soviets were similar to Bonesmen, the critical question Stimson had for Harriman over lunch was whether there were any signs the Soviets were ready to open up their society. Harriman's response, Stimson noted, was "gloomy." The seeds of liberalism, Harriman insisted, did not exist in Russia.

The news about the bomb did not alter Harriman's desire for an early summit nor make the problem of Poland seem any less pressing. It did, however, add a new element to the question of what concessions the U.S. should make in order to get Soviet support in the Japanese war. The bomb, he realized, made Red Army participation less necessary. Before going back to Moscow, Harriman wanted to know whether Washington felt it was still worth the price. "I tried to stimulate thinking in the State Department about ending the request to the Russians to come into the war and ending any obligations to them for doing so," he later recalled.

So early on the morning of May 12, a Saturday, Harriman, McCloy, Bohlen, Grew, and Forrestal gathered at the State Department. Harriman asked his questions. Should the concessions made at Yalta for Red Army participation in the war against Japan (which included such things as rights to ports in Manchuria and control of Sakhalin Island) be re-examined in light of Moscow's apparent violation of the Yalta pledge that there would be free elections in liberated Europe? How urgent was the need for Soviet support? "Our conduct toward Stalin," he told the group, "would obviously be greatly conditioned by the degree of urgency."

It was decided that Harriman and Bohlen should write a memo officially posing these questions, which Grew would send to the War, State, and Navy departments for formal responses. Their two-page product was very specific. But its significance lay not in the narrow questions regarding the Japanese fighting; there was little doubt that the Soviets would enter the Pacific war when and if they desired. The true importance of the memo was that it would provoke a formal discussion, one that would dominate the coming Monday and Tuesday, about the ominous drift in America's policies toward the Soviet Union.

•   •   •

Upon Harriman's arrival from San Francisco, the Administration had stumbled through a clumsy pirouette on the question of aid to the Soviets. The Lend-Lease program for Britain and Russia was supposed to end with the war, and Congress had been promised that it would. But when the pipeline was abruptly plugged within days of the German surrender in early May, howls of protest erupted—particularly from the Soviets. They interpreted the cutoff as a political bludgeon designed to intimidate them.

The imbroglio was not exactly Harriman's fault. He had long felt that aid to the Russians should be used as a form of leverage, but he knew that this could work only if handled deftly. He emphasized this when he recommended that Lend-Lease be curtailed judiciously, with exceptions made for shipments to factories under construction and for material that might help the war in the Far East. Nor was it exactly

Truman's fault. He barely glanced at the vaguely worded termination order which Harriman and others had approved.

Most everyone, including Harriman and Truman, ended up blaming the ensuing uproar on overzealous bureaucrats, who indeed had acted more zestfully than intended when they ordered that even ships already sailing toward Soviet ports be immediately turned around. Harriman rushed to the White House to get the heavy-handed approach reversed. But the incident became a symbolic milestone marking the end of wartime cooperation between the two powers.

It also reinforced Truman's growing doubts about the hard line that his advisers had pressed in April. Among those Truman confided in was his old poker crony Joseph Davies, the dean of the soft liners, whose memoirs of his mission as ambassador to the Soviet Union during the 1930s, titled *Mission to Moscow*, had been dubbed by Bohlen and Kennan "Submission to Moscow." On May 13, after a morning spent fretting with Felix Frankfurter over the course of Soviet-American relations, Davies decided to pick up the phone and call the White House.

He was promptly invited over for a glass of Bourbon and Sunday supper. The President unloaded his worries, laying blame on the "get tough" advice of the State Department and the distortions of the "damn" newspapers. Davies then read a letter he had written to Truman the day before but not mailed. "I have found that when approached with generosity and friendliness, the Soviets respond with even greater generosity," he said. "The 'tough' approach induces a quick and sharp rejoinder that 'out toughs' anyone they consider hostile."

"It is a terrible responsibility," Truman lamented at the end of the discussion, "and I am the last man fitted to handle it." Having either forgotten about or shelved the idea of sending Hopkins to Moscow, Truman suggested to Davies that he might want to undertake such a trip. Davies demurred.

His conversation with Davies did not prompt an abrupt reversal of policy, but Truman did become more skeptical of what had become known as the Harriman hard line. The "get tough" policy had been a mistake, Truman conceded to Roosevelt's daughter, and he claimed as an excuse that it had been foisted on him by "all my advisers." Part of this was merely Truman's penchant for telling listeners what he thought they wanted to hear. But it also represented a real worry.

What Truman did not know was that Harriman and Bohlen shared similar concerns. Washington, they feared, was confusing pragmatic firmness, which was certainly justified, with outright belligerency, which could only be counterproductive. That is why they favored sending Hopkins to Moscow and why they hoped a Truman-Stalin-Churchill summit could soon be held to work out a solution on Poland and other questions.

Stimson, of course, also favored a lessening of tensions, and consequently so did McCloy. The dispute that was to dominate the first few days of the third week in May mainly concerned timing: when would the U.S. be in the best bargaining position?

Harriman and the relative hard liners favored a conference as soon as possible. Along with Churchill, they argued that the best leverage the U.S. had was the presence of its soldiers in Central Europe, many of whom would soon be withdrawn. In addition, with each passing week the Kremlin was tightening its grip on the areas it occupied. As Harriman told Forrestal as they cruised the Potomac, "We must face our diplomatic decisions from here on with the consciousness that half and maybe all of Europe might be communistic by the end of next winter."

Stimson, on the other hand, favored delay. The most important factor, he knew, was the atomic bomb, and Washington would not know whether the thing worked until mid-July. He now faced the task of converting Truman to his view that the bomb would be a powerful persuader and that the prospect of being made a partner in its control could entice the Kremlin into opening up to the world community. Perhaps in deference to the President's favorite pastime, the players began to talk in poker metaphors as they argued over when America would hold the best hand.

While Davies was drinking Bourbon at the White House on May 13, Stimson was returning from a restful weekend at Highhold, his rambling Long Island estate. McCloy met him when he arrived in Washington and handed him the questions that Harriman, Bohlen, and Grew had prepared about the need for Russian support in the Japanese war. As the Secretary noted in his diary that night: "These questions cut very deep, and in my opinion are powerfully connected with S-1." That was the code name the War Department had given to what the British called "tube alloys" and the scientists at Los Alamos called "the gadget."

After sleeping on the situation, Stimson came to the conclusion that it was foolish to force any issues with the Soviets until the new weapon was in hand. On Monday he called in McCloy for another discussion. "I told him this was a place where we really held all the cards," Stimson wrote in his diary. "I called it a royal straight flush and we mustn't be a fool about how we play it." What was important now, he added, was "not to get into any unnecessary quarrels."

Stimson and McCloy met with Harriman, Forrestal, and Grew on Tuesday morning. The subject was supposed to be Russia and the Japanese war. But Stimson, saying he thought it "premature" to answer such questions, broadened the discussion to include the timing of a summit. "It might be necessary to have it out with Russia," he noted in his diary. "Over any such discussion the S-1 secret would be dominant." Thus it was best to wait until the bomb was tested. "It seems a terrible thing to gamble with such big stakes without having your master card in your hand."

It turned out to be, in Stimson's words, "a pretty red hot session." Harriman remained skeptical about any delay. But he agreed to postpone his return to Moscow until they had more time to consider what course to take.

Later that day Harriman, along with Bohlen and Grew, went to see the President. Harriman told Truman that he shared his concern that the new eagerness to challenge the Soviets might be leading to an irreparable breach. "The problem of our relations with Russia is the number one problem affecting the future of the world," the ambassador warned. "At the present moment we are getting farther and farther apart." Recommending a summit, he urged that it be scheduled before too many American troops had been withdrawn from Europe. "If the meeting could take place before we were in a large measure out of Europe," he advised, "the chances of success would be increased."

Truman then turned to Bohlen. The Soviets were getting the impression that the U.S. and Britain were "ganging up" on them, the President said. Would this be exacerbated if Truman agreed to Churchill's request to visit London on the way to a tripartite conference? To Bohlen this was silly. "The Russians considered it in the logic of things that Britain and America would be very close together," he replied. A Truman-Churchill meeting beforehand "might on the contrary have a salutary effect and make Stalin more reasonable."

Stimson had his turn the next day. The redeployment of American troops from Europe would take many months, he told the President, and thus provide "more time for your necessary diplomacy than some of our hasty friends realize." Above all, he thought it would be an advantage to have any summit coincide with the first test of the atomic bomb. "We shall probably hold more cards in our hand later than now," he said.

Despite Harriman's and Bohlen's arguments, Truman remained wary about creating the impression of an Anglo-American alliance against Russia. Nor was he willing to leave Washington before completing his new budget and knowing more about the progress of the bomb. He finally decided to postpone a summit until mid-July and to spurn Churchill's entreaties to meet privately with him on the way.

The flurry of discussions had as its backdrop a growing fear, indeed a hysteria, that the tensions were careening toward an uncontrollable showdown. As the U.N. session continued to erupt in a series of disputes, Vera Micheles Dean of the Foreign Policy Association said in a well-publicized speech: "The most disquieting development at the conference was the tendency to believe that a conflict between the U.S. and Russia is becoming more inevitable." *Time* magazine was far less circumspect. "Last week the possibility of World War III was more and more in the horrified world's public eye," it reported. "That there were those who looked upon war between the democratic, capitalistic U.S. and authoritarian, Communist Russia as 'inevitable' was no longer news."

Perhaps the most gloomy among Washington's inner circle was Under Secretary Grew. After forty years in the State Department, in which he had served as mentor for Bohlen and Kennan and other Soviet specialists trained in Riga, he was about to be shunted aside by Truman's appointment of Byrnes as Secretary. After a sleepless Friday night the erect old-school diplomat came down to his desk at 5 A.M. and put his thoughts to paper. As soon as he knew they would be awake, Grew telephoned Harriman and Bohlen, the two men who had been his allies during the debates of the previous week, and invited them to come hear what he had written.

The result of the war just ending, Grew predicted, "will be merely the transfer of totalitarian dictatorship and power from Germany and Japan to Soviet Russia, which will constitute in future as grave a danger to us as did the Axis." It would be fatal to place any confidence "whatever" in Soviet sincerity, he said. "A future war with Soviet Russia is as certain as anything in this world can be certain."

Bohlen and Harriman shared many of the older man's worries. Despair, however, was not their style. There was a problem to be solved, a balance to be restored, and they were determined it could be accomplished. That very day, in fact, their plan to have Harry Hopkins sent to Moscow was officially approved.

Even though Truman had briefly considered a Hopkins mission before Bohlen and Harriman suggested it, some sensitive shuttle diplomacy by Hopkins's two protégés was necessary to bring the plan to fruition. Hopkins, though still ghastly sick with cancer, was no longer reluctant to undertake the trip when Harriman and Bohlen broached the idea on a visit to his Georgetown bedside. "Although he appeared too ill even to get out of bed and walk across N Street," Robert Sherwood reported, "the mere intimation of a flight to Moscow converted him into the traditional old fire horse at the sound of the alarm."

His only worry, Hopkins said, was that Truman might no longer be in favor. Indeed, the President alternated between liking the idea, resisting it, and conjuring up other alternatives, such as sending Davies. Harriman later recalled that when he first suggested the Hopkins mission to Truman, "he was quite opposed to it." The President finally decided to give the go-ahead on May 19, jotting down on his appointment calendar that the plan had been hatched "after some discussion with Mr. Harriman." He also noted the marching orders he gave. "I told Harry he could use diplomatic language or he could use a baseball bat if he thought that was the proper approach to Mr. Stalin."

Hopkins, the consummate conciliator, clearly preferred the former approach, and said as much the following day when Harriman, Bohlen, and Forrestal came to visit. "He thought it was of vital importance," Forrestal recorded, "that we not be maneuvered into a position where Great Britain had us lined up with them as a bloc against Russia."

• • •

As they looked down on the scorched landscape during their flight from Paris to Moscow, they were painfully reminded of the difficulties that confronted a war-weary world and of the dire consequences of a failure to preserve the new peace. With this in mind, Hopkins and Harriman and Bohlen, each harboring different degrees of hope that Soviet-American cooperation could be restored, came to the baize-covered table in Stalin's cavernous Kremlin meeting room. Their remarkable series of six meetings, extending into early June, represented perhaps the last full-fledged effort to salvage the shaky alliance.

Poland had become a "symbol of our ability to work out problems," Hopkins emphasized to Stalin. Instead of trying to explain to the dictator why a free and independent Poland was central to American ideals, he cast the issue in terms of placating public opinion. As usual, that argument fell on deaf ears. But when Hopkins spoke of Moscow's security interests, Stalin perked up. The Soviets had a right to have "friendly countries" along their border, Hopkins conceded, and Truman knew that as well as Roosevelt. "If that be so," said Stalin, "we can easily come to terms in regard to Poland."

Just as Hopkins had cast the problem in symbolic terms, Stalin's concessions were mainly symbolic. He gave his personal assurances, which Harriman had heard before, that the Soviet system "was not exportable." There were no plans to collectivize other countries, he promised. If the Poles wanted a parliamentary system, so be it. Mikolajczyk and perhaps four other non-Communists, he once again pledged, could become part of a reconstituted Warsaw regime.

With such a solution in mind, Hopkins decided to call in for consultations a man he had only fleetingly met but whose dispatches were gaining renown. Kennan's summons to Spaso House baffled the insecure diplomat. Although he was ever eager to pour out his opinions, he was nonetheless deferential to hierarchy and feared that his intrusion might annoy Harriman. But the ambassador, quite oblivious to such things, seemed not to mind in the least.

Kennan had long since concluded that it was best for the U.S. simply to abandon the whole hopeless business of Poland. "We are never going to have at this juncture anything like a free Poland," he had told Harriman in a long personal cable a few weeks earlier. "If we join with the Russians in cooking up some façade government to mask NKVD control," he went on, "we shall have tacitly given the stamp of approval."

Kennan had just completed another of his periodic outpourings, this one entitled "Russia's International Position at the Close of the War with Germany." Swathed in Kennan's usual florid prose ("Peace, like spring, has finally come to Russia," it began), the essay assailed the belief that collaboration with the Soviets was either desirable or possible. It urged instead "a realistic understanding as to the mutual zones of vital interest."

Hopkins took a copy of Kennan's paper, but did not read it before soliciting his opinion on the Polish settlement that was emerging. Did Kennan think, Hopkins asked, that the U.S. could do any better? No, replied Kennan, he didn't. In that case, did he think that Washington should agree to the terms? Again Kennan said he didn't.

"Then you think it's just sin," Hopkins asked, "and we should be agin it?"

"That's just about right," replied Kennan.

"I respect your opinion," said the elderly envoy, "but I'm not at liberty to accept it."

And so Hopkins proceeded to settle temporarily, if not solve, the Polish problem, that "touchstone" of Soviet-American relations. More than any other issue, it had served to poison the meager reservoir of friendship between the two powerful nations. Harriman's two-year effort to stand firm for democracy and self-determination, albeit a genuine and laudable crusade, had proved to be fruitless, indeed perhaps counterproductive, in the face of Russia's even stronger desire to make secure at long last its vulnerable European frontier.

Stalin's empty pledges of free elections and a role in Warsaw for Mikolajczyk and other non-Communists did not prevent Poland, like the rest of Eastern Europe, from sliding inexorably into the Soviet sphere. The free elections would never take place, and Mikolajczyk would soon flee into exile.

When Hopkins asked Stalin whether Moscow would keep its commitment to enter the war against Japan, Stalin replied testily. "The Soviet Union always honors its word," Pavlov translated. As the conversation was about to continue, Bohlen broke in. "I believe there is a little more, Pavlov," he said. The Russian translator reluctantly mumbled a qualifying phrase Stalin had added: ". . . except in case of extreme necessity."

As usual the meetings were accompanied by Soviet effusiveness. When Hopkins's wife, Louise, who had charmed the Soviet high command, casually expressed interest in taking home some gifts, a truck pulled up to Spaso House the next day carrying precious stones and furs of fox and ermine. Her husband, however, sternly forbade her to accept anything of value; keeping one small Ural stone, she returned the rest.

Harriman had fewer compunctions. During the showing of a newsreel at one of the dinners, the polo-playing diplomat complimented one of the horses on the screen. With a great flourish, Stalin announced that the stallion was his. When the animal arrived at Spaso House shortly thereafter, another was included for Kathleen. The two horses were used by the Harrimans for the remainder of their tenure in Moscow, and they spent their later years prancing the fields of the Harriman estate at Arden.

Neither Kennan nor Bohlen believed that cozying up to world leaders was the way to influence policy. They were professional Foreign Service officers, and in Kennan's case, a bit of an egghead to boot. But Harriman was a businessman. He and his friends—Lovett, McCloy, Acheson, even Hopkins—viewed history as the actions and decisions of great men, rather than an inevitable unfolding of grand forces. And their way of doing things—especially Harriman's—was to deal with those in charge.

The fascination that the Riga alumni had with cultural forces seemed to Harriman somewhat irrelevant. Give him a few minutes in the gilded rooms of the Kremlin, he thought, and the forces of history could be moved. Like many of Harriman's conceits, this one was self-serving, occasionally illusory—and often correct. At the juncture of historic forces are people in rooms making decisions. Harriman made it his business to be in those rooms.

"Harry's visit has been even more successful than I had hoped," he wired the White House, expressing an unwarranted optimism that the coalition government in Warsaw would turn out to be "friendly" to Moscow without ending up totally subservient. Although he had long struggled to make Poland an issue, Harriman now ventured to tutor the President on the need to see the situation from the Soviet perspective. "Stalin is a realist in all of his actions," he explained. "It is difficult for him to understand why we should want to interfere with Soviet policy in a country like Poland, which he considers so important to Russia's security, unless we have some ulterior motive."

The perceived success of the Hopkins mission, however, left unresolved the question of where a sphere-of-influence policy might lead. Optimists, including Stimson, thought that a frank recognition by Washington and Moscow of each other's security interests would permit a new era of global harmony. Pessimists, of which Kennan was the exemplar, felt that it was simply an unavoidable step toward the division of Europe, and indeed much of the world, into two hostile blocs—a course that would require the U.S. to shore up its own sphere and contain that of the enemy.

The American people were, for the moment, surprisingly receptive to the idea of permitting the Soviets latitude in their geographic region. In retrospect, faith that the compromise would lead to an independent Poland and free elections would seem naïve. Stalin would turn out to be less benign, and increased East-West tensions would cause Soviet leaders to feel that they had to control rigidly the countries within their sphere. At the time, however, any solution to the gnawing problem of Poland, even one that would later seem a flimsy defense against eventual Communist domination, was a welcome relief for the vast majority of Americans who sincerely hoped to avoid a confrontation with the Soviets. A State Department survey of public opinion in the wake of the Hopkins mission reported: "There is considerable acceptance of the necessity for establishing a Polish government able to get along with the Soviet Union, even one at least partly subservient to it."

So too, in fact, was Truman. "I don't feel like falling out with Russia," he told a group of editors, "over the fact that they want friendly people around them." Particularly pleasing to the President, now that the difficult hand of Poland was behind him and the prospect of holding a "royal straight flush" lay ahead, was that Stalin had agreed to attend a summit scheduled for mid-July in the Berlin suburb of Potsdam. Just as Harriman tended to view Soviet leaders as wily businessmen, Truman fancied them as fellow machine politicians, Communist counterparts to his Missouri mentor, Boss Tom Pendergast. It was necessary to be tough with them, the President had learned, yet there were moments he thought it still possible to preserve a workable alliance. "I'm not afraid of Russia," he wrote in his diary. "They've always been our friends and I can't see any reason why they shouldn't always be."

Bohlen was far less sanguine. On the way home from Moscow, he held another long discussion with Hopkins, one that echoed his first. The nature of the Soviet system, Bohlen said, precluded the development of normal international relations, even with a country as powerful as the U.S. For the first time, despite the fact that others seemed anxious to regard his mission as an apparent success, Hopkins seemed to agree.

At a stopover in Germany, Bohlen also discussed the situation with Lucius Clay, who had been appointed to oversee the German occupation. The general put forth Stimson's maxim, that to gain the Soviets' trust the U.S. would have to show trust. "I told Clay that within a few months, or certainly within a year, he would become one of the officials in the American government most opposed to the Soviets," Bohlen recalled. "Anyone who started with too many illusions about the Soviets came out totally disillusioned."

CHAPTER 10

LINE DOWN
THE MIDDLE

Splitting Germany
and the atom

John McCloy had just finished a tour of occupied Germany in April of 1945 when he heard of Roosevelt's death and cut short his trip. He had been appalled by the "near anarchy" he saw: entire cities burned out, hordes of hungry children roaming the streets, sporadic outbreaks of epidemics, neither currency nor the rudiments of a distribution system to help restore a subsistence level of commerce. Given his own ties to the country and his wife's heritage, it was understandable that McCloy, a sage man who usually chose his words with great care, told Stimson it was "something that is worse than anything probably that ever happened in the world."

McCloy and Stimson had an appointment to see the President on April 23, but it was abruptly canceled when Truman summoned Stimson and others to solicit their advice about his impending meeting with Molotov. Instead, McCloy sent his thoughts over on paper later that week. By that time he had come up with a historical analogy. "There is complete economic, social and political collapse going on in central Europe, the extent of which is unparalleled in history unless one goes back to the collapse of the Roman Empire," he wrote. After reading the memo, Truman sent for McCloy to hear his report first-hand. The "chaotic conditions," McCloy informed him, might result "in actual starvation on a widespread scale."

Less than a year later, the idea would take hold that Germany and Western Europe must be strengthened in order to provide a bulwark against Soviet expansion. In his April 1945 memo to the President, however, McCloy emphasized cooperation. "We are going to have to work out a practical relationship with the Russians," he said. In his journal, McCloy summarized a talk he had with Stimson at the time: "Our geographical situation with respect to Russia, as well as our position in the world, made it perfectly possible for us to get along without fighting."

But the two Wall Street lawyers did share the view, common after the First World War as well as the Second, that economic instability created fertile territory for the spread of Bolshevism. Rebuilding the industries of Germany was important, Stimson told the President in May, because economic misery in Europe was "likely to be followed by political revolution and Communist infiltration." McCloy recalls that he and Stimson were struck by the reception this argument received. "People sat up and listened when the Soviet threat was mentioned," he later said. It taught him a valuable lesson: One way to assure that a viewpoint gets noticed is to cast it in terms of resisting the spread of Communism.

The debate over how to treat Germany had not yet been framed in East-West terms partly because officials were still thinking that there would be a joint occupation, with the U.S., Britain, and Russia cooperating in the administration of a unified German nation. Until policy makers began to accept the inevitability of the division of Europe and possibly Germany itself into two competing blocs, there was little reason to emphasize fears of Soviet expansionism as a factor in deciding whether to reindustrialize the Western sectors.

• • •

One of the few who did foresee the division of Europe into hostile East and West spheres was George Kennan. Running the embassy in Moscow while Harriman was spreading the gospel of firmness, Kennan peppered the State Department with warnings that the U.S. must dedicate itself to rebuilding Germany and the other areas of Europe under Western control in preparation for the coming competition with the Soviet bloc.

Kennan's views on Germany were somewhat quirky. In his unsolicited comments on some State Department policy proposals, for example, he took strong exception to a seemingly innocuous recommendation for "the establishment of a democratic government." Wrote the die-hard anti-idealist: "The only reasonably respectable tradition of orderly and humane government in Germany is actually that of a strong monarchial government."

More persuasive was Kennan's constant refrain that policy makers must face the likelihood that there would soon be two opposing blocs in Europe. "The idea of a Germany run jointly with the Russians is a chimera," he wrote in one paper. "We have no choice but to lead our section of Germany—the section of which we and the British have accepted responsibility—to a form of independence so prosperous, so secure, so superior, that the East cannot threaten it." At the time this was somewhat of a radical idea. "Admittedly, this is dismemberment," he conceded. But to Kennan it reflected the harsh realities. "Better a dismembered Germany in which the West, at least, can act as a buffer to the forces of totalitarianism than a united Germany which again brings those forces to the North Sea."

Although this outlook would not be adopted by most American officials until the forthcoming summit in Potsdam, there was one world leader whose orotund warnings were sounding quite like Kennan's. "What is to happen about Russia?" Winston Churchill cabled Truman in May. Using for the first time the striking metaphor he would later make famous, the Prime Minister continued: "An iron curtain is drawn down upon their front. We do not know what is going on behind... Meanwhile the attention of our peoples will be occupied in inflicting severities upon Germany, which is ruined and prostrate, and it would be open to the Russians in a very short time to advance if they chose to the waters of the North Sea and Atlantic."

· · ·

For slightly different reasons, Stimson, McCloy, Kennan, and others had come to the same conclusion: Germany (or at least the part under Western control) should be rebuilt. Rather than pastoralizing the country or letting its inhabitants starve, it should become a key part of a revived world trade system and, perhaps, a bulwark against Bolshevik expansion. That way the U.S. would not be forced to foot the bill for the postwar peace. Soviet leaders, supported by many American liberals, had other ideas. They believed that German industries should be dismantled for reparations and used to rebuild the economy of the Soviet Union and other Allies. It was an issue destined to replace Poland as the primary source of Soviet-American friction.

At Yalta, a vague agreement had been reached that a large amount of German equipment and future production would be confiscated by the victors. At the Soviets' insistence, a figure of $20 billion, half of which would go to them, was accepted by the U.S. as "a basis for discussion." But that had been long weeks ago, way back in February, before the problems of Eastern Europe seemed so unsolvable and before Harriman had brought his alarming message from Moscow. Suddenly, the idea of dismantling the mighty factories of the Ruhr and packing half of them off to Russia no longer seemed like such a good idea.

From Moscow, Harriman and Kennan bombarded Washington with reasons to resist Russian demands for reparations from the Western zones of Germany. The U.S., Harriman said in early April, should follow a "policy of taking care of our Western Allies and other areas under our responsibility first, allocating to Russia what may be left."

What particularly upset Harriman was that the Russians, without waiting for any agreement on reparations, "are already busily removing from Germany without compunction anything they find it to their advantage to remove." Kennan, perhaps because he had been drafting Harriman's telegrams, used virtually identical language in his own missives from Moscow after Harriman had headed home to meet the new President.

Truman was easily persuaded. While Harriman was making his rounds in Washington, the President appointed as U.S. negotiator on the reparations issue Edwin Pauley, a conservative oilman and Democratic fund raiser. He was, Truman said, "someone who could be as tough as Molotov." No longer was it the U.S. aim to rebuild the Allied victors at the expense of Germany; now the goal was to stand firm against Soviet demands. Pauley's appointment was evidence, said U.S. News & World Report, "of this country's changing attitude toward Russia."

In Washington, Robert Lovett took over the task of representing the War Department on the committee that was drafting Pauley's instructions. Treasury Secretary Henry Morgenthau, who had been arguing that Germany should be "pastoralized," wanted to begin dismantling German industry as soon as possible. Delaying any such action, Lovett concluded, was the best way to prevent large-scale reparations. Nothing should be done, he argued, until a "complete survey" was made of the German economy and the direction it was likely to take. Only then could it be decided what equipment ought to be removed. It was hard to dispute the logic of such a judicious approach, and even Morgenthau seemed to accept it.

Kennan, slow to realize that his own views were being adopted, expressed "anguish" when informed that Pauley was heading for Moscow in June with a flock of thirty delegates to begin talks. Once again, he sent a personal wire to Harriman. Instead of taking Moscow's demands seriously and trying to quantify a program, Kennan argued the U.S. should face the fact that the Soviets would loot whatever they wanted from their own zone. America and Britain should ship them excess equipment from the Ruhr and other Western areas only in exchange for food and products the Soviets were willing to swap. "In the end it will come down to a simple horse trade," he predicted. "How much are we going to make available to the Russians from our zones, and what price are we going to demand for it?"

Harriman knew there was little danger that Pauley and his cohorts, many of whom were along only for the ride, would start calculating $10 billion worth of equipment to give away. "Pauley's instructions are firm," he cabled from Washington to his anxious counselor. "I have no fears about us giving in." Harriman hardly suspected, however, that Kennan was right in predicting that it would come down to simple horse trading. Virtually every American policy maker still believed that Germany would remain unified and that any economic policy would be imposed by the Allied Control Council on the country as a whole.

With Kathleen Harriman acting as hostess to the large delegation, and her father and Kennan keeping a watchful eye, Pauley and his group held a fruitless series of reparation talks in Moscow in late June and early July. Pauley immediately backed away from the $20 billion total suggested at Yalta and indeed from any fixed figure at all. Instead he insisted in dealing only in percentages: the Soviets could have 55 percent of whatever was taken from Germany. But it would be up to the commanders in each zone, he insisted, to decide what if anything could be removed.

Given the growing American feeling that Germany should be allowed a reasonable standard of living and even some industrial revival, it seemed quite possible that the Soviets would get 55 percent of very little under the U.S. formula. Molotov for once found himself forced to retreat. Some figure must be set, he argued, otherwise the percentages were meaningless. If $10 billion for Russia was too high, he could accept $9 billion, even $8 billion. But Pauley held firm. He would bargain away a percentage point or two, but not set a fixed total. It was an impasse that was left for the Allied leaders to resolve at their summit in the Berlin suburb of Potsdam, if they could.

• • •

By June 17, 1945, after ten bloody weeks of fighting, General Douglas MacArthur's forces had just about won the battle for Okinawa, a small island between Iwo Jima and the Japanese mainland. Some forty-nine thousand American men had been killed or wounded, and four hundred ships had been struck by kamikazes. As he sailed on the Potomac with a handful of cronies that muggy Sunday, Harry Truman was less than enamored with the man he called "Mr. Prima Donna, Brass Hat, Five Star MacArthur." As the President put it in his diary: "He's worse than the Cabots and the Lodges—they at least talked to one another before they told God what to do." What worried Truman more, however, was a decision that could no longer be put off. "I have to decide Japanese strategy," he wrote. "Shall we invade Japan proper or shall we bomb and blockade? That is my hardest decision to date. But I'll make it when I have all the facts."

That same Sunday, after an all-night meeting, J. Robert Oppenheimer finished his final, top-secret "recommendations for the use of nuclear weapons." The decision had been made and reaffirmed, by both the civilians and scientists on the Interim Committee, that Japan would be bombed "at the earliest possible date," without warning and without an attempt to provide a demonstration blast that might cow the warlords into surrender.

In a stuffy room at the Pentagon, Colonel Paul Tibbets, the commander of the 509th Composite Group who had christened his B-29 Superfortress *Enola Gay*, after his mother, was studying maps and aerial photographs. General Curtis LeMay was flying in from Guam, and Tibbets was preparing to show how he could use certain waterways to find his designated target at Hiroshima.

John McCloy was also thinking about the bomb and Japan that Sunday. After arriving back from a weekend with his wife's family in Hastings-on-Hudson, he had been called by Stimson. The Secretary wanted to discuss a meeting the President had scheduled for the next day regarding plans for an invasion of the Japanese mainland.

"We ought to have our heads examined if we don't think of the possibility of bringing the war to a conclusion without the further loss of blood," said McCloy. America was in a position of great military superiority, he added. Now was the time to modify the conditions of unconditional surrender and offer to allow the Japanese to retain their emperor. The message, he added, might also include an explicit warning that the U.S. had developed a devastating new atomic weapon and would use it if the Japanese continued their struggle.

At a meeting at the end of May, the idea of offering to allow the Japanese to keep their emperor had been pressed on Stimson and McCloy by Under Secretary of State Grew, who had served as ambassador to Japan. But the issue of the bomb, which Stimson in his diary that day called "the real feature that would govern the whole situation," had not been raised, partly because Grew was not privy to the full secret. After Grew left, McCloy and Marshall discussed how the bomb might be used. Marshall suggested that the first target should be a naval installation. "If no complete result was derived from the effect of that," McCloy recorded in his notes, "he thought we ought to designate a number of large manufacturing areas from which people would be warned to leave."

There was a vague awareness that the atomic bomb was unique. Stimson, in fact, had told the Interim Committee that he did "not regard it as a new weapon but as a revolutionary change in the relations of man to the universe." Yet in fact, Stimson did regard the bomb primarily as a weapon. Even the scientists were not fully aware of the effects of the radioactivity the device would release, and they certainly did not stress to Stimson or other officials that a mysterious fallout might make it a far more sinister weapon than even gas or chemicals. Truman and his advisers thought, for the most part, that they were faced with a bomb of incredible force—J. Robert Oppenheimer, the wizard of Los Alamos, estimated that it would equal twenty thousand tons of TNT, an explosive power greater than could be carried by two thousand fully loaded conventional B-29 bombers—but not necessarily one that was more morally abhorrent than the massive fire-bombing raids that General LeMay was using to cremate much of Tokyo. As Stimson later noted, there was no reason not to consider the atomic bomb "as legitimate as any other of the deadly explosive weapons of modern war."

Thus the plan to use the bomb against Japan had acquired a momentum of its own. From Truman and Stimson on down, American policy makers considered it a foregone conclusion that it would be wrong, politically and morally, not to use the new device if it could shorten the war and save the lives of American boys. The Interim

Committee, spurred by Byrnes and Oppenheimer, had made a clear determination that this was the case. Nevertheless, top U.S. officials still had a chance to consider the issues McCloy raised with Stimson. Should the Japanese be offered a political solution first? Should they be given advance warning about the new weapon?

When McCloy and Stimson discussed the matter on June 17, the Secretary's primary concern was in finding some way to avoid an invasion of the Japanese mainland. He did, however, tell McCloy that all of the options should be raised at the meeting with the President the next day. Because he was suffering from a migraine, Stimson added, McCloy might have to carry the ball.

Washington was filled with excitement that sunny Monday: Dwight Eisenhower, the returning hero, was greeted by the largest crowds in the city's history as he paraded down Pennsylvania Avenue. Wedged into Truman's afternoon schedule—between lunches and dinners and other ceremonies honoring Eisenhower—was the meeting on Japanese strategy.

Despite his illness, Stimson showed up for work that day. He conferred with McCloy on the bothersome squawk box, and along with Lovett and Marshall they attended a morning reception in the Pentagon courtyard for Eisenhower. The Secretary, however, still wanted McCloy to come to the presidential meeting that afternoon, so McCloy checked with Harry Vaughan at the White House to make sure Stimson could bring him along.

At the White House session, McCloy took a back seat while Truman grilled Stimson, Forrestal, and the Joint Chiefs about plans for a mainland invasion. When Stimson's turn came, he expressed his approval of the strategies, adding only as a vague afterthought that he "still hoped for some fruitful accomplishment through other means."

McCloy was stunned. Stimson had not mentioned any of the options they had talked about the day before. As everyone was gathering his papers, Truman noticed that McCloy seemed to have something on his mind. "McCloy, you didn't express yourself," said the President. "Nobody gets out of this room without standing up and being counted." McCloy glanced over at Stimson. "Say what you feel," the Secretary prompted.

"I do think you've got an alternative," McCloy began. Repeating the conversation of the day before, he outlined terms for a political solution, among them being "that we would permit them to choose their own form of government, including the retention of the Mikado."

"Well, that's what I've been thinking about," said Truman. He asked McCloy to put his thoughts on paper. Added Stimson: "I'm very glad the subject was brought up."

But McCloy had more to say. "I think our moral position would be better if we gave them specific warning of the bomb," he argued. Years later, he recalled the scene: "As soon as I mentioned the word 'bomb'—the atomic bomb—even in that select circle—it was sort of a shock. You did not mention the bomb out loud. It was like mentioning Skull and Bones in polite society at Yale. It just wasn't done."

Neither Stimson, the only Bonesman in the room, nor any of the others was ready to back McCloy. What would happen, he was asked, if the bomb turns out to be a dud? It was a risk worth taking, McCloy insisted. Then he backed down a bit: "If you don't mention the bomb, at least mention in general terms what its capacity is."

Again Truman asked McCloy for a memo on the subject. "We'll explore this," the President promised. Thus began the process that would eventually result, with many crucial revisions, in the Potsdam proclamation to the government of Japan.

•   •   •

During the next two weeks, McCloy, Stimson, Grew, and Forrestal all worked together in formulating a proposal for seeking a solution to the Japanese war along the lines the President had requested. Their focus, however, was not on the atomic bomb. One reason was that McCloy and Stimson, men of extreme discretion, were reluctant to talk much about the secret project, especially in the presence of Grew, who was only the Acting Secretary of State and was due to be replaced by Byrnes. Nor did they feel any great urgency about avoiding the use of the bomb; there was, in their minds, no reason to make that an overriding goal. The primary issue was avoiding an American invasion of the mainland. Thus the core of their proposed declaration was letting the Japanese know they could keep their emperor if they surrendered.

In fact, when the four men met one Tuesday in late June, after McCloy had worked until midnight drafting his memo, the "warning" was still considered something that might be issued after the bomb was dropped. "I took up at once," Stimson wrote in his diary, "the subject of trying to get Japan to surrender by giving her a warning after she had been sufficiently pounded possibly with S-1." The main priority, he said, was to make sure that "every effort is made to shorten the war." The next day the Secretary flew up to his Long Island estate, leaving McCloy behind to draft the proposal.

At the June 18 meeting with the President, McCloy's intention may have been to provoke a discussion of the bomb and the need to warn Japan before it was used. But when others failed to go along, he did not press his case. In fact, even questioning the accepted wisdom in the first place, particularly on moral grounds, was quite rare for him. In any event, McCloy did not make the matter into a crusade or raise it again. Behind the scenes, while Stimson vacationed on Long Island, his loyal assistant began efficiently shaping a consensus without challenging the basic course on which the country was heading.

McCloy sent Stimson a version of the proposed proclamation by courier later in the week, and on Saturday he arrived at Highhold himself. As drafted, the statement proclaimed that the postwar government of Japan "may include a constitutional monarchy under the present dynasty." Yet nowhere in McCloy's proposed "warning," or in the memo to the President that was to accompany it, was there a mention of the atomic bomb. The first test of the weapon was scheduled for mid-July, just over two weeks away, and Colonel Tibbets was already on the island of Tinian with plans for a mission in early August.

Once again, the omission was partly prompted by discretion. Very few people were supposed to know about S-1, so it was difficult to mention it in a document that might be widely read before it was approved or released. Consequently, no one had actually decided on the exact purpose of the proposed proclamation. Was it intended partly as a way to avoid using a fearful new weapon? That seemed to be what McCloy implied two weeks earlier. Or was it simply designed to prevent an invasion? In that case it might be more effective if issued after the bomb was dropped. Because of the understandable premium placed on secrecy, the key issue—whether or not the Japanese should be explicitly warned and given a chance to surrender before the terrifying new forces of the nuclear age were unleashed for the first time— was decided by an Interim Committee but never fully discussed by the country's top policy makers.

The fuzzy relationship between the proclamation and the bomb was evident in a private letter Stimson handed the President along with the draft. "You will note that it is written without specific relation to the employment of any new weapon," he said. "Of course it would have to be revamped to conform to the efficacy of such a weapon if the warning were to be delivered, as would almost certainly be the case, in conjunction with its use." The precise nature of such a "conjunction" Stimson did not explain.

Stimson did, however, raise one particular concern. He had not been invited to Potsdam. Was it because the President was worried about his health? Truman laughed and said yes, but did not immediately extend an invitation. Stimson brooded in his diary that he was faced with "two of the largest and most important problems that I have had since I have been here," namely "the effort to shorten the Japanese war" and "to lay the foundations of a new Germany." The next evening he raised both of these issues with the President again, concluding with another request to go to Potsdam and "bring McCloy with me." With a curt "all right," Truman invited them along.

• • •

Averell Harriman was among the first to arrive in Potsdam for the third and final summit of the Grand Alliance. Once again he had been somewhat anxious about whether he would be invited. "Have assumed the President and you wish me to be present," he wired Stettinius somewhat plaintively in June. By early July, he had had no reply, and Stettinius was no longer the Secretary. Harriman did not know James Byrnes well, nor like what he did know. So he sent a personal cable to Chip Bohlen asking him to straighten things out, noting for good measure that the British ambassador to Moscow had been invited. "I would appreciate an urgent reply," he added. Bohlen wired back the same day that he had checked with Byrnes and, yes, Harriman would be most welcome.

Despite the compromise worked out by Hopkins, there was still a sticky Polish problem Harriman knew had to be resolved. The Soviets had refused to rescind their transfer of a slice of Germany to Poland, the action that had prompted Kennan's anguished cries two months earlier. Moscow thought it had gotten tacit Allied approval during the war to "shift" Poland westward by paring off a portion of that nation for itself and adding a piece of Germany to Poland's western frontier. But by imposing this border change unilaterally, the Soviets had, among other sins, complicated the calculations of German reparations.

Harriman had never seen much sense in the whole idea of reparations, except perhaps as a bargaining chip that could be used with Moscow. The flight to Berlin made him even more skeptical. Peering out over the devastated landscape, he was struck by signs of wholesale Soviet looting. "I decided after seeing the situation for myself," he recalled, "that while there was nothing we could do to stop the Russians from taking whatever they wanted out of their zone, we ought to give them nothing from the Western zones."

When McCloy landed at the Potsdam airfield on Sunday, July 15, Harriman was on hand to meet him. Actually, Harriman was there to greet the President, whose plane was due at about the same time. The two of them waited, along with Soviet Ambassador Andrei Gromyko and a large crowd of spectators, for Truman to arrive.

Among those traveling with the President was Chip Bohlen, who felt somewhat excluded from the inner circle. No one could match Bohlen's grace and charm at a poker table, but he was not invited to the presidential games that dominated the evenings on the heavy cruiser *Augusta*. Harry Vaughan, James K. Vardaman, Matthew Connelly, Charlie Ross: mostly Missourians and backslapping rapscallions, the players were not exactly Bohlen's type, nor he theirs. At Teheran and Yalta, where Bohlen's official duties were mainly supposed to be those of a translator, he had served as a de facto adviser. On the trip to Potsdam, he found that he was now being treated mostly as a mere translator.

The man who caused Bohlen to feel most excluded, at least at first, was Jimmy Byrnes. The new Secretary of State, once a master wielder of patronage and power as a South Carolina senator, had been made a Supreme Court justice by Roosevelt, and later served as virtually an "assistant president" as head of the Office of War Mobilization. But Roosevelt stunned Byrnes in 1944 by passing him over for the Vice-Presidency. The dark horse picked instead had originally promised to nominate Byrnes for the post; when Truman ascended to the Presidency, Byrnes seemed to have trouble shaking the feeling that he should be there instead. Truman also harbored a vague sense that he owed Byrnes something. Not enamored with Stettinius, and concerned that the Constitution made the Secretary of State next in the line of succession, Truman quickly offered the job to Byrnes.

Upon becoming Secretary in July, Byrnes promptly told Bohlen that the department no longer needed a "liaison" to the White House; Byrnes would henceforth handle all dealings with the President. Later, after he had once again become a top policy maker, the amiable Bohlen came to view Byrnes as friendly and "underrated." But others were not so charitable. "Mr. Byrnes is not sensitive or lacking in confidence," wryly noted Acheson, who shared only the latter of these attributes. Acheson promptly decided to resign, and would be dissuaded only when flattered by a promotion.

Harriman, similarly disgruntled, also made plans to leave government. "I didn't like the relationship with Byrnes," recalled the ambassador, who was not used to being subservient to Secretaries. "Byrnes thought Harriman, a liberal, to be prejudiced against him," wrote Herbert Feis, who knew them both, "and Harriman thought Byrnes was set against his admission to the top inner circle." The real problem was that the new Secretary was not solicitous of advice. "He would seldom consult me," Harriman complained.

Stimson, already annoyed by reports from McCloy that Byrnes did not support the proclamation to Japan they had drafted, also felt left out. "He gives me the impression that he is hugging matters in this conference pretty close to his bosom," Stimson wrote in his diary, "and that my assistance, while generally welcome, was strictly limited." Years later, McCloy and Harriman still remembered how they used to sit outside Stimson's villa in Potsdam after Byrnes made it clear the three of them would play little role. "Byrnes threw me out," complained Harriman. Agreed McCloy: "It was rather pathetic."

Delegates to the conference were housed in a lakefront compound of stucco houses that had been the colony of the German film industry. Bohlen and Byrnes lived on the first floor of the President's "Little White House," a yellow three-story manor that once housed a prominent German publisher. Harriman lived in a bungalow down the road, with reparations negotiator Edwin Pauley next door and the "unpretentious" house shared by Stimson and McCloy nearby.

Everyone agreed that, except for the mosquitoes, the accommodations were comfortable. Yet there was something about the atmosphere that bothered the Americans. Berlin was in the part of Germany occupied by the Red Army and, as Bohlen recalled, "most of the security guards were green-hatted Soviet frontier troops with Oriental faces." Stimson was particularly upset with the rigid control they imposed. "The Russians let us know very well it was their zone," he grumbled on his arrival. Their guards tightly patrolled the perimeter of the American compound and, Stimson complained, "we could not walk out of it without being stopped."

The atmosphere within the American area, on the other hand, was collegial and relaxed, in fact even more so than in Washington. The informal interplay began as soon as the American motorcade arrived. Harriman and McCloy discussed the Polish situation over lunch, and later that afternoon sat down with Stimson to talk about the situation in the Far East. Bohlen had an early dinner with the President and two other aides, after which Harriman and Pauley dropped by to talk about the reparations question.

With an opportunity to spend more than two weeks thrashing out the problems of the world, the American delegates, especially those not caught up in the day-to-day operations of the conference, began to formulate a consensus that was to become the foundation for America's role in the postwar world. While Byrnes concentrated, with some success, on bargaining and dealing at Potsdam, McCloy and Stimson and Harriman had time to consider some of the larger questions, including the most important of them all: how to deal with the new atomic bomb.

•   •   •

On Monday morning, while Truman and most of the others awaited Stalin's delayed arrival, McCloy and his War Department colleague Harvey Bundy sat down with Stimson in the garden of their villa to put their thoughts on paper. They began by composing a memo to the President reiterating the need to issue "a warning to Japan." McCloy and Stimson had by then concluded that the proclamation should definitely come before the bomb was used, but they were still murky on whether it should specifically mention the bomb. In fact, they suggested that a second, more explicit proclamation might come later. "If the Japanese persist," they wrote, "the full force of our newer weapons should be brought to bear in the course of which a renewed and even heavier warning... should be delivered."

Even as McCloy and Stimson were writing their memo, a group of scientists and technicians had gathered in a remote desert near Alamogordo, New Mexico, where it was still just before dawn. Suddenly, from the direction of a distant steel tower, a spectral turquoise column of light shot up toward the heavens and mushroomed into a ball of fire, its temperature ten thousand times hotter than the surface of the sun. Even from twenty miles away, the blinding light seemed as bright "as several suns at midday." It could be seen from El Paso to Albuquerque to Sante Fe, and 125 miles away a window shattered.

The scientists, who had predicted the blazing cloud would reach seventeen thousand feet, watched in awe as it burst into the substratosphere at twice that height. Some danced a jig that was, in the words of *New York Times* reporter William Laurence, "like primitive man dancing at one of his fire festivals." Klaus Fuchs, a refugee German physicist, stood off by himself, silent and erect. J. Robert Oppenheimer

thought of a passage from the Bhagavad-Gita referring to the transformation of Vishnu the creator into his avatar of destruction: "I am
become death, the shatterer of worlds." Others simply muttered, "My
God, it works."

"Operated on this morning," said the cryptic message that reached
Stimson's villa that evening. "Diagnosis is not yet complete but results
seem satisfactory and already exceed expectations." McCloy recorded
in his diary: "The Secretary cut a gay caper and rushed off to tell the
President and Jimmy Byrnes about it." The next day brought more
news about the "husky" little boy: "The light in his eyes discernible
from here to Highhold, and I could hear his screams from here to
my farm." Stimson knew what that meant: the blast could be seen for
250 miles and its thunder heard 50 miles away.

News of the atomic test visibly buoyed the President's performance
at the conference, giving him the assured air of a Christian with a
straight flush. After getting the reports from Los Alamos, McCloy
reported, Truman and Churchill "went to the next meeting like little
boys with a big red apple secreted on their person." To McCloy,
however, the situation was filled with what he often called "imponderables." "I hope it does not augur the commencement of the destruction of modern civilization," he wrote in his diary. "In this
atmosphere of destruction and the callousness of men and their leaders,
the whole thing seems ominous."

By the end of the week, a full report from Los Alamos had been
flown to Potsdam by courier. From Washington came a final request:
"Patient progressing rapidly and will be ready for final operation first
good break in August. Complicated preparations for use are proceeding
so fast we should know not later than July 25 if any change in plans."

•   •   •

The midday heat was beginning to subside on Thursday of the first
week of the conference when McCloy, Bundy, and Stimson sat down
to discuss the bomb and the Soviets. Their focus was not on whether
the bomb should be dropped. The Interim Committee had already
decided that the weapon should be used when ready; in the absence
of a specific decision to do otherwise the process had a momentum
of its own. Instead, Stimson focused on the next stage of the drama:
the pressing need for the U.S. and the Soviets to find some way to
control the new atomic monster once the war was over.

Stimson still believed that trust of the Soviets could be a two-way
street. But Harriman's gloomy reports, and the evidence of Russian

repression he was seeing with his own eyes, were beginning to worry him. "While the Russian soldiers and the American soldiers seem to like each other individually when they meet," he wrote in his diary, "the people who have to deal with the Russian officials feel differently."

The basic obstacle to East-West cooperation on atomic weapons, as Stimson saw it, was "that a nation whose system rests on free speech and all the elements of freedom, as does ours, cannot be sure of getting on permanently with a nation where speech is strictly controlled and where the government uses the iron hand of the secret police." It would be impossible, Stimson felt, to share control of the atom with a country that relied on repressive police tactics. But America's "head-start" in atomic research, when combined with the Kremlin's "desire to participate," might be used as a lever to force basic changes in the repressive nature of Russian society.

McCloy tended to think Stimson was being a bit naïve. His own assessment was that it would be tough to get along with the Russians; their outlook was very different from that of Americans. But he was not sure that abstract worries about freedom in the U.S.S.R. really went to the heart of the matter. "Personally," he noted, "I think they have their political religion and we have ours."

Both men agreed, however, that it was essential to achieve a more stable relationship with Russia. "We must not accept the present situation as permanent," they wrote in their memo that evening, "for the result will then almost inevitably be a new war." With their concern for secrecy, they were circumspect about mentioning the bomb. "The foregoing has a vital bearing upon the control of the vast and revolutionary discovery of ————."

The next afternoon, Stimson and McCloy invited Harriman to come by to read their latest paper. They had discussed the same topic many times before, most recently in May, when Harriman had insisted that there was little that could be done to liberalize the internal Soviet system. Once again he made the argument. They had put their finger on the heart of the problem, the ambassador agreed, but he did not think that dangling the prospect of a nuclear partnership in front of the Soviets would cause them to alter their disregard for freedom. The Russians are different from us, said Harriman, and not merely because they have less money or freedom.

Harriman had made a point of seeing Stalin upon his arrival. It must be gratifying, Harriman politely noted, to be in Berlin after four bloody years of battle. The dictator hesitated for a moment, thought of other Russian imperialists who had pushed even farther west, and replied: "Czar Alexander got to Paris." In retelling the story, Harriman commented: "It didn't take much of a clairvoyant to guess what was in his mind."

A workable relationship might be forged, Harriman told Stimson, but it would have to come through firmness rather than a dreamy faith in reciprocated trust. "He has been in Russia now for nearly four years and has grown evidently depressed and troubled by the situation," Stimson wrote in his diary. "I talked with him a long time regarding the matter and, in view of his intelligence and capacity, such a despairing view from him troubled me a great deal."

When they continued their discussion early the next week, Harriman mentioned to Stimson and McCloy "the increasing cheerfulness" caused by the reports of the successful atomic test. Yet the Soviets were being no more malleable. Not only were they insisting on having their way on the Polish border dispute and the recognition of their subservient governments in Eastern Europe, they were also pressing for bases in Turkey. McCloy, with his avid interest in history, fully grasped the strategic threat posed by such a demand, and he was determined to see it opposed.

When Stimson took his memo on atomic control to Truman, he found him generally supportive. Yet by then the President was enjoying his powerful new wild card. Stalin was making increased demands. Truman, Stimson reported, "told me that the U.S. was standing firm and he was apparently relying greatly upon the information as to S-1."

McCloy and Stimson felt quite strongly that Truman should tell Stalin about the bomb before it was used. He was, after all, ostensibly an ally. Taking him by surprise would scuttle any chance of future atomic cooperation. The Interim Committee, after much to and fro, had also recommended such a course.

Truman agreed. But his approach was resolutely casual. He was determined to downplay the significance of the information and avoid being forced into yielding any details. On July 24, Truman strolled over to Stalin at the end of the day's session. Bohlen, who ordinarily followed at his side to translate, was ordered to keep his distance and leave the job to Pavlov. "He did not want to indicate that there was anything particularly momentous," Bohlen recalls.

The U.S. had developed "a new weapon of unusual destructive force," said Truman, avoiding mention of the atom. Bohlen carefully watched Stalin's face from across the room. As poker players he and the President marveled at the Russian's ability to match the offhand manner. Bohlen was in fact unsure whether Stalin fully understood what Truman was telling him. "All he said," Truman later reported, "was that he was glad to hear it and hoped we would make good use of it against the Japanese."

It was not simply the old Bolshevik's stony style that allowed him to seem so complacent. Unbeknownst to the Americans, Klaus Fuchs, the physicist who watched in solitary silence the Alamogordo test, had seven times fed detailed information about the workings of the device to Moscow. The fervent dedication to secrecy of McCloy and Stimson, which did so much to prevent a full consideration on whether and how the bomb should be used, had done nothing to keep the Soviets in the dark.

Nor did Fuchs's betrayal augur well for the hope that American willingness to share control of the atom might encourage the Soviets to be more open and cooperative. As Marshal Georgi Zhukov, the Soviet commander, would later reveal in his memoirs, Stalin that day sent a telegram back to Moscow ordering those working on the weapon in Russia to speed up their efforts.

•   •   •

Wandering through the ravaged streets of Berlin, McCloy was faced by the enormity of the reconstruction challenge. Hitler's box at the old Olympic stadium, where as a driven young lawyer McCloy had sat with his wife, Ellen, during the Black Tom negotiations, was torn by a bomb blast. The streets were filled with barefoot survivors trudging aimlessly, women sorting out piles of rubble, pale men gathering to exchange meager goods. During one ride he passed a dead horse on the road. On the way back, women and children were pulling it apart bit by bit with their bare hands. "It is all a very depressing sight and gives evidence of the crazy character of man," he wrote of Berlin. "The future for these people is nothing less than terrible and one continually is sympathizing with them."

Along with an American general, McCloy convinced a Russian sentry guarding Hitler's bunker near the chancellery to let them take an eerie tour. Using flashlights, they made their way past gas masks and oxygen tanks to Hitler's study and Eva Braun's "spectacular" bedroom. Two military policemen, acting on orders of the general, took a chair from Braun's room and presented it to McCloy. "I feel as if I were very much of a looter," he wrote in his diary. But since the general took two others, McCloy rationalized, "I felt less guilty."

On one occasion, McCloy watched as a young German fräulein

tried to sell some cloth "to a buxom Russian girl soldier." Neither could understand the other, but it was clear that the Russian wanted the material and, noted McCloy, "the German girl did not know just how stiff to go with her bargaining for fear the Russian would take it from her if she became vexed."

The U.S., McCloy came to feel, must be more energetic in touting the strength of its own ideals. "The Russians," he wrote in his diary, "are actually posing as 'democrats' in spite of practicing totalitarianism in its most complete form (and getting away with it even in our own press!)." Countering Communism need not require confrontation; the U.S. could prevail by example, by embarking on an aggressive policy of involvement in the international economy. "We help create the vacuums in which the Russian methods best prevail," he noted, "by failing to install our own system."

McCloy's recommendations for rebuilding Germany were mainly motivated, at least at first, by a desire to help that country for its own sake. He and Stimson had begun to realize, however, that their ideas got more attention if they were related to the goal of resisting Soviet expansionism. Increasingly, the ideas that would come to fruition in the Marshall Plan two years later were being cast in terms of the strategic interests of the Western world.

On their first day at Potsdam, McCloy helped Stimson draft a memo arguing that the destruction of German industry could produce an "infection which might well destroy all hope we have of encouraging democratic thinking and practices in Europe." A week later, they urged that "a completely coordinated plan be adopted for the economic rehabilitation of Europe as a whole." Distressed conditions, they emphasized, would only serve to spark revolution. On the other hand, "an economically stable Europe, with the impetus it can give to free ideas, is one of the greatest assurances of security and peace we can hope to obtain."

This outlook, of course, made McCloy and Stimson ardent opponents of conceding on the reparations issue. "The Russian policy on booty in eastern Germany," they declared, "is rather Oriental. It is bound to force us to preserve the economy in western Germany in close cooperation with the British." At a dinner he and General Clay had with the President, McCloy raised the idea that Russian actions might force Britain and America to pursue a separate course in their own zones. The argument was not new to Truman. Harriman and Pauley were also pressing it, and even more forcefully.

The morning after Stimson and McCloy finished their second paper on Germany, Byrnes went to see Molotov, taking only Bohlen with him. Bohlen marveled at the former senator's cloakroom tactics. The reparations issue seemed to be inextricably tangled with the Polish border question, Byrnes told the Soviet Foreign Minister. If the Soviets did not want to back down on Poland, he suggested, perhaps the best solution was simply to let each side handle reparations in its own zone separately.

Throughout the next week, Molotov kept pressing for some set figure for manufacturing equipment, especially from the industrialized Ruhr region. But Byrnes said no. The Western commanders would decide on their own what equipment could be spared in their areas, and the Soviets would get a percentage. If they wanted more, they could work out a trade for agricultural products from their sector.

By the end of the conference, Byrnes had tied things together into a neat package plan that would have done credit to the wiliest majority leader. The U.S. was willing to concede the Polish border issue. As for the Soviet desire to have their friendly regimes in Eastern Europe recognized, which the British were strongly resisting, Byrnes said (according to Bohlen's minutes) "a compromise between his British and Soviet friends" could be arranged. For its part, Moscow would have to accept the U.S. plan on reparations. All three elements came as a package; the Soviets could take it or leave it. The Americans were ready to go home. With little alternative, Stalin accepted the deal.

The package deal at Potsdam transformed the contours of the postwar world far more than the participants imagined at the time. When the Allied armies had arrived in Berlin less than three months earlier there was hope that a joint control of a unified Germany would be the cornerstone of an enduring peace. The decision to divide Germany into sectors for the purpose of reparations, however, marked the first step toward the division of that country on other related economic issues.

The Western Allies would embark on a program to rebuild their sectors, and the Soviets would be unwilling or unable to work out even the limited arrangements agreed to at Potsdam for the exchange of agricultural products for industrial reparations. In addition, the Kremlin would insist, as it had with Poland, on complete domination of the areas under its control. Almost inexorably, Europe was being divided into hostile rather than cooperative blocs. And as a result, the U.S. would find itself faced with a far-reaching new commitment to rebuild and protect what had become—intentionally or not—part of its new global sphere.

McCloy, like most Americans, had originally assumed that Germany would be treated as a unified nation. But he soon began to agree with the de facto partition. "This situation," he concluded, "is better than the constant distrust and difficulty we would have with the Russians over their being in our zones." He knew full well the implications. Upon hearing of the final outcome, he wrote in his journal: "We are drifting toward a line down the middle of Germany."

The inability of any of the statesmen to find an alternative to this division depressed McCloy. "In the discussion there was no clear evidence of an outstanding mind," he complained. He shared his despair with Harriman and Bohlen, who visited his villa on one of the last evenings of the conference. Together they watched *Devotion*, a movie about the Brontë sisters, and discussed the failure to reach any lasting understandings. Before leaving on an inspection tour of Frankfurt and Munich, McCloy recorded his bitter feelings about Potsdam. "The misery of the place and the conflict between the East and the West," he wrote, "hangs over you all the time."

Harriman confided his own fears to Forrestal, who had arrived uninvited just before the conference closed. "Averell was very gloomy about the influx of Russia into Europe," Forrestal wrote in his diary. "He said the greatest crime of Hitler was that his actions had resulted in opening the gates of Eastern Europe to Asia." The intense Navy Secretary tended to overdramatize reports of problems, particularly when they concerned Russia. Even allowing for that, Harriman's mood was as dark as it had ever been.

Bohlen too was abandoning his vestiges of Roosevelt optimism. Flying home with his friend and fellow Soviet expert Llewellyn ("Tommy") Thompson, who had helped with the translating duties at Potsdam, he discussed whether the bomb would help make Moscow more compliant. "It seemed obvious to us that wherever the Soviet armies were, the Soviet system, with its highly structured authoritarian control, would be imposed," Bohlen recalled. "We recognized the fact that the Soviet Union would not respond to anything except measures endangering the country."

Only Stimson seemed compelled to hope for an improvement. The day before leaving Germany, he had his first private meeting with Stalin. Their two nations "had no reason for dispute," Stimson said. "Their natural objectives were the same." Stalin, as might be expected, agreed. Stimson was no more complacent about Soviet evils than his younger colleagues. In fact, he was perhaps the most genuinely concerned, in a deep moral way, about the clear differences between the

Soviet and American systems. But in his mind there was a critical new factor that loomed larger than all of the ideological differences and border disputes, one that by its very nature should serve to insure that the two countries would henceforth find no reason for dispute.

• • •

The formal order to proceed with plans to drop the atomic bomb was approved by Stimson early on the morning of July 25, the day he left the conference. There were no agonized discussions of the issue among the President and his policy makers at Potsdam, nor was there even a single final high-level decision. There was merely the lack of any decision to do otherwise. As Stimson later explained: "No effort was made, and none was seriously considered, to achieve surrender merely in order not to have to use the bomb."

In retrospect, at least, it is clear that there were alternatives. Back in Washington, Lovett was preparing a conventional strategy he believed could end the war. Although he knew about the atomic bomb, he was not involved in deciding whether it should be used. Nor did he think it all that important. In his assessment, which he prepared for Marshall in late June, an invasion could be avoided by a combination of "bombardment and blockade." His idea was to "bomb the daylights out of the Japanese homeland" and use planes to drop mines that would block shipping routes. This would "nail them down until they sued for peace."

In addition, a prompt declaration of war by Moscow would likely have hastened a Japanese surrender and precluded the need for dropping the bomb. By the time of the Potsdam Conference, moderate members of the Japanese Cabinet were anxiously looking for an honorable way to end the fighting, as the Americans knew from intercepted cables, and were asking the Soviets to act as mediators.

Soviet leaders had repeatedly reaffirmed their pledge made at Yalta to send troops into Manchuria and declare war on Japan. President Truman proclaimed, both publicly and in his letters to his wife, that securing this Soviet assistance was his primary goal at Potsdam. When Stalin at Potsdam once again affirmed that the Red Army would attack by mid-August, Truman jotted in his diary: "Fini Japs when that comes about."

But the bitter disputes over occupied Europe, along with Moscow's clear designs in the Far East, made another military partnership with Russia seem less and less attractive to the U.S. Now that it was clear that Germany was being inevitably divided, with the Soviet sectors competing rather than cooperating with the Western ones, the prospect of a joint occupation of Japan seemed untenable. As the situation in Poland made clear, any area where the Red Army marched would be difficult to remove from the clutches of the Kremlin.

The final results from Alamogordo served to lessen U.S. eagerness for Soviet support even further. "Neither the President nor I," Byrnes wrote in his memoirs, "was anxious to have them enter the war after we learned of this successful test." Stimson seemed to agree. "The news from Alamogordo," he later wrote, "made it clear to the Americans that further diplomatic efforts to bring the Russians into the Pacific war were largely pointless." He and McCloy discussed the issue with Marshall at their villa one evening. "Marshall felt," Stimson recorded in his diary, "that now with our new weapon we would not need the assistance of the Soviets to conquer Japan." Bohlen later added his own unsolicited opinion. "We should not put ourselves in the position of the suppliant begging the Russians for help."

As the conference was ending, Molotov asked for "a formal request to the Soviet government for its entry into the war." Truman demurred. Finally, the U.S. produced a vague letter citing Soviet obligations under the United Nations Charter, which had not yet been ratified. At Harriman's insistence the U.S. and Nationalist China held firm in the negotiations over the final disputed details regarding concessions made at Yalta for Soviet support.

Instead of viewing Soviet entry into the war as a way to avoid the need to use the atomic bomb, American leaders seemed to view the bomb as a way to avoid the need for such Soviet assistance. Their reluctance to have the Soviets help finish off Japan was stronger than their reluctance to use the bomb.

The day after the order was given to proceed with final plans for using the bomb, Truman issued the proclamation to Japan that Stimson and McCloy had worked on for more than a month. But against their advice, the President agreed with the Joint Chiefs of Staff that the direct reference to retaining the emperor should be dropped, so as not to show any signs of weakness.

More importantly, nothing was added to make clear that the ultimatum was a warning about the impending use of an atomic bomb. Once again, the issue was never fully discussed by top officials after the Interim Committee had made its recommendation in June. The Japanese militarists, Stimson and others felt, would be contemptuous of any warnings about a mysterious new atomic force they presumably knew nothing about unless a convincing demonstration of the weapon could be arranged; the scientific advisers to the Interim Committee, however, had reluctantly concluded that they could come up with no method of staging such a public demonstration, other than on a real target, that would persuasively show its full force. Besides, it might turn out to be a dud, thus encouraging the Japanese to fight even more fiercely.

An explicit warning, with or without a demonstration, would also dissipate one of the most potent attributes of the bomb, its shock value. To extract a surrender from the Japanese, Stimson said, "there must be administered a tremendous shock." General Marshall, he added, "was emphatic in his insistence on the shock value of the new weapon." Those who suggested that the U.S. would be in a better moral position if it warned the residents of the target city about the atomic force were rebuffed by military arguments. As one general asked a worried scientist: Would you like to pilot the B-29 after such a warning was given? The Japanese would no doubt go all out to down the plane, and they might also bring large numbers of American prisoners into the potential target areas.

Consequently, the only vague clue in the Potsdam proclamation about the atomic bomb was a reference to "immeasurably greater" powers and a concluding sentence that "the alternative for Japan is prompt and utter destruction." This was hardly an explicit warning. Indeed, even Dean Acheson did not know what it referred to. Back at the State Department in Washington, he and Archibald MacLeish, adopting what was considered the "liberal" line, were fighting a rearguard action against the proclamation. In a rare concession, Acheson later wrote that he had been "quite wrong" in opposing it, saying he had done so because he did not know that it was supposed to warn of America's atomic might. "This was not referred to," he wrote. "Neither I nor the rest of the world knew what the authors of the proclamation were talking about."

Harriman likewise later noted that the ultimatum was at best obscure. "There was reason to doubt that the Japanese understood the awful alternative," he wrote. "The hint of destructive powers 'immeasurably greater' than those which had leveled Germany may have been overly subtle."

Neither McCloy nor Stimson, however, argued for a more explicit warning. McCloy, in fact, noted that he was happy with the final document, calling it "a real accomplishment" for the War Department. Even after the bombs were dropped, McCloy would have no real doubts about the wording. Quite the contrary: In his diary he would credit the document—once vaguely conceived as a "warning" about a powerful new weapon—with helping persuade Japan to surrender so quickly. "The bomb, of course, played a large part," he would add, "but it was part of all the planning, and it all tied in."

Faced with an ultimatum that mentioned neither emperor nor atom, the Japanese government said it would *"mokusatsu"* it, which roughly translated meant "treat with silent contempt." Despite the peace feelers that the emperor had gladly authorized at the urging of moderates in his government, the militarists still seemed to be firmly in control, and more than two million soldiers were being deployed for a last-ditch defense of the homeland. On Tinian that day, a three-hundred-pound lead cylinder with a core of enriched uranium was transferred to the headquarters of Colonel Paul Tibbets's 509th Composite Group.

Some revisionist historians (as well as official Soviet ones) have gone so far as to say that American leaders were not only willing to use the atomic bomb rather than rely on Soviet help, but in fact were anxious to drop it as a way to cow the Soviets into being more compliant on Eastern Europe and other issues. Thus there was no desire to have the Japanese surrender and deprive the U.S. of the opportunity to demonstrate its fearsome new military and diplomatic weapon.

That interpretation seems, at best, to be farfetched. In truth, the American motives were less sinister, though hardly more edifying. Creating the bomb had been a difficult and costly scientific miracle. It offered the chance of saving lives, both American and Japanese, and ending the grotesque fire bombings. It would likely spare a gruesome invasion of the Japanese mainland. It would avoid the need for a new military alliance with the Soviets. A sudden decision to forsake the new $2 billion weapon would be difficult to justify politically, and perhaps even morally. How would the President be able to explain such a decision to the families of the boys who would have subsequently died, be it forty thousand of them or a million? To the top U.S. officials at Potsdam, there seemed to be no compelling reason to make avoiding the use of the bomb a primary goal of American policy. "I regarded the bomb as a military weapon," Truman wrote in his memoirs, "and never had any doubt that it should be used."

Even McCloy and Stimson, who at one point had worried about the historic impact of unleashing such a new force, simply felt no overriding need to re-examine the long series of decisions that had culminated with the order to use the bomb. The process had a momentum of its own, and no one felt compelled to step back at the last minute and reconsider the imponderables, to wonder about the new age that would be unleashed. As Stimson explained in an article a year and a half later: "No man, in our position and subject to our responsibilities, holding in his hands a weapon of such possibilities for [ending the war] and saving those lives, could have failed to use it and afterwards looked his countrymen in the face."

CHAPTER 11

*Acheson and Baruch in
Lafayette Park*

THE BLINDING
DAWN

Diplomacy in
an atomic age

The heavily laden B-29 Superfortress had been lumbering toward Japan for almost five hours when the voice of its captain, Colonel Paul Tibbets, came over the intercom. "We are carrying the world's first atomic bomb," he said. The copilot, Robert Lewis, gave a low whistle. Several crew members gasped. They had been briefed on the appalling power of the weapon they carried, but this was the first time that many on board had heard the word "atomic" used. It was just after 8 A.M. Japanese time on August 6, 1945, when Tibbets gave his orders: "Put on your goggles."

And then there was light, a flash so bright that for a moment it suffused the plane. The tail gunner peered out. It looked like a "ring around some distant planet had detached itself and was coming up toward us," he said into his recorder. "Target visually bombed with good results," Tibbets radioed back to base. Copilot Lewis was far less restrained. "Look at that! Look at that!" he shouted, pounding Tibbets on the shoulders. "My God, look at that sonofabitch go!" But when he turned to his logbook to record what they had wrought, Lewis could think of nothing more original than the words gasped by the scientists at Alamogordo. "My God," he wrote. "What have we done?"

At the Pentagon, there was a discussion about whether the press release announcing the attack should claim that Hiroshima had been completely destroyed. Robert Lovett, who as Assistant Secretary of War for Air was the civilian in charge of making the decision, counseled caution. He reminded the generals that they had more than once claimed the destruction of Berlin. "It becomes rather embarrassing after about the third time," he noted dryly. What they wrote nevertheless quickly caught the attention of reporters. "It is an atomic bomb," the statement said. "It is a harnessing of the basic power of the universe."

In Rome, a general asked upon hearing the news, "Is this all it's cracked up to be?" "Yes," replied John McCloy, who was making an inspection tour on his way back from Potsdam. "It's bigger than anything you've ever thought about." In Washington that night, Dean Acheson wrote a letter to one of his daughters. "The news of the atomic bomb is the most frightening yet," he said. "If we can't work out some organization of great powers, we shall be gone geese for the fair."

Slowly, as if feeling their way in a blinding light, people tried to understand what it all meant. As Stimson soberly proclaimed: "The world is changed and it is time for sober thought."

"Yesterday another chapter in human history opened," wrote Hanson Baldwin in *The New York Times*, "a chapter in which the weird, the strange, the horrible becomes the trite and the obvious." In its next issue, *Time* magazine introduced a new section, "The Atomic Age." A writer named James Agee was called upon to compile the cover story. He wrote:

In what they said and did, men were still, as in the aftershock of a great wound, bemused and only semi-articulate, whether they were soldiers or scientists, or great statesmen, or the simplest of men. But in the dark depths of their minds and hearts, huge forms moved and silently arrayed themselves: Titans, arranging out of the chaos an age in which victory was already only the shout of a child in the street. With the controlled splitting of the atom, humanity, already profoundly perplexed and disunified, was brought inescapably into a new age in which all thoughts and things were split—and far from controlled. . . .

The bomb rendered all decisions made so far, at Yalta and at Potsdam, mere trivial dams across tributary rivulets. When the bomb split open the universe and revealed the prospect of the infinitely extraordinary, it also revealed the oldest, simplest, commonest, most neglected and most important of facts: that each man is eternally and above all else responsible for his own soul . . .

The last great convulsion brought steam and electricity, and with them an age of confusion and mounting war. A dim folk memory had preserved the story of a greater advance: the winged hound of Zeus tearing from Prometheus' liver the price of fire. Was the world ready for the new step forward? It was never ready. It was, in fact, still fumbling for the answers to the age of steam and electricity.

Man had been tossed into the vestibule of another millennium. It was wonderful to think of what the Atomic Age might be, if man was strong and honest. But at first it was a strange place, full of weird symbols and the smell of death.

• • •

On August 9, the day that America's second and sole remaining atomic weapon was dropped on Nagasaki, Stalin summoned Harriman to the Kremlin. Events were moving quickly. Japan might surrender at any moment, and Stalin wanted to get his oar in before that happened. But the Chinese, under Harriman's tutelage, had been dragging their feet in the talks with Soviet leaders since the end of the Potsdam Conference. Details had still not been worked out about the precise concessions Moscow thought it would get in China for joining the fighting.

The Soviets, unwilling to wait any longer, had declared war, Stalin told Harriman. Its troops at that moment were moving into Japanese-occupied Manchuria. This was not, of course, what Harriman wanted to hear, but he had to feign at least a semblance of happiness that the U.S. and the U.S.S.R. were once again allied against a common enemy.

Stalin also had another subject on his mind, but he was careful not to appear overly concerned about it. "He showed great interest in the atomic bomb," Harriman reported, "and said that it could mean the end of war and aggression but that the secret would have to be well kept." As Kathleen, still serving as her father's hostess in Moscow, wrote to her sister: "Ave's just returned with the news that Russia is at war with Japan. I wonder how many people will attribute it to the atomic bomb."

When Japan offered to surrender the following night, Harriman was called back to the Kremlin by Molotov to discuss the proposed terms. The only concession the smoldering nation requested was the right to keep its emperor. The Soviets, Molotov said, were skeptical. Their troops were continuing their advance in Manchuria, and there was no reason to settle for less than complete capitulation.

After midnight, while the discussion was still under way, Kennan burst in with a message. Washington wanted to accept the Japanese surrender offer immediately, he exclaimed, and sought Moscow's concurrence. When Molotov promised that his government would have a reply ready the following day, Harriman declared that would be too late. A decision must be reached before the night was over.

After two hours of waiting at Spaso House, Harriman was called back to the Kremlin for a predawn conference with Molotov. The Soviets would join in accepting the surrender. But the message he brought from Stalin had a second sentence. The Allies, it said, should jointly "reach an agreement" on which commander or commanders should control the occupation.

Harriman was incensed. Russia had been fighting for all of two days, he thought to himself, and there was no question that General MacArthur would be the Supreme Commander. Even if the Soviets would accept this choice, it was a decision in which they should have no say. Although he lacked any instructions from Washington, he knew what the response would, or should, be. "I reject it in the name of my government," the ambassador solemnly decreed. After an hour, Molotov telephoned back to say that Stalin had agreed to withdraw the request for a joint say in who should command the occupation.

Years later, McCloy would praise Harriman for taking the matter in his own hands. It was a good thing he had decided to be firm without consulting Washington, McCloy confided, because the U.S. was so keen to see the war ended it would have accepted almost anything the Soviets requested. Harriman later recalled he had been adamant about rejecting the Soviet demand "because I knew that it would lead to the Russians having a major say in the future of Japan."

When the final announcement of V-J Day reached Spaso House a few nights later, a raucous reception was under way for General Eisenhower. "After that," wrote Kathleen, "we had a hard time getting rid of some of our drunker Soviet guests."

"I took a great shine to Marshal Zhukov," Kathleen added in describing the affair to her sister. Eisenhower's visit had produced a massive outpouring of public affection, which impressed Harriman as genuine. When Eisenhower and Zhukov, the two great Allied commanders, were introduced at a soccer game, the cheers "surpassed anything I had ever heard," Harriman reported. Eisenhower was a living symbol of Soviet-American cooperation, and Harriman sensed a fervent yearning, among the people if not their leaders, for it to continue.

The spirit infected Eisenhower, who assured Harriman that his friend Zhukov, who called him "Ike," would succeed Stalin and usher in a new era of friendly relations. He and Zhukov had linked arms in repeated toasts to peace, Eisenhower explained. Alas, the ambassador argued, such hopes were "unrealistic." Military leaders, Harriman had discovered, were the last to realize that the era of wartime cooperation was over. The greater the hopes, he knew, the greater would be the eventual disillusionment. "Like General Marshall," he later wrote, "Eisenhower was slow to understand the crucial importance of the Communist Party in setting Soviet policy."

•   •   •

On August 12, the very morning that Stimson arrived at the Ausable Club, he began phoning his assistant back in Washington to talk about atomic control. The doctors had ordered the old colonel to take an unbroken rest, so he had headed up to the private retreat in the Adirondacks where both he and McCloy owned summer cabins. Yet he could not take his mind off the bomb. Each day he would call McCloy to talk about it, to say he had been rethinking his views on the Soviets. Russia's totalitarian system still repulsed him, Stimson admitted. But he had begun to agree with McCloy: working with the Kremlin to control atomic weapons must take precedence over any dreams of forcing that regime to liberalize its rigidly repressed society.

Finally, McCloy flew up to the Ausable Club to help write a recommendation for controlling the bomb. They both believed strongly that Washington should approach Moscow with an offer to share scientific knowledge as a first step. But the news that McCloy brought to the mountain bungalow was dispiriting. Byrnes was ready to leave for London to meet Molotov and other Allied Foreign Ministers at their first postwar conference and, McCloy lamented, "wished to have the implied threat of the bomb in his pocket."

During the war, McCloy made a habit of working seven days a week, many times past midnight. Now he felt he deserved a vacation and hoped to spend some time in the Adirondacks fishing with his wife and son. But he found it hard to have a peaceful holiday. Ellen slipped on some rocks and badly wrenched her leg. Moreover, Stimson was anxious to finish their memo before Byrnes left for London. They polished it off during the week before Labor Day, but Stimson's sense of urgency prevented McCloy from spending the long weekend with his family. He was dispatched back to Washington to explain the plan to Byrnes and inform him that Stimson planned to propose it directly to the President.

When he arrived in the Secretary of State's office that Sunday morning, McCloy emphasized that the proposals for atomic control he had worked out with Stimson at the Ausable Club would not mean disclosing any technological procedures to the Soviets. But his worst fears about Byrnes were confirmed. The Secretary of State was still adamantly opposed to seeking any form of atomic cooperation. The Russians were "only sensitive to power," Byrnes explained, and they were especially "cognizant of the power of this bomb." McCloy noted in his diary: "With it in his hip pocket, he felt he was in a far better position to come back with tangible accomplishments."

When Stimson got back from the Adirondacks that day, he cornered Byrnes in a White House corridor and discovered McCloy's pessimism was justified. As Byrnes prepared to sail for his showdown with Molotov in London, carrying his nuclear bludgeon, a disheartened Stimson submitted his resignation. In reluctantly accepting it, Truman had one request: that the Secretary stay on for another two weeks so that he could present to the Cabinet his ideas on the postwar atomic age.

Over the next week, McCloy worked late into the nights fleshing out the Ausable Club paper into the first formal proposal for a Soviet-American atomic arms control "covenant." For more than forty fruitless years, this quest would be pursued. The core of the recommendation, which Stimson signed and took to the White House on September 12, was that the U.S. should approach the Soviet Union with a plan "to control and limit the use of the atomic bomb." Washington would pledge to "stop work" on atomic weapons and "impound what bombs we now have." The offer ought to be made directly to the Soviets, not through the U.N. "Action of any international group of nations," they wrote, "would not be taken seriously by the Soviets."

The alternatives were ominous. "Unless the Soviets are voluntarily invited into the partnership," they warned, "a secret armament race of a rather desperate character" would ensue. The bomb "virtually dominated" other diplomatic issues. "If we fail to approach them now and merely continue to negotiate with them, having this weapon rather ostentatiously on our hip, their suspicions and their distrust of our purposes and motives will increase." A covenant for control, on the other hand, would be a "vitally important step in the history of the world." And thus, the seeds of nuclear arms control were planted by McCloy and Stimson even before the race began.

The rationale behind this approach, and indeed its philosophic foundation, was contained in a sentence at the heart of the long memo. There, once again, Stimson quoted his favorite Bonesman maxim. "The chief lesson I have learned in a long life," he said, "is that the only way you can make a man trustworthy is to trust him."

After Stimson explained the paper paragraph by paragraph, the President wholeheartedly concurred. "We must take Russia into our confidence," he said. Truman also raised this radical proposal at the next Cabinet luncheon, which was intended as an informal farewell for the departing Secretary, and announced that he would make it the sole topic on the agenda for the next Cabinet meeting. Would Stimson stay on for a few more days, Truman asked, to give the Cabinet one last benefit of his wisdom? "I will be there," Stimson replied, "if I can walk on my own two feet."

• • •

Friday, September 21, was a busy day at the Pentagon. It was Stimson's seventy-eighth birthday, and wherever he went a song and a cake seemed to follow. It was also his last day in office, and his plane was at the airport waiting to make the last trip to Highhold. But most importantly, that Friday was the day of the special Cabinet meeting, the one that Truman had dedicated to a single topic, the aging warrior's final and most critical crusade.

When the President called on him that afternoon, Stimson spoke eloquently and off the cuff. The only way to avoid a devastating arms race, he argued, was a direct offer to the Soviets to share control of the atomic bomb. The Russians had "traditionally been our friends," he said, harking back to the Civil War and the sale of Alaska. There was no "secret" at stake, for the scientific principles were common knowledge. And once again he imparted his gentleman's faith that trust was the way to beget trust.

As the discussion worked its way around the table, the Cabinet was split. Most forcefully opposing Stimson's plan was Navy Secretary Forrestal, whose misgivings about spreading Bolshevism had steadily deepened. The Russians "are essentially Oriental in their thinking," he stated. "It seems doubtful that we should endeavor to buy their understanding and sympathy. We tried that once with Hitler. There are no returns on appeasement." The bomb, he insisted, "was genuinely the property of the American people."

At the other extreme was Commerce Secretary Henry Wallace, the man Roosevelt had dumped as Vice-President and the most starry-eyed of those who still believed that Soviet-American friendship was possible. The question, as he put it, was whether the U.S. would "follow the line of bitterness" or "the line of peace." The secrets of the atom were not exclusive U.S. property, and to try to withhold them from the Russians would make them "a sour and embittered people." Forrestal, putting his usual alarmist spin on whatever he heard, in his diary accused Wallace of being "completely, everlastingly and wholeheartedly in favor of giving it to the Soviets."*

Had Wallace been his only strong ally, Stimson may have retreated to Highhold with his hopes shattered. Instead, however, he found reassuring support from an important new quarter. With Byrnes away in London having a conspicuous lack of success achieving anything with a weapon he could not pull out of his hip pocket, the State Department chair at the Cabinet table was being filled by Dean Acheson.

•   •   •

Acheson, anxious to return to private life, had submitted his resignation as Assistant Secretary, and it had been accepted "with reluctance" by Truman and Byrnes back on August 9, the day the second bomb was dropped. He and Alice then took a train up to Saranac, New York, where their daughter Mary was recuperating from tuberculosis. Next on their agenda was a long-awaited jaunt with friends through the backwoods of Canada. After some warm embraces, Mary remembered to mention to her father that Secretary Byrnes had been trying all day to reach him on the phone.

It turned out that Byrnes and Truman, preoccupied by the bomb and the Japanese surrender, had not meant to accept the Assistant Secretary's resignation after all. As Acheson explained to his confused friend Frankfurter: "The Hon. Jimmy brought me back to Washington by air and told me I had caught him in a weak moment and he didn't mean any of it. I had not escaped, I was not to be allowed to and that

---

*Most of the other Cabinet members seemed somewhat baffled. Treasury Secretary Fred Vinson said he did not see how the U.S. could "give away" certain secrets and try to keep others. Attorney General Thomas Clark agreed. Robert Hannegan, the Postmaster General and chairman of the Democratic National Committee, said the issue was too complex for him, but that he respected and trusted Stimson's wisdom.

the President would draft me by virtue of Title something Section something if I resisted." Instead of his freedom, Acheson was offered a promotion to Under Secretary, replacing his fellow Grotonian Joseph Grew.

Acheson wavered at first. One of his worries was money. Now fifty-two years old, he had cultivated a gracious style and longed to become accustomed to the manner in which he was living. His Georgetown home had been expanded into a right-sized little mansion, and Harewood Farm had been renovated and decorated in a simple yet comfortable manner. The promotion would raise his salary only from nine thousand dollars a year to ten thousand dollars, a fraction of what he could make as a senior partner at Covington & Burling, his prosperous old law firm. Nor was he particularly fond of Byrnes.

On the other hand, he was acutely aware of history and the fact that he might play a role in it. The new job would put him at the very epicenter of power, a notion that no protégé of Peabody and Brandeis could easily resist, and give him a chance to be present at the creation of a whole new era.

At his wife's suggestion, Acheson spent one night pretending he had accepted the job and the next night pretending he had rejected it. "The experiment did not help," he reported. "Both assumptions depressed me." But with the aid of Byrnes's flattery, to which Acheson was quite susceptible, he finally decided to sign on. "I have no strength of character anyway," he wrote Frankfurter, "and certainly not when anyone is as charming to me as His Honor was."

Acheson was still considered, by himself and others, a traditional "liberal," one of the Frankfurter–New Deal crowd that believed strongly in both America's global role and the need for good relations with Russia. I. F. Stone wrote in *Nation* magazine that Acheson was "friendly to the Soviet Union" and represented "by far the best choice for Under Secretary."

Yet even though Acheson still thought friendly relations with the Soviets were quite possible, he had begun to be swayed by his old friend Harriman's constant refrain in State Department discussions and Georgetown dinners that friendliness must be mixed with firmness. Peabody's Groton did not breed softness. Allowing itself to be pushed around, Acheson believed, was certainly no way for the U.S. to win the respect of the Soviets.

The pattern of his thinking was clear within his first few weeks on the job: although a leading advocate of working with the Soviets, he visibly bristled when Prague and Moscow demanded the removal of

U.S. troops from Czechoslovakia. Washington must never flinch or retreat from a test of its resolve, he argued in stiffening Truman's backbone. American military presence, said the new Under Secretary, was "the most concrete and telling evidence of our interest in the restoration of stable and democratic conditions." The GIs would stay, Truman and his State Department subsequently decided, until a deal could be worked out for Soviet troops to withdraw simultaneously.

Acheson's outlook was not primarily motivated by a belief in the wickedness of the Soviets, at least not yet. Mostly it was guided by his anti-isolationist instincts. In the postwar world, with Britain on the ropes, America would have to be the champion of order and the paladin of a new Pax Americana. Even before his confirmation, Acheson entered into a contest of will with Douglas MacArthur, who had suggested that demobilization could be hastened. While other officials prudently ignored the general, Acheson called a press conference to decry the growing "bring the boys home" mentality and to remind MacArthur that policy was made in Washington. Thus while most liberals regarded him with favor, Acheson found his nomination most vigorously challenged by the old America First gang, the former isolationists who applauded MacArthur's unilateral approach to American interests in Asia and looked suspiciously at the European internationalists of the East Coast Establishment.

Acheson was very much a practical man, one who eschewed visionary schemes. The U.N. could play a useful role, he believed, but the hope that it could preserve peace among the Great Powers he treated with the same contempt that Brandeis heaped on "universal Plumb Plans." Its charter, Acheson pronounced, "was impractical." Peace could be maintained only by the Great Powers working in concert. That was why he thought there must be some modus vivendi with the Soviet Union.

This pragmatism was also one reason Acheson never saw much point in cloaking America's overseas interests with idealistic phrases about democracy and self-determination. The U.S. had important strategic and economic interests in such places as Iran, Turkey, and Greece—hardly paragons of electoral enlightenment—and these interests should not be obscured by what Acheson took to calling "messianic globaloney." When faced with the "evangelical enthusiasm" of those who believed in world government and universal democracy—and who disparaged the need for power diplomacy—Acheson would cite the admonition of Andrew Jackson at the Battle of New Orleans: "Boys, elevate them guns a little lower."

Yet there were traces of a new mellowness in Acheson's personality. No less sure of himself, he nonetheless felt less need to assert his self-confidence. Partly this was a result of his job as Assistant Secretary, which involved dealing with Congress and placating the likes of Arthur Vandenberg. Perhaps even more important was his daughter's prolonged recuperation from tuberculosis up at Saranac. He was deeply attached to Mary, who had served as a code breaker during the war and married Harvey Bundy's son William. Every evening he would write her long chatty letters on everything from national policy to the foibles of his secretary. "Mary's illness marked a tremendous crisis in Dean's life," a friend said. "He became reconciled to slow, hard answers to difficult questions."

Shorn of some of its brashness, the force and elegance of Acheson's intellect came through more vividly. Fuzzy abstractions annoyed him. Despite his reputation as a complex man, he approached problems actually quite simply. "His method," Mary recalled in an interview years later, "was to sift through all the complications and find a way to solve a problem, not make it more complex. If the problem just could not be solved, he would recognize that and simply do the best he could." He adopted the favorite sayings of two of his friends: Lovett's "To hell with the cheese, let's get out of this trap," and Marshall's "Don't fight the problem, decide it."

The new job as Under Secretary brought Acheson real power. Byrnes tended to ignore the department, handling some of the big problems on his own as a roving troubleshooter while delegating Acheson to make the day-to-day decisions at his nine-thirty staff meetings. For 350 out of his 562 days in office, Byrnes was out of town at foreign minister meetings or other excursions, leaving Acheson as Acting Secretary. In fact, Byrnes departed for the London Foreign Ministers' Conference before Acheson was even confirmed.

And so it was that Acheson, having made a conscious decision to seek his place in history, was the Acting Secretary of State when Henry Stimson telephoned to lay the groundwork for the critical September 21 Cabinet meeting and to argue his case for making a direct offer to the Soviets to share control of the atom.

•   •   •

The topic was already familiar to Acheson; for almost a month he had been working with McCloy on legislation that would set up a new domestic atomic energy agency. Discussing the issue late into the evenings in the cozy study of Acheson's Georgetown home, the two men had concluded that it was difficult to divorce domestic issues from international ones.

After hearing Stimson explain his proposal on the telephone, Acheson expressed some reluctance about breaking with Byrnes, who he knew opposed any approach to the Soviets. Yet the new Under Secretary deeply sympathized with Stimson's perspective and asked to see his memo to Truman. "Acheson is evidently strongly on our side," Stimson wrote in his diary that evening.

When Acheson's turn to speak came at the Cabinet session on September 21, Stimson could not have written a better script himself. There was "no alternative," Acheson said, to sharing atomic information with Russia. He could not "conceive of a world in which we were hoarders of military secrets from our Allies, particularly this great ally" whose cooperation was essential for "the future peace of the world." The exchange must be done on a "quid pro quo" basis, but above all the Grand Alliance must be kept intact—especially when it came to atomic weapons.

The President, at the conclusion of the Cabinet meeting that Friday morning, requested memos on atomic control from Acheson and Robert Patterson, the former judge who had served with McCloy, Lovett, and Bundy in the War Department and was replacing Stimson as Secretary. Patterson's product was a limp and fuzzy recap of Stimson's ideas. Acheson, however, was determined to impress the President with the eloquence and elegance of his arguments. He did.

The theory behind atomic power was widely known, Acheson wrote, and it was futile to believe that it could be treated as a "secret." Any attempt to exclude the Soviets would be seen as "evidence of an Anglo-American combination against them." Moscow would soon have the ability to make its own bomb. "The advantage of being ahead in such a race," he said, "is nothing compared with not having the race."

Acheson conceded that tensions with the Soviets were increasing. "Yet I cannot see why the basic interests of the two nations should conflict." His recommendations were similar to those Stimson and McCloy had made: The U.S. should make a direct approach to the Soviets—not through the U.N.—offering a step-by-step plan to share scientific information and adopt verifiable safeguards against the production of atomic weapons by any country. If cooperation fails, Acheson warned, "there will be no organized peace but only an armed truce."

So impressed was Truman with the power of the Acheson-McCloy-Stimson position that he asked the Under Secretary to prepare a presidential message to Congress linking domestic and international control of atomic energy. With his assistant Herbert Marks, Acheson put together a statement that was sent to Congress on October 3. Using Stimson's phrases about "a new force too revolutionary to consider in the framework of old ideas," Acheson wrote a resounding clarion call for "the renunciation of the use and development of the atomic bomb" and for a system in which "cooperation might replace rivalry in the field of atomic power."

Before the Soviets could be persuaded to accept such a program, however, it was necessary to persuade Congress. Leaders of both parties reacted skeptically, at best, to the President's message. "I think we ought to keep the technical know-how to ourselves as much as possible," said Senator Richard Russell, a conservative Georgia Democrat. The American monopoly should be retained, added Republican Arthur Vandenberg, until there was "absolute free and untrammeled right of intimate inspection all around the globe." A poll of sixty-one congressmen showed that fifty-five opposed sharing knowledge of the bomb with any country. And 85 percent of the public, according to a National Opinion Research Center survey, wanted the U.S. to retain exclusive possession of the weapon as long as possible.

•   •   •

Among those who thought it folly to share control of atomic weaponry with the Russians was Kennan, once again temporarily in charge of the embassy while Harriman traveled through Europe. What particularly grieved him was that news of the proposals circulating in Washington came to him from a delegation of traveling congressmen. Their visit not only reminded the moody diplomat about how little Washington understood the Soviet Union, it also reinforced his disdain for politics and politicians.

Surprised that he was able to obtain an interview with Stalin for the delegation, Kennan nervously waited at their appointed rendezvous for the congressmen to finish their obligatory tour of the Moscow subway system. The visitors, however, were being treated to a lavish late-afternoon "tea," with the usual abundance of vodka toasts, somewhere in the subterranean bowels of the city. Just before 6 P.M., the scheduled time of the interview, the well-lubricated group finally emerged.

As they tore off toward the Kremlin in two limousines, the members got a bit rowdy. "Who the hell is this guy Stalin anyway?" bellowed one of the drunker congressmen, who proceeded to threaten to jump out of the car. "You'll do nothing of the sort," Kennan sternly reprimanded. "What if I biff the old codger one in the nose?" came the drunken cry.

Kennan was mortified. "My heart froze," he recalled. In the end, however, the interview came off relatively smoothly, although Kennan noted that the drunken member did "leer and wink once or twice at the bewildered dictator."

For his part, Stalin was on his most charming behavior. When Senator Claude Pepper of Florida asked about Soviet intentions, the Generalissimo replied: "Our people are tired. They couldn't be induced to make war on anybody anymore." Afterwards, he pulled Kennan aside for a private word. "Tell your fellows not to worry about those Eastern European countries," the Soviet dictator told the skeptical diplomat. "Our troops are going to get out of there and things will be all right."

The visit of the unruly legislators, Kennan later wrote, was one of the many small episodes that "bred in me a deep skepticism about the absolute value of people-to-people contacts." In addition, Kennan's contempt for the intrusion of domestic politics into foreign policy jumped another notch. What bothered him most, however, was the information imparted by Senator Pepper, then a strong advocate of Soviet-American friendship, that plans were being considered for sharing with the Kremlin control of atomic weapons.

His message to Washington was among his most impassioned to date. "There is nothing—I repeat nothing—in the history of the Soviet regime," Kennan proclaimed, "which could justify us in assuming that [Russian leaders] would hesitate for a moment to apply this power against us if by doing so they thought that they might materially improve their own power position in the world." Proposals based on other assumptions "would constitute a frivolous neglect of the vital interests of our people."

The world, Kennan had learned, was not run by Stimsonian gentlemen who lived according to social club codes of reciprocated trust. Certainly the Kremlin was not. So Kennan decided to suggest something that would help lay the groundwork for what would become the present-day Central Intelligence Agency: the establishment of a new espionage apparatus to spy on the Soviets' atomic facilities.

Appended to Kennan's missive about the folly of sharing atomic secrets was a report from an embassy attaché speculating on the Soviet Union's atomic potential. "It is vital to U.S. security that our gov-

ernment should be adequately and currently informed on this subject,"
Kennan urged. It was "out of the question that adequate information
can be obtained through the normal channels." His conclusion was
discreetly worded but very clear. "Large-scale special efforts on various
lines in this direction are therefore justified," he said. "I consider it
the clear duty of the various interested agencies of our government to
determine at once in Washington the measures which our government
should take to obtain information with respect to Soviet progress in
atomic research."

This was too hot for even the coded communication facilities of
the embassy. Kennan gave his message to General Deane to carry to
Washington by hand. In a covering letter to Harriman, Kennan added
a personal plea "to see that everything possible is done to obtain
information on Russian progress along these lines."

When he read Kennan's memo, Acheson dismissed the parts about
the danger of trying to bring the Soviets into a partnership for atomic
control. But the proposals for an intelligence-gathering system caught
his eye. Kennan had mentioned that he thought his message was not
the proper "vehicle" for "detailed recommendations," but added that
he had other ideas he would be willing to discuss. In the margin next
to these words, the acting Secretary scribbled a note: "This would be
asked for. D.A."

The Office of Strategic Services, the wartime intelligence agency
headed by William Donovan, had been disbanded by Truman at the
end of September. There was at the time no specified agency designated to spy on the Soviet Union. When the CIA was being formed
a year later, shortly after Kennan returned from Moscow, he quietly
spent a month on its payroll as a "special consultant" to the new
director of Central Intelligence, General Hoyt Vandenberg.

•   •   •

The London Conference ended up as a disaster for Byrnes. The
Americans, Soviets, and British could not even agree on a final communiqué about the postwar governments of Europe. Byrnes's "bomb
in his pocket" did little more than provoke what was in all likelihood
a clumsy Soviet charade. At the end of a long reception, Molotov got
up, appearing drunk, and made a toast: "Here's to the atomic bomb.
We've got it." An aide grabbed him by the shoulders and quickly led
him from the room.

Byrnes had curtly dismissed Harriman's request to come to London
for consultations. He would be too busy to see him before the start

of his meetings with Molotov. This was more than just a personal insult to Harriman; it was a denigration of his duties as ambassador to Moscow. Harriman had wanted to discuss his own resignation, and the brusque lack of regard for his advice only strengthened his resolve. So Harriman went to London anyway, and at the end of the conference, in early October, the two men finally had dinner.

"Now that we're in this jam," said Byrnes, mixing his metaphors, "you'll have to wait and get the train back on the rails."

Harriman, in fact, was actually considering going back to his own rails, the Union Pacific. But he was not, if truth be told, all that anxious to leave his rarefied work for a return to private life in New York. He enjoyed his growing fame throughout Europe and his surprising celebrity wherever he traveled in Russia.

Although he was very close to his bright and charming daughter Kathleen, who had been a great hit as Spaso House hostess, Harriman rarely saw much of his wife, Marie, who had stayed back in New York. During his tenure in London and his frequent visits there after moving to Moscow, he had enjoyed a noted friendship with Pamela Churchill, or at least one that was noted by the gossip columnists.

Pamela, the daughter of the 11th Baron Digby, had married Winston Churchill's son, Randolph, shortly after the war began, when she was nineteen. A brilliant woman of striking beauty, she and her newborn son, Winston II (later a member of Parliament), had graced the cover of *Life* magazine about a year later. But the marriage soon soured, and in 1946 she sought a divorce, charging that Randolph "seemed to prefer a bachelor's existence." Her name was subsequently linked with a wide array of prominent men, among them Ali Khan, Fiat heir Giovanni Agnelli, Baron Elie de Rothschild, and newsman Edward R. Murrow. Averell Harriman especially caught her eye. "He was the most beautiful man I ever met," she recalled forty years later. "He was marvelous, absolutely marvelous-looking, with his raven black hair. He was really stunning."*

Byrnes found Harriman somewhat easier to re-enlist than Acheson had been, though neither proved all that difficult once properly stroked. The one thing Harriman wanted was another chance to deal with Stalin directly. So Byrnes promised him a letter from Truman, for

---

*Pamela, in 1960, married the theatrical producer Leland Hayward (*South Pacific, Call Me Madam*). In 1971, shortly after both Hayward and Marie Harriman died, Averell, seventy-nine, and Pamela, fifty-one, married at a tiny ceremony with Ethel Kennedy as one of their witnesses. Pamela became an important fund raiser and activist for the Democratic Party, and the two were still happily together some fifteen years later.

delivery to Stalin personally, that would serve as a basis for meeting. That accomplished, Harriman set out for a visit to Germany and Eastern Europe on his way back to Moscow.

Traveling with him was his friend McCloy, who had embarked on a six-week round-the-world tour that would be his final official act as Assistant Secretary of War. The two men met in London at the tail end of the Foreign Ministers' Conference, discussed their mutual worries about Byrnes and the bomb and the Soviets, then took off together for the Continent.

In Vienna, Harriman and McCloy were feted at a lavish reception attended by Marshal Ivan Koniev, the commander of Soviet forces in Austria. Once again the American military's rosier view of relations with Russia was evident. In his notes at the time, Harriman derided the "exaggerated importance" that the U.S. military put on the co-operation they had received on "relatively small issues." There was a tendency, Harriman noted, "to think that the politicians were making their work more difficult."

McCloy found himself caught between Harriman and the military. Everywhere they went, the Russian officers seemed so friendly, so profuse in their claims of comradery. From Eisenhower on down, American officers assured McCloy that given the chance, cooperation was possible. Yet he could not escape the gloomier talk, the worries about Soviet motives expounded not only by Harriman but in almost every conversation with foreign officials and American diplomats.

It was a profound enigma, but one perhaps better left to more profound men. So McCloy simply recorded the riddle in his notebook, noting that it was of "prime importance" for statesmen to figure it out. McCloy was not a conceptualizer. He was an implementer. The problems of coal distribution and communication services were to his mind even more pressing, and these were things he could get on with.

There was one thing on which Harriman and McCloy heartily agreed: America could not avoid the global involvement that had come with victory. They were shaken by the destruction in Budapest, that once-glorious gem on the Danube which had been ravaged by weeks of street fighting. Yet there was jubilation in the city when they arrived: a free election had been permitted by the Soviet occupiers and the anti-Communist Smallholders Party had won an unexpected majority.

As McCloy and Harriman headed for the American mission, they found their way blocked by jubilant Hungarians. "There was an enor-mous crowd celebrating the victory under the American flag," Harriman recalled. "It made me feel very humble to recognize how much these people looked to the U.S. as the protector of their freedom." As the crowd surged up to their car and cheered, the two men were awed, even slightly scared by the responsibility such a role would carry. "Here was the hope of the world," McCloy remembers thinking, "the American flag."

Harriman and McCloy agreed as they surveyed the crowd that the American sentiment to pack up and go home, to demobilize and wash hands of European entanglements, must be mightily resisted by people like themselves, those who shared a unique understanding of the role America should and must play. The global duties that the American public, with its insular perspective, had forsaken after the last war could not be shirked once again.

The experience stiffened Harriman's resolve that Eastern Europe should not be abandoned. "I simply could not accept the view that we ought to walk away and let the Russians have their sphere," he said, recalling the incident. Kennan might advocate such a course, Harriman thought, but only because he was insensitive to the plight of those in the helpless nations involved.

To McCloy, there was something "terrifying" about the incident. It showed how dependent Europe was on the U.S. for its future stability. "We give the population hope against the Russian fear," he cabled in a long report to Washington. His own eyes finally convinced him of what Harriman had long been insisting: the Soviets were embarked on a "determined" policy of dominating the economies and societies the Red Army controlled. In a recommendation that could have been written by Harriman, McCloy urged that U.S. loans and reconstruction aid to Eastern Europe be held up until the Soviets reduced their presence. In addition, American troops should remain in Austria pending the Soviet withdrawal. "Opposition to Russian pressures gains encouragement," he said, "by our mere presence."

• • •

While McCloy continued on to the Far East, Harriman headed back to Russia, determined to go straight to the source to determine what the Soviets were really up to. Armed with his letter from Truman, the ambassador called on Molotov to request an interview with Stalin.

The Soviet leader was on a long vacation, said Molotov, who offered to pass the letter on himself. "Where is he?" Harriman asked. "I can join him." Molotov, finding the suggestion somewhat incredible, said he would see if that was possible. It was a testament to Harriman's unique stature in the Soviet Union that the word soon came back that he was invited to Stalin's secluded dacha in the Black Sea resort of Gagra.

The basic question, as Harriman saw it, was whether the U.S.S.R. wanted to follow a policy of international cooperation, which involved working out some form of "collective security" arrangements with the West, or whether it had decided to pursue a unilateral policy (often referred to in the Soviet Union as "isolationism"), which would entail an aggressive expansionism in pursuit of its own security goals. He found that Stalin seemed to be of two minds on the question, but that he was leaning toward the latter course.

Welcoming Harriman to his white stucco villa, Stalin led him into a mahogany-paneled office where they had two days of talks in late October. International cooperation was still possible, Stalin seemed to indicate on the first day, but it had to be a two-way street. The Americans, he said, were demanding a voice on Soviet-dominated control commissions in Eastern Europe. Yet the U.S. had been adamant in refusing the Soviets any say in the occupation of Japan, a country that had historically been a security threat to them.

Harriman, who took pride in having resisted Stalin's demands on the night Tokyo surrendered, was not anxious to permit the Soviets a toehold in Japan. But he did believe they should be given some voice, subject to General MacArthur's final authority, if only as a way to strengthen American claims in the Balkans and Eastern Europe. "We can't get away with this brush-off," Harriman had scribbled to Byrnes at the London Conference when the Secretary refused to discuss the issue. Byrnes finally agreed to let Harriman and Bohlen draft a note to Molotov saying that the U.S. would discuss the Japanese occupation after the conference ended.

Although he had no authority to do so, Harriman assured Stalin that an arrangement could be worked out for an Allied control council or commission under MacArthur's authority. As Harriman pointed out to Washington: "Japan has for two generations been a constant menace to Russian security in the Far East and the Soviets wish now to be secure from this threat."

On their second day of talks, however, Harriman found Stalin to be far less agreeable. Maybe, the Soviet leader said, it did not really matter what happened in Japan. He had never favored a policy of unilateral action, he claimed, but now it might be inevitable. "Per-

haps," Stalin added, "there is nothing wrong with it." Harriman concluded that the Soviets had decided that postwar cooperation with the
West was not to their advantage. "The Soviet leadership," he later
speculated, "had discussed and settled on a new policy for the postwar
period, a policy of increased militancy and self-reliance."

Even though he had long been an advocate of firmness, the prospect
of a complete breakdown in cooperation upset Harriman. So too did
Washington's dithering about setting up a joint control commission
for Japan. Despite the reluctance of the State Department to take up
the matter, Harriman immediately embarked on a series of discussions
with Molotov designed to allow the Soviets some say in the occupation
in return for greater American involvement in Eastern Europe.

• • •

What Harriman did not know was that Truman and his advisers
were enmeshed in their own negotiations on the issue of Japanese
control—not with Moscow but with their own imperial commander
there, Douglas MacArthur. Many of the isolationists who before the
war resisted American entanglement in the affairs of Europe had
evolved into Asia Firsters, advocates of forceful and unilateral American actions to control the Pacific. Their new hero was General
MacArthur, who wanted nothing to do with the Soviets in his Pacific
theater and cared little for what effect this would have in Central
Europe.

In the first of many efforts by the Truman Administration to rein
in its high-handed Pacific commander, John McCloy was given the
mission of negotiating with MacArthur. When he arrived in Tokyo
on the last leg of his global tour, McCloy found that MacArthur
had graciously driven for two hours to meet him at the airport. But
in a series of long sessions over the next three days the general's
short temper was snapped by McCloy's arguments that the Soviets be
given some voice in the control of Japan. "He became very agitated,"
McCloy wrote in his diary. "He talked of the great opportunity we
had in the East, of the God-given authority we now had here, of
what a mess things were in Europe, of the threat of the Russian
Bear."

The Assistant Secretary, courtly and calm, found it hard even to
get in words edgewise. "It became a sort of shouting contest," he noted.
"I told him that the Russian relation was one that had to be looked
at from a world point of view. We had great interests in middle Europe.

We could not take a unilateral position in the Pacific and still press for a satisfactory solution elsewhere in the world."

McCloy discussed MacArthur's stubborn attitude in a teletype conversation with Acheson and Bohlen in Washington. Acheson began by arguing that a "face-saving" solution giving the Soviets some voice in the occupation of Japan "may be determinative of future cooperation" between Washington and Moscow. Harriman was discussing this very issue with Stalin, Acheson added, so the dispute with MacArthur must be cleared up quickly.

McCloy wired back that he and MacArthur may have found "an arrangement that would be satisfactory." Representatives of Allied countries, including the Soviet Union, could be invited to join a "Council of Political Advisers" that would recommend to MacArthur policies for the treatment of occupied Japan.

Would the general, Bohlen asked, be willing to be a member of the "council" rather than treating it as merely an outside advisory group? "As Bohlen puts it," McCloy teletyped back, the idea "carries with it just the implication that MacArthur wishes to avoid." The general, he said, was willing to accept only an "advisory" panel that would send him recommendations. Replied Acheson: That was even less than the Russians were granting American officials in the Balkans.

In the end, the Soviets were given no real authority. As Harriman discovered in his conversations with Stalin, this was perhaps all for the best: the Kremlin had by now clearly decided to pursue a unilateral policy of asserting its own power without regard to considerations of international cooperation. The U.S., he concluded, would simply have to adjust itself to this new reality.

•   •   •

When McCloy returned home, he felt for the first time the need to speak out. No longer could he serve as merely an administrator of Stimson's ideas; Stimson was gone and people were looking to McCloy for insights of his own. His brother-in-law Lew Douglas, who was then president of the Mutual Life Insurance Company and would later become ambassador to Britain, asked him to talk about his world trip at the annual dinner of the Academy of Political Science in New York. NBC radio offered him air time for a similar report.

McCloy had none of the eloquence of an Acheson. Even though he had stayed up past 1 A.M. one night to compose his speech, his remarks tended to ramble. Yet there was a crucial point he wanted to make, and he hammered it home: "the need for American leadership to bring this world into some semblance of balance again." People all over looked to the U.S. as "the one stabilizing influence" that could protect their freedom. "A shudder runs through them when they hear the increasingly loud demand for the removal of our troops, which they consider the abandonment of our interest in their parts of the world."

The isolationism that followed the last war, McCloy emphasized, gave rein to forces hostile to democracy. This time America should not retreat from involvement, either militarily or politically. "The people of the world will not believe, unless we convince them, that we have what it takes to carry through in peace."

McCloy also touched on the other topic troubling him: the Soviet Union. "Everywhere you go, that topic is up," he reported, "the concern over Russia's ambitions, how far she is going to go, how to deal with her." He offered no judgments, no solutions, just an admonition: "It is quite clear that this is the A-1 priority job for the statesmen of the world to work out."

A crucial personal decision now faced McCloy: What role would he play in this A-1 priority job? His friends who had left their lucrative careers to join the wartime effort were all considering a return to private life now that the fighting was over. Acheson had made an attempted break from Washington only to be dissuaded after three days. But Acheson had a greater taste than McCloy for the public spotlight; he also had a bit more money saved up from his days as a lawyer as well as a wife with some wealth of her own. Harriman, likewise, had made rumblings about leaving, and insisted that he still planned to in the near future.

Upon returning from his world tour, McCloy was presented with a surprising offer from Byrnes. Now that Harriman was talking about resigning, the Secretary said, McCloy was the President's choice to be the next ambassador in Moscow. "It was most flattering and disturbing," McCloy noted in his journal, "for no one can deny the challenge that lies ahead." Another offer came from Amherst, which wanted him to be its next president.

Throughout the fall, McCloy agonized about his future. It would be difficult, he wrote, "to get back to humdrum things." But he badly needed to make money again, to support his family better; perhaps as a legacy of his childhood poverty, McCloy always seemed worried about not having enough money. Extremely lucrative offers were coming in from the top law firms of Wall Street, including one from Milbank, Tweed, Hope and Hadley to become a name partner.* He wanted to spend more time with his son and daughter. "Now that the war is over," little Johnny had said at dinner one night, "can I have my daddy back too?"

Finally he decided to reject the chance to become Spaso House's next ambassador and to return to the practice of law, adding his name to the partnership of Milbank, Tweed, which handled the affairs of the Rockefeller family and the Chase Bank. "We are at a windy corner of history," he wrote in his journal. "As interesting as it is, I must make my living again." But he would do so, he vowed, in the tradition of such people as Root and Stimson, men who had distinguished themselves in private careers while continually answering the call of public service.

The emulation was quite conscious. That September, when Stimson presented him with the Distinguished Service Medal, McCloy had noticed "the steady gaze of Elihu Root" from the portrait hanging behind the Secretary's desk. "I felt a direct current running from Root through Stimson to me," he wrote in his diary. "They were the giants."

Thus it was hardly surprising that as he re-entered private life, McCloy became actively involved in the Council on Foreign Relations. Founded in 1921, this respected bastion of top lawyers and bankers and statesmen was the wood-paneled reification of the Root-Stimson tradition. During the war, McCloy and Lovett used to flip through the club's roster to come up with names of people who might be called upon to serve their government. Now it would serve as a perfect base for his own special talents.

The council was not suited to those who sought an ideological pulpit; it was, instead, a place where stable bipartisan consensus could be forged, where behind-the-scenes discussions could be held, where wise counsel could be sought. Such was an atmosphere in which McCloy could thrive. He had none of Acheson's brilliance, nor Kennan's conceptual vision, nor Harriman's boldness as a top-level bargainer, nor Forrestal's philosophical fervor. Yet though he was only an outgoing Assistant Secretary, McCloy was already revered for his discreet counsel, his rocklike wisdom, his reassuring steadiness.

At the end of his European tour, McCloy was feted at a black-tie

---

*The Cravath firm also sought him back, but it did not offer to make him a name partner. McCloy resented the attitude of senior partner Robert Swaine that service in the War Department did not qualify McCloy for a promotion.

dinner in the council's newly acquired Park Avenue home, a 1919-vintage English Renaissance marble mansion. There he outlined his vision of America's righteous mission in the emerging global era. "Thus far we have gotten along with Russia fairly well," he said in response to a question. The Soviets could never hope to match America's economic and moral might in the world. "Russia's concepts and example will wilt before ours," he had concluded, "if we have the vigor and farsightedness to see our place in the world."

· · ·

Robert Lovett received his Distinguished Service Medal from Stimson at the same time as McCloy. Despite the weighty gaze of Elihu Root, it was a jovial occasion, with the two Imps of Satan recalling old tales, joking with their departing mentor, and posing for countless photographs. For Lovett, secure in the knowledge that he had done his job well and that the government could function without him, there was no hesitation about leaving public service for the time being. He was already making arrangements to resume his partnership in Brown Brothers Harriman.

Lovett's Distinguished Service citation, which Stimson personally wrote, spoke of the fact that "he early envisioned the vast possibilities of air power." Lovett's contribution had been far more than that of an able administrator. He had come to represent an important yet intangible quality, one that Stimson alluded to in lauding his "diplomatic tact and wise counsel."

With his great sense of inner security, Lovett seemed devoid of personal ambition or ulterior motives. His discreet and selfless style of operating came to be idealized by others as the bench mark for a certain breed of public servant. It was a standard that had long been associated with Stimson and was now coming to be known, in newspapers and conversation, as that exemplified by Lovett. "The problem is to keep such men in public service in peace as well as war," *The New York Times* wrote in marking Lovett's departure that November. "The more prosaic tasks of government in peace also need men of knowledge, of courage, of vision, qualities Mr. Lovett has shown in such full measure."

The impact of a "classic insider's man," as journalist David Halberstam would later call Lovett, is generally harder to quantify than that of more assertive personalities, such as Harriman or Acheson. But within certain circles, Lovett was already considered to be a man of enormous influence. More than any of his colleagues, he had come to be regarded by those within the Wall Street and Washington Establishment as a touchstone of things safe and sound. Because of the respect others had for his impeccable credentials and motives, he imparted a seal of approval upon people and policies he supported. When Lovett brought people together, there was the unspoken sense that they were the right sort of people, ones who could be trusted to put aside personal or partisan considerations for the good of the country. Consequently, part of his importance in Washington by 1945 was his role as the reliable focal point for a group of bankers, lawyers, journalists, and public officials who viewed themselves as the backbone of a nonpartisan foreign policy elite.

As he had promised his wife the day the war ended, Lovett moved back to New York in time for Thanksgiving. The accumulated exhaustion of seven-day work weeks had taken a toll, as did the ailments, both real and imagined, on what he called his "glass insides." That winter he underwent gallbladder surgery, which was followed by a month of recuperation at his vacation home in Hobe Sound, Florida.

After he finally returned to his rolltop desk in the Brown Brothers Harriman Partners' Room, Lovett settled into the comfortable life of a prominent Wall Street banker. He served on the boards of such companies as the Union Pacific and New York Life Insurance and was a trustee of the Carnegie Foundation and the Rockefeller Foundation. His clubs included the Century Association and the Links in New York and the Creek in Locust Valley. Yet he discovered that his advice was still much sought in Washington. He would find himself making frequent trips down there at the behest of Acheson or Harriman or occasionally the President. His apparent lack of desire to re-enter government served only to make him seem more indispensable to those who would eventually see that he did.

· · ·

"I can state in three sentences what the 'popular' attitude is toward foreign policy today," Acheson told the Maryland Historical society in November of 1945. "1. Bring the boys home; 2. Don't be a Santa Claus; 3. Don't be pushed around."

On the first two counts, Acheson's own attitude was clear: he was against the rush to demobilize and felt that America's involvement in rebuilding a prosperous Europe was in its own economic and political interest. On the third point, however, his ideas were still a bit hazy. He resisted the growing anti-Communist truculence sweeping parts of the country, yet he was just as certainly opposed to having the U.S.

pushed around. McCloy's "A-1 priority job," figuring out what the Soviets were up to, was still quite a nagging riddle for the new Under Secretary.

Acheson got a taste of how explosive the issue could be when he agreed to address a New York meeting of the Soviet-American Friendship Society in November. Armed with a speech suitable for a Frankfurter seminar, he arrived at Madison Square Garden to find a vociferous and crowded rally ready to be inspired. And inspired they were: An orchestra played revolutionary marches, the crowd stomped and chanted, and Paul Robeson, the great bass singer who later became a Soviet citizen, boomed forth a rendition of "Ole Man River" that just kept rolling through a crescendo of protest to a defiant finale. The Very Reverend Hewlett Johnson, the "Red" Dean of Canterbury Cathedral, also received a thunderous ovation. "He sashayed around the ring like a skater," Acheson reported, "his hands clasped above his head in a prize fighter's salute."

Acheson was eloquent in conveying his sympathy for the Soviets' security aims. To understand them, he said, an American would have to imagine what it would be like if Germany had invaded the U.S., destroyed industrial centers from New York to Boston to Pittsburgh, ruined a large part of the Midwest's breadbasket, and killed a third of the population. To Acheson this made a compelling case for allowing the Soviets at least some form of sphere in Eastern Europe. "We understand and agree with them," he said, "that to have friendly governments along her borders is essential both for the security of the Soviet Union and the peace of the world."

But the situation was not all one-sided. Although Acheson, out of deference to his audience, toned down the growing qualms he had about Soviet police-state tactics, he did not omit them altogether. "Adjustment of interests," he said, "should take place short of the point where persuasion and firmness become coercion, where a knock on the door at night strikes terror into men and women." Amid a rising chorus of boos and catcalls, Acheson hurried on through his speech, tossing quotations from Molotov and Stalin in hopes of calming the fury he had ignited. "But I had shown my true colors," he later wrote. "Those who took their red straight, without a chaser of white and blue, were not mollified."

When he finished, a policeman touched him on the arm. "Come," he said, "I can show you a quiet way to your car." At a friend's house, a glass of Scotch was waiting. Acheson had learned a valuable lesson: The difficulty of figuring out the Soviet riddle paled in comparison to facing an American audience—on either side of the issue—without a clear and forceful answer to their liking. The hissing that came from the left that evening would later be matched by that from the right. In fact, his presence at the Madison Square Garden rally would, ironically, be cited during the McCarthy era as evidence of his softness on Communism. "This seemed to me," he later mused, "to add a companion thought to Lincoln's conclusion of the impossibility of fooling all of the people all of the time, the difficulty of pleasing any of the people any of the time."

•   •   •

What Acheson had been trying to express, and indeed what he had come to believe, was the new State Department line formulated by Chip Bohlen. As the department's Soviet expert, Bohlen had been wrestling with the idea of Eastern Europe as a Soviet sphere. He still could not buy Kennan's view that the area should be written off totally to the Soviets. The U.S., Bohlen and others genuinely believed, had a moral interest in protecting freedom and encouraging democratic ideals. Yet he had come to accept, as had officials ranging from Stimson to Harriman, that the Soviets' insistence on protecting their security interests along their borders had some merit.

To that extent, Bohlen concluded, Moscow was entitled to some sort of sphere of influence, despite the high-minded rhetoric of the Atlantic Charter, and to "friendly" states next door. The problem was defining what "friendly " meant.

The difficulty, as Bohlen saw it, came when the Kremlin insisted "on complete Soviet domination and control over all phases of the external and internal life" of countries within its sphere. Such police-state repression was an anathema not only to Americans, but to principled and freethinking people everywhere. Besides, this total domination (at least in Bohlen's eyes, if not the Kremlin's) was unnecessary for Soviet security purposes. Somehow, he figured, there must be a way to establish governments in Eastern Europe that were "friendly" to the Soviets and yet did not depend on repressive Stalinist tactics to stay in power.

Thus Bohlen proposed making a distinction between "open" spheres, in which the Soviets exercised "legitimate influence" over matters relating to their security, and "closed" spheres, in which there was "illegitimate extension of such interest in the direction of domination and control." He explained it all in a memo to Byrnes and Acheson in October of 1945. "The U.S. should not and indeed could not assist or even acquiesce in the establishment by the Soviet Union of exclusive spheres of influence in Central and Eastern Europe by means of complete domination," he wrote. "On the other hand, we should not in any sense attempt to deny to the Soviet Union the legitimate prerogatives of a great power in regard to smaller countries resulting from geographic proximity."

The distinction was immediately embraced by Byrnes as the new definition of American policy, which he enunciated in a major New York speech. Truman proclaimed it too, as did Acheson at Madison Square Garden.

There were, however, some sticky problems with the policy. First of all, how could the U.S. convince the Soviets that the regimes being set up by the Red Army should permit the people some semblance of personal freedom? Bohlen hardly provided much of an answer when he wrote that the U.S. "should leave the Soviet Government in no doubt as to the automatic and inevitable results" of imposing a closed sphere. That seemed to be a prescription for further fiascoes like the two-year wrangle to get four token ministers temporarily into the Polish Cabinet.

Another drawback was that Bohlen's two-pronged policy would be difficult, at best, to sell to the American public. It certainly had not played well before the Soviet sympathizers in Madison Square Garden. Byrnes was already running into criticism from diehards in the Senate who thought he was too willing to give away the Balkans and Eastern Europe to the Soviets, along with the bomb. Indeed, the middle approach appealed neither to the left nor the right, neither to Wilsonian idealists nor even fervent realists like Kennan.

The thorniest problem of all was Harriman's old domino dilemma. Given a friendly sphere (either "open" or "closed"), would the Soviets set their sights on the next layer of countries? Would a sphere that included Russia's Balkan neighbors soon swallow Greece? Bohlen's middle road did nothing to answer the A-1 question: How much did the Soviets want and how far were they planning to go?

The hard-line attitudes of Harriman and Kennan had been spawned by their revulsion over the Kremlin's fanatic insistence on imposing rigid controls on its own society and those that fell into its orbit. Officials who still hoped for closer Soviet-American friendship, such as Acheson and Bohlen, and those who had not yet sorted out the complex questions, such as McCloy and Lovett, would likewise soon see the need for a firmer stance. For them the catalyst would be evidence that Moscow was setting its sights on areas that lay beyond the countries its armies had liberated during the war, areas that were of clear strategic importance to the West.

*   *   *

At the theater in Moscow one evening in late November, Harriman had a depressing conversation with former Foreign Minister Maxim Litvinov, who was brooding about his own ouster from the Kremlin inner circle and the abandonment of the policy of cooperation he had once advocated. When Harriman asked what could be done about the breakdown in relations, the former Foreign Minister gloomily replied, "Nothing."

In a cable to the State Department about his chat with Litvinov, Harriman sketched out the evidence, accumulated since his Black Sea meetings with Stalin, that the Soviets were pursuing a unilateral expansionist policy. Their attitudes toward Bulgaria and Rumania had hardened, he reported, and the Chinese Communists had been invited by the Red Army into Manchuria. Even more troublesome was evidence that they were probing into other areas. They were fomenting the revolt in northern Iran, he said, and putting new pressure on Turkey for naval bases on the Dardanelles.

The question was why. As he sat down to consider the causes of the apparent Soviet decision to go it alone, Harriman's mind began to focus on an important new element: the atomic bomb. In a long analysis for Washington, he explained that Soviet leaders should feel more secure than ever. "With victory came confidence in the power of the Red Army and in their control at home, giving them for the first time a sense of security." What had happened? "Suddenly the atomic bomb appeared," Harriman wrote "This must have revived their old feeling of insecurity... As a result it would seem that they have returned to their tactics of obtaining their objectives through aggressiveness and intrigue." Even though the link between Moscow's growing orneriness and the atomic bomb might have seemed somewhat tenuous, both Kennan and Harriman had long believed that paranoia and insecurity were the major sources of the Soviets' expansionist instincts.

Harriman had no suggestions to make. His message, he noted, was only meant as "a partial explanation of the psychological effect of the atomic bomb on the behavior of Soviet leaders." But it reached Washington at a very critical time.

In mid-November, shortly before Harriman sent his analysis, Truman had held a summit with the Prime Ministers of Britain and

Canada, America's two partners in developing the bomb. Contrary to what Stimson had urged, and contrary to what Acheson and Bohlen were recommending, the three leaders decided to submit the issue of atomic control to the U.N., rather than first approach Moscow with a plan.

But by later in the month, even Byrnes had come to realize that it was best to bring the matter up directly with the Soviets before any U.N. meeting. He proposed to Molotov a late-December conference of the American, British, and Soviet Foreign Ministers in Moscow. The bomb would be the first order on the agenda, followed by a discussion of the problems in Eastern Europe, Japan, and elsewhere.

A committee was formed to flesh out the American proposals for atomic control along the lines that Stimson, McCloy and Acheson had advocated in September. Bohlen and Acheson's assistant Herbert Marks were designated as the State Department representatives. The Soviets, they proposed, should be asked to cosponsor the U.N. resolution setting up an atomic commission. Control would be accomplished through a series of related steps that included exchanging scientific information, sharing data on natural resources such as uranium, and establishing safeguards to prevent any nation from producing nuclear weapons on its own.

One important element was that there was no firm link in timing between the acceptance of verifiable safeguards and the sharing of information. That was too much for Forrestal. "The proposed basis for discussion goes too far," he phoned Byrnes. No information should be shared until guarantees had been adopted to prevent any country from building its own bomb. When the plan was finally presented to Senate leaders they were even more outraged. "We are opposed to giving any of the atomic secrets away," said Senator Vandenberg, "unless and until the Soviets are prepared to be policed by the U.N." Expressing little regard for their concerns, Byrnes departed for Moscow.

Even as Byrnes was in the air, the horrified senators were demanding a meeting with the President. Acheson, who had earned the dubious duty of being Vandenberg's handler, was summoned to the White House to mediate. Truman was convinced that Soviet cooperation was crucial, and he showed little interest in the disputed details of the step-by-step approach. But after the showdown he instructed Acheson to convey the senators' concerns to Byrnes.

The entire issue seemed to hold surprisingly little interest to the Soviets. Molotov, in fact, insisted that atomic control be placed last on the agenda at the Foreign Ministers' meeting. He even attempted a feeble barb about the bomb at one of the banquets, but Stalin peremptorily put him down. "This is too serious a matter to joke about," he said. "I raise my glass to the American scientists and what they have accomplished. We must now work together to see that this great invention is used for peaceful ends."

With little debate, the Soviets accepted a vague proposal to set up a U.N. commission on atomic control. There was no discussion of what steps would come in which order. The only Soviet demand, which the Americans and the British accepted, was that the commission should report to the Security Council, where the Soviets had a veto, and not to the General Assembly.

The Soviets were far more interested in winning Western recognition for their "friendly" regimes in Eastern Europe. When the Foreign Ministers could not reach an agreement on this issue, Stalin invited Byrnes, Harriman, and Bohlen to the Kremlin to see what could be worked out. The cosmetic concessions offered by the Soviet leader mirrored what he considered to be the token ones the U.S. had made regarding Soviet participation in the occupation of Japan. A few non-Communists could be added to the Bulgarian and Rumanian governments, Stalin said, in return for Western recognition.

Byrnes, who was anxious to bring home some sort of an agreement, leaped at the proposal. But neither Bohlen nor Harriman thought that it amounted to much. Stalin's concessions, Harriman later said, "did not alter the brute facts or in any way loosen his grip on Eastern Europe." They were also dismayed by Stalin's cavalier attitude about Iran. Warned that if Soviet troops did not stop fomenting unrest in the northern region of that country the matter would be raised at the U.N., Stalin replied with a shrug: "This will not cause us to blush."

While his colleagues were at the Kremlin, Kennan was nervously pacing and awaiting their arrival at the Bolshoi Theater. A special performance of Sergei Prokofiev's new ballet *Cinderella* had been scheduled, and it was being delayed pending the appearance of the Americans. Just as Kennan was about to phone the embassy, a Soviet secret policeman, knowing full well what was agitating Kennan, told him the party was on its way.

More than ever, Kennan felt excluded and ignored. He had handed Byrnes his secret memo on the folly of sharing atomic secrets with the Soviets, but the Secretary seemed to have no interest in his views. "His main purpose is to achieve some sort of an agreement," Kennan noted in his diary. "He doesn't much care what." The accords being worked out on Eastern Europe, Kennan pronounced, were "fig leaves of democratic procedure to hide the nakedness of Stalinist dictatorship."

Dismayed by the unprofessionalism of the politicians who thought they could handle diplomacy, Kennan began setting down a series of rules for dealing with the Russians. "Don't act chummy with them," he began. "Don't assume a community of aims with them which does not really exist. Don't make fatuous gestures of good will." When the topic was brought up at a lunch with Alexander Cadogan and other members of the British delegation, Kennan and Bohlen unleashed their shared views. Noted Kennan: "I think he and I rather shook Cadogan's composure with our observations on the techniques of dealing with the Soviet government."

Harriman, who was always scrupulous about stroking the Presidents he served, was surprised when Byrnes announced that he was not planning to send regular cables back to Washington. "I can't trust the White House to prevent leaks," said the Secretary. When Bohlen brought up the same matter, Byrnes sharply said that he knew when it was necessary to report and when it was not. "I was put in my place," recalled Bohlen, "and I stayed there." Little did Byrnes realize that, back in Washington, Acheson was facing an annoyed President and some disgruntled senators anxious that Byrnes be the one who was put in his place.

•   •   •

Senator Vandenberg found out what Byrnes had done in Moscow by reading the newspapers. Worse yet, so did Truman. Neither was happy. The nebulous agreement on atomic energy contained no commitment to share information until the U.N. had somehow worked out a system of inspection and control. But Vandenberg, determined that this point be made more explicit, howled in protest to Acheson before Byrnes had even arrived home.

Off to the White House the two men marched to hear Truman's assurances once again. This time the senator wanted them in writing. Truman sent him back to the State Department with Acheson, and there the two men negotiated an acceptable clarification. "Complete and adequate security must be part of each stage" of a plan for joint atomic control, it emphasized. Feeling somewhat humiliated, Truman agreed to issue the statement.

Thus the President was not in the best of moods when Acheson had to irritate him even further. Overjoyed with what he considered a great set of breakthroughs, and oblivious to the mood in Washington, Byrnes cabled home to arrange time on the radio networks so that he could tell the nation of his triumphs.

Acheson was acutely aware of the need to show proper respect for the Presidency, especially when it was held by a man like Truman, who was sensitive about slights to the office. Without consulting Byrnes, who was then somewhere over the Atlantic, the Under Secretary suggested to the President that the broadcast could be delayed for a day. This was heartily endorsed by Truman, who was taking a pleasure cruise down the Potomac on the yacht *Williamsburg*. Admiral Leahy, crusty as ever, and Clark Clifford, the smooth Missouri lawyer who was then a rising aide in the White House, convinced Truman that Byrnes should be ordered to come promptly to the yacht upon his arrival and report to the President first.

It was Acheson's unhappy task to meet Byrnes at the airport, tell him of the change in plans, and gently pass along word of the President's displeasure. Byrnes and Truman provided differing accounts, both to Acheson and in their memoirs, of the tongue-lashing that occurred on the *Williamsburg*. Whether or not it was as harsh as the President claimed, it was clear that Truman was no longer interested in finding some middle ground regarding Soviet spheres in Eastern Europe. "I'm tired of babying the Soviets," Truman told Byrnes. At his next press conference the President emphasized that he had no plans to recognize the regimes in Rumania or Bulgaria until free elections were held.

Lacking any coherent theory of why Moscow behaved the way it did, Truman and his top policy makers had spent much of 1945 floundering from situation to situation, vacillating in their attitude toward Moscow and adopting new strategies and approaches as they stumbled along. But neither firmness nor friendliness seemed to work with the Russians. Their underlying motives, their goals, the sources of their conduct all remained a mystery.

So this was the task for 1946: shaping a new framework that would explain Soviet conduct. Only then could the U.S. figure out how to respond to each challenge. Only then could it be determined what element of trust could be included in a program for control of the atomic bomb.

CHAPTER 12

Kennan on the farm

CONTAINMENT

Sensitive to
the logic of force

I t was time for Harriman to come home. His mission of securing wartime collaboration with the Soviets had long since been accomplished. His subsequent mission of sounding the alarm about the need for a policy of firmness had also been accomplished—perhaps, as it seemed to him at times, a bit too successfully. Harriman knew that his strength, the role for which he was best suited, was as a personal fixer, one who could deal at the top. Now it was time for studied analysis, sitting back and figuring out the underlying explanations of Soviet conduct. That, Harriman felt, was a task for others.

When he called on Stalin in January of 1946 to bid him a final farewell, Harriman found himself as unsure as ever about the real motivations of Soviet actions. Despite the sharp differences between their social systems, the Soviet dictator insisted, the two countries "could find common ground." They even discussed the possibility of a postwar loan and reminisced about Harriman's old manganese concessions. Yet Harriman left the Kremlin baffled by the enigmatic character of the brutal Bolshevik and his policies. "Stalin," he later confessed, "remains the most inscrutable and contradictory character I have ever known."

"Those who place greater emphasis on unilateral action rather than collective security are in ascendancy in the Soviet government," Harriman told his embassy staff in his valedictory talk. Using the Red Army, they wanted to control as large an area as possible. The new situation required a realistic understanding of Soviet goals and of America's role in resisting them. "I am not discouraged," Harriman said. "But I think we have a long, slow scrape ahead."

Americans had grown weary of global responsibilities, he continued, and wanted nothing more than to "settle all our difficulties with Russia and then go to the movies and drink Coke." They must be made to realize that "there is no settlement with Russia and that this is a continuous thing." There were, in fact, signs that this was beginning to sink in. It was "interesting and encouraging," Harriman said, that Byrnes was being criticized for being too conciliatory. "The boys coming home don't want it to happen again."

As he was leaving, Harriman pulled aside his studious and intense counselor at the embassy. "You're in charge now," he told Kennan. "Now you can send all the telegrams you want."

Harriman and his friends from his Wall Street days, such as McCloy, Lovett, and Acheson, occasionally differed over the best tactics for dealing with Moscow. But they did share a common outlook. First of all, they were pragmatic businessmen and negotiators, the type who felt that deals could be made and problems solved by getting the right people around the right table to strike a mutual bargain. In such an atmosphere, a forthright firmness engendered respect, whereas trying to buy friendship with concessions tended to be treated as a reason for suspicion. It was important not to be pushed around.

They were also disciples of the multilateral ideal. A system of free and vibrant world trade, they believed, would lead to greater prosperity and a greater chance of lasting peace. By background and breeding their natural ties were with England and Europe, and they were fully aware that the culture and commerce of the Old World, however decaying, were the bases of their own heritage.

They were also firmly convinced that, in the global age that would arise from the ashes of World War II, the U.S. should not retreat from the struggle for freedom as it had following World War I. In an era of air power and nuclear weapons, security could not be protected by territorial control or by vast oceans. The best guarantee of America's security—and that of the world—would be the establishment of democratic and representative governments everywhere, ones that by their very nature would be peace loving rather than aggressive.

In addition they were imbued with a special sense of destiny involving both America's role and their own. Safety in the atomic age would demand some sort of Pax Americana in which the U.S. accepted the obligations of leadership. People like themselves, who understood the need for American resolve and involvement, would have to take the lead. McCloy liked to speak of a "Periclean age," in which a great nation with selfless ideals was led by great men with equally selfless motives.

This outlook was a very genuine one, indeed a righteous and laudable one. This is what made it particularly hard for a Harriman or an Acheson or a McCloy to understand why Stalin seemed so reluctant to go along.

The Soviets, however, had a starkly different outlook. Rather than embracing free-trading prosperity, they viewed the goal as an insidious form of U.S. economic imperialism. The natural affinity some Americans felt for the English and other Europeans appeared to be evidence of a Western alliance dedicated to the hostile encirclement of the Soviets. The vision of an American-led peace seemed like threatening atomic diplomacy. And the political ideals that Americans considered self-evident were seen by the Kremlin as antithetical to its security interests. Having been invaded so often, Russia tended to view security in terms of dominating and occupying as much territory as possible.

There were those who realized the inherent conflicts involved, ranging from conservatives such as Kennan, who warned against assuming a "community of interests" with Moscow, to liberals such as Lippmann and Wallace, who urged Americans to try to see things from the Soviet perspective. But for most U.S. policy makers, the root causes of Moscow's belligerent attitude remained an enigma. That is why Stalin's speech at the Bolshoi Theater on February 9 caused such a stir.

At an election rally on the eve of voting for the Supreme Soviet, Stalin mixed orthodox Marxist dogma with exhortations on behalf of the new five-year plan for economic development. World War II, he contended, had been caused by the inherent contradictions of capitalism. He conceded that the Soviets and their "freedom-loving" Western allies had been fighting for a common cause, the elimination of fascism. But what caught the most attention in the West were his references to the "hostile" international system and "capitalist encirclement." The incompatibility between Communism and capitalism, he ominously warned, could lead to another war.

Reaction in the U.S. ranged from bafflement to alarm. Justice William Douglas told Forrestal that the speech was "the declaration of World War III." Said commentator Eric Sevareid: "If you can brush aside Stalin's speech of February 9, you are a braver man than I am." *Time* magazine described it as "the most warlike pronouncement uttered by any top-rank statesman since V-J Day" but noted that Stalin may have made it "for purely Russian reasons."

When reporters asked Harriman, just back from Moscow, for his assessment, he downplayed the speech as being "directed primarily" to the Soviet public. "They are now being asked to support another five-year plan and that plan will mean hard work." Americans had already awakened to the Soviet threat, he knew, and there was no cause to rile them further. But Harriman was less sanguine in his private thoughts, which he confided to Admiral Leahy. The first objective of the Kremlin's policy, he said, was to extend Communist ideology to other parts of the world.

One of those who reacted strongly to the speech was Paul Nitze. The son of a Romance languages professor at the University of Chicago and the grandson of the banker for the Baltimore and Ohio Railroad, Nitze had gone on to distinguish himself at Harvard, where he was a member of the Porcellian with Bohlen, and on Wall Street, where he teamed up with Forrestal at Dillon, Read. He and Forrestal had joined with Harriman and Lovett at one point to handle Paramount's sale of Columbia Pictures. Clarence Dillon had pulled out of the deal at the last minute, because he did not want to play second fiddle to Brown Brothers Harriman, but the working relations between the two financial houses remained cordial. During the war, Nitze by chance met George Kennan in the dining car of a train to New York. They discussed mutual friends, Bohlen in particular, and Kennan imparted his hard-line views about the Soviets. "I was really taken by what he said," Nitze later remembered.

Upon reading Stalin's remarks, Nitze, then a mid-level official at the State Department, immediately went to see Forrestal at the Pentagon, telling him the speech was a "delayed declaration of war on the U.S." Forrestal of course needed no convincing, but he sent Nitze off to see Acheson, who did. Such fears, said the Under Secretary, "were all nonsense, Paul."

Yet Acheson, involved once again in the problem of controlling the atom, was depressed by both the speech and the uproar. His unfocused broodings about the dimming prospects for Soviet cooperation prompted him to ask Bohlen for a memo on the subject. In addition, he instructed, the State Department should solicit opinions from its experts in the field, people like George Kennan.

Bohlen was stymied in his attempt to come up with any new handle on the problem. Creative strategic thinking was not his strong point. In his memo for Acheson he listed three alternatives: frankly recognizing Soviet and Western spheres of influence, embarking on a policy of military firmness to challenge Soviet expansionism, and pursuing a Wilsonian "universalist" approach based on the ideals embodied in the U.N. Charter regarding each nation's right to freedom and self-determination.

The first two of these options, Bohlen argued, lacked domestic support. Adhering to the principles of international law as proclaimed by the U.N., especially if efforts were made to consult with the Soviets directly on any issue, was consequently the wisest course. At least if the U.S. was involved in any dispute, it "would be on a clear moral issue and not as a result of conflict of national interests between the great powers which would tend to divide world opinion."

Bohlen conceded that this approach had one difficulty, "that of integrating the policies of a dictatorship, directed virtually exclusively towards the furtherance of the national interest of the Soviet state, with the principles of world cooperation and international morality." This, of course, was not an insignificant problem. Indeed, that was the crux of the whole problem.

The Kremlin was simply showing no interest in international cooperation. Bohlen's framework, a mixture drawn from Wilson and Roosevelt, did not help explain the apparent hostility of Stalin's speech. Nor could many in Washington genuinely understand why the Soviets were not eager to work with agencies that promoted international cooperation and free trade, such as the World Bank or the International Monetary Fund.

As a result of such confusion, two inquiries, one from the State Department and another initiated by the Treasury, were dispatched to Moscow. There they landed on the desk of a man who was seething with pent-up opinions and had just been given the freedom to unleash them, a man who favored more fervently than anyone the first two of Bohlen's options, a man whose mind was not clouded by well-intentioned assumptions that Russia somehow shared the same values or goals as the U.S.

•   •   •

Ever despondent about Washington's feckless attitude toward the Soviets, George Kennan was once again threatening to resign. And once again, Bohlen was begging him "don't do anything foolish." Adding to Kennan's dolors was yet another spate of minor ailments (the flu, sinus congestion, tooth trouble), which had forced him to take to bed for a few days in his rooms at the Mokhovaya Street embassy. Thus it was hardly surprising that the latest set of naïve queries brought to his bedroom only served to reduce Kennan to, in his words, "a new level of despair."

Instead of resigning, however, Kennan decided to unload his frustrated thoughts. "For eighteen long months I had done little else but pluck people's sleeves, trying to make them understand," he later recalled. "So far as official Washington was concerned, it had been to all intents and purposes like talking to a stone."

It was Washington's Birthday. The embassy, closed for the holiday, was quiet and desolate. But Kennan, resisting the temptation to "brush the question off with a couple of routine sentences," had been galvanized into action. Having produced reams of unsolicited explanations of Soviet behavior, most of which were destined to languish unappreciated in the files of Harriman or others, his opinions had finally been officially sought. "They had asked for it," he thought. "Now, by God, they would have it."

He telephoned his secretary, sent for two military attachés, and gathered the small group in his upstairs bedroom at the embassy. Composing his thoughts as he went along, and dividing them neatly into five sections like a Puritan sermon, Kennan proceeded to dictate a 5,540-word analysis that became known as "the Long Telegram." Its purpose was to awaken as well as to enlighten, to make official Washington sit up and finally listen to its anxious author. Simmering beneath its sober tone were sentences susceptible to quite alarmist interpretations. Both through what it said and the way it was interpreted, Kennan's analysis was to become the most influential cable in the history of the American Foreign Service.

What caused the Soviets to behave the way they did in international affairs? According to their Marxist propaganda, Kennan reported, they claimed to be motivated by a belief that the inherent conflicts of capitalism would cause Western countries to launch "wars of intervention" against the Soviets. Of course, such "baseless and disproven" rationales were "simply not true." In reality, "the Soviet party line is not based on any objective analysis of the situation beyond Russia's borders." What actually motivated Russia's rulers, Kennan argued, was a "centuries-old" outlook: "At the bottom of the Kremlin's neurotic view of world affairs is traditional and instinctive Russian sense of insecurity."

What role, then, did ideology play? Marxism was mainly a "fig leaf" for Russia's current rulers, one that served to justify police-state tactics, a closed society, and expansionist ambitions. "In this dogma, with its basic altruism of purpose, they found justification for their instinctive fear of the outside world, for the dictatorship without which they did not know how to rule," Kennan explained. "This is why Soviet purposes must always be solemnly cloaked in trappings of Marxism, and why no one should underrate the importance of dogma in Soviet affairs." Marxism was not the cause of Soviet expansionism, Kennan contended, but "its honeyed promises" made traditional Russian instincts "more dangerous and insidious than ever before."

What did this mean for the Kremlin's foreign policy? Kennan predicted that "efforts will be made to advance official limits of Soviet power." The first signs of this expansionism will come in neighboring areas, such as Iran and Turkey. In addition, an international Communist network would attempt to undermine Western resolve by penetrating "labor unions, youth leagues, women's organizations, racial societies . . . liberal magazines, publishing houses, etc."

Kennan's conclusions were dire. The Soviets considered it necessary, he said, that "our traditional way of life be destroyed." The question of how the U.S. should cope with such a challenge was, therefore, "undoubtedly the greatest task our diplomacy has ever faced and probably the greatest it will ever have to face."

Within a couple of years, after his warnings had been heeded and more, Kennan would complain that he did not intend his theory of Soviet "containment" (as it was later dubbed) to be interpreted as primarily a military response. In the Long Telegram, however, that was the first strategy he discussed. "Soviet power," he wrote, is "impervious to the logic of reason, and it is highly sensitive to the logic of force." The Kremlin was likely to back down "when strong resistance is encountered at any point." A Soviet adversary would "rarely" have to use force as long as he "makes clear his readiness to use it."

The additional strategies he advocated—better propaganda programs, efforts to build up the economic and spiritual vitality of the West—drew little attention when Kennan's ominous opus landed in Washington. Nor did the "encouraging" parts of his message: that Soviet leaders were basically cautious, that Marxist theory did not require launching wars against capitalist countries, that Western strength could deter military conflicts. Partly because Kennan, ever anxious to be heard, cloaked his thoughts with portentous prose, the Long Telegram was viewed by those who read it in February of 1946 as having two main messages: the U.S. must forcefully draw the line against further expansion of Soviet influence, and it should unabashedly forge an alliance with Britain and other Western nations for this purpose.

What made the Long Telegram so immensely influential was not what Kennan said (for he had said the same often before) but what Washington was willing to hear. "If none of my previous literary efforts had seemed to evoke even the faintest tinkle from the bell at which they were aimed," he noted, "this one, to my astonishment, struck it squarely and set it vibrating."

For ten years he had been ineffectively fretting about the dangers of American mellowness toward the Soviets. Within three years he would be fretting about the dangers of American militarism. But for a brief and critical period, Kennan's outlook and the pendulum of official U.S. thinking coincided. He had given a resonant voice to the unarticulated unease that was growing in Washington. Kennan, for once, was delighted. "My reputation was made," he said. "My voice now carried."

"This telegram from George Kennan in Moscow is not subject to condensation," a State Department aide wrote in passing it on to Byrnes and Acheson. A "splendid analysis," Byrnes cabled back. Particularly pleased were the veterans of the Riga-Moscow days of the early 1930s. "It hits the nail on the head," proclaimed Loy Henderson. "It has been very gratifying for Chip and me and others who have been associated with Russian matters for a long time," noted Elbridge Durbrow, "to see the thing come into its proper perspective."

Bohlen and Harriman had long shared Kennan's basic beliefs about the difficulties of dealing with Moscow. But they had resisted his harsh prescription that the world be split into rival spheres. Their own hard-line attitude was primarily engendered by the contempt Moscow showed for self-determination and freedom, particularly in places like Poland. George Kennan, the indignant Presbyterian elder, could undoubtedly work himself into a moral frenzy about Soviet totalitarianism, just like

Harriman and Bohlen; but George Kennan the Bismarckian realist cared little for Wilsonian idealism and was perfectly prepared to concede Poland and other hapless places to the Soviet sphere.

One significant result of the Long Telegram was that it unified the thinking of the various advocates of firmness. Only after people like Bohlen and Harriman began to adopt Kennan's view of the Soviets and their satellites as a rival power bloc—one that was implacably resistant to accommodating Western democratic ideals—could the attitude of firmness evolve into a policy of containment.

Bohlen, uneasy about the vacuity of his own recent memos, eagerly embraced Kennan's "exhaustive and excellent analysis." In a memo to Acheson, the State Department's Soviet expert proclaimed that Kennan's cable meant that "there was no need to examine further the motives or the reasons for present Soviet policy." The U.S.S.R. was "an expanding totalitarian state," Bohlen added, and the world was being divided into "two irreconcilably hostile camps." He proposed that the U.S. "should use every method at its disposal" to counter the Soviets.

Harriman, who had seen such outpourings from Kennan before, wired his former aide "congratulations on your long analytical message." Far more significantly, he sent along a copy to his friend Forrestal. Given your "interest in the philosophy of the present Soviet leaders," Harriman wrote the Navy Secretary, Kennan's dispatch was "well worth reading."

A month before Kennan's telegram arrived, Forrestal had written Walter Lippmann to argue that the fundamental question facing America was whether it was dealing with a traditional nation-state or a fanatic religion. Forrestal was inclined to believe that Russia was the latter. Convinced that the free world was under siege from international Communism and that the Kremlin's actions could be explained by its devotion to this dogma, Forrestal had immersed himself in philosophical tracts about Marx, Lenin, and the Bolshevik Revolution.

In Kennan's telegram he thought he found the intellectual confirmation he so ardently sought. Thus he was prone to miss not only the nuances of the Long Telegram but much of its basic thrust. The way Forrestal read Kennan's cable, it confirmed his own fervent belief that Marxism was the cause of Soviet expansionism and that halting the spread of international Communism would likely demand a resort to force.

Forrestal hardly knew who Kennan was, but he began spreading his gospel like an evangelist. He entered the Long Telegram in his diary, had scores of copies distributed, and made it required reading for his staff and top officers. By taking him under his wing, Forrestal assured that Kennan's voice would be loudly heard. In the amplification, however, there was bound to be some distortion.

• • •

The telegram was on Dean Acheson's desk when David Lilienthal, the head of the Tennessee Valley Authority, arrived in Acheson's State Department office. The two men were in charge of shaping the atomic control plan that the U.S. would submit to the U.N., and Lilienthal had walked across Lafayette Park that morning in early March to go over the draft they would present to their full committee the next day. But he found his colleague distracted, almost agitated. For more than ninety minutes, Acheson agonized about foreign policy problems, handing Lilienthal Kennan's Long Telegram to read. "The atomic bomb," Lilienthal said when he finished the dispatch, "will be one of the first real tests of our ability to understand the Russian problem."

Acheson agreed. But he had begun to realize that the task would be harder than he and Lilienthal originally hoped, that it would demand a greater emphasis on safeguards and less reliance on trust and faith. Kennan's telegram was far too abstract for Acheson's practical tastes, and its vague recommendations were hardly much help for an action-oriented policy maker. But its warnings resonated. Acheson, as he considered atomic energy and a broad range of other problems, slowly began to grapple with Kennan's forebodings.

The morning that Acheson and Lilienthal sat reading Kennan's telegram—Wednesday, March 6, 1946—was one of those moments when a variety of events and ideas seem to collide:

• Just minutes before their meeting began, a cable arrived from the American consul in Tabriz reporting "exceptionally heavy Soviet troop movements" in northern Iran. In a nearby office, a large map of that country was being prepared with red arrows sweeping down from Russia toward Teheran and the Turkish border.

• Newspapers were headlining an address given the previous day in Fulton, Missouri, warning of an "iron curtain" descending across Europe. Already worried about British demands for preferential treatment on atomic energy matters, Acheson decided that the State Department must distance itself from Winston Churchill's warlike cry. But he feared that the former Prime Minister's appraisal might in fact be pretty realistic—and he knew for certain that it reflected a sentiment that was growing in Washington.

• The front pages also contained the latest news of the Canadian spy scandal. Twenty-two scientists and technicians had been arrested as part of an intelligence ring providing atomic secrets to the Soviet Union, and Moscow had not even denied the charges. Even as Acheson was considering ways to share control of the atom, there were rumors that the espionage efforts extended into the U.S.

• The previous week had seen a spate of speeches—including ones by Jimmy Byrnes, Arthur Vandenberg, and John Foster Dulles—calling for a firmer American line toward the Soviets. Each had contained the requisite lines about hope for closer cooperation and adherence to the ideals of the United Nations, but their basic thrusts echoed Kennan's telegram: the world was being divided into hostile East-West blocs and the U.S. must act forcefully to prevent the further spread of Soviet influence.

All of these were new elements in the equation being considered by Acheson that morning. This rapidly changing environment, he told Lilienthal, was bound to affect the outlook for the plan they were trying to shape.

Acheson had been brought back into the effort to control atomic weapons early in January. As Byrnes was leaving for the U.N. meeting in London, he caught Acheson at home in bed with the flu. Now that everyone—from Truman to Vandenberg to Stalin—had agreed that Washington should submit a proposal on atomic development to the U.N., a committee was being formed to draw one up. Acheson was going to be its chairman, the Secretary informed him over the phone.

Acheson's protests that he knew nothing about the technical side of the subject were brushed aside. There would be, said Byrnes, plenty of help: James Conant, the president of Harvard; Vannevar Bush, the President's former scientific adviser; General Leslie Groves, commander of the Manhattan Project; and John McCloy, who had sat with Stimson at Potsdam and in the Adirondacks drafting the first proposals for atomic control. They were all nice fellows, said the Secretary, and would be fun to work with. Acheson tried one more meager protest, but Byrnes said he had to rush for his plane. Acheson recalled, with perhaps a bit of exaggeration, that his temperature rose six points before he recovered.

When the group started its work, McCloy was among the most

optimistic that a plan could be devised that was acceptable to the Soviets. Part of his mandate, as he saw it, was to carry the torch passed to him by Stimson. He eagerly accepted his appointment, flew down from New York, and took the Achesons' offer to be their house guest.

The first thing Acheson and McCloy decided was that the committee needed the help of a board of technical consultants. To chair that group Acheson chose Lilienthal, a fellow member of the Brandeis-Frankfurter coterie from the Harvard Law School. Without such a panel of experts, Acheson explained, it would be like telling a South Sea Islander to do something about the problem of cows being killed on railroad tracks: no matter how well-intentioned the islander, he could be of little help if he did not know what a cow or a railway was.

The star of the panel was J. Robert Oppenheimer, the mastermind of Los Alamos, the troubled father of the atomic bomb. He too stayed with the Achesons. After dinner each night, a borrowed blackboard was set up in Acheson's library, where a picture of Stimson had joined the family pictures and silver rowing cup from his Yale freshmen crew along the cluttered walls. There the intense physicist would lecture Acheson and McCloy about the inner working of the atomic bomb.

"He drew little figures representing electrons, neutrons, and protons," Acheson recalled, "bombarding one another, chasing one another about, dividing and generally carrying on in unpredictable ways." McCloy and Acheson would pepper Oppenheimer with questions. "It's hopeless," their tutor occasionally lamented. "I really do think you two believe neutrons and electrons *are* little men." Noted Acheson: "We admitted nothing."

Throughout February—while Stalin spoke, Kennan analyzed, Soviet troops shifted, and Churchill flew across the Atlantic—the Lilienthal-Oppenheimer panel was off on its own, flying to Oak Ridge and other laboratories, gathering information, and piecing together the details needed for a plan to control atomic energy. The proposals they came up with were innovative, exciting, far-reaching—and perhaps, alas, somewhat naïve.

No cooperative international system, Lilienthal and Oppenheimer concluded, could be based simply on restrictions enforced by a cadre of atomic policemen roaming the globe like Prohibition agents. Instead, a new International Atomic Development Authority should be created and given an active and positive role. It would be responsible for owning and mining the world's limited number of deposits of uranium and thorium, providing "denatured" material for smaller power plants, and operating on its own all atomic facilities, anywhere in the world, that could be considered dangerous. With its virtual monopoly, the agency could easily discover if any country tried to pursue its own independent weapons program. Other nations would then have ample warning that forceful measures must be taken.

This was the program that Lilienthal brought to Acheson on March 6 and which the Under Secretary asked him to present to the full committee at Dumbarton Oaks the following day. The conference room of that Georgetown mansion provided a setting befitting the historic grandeur of the plan. The three-story-high chamber was graced by carved and painted wooden beams, and priceless tapestries covered the walls. Catching the light from the French doors to the garden was El Greco's *The Visitation*.

The scientists took turns reading parts of the proposal. When Lilienthal finished the final section, he dramatically placed the report on the table and announced: "This, gentlemen, is our recommendation of a plan for security in a world of atomic energy." At the other end of the long table, Acheson put down his copy and took off his glasses. "This is a brilliant and profound document," he announced in a warm, low tone.

And yet he had qualms, and so did the rest of his committee, qualms prompted by the growing worries about Russia's motives. So for more than a week the members and their experts worked on the plan, together and separately, debating revisions under Acheson's careful guidance. There must be more emphasis on inspection, the scientists were told, and on a timetable of clear steps that would protect the U.S. from giving away too much if Russia showed bad faith. The scientists, who had not been reading the cables from Moscow and Teheran or agonizing about Soviet intentions, were reluctant. But they went along.

McCloy, along with Acheson, was among the most fervent supporters of the overall scheme. Its affirmative tone went beyond what he and Stimson had dared to envision. But it appealed to his sense of action, of grasping ahold of the imponderables. There must be no delay, he emphasized. America could not push ahead with its own atomic plants while trying to prevent other nations from doing so. What made the plan so admirable, he said, was that it could be accepted by the Soviets and everyone else. It was workable without being softheaded.

There was, however, in the back of McCloy's mind, a notion that had captivated Stimson. No plan could fully succeed if the Soviet

Union remained a closed society. The grandiose scheme would no doubt mean that the international agency would build atomic plants inside the U.S.S.R. Perhaps this could be used as an inducement or a lever to get the Kremlin to loosen up its police-state society. Perhaps even a broad program of disarmament could be part of the price for sharing in America's atomic monopoly.

Acheson was somewhat startled by his friend's naïveté and quickly moved to quash the notion. There was no use "chasing a will-o'-wisp," he said, nor in trying to solve the Soviet problem in one fell stroke. It would take time and patience if America hoped to achieve Russia's gradual "civilization."

After nine days of concentrated work, Acheson called both his committee and their consultants for a final Sunday morning meeting at Dumbarton Oaks. He and McCloy were both anxious that the plan be finished as quickly as possible, fearing that events would overtake them. (There were a few personal considerations as well. McCloy had cabled Acheson before coming down: "Atom bomb has no terrors compared to what will happen to me if I cannot get to Providence for young Douglas's wedding.")

Yet the members were still bickering over details. Anne Wilson, who was then Herbert Marks's secretary and later his wife, passed Acheson a note saying that a coffee break might relieve the tension. It did. Acheson circulated among the members stitching compromises back together, securing agreement on words and phrases. When everyone had retaken his seat, the Under Secretary posed the question: Should the plan be approved? Agreement was unanimous.

Taking no chances on a renewed debate, Acheson personally drafted the letter of transmittal while the others went out for lunch. All of the carefully crafted agreements on timing and stages and safeguards were deftly woven together. "We are impressed," Acheson wrote, "by the great advantages of an international agency with affirmative powers and functions coupled with powers of inspection."

In a CBS radio interview the next week, Acheson was asked if the plan was "like a road map showing a safe national highway toward international control?" Replied Acheson: "Yes, except this is no vacation jaunt. It is deadly serious and we must start moving at once."

Byrnes and Truman, however, felt the need for a more prestigious driver. Selected to present the plan at the U.N. was Bernard Baruch, the seventy-five-year-old "adviser to Presidents," self-styled park-bench philosopher, and retired stock market speculator. Acheson vigorously protested: Baruch was a pompous man with a reputation for wisdom earned mainly by the dispensation of campaign contributions and the careful image polishing of his publicist, Herbert Bayard Swope. Lilienthal pronounced himself "quite sick" over the appointment of the "vain" self-promoter.

McCloy had helped talk Acheson out of releasing the report publicly, arguing that it should serve as a basis for the U.N. delegate to use as he pleased. But after Baruch's appointment, Acheson felt little compulsion to keep the plan secret. He wanted a public debate, which he was sure would show the soundness of the package they had put together. So he provided a copy to a Senate committee and, not unexpectedly, its essence appeared in the next day's newspapers. The State Department then formally released the document.

Approval came from a surprisingly broad spectrum, ranging from liberal commentators to conservative senators. Both *The New York Times* and the Washington *Post* endorsed the plan in editorials, and a Senate resolution was immediately introduced to make it the basis for negotiations. (I. F. Stone was among the few liberal dissenters, commenting that the only one of the authors "who is at all progressive in his thinking is Acheson." Sending along a copy of the article to McCloy, Forrestal joked that he was "glad to note that you do not qualify in the Acheson school of progressivism.")

Baruch summoned forth all of his great pride to announce that he was too old to be a "messenger boy" and to demand the right to make revisions as he saw fit. Both McCloy and Acheson worked with him closely, hoping to preserve the basics of their plan. But Baruch insisted on elements that would, in Acheson's words, "almost certainly wreck any possibility of Russian acceptance." These included automatic penalties for any country violating the final agreement and no veto power for the Soviets or other members.

Carrying his own alternative to the White House, and threatening to resign if the Acheson plan were chosen instead, Baruch got his way. At the U.N., he was able to excite his audience and pave the way for a propaganda victory by opening with a sentence Swope had written for him: "We are here to make a choice between the quick and the dead." Andrei Gromyko was also able to score propaganda points with a Soviet proposal for a complete ban on nuclear weapons. Neither side, however, presented a plan that had a chance of being accepted by the other.

McCloy and Acheson would surely have found it difficult to get their program accepted by the Soviets. Stalin was hardly likely to sit still for a plan that allowed Americans to inspect facilities and mines

in the U.S.S.R. and approve each step toward joint control. Nor was
such a grand vision of an atomic authority, one that would own mines
in various countries and be run by international bureaucrats, a very
practical prospect. In retrospect, too, it is clear that the Soviets were
secretly determined to spy and build on their own, and would likely
have exploited any deal for their own cynical purposes.

At the time, however, there seemed to be a chance, albeit quite
small, that the plan could have established an effective framework for
international cooperation, an alternative to a frenzied and uncon-
trolled race for destructive atomic capacity. Such was the sincere dream
that Stimson had bequeathed to McCloy and Acheson and many
others, one that now slowly began to fade.

•   •   •

The conversion of Dean Acheson to a hard-line stance on dealings
with the Soviets was perhaps the most dramatic and significant of any
postwar American statesman. In early March he had held the highest
of hopes that a system of atomic cooperation could be accomplished.
But even as those hopes died, so too did Acheson's faith that friendly
relations could be worked out with America's lapsed ally.

A sureness of manner, a firmness of outlook, a clarity of vision—
these were all part of Acheson's authoritative, some would say imperious, style. A Hamlet-like attitude toward the Soviets did not suit
him well, nor was it to burden him for long. As he later put it: "The
year 1946 was for the most part a year of learning that minds in the
Kremlin worked very much as George F. Kennan had predicted they
would."

Acheson's attitudes—unlike those of Harriman, Bohlen, and Kennan—were not shaped by personal exposure to the perfidy of Kremlin
leaders or the infirmity of Soviet society. Nor was he prone to Kennan-
style abstract agonizing about the forces of history and ideology. Brandeis's prized pupil was influenced by solid evidence and concrete
situations. Even as the maneuvering over atomic control was under
way, the early days of spring were providing two such lessons.

Back in December, when Acheson first began work on an American
loan to the British, the action was not conceived as an Anglo-American
effort to counter Soviet strength. In fact, Acheson harbored hopes,
along with Bohlen and Harriman, that it would be followed by a loan
to Moscow; they all still believed, at the beginning of 1946, that
economic assistance could be used as a lever with the Kremlin and
might even pave the way for Russia's gradual evolution into a coop-

erative member of the world community. In putting together the $3.75 billion package for Britain, Acheson mainly concentrated on winning concessions from London that would reduce imperial tariff barriers and promote the goal of global free trade.

Perhaps what insured that the loan would be cast in East-West terms was Winston Churchill's visit to the U.S., as a private citizen, in early March. Less than two weeks before the Senate was due to consider the measure, Churchill made his "iron curtain" pronouncement in Missouri. What aroused the most controversy, however, was not his description of the problem but his solution to it: an unabashed Anglo-American alliance against the Soviets. "I am convinced that there is nothing they admire so much as strength," the former Prime Minister rumbled. And this, he added, required a "fraternal association of the English-speaking peoples."

The result was a polarizing uproar. The U.S. (like Britain) was still officially an ally of the Soviet Union. President Truman, feeling the need to distance himself from the man he had shared a stage with, lamely contended that he had not read the speech beforehand. "I think it did some good," he wrote his mother, "but I am not yet ready to endorse Mr. Churchill's speech." Claude Pepper and a handful of other senators issued a statement accusing Churchill of being unable to divorce his thinking "from the roll of drums and the flutter of the flag of empire." Liberals such as Henry Wallace and Walter Lippmann again railed against the appearance of an Anglo-American coalition, which they claimed would serve only to increase Soviet insecurity and hostility.

The night of the speech, the Achesons happened to give a dinner party to which Lippmann and Wallace, as well as Chip Bohlen, were invited. There the argument raged. Acheson, articulate and aggressive as usual, dominated the conversation. Churchill had a point, he said. It was time to stand firm with the Soviets. Bohlen belittled the Soviets' fears of encirclement; they were the ones on the offensive, not the U.S. Wallace, on the other hand, warned that this could lead to war. "Well, Chip," Mrs. Lippmann told Bohlen, "all I can say is that in your war I will not be a nurse's aide." Her husband for the most part brooded quietly, but in the column he wrote the next day he warned: "The line of British imperial interest and the line of American vital interest are not to be regarded as identical."

Bohlen relayed such sentiments to the friend in Moscow whose outlook he had come to share, and Kennan responded with his usual "concern and alarm." Citing Lippmann and Wallace by name in a cable back to Washington, Kennan reiterated his contention that Moscow's view of the world was based not on facts but on internal necessities. "Nothing short of complete disarmament, delivery of our air and naval forces to Russia and the resigning of powers of government to American communists would even dent this problem," he cabled. "And even then we believe—and this is not facetious—that Moscow would smell a trap." In short, Britain and American should work together and not worry about how this would be interpreted in the U.S.S.R.

Harriman was also in substantial agreement with his friend the former Prime Minister. In Washington a few days after the Fulton speech, the two men had a long, private talk. The Russians, Churchill said, will try all the rooms in a house, enter those that are not locked, and when they come to one that cannot be broken into, they will withdraw and invite you to dine genially that same evening. Harriman, a far less felicitous thinker and talker, was as impressed by the glories of Churchill's rhetoric as he was by the gloominess of his outlook.

Acheson had his own chance to dine with Churchill at the British Embassy in Washington. He too was swayed by the Briton's gruff charm. Alice Acheson could hardly restrain her outpouring of personal praise, both for Churchill's statesmanship and his paintings. An accomplished artist herself, she engaged in a spirited but friendly argument over whether the tones and hues of Churchill's palette might be too high-keyed for his artistic style. "A woman of conviction, your wife," Churchill said to Acheson, thus earning his lasting affection.

Yet Acheson, despite his argument with Wallace and fondness for Churchill, was worried about whether American policy should be so closely tied to Britain in defiance of Moscow. On the advice of his colleagues at the State Department, he decided not to attend an official reception being given for Churchill in New York. And when the Senate began its hearings on the British loan, Acheson tried to walk a fine line.

The loan, as Acheson tried to cast the issue, represented American support for the principles of freedom, but it should not be seen as an effort to combat the spread of Communism. "We are interested," he proclaimed, "in an economic system which is the very basis of our life—the system of free individual enterprise." Senator Vandenberg, however, was more interested in the strategic implications. "If we do not lead," proclaimed the new convert to internationalism, "some other and powerful nation will capitalize on our failure."

After passing the Senate on a close vote, the measure went to the

House, where even more anti-Communist rhetoric proved necessary. "The economic arguments," explained Congressman Christian Herter, a respected Republican internationalist from Massachusetts, "are on the whole much less convincing than the feeling that the loan may serve us in holding up the hand of a nation whom we may need badly because of impending Russian troubles." Added Speaker Sam Rayburn, a Texas Democrat: "I do not want Western Europe, England and all the rest pushed toward an ideology I despise."

Acheson concluded that the anti-Communist rhetoric was necessary to win support for the British package. And that, of course, meant abandoning any plans for a loan to the Soviets. In a March poll, citizens were asked if "the U.S. is being too soft or too tough in its policy toward Russia." In a dramatic swing from previous surveys, 60 percent answered "too soft," while only 3 percent said "too tough." Acheson was already becoming convinced of the same thing. Just as importantly, he had learned that such sentiment could be tapped to rally support for the critical responsibilities that America would have to shoulder in a changing and dangerous world.

• • •

A crucial factor in Acheson's outlook, during the debate over both the British loan and atomic energy, was the crisis in Iran that was coming to a head at the same time. It vividly illustrated all of the tactics that made Americans most fearful about the Soviet Union. Contrary to what had been agreed just months before, Moscow refused to honor the March 2 deadline for withdrawing the Red Army from the parts of Iran it occupied during the war. It also encouraged a Communist-led separatist movement in the northern province of Azerbaijan—and helped impose Soviet-style secret police there. And finally, Moscow seemed to be involved in toppling the Prime Minister in Teheran and replacing him with an enigmatic man who acted, at least for a while, like a Soviet sympathizer.

Worst of all, this was happening not in Eastern Europe, where it could be argued that Russia had a legitimate interest in establishing a security belt. The only logical explanation was that Moscow's moves were blatantly expansionist. To Acheson and other students of history, the region at stake was vital to the economic and strategic interests of the West.

Posing the question that everyone now seemed to be asking, *The New York Times* printed a hard-hitting editorial on "What does Russia want?" Conceding that the Soviets had security needs, it went on to

list the places "annexed" since the end of the war. The territory stretched
from Eastern Europe to Manchuria, a total of 273,947 square miles.
"Where does the search for security end," asked the editorial, "and
where does expansion begin?"

While Byrnes served as the front man, Acheson took on much of
the day-to-day authority at the State Department once the Iranian
crisis erupted in mid-March. The committee he convened concluded
that the challenge must not be minimized: continued occupation of
northern Iran by Soviet troops would soon mean that the West would
face a fait accompli.

With maps of Red Army movements as an ominous backdrop,
Acheson's committee at first decided to confront the situation as a
violation of a 1942 treaty that the Soviets had signed guaranteeing
Iran's sovereignty. But Chip Bohlen objected: the U.S., he pointed
out, was not a party to the pact, which had been negotiated by Britain.

What worried Acheson more, however, was that he had been waging
a losing battle against American military demobilization; any threat
not backed by strength might be called as a bluff. He concluded that
for the moment the best approach was to protest to the Kremlin but
"leave a graceful way out" if it did not want a showdown. A department
official named Alger Hiss, then director of the Office of Special Political Affairs (forerunner to the Policy Planning Group that Kennan
and Nitze would later head), drafted the note for Acheson, which was
sent to Kennan for delivery to Molotov.

Truman was aware that the crisis represented a critical shift to the
U.S. of Britain's traditional role as the guardian of Western interests
in Iran. It was a transition that must be handled gingerly. Harriman,
he decided, was the man who could help.

In the taxi on the way to the White House, the recently retired
ambassador to Moscow marshaled his thoughts on how to decline the
pending appointment as ambassador to London. Some of Harriman's
considerations were professional: he had no desire to work for a Secretary of State he had taken to calling "the damn fool." Other considerations were personal. He and Marie had just spent an enjoyable
couple of weeks down at Hobe Sound in Florida with Adèle and Bob
Lovett, who was at the time recuperating from his gallbladder operation
and about to rejoin Brown Brothers Harriman. Yet tugging at him
from the other side was his enjoyable friendship with both Churchill
and his daughter-in-law, Pamela. When he reached the Oval Office,
his resistance dissolved.

"I want you to go to England," Truman said. "There is a very dangerous situation developing in Iran." He explained that the Russians were refusing to pull their troops out, as they had promised the British they would do. "This may lead to war," said the President. "I must have a man in London who knows the British, a man I can trust."

"When do you want me to go?" Harriman replied.

In the end, there was little for Harriman to do. American policy makers decided that the Iranian situation was so critical that Britain's sensitivity about its own role in its historic sphere of influence could be ignored.

From Moscow, Kennan's cables painted a dire picture. The Soviets, he said, had designs on the whole region. "The U.S.S.R. aims not only at acquiring a privileged position in northern Iran," he wired at the height of the crisis, "but at virtual subjugation, penetration and domination of the entire country, and Bahrein and Kuwait as well." Nor, he added, were Turkey or other neighbors, stretching as far as India, immune from Russia's drive for "ultimate political domination of the entire Asiatic mainland."

The Soviets indeed had their eyes set on controlling parts of Iran. But as Kennan's Long Telegram had predicted, they were reluctant to press too hard when faced with strong resistance. After securing Iranian agreement for joint ownership of some important oil concessions, Moscow agreed in late March to pull back its troops.

The U.S. nevertheless insisted that the issue remain on the U.N. agenda until the troops were actually withdrawn. This prompted Andrei Gromyko to stage the first in a long series of dramatic Soviet walkouts form the Security Council. But the continued pressure also helped assure that the troops would in fact depart. By May they had.

Although the U.N. had served nicely as a source of moral support, it was already clear that it would never be, as some of its founders had dreamed, a force in its own right against aggression. It was American resolve, Acheson and others believed, that had caused Moscow to back down. In response to the showdown occurring in Iran, and one that seemed brewing in Turkey, the U.S. had sent the battleship *Missouri* to fly the flag in the eastern Mediterranean. In addition, Washington soon began supplying aid and pledges of support as a way of encouraging Teheran to secure its control over Azerbaijan.

The successful conclusion of the Iranian crisis illustrated to Acheson, more clearly than any Long Telegram could, the importance of firmly confronting any Soviet probe. Moscow was clearly enticed by weakness and deterred only by strength. With Britain no longer able to protect traditional Western interests in places like Iran, that duty was now inevitably in U.S. hands.

This was a bold new vision of America's role, one that would be hard for a sheltered nation to accept. But men such as Acheson knew it was necessary. That June, at the urging of Bohlen and other friends, he spent a couple of late nights at his desk at home, a glass of Scotch by his side, writing a discursive speech entitled "Random Harvest" which he delivered at the Harvard Club in Boston. "Our name for problems is significant," he concluded. "We call them headaches. You take a powder and they are gone. The pains about which we have been talking are not like that. They will stay with us until death. We have got to understand that all our lives the danger, the uncertainty, the need for alertness, for effort, for discipline will be upon us. This is new to us. It will be hard for us."

McCloy, a less felicitous speaker, struck the same theme that month when he spoke at the Amherst commencement. "There is no war to end all wars," he told the students. "No war to make the world forever safe. Men who fight for freedom merely win the opportunity to continue the peacetime struggle to preserve and advance it."

•   •   •

"When the facts seemed to him to merit a change—as he seems to think they now do in the case of the Soviet Union—he switched with the facts," wrote James Reston in a lengthy *New York Times Magazine* profile of Acheson in the summer of 1946. Certainly Acheson by then had facts to go on, facts that pointed to a clear conclusion. The Soviets and their satellites could be dealt with in a businesslike way—perhaps even Poland could get coal credits—but any aggressive step, any probes for new areas to dominate, must be dealt with firmly.

If George Kennan's mind was like that of a Puritan elder—drawing anguished abstractions from a few shards of painful experience—Dean Acheson's mind could be compared to that of an elegantly cloaked Anglican archbishop. Resounding in its buttressed, soaring chamber were great moral certitudes, dressed in righteous words like "honor" and "duty," lessons deduced from the evidence of history, such as the failure of appeasement at Munich and the duplicity of the Soviets in Iran.

His world order, once shaped by the needs of the wartime alliance, had crystallized now around a new set of premises. Prime among these was an awareness, based on Kennan's theories and concrete events, that the Soviets were bent on expansion. If there was to be order and balance in the postwar world, and a renewed system of commerce and prosperity, America would have to assume the role once played by the British. This would demand farsighted commitments by a people quite content to retreat back to their own shores. The one thing that proved capable of galvanizing them was the fear of Communist expansion. By casting the power struggle against the Soviets in terms of a holy crusade against Communism, all elements of Acheson's package held neatly together.

Thus there was no hesitation, no indecision this time around, when Acheson was handed a note from the Soviets in early August. Addressed to Turkey, with a copy to the U.S. and Britain, it demanded a joint Soviet-Turkish defense system for the Dardanelles and the Turkish Straits. The Foreign Service, the State Department staff, and the War Department staff all agreed: what the Soviets were requesting would mean giving Moscow military bases on the Straits and a major toehold in the eastern Mediterranean.

On its own, this may have been acceptable. The Soviets made a valid point: during the war, German warships had been allowed into the Black Sea by a defenseless Turkish regime. At the Potsdam Conference, the Allies had agreed that the Montreux Convention governing the Straits needed revision; Britain and the U.S. made a generous proposal that would have given Soviet ships special priority during wartime. The whole issue, unfortunately, got somewhat tangled in a pet notion of Truman's, one the other Allies saw fit to ignore, to internationalize all European inland waterways.

The problem with the Soviet demand was that in August of 1946 it could no longer be considered just on its own merits. For a year Moscow had been exerting clumsy pressure on the Turkish government. Red Army movements in Bulgaria and Iran seemed partly aimed at the Turkish border, and *Pravda* prominently printed claims by Soviet strategists that the U.S.S.R. had rights to territory in northeastern Turkey. Domination of that critical country, rather than defense of the Dardanelles, seemed the main reason Russia wanted bases there. In addition, the Soviets had created a crescent of crises stretching from Trieste to Teheran, sparking brush fires that made their expansionist motives seem quite clear.

With Byrnes away, Acheson was in charge. As he pored over his maps, he had no doubt what the Soviets were up to. History offered many examples of an emerging power moving into the regions that a waning one could no longer influence. The Soviets saw the entire Middle East as ripe for the picking. Britain was retrenching, and the

U.S. had expressed no strategic "interest" in the area. In 1946 it seemed quite conceivable, certainly to Moscow and even to some in the West, that Russia was destined to become the dominant power there.

To Acheson, with his strategic vision and new understanding of Soviet intentions, it was clear that this could result in Russian domination of a vast area of critical importance to the West. If Britain could no longer exert her traditional influence in the Mediterranean and Middle East, the U.S. would have to step forward and assert for the first time that it had a strategic interest in the region.

Acheson summoned Forrestal and a handful of top military aides to the State Department to devise a forceful response. At the outset, they agreed that the Soviet request was not dictated by defensive needs; in times of war, Soviet air power could easily defend access to the Black Sea. Instead it was clearly intended as a step toward dominating Turkey and achieving the old czarist goal of having unfettered access to the high seas—a goal which, however understandable, would eventually lead to Soviet pressure from the Aegean to Gibraltar to the Red Sea.

In the memo for Truman he drafted at the meeting, Acheson bluntly summed up the fear of falling dominoes that had haunted Harriman. "For global reasons," Acheson wrote, "Turkey must be preserved if we do not wish to see other bulwarks in Western Europe and the Far East crumbling at a fast rate." With these words, the first concrete steps were taken toward what would soon be known as the Truman Doctrine and the policy of containment.

There were no illusions, certainly not in the minds of Acheson or Forrestal, that the Soviets would be swayed by diplomatic pressures alone. "The only real deterrent to Soviet plans for engulfing Turkey and the Middle East," Acheson declared at the meeting, "will be the conviction that the pursuance of such a policy will result in a war with the United States." This risky course, he boldly added, would test whether Kennan was right in predicting that the Soviets were reluctant to go to war to achieve their aims. "We shall learn," he said, "whether the Soviet policy includes an affirmative provision to go to war now."

At three-thirty the next afternoon, August 15, they gathered around Truman's desk to present the most forceful U.S. proposal for dealing with the Soviets since American forces were withdrawn from Siberia twenty-six years earlier. Next to Acheson stood Forrestal and the Pentagon's top military officials. "In our opinion," Acheson informed the

President, "the establishment by the Soviet Union of bases in the Dardanelles or the introduction of Soviet armed forces into Turkey on some other pretext would [result] in Greece and the whole Near and Middle East, including the eastern Mediterranean, falling under Soviet control and in those areas being cut off from the Western world."

Sixteen months earlier, Harriman had stood in the same spot and urged Truman to lay it on the line with Molotov. Now Harriman's longtime colleague was insisting that mere words were not enough. "The only thing that will deter the Russians," Acheson solemnly told the President, "will be the conviction that the U.S. is prepared, if necessary, to meet aggression with force of arms."

"We might as well find out," Truman replied, "whether the Russians are bent on world conquest." Agreeing with the conclusion reached by Acheson and Forrestal the previous day, the President noted that it was best to figure out the answer now rather than in five or ten years. Thus, he said, he was prepared to pursue the policy "to the end."

One of the generals whispered a critical question to Acheson. Had he made it sufficiently clear that the policy might lead to war? Before Acheson could answer, the President asked what had been said. On hearing the question, Truman opened a desk drawer and pulled out a large map of the region. A hush came over the room as Acheson and the others huddled to look over the President's shoulder. Then the self-taught history buff from Independence launched into a lecture about the strategic importance of the eastern Mediterranean and the critical need to keep it free from Soviet domination.

"When he finished," Acheson recalled, "none of us doubted he understood fully all the implications of our recommendations." The educational backgrounds of the two men could hardly have been more different, but Acheson was deeply impressed—"awed" he told a friend—by Truman's grasp of history. The President's no-nonsense style was also appealing: he understood well, Acheson thought, the need for decisive action.

The battleship *Missouri* was already in Istanbul. With the President's approval, a task force led by the new supercarrier *Franklin D. Roosevelt* was dispatched to join it. In the note Acheson prepared for the Soviets, the U.S. formally declared that the Turkish Straits was a matter of concern to its own strategic interests. The Montreux Convention could be revised, but Turkish sovereignty over the waterway could not be compromised. The American ambassador in Ankara was instructed by Acheson to tell the Turkish government to be "reasonable but firm" in its own response to the Soviets.

At Forrestal's suggestion, Acheson gave a background briefing to eighteen influential reporters. The Soviets, Acheson told them, "are not trying to control the Straits, but Turkey." He also held a press conference on what was seen as a related issue: the downing by Yugoslavia of two American planes that had strayed off course. Calling it an "outrageous" act, Acheson acidly proclaimed: "Nobody shoots down planes that are lost between clouds and are trying to get home. That isn't the ordinary aid to navigation with which they are familiar."

Even the British, whose traditional sphere of influence the U.S. was suddenly seeking to support, found themselves unnerved by Washington's tough line. Lord Inverchapel came by the State Department to tell Acheson that the tensions were causing "quite a bit of excitement" both at his embassy and in London. What did the U.S. have in mind? Was it truly prepared to resort to war? The ambassador was a friend, but Acheson responded in formal phrases. The U.S., he said "realized fully the seriousness" of the matter and "was prepared to conduct itself in a manner appropriate to that realization."

Firmness worked. A few weeks after receiving Turkey's response to their demands, the Soviets sent back another note, which Litvinov had been called out of retirement to write. It was considered "extraordinarily mild," and though the Soviets did not drop their desire for some military control of the Straits, they were willing to shelve the issue. Marshal Tito went even further: he actually apologized for Yugoslavia's attacks on the American planes.

Acheson felt he had learned how to deal with the Soviets; just as importantly, he had discovered how to please the man who shared his taste for action. In addition, when others took to belittling Truman—not an infrequent occurrence at Georgetown dinner parties—the proper Grotonian would stoutly defend him.

Acheson could be condescending, but not to the office of the Presidency or the no-nonsense man who properly insisted on respect for its authority. In Acheson's presence, Byrnes once addressed the President over the phone as "Harry." Acheson later scolded him gently. "Mr. Secretary," he said, "he is Harry to no one except Mrs. Truman." Byrnes ignored the advice, but Acheson, much to Truman's liking, never failed to call him "Mr. President."

•   •   •

Chip Bohlen was among the many who suggested it: now that Kennan had returned from Moscow, he should take a leisurely trip across the U.S., getting reacquainted with the country that often seemed so alien to him. In the process, he might help provide the public with a much-needed education about the Soviet threat.

Kennan had spent a few weeks consulting with the newly formed CIA about information gathering in the Soviet Union and in September was scheduled to become, thanks to Forrestal, the Deputy Commandant for Foreign Affairs at the National War College in Washington. The summer months in between, he agreed, would offer a good chance for a cross-country speaking tour.

American attitudes had changed quite a bit since Kennan was last in the country. Instead of running stirring picture spreads on the "valiant" Russian allies, *Life* was printing such articles as a long, two-part warning by Republican John Foster Dulles on the dire threat of the spread of international Communism. A new breed of politician, just back from the war, was finding ways to tap into a powerful new sentiment. A circuit judge named Joseph McCarthy, who had served as a desk-bound bombing analyst in the Pacific, was stumping on the slogan "Wisconsin needs a tail gunner in the Senate." Lyndon Johnson, back in Congress after a stint in the Navy, proclaimed: "We must have military strength to fulfill our moral obligations to the world." Knocking on doors in Boston, another former Navy man, John Kennedy, was finding that voters seemed to respond to his talk about America's new burden of leadership. And in southern California, Richard Nixon was discovering that these nebulous sentiments could be focused and aroused when the menace of international Communism was raised.

Even though public pressures to demobilize and "bring Daddy home" continued, Americans were bracing for the new challenge. Stalin, Molotov, Iran, Turkey, Communist spies, an iron curtain, the menacing mystery of Marxism: it all added up to a growing anxiety, one that was arousing a new sense of America's global role and, to an even greater extent, an outpouring of impassioned rhetoric about it.

Kennan began to feel more like a Janus than a Cassandra, casting his wary glances both at the anti-Communist zealots in his audience as well as the naïve Soviet sympathizers. He was particularly anxious that a distinction be made between socialism and Sovietism, the latter being the true danger. It is important, he explained, "to distinguish what is indeed progressive social doctrine from the rivalry of a foreign political machine which has appropriated and abused the slogans of socialism."

In his report to the department at the end of the tour, Kennan lamented that academic and scientific audiences seemed particularly naïve in their hopes for Soviet collaboration. "In trying to explain things to them I felt like one who shatters the pure ideals of tender youth," he noted. "Fortunately for them, they didn't believe much of what I said."

On the other extreme, Kennan found wild-eyed anti-Communists who spouted fears that the insidious ideology was seeping out from under every bed. Too many people, he reported, "sustained a false sort of hope from the beginning about collaboration and now they are drawing false conclusions from false disillusionment."

When he took up his duties at the War College, Kennan strove to put forth "a little clearer and more hopeful view" in a sixteen-page lecture. He still had sharp words for "the preposterous and fantastic distortions" of liberals "like Mr. Wallace" who felt a friendlier American attitude could induce the Russians to be more cooperative. It was important to remember, he said, that the "fanatics" who ruled Russia had "inherited many of the traditions of the old czarist state" and had come to power "breathing venom and hatred and implacable hostility toward the entire capitalistic world." Any attempt at appeasement, he argued, would be met "with unabashed demands for further concessions at every point."

This naïve liberal line, however, was only one of "two aberrations" that infected the public mind, Kennan added, "and personally I don't know which of the two is more dangerous." As he explained it: "The other aberration—into which even more Americans seem to fall—is to throw up the sponge at this point and to conclude that war with Russia is inevitable."

Russians would probe into areas of weakness, but they had no compulsion to wage wars of aggression when faced with resolute opposition. Propounding a doctrine that would soon become famous, Kennan concluded in his War College lecture: "There is no reason, in theory, why it should not be possible for us to contain the Russians indefinitely by confronting them firmly and politely with superior strength at every turn."

Despite his subsequent protests that his theories were not intended as a military doctrine, Kennan's lectures in the fall of 1946 emphasized that component quite heavily. Citing the troubles the U.S. was having with Yugoslavia at the time, he said that a better approach would be if "our negotiations over the future of the port of Trieste would be backed up by quiet but effective augmentations of our military and air strength in that area."

Coping with the Soviet sphere was possible, Kennan explained in his lectures, "as long as you have the superior force." The approach must be two-pronged: "It is the question of the manipulation of our political and military forces in such a way that the Russians will always be confronted with superior strength." To an audience of Foreign Service officers, he said of Soviet leaders: "While they are political gamblers, they are not gamblers when faced with the reality of military force."

Kennan was coming to the realization that because of the bomb, the concept of total war, which sought the unconditional defeat and occupation of an enemy country, was no longer realistic. Future wars would necessarily be more restricted in scope, conducted by small flexible strike forces to achieve limited political ends. Nuclear weapons were necessary for deterrence, but must not be considered a usable tool in a military confrontation. The U.S. should make it clear that it would never be the first to use the bomb, and it must restructure its military strategies to take this into account. Kennan, who felt somewhat out of his element on the subject, did not press these views strongly at the time. But over the years these convictions would grow.

Kennan's most direct involvement with national policy during this period was his contribution to a top-secret report prepared by Clark Clifford. The son of a Missouri railroad executive, Clifford, a suave and persuasive lawyer, had just begun what would be a long career in the inner circles of the American foreign policy Establishment. After serving in the naval reserve during the war, he was recruited into the Truman White House as a naval aide. With his felicitous writing style and shrewd common sense, Clifford was soon shifted from military work to serve as a speech writer, legal counselor, and multipurpose political adviser.

For a proposed speech reflecting America's new hard line, Truman asked Clifford in the late summer of 1946 to prepare a list of international agreements the Soviets had violated. Clifford enlisted the help of his own aide, George Elsey, who argued that the report should be expanded to explore the entire realm of Soviet conduct and its motivations. The starting point for his research, not surprisingly, was Kennan's Long Telegram.

Indeed, much of Elsey's final product was a compilation of Kennan's telegrams and memos interwoven with some written by Bohlen and

Harriman. "We should be prepared to join with the British and other Western countries in an attempt to build up a world of our own," the report declared, "and recognize the Soviet orbit as a distinct entity with which conflict is not predestined but with which we cannot pursue common aims."

That much Kennan could agree with. But the report represented the first small step in pushing Kennan's ideas beyond nebulous theory. "The language of military power is the only language which disciples of power politics understand," the Clifford-Elsey report emphasized. The U.S. must be prepared "to wage atomic and biological warfare" and establish a global doctrine designed to "support and assist all democratic countries which are in any way menaced or endangered by the U.S.S.R."

Perhaps out of pleasure at seeing the ideas he had once shouted from the wilderness now being officially embraced, Kennan was reticent about resisting those who would extend them a bit further. "I think the general tone is excellent and I have no fault to find with it," said the flattered analyst when Elsey sent him a draft in September. He suggested only minor modifications: successful containment might alter the Soviet system for the better, and the use of atomic weapons was something that would require "careful consideration" given the conditions prevailing at the time. These and other little fixes were promptly made by Elsey and Clifford.

"How many copies of the report do you have?" Truman asked Clifford after reading it.

"Ten," replied Clifford.

"I want them all," the President ordered. "Go to your office and get them." They must be locked up and kept secret, Truman explained, otherwise any further efforts to work with the Soviets at all would be impossible. "If this got out it would blow the roof off the White House, it would blow the roof off the Kremlin."

•   •   •

Averell Harriman was lunching with Churchill at Chartwell when the butler announced that a telephone call for the new ambassador was coming through from the White House. As they waited for the connection to be completed, the former Prime Minister asked what the President might want.

Harriman speculated about the recent flap over Commerce Secretary Henry Wallace's speech decrying the emerging "get tough with Russia" policy. Arguing for a realistic recognition of spheres, but coming to the exact opposite conclusion of Kennan, Wallace had declared: "The tougher we get, the tougher the Russians will get." Byrnes and others demanded that Wallace be fired, Truman did a clumsy twist about whether he had approved the speech, and finally Wallace was forced to resign.

It was likely, Harriman said, that Truman wanted him to replace Wallace in the Cabinet. Should he accept?

"Absolutely," said Churchill. "The center of power is in Washington."

That argument had special appeal for Harriman, who had begun to harbor political ambitions of his own. When the President came on the line and made the predicted offer, the well-traveled envoy flatly responded: "When do you want me there?"

"You don't seem to understand," said the perplexed President, who was expecting to face a tough sales job. "I want you to be Secretary of Commerce."

"Yes, sir," said Harriman. "I understand. When do you want me there?"

"Just as soon as you can conveniently do it," Truman happily replied. Within two weeks, by the beginning of October, Harriman was home.

Like Kennan, Harriman was becoming somewhat concerned about the swing of the pendulum. Not that he felt any softer toward the Soviets: Stalin himself made it clear that the Kremlin had opted for a unilateral policy, which could only mean further expansionist probes that the West would have to resist. Yet Harriman was beginning to fear the anti-Communist hysteria was serving no useful purpose. After all, it was a small planet. The U.S. would have to find some way to live with the Russians. And Harriman had always believed that this would require a realistic and businesslike approach.

Forrestal noticed the shift when Harriman dropped by soon after his return. "He was not overpessimistic" was the way Forrestal carefully phrased it in his diary. "He said that he did not believe the Russians would provoke war in the near future, but there was a chance of finding an accommodation which would be the foundation for peace provided they realized we would not make an unending series of concessions."

Even Forrestal, the firmest of the firm, gave a few indications—at least on occasion—that the pendulum could get out of control. "Just as you and I felt there was too great a swing pro-Russia three years ago," he wrote Harriman, "I am a little fearful that it may swing too strongly the other way now." The tendency to "see things precisely in black and white terms," he added was "the great American temptation."

Such moments of moderate reflection were rare for Forrestal. As he became increasingly obsessed with Communist expansion—indeed eventually paranoid about it—he viewed the Soviet threat more and more as an ideological one, a Marxist-Leninist apocalyptic peril. But he and Harriman were both, by profession, men who knew how to deal with competitors and adversaries. At least for Harriman, and occasionally for Forrestal, this could provide a context for the Soviet problem.

This was, in fact, one of the things that attracted Kennan to these two men. Conservative and introspective by nature, he admired people who could cope in the world of commerce and industry. "The stag groups of businessmen," he said of his cross-country tour, were "hard-headed, thoughtful, schooled in the sort of dialectical approach that permitted you to oppose a competitor without finding it necessary, or even desirable, to destroy him." Thus they were uniquely "capable of understanding that the Soviet-American antagonism might be serious without having to be resolved by war."

Harriman's main failing, in Kennan's eyes, was that he was not very reflective. Seldom did he articulate his own philosophical beliefs with any depth. One of the few times he did was as a favor to Kennan. Shortly after returning from England, Harriman gave a guest lecture at Kennan's War College class, an off-the-cuff and off-the-record hour talk that provided a rare and cogent explanation of his outlook.

"I know of no one," a proud Kennan told his students, "literally no one in this country, who is better acquainted with the international environment in which we live." Harriman in turn cited the two people who helped shape his outlook: George Kennan and Chip Bohlen, men who were less optimistic than others about the prospects for Soviet cooperation and, he said, turned out to be right.

Harriman's basic thrust was similar to Kennan's. "The Soviets have declared ideological warfare on us," he said. Yet at least for the present, they "have no intention to become involved in a shooting war." Hopes for cooperation failed, said Harriman, because the Kremlin consciously decided to pursue a unilateral policy, which may have been "just as well." Otherwise America might have been "lulled to sleep" by a façade of Soviet reasonableness. "The warmth of feeling in the hearts of the American people toward the Russian people would have led to all sorts of things, large loans, political agreements." The result would have been that the West would be faced with "a much more serious situation later."

In discussing ways to confront the "menace" of Soviet expansion, Harriman gave priority to military force. "It is of paramount importance that we maintain and let the Russians know we have maintained a strong military establishment," he said. Echoing Lovett, he emphasized that the "most effective" military tool would be a large "air striking force," one that could "penetrate the centers of their industry." The U.S. must have "guts enough to face the fact" that the atomic bomb must be developed. "There is no indication so far," he said, "that we would be any safer in giving Russia the atomic bomb than we would have been in giving it to Hitler."

Harriman showed himself quite different from Kennan in one respect: rather than dwelling on the forces of history, he focused instead on the actions of people. Whereas Kennan could (and often did) analyze a situation endlessly without mentioning any individual by name, Harriman (by habit a name-dropper) studded his remarks with such phrases as "when I went with Churchill to see Stalin" and "as Litvinov once told me."

More importantly, Harriman had a keener awareness than Kennan that the lives of real humans with real values were at stake. Kennan's dark realism about the division of Europe was now generally accepted by American policy makers. Harriman, however, rose to rare heights of eloquence in explaining the moral reasons why America should not rest easy with this outcome. "It is my firm conviction," he said, "that man is destined not to live under a Communist dictatorship but in a free society. The struggle through the centuries of man for freedom is not going to be overthrown by these people." This could cause serious problems for the Soviets in Eastern Europe. "They have a lot of difficulties in those countries, particularly if we keep hope alive in them."

Should "some method of checking Communism" within the U.S. be taken? asked a student. The problem, Harriman replied, was not with people who were attracted to "the humanitarian side of the theoretical Communist doctrine." The real threat came only from those Communists whose allegiance was to Moscow. Why did the Soviets decide to abandon a policy of cooperation? Such a policy, Harriman explained, "wasn't to their advantage. The hunting was too great."

The dispute over why Soviet-American cooperation failed—or more broadly why the Cold War began—has been debated ever since. Did

Stalin and the Soviets represent a deceitful, dangerous expansionist threat? Or were they mainly motivated by understandable security concerns which prompted them to seek control over a ring of neighbors that had historically been a corridor for invasions? Were their actions— in Poland and Iran and Manchuria and elsewhere—manifestations of aggression, or were they reactions to a Western bloc attempting to impose its own influence while flaunting the bomb on its hip?

Those who dealt with the Soviets firsthand—most notably Harriman and Kennan and Bohlen—were generally unanimous in their assessments by 1946. "It isn't a question of wisdom," Harriman told Kennan's class. "It is a question of having been exposed to the disease." At stake was more than merely a power rivalry between traditional nation-states. "The issue," said Harriman, "is a free society as against dictatorship."

Some attributed Harriman's and Kennan's outlook to the personal slights and inconveniences they suffered in Moscow. But in fact their sentiments were far more genuine and deep. They saw the Soviets were different in a fundamental moral way, and felt this factor was too often ignored by detached politicians and revisionist historians seeking to apportion Cold War blame. Using the terror tactics of a secret state-police force, the Kremlin had brutally imposed, both on its own citizens and those of hapless neighboring countries, a rigid control over all aspects of life and thought and speech.

For Harriman and others who served in Moscow and Eastern Europe, fear of the "dreaded knock on the door" was something they had seen up close. So too were the ruthless tactics used to impose party control, purge any dissent, kill or exile any opposition—be it in Poland or Bulgaria or Russia itself.

Some on the American left have argued that the Soviets initially tried to cooperate with the West by establishing governments in Eastern Europe that tolerated representative democracy. Harriman and Kennan took a more flinty-eyed view, and the subsequent memoirs of those involved in such regimes tend to prove them right. "Wherever they have taken over domination of neighboring countries," Harriman said at the time, "the brutality of the Red Army and the methods of the secret police in the governments set up have alienated almost all the population."

The outlook of the Americans who had served in Moscow was not monolithic. Kennan believed that the division of the world into hostile spheres was inevitable, while Harriman and Bohlen clung to the view that the American struggle should include fostering hopes for freedom in Eastern Europe. Harriman and Bohlen, who had believed in the high-minded public pledges signed by Stalin and Roosevelt at Yalta, also attributed the Cold War to a conscious Soviet decision in early 1945 to abandon those agreements and pursue a course of expansion. Kennan, on the other hand, scoffed at dating the Cold War at all; the sources of the tensions that arose after the war, he felt, were no different from those that existed before the war, or during the sixteen years that the U.S. refused to recognize the Bolshevik regime—or for that matter from the tensions that existed before the revolution.

Yet these men, and most who served in Moscow with them, agreed on one essential point in 1946: because of what they knew firsthand about the nature of the Soviet Union, its fanatic ideology and even more fanatic dictator, it would not be a fit ally for the West, and in fact would be a dangerous adversary.

• • •

Like Harriman, James Forrestal had triumphed in the competitive world of Wall Street. Such hard-nosed instincts were one of the things that prompted Kennan's admiration. Although he was prone to carry his views to extremes, Forrestal's early awareness of the Soviet threat also impressed Kennan. But above all, Forrestal had a quality that was, to Kennan, disappointingly lacking in Harriman: a willingness to wrestle with ideas. "Forrestal was not so much a man of reflective and refined intelligence," Kennan explained in a letter to a friend, "as he was a man who appreciated those qualities in others."

It was hardly a dispassionate compliment. What made this trait so appealing to Kennan was that it was his own "refined intelligence" that Forrestal began to dote on in the fall of 1946. Taking Kennan under his wing, the Navy Secretary sponsored him for his position at the War College, avidly distributed copies of his cables and speeches, and set up Pentagon lunches for him with top policy makers.

Such flattering patronage, in turn, made the once-alienated diplomat even more eager to please. In fact, Kennan later admitted that a paper he wrote for Forrestal, which became the most famous and important article of his career, had serious shortcomings—ones that he said originated because of "what I felt to be Mr. Forrestal's needs at the time."

Forrestal was as eager to pick Kennan's brain as Kennan was to have someone finally eager to pick it. On a leisurely cruise down the Potomac on the Navy yacht *Sequoia*, they spent an evening with Chip Bohlen discussing Soviet motives. Kennan became a frequent visitor to Forrestal's office, and was invited to a dinner party at the Secretary's Georgetown home.

Kennan did not fit in well at the Georgetown dinner, and his relationship with Forrestal never became a social one. Although their intellectual interests were similar, their personal styles were not. Forrestal had come to Princeton as an Irish-Catholic outsider and resolutely worked his way into the top ranks of campus life. Kennan had arrived nine years later just as much of an outsider and resolutely remained that way. A good friend of the Lovetts and Bohlens and McCloys, Forrestal had earned a prominent position in the Washington social scene. His marriage, to a vivacious and heavy-drinking former fashion editor at *Vogue*, Josephine Ogden, was an unhappy one. The Kennans, on the other hand, were a close and inward family and unfailingly retreated to their Pennsylvania farm for weekends, occasionally bringing hapless guests who later privately complained about spending the entire time doing chores and listening to abstract geopolitical discourses.

While others in Washington wondered about Soviet motives, Forrestal was plagued by neither nuances nor doubts. Marxist-Lenin dogma, treacherous and insidious and evil, was dedicated to the destruction of the capitalist world and would do so unless forcefully checked. He had searched for a document that would expose the "whole truth" about Communism, and thought he had found it with his overeager reading of the Long Telegram. Now he wanted to enlist Kennan as his philosophical aide-de-camp in the crusade.

Although pleased to be graced by such a powerful patron, Kennan faced a problem. He despised the Soviet system with a fervor approaching Forrestal's, and he was alarmed by the threat of Russian expansionism. But he did not see Communist dogma as the primary source of the menace. Ideology was important. It explained some things and acted as a "fig leaf" to justify others. But Communism was not the real enemy. Russia was. Its perverse paranoia and historical expansionism had been abetted and amplified, but not caused, by the Marxist doctrine usurped by its new Bolshevik czars.

The distinction was partly an academic one, but it had certain ramifications. Like Harriman, Kennan was not convinced that war with the Soviets was inevitable. Because the security of their country took precedence over considerations of a global Communist crusade, Kremlin leaders were unlikely to embark on reckless wars of aggression. Strengthening the free world, economically and militarily, could serve to contain Soviet expansionism.

Forrestal never quite seemed to grasp these nuances, and Kennan, gratified by his patronage, seemed reluctant to press them. He did, however, take the opportunity to make some of his points (although hardly in a manner designed to shake Forrestal's convictions) when Forrestal sent along a study he had commissioned earlier in the year.

In his effort to find a paper that explained the dire nature of the Communist threat, Forrestal assigned the subject to Edward Willett, a Smith College professor. The forty-three-page product, entitled "Dialectical Materialism and Russian Objectives," heavily emphasized the role of ideology. "The basic philosophy of communism," the professor wrote, "not only is conducive to, but indeed demands, an ultimate conflict between communism and Capitalistic democracy."

Kennan sent Forrestal five pages of detailed comments. "If we can maintain a state of affairs in which the chances of a violent effort to overthrow our system of society are unfavorable," Kennan argued, "then such an effort may not be made." Yet Kennan did concede that containment might involve a military showdown. "I do not think it at all out of the question that this government should take up arms in defense of the political independence of nations outside the Western hemisphere."

The most prescient part of Kennan's analysis was his awareness, not shared by Willett or Forrestal or many others, that the real threat from Moscow was not the ideology of Marxism. What the Kremlin sought, he said, was not more Communism but more Soviet control, the establishment of "governments amenable to their own influence and authority." They had "no desire" to see countries move toward a socialist system "except under the guidance of persons who recognize Moscow's authority." Even if there were a Communist revolution in the U.S., Kennan argued, "the only reaction of the men in the Kremlin would be to stamp it as a form of fascism" unless it was led by people acting under their control.

Gently correcting a professor's mistakes was hardly an edifying task, so Kennan asked Forrestal whether he "would mind my writing on the same subject in my own way." The resulting paper, which Kennan titled "Psychological Background of Soviet Foreign Policy," attempted to lay out the subtle relationship between "ideology and circumstances" that accounted for the Kremlin leadership's "particular brand of fanaticism."

Much in his essay Kennan had written before: Soviet belief in the hostility of the outside world, originally a product of Marxist ideology and "the powerful hands of Russian history and tradition," was now being fostered by leaders who found it "necessary to justify the retention of their dictatorship by stressing the menace of capitalism abroad." Despite Communist preachings, there was no reason to believe that Moscow would embark on "a do-or-die program to overthrow our society by a given date," Kennan explained. "The theory of the inevitability of the eventual fall of capitalism has the fortunate connotation that there is no hurry about it."

Although he stressed once again that the Soviet Union must be regarded as "a rival not a partner," Kennan struck a more hopeful note than he had before. The Soviets were "a tired and dispirited population," economically crippled and facing severe leadership problems. Perhaps it was on the wane. Certainly its power should not be hard for the West to counter.

This task could be accomplished by "firm and vigilant containment." It was a word Kennan had used before in his speeches, but in his paper for Forrestal he returned to it three times. He left vague the exact nature of the "force" that would be used to accomplish this containment, but he phrased the idea in a way that inevitably appealed to the action-oriented Navy Secretary. The goal, Kennan said, was "a policy of firm containment, designed to confront the Russians with unalterable counter-force at every point where they show signs of encroaching upon the interests of a peaceful and stable world."

The prospects for such a policy elicited a rare sense of elation in Kennan. The "vigilant application of counter-force at a series of constantly shifting geographical and political points" would involve massive global commitments. Yet this should cause no "thoughtful" American to complain, Kennan declared. "He will rather experience a certain gratitude to a Providence which, by providing the American people with this implacable challenge, has made their entire security as a nation dependent on their pulling themselves together and accepting the responsibilities of moral and political leadership that history plainly intended them to bear."

Certainly this ideal played well with Forrestal, who printed up copies of Kennan's paper and showed them all over town. He still missed some of the nuances. "Nothing about Russia can be understood without understanding the implacable and unchanging direction of Lenin's religion-philosophy," Forrestal explained to his old boss Clarence Dillon in a letter accompanying the essay. Yet Kennan's basic idea was something Forrestal understood well: the need for forceful containment of Soviet probes around the world.

A study group at the Council on Foreign Relations, which had been grappling with the Soviet issue without much success, invited Kennan up to New York to lead a discussion there in early January. Drawing from the essay he was just completing, he explained the "diversity" of factors that motivated Soviet conduct. Ideology, cultural traditions, and the insecurity of Russian rulers all played a role. Yet it was "perfectly possible," he added, "to contain Russian power" in a "non-provocative way."

Why was it reasonable to believe, one council member asked, that a policy of containment could work? "They are very cautious in a military sense," Kennan replied, "never allowing their commitments to exceed their capabilities." Would the Soviets accept a plan for international control of atomic energy? Perhaps, said Kennan, but only very slowly, because inspection ran counter to "their most deep-seated inhibitions." The Soviets, he added, did not "have any intention to use the bomb" because they knew an atomic exchange would defeat all of their aims. "They are wiser than we are in that sense."

What turned out to be the most important question came after the discussion. Hamilton Fish Armstrong, editor of the council's authoritative magazine *Foreign Affairs*, asked if Kennan had a copy of his speech. No, Kennan replied, but there was a paper he was finishing for Forrestal that covered the same ground.

After getting Forrestal's consent and clearing the essay with the appropriate State Department committee, Kennan wrote Armstrong that he would be pleased to have him publish it. There was one qualification: since he was about to become the head of a new policy planning unit at the State Department, he would prefer that the article be anonymous. That would be no problem, replied Armstrong. He would schedule the article for the July issue. So Kennan scratched off his name, replaced it with an "X," and sent the paper up to New York.

CHAPTER 13

ORDER FROM CHAOS
"Like apples
in a barrel"

In Berlin, before the ground froze in the autumn of 1946, the methodical Germans dug thousands of graves for their neighbors who would starve to death by spring. By February of 1947, more than nineteen thousand Berliners had been treated for frostbite; on the walls of the bombed-out Reichstag, someone scrawled, "Blessed are the dead, for their hands do not freeze."

Europe was "a rubble heap, a charnel house, a breeding ground of pestilence and hate," said Winston Churchill. The German factories that had survived Allied bombing were being looted by the Russians. All across Europe, canals were plugged, bridges broken, rail lines torn up. Farmers were consuming their produce, while city workers starved.

In London, the weather forecast for January 6 was "cold or very cold." By January 26, England was virtually paralyzed by blizzards, the worst since 1881. Lights flickered on for only a few hours each morning. Factories shut down, unemployment soared, rations fell below wartime levels.

Drained by two world wars, Britain began divesting itself of empire. On February 14, the government referred the Palestinian dispute to the U.N. On February 18, it announced the impending end of the Raj in India. On February 21, a Friday, Britain sought a successor for its traditional responsibilities of preserving stability in Greece and Turkey, a task that required half a billion dollars a year in financial aid and a garrison of forty thousand troops. It turned to the United States.

• • •

At the State Department that gray Friday, junior officials and secretaries wandered through the hallways, cluttered with packing boxes, making plans for the weekend and grumbling about the move. The department had outgrown its quarters, a marble Victorian pile next to the White House, and was moving to a new building a few blocks away, in Foggy Bottom. James Reston said in *The New York Times* that the new building had "about as much character as a chewing gum factory in Los Angeles," and most State Department officials agreed. They would miss Old State's high-ceilinged rooms, the wainscoting and elaborate moldings, the white-gloved messengers dozing in their swivel chairs in the hallways.

Dean Acheson's nostalgia for Old State was tempered by his low regard for its heating and cooling system. His office was drafty in the winter and a steam bath in Washington's oppressive summers. At least New State was air-conditioned.

Shortly before noon, Acheson received word from the British Embassy that the ambassador, Lord Inverchapel, wished to deliver a "blue piece of paper," diplomatic cant for an important message. The aide-mémoire, he was told, concerned Greece. There was, however, a protocol hitch: the ambassador could be received only by the Secretary of State, and General Marshall had already left for the weekend to make a speech at Princeton's two hundredth anniversary.

Acheson, who felt that he could not afford to wait until Monday to act, devised a small ruse: he had a carbon of the message delivered to him, so that "staff work" could begin. Within an hour H. M. Sichell, First Secretary of the British Embassy, had arrived with a dispatch case containing two documents. They were "shockers," Acheson later wrote. One stated: "His Majesty's Government, in view of their own situation, find it impossible to grant further financial assistance to Greece," and declared that Britain would pull out of Greece by the end of March, little over a month away. A second told of the same fate for Turkey.

The Greek government was corrupt, repressive, and incompetent, as Acheson knew. It was also on the verge of collapse in a civil war waged by rebels who were, Acheson believed, supplied and controlled by the Soviet Union. The U.S. ambassador to Greece, Lincoln MacVeagh, Acheson's fellow Grotonian, had told him so; a delegation sent by the State Department to examine the scene cabled back on February 18—just three days before the aide-mémoire arrived—that the "Soviets feel that Greece is ripe plum ready to fall in their hands in a few weeks... After having been rebuffed in Azerbaijan and Turkey, Soviets are finding Greece surprisingly soft... matter has gone beyond probing state and is now all-out offensive for the kill."

The Turkish Straits crisis six months before had hardened Acheson's view of Soviet designs. He believed that the Kremlin was not content to sit on its sphere of influence in Eastern Europe, but rather sought to dominate the eastern Mediterranean, if not all of Europe. After wrestling so long with McCloy's "A-1 priority job," he had come to a simple, perhaps simplistic, conclusion. He believed that Russia was behaving like a classic empire: expansionist, insatiable, controllable only by force.

The fact that Britain was abandoning the field, no longer able to fulfill its centuries-old role of preserving a balance of power in Europe and opposing Continental aggressors, left no doubt in Acheson's mind that the United States must move to fill the void. Before the war, he had envisioned a Pax Anglo-Americana. But now a shared hegemony was out of the question. Acheson was not such an Anglophile as to be sentimental about the loss of empire. He knew that the end of Pax Britannica meant the beginning of Pax Americana.

The World War had left the U.S. by far the strongest Western country; indeed, it was the only major power not verging on famine and bankruptcy. With immense natural resources and limitless confidence in the righteousness of its ways, America, Acheson firmly believed, was the natural successor to Britain. Yet, as he was equally well aware, the American republic's tradition since its founding had been to avoid European entanglements. After saving Europe twice in half a century, most Americans, secure in their monopoly over the atomic bomb, were content to keep the troubled Continent an ocean away. The most powerful military machine in the history of mankind in 1945, the United States by 1947 had almost totally demobilized; its armed forces had withered from twelve million men to fewer than two million. Certainly Americans were in no mood to rescue Greece and Turkey, two countries they associated more with ruins and rugs than shared destiny. These obstacles, however, only heightened Acheson's's sense of urgency.

Most men when they make history are too busy, too overwhelmed, to know it. But there is every indication that Acheson understood precisely the full portent of the British ambassador's "blue piece of paper." Acheson's words and actions at the time show a clarity of vision, a certainty of historic purpose unclouded by the fog of war or the ambiguity of crisis. His country was faced, he believed, with "a task in some ways more formidable than the one described in the first chapter of Genesis." For Acheson, this was the moment of Creation. His job, and the job awaiting his countrymen, was nothing less than to restore order from chaos.

All week, Acheson had been stirring. On Tuesday, speaking off the record to journalist Louis Fischer, he had said, "What we must do is not allow ourselves to be set back on our heels by [the Russians'] offensive strategy." So far, the U.S. had merely reacted to the Soviets. "They throw bricks into the window and we push a newspaper in that hole and try quickly to plug another hole, and so on." Now, Acheson insisted, the U.S. must take the initiative from the Soviets and "keep on the offensive about it." On Thursday, he had rephrased and strengthened a memorandum entitled "Crisis and Imminent Possibility of Collapse," authored by the director of Near Eastern Affairs, Loy Henderson, which urged an immediate program for economic and military assistance to Greece. "Unless urgent and immediate support is given," the memo bluntly warned, "it seems probable that the Greek government will be overthrown and a totalitarian regime of the extreme left will come to power."

The British aide-mémoire was only the final spur. As soon as he had finished reading it, Acheson assembled his staff in his office. "We're right up against it now," he announced. He ordered them to work through the weekend in order to have position papers, arguing for U.S. assumption of aid to Greece and Turkey, prepared for the Secretary by Monday at 9 A.M. His instructions were brief: "Work like hell."

Only then did Acheson pick up the phone and call the Secretary of State and the President and tell them what had happened and what he had done. Their reaction was the same. Both assented, without comment.

•　•　•

It is characteristic of George Marshall and Harry Truman, and of their relationship with Dean Acheson, that they told him simply to carry on. Marshall, to Acheson's immense relief, had replaced Byrnes as Secretary of State in January. Truman had finally tired of Byrnes's free-lancing and grown suspicious of his presidential ambitions. General Marshall, Organizer of Victory, was everything Byrnes was not: utterly loyal, self-effacing, ambitious only for his President and his country.

Acheson had served Marshall before. In 1946, Truman had sent Marshall as his special envoy to see if he could bring a peaceful solution to the civil war raging in China between Chiang Kai-shek's Nationalist government and the Communist insurgents under Mao Tse-tung. Marshall, in turn, had appointed Acheson to be his "rear echelon," his agent in Washington to make sure his orders were carried out. Marshall reported directly to Truman, sidestepping Byrnes, with Acheson serving as the go-between to the White House. "A design for living dangerously" was Acheson's description of the arrangement; it did not bring him closer to Byrnes.

Despite Marshall's best efforts, the mission was a failure, doomed by mutual mistrust between the warring Chinese factions. The experience confirmed Acheson's respect for Marshall's forbearance and wisdom. It also left him with an impression of China as a quagmire to be avoided.

On the morning of his swearing in as Secretary of State, Marshall walked back across the street to Old State with Acheson. "Will you stay?" Marshall asked. Certainly, Acheson replied, but he wanted to get back to his law practice before long. Six months? asked Marshall. Acheson agreed. Marshall told Acheson that he would be his chief of staff—and the only channel to the Secretary of State. Acheson could barely contain a smile. Byrnes had consistently short-circuited State Department channels as he traveled about from one peace conference to another. Now Acheson would not have to guess what the Secretary was up to. Marshall continued: he wanted complete and brutal candor from Acheson. "I have no feelings," the general declared, "except those I reserve for Mrs. Marshall."

Marshall was an icon to Acheson, as he was to Lovett, and to Bohlen and Kennan, Harriman and McCloy. Like Stimson, he was as important for what he inspired in others as what he accomplished himself. Acheson described General Marshall entering a room: "Everyone felt his presence. It was a striking and communicated force. His figure conveyed intensity, which his voice, low, staccato, and incisive, reinforced. It compelled respect. It spread a sense of authority and calm."

Marshall was far from brilliant. His mind was more conventional than imaginative. He was wise, but his judgment was hardly infallible, as Acheson was to discover to his everlasting chagrin in November of 1950. Yet he had about him an aura of absolute integrity.

He had learned self-control by trial: as a cadet at Virginia Military Institute, ordered to squat over a bayonet for hours, he had fainted and nearly lost his manhood. More patience was acquired sitting on dusty posts in the peacetime Army, passed over for promotion. In wartime, he dealt with martial egos with fairness, while utterly suppressing his own.

Marshall held himself aloof. When President Roosevelt called him George, Marshall gently remonstrated that only his wife called him by his first name. Although his only discernible weaknesses were a fondness for pulp fiction and maple-sugar candy, he was not a prig. He enjoyed telling dryly funny stories, and could be caustic and blunt. He rationed his energy and emotions. "I cannot allow myself to become angry," he told his wife. "That would be fatal. It is too exhausting."

When Marshall became Secretary of State, he was sixty-six years old, silver-haired, pink-faced, erect. Highly competent at running a war machine, he knew less about peacetime diplomacy. He believed in delegating responsibility, which in practice meant letting Acheson run the State Department. Yet he also had "the capacity for decision," Acheson noted, a quality that was to Acheson "surely God's rarest gift of mind to man." Marshall had little use for "kicking the problem around," a State Department pastime. Acheson relished quoting Marshall to his subordinates: "Don't fight the problem; decide it!"

Four days after Marshall's swearing in, Acheson reported to Henry Stimson—writing to one icon about another—"General Marshall has taken hold of this baffling institution with the calmness, orderliness, and vigor with which you are familiar. We are very happy and very lucky to have him here." At a dinner party at P Street in March, Acheson "spent a good deal of time bubbling over with enthusiasm, rapture almost, about General Marshall," a guest, David Lilienthal, noted in his diary. "To work with [Marshall] is such a joy that he can hardly talk about anything else," Lilienthal continued. "It has made a new man of Dean and this is a good thing for the country right now."

• • •

Acheson's respect for Marshall was matched by his regard for Truman. From the first he had admired Truman's grit. He had been heartened by the President's depth and decisiveness ever since the August morning in the Oval Room when the self-taught history buff had displayed his firm grasp of the strategic significance of the Dardanelles. Since then, Acheson had impressed Truman with his own forcefulness and, equally important, with his loyalty.

Truman was a virtual pariah in Washington in the late autumn of 1946. His low standing had been blamed for the Democrats' loss of Congress in the November elections. After the drubbing, when the President's train pulled into Union Station from Independence, Missouri, the platform was empty of greeters. Save one: Dean Acheson. Formally dressed in cutaway and striped pants, mustache clipped, homburg in hand, Acheson cut a resplendent figure to the downcast President slinking back into town to sift through the political ruins.

Acheson was there out of dutiful innocence. In FDR's time, it had been a Cabinet custom to greet the President's train after elections. Acheson recalled the "triumphal processions" from Union Station up Pennsylvania Avenue, and assumed Truman would at least warrant a procession, albeit a subdued one. He was quite aghast to find himself standing alone in his solemn finery on a dark platform, like an undertaker awaiting delivery of a casket.

Truman never forgot Acheson's show of loyalty. That evening, he invited the striped-pants Grottie back to the family quarters in the White House, sat him down in his small upstairs study, and asked him his advice about politics. Truman's aides were urging him to call a lame-duck session of Congress to ram through a last batch of legislation before the GOP took over. Acheson, emboldened by intimacy and Bourbon, counseled against it. A "good sportsman," he stated in terms that would have pleased the Rector, would face up to defeat and not try to bend the rules. Truman agreed. Acheson even helped him draft a statement graciously accepting the judgment of the American people.

Acheson further impressed Truman with his fealty by exposing the lack of it in James Forrestal, who had taken to holding lunches with other Cabinet members to discuss policy—without the presence or even the knowledge of the President. Though Acheson felt uncomfortable about "tattling" on Forrestal, he strongly believed that these lunches undermined the President's rightful authority. Truman promptly ordered Forrestal to cease his rump lunches. Acheson's standing at the White House rose another notch; Forrestal's fell.

By February, Acheson felt secure in the President's trust. He felt equally sure of Marshall's. He did not hesitate to act on their behalf.

•   •   •

Early Sunday evening, Loy Henderson arrived at Acheson's house on P Street in Georgetown to report on the staff work that Acheson had ordered up on Friday in response to the British aide-mémoire. All weekend, the State Department staffers had sorted through policy implications and the costs of taking over from Britain the burden of supporting Greece and Turkey. "Henderson asked me whether we were still working on papers bearing on the making of a decision or the execution of one," Acheson recalled in his memoirs. He did not hesitate with the answer: "Loy, we're going to do it. You proceed on that basis." Mission clear, they sat back in the overstuffed chairs in Acheson's cozy study and drank a martini "to the confusion of our enemies."

Acheson handed the recommendation for Greek and Turkish aid to General Marshall at 9 A.M. Monday. He told the Secretary that the papers contained "the most major decision with which we have been faced since the War." Marshall asked a few questions, and—in an extraordinary delegation of authority—informed Acheson that the responsibility for carrying through the plan would be Acheson's. The Secretary was leaving in a week for a Foreign Ministers' meeting in Moscow. Acheson had not expected anything other than approval from Marshall. But he was already worried about selling the plan to Congress, a less trusting authority.

At noon on Monday, journalist Louis Fisher came to Acheson's office to keep a lunch date. He noticed that Acheson was agitated. The phone rang repeatedly; Acheson seemed very tense. Swearing Fisher, an old friend, to secrecy, Acheson told him what was afoot. The two departed in the Under Secretary's limousine for the Metropolitan Club. Acheson immediately cranked up the window behind the driver. "The British are pulling out everywhere," he said, "and if we don't go in the Russians will." At the club, Acheson ordered exactly what Fisher did and showed little interest in his food. "There are only two powers left," he said. "The British are finished. They are through. And the trouble is that this hits us too soon, before we are ready for it. We are having a lot of trouble getting money out of Congress." Acheson grimaced and threw his hands in the air. "If the Near East goes Communist, I very much fear for this country and for the world."

Though the polls showed growing awareness of Soviet aggressiveness, most Americans were still not ready to undertake the dangerous, expensive job of opposing Russia. In the last few weeks, Capitol Hill had already repudiated requests by Marshall and Forrestal for increased foreign aid and defense spending; most congressmen were more interested in cutting taxes by 20 percent. The Republicans had gained control of Congress in November by promising a return to normalcy, not an assumption of Britain's empire.

Acheson was no neophyte at dealing with Congress, despite his distaste for jollying up to hacks and claghorns. As an Assistant Secretary of State for congressional liason during the war, he had manfully tried to be one of the fellows. "This is a low life but a merry one," he wrote his daughter Mary in the summer of 1945. "I've had a fine lunch in the office of the Secretary of the Senate with House and Senate members. A real Texas ham was offered and whiskey. I'm getting to be a real politician." But one pictures Acheson poking about the halls of Congress like an anthropologist sampling native customs. He had at least learned an essential lesson while selling the British loan to skeptical congressmen: fear of Communism was a better goad than concern for allies.

The first real test for the Greek-Turkish aid package came on Thursday, February 27, when Truman summoned congressional leaders to get their private, informal reaction. Acheson viewed the meeting with tremendous apprehension: "I knew we were met at Armageddon."

Marshall outlined the case. He mouthed the right words: "It is not alarmist to say that we are faced with the first crisis in a series which might extend Soviet domination to Europe, the Middle East, and Asia. . . ." But his delivery was flat, uninspired. Joseph Jones, a young State Department official who attended the meeting, later wrote, "He conveyed the overall impression that aid should be extended to Greece on the grounds of loyalty and humanitarianism." The congressmen listened sullenly. The grumbling began: "What are we getting in for?" one asked. "How much is this going to amount to?" asked another. "Does this mean pulling the British chestnuts out of the fire?"

Acheson fretted silently. Marshall, he later wrote, had "flubbed his opening statement. In desperation, I whispered to him a request to speak." Marshall assented. In recalling the scene Acheson spared no sense of drama: "This was my crisis. For a week I had nurtured it. These congressmen had no conception of what challenged them; it was my task to bring it home." Like a bold lieutenant in a wavering charge, Acheson grabbed for the fallen standard and plunged onward.

"Never," he recalled, "have I spoken with such a sense that the issue was up to me alone."

Acheson's rhetoric was the product of emotions that had been welling up within him for months. The situation, he declared to the doubting congressmen, was unparalleled since ancient history. Not since Athens and Sparta, not since Rome and Carthage, had the world been so polarized between two great powers. The U.S. and the U.S.S.R. were divided by "an unbridgeable ideological chasm." The choice was between "democracy and individual liberty" and "dictatorship and absolute conformity." What is more, the Soviets were "aggressive and expanding." If Greece fell, "like apples in a barrel infected by one rotten one," Iran, Asia Minor, Egypt, then even Italy and France would fall prey. Before long, two-thirds of the world's population and three-quarters of its surface would be Red. This was not an issue of "pulling British chestnuts out of the fire," but of preserving the security of the United States, of Democracy itself.

A long silence followed. Finally, Acheson recalled, Arthur Vandenberg spoke up: "Mr. President, if you say that to the Congress and to the country, I will support you, and I believe most of the members will do the same." Loy Henderson recalls Vandenberg putting the message more bluntly: "Mr. President, the only way you are ever going to get this is to make a speech and scare the hell out of the country."

Work on such a speech began immediately. At a meeting with State Department officials the next day, Acheson recounted the session at the White House (not omitting his own prominent role) and instructed his minions to begin drafting a presidential message that would stress the "global struggle between freedom and totalitarianism." The message could not be restricted to Greece and Turkey, or even the Near East. It must stress the "protection of Democracy everywhere in the world." The speech should not be "provocative" in the sense of accusing the Soviets directly, but rather address the spread of totalitarianism generally. The men listening thought Acheson seemed unusually grave. "There is a great job to be done," he concluded, and it must be done "with great speed."

Within a couple of days, the drafters had churned out a report called "Public Information Program on United States Aid to Greece." The report stated the objective of the United States as broadly as possible: "It is the policy of the United States to give support to free peoples who are attempting to resist subjugation from armed minorities or from outside forces." At Acheson's direction, this passage was lifted almost verbatim from the report and put in the President's address. It became known as the Truman Doctrine.

•   •   •

For months, George Kennan had been preaching the doctrine of containment to select audiences at the National War College and other forums. Now Acheson asked him to join the process of implementing it. On the Monday that State Department staffers began working on the Greek-Turkish aid proposal, Acheson summoned Kennan to his office and told him of the crisis. Would he sit in and lend his voice? Kennan accepted with alacrity.

Kennan's reputation as a seminal thinker was by now well established in the State Department bureaucracy. When he appeared at the meeting at the State Department, Loy Henderson immediately turned over the chair. By midnight, a first draft outlining the need to prop up Greece and Turkey against the Communist threat was completed for the President's review. Kennan recorded in his memoirs that as he drove home through the streets of Georgetown that night, he was filled with a sense of having participated in the making of history.

Kennan was not, however, asked to participate in drafting the President's speech. This was a chore to be entrusted to the more politically minded. It was not until March 6, the day before the draft went to the President, that Kennan came over from the War College to the State Department to have a look. He was appalled. He immediately seized on the open-ended commitment to aid "free peoples" everywhere. He protested to Acheson: This was going too far. "The Russians might even declare war!" Acheson listened unmoved.

Kennan repaired to his office and hurriedly cranked out a draft of his own, a much more finely calibrated effort focused on the particular problems of Greece and Turkey. Acheson rejected it out of hand. When another State official asked Acheson if the U.S. planned to bail out every imperiled democracy, Acheson leaned back in his chair, looked across the street at the White House, and replied: "If FDR were alive today, I think I know what he'd do. He would make a statement of global policy but confine his request for money right now to Greece and Turkey."

At a dinner party at Acheson's house later in the week, Kennan brought up the matter again. He was anxious about overstating the case and making commitments that the U.S. could not realistically honor. Acheson reiterated the need to convince Congress. A hint of tension crept into the conversation. Kennan, shy in Georgetown society and unable to enjoy argument as sport, backed off. The evening resumed its pleasant course.

But Kennan could not rid himself of his doubts, which poured out in a letter to his old comrade Chip Bohlen. "There is a complete lack of intelligent public liaison here on the Greek question," Kennan wrote. "Most of Congress and the press are still running around bleating elemental questions which any child could answer." Kennan felt like a lone voice. As he told Bohlen: "Your presence is badly needed."

Bohlen too had qualms. He was on his way to Moscow for the Foreign Ministers' meeting with General Marshall when he saw a cable of the speech draft. "It seemed to General Marshall and me that there was a little too much flamboyant anti-Communism in that speech," Bohlen later recalled. Marshall and Bohlen sent a cable back to Washington asking that it be toned down. The reply came back from Truman: without the rhetoric, Congress would not approve the money.

There were other, muted voices of concern, even within the White House. Presidential aide George Elsey wrote Clark Clifford, "There has been no overt action in the immediate past by the U.S.S.R. which serves as an adequate pretext for an 'all-out' speech." But Clifford thought like Acheson, only more so. He saw the speech as "an opening gun in a campaign to bring people up to the realization that the war isn't over by any means."

Clifford, whose polish and ego were a match for Acheson's, had been working closely with the Under Secretary for some months. Clifford handled national security matters for Truman; Acheson was the State Department's day-to-day contact with the White House. Acheson had come to appreciate Clifford's political savvy and art of persuasion. A few years later, Acheson would try to recruit Clifford for his law firm. They were social friends as well. In 1949, Acheson would second Clifford for membership in the Metropolitan Club.

"I viewed my role as asking, 'Is the speech saleable?'" Clifford later recalled. He understood that to grip the American people the issue had to be framed as a contest between the forces of darkness and light. Clifford made the speech simpler and more dramatic, as did Truman himself. In fact, the President bounced the first State Department draft as sounding "too much like an investment prospectus." As he explained in his memoirs, "I wanted no hedge in this speech. This was America's answer to the surge of communist tyranny." To the crucial sentence stating the Truman Doctrine, the President changed "I believe it should be the policy of the United States" to "I believe it *must* be..."

Truman stepped to the rostrum to address a Joint Session of Congress at 1 P.M. on March 12, 1947. His voice was flat and high-pitched, but forceful; his speech, as Robert Donovan wrote, "was probably the most enduringly controversial speech that has been made by a president in the twentieth century." When he finished announcing that the United States was undertaking the role of world defender of democracy, he was greeted not with applause but with stunned silence. Robert Taft, the isolationist Republican leader, took off his glasses, rubbed his face, and yawned prodigiously. The public reaction was equally unmoved, according to *Time*. The magazine quoted an anonymous Chicago commuter as scoffing, "More sand down the rat hole."

In later years, the Truman Doctrine would be described as a pre-scription for tragedy and blamed ultimately for the Vietnam War. At the time, its drafters had hardly an inkling of where it might lead. Clifford recalls that as he rode down Capitol Hill in the President's limousine after the speech, he felt, "Well, we hit that a good stiff lick." The only prospect he envisioned was a vacation at the President's winter getaway in Key West.

Kennan, with his prescience, did worry that the Truman Doctrine was potentially mischievous. But his own narrow and overly detailed speech would not have squeezed a nickel out of Congress for the defense of Greece and Turkey. Acheson did not take the Truman Doctrine literally. He was highly sensitive to the limited resources of the United States, and had no intention of intervening around the globe. He particularly wanted to avoid the China quagmire. At the same time, he genuinely believed the Soviets had aggressive designs on Europe and the Near East, and he wanted to signal U.S. resistance. Overstatement was to him merely a tool for manipulating balky, un-sophisticated congressmen into paying for legitimate policies.

The problem was that those unsophisticated congressmen, not to mention the public, took sweeping language literally. Congressman Lyndon Johnson of San Marcos State Teachers College, sitting in the audience that day, had no way of knowing that Truman did not really mean what he said. It was undoubtedly necessary to make arguments "clearer than the truth," as Acheson later put it, in order to strike a deal with Congress. Unfortunately, the bargain proved Faustian.

Already, the Communist bugaboo was beginning to roil domestic politics. Red-baiting had been a major issue in the 1946 congressional elections. When Congress returned, John Taber, the hulking chair-man of the House Appropriations Committee—and thus controller of purse strings on foreign aid—announced that he was bent on getting subversives out of government. Forrestal was not unsympathetic. He wrote to Clifford on January 31 that at a private dinner Taber had told him that he planned to "go after" Communist personnel "hammer and tong." Kennan sensed the coming darkness. "I look personally with some dismay and concern at many things we are now experiencing in our public life," he stated in a lecture. "In particular, I deplore the hysterical sort of anti-Communism which, it seems to me, is gaining currency in this country."

Truman also disdained Red-baiting. But he believed he had to head off the Red-baiters with a concession. He could not very well afford to ask Congress to get "tough" on Communism abroad if he was "soft" on Communism at home. Ten days after he announced the Truman Doctrine, the President promulgated an Employee Loyalty Program. Henceforth, all government workers would undergo loyalty tests.

Acheson would himself become a target of the hysteria. But in March of 1947, he was too preoccupied with cultivating a single senator, Arthur Vandenberg, to notice the still shadowy figure of Joseph R. McCarthy of Wisconsin.

It is easy to make fun of Vandenberg, the isolationist turned internationalist. And Acheson did. Son of the American Revolution, thirty-third-degree Mason, and an Elk, Vandenberg craved recognition. He had composed a popular ballad to a movie queen of the 1920s, Bebe Daniels, entitled, "Bebe, Bebe, Bebe—Be Mine." Big, pink, and lumbering, waving a trunklike arm, he indulged his love of phrase making with such clinkers as "our merific inheritances," "marcesant monarchy," "nautical nimbus."

Vandenberg, Acheson later wrote, "did not furnish the ideas, the leadership, or the drive to chart the new course or to move the nation into it. But he made the result possible." As a practical matter, in those days before Watergate and congressional reform, "advice and consent of the Senate" meant "consult with Vandenberg." As chairman of the Senate Foreign Relations Committee, he exercised enormous sway over his colleagues, who knew little about foreign affairs and deferred to his judgment. Vandenberg was a Republican. But since 1945, when he had made a famous speech confessing his conversion to internationalism, he had been a sincere believer in bipartisan foreign policy. In Congress, he was the creator of the internationalist consensus that future Presidents would look back upon with wistful longing.

In the Truman Administration, most Democrats could be counted on to stick with the White House, despite their grumbling about its occupant. If Vandenberg was on board, he would bring along most of the Republicans. His approach to the isolationists and strident right-wingers was to "kill them with kindness." He would invite them to hearings and let them posture for hours until they had sufficiently ventilated and cooled down.

Acheson's approach to Vandenberg was large doses of flattery. "Each move and speech you make seems to me the perfect one," Acheson wrote in one typically effusive note. "I marvel how you maintain your good humor, your strength, and your zest for the fray." Another tactic was known as "applying the trademark" or "determining the price." Explains Acheson: "This meant either stamping the proposal with the Vandenberg brand, or exacting from the Administration a concession which he thought politically important."

It did not take Acheson long to find the Vandenberg brand for the $400 million Greek-Turkish aid bill that the Senate was scheduled to consider in the spring of 1947. In the Administration bill, there was no mention of a role for the United Nations. There had been one in early drafts, but Acheson, who considered the U.N. to be weak and irrelevant, struck it out. Vandenberg, who believed in the U.N. with a convert's zeal, pounced on the omission and insisted that the bill should provide for the cessation of U.S. aid if and when the U.N. should take charge of the situation. Acheson was sure this would never happen, since the Soviet Union would prevent it, so he went along. It was, he said, "a cheap price for Vandenberg's patronage." The change was proposed as the "Vandenberg Amendment." Acheson wrote: "The brand had been applied."

Acheson was not quite home free. During the lengthy hearings on the bill, he was asked some awkward questions. Karl Mundt, a literal-minded congressman from South Dakota, demanded to know if the Truman Doctrine was a "first step in a consistent and complete American policy to stop the expansion of Communism." Acheson hedged. The U.S. was not, he answered, embarking on a "crusade against ideology." Aid would be dispensed "according to the circumstances of each specific case"—depending on need, American interests, and the likelihood that it would be effective. This was a commonsense approach, but it did not satisfy all his questioners. The China specialists, such as Walter Judd of Minnesota, asked the inevitable: If Greece and Turkey, why not China? Different circumstances, answered Acheson, somewhat cryptically and, to the China-lobby crowd, unconvincingly.

Acheson's skeptics were not just congressmen he could dismiss as know-nothings. One evening in April, while the Greek-Turkish aid bill was still languishing in committee and Acheson was weary from grinding out testimony on the Hill, he went to a dinner party with Walter Lippmann. The distinguished columnist, sniffing the flaw in the Truman Doctrine, had warned in a column that the U.S. was in danger of violating one of his favorite precepts, the balance of resources and commitments. The U.S. would face the Soviets, Lippmann feared, with "dispersed American power in the service of a heterogenous collection of unstable governments." The column, widely read, was not helping the Administration's cause on the Hill.

Fortified by a martini or two, Acheson launched into a fierce defense of the Truman Doctrine. As his passion grew, he turned on Lippmann and accused him of "sabotaging" American foreign policy. The columnist hit back. "Words flew, fingers were jabbed into chests, faces grew red," Lippmann's biographer Ronald Steel recounts. The dinner guests delighted in this battle between titans, but Lippmann later described the evening as "very unpleasant." (His nicotine hangover was so great the next morning that he quit smoking.) Acheson, whose scorn could be quite lethal, called Lippmann before noon to apologize, but the friction between the two men would continue to grow.

Despite such unpleasant moments, the Greek-Turkish aid package passed in April 1947 by more than two to one margins in the Senate and the House. Lippmann ultimately supported the bill in his column; even Bob Taft voted for it. Both liberals and Republicans were trapped: neither could afford to appear soft on Communism.

In the end, American involvement in Greece and Turkey proved effective. By the summer of 1949, the Communist-backed insurgency in Greece was finished; the American-backed government troops had won. No dominoes fell. The engagement eerily foreshadowed Vietnam, except in its outcome. American "advisers," trained in counterinsurgency, bolstered a corrupt right-wing government against Communist rebels. Napalm bombs were extensively used for the first time.

One major reason for this first great success of America's willingness to assume global responsibilities was that the rebels did not enjoy quite the Soviet backing Acheson thought they did. Stalin, it later emerged, was ambivalent about the insurgency from the outset, and offered the rebels little support. In early 1948, he angrily told the Yugoslavs, who were providing sanctuaries for the Greek rebels, that the insurrection had "no prospect of success at all." The Soviet dictator exclaimed to a pair of Yugoslavian diplomats, "Do you think Great Britain and the United States—the United States, the most powerful state in the world—will permit you to break their line of communication to the Mediterranean? Nonsense."*

Stalin was right, but American firmness was hardly such a foregone conclusion. Had it not been for Acheson's resolve, and the strong support of Marshall and Truman, the U.S. would have almost surely abandoned Greece to its fate. And regardless of Stalin's doubts about fomenting rebellion in Greece, he would have moved in an instant to declare the rebels' victory as his own. Though paranoid, Stalin was opportunistic; he took what he perceived he could get away with. Had the Greek rebels won, there is little doubt that the Kremlin would have quickly folded the country into the Soviet bloc.

•   •   •

Deep into a drunken dinner at the Kremlin in early April 1947, Molotov, the Soviet Foreign Minister, turned to General Marshall and asked: "Now that soldiers have become statesmen in America, are the troops goose-stepping?" The U.S. Secretary of State, his eyes icy gray, turned to Bohlen, who was translating for him, and said quietly: "Please tell Mr. Molotov that I'm not sure I understand the purport of his remark, but if it is what I think it is, please tell him I do not like it."

The Foreign Ministers' meeting that had begun in Moscow in early March was not going well. There were toasts and more toasts, but no progress toward settling the disputes dividing postwar Europe. As March dragged into April, the proceedings became oddly punchy. The American ambassador to Moscow, Walter Bedell Smith, asked for hair tonic in a Moscow barbershop and got hair dye; his hair turned slightly pink. When the Foreign Ministers decided to give up in mid-April and go home, Britain's irrepressible Ernest Bevin was so delighted to be leaving Moscow that he warbled a song to Andrei Vishinsky, Molotov's deputy: "The more we are together, together, the more we are together, the merrier we shall be!" Vishinsky eyed him curiously. "What a jolly man," he said.

Marshall, trying to glean some indication of what the Soviets really

---

*Stalin's split with Yugoslavia's Marshal Tito was the final blow to the Greek insurgency. When the Greek Communists followed their Kremlin masters by denouncing Tito in 1948, the Yugoslavs cut off supplies to the rebels and no longer provided them with safe haven.

wanted, requested a private audience with Stalin on April 18. In Stalin's netherworld, day was night. The dictator, who preferred to work after dark, granted Marshall an appointment at 10 P.M.

Through the empty, dark Moscow streets the American limousine sped, through traffic lights synchronized to turn green (the Americans were accorded "Kremlin privileges," though their hotel rooms were bugged), into the massive stone fortress. Marshall and Bohlen were ushered down a long, narrow corridor, past a high double door, through a succession of reception areas, to a sparsely furnished room. There they found Stalin, with his withered arm, pockmarked face, bad teeth, and calm slow manner.

Bohlen was struck by how Stalin had aged. He was gray and worn. For an hour and a half, he engaged Marshall in desultory conversation. Stalin, who had become Soviet dictator when Marshall was still an assistant commandant of the Army Infantry School at Fort Benning, seemed quite unperturbed by the lack of progress. The conference was but an opening skirmish. "We may agree next time, and if not, the time after that." As he talked, Bohlen noticed, he idly doodled wolves' heads with a red pen, just as he had done during Harriman's first visit at the outset of World War II.

On the long flight home to Washington, Marshall laid out the gloomy lessons he had learned in Moscow. Stalin wanted drift. He preferred an unsettled Europe. Chaos, as Harriman and McCloy had both warned, was working to the Soviets' advantage. Now, said Marshall, it was time for the U.S. to act, without the Soviets if necessary. Bohlen, who had accompanied Marshall as his special assistant for Soviet affairs, did not dispute his new chief's conclusions. He too believed that diplomacy was not enough; some kind of bold stroke was needed.

Acheson, kept abreast of the Moscow stalemate by daily cables, was coming to the same conclusion back in Washington. "I think it is a mistake to believe that you can, at anytime, sit down with the Russians and solve questions," he told the Senate Foreign Relations Committee in early April. Senator H. Alexander Smith asked him: "You are not planning any early participation for settlement of these issues?" Acheson replied: "You cannot sit down with them."

Then what? If Europe was not to be rescued by talk, then how? "The patient sinks while the doctors deliberate," Marshall told a national radio audience on April 28, the day of his return from Moscow.

•   •   •

James Forrestal had been agitating for the cure for more than a month. He had always seen the face-off against the Soviets as a Manichaean struggle. Now he wanted to pit capitalism against Marxism, our system against theirs. In early March, the Navy Secretary had moved to enlist Clark Clifford in his cause.

Clifford was careful to stay in touch with Forrestal; the two breakfasted every Wednesday at Forrestal's home in Kalorama. Forrestal, like Acheson, saw Clifford as an invaluable ally within the White House. "Clark continues to be a great help," he wrote Assistant Secretary of War for Air Stuart Symington in April. "He is the greatest single asset to the White House, both to the President and to the people working for him."

Forrestal urged Clifford to draft a memorandum that would "bring into focus the central problem, which is: which of the systems currently offered in the world is to survive?"

Forrestal had a prescription: "economic leadership." He wanted to form a "group of our most competent citizens" to design and push a plan to rebuild the economy of Europe. "Only by an all-out effort on a worldwide basis can we pass over from the defense to the attack."

General Marshall was his next target. At a Cabinet lunch on April 28—only a few hours after Marshall had stepped off the plane from Moscow—Forrestal cornered the Secretary and delivered his Capitalist Manifesto: the United States had everything it needed to restore the world to strength. The Soviets had nothing, neither capital, nor goods, nor food. Russia could export only anarchy and chaos. But the U.S. had to move quickly; time was on the Russians' side. It was fortunate, Forrestal went on, that the Secretary was creating a planning staff at the State Department to look into such long-range policy questions.

The next morning, Marshall summoned the chief of this new planning staff, George Kennan, to his office. He had chosen Kennan for the job at the urging of Forrestal, who had taken it upon himself to promote the author of the Long Telegram. In many ways, Kennan was the obvious choice to become the State Department's chief planner; he was the most creative, penetrating thinker in the department. Acheson too had suggested Kennan's name, though his explanation was somewhat more whimsical. To Loy Henderson, Acheson said merely, "There's no one quite like George."

Kennan's original arrangement was that he would complete the academic year lecturing at the War College before coming over to State to set up the Policy Planning Staff. The failure of the Moscow conference, however, hastened his move. General Marshall briskly told Kennan that his services were required, that he would have to come over to State "without delay." Europe was a mess. Something had to be done. If State did not take the initiative, others would, notably Congress. Marshall did not want to be on the defensive. Kennan was to assemble a staff, produce an answer. He had ten days to do it. Marshall had only one piece of advice: "Avoid trivia."

The staccato commands left Kennan reeling. He had no office, no staff, and three out-of-town speaking engagements on his calendar. The "whole great problem of European recovery in all its complexity," Kennan confessed, was quite daunting to him.

Management was not Kennan's forte. But he was able to secure a suite of offices—prime ones, next to Marshall's own—and an able staff familiar with Europe and its woes. Then he began holding forth, pacing about and expounding, night and day, restlessly and relentlessly. "We'd all gather round the table and George would start talking," recalled a slightly awed Policy Planning staffer. "Very often none of us would say a word, but we'd just be looking at him. And he, by watching us, seemed to know just what we were thinking."

The emotional strain was, as ever for Kennan in moments of intellectual ferment, almost unbearable. Late one night he startled his staff during a particularly intense discussion by welling up with tears. He fled the office and walked around the building several times, trying to regain his composure.

Kennan was seized with anticipation. Here was an opportunity both to rectify the excesses of the Truman Doctrine and to rescue Europe. The U.S. should offer massive economic aid to its struggling allies on the Continent. But its avowed purpose, he felt, must be to restore health to Europe's economy and society, not to "combat Communism." Washington would put up the money, but the plan itself must come from Europe. While supplying the means, the U.S. must not be seen as dictating the results.

Instead of wide-open military commitments, Kennan concluded, the U.S. should undertake a finite, albeit huge, obligation to help Europe help itself. By this act, the U.S. would help save thousands of lives, indeed an entire society. It went without saying that a revitalized Europe would be an active trading partner for the U.S. and a bulwark against Soviet encroachment.

The idea was simple. It launched the U.S. on what Acheson later described as "one of the greatest and most honorable adventures in history"—the Marshall Plan.

The plan was not Kennan's alone, by any means. Forrestal, Acheson, Bohlen, McCloy, Stimson, Harriman, and a few others, including General Marshall himself, all share paternity. The members of their insular circle had been talking and thinking about a huge aid plan to restore Europe since the last days of the war.

A precise moment of creation is difficult to pinpoint, though Harriman may have been the first to commit the idea to paper. He had urged massive reconstruction aid for the West in one of his final cables to FDR and reiterated that advice when he flew to Washington to meet Harry Truman. From Potsdam in 1945, McCloy and Stimson had called for a "completely coordinated plan to be adopted for the economic rehabilitation of Europe as a whole." Even as he drafted the Truman Doctrine, Acheson had warned Truman that Greece and Turkey were part of a much greater problem, that all Europe needed to be restored. In the meantime, the notion of a European Recovery Plan had been nurtured and bruited about within the intimate precincts of Georgetown and Foggy Bottom, at tony dinner parties and in drab government hallways. Individuals added nuance and refinement, but the genesis was collective.

None of this ferment took place on Capitol Hill. To an ordinary congressman, determined to cut budgets, spending billions and billions to rebuild a war-ravaged foreign continent was political madness. Most of their constituents had barely recovered from sacrificing their sons to save Europe; foreign aid was widely viewed as "Operation Rat Hole."

Yet to a small, tightly knit group of men in postwar Washington the restoration of Europe seemed not only right, but natural, even obligatory. They saw the world differently, and they felt within themselves the duty and power to save it.

To undertake the rescue of Europe was an act of supreme self-confidence. Such boldness has diverse wellsprings; no single source suffices to explain why this particular set of men showed breathtaking initiative, while others, seemingly just like them, sat back. It is true that the social class into which they were born or later assimilated, America's tiny turn-of-the-century aristocracy, instilled in some a sense of remarkable well-being and certainty. Yet for many more of the gentry it also bred complacency and idleness. Schools and colleges like Groton and Yale tried to imbue a sense of duty and merit, though they succeeded with more of their graduates in inspiring conformity and snobbery.

Those who did choose public service felt a sense of duty that was truly cosmopolitan. It was not just the United States they sought to serve but, in a broader sense, the culture and civilization of the West. Europe was not to them an abstraction, dimly portrayed by high-school history books as an entanglement to be avoided. As children, they had strolled with their parents through Europe's Edwardian autumn; as young men they had immersed themselves in the tangled economies and politics of the Continent on the eve of its Nazi ordeal. By upbringing and experience they were intensely aware of Europe's worth.

When the men who created the Marshall Plan came of age, the U.S. was vibrant and raw, poised to touch more of the globe with its power than any nation ever. Yet for another two decades it remained isolationist and preoccupied with its own surges of boom and bust. As individuals, Acheson and Harriman, Lovett and McCloy, Kennan and Bohlen, each had his own blind spots and shortcomings; alone, no single one of them could have guided the country to its new role as world power. Yet collectively, this small group of men, and those who emulated their example, brought to the immense task just the right mixture of vision and practicality, aggressiveness and patience. They came together at one of those moments in history when time and place, upbringing and character, fuse into a kind of critical mass, and give ordinary men the power to forever change the way things are.

It has been argued by revisionist critics that the so-called Establishment's interest in European recovery was primarily self-interest, that these ardent capitalists sought to rebuild Europe to provide a market for American goods. Charles Bohlen conceded years later that "self-interest" was an "element" of the Marshall Plan. But he spoke as well of a "feeling of duty toward the civilized world." Such words were not empty or guileful; there is every reason to believe that Bohlen and his colleagues felt morally compelled to save Europe from hunger and the Russian night.

Their aim was not dreamy or hopelessly idealistic. They did not want to save souls or "make the world one," like earlier, and less successful, American internationalists. Rather, they were intensely pragmatic; they wanted to supply capital, tools, sustenance; they wanted to restore Europe, not change it. Nonetheless, their vision was spectacularly bold; it demanded a reshaping of America's traditional role in the world and a restructuring of the global balance of power. By seeking change in order to preserve, these men were, in their own way, revolutionaries in the cause of order.

Almost four decades later, the creators of the Pax Americana remain partially obscure figures, semiprivate men who preferred to exercise power discreetly and shunned the glare and tumult of politics. There are fifty-two monuments or outdoor statues in Washington honoring a wide assortment of long-forgotten as well as famous figures, but in the public spaces of the capital there is not so much as a park bench named after Dean Acheson.* Indeed, Acheson is remembered, if at all, as an exemplar of the old Eastern Establishment, a term that is to many not merely descriptive but pejorative.

The motives and wisdom of the old foreign policy elite can be fairly debated, but its impact is undeniable. More than any others, this small group of men made the U.S. assume the responsibility of a world power and defined its global mission. And without doubt the Marshall Plan remains their purest and greatest achievement, power used to its best end.

•   •   •

When they wished to communicate with the public at large, the Washington elite often spoke through a small band of like-minded reporters and columnists, men who were often schoolmates or social friends and who could be trusted to grasp nuance and exercise discretion. The High Priest of this journalistic order was Walter Lippmann, the widely read columnist who was such a Washington insider that he was almost a minister without portfolio in government. He willingly lent his pen to causes he endorsed and, not infrequently, helped design. For Administration policy makers, interviews with Lippmann were less question and answer than advice and consent.

Forrestal, the tireless polemicist, sent Lippmann to see Kennan in April. Over a long lunch at the War College, the columnist and the planner, both shy and sensitive men, matched intellects. Lippmann, who had a less severe view of the Soviets than Kennan, would later become a severe critic of the containment doctrine. But at this meeting the two found much to agree upon. They shared a distaste for the overcommitments and stridency of the Truman Doctrine; they both wanted a recovery plan that would not seem like an American bid to dominate Europe or a blatantly anti-Soviet manuever. It was Lippmann who first suggested that the U.S. invite the Europeans to draw up a plan of their own, according to his biographer Ronald Steel. The

*Needless to say, there are no Dean Acheson high schools or highways either. The State Department did name its auditorium after him.

columnist continued to do his part by pushing hard for a massive economic rescue plan for Europe.

Lippmann's rival, Arthur Krock of *The New York Times*, was regularly fed secret cables and memoranda by Forrestal, Krock's old Princeton clubmate. James Reston, the *Times's* star young reporter, was kept informed by Acheson, who was more forthcoming with good reporters than with congressmen. Junior State Department officials began to notice that every time Acheson went to lunch with "Scotty" Reston at the Metropolitan Club, the next day the front page of *The New York Times* would hint broadly at "big planning at State." The stories gave Policy Planning staffers, as one put it, the "jimjams." They were afraid they would be blamed. Kennan, a remarkable innocent in this arena, went so far as to write Acheson in May that he was not leaking to New York *Herald Tribune* columnist Joseph Alsop. (Actually, Chip Bohlen was; he and Alsop shared the bond of membership in Harvard's Porcellian.)

•   •   •

The Administration's first formal declaration of intent was a speech delivered by Acheson on May 8 in a hot, crowded gymnasium at Delta State Teachers College in Cleveland, Mississippi. The forum was "a far cry from the conventional setting for striped-pants diplomatic utterances," Acheson recorded, "but the people in the gymnasium are serious." Truman was supposed to speak there, but had to bow out in order to avoid getting sucked into a local political squabble involving Senator Theodore (The Man) Bilbo. It was announced that Acheson, his replacement, would make "an important foreign policy speech." To the Under Secretary, who had appointed himself as chief promoter for European recovery, it was an opportunity to "sound reveille," he later recalled, "to awaken the American people to the duties of that day of decision."

With his sleeves rolled up and his jacket off, Acheson played the unfamiliar role of stump speaker. Europe was in its death throes, Acheson told his listeners, who overflowed the gym and sprawled on the grass outside, drinking Cokes and minding their children. Not just subsistence, but "human dignity, human freedom" was at stake. Europe had to become self-supporting again, and it could not do it without the help of the United States.

Whether or not the farmers understood, James Reston did. He asked Acheson at a press conference in Washington after the speech, "Is this a new policy that you are announcing or just a bit of private kite flying?" Acheson grinned. "You know this town better than I do. Foreign policy is made at the White House. You must ask the President." Reston asked Truman if Acheson spoke for him. "Yes," the President answered.

In his Senate office, Arthur Vandenberg was reading the newspapers and stewing. Upon digesting the Delta State Teachers College address, he demanded an audience at Blair House, where the President had moved while the White House was being restored. Vandenberg waved the speech at Marshall. Acheson had publicly declared that the U.S. was about to spend huge amounts on foreign aid! What was going on? Things were getting out of hand! Marshall tried to calm him. The Administration would not ask any more money from Congress this session. But sooner or later, yes, there would have to be an aid bill. He reassured him that Congress would not be ignored in the planning. Vandenberg remonstrated to Truman: "Harry, I want you to understand from now on that I'm not going to help you with crash landings unless I'm in on the takeoff." Acheson just listened. It was a warning to him; Congress would need to be treated gingerly. He thought to himself, he later recalled, that it was time to find the Vandenberg brand.

Truman's own involvement in the creation of the Marshall Plan was at once minimal yet essential: he simply trusted Marshall and Acheson, and backed them. The one contribution the President made on his own was characteristically shrewd and humble. Clifford, who played the courtier at times, suggested to the President that the plan for European recovery be named the Truman Plan. "Clark," Truman answered, "if we try to make this a Truman accomplishment, it will sink. It will never see the light of day." Truman had a better idea: name the plan after Marshall, "the greatest living American." It would sell "a whole hell of a lot better in Congress."

The plan needed but one more boost. On May 19, Will Clayton, the big-boned, square-jawed, six-foot-three Assistant Secretary for Economic Affairs, returned from an inspection trip of Europe. A soft-spoken, courteous teetotaler, Clayton was a hard businessman, a founder of the largest cotton trading company in the world. American cotton was in very long supply in the spring of 1947. Clayton was blunt about it: "Let us admit right off that our objective has as its background the needs and interests of the U.S. We need markets—big markets, in which to buy and sell."

Clayton painted a horrific picture of the economic collapse of Europe in a memo for Marshall. Distrusting the currency, farmers were no longer going to market. They were feeding produce to their cattle while city workers starved. If anything, Clayton warned, the State Department had underestimated the seriousness of the situation.

The memo moved Acheson, who felt that Kennan's efforts at Policy Planning had not been phrased forcefully enough. Clayton's memo also energized Marshall. When an aide asked him if he wanted to confirm a tentative appointment to speak at Harvard's commencement, Marshall answered yes. The next day he summoned Chip Bohlen to his office, handed him Kennan's Policy Planning paper and Clayton's memo, and told him to write a speech that would invite Europe to ask for American aid.

Marshall had inherited Bohlen from Byrnes as his special assistant for Soviet affairs. He was impressed by Bohlen's professionalism, his steadiness and sound instincts, so much so that he promoted him to the title of State Department Counselor in early summer. The two were well matched. Henry Kissinger later described Bohlen as "quite conventional, quite predictable, and thus quite reliable," a description that could apply equally to Marshall.

Bohlen revered Marshall. "I have never gone in for hero worship," he later wrote, "but of all the men I have been associated with, including presidents, George Catlett Marshall is at the top of the list of those I admire." The two became personally close. "Bohlen was like a son to him," recalled a State Department colleague. Though Marshall was known for his aloofness, he showed his affection for Bohlen in small ways. When his counselor had been gone for some weeks on a trip to Europe without seeing his two-year-old boy, Marshall summoned little Charlie to his office, sat him on his knee, and directed the State Department photographer to take a picture, so that Bohlen could at least see what the child looked like.

For two days after receiving his speech-drafting assignment, Bohlen closeted himself in his office. His aim, like Kennan's, was to present the recovery plan not as an anti-Soviet maneuver but as a humanitarian gesture. He wrote that U.S. policy was directed "not against country, ideology or political party, and specifically not against Communism," but rather "against hunger, poverty, and chaos." Bohlen thought he was being clever; if the Soviets opposed the plan, he later wrote, they would be perceived as the "partisans of hunger, poverty, and chaos." This would be an important propaganda point in Western Europe, where the Communists were vying for control of government.

As a diplomat, Bohlen was more concerned with what European allies would think of the speech than how it would play in the U.S., where his subtleties were apt to be lost. His prose was, as usual, bland and stolid. Marshall's speech, while noble, is hardly memorable for its eloquence.

Marshall, no great draftsman himself, accepted most of Bohlen's language, but he was still fiddling with the speech as he flew to Boston on June 4. He had not even left an advance text at the State Department press office. Indeed, afraid of the angry reaction of right-wingers and isolationists, he had told the press office that he wanted no advance publicity. He had already ducked a foreign policy speech at the University of Michigan for fear of what Colonel McCormick's isolationist Chicago *Tribune* would say about it.

Acheson was not so chary of publicity. He was dubious about the Harvard idea, perhaps because he had sat through too many graduations as a Yale trustee. "No one listens to commencement speeches," he told his boss. To make sure the press paid attention, he planted a story with Reston revealing that the State Department was considering a four-year, $16 billion program to revive Europe.

The interest Acheson most wanted to arouse was Europe's. It was essential that European leaders respond positively, and at once. So he decided to have lunch with three influential British journalists: Leonard Miall of the BBC, René MacColl of the *Daily Express*, and Malcolm Muggeridge of the *Daily Telegraph*. The date was set for June 4, the day before Marshall's speech.

That morning, Acheson was badly hung over from an excessively convivial dinner party the night before. On his way out the door to meet the three Britons, Acheson gravely remarked to Lincoln White, a press aide: "If these limeys offer me sherry, I shall puke." Muggeridge greeted him in a private room at the United Nations Club. "Now," began Muggeridge, "we won't have this horrible bad habit of having some strong liquor before lunch." He turned to Acheson. "Sherry?"

Acheson ordered a dry martini. At lunch, he made his pitch. The Administration had "rather oversold" its case for European recovery in Congress by asking for piecemeal bailouts, individual loans to Britain, France, Italy, and the UNRRA. Now what was needed was "some kind of cooperative and dramatic move from the European side in order to capture the imagination of Congress" which was "in a very economic frame of mind." Marshall was about to make a major speech inviting such a request. "Don't waste your time writing about it," he said to Muggeridge. "As soon as you get your hands on a copy, telephone the whole thing to London. Ask your editor to see that Ernie

Bevin gets a copy of the text at once. It will not matter what hour of the night it is; wake Ernie up and put a copy in his hands."

On the steps of Memorial Church in Harvard Yard, under a leafy canopy of elms, General Marshall, dressed in a plain gray suit amidst the brightly colored academic robes, delivered his simple speech on the afternoon of June 5. "Our policy is not directed against any country or doctrine," he said (he had crossed out "Communism" in Bohlen's draft), "but against hunger, poverty, desperation and chaos.... Any assistance that this country should render in the future should provide a cure rather than a mere palliative. Before the U.S. government can proceed much further there must be some agreement among the countries of Europe as to the requirements of the situation.... The initiative, I think, must come from Europe."

Acheson's prediction about the interest paid to commencement speeches was correct. The next day, The New York Times led the paper with Truman's press conference denouncing a Communist coup in Hungary. The Secretary's speech received a tepid headline ("Marshall Pleads for European Unity"). So "Platonic a purpose as combating 'hunger, poverty, desperation and chaos,'" Acheson noted, utterly failed to move the public.

Yet to Bevin, listening to Leonard Miall read the address over the BBC shortly after dawn, it was "like a lifeline to a sinking man. It seemed to bring hope where there was none." Before the U.S had a chance to renege, the British Foreign Minister raced to accept. He cabled the State Department that he was "taking the initiative" by visiting Paris, and hurried off to see what he could hastily put together with the French.

Marshall's invitation had been open-ended. It was not limited to Western Europe. The Soviet Union and their satellites were free to join in the recovery plan, if they so desired. Inviting Russia was "a hell of gamble," Bohlen realized; Soviet acceptance would doom the whole exercise. The chances of Congress paying for Soviet recovery were nil, and their participation would mean the kind of endless bickering that had characterized those hopelessly stalemated Foreign Ministers' meetings.

When Marshall asked Kennan what to do about the Soviets, he had replied, "Play it straight." Invite them to join. The Soviets, Kennan explained, could not afford to accept. They would not dream of opening up their books to an international recovery plan, or of loosening control over their satellites by letting them trade freely with the

West. By participating, the Soviets would have to give up their claims to reparations; instead of draining Germany of resources, the flow would be the other way around. Though the Soviets had been ravaged by war and desperately needed reconstruction aid themselves, Kennan's plan called on the Kremlin to help restore conquered Europe. But the Soviets must be allowed to discover all this for themselves, Kennan warned. They must not be explicitly cut out. The onus for dividing Europe should not fall on the United States.

Kennan's reasoning was clever and persuasive. Yet within the inner councils, there was considerable uneasiness about the Soviet response. Forrestal, particularly, feared that Russia would wreck the Marshall Plan by joining it. Even after he had delivered his speech, Marshall himself anxiously asked Kennan and Bohlen whether he should really say yes when asked if the Soviets were included in the offer. "Kennan and I looked at each other," Bohlen recalled, "and said we were convinced that the Soviet Union could not accept the plan"; they reiterated the reasons Kennan had already outlined.

Another worried voice in the inner sanctum that early summer of 1947 was Robert Lovett's. Absent from the realm of policy making during the formulative stages of the Cold War, he had been lured back into government from his comfortable niche in Wall Street by General Marshall, who was eager to have his old "copilot" from the War Department. Lovett was to be Acheson's successor, slated to take over as Marshall's number two when Acheson returned to his law firm at the end of June. Through half of May and most of June, Lovett served as the Under Secretary's understudy, shadowing him everywhere, sitting in his office, attending his meetings, and often going home to dine with him at night. In this unofficial capacity, he was a participant in the debate over whether to invite the Russians to join the Marshall Plan.

"I questioned Kennan about it quite a bit," Lovett later recalled. "How will the Russians react? Will they be tempted? Will they treat it as something aimed at them?" Kennan tried to reassure Lovett, but the Wall Street banker was skeptical of diplomats, particularly egg-headed ones like Kennan. He turned to one of his own kind for further counsel. Flying to New York, he handed a draft of Marshall's speech to Russell Leffingwell, a Morgan partner and chairman of the Council on Foreign Relations. Leffingwell considered for a moment and told Lovett, "You'd make a mistake by not offering the Russians to go in on it. They would never agree to the provisions on inspection." It is noteworthy that Lovett recalls being convinced by Leffingwell, a private banker, and not by Kennan, the Soviet expert.

Kennan and Bohlen used their diplomatic skills to enlist the British government in their scheme to keep the Russians out. They rather casually dropped in on Lord Inverchapel, the British ambassador to the U.S., to inform him, in gingerly and discreet fashion, of their "expectations" concerning the U.S.S.R. They told Inverchapel that they doubted that the Soviets would want to join, but if the Russians did, they would be expected to contribute money to the plan, not withdraw it. The British ambassador got the message: that night, he cabled London that the Americans were counting on the British to help keep the Russians out.

Kennan's disingenuous "play it straight" gambit worked. "In a sense we put the Russians over a barrel," he later recalled. "When the full horror of [their] alternatives dawned on them, they were suddenly left in the middle of the night." To be encircled by capitalist countries was in fact Stalin's worst nightmare. He reacted with the usual paranoia, by clamping down the iron curtain a little tighter. Foreign Minister Molotov actually came to the first meeting on European recovery in Paris, and seemed to show a sincere, if skittish, interest in Soviet participation. But his superiors in Moscow were rightly suspicious of Western motives. Molotov was instructed to offer a Soviet plan—that each country submit individual shopping lists to be filled by the U.S. This he did and stalked out, denouncing American imperialism.

To Averell Harriman, watching from the wings as an old Soviet hand and Commerce Secretary, Molotov's walkout was a blunder. "He could have killed the Marshall Plan by joining it," Harriman later stated. The fact that he missed this opportunity proved to Harriman that Molotov was "essentially a dull fellow."

For the Eastern-bloc countries, the Soviet *nyet* was a tragedy. Poland and Czechoslovakia wanted desperately to accept the Americans' invitation to participate in the recovery program. Warsaw was in ruins, with thirty thousand of its war dead still buried beneath the rubble of the bombed-out ghetto, while the remaining moderates in the Prague government, trying bravely to maintain their independence from Moscow, were eager to resume trading with the West. After Molotov walked out, however, the Kremlin quickly brought the Czechs and Poles to heel. The Poles abruptly announced that they would not be attending the recovery meeting in Paris; the Czechs were forced to renounce their earlier acceptance when Stalin informed them that participation would be regarded as "an act specifically aimed against the U.S.S.R."

It was the inevitable but nonetheless unfortunate fallout of the Marshall Plan that it hastened the permanent division of Europe. Western Europe saw the Marshall Plan as a selfless act of humanitarianism, a bold stroke that restored its chances for prosperity and saved it from Soviet domination. But, as Daniel Yergin put it in his Cold War study, *Shattered Peace*, "the Russians saw [the Marshall Plan] as a declaration of war by the U.S. for control of Europe." FDR's vision of the wartime Allies acting in concert to guarantee peace and security was now irrevocably shattered. Though the Marshall Plan was entirely an economic initiative, its long-term result was to further drive East and West into tense and hostile armed camps.

It is tempting to speculate what might have happened if the U.S. had sincerely invited the Soviets to join the Marshall Plan, and Stalin had accepted. Though Kennan and Bohlen pointedly insisted in their discussions with France and Britain that the Soviets would have to be contributors, rather than beneficiaries, under any recovery plan, conceivably a compromise could have been worked out. Russia, after all, had been just as ravaged by war as Western Europe, if not more so. In hindsight, it can be wished that the U.S. and U.S.S.R. had tried harder to find a way to cooperate on economic recovery. But to the pragmatists in Washington in the summer of 1947, the prospect of just trying to bring a balky Congress and the historically feuding governments of Europe together was daunting enough, without involving an obdurate and paranoid Stalin. Further isolating and antagonizing Russia was a price Washington was willing to pay to achieve European recovery. Indeed, to isolate Russia was to contain her, which was precisely the point.

Bohlen watched the rift grow with foreboding, if not surprise. "There are, in short, two worlds instead of one," he stated at a high-level State Department meeting in August, predicting a crisis between the superpowers. "There is virtually no chance of any of the problems between the two worlds being settled until that crisis comes to a head. It is not a matter of several years in the future. It is more likely several months... It will obviously contain in it the very real danger of outbreak of hostilities."

•   •   •

At first, Robert Lovett had resisted coming back to Washington. The White House had reached him at home in Locust Valley at 6:45 A.M. one February morning in 1947 as he was trying to rush out the door to catch a commuter train to Manhattan. Lovett thought the White House operator was a crank call. Truman finally came on the line and reassured him, "No, this really is the President..."

The President told Lovett that General Marshall had insisted on bringing his "old copilot" to the State Department. Lovett found it extremely difficult to turn down General Marshall, much less the President, yet he worried that it would be difficult for him to disengage from his partnership in Brown Brothers Harriman for a second time in less than seven years. Membership in the Wall Street bank involved a shared ownership with unlimited liabilities for all the partners.

It was Averell Harriman who resolved his doubts. When Lovett called his old partner to discuss the situation, Harriman called him a "damn fool" and told him to go ahead and take the job. Lovett called Truman and accepted with two conditions. He wanted two months in Florida to recover from yet another operation on his "glass insides" (more gallbladder surgery), and a month of "dual instruction" with Acheson before "flying solo."

Acheson welcomed this unusual intimacy with his replacement. He told Marshall that he had "known Bob since Yale" and was "all for it." The two stayed in close touch throughout the spring. Acheson took Lovett to meet Vandenberg ("I've known Bob since college and I hope you will be agreeable to accept his services," said Acheson. Replied Vandenberg: "I welcome you to the job of Under Secretary of State and may God have mercy on your soul.") While ministering to his gallbladder with large doses of paperback murder mysteries and a reduced intake of Lovett Mists, a Bourbon concoction, at Sea Change, his Hobe Sound cottage, Lovett faithfully wrote Acheson every week. "I am sticking to that damned health building regime and, somewhat to my surprise, it seems to be working. I've gained a little weight and am almost beginning to feel human," he said in one letter. "I'm going to work very hard at it because I want to do my damndest to be everything you want me to be when I get back." On April 5, when Acheson was fencing with the popular press and its mavens such as Walter Winchell over Greek-Turkish aid, Lovett tried to cheer him up with his peculiar childlike whimsy: "Do you suffer from backache?," he began. "Do you wake up in the morning feeling groggy? You do-o-o? Then try Dad's Ruin. Just drop one Winchell in hot water, gargle, and forget your troubles. . . . Good evening folks, this is your announcer Turgid D. Pepperwhistle with up-to-the-minute news . . ."

Lovett and Acheson were affectionate friends who immensely enjoyed each other's company. Yet despite their common schooling and tradition of public service, the two were quite different men who brought contrasting talents and liabilities to the job. Though both were elegant and polished, Acheson was bristling and erect, while Lovett was slouched and somewhat shy. Acheson, with his hauteur, could unintentionally offend by his mere presence; Lovett, gentle and amiable, was more soothing to ordinary politicians. Acheson had the "capacity for decision"; he never hesitated to act, even when patience was called for. Lovett was not one for bold strokes; he was cautious, sometimes overly so. His great strength was in getting others, particularly congressmen, to do what had already been decided.

The timing of their job switch could hardly have been more fortuitous. With the pronouncement of the Truman Doctrine and the Marshall Plan, the task became to implement these grand gestures. The transformation of America's global role took Acheson's force to create it, but Lovett's tact to sell it.

Acheson was not happy to relinquish power, even to Lovett, despite the fact that he had told Marshall back in January that he was eager to return to his law firm and make some money. The past six months had been almost giddy. Under Marshall, he had, for the first time in his life, tasted real responsibility in a moment of extraordinary ferment. After wrenching America from isolationism, facing down the Soviets, and launching the rescue of Europe, practicing law began to look pretty pedestrian. "I feel very sad and somewhat panic stricken at going back to the Union Trust Building," he wrote his daughter Jane. "I like what I am doing and now have some sense of sureness of touch and of a willingness on the part of others to let me drive." He did not know that his greatest and hardest tour of duty lay ahead.

CHAPTER 14

Kennan and Lovett at State

"SIMPLE
HONEST MEN"
The selling of
the Marshall Plan

"This is a terrific business," Lovett wrote his old Wall Street compatriot Ferdinand Eberstadt in June of 1947. "I now refer to the wartime problems as the 'good old days.'" To Thomas Lamont at Morgan Bank, he wrote, "At no time in my recollection have I seen a world situation which was so rapidly moving toward real trouble." At lunch with Forrestal, he worried that England was on the verge of bankruptcy and that Congress would balk at assuming the costly burden of her global role.

Lovett was less enthusiastic and confident about a Pax Americana than his predecessor. He had been reading the Lippmann columns that Acheson attacked so bitterly, and he found himself more often than not in agreement with the columnist. Lippmann's classic definition of a viable foreign policy—the balance of resources and commitments—appealed to the cautious banker's mind. At a private session at the Council on Foreign Relations in May, when he was still quietly serving as Acheson's "understudy," Lovett offered his world view to a small circle of insiders, including *Foreign Affairs* editor Hamilton Fish Armstrong and *The New York Times* military correspondent Hanson Baldwin. Quoting Lippmann with approval, Lovett said that he had been trying to draw up a balance sheet of U.S. commitments and resources. Not surprisingly, he was having difficulty with this literal-minded exercise. The experts at the Council chided him for being too much of a banker, but Lovett was uneasy. It was apparent, he argued, that the U.S. was not planning carefully, that it was already spread too thin around the globe. He had no doubt about the Soviet threat, however, or the need to meet it. Lovett's preference was for building up resources rather than paring down commitments. He wanted the U.S. to be prepared for "swift sure retaliation."

When Lovett formally took over from Acheson on July 1, he knew that despite all the spring ferment at the State Department, he was starting virtually from scratch on European recovery. Kennan made this perfectly clear in a memorandum that began: "Marshall 'Plan': We have no plan."

The plan was supposed to come from Europe, but the Europeans, despite their terrible needs, quickly fell to squabbling. From the outset, the French equivocated, continuing to insist that Germany be kept weak. Truman had to send his most experienced negotiator, Averell Harriman, to bring the balky French leaders into line. The U.S. Military Governor of Germany, General Lucius Clay, relentlessly sniped back at the French. Lovett finally had to remind the general firmly that policy was set in Washington, not Berlin. Clay promptly threatened to resign. This was normal procedure for Clay, who threatened to resign almost a dozen times. Accustomed to dealing with the egos of generals from his days in the War Department, Lovett carefully maneuvered to keep Clay satisfied but under control.

Lovett could be self-deprecating, cautious, bland. He could also be wickedly funny, forceful, and effective. More important, he knew when to be which. At meetings of foreign representatives on the Marshall Plan held at the State Department, he refused to sit at the head of the table as chairman: he did not want it to appear as if Washington was running the show. In private, however, he mimicked his stuffier

European counterparts to the great amusement of his State Department colleagues. He enjoyed replaying the morning when Henri Bonnet, the *très grave* French ambassador, arrived at a meeting with his fly open. Bonnet immediately sat down and zipped himself, but he somehow managed to catch his necktie, which had been tucked into his pants, so that the tip protruded from his fly. After much standing up and sitting down again, Bonnet finally had to ask for scissors to cut off his tie. Lovett, in his franglais, would imitate Bonnet struggling to maintain his dignity through this ordeal. Lovett could also be withering about his own associates, especially inflated generals such as Clay. When diplomats sent him impenetrable cables, he would hold them up to the window and, squinting hard, recite nursery rhymes.

Lovett patiently listened to the entreaties of Bonnet and the other European diplomats who came, silk hat in hand, to Washington that summer of 1947. By August, his patience was waning. All the Europeans had produced so far, he told Marshall, were "sixteen shopping lists." In his speech, the Secretary had offered the Europeans "friendly aid" in putting together a package. Now, Lovett believed, the U.S. would have to do more than gently cajole.

Kennan was coming to the same conclusion. Dispatched to Paris in August to monitor the bargaining sessions between the European countries, he came home within a week predicting that the U.S. would, as he put it to Marshall, "listen to all the Europeans had to say, but in the end, we would not *ask* them, we would just *tell* them what they would get."

In Paris Kennan had been the perfect diplomat. He explained to the Europeans that they were dealing with "a new set of men in Washington with simple honest minds," by whom he presumably meant Truman, Marshall, and Lovett. Subtlety must "at all costs be avoided" when dealing with these men, he emphasized as he made the rounds of diplomatic receptions and cocktail parties. The Europeans must send "simple honest men" back to Washington to represent them. This approach seemed to soothe the sophisticated European diplomats, and it apparently did not offend the "simple honest men" back in Washington. One of them, Bob Lovett, told Senator H. Alexander Smith that while the Paris sessions were still "unsatisfactory" because they lacked "realism," Kennan had been "extremely effective."

Kennan, for so long an ignored and awkward analyst, was now a public celebrity. The X-Article had appeared in the July *Foreign Af-*

fairs. The mysterious "X" was quickly unmasked by Arthur Krock of *The New York Times*, who had been slipped a copy of it by his fellow Princetonian Forrestal when the article was merely a memorandum for Forrestal's private use. When Krock read "The Sources of Soviet Conduct," it did not take him long to deduce the identity of "X." The obscure diplomat was suddenly seen as the visionary behind the Administration foreign policy; the *Times* dubbed him "America's global planner." The publication of the X-Article was seen as an official pronouncement, "an event," wrote Lippmann, "announcing that the State Department had made up its mind." Kennan had even given the new policy a name: containment.

Reader's Digest and *Life* reprinted long excerpts of the X-Article. Mr. "X" himself was feted at a whirl of parties in Paris, where his appearance caused a minor sensation. Kennan, naturally enough, was quite overwhelmed. It was beginning to dawn on him that the article was taking on a meaning and a life of its own, one disturbingly different from the intent of its author. He "felt like one who has inadvertently loosened a large boulder from the top of a cliff and now helplessly witnesses its path of destruction in the valley below, shuddering and wincing at each successive glimpse of disaster."

The most painful twinges came from reading Lippmann. In twelve consecutive columns beginning while Kennan was in Paris, Lippmann attacked the "containment doctrine" as a "strategic monstrosity." To try to "confront the Russians with unalterable counterforce at every point" was folly. It would mean propping up puppet regimes all along the Soviet periphery. The result would inevitably be to "squander our substance and our prestige." The U.S. should devote its resources to restoring Western Europe, not mucking about in Asia or the under-developed world. The columns were reprinted later that fall in a book whose title popularized another new phrase: *The Cold War.*

Kennan read the columns with horror. He later described Lippmann's series as a "misunderstanding almost tragic in its dimensions." He had not meant the X-Article to be a prescription for U.S. policy but rather an analysis of Soviet character. But he had, as had happened before, become overwrought and been betrayed by hyperbole, by what he later admitted was his "careless and indiscriminate language."

Still, Kennan felt unjustly accused. He had, in fact, strongly and repeatedly opposed the sweeping language of the Truman Doctrine, both to his students at the War College and to Acheson personally. In May, for instance, he had complained to Acheson that "the Truman

Doctrine is a blank check to give economic and military aid to any area of the world where the Communists show signs of being successful." The next month he admitted to a National War College audience, "It may be that we have undertaken too much." Kennan in that speech had warned against violating Lippmann's equation of resources and commitments.

Yet here was the famous columnist accusing him of authoring, in Kennan's words, "precisely those features of the Truman Doctrine which I had most vigorously opposed." Even worse, Kennan noted, Lippmann had cited as corrections to the excesses of the Truman Doctrine precisely "those features of General Marshall's approach, and those passages of the Harvard speech, for which I had primary responsibility." Lippmann's ignorance of Kennan's true role was doubly perplexing to Kennan, since he had sat down with Lippmann for their long lunch at the War College that past spring and felt quite in agreement with the famous columnist. If Lippmann, with his sophistication and inside knowledge, was so misreading the X-Article as an official State Department pronouncement of global containment, what must his many readers think?

Kennan longed to clear up the misunderstanding, to set the record straight. But he could not. He had violated a precept of General Marshall's: "Planners don't talk." Marshall had been shocked to see the head of his Policy Planning Staff become an international celebrity. He summoned Kennan to his office and with raised eyebrows ("eyebrows before whose raising better men than I had quailed") demanded an explanation. Kennan stammered that the article had been cleared for publication by a State Department committee, which was true enough. Marshall, who believed in proper channels, was satisfied, but he repeated his injunction against talkative planners.

Kennan was hopelessly insecure in the presence of someone so secure as Marshall. "I have a feeling that I puzzled him," he wrote in his memoirs. The General, never one for praise, had been sparing with Kennan as well. Once, while the diplomat was nervously pouring drinks in his office, Marshall had exclaimed, "Kennan, they tell me you are a good head of a planning staff, and for all I know you are, but who the hell ever taught you to put the ice in before the whiskey?" Kennan was not about to jeopardize even such faint praise. While his colleagues were jabbering away with their favorite reporters, he became virtually mum to the outside world. His gag was not just self-enforced. Lovett turned down speaking requests for Kennan by explaining that the department's chief planner was "under directive from Marshall" not to speak publicly. *

• • •

Lovett was far too busy cajoling congressmen to worry about Kennan's misunderstandings with Lippmann, no matter how fundamental they appeared. He told Jim Forrestal at lunch that he doubted Congress would "produce the sums necessary" to rescue Europe. Forrestal shared his worry. He warned a Cabinet meeting that a new isolationism and a "let Europe go" mood was developing in the country. The result, he said, would be "Russians swarming over Europe."

In September, the President met with a group of congressional leaders and told them that he planned to call an emergency session of Congress. He wanted Congress to pass an "interim aid" bill to tide Europe over until a full recovery plan could be approved in the next session. The congressmen were unenthusiastic. "Mr. President, you must realize there is growing resistance to these programs," the Republican House Leader, Charles Halleck, said. "I've been out on the hustings and I know. The people don't like it."

The courtship of Arthur Vandenberg was renewed with ever greater ardor. "Politicians were a race that Marshall got along with but did not understand," Chip Bohlen recalled. "Their motivation mystified him." When Lovett and Bohlen urged Marshall to cultivate Arthur Vandenberg, the general resisted at first, replying that he assumed the senator was motivated by the national interest and therefore required no cultivation. But Lovett and Bohlen prevailed; Marshall began devoting hours to the company of the chairman of the Senate Foreign Relations Committee. "We could not have gotten much closer," Marshall later recalled, "unless I sat in Vandenberg's lap or he sat in mine."

Acheson's last contribution before he returned to his old Washington law firm of Covington, Burling in June had been to find the "Vandenberg brand" for a European Recovery bill. The senator had suggested that a "bipartisan committee" would be necessary to soften up Congress, and made it clear that unless Acheson followed his

---

*Kennan did speak out at least once more to the War College that December. "We must not hope to hold everything everywhere," he said to his audience of military officers. "We must decide which areas are key areas, and which ones are not, which ones we must hold with all our strength and which we may yield tactically." But Kennan's off-the-record warnings never surfaced in the press, and they seem to have had little impact in official circles.

advice, his help would not be forthcoming. Acheson readily agreed, but made sure that the appointments were tightly controlled by the White House. The committee was packed with industrialists, many chosen by Lovett, to ease congressional qualms that the Marshall Plan was a "socialist idea."

Acheson recommended his old schoolmate and rowing coach, Averell Harriman, to be chairman of the Administration's Committee on Foreign Aid. Disappointed at not being chosen Secretary of State, Harriman had dutifully toiled as Commerce Secretary, but he felt peripheral. This appointment made him a player again. It also pleased Forrestal, who had always believed that essential questions were best decided by a committee of his friends. "I don't know how much I can do," he wrote Harriman, "but one thing I do know: that between Bob, you, and myself we may be able to tie a few strings together that will not come unstuck." Forrestal, who was feeling battered by interservice rivalries at the Pentagon, added, "I also know that it is a relief to be working in an atmosphere in which one's associates are hoping for his success rather than the contrary."

Harriman undertook the foreign-aid job with his usual single-minded intensity. A plodding public speaker, however, he was not particularly well suited to congressional testimony. Indeed, after one deadening performance before the House Foreign Affairs Committee, a House staffer sympathetic to the Administration cause, Charles Burton Marshall, tore up the transcript of Harriman's rambling and tentative remarks and substituted a crisper, more upbeat version for the official record.

It was Bob Lovett who really understood how to stroke Congress. He soon discovered, not much to his surprise, that many members had found his predecessor condescending. Forrestal informed him that, at a dinner for Averell Harriman in June, Congressman John Lodge had confided that his colleagues "had the impression they were being talked down to" by Acheson.

Lovett liked to joke to his friends that dealing with Congress was "like getting a shave and having your appendix taken out at the same time." But if Lovett felt uncomfortable, he did not show it. His disarming friendliness and old-boy politesse came naturally. Whereas Acheson had to feign friendship with Vandenberg, Lovett really became Vandenberg's friend.

The two spent more waking hours together in the fall of 1947 than they did with their wives. (Lovett worked so hard that at Christmas Truman personally ordered him to take some time off.) The Under

Secretary's daily diary logs numerous long phone conversations with Vandenberg. Almost every evening on his way home from work, Lovett would stop off at Vandenberg's apartment at the Wardman Park Hotel, just across Rock Creek from his own house. There, over cocktails, the Under Secretary would show the senator the day's most illuminating classified cables. Typically, those dispatches would describe unrest in Europe, where the local Communist parties in France and Italy were making an all-out push to disrupt and, if possible, bring down government.

The offensive was Stalin's reaction to the Marshall Plan. Not unreasonably, given Soviet history, he saw a restored Europe, and especially a rebuilt Germany, as a threat to Soviet security. In September, he created the Cominform, a more restrictive, more tightly controlled version of the old Communist International, to assert his control over local Communist parties, which he ordered to stage a wave of general strikes in France and Italy.

The tactics did succeed in disrupting already fragile economies. But they also alienated public opinion, and in retrospect appear to have been the death gasp of Stalinism in Western Europe. At the time, the agitation seemed threatening. Forrestal was so worried that he wondered to Lovett over the phone whether the U.S. should land troops in Italy to quell the disorders. Not until the Italian government asks us, replied Lovett, who was less excitable than his old neighbor from Locust Valley.

In Europe, government and business leaders were not above exploiting this scare. Said Pierre Mendès-France, the French executive director of the World Bank: "The Communists are rendering a great service. Because we have a 'Communist danger,' the Americans are making a tremendous effort to help us. We must keep up this indispensable Communist scare."

Back in the U.S., certain segments of the Administration were fueling a Red scare of their own. Politicians seemingly indifferent to the spread of Communism abroad were determined to root out subversion, real or imagined, at home. Republican isolationists were the fiercest Red-baiters of all. For fiscal conservatives, domestic Red hunts had the virtue of being far cheaper than massive rearmament or reconstruction programs. Truman grudgingly felt the need to pacify the right by showing that he too was vigilant. Some of his lieutenants were overly so. Attorney General Tom Clark, along with FBI Director J. Edgar Hoover, dreamed up a "nationwide patriotism campaign" to stamp out subversion. A "Freedom Train" containing the Declaration of Independence, the Magna Carta, and the Constitution toured the country, while mass demonstrations of government employees took a "freedom pledge" and sang "God Bless America." The celebration culminated with a mock bombing run on the nation's capital at Thanksgiving time.

Some of the activities were not so harmless. In November, the Attorney General published a list of eighty-two subversive organizations, including the National Negro Congress and the Walt Whitman School of Social Science in Newark; membership in any of these was generally a bar to government employment. On Capitol Hill, meanwhile. The witch-hunts had begun. The House Un-American Activities Committee trumpeted its investigation of subversion in Hollywood, with Gary Cooper declaring that while he had not actually read Marx, "from what I hear, I don't like it because it isn't on the level."

Most Administration officials, from Truman on down, thought this was mostly nonsense, perhaps even dangerous, but they kept quiet. Forrestal, who genuinely feared subversion from Soviet fifth columnists, floated the idea of requiring journalists to take loyalty tests, but the scheme predictably leaked and sank. Lovett discussed the list of subversive organizations with the Attorney General, but his only contribution was to ask Clark to call them "subversive" rather than "Communist."

Lovett could ill afford to say or do anything that might distract from his lobbying campaign for the so-called Interim Aid plan designed to tide over Europe until the Marshall Plan could be put in place. Along with Marshall and Harriman, he appeared repeatedly on the Hill to warn of the Communist threat in Europe; he testified every day from November 17 to November 30. Some moments were rocky. Congressman John Vorys of Ohio badgered him one morning with a question Acheson had found uncomfortable (and would again): If Europe, why not China? Lovett was taken aback by his questioner; Vorys had been Skull and Bones at Yale and a flier in Lovett's beloved Yale Unit during World War I; his wife had invited Adèle Lovett to watch the session with her. As Vorys bore in, a page handed Lovett a note: it was an invitation from Vorys to Lovett to have lunch. In the more private precincts of the House dining room, Lovett was able to calm Vorys down with Yale chatter. Lovett passed off China as "General Marshall's specialty," a reference to Marshall's fruitless mission to China in 1946.

"Never before has Congress been bombarded with such propaganda," grumbled Congressman Fred Busby of Illinois, but the lobbying worked; the Interim Aid package passed overwhelmingly. When the Senate Foreign Affairs Committee approved the package on November 20, Vandenberg called Lovett to tell him that passage for Interim Aid looked safe, but "we're headed for the storm cellar on the Marshall Plan," which Republicans were already denouncing as an "International WPA" and a "bold socialist blueprint." Averell Harriman dropped by the British Embassy to give a progress report to Lord Inverchapel. Congress, he informed the ambassador, had seen nothing "compared to the flood of organized propaganda which the Administration is about to unloose."

●   ●   ●

It was a characteristic of the old foreign policy Establishment that its members could come and go between government and their banks or law firms. Indeed, over time, they constantly seemed to be substituting for each other, like lines in a hockey game changing on the fly.

Everyone, in or out of government, jumped into European recovery. In July of 1947, pending the merger of the old Navy and War departments in September, Forrestal had been nominated to be the first Secretary of Defense, but he found time to agitate for the Marshall Plan, knowing full well that a revived Europe would enhance national security. Acheson took time out from his law firm to form the Citizens' Committee for the Marshall Plan, patterned after the Committee to Defend America by Aiding the Allies, the group that had lobbied for U.S. intervention in World War II. His codirector was former War Secretary Robert Patterson. The committee's honorary chairman was, inevitably, Henry Stimson. Acheson performed such chores as making speeches to the National-American Wholesale Grocers' Association in Atlantic City and ghostwriting congressional testimony for the National Farmers Union. Testifying himself, he could not refrain from twitting a congressman or two. "If you didn't talk so much and listened more," he lectured one, "I think you would understand better what this is all about."

John McCloy had become president of the International Bank for Reconstruction and Development—better known as the World Bank— at the end of February 1947, leaving once again his lucrative law practice with Milbank, Tweed. "When he took over," according to *The New York Times*, "the bank was eight months old, split by dissension, sadly lacking in prestige, and had not lent one dime." In McCloy's view, the bank's weakness was "too much politics, too little finance." In a series of meetings and speeches with businessmen and financiers, many of them his friends, he made the case for investing in Europe: to create markets for U.S. trade, to cure the dollar surplus, to stop Communism. His more subtle purpose was to convince Wall Street that the Bank was not full of New Dealers seeking to finance their mushy ideals by making bad loans. He succeeded; the first loan, $250 million to France, was oversubscribed by private investors.

McCloy believed that, in the long run, private investment was Europe's salvation. The Bank, he said, would be around long after the Marshall Plan was finished. The Bank was the perfect vehicle for McCloy, who over his long career would weave private and public concerns so skillfully that it became difficult to tell where one ended and the other began. He worked closely with his State Department friends; his announcement of the loan to France came, not coincidentally, only hours after the French government forced Communists out of the Cabinet. At the same time, he protected private investment in World Bank securities with some quiet lobbying of his old "Heavenly Twin" at the War Department, Bob Lovett. The Under Secretary's phone logs show McCloy checking in with Lovett in December of 1947 to make sure that Congress would not cut $3 million out of the Administration's aid package to France that was to be used to repay loans from the World Bank. McCloy also floated the idea of a loan to finance renewed coal development in the Ruhr. His memory of Germany's shattered landscape still fresh, he was convinced that Germany had to be rebuilt for Europe to recover. In his disarmingly direct manner, he stated, "Most of Europe's problems can be broken down in terms of coal. The Ruhr's got most of it." German power was still too vivid a memory to others, however. The idea of refueling the source of German power with American dollars was spiked by the Administration.

In its attempts to implement a European recovery plan, the U.S. was getting some discreet help from an old friend of Lovett's and McCloy's, and Acheson's and Harriman's—Jean Monnet, the French investment banker who had been a regular participant in government and business deals, as well as Washington dinner parties, in the thirties. Monnet was well placed as cochairman of the Committee on European Economic Cooperation, the organization that put together those "laundry lists" for U.S. aid that had so discouraged Lovett in August of 1947. Monnet, in turn, worked with two future paragons of the foreign policy Establishment, George Ball and Paul Nitze. Advised secretly by Ball, a Chicago lawyer who had succeded McCloy as his American counsel, Monnet leaked a copy of a $28 billion shopping list to Nitze, then an up-and-coming young State Department economic adviser. The adverse reaction in Washington helped Monnet persuade his European colleagues to draft a more reasonable request. Monnet did make one gaffe; he joked to a congressman that French peasants had stashed $2 billion in gold bullion in their mattresses. Averell Harriman spent most of a day explaining that old French joke in a congressional hearing.

The intimacy of decision making in Washington during the early postwar years was remarkable. The National Security Staff, which in 1985 had fifty specialists, hardly existed in 1947. Clark Clifford was a de facto national security adviser, but he also counseled Truman on domestic affairs, politics, and a whole range of issues. The National Security Council had been created that summer, but it was rarely used; national security meetings, such as they were, consisted mostly of Clifford having breakfast with Jim Forrestal at his home in Kalorama on Wednesday mornings. It is fair to say that almost everyone knew everyone else; they had gone to school together, gone to war together, and gone out to dinner together at least once a month. Not everyone was Ivy League, by any means, but Yale's secret societies were better represented in the inner councils than any state university. Government was hardly a Masonic order; an Averell Harriman or a Bob Lovett cared far more about a colleague's ability than the pin in his cravat, and Dean Acheson boasted about the diversity of the State Department. Still, friendships and old ties blurred boundaries between government agencies, between government and business, even between nations.

Chip Bohlen thrived in a world where business could be done face-to-face with like-minded men. He was a poor writer who had as much difficulty composing his prose as others had reading it. He could also be caustic, even cruel to dimmer lights than himself. Foreign Service officers had winced as he publicly dismembered a colleague, Charles Yost, at the Potsdam Conference on some minor matter. He described his sister-in-law's husband, within his earshot, as "all body and no brains." But he was more often charming, inquisitive, funny, and hugely persuasive in conversation.

Bohlen's assignment was to help with congressional liaison and to handle public relations for the selling of the Marshall Plan. He did not much enjoy stroking congressmen, but he was effective at it, and he got on very well with the press. He loved staying up all night playing cards and talking to journalists; he was blunt and honest, and the good ones, such as Reston and the Alsop brothers, the syndicated columnists Stewart and Joseph, swore by him.

Bohlen's appointment as State Department Counselor in the summer of 1947 was "certainly welcome as it may keep the Bohlen family from the poor house," he wrote a friend. He was as usual broke, but poverty was highly relative in postwar Washington. He owned a small, charming Georgetown house, book-lined, with Oriental rugs and a garden out back, of the type later bought by successful lobbyists for several hundred thousand dollars. Bohlen purchased it in the thirties when Georgetown was being gentrified by New Dealers. (Their neighbor, when the Bohlens moved into 2811 Dumbarton Avenue, was an old black man with dozens of cats.) Bohlen always felt slightly pinched, unable to afford a summer home or a new car, and he sometimes had to borrow from friends, but he did not greatly suffer, or complain. He loved to gamble, and would fleece suckers at poker unashamedly.

He lost too. "Don't tell Avis," he would implore his gambling partners. "He was scared of her," recalls Cecil Lyon, Bohlen's friend through St. Paul's, Harvard, and all the State Department years. "And he was absolutely devoted to her, and she to him." Avis calmed and soothed Bohlen, moderated his late-night hooting and love of contentious debate. Avis was also astute. "She could get along with men like Joe Alsop and Averell Harriman, men who wouldn't tolerate butterflies," recalled Lyon.

Once a week, the Bohlens partook in an institution known as the Sunday Night Supper (called by Joe Alsop, perhaps more aptly, the Sunday Night Drunk). It was servants' night out; the Bohlens, the Stewart Alsops, Joe Alsop, the Frank Wisners (he was later head of the CIA's department of dirty tricks and a tragic Cold War suicide), the Bob Joyces (he was a veteran FSO), and the Tommy Thompsons (he was soon to become Bohlen's and Kennan's equal as a Soviet expert) would have well-lubricated potluck dinners, often inviting the Lovetts, Harrimans, Achesons, or Kennans to join them. Bohlen, in his baggy suits and spotted ties, sipping on Scotch and puffing Camels, would hold forth and argue with his friends, sometimes past three in the morning. "They would all argue at the top of their lungs," Mrs. Stewart Alsop recalls. Joe Alsop would fish for information, offering up rumors and wheedling, "That's right, eh? Eh?" If Bohlen remained silent, Alsop would infer confirmation. Bohlen would tire of Alsop from time to time, and the dinner would be off for a few weeks. But it would always resume. Bohlen, in the midst of one debate, yelled at Alsop, "Get out of my house!" Alsop yelled back, "I will not! This is *my* house!" (It was.) The two remained close friends; the Alsops' column was particularly knowing that winter.

Bohlen's coziness with the press was matched by Lovett's. When *Time* decided to run a cover on Lovett in the spring of 1948, Lovett protested that he did not want any publicity, but ended up entertaining Jim Shepley, the magazine's Washington bureau chief, over Lovett Mists at Sea Change, in Hobe Sound. When the glowing profile appeared, praising Lovett as the "New Broom at State," Lovett's diary recorded a call to Shepley: "Thanks for his restraint in article in *Time*. Very appreciative." Lovett was even tighter with *The New York Times*. After one press conference in March, Lovett called Lester Markel, an editor. Lovett's secretary recorded: "Mr. L thanked him and asked him to thank Reston. L said there ought to be assurance from outside the Department that the Dept. is an extremely competent organization. Mr. Markel will see what he can do to bring this about." Arthur Krock shamelessly catered to Lovett, phoning him once with reassurances after some leaks from the White House had been critical of his performance. Krock promised to put an end to it, in the *Times* at least, and read Lovett a column praising him, as well as their mutual friend Jim Forrestal.

With such friends, Lovett was not above propagandizing. When the State Department uncovered evidence that the Soviets had agreed with the Nazis to carve up Europe as part of their infamous non-aggression pact in 1939, Lovett decided to make good use of the embarrassing documents. "Mr. L thinks it would be a good idea to have printed up the Molotov-von Ribbentrop agreement," his secretary recorded, "and publish it as a white paper when the opportunity offers. Mr. Forrestal heartily agrees." The opportunity offered in early January, when *Time* printed a gloomy piece warning that support in Congress for the Marshall Plan was soft. By this time, any pretense that the European Recovery Program was not intended as an anti-Soviet measure was dropped. Before publicizing documents that showed the Soviets taking great delight in the Nazi invasion of Norway, Holland, and Belgium in 1940, Lovett called Acheson at his law firm. Did Acheson think it would be considered "propagandizing" for the European Recovery Plan? Acheson said maybe, but it was a chance worth taking.

The Establishment laid siege to Capitol Hill that winter of 1947-48. General Marshall, usually understated, told Congress that the vote on the ERP was "the greatest decision in our history." He warned

Congress that if the U.S. decided it was "unable or unwilling effectively to assist in the reconstruction of Western Europe, we must accept the consequences of its collapse into the dictatorship of police states... there is no doubt in my mind that the whole world hangs in the balance." Harriman's bipartisan committee examined the Marshall Plan objectively and delivered to Congress a three-inch-thick report. It heartily approved every aspect.

Actually writing the ERP was a logistical nightmare. The groundwork fell largely to Paul Nitze, Forrestal's former partner at Dillon, Read and Chip Bohlen's old Porcellian clubmate. Nitze worked up a series of "brown books" on every country, measuring their balance of payments, needs and requirements down to the smallest detail. To accomplish this feat Nitze had to borrow all the calculating machines of the Prudential Life Insurance Company in Newark, the same ones that he and Lovett had used right after the war for an inventory of the Air Force. The "brown books" were presented to John Taber, chairman of the House Appropriations Committee and the first and largest hurdle.

Taber was a small-town lawyer and farmer from upstate New York. Nitze was a smooth Harvard Wall Streeter. Taber decided to teach Nitze a lesson. "Mr. Nitze," he said at the outset of the first hearing, "I have seen your brown books and we're not going to use them. We're going to go country by country alphabetically, and you're going to justify every commodity you want to ship." Nitze winced. The laborious process got as far as "P" in the first country, Austria. The item at issue was twenty-five thousand tons of pulse beans. Taber peered down at Nitze and asked him, "Have you ever grown pulse beans?" Nitze conceded that he had not. "Well, I have," said Taber. He had also been to Austria and the climate was perfect for growing pulse beans. "So why should we send them twenty-five thousand tons?" the congressman inquired. Nitze was feeling lower and lower. "Can I call experts from the Agriculture Department?" he asked. "No," replied Taber. "You tell me." Nitze took a deep breath and began to mumble something about nutritional levels and caloric intake. Taber rose from the table, literally pulling his hair. "This man knows nothing! I'm going to call Bob Lovett and tell him that this whole exercise is going to have to be put off one full year until the Department of State finds out what it is doing!" He stalked out. Nitze sat there, slumped over in his chair, watching six months of twelve-hour days, not to mention European recovery, go down the drain.

A half hour later, Taber returned. To Nitze's surprise he was calm.

He told Nitze quietly that he could call his experts and proceed. Nitze, relieved, went back to Lovett's office and asked him what happened. "I couldn't get a word in edgewise for about fifteen minutes," Lovett answered, "but when he finished I said, 'You know, I could ask you a question that I bet you couldn't answer. How many rivets are in the wing of a B-29?' Taber replied, 'You used to be Assistant Secretary for Air. You know that, not me.' I said, 'That's just the point. Now why don't you let Nitze call those experts. I've got another question you can't answer.' Taber said, 'What's that?' I said, 'If it takes eight yards of pink crepe to tie around an elephant's leg, how long does it take to swat a fly?' Taber said that was a ridiculous question. I said, 'Well, why don't you stop asking Paul Nitze ridiculous questions!'"

Only Lovett could have so teased and scolded a self-inflated congressman and gotten away with it. Nitze went back to testify for forty-three sessions. He lost fifteen pounds. By early March 1948 the Marshall Plan was still in trouble, denounced by Republican leader Robert Taft as a "European TVA." As Bohlen reported to Lovett early that month, "Taber had telephoned him and torn the Department apart . . . Communists in the State Department, etc." All the testimony, all the good press, all the cajoling and jollying, still had not convinced Congress. The Administration needed something more persuasive. It needed a war scare.

• • •

George Kennan watched the lobbying effort with distaste. To a journalist who chastised him for failing to help sell the Marshall Plan, he replied that he was a diplomat, not a salesman. He resented having to curry favor with Congress. "My specialty," he recalled telling the reporter, "was the defense of U.S. interests against others, not against my own representatives."

Kennan felt uncomfortable in the social world of Chip Bohlen. He did not enjoy boozy debates; he took invective personally, and would sulk. At one of the Sunday Night Suppers, while Bohlen and the Alsop brothers were having at it in the next room, Kennan sat on the couch for most of the night with Mrs. Stewart Alsop, talking morosely about his unfortunate youth, the maiden aunts, the military academy, the social slights at Princeton. On weekends, Kennan would invite friends out to his Pennsylvania farm, but few relished the prospect. A ramshackle affair, it was in constant need of repair. Guests were pressed into service. Mrs. Alsop, who was very fond of Kennan but not his farm, recalls a weekend spent on her hands and knees painting radiators.

Kennan's bond with Bohlen was intellectual, which was the most that the alienated loner could hope for in a relationship. His friendship with Chip, he wrote Charlie Thayer, "represents the maximum of what I am destined to have." It had been forged in the isolation of Moscow; in social Georgetown, it began to wither.

Kennan, feeling increasingly isolated during the early months of 1948, was beginning to sense that the pendulum he had shoved so mightily with the Long Telegram and the X-Article had swung too far. The dire warnings that were being passed on to Capitol Hill and that Lovett was sharing with Vandenberg over cocktails made Kennan feel uneasy. His own view, expressed in a "Resume of World Situation" to Marshall, was that the worst was already over in Europe. "The danger of war is vastly exaggerated in many quarters," he began. Containment was working. True, the Soviets should be expected to try to consolidate their power within Europe. This was perfectly natural (and to Kennan, who believed in spheres of influence, acceptable). Kennan specifically warned Marshall that the Soviets would "clamp down completely on Czechoslovakia," a predictable defensive reaction to the Marshall Plan. In February, Kennan went further, suggesting that the time was approaching to "talk turkey" with the Soviets about a mutual reduction of forces in Europe. He also offered a characteristically prescient warning: "To oppose the efforts of indigenous Communist elements within foreign countries must generally be considered as a risky and profitless undertaking, apt to do more harm than good."

Kennan was beginning a long journey back into the wilderness. The diplomat who had done so much in 1946 to convince official Washington that the Soviets had to be contained—by the threat of force as well as political and economic pressure—felt by 1948 that he had created a monster. He believed that his ideas had been not so much adopted as vulgarized, coarsened, and distorted by the failure of policy makers to understand essential nuance. But more than that, his own views had begun to change.

The Soviets were still a threat, to be sure, and the fate of Europe still hung "in the balance." But Kennan began to argue in 1948 that—contrary to many of his earlier warnings—it was possible to bargain with the Soviets. Their behavior could be modified; they could be made to see "situations, if not arguments." Not right away, perhaps, and only through painstaking and careful diplomacy. But an effort should be made to lessen Stalin's paranoia, to defuse the tensions that could lead to war.

Significantly, Kennan understood that Communism was not monolithic. In his Policy Planning memos, he predicted that fissures would show in Stalin's bloc (already Tito was showing independence in Yugoslavia), and he early on foretold that China and Russia would fall out, that Chinese Communism would be peculiarly adapted to China. "We may doubt that Communism—itself a rather vague concept—will be the right thing for the Chinese," he wrote that winter. "We may be sure it will be given a distinctly Chinese flavor."

Kennan's mellowing was partly due to his belief that containment was working and that it was time to look to the next phase, a mutual reduction of forces. As he later explained in his memoirs, he believed that by standing up "manfully but not aggressively" to Soviet leaders, "they could be brought to a point where they would talk reasonably about some of the problems flowing from the outcome of the war . . . Formidable as they were, they were not supermen. Like rulers of all great countries, they had internal contradictions and dilemmas to deal with." As Kennan watched Europe coalesce around the Marshall Plan and the Kremlin struggle with emerging Titoism, he felt the time had come to talk, or at least to sound out the Soviets about establishing some sort of dialogue aimed at reducing tensions and heading off the arms race.

There is a certain logic and consistency to Kennan's account of his evolving views. Yet his retrospective explanation is somewhat too tidy and rational. It glosses over what appears to be a true change of heart, and it fails to account for Kennan's own human quirks.

The fact is that Kennan throughout his own career was more intuitive than logical. Over the years, as Barton Gellman notes in *Contending with Kennan*, scholars have vainly tried to reconcile his apparent contradictions, to make coherent sense of his philosophy. Some, like Eugene Rostow, simply throw up their hands. Kennan is "an impressionist, a poet, not an earthling," sneers Rostow. More understanding critics recognize in Kennan what John Lewis Gaddis calls "noncommunicable wisdom"—a play on Dean Acheson's frustrated plaint that what Kennan's superiors really needed from him was "communicable wisdom, not mere conclusions, however soundly based in experience or intuition."

Kennan was a thinker, not a warrior. However hardheaded he professed to be about standing up to the Soviets, he never lost a statesman's innate preference for words over weapons. Though he recognized that a strong, alert military force is "probably the most important single instrumentality in the conduct of U.S. foreign policy," he deeply mistrusted the ability of U.S. leaders to use it wisely and sparingly.

Between 1946 and 1948, his doubts on this score hardened into near despair. Asked at the War College in 1946 if the U.S. did not have something more constructive to offer than military force, Kennan groped uneasily. "I would be happier," he said, "and I think we would be on sounder ground if we had things that were constructive to offer people in fields beside the military fields. I am still trying to think it out. . . . I just don't know." By the winter of 1947–48, he was increasingly convinced that the military men and the politicians were heedlessly shoving the diplomats aside. Kennan's essential elitism, his disdain for government by the masses, figured heavily in his deepening disenchantment. It made him exceedingly leery of popular passions that were hardening the government's anti-Communist line. As he wrote in his private notes:

> When I returned from Russia a year and a half ago . . . I was conscious of the weakness of the Russian position, of the slenderness of the means with which they operated, of the ease with which they could be pushed back. It was I who pressed for "containment" and for aid to Europe as a form of containment.
>
> Today I think I was wrong. Not in my analysis of the Soviet position, but in my assumption that this government has the ability to "operate" politically at all in the foreign field.

Kennan had profound doubts about the capacity of democracy to use force as an effective tool of foreign policy. Not only was the military chain of command "addicted to doing things only in the most massive, ponderous, and unwieldy manner," but so was the American public. "A democracy," Kennan wrote in a note to himself, "is severely restricted in its use of armed forces as a weapon of peacetime foreign policy. It cannot manipulate them tactically on any extensive scale, for the accomplishment of measures short of war." A democracy is suited only to all-out wars. "It soon becomes a victim of its own propaganda. It then tends to attach to its own cause an absolute value, which distorts its own vision of everything else. Its enemy becomes the embodiment of all evil. Its own side, on the other hand, is the center of all virtue."

Kennan's philosophy of cool realpolitik was not matched by inward dispassion. He was moody and emotional, and ever insecure. He could not help but feel that he was partly to blame for the overreaction to his at times overwrought and imprecise X-Article. Yet mindful of Marshall's injunction that "planners don't talk," and both repulsed by and inept at bureaucratic maneuvering, he felt helpless to redress the balance. In a way, one senses, he almost preferred his lonely intellectual existence. There was in Kennan an essential contrariness, a need to play the misunderstood iconoclast, to cast himself as a remote Cassandra in the long-running tragedy of U.S.-Soviet relations.

On February 25, 1948, Kennan handed General Marshall his paper calling for peace feelers to the Soviets and departed on a tour of Japan. His timing was unfortunate. That same day, Washington plunged into crisis, the first real war scare of the Cold War. Kennan's moderation, his call for restraint and accommodation, would be overwhelmed by events.

CHAPTER 15

CRISIS

"Will Russia move first?"

The "clampdown" on Czechoslovakia came on February 25, 1948. Pro-Western politicians were purged; a Kremlin puppet, Prime Minister Klement Gottwald, installed a Communist-dominated government. "National Police Week" was proclaimed; arrests and executions swept Prague. The last link with the West, Foreign Minister Jan Masaryk, fell, or was pushed, from his office window on March 10.

It may have been predictable to Kennan, but to official Washington, Prague in 1948 looked just like Munich in 1938. "We are faced with exactly the same situation with which Britain and France were faced in 1938–9 with Hitler," Truman wrote to his daughter, Margaret, on March 3. "Things look black. A decision will have to be made and I am going to make it."

The war scare deepened on March 5 with a telegram from General Lucius Clay, the Military Governor of Germany. Clay reported a "subtle change" in Soviet attitudes. He feared that war could come "with dramatic suddenness." Truman jotted on a note from Marshall,

"Will Russia move first? Who pulls the trigger? Then where do we go?"

The Pentagon was in a state of alert. The CIA reported that it could not "guarantee" against war for more than sixty days. The Chief of Naval Operations proposed steps to "prepare the American people for war." The Secretary of the Army asked how long it would take to move the "eggs"—atomic bombs—to the Mediterranean. (The U.S. had at the time about two dozen in its arsenal.) The Secretary of the Air Force suggested privately that the U.S. drop several "atomic bombs" on Russia if the Soviets refused to withdraw from Central Europe.

Forrestal's reaction to the Clay telegram was to broadcast it all over town. In his diary he wrote that it was "inconceivable" that the Soviets would start a war, but he added that the same could have been said about Hitler.

The press fed the tension. A front-page map in the Washington *Post* showed Europe with the area under Soviet domination shaded. "Where next?" the headline asked. Arrows pointed to Italy, France, Finland, and Austria. "The U.S. had stopped kidding itself," the lead story of *Time* magazine began on March 15. "The hard facts were plain enough now: dollars alone would not stop the Russians." A week later the *Time* lead declared: "All last week in the halls of Congress, on the street corners, U.S. citizens had begun to talk of the possibility of war between the U.S. and U.S.S.R." The Alsop brothers reported: "The atmosphere of Washington today is no longer postwar. It is a prewar atmosphere."

The worry was genuine. But even as they fretted, Washington officials could sense that the crisis was serving a useful purpose with Congress. Not only was it helping in the selling of the Marshall Plan, but it was aiding the Administration with such aims as getting more money for the military and restoring the draft. Actually, Clay's chilling telegram had little to do with Russians, and everything to do with Congress. According to Clay's biographer: "The primary purpose was to assist military chiefs in Congressional testimony; it was not Clay's opinion related to change in Soviet strategy." Clay, it later turned out, had been asked by Army Intelligence for some propaganda for the Hill.

Forrestal was not nearly so cynical. But at a meeting on March 2 with Lovett, Marshall, and McCloy (who had a way of showing up at crucial meetings quite unrelated to the World Bank), the Defense Secretary observed that the atmosphere was right in Congress to "capitalize" on "present concern of the country over events of the last week in Europe."

The White House did not miss the opportunity. Truman faced a hard re-election campaign. Clark Clifford had written in a campaign strategy memo that "the worse matters get, up to a fairly certain point—real danger of imminent war—the more there is a sense of crisis. In times of crisis, the American citizen tends to back up his President." On March 17, Truman addressed a Joint Session of Congress to ask for passage of the European Recovery Program, selective service, and universal military training. He denounced the Soviets' "ruthless action" and warned that the Soviets had a "clear design" to extend their domination to the "remaining free nations of Europe."

The histrionics worried Marshall and Bohlen, just as the sweeping language of the Truman Doctrine had concerned them a year earlier. Bohlen went to Clifford to tell him that Marshall wanted "a weak message, drop intemperate language . . . simple, businesslike, no 'ringing phrases'—nothing warlike or belligerent. Don't denounce, just state the facts." Clifford replied: "It has to be blunt to justify the message! He asks for legislation—how does he explain it?" Marshall warned Truman directly that a hotheaded speech might "pull the trigger—start the war."

The speech, and the crisis, worked just the way Clifford hoped. Two days after Truman addressed Congress, the House Appropriations Committee, which had been sitting on the European Recovery Program, sent it to the floor recommending passage "to reverse the trend of Communism in Europe." The bill sailed through the House and Senate, literally shouted through by Republican isolationists who had never voted for a foreign-aid bill in their lives.

Within days, the first ship set sail from Galveston, Texas, with nineteen thousand tons of wheat. Before long, at any given moment, there were 150 ships at sea carrying American goods and produce and know-how to Europe.

To head the ERP in Washington, Truman decided to pick Dean Acheson. "Van," the President told Arthur Vandenberg, "I've got just the man for the job and he's willing to take it at great personal sacrifice." Vandenberg promptly vetoed the President's choice. He told Truman that Acheson could not be confirmed by the Senate. Vandenberg personally disliked Acheson and knew that many of his colleagues resented Acheson's imperious manner. So Truman picked a

Republican auto salesman, Paul Hoffman, the president of Stude-baker.

To administer the ERP in Europe, Truman chose the ubiquitous Averell Harriman, whose committee had done so much to shape the Marshall Plan and ram it through Congress. Harriman was given the title of U.S. Special Representative in Europe and the rank of ambassador. But a more accurate description of his job was Theater Commander.

During World War II, President Roosevelt and General Marshall had given tremendous latitude to General Eisenhower, the Allied commander, to go about liberating Europe. Truman and Hoffman gave equal license to Harriman to restore the Continent.

There is no equivalent in today's foreign policy bureaucracy to Harriman's position or his power. The immensity and urgency of the task demanded a benevolent despot, and Harriman's authority was unquestioned in Washington as well as in the sixteen European capitals dependent on ERP's beneficence. He did not report to the State Department but rather to Hoffman and the President. Harriman used all the authority he was given, and then some. "Harriman was used to being head of his own show," said Hoffman's assistant, Richard Bissell. "It doesn't come naturally to him to report fully to someone else, to negotiate on behalf of someone at the other end of the line."

In Paris, the U.S. representative was posted to the Hotel Talleyrand, on the Place de la Concorde, where Napoleon's Foreign Minister had conducted his love affairs and outfoxed France's enemies. Harriman ensconced himself in a gilt-edged chamber beneath a bust of Benjamin Franklin, the first U.S. minister to France. But he immediately had second thoughts about his furnishings. "What will congressmen think when they see this stuff?" he asked an aide. "Can't we put a little card up somewhere, the way they do in museums, telling where the furnishings came from?" The solution he finally settled on was a preemptive strike: a letter to Washington scandalmonger Drew Pearson to explain how it was that the U.S. ambassador to the Marshall Plan came to have such lavish offices.

Theodore H. White, then a journalist covering Harriman and the Marshall Plan, bluntly reported that "people, and newsmen in particular, thought he was stupid. This was an impression one might easily gather from his mumbled diction, his apparent inattention to conversation, his groping for the proper figures when making a point." As White added, however, Harriman was "not stupid—only single-minded. . . . once [he] was wound up and pointed in the direction his government had told him he must go, he was like a tank crushing all opposition." Harriman would occasionally drop a tread. In the course of a whirlwind tour of Scandinavia in the spring of 1949, he gave a stirring tribute to the wartime gallantry of Danish seamen—while he was in Norway.

"Averell was not quick or gifted with words," recalled his deputy and later successor as ERP administrator, Milton Katz. "Yet he had great intuition. His conclusions were right even when his reasoning was not persuasive." Harriman had been among the first to seize on a solution to the vexing question of German reindustrialization. The wartime Allies, particularly France, were not eager to see Germany rebuild the industrial base that had been so efficiently transformed into a war machine. Yet without Germany's great coal and steel production capacity, the recovery of all Europe would be retarded. It was Jean Monnet, the great visionary of European integration, who first suggested a compromise solution: that France and Germany pool their coal and steel resources. The radical idea was strongly opposed by economic experts and State Department bureaucrats who warned that such an arrangement would lead to the creation of a gigantic European cartel. The British, who saw their own coal and steel industries threatened, were vehemently opposed. "But Harriman knew immediately and intuitively that it was the right move," recalled Katz. "He knew it was the best way to create a stable and secure Europe. He just whooped right through the intricacies of the economics to the essential point." Joining forces with Monnet and McCloy, who by then (1949) had become High Commissioner of Germany, he helped sell the plan, named after French Foreign Minister Robert Schuman, to the doubters in Washington and London. Harriman's judgment proved correct: the European Coal and Steel Community was at the core of Europe's astounding recovery.

Though gruff and at times stiff, Harriman was an effective diplomat. As a creature of both Wall Street and Washington, he was uniquely able to understand the different and often opposing perspectives and needs of business and government officials. By the shrewdness of his judgment, if not always the art of his rhetoric, he served, Katz recalled, "as a full-scale interpreter" between the public and private sectors— in sixteen different countries.

Harriman's efforts notwithstanding, the American presence was not always entirely welcome in Europe. A ditty making the rounds of London salons began, "Our Uncle who art in America, Sam be thy name/ Thy Navy come, Thy will be done... give us this day our

Marshall aid, and forgive us our un-American activities...." The National Assembly in Paris, meanwhile, voted in 1949 to "prohibit the import, manufacture, and sale of Coca-Cola in France, Algeria, and the French Colonial Empire."

American aid was not at all times altruistic. The tobacco lobby insisted on Congress paying to send Europe forty thousand tons of tobacco, even though none had been requested, and 177 million pounds of unpalatable spaghetti were shipped to Italy. Foreign currency soaked up U.S. products. Despite the French prohibition, Coca-Cola was selling 50 million bottles a day to Europe, enough to float a light cruiser.

Nonetheless, the Marshall Plan was an incredible success. The United States poured $13 billion into Europe (about $70 billion in 1985 dollars). It sent 100,000 tractors to France, rebuilt entirely French harbors that had been 70 percent destroyed, bought new nets for Norwegian fishermen, and sent one thousand baby chicks for the children of Vienna from the 4-H Clubs of America. It provided thousands of tons of coal to keep steel factories running, bread to eat, and hope.

The Marshall Plan was, said Winston Churchill, the "most unsordid act in history." Bob Lovett said he was proud of the Marshall Plan on other grounds: it was a government program that stayed within its original cost estimates, and when it had outlived its usefulness, it ended.

• • •

The war scare of March 1948 quickly evaporated. On March 25, General Clay, whose telegram had done so much to inflame Washington, held a press conference to say that he was "not the least bit apprehensive" and that "much too much is being made of this." Lovett spent the last two weeks of March in Hobe Sound, sipping Lovett Mists and pretending to read whodunits while he mulled over State Department problems. Forrestal wrote a friend on March 17, "I feel better about the world situation than I have for two and half years."

But for Forrestal there was no easing up. There never was. On March 30, he demanded that the recently formed National Security Council prepare a report on "subversive elements" in the U.S. and "propose countermeasures" in the event of an emergency. The same day he asked the Air Force, "How soon and at what rate can we get B-29s [atomic bombers] out of storage?" Forrestal was no warmonger. "Anyone who thinks in terms of the concept of preventive war ought to get his head examined," he wrote a friend on March 3. But he was obsessed with U.S. preparedness, or the lack of it.

Forrestal had become the first Secretary of Defense in September of 1947. The War and Navy departments had been merged into a National Military Establishment. As Secretary of the Navy, Forrestal had successfully opposed a strong Defense Secretary, in order to preserve the Navy's independence. As Secretary of Defense, he would deeply regret it. "This office will probably be the greatest cemetery for dead cats in history," he wrote playwright Robert Sherwood.

Forrestal was caught in a withering cross fire among the services. The Air Force wanted to rely on the Bomb and build ever larger bombers; the Navy wanted more and bigger carriers; each side tried to sabotage the other. Air Force Secretary Stuart Symington was out of control. He simply refused to support the share of the budget that the Administration had assigned the Air Force, and lobbied Congress to give him more. "Then quit," Forrestal told him.

"I won't support it and I won't quit," Symington replied. Forrestal took Symington's disloyalty hard; he had felt that Symington, a Yale man and social friend from Locust Valley, was "one of us."

Truman was unsympathetic with Forrestal. While the U.S. had a monopoly on the atomic bomb, he did not feel the need to spend heavily on the military. When Forrestal asked him to authorize a "careful analysis of existing and potential dangers to our security" and "a comprehensive statement of national security policy," Truman snapped, "The proper thing for you to do is get the Army, Navy, and Air Force people together, and establish a program within budgetary limits which have been allowed. It seems to me that it is your responsibility."

Truman was losing confidence in Forrestal. He believed his Defense Secretary was getting "bulldozed" by the services, who were preying on Forrestal's obsession with preparedness. After a budget meeting on May 7, Truman ranted, "the Air Force boys are for glamour," while the Navy is "as always a propaganda machine." General Marshall was a "tower of strength." But "Forrestal can't take it. He wants to compromise with the opposition."

Forrestal was always candid with himself. "I am frank to say I have the greatest sympathy with [Truman] because he is determined not to spend more than we take in in taxes." Forrestal admitted that it was quite possible to "wreck the economy in the process of trying to fight the cold war." He was also justified in his feelings that the U.S. had to begin building up conventional forces in a steady and rational way.

But Forrestal worried too hard and spread himself too thin. When he wasn't fighting with service chiefs, he was lobbying for the Marshall Plan or catering to senators ("Jim, I would like to get your help on a matter," Tydings of Maryland wrote on February 17. "I am very anxious to have Navy play the University of Maryland in football in 1949"). Aides began to observe that Forrestal had a strange habit of dipping his finger into a water glass and rubbing his lips. Clark Clifford noticed that at meetings Forrestal rubbed a spot on the back of his head so persistently that it became a raw wound.

•   •   •

In early April 1948, Kennan lay in bed on the sixteenth floor of Bethesda Naval Hospital, sick with duodenal ulcers, "very bleak in spirit," he recorded in his moody way, "made bleaker still by the whistling of the cold spring wind in the windows of that lofty pinnacle." He had returned in March from his trip to Japan to find Washington still stewing with war rumors. The jittery talk depressed him. For months he had wanted to set the record straight about his X-Article. He continued to fear that "containment" was being perverted into a dangerous goad to the Soviets. As he lay ill, he finally poured out his frustrations in a letter to Walter Lippmann. "The Russians do not want to invade anyone. It is not in their tradition. They tried it once in Finland and got their fingers burned. They don't want war of any kind." The threat, he tried to explain, was political, not military. "They far prefer to do the job politically with stooge forces. Note well: when I say politically, that does not mean without violence. But it does mean that the violence is nominally *domestic*, not *international* violence. It is, if you will, a police violence . . . not a military violence."

Kennan, typically, did not mail the letter. He still felt the force of Marshall's admonition against talkative planners. Two years later, after he had left government, he finally confronted Lippmann in the parlor car of a train to New York and unburdened himself with a long monologue. By then, it was too late to do any good.

Kennan's distinction between political and military violence was not just an academic nuance. If the real threat was subversion, not invasion, then the way to meet it was by strengthening political institutions, not by engaging in an arms race. But official Washington was not listening. When Kennan finally returned to the State Department on April 19, he discovered that Robert Lovett and his minions were already well along the way toward concluding a (still secret) military alliance with Western Europe.

The idea had been germinating since December. Britain, France, and the Benelux countries were talking about forming their own "Western Union," but they needed U.S. power to make it a meaningful deterrent to the Soviets. Marshall and Lovett, preoccupied with the Marshall Plan, were at first hesitant. But a skillful State Department bureaucrat, John Hickerson, chief of the Office of European Affairs, was determined. A Texan and a staunch Cold Warrior, Hickerson stumbled into the State Department on New Year's Eve, drunk on Fish House Punch from the Metropolitan Club, and declared to his deputy, Theodore Achilles, "I don't care whether entangling alliances have been considered worse than original sin since George Washington's time. We've got to negotiate a military alliance with Western Europe in peacetime, and we've got to do it quickly."

Hickerson soon persuaded Lovett to begin private talks with the Europeans at the State Department, where a parade of military experts warned that the Soviets could reach Cherbourg in forty-eight hours. In these State Department meetings during the early months of 1948 the alliance later known as the North Atlantic Treaty Organization— NATO—was born. Elaborate precautions were taken to insure secrecy; the participants had to slip in through the State Department garage. The precautions were not quite enough, however. One of the members of the British delegation was Donald Maclean, a Soviet spy.

Kennan thought a formal military alliance was a terrible idea. It would merely divert resources away from economic recovery and provoke the Soviets. He had no feel for military realities. He believed that a small, elite mobile corps—a couple of divisions of marines— would suffice to deter the Soviets. To military men this was laughable.

When he considered the Soviet mind-set, Kennan was on surer footing. A military alliance would strike at the heart of Soviet paranoia: Stalin feared nothing so much as encirclement by capitalist nations, which is precisely what the alliance meant. "We are like a man who has let himself into a walled garden and finds himself alone with a dog with very big teeth," Kennan argued. "The dog, for the moment, shows no signs of aggressiveness. The best thing for us to do is surely to try to establish, as between the two of us, the assumption that teeth have nothing to do with our mutual relationship."

Kennan may have been right. But it is still far from clear that Stalin would have been kept at bay by pats and biscuits. Most policy makers understandably preferred not to take the risk and to instead enter the garden with a large stick. Bohlen too had balked at a military alliance, but he later came to recognize NATO as "simply a necessity." It was certainly a natural response in the jittery atmosphere of 1948. "Whether or not European fears of an armed Soviet attack were exaggerated," Bohlen wrote, "they were genuinely felt."

Kennan, though a good debater, was a poor bureaucratic infighter, and he was soon trumped by Hickerson. While the State Department's chief planner was off in Japan during March, Hickerson was using the Czech crisis to prod Marshall and Lovett. "A general stiffening of morale in Free Europe is needed," he wrote Marshall on March 8. The Czech crisis "scared the bejesus out of everyone," Hickerson later recalled with some satisfaction. Marshall signed on.

Kennan, despite his growing doubts about the military, had not suddenly changed into a closet pacifist in 1948. On at least two occasions, he had considered the need to send U.S. troops to aid European countries in the throes of Communist insurrection; in December, to Greece; and in March, to Italy. If the Communists won the Italian elections in April, he suggested to Marshall on March 15, civil war would break out and the U.S. should be prepared to reoccupy the Foggia oil fields.

He also continued to be an advocate of covert operations. Feeling that since the Soviets play that way, the U.S. should too, that spring he recommended a small directorate for overt and covert political warfare. On June 18, the National Security Council created within the CIA an "office of special projects." Its first efforts were tame: dropping leaflets from balloons in Italy, putting up posters linking the bread supply to American aid. Paul Nitze later noted that the first "Department of Dirty Tricks" was run by the Sunday Night Supper: Kennan proposed it, Frank Wisner ran it, and Bob Joyce, another Bohlen friend, was the State Department liaison. It is doubtful, however, that they contemplated where all this might one day lead.

Though more pragmatic and less histrionic, Bohlen shared Kennan's worries about provoking the Soviets. While Kennan had been touring the Far East or lying sick at Bethesda, Bohlen had tried to represent his views within the Policy Planning Staff, with notable lack of success. Bohlen's concern about Soviet paranoia had been heightened by a meeting in April with the Soviet ambassador to the U.S., Alexander Panyushkin, who had expressed his fear of a preemptive strike by the U.S. At the same time, Panyushkin seemed confused by the rhetoric of Henry Wallace, the liberal presidential candidate who was calling on Truman to sit down with Stalin and formulate a world peace plan. Discouraged by the drift of events, Bohlen and Kennan joined forces in May to slow the momentum of militarization and to reassure the Soviets of American steadiness. With Marshall's approval they sent the Kremlin a message stating: "the door is always wide open for full discussion and the composing of our difficulties." Much to Washington's amazement, the Soviets responded by publicly asking for a high-level parley. The Western European countries panicked, as Stalin no doubt intended, and besieged Marshall: What was going on? Was the U.S. trying to negotiate behind their backs? The Administration had to back down sheepishly and announce that a high-level parley was not what it had in mind after all. The press had a field day with this waffling. Herblock, in the Washington *Post*, drew a cartoon of Truman swinging and wildly missing a pitch.

Kennan was mortified. For two evenings, he walked his neighborhood of Foxhall Village, a government employees' enclave on the fringe of Georgetown, trying to figure out what he had done wrong. On the third day, he went to Marshall with his anguish. Marshall fixed him in his cool gaze and replied, "The decision had my approval; it was discussed in the Cabinet; it was approved by the President. The only trouble with you is that you don't have the perspicacity of a columnist. Now get out of here."

Marshall had been Kennan's patron. He had installed him next door, listened to him, been educated by him. But the great war hero was old and getting sick; a pair of tumors the size of tennis balls were growing on his kidneys. Always one to delegate and ration his energies, Marshall became increasingly remote in the winter and spring of 1948. As early as November 1947, Dean Acheson had remarked to Felix Frankfurter on one of their morning walks, "Marshall is a four-engine bomber going on one engine. I don't know what's the matter with him. He doesn't seem to bring his full force into action."

Increasingly, "Marshall just gave the ball to Lovett," recalls Hickerson. Lovett was considered much warmer, more approachable than Marshall. Hickerson once called Lovett's office and thought he had reached Lovett's assistant, Bob Reams. Hickerson joshed Reams, "Bob, you old bald-headed bastard, how did you get to be Under Secretary of State?" Hickerson did not realize that he actually had Lovett, who was also bald, on the line. "That's a good question," Lovett answered deadpan. "I don't know." The story quickly made the rounds of the department.

Kennan regarded Lovett as a good man, personally charming, but not very deep and much too eager to please Congress. "A simple good man," he had told the Europeans in August. Lovett, however, had little use for Kennan. As he later put it, "I liked him more as Mr. X."

He thought that Kennan was too much of an egghead and too indecisive. He agreed with McCloy that Kennan was "too damn esoteric"
and cited Acheson's description of Kennan as a "horse who would
come up to a fence and not take it."

Lovett did not ponder long over Soviet motives. He expected the
worst from Stalin. McCloy recalls that Lovett never trusted the Soviets
in World War II. When the Russians were shopping for warplanes,
the Soviet test pilot dispatched to Washington chose the least stable
bomber the U.S. had to offer. McCloy wanted to warn the Russian,
but Lovett just shrugged; "Let the SOB break his neck." The Cold
War did not come as a surprise to Lovett. He regarded the Czech
crisis in March as "only one more guidepost on the road to war."

Lovett's concern, like Forrestal's, was with preparedness. A military
alliance with Europe made more sense than having to rebuild the Air
Force from scratch, as he had during World War II. To Lovett, the
real issue was not whether the Western Alliance should exist, but
whether Congress would go along.

Once again, Lovett found himself spending his cocktail hour with
Arthur Vandenberg. They were known as the "500 G meetings," after
Vandenberg's apartment number at the Wardman Park. The result
was the Vandenberg Resolution, committing the U.S. to the defense
of Europe. After several sessions, Lovett brought Vandenberg the State
Department draft, three legal-sized pages long. "Too long," said Vandenberg. "There are so many whereases in there you've forgotten what
it is you're going to resolve." Lovett agreed. "I'll take a crack," said
Vandenberg. "You go talk to my wife, Hazel." He emerged twenty
minutes later with the resolution that ultimately passed.

What Vandenberg had produced was carefully vague. Listening to
the final hours of debate on June 11, Francis Wilcox, Vandenberg's
chief aide, realized that "most Senators don't know what they're voting
on." Only later did they begin asking questions, such as: Does an
attack on Paris mean the same thing as an attack on Chicago? By then
it was too late. Vandenberg was able remind them that they had already
voted to commit the U.S. to the alliance.

Whether or not the senators realized it, they had endorsed a radical
transformation by passing the Vandenberg Resolution, or as Bohlen
preferred to call it, "the Vandenberg-Lovett Resolution." Formalized
a year later, in the spring of 1949, as the North Atlantic Treaty
Organization, the Western Alliance was a "substantial departure from
the former foreign policy of this country," Lovett stated in the summer
of 1948. "The United States had sought peace through weakness. . . .

After many heartbreaks, it had reversed its policy and was seeking to deter aggression by proof of determination. The only question was how its determination should be implemented."

• • •

While Lovett was quietly working to tie the U.S. to Europe in the spring of 1948, he was trying equally hard to avoid getting the U.S. entangled in the creation of Israel.

"The Palestinian issue," as it was known at the State Department, had been long festering. Survivors of the Holocaust were pouring into their biblical homeland and demanding the creation of an independent Zionist state. The British, rapidly jettisoning their empire, had tossed Palestine to the U.N., which was in turmoil over what to do about it. The British were scheduled to pull out of Palestine on May 15; fighting between Jewish settlers and Palestinian Arabs was escalating.

For reasons both political and humanitarian, Truman wanted to help create a new state of Israel. He believed that after so many years in the wilderness, so much suffering and persecution, the Jews deserved a homeland of their own. He was, as well, under tremendous pressure from Jewish groups, whose support he badly needed to stay in the White House. In early 1948, Truman was a decided dark horse to win re-election the next November against Thomas E. Dewey, the popular governor of New York.

His most trusted foreign policy advisers, on the other hand, were all dead set against the birth of Israel. Marshall, Lovett, Forrestal, Kennan, Bohlen, and Acheson formed a united front. However humanitarian a Jewish homeland might seem, they argued, it posed a real risk to U.S. national security. It was absolutely vital that the U.S. maintain its pipeline to Mideast oil. Supporting the Zionist cause would only antagonize the Arabs; worse, it might drive them into the arms of the Soviets. In any case, if the U.S. supported the creation of Israel, it would inevitably be drawn into a vicious war. All the top officials believed—wrongly as it turned out—that the Jews would not be able to go it alone, that they would need U.S. soldiers fighting alongside to survive. To Lovett, who carefully weighed the balance of resources and commitments and saw the scale tipping dangerously, Israel was one ally too many.

It is easy to look at these arch WASPs writing off Israel and sense more than a whiff of prejudice. But it is probably more accurate to describe the attitude of Lovett and the others as intellectually unsympathetic, not viscerally anti-Semitic. Pragmatists all, they were really

quite bloodless about an issue that aroused such passion in others. As
Forrestal, the most hard line, bluntly put it to Clark Clifford, who
was pro-Israel: "You just don't understand. There are four hundred
thousand Jews and forty million Arabs. Forty million Arabs are going
to push four hundred thousand Jews into the sea. And that's all there
is to it. Oil—that is the side we ought to be on."

Truman almost invariably took the advice of his foreign policy
advisers, but Israel was an exception. Though the fear that the Soviets
would make common cause with Arabs gnawed at him, he felt, both
for political reasons and out of genuine sympathy, that he must support
the Jews. He decided that when the British mandate expired on May
15, the U.S. should recognize the new state of Israel.

General Marshall was indignant. He thought that Truman was
buckling under to political pressure, an unpardonable sin to the upright
old general. At a meeting at Blair House on May 12, he listened with
rising anger to Clark Clifford make the case for recognition. He was
furious that Clifford, whom Marshall regarded as a political operator,
was even allowed into the meeting to discuss such a sensitive national
security issue. Clifford recalled uneasily watching the color rise in
Marshall's pink face.

"In the first place, I don't even know why this man is here," Marshall
said to Truman, gesturing at Clifford. The old general was harsher
than anyone in the room had ever heard him be. "If you follow
Clifford's advice," he coldly told Truman, "and in the election I were
to vote, I would vote against you." From a man Truman regarded as
the "greatest living American," this was bitter medicine.

Lovett spoke out strongly against recognizing Israel. It would be
"buying a pig in a poke," he stated in his colloquial way. But as soon
as the meeting broke up, he called Clifford and asked him to come
by his home for a drink at seven that evening.

"I've been uneasy since that meeting," Lovett told Clifford when
the two men had settled down with a cocktail. Clifford couldn't resist
twitting him: "You didn't show your uneasiness *at* the meeting." Lovett
pressed on: "I hate there to be such a sharp difference of opinion.
We've got to straighten this out. It's going to lead to a breach between
the President and General Marshall, and I'm afraid that Marshall
could resign."

Lovett had opposed the recognition of Israel on pragmatic grounds.
But having made his case, he could see that he had lost. Inevitably,
the U.S. would support an independent state of Israel, and all that
remained to be determined was the timing. Since he was not emo-

tionally engaged, he was able to accept the President's decision and, without hesitation, turn to implementing it. Rather than sulk or wage a campaign of leaks to pin the blame, he immediately turned to patching up differences. The next day, Lovett called Clifford. "I've had a good talk with General Marshall," he said; the President's policies would be supported, whatever Truman decided to do. Asked years later what he said to convince General Marshall, Lovett replied simply, "I told him that it was the President's choice." This was a reason that Marshall could accept without complaint. Like Lovett, he was duty-bound to his chief; having argued and lost, they must now carry out the President's orders.

Lovett even had lunch with Clifford the next day at the F St. Club to draft the press release announcing U.S. recognition of Israel. Lovett made a last pitch for more time, to at least warn the U.S. delegation at the U.N., but Clifford did not want to risk a leak. Lovett accepted his judgment; the decision remained secret until it was formally announced. The next day Arab armies invaded Israel, but a nation had been born. If the U.S. had not exactly been the father, Lovett sardonically noted a few days later, it had at least been the midwife.

• • •

Bohlen wondered: What did the Soviets want? He was the counselor to the Secretary of State, the Soviet expert, but he had no clear idea what Stalin was really up to in Europe, particularly Germany. He shared Kennan's concern that Washington was overreacting to Soviet bellicosity, that the Cold War was becoming too "militarized." But he had not gone so far as Kennan. Indeed, he was coming increasingly to accept the need for military deterrence. In conversation with Joe Alsop, he would say, "Stalin believes you have to probe with a bayonet. If you meet mush, you push farther. If you meet steel, you pull back."

And he was more of a centrist than Kennan, more a conformist. Bohlen was not nearly the grand strategist, the facile conceptualizer who could divine coherent themes from jumbled facts. But in his close attention to nuance and his commonsense feel for the uncertainty and fluidity of the situation, he was probably more wise about the Soviets. Western belligerence did spook Stalin and make him "bare his fangs," as Kennan put it. Yet it is unlikely that reason or diplomacy could have persuaded Stalin to withdraw his troops from Germany or to cease fomenting unrest in Italy or France by stirring up local Communist parties. The Soviets were too suspicious to deal with the West. Stalin acted unilaterally, and it was probably not clear in his own mind how far he would probe in his quest to find "security" for his empire.

Germany was the great unanswered question, the potential flash point. Throughout the spring and into the summer of 1948, Bohlen puzzled: Did the Soviets want a unified Communist Germany? A ruined, impotent Germany? To punish Germany and milk it with reparations? Soviet behavior was contradictory. The Russians were still looting factories and sending equipment on flatcars to the U.S.S.R. (where it sat and rusted in the snow)—yet permitting former Nazis to hold high positions in the Eastern zone.

Whatever the Soviets wanted, the U.S. did not want a united Germany under Soviet domination. Such a development would constitute "the greatest threat to the security of all Western nations, including the U.S.," General Marshall testified in February. A weak Germany, on the other hand, would frustrate European recovery. Lovett, along with his other Wall Street colleagues, Forrestal, McCloy, and Harriman, was determined to rebuild Germany as a bastion of the West, even if that meant partition.

This could not be done without currency reform. The Deutsche mark was worthless; real currency was measured in Lucky Strikes sold on the black market. Back in August of 1947, Harriman had flatly stated to Truman, "Monetary reform is overdue. It is hard to understand how business is now being transacted with a worthless currency." Harriman added, however, that he had grave doubts that currency reform could include the Soviets "as the Soviet methods are so completely different from ours."

Currency reform may sound like a technical exercise, but it meant the end of any semblance of U.S.-Soviet cooperation in Germany. It signaled the great divide between East and West.

Lovett, as usual, was the expediter. On March 10, at the height of the Czech crisis, he received a memo from Bohlen's friend and colleague Frank Wisner summing up the situation: currency reform would "represent a very definite move toward East-West partition of Germany." But it "would also move toward much needed economic stability in Germany." Wisner recommended it. Lovett agreed. He scribbled on the memo: "Better act fast."

The Soviets were not as mystified about Western intentions as the West was about theirs. Their British mole, Donald Maclean, had been providing regular progress reports on the creation of the Western Alliance. The Soviets had only to read the newspapers to know about war hysteria over Czechoslovakia. Now, they learned, printing presses in the Western zones were churning out new currency to rebuild a capitalist Germany.

By the spring of 1948, the Four-Power Control Council nominally governing Germany had become a farce. The Soviet representative, who normally took copious notes, now merely doodled. On March 20, he walked out. To the Soviets, it must have seemed like their worst fears realized. A powerful capitalist Germany rebuilt on their border. Capitalist countries allying to encircle them. Local Communist parties in France and Italy losing power, renounced by the public. In Yugoslavia, Marshal Tito asserting his independence. Stalin may have been the cornered animal of Kennan's imagery, but he was as well a predatory creature. In the summer of 1948, he lunged for Berlin.

• • •

The Berlin blockade began slowly. In mid-June, the Soviets started turning away freight trains carrying coal from the Western zones to West Berlin, 110 miles inside Soviet-controlled territory. The explanation given was "defective cars." Next came the passenger trains: Red Army guards along the border began sending back every other one because of "crowded stations." Finally, the autobahn was closed for "urgent repairs."

On June 23, the West announced new Deutsche marks for its sector of Berlin and West Germany. Lucky Strikes had reached an all-time high of $2,300 a carton at the official exchange rate; a German reporter asked a U.S. official if the West planned to stabilize the economy with a loan of 50 million cartons of Luckies.

Within twenty-four hours, the Soviets had cut all overland routes between West Germany and West Berlin and shut off electricity in the city. The two million citizens of West Berlin had enough food to last thirty-six days. The squeeze was on.

• • •

On the fifth floor of New State, just across the marbled elevator well from Bob Lovett's office, was the Overseas Communications Room. At the door behind the locked gate stood an armed guard; the sign on the gate read: "Authorized Personnel Only." Inside was a small, plain fifteen-by-twenty-five-foot room with a walnut conference table. Built into the wall were two backlighted screens. Onto those screens flashed Telexes, twenty-four hours a day, secret cables bearing news of upheaval and crisis from American embassies around the world.

Here Lovett, Bohlen, and Kennan spent many long and fretful nights in the summer of 1948. Kennan later recalled the terrible feeling of uncertainty, sitting in the darkened room, watching the ominous cables flash up on the screen, wondering which one would bring the news that shots had been fired, that tanks were rolling. "The situation," he remembered, "was dark, and full of danger."

At the other end of one Telex line was General Lucius Clay. At West Point, he had been at the top of his class in English and history but near the bottom in conduct and discipline. He was an able soldier with a huge ego, inflated further by his position as Military Governor of Germany. "Military Governor was a pretty heady job," Jack McCloy, who succeeded him, later remarked. "It was the nearest thing to a Roman proconsul the modern world afforded. You could turn to your secretary and say, 'Take a law.'" Harriman, who as administrator of the Marshall Plan often tangled with Clay, considered the general to be a "natural-born Tsar," so excitable that he "typically ran a temperature of 106 degrees."

Clay wanted to stand up to the Soviets, to ram through an armored column, like the cavalry rescuing a wagon train. He believed the Soviets could be bluffed, that they would back down.

Lovett thought Clay's idea was "silly." By cutting a couple of bridges, one before, one behind, the Red Army could strand even the most heavily fortified convoy. "The Soviets would just sit up on the hillside and laugh," Lovett told his colleagues in the darkened room. Or worse they would start shooting. Either way, the convoy would never make it.

Clay persisted. "I am still convinced that a determined movement of convoys with troop protection would reach Berlin," he cabled on June 25, "and that such a showing might prevent rather than build up Soviet pressures which could lead to war."

Lovett had wrestled with Clay before. The general had threatened to resign the past summer over Marshall Plan squabbles at least eleven times. The State Department did have an ambassador in Berlin, Robert Murphy, a poor Irish Catholic boy from the Midwest who had become "Grottier than the Grotties," according to Felix Frankfurter. But Murphy was on Clay's side, not Lovett's.

Lovett worried that the general might try something precipitous. At 10:50 A.M. on June 26, Forrestal called Lovett and asked, "Any news?"

Lovett answered that the cable traffic indicated that Berlin was now "hotter than a firecracker." There was "no orderly operation," he added, "and nobody exercises any influence over Clay." Was it time to relieve Clay? asked Forrestal. No, answered Lovett, at least not yet. At the moment such a move would be interpreted as a "sign of weakness."

Although Lovett knew that an armed convoy was a bad idea, he was stumped in his efforts to come up with a better one. Other ideas being bruited about—like closing the Panama Canal to Soviet ships or blockading Vladivostok—seemed impractical or ineffective. The U.S. did not want war, yet if it abandoned Berlin, some two million more people would be consigned to Soviet domination and all of Europe would lose faith in the U.S. as an ally. The Western Alliance would be stillborn.

At a meeting on the twenty-fifth, Lovett, Forrestal, and Truman agreed that "determined steps must be taken by the U.S. to stay in Berlin." But what? The following day, American military police arrested General V.D. Sokolovsky, the Soviet commander, for speeding through the Western zone of Berlin on his way home to a suburb in the Eastern zone. A U.S. soldier put a tommy gun to the Soviet marshal's stomach. Soviet guards reached for their guns. The tense moment passed, Sokolovsky was released, but nerves stretched tighter.

• • •

Jack McCloy hated playing tennis with Jim Forrestal. Forrestal was constantly calling him up on the assumption that he could just drop everything any time. McCloy was a far better player, and that, McCloy knew, was precisely why Forrestal wanted to play. Forrestal was as humorless and driven on the tennis court as he was on the golf course.

Forrestal was particularly intense as he lost to McCloy at the Chevy Chase Club on Saturday afternoon, June 26. To Forrestal, the Berlin crisis was exactly what he had feared and warned against. The U.S. was not ready. The Soviets could drive the American Army to the Pyrenees. The U.S. had the bomb, but not enough bombs, in Forrestal's view, to guarantee a strike destructive enough to knock the Soviets out of war.* The U.S. had allowed its conventional forces to shrink, and now it had no leverage to face down the Soviets. Forrestal

---

*The war scares of 1948 caused a rapid buildup in the U.S. nuclear stockpile. In 1947, the U.S. had only 13 bombs; in 1948, 50 bombs; in 1949, as military planners began to realize that the bomb was a cost-effective form of deterrence, 250.

often confided in McCloy, and that weekend he shared his doubts. If Clay sent his column through and the Soviets fought back, the U.S. would be helpless. McCloy listened. Though tank columns had nothing to do with the World Bank, he was a trusted adviser to Forrestal and Lovett both; he would soon have a role to play in dealing with General Clay.

On Monday, Forrestal and Lovett met again with Truman at Blair House. Truman had become impatient with Forrestal. He thought that the Defense Secretary was growing irresolute and indecisive, cardinal sins to the President. "Jim wants to hedge—he always does," Truman wrote in his diary a few weeks later. "He's constantly sending me alibi memos, which I return with directions and the facts." Truman liked to make decisions, and Berlin was no exception. Bravely Truman cut into the conversation swirling around the Cabinet table: "We stay in Berlin, period."

As the discussion continued, no means of staying in Berlin occurred to anyone. Even Truman began to hedge. The next day he announced that the U.S. would stay in Berlin "as long as possible." As a show of force, sixty B-29 "atomic bombers" were dispatched to England, and the news was carefully leaked. It was all a bluff. The planes were not configured to carry atomic bombs, and they lacked the fueling capacity to reach Soviet cities and return.

But a real solution was slowly coming clear to Lovett and others. Lovett was an airman. He knew from his days as Assistant Secretary of War that the Air Force had flown seventy-two thousand tons of equipment over the Himalayas from Burma to China. Now he began to talk to two of his old generals, Curtis LeMay and Albert Wedemeyer, both veterans of the Burma Hump. Lovett became convinced that an airlift could at least keep Berlin fed. (How to keep it heated was another problem, but winter was months away. On June 30, his phone log shows, he told Forrestal, "Can feed by air; cannot furnish coal.") Lovett went to his old partner in manipulating the Pentagon, Jack McCloy, to explore privately the practicality of an airlift. McCloy made a back-channel call to General Henry "Hap" Arnold, an old friend who had been chief of the Army Air Forces during World War II, to inquire whether the runways in Berlin could be extended to handle a steady stream of heavy cargo planes. The answer was yes.

Lovett made his inquiries discreetly, without engaging—or warning—the normal military chain of command. He knew from his War Department days that the military tended to worry more about future contingencies than present crises and would almost certainly balk at diverting its entire airlift capacity to a single route. Lovett's suspicions were later confirmed: the Air Force Chief of Staff, General Hoyt Vandenberg, strongly objected to diverting more planes to the Berlin run in mid-July. But by then it was too late. The President had been persuaded to support the airlift.

Lovett was scornful of General Clay as a "ground soldier." This was unfair; Clay himself had asked LeMay on June 24 to put all his C-47s on the Berlin run. But Clay also persisted in pressing for his armored column. Again Lovett called on McCloy. He knew that McCloy was Clay's old friend and had in fact gotten him the job of Military Governor in 1945 after turning it down himself. McCloy quietly called Clay in Germany and told him the plain truth: the convoy was a nonstarter in Washington, and no amount of arguing was going to help him.

Clay did not entirely give up. But when he flew home to see Truman in mid-July, he grudgingly acknowledged that the time for an armed column was probably past. Indeed, Truman by then was feeling the need for moderation. He decided to make a diplomatic overture to Stalin, to see if the two superpowers could settle the crisis without an armed confrontation.

Bohlen was sent to Berlin to coordinate the peace offensive. He flew back with Clay, who had such severe lumbago that he could not turn his head. The proud general was embarrassed when he had to be carried from the plane in a chair. He did not think it suitable for a commander to be incapacitated in battle.

Before he left Washington, Bohlen had advised Marshall that he doubted Stalin would even respond to the peace feeler, though there was no harm in trying. As Bohlen had predicted, the Soviet leader was said to be "on vacation." The Soviets finally agreed to talk, but the negotiations were mired in suspicion and deceit. "This is the seventy-fourth day since the blockade," Forrestal wrote in his diary on Labor Day. "The sheer duplicity of the Soviets is beyond the experience of the experts in the State Department. . . . It is Lovett's hunch . . . that the Soviets do not want an agreement. They would just as soon have a break now unless they can get an agreement on their own terms." Lovett "stressed," Forrestal added, "the difficulty of dealing with someone 'whose head is full of bubbles.'" Stalin's terms were simple: the West must not create a separate West German state. This, Bohlen recorded, "was a price we would not pay."

Bohlen's diplomatic energies were devoted less to the Soviets than to persuading the Allies that the U.S. would not start World War III.

"I know all you Americans want a war," British Foreign Minister Ernie Bevin chided the American diplomat, "but I'm not going to let you 'ave it."

The U.S. was in fact readying its forces for the outbreak of war. Forrestal anxiously asked Truman whether he would be willing to drop the atomic bomb on the Soviets if their tanks rolled into Western Europe. "The President said he prayed that he would never have to make such a decision, but that if it became necessary, no one need have misgiving but what he would do so," Forrestal recorded in his diary on September 13. Truman wrote in his: "A terrific day. Berlin is a mess. Forrestal, etc., brief me on bases, bombs, Moscow, Leningrad, etc. I have a terrible feeling afterwards that we are very close to war."

The cables kept coming in, relentlessly flashing their warnings onto the screen in the darkened room. Lovett would try to relieve the pressure by making cracks about General Clay's unyielding negotiating stance. ("I wish the general would realize that our policy is open sewers, openly arrived at.") But the strain was grinding on the participants, particularly Forrestal, who was chiefly responsible for war preparations and lay awake at night unhappily contemplating the military's grim choice between fighting with weak conventional forces or dropping the atomic bomb.

Since the war scare over Czechoslovakia in March, the U.S. had entered a strange new era, an age of perpetual crisis. Because of the bomb, the superpowers remained always on edge, always probing and testing, but never attacking. They would creep up to the precipice and then, after peering into the abyss, shudder and pull back. For the men in the darkened room, the moments at the brink could seem endless and exhausting. Washington's policy makers were caught; as *Fortune* magazine put it that autumn, "the only way to avoid having American policy dominated by crisis is to live by crisis—prepared for war." With the Berlin blockade of 1948 East and West entered "an armed truce, a precarious balance," wrote Daniel Yergin, "a crisis always just short of catastrophe."

The Berlin blockade was saved from catastrophe by the airlift. Standing in the street in Berlin, Bohlen recalled his amazement at the sight of C-54s swooping into Berlin one after the other, landing at Tempelhof Airport every four or five minutes. The airlift just kept growing. Keeping Berlin alive required 4,000 tons a day, or a C-54 every three minutes and forty-three seconds. In June and July, the airlift averaged

1,147 tons; but by autumn, it had reached the 4,000-ton minimum. The planes were even able to transport coal. To accommodate more transports, another airfield was built by twenty thousand Berliners with their bare hands. Stalin had blundered. The Soviets began to look like barbarians, bent on starvation, while the Americans seemed like saviors. The crisis eased, at least for a while.

•   •   •

Truman seemed a sure loser in the 1948 presidential election. "He's a gone goose," said Clare Boothe Luce, and the polls agreed.

Lovett did not question the conventional wisdom, nor did he worry much about it. He considered himself apolitical, a nonpartisan, a "mugwump," as he liked to call himself. Although Lovett admired Truman, he was perfectly content to see Tom Dewey, a moderate East Coast Republican, as his successor. Lovett was not personally fond of John Foster Dulles, the stiff-necked lawyer who would no doubt be Dewey's choice for Secretary of State, but Dulles was certainly familiar, a Wall Street Princetonian and member of the Council on Foreign Relations.

Lovett's chief concern was maintaining a bipartisan foreign policy, not getting Harry Truman re-elected. After Truman lambasted the Republican-controlled "do-nothing Eightieth Congress" at the Democratic Convention in July, Lovett secretly summoned Foster Dulles to his office and confided his chagrin over the Democratic platform on foreign policy. He had tried to get a platform that would not claim all the credit for the results of bipartisan cooperation, he told Dulles, but the White House had insisted. Such partisanship was bad for the country, Dulles and Lovett agreed.

So that Dulles would not take over unprepared, Lovett allowed him to see important State Department cables that summer and fall. They were delivered through GOP Congressman Christian Herter (an old St. Paul's friend of Bohlen's) as well as through Foster Dulles's brother, Allen, and a young Dewey aide named McGeorge Bundy in New York. There was nothing particularly unusual about sharing State Department secrets with Dulles; he had been a Republican observer at several Foreign Ministers' meetings and enjoyed a quasi-official status at the State Department. Nonetheless, this back channel during an election campaign would have infuriated Truman had he known about it; it proved that Lovett's allegiance clearly lay to the bipartisan foreign policy Establishment over his President. "You have to understand the mood of the time," recalled Bundy. "It seemed sure that Dewey would win. Bipartisanship was seen as a jewel, achieved against odds, that must be preserved."

Lovett had some reason to believe that Dewey wanted him to serve as his Secretary of Defense; Dean Acheson had told him so in a phone call on June 29. But there is no record of any overture from the Dewey camp and no mention of Acheson's source of information. At any rate, it is far more likely that Lovett was motivated to cooperate with Dewey by a desire to maintain continuity in foreign policy rather than out of his own personal ambition. After a second stint in Washington, Lovett was eager to return to Wall Street, and was once again plagued by his usual anxieties about precarious health. On election day, as Truman was staging his upset, Lovett was on the phone with Clark Clifford stressing the need for an orderly transition so the Soviets would not take advantage of a "spectacle of terrible uncertainty" over the next three months.

Lovett's boss, General Marshall, went even further. A week before the election he suggested that because of the "emergency character" of the world situation, Dulles should replace him immediately after the election, while Truman still had three months to serve. Dulles had to remind Marshall that under the Constitution, the President, even a lame duck, has responsibility for foreign affairs.

• • •

Unlike Lovett, Dean Acheson was a true Democrat. He stayed up all election night at his friend Gerhard Gesell's listening to the astonishing returns. By dawn he was overjoyed and quite drunk. He and Gesell, his law partner, had to catch a train to New York at 8 A.M. At the station, Acheson announced solemnly, "I'm going to do something I've never done. I'm going to have a highball for breakfast." Together, they toasted the President.

Acheson was living a good life. On the weekends out at Harewood, he raised gladioli, one summer thirteen hundred of them. He tended to "Adèle's dahliaretum," his dahlia garden given him by Bob Lovett's wife. He cleared brush, followed by Alice picking up firewood (Acheson referred to her as his "Fire Goddess" to a visiting *Time* reporter). He built furniture in his woodworking shop. He read Trollope and Twain and drank the powerful cocktails made by his faithful butler, Johnson. But he missed the power of public life. "To leave positions of great responsibility and authority," he said, "is to die a little."

General Marshall was retiring, his kidneys shot, his energy exhausted. At the White House, the short list for Secretary of State was drawn up: Chief Justice Fred Vinson, Ambassador Lewis Douglas, Justice William Douglas, Averell Harriman, and Dean Acheson. At the end of November the list was narrowed down to Harriman and Acheson. Truman eliminated Harriman, as Clifford explained over the phone to Acheson on December 8, "on the ground that, though Averell had many qualifications, his gifts were not those required in the administration of the department and on dealing with the problems which the next few years would present."

Clifford's explanation to Acheson of why Truman did not choose Harriman was deliberately terse and ambiguous. "Truman did not want to appear to downgrade Averell by giving a detailed reason," Clifford later explained. In fact, Truman was "very fond of both Averell and Dean," said Clifford. "It was natural that the choice would narrow to those two. It was, I believe, a close call." Truman did not explain just why he chose Acheson, even to Clifford, his closest adviser.

Harriman lacked Acheson's obvious, almost flashy brilliance. He had little of Acheson's wit; indeed he mumbled so gruffly and inarticulately that others commonly underestimated his intelligence. "Acheson has more brains at the end of his little finger than Harriman does in his whole body," Stuart Symington huffed at a dinner party at Joe Alsop's one night. Harriman would certainly have made a less artful spokesman for the Department of State than Acheson proved to be.

Plodding and stolid though Harriman appeared, he was nonetheless an effective diplomat, vastly experienced and utterly indomitable. There is every reason to believe his judgment would have been as sound in moments of crisis as that displayed by his old rowing pupil. Though he did not think in sweeping geopolitical terms, preferring to deal with men face-to-face and problems as they arose, he was equally committed to an activist role for the U.S. in world affairs. He would as well have taken a tough stance toward the Soviets. It is likely, however, that Harriman would have put more store in negotiating with the Kremlin than Acheson did; it is possible, though highly speculative, that better long-term relations would have been the result. Certainly, Harriman was every bit as forceful a man as Acheson. Years later, they are both remembered by many long-term State Department observers as the most formidable, naturally powerful men ever to serve in Foggy Bottom. "Topflight" is Clifford's assessment of the Secretary Harriman might have been. "He was in every way trained and suited for the job."

But it was not to be. The one job Harriman sought above all others he barely missed attaining in 1948. He would never again come so close.

Truman called Acheson to Blair House at the end of November. "You better sit down when you hear what I am going to say," said the President. "I want you to be my Secretary of State. Will you?" Acheson said that he would ask his wife, which meant yes. In later years, Acheson would like to recount how Truman explained his decision: "You know, twenty guys would make a better Secretary of State than you, but I don't know them. I know you."

• • •

They were one of history's odd couples. Truman the dirt farmer and failed haberdasher, product of the Pendergast machine in Kansas City, wearer of loud sport shirts in Key West. Acheson the Episcopal bishop's son, the Grotonian, the dandy in his double-breasted English suits. Yet they shared a sense of history, irreverence, moral courage, and impatience with waffling. They admired each other, and enjoyed each other's company.

Acheson was immensely loyal. "I have a constituency of one," he liked to say. "Truman was the boss and Dean played it that way," Chip Bohlen told Truman's biographer Bob Donovan. Though he was sensitive to their vastly different roots, Truman felt honored by Acheson's devotion and friendship. When the two parted four years later, Truman wrote his patrician adviser, "I would be proud to appear anywhere with you from Yale to 1908 Main in Kansas City (that's the address of the Pendergast Club)."

Acheson's outward hauteur was, like most such demeanors, a mask. He was capable of gentleness and kindness. When Gesell's son was stricken with polio, Acheson invited the eight-year-old to lunch with him at the State Department. He sent around a big black limousine for the crippled boy, dined with him alone in the Secretary's dining room, and let him stay in the afternoon for a briefing, having duly sworn him to secrecy. Acheson's secretary, Barbara Evans, served him happily and faithfully for thirty-five years. (She was almost as formidable as he was, says Acheson's son-in-law Bill Bundy; "She *loved* to say no.") Despite his obvious joy in flirtation, his devotion to his wife, Alice, was deep, lasting, and reciprocated; her stability and strength sustained him through the ordeals of office.

Acheson was not a social snob. His best friend, Felix Frankfurter, was an immigrant Jew. Though he could get on with the highborn (Anthony Eden, the high-toned Tory from Eton, exclaimed, "I would not hesitate to go tiger hunting with him"), he almost seemed to prefer self-made, original men. He tremendously enjoyed Ernie Bevin, the bastard son of a serving girl who became the Labour Party's Foreign Secretary. Bevin, "short and too fat," as Acheson described him, was well read, blunt, and honest, not unlike Harry Truman. Bevin called Acheson "me lad." Together, Acheson and Bevin once linked arms to enter a Foreign Ministers' meeting singing simultaneously the words to "The Red Flag" and "Maryland, My Maryland," which shared the same tune.

Acheson's irreverence was provoked by dreary Foreign Ministers' meetings. As he sat there appearing to take notes he was often writing ribald limericks about the speakers ("The Iraqi is really not whacky/ Toady, perhaps, even tacky/When they gave *him* the word/He gave *us* the bird/And joined with the Arabs, by cracky!").

Acheson loathed the diplomatic circuit. It was an immense effort for him to pretend to be civil to dull foreigners in striped pants. His wife, Alice, says that he did not like to go out to dinner, unless it was with close friends, and that he disliked traveling and small talk. His stomach was sensitive and would react badly at banquets. His real pleasure, according to Mrs. Acheson, was to "curl up with a book." For all his wit and charm, he was a very private man. Once when he and Gesell were walking from their law firm to lunch at the Metropolitan Club, Gesell grabbed Acheson's elbow to make a point. Acheson flinched visibly from the touch of his old friend.

He could not suffer fools; he freely admitted it. But Acheson could also be intolerant of the insecure, the dull-witted, the too-eager-to-please. His shows of impatience were a terrible failing, cruel at times, and they were nearly his undoing. "He had a low boring point," says his secretary, Miss Evans. Forrestal's aide, Marx Leva, said: "You really could never talk with Dean Acheson without getting a put-down feeling." The people he really looked down on were congressmen. He would describe their less enlightened questions as "silly" or "nonsense," sounding like a schoolteacher scolding a fourth grader. The Guardsman's mustache and Groton accent did not soften the impression.

Lovett could be just as contemptuous of congressmen, but he never showed it. Congressman Walter Judd of Minnesota, a Republican on the House Foreign Affairs Committee at the time, contrasts the two: "Acheson was always dignified, but there was a certain condescension. It was like he was sorry for us hayseeds, that he was casting pearls before swine. Lovett was different. He was not schoolteacherish. He was so much more convincing." Lovett himself was frank about Acheson's failing. "Dean had a contempt for ignorance," he recalled. "He gave the impression of being arrogant before Congress."

• • •

The Republicans in Congress were bitter in the winter of 1949. They had expected to control both Congress and the White House after the 1948 elections; now they controlled neither. The Democrats had taken the high ground by opposing Soviet aggression in Europe; both the Marshall Plan and the Berlin airlift were working. With isolationism roundly discredited, the conservative Republicans needed a new issue, a way to deflect attention from the Administration's current success in Europe.

In retrospect, the issue the GOP right-wingers chose seems fantastic, ludicrous on its face. They charged that the Administration was "soft" on Communism; that it had sold out Eastern Europe at Yalta, was in the process of "losing China," and was riddled by Communists at home. At its most crazed, the Republican right accused Dean Acheson of actually *being* a Communist, or at least a pinko fellow traveler.

Incredibly this political strategy worked, in a destructive, deadening sort of way. It is hard to explain why, except to understand how inexplicably frightening the world seemed to a country that had just won World War II and yet now seemed faced with a threat to its own survival. Senator Joe McCarthy of Wisconsin, at the height of his dark power three years later, put the question precisely: "How can we account for our present situation unless we believe that men high in this government are concerting to deliver us to disaster? This must be the product of a great conspiracy on a scale so immense as to dwarf any previous venture in the history of man." It *must* be. Therefore it was.

The force of this madness was just beginning to be felt in January of 1949. Alger Hiss, a former high-ranking official at the State Department, had been indicted the month before, accused of lying to a congressional committee by denying that he had passed classified documents to a Communist agent. Hiss was the perfect target for the Republican right: a cultivated, patrician New Dealer who had clerked for Oliver Wendell Holmes after Harvard Law School. His principal prosecutor was Congressman Richard Nixon.

At a House Un-American Activities hearing in August, Acheson's name had been linked with Hiss's. Now, at his confirmation hearings in January, Acheson explained that Hiss had not been his personal assistant, as alleged, but that Alger's brother, Donald, was his law partner and Alger was his friend. Acheson added coolly that his friendship was "neither easily given nor withdrawn."

When this response was reported in the papers, Mac Bundy wrote "Uncle Dean" that "the people will know that the Secretary of State is a man." Arthur Vandenberg was less sanguine. In a closed "executive session" of the Senate Foreign Relations Committee, he bluntly told Acheson that he had a public relations problem. He needed a statement to show that he was a good anti-Communist. So Vandenberg wrote one for him: "Communism as a doctrine is economically fatal to a free society and to human rights and fundamental freedoms. Communism as an aggressive factor in world conquest is fatal to independent governments and to free peoples." Ten years earlier, Acheson had persuaded a reluctant Felix Frankfurter to read a similar statement at his confirmation hearing for the Supreme Court. Now he was being forced to swallow some of the same distasteful medicine. With obvious discomfort he read the prescribed drivel and told Vandenberg, "I shall be perfectly happy to have you say that is what I said." Grimacing, he turned to Francis Wilcox, Vandenberg's aide, and asked for a cigarette. Acheson rarely smoked.

The Hiss case would come back to torment Acheson. As it turned out, Alger Hiss was found guilty, and, history suggests, rightfully so. There had in fact been Communists in government in the 1930s— not enough to truly jeopardize national security, but just enough to lend credence to a Red scare. By staking his integrity on his friendship with Hiss, Acheson would in later years find himself a target of anti-Communist hysteria.

"I am frank to say that Mr. Acheson would *not* have been my choice for Secretary of State," Vandenberg wrote a friend in January of 1949. His own choice was Bob Lovett, he told one newsman off the record. He added: "If Acheson's confirmation had been left to a secret ballot, he would have been badly beaten." Acheson, Vandenberg privately predicted, would be "another Anthony Eden—flashy, brilliant, but soft at the core."

In May, Vandenberg described in his diary a visit that Acheson paid to his apartment after work for a drink. "It was *slightly* reminiscent of the old Lovett days. He is entirely surrounded by baffling problems. . . . I didn't let him unload on me in any such fashion as Marshall and Lovett did." Vandenberg was sick, in fact, though he did not know it yet, was dying from a lesion on a lung. The bipartisan foreign policy consensus he had forged with Lovett was dying too. Acheson made fun of Vandenberg, but in fact the vain old politician had turned out to be shrewd and steadfast. As Secretary of State, Acheson would sorely miss such a loyal and steadying hand in Congress.

•   •   •

On January 11, a newspaper reporter asked Forrestal if he planned to stay on as Secretary of Defense. "Yes," he answered. "I am a victim of the Washington scene."

In December, Forrestal had talked of retiring. He was weary, and he did not look forward to working with Acheson, whom he described to his aides as a "stuffed shirt." The notion of buying a New York newspaper and devoting himself full time to a career as polemicist intrigued him, at least for a while. He had talked to his family about it and begun to make the necessary financial preparations, but, at about Christmastime, the talk abruptly stopped. Forrestal was an addict. He had been in Washington, in a state of perpetual crisis, for eight and a half years. He could not leave.

For those who looked for them, there were signs that Forrestal was troubled. He did not try quite so hard to beat his son Michael at squash anymore. He thought his phone was tapped. In long conversations with J. Edgar Hoover he brooded about subversion; in January, he mailed the FBI director a copy of *Darkness at Noon*, Arthur Koestler's bleak tale of the Soviet police state. He had always called his friends at odd hours, but the late-night calls became more common. Jack McCloy recalls that Forrestal began calling him at 2 A.M. and asking him to come over. When McCloy would say that he couldn't, it was much too late, Forrestal would ask, "Well, can I come 'round to see you?" McCloy, with his accommodating attitude to powerful personalities, found it difficult to fend him off. Lovett, characteristically methodical, had a standing rule: only if the light was shining in his study could Forrestal come on up.

In the office, Forrestal's aides had an increasingly difficult time getting the Defense Secretary to make decisions. Palestine particularly troubled him. Forrestal had led the opposition to creating the state of Israel. Although not overtly anti-Semitic (his closest aide, Marx Leva, was Jewish), Forrestal believed that the U.S. had to preserve its pipeline to Arab oil for the sake of national security. His stand had been bitterly controversial, and now the Defense Secretary began to repeatedly ask friends and advisers, "Did I take the wrong position on Israel?"

Forrestal had always been painfully honest with himself. It was a quality that endeared him to his friends and colleagues. His sense of duty was unmatched in Washington. But now he seemed staggered, ridden with self-doubt. He could not unburden himself at home; his wife was drinking heavily. At parties, Forrestal would leave without her and ask a naval aide to take her home. After work, Forrestal would sometimes ask his young assistant, John Ohly, to come home with him for a drink. Ohly remembers the house, large, dark, and empty. Mrs. Forrestal was always "upstairs" or "out."

The muckrakers and gossip columnists bore in. Drew Pearson and Walter Winchell had long attacked Forrestal for his connections with Wall Street, insinuating corruption and conflict of interest. They liked to note, for instance, that Dillon, Read did business with Arab countries. The lowest blow came in early January, when both columnists reported that back in 1937, Mrs. Forrestal had been held up outside their Manhattan town house at 27 Beekman Place and suggested that Forrestal had run away, leaving his wife defenseless. The stories were false and cruel (he had been asleep upstairs at the time), and Forrestal brooded over them for days.

Truman had heard rumors and reports that his Defense Secretary was disloyal. Two or three times that fall Forrestal had met with Dewey to discuss defense problems. Drew Pearson had begun to whisper that Forrestal was fishing for a job in the Republican Administration. In truth, Forrestal had done little different than Marshall and Lovett. Like them, he had wanted to arrange an orderly transition, but unlike them, he had been indiscreet about it. Louis Johnson, Truman's chief fund raiser, complained that Forrestal had not done enough to raise money for Truman's campaign from his Wall Street connections. Johnson also made it known that he wanted Forrestal's job.

Shortly after noon one Tuesday in early March, Forrestal was summoned to the White House. With no warning and few niceties, Truman demanded his immediate letter of resignation. Forrestal returned to his office and just sat there, stunned.

For the next month, Forrestal slept little. He was bitterly disappointed with his successor, Johnson, who represented everything that Forrestal opposed. He was a political hack who wanted to use the Defense Department to further his own presidential ambitions. He hoped to curry popular support by cutting the defense budget. He was a tool of the China lobby. He was a braggart.

When Truman presented him with the Distinguished Service Medal shortly after he left his post, Forrestal was visibly flustered, speechless, and exhausted. A day later, his aide, Marx Leva, found him sitting in a Pentagon office that had been set aside for him while he wrapped up his affairs. Forrestal was wearing his hat, and staring straight ahead at the blank wall. "Is there something the matter?" Leva asked. "You are a loyal fellow," Forrestal replied.

Leva managed to get him home and called Forrestal's old friend Ferdie Eberstadt. When Eberstadt rushed to the house, Forrestal poured out his twisted emotions, telling him that he was a complete failure, that Communists, Jews, and White House aides were out to "get" him, and that some of "them" were in his home right that moment. To prove his point, he began looking in closets. Leva and Eberstadt were able to get him on a military plane that night for Hobe Sound, where Bob Lovett could take care of him.

Lovett was shocked by his friend's appearance. His lips were so tightly drawn they were invisible. "Jim," said Lovett, "I hope you brought your golf clubs because the weather down here is perfect for golf." Forrestal stared at him. "Bob," he said, "they're after me."

On April 2, Forrestal was flown to Bethesda Naval Hospital and was admitted for "involutional melancholia." At 1:45 A.M. on May 22, he was seen at his night table copying Sophocles' "Chorus from Ajax" onto several sheets of paper:

> ... Worn by the waste of time—
> Comfortless, nameless, hopeless save
> In the dark prospect of the yawning grave. ...

Breaking off his copy in the middle of a word, he walked across a corridor to a small diet kitchen with an unbarred window, tied one end of his dressing-gown sash to a radiator, and the other end around his neck. Then he leaped into the night.

• • •

Kennan's qualms about Washington's militaristic containment policy, for which he had been unfairly credited and blamed, markedly increased in early 1949. "We must refrain as much as possible from making the present East-West line a hard and fast one," he told a private meeting of the Council on Foreign Relations that winter, "and should continually engage in negotiations with the Russians, even though we must recognize that they will consume needless time and that we cannot hope for success in terms of years."

Kennan was particularly farsighted that evening. He predicted that Russia and China would become enemies. He worried about the growing hubris of a Pax Americana. "We must be careful about talking in big words, about using too carelessly such words as 'world leadership' and 'raising the world's standard of living.'" Kennan was picturing the world as it would seem about two decades later, in 1969. He was, as usual, out of synch with his own time.

He was beginning to feel restless, tired of losing bureaucratic battles. If the infighting continued, he wrote Acheson in January, "I'd rather be at Yale, or where-you-will—anyplace where I can sound off and talk freely to people—than in the confines of a department in which you can neither do anything about it or tell people what you think ought to be done." Kennan offered some suggestions to the new Secretary. "There—dear Dean—are some of the things I think would have to be done to the hull of the ship of state."

Kennan particularly wanted Acheson to consider an idea he had been working on all fall. Known as Plan A, it called for both the U.S. and the U.S.S.R. to withdraw their troops from Germany and create a united, demilitarized country. It was the bold stroke Kennan longed for to defuse the Cold War, to avoid an East-West Armageddon.

Coming from Kennan, the plan was breathtaking. After all, it was Kennan who had insisted that a divided Germany was inevitable back when his colleagues were still hoping for a unified state. Indeed, he had urged the creation of a strong West Germany as a bulwark against the Soviets. Now, stricken by what he had wrought, he cast about for an alternative, even if it entailed a total about-face. It is no small irony that the idea of a mutual withdrawal and the reunification of Germany had been first suggested by Walter Lippmann in his series of columns attacking Kennan's X-Article. In later years, Kennan acknowledged that Lippmann's articles had at least a "subliminal effect" in the evolution of his own views. Kennan's progression was not altogether illogical; it was dictated in part by the very success of containment. Yet such a sharp reversal did not enhance Kennan's credibility.

Still, Acheson seemed to listen carefully to Plan A. At the time, he knew little about Germany, and Kennan, his chief planner, was an authority on both Germany and the U.S.S.R. In March, he told Kennan that he was "almost persuaded by the cogency of his argument," and asked him to go to Germany to study the situation on the ground.

Upon his arrival Kennan sank into one of his periodic glooms. He was disgusted by the garish high living of the U.S. occupiers amidst the squalor of defeated Germany. In the officers' club, he tossed and turned at night, listening to the honky-tonk music, drunken babble, and the constant drone of planes, one every two or three minutes.

Rather than feel heartened by the audible pulse of the Berlin airlift, he preferred to dwell on the past, to think of Allied planes bearing bombs, not food. He was appalled by the rubble still left in Berlin by three days of saturation bombing in 1945. It stirred within him a loathing of the instruments of war that would evolve into a lifelong crusade against nuclear weapons. "Here, for the first time," he wrote in his memoirs, "I felt an unshakable conviction that no momentary military advantage could have justified this stupendous, careless destruction of civilian life and material values."

Returning from Germany in March of 1949, he was more convinced than ever that unless the invaders withdrew and Germany was reunited, the country would become a war zone once again. In Washington, however, his Plan A was being gutted. General Clay attacked it as "suicidal to our objectives" and accused the State Department planners of trying to lose the war he had won in Berlin. At the Department of State, Kennan's bureaucratic foes on NATO leaked Plan A in order to kill it. As Kennan knew they would, the European countries loudly objected, thinking they were being presented with a fait accompli. Even Bohlen turned against his old colleague, arguing that the Soviets would never agree to withdraw from Germany. His opinion was confirmed when he dined with the Soviet Military Governor of East Germany, General Vasily Chuikov, in May at a Council of Foreign Ministers' meeting in Paris. "There are those who think we should remove our troops," Chuikov told Bohlen. "They don't understand: the Germans hate us."

Bohlen was more realistic than Kennan. Kennan himself later admitted that his idea was flawed, that he had overreacted to the suffering of the Germans and the vulgarity of the occupiers, and underestimated the West German recovery. To Acheson, the choice was not all that difficult. Perhaps the Soviets would withdraw, perhaps a peaceful, unified Germany could be resurrected. This was all well and good for planners to envision. But Acheson bore the responsibility for such decisions. He could not afford to take the risk that Kennan, alone, had guessed right.

●   ●   ●

As Kennan was pushing his vision of an East-West military disengagement in Germany, Bohlen was tending to the more practical matter of seeking to extricate both sides from the showdown over Berlin. The blockade had become a debacle for the Russians, "the stupidest move they could make," General Clay said. The airlift had made a mockery of the Soviet attempt to strangle the city. The Kremlin, Bohlen believed, was looking for a way out.

The signal Bohlen was looking for came on January 31. A wire-service man in Paris had sent Stalin a list of questions, a common fishing expedition that usually produced nothing. But Stalin answered. To a question about whether Stalin attached great importance to money matters in Berlin, the Soviet dictator mentioned nothing about money, but acknowledged that the prolonged standoff was hurting the development of Germany.

Since currency reform had precipitated the eight-month-old Berlin blockade, Bohlen's interest was piqued. He went to Acheson and told him something was stirring inside the Kremlin. They agreed that it was time to start sending out feelers. In the delegates' lounge of the United Nations, the U.S. ambassador, Philip Jessup, stopped the Soviet ambassador, Yakov Malik, to chat about the weather. Jessup casually asked Malik if Stalin's failure to mention currency reform was accidental. Malik was noncommittal, and the conversation broke off. A month passed, and Bohlen began to have doubts. But then on March 14, Malik called Jessup and told him to meet him at an apartment on Park Avenue. Bohlen had been right; Stalin had been signaling.

For the next two months, the Soviets squirmed and tried to exact a price—that the Allies not establish a West German government—but Acheson held fast. On May 5, the Soviets gave up. The blockade was over. When the news chattered over the teletype in the State Department, Acheson and Bohlen broke out champagne. They sensed that the crisis of Europe had passed, at least for the moment. The Communist revolution in Greece had failed; the Marshall Plan was working; Berlin had been relieved; the West was allied against the Soviet threat. "America," Winston Churchill proclaimed, "has saved the world."

· · ·

Increasingly through his first year as Secretary of State, Acheson came to regard Kennan and Bohlen as devil's advocates. He was charmed by Bohlen, and he agreed with him far more than he did with Kennan, but he felt that Bohlen was too in love with argument for argument's sake.

Bohlen was tiring of Washington. He had been there seven years; he wanted to go back abroad. In the summer of 1949, Acheson sent him to Paris as minister, the number-two position in the embassy.

Kennan succeeded Bohlen as department counselor, while keeping his position as director of Policy Planning, but his responsibility actually diminished. Acheson was growing impatient with his mercurial seer, the abstract theoretician who seemed to feel that anything practical and workable was, almost by definition, flawed. In later years, Kennan remained mystified that he was unable to get across his argument that the main Soviet threat was political, not military. But to Acheson, Kennan was obsessed with distinctions without difference; his nuances were trifles. Curiously, Kennan was not helped by his writing, for though his missives were often eloquent, they were also at times rambling and, to Acheson, convoluted. Acheson refused to be seduced by Kennan's intuitive powers. The Secretary liked to tell friends that he had once spent hours puzzling over a Kennan memo, sure that its advice was wrong-headed but unable to put his finger on the flaw. To strip the memo of its veneer, Acheson called in a mid-level State Department bureaucrat and asked him to redraft the document. Translated into bureaucratese, the weakness of Kennan's logic became instantly apparent. David Bruce, Acheson's ambassador to Paris and a close friend, told journalist C. L. Sulzberger that Acheson "got to the point where he simply could not read Kennan's reports and telegrams because they were so long-winded and so blatantly seeking to be literary rather than to provide information." Furthermore, Acheson had little use for the Policy Planning Staff. He preferred to be advised by people, not institutions.

By the summer of 1949, Kennan had begun to feel "like a court jester, expected to enliven discussion, privileged to say shocking things, valued as an intellectual gadfly on the hides of slower colleagues, but not to be taken fully seriously when it came to the final, responsible decisions of policy."

The breaking point came in mid-September. Kennan was informed that Policy Planning memos would no longer go directly to the Secretary of State but to Assistant Secretaries. The message was clear to Kennan: he no longer had direct access to Acheson, even though his office was right next door. Later that month, Kennan informed the Secretary that he wanted to be relieved of his PPS duties as soon as possible, and that he would take an indefinite leave from the State Department in June of 1950.

•   •   •

On the day Acheson was sworn in as Secretary of State—January 21, 1949—Chiang Kai-shek turned over the command of his unraveling Kuomintang forces and departed from the mainland to establish a sanctuary on Formosa. "We passed," Acheson later recalled, "I coming in, Chiang going out." But Chiang, and China, would stay with Acheson for years, like a persistent sore.

Acheson was a Europeanist. He neither knew much about China nor cared much about it. In his introduction to the 1948 edition of the Council on Foreign Relations' annual survey, *The United States and World Affairs*, he had not even mentioned the world's most populous nation, even though it had reached the critical stage of its two-decade-long civil war.

Acheson was atypical. Many Americans had a long-standing fascination with China. They had been told for years about the special comity between the two countries, the steady stream of missionaries, the Open Door policy. They had read *The Good Earth* and been indoctrinated by the Luce publications. Henry Luce's obsession with China that began with his childhood as the son of a missionary now translated into lurid headlines warning of the consequences of a "lost" China: "MACARTHUR SAYS FALL OF CHINA IMPERILS U.S.," *Life* proclaimed in December 1948. To many, Generalissimo Chiang, with his Wellesley-educated wife (the "Missimo") and his overt Christianity, seemed like a hero worth rooting for.

The "G'mo" had powerful friends. The China lobby, financed by Chiang's bullion and Alfred Kohlberg, an importer of Chinese textiles, won (and bought) allies in Congress. Senator William Knowland of California, who would become known as "the Senator from Formosa," liked to end congressional meetings on China with the KMT toast, "Back to the Mainland!" When Knowland spoke about China, Acheson observed, he took on a "wild, stare-y look." Senator Kenneth Wherry, a former mortician from Pawnee City, Nebraska, vowed to "lift up Shanghai and make it like Kansas City." Congressman Walter Judd, a former China missionary and member of the America-China Policy Association, an arm of the China lobby, charged, "Since 1945, our policy in Asia, in fact if not in words, has been one of abandonment of the Chinese government."

Judd was not far wrong. Acheson, vividly recalling the frustration of General Marshall's mission in 1946 to work out a peaceful solution to the civil war, now wanted to cut off aid to the Nationalist government altogether. He believed the aid would simply fall into the hands of the Communists, or make its way into the bank accounts of Chiang or his wife's rapacious family, the Soongs.

When Acheson tried to explain U.S. policy to thirty-five congress-

men at a private session on Capitol Hill in February 1949, he told
them that any new initiatives must wait until the "smoke and dust of
the Chinese civil war cleared." It immediately leaked that Acheson's
policy was "to let the dust settle." The reaction was furious. It was
"common knowledge," charged Senator Wherry, that "Mr. Acheson
had . . . been considered as one who has gone along with the appeasement policy toward Russia." Styles Bridges of New Hampshire accused
Acheson of having sabotaged "the valiant efforts of the Chinese Nationalists to keep at least a part of China free."

In fact, Acheson was considering accepting the inevitable and recognizing Red China. Tentative feelers came in from Chou En-lai,
the Communist Foreign Minister, and were quietly encouraged by
the State Department. But the political atmosphere doomed such talk.
"We can't make a deal with the Commies," Truman flatly told Acheson. The Red Chinese did not help matters by announcing in July
that they would "lean" toward Moscow and by abducting the U.S.
consul in Mukden and holding him incommunicado for months.

  The inevitability of Chiang's final defeat, and the stridency of Con-
gress, made Acheson want to educate the public. On August 5, the
State Department published a 1,054-page white paper, *United States
Relations with China, with Special Reference to the Period 1944–1949.*
The white paper was a model of candor. It included secret cables,
internal memoranda, virtually the entire record. Few people actually
read it, however. The press just reported the conclusion: that the
Communist victory was "beyond the control" of the U.S.

The white paper backfired. It was called a "whitewash of a wishful
do-nothing policy," by Knowland, Wherry, and Co. The China lobby
printed its own white paper attacking Acheson for making the noble
Chiang the scapegoat for Washington "blunders." Worse, *The New
York Times* and Walter Lippmann criticized the document as a record
of failure. Acheson was flabbergasted. As he fretted on his morning
walk with Felix Frankfurter, the justice told him that he was a "frustrated schoolteacher, persisting against overwhelming evidence to the
contrary in the belief that the human mind can be moved by fact and
reason." Acheson later said that the white paper helped teach him to
make his education efforts "clearer than the truth."

The Chinese Communist victory over the remnants of the Nationalist Army in the fall of 1949 did not resolve the issue. The U.S. now
had to worry whether the Reds would invade Formosa and drive
Chiang from his sanctuary. The China lobby, meanwhile, agitated
for a U.S.-backed invasion of the mainland. Acheson told Truman

that the whole affair should be regarded as "a row between two Chinese factions about Chinese territory," but he knew the public would not agree. "Formosa is the subject which seems to draw out the boys like a red-haired girl on the beach," he wrote his old friend Archibald MacLeish in January of 1950. "It appears that what you want most is what you ain't got."

Kennan's aversion to the Generalissimo was even greater than Acheson's. But unlike Acheson, who favored benign neglect, Kennan wanted to resolve the Formosa issue by actually driving Chiang off the island— using American forces—and setting up an independent regime on Formosa. Somehow, he thought, by eliminating Chiang the U.S. would eliminate congressional demands to support the G'mo. This remarkable and harebrained scheme from a man who fancied himself as a realist and nonmilitarist had been laid out in a memo to Acheson in July of 1949. Kennan's model for action was Teddy Roosevelt, a man as unlike Kennan as any human imaginable. The old Rough Rider might have done it, Kennan wrote, with "resolution, speed, ruthlessness, and self-assurance." Acheson wisely chose to ignore his ethereal analyst's call to send in the marines.

In his more rational moments, however, Kennan clearly influenced Acheson's Far Eastern policy. Kennan had consistently pushed the notion that Peking was not likely to become Moscow's stooge. In February of 1947, he had predicted that "the men in the Kremlin would suddenly discover that this fluid and subtle oriental movement which they thought they held in the palm of their hand had quietly oozed away between their fingers and that there was nothing left there but a ceremonious Chinese bow and a polite giggle."

In January 1950, Kennan drafted a speech for Acheson arguing that the U.S. should let nature take its course in Asia. China would eventually perceive the Soviets to be its true enemy unless the United States made China her enemy first. Acheson's speech, delivered from notes at the National Press Club, was a model of enlightened flexibility. Unfortunately, it was ignored at the time and later remembered for an altogether different reason. In the course of his remarks, Acheson drew a "defensive perimeter" in the Pacific that excluded South Korea. As a consequence, he was blamed for inviting the North Korean invasion of South Korea less than six months later, aggression that would ultimately cost more than fifty thousand American lives. The criticism of Acheson ignores the fact that the North Koreans got Stalin's blessing for the invasion *before* the speech; that General MacArthur had drawn the same defensive perimeter a year earlier; that Acheson had also made clear that an attack on Korea would be viewed as a violation of the U.N. Charter.

The real tragedy of Acheson's speech was that it was premature. China and Russia would indeed fall out, but not before China attacked U.S. forces in Korea as they pressed to the Chinese border in November of 1950. Acheson was horribly shocked when they did. In later years, his bitterness over this catastrophe hardened his attitude toward Communism in Asia.

•   •   •

Acheson took a hard line toward Vietnam, China's southern neighbor, almost from the first. He did for a moment in 1949 entertain the "theoretical possibility" that Ho Chi Minh was another Tito. But by May he had written off the charismatic Vietnamese leader as a Kremlin pawn. The question of whether Ho "was as much nationalist as Communist" was "irrelevant" since "all Stalinists in colonial areas are nationalists." The political reverberations from the fall of China may have hardened his view. The Soviets' formal recognition of Ho in February 1950, Acheson declared, "should remove any illusions as to the 'nationalist' nature of Ho Chi Minh's aims, and reveals Ho in his true colors as the mortal enemy of native independence in Indochina."

Acheson's view of Vietnam was heavily influenced by his concern for France. Franklin Roosevelt had wanted to force France to give up her colonies, including Vietnam. Acheson, whose vestiges of old-fashioned liberalism made him similarly wary of colonialism, nevertheless wanted to do whatever was necessary to strengthen France as a member of the Western Alliance. France was a shaky, tentative ally in these years, fearful of a revived Germany, preoccupied with her own problems, including her crumbling empire. If the price of a strong France was propping up her colony in Southeast Asia, Acheson believed, then so be it. It was France, not Vietnam, that occupied Acheson's attention in 1949 and 1950. Vietnam was a minor irritant, one more in a long list of such trouble spots. What is more, he made it clear that he wanted France, not the U.S., to deal with Ho. In March of 1950 he told Congress: "We do not want to get into a position where the French say, 'You take over; we aren't able to go on with this.' We want the French to stay there."

On May 7, 1950, the day that France agreed to the Schuman Plan to share coal and steel with Germany—an essential step in rebuilding Europe—Acheson advised the President to begin the flow of $10 million in military supplies to France for use in Indochina. Acheson's special assistant, Lucius Battle, later explained that Congress was determined to spend money to combat Communism in the Far East, and Acheson figured that the U.S. might as well send the money to Vietnam, where it would at least do some good with France. So, with loose rocks, do avalanches begin: In the next four years, the U.S. would spend $2.5 billion to finance France's losing war in Southeast Asia, more than it spent through the Marshall Plan to rebuild France itself. And that, of course, was just the beginning.

CHAPTER 16

"A DIFFERENT WORLD"

Of Super bombs and primitives

On September 3, 1949, an American B-29 weather reconnaissance plane recorded a higher than normal radioactive count eighteen thousand feet over the northern Pacific. Two days later, a second weather plane flying between Guam and Japan picked up another dose of radiation. As the winds swept the cloud eastward, more planes were sent aloft to collect samples. Their air filters absorbed fission isotopes of barium and cerium. By mid-September, U.S. scientists were convinced: there had been an atomic explosion in Russia.

Truman was incredulous at first. "Are you sure?" he asked. "Are you *sure*?" The President did not believe the Soviets were capable of building a bomb so quickly. But the Pentagon had no doubt. The Air Force called the explosion Operation Joe, after Stalin, and immediately pressed to increase U.S. A-bomb production. In Congress, Arthur Vandenberg believed the news. "This is now a different world," he said.

America was no longer an island, protected by two oceans from the ravages of war. What had happened to London and Berlin, Tokyo and Stalingrad—or more precisely and unthinkably, Hiroshima and Nagasaki—could now happen to New York and Chicago. A quiet sense of dread spread through the country when Truman announced on September 23, "We have evidence that within recent weeks an atomic explosion has occurred in the U.S.S.R." In London, Lloyd's gave peace less than an even chance.

Without its monopoly on the bomb, the U.S. could no longer feel complacent about military superiority. Truman had been able to ignore Forrestal's pleas for more and better conventional forces because he believed that the bomb alone would check Soviet aggression. Now he could not be so sure.

To George Kennan, the news gave a terrible urgency to his own cause. He began to see his mission as not merely defusing tensions along the East-West divide in Europe, but taking the first steps toward nuclear disarmament. He had already given notice that he would step down as head of PPS "as soon as possible," but now he undertook one last assignment: exploring the ramifications of the Soviet bomb for U.S. national security planning. He began planning, as it were, against doomsday.

Kennan had increasingly lost touch with, and control over, his own Policy Planning Staff. Its members had ignored his qualms about creating a Western Alliance in 1948. By the fall of 1949, a member of the staff recalls, Kennan had stopped trying to shape consensus. In meetings, he would be "wholly frank" and "listen closely." But after the discussion around the table had gotten to the point where Kennan had "heard all he wanted to," he would go off with his secretary to a little office he kept in the Library of Congress. There, undisturbed, he would write. Once done, the staffer recalls he was locked in; he would not compromise. Any tinkering, he believed, would ruin his document's essence, its "inner worth." He wanted the paper to be "pure Kennan, or nothing."

The staffer who offers this description of Kennan's modus operandi in the fall of 1949 is Paul Nitze. He was, at the time, Kennan's deputy. He was about to become his successor as the State Department's chief planner.

Paul Nitze was in many ways better suited than Kennan to the small world of postwar foreign policy makers. Urbane, fit, impeccably dressed, a slight patrician lilt to his voice, Nitze came by way of Harvard and Wall Street. He shared none of Kennan's insecurity, and little of what Acheson called Kennan's "sweetness of spirit." He was, like Kennan, intense at times, and he had the same high sense of public duty and honor. One essential difference set them apart: whereas Kennan was tentative, beset by complexity and nuance when it came time to decide, Nitze went flat out. He was far more of a doer; he brought his intensity to carrying through on his ideals, even if at times that meant making them "clearer than the truth."

•   •   •

As a boy growing up on the South Side of Chicago, the young Paul Nitze was sent off to school every day wearing a Buster Brown suit. Mocked and beaten up by local toughs, he joined an Italian street gang in self-protection. It was an early lesson, he later recalled, in power relationships.

Nitze's father, scion of a well-to-do German family that had immigrated to the U.S. after the Civil War, was a professor of Romance languages at the University of Chicago. His mother loved young Paul "in a totally intense way," he recalls. A flamboyant beauty, she shocked Chicago society by smoking cigarettes and cavorting with liberal and outrageous friends, including Sally Rand, the fan dancer, and Isadora Duncan.

Nitze grew up in the most intellectual of worlds, amidst the creative ferment surrounding the University of Chicago in its heyday. He later recalled, however, that as he grew older he found the endless discussions among Chicago professors vapid and ineffectual; the relentless talk made him yearn for a sense of accomplishment, for matters more concrete and tangible than, say, his father's expertise in philology. The monotony was greatly relieved by long trips to Europe—for six months every two years during his boyhood. He was in Germany when World War I broke out; the Germans hissed at him for speaking English and his father had to sew an American flag on his sleeve.

A prodigy at the University of Chicago High School, Nitze was packed off to Hotchkiss at sixteen. "I enjoyed it," he recalled. "I developed bad habits. I did not work but I played football and made friends." His father wanted him to go to Yale along with most of his Hotchkiss classmates, but an "unattractively drunken" Yale alumni dinner in Chicago queered him on Old Eli. He went to Harvard instead.

There he began by rowing and getting A's but soon fell in with a fast crowd of white-shoe boys, including Chip Bohlen. Bored with an economics course, he skipped the final exam to go to a house party in Newport, and received a zero. "In those days, grades didn't count. Harvard was more like a European university. You just tried to absorb wisdom. We all drank too much, had girls, and a rich glorious life." Exertions included paddling a small craft from Ipswich, Massachusetts, to New York City with a Porcellian chum, Freddie Winthrop, on a drunken dare after Nitze had just recovered from a bout of hepatitis. They made it in eight days and Nitze ended up back in the hospital. He almost died.

Nitze was, he likes to recall, the last man hired on Wall Street before the Crash of '29, joining Dillon, Read two weeks before Black Thursday. Despite the hard times, he became the pet of Clarence Dillon and flourished as an investment banker. Then, he recalls, "I did a deal badly." It appeared that the firm was out $1.7 million, and as a result "Mr. Dillon ceased to know my name." His downfall did serve, however, to bring him close to another Dillon, Read partner, James Forrestal, who appreciated Nitze's new humility.

Nitze's first meeting with Forrestal had given him a sense of the future Defense Secretary's intensity as well as his priorities. Forrestal had burst into the partners' dining room where Nitze was eating lunch with old man Dillon to announce that he had come up with a plan to trump a competitor in a complex business deal. He said that he would act on the plan "the day after tomorrow." Dillon told him to do it "tomorrow." Forrestal had hesitated for a moment and come back with "Tomorrow afternoon." "Why not tomorrow morning?" asked Dillon. "I'm getting married," Forrestal ruefully explained. The next morning he married Josephine, and in the afternoon he arranged a bank merger.

Nitze himself worked too hard. He took no vacations for almost eight years. Finally, in the spring of 1937 the market turned slack, and he felt he could afford to take his wife, Phyllis (née Pratt, a Standard Oil heiress), and his children to Europe for a vacation. The trip was not relaxing. In Germany, he tried to find a Jewish business associate, but, it turned out, the man had been taken in by the Gestapo. He waved to another Jewish businessman he knew on the Parisplatz, but the man nervously scuttled away. He saw Hitler Youth, "arrogant and disdainful." He became acutely aware of, and uneasy about, his own national origins.

When he returned to New York, instead of going back to Wall Street, he decided to take a full year off to study sociology, religion, and history at Harvard. Clarence Dillon told him that his sabbatical was "asinine, crazy." But Nitze felt a strong need to understand the terrible forces loosed in Europe. Tutored by a White Russian émigré, he learned to "understand Communism" and grappled with Oswald

Spengler's *The Decline of the West,* an opaquely written and ardently Germanic study of historical determinism. The cumulative effect of visiting Germany and studying at Harvard was to make him an America Firster. He wanted to keep the U.S. out of the "coming apocalypse," as much to avoid Stalinism as Nazism. The German-Soviet pact in 1939 and Russia's invasion of Finland made him fearful of a most unholy alliance. Even after the Soviets switched sides and became an ally, Nitze says, he remained highly suspicious.

Upon his return to Wall Street in 1939, Nitze began having long talks with Jim Forrestal about Communism, even sharing his Harvard reading list with him. Both had a typical Wall Street aversion to Bolshevism, but also an uncharacteristic desire to read and think about it. The two further defied Wall Street convention by approving of FDR's Keynesian economic policies; they understood better than their hidebound Republican friends that the economy desperately needed liquidity.

It was Forrestal who recruited Nitze to government. Nitze was fishing in Louisiana with August Belmont in June of 1940 when he received a telegram: "Be in Washington Monday morning. Forrestal." When Nitze dutifully showed up in the office Forrestal occupied as one of FDR's "Silent Six" advisers and asked what he was there for, Forrestal replied simply, "To help me." "Who pays my salary?" Nitze asked. "Dillon, Read" was the reply. "Where do I live?" he asked. "With me," said Forrestal. The working arrangement was "all totally illegal and improper," Nitze recalls but it was a trifle compared to some of the shortcuts Forrestal would take in wartime Washington. Nitze quickly abandoned his isolationism; Neville Chamberlain's appeasement, he later recalled, was "a rude but enduring lesson."

War's end found Nitze working on the U.S. Strategic Bombing Survey with John Kenneth Galbraith and George Ball. The experience made them all doubtful about the efficiency of conventional long-range bombing, a skepticism that would affect their attitude toward the Vietnam War. But whereas Galbraith and Ball also developed a low regard for the military, Nitze became quite fascinated by it. In Galbraith's acerbic view, Nitze became a "Teutonic martinet happiest in a military hierarchy." It is more charitable to say that Nitze admired and befriended General Douglas MacArthur, the U.S. Supreme Commander in Japan. America's Caesar even tried to hire Nitze to rebuild Japan's economy after the war. The arrangement fell through when Nitze insisted on getting help from Washington, and MacArthur exploded, "I have absolutely no use for Washington at all, including the President!"

As a director of the Strategic Bombing Survey, Nitze was one of the first Americans to see the rubble of Hiroshima and Nagasaki. Curiously, however, he was not overwhelmed by the devastation. His task, he later recalled, was to "measure precisely" the impact of the bomb—"to put calipers on it, instead of describing it in emotive terms." While others saw the bomb as the ultimate proof of the futility of war, Nitze saw it as a weapon that could and probably would be used again. The damage in Hiroshima, he reckoned, was simply the equivalent of an incendiary bombing raid by 210 B-29s.

When Nitze returned home he sought to prepare America to survive a nuclear attack. In his report on strategic bombing, he recommended that the U.S. disperse its vital industry and medical facilities and consider adopting a nation-wide bomb shelter program. The country, he soon discovered, was more interested in returning to peace-time normalcy. When Nitze tried to convince New York City masterbuilder Robert Moses to construct civil defense shelters, Moses cut him off: "Paul, you're mad, absolutely mad. Nobody will pay attention to that."

Unsure what else to do, Nitze after the war drifted back toward Wall Street. He was about to take a job in 1946 running J. H. Whitney and Company when he was drawn back into government by Assistant Secretary of State for Economic Affairs Will Clayton. Nitze turned his formidable talents to European recovery. He recommended to Clayton a massive American aid program to restore Europe in December of 1946—four months before the Marshall Plan became a serious item on the agenda for Acheson, Kennan, and others.

Kennan was quick to spot Nitze's brilliance. In the spring of 1947, he tried to hire Nitze as deputy of the Policy Planning Staff to handle economic questions. Ironically, in light of their later close alliance, Acheson vetoed Nitze. The two had sparred for bureaucratic reasons at the State Department during the war, and Acheson regarded Nitze as a "Wall Street operator." Nitze's performance in helping to write and sell ERP changed Acheson's mind, and when Kennan asked again if he could have Nitze as his number two at PPS in the summer of 1949, Acheson assented.

One of Nitze's chores was work as liaison with the Pentagon on military preparedness. It was from an Air Force colonel in the Pentagon, in October of 1949, that Nitze first heard about the Super bomb.

• • •

Edward Teller, the scientist who had helped create the atomic bomb for the United States, was furious to learn that the Soviets now had one too. His answer was to build a bigger bomb—much bigger, one thousand times bigger, a hydrogen bomb detonated by nuclear fusion. In the fall of 1949, Teller made a crusade of the Super, as the H-bomb was then called, trying to convince any policy maker he could find that the U.S. could regain the nuclear edge over the Soviets with this fantastic weapon of destruction.

Teller was only too happy to tutor Paul Nitze. The State Department planner was a good pupil, with a technical mind and an easy grasp of numbers. Teller had a much simpler time with Nitze than Robert Oppenheimer had had trying to teach atomic physics to Acheson and McCloy in 1946. (Nitze did not need to pretend that neutrons and electrons were "little men.") As Nitze watched Teller's chalk race across the blackboard, he became convinced that the Super would work.

Other scientists were not so sure the Super could be built, and even less sure it ought to be. On October 10, David Lilienthal, the chairman of the Atomic Energy Commission, wrote in his diary, "We keep saying, 'we have no other course'; what we should be saying is 'we are not bright enough to see any other course.' The day has been filled, too, with talk about Supers, single weapons capable of desolating a vast area. . . . Is this all we have to offer?" Oppenheimer was, if anything, more troubled. As the head of a special advisory committee to the AEC asked to recommend whether or not to go ahead with the Super, he counseled other members to vote no. He saw technical problems: the Super was too big, it would use up too much fissionable fuel. But his real reservation was moral. He warned that "by its very nature [the Super] cannot be confined to a military objective but becomes a weapon which in practical effect is almost one of genocide." In late October, Oppenheimer's committee voted unanimously against developing the new bomb.

It fell to a special three-man national security committee created by President Truman to finally decide. One member, Secretary of Defense Louis Johnson, was in favor of the new bomb. Another, AEC chairman Lilienthal, was against. The swing vote was the Secretary of State.

Acheson had great regard for both Oppenheimer and Lilienthal. He had shared their desire to neutralize and control the bomb by sharing it with the Russians back in 1946. On November 1, Lilienthal came to him and gave him the moral and practical arguments against taking a new leap in the arms race.

Two days later, Acheson went to the Policy Planning Staff to ask their advice. Kennan was aggressively opposed to the new bomb. He had already allied himself with Oppenheimer, traveling up to Princeton in October to tell the scientist that the Soviets were paranoid and that a bigger bomb would just make them feel cornered and more dangerous. Now, with Acheson, he questioned what would be accomplished by building the Super "without showing the Russians any ray of light as far as their own [nuclear] policy is concerned." Instead, Kennan wanted to investigate further possibilities for international control.

Acheson had some sympathy for this view. At the PPS meeting he at least toyed with the idea of an eighteen-to-twenty-four-month moratorium on testing the bomb "during which time," as he put it, "you do your best to ease the international situation, come to an agreement with the Russians, put your economic house in order, get your people's minds set on whatever is necessary to do, and if no agreement is in sight at the end of that time . . . then go ahead with overall production of both the Super bomb and the atomic bomb."

But the Acheson of 1949 had himself evolved in his view of how to handle the Soviets, and in a direction entirely opposite from Kennan's. He could understand how his friends Lilienthal and Oppenheimer would, for visceral reasons, not want to bring any more evil into the world and indeed would want to stuff the genie back into the bottle. But he could not understand "the logic" of their view. The Soviets, he believed, were sure to build the Super bomb if the U.S. did not. Acheson's liberalism was by now all but eclipsed by his distrust of the Soviets. He told a Policy Planning staffer, Gordon Arneson, "You know, I listened as carefully as I know how, but I don't understand what Oppie was trying to say. How can you persuade a paranoid adversary to disarm 'by example'?"

As Acheson's own thinking moved him closer to endorsing the Super, Kennan's mind raced with the larger implications of U.S. nuclear policy. Vanishing into his hideaway at the Library of Congress, he began drafting a seventy-seven-page *cri de coeur* about nuclear arms. The paper became an obsession; in November and December he could work on little else. He later called it "one of the most important, if not the most important, of all the documents I ever wrote in government."

The cold realism Kennan brought to big-power relationships left him totally when he considered nuclear bombs. He regarded them as instruments of genocide and suicide. They were in no sense ordinary weapons that could conceivably be used in a war. They would not "spare the unarmed and helpless noncombatant . . . as well as the combatant prepared to lay down his arms." By building the Super, Kennan feared, the U.S. would escalate the arms race to a point of no return. He pleaded for a serious effort at international control, doubting that more than lip service had been paid to the idea, despite the earlier labors of Stimson, McCloy, Acheson, and Lilienthal. At the very least, he argued, the U.S. should forswear first use of nuclear weapons.

Kennan's arguments were, as usual, farsighted. His discussion of "no first use" (the idea that the U.S. should exclude from its contingency planning the possibility or threat of being the first to use nuclear weapons) anticipated a debate that would pick up in the Kennedy Administration and rattle on into the 1980s. But, as usual, Kennan was out of kilter with the times. His paper had no discernible impact on policy making. Indeed, it was a tangent; the issue before Acheson was more narrowly whether or not to build the Super, not international control or "no first use." And, as usual, Kennan harmed his case by showing his fragile emotions.

He was touchy even with Chip Bohlen. When Bohlen mildly accused him of "engaging in polemics," Kennan wrote back with wounded feelings: "We have always argued warmly, with our gloves off. You know me well enough to take into account my polemical temperament. . . . I find my estimate of my own political usefulness here shaken by the depth of this disagreement, and others I have had with numbers of worthy people. I would be happier than ever if, as I hope, it will be possible for me next June to subside quietly into at least a year or two of private life." This time Bohlen agreed; in December, he wrote Bob Lovett that he had had "for some time a feeling that a breathing spell for a year or so would not be at all a bad thing for his [Kennan's] case."

Acheson had genuine affection for Kennan. "I have rarely met a man the depth of whose thought, the sweetness of whose nature combined to bring a real understanding of the problems of modern life," he told a War College audience in December. The speech lifted Kennan out of a deep funk; that night he wrote Acheson that he had badly needed some cheering up, because when he had awakened that morning he had been tempted to go into his baby's room and say, "Go on, get up. You're going to work today. I'll get in the crib." Yet this was just the sort of self-pity Acheson could not abide. In private with Kennan, Acheson was a good deal less sympathetic. When Kennan kept after him with his antinuclear screed, Acheson finally snapped at him, "If that is your view you ought to resign from the Foreign Service and go out and preach your Quaker gospel, but don't do it within the department."

Acheson was hearing an entirely different message from Kennan's number two that fall. To Paul Nitze, the issue was not moral but practical: Would the Super work? He was convinced from his lessons with Edward Teller that the new bomb could be "weaponized." Unlike Kennan, Nitze did not regard nuclear war as unthinkable. His experience with the Strategic Bombing Survey had taught him that the bomb was just one more weapon, more devastating perhaps, but not qualitatively different from other bombs. What is more, he told Acheson that the real lesson of the Soviet bomb was not merely that the U.S. should proceed with the Super, but that it should build up conventional forces. The bomb was no longer enough to keep the Soviets in check. Nitze had gone to Europe with a group from the Pentagon that summer at the invitation of British military planners. The expedition had been a revelation. The British showed him their working sheets. To stop the Soviets at the Rhine, they estimated, would cost NATO $45 billion, or three times the cost of the Marshall Plan and three times current U.S. spending on defense. To Nitze, the real mission became clear; to wake up the Administration and Congress and make them spend more money, much more money, on defense.

Nitze shared his views with Acheson, who was of like mind. Acheson knew full well that NATO was a shell. At the signing ceremony for the North Atlantic Treaty that spring, Acheson had sardonically noted that the band's selection of show tunes from the Broadway hit *Porgy and Bess* was appropriate: "I've Got Plenty of Nothin'" and "It Ain't Necessarily So." Acheson was tired of hearing morality lectures. Here was a planner who would give him the facts, a realist who understood power, who spoke clearly and to the point. In November, Acheson decided to make Nitze the new head of PPS.

State's new planner was a technician and a numbers man, a pragmatist, who understood the military and liked it. Military considerations had been almost missing from Kennan's planning. Kennan was emotional, intuitive, he understood broad forces that swept nations, but little about the physical requirements of stopping Soviet tanks at the Rhine. Personally, Kennan and Nitze were friends—true friends.

More than three decades later, the warmest toast to Kennan at his eightieth birthday party would be spoken by Paul Nitze. But in the intervening years, they came to represent opposing points of view on how to deal with the Soviet Union.

Kennan did not formally turn over PPS to Nitze until January 1, 1950, but in fact Nitze held sway by mid-November. Significantly, when Acheson had to pick a staffer to run his working group for the special committee appointed by Truman to decide on the Super, he chose Nitze, not Kennan. The committee's conclusion was foregone. It recommended to Truman that development proceed. The committee also urged that the U.S. undertake a comprehensive study of U.S. national security policy. On January 31, the President agreed.

In death, James Forrestal's wish was fulfilled. The study, known as NSC-68, would be a memorial to Forrestal's unrelenting demand for military preparedness. In addition, it would come to be regarded as a blueprint for U.S. national security policy through the 1960s. To run a special interdepartmental group to write NSC-68, Acheson naturally picked his new planner, Nitze. At the same time, Kennan was dispatched on a fact-finding tour of South America.

• • •

The long-simmering and tragic case of Alger Hiss came to a head that winter. On Saturday, January 22, 1950, the prim young Brahmin was convicted of perjury. His first trial six months earlier had ended in a hung jury, but a second jury found that he had lied when he denied having given classified documents to a Communist agent. For the Republicans, the Hiss tragedy was a political deliverance.

By unfortunate timing, Acheson was scheduled to give a press conference on Tuesday, the day Hiss was to be sentenced. On Sunday, Acheson read the newspapers, full of gloating by Richard Nixon, Hess's chief congressional prosecutor, and Republican insinuations that Hiss was barely the tip of a vast New Deal–Harvard–State Department conspiracy to surrender to Russia. From Hiss's colleagues in the Administration came a resounding silence. But the man who had been taught by Brandeis that loyalty and honor are inseparable decided to speak out.

Acheson was not particularly fond of Alger Hiss, but he had worked with him and counseled him. As director of the State Department's Office of Special Political Affairs, dealing with U.N. matters, Hiss had attended Acheson's nine-thirty meetings back in 1946; a silver tray on Acheson's desk bore Hiss's signature, alongside those of other members of the "Nine-Thirty Club—or Prayer Meeting," including Chip Bohlen and Dean Rusk, then a young State Department official. Hiss had clerked for Justice Holmes, an important credential to Acheson, and his brother, Donald, was Acheson's law partner. As a favor to Donald, Acheson had secretly helped Hiss prepare his defense before the House Un-American Activities Committee a year and a half before.

In a reflective speech in 1946, Acheson had stated, "If one is to spin from his own visceral wisdom, he must say first, 'I shall not be a fake.'" Acheson would not be a fake to himself, nor to Alger Hiss.

The night before his press conference, Acheson told his special assistant, Lucius Battle, that he would defend Hiss. Battle, who sensed the risk immediately, told Paul Nitze, "We've got to stop him." At the morning meeting, the two men warned Acheson to be careful. He replied that he merely intended to read from the Sermon on the Mount. They were not entirely reassured.

At breakfast that Tuesday, Acheson had told his wife that he was sure he would be asked about Hiss. "I'm going to reply that I will not forsake him," Acheson said. Alice, made of stoical stuff, had replied: "What else could you say?" "Don't think this is a light matter," he warned. "This could be quite a storm and it could get me in trouble." Alice asked if he was sure he was right. Acheson, heading for the door, replied, "It is what I have to do."

Homer Bigart of the New York *Herald Tribune* asked the question: "Mr. Secretary, have you any comment on the Alger Hiss case?"

Acheson began by stating that the case was still before the courts so it would be improper for him to discuss it. Before his aides could breathe a sigh of relief, however, Acheson plowed forward: "I take it the purpose of your question was to bring something other than that out of me." Then he stated: "I should like to make clear that whatever the outcome of any appeal which Mr. Hiss or his lawyers might take in this case I do not intend to turn my back on Alger Hiss."

The words were to become permanently engraved next to Acheson's name, a taunt to the Republican right, further proof of the terrible conspiracy at Foggy Bottom. As the reporters scribbled, Acheson went on to quote the words Jesus Christ spoke on the Mount of Olives according to Matthew: "'. . . I was hungry and you gave me food, I was thirsty and you gave me drink, I was a stranger and you welcomed me, I was naked and you clothed me, I was sick and you visited me, I was in prison and you came to me.'"

On the Senate floor at that moment, the right-wingers were avidly chewing over the Hiss case. Karl Mundt, a HUAC member in his

House days, fulminated about how Hiss and his "Harvard accent" had brought about the "entire subjugation of China by Communist forces directed from Moscow." Senator William Knowland threatened to withhold State Department appropriations until Foggy Bottom disgorged its traitors. Senator Kenneth Wherry had just dug into the "secret agreement of Yalta" when Joe McCarthy burst onto the floor and interrupted.

"I wonder," asked McCarthy, "if the senator is aware of a most fantastic statement the Secretary of State has made in the last few minutes?" McCarthy with feigned indignation and barely restrained glee read Acheson's refusal to turn his back on Alger Hiss. Then he wondered aloud if the statement meant that Acheson would not turn his back on other Communists as well.

Expecting the worst, Acheson had asked for an appointment with the President. He found Harry Truman in his office reading the wire stories about his remarks. Truman smiled as Acheson entered the room. Acheson offered to resign, but the President would not even hear of it. As one who had been roundly criticized for going to the funeral of a "friendless old man just out of the penitentiary," Truman said, referring to his own attendance at Kansas City Boss Tom Pendergast's funeral in 1945, he had no trouble understanding what Acheson meant or approving of it.

That evening, Acheson delved into his feelings in a long letter to his daughter Mary:

> Alger's case has been on my mind incessantly. As I had written you, here is stark tragedy—whatever the reasonably probable facts may be. I knew that I would be asked about it and the answer was a hard one—not in the ordinary sense of do I run or do I stand. That presented no problem. But to say what one really meant—forgetting the yelping pack at one's heels—saying no more and no less than one truly believed, this was not easy. I felt that advisers were of no use and so consulted none. I understood that I had responsibilities above and beyond my own desires.

· · ·

The uproar swelled. "Disgusting," sneered Nixon. Senator Bridges of New Hampshire announced that he would "go after" Acheson. Wherry insisted that Acheson "must go" as a "bad security risk."

China was lost, and Russia had the bomb. Six days after Acheson's press conference, Truman announced that the U.S. would develop a bigger bomb, the Super bomb. Albert Einstein went on television to say that "annihilation of any life on Earth has been brought within the range of possibilities. . . . General annihilation beckons." Two days later, Klaus Fuchs, a scientist who had worked on the Manhattan Project, was arrested for giving the secret of the atomic bomb to the Soviets.

Joe McCarthy was still an obscure hack, voted the worst U.S. senator in one poll of the press corps, linked to a minor housing contractor's scandal, more visible to Washington barflies than to his Wisconsin constituents. But on February 9, two weeks after Acheson's press conference, McCarthy delivered a speech in Wheeling, West Virginia, that, to many, seemed to explain everything. Waving a piece of paper, he insisted in his high-pitched whine that he had in his hand a list of fifty-seven Department of State employees who were Communists.

The headlines began rolling, and McCarthy never looked back. He kept up the attack from the libel-proof precincts of the Senate floor, ranting about the "twisted bunch of intellectuals" who kept the President in thrall, the State Department "infested" with "vast numbers" of Reds and "espionage rings." It was all smoke; the number of Reds in the State Department changed from day to day—57, 205, 81—and McCarthy never did catch a real Communist. But no matter. He had started up a strange and terrible machine: he charged, the press printed; he charged, the press printed. By the time the denials caught up they were buried inside the paper; on page one were new headlines, like "Jessup pal of Reds—McCarthy," a slur on Acheson's irreproachable ambassador-at-large, Philip Jessup. Many readers knew better, of course, but just as many did not. McCarthy tapped into an old and deep know-nothing vein of American nativism, a virulent blend of FDR haters, Harvard haters, Wall Street haters, Washington haters, and just plain haters. Many who did know better kept quiet out of fear. The Repubican leadership formally backed McCarthy on March 22, stating "the pro-Communist policies of the State Department fully justify Joe McCarthy." Senate GOP leader Bob Taft, in a shabby moment of an estimable career, whispered to McCarthy, "If one case doesn't work, try another."

Acheson's friends—his oldest friends, the ones who really counted—rallied around. On the night of the press conference at which he vowed not to turn his back on Hiss, Acheson was applauded at dinner by Jack McCloy; the next night at dinner by Chip Bohlen. Bob Lovett sent him a typically whimsical letter blaming snowfall on card-carrying Communist weathermen ("whoever is responsible for it is a nasty, double-jointed traitor to his country and his class and I hope he finds lumps in his mashed potatoes. If he does, and opens them up, he is quite apt to find either Bridges or Wherry in them"). Lovett also thoughtfully offered Acheson his house in Hobe Sound for the month of April to rest up and wrote, "I pray for you—quite literally." The congratulatory letters poured in; from the headmaster of Groton, from Yale classmates ("You have plenty of guts!"), from his brothers in Keys. One, Boylston Adams Tompkins, assured him that his "real friends" would protect him from the "jackals." Clark Clifford wrote, "The statements of McCarthy and his ilk remind me of curs snapping at the heels of a thoroughbred."

At first, Acheson felt fairly pleased with himself about the Hiss statement, recalls his assistant, Lucius Battle. He considered Mc-Carthy, Wherry, Bridges and Co. beneath his contempt. He began calling them "the primitives." When Alice was dragged in because she had joined a "leftist" organization called the Washington League of Women Shoppers, which boycotted stores that were unfair to their employees, Acheson made light of it, in his slightly haughty way. He explained to reporters that he had read to her the list of the other sponsors and she had said that it rather sounded like the Social Register and that her standing was going up. To the American Society of Newspaper Editors, Acheson was brusque. He stated: "I don't ask your sympathy. I don't ask your help. You are in a worse position than me." He said that he was merely a "victim" while the press was a "participant." He quoted John Donne at them: "'Never send to know for whom the bell tolls; it tolls for thee.'"

Truman was equally, if less eloquently, contemptuous. "Privately, I refer to McCarthy as a pathological liar, and Wherry as the block-headed undertaker from Nebraska," he wrote Acheson on March 31. "Of course we can't do that publicly but that's exactly what they are." Truman, like Acheson, refused to take them seriously. "I think we have those animals on the run," he told Acheson in March.

The President and his Secretary of State underestimated the rabid pack. They would find the baying and howling harder and harder to ignore in the year ahead. It has become fashionable for historians to assume that Acheson was embittered and hardened by the vili-fication, made more inflexible and rigidly anti-Communist. Some of his friends share this assessment; Chip Bohlen, for one, asserts it in his memoirs. Acheson would deny that the primitives had any effect on him whatsoever, and it is impossible to know for sure what impact the right-wing assaults had on his innermost thoughts. Thirty years later, however, Alice said that the "attack of the primitives" took ten years off her husband's life.

Acheson himself acknowledged in 1954 that his Hiss statement had hurt the department. In discussing the period with Nitze and other old colleagues, he realized that he had "brought down the lightning on their shoulders." He added that "turn my back" was an "awful phrase" thought up "at the spur of the moment."

Indeed, McCarthy's witch-hunt tore through the Department of State. In February the department announced that it had fired ninety-one employees, mostly homosexuals, as security risks in the last three years. Over the next three years, the Loyalty Boards set up by Truman as a sop to the right wing in 1947 would fire hundreds more, of all types of innocents. Acheson tried fitfully to defend his troops, and he certainly did a better job of it than his successor as Secretary of State, John Foster Dulles. But he could not afford to take a high profile, to make a crusade out of protecting his underlings. He was damaged goods; he had exhausted his moral capital. By showing his courage in the defense of Hiss, he lost some of his ability to protect other State Department officials far more innocent of Communist ties than Hiss. Acheson was true to himself, and brave. But integrity can be an oddly selfish quality.

• • •

George Kennan was dead set against the writing of NSC-68. He did not believe there was a need for a massive military buildup. He did not believe that the Soviets would attack the U.S. unless provoked. The document would be clumsy and overstated, he feared, and serve only to inflame politicians who interfered with the successful conduct of diplomacy.

Kennan had his doubts about Nitze as well. The ex-Wall Streeter was fine for economic questions, but not for grand strategy. He was, like Lovett, too much of a banker, too much of a numbers man— only more intense than Lovett. Kennan had noticed that Nitze was not content until he could get numbers down on paper. He was so intense, Kennan later recalled, that when he wrote down numbers his pen would sometimes drive right through the paper.

In Kennan's view, Nitze had succumbed to the seduction of military planning, to the "planner's dummy." The military always assumed the worst in its hypotheticals. Too much emphasis was put on the enemy's *capacity*, not enough on his *intentions*.

Before leaving for South America in February Kennan wrote a last memo pleading for moderation. "There is little justification for the impression that the 'cold war' . . . has suddenly taken some turn to our disadvantage," he wrote in a draft that he delivered orally to Acheson. The Soviet A-bomb "adds no new fundamental element to the picture ... insofar as we see ourselves in any heightened trouble at the present moment, that feeling is largely of our own making." He argued for "drastic measures to reduce the exorbitant cost of national defense."

That was precisely the opposite of what Nitze was saying. At one of the Secretary's morning meetings that month, Nitze stated that the risk of attack by the Soviet Union was "considerably greater" than it had been in the fall. There were increasing "signs of toughness" from the Soviets, he added, and the Joint Chiefs of Staff believed that the Red Army could attack Europe from a "standing start" without the usual signs of mobilization. As he expressed it in a memo: "Recent Soviet moves suggest a boldness that is essentially new and borders on the reckless."

Actually, as Nitze later conceded, he was less concerned with Soviet intentions than capacity. The CIA reports of early February had shaken him. They forecast a Soviet stockpile of ten Nagasaki-size bombs by 1953, 200 by 1955. The intelligence agency estimated that roughly twenty bombs could put the U.S. out of war.

As Nitze saw it, maybe Kennan was right, maybe the Soviets would not attack. But how could he be so sure? What was really eating at Kennan, Nitze suspected, was that he believed a diplomatic elite should run foreign policy, without any interference from politicians or generals. To Nitze, Kennan was a diplomat only. He knew nothing about the military or defense strategy. That summer, Kennan had told Nitze that two divisions of marines would be enough to defend Europe. Nitze thought this was a ridiculous assertion and a mark of Kennan's naïveté.

Nitze understood that the U.S. had to be prepared to fight a total war. It had to be able to control the skies, transport troops by air and sea, blunt armor attacks with armor. The minimum price tag for total preparedness Nitze knew from examining British and U.S. estimates was $40 to $50 billion. That was roughly three times what the Administration currently allotted to defense, but Nitze believed that the U.S. economy could afford the cost. As a Keynesian, he believed that deficit spending could fuel the economy enough to sustain much greater military spending. He had consulted with Leon Keyserling of the President's Council of Economic Advisers, who privately agreed.

The real question was whether Congress and the Administration would pay for it. The public had to be persuaded. The way to do that,

Nitze knew from experience was to scare them: to tell them that the Soviets were intent on world domination, that they were poised to attack, and that the U.S. had to meet them everywhere. That was the message that Nitze gave to the drafters of NSC-68: he told them to "hit it hard."

Joining Nitze in urging this course was a special consultant brought in to speak to the interdepartmental group working on NSC-68: Robert Lovett. Since leaving Washington a year earlier, Lovett had been quietly working as a banker and resisting Acheson's attempts to bring him back into government, most recently as ambassador to England. In mid-March, Lovett flew down and delivered the drafters a pep talk that sounded a great deal like their final product. "We are now in a mortal conflict," Lovett said, abandoning his usual caution. "We are in a war worse than we have ever experienced. It is not a cold war. It is a hot war. The only difference is that death comes more slowly and in a different fashion."

This urgency had to be conveyed in the document, Lovett insisted. The conclusions should be written "in almost telegraphic style" with "Hemingway sentences." Lovett added: "If we can sell every useless article known to man in large quantities, we should be able to sell our very fine story in larger quantities." His almost desperate effort to build an Air Force from scratch as Hitler was rolling through Europe had forever convinced Lovett that the U.S. should never again be unprepared. He agreed with Nitze that the country could afford to spend much more for defense. "There is practically nothing that this country can't do if it wants to."

Like the Truman Doctrine pledging to defend freedom everywhere, NSC-68 was written quickly and by committee. It was a selling job, not a precise delineation of U.S. commitments. The language was ominous and lurid. "The grim oligarchy of the Kremlin . . . is seeking to demonstrate to the Free World that force and the will to use it are on the side of the Kremlin. . . . The implacable purpose of the slave state is to eliminate the challenge of freedom." The document stressed Soviet ideology: "The Soviet Union, unlike previous aspirants to hegemony, is animated by a new fanatic faith, antithetical to our own, and seeks to impose its absolute authority over the rest of the world."

The most important new idea was a concept later to be known as "flexible response." The Soviets, NSC-68 argued, are expansionist everywhere. The Free World lacks the resources to thwart such expansion locally.

The U.S. will therefore be confronted more frequently with the dilemma of reacting totally to a limited expansion of Soviet control or not reacting at all (except with ineffectual protest and half measure). Continuation of present trends is likely to lead, therefore, to a gradual withdrawal under the direct or indirect pressure of the Soviet Union, until we discover one day that we have sacrificed positions of vital interest.

This was the nub: The U.S. had to be able to fight small conventional wars, and fight them anywhere, or one day it would find the Red Army in Paris. There was no effort to distinguish between vital and peripheral interests. "The assault on free institutions is worldwide now, and in the context of the present polarization of world power, a defeat of free institutions anywhere is a defeat everywhere."

                              •   •   •

In April Bohlen was flown back from Paris, where he was still serving as minister in the U.S. Embassy, to comment on the draft. Already he was worried about the hawkish drift in Nitze's thinking. When his old clubmate had visited Paris five months before, they had engaged in "long and gloomy debates." Bohlen, meanwhile, had patched up his differences with Kennan, and on a trip to Washington in January had enjoyed, as he wrote his wife "many long and on the whole satisfactory talks with George."

Bohlen found himself, as he often did, somewhere between Kennan and the current consensus. He agreed that it was necessary to build up conventional forces, though perhaps not quite as much as Nitze had in mind. But he did not agree that the Soviets intended to "dominate the world," or that war was "inevitable." Worried that the U.S. was overstating its commitments, he wrote Nitze that NSC-68 "oversimplifies the problem."

Nitze could not understand what Bohlen was so riled up about. He believed NSC-68 was essentially restating what Kennan himself had written about the Soviets in the X-Article and a host of PPS papers. At Bohlen's insistence, Nitze made some changes that he regarded as purely cosmetic, but which Bohlen regarded as essential. As Soviet aims, Nitze had originally listed world domination first. Bohlen persuaded him to describe "protecting their own borders" as the Soviets' top priority. Second came controlling their satellites. Then only third came global expansion.

As he had with Kennan, Nitze attributed his differences with Bohlen to his adversary's ignorance of military capability. As Nitze later recalled their conversations, Bohlen did not believe that the Soviets were technically capable of mounting a modern offensive blitzkrieg. He thought the Soviet bureaucracy was so incompetent that it could do little right. The fallacy of Bohlen's judgment came clear to Nitze that spring. When the CIA reported that the Soviets were building 315 MiGs a month, while the U.S. was producing only half a dozen F-86s, Bohlen said the estimates were preposterous, that the Soviets could never produce so many. The CIA estimate was based on the square footage of certain Soviet factories, not on actual sighting of planes. Nitze decided to try a test case. He got the CIA to photograph a Soviet base on Sakhalin Island north of Japan. The CIA had predicted that it would find thirty to forty MiGs there. In fact, the U.S. spy plane photographed fifty. Nitze felt vindicated. "Chip," he later recalled, "didn't know what he was talking about."

Nitze was careful to involve the Secretary of State in these discussions. Acheson talked to Nitze almost daily about the report through the late winter and early spring; from time to time, the Secretary would slip through the back door of his office into Nitze's and sit in on the discussion as the drafters worked around the table.

Acheson was pretty well fed up with Kennan's advice, but he liked and admired Bohlen and, though he regarded him as somewhat a devil's advocate, he listened to his views. Through three long sessions with Acheson and Nitze, Bohlen tried to explain his objections. Finally Acheson threw up his hands and exclaimed that he could not understand what Bohlen was talking about. As far as he could tell, the document already said what Bohlen wanted it to say, which was what the Soviet experts had been saying all along. The Secretary didn't have time to quibble over nuance.

Like Nitze, Acheson was more worried about selling the critical U.S. military buildup. Initially, Nitze and his PPS staff had intended to make large portions of the document public. Indeed, that was why the language was so loud and simplistic. The staff referred to the project as "Operation Candor." Acheson, however, objected to full disclosure. He wanted to keep the document classified, for distribution only to those with top-secret classification, and he wanted to leave out any mention of cost altogether. When Nitze showed him the "back of the envelope figure" of $50 billion, Acheson replied, "Paul, don't put that figure in the report. You're right to tell me and I'll tell the President, but don't put any figure in the report."

Acheson explained that he wanted to get the President and the top bureaucracy on board before he began selling to Congress and the public. The goal of NSC-68, he later stated, was "to bludgeon the mass mind of 'top government' so that not only could the President make a decision but that the decision could be carried out."

Persuading the President would not be easy. Truman, wedded to balanced budgets, had steadfastly resisted the importuning of Forrestal for the previous three years. The new Secretary of Defense, curiously enough, would be an obstacle rather than an ally. Louis Johnson was more interested in his own political ambitions than in rebuilding the military. He had hitched himself to the balanced budget. He believed, incredibly, that he would be viewed as a savior by the public for holding down defense spending, and that in gratitude the people would elect him President in 1952.

Acheson loathed Johnson. He thought the Defense Secretary was loud, unprincipled, obnoxious, and a tool of the China lobby. Acheson's judgment, subtracting slightly for his prejudice against politicians who reminded him of congressmen, was pretty nearly accurate.

Handling Johnson was difficult. He could not be allowed to know too much about NSC-68 while it was still in the drafting stages, or he might try to kill it. On the other hand, he could not just be presented with a fait accompli. On March 22, Acheson invited the Defense Secretary and the Joint Chiefs of Staff over to State for a briefing. So as not to attract newsmen, the Pentagon contingent entered by the basement, and came to Nitze's office. Acheson started to explain the report when Johnson interrupted and asked if he, Acheson, had read it. Acheson said that he had. Johnson said that he had not and indeed had only heard of the report that morning. He told Acheson that he did not like being called into conferences without a chance to read the appropriate material, and added that this was the fourth time the Secretary of State had done this to him. He wanted no more of it.

Suddenly, he lunged forward with a crash of chair legs, pounded his fist on the table, and began accusing Acheson and Nitze of keeping him in the dark and trying to end run him. "I'm not going to be subjected to this indignity!" he stormed. "This is a conspiracy being conducted behind my back in order to subvert my policies! I and the chiefs are leaving now!" He stalked out. The meeting had lasted fourteen minutes. The Department of Defense representative on the committee, Major General James Burns, was so unnerved that he wept. Acheson decided that Johnson was "brain damaged."

In later years, Nitze would concede that the language of NSC-68 "sounds extreme." At the time, however, he thought he was squarely in the center. Acheson agreed with him, as did Lovett. Despite quibbles, he believed that Bohlen did too. Kennan—well, he was over-wrought. But hadn't he written the Long Telegram warning of the Soviet menace in the first place?

Acheson likewise hardly felt like a radical. From Europe, both McCloy, then U.S. High Commissioner in Germany, and Harriman, the U.S. administrator of the Marshall Plan, had weighed in to argue that European security depended on U.S. military might as well as economic aid. Indeed, Acheson thought he was holding off the true hawks, like one right-wing Republican senator, who at an off-the-record session with Acheson in January had urged a preemptive strike against Moscow. "Why don't we get into this thing and get it over with before it is too late?" the senator demanded. Acheson responded bluntly that if preventive war was the policy of the United States he would resign.

Though Acheson wanted to keep NSC-68 itself under wraps, he began a PR campaign in February to lay the groundwork for the inevitable lobbying campaign of Congress. He felt beset by idiocy on all sides. There were the McCarthyites accusing the Administration of coddling Communists. At the same time, Senator Brien McMahon, chairman of the Joint Congressional Atomic Energy Committee, was urging the abolition of all nuclear weapons to be achieved by a "moral crusade for peace" and a $50 billion "global Marshall Plan." Millard Tydings, the chairman of the Senate Armed Services Committee, proposed that the President convene a worldwide disarmament conference. U.N. Secretary-General Trygve Lie insisted that it was time for the U.S. to "sit down" with the Russians.

To Acheson, this was all poppycock. The Soviets, he told the press, understand only "situations of strength." He warned against the "Trojan doves" of the Communist movement and called for an arms buildup. The U.S. could not afford to rely solely on the bomb; it could not, he told a Dallas audience, "pull down the blinds and sit in the parlor with a loaded shotgun, waiting." After hearing Acheson talk at an off-the-record session at the Conference of State Governors in White Sulphur Springs, West Virginia, one governor remarked, "He scared hell out of us."

Despite the global sweep of NSC-68's rhetoric, its drafters and supporters were hardly unmindful of Lippmann's injunction against skewing the balance of resources and commitments. They saw NSC-68 as a means of fulfilling existing commitments, not undertaking new ones. Testifying before the drafters in private session, Lovett urged that the U.S. "refrain from making commitments which are neither absolutely necessary nor within our capacity to fulfill." Acheson himself told a congressional hearing that spring that the U.S. had to be careful not to take on more than it could afford. "I think we have to start out with the realization that the main center of activity at the present moment has got to be in Europe. We cannot scatter our shots equally all over the world. We just haven't got the shots for that."

This was hardly global intervention run amok. Indeed, Acheson had been widely criticized for excluding Korea from the U.S. defense perimeter in January. When John Foster Dulles came to Nitze in the spring and urged that the U.S. commit itself to defending Formosa from Chinese Communist invasion, Nitze disagreed. The U.S., he said, lacked the resources. (It is perhaps also worth noting that Nitze, the principal drafter of NSC-68, would be one of the few men in government to oppose U.S. involvement in Vietnam at the outset.)

The problem is that the cautionary, private views of men like Acheson and Nitze are quickly forgotten. Their bolder, simpler pronouncements, however, are remembered, and believed by ordinary citizens and their congressmen. In later years, NSC-68 would be held up by revisionist historians as the inevitable extension of the Truman Doctrine and a blueprint for disaster, responsible for the next two decades of East-West tension and the Vietnam War itself.

Acheson and Nitze hardly bear all the blame for a U.S. policy that pitted itself against global, monolithic Communism. Dulles, when he took over from Acheson under Dwight Eisenhower in 1953, would make a moral crusade of taking the Russians to the "brink," and right-wing congressmen like McCarthy had all along fanned fear of Communism into a kind of hysteria, making it almost impossible for politicians to be reasonable about Communism and still get re-elected.

While Acheson found it necessary to make things clearer than the truth, he was not a cynic. He believed the U.S. had to arm to face down the Soviets, that the Kremlin understood only "situations of strength." Still, propaganda can be insidious. It can convince even the propagandists, if they repeat the rhetoric often enough. When Truman asked Acheson, Lovett, Nitze, and Averell Harriman to update NSC-68 for the incoming Eisenhower Administration at the end of 1952, the group made only one significant change. Mindful of the Korean War, they argued that the U.S. should put more emphasis on stopping Communism in the Middle East, Africa, and Southeast Asia.

NSC-68 was flawed in another respect. Not only did it put too much emphasis on Soviet capability, and too little on the Kremlin's intentions, it overestimated Soviet strength. As Nitze later acknowledged, of the 175 Soviet divisions cited in NSC-68, only a third were at full strength. One-third were undermanned and one-third were "cadres," or ill-equipped militia. Nitze blamed poor intelligence.

In fact, the U.S. had consistently overestimated Soviet forces after the war. In 1948, it was widely believed that the Red Army numbered between four and five million men. It now appears that the Soviet forces did not exceed three million, and most of the troops were engaged in occupation duties. The British and Americans had between them about 2.5 million soldiers and the atomic bomb as well. The Soviets would have had difficulty mounting an invasion because in 1946 they had torn up most of the railroad track between Germany and Russia; with 20 million war dead, they wanted no more invasions from the west.

Frightened by the Western Alliance, the Soviets began to rebuild their forces after 1948 and to develop their own nuclear weapons. Clearly, by 1950 the U.S. needed to modernize its nuclear arsenal and expand conventional forces to back up its vast commitments. But it seems just as clear that NSC-68 greatly exaggerated Soviet superiority. Henry Kissinger, though generally approving of Acheson's strategy of containment, asserts that "it was based on a flawed premise; that we were weaker than the Soviets and had to build from positions of strength. In fact, we were stronger than they were."

• • •

It is one of the final ironies of NSC-68 that it did not work—at least right away. It failed to "bludgeon the mass mind of top government" sufficiently to make its members want to spend $50 billion more on defense. Some were properly shocked by the statistics on the Soviet arms buildup and American vulnerability. When Charles Murphy, who had replaced Clark Clifford as Truman's aide handling national security matters, took the document home one night in April, "what I read scared me so much that I didn't go into the office at all. I sat at home and read this memo over and over wondering what in the world to do about it." Others were less impressed. Senator Walter George, a power on the Finance Committee, was given a peek and shrugged. "I see the logic, but..."

Truman came around only slowly and grudgingly. In January, eyeing the "Buck Stops Here" sign on his desk, he mused with Gordon Arneson, a PPS staffer, about how many "bucks" he had stopped.

"The Truman Doctrine, good. Greece and Turkey, good. Berlin airlift, right again. Marshall Plan, a ten strike." Overall a pretty good batting average. But he wondered aloud whether his decision to reduce the defense budget was so wise. True, it worked politically with the voters and Congress. But considering the shaky state of the world and the uncooperative Russians, was it prudent? He sighed.

When it came to acting on NSC-68, Truman equivocated. He endorsed it in principle in late April but called for a study of the cost; in other words, he begged the all-important question. As late as June he told Arthur Krock of *The New York Times* that he still wanted to hold down the defense budget. Once again, Acheson and the State Department warriors needed a crisis to shake the listless body politic. As Acheson later remarked, "Korea saved us."

CHAPTER 17

WAR

"No weakness
of purpose here"

After an afternoon of gardening and a good dinner, Dean Acheson put on a pair of blue pajamas and turned in to read himself to sleep. It was a Saturday evening—June 24, 1950—and at Harewood Farm all was quiet, except for the creaking footfalls of security agents pacing through the house. Acheson had been getting crank mail from McCarthyites, and his home was kept under twenty-four-hour guard.

Shortly after 10 P.M., he was stirred by the ringing of the white telephone beside his bed that was tied into the White House switchboard. The State Department duty officer was calling; he read Acheson an urgent cable from the U.S. ambassador to South Korea, John Muccio. After issuing some instructions, Acheson hung up and called Harry Truman in Independence, Missouri, where the President had gone for the weekend. "Mr. President," he said, "I have very serious news. The North Koreans have invaded South Korea."

• • •

Korea was an unlikely place, in Acheson's view, for the Cold War
to turn hot. He considered Asia to be a nuisance and a distraction.
Urged by General MacArthur to visit the Far East the year before, he
had replied that he had no time (he visited Europe eleven times). He
had passed off Korea as outside the periphery of vital U.S. interests
in his Press Club speech in January.

To the Communists, South Korea looked like a soft spot to be
probed. Although it was widely assumed that the North Koreans were
merely Soviet surrogates, Stalin did not take the initiative, according
to Nikita Khrushchev's memoirs. The fanatic North Korean dictator,
Kim Il Sung, pressed him for backing and permission. Stalin and his
Chinese ally, Mao Tse-tung, went along, hoping that the U.S. would
consider it only a local affair.

To Washington, however, the invasion would look like Japan's
invasion of Manchuria all over again; a warning sign on the road to
world war.

Yet Washington was surprisingly unprepared. Intelligence failed
totally; the CIA was still too small and unformed, Army G-2 was too
unwieldy and too uncritical. Asked four days before the attack if North
Korea had any invasion plans, the State Department's Assistant Secretary for Far Eastern Affairs, Dean Rusk, told a congressional hearing,
"We see no present intention that the people across the border have
any intention of fighting a major war for that purpose."

•   •   •

Acheson rose to crises. At eleven-thirty Sunday morning, after a
long night of phone calls back and forth between the State Department
and Harewood Farm, he sped into Washington in his convertible, top
down, jacket off, tie flying. Reporters waiting at Foggy Bottom for
scraps of information duly recorded the Secretary's urgency. Acheson,
voted one of the Ten Best-Dressed Men of 1949 by several tabloids,
was rarely seen out of pinstriped uniform.

The early reports were grim. A North Korean tank column was
driving toward Seoul; fighters were strafing Kimpo Airfield outside the
capital. The South Korean soldiers, Acheson believed, were "clearly
outclassed." At 3:30 P.M., he shooed everyone out of his office to sit
alone and think. His head swirled with ideas, as he later recalled,
"like glass fragments in a kaleidoscope." On a yellow legal pad he
scrawled little notes: What were the Soviets up to? Where else would
they probe? Berlin? Greece? Turkey? Iran?

Clearly the invasion of South Korea could not be stopped without force. But Seoul's troops were not up to it. Only the U.S. could do the job. Acheson had already obtained a U.N. resolution condemning the North Korean aggression, but talk would not suffice. The U.S., he decided, would have to fight, to commit ground troops if necessary. To back away from this challenge, he thought, would be highly destructive to the prestige and power of the United States. The true stakes were not South Korea, a wretched little country, nor even the U.S. strategic position in the Far East. The real reason Acheson decided that the U.S. should go to war that Sunday afternoon, he later told Walt Rostow, was to save the Western Alliance in Europe.

Korea was an old war zone between Russia, China, and Japan, "a shrimp crushed in the battle of the whales," according to a Korean proverb. To Acheson, Korea was to be the source of tremendous anxiety and pain; it was the crisis of his working life. Exasperated by the war's unpredictable turns some months later, Acheson slammed down his hand on his desk and exclaimed, "If the best minds in the world had set out to find us the worst possible location to fight a war, the unanimous choice would have to have been Korea." It was to be, Averell Harriman would say, "a sour little war."

* * *

America's premier authority on the Soviet Union was unaware that war was breaking out that weekend. George Kennan, who had just begun his leave from the State Department that June, had gone to his farm in Pennsylvania; among its deliberate lack of conveniences was a telephone. Kennan only learned what was happening when he returned to Washington late Sunday afternoon and saw the block-letter headlines. He was irked that the State Department had not found a way to notify him; General Marshall, he thought somewhat petulantly, would not have failed to track him down.

Kennan rushed to Foggy Bottom, where he found Acheson talking to his aide about possible U.S. moves. The Secretary welcomed Kennan and asked his advice. Kennan, somewhat atypically, was direct: the U.S. must use all necessary force to push the Soviets out of the Korean peninsula. The U.S. global position demanded it, he said. Kennan, for once, was thinking exactly like Acheson. The hard liner turned dove had turned hawk again; there were no doves in Washington's inner circle that night.

At 6 P.M., Acheson excused himself to meet Truman's plane due in from Independence. Sitting next to Acheson in the limousine returning from Andrews Air Force Base, the President was brimming with defiance. He had been thinking about Mussolini and Hitler on the plane, he said. Now the Soviets... "By God," he exclaimed, "I'm going to let them have it!"

The senior officials from the Pentagon and State Department assembled for dinner at Blair House. When the mahogany table had been cleared and converted into a conference table, Truman turned to Acheson. There was little question who was the dominant voice in this makeshift war room. Not the Secretary of Defense, nor the chairman of the Joint Chiefs of Staff, but Acheson, a diplomat. Acheson briskly recommended that General MacArthur in Tokyo supply the South Koreans with arms and equipment and position the Seventh Fleet between Formosa and the mainland. Defense Secretary Louis Johnson began to fulminate about the necessity of protecting Formosa from attack, but Acheson brushed him off. "The U.S. must not get tied up with the Generalissimo," he said; he wanted the fleet there as much to keep Chiang from launching an attack on the mainland as to protect him from invasion. Without hesitation, Truman accepted Acheson's recommendations; by now, the President's faith in his Secretary's crisis judgment was absolute. As the military and Johnson left, the President asked Acheson to stay. The two friends drank a Bourbon together, and Acheson slipped out the side door, dodging reporters.

•   •   •

The decision to commit U.S. troops to combat came quickly, and after little debate. Only the chairman of the Joint Chiefs, General Omar Bradley, raised any concern about the advisability of committing ground troops. Each day, the situation on the ground deteriorated further; each night, Truman's war council, meeting at Blair House, escalated U.S. involvement from supplies and equipment, to air cover and naval bombardment, to ground troops. Truman gave the order to General MacArthur to engage the North Koreans in combat at 4:57 A.M. EST, on Friday, June 30.

A week earlier, Kennan had given columnist Joe Alsop a gloomy lecture about the failure of democracies to stand up in time of crisis. On Tuesday, after it was clear that the U.S. would back South Korea all the way, Alsop saw Kennan again on a Georgetown sidewalk, walking to a dinner party. Kennan whacked him on the back and did a little jig. "What do you think of democracies now?" he exclaimed.

It was hard to find a dissenting voice in Washington, or around the country. Truman, Louis Johnson, Dean Acheson, Bob Taft, the Republican right, MacArthur, the Joint Chiefs of Staff, *The New York*

Times, and Walter Lippmann were all in agreement: the U.S. had to intervene to save South Korea from the Communists. So total was the support that the Administration did not even bother to get any congressional resolution or declaration of war. Republican leader Bob Taft complained about "a complete usurpation by the President of authority to use the armed forces of the country," but Acheson counseled against seeking formal congressional approval. He told Truman that the Administration would just get bogged down in hearings and idle talk when time was of the essence.

In retrospect, this was questionable advice. Sentiment for intervention was so strong that a resolution would have been shouted through Congress. Without one, when the war turned sour some months later, congressional critics were able to inveigh against "Truman's war." Acheson's advice also set an unfortunate precedent of presidential authority for Vietnam. But at the time, it merely appeared that he was being decisive and bold. Truman honored and valued these qualities in Acheson. On July 19, the President sent his Secretary of State a handwritten note stating "for the record" that "the whole action was your initiative. . . . Your actions on Korea show that you are a great Secretary of State. . . . Your handling of the situation since [the invasion] has been superb."

•   •   •

Averell Harriman hated feeling out of the loop. By June of 1950, he had decided that his work implementing the Marshall Plan was done. He longed to leave Paris and return to Washington, and he let his desire be known through the back channel of Bob Lovett.

Acheson agreed that it was time to bring Averell home, but he told Lovett that he was not sure what to do with him. Harriman had immense prestige, which he carried in a somewhat stiff patrician manner that engendered as much jealousy as admiration. When Harriman abandoned Washington to run the Marshall Plan, the power vacuum had been quickly filled. "Washington is like a self-sealing tank on a military aircraft," Acheson said to Lovett. "When a bullet passes through, it closes up."

Still, Acheson had an idea. He thought it would be useful to have a White House official to oversee national security affairs. Clifford had performed this role informally, but he had gone back to his law practice, and his successor as counsel to the President, Charles Murphy, was not quite so comfortable with foreign policy questions. Acheson knew that he needed an insider in the White House to convince

Harry Truman of the need to pay for the massive military buildup called for by NSC-68. Though Acheson and Truman were in synch on most issues, they were not on this one. Truman's desire to balance the budget was stronger than his convictions about rearming against the Soviets. Harriman, however, was all for NSC-68, and had told Acheson so during a home leave that spring. Finally, the Secretary of State had one more use for a friend in the White House: to keep an eye on the Secretary of Defense. Louis Johnson by now was openly conspiring against Acheson.

Truman was amenable to taking on Harriman, but he warned Acheson that if he did, there would be gossip that Harriman was being primed to succeed Acheson at State. Long knives, he said, would be sharpened to fulfill that prophecy. Acheson was unfazed. He knew that his old schoolmate regarded him as a rival, but he knew as well that Harriman was an honorable man. He had known Averell for forty-five years, Acheson told Truman, and he trusted him.

•   •   •

Chip Bohlen was at his weekend cottage in Thiers, north of Paris, when the embassy called with news of war. He returned to Paris that night and met with Harriman in the morning. The two shared a discouraging prognosis. They saw no signs that the U.S. would take vigorous action to stop the Communist advance. Such inaction would dishearten the Allies, hurt U.S. prestige, and invite further Soviet adventurism.

While they were sitting in the American Embassy, mulling over this depressing prospect, a cable arrived from Truman: the U.S. was intervening in South Korea by air and sea. Bohlen and Harriman were exultant. Along with Ambassador David Bruce, they went to tell the news to Robert Schuman, the French Foreign Minister. To the French, appeasement carried a special shame. Schuman's eyes filled with tears. "Thank God," he said, "this will not be a repetition of the past."

That night, Bohlen wrote Kennan:

This is the clearest case of direct defiance of the United States, plus for the first time overt violation of the frontier that has occurred since the end of the war and you may be sure that all Europeans to say nothing of Asiatics are watching to see what the U.S. will do. It is a situation requiring maximum firmness, and even willingness to take major risks in order to convince the Kremlin that we mean business.

Harriman was not about to wait until August, his scheduled date of return to Washington. He was "carried away," Acheson later recalled, with enthusiasm for Truman's firmness. He could not stand delaying his return by even another hour, he told Acheson by transatlantic phone, while Washington was "electrifying the world." He wanted to go to the airport at once. Would Acheson "square it with the boss?"

Bohlen was instructed to fly back with Harriman in order to advise the State Department on possible Soviet moves. The two took off from Paris on a stormy night. "Everything was uncertain, and the bumpy plane ride symbolized our emotions," Bohlen later recalled. "In the early morning before arriving in New York, we ran into a thunderstorm. Suddenly the airliner dropped perhaps a thousand feet. As the plane lurched, sugar, dishes, and other kitchen supplies poured in the aisles. Unperturbed, Harriman, shaving with his hat on in the men's room, kept right on scraping away."

The two men were immediately sucked into the war effort. "It has been day and night, weekends, etc. . . . We did the right thing and God willing continue to do so," Bohlen wrote Avis in Paris. "Washington is a madhouse. There is no weakness of purpose here."

• • •

Where would the Soviets move next? The question gnawed at official Washington, undercutting the buoyant mood. The U.S. Embassy in Moscow could offer no clue; the ambassador reported that top Soviet officials were "out of town."

The question was asked, but not answered, at the war councils at Blair House. The one man who could have given the best estimate was not there. Acheson had specifically instructed that Kennan be invited to the Blair House meetings. But when department officials readied to go to Blair House on the first night, Barbara Evans, Acheson's secretary, awkwardly informed Kennan that there had been a mistake, his name had been omitted from the guest list. Kennan never found out why. It is possible that the oversight was inadvertent, or that White House staffers trying to hold down the size of the meeting had arbitrarily lopped his name off the list. In any case, it was too late to get him in to the dinner. Kennan, naturally, was quite put out. He later sarcastically wrote: "The dinner had the effect of defining—by social invitation, so to speak—the group that would be responsibly engaged in the handling of the department's end of the decision in the ensuing days." Kennan felt himself "relegated to the sidelines," a "floating kidney" in Bohlen's phrase, outside the chain of command and one step removed from real decisions.

Kennan exaggerates. Acheson did seek his advice, though whether he really listened is less clear. The next morning, Kennan was summoned to the Secretary's office. Acheson's great fear was that Korea was a fake, a diversionary move from a true Soviet onslaught in Western Europe. Kennan tried to reassure him. He told the Secretary that he did not believe the attack presaged further Soviet moves, that it was a local affair. "The Kremlin did not intend to bring about a general war or to involve itself in a showdown with the U.S.," he wrote Acheson a few days later. Rather, the Soviets preferred to see the U.S. get bogged down in a "profitless and discreditable war" or to "acquiesce in Communist seizure, thus suffering a tremendous prestige defeat everywhere." There was not likely to be "a new world war." The risk of conflagration was not in Europe—it was in Korea itself. With great foresight, he predicted that the Soviets would try to get the Chinese involved in Korea. Nervous about the U.S. rolling back up the peninsula toward Vladivostok, the Russians might, he warned, "introduce into North Korea their own puppet Chinese forces from Manchuria."

Yet, as he so often did, Kennan fogged up his insights by offering judgments that seemed contradictory. Perhaps hedging his bets, he warned that the Soviets "will make every effort to probe the firmness of our purpose and our nerves at other sensitive points, above all Germany and Austria, where their forces come in contact with ours."

Bohlen's waffling was even worse. At first he discounted the threat to Europe and worried about the Chinese. At a State Department meeting on June 30, six hours after Truman ordered in U.S. troops, Bohlen stated: "The Russians have a tradition of probing soft spots. Now they found a hard spot and probably would not directly intervene. They *would* however try to get the U.S. tied up in an Asiatic Communist trap—particularly with the Chinese."

Yet two weeks later, he wrote that the world situation was "one of extreme danger and tension" and that Korean fighting could lead to "new outbreaks of aggression possibly up to and including general hostilities." It was urgent, wrote Bohlen, that the U.S. build up its forces and not siphon off too many troops from Germany, or it would risk "invit[ing] another Berlin blockade."

Presented with conflicting analysis, Acheson, like other policy makers, was able to read into Kennan's and Bohlen's memoranda what he wanted to believe. And as always his eyes were on Europe. That was where the real Soviet threat lay; that was the part of the world that really counted. As in the past, he felt that Kennan might be right, the Soviets might not have any intention of attacking Europe, but he as policy maker could not afford to take the risk.

In his memoirs, Bohlen wrote that Acheson was misled "by those in the State Department who did not know Soviet Russia" into making too much of the Soviet threat in Europe at this time. This may well be. But the fact remains that Acheson read from *Bohlen's* memorandum when he warned a Cabinet meeting on July 14 that there were "real risks of the Soviets moving elsewhere" besides Korea.*

Acheson had another reason to argue that the Soviet menace was global and not confined to Korea. NSC-68 was little more than a piece of paper until the North Koreans attacked South Korea. The fear that this invasion was just the first step in a broad offensive by the Soviets proved highly useful when it came to persuading Congress to increase the defense budget. The total budget for defense and international security tripled—from $17.7 billion in fiscal year 1950 to $53.4 billion in FY 1951, a larger amount than Acheson had even dared mention in NSC-68.

• • •

The most dire warning of Soviet moves in Europe came from Jack McCloy, now the U.S. High Commissioner of Germany. In mid-July, McCloy sent Acheson a cable flatly stating that the U.S. would lose Germany, politically as well as militarily, unless it gave the Germans the means to fight.

McCloy was engaging in hyperbole, but he had reason to be concerned. The East Germans had built a large "police" force of at least fifty thousand men, the Volkspolizei, and the Kremlin had been making threatening noises toward West Germany that summer. After a year or so of relative calm following the Soviet humiliation of the Berlin blockade, West Germany again appeared in jeopardy. Its people were divided. A large body of neutralists, fearing that Germany would become the battlefield in an all-out war, believed it would be "better to be ruled by Bolsheviks than to live in caves."

Germany's new chancellor, however, looked west. Konrad Adenauer had been an obsure *bürgermeister* in the city of Cologne who

---

*What, in fact, were the Soviets' true intentions? The best evidence—from Khrushchev's memoirs—is that the Soviets had hoped to quickly snatch South Korea for the Communist orbit, and were surprised by the ferocity of the U.S. reaction. It is highly unlikely that the Kremlin had any plans to strike in Europe, though the Soviets were opportunists, and might have interpreted weakness in Korea as an invitation to meddle in Europe.

had been imprisoned during World War II for opposing the Reich. Now seventy-four, he conserved energy even more carefully than George Marshall, chuckling rather than laughing, speaking quietly, gesturing almost not at all. But *Der Alte* (the old man) was shrewd, and he had a clear vision of Germany's future. He had moved Acheson by speaking of the need for European unity when the two men had met for the first time in November of 1949. "Here was a man," Acheson later wrote, "whose mind—once the yeast of reconciliation began to work in France and Germany—could travel the road along which all our measures for the recovery and security of Europe had been moving."

Germany's democracy was still newborn; both Acheson and McCloy were touched by the sight of crowds yearning to see *Der Alte* as they traveled through the streets of Bonn with the German Chancellor at the conclusion of a visit by the American Secretary of State in 1949. Acheson suggested that Adenauer and he step out and shake some hands, as American politicians do. The two men walked into the town square and "everything exploded," Acheson recalled. "The police lines broke; we were picked up and carried to our train." Acheson was pleased for Adenauer's "popular triumph." But the people were cheering for him too. In later years, the Secretary of State would be denounced on American street corners, castigated in editorials, and hung in effigy from lampposts for being "soft" on Communists. He certainly would not be carried around, shoulder high, like a victorious football captain. Inevitably, Acheson's lifelong devotion to protecting Germany and the Western Alliance was made more visceral by the outpouring of feeling that day in November 1949. McCloy, swept up by the crowd as well, was equally overwhelmed by the roaring throng. For a discreet, behind-the-scenes operator to be the subject of such public adulation was a deeply affecting experience.

Personal emotions aside, Germany was of immense strategic importance to the U.S. The B-29 bomber, the Air Force delivery system for nuclear weapons, had a range of two thousand miles; midair refueling was still somewhat experimental. To be able to strike cities deep in Russia, the U.S. needed staging bases in Germany. U.S. war plans had originally called for pulling out of Europe and then reinvading in the event of Soviet aggression, but now the Pentagon was giving serious thought to keeping a permanent force on the Continent. In 1948, the U.S. began stockpiling ammunition and fuel at depots in eastern France (under the guise of the American Graves Registration Command). There was no question that the best way to defend Europe was to take on the Russians before they had rolled to the Rhine. But that meant rearming Germany. Five years after Hitler shot himself in his bunker, this was not an easy thing to persuade the Europeans to do.

The rearming of Germany was the last great question of the postwar Western Alliance and the rebuilding of Europe. It was a highly delicate issue; having been invaded three times by Germany in less than a century, the French were loath to see Germany under arms once more. In the face of such passion and deep suspicion, the most careful, gingerly diplomacy was required. In the end, the rearming of Germany was achieved less by cogent arguments than by close friendships.

Acheson had recommended McCloy as German High Commissioner in the spring of 1949. He had picked McCloy because he knew him and trusted him, and because he had to find someone who was acceptable both to Averell Harriman and the U.S. Army, two roughly equivalent forces. Harriman, the administrator of the Marshall Plan in Paris, had squabbled with General Clay, the Military Governor of Germany. Harriman thought Clay was building Germany at Europe's expense and Clay thought Harriman was milking Germany for Europe's benefit.

McCloy knew both men. He had gotten Clay his job as Military Governor, after turning it down himself when FDR first offered it in 1945. McCloy had told FDR that Germany needed to be run by a military man so soon after its conquest. By the spring of 1949, however, he felt that Germany was ready for civilian government. Clay by then was ready to step down as Military Governor, and the title was to be dropped; a civilian "High Commissioner" would administer still-occupied Germany. In April, when Truman asked McCloy to take the post ("the toughest job in the Foreign Service," the President warned), McCloy accepted.

McCloy was careful to make sure he had absolute authority—including control over the money meted out to Germany by Harriman's ECA. Friendship quickly served to overcome turf struggles. As soon as Harriman heard that McCloy had been appointed High Commissioner, he ceased to insist on control of ECA funds in Germany. McCloy could "write his own ticket," Harriman told Robert Murphy, who had served as the top State Department official under Clay.

McCloy was largely left alone by his bosses in Washington to do as he pleased in Germany. When McCloy asked for instructions from Truman on one occasion, the President replied, "Now look, I sent you over there to run it and you're doing a good job. You'll hear from me when you aren't. Now let's talk about the Civil War." (Truman knew the western campaigns, McCloy knew the eastern ones.)

In later years, McCloy would liken the dictatorial power that his predecessor, General Clay, had enjoyed as Military Governor to that of a "Roman proconsul." But as High Commissioner, McCloy devoted himself most strenuously to returning power to the Germans. He was, to be sure, a hands-on administrator at times. He enjoyed such exercises as persuading Sweden to provide Germany with wooden pit-props to get German coal mines going again. Yet he brought to his job great sensitivity to the devastated psyche of the German people. He wanted to restore their self-respect and sense of worth, to remind them, as historian Alan Brinkley has noted, that they were the people of Beethoven and Goethe as well as Hitler. When he saw signs in the American colony in Frankfurt that read "Entry Forbidden for Civilians," he demanded that the signs be torn down right away. He told American officials in Bonn to speak German, or learn it as fast as possible.

By making common cause with Adenauer, whom he greatly admired, he slowly transformed the U.S. role from occupier to partner. They were an unlikely couple in some ways, the buoyant, athletic American who lived in a big house above the Rhine with his own tennis court, and the modest, restrained German who had spent much of World War II in hiding or in prison. Yet McCloy listened closely to Adenauer; so much so that some wags began calling the German Chancellor the "real McCloy."

The Nuremberg trials were over by the time McCloy arrived, but the U.S. government was still committed to purging Germany of its evil past. McCloy criticized "the amazing docility and acquiescence of the greater part of the German people toward Nazi outrages." But as ever a pragmatist, he preferred restoring Germany to punishing it. He continued the denazification program to rid government of all former Nazis, but eliminated its excesses, such as removing the children of Nazi parents so they would not become "infected."

When McCloy began reviewing and reversing sentences meted out to war criminals, he inevitably aroused controversy. American liberals like Eleanor Roosevelt and Supreme Court Justice Robert Jackson, the Nuremberg prosecutor, were particularly indignant when McCloy released an important cog in the German war machine, Alfred Krupp, who was serving a long sentence for employing slave labor in his family's armament factories. In the Washington *Post*, cartoonist Herblock drew a smiling Jailer McCloy opening Krupp's cell, while in the distance Stalin snapped a photo for his propaganda album.

McCloy believed that Krupp was a "weakling" and a "playboy," and that he was a "scapegoat" for his father's crimes. Others insisted, however, that the younger Krupp was both in accord with Nazism and fully in control of Krupp armaments in the last years of the war. Nonetheless, McCloy was bothered by the arbitrary confiscation of the Krupp property; it offended his strong Wall Street lawyer's belief in property rights. In 1951 Krupp walked out of prison to a champagne breakfast and resumed control of the family armaments industry.

For years thereafter, critics charged that McCloy had released Krupp in order to ease the path of German rearmament. "A damnable lie," McCloy responded, and in fact there is no basis to believe that McCloy cynically set out to "buy" German rearmament by freeing war criminals. Still, there can be no question that by 1951 McCloy was worrying far less about Nazis than about making Germany strong enough to resist the Soviets.

The Korean War hastened his sense of urgency. "Korea brought Europe to its feet," he later wrote. "The realization that the Soviets were prepared to unleash armed forces to extend their power aroused Europe and particularly Western Germany, whose situation presented a parallel unpleasant to contemplate."

The interested parties were badly divided over the question of German rearmament. The Pentagon was unwilling to send U.S. soldiers to defend Europe unless the Germans contributed their share. The French bitterly resisted any German Army. McCloy too was wary of resurgent German militarism. Indeed, until the shock of the Korean War, he had opposed German rearmament. To McCloy, the challenge was to make Germany secure without arousing once more German bellicosity—as historian Thomas Schwartz phrased the dilemma, "to reconcile the West's need for Germany with her fear of it."

The way to overcome old nationalist hatreds, McCloy believed, was to nurture within Europe a sense of unity, of common needs and purpose. Throughout the chaotic postwar years, McCloy never lost sight of his overriding goal: to create a unified, economically sound Europe that could stand secure against the Soviets. McCloy was fond of telling Adenauer that he had come over to Europe twice in his lifetime because of a Franco-German war, and that as the representative of the United States, he was "determined to end hostilities for once and for all."

To achieve such a goal, to mediate between fractious and suspicious historic rivals, required an honest broker of exceptional judgment and patience. McCloy was one of the few men—if not the only man—whose word was taken with equal faith in Bonn, Paris, and Washington. His sincerity was so evident, his manner so amiable, his optimism so persistent that he was able to overcome deep and long-standing animosities in European capitals.

McCloy was fortunate to have as his mentor and ally in the cause of European unity his old friend and law client Jean Monnet, "the inspirer." Monnet's vision was of a United States of Europe, and although he never realized it, he did much to break down enmities and make European nationals work closely together after the war. McCloy and Monnet collaborated in 1950 to help create the European Coal and Steel Community, pooling the coal-mining resources of France and Germany, a great diplomatic feat for two countries so recently and so often at war. In the early autumn of that year, Monnet proposed to McCloy that they try something of the same with an army, a European Defense Community into which German soldiers would be gradually integrated.

To Monnet's delight, McCloy agreed to push the idea. The French statesman later wrote, "McCloy brought with him the contrasting views of Acheson and Adenauer, both of whom trusted him implicitly as we did ourselves. I knew that he would believe what we had to tell him, and that in turn he would be believed in both Bonn and in Washington, so great was the respect he inspired by his independence and goodwill." McCloy worked easily with the U.S. embassies in Paris and London as well: his brother-in-law, Lew Douglas, was ambassador to England, while David Bruce, the able U.S. emissary to France, was an old friend. In Washington, another of McCloy's old colleagues, Averell Harriman, was "absolutely convinced" as well that Germany had to be brought into a military alliance; his strong voice was sure to be heard in the White House.

This "cabal" of friends, as Acheson called them, had an exceedingly arduous time persuading France and Germany, not to mention Congress and the Pentagon, to agree on a European Army. The infighting and political posturing at times discouraged even the irrepressible McCloy. In January of 1951, for instance, he wrote Felix Frankfurter, "Things are at sixes and sevens again and I am almost depressed." Not until 1955 would German soldiers actually take the field, and in the end, the French Assembly rebelled against the idea of a truly "integrated" army, preferring to maintain separate forces under a NATO banner. Nonetheless, France was persuaded to accept what it had long dreaded: German rearmament. Bound by economic and military ties, France and Germany embarked on two decades of secure prosperity, the "economic miracle" of the fifties and sixties. McCloy was able to claim without boasting: "We made unthinkable another European civil war. We ended one of history's longest threats to peace."

McCloy's goal had been to rebuild an independent Europe. He even hoped—naïvely, it turns out—that one day the U.S. would be able to withdraw its troops from the Continent and let Europe defend itself. But inevitably and inextricably, the activist role played by McCloy, as well as the other distinguished emissaries recruited by Acheson, bound together the security of America and Western Europe. For a nation so steeped in isolationism, that was a breathtaking departure. It required, Acheson told the British and French Foreign Ministers in September of 1950, "a complete revolution in American foreign policy and in the attitude of the American people."

•   •   •

In July of 1950, Truman summoned his new special assistant for national security affairs, Averell Harriman, to his office and gave him his first assignment. "Help Dean," the President instructed. "He's in trouble."

Harriman was in essence the first in a long line of National Security Advisers. But he viewed his role differently from his more modern successors, like Henry Kissinger and Zbigniew Brzezinski. He had a tiny staff. He was anonymous. More importantly, he was not the Secretary of State's rival. Indeed, he saw his job as *defending* the Secretary.

He was, at first, a bit of a fifth wheel around the White House. He did not fit in at all well with Truman's cronies. He was too stiff; he did not play poker; in Key West he wore plain white shirts, rather than loud, flowered ones. He was, Bob Lovett recalls, a little disheartened by it all.

He did have good political instincts, at least better ones than Acheson. Harriman had recommended that the President get a resolution out of Congress backing U.S. engagement in Korea. Acheson had scoffed at the idea. Asking Congress for support, the former lawyer huffed, was like asking one more question of a hostile witness, the question that destroys you. Truman had agreed with Acheson, and publicly described the conflict not as a real war, of the sort that required congressional declarations, but rather as a "police action." Later, after he had been held solely responsible for a "police action" that cost more than fifty thousand American men, Truman would have more respect for Harriman's political judgment.

Acheson's enemies were beginning to circle by that summer, chief among them the Secretary of Defense, Louis Johnson. Already, Johnson had been leaking stories to reporters that U.S. intervention in Korea had been slow because of Acheson's foot dragging (quite the opposite was true) and that Truman was thinking of dumping his Secretary (equally false). Harriman's job was to keep an eye on Johnson and to keep Acheson out of harm's way.

Harriman could hardly have been blamed if he felt a twinge of ambivalence. The job he wanted more than another other was Dean Acheson's, and he had reason to believe that his old schoolmate had barely edged him out for the post eighteen months earlier. Always tight, he had given Truman's re-election campaign only five hundred dollars in 1948. If he had given more, he later grumbled, half jokingly, he might have been Secretary of State. Harriman did not have to wait long to be tempted. Only three days after he had arrived in Washington, he was in Louis Johnson's office for a chat. Johnson got on the phone to Bob Taft, the Republican leader, and in Harriman's presence congratulated Taft for calling for Acheson's resignation on the floor of Congress. "That was something that needed to be said," Johnson exclaimed to Taft. Hanging up the phone, he said directly to Harriman that if Acheson was fired, then he, Johnson, would personally "see that Harriman was made Secretary of State."

Harriman's response was to go directly to Truman and tell him of Johnson's sedition. He gruffly told the President, "I can't be bought that easily." Harriman suggested that Acheson fight back with leaks, but Acheson shrewdly refused. He knew that Johnson would sink himself in due course.

•　•　•

While Harriman had been rebuilding Europe as administrator of the Marshall Plan, postwar Japan was being restored by another high sovereign, General of the Army Douglas MacArthur, the supreme commander of U.S. forces in the Pacific.

MacArthur had single-handedly introduced democracy to Japan after the war. Though careful to respect the symbolic authority of the emperor, he ruled like a *genro*, the senior statesmen who had steered Japan from behind the throne during the nineteenth century. In a stream of edicts, MacArthur legally emancipated women, empowered labor unions, and began to break up the feudal *zaibatsu*, the ruling oligarchy that had dominated Japan's commerce for centuries. His administration "is a model of government and a boon to peace," pronounced *The New York Times*.

MacArthur's reformism, however, had disturbed the Cold Warriors in Washington. The wrenching changes, especially the attack on the *zaibatsu*, had in the view of men like Forrestal and Kennan left Japan unstable and thus vulnerable to Communist subversion. In February of 1948, the author of containment had been dispatched to set MacArthur straight.

Kennan found relations between Washington and MacArthur "so distant and so full of mistrust that my mission was like nothing more than that of an envoy charged with opening up communications and arranging the establishment of diplomatic relations with a hostile and suspicious foreign government." Surprisingly, however, the shy diplomat and the bluff general got along quite well, perhaps because both were in their own way visionaries. MacArthur, as it turned out, needed little convincing that Communism was a threat to the Far East as well as Europe. Kennan was able to persuade MacArthur to shift his emphasis from political reform to economic restoration. Thus was launched Japan's economic miracle. "I consider my part in bringing around the change to have been, after the Marshall Plan, the most significant constructive contribution I was able to make in government," Kennan later wrote. Japan was firmly established as a bulwark against Communism. But it was to be the last time MacArthur politely heeded Washington's advice.

Entering his eighth decade, the old warrior was not content to serve out his days as a peacetime preconsul. Though he knew war well enough to abhor it, he was exhilarated when North Korea attacked the South. Assuming command of U.S. forces, he did not regard the war as a local "police action" but rather as his final and greatest battle, fought not just against the North Koreans, but against Communism itself.

Envisioning a wider war for the control of all Asia, he did not share Acheson's reluctance to "tie up with the G'mo." He saw Chiang Kai-shek as a potential ally, a useful tool in turning back the Communist tide. At the end of July, he set out to court the Generalissimo at his island sanctuary.

He was effusively welcomed. He kissed the hand of Madame Chiang and called Chiang "my old comrade in arms," even though they had never met before. Considerable toasting and banqueting and reviewing of troops followed. State Department officials along for the trip were conspicuously frozen out of all discussions. When he had had his fill, MacArthur issued an effusive release in praise of the G'mo and returned to Tokyo.

Truman and Acheson sensed distant trouble, especially when back-channel sources told them that MacArthur, seventy years old and approaching Valhalla, was itching to fight Communists anywhere and everywhere, including the mainland of China. It was a hint of the coming disaster, though at the time Acheson was distracted by his belief that MacArthur was mainly posturing for the Republican Right. Like many in Washington, Acheson assumed that MacArthur wanted to retire from the Army into the White House.

Truman got on the phone to Bob Lovett in New York, where Lovett was still quietly working at Brown Brothers, Harriman and resisting government employment (most recently turning down the post of ambassador to NATO). Truman knew that Lovett was the best source on Harriman. "What kind of investigative reporter do you think Averell would make?" the President asked. Lovett, knowing Harriman's doggedness, answered that he would be a shrewd and aggressive one.

In early August, Truman dispatched Harriman to Tokyo as his personal envoy to the general. "Tell him two things," Truman instructed. "One, I'm going to do everything I can to give him what he wants in the way of support; and secondly, I want you to tell him that I don't want to get into a war with the Chinese Communists." Truman also told him to ferret out just what MacArthur had promised to Chiang.

"Hello, Averell," said the general, as Harriman stepped off the plane in Tokyo. "Hello, Doug," said Harriman. Reporters noticed that MacArthur seemed somewhat taken aback by the informality of Harriman's greeting; the general had been running Japan for five years and was not accustomed to being called by his first name. Harriman refused to be intimidated by MacArthur. He had duck hunted with him at Arden when MacArthur was superintendent of West Point in the early twenties. (And, as Harriman later recalled, "his first wife was a prom girl in New Haven, so I knew her.") In 1945, drawn as ever to "collecting" great men, he had gone to see MacArthur in Tokyo on his way back from Moscow. The two had gotten on well at the time; MacArthur now told Harriman that he had been the first to warn him about the Russians.

Over eight hours, not counting meals, the two talked about fighting wars in Asia. MacArthur was dramatic about the fatalism of the enemy.

He described Orientals "folding their arms as a dove folds his wings, relaxing and dying." With that, MacArthur folded his arms and sighed.

MacArthur assured Harriman that the Russians and the Chinese would not intervene, and that he would not provoke them. Harriman got down to the real purpose of his trip. "The President wanted me to tell you," he declared in his stiff, gruff way, "that you must not permit Chiang to be the cause of starting a war with the Chinese Communists on the mainland, the effect of which might drag us into world war." MacArthur's reply was predictable, if not altogether sincere: "As a soldier, I will obey any orders that I receive from the President."

Harriman was not convinced. In his report to Truman, he wrote:

> For reasons that are rather difficult to explain, I did not feel that we came to a full agreement on the way we believed things should be handled on Formosa and with the Generalissimo. He accepted the President's position and will act accordingly, but without full conviction. He has a strange idea that we should back anybody who will fight Communism, even though he would not give an argument why the Generalissimo's fighting Communists would be a contribution toward the effective dealing with the Communists of China.

Before saying goodbye to him, MacArthur had burst out to Harriman, "We should fight Communists everyplace—fight them like hell!" As they walked to the plane, MacArthur exclaimed, loudly so the reporters could hear, "The only fault of your trip was that it was too short!"

Truman had quietly given Harriman another reporting assignment: to see if he thought MacArthur was mentally and physically capable of command. There is no mention of MacArthur's health in Harriman's written report, perhaps because what he had to say was too delicate to commit to paper. He must have said something to alarm the President, because almost immediately Truman dispatched a doctor he trusted, Major General Frank Lowe, to "report on MacArthur's physical condition and ability to withstand the tremendous stresses incident to his duty." The doctor, failing to diagnose megalomania, pronounced MacArthur "hale and hearty."

MacArthur held his tongue for barely two weeks before he defied the Administration on Formosa. On August 25, the U.S. ambassador to the U.N., Warren Austin, declared that his country would not use Formosa as a base to attack China. The same day, Acheson got a call that the news wires were moving the advance text of a message from MacArthur to be read to the Veterans of Foreign Wars celebrating the strategic importance of Formosa as an "unsinkable aircraft carrier." In his prepared remarks, MacArthur fulminated: "Nothing could be more fallacious than the threadbare argument by those who advocate appeasement and defeatism in the Pacific that if we defend Formosa we alienate continental Asia."

This was a direct slap at Acheson. He immediately asked Harriman to show the wire to Truman. Truman was even more furious; when he met with his top advisers the next morning, Acheson recalled, his lips were white and compressed. The President told Defense Secretary Louis Johnson that he wanted MacArthur to retract his statement. Johnson agreed but quickly got cold feet. After the meeting he called Acheson and told him that the Joint Chiefs feared that MacArthur would be embarrassed. Couldn't MacArthur just say he was expressing his own views? Acheson said no, that the issue was clear, and that Johnson should do as the President had ordered. Johnson said that it was not clear to him what the President had ordered. Acheson had no patience with equivocation. "Louis," he said angrily, "don't argue with me as to whether the President's order makes sense or not. I heard him give it, and you accept it. Whether it can be done or not, you better do it."

Johnson quickly tried to recruit Harriman as an ally against Acheson in this dispute, but by now he should have known better. In fact, Harriman, with his strong sense of loyalty to the President, argued that MacArthur should be sharply reprimanded, even if the effect was to make him resign.

Truman himself finally called Johnson and dictated an order to MacArthur. Incredibly, Johnson still waffled. Truman had to order Johnson as his commander in chief to carry out his instructions.

In his memoirs, Truman says that he considered firing MacArthur at this time, but decided against it, fearing a Republican uproar. He later regretted having missed his chance. The incident did at least give him an excuse to fire Louis Johnson, whom he had wanted to unload for months. The Defense Secretary's machinations against Acheson had become too open; on August 25, Marquis Childs had reported that Johnson was feeding the Republicans damaging information about Acheson. On September 12, Truman forced Johnson, weeping, to sign the letter of resignation.

·   ·   ·

Mrs. Stewart Alsop heard the news of Johnson's resignation on the radio just as Averell Harriman was arriving at her house for a dinner party. "Did you hear the news, Ave?" she asked as he came in the front door. Harriman, normally not the most demonstrative of men, swept her up in his arms and spun her around the hall.

Harriman had begun thinking about Louis Johnson's replacement as Secretary of Defense almost the moment Johnson tried to importune him into betraying Acheson at the end of June. The very next day, July 1, Harriman and Acheson had driven down to Leesburg to visit George C. Marshall. They found the old general alert and back in good health. At Harriman's suggestion Truman went to see Marshall later that month; in August, while Johnson was still Secretary, Truman had asked Marshall if he would be willing to come back and take over the Defense Department in its wartime hour of need. Marshall had dutifully said yes. Harriman's last mission in these quiet negotiations was to make sure Mrs. Marshall was agreeable. On September 7, five days before he fired Johnson, Truman recorded in his diary, "Harriman went to Leesburg today and had lunch with him, and they talked it out. Wonder of wonders, Mrs. Marshall is for it!"

As his number two, his chief of staff, Marshall wanted Bob Lovett. But he was worried that Lovett would not want to untie his complicated financial strings to his banking partners for yet a third time in ten years. Marshall expressed his concern to Acheson, who dismissed it. He predicted that Lovett would be waiting by the phone for Marshall's call.

At 7 A.M. on September 14 the phone rang beside Lovett's bed at his house in Locust Valley. Lovett rolled over and said to his wife, "It must be the White House, only the White House calls at seven A.M." Adèle heard him say, "Yes, sir, yes, sir," and hang up. "Well?" she asked. Lovett replied that the President had told him that General Marshall had been asked to take the job as Secretary of Defense and agreed to do it only if he could have Bob Lovett as his deputy. "I said yes. What else could I say?" "How about no?" answered Adèle.

In the last year, Lovett had turned down Truman when he asked him to be ambassador to NATO, Acheson when he asked him to be ambassador to London, and McCloy when he asked him to be his number two and designated successor at the World Bank. He liked to say that there were only three people he could not say no to, his wife, Henry Stimson, and General Marshall. In fact, the list was shorter.

Louis Johnson had been sworn in as Secretary of Defense at a large celebration in the Pentagon courtyard. Attendance had been required for Pentagon employees. When Marshall was sworn in, he refused to have his picture taken; his counsel, Felix Larkin, had to cajole him by saying that a proper record was necessary. Lovett moved into the office next door without any public stir at all. But he spent three nights picking Larkin's brain to find out who were the troublemakers in the Defense Department.

• • •

The war in Korea went badly at first. The North Koreans were effective and ruthless soldiers who were known to tie up their captives and bayonet them. The American Army, softened by Japanese occupation duty, developed "bug-out" fever. Defeatism set in among senior officers, and U.S. correspondents began writing about an "American Dunkirk." By mid-July, the North Koreans had nearly driven U.S. forces off the end of the peninsula and into the sea. Hanging on to a small perimeter at Pusan, the Army was finally ordered by General Walton "Johnny" Walker to "stand or die."

In Washington, however, Kennan and his successor as Policy Planning director, Paul Nitze, were already trying to figure out what to do after North Korea was defeated. It might seem remarkable that these two men were able to work together at all, given their fundamental divergence over national security strategy. But it was a hallmark of their relationship that Nitze and Kennan, so different in their world views and personalities, remained respectful friends. Invited by Acheson to have lunch with Nitze at P Street shortly after he returned to Washington during the first week of the war, Kennan quickly dispelled any awkwardness that might have lingered from their battle six months earlier over the Super bomb and NSC-68. "When I left Washington," Kennan drolly greeted the Secretary and the Policy Planning director, "it never occurred to me that you two fellows would go ahead and make policy on behalf of the United States without consulting me."

In fact, it turned out, Kennan and Nitze were of like minds on Korea. Although Kennan had strongly backed intervention, he believed U.S. war aims should be sharply limited: the U.S. should merely try to restore the status quo between North and South. Trying to reunite all of Korea under non-Communist leadership ran too great a risk of provoking the Soviets or the Chinese. Nitze shared this view. Despite the sweeping rhetoric of NSC-68, Nitze was acutely conscious of how ill equipped the U.S. was to fight distant wars. In late July,

Nitze and Kennan drafted a paper advising the Secretary that the U.S. forces should push north of the 38th parallel dividing the two Koreas only for the purpose of driving the North Koreans out the South. If possible, fighting should be restricted to south of the parallel.

Nitze and Kennan were astute about the Russians and the Chinese, but they failed to consider U.S. politics. Here was a chance to roll back the Reds, prove that the Administration was not "soft" on Communism, and avenge, at least symbolically, the loss of China. John Foster Dulles, who had taken a somewhat vaguely defined job as "consultant" to the State Department that spring after a brief term as senator from New York, and who was acutely sensitive to the Republican right, was already pushing: on July 14, he wrote Nitze that the U.S. should "obliterate" the 38th parallel.

There was another State Department official who could sense the politics of the moment, a bald, round-faced, chain-smoking former army colonel from Cherokee County, Georgia, named Dean Rusk.

• • •

Rusk, often dour and bland, at other times quietly wry, was an unusual bureaucrat. He had that spring volunteered for a demotion, from Deputy Under Secretary of State to Assistant Secretary for Far Eastern Affairs, or FE as it was called in the department. The McCarthyites had hounded the last head of FE, W. Walton Butterworth, out of the job for being unduly soft on Communism. To protect him, Acheson had quietly packed Butterworth off to a diplomatic posting in Sweden. To Acheson's amazement, Rusk offered to take this highly exposed thankless job. Acheson was so grateful that years later he cited Rusk's selfless willingness to take on FE when John Kennedy asked him who would be a good Secretary of State.

Rusk took the job because he was the consummate good soldier, but for other reasons as well. One was a fascination, which would grow into an obsession, with China and the Far East. Unlike Acheson and most of his peers, Rusk was not a Europeanist. Also unlike Acheson, Rusk was able to get along with congressmen, even right-wing Republicans. In fact, Rusk later said that he knew he would be immune from attack if he took on FE. He had made a point of cultivating conservative senators, knew what they wanted, knew that in return they would tell McCarthy to lay off him. Rusk had also grown close to Dulles, who he accurately guessed would be the next Secretary of State. It was Rusk who persuaded Acheson earlier that spring to give

Dulles a job in the State Department. By making Dulles an insider he knew that the department was buying a measure of protection against the right.

Rusk would remain an anomaly through his long career, secretive, often misunderstood, both over- and underrated. He was adopted by the Establishment, not born into it. Rusk had grown up dirt poor in rural Georgia, the son of a Presbyterian minister whose voice had failed him. Young Rusk was intensely religious, but he quit Sunday school because his clothes were shabbier than those of the other children. At times, he went barefoot, and his underwear was made from flour sacks. His ambition, as a boy, was plain: at age twelve, he wrote "What I Plan to Do for the Next 12 Years"; the list of achievements culminated at Rhodes scholar. Rusk went to Davidson College in North Carolina, which he dubbed a "poor man's Princeton." After a career as campus Big Man, he won his Rhodes. At Oxford, he was polished up in the junior common room and permanently seared by watching the Oxford Union resolve not to "fight for King and Country." He would through all his life cite the misbegotten pacifist Oxford Movement as a lesson in preparedness.

He became, briefly, an academic, dean of Mills College, a proper women's school in California. During the war, he was a superb staff officer in the China-Burma-India theater. When it was over, he came to the State Department, where he eventually handled U.N. matters. He was much more of a believer in the U.N. than Acheson. Indeed, he had a strong streak of universalist idealism. He was at heart an internationalist do-gooder, but his idealism was well concealed beneath the self-effacing exterior of an efficient, hardworking staff man.

•   •   •

As the head of the Office for Far Eastern Affairs, Rusk pressed hard to allow U.S. forces to cross the 38th parallel into North Korea in the summer of 1950. He wanted to show the Republican right that the Administration was not "soft" and the Soviets that the U.S. had learned the lesson of Munich. "We must now make it clear to an aggressor that aggression carries with it their certain destruction," he said in a speech on September 9. Joined by his subordinate, John Allison, head of the Northeast Asian Affairs desk, Rusk was able to gradually swing of weight of bureaucratic Washington to his side, despite the warnings of Kennan and Nitze about the risk of Soviet or Chinese intervention. By the end of August, the State Department draft of U.S. war aims called for crossing the 38th. The document conceded that intervention by the Chinese was "possible but not probable."

Increasingly isolated in this slow-moving bureaucratic process, Kennan continued to warn of the dangers. In late August, he wrote Acheson that the Russians would not tolerate the U.S. drawing too close to their borders and that "we must be prepared at any time for extreme Soviet reaction." He even had the temerity to suggest that the U.S. calm the Chinese Communists by admitting them to the United Nations. Had his advice been accepted, the U.S. could have averted a terrible military defeat in the months ahead, punctured the myth of monolithic Communism, and begun the process of recognition that, instead, had to wait more than two decades. As it was, Kennan wrote, "Our policy toward the rival Chinese regimes is one almost sure... to strengthen Peking-Moscow solidarity rather than weaken it." Kennan accurately warned that the Administration was giving MacArthur too much latitude to set policy. While he was at it, he threw in a caveat about Vietnam that, ignored at the time, would be hauntingly accurate: "We are getting ourselves into the position of guaranteeing the French in an undertaking which neither they nor we, nor both of us together, can win."

As usual, Kennan's prescience was lost on the policy makers, and, as usual, his sense of futility became unbearable. "The nervousness and consciousness of responsibility is so great around Washington that it is impossible to get people to set their signatures to anything as risky and as little founded in demonstrable fact as an analysis of Soviet intentions based on the subjective experience of persons like Chip and myself," he wrote in his diary on July 12. He was even more gloomy a month later, noting: "Never before has there been such utter confusion in the public mind with respect to U.S. foreign policy. The President doesn't understand it; Congress doesn't understand it; nor does the public, nor does the press. They all wander around in a labyrinth of ignorance and error and conjecture." To Bohlen, the melancholic Kennan said simply, "We're lost." At the end of August, Kennan packed up his family and began an indefinite leave from the State Department. He left Washington for Princeton, to study and write history at Robert Oppenheimer's Institute for Advanced Study.

Acheson had made a renewed effort to listen to Kennan and Bohlen that summer but he was again exasperated. "There is something about Soviet experts which makes them... dangerous reporters and advisers," Acheson later wrote a friend. "Their hunches are uncommunicable and must be accepted by those who have not the same occult power of divination. Chip as much said this to me, 'Dean, you came to this field too late to be able to get the feel for it.'" Acheson was hardly alone in his resentment; others at State felt "a certain intolerance" from Kennan and Bohlen "of views differing from their own." One colleague joked that Kennan probably disliked NATO because he failed to invent it.

Acheson returned from a one-week holiday in the Adirondacks at the end of August to find the decision on whether to cross the 38th parallel awaiting him. He dutifully read Kennan's memo advising him to say no and making such recommendations as admitting China to the U.N. The memo, Acheson recorded in his memoirs, was "typical of its gifted author, beautifully expressed, sometimes contradictory, in which were mingled flashes of prophetic insight and suggestions, as the document conceded, of total impracticability."

Acheson at first had favored merely restoring the status quo in Korea. He had explicitly stated this in a speech at the end of June. Two weeks later, he wrote Paul Nitze that the aim was to drive the North Koreans out of the South, not to reunite Korea. Still, he was uneasy about what the U.S. would do after the invaders had been driven out. Would its troops have to stand permanent guard on the border? He could not, as he wrote Nitze, "see the end of it, in other words, as the Virginians say, we have bought a colt." He also recognized the realities of warfare, that battlefields are fluid and difficult to control. MacArthur's troops could not be "expected to march up to a surveyor's line and just stop."

Acheson, though he did not like to admit it, was sensitive to political forces. Already, the Administration was being blamed for the war. Four members of the Senate Foreign Relations Committee charged that Truman had "sold out" Chiang at Potsdam and that his fall had led directly to the Korean War. Even Vandenberg endorsed the statement. Senator Wherry charged that "the blood of our boys in Korea" was on Acheson's hands. Congressman Hugh Scott accused the State Department ("the Hiss Survivors Association") of planning "to subvert our military victory by calling a halt at the 38th parallel. The scheme is to cringe here behind this line. . . ."

Acheson needed a clear-cut victory, not a protracted stalemate. His friends and aides began to sense that he was worried about political pressure and eager to find some way of winning over public support. "This was worry number one with him," recalls C. B. Marshall, a Policy Planning staffer at the time and later a close friend. In August, for instance, Acheson wrote to his deputy, Jim Webb, fretting that

"Wherry et al." would attack him for "giving the Communists the green light for aggression."

On September 7, Acheson tentatively decided that MacArthur should be allowed to push north over the 38th parallel. Yet he was still uneasy. He worried aloud about provoking the Soviets and told staffers working on the National Security Council draft of war aims to make it clear that MacArthur was not to actually drive across the border until he had specific orders from Washington.

•   •   •

In early September, MacArthur's forces were nowhere near the 38th parallel. They were still fighting a slow, hard battle up the peninsula. MacArthur, however, had been plotting one of the most audacious gambits in military history: as he described it, "a turning movement deep into the flank and rear of the enemy that would sever his supply lines and encircle all his forces south of Seoul."

MacArthur wanted to land twenty-five thousand men two hundred miles behind enemy lines and swiftly cut off the North Korean invasion by its tail. For his landing site, he picked the port of Inchon. The choice broke every rule for amphibious operations: there were no beaches, just seawalls; the landing would be into the heart of a city; an enemy fortress commanded the approach; the landing craft would have to maneuver through rocks and breakwaters in passages that were easily mined; a thirty-two-foot tide left mud flats at low water. Indeed, a landing was physically impossible for all but two days a month. MacArthur himself called the operation a "5,000 to one shot." The plan had going for it only the most essential element: surprise.

Averell Harriman played a crucial role in persuading MacArthur's superiors to approve this outrageous scheme, which the general had outlined for him when the two met in Tokyo in early August. Though Harriman knew little about military tactics, grand and audacious moves appealed to him. CHROMITE, as the plan was code named, was no more bold than some Harriman business ventures, like E. H. Harriman's scheme to build an around-the-world sea and rail line.

Harriman enthusiastically described MacArthur's strategy to Truman, another lover of bold strokes. Truman said he was persuaded, but added "you better get over to the Pentagon as fast as you can to convince Bradley and Johnson." The military establishment had already gone on record firmly opposing CHROMITE as far too risky.

At the Pentagon, Defense Secretary Johnson was in his last days on the job, on the verge of getting sacked by Truman, though Johnson did not know it. Harriman found the Defense Secretary steaming over Truman's decision to buck both him and the Joint Chiefs and approve CHROMITE. The Defense Secretary was becoming somewhat suspicious of Harriman, who had turned out not to be an ally but an adversary in his campaign against Acheson. Johnson angrily accused Harriman of poaching on military turf by persuading Truman to buy MacArthur's plan. "What have you done to the President?" he demanded. Harriman mumbled that he had just offered political advice. Johnson was highly doubtful, but he was trapped; he had his marching orders from Truman. "Well," Johnson spluttered, "the President has told me he wants this plan of MacArthur's supported."

It was up to MacArthur himself to convince the Joint Chiefs with a rousing peroration: "I can almost hear the ticking of the second hand of destiny," McArthur orated to a meeting of the top brass in mid-August. "We must act now or we will die. Inchon will succeed. And it will save a hundred thousand lives."

By brilliance and luck, CHROMITE turned the war around. On September 15 MacArthur's lightning strike routed the North Koreans, quickly recaptured Seoul, the South Korean capital, and left U.S. forces at the border, ready to drive north.

"There's no stopping MacArthur now," Acheson told Harriman after Inchon. The public clamor was uniform: to stop now, warned Senator Knowland, would be "appeasement of the Communists." Not only right-wing senators but *The New York Times* called for an all-out push to reunite Korea.

MacArthur's orders from Washington were somewhat ambiguous. They were designed at once to encourage him to wipe out the North Korean Army and at the same time be wary of the risk of Soviet or Chinese intervention. In general terms he was to push north of the 38th parallel, but he was to use only South Korean troops close to the Chinese border, and he was to break off contact if he encountered Russian or Chinese troops. One of the drafters, C. B. Marshall, recalled, "I was full of awareness that we were kidding ourselves with the neatness of the phrasing."

Acheson's young special assistant, Lucius Battle, was also worried that the orders were too vague. As he handed them to Acheson for his signature on September 27, he told the Secretary that the Joint Chiefs had already approved them, but he blurted that the orders were too broadly drawn, that MacArthur should be given more precise guidance. Acheson was at the moment standing in a suite at the Waldorf Astoria in New York, preoccupied with NATO matters. He turned to Battle and snorted, "For God's sake, how old are you?" Battle self-consciously answered that he was thirty-two. "Are you willing to take on the Joint Chiefs?" asked Acheson, as he scribbled his signature and went back to worrying about NATO.

Unbeknownst to Acheson, his idol, General Marshall, was making matters worse. The newly sworn-in Defense Secretary sent MacArthur an EYES ONLY cable with Truman's approval—but without showing it to Acheson—that told MacArthur, "We want you to feel unhampered tactically and strategically to proceed north of the 38th parallel." Marshall later explained that he was just trying to reassure MacArthur that he was free to cross the border into North Korea, despite the fuzziness of his formal orders. MacArthur, however, took Marshall's cable as a license to roam anywhere he pleased. He wired back, "I regard all of Korea open for military operations." No one in Washington contradicted him; indeed, a week later the U.S. pushed a resolution through the U.N. calling for the reunification of Korea.*

The warnings from China began immediately. India's ambassador to China, K. M. Panikkar, was the message bearer. A Chinese general told him on September 25 that the "Chinese did not intend to sit back with folded hands and let the Americans come up to their border." A more direct and highly placed message followed: at 5:35 A.M. on October 3, Acheson was awakened with a cable coded NIACT (meaning call to the Secretary's attention day or night) informing him that the Chinese Foreign Minister, Chou En-lai, had told India's Panikkar that if U.S. forces pressed north across the 38th parallel China would have to intervene.

The British were worried by Panikkar's reports and advised Acheson not to ignore them. Acheson was contemptuous. He dismissed the Indian ambassador as a Communist stooge and his warnings as the "mere vaporings of a panicky Panikkar." He told the British that "we

---

*Nominally, Korea was the U.N.'s war. With the Soviets cynically (and stupidly) boycotting the Security Council, the U.S. had been able to win U.N. resolutions denouncing the North Korean invasion and calling on U.N. members to collectively raise an army to drive out the invaders and restore peace. Indeed, fifteen member nations contributed 25,000 troops to the half-million-man main force (the South Koreans supplied 250,000), and MacArthur himself was designated Supreme U.N. Commander. To Harry Truman, Korea was the first test of the world organization's ability to enforce collective security. "We can't let the U.N. down!" Truman had sworn aloud the day after the war broke out. Acheson was perfectly willing to use the U.N. to harness world opinion. Even before he called Truman to tell him of the North Korean invasion on the night of June 24, he had summoned a special session of the U.N. Security Council. But Acheson had little faith in world government and privately regarded Korea as a test not of the U.N. but of America's ability to stand up to the Soviets.

should not be unduly frightened at what was probably a Chinese Communist bluff."

President Truman, meanwhile, was making plans to visit with General MacArthur on neutral territory, tiny Wake Island in the mid-Pacific. The purpose was partly political: Truman's advisers, with an eye on congressional elections only a month away, felt that MacArthur might be less useful to the Republican right if he was seen chatting amiably with Harry Truman. Nor could it hurt the President to bask in the hero of Inchon's reflected glory.

Acheson was skeptical. He said to Truman in his arch manner that while MacArthur had many of the attributes of a foreign sovereign and was quite as difficult as any, it did not seem wise to recognize him as one. He refused to go to Wake Island himself. Harriman, however, supported the trip as a necessary political gesture, and even brought Mrs. MacArthur a five-pound box of chocolates. When his plane landed on the remote island, Harriman hurried to intercept MacArthur before he got to Truman. The general gruffly asked him, "What's this meeting about?" Harriman said that Truman wanted to discuss how a political victory could be won in Korea now that MacArthur had won such a brilliant military victory. MacArthur seemed relieved. He grabbed Harriman's arm and told him that he had taken "an awfully big risk" at Inchon. Harriman reminded him that the President had taken a big risk in backing him.

MacArthur failed to properly salute his commander in chief, but was otherwise civil to the President. Truman got right to the point: Will the Chinese come in? No, MacArthur reassured him. The war would be wrapped up by Thanksgiving.

CHAPTER 18

Acheson and Lovett testify before Congress

NADIR

Disaster at the Yalu

In late October of 1950, U.S. and South Korean troops made sporadic but murderous contact with Chinese Communist troops in the barren hills of North Korea. Chairman Mao announced on November 2 that they were "volunteers" who had joined the North Korean Army to protect their homeland's hydroelectric plants along the Yalu River between Korea and China. Carrying old Japanese rifles and wearing cloth shoes, the Chinese were dismissed by MacArthur in a cable to Washington as "not alarming." Field commanders, however, reported that while the Chinese troops were poorly equipped, they were well disciplined. As a precautionary measure, MacArthur decided to take out the bridges over the Yalu. Washington was routinely informed.

Lovett saw the cable less than four hours before the first bombs were scheduled to fall. Looking at a map, he decided that the air strikes were a terrible idea. They might provoke the Chinese, but they would not stop the flow of troops, since the river was shallow and easily forded. He moved quickly to stop the mission, enlisting Acheson and Marshall.

MacArthur was indignant. He protested that Washington's interference "threatens ultimate destruction of forces under my command." He demanded that his cable be shown to the President, "as I believe your instructions may well result in a calamity of major proportions."

Such dire warnings, coming from someone who only a few days earlier had dismissed the Chinese incursions as "not alarming," made Washington wonder—not so much about the Chinese, who had suddenly broken off fighting and vanished back into the hills, as about MacArthur.

Lovett, in particular, was worried. He lost his usual geniality when he talked about the vainglorious general; his humor became more wicked. At meetings Lovett would imitate MacArthur flipping the hairs of his head to cover his bald spot. "You know those wisps of hair he so carefully combs over the crown of his head?" Lovett would ask. "Actually, he has no hairs on his head. It grows out his back and curls up around over his head."

General Marshall, too, was uneasy. He thought MacArthur's strategy for conquering the North was ill-conceived. He believed that MacArthur had wasted valuable time mounting another landing after Inchon, and allowed too many remnants of the defeated North Korean Army to slip out of the South. Then MacArthur had split his command into two forces, the Eighth Army and X Corps, driving up either side of the long spine of mountains running north–south through the country. It was difficult for the two columns to communicate, much less relieve each other. At nine-thirty meetings in the Pentagon, Marshall bore in on his subordinates with specific questions about troop movements and logistics. "How many men are in that unit?" he would demand. The Pentagon officers, never too sure of what MacArthur was up to, would give vague answers, and Marshall would say, "Never mind *about* how many. How many?"

Washington had no way of knowing what was really happening on the ground. The Pentagon did not learn the extent and nature of the firefights with the Chinese "volunteers" for almost a week. CIA reports about the enemy were so contradictory as to be meaningless. MacArthur was suspicious of the fledgling agency and sought to keep it uninformed. His own intelligence network was run by sycophants. General Charles Willoughby, head of the Far East command's intelligence, was inundated with raw data, but he had trouble accurately sorting through it. He knew, for instance, that the Chinese had half a million soldiers in Manchuria, just across the Korean border, but somehow never quite grasped the significance of this statistic, or called it to Washington's attention. He was also distracted that fall: he was writing a eulogistic history of MacArthur's Pacific campaigns against the Japanese.

Despite the intelligence lapses, Dean Acheson later said, "We had the clearest idea among ourselves of the utter madness and folly of what MacArthur was doing up north." Yet, as he later wrote Richard Neustadt, "We sat around like paralyzed rabbits while MacArthur carried out this nightmare."

Why? The question would gnaw at Acheson the rest of his life.

The written record discloses no shortage of discussion in Washington about MacArthur and his war plans. Between November 10 and December 4, the Secretaries of Defense and State and the Joint Chiefs of Staff met three times in the Pentagon War Room, the two Secretaries met five times with the President, and Acheson himself talked five more times with the President. The minutes of the meetings repeatedly reflect concern with MacArthur's moves, yet there is about them a sense of drift, almost helplessness. Acheson acknowledges in his memoirs, "Not one of us, myself prominently included, served [the President] as he was entitled to be served."

The Joint Chiefs were cowed by MacArthur. They had opposed CHROMITE and were now reluctant to second-guess the "Sorcerer of Inchon," as Acheson called him. The JCS did send MacArthur a "request for information" about the gap between the Eighth Army and X Corps, in military etiquette a broad hint from headquarters that the field commander was taking unnecessary chances. But MacArthur merely ignored the request. When the Army Chief of Staff, General J. Lawton Collins, went out to see MacArthur in December, he saluted and said, "Hello, General," as he stepped off the plane. MacArthur, nominally Collins's subordinate, just said, "Hello, Joe."

Acheson was scornful of the Chiefs' paralysis. But as he later said, he was faced with a dilemma. "Should I sit there uttering amateur questions to the Chiefs? Or go to the President and say, 'Look, I don't know anything about soldiering, but for heavens' sake, this is very bad.'" Acheson dismissed the second alternative because he could not advise the President to *do* anything. He would thus not be offering a solution, but merely passing the buck, a cardinal sin.

Acheson did go to General Marshall. Almost twenty years later, in

1967, Acheson wrote Marshall's biographer, Forrest Pogue, to say that he had privately asked General Marshall why, if he was dissatisfied with MacArthur's strategy, he did not order him to employ a different one, and if he refused, relieve him of command? Marshall replied that he was no longer Army Chief of Staff and that he must bend over backward to maintain a "civilian attitude." Marshall firmly adhered to a principle first established by Lincoln with Grant in the Civil War: that once a field commander has been assigned a mission "there must be no interference with his method of carrying it out."

This tradition of noninterference with the theater commander is usually cited by historians as the reason why Washington allowed MacArthur to plunge on heedlessly in the fall of 1950. Yet it did not satisfy Acheson. When he was writing his memoirs in the late sixties, he probed for a better understanding of what, in a letter to Paul Nitze, he called General Marshall's "curious quiescence." As Acheson wrote Pogue, Marshall's hands-off approach "never seemed very sensible to me, especially when MacArthur was violating military discipline and bullying his superiors." Acheson added, however, "I would rather say nothing than reflect [critically] on General Marshall."

Marshall was hardly blameless for Washington's paralysis that fall. Naturally cautious, by now old and careful to conserve his energy, he was not quite up to speed at the Pentagon, which he had taken over only at the end of September. He was made even more circumspect by his personal relationship with MacArthur. At his confirmation hearings, he had been badly abused by congressional fanatics who he knew were in league with MacArthur. If he were to remove MacArthur, he knew, he would set off a congressional fire storm and possibly even precipitate a constitutional crisis.

For more than three decades, ever since MacArthur had been the dashing battlefield commander in World War I and Marshall the brightest staff officer at headquarters, the two men had been rumored to be deadly rivals. Though Marshall did not much like MacArthur, the rumors were way overblown. Still, Marshall felt that he could not afford to show any trace of ill will toward his alleged foe in their official dealings. It was a characteristic response from someone so selfless and stoic, but it did not serve him well. In the fall of 1950, Marshall bent over so far backward to be neutral that he fell down, and abnegated his responsibility.

Marshall's failure hardly absolves Acheson. The Secretary of State had a policy-making responsibility that transcended military questions. Acheson may not have known much about soldiering, but he knew more about Chinese intentions than Marshall, having been warned by the Indian ambassador to Peking via the British. Later that fall—*after* disaster struck—Acheson would not hesitate to forcefully and repeatedly override the Pentagon on military matters. But in October and November of 1950, he was strangely paralyzed. His indecision can be explained only by the failure of government among friends.

So taken was Acheson with Marshall, so transfixed by his essential goodness and honor, that Acheson could not see that his former mentor was not up to the challenge of taming MacArthur. In his memoirs, Acheson writes how conscious Marshall was of protocol, refusing to enter rooms before Acheson and always sitting on his left. "To be treated so by a revered and beloved former chief was a harrowing experience," he records. Acheson goes on to write glowingly that for the first (and last) time the State and Defense departments were able to work as a team. Yet one has the sense that the relationship was almost too cozy; Acheson was too awed and Marshall too polite to disagree with each other.

Lovett was equally blinded by Marshall's halo. The aging general and his favorite "copilot" had grown so close that aides began to notice that they no longer needed to say much to each other; a few dozen words sufficed to resolve issues that would entangle normal bureaucracies for a day. "They communicated by osmosis," recalled Felix Larkin, the Pentagon's chief counsel. If his revered general refused to second-guess MacArthur, Lovett was not about to force the issue. He did not hesitate to entertain the Joint Chiefs with his imitations of MacArthur vainly combing his hair over his bald spot, but he made no effort to persuade them to stop MacArthur's suicidal trek to the Yalu. Lovett did fret with his friend Acheson over the general's foolhardiness, but he did not urge him to intercede with Truman or Marshall. Lovett regarded Acheson with an almost childlike affection. In mid-October, as Washington brooded over MacArthur's mad march a half a world away, the Deputy Secretary of Defense sent the Secretary of State one of the more peculiar notes ever to travel by interoffice mail: "Dear Stimme, I am tired. Will you please carry me? Gesundheit, Bobchen."

Ironically, Truman might have been better served if Louis Johnson had *not* been canned and replaced with Marshall. Had Johnson stuck up for MacArthur, as he surely would have, then Acheson, Lovett, and Harriman might very well have lobbied Truman to have them both fired.

It is likely that Acheson's independence of judgment was further clouded by his immense loyalty to Truman. The Secretary had become a genuine political liability to his boss and to the Democratic Party. McCarthy was in full cry that fall, stumping on behalf of Republican candidates in the November congressional elections, howling about "the Korea deathtrap we can lay to the doors of the Kremlin and those who opposed rearming, including Acheson." The Big Lie worked: The Democrats lost six Senate seats and two-thirds of their House majority. Truman was disconsolate; the only time his aide George Elsey recalls seeing him drunk was after the 1950 midterm elections.

Acheson wanted to help Truman. He was well aware of what McCarthy and the whole Republican Party would say if word got out that a striped-pants diplomat had tried to rein in the great Douglas MacArthur. Furthermore, Congress in January was scheduled to begin what was billed as "the Great Debate" over whether to station U.S. troops permanently in Europe. Acheson risked jeopardizing his beloved Western Alliance if he looked like an appeaser in Asia.

At the White House, Harriman was just as sensitive to the politics of the moment, if not more so. Years later, he said about the decision to cross the 38th parallel and conquer all of Korea, "It would have taken a superhuman effort to say no. Psychologically it was almost impossible to not go ahead and complete the job."

Harriman was an admirer of MacArthur's boldness. He had, after all, helped sell the general's daring plan to invade Inchon to the President when the Joint Chiefs were all timidly opposed. Yet, like his friends Lovett and Acheson, he too had qualms about MacArthur's plunge north. He thought MacArthur's staff was "third-rate," he later recalled, and felt that MacArthur's field commander, Walton Walker, was "incompetent." On November 24 at a meeting Acheson would later describe as "the last clear chance" to stop MacArthur, Harriman joined the chorus of doubters, worrying aloud that U.S. probes toward the Yalu would provoke the Chinese. At most discussions between the President's advisers and the top military brass that November, however, Harriman rarely spoke out. Inarticulate and ponderous in debate, Harriman was not much for holding forth at meetings. Furthermore, he felt that he had done all he could by helping to get rid of Louis Johnson and to replace him with Marshall. He saw his own role more as a fixer than a strategist, as the President's enforcer to make sure that orders were followed and that policy was not disturbed by rivalry and needless bickering. With Johnson gone, and Marshall and Lovett in the saddle, he felt Acheson had no more need for a

White House go-between to the Pentagon. He began attending fewer meetings between the two Secretaries.

Like Acheson, he was to regret his failure to loudly speak out against MacArthur's folly for the rest of his career. Questioned about his role almost two decades later, he fretted, "When I saw those divisions moving up to the Yalu River, I don't know why I didn't move."

•　•　•

On November 24, MacArthur launched what he called his "massive compression envelopment" to "close the vise" around the enemy. He told reporters that he would "have the boys home by Christmas."

The next day, 300,000 Chinese Communists, hidden in mountain gorges and ravines, exploded around the Eighth Army and X Corps with eerie cymbals, bells, whistles, shrieks, and cries of "Son of a bitch marine we kill! Son of a bitch marine, you die!" With heavy casualties, the American Army turned and fled south.

"We face an entirely new war," MacArthur cabled Washington. He blamed "conditions beyond control." "The Chinese have come in with both feet," Truman said to his shocked advisers. He asked for suggestions. General Marshall admitted that he had no answer. "We want to avoid getting sewed up in Korea," he said, but "how can we get out with honor?" Acheson, exhausted from passing the dreadful news to congressional leaders, who were less than gracious about it, said he was fearful of a world war. But he was against getting out. "We must find a line we can hold and hold it," he declared.

Acheson was thunderstruck. He later described what had happened as "the greatest disaster of the Truman Administration, of colossal importance to the history of the U.S." For him it was a time of great personal crisis. He knew that he had failed his President by not pressing him to stop MacArthur before it was too late. His wife, Alice, later said that she had never seen him so depressed, so fearful for the world. Characteristically he did not reveal his anguish to others. Instead, he kept an even temperament and faced up to the disaster.

Throughout the gloomy meetings of the next few days, Acheson's voice alone kept up one refrain: the U.S. must not withdraw from Korea. It had to hold. The military was in a state of near panic. MacArthur's army had suffered one thousand casualties in the first forty-eight hours and was now desperately fighting its way out of the Chinese trap. MacArthur himself had plunged into despair and was warning of the "complete destruction" of his command. To reporters he bitterly blamed Washington for restricting him from bombing Manchuria, "an enormous handicap, without precedent in history." Lovett read the cables with utter contempt. He told Acheson that MacArthur was "issuing posterity papers" to cover up his blunder. "He's scared," said Lovett.

The Joint Chiefs had virtually given up. They told Acheson that they needed to obtain a cease-fire to withdraw U.S. forces. Acheson answered, "There is a danger of our becoming the greatest appeasers of all time if we abandon the Koreans and they are slaughtered; if there is a Dunkirk and we are forced out, it is a disaster, but not a disgraceful one." General Bradley, the chairman of the Joint Chiefs, wondered mournfully whether "we could come home and just forget the matter." Acheson snapped, "Certainly not."

Yet Acheson could not order the Army to stand or die. He confessed to Truman that the U.S. might have to evacuate, or be driven into the sea. *"It looks very bad,"* the President wrote in his diary.

On the evening of December 3, Acheson, after a day of relentlessly gloomy meetings, was sitting in his office, feeling his strength ebb, when he received a lift from the most unlikely quarter.

•   •   •

Bohlen had watched the debacle from Paris with horror. "MacArthur got caught with his pants down," he told Cy Sulzberger of *The New York Times*. The old Russian hand worried that Acheson had no Soviet specialist to advise him during the crisis. So on December 1, he called Kennan by transatlantic phone at his farm in Pennsylvania and urged him to go to Washington and help.

Kennan arrived the next day and was briefed by Jim Webb, Acheson's number two. The briefing left "substantially no hope that we could retain *any* position on the peninsula," Kennan wrote Bohlen. The next evening, after the busy corridors of New State had emptied for the night, Kennan slipped down the hall and stuck his head inside the Secretary of State's office.

Its occupant, his proud bearing slightly sagging at the end of the another grueling day, rose to greet him. Kennan was shocked to see how exhausted the Secretary looked. Yet Acheson was as ever gracious to the old colleague whose advice he had so often spurned but whose friendship he still valued. "George," he said with a weary smile, "why don't you come home and stay with me?"

The two repaired to P Street. Acheson seemed so worn that Kennan did not want to even bring up the war with him. Yet as they settled down with a drink, the shy diplomat found Acheson charming, witty, and quite unbowed. Kennan reflected that he rarely agreed with Acheson anymore, their minds no longer meshed. Yet he could not help but admire his courage.

Inevitably they got to talking about MacArthur's erratic behavior, the wild and jittery mood of Washington, particularly in Congress and the military. Mrs. Acheson, listening to the two as they conversed across the kitchen table (it was maid's night out), recalls that Acheson, fidgeting, stood up. He and Kennan went out into the gallery and paced along the long stone passage by the French doors, frosted over this December evening, and into the front parlor. There, beneath the portrait of Bishop Acheson and the photos of Brandeis and Stimson, beneath the Yale rowing cup on the mantel, they talked of the need for staying power, for grit over the long haul.

Before Kennan went to bed that night, he sat down and wrote Acheson a longhand note.

In the morning, Acheson met the plane of Clement Attlee, the Labour Prime Minister, arriving from England in a huff because Truman, at a press conference, had refused to rule out the use of nuclear weapons in Korea. Then he went to his nine-thirty staff meeting. He found there Kennan's note.

DEAR MR. SECRETARY:

There is one thing I would like to say in continuation of our discussion of yesterday evening. In international, as in private, life what counts most is not really what happens to someone but how he bears what happens to him. For this reason almost everything depends from here on out on the manner in which we Americans bear what is unquestionably a major failure and disaster to our national fortunes. If we accept it with candor, with dignity, with a resolve to absorb its lessons and to make it good by redoubled and determined effort—starting all over again, if necessary, along the pattern of Pearl Harbor—we need lose neither our self-confidence nor our allies nor our power for bargaining, eventually, with the Russians. But if we try to conceal from our own people or from our allies the full measure of our misfortune, or permit ourselves to seek relief in any reactions of bluster or petulance or hysteria, we can easily find this crisis resolving itself into an irreparable deterioration of our world position— and of our confidence in ourselves.

GEORGE KENNAN

Acheson was so moved that he read the note aloud to the small group gathered in his office. Then he spoke for himself. We are being infected with the spirit of defeatism emanating from MacArthur's headquarters in Tokyo, he said. How, he asked, should we begin to inspire a spirit of candor and redoubled effort?

Dean Rusk, with words that lodged in Acheson's mind, spoke of the British example, of how they soldiered on through their darkest hour. Rusk suggested that the President fire MacArthur. Kennan, present at the meeting, also spoke of the British rallying in the desert of North Africa in World War II, and suggested that this was a poor time to negotiate with the Soviets, that the U.S. should never negotiate with the Communists from defeat.

The group concluded that they needed to recruit General Marshall as an ally in their effort to stiffen U.S. resolve. Acheson called Marshall and told him that the Korean campaign had been plagued by wild swings between exuberant optimism and despair, that what was needed was "dogged determination." Rusk and Kennan then went personally to see Marshall to enlist his support for a stand-fast policy. Marshall was quickly persuaded. He responded that MacArthur should be ordered to "find a line he can hold and hold it." Meanwhile, Lovett arrived from Capitol Hill to report pervasive defeatism in Congress and a growing feeling that the U.S. should pull out. The effect of this news, predictably, was to increase the determination of Acheson's rump group. By lunch, they had obtained Truman's vow: "We stay and fight."

Truman was haunted by broader fears of world war. He wrote in his diary, "It looks like World War III is here. I hope not—but we must meet whatever comes—and we will." Others shared his dread. The JCS warned all U.S. commanders worldwide that the possibility of general war had "greatly increased." The night of his long and brooding chat with Kennan, Acheson had gone to bed thinking that he would not be surprised to be awakened by an announcement of global war.

For a moment on the morning of December 6, he thought his nightmare had come true. At 10:30 A.M. Bob Lovett called him from the Pentagon and abruptly informed him in his laconic voice: "When I finish talking to you, you cannot reach me again. All incoming calls will be stopped. A national emergency is about to be proclaimed. We are informed that there is flying over Alaska at the present moment a formation of Russian planes heading southeast. The President wishes the British ambassador to be informed of this and be told that Mr. Attlee should take whatever measures are proper for Mr. Attlee's safety. I've now finished my message and I'm about to ring off." Acheson cut in. "Now wait a minute, Bob, do you believe this?" "No," Lovett replied, and hung up. Acheson sat in his office and waited. The Air Force scrambled. A senior official burst in asking permission to telephone his wife to get out of town and wondering if he should begin moving files to the basement. Acheson tried to soothe him. A few minutes later Lovett calmly called back. The radar blips were not Soviet bombers after all. They were flocks of geese.

•   •   •

The attacks on Acheson in Congress reached new extremes. He was vilified not only for his policies, but for his aristocratic hauteur and noble but unfortunate defense of Alger Hiss. On December 15, Republicans in the House voted unanimously and in the Senate by 20 to 5 that Acheson had lost the confidence of the country and should be removed from office.

Outwardly, Acheson was either stoical or mocking about his critics. Archibald MacLeish recalled hearing Acheson whistling bravely while listening to Fulton Lewis's diatribes against him on the radio. After Bob Taft refused to stand next to Acheson in a procession of Yale trustees, Acheson was greatly amused when the two antagonists were pushed together by accident as they came through an archway into public view, setting off an explosion of flashbulbs. To cabdrivers who would ask "Aren't you Dean Acheson?" he would reply, "Yes. Do I have to get out?"

Yet Acheson was wounded, his wife recalled, when he was abandoned by his friends in the press. Acheson himself recognized that his relations with the press had deteriorated after he became Secretary. He later described the relationship as "one of baiting them and making up: I thought they were spoiled; they thought I was irritable; we're both probably right." He admitted that he tried to "put a little fear of God into the press" and boasted that "you can really get it into them if you snap their heads off." He succeeded in alienating not just the press-room hacks but the insiders like Reston and Lippmann. Lippmann, who had once nominated Acheson for the Century Club in New York, even called for Acheson's resignation that fall. Acheson was particularly irked at the Alsop brothers, fellow Grotonians, who had reported what was probably the truth: that Acheson had been slow to rein in MacArthur because he feared being accused of "softness" on Communism.

Acheson did finally lash out at one of his most consistent congressional baiters. During August 1950, Senator Kenneth Wherry, the Nebraska mortician, leaned over a narrow table and started shaking his finger at Acheson during a hearing. Acheson jumped up and shouted at him not to "shake his dirty finger in my face." Wherry bellowed that he would. "By God you won't!" roared Acheson. As other senators looked on in amazement, Acheson reared back and started to launch a haymaker punch. Adrian Fisher, the State Department counsel and a former Princeton football player, had to grab the Secretary of State and push him down in his chair. Later, telling of the incident, Acheson tried to make it appear that he had never lost control. As he listened to Wherry fulminate, he said, "I wondered even if I had lost the capacity for rage, a chilling thought. So I began to work up a temper by murmuring hair-raising imprecations. To my delight, I felt the blood rising along the back of my neck and my ears getting hot." Acheson's explanation is too arch; one would prefer to believe that he just lost his temper.

As usual, Acheson was protected by devoted friends. Lovett always seemed to be there with some small cheering touch. At Christmas he sent Acheson a bottle of wine with a silly verse, "Some Pomery Rose, to pink your nose, to dull your woes, to make your life cosy." On January 21, he wrote him more seriously, "I don't know from what source you draw your courage, but whatever it is, hang on to it—and go on sharing it with the rest of your friends." To reporters Lovett said of Acheson: "He's no cookie pusher. He's a giant."

In his own mind, Harriman was critical of Acheson. In later years, he would tell his friends that Acheson had foolishly tempted the Kremlin by placing Korea outside the U.S. strategic perimeter. He felt that Acheson's defense of Alger Hiss had been a blunder that exposed the State Department to right-wing fanaticism. "I think the Secretary of State *should* turn his back on a man who has been convicted," Harriman would say to intimates. But to reporters and official Washington that autumn of 1950, Harriman stoutly and loudly defended Acheson. In November, he told a press conference, in his blunt, unartful way, "I don't believe we have had in our history many Secretaries of State with the guts to deal so forcefully with the issues with which he has been faced."

Harriman could barely tolerate the men attacking Acheson. After the 1950 elections, Joe Alsop had too much to drink at a dinner party and invited Richard Nixon to a Sunday Night Supper. Fresh from defeating Helen Gahagan Douglas with Red-baiting ("she's pink right down to her underwear"), Senator Nixon arrived at the Stewart Alsops' house in a shiny new suit just as another guest, Averell Harriman, was coming through the door. Harriman turned around to walk out.

"I will not eat dinner with that man," he told his hostess. Mrs. Alsop begged him to stay, but at dinner he turned his plate over, switched off his hearing aid, and refused to speak.

Harriman was almost as brusque with Acheson. He knew that many congressmen found Acheson's bristling Guardsman's mustache an offensive reminder of class superiority. "Shave it off," he instructed Acheson, as a sixth former to a fourth former. "You owe it to Truman." Acheson, ever the vain nonconformist, declined. Privately, Harriman faulted Acheson for not standing up to his political foes. Dining at the Achesons' in the spring of 1950, Harriman had listened with growing impatience while Acheson outlined a series of speeches that he planned to make on U.S. foreign policy. "Dean," Harriman finally interrupted, "do you want to write three speeches that can be put into the collected addresses of the great Secretary of State Acheson for future historians to read, or do you want to have some impact on the political situation?" Acheson began to argue with Harriman, until Alice interjected, "I think Averell's got something." But Harriman mixed his gruff lectures to his former rowing pupil with moral support. He tried to buck up Acheson by sending him a quote from Swift: "Whomever could make two ears of Corn or two Blades of grass to grow upon a Spit of Ground where only one grew before, would deserve better of Mankind, and do more essential Service to his Country, than the whole Race of Politicians put together."

Acheson was bemused by Harriman, and deeply grateful to him. A year later, in November of 1951, he went to Harriman's sixtieth birthday party in Paris, a glittery black-tie affair in Marie's soignée apartment on the Right Bank. After Harriman had blown out the candles on his cake, Acheson stood up and gave a toast on behalf of "all of us around the table who have come together this evening because we are so fond of Averell." He recalled first meeting Harriman as a schoolboy at Groton, how awed he had been by him then, how many years they had worked together, how Harriman had become one of the nation's great public servants. Touched, Harriman rose from his seat and told of how Acheson was the lightest oarsman, at 149 pounds, ever to row for the Yale freshmen, how the two of them had been fired as coaches of the crew, but how they had both survived to row in swifter waters.

Beneath the chandeliers, the small party gathered around a piano and sang sentimental songs while waiters passed around trays of champagne. Lydia Kirk, the wife of Admiral Alan Kirk, old and dear friends of Acheson's, felt emboldened by the champagne and the intimacy to suggest to Acheson that Averell had always wanted to be Secretary of State, much as he liked Dean. Acheson replied that he had always known this, and that even though they had never been really close friends, Averell had "always been the most loyal friend and faithful servant a Secretary could ever ask for."

• • •

Still reeling from disaster at the Yalu, the Administration was no longer talking about "rolling back" Communism and reuniting Korea as the new year began in January 1951. The U.S. war aim had become the one urged by Kennan and Nitze from the outset: restoration of the status quo at the 38th parallel. Actually, Acheson, Marshall, and Lovett were having difficulty simply persuading the Joint Chiefs that U.S. forces should not quit Korea altogether.

General MacArthur, meanwhile, was preparing for Armageddon. "He simply could not bear to end his career in checkmate," wrote his biographer, William Manchester. Acheson in his memoirs quoted Euripides: "Whom the gods destroy they first make mad."

MacArthur wanted to stomp out Communism in the Far East, if not the entire globe, in one last apocalyptic battle. At the end of December, he proposed to the JCS that he blockade the coast of China, destroy China's industrial capacity with air strikes, and unleash Chiang Kai-shek to attack the mainland. When the Joint Chiefs replied that they were not interested in starting World War III, MacArthur came back complaining that the morale of his troops was suffering and that unless "the extraordinary limitations and conditions imposed" upon him were lifted, "complete destruction" beckoned. The blood, he implied, would be on Washington's hands. General Marshall dryly observed to Dean Rusk that "when a general complains of the morale of his troops the time has come to look to his own." Acheson angrily summoned a war council to his house in Georgetown on January 10 and demanded that the military stop bickering and get on with the war.

Fortunately, while Washington and MacArthur talked, General Matthew Ridgway was rallying the tattered U.S. forces in Korea and slowly recapturing lost ground. His plan of attack, code named Operation Killer, was simple and brutal; the objective was not to win territory but to kill as many of the enemy as possible. This attrition strategy relied on superior U.S. firepower; fifteen years later, it would work less well in Vietnam.

In early December, Truman had tried to muzzle MacArthur's statements to the press by ordering that military commanders should use "extreme caution in public statements." MacArthur had flouted this directive. He told reporters about the conspiracy against him at the State Department: "This group of Europhiles just will not recognize that it is Asia which has been selected for the test of Communist power and that if all Asia falls Europe will not have a chance."

He openly criticized the decision to restore the status quo at the 38th parallel. Finally, he intentionally sabotaged peace feelers with a statement denigrating the Chinese as an "exaggerated military power." If Washington would only remove the "inhibitions" on him, he vowed, China would be "doomed." The peace initiative was stillborn. The Kremlin called MacArthur a "maniac, the principal culprit, the evil genius" of the war.

Lovett brought the text of MacArthur's remarks to Acheson's home at eleven o'clock at night on March 23. Lovett, "usually imperturbable and given to ironic humor under pressure, was angrier than I have ever seen him," Acheson later wrote. MacArthur, Lovett insisted, should be removed, and removed at once.

Acheson and Truman were almost as angry, but MacArthur was issued more rope with another, more explicit gag order. In fact, he had already sealed his doom. On March 20, he had written the Republican leader of the House, Joseph Martin, that he entirely agreed with the right-wing Republican view that Chiang should be unleashed to open a "second front." "There is no substitute for victory," he concluded. The letter was off the record, but the secret was too good to keep. On April 5, Martin read the statement on the floor of the House.

• • •

Dean Acheson adored the actress Myrna Loy. He had gone with her and her husband, a State Department official named Howland Sergeant, to a play at the National Theater on the night of April 5 and had returned home in high spirits. He found Lovett again sitting in his living room, with a long hound's face. "He's gone too far," said Lovett. Acheson agreed. Harriman, with his enormous sense of loyalty to the President, was outraged and adamant. MacArthur must be relieved, without delay.

Truman had finally had enough with his megalomaniacal commander. The next night he wrote in his diary, "This looks like the last straw. I've come to the conclusion that our Big General in the Far East must be recalled."

General Marshall, however, balked. He was worried about congressional reaction, about getting military appropriations passed, about his Joint Chiefs. He just could not bring himself to fulfill MacArthur's paranoid prophecy of three decades that his downfall would come at Marshall's hand. The old general had the flu. He was wheezing, and his deafness was becoming more noticeable. He wanted more time.

A curtain went down over the White House. The press secretaries were mum, limousines passed back and forth through the private gates to the North Portico, no public schedule was listed for the President. Reporters waiting outside wondered at the crisis.

Over the weekend, Marshall carefully reviewed the cable traffic between MacArthur and Washington. When he finished he was his old decisive self. "We should have fired him two years before," he told Truman.

MacArthur was fired on Tuesday. Because of a communications snafu, he first heard about it on the radio. The apparent shabbiness of this treatment left a bitter taste that for many welled into a kind of hysteria. Within forty-eight hours, the White House had received 125,000 telegrams: "Impeach the imbecile"; "Impeach the Judas"; "Impeach the bastard who calls himself President"; "Impeach the little ward politician"; "Impeach the red herring." The Republican right went mad. "This country is in the hands of a secret inner coterie which is directed by agents of the Soviet Union. Our only choice is to impeach President Truman," said Senator William Jenner of Indiana. "The son of a bitch should be impeached," snarled McCarthy. He declared that the decision to fire MacArthur had been made by Truman while he was "drunk from Bourbon and Benedictine."

Around the country, flags flew upside down at half-staff, the President was denounced as "a pig." A Denver man started a Punch Harry in the Nose Club. Acheson was hung in effigy from streetlamps; posters were painted pleading "God save us from Acheson."

MacArthur came home to one of the greatest greetings ever given a returning hero. Crowds overwhelmed the police barricades in San Francisco. In Washington, General Marshall dutifully went out to meet MacArthur's plane. MacArthur, remembering that Marshall preferred to be called by his last name by everyone but his wife, stepped off and said, "Hello, George, how are you?" Before a Joint Session of Congress he attacked appeasement and defeatism, and brought tears with his famous valedictory ("Old soldiers never die, they just fade away...."). "We heard God speak today, God in the flesh, the voice of God!" cried Congressman Dewey Short. At the White House, Truman said to Acheson, "It's nothing but a bunch of bullshit."

Acheson called MacArthur "pathetic." Then he told the story of a family with a beautiful daughter living at the edge of an army camp. The mother worried constantly about her daughter's virtue and relentlessly badgered her husband with her anxiety. One day the daughter showed up weeping and confessed that the worst had happened, that she was pregnant. The father wiped his brow and declared, "Thank God that's over."

It wasn't quite. Congress launched a massive investigation that the Republicans devoutly hoped would expose the State Department in all its perfidy. Acheson alone testified for eight days. He was asked about everything imaginable, not just about Korea, but Yalta, loans to Mexico to develop oil, soybean speculation by renegade refugees of the Chinese Nationalist regime, and the fact that one of his aides was married to an international oil geologist. He was totally prepared, brilliant, and for once, he held his tongue. One senator complained that Acheson had an unfair advantage because he had greater knowledge of the subject matter. When Acheson was done, on a Saturday, June 9, at 5 P.M., he was asked what he planned to do now. He replied, "I have a plan that will test my capacity for the consumption of alcohol, and if another war erupts before I finish, it must be waged without my services."

The uproar did not die, but it faded away over the summer. Very shortly, General MacArthur was just an old warrior sitting in his West Point bathrobe in a fancy hotel in New York, dreaming of old battles and the last great one he never got to fight.

• • •

With MacArthur out of the way, and Ridgway's men once more closing in on the 38th parallel, Washington began to search in earnest for a peaceful settlement of the war. Bohlen had begun planting the idea of a cease-fire along the old border with Soviet diplomats in Paris as early as January. By May, Acheson felt that "if hostilities were going to end, this was a good time to see about ending them."

Kennan had gone back to Princeton before Christmas in a sulk, feeling like a "fifth wheel" and not realizing how much he had helped Acheson with his inspirational letter. Acheson had not forgotten, however, and in May he turned to Kennan again. He knew that Kennan had excellent contacts and was trusted by the Kremlin. He asked Kennan to quietly approach the Soviets and feel them out on a peace offer: a cease-fire along present dispositions, roughly the status quo ante.

Kennan wrote a longhand note to Yakov Malik, the Soviet ambassador to the U.N., asking to see him. Malik promptly invited him to the Soviet mission's summer compound in Glen Cove, Long Island, on May 31 for lunch. Malik was nervous—he dumped a tray of fruit and wine into his lap—but Kennan, polished and fluent, gingerly laid out the offer and asked that Malik let him know his answer after he had time to consider it, i.e., after he obtained instructions from Moscow. Less than a week later he got his answer: the Soviets wanted a settlement.

The negotiations would drag on for two more years, and thousands more Americans would die in the fitful fighting as both sides maneuvered for better position. Part of the problem was that the U.S. did not recognize the Chinese government, which made diplomatic contact difficult. It was all baffling and frustrating to Acheson. He quoted Bret Harte: "That for ways that are dark/And for tricks that are vain,/ The heathen Chinee is peculiar."

•   •   •

Academic life suited Kennan. He lived in a comfortable house on a sycamore-lined street in Princeton, students flocked to his lectures, and one of his scholarly works, *Russia Leaves the War*, would win the Pulitzer Prize. Yet, still in his late forties, he was unable to reconcile himself to leaving public life. He was characteristically ambivalent, unable to commit himself wholly to academe, yet shy of Washington.

Dean Acheson's respect for Kennan had been partly restored by his stoicism during the grim days of December 1950. Kennan's deft handling of Malik to launch the Korean peace negotiations further reminded the Secretary of Kennan's diplomatic skills. When Acheson's friend Alan Kirk decided to step down as ambassador to the Soviet Union at the end of 1951, Acheson once again looked to Kennan. The Sovietologist could hardly say no. "It was," he wrote in his memoirs, "a task for which my whole career had prepared me, if it had prepared me for anything at all."

Kennan, buoyant and curious, had lunch with Acheson in April 1952 to receive instructions. He found the Secretary cordial, but reserved and weary. Kennan left the meeting unsure of his role; further rounds of the State Department and other familiar precincts left him chilled. The spirit of the day was NSC-68. Even his closest friends, he wrote, had been captivated by "the flat and inflexible thinking of the Pentagon." He began to sense that he was being sent to Moscow to "play a game which I could not possibly win."

And yet, Kennan could not help harboring a vague sense of hope. Despite his belief that personal diplomacy could do little to sway historical tides, despite his feeling that Russia had never been "a fit ally" for the U.S., he could not help but think that, perhaps, he could make a difference. His return to Russia was "at once a sentimental journey and a diplomatic mission to which he brought a mystical sense of purpose," recorded Harrison Salisbury, the *New York Times* correspondent in Moscow who often invited Kennan out to his week-end dacha at Saltykovka.

In his contrary but perhaps insightful way, Kennan sensed that the Soviets, despite their harsh rhetoric, would be receptive to diplomatic overtures to ease tensions and slow the escalating arms race. Brutal, hostile, and paranoid though he was, Stalin was also a pragmatist, Kennan believed. In the opinion of its author, containment had worked: the Soviets had been frozen out of Western Europe, their aggression by proxy met resolutely in Korea. Since Stalin put pragmatism ahead of all else—precedent, ideology, consistency—he would be perfectly willing to abandon belligerence and, without embarrassment, seek peaceful solutions with the U.S. to their mutual problems.

Such was the vision Kennan spun out to Salisbury as he lolled beneath the pines in Saltykovka in the summer of 1952. Kennan hoped for some sign, some small hint from the Kremlin of a change of heart. It was vital, he felt, that someone with particularly sensitive antennae be on hand to catch the first signals. He was prepared, wrote Salisbury, "like a good obstetrician coping with a difficult birth to use the forceps a bit."

Before he left Washington, he had persuaded the Voice of America to refrain from ad hominem attacks on Stalin and beseeched Henry Luce's *Time* and *Life* to ease up its Kremlin bashing. Yet Kennan gloomily conceded to Salisbury that it was probably too late; that Washington was so deeply committed to stocking its arsenal, rearming Germany, and stiffening its allies that the prospects for diplomacy were slight indeed.

Kennan's return to Spaso House did not improve his mood. Leaving Annelise, who was about to have a baby, in Bonn, he found the embassy "barnlike, empty, and a little sad." Servants with whom he had once gotten on pleasantly were now sullen; the outer walls of the grounds were "now floodlit, like those of a prison, and patrolled day and night by armed guards." He was followed wherever he went, even swimming (the KGB agents would paddle alongside). The "tame Russians," those with whom he had been allowed to have normal contact in the thirties and forties, "ceased to exist." At night, he began to wander around the great empty rooms of Spaso House in the darkness, alone. In the dimly lit white ballroom he would play the grand piano or "establish myself in one of the gilded chairs of the several living rooms and read Russian aloud to myself just to indulge my love of the language." Isolated, uneasy, he began to feel, he wrote home, "like sort of a phantom of the opera."

Stalin, in his last demented days, had launched a lurid "Hate America" campaign. Moscow was festooned with grotesque propaganda. "Placards portraying hideous spiderlike characters in American military uniform, armed with spray guns and injection needles for bacteriological warfare, stared down at us from every fence throughout the city," Kennan wrote.

He cabled Acheson that the U.S. was in part to blame for this nadir in the Cold War, that traditional Soviet paranoia had been terribly exacerbated by the growing militarism of the West. The dispatch turned out to be Kennan's "swan song," his final dejected piece of reporting on a subject "to which I had now given just twenty-five years of my life."

In the end, Kennan the dispassionate analyst succumbed to Kennan the tortured man. A small unpleasantry, a minor reminder of his isolation and the Kremlin's ceaseless paranoia, shattered him.

On a pleasant summer's day at the end of August, after his family had rejoined him in Moscow, he was watching his two-year-old boy play in the garden. Through the iron fence, some Soviet children smiled at the American child, who "squealed with pleasure" and reached out through the bars to touch them. Guards rushed up and shooed the children away. "Something gave way, at that point," Kennan recorded, "with the patience I was able to observe in the face of this entire vicious, timid, medieval regime of isolation to which the offical foreigner was still subjected."

Kennan lost his diplomatic poise altogether. Summoned to a meeting of ambassadors in London, depressed that the mood in Western capitals would be no less suspicious than in Moscow, Kennan was silent and withdrawn as he boarded a plane at Vnukovo airport on September 19. Passing through Berlin, he was asked by a reporter at the airport if he had had many social contacts with the Russians. His answer was to compare serving as ambassador to Russia with being interned during World War II in Nazi Germany.

Stalin, not surprisingly, was enraged to be compared to Hitler. The American ambassador had "lied ecstatically," declared *Pravda*. Kennan was promptly pronounced persona non grata by the Soviet Union and barred from returning.

Kennan was "deeply shamed and shaken." The American High Commissioner in Germany, Jack McCloy, found him in a "state of shock." McCloy was not very sympathetic. He felt that Kennan looked down on him as an amateur. "I thought he was the bright boy and I was anxious to be tutored by him," McCloy later recalled, but Kennan snubbed him. The moody diplomat turned down the High Commissioner's offer of a ride from the airport so that he could "think by myself." McCloy later scoffed, "He didn't want to be contaminated by conventional policy." When Kennan was declared PNG by the Soviets, recalled McCloy, "I smiled. Here he was criticizing *me* for being a lousy diplomat."

•   •   •

Robert Lovett kept a cartoon in his office at the Pentagon that showed him wearing an aging maiden's nightgown and mournfully reading three telegrams: "Come be *assistant* secretary of War. Stimson. Come be *under* secretary of state. Marshall. Come be *deputy* secretary of defense. Truman." The caption read: "Often a bridesmaid, never a bride."

In 1951, Marshall and Truman finally did right by Lovett and made him Secretary of Defense upon Marshall's retirement. He was a very good Secretary, one of the few who actually gained some control over the Pentagon bureaucracy. With his great attention to detail, he refused to let the different services simply present him with a request for a lump sum of money every year. He insisted on seeing the figures that demonstrated how they had reached those totals. He was as usual diplomatic about his scrutiny. "We're not questioning your assumptions," he told the brass. "We just want to know the basis for your decisions." Yet he did not hesitate to scratch out the more extravagant items on the wish lists.

He was able to withstand the constant pressure for new high-tech weapons (he thwarted, for example, a "snorkle jeep," to travel underwater), and forced his way through the layers of obfuscation. "I

don't want a briefing," he would say. "I just want the facts." He brought
to the job his endearing humor: at one high-level conference, he held
up a picture of a melancholy beagle and remarked, "This is exactly
how the Secretary of Defense feels this morning."

Lovett's greatest capacity as a thinker was to look ahead, to prepare
for the next war while the generals were still readying to fight the last
one. When the brass had urged more battleships early in World War
II, Lovett insisted on bombers. Now that the Pentagon was clamoring
for bombers, Lovett wanted to build missiles. He was able to look past
the bitter bureaucratic feuding between the Navy (bigger carriers) and
the Air Force (more bombers) at what the Russians were doing: building powerful rockets. At his insistence, production on the Atlas in-
tercontinental ballistic missile, abandoned in the late 1940s, was
resumed.

Carefully balancing resources and commitments, Lovett resisted
potentially costly entanglements. His caution sometimes irked Acheson. When Lovett objected to the cost of advancing oil credits to the
shaky government of the Shah during the 1952 Iran crisis,* Acheson
scoffed to his aides, "What do you expect from an investment banker?"

•   •   •

Acheson was finding it harder and harder to fend off the Mc-
Carthyite attacks on the State Department. In April of 1951, Truman,
bending to McCarthyism, had expanded the grounds for dismissal of
government employees under the pernicious Loyalty Boards system
he had set up back in March of 1947. Now the boards could sack
employees on a mere showing of "reasonable doubt" about their loyalty. The burden of proof switched from the government to the employee. Witch-hunts abounded.

One by one, the McCarthyites picked off the old China hands, the
State Department experts who had been so enlightened, and so mis-
understood, about U.S. policy in the Far East. Acheson had been

---

*In Iran, the Prime Minister, Mohammed Mosadeq, wanted to nationalize the British
owned oil fields. A mission in 1951 by the ever-available Averell Harriman to bring
peace between the British and Iranians failed. In 1952, the Shah's regime appeared in
jeopardy, and Acheson wanted to advance the Iranian government $100 million against
future delivery of oil under the Defense Materials Procurement Act. Lovell objected but
Truman went ahead and ordered the oil credits. Mosadeq, however, rejected the U.S.
offer, and Iran plunged into riots. The CIA stepped in to overthrow Mosadeq and restore
the Shah in 1953.

trying, fitfully, to protect them, but he was running out of room and energy.

He stood up for John Carter Vincent, a gracious Southerner who had warned in 1946 that the Kuomintang was a rat hole for U.S. aid. With the China lobby in hot pursuit, Acheson had tried to hide Vincent in Switzerland, though not as ambassador because the Senate would not confirm him. (Vincent had asked for Czechoslovakia, but he was philosophical about not getting it; he knew he'd be blamed for losing that country too.) McCarthy was so determined to get Vincent that he tried to have him framed as a Communist agent in 1950. Acheson sent Vincent off to Tangier, but that still was not far enough away. A Loyalty Board found "reasonable doubt" about him in 1952. Acheson refused to fire him, but rather set up a commission under retired U.S. Court of Appeals judge Learned Hand (McCloy was a member) to look into the case. Just before leaving the State Department in January 1953, Acheson wrote his successor, John Foster Dulles, "It seemed to me that the opinion of the loyalty review board had passed judgment not on Mr. Vincent's loyalty but on the soundness of the policy recommendations he had made. If disagreements on policy were to be equated with disloyalty, the Foreign Service would be destroyed."

Other old China hands received less protection. John Stewart Service had first been shuttled off to Calcutta and then, when McCarthy bore in, sent to the Office of Operating Facilities, where he kept track of typewriters. Smeared with the somewhat contradictory charge that he was a homosexual who had fathered an illegitimate child, he was declared disloyal in late 1952. Acheson let him go. Kennan was unhappy with the decision; he wondered why the Secretary was not helping Service with exculpatory material he knew to be in State Department files. Kennan vainly testified on Service's behalf, and also went to bat for a PPS expert on China, John Paton Davies, even flying back from Europe at his own expense to appear before Davies's loyalty hearing. Davies's crime was doubting Chiang Kai-shek. He was dragged half a dozen times before loyalty boards, cleared each time, and promptly recharged.

By 1952, Acheson was too worn out to make a crusade of defying Joe McCarthy and his ilk. He was himself too much of a target to argue that he was simply trying to uphold procedural safeguards. Korea, the attack of the primitives, a crisis in Iran, Moscow's Hate America campaign, and a decade of service through hot and cold war had left him drained. He was sick; he had picked up an intestinal amoeba traveling through South America and had chronic diarrhea. He had, at least, not lost his sense of humor. Shortly before he left office, he penciled himself a ditty:

> Can't drive car
> Can't order lunch
> Got no program
> Don't have hunch
>
> Got no brains
> Got no mem'ry
> Call his friends
> Tom, Dick, or Henry
>
> Can't read cables
> Can't write name
> As to speeches
> 'Bout the same

CHAPTER 19

EXILE

The wilderness years

Though Douglas MacArthur himself quickly faded away, the general's impulse to take on Communism, to not merely restrain it but smash it, had touched a public nerve. Many ordinary people were impatient with containment, a strategy that required half measures, patience, steadiness, endurance. Kennan's prescription for fencing in the Soviets with vigilance and care, but without provocation, did not sit well with an American public that demanded unconditional victories.

The Republican platform for 1952 reflected these reckless sentiments. The next administration, it vowed, "will mark the end of the negative, futile, and immoral policy of 'containment,' which abandons countless human beings to despotism and Godless Communism . . . the policies we espouse will revive the contagious, liberating influences which are inherent in freedom."

The champion of this new policy was John Foster Dulles. He had written the foreign policy plank of the GOP platform, and he would carry it out as the next Secretary of State, assuming, as most correctly did, that Dwight Eisenhower would defeat the Democratic nominee, Adlai Stevenson, in November.

On the surface, Dulles seemed the perfect member of the eastern foreign policy Establishment. His résumé could not have been more impeccable: Princeton and the Sorbonne, senior partner at Sullivan & Cromwell, Council on Foreign Relations, the Century and Piping Rock. He had been both a "symbol and an agent" of bipartisan foreign policy, writes his biographer Townsend Hoopes; he worked with Vandenberg to maintain Republican support for the postwar policies of the Truman Administration.

But in fact he did not fit in well with the inner circle of postwar foreign policy makers, and was regarded by its members with distrust and personal dislike. Suspicious, preachy, and righteous, Dulles was not a very agreeable man. He had Kennan's sensitivity without his insight, Acheson's coldness without his wit, McCloy's simplicity without his wisdom, Forrestal's dogmatism without his self-honesty, and very little of Lovett's or Bohlen's grace and charm. "He gave the impression that he had a direct line to the Almighty," Lovett later recalled. "He had no humor or lightness. He was all pontifical and actually sounded as though he was delivering the Sermon on the Mount."

As a boy growing up in upstate New York, Foster Dulles had been fed large doses of A *Pilgrim's Progress*; as a Princeton student, he was a shy grind and social outcast. His ambition was to be a "Christian lawyer," which, after a fashion, he became. A stolid, relentless practitioner, he built a large international practice for Sullivan & Cromwell, one of Wall Street's best law firms. Many of his clients were German. When Hitler's persecution of Jews became undeniable in 1935, Dulles came under great pressure from his partners to drop his German clients. He resisted and finally capitulated in tears; he regarded Hitler, Thomas E. Dewey later recalled, as a "passing phenomenon." McCloy later recalled, "I was always puzzled to see where Foster stood with the Nazi business, and what his feeling was about the oncoming menace from Germany. I rather gathered the impression that he was not particularly concerned about it."

Though a closet Sybarite who liked Cognac and cigars, Dulles did not cultivate the stylishness of his predecessor as Secretary of State, Dean Acheson. He stirred whiskey with a thick forefinger, his socks drooped, his suits were green-hued, his ties were indifferent, and his breath was chronically bad. Hunched forward as he talked, he droned on in a flat voice, pronouncing Anthony Eden "Ant-ny."

He was sincerely devout. He had "rediscovered" religion in 1937, and applied it to his anti-Communism. In a famous *Life* article in May 1952, he defined the Cold War as a moral rather than an economic or political crusade, a struggle that pitted Christianity against Godless Communism. His speeches had titles like "Spiritual Bases of Peace," "Christian Responsibility," and "A Diplomat and his Faith." He carried around a well-thumbed, heavily underlined copy of Stalin's *Problems of Leninism*, which he regarded as an atheist tract.

To Dulles's credit, he had worked to maintain a bipartisan foreign policy after the war, going as a Republican observer to various Council of Foreign Ministers' meetings and behaving in a generally responsible and supportive manner. Brought into the State Department in 1950 as a consultant to help insulate Foggy Bottom from the Republican right, Dulles had performed admirably in working out a sensible peace treaty with Japan, a last bit of unfinished postwar business.

But as the 1952 elections approached, Dulles became bitterly partisan. Attacking the "treadmill" policies of Acheson, he called for a "policy of boldness," declaring that the U.S. should seek not to merely contain but "roll back" Communism. He wanted to "liberate" areas under Communist dominance, like Stalin's Eastern European satellites. How this was to be accomplished, he did not say.

•   •   •

In a characteristically bold, if unrealistic gesture, Averell Harriman tried to run for President in 1952. He was drawn into the fray in March, on the night Harry Truman announced at the Democrats' annual Jefferson-Jackson Day dinner in Washington that he would not seek a third term. In the confused uproar that followed Truman's declaration, New York Democratic Chairman Paul Fitzpatrick grabbed Harriman, who was seated at the head table, and pleaded, "Averell, you've got to be a candidate to hold New York together." Harriman assented on the spot to be his state's favorite son.

Harriman was, as usual, lured by his twin mistresses of duty and ambition. He felt obliged to carry on Truman's programs, particularly the Administration's commitment to a strong Western Alliance, and to accept the bidding of New York Democrats, who had already urged him to run for Governor. At the same time, he felt perfectly suited to be President of the United States, even though he had not been elected to anything since Skull and Bones.

Despite a total unfamiliarity with the hustings, Harriman plunged right into the campaign that spring, to the bemusement and mild

horror of Acheson, Lovett, and other friends. He dropped the "W."
before Averell and picked up a corny nickname, "Honest Ave" (reporters took to calling him "Available Averell"). Gamely, he rode on
a jolting buckboard escorted by fifty cowboys and Ute Indians through
Salt Lake City, declaring, "This is the nicest time I've had since
becoming a candidate." His platform was predictable: he "clung closely
to the Fair Deal party line," according to *Time*, and bluntly reminded
voters that if the U.S. wanted security, the taxpayers would have to
pay for it. "Foreign and domestic politics are indivisible," the old
internationalist told a $100-a-plate testimonial dinner at the Waldorf
in April. "If the voice of hesitation prevailed, we would destroy what
we have built and we would be on the road to World War III. . . .
The Republicans never change. They voted against everything that
has made this country strong for twenty years."

As he crisscrossed the country in his private railway car, Harriman
began to fancy himself as more than New York's favorite son. "I am
the Democrat to beat," he declared. But dull, stumbling and stolid
on the stump, he could not hope to match the popular appeal of Adlai
Stevenson, who was still pondering whether to run, and waiting coyly
to be drafted.

Harriman did have some support from Truman, but the President
described Harriman's fatal image in a diary entry in June: "He is the
ablest of them all. But he has been a Wall Street Banker, is the son
of one of the old-time pirates of the first years of this century. . . . Can
we elect a Wall Street Banker and railroad tycoon President of the
United States on the Democratic ticket?" At Truman's request, Harriman withdrew from the race in favor of Stevenson at the Democratic
Convention, guaranteeing the Illinois governor the nomination.

Harriman had to content himself with the knowledge that he would
finally realize his ambition to become Secretary of State if by some
miracle Stevenson defeated Dwight Eisenhower in November.

"Averell hates Dulles and thinks he is ambitious and dishonest,"
Cy Sulzberger wrote in his diary on August 21, 1952, after a chat
with Harriman. That night Harriman debated Dulles over national
television with typical bluntness:

DULLES: The first thing I would do would be to shift from a purely
defensive policy to a psychological offensive, a liberation policy, which
will try to give hope and a resistance mood inside the Soviet empire. . . .
HARRIMAN: Those are very fine words but I don't understand the meaning of them. . . . There can be nothing more cruel than to get people

behind the Iron Curtain—I have been there and I know what it is—to try to revolt and have a tragedy and a massacre. . . .

The moderator, Walter Cronkite, asked Dulles if the Republicans supported such an insurrection. Dulles replied that he did not want to start a massacre but that he had written "quite a little piece in *Life*. . ." Harriman cut in, "I read it twice, but I couldn't understand what you meant." Dulles: "You should have read it a third time." Harriman: "I did. I still didn't understand it. . . ."

Harriman was frustrated. He knew that Stevenson had little chance in November and that he, as a staunch Democrat, was about to be out of power.

• • •

Acheson's contempt for Dulles was, if anything greater than Harriman's. To a pragmatist like Acheson, Dulles's moralism was offensive. Like Harriman, Acheson also thought Dulles dishonest. Though Dulles had been among the first to urge ground troops for Korea in June of 1950, when the war turned sour in December he began publicly declaring that he had always opposed sending in the troops. Worst of all, perhaps, Acheson believed that Dulles was a coward who would cave in to the primitives.

Acheson so loathed Dulles that he resigned as Secretary of State one day early in order to avoid having to sign Dulles's commission. From under a palm tree in Antigua, where he had gone on an extended vacation, Acheson watched Dulles permit the destruction of the Foreign Service, just as he had feared. As he wrote Harry Truman that spring: "The studied appeasement of the Hill which is now going on at the expense of the best civil servants we have—certainly in State— is not only criminal but frightening." To his former special assistant Lucius Battle he wrote: "Dulles's people seem to me like Cossacks quartered in a grand city hall, burning the paneling to cook with."

• • •

For Acheson, as well as the other architects of America's role in the postwar world, these would be years of exile. After seven years of extraordinary global power, these men suddenly found themselves engaged in lonely scholarship or attending to the narrow concerns of private clients, a lucrative but not altogether rewarding existence.

In part, they were victims of a revolution of the Outs against the Ins. Excluded from power for two decades, the Republicans understandably wanted to start fresh. That meant purging even the most resolutely nonpartisan appointees, apolitical diplomats like Kennan as well as Truman's cronies.

Yet in this twisted era, Acheson and his kind found themselves not only rejected but scorned. Incredibly, these men, who were the first to warn against the Soviet threat and were themselves the sturdiest pillars of capitalism, were cast as Communist sympathizers. Jack McCloy's career as president of the World Bank and High Commissioner of Germany, for instance, was luridly described by McCarthy as "the unbelievable, inconceivable, unexplainable record of the deliberate, secret betrayal of the nation to its mortal enemy, the Communist conspiracy." The demagogue's remarkable success at peddling this Big Lie can be explained only by resentment not just against what McCloy did but against who he was and what he stood for.

To many ordinary people, Wall Street itself was a conspiracy. Especially in the South and the West, poor farmers and common workers suspected that their hardships were inversely proportional to the life of ease enjoyed by the tycoons and fat cats of the East Coast. A long line of demagogic politicians preyed on this resentment, darkly accusing the "malefactors of great wealth," in the phrase Teddy Roosevelt once used to describe E. H. Harriman, of greed and self-interest. McCarthy just took the old conspiracy notion and gave it a sinister new twist.

At first the Achesons and McCloys could not take these allegations seriously; later when they found themselves back in private life with a slight case of leprosy they were hurt and indignant. Years later, Paul Nitze still marveled that McCarthy attacked him—successfully—not for his policy views, or even as a Communist appeaser, but rather simply because he was a "Wall Street operator."

·   ·   ·

John Foster Dulles did not want just loyalty; as he told State Department employees in a memo on the day he took office, he wanted "positive loyalty." Anything less was "not tolerable at this time." In his maiden address he announced that department policy would be based on "simplicity and righteousness."

As Under Secretary for Administration, Dulles hired Donald Lourie, a manufacturer of breakfast cereal. "A few years ago he was an all American quarterback," Dulles explained at a mandatory meeting of department employees, "and I think that is the kind of thinking and creative action we're going to see." Lourie hired as his

Special Assistant for Internal Security Scott McLeod, a former reporter for the Manchester (N.H.) *Union-Leader* and an investigator for Senator Styles Bridges, an extreme right-winger. Vindictive and shrewd, McLeod hired 350 inexperienced but zealous investigators who quickly went to work ferreting out Foreign Service officers deemed drunkards, homosexual, incompetent, or "incompatible," a flexible category. They were replaced by true believers. To run the Far Eastern Affairs division, Dulles picked Walter Robertson, a Richmond banker and protégé of Congressman Walter Judd, who was devoted to Chiang Kai-shek. When the CIA estimated that the Chinese Communists had increased steel-making capacity, Robertson told the agency briefer that he was wrong—"no regime as malevolent as the Chicoms could ever produce five million tons of steel."

Dulles moved quickly to finish off the old China experts. He simply dismissed the Hand commission established by Acheson to look into John Carter Vincent's case and forced Vincent to resign. When the Loyalty Boards still could not find "reasonable doubt" about John Paton Davies, Dulles fired him for "bad judgment."

For the department's leading Soviet expert, George Kennan, Dulles could find nothing at all to do.

The moralizing Dulles had long distrusted the pragmatic Kennan. He had told journalists in the summer of 1950 that Kennan was a "very dangerous man" because he advocated the admission of Red China to the U.N. and warned against crossing the 38th parallel. Dulles's suspicion of Kennan deepened further when the career diplomat made a rather impolitic speech in mid-January, just before Dulles took office, attacking the new Secretary's liberation doctrine as imprudent and futile.

In his self-imposed exile on his farm in Pennsylvania, still horrified by the blunder that had cost him the Moscow embassy, Kennan waited anxiously to learn his place in the new order. He was particularly worried because under the Foreign Service rules an ambassador not reassigned after ninety days is automatically retired. Kennan had little savings and could not afford to be jobless. (When his daughter Grace, a Radcliffe student, applied for a scholarship, she listed her father's income as "o.")

"With regard to my reassignment," Kennan wrote his sister Jeannette on January 26, "there simply hasn't been any." He had "not even an inkling of what is in store for me." Anxiously, he added that "meanwhile the McCarran committee has stumbled over me in its pursuit of Davies, and there is plenty of trouble ahead for me there...."

McCarthy and McCarran will do a job on me in this coming period, and whenever they're through, whatever reputation I had will be pretty well shattered." Kennan was unsure of his standing even with old colleagues. "I find myself treated with the elaborate politeness and forbearance one reserves for someone who has committed a social gaffe too appalling to discuss," he moaned to Jeannette.

Dulles's hand was forced when *The New York Times* began pointedly wondering whatever had become of the former ambassador to the Soviet Union. Summoned to the Secretary's office in late March, Kennan was matter-of-factly informed by Dulles that the department had "no niche" for him. Incredibly, as Dulles fired Kennan, he picked his brain, asking his opinion of the current mood in the Kremlin. "You know, you interest me when you talk about these matters," Dulles blithely observed as he ushered Kennan out the door and out of the Foreign Service. "Very few other people do," the Secretary prattled on. "I hope you'll come in from time to time to let us have your comments on what is going on." That night a hurt and bewildered Kennan wrote his wife that Dulles's parting solicitude was as if a husband had said to his wife, "You know, I'm divorcing you today, and you are to leave my bed and board at once. But I love the way you cook scrambled eggs, and I wonder if you'd mind fixing me a batch of them right now, before you go."

On a warm spring day a few weeks later, Kennan cleared out his office and walked sadly down the halls, looking at the new faces, impassive, guarded, coldly polite. Unable to find anyone to say good-bye to, he finally bade farewell to the fifth-floor receptionist and left the department he had served for twenty-seven years.

• • •

President Eisenhower was not a zealot like Dulles, and was not quite so cowed by the Republican right. As Supreme Commander of NATO he had admired Chip Bohlen's diplomatic skills at the Paris embassy, and he wanted Bohlen to be his ambassador to Moscow.

Dulles opposed the appointment and worried about it. When Congressman Judd called him with reservations, Dulles quickly assured Judd that the appointment was "not a promotion," that Bohlen would be "removed from policy making" and would be "merely a reporter." Dulles was unamused by Bohlen's irreverent humor, especially after Bohlen "half jokingly" said, and Dulles overheard, that the State Department had become like a wagon train in hostile Indian territory, circling at night and posting guards.

Bohlen was not about to equivocate at his confirmation hearings to suit Dulles. He told the Secretary that he would not be able to go along with the Republican platform's charge that at Yalta Roosevelt had sold out Europe and China to the Russians. Dulles asked wishfully if Bohlen could just pretend that he had been a translator at Yalta and had no views of his own. Bohlen declined.

Meanwhile, the resourceful Scott McLeod, the State Department's new security man who had an autographed photo from Joe McCarthy on his desk ("To a great American"), was digging. He at first told Dulles that he could find no security reasons to oppose Bohlen, but then told his former mentor, Senator Bridges, that Bohlen's personnel folder contained "derogatory information." On March 13, Bridges held a press conference to say that "top officials" in the Administration opposed Bohlen's nomination and that he would face heavy opposition in the Senate. Knowland, Wherry, and McCarthy joined the pack. Dulles squirmed; he dreaded a confrontation with the Right. Eisenhower, however, refused to back away from his choice.

Dulles summoned Bohlen to his office. Was there anything in his record that could possibly be used to embarrass him? Bohlen answered that there was not. "I'm glad to hear this," the Secretary responded. "I couldn't stand another Alger Hiss."

Bohlen was at first a little taken aback to be a target. He guessed that Dulles was unnerved because Alger Hiss had once worked for him in the U.S. delegation to the first U.N. conference in San Francisco, and Dulles had even recommended Hiss for a job as head of the Carnegie Endowment for International Peace. Bohlen knew that Dulles had been aware all along of Whittaker Chambers's allegations against Hiss because both Dulles and Bohlen had been shown the same file on Hiss by Jimmy Byrnes. At the time, both men had dismissed the allegations as preposterous. Now, Bohlen figured, Dulles was deathly afraid that the press would find out that the new Secretary of State had been soft on Alger Hiss.

This was all vaguely amusing to Bohlen. But his chuckles turned to outrage when Dulles's henchmen pilloried Bohlen's old friend and brother-in-law, Charlie Thayer. McLeod's intrepid investigators had discovered that Charlie had been a Lothario in Moscow. To spare his mother the embarrassment of a public controversy over his morals, Thayer resigned from the Foreign Service.

The weekend before his confirmation hearings, Bohlen sat at home, quarantined with German measles. As he lay on the couch in his living room, recuperating, he tried to make light of his predicament to his family. "It's a good thing I have the German measles," he joked, "and not the Red ones." But he was slowly realizing that his case was becoming a matter of principle, a test of whether the yahoos were going to be able to ride roughshod through the Department of State. He became, he recorded in his memoirs, "exhilarated."

On Monday night, Dulles called Bohlen at home and told him that Eisenhower wanted to stand by him, but that he, Dulles, did not want Bohlen to do anything that would embarrass the President. Did Bohlen intend to quit? Bohlen said he had no intention of quitting, "none whatsoever." The next day, the day of his hearing, Bohlen went to Dulles's office to ride with him to Capitol Hill. Dulles uneasily informed him that they should ride in separate cars. He added that it would be better if they were not photographed together.

Bohlen could be twinkly and charming, and he could be chillingly correct. He was a discreet and obliging staff man, but he brooked no condescension. He fixed on the Secretary with ice-blue eyes. "I have no desire to be photographed at all," he said coolly, "but I'm not sure I understand you." Dulles said nothing and walked out the door.

The Senate Foreign Relations Committee proved no obstacle, sending Bohlen's nomination to the floor by unanimous vote. But the McCarthyites were agitating hard to see Bohlen's file with its supposed "derogatory information." On March 21, McCarthy rose to say that he had obtained sixteen "closely typed pages" of damning allegations from the file, though he declined to offer any specifics. The rumors picked up. From his farm in Pennsylvania, George Kennan had already felt compelled to write his sister Jeannette on March 20, "No matter what you read or hear on the radio, you can take it from me that Bohlen is not a homosexual, nor is he disloyal. That these things can be seriously suggested fills me with horror and foreboding."

McCarthy ranted and raved, whined that Bohlen's is "an ugly record of Great Betrayal," and linked him with "that elusive statesman of the half world whose admiration for everything Russian is unrivaled outside the confines of the Communist Party"—Averell Harriman.

But then McCarthy went too far. He began attacking the new Administration as well, insinuating that Dulles had lied to Congress and demanding that the Secretary be put under oath. This was the sort of self-inflicted wound that would eventually doom McCarthy, and the effect this time was to anger the Senate majority leader, Bob Taft.

Taft decided to put an end to the nonsense. He and Senator John

Sparkman of Alabama were permitted to see Bohlen's file. They found a charge by someone claiming to have a "sixth sense for moral terpitude" that Bohlen was guilty of same and a report that Bohlen sometimes entertained left-wing houseguests. The report was stuffed with testimonials to his honor and morality from a variety of Republican eminences, ranging from Douglas MacArthur to Henry Cabot Lodge (who said that he had known Bohlen since he was twelve years old and that "there is no one about whom any question of morals is less probable in my whole acquaintanceship").

The truth about Bohlen is that his marriage was remarkably strong. A very handsome man with no shortage of opportunities to stray, he felt the pull of temptation but resisted. Even alone in Eden—in Paris after V-E Day—he reached out to his wife for moral support: he wished she were there, he wrote, because "we could have lots of fun and you could keep me out of trouble. I am frightened of all these pretty corrupt French babes."

Bohlen was confirmed by a vote of 74 to 13. Reston, Lippmann, and the Alsops, his friends in the press elite, gave him a victory lunch at the Metropolitan Club, at which he pretended to be embarrassed and could barely conceal his exultation and feeling of triumph over cowardice and paranoia. Justice Felix Frankfurter wrote Avis, "You must let me tell you how exhilarating it is to have Chip's forthrightness pierce through the *nacht und nicht* of Washington's 'prudence' and cowardice." Only J. Edgar Hoover, who refused to give Bohlen a full security clearance, and Donald Lourie, who told Dulles over the phone that "those who study this sort of thing feel he is one of them [meaning homosexual]," continued to hold out in opposition to Bohlen.

Dulles himself remained uneasy. Before Bohlen left for Russia, he dropped by Dulles's office and told the Secretary that he planned to stop over in Paris for a few days before joining up with Avis, who had to wait until the children finished school in Washington. Dulles responded, "Don't you think it would be wise for you and your wife to travel together?" Bohlen snorted, "For God's sake, why?" Dulles went on awkwardly, "Well, you know there were some rumors in some of your files about immoral behavior and it would look better if your wife was with you." Bohlen icily replied that he would do no such thing.

On April 4, Bohlen left for Moscow, well pleased with his victory, feeling that McCarthy had finally been put in his place. The victory for the Administration, however, was Pyrrhic. Taft, though he had defended Bohlen, disliked controversy. He said to Dulles: "No more Bohlens."

• • •

Dulles summoned Paul Nitze to his office the afternoon of Eisenhower's inauguration. He was cordial; he told Nitze that he approved of his work. He was sorry to say, however, that he could not afford to keep on Dean Acheson's chief planner. It would not look right. In a letter to Harry Truman, Acheson described Dulles's treatment of Nitze as "plain cowardice and utter folly."

As a consolation prize, Nitze was allowed to work for the new Secretary of Defense, Charles Wilson, the former president of General Motors. Nitze started up the Pentagon's Office of International Security Affairs, ISA, its "little State Department," to ponder the broader national security implications of military planning. But then McCarthy moved in, charging that Nitze was a "Wall Street operator," while Senator Knowland claimed that Nitze was one of "Acheson's architects of disaster." In June, Charlie Wilson sheepishly told Nitze that he was sorry but that his presence at the Pentagon made it difficult for the Defense Department to win appropriations from Congress. He had, he went on, received his orders from the White House: "No more Bohlens."

Nitze was forced out of government. He established a "PPS in exile" at Johns Hopkins School of Advanced International Studies, but he was quickly bored by the theorizing of academicians. After visiting Groton one weekend in 1954, he confided to Acheson that the "thought and talk" of the Groton sixth formers was "infinitely better" than what he had heard "at meetings of political scientists." His bitterness at being sacrificed to the primitives was only slowly assuaged. He recalls not quite feeling right until he had ridden in a steeplechase in Maryland in the autumn of 1953 and looked back, as he crossed the finish line in first place, to see mud splattered all over the also-rans.

• • •

President Eisenhower had had misgivings about choosing Dulles as his Secretary of State. He rather preferred John McCloy, whom he had known well since McCloy was Assistant Secretary of War and he was Supreme Commander of allied forces in Europe. McCloy was much more easygoing and pragmatic than Dulles, more Ike's sort. Eisenhower's advisers, however, had warned that McCloy was too closely tied to Acheson and his crowd (it did not help McCloy that Harriman was telling reporters that McCloy was *his* choice to be Secretary). McCarthy, meanwhile, was roiling about, ranting at McCloy's "unbelievable, inconceivable, unexplainable record of deliberate, secret betrayal."

Eisenhower tried another idea: He would make McCloy Under Secretary and then, after a year or so, bring Dulles over to the White House as his National Security Adviser and make McCloy the Secretary. Dulles, after all, did not want to be bothered with administration or personal diplomacy; he was more interested in policy making.

Dulles volunteered himself to broach this idea to McCloy. Dulles was at first oblique (he began by asking whom McCloy would recommend), and McCloy was reluctant. He told Dulles that he was broke and wanted to make money. McCloy was also suspicious. "What are *you* going to do, Foster?" he asked. As he listened to Dulles explain, he got the feeling that Dulles would remain as policy maker, leaving McCloy to "act as caretaker and do dirty jobs." McCloy refused.

Years later, after talking to Eisenhower and his longtime aide Walter Bedell Smith, McCloy was convinced that Dulles had intentionally misrepresented Eisenhower's true desires. Both men indicated that McCloy's role was to have been larger than Dulles described it. McCloy became convinced that when Dulles got wind of Eisenhower's scheme, he had said to Ike, "Let me handle it," and in his own fashion, he had.

McCloy returned to Wall Street. He would never hold public office again, save for a brief tour as Kennedy's special assistant for disarmament. Yet in many ways, he would wield more power out of government than in. As chairman of the Chase Manhattan Bank, he became a kind of private statesman, an emissary of American capitalism. At the bank itself, he was characteristically disarming, starting on the first floor and working his way up, introducing himself to every employee ("Hello, I'm Jack McCloy"). At the same time he aggressively pushed the bank into international markets, lending billions of dollars and picking up myriad IOUs. *Fortune* gushed that the "Chase Chairmanship—vast, varied, statesmanlike—symbolizes the something more in commercial banking." He had total access, not just in Washington but in European and Middle Eastern capitals. Foreign leaders, when they came to the United States, paid homage to him, as if he were a sovereign in his own right. McCloy leveraged his power by joining boards; he became a director of, among other companies, Westinghouse, Allied Chemical, United Fruit, each with its own vast international empire; he also became chairman of the Ford Foundation, the richest dispenser of philanthropy.

He became a sage. In 1953 alone, McCloy took honorary degrees from Princeton, Columbia, Smith, Dartmouth, and New York University. That year he published *The Challenge to American Foreign Policy*, based on the Godkin lectures he had given at Harvard; the tract was straightforward containment, but the emphasis was on management, on making bureaucracy work, on the need for pragmatism over philosophy. He became chairman of the Council on Foreign Relations, the incubator of foreign policy ideas and a farm club for policy makers. In 1956, it was McCloy who picked Henry Kissinger, then an obscure Harvard government professor, to chair a study on Soviet-American relations. For Kissinger, this was his first break into the foreign policy elite; McCloy later helped Kissinger get a job on Nelson Rockefeller's payroll as a speech writer.

McCloy never lost touch with government. He assumed the role of elder statesman, advising Eisenhower and Dulles from time to time on foreign policy questions. On the eve of the Suez crisis, for instance, Dulles phoned McCloy in the middle of the night and asked him to call the heads of every major bank to determine if there was an unexpectedly large flow of funds to Europe or Israel that might signal a buildup for war.

McCloy was disturbed that Dulles seemed so panicky and uninformed. But in fact, Dulles's ignorance about developments in the Middle East was not so surprising. Ever since World War II, the U.S. government had preferred to leave Middle East diplomacy to the oil companies and the bankers who financed Big Oil—now chief among them John McCloy.

Washington was torn by conflicting aims. An abundant supply of cheap oil was essential to the economy and national security. Friendly relations with the Arabs were necessary to keep them out of the Soviet orbit. Yet no Administration could politically afford to offend American Jews by appearing to help Israel's mortal enemies in the Middle East. The solution: Let the oil companies take care of the Arabs, with the discreet aid or at least noninterference of the U.S. government.

Acheson had been perfectly frank about the oil companies' role. "American oil operations are, for all practical purposes, instruments of our foreign policy towards [Middle Eastern] countries," he declared before leaving office in 1953. Eisenhower and Dulles simply maintained the Truman Administration's benign hands-off policy toward the oil companies. The U.S. continued to regard royalties paid to

Arab countries by the oil companies as income tax, saving the oil companies billions in U.S. taxes. This so-called "golden gimmick," first conceived in 1950 and kept secret for the next six years, allowed the U.S. to in effect funnel foreign aid to Arab countries without admitting it.

The only real dissent came from the trustbusters at the Justice Department, who charged that the oil companies were joining to arbitrarily fix prices and production levels to guarantee profits. The Justice Department initiated a criminal action against the oil companies in 1952, but Acheson was able to intercede with Truman and head off the investigation.

As the Rockefellers' banker, McCloy was heavily involved in financing oil production in Arab countries. The Rockefellers held a controlling interest in the Chase; three of the so-called Seven Sisters (Esso, Socal, and Mobil) were offshoots of John D. Rockefeller's Standard Oil. McCloy regularly found himself shuttling back and forth between New York and Middle Eastern capitals, handling multibillion-dollar oil deals and hobnobbing with the Shah of Iran, the king of Jordan, and various Arab sheiks.

Eisenhower and Dulles were only too happy to make McCloy their unofficial emissary to the Arab world. When the British worried that Arab oil money was being used to foment revolution in Iraq, for instance, it was McCloy who was dispatched to implore King Ibn Saud to not finance Iraqi dissidents. In 1957, after the Suez crisis, it was McCloy who was asked to head the U.N. mission to negotiate the salvaging and reopening of the Canal. Along the way, McCloy added Nasser to his list of friendly Arab potentates.

McCloy was perfectly suited to his public-private role. The U.S. government felt it could trust him to look after the national interest as well as the Rockefellers', and in fact the two seemed perfectly congruent. By maintaining close personal relationships with Arab rulers, McCloy helped guarantee stability, a steady supply of cheap oil, and a buffer against the Soviets. It was the sort of practical diplomacy that McCloy could practice better than anyone. At the time, it was still possible to conduct business in the Middle East face-to-face, by reasoning and bargaining with leaders who had developed a taste for certain Western temptations, like Rolls-Royces. Though the forces of nascent nationalism could be felt, they could be dealt with, smoothed over, contained. The really tempestuous revolution—the rise of Islamic fundamentalism—had not yet stirred. In the late 1950s, OPEC was not even an acronym; Muammar Qaddafi was an impoverished

Libyan teen-ager; Ruhollah Khomeini was an obscure middle-aged mullah praying quietly in Iran.

• • •

Determined to cut spending for conventional forces and rely almost totally on the Bomb, the Eisenhower Administration had no place for Bob Lovett, the Defense Secretary who wanted to spend more, not less, on overall preparedness. Lovett was not entirely unhappy to leave his ulcer-inducing responsibilities behind, however, and take his "glass insides" back to Wall Street.

Lovett's advice and experience were too valuable for the New Administration to lose altogether. Like McCloy, he became an elder statesman. He advised Dulles on disarmament, and at Eisenhower's request joined the President's Board of Consultants on Foreign Intelligence Activities in 1956.

His principal task was to look into the covert operations of the CIA. The agency, run by Foster Dulles's brother, Allen, was in the 1950s in its freebooting heyday. It organized the overthrow of the governments deemed to be pro-Communist in Iran in 1953 and Guatemala in 1954; helped install supposedly pro-Western governments in Egypt in 1954 and Laos in 1959; tried and failed to overthrow the government of Indonesia in 1958; infiltrated refugees to disrupt Soviet-bloc governments in Eastern Europe and ran sabotage operations against China from Laos and Burma; plotted assassination attempts against Chou En-lai of China, Patrice Lumumba of the Congo, Fidel Castro of Cuba, and Rafael Trujillo of of the Dominican Republic.

Lovett was disturbed by the agency's interventionism. In 1956, Lovett and David Bruce, Acheson's former ambassador to France, wrote a report to Eisenhower sharply denouncing "King Making" by the CIA. It warned that all those bright young men being recruited by the CIA out of Yale were becoming freewheeling, well-financed buccaneers. Lovett and Bruce cautioned Eisenhower that the agency was out of control, that it needed formal oversight and asked, "where will we be tomorrow?" In 1960, Lovett particularly objected to the plans for the Bay of Pigs invasion, then in the planning stages, and demanded a total reassessment of covert policies. His recommendations were resisted by Allen Dulles and ignored by the Eisenhower White House. The Kennedy Administration heedlessly plunged ahead with the harebrained scheme to land fifteen hundred Cuban exiles on the Cuban coast in April of 1961; lacking air cover or reinforcements, they were quickly driven into the sea by Castro's army. After the Bay of Pigs, Lovett angrily demanded before a board of inquiry: "What right do we have barging into other people's countries, buying newspapers and handing out money to opposition parties or supporting a candidate for this or that office?" Lovett was too discreet to take the one step that might have reined in the CIA before it was too late: leaking to the press. Actually, the editors of *The New York Times* knew of the Bay of Pigs, but, as faithful members of the Establishment themselves, printed nothing.

• • •

Bohlen arrived in Moscow as the U.S. ambassador to the Soviet Union on April 11, 1953. He found the city "grim, brooding, and drab," the neo-Stalinist architecture rising over the city "a rather bad combination of classical and Moorish and some indefinable elements." Unlike Kennan, the more ebullient Bohlen was not depressed by the ambience. Among his first official acts was to bring in a French chef from the American Embassy in Paris; Bohlen's dining room was thereafter the best in Moscow.

Washington badly needed accurate reporting from Moscow. While the U.S. Senate had been trading rumors about Bohlen's moral turpitude and tying up the appointment of the American ambassador, Stalin had died. He had ruled Russia with absolute authority for nearly three decades. Without his iron grip, the direction of Russia was a huge and essential mystery.

Except that he should travel with his wife, Bohlen had been given no instructions by Dulles upon leaving for Moscow. Eisenhower told him only, "Watch your stomach and don't let them get you." Bohlen did not even attempt to see the new Premier, Malenkov; Dulles disapproved of personal associations with Soviet officials. The U.S. ambassador was never invited to a private home in Moscow, and, like Kennan before him, he was followed everywhere by four KGB agents, or "angels," as they were known by embassy staffers. In the new chancery under construction that spring the Soviets installed forty-three listening microphones in rooms that were thought by the Americans to be "secure." (They were years later discovered by the CIA.) Bohlen just assumed his office was wired by the Soviets and wrote all his analyses in longhand.

According to the *Times*'s Harrison Salisbury, Bohlen arrived "bruised, shaken and spooked" by his confirmation ordeal and hardly dared to report what he saw. Actually, Bohlen could see significant change in the Kremlin's mood, and he did report it. Upon Stalin's death, the

Hate America campaign was abruptly dropped and the purges ended. The cult of personality that had deified Stalin was denounced in *Pravda*; Malenkov seemed more moderate than his predecessor (Bohlen took to calling him Warren G. Malenkov; his return to normalcy à la Warren G. Harding included doing business by day, rather than at night as Stalin had demanded). Bohlen wrote Dulles on July 7 that he was convinced that these moves could not be dismissed as "simply another peace campaign designed solely or even primarily to bemuse and to divide the West. The events that have occurred here cumulatively add up, in my opinion, to something considerably more important, offering on the one hand more opportunity and on the other considerably more danger than the standard propaganda gestures which we have seen since the end of the war." He said that he believed the Soviets were interested in using diplomacy to further their interests, especially preventing German rearmament and averting a general war.

Dulles did not even bother to respond. Then, a few days later, Beria, the chief of police, was arrested. Dulles's interest suddenly perked up; Bohlen was summoned home to report. At the airport he was taken directly to Dulles's house and ushered into the Secretary's study.

Dulles was convinced that the Kremlin was on the verge of a bloody power struggle that would lead to the downfall of the regime. Bohlen disagreed; he said that Beria had been arrested because the new man wanted to put the police under collective leadership. Dulles ignored him. He picked up his copy of Stalin's *Problems of Leninism*, lying open on the desk, and began reading underlined passages about seizing power. Bohlen remarked that Stalin's writings bore little relevance to the Soviet Union now that Stalin was dead. Dulles dismissed him.

Bohlen had hoped to have some influence on Eisenhower. Ike liked to play golf with Bohlen. He was rarely interested in discussing the Soviet Union in any depth. The President's seeming indifference could be deceiving; he was more alert, more in charge, than his bland, amiable style let on. But Dulles stood between Bohlen and the President. The ambassador could barely abide the Secretary, but he had too much respect for Dulles's office to try to go behind his back to the White House. Bohlen's lost opportunity to educate Eisenhower on the intricacies of the Soviet Union is history's loss. A chance to truly ease the Cold War was lost as well.

In later years, Bohlen would regret that he had not done more, that he had not tried harder to make Washington warm up to the Soviets after Stalin's death. In particular, he rued that he did not urge the

Administration to heed Winston Churchill's call for a "meeting at the summit" when Malenkov succeeded Stalin in 1953 (the first time the phrase was used). Dulles probably would not have listened; still, Bohlen would muse in later conversations with friends that Stalin's death had offered a last chance for a real breakthrough—a reunified Germany: an arms control agreement?—at least an opening to start talking.

Later thaws were regarded with suspicion by Dulles. When the Soviets agreed to a Foreign Ministers' meeting in 1954, Dulles employed a Russian-speaking lip-reader to watch the Soviet delegation; he hoped to spy on the Soviet "huddle." Bohlen was delighted when Eisenhower, pressed hard by England and France, agreed to a summit meeting with the Soviets in 1955, overriding Dulles's objections. On the eve of the Geneva summit, Bohlen advised Dulles that the Kremlin genuinely wished to relax tensions, that the Soviets feared that an arms race would strain their economy, and they they might even be interested in arms control. Dulles again paid little heed, though he did ask Bohlen to stay in Washington to help him prepare for the summit. Bohlen by now was quite cynical; he wrote Avis at the end of June, "His Nibs in telling me his wish said, 'You better stay. There might be something you could help me out on,' which for him to me is almost gracious." The summit itself was a disappointment, doomed by mutual suspicion.

Bohlen began letting his disgust with Dulles show during Sunday-night poker games or drinking bouts with reporters he trusted. (It was at one such affair that Bohlen dubbed the Secretary with an enduring nickname: "dull, duller, Dulles.") Inevitably, word got back to the Secretary. When Sherman Adams, Eisenhower's chief aide, asked Dulles in April of 1956 if Bohlen should address the Cabinet, Dulles replied that the Cabinet "might enjoy it but rather not—it would build him up too much—he is not working with us."

Dulles informed Bohlen by letter in December of that year that he was relieving him as ambassador to Moscow "knowing your desire to take up writing as a profession." Bohlen was flabbergasted; he had not "the foggiest idea" where Dulles had gotten the notion he wanted to write; the Secretary's letter just seemed to him a dishonest way of removing a diplomat from his post. When Bohlen said he had no intention of retiring to write, Dulles offered him Pakistan. Bohlen refused. The Philippines? Bohlen, in a quandary, called on Acheson and Lovett for advice. They urged him not to leave the Foreign Service, but to stay on and simply outlast Dulles.

Reluctantly, Bohlen accepted the Philippines, a country he knew very little about. Dulles promptly leaked that Bohlen had been trying to leave Moscow for four years and that he, Dulles, had only reluctantly agreed to let him. Before leaving for Manila, Bohlen stopped by to see Eisenhower. The President said he was sorry to see Bohlen leave Moscow, that he had debated a long time before agreeing to his request to transfer, but that since it was Bohlen's wish to leave Russia, he had reluctantly accepted. Bohlen said he had no desire to leave Moscow at all. Eisenhower exclaimed, "Oh, is that true?"

From Manila, Bohlen was asked by Dulles to comment on developments in the Soviet Union. Bohlen responded that it was impossible for him to do so "at this great distance." Bohlen's golf game improved markedly in Manila, but he caught an intestinal disease and had to go on the wagon—for the first time ever. "You can imagine what that means," he wrote Avis. Financial problems gnawed; he could not cover embassy entertaining with private funds and fell five thousand dollars short, forcing him to borrow from friends. He began to regard Manila as his last tour, and to think of retiring to make money. At times, he felt that he wanted nothing more to do with public life. If her husband were to quit, Avis wrote her brother, Charlie Thayer, in April of 1958, "we shall certainly not do anything that means any connection with foreign affairs or Washington, and preferably will have some connection with some DOUGH."

·   ·   ·

Kennan had considered fleeing the U.S. altogether after his forced resignation from the State Department in 1953. "There is nothing much that any of us can do to oppose the McCarthyite trend or to escape it," Kennan wrote Thayer, who was himself living abroad in Majorca after being purged by McCarthyites. "And in these circumstances I can imagine that life might be pleasanter or more productive somewhere else."

Rather than become "in effect an exile," however, Kennan retreated to the Institute for Advanced Study in Princeton, Robert Oppenheimer's oasis for gifted thinkers. From his cloister, Kennan peered out into the dark age. His heyday—the first two years after the war—he regarded as a rare moment of integrity in foreign policy. Thereafter, he said, "normalcy took over." He came to believe that he would have been compelled to resign even if the Democrats had won in 1952. His different views on how to handle the Soviets now set him apart not just from John Foster Dulles "but the entire ruling establishment of American political life."

Still, Kennan could not stay out of public life. One night late in the winter of 1954, he answered his door in Princeton to find a farmer and his wife standing outside. They had driven 150 miles in the hopes of seeing him. Would he, they asked, consider running for Congress? Kennan gaped. "Which party?" he asked. "Democratic," they answered. (He added in his memoirs that "it would have made no difference to me if it had been the other one.")

"I was really rocked by this approach," he wrote his sister Jeannette, "partly for its sincerity and ingenuousness, partly because I realized that having spoken out critically in so prominent a way about the shortcomings of our government, I had no right to decline such an offer, if it were genuine." So Kennan said yes. After some debate among the party elders ("Why he ain't even registered as a Democrat!" "Yeah, but his wife is.") he received the party nomination. But when he returned to Princeton he was "horrified" to discover that the Institute for Advanced Study could not continue to pay his salary if he were to run for Congress. Lacking independent means, unwilling to turn to "some big dairy owner or other local tycoon," and "feeling an awful fool for it," he withdrew his name from the race. The experience left him believing that congressmen should all be "men of means" and thus "above petty corruption."

Britain's pre-Reform Parliament was closer to his ideal of enlightened government than the U.S. Congress of the 1950s. A self-described "natural-born antiquarian," Kennan harbored nostalgia for England's eighteenth-century ruling aristocracy. In 1957, he was offered the opportunity to indulge his Anglophilia as Eastman Visiting Professor at Oxford for a year.

He was disappointed. Oxford seemed to him a grim industrial town, its elegance tarnished by automobile fumes and the working classes. At the same time, Kennan felt socially insecure among the residual gentry. He confided to Isaiah Berlin that he would "never fit into an Oxford common room: the people there would be too urbane, too witty, too quick in repartee; I was only a gloomy Scot." Berlin tried to reassure him, in a British sort of way: "Think nothing of it. Balliol's full of gloomy Scots."

Kennan was invited that year by the BBC to give the Reith Lectures, a prestigious, widely heard annual series of six radio addresses. He was panicked to be alone ("alone as I have ever been") before a radio microphone for twenty-eight minutes, but he settled down and spoke lucidly with a kind of controlled passion. His lectures caused a sensation, not just in England, but in the U.S. as well. *Life* declared:

"The unofficial words of a retired U.S. diplomat have become a major political issue throughout the Western world."

Kennan had urged publicly what he had suggested privately within the State Department eight years earlier: that the U.S. and Soviet Union disengage from Germany and leave a demilitarized, unified country. But he had added, significantly, that all nuclear weapons should be withdrawn from Europe. His rhetoric was vivid, if at times slightly contorted ("until we stop pushing the Kremlin against a closed door, we shall never learn whether it will be prepared to go through an open one"). And his timing was propitious. The Soviets had just launched Sputnik, causing fear throughout the West that war could come raining down from the heavens.

To hear Mr. "X," the author of containment, plead for disengagement shocked many who knew nothing of his quiet evolution at the State Department. (And startled even some who did: "Dear George sure has gone off the deep end," Avis Bohlen wrote Charlie Thayer upon reading about the lectures.) Kennan's words were heartfelt, and they reached beyond ruling circles to common people; Kennan was astonished to see a radio technician, a small Cockney woman, pounding the table in approval as he spoke from the glass broadcasting booth. The acclamation had its predictable effect on Kennan: he collapsed with ulcers and an acute sinus infection.

• • •

Dean Acheson was outraged by Kennan's Reith Lectures. He put out a press release explaining that Kennan had "never grasped the realities of power relationships" but instead had taken a "rather mystical attitude towards them." Acheson followed that swipe with a long article in *Foreign Affairs* warning that without American military might, Europe would be a prime target for the Soviets, that unless Europe and the United States teamed up, Soviet tanks would roll and West Germany would fall.

Acheson was fond of Kennan, though he did not usually agree with him, and he softened this public assault with private reassurances of friendship. "We have differed on this subject for too long for it to affect my deep regard and affection for you," he wrote Kennan, enclosing the proofs of the *Foreign Affairs* article. "I hope the same is true for you, although I am more accustomed to public controversy and criticism than you are. So you are entitled to a few earthy expletives." Kennan responded a week later, "No hard feelings . . . a very good article; rarely if ever have I seen error so gracefully and respectably clothed." The ability of gentlemen to remain close while carving each other up in public debate was a revelation to Kennan's daughter Grace. She later recalled, "Even though I got very upset by the things he said about my father, I remember that the Achesons were invited to my wedding and sent me a present. I didn't write them a thank-you note, even though I knew it was rude. I was too young to realize that you can disagree bitterly on policy and still be friends."

Yet others began to notice that Acheson's invective was getting more bitter, more cruel. This was especially true when aimed at those he did not like, particularly John Foster Dulles.

To Gerhard Gesell, his law partner at Covington, Burling, he repeatedly referred to Dulles as a "coward." Acheson positively enjoyed Dulles's fiascoes. In 1956, after Dulles had precipitated the Suez crisis by driving Egypt's Nasser into the arms of the Soviets, Acheson wrote his son, David, "Dulles really got his comeuppance there, didn't he?" After Dulles told *Life* magazine that "the ability to get to the verge of war is the necessary art... if you are scared to go to the brink, you are lost," Acheson wrote the Lovetts a New Year's card: "Our love to you both, and stay away from Foster's verge." Lovett joined in the fun. He sent Acheson a photograph of Dulles in a cub scout uniform that had appeared in a New York paper. Acheson responded, "Oh, God! I can't bear it. I'm too old to stand shocks like the one you just gave me. What in the world do you think the man—if that's what he is—was thinking of?" A few days after Dulles died of cancer in May 1959, Acheson silenced a dinner party at Harewood by announcing "Thank God Foster is underground."

Acheson wrote acerbic notes, practiced law, devoted days of his time to Yale, where he was a trustee (among his causes was resisting the introduction of sherry to university functions. "I have bitterly opposed it in favor of the coarser but quicker cocktail," he wrote a friend). And he fretted over his loss of influence. "Thanks for the note," he wrote Joe Alsop, whose hard-line views Acheson shared. "It has cheered me out of the frustrated feeling I sometimes have that I am talking only to myself."

Acheson knew that he was earning a reputation as a curmudgeon. "They tell me in the press that I am getting rigid. Perhaps they are right," he wrote a Yale friend in 1959. "At any rate I still believe that we are not going to get very far in our dealings with the Russians unless they realize that the Free World has a basis of power to which they have got to adjust themselves."

He longed to return to power himself. In the late fifties he became increasingly involved in building a shadow government, in generating new ideas to challenge the Republicans. In 1957, he read with great interest a new book by McCloy's discovery at the Council on Foreign Relations, Henry Kissinger, called *Nuclear Weapons and Foreign Policy*. Acheson was a bit unnerved by Kissinger's argument that limited nuclear war should be considered a strategic option, but he was struck by his attack on Dulles's massive retaliation doctrine. In part to save money by skimping on conventional forces, the Eisenhower Administration relied on the Bomb ("more bang for the buck") as virtually its sole deterrent to the Soviets. Kissinger perceived that it was foolhardy to "go to the brink" at every international crisis, that the U.S. needed to be able to calibrate its response. The book, among several others, nurtured the germ of a new idea that would become the policy of the Kennedy and Johnson Administrations—"flexible response," the capacity to fight small, limited "brush-fire" wars. Kissinger's book "has shaken me," Acheson wrote a friend. "It is a hard book to read because of its repetitive Germanic style and the first section is infuriating because of its academic superiority. But the damned cuss has brains and has thought a lot." Acheson was so impressed by Kissinger that he tried to recruit him to formally declare himself a Democrat. Kissinger, preserving his options, declined, though his letters to Acheson in this period spare no flattery.

Acheson was also impressed by another comer, General Maxwell Taylor, whom he had admired since meeting him in Germany in the early fifties. When Taylor resigned as Army Chief of Staff in 1959 in opposition to the diminished role massive retaliation gave to the Army, Acheson was among the first to ask him to lunch.*

Acheson's fomenting was formalized and given direction by the creation of the Democratic Advisory Council in 1956, a sort of government-in-exile for the party out of power. Acheson chaired the Foreign Policy Committee; his chief planner, out of government as in, was Paul Nitze.

Nitze had forever endeared himself to Acheson by a small gesture of friendship. A couple of months after the change of Administrations, he called Acheson and asked him to lunch at the Metropolitan Club. Acheson told him, "You know, you're the first person in Washington who has asked me to have lunch since I was Secretary of State." For

---

*The admiration was mutual. Taylor was so impressed by Acheson and McCloy that he believed they should be established as permanent *genro*, like Japanese noblemen, to guide U.S. national security policy.

the next two decades, the pair ate lunch together every week at the same table reserved in the Metropolitan Club dining room.

Together, Nitze and Acheson wrote the foreign policy plank of the Democratic platform in 1956. Neither was enamored, however, with the party's nominee, Adlai Stevenson. They considered him brilliant, but fatally indecisive and too "soft." Acheson and his cohorts shared a mean little joke about Stevenson, that as he was about to give a speech, he asked an aide, "Do I have time to go to the bathroom?" Assured that he did, he would ask, "Do I want to go to the bathroom?" Acheson was equally caustic about Stevenson's liberal foreign policy advisers, particularly Chester Bowles, a former advertising executive who had served as ambassador to India and became a congressman from Connecticut in 1959. He thought Bowles was a garrulous windbag and an ineffectual do-gooder. "Time spent in the advertising business seems to create a permanent deformity, like the Chinese habit of footbinding," Acheson wrote Eugene Rostow about Bowles in 1958.

Stevenson's admirers, in turn, thought that Acheson was too rigid, too hard line. Bowles, along with John Kenneth Galbraith, Arthur Schlesinger, and other members of the liberal wing, believed that Acheson had been made more rigid by right-wing attacks. Though Acheson denounced Dulles for selling out to McCarthyism, the liberals were convinced that McCarthy's attacks had made Acheson and his cohorts overly afraid of appearing "soft" on Communism. The Achesonians would never come out and say this, recalls Galbraith. Rather, they would say, "We've got to maintain our credibility."

•   •   •

Only one figure in the Democrats' inner council was able to "maintain credibility" and still insist that it was possible to reason with the Soviets. Averell Harriman, recalls Galbraith, would begin discussions by talking about "what a bunch of bastards the Soviets were" but then he would say, "but we've got to deal with them." Like his tutors in Kremlinology, Kennan and Bohlen, Harriman believed that the Soviets were paranoid, dangerous, yet ultimately conservative and not eager to start a war by invading Europe. Harriman argued that it was possible, by diligence and patience, to negotiate agreements with the Soviets, especially if he was the negotiator.

There was nothing "soft" about Harriman, and Acheson, at first, trusted him to brace up Stevenson, to "keep him pointed close to the wind and not let him fall off with phrases like 'the relentless pursuit of peace,'" he wrote Truman in November of 1955. Harriman, however, was becoming irritated with Acheson. He felt that his old schoolmate was becoming fixed and dogmatic in his old age, and he let his disenchantment show. "You know, Dean," he would growl at meetings of the Democratic Advisory Council, "I don't agree with your declarations of war." He would tell friends how fortunate it was that his own mind had not aged so.

There was some real truth in this arrogant remark. Harriman was thought of as a stolid man, not particularly creative or bright. But the truth is that he retained all through his life the capacity to change, to grow and adapt. He was able to change careers, change political parties, change his point of view. He was never dogmatic and often restless. The only real constant was his desire to fulfill his father's wish that he "be something and somebody."

To his friends, Harriman's ambition had always been a source of bemusement. But they had difficulty accepting the latest turn in a career that had spun from business tycoon to statesman and now to politician.

After his abortive attempt to run for President in 1952, Harriman returned to Europe, where along with Jean Monnet he beefed up NATO by building a European Defense Community. But he had been bitten by politics. In 1954, he decided to run for governor of New York.

A wooden speaker, graceless at small talk, and about as far removed from the common man as it is possible to be in a modern democracy, Harriman was an unlikely politician. Caustic, socialite Marie was an even more unlikely politician's wife. Harriman had actually been approached about running for governor of New York in 1950 by Carmine De Sapio's Democratic machine, "told that he could have the nomination if he wanted it," but Marie had balked. She told her husband that she would "jump off a bridge" if he ever ran for elective office. "How do you think Marie would fit in in Albany?" Harriman asked Cy Sulzberger with a smile in November 1951. "We both agreed that it was not her type of town," Sulzberger recorded in his diary.

Marie, who did not like to rise before noon, found herself giving morning teas for the ladies of Albany as of January 1, 1955. A driven worker (he awakened one aide before 7 A.M. and grumbled, "I see you've taken to snoozing before breakfast"), Harriman was a conscientious governor. He ordered his staff to move to Albany from New York City and dutifully cut ribbons, kissed babies, and wrangled with the legislature. His agenda was ambitiously liberal in that pre–Great

Society era; he pushed programs for the elderly, mental health patients, and minorities. As a tightwad, however, he did not want to spend heavily to pay for social programs, and his were rather modest.

Harriman's real aim was the White House. The 1956 presidential race found him far from Albany, whistle-stopping in his private railway car. He had Harry Truman's support, but at the convention Stevenson had Mayor Daley's, which counted for much more. "You know," one of Harriman's floormen told Theodore H. White, then covering his first convention, "I hear you can buy all the delegates from the Canal Zone, Puerto Rico, and the Virgin Islands in one package, all twelve of them, but you have to deal with a fellow named Benitez." He went off in search of Benitez, but Daley's operatives got there first. Stevenson won 905½ delegates (including the Caribbean contingent) to Harriman's 210.

Harriman did not enjoy the heartfelt support of his old friends in these endeavors. Acheson, despite his impatience with Stevenson and his deep ties to Harriman, supported Stevenson for President in 1956. Most of Harriman's old colleagues—including Lovett, Acheson, McCloy, and Nitze—felt that he was cheapening himself, letting hubris compromise his principles. They believed that his moderate views on the Cold War came not from a sophisticated understanding of Soviet behavior but rather out of a desire to win over the liberal wing of the Democratic Party. Years later, discussing the evolution of Harriman's views, Nitze's face took on a sour expression, as if he had bitten into a clove. "He picked up crazy ideas when he started to run for office," said Nitze. McCloy attributed a "definite change in [Harriman's] attitude" on the Cold War largely to "political ambition." He had been dubious about Harriman's political integrity ever since hearing him boast that he had contributed to both parties in 1932 to be sure of getting into government. Lovett, determinedly apolitical himself, was privately contemptuous of his old friend's desire for elected office. "Averell's a Democrat," he would say, "and a fool." Acheson would tease Harriman about his career in politics, but, recalls his son-in-law Bill Bundy, there was a slight edge to his voice.

In 1958, Harriman was stunned by Nelson Rockefeller in his race for re-election as governor. Harriman's leaden campaigning was no match for Rocky's flamboyant blintzes-and-pizza, "Hihowaya?" juggernaut. He lost badly, by four hundred fifty thousand votes.

Harriman was sixty-seven years old, and finally slowing. He had quit taking cold baths in the morning, thereby shedding a last bit of Groton asceticism, and quit smoking, on a dare from his family doctor and John Kenneth Galbraith. He began nodding off after dinner, though friends noticed that he woke up quickly when the ladies left and the male conversation turned to politics or foreign affairs. His hearing, ruined by too much flying on unpressurized airplanes to remote spots around the world, began to deteriorate noticeably. After losing to Rockefeller he seemed downcast, as if he had tried everything that private and public life had to offer, and could think of nothing else. Even his close friends began to think he was all done in. They underestimated him.

PART THREE

WISE MEN

I thought to myself that what began in the spring of 1940 when Henry Stimson came to Washington ended tonight. The American Establishment is dead.

WALT ROSTOW, AT THE LAST SUPPER OF THE WISE MEN, MARCH 25, 1968

CHAPTER 20

Lovett and President-Elect Kennedy

PASSING
THE TORCH

"No, sir, my bearings
are burnt out"

Dean Acheson was waiting on a platform in New York's Penn-sylvania Station on a snowy March evening in 1958 when a porter ushered him to the stationmaster's office. He found there an elegant, soft-voiced young woman whom he knew from Georgetown society, Jacqueline Kennedy. He knew her stepfamily, the Auchinclosses, from school days; the Auchincloss men were well represented at Groton and in Scroll and Key at Yale. He greeted her cordially. She gave him a rather frosty hello.

The stationmaster apologized. A late-winter blizzard had delayed the train to Washington, and he was afraid it might take all night to get there. Acheson said that he would board anyway; so did Mrs. Kennedy.

By chance, their seats were together in the parlor car, and as soon as they settled down, Mrs. Kennedy lit into Acheson. How could he attack her husband so in his book? Acheson sighed and recalled that in *Power and Diplomacy* he had harshly criticized a speech by Senator Kennedy that called on France to grant independence to Algeria immediately. "This impatient snapping of our fingers," Acheson had written in *Power and Diplomacy*, was a poor way to treat an old and valued ally. Acheson turned to her and remarked that they could spend the rest of a long train ride fighting, or they could be pleasant. "All right, let's be pleasant," she said, but continued to sulk. They passed the night, Acheson later recalled, with "desultory conversation and troubled sleep." Mrs. Kennedy did not let go after they finally arrived in Washington. She wrote Acheson demanding to know "how one capable of such an Olympian tone can become so personal when attacking someone for political differences." Acheson responded dryly in a note to "Jacquie" that "the Olympians seem to me to have been a pretty personal lot."

Dean Acheson did not have easy relations with the Kennedys. He had occasionally shared a ride with Senator Kennedy from Capitol Hill to Georgetown after Democratic Party meetings, but the conversation was never all that warm. "I would not say that we were in any way friends—we were acquaintances," Acheson later recalled of their relationship. He distrusted the Kennedys, or more precisely Joe Kennedy. At lunch at the Metropolitan Club, he would dismiss Joe as a social-climbing bootlegger who had bought his spoiled son a seat in Congress. Acheson could not forgive the father for siding with Neville Chamberlain and appeasement in World War II.

John Kennedy, who believed in the existence of an American Establishment, very much wanted its approval. The Kennedys had overcome much of their social insecurity, they had conquered Harvard, including its Brahmin sanctuaries. But the family felt slightly cowed by the disciples of Stimson and Marshall, the Achesons, Lovetts, and Harrimans who had come from Wall Street and the great law firms. John Kennedy himself had more admiration for the cool toughness and unflinching pragmatism of Lovett and Acheson than he did for his more liberal advisers, men like Bowles and Galbraith, whom he considered idealistic but slightly mushy.

Acheson was the most intimidating exemplar of the Stimsonian tradition. Young Kennedy, perhaps sensing Acheson's dislike of his father, was stiff and ill at east around the old statesman. Acheson later recalled that Kennedy was so deferential to him that he made him feel old. It is too bad; the two had a common irreverence and might have enjoyed each other's company.

Acheson had hoped to block John Kennedy's nomination for President in 1960 by backing Senator Stuart Symington, a fellow Yale man. "Maybe we should all give Jack a run for his money—or Joe's," Acheson wrote Harry Truman in April of 1960. Like Acheson, Clark Clifford backed Stuart Symington, a fellow veteran of the Truman days when Clifford had been a presidential adviser and Symington Secretary of the Air Force. But Clifford was a flexible man, a skillful, discreet operator who knew how to smooth over strained relations and who by nature gravitated to power. He had handled touchy legal problems for the Kennedys, suing columnist Drew Pearson for alleging that Kennedy had not been the true author of *Profiles in Courage*, and, more recently, quietly disposing of an even more delicate matter, a charge by a woman that she had once been engaged to marry JFK. In the late spring of 1960, the Kennedys called on Clifford again. Harry Truman had been openly denouncing Kennedy, in part for his Catholicism. Could Clifford restrain the former President? Clifford went to Acheson, pleading the need for party unity. Acheson, a good Democrat, agreed to intercede with Truman. On June 27, before the Democratic Convention, he wrote "the Boss": "Could we make a treaty on what we shall *not* say?" He laid out a list of "It's not dones": "I. About other Democratic candidates: (a) Never say any of them is not qualified to be President. . . ." Later he asked Truman, "Do you really care about Jack's being a Catholic? I never have. It hasn't bothered me about de Gaulle or Adenauer or Schuman or DeGasperi, so why Kennedy? Furthermore, I don't think he's a very good Catholic. . . ." Still, Acheson remained dubious about JFK. In mid-September, he wrote Archie MacLeish, "The best campaign cheer I know is the current gag, 'anyway, they can't elect *both* of them.'" In October, Acheson bowed to the modern age and rented a television set to watch the presidential debates. He was so put off, however, by television as well as the candidates, that he returned the TV set before the second debate.

Almost immediately after his election, John Kennedy called on Acheson at P Street. Acheson offered him a martini, but Kennedy took tea, setting a precedent that did not particularly please Acheson. The cameramen tromping through his parlor to record the young President-elect seeking the counsel of the elder statesman further irritated Acheson.

Kennedy said that he needed Acheson's advice on three positions in his Cabinet: State, Defense, Treasury. He quickly assured Acheson that he had no intention of appointing a "soft" liberal for State; he ruled out Stevenson and Bowles. But he had no one else clearly in mind. He knew Bill Fulbright, chairman of the Senate Foreign Relations Committee, from the Hill. Acheson dismissed Fulbright. The Arkansas senator was a "dilettante" who liked to "call for brave bold new ideas but doesn't have any brave bold new ideas." Acheson then made his own nomination: Paul Nitze. He realized that Nitze was still too unknown, so he suggested a two-step process: initially, Kennedy should name as Secretary David Bruce, a well-bred, Princeton-educated diplomat who had served Acheson well as ambassador to Paris, with Nitze serving as the State Department's number two. Then, after Nitze had gained visibility and experience, he would take over from Bruce—in a year or so. Looking diffident, Kennedy made no comment.

How about Jack McCloy? asked Acheson. Though Acheson was a loyal Democrat—indeed, an important party figure—it apparently did not bother him that McCloy was a Republican. McCloy's party affiliation, however, did put off Kennedy. The President-elect interrupted to say that he wanted a Democrat.

Acheson tried a third name: Dean Rusk. Kennedy replied that he did not know Rusk. Acheson told him the story of how Rusk had volunteered for a demotion to take over the hot seat in Far Eastern Affairs, that he deserved "the Medal of Honor" for it. He recalled that Rusk had been steadfast on Korea, and remarked that he was "strong and loyal and good in every way." He had heard from Bob Lovett and Jack McCloy that Rusk had made a fine president of the Rockefeller Foundation, his job since leaving State in 1952. Acheson recommended him "without reservation." True, the old statesman added, there was always the risk that a number two or three would not work out as a number one, but one had to try in order to find out. Kennedy seemed to listen with interest.

The President-elect moved on to Treasury. He said that he had dispatched Clifford to New York to ask Bob Lovett. This brought a guffaw from Acheson. He told Kennedy that he was wasting his time. Lovett would never do it; he was not that well suited; he spent his time on Union Pacific matters and "a lot of fooling around with trains." "Anyway," Acheson continued, "if you want him why don't you ask him yourself? If you give warning by sending Clark up, the old rascal will have affidavits from every doctor in New York saying that he's going to drop dead." Acheson added, "If you really want to put Lovett to work, make him reorganize the Defense Department. By the time he offended everyone in Washington, you'd have to let him go home."

As the jaded older man sat back in his overstuffed chair, and the overeager younger man sat stiffly in his, the winter twilight dimmed in the parlor, the tea cooled, the conversation turned desultory. Kennedy perked up briefly when Acheson suggested C. Douglas Dillon for Treasury; JFK and Dillon were members of the same Harvard final club, the Spee; they had met there, Kennedy self-consciously revealed, several years before at reunion time.

Finally as night fell over Georgetown, Kennedy rose to leave. He had one final request for the old statesman: Would Acheson serve as his ambassador to NATO? The former Secretary of State demurred, saying there was no need to worry about him, that there was nothing he wanted, that he was glad to be of help, but as Churchill had said, "I've had enough responsibility." In truth, the only job that interested Acheson was his old one.

• • •

Acheson was right about Lovett. When Clifford told him that his experience at State and Defense had made him a "rather unique package," Lovett replied that he could not keep up with a bunch of forty-year-old touch-football players. At any rate, he would have to consult his doctors. That afternoon he hastened up to Presbyterian Hospital and came back with a letter stating that, in light of his medical history of bleeding ulcers and a good possibility of corrective surgery, the rigors of government service would be out of the question.

Still, Kennedy pressed. The more he learned about Lovett—his pragmatism, his common sense, his ability to get on with senators, his discretion—the more determined he was to bring him into his Cabinet. In fact, his brother Robert later recalled, Lovett was JFK's first choice for all *three* top spots—State, Defense, and Treasury. Kennedy called Lovett out of a board meeting in New York on the morning of December 1 and asked him to come to Washington. "Is it urgent?" asked Lovett. "I'd like you to come for lunch," the President-elect replied. Lovett took the first plane.

He encountered Caroline, aged three, in Kennedy's front hall. She was wearing overalls emblazoned with an "H" and carrying a football. "That's a hell of a way to treat a Yale man," Lovett said to Kennedy as his host appeared. Lovett recalled that he was immediately charmed by Kennedy's amused tolerance and affection toward his daughter. The young man and the old man sat by the fireplace; their conversation was both light and blunt. When Lovett mentioned that he had not voted for Kennedy, the President-elect just smiled. What did Lovett think of Ken Galbraith as an economist? "He's a fine novelist," answered Lovett.

Kennedy made the offer: State, Defense, or Treasury. "No, sir, I can't," Lovett replied. "My bearings are burnt out." Lovett went on that every time he took a new job in Washington, the doctors took another slice out of his innards. Kennedy was understanding; he said he knew about working in physical pain. He asked Lovett for his recommendations.

Lovett said that Secretary of State was easy: Dean Acheson. Kennedy shook his head. Too many enemies in his own party, much less among the Republicans. Lovett paused and tried another name: Dean Rusk.

Kennedy and Lovett agreed that Dulles had been given too much license by Eisenhower. Kennedy said that he would be different. He wanted to make foreign policy himself. Lovett asked, "Do you want a Secretary of State, or do you really want an *Under* Secretary?" Kennedy laughed and said, "Well, I guess I want an Under Secretary." Then Rusk would be perfect, said Lovett. He was the ideal staff man.

Kennedy asked if Lovett would serve him as an "unofficial adviser," and the aging statesman nodded his agreement.* After a pleasant lunch, Kennedy walked his guest to the door. Newsmen were clustered outside. Lovett enjoyed having a drink with an Arthur Krock or a Joe Alsop, but he was shy of confronting the pack. Kennedy, coatless, escorted the old gentleman out into the snowy street, fended off the reporters, and put him in the President-elect's personal limousine. "Take off," he instructed the driver. Lovett was touched by the young man's graciousness; the gesture was just the sort of thing Bob Lovett himself would have done.

• • •

Dean Rusk's name kept coming back to the Kennedys. He was an unknown to the public, but he had the endorsement of both Lovett and Acheson. McCloy too backed him: "He has a fine mind and is

---

*He was to learn that this was not an honorific post. Kennedy truly believed that Lovett spoke for the Establishment. When Wall Street tumbled in May of 1962 after the Steel Crisis on the perception that the President was antibusiness, Kennedy called Lovett and asked him how to repair the damage. Lovett took the opportunity to advise Kennedy to lower taxes to encourage capital accumulation. Kennedy listened; a month later, against the strong opposition of liberals such as Galbraith, the Treasury liberalized depreciation allowances.

experienced," the Council on Foreign Relations chairman wrote the President-elect. Summoned to lunch with Kennedy, Rusk had seemed somewhat bland and unforthcoming to the President-elect, but perhaps his diffidence was simply humility.

On December 4, Rusk, Lovett, and McCloy were all at a board meeting of the Rockefeller Foundation at Williamsburg, in Virginia, when Kennedy called Lovett. The President-elect told Lovett that the list for State had narrowed to three: Bruce, Fulbright, and Rusk. Lovett strongly backed Rusk. He told Kennedy that Rusk had written an article in *Foreign Affairs* stating that the President himself should make foreign policy. Had Kennedy read it? He had.

The phone call to Lovett cinched it, according to Bobby Kennedy. The President-elect asked Lovett to approach Rusk about becoming Secretary of State.

The dour Georgian was suitably humble and grateful. But there was a hitch; he had no money, and he had children and a big mortgage. Lovett told him to rest easy; both he and Jack McCloy were on the board of the Rockefeller Foundation. They would make sure he received a comfortable termination bonus.

Acheson, Lovett, and McCloy would come to be disappointed with their choice. But in December 1960, both Lovett and Acheson had clear memories of a day, exactly ten years earlier, when Dean Rusk had stood up in the Secretary's office, on December 4, 1950, and argued that the U.S. must not quit Korea, that it must follow the example of the British against the Nazis in 1940. In mid-December, Lovett described Rusk's steadfastness to some reporters trying to learn about the new Secretary-designate: "If Rusk hadn't been absolutely and immediately firm that we had to honor our word, that any cave-in on our part would be disastrous, who knows how the Korea business would have turned out? My impression is that Rusk picked up the loose ball and ran with it." Lovett added, "I think you'll find Dean Acheson saying the same thing."

Unlike its earlier European counterparts, the American Establishment of the time was largely meritocratic, despite its web of schools and clubs; it positively relished finding and shaping promising poor boys like Dean Rusk. The willingness, even eagerness, to reach out to fresh talent from every quarter insured that certain values would be passed on along with power.

Rusk was considered a prize pupil. Unlike Kennan and Nitze, he had not been purged from the Dulles State Department, but rather promoted out of it. In 1952, Foster Dulles told Bob Lovett that he was "so impressed by Rusk" that he was "going to have to take him out of government and send him to the Rockefeller Foundation." Lovett replied, "Damn it, Foster, you can't do that. We need this man in Washington." Dulles responded, "True, but I'd like him to fly a slightly wider radius."

The polishing of the Cherokee County dirt-farm boy that began at Oxford continued in a boardroom at Rockefeller Center. Rusk was adept at expressing consensus; at the end of a contentious meeting, he could ably summarize the middle ground. "Rusk is the best explainer of things I know," Lovett told Kennedy. Lovett particularly appreciated Rusk's skills placating conservative congressmen ("If the Secretary of State gets on a white charger and starts making too much news," Lovett would say, "he creates a lot of jealousy—notably where he can least afford it, in the Senate Foreign Relations Committee").

These qualities, of course, appealed to Kennedy, who knew well what problems Dean Acheson had stirred on the Hill, and who wanted to be his own Secretary of State. If he could not have Bob Lovett, then Dean Rusk seemed like a handcrafted imitation.

Rusk was a reasonable facsimile. But there were some critical differences. Lovett was quiet and discreet and cautious, but he was ultimately a doer. Rusk was not. He lacked Lovett's inner confidence, his sense of when to move, to carry through. Rusk was even in his own mind an imitation. He self-consciously modeled himself after Lovett's patron, General Marshall. He did in fact share Marshall's humility and stoicism, as well as his innate decency. Yet he utterly lacked Marshall's decisiveness.

Lovett did have a few reservations about Rusk, though they seemed fairly minor at the time. He worried about Rusk's "executive ability," his capacity to make the jump from chief of staff to chief executive. He also thought Rusk was unduly obsessed with the Far East. These concerns, in the hard years ahead, would turn out to be not so minor after all.

•   •   •

At a three-hour lunch on November 28 with Clark Clifford (who had become the head of Kennedy's transition team), Lovett was asked for his recommendation for Secretary of Defense. Lovett surprised Clifford by suggesting someone quite out of the Wall Street–Truman-era loop: Robert McNamara, the California-born, newly named president of Ford Motor Company. Lovett had discovered McNamara during World War II and brought him in from Harvard Business

School, where he had been teaching, to help make the war machine more efficient. Using calculators borrowed from an insurance company, McNamara had set up a statistical control unit in the Pentagon to keep a daily record of all the Air Force's warplanes, fuel, bombs, and ammo. Lovett had been enormously impressed with McNamara's brilliance and intensity. When Henry Ford, whose mother owned a house nearby the Lovetts' in Hobe Sound, called him after the war looking for able men for his auto company, Lovett sent him McNamara.

Lovett was struck by how unwieldy the Pentagon had become. He believed it needed a man who was both a numbers wizard and a forceful manager. He noted with approval that McNamara was an iconoclast, who chose to live in the university town of Ann Arbor rather than the corporate bedroom of Grosse Pointe, who was openminded enough to join the ACLU and the NAACP. Lovett felt such independence of mind would be useful in tackling the bureaucracy. To Lovett, McNamara was just about right: a humanist technocrat with a strong will. He overlooked McNamara's fixation with numbers and forgot, perhaps, the definition of a statistician he had given Harry Truman in 1952: "a man who draws a straight line from an unwarranted assumption to a foregone conclusion."

When Sargent Shriver, Kennedy's chief headhunter, called Lovett about the Pentagon job, he again recommended McNamara as "the best of the lot." Lovett's voice counted heavily with Kennedy; he told Shriver to gather the particulars on McNamara. The auto executive passed muster; he had even read and admired *Profiles in Courage*. After McNamara had been chosen for Defense, he went to see Lovett in New York, to seek his counsel. Lovett told him that his first order of business was to visit the chairmen of the Armed Services Committees, that without their support he was helpless. McNamara listened closely; as Lovett spoke, he took notes.

• • •

Sitting on his verandah in West Palm Beach, John Kennedy asked Paul Nitze if he would be interested in serving as National Security Adviser. Nitze said no. He wanted to be at Defense, where the buildup would come, where flexible response would actually be implemented. Nitze hoped that Kennedy would pick Lovett as Secretary of Defense with Nitze as his number two—with the understanding that Nitze would take over after a year or so.

McNamara's appointment ended that idea. McNamara picked

Roswell Gilpatric (Nitze's old classmate at Hotchkiss) as his deputy. When Nitze heard the news, he hastily called Kennedy on his private number in West Palm to change his mind and accept the job as National Security Adviser. Kennedy did not return the phone call. Nitze had to settle for Assistant Secretary for International Security Affairs, ISA, the "little State Department" he helped create before getting purged from the Pentagon in 1953. As Nitze watched the White House make its own foreign policy in the years ahead—through the office of National Security Adviser—he would kick himself.

The National Security Adviser Kennedy did pick could hardly have been more acceptable to the old guard. McGeorge Bundy was the "next generation" par excellence. At Groton he had been the brightest boy; at Yale he was Skull and Bones. He had coauthored Colonel Stimson's memoirs, *On Active Service*; he had edited Acheson's collected speeches. He was Harvey Bundy's son; he called Acheson, whose daughter was married to his brother, "Uncle Dean."

He was a Brahmin ("Mahatma Bundy," quipped the Yale *Daily News*), yet a true believer in meritocracy. He would scoff at the suggestion that he had been shaped by Endicott Peabody, whom he found a trifle quaint. The biggest influence on his life, he would later say, was Robert Oppenheimer. In this respect, he was just like Uncle Dean, who saw as his mentor not the Rector but a brilliant Jew, Louis Brandeis. Bundy shared as well some of Acheson's intimidating acerbity and his incisive logic. He hewed to the same simple principles. ("Let me put my whole proposition in one sentence," Bundy, a Yale senior, declared in 1940. "I believe in the dignity of the individual, in government by law, in respect for the truth, and in a good God; these beliefs are worth my life and more; they are not shared by Adolf Hitler.") He approached problems with the same cool pragmatism.

Acheson was delighted to hear that "Mac" had been chosen as National Security Adviser. Acheson's model for the job was the loyal, discreet Averell Harriman in the Truman White House. In fact, Bundy tried hard to keep a low profile and get along with Dean Rusk. But the focus of foreign policy making moved from the State Department to the White House during his tenure, and Bundy, forceful and incisive, unavoidably at times edged aside the more tentative Rusk. In the late sixties, Acheson was asked what he would have done if Mac Bundy had been National Security Adviser when he was Secretary of State. "Resign," he answered.

•   •   •

Jack McCloy got his call in the midst of a dinner party in New York in early December. Arriving at Kennedy's suite at the Carlyle, the newly retired chairman of the Chase Manhattan Bank sat and listened as the President-elect paced barefoot around the room. Kennedy told him that Lovett had suggested him for the Pentagon. "I've already done that," grunted McCloy. How about Treasury then? "I'm not qualified," said McCloy. Kennedy laughed, reminding him that he had been chairman of Chase Manhattan and president of the World Bank. McCloy said that he had done badly in economics in college. Kennedy had another offer. He wanted an arms control agreement with the Soviet Union. Would McCloy take on the task as his special adviser for arms control?

McCloy said yes. He had just become a senior partner at Milbank, Tweed, and it would be awkward to back out of his new arrangement. But he later recalled, "I had spent so much time organizing the destruction of things that I wanted very badly to do something constructive in terms of peace. Stimson was very concerned about the Bomb, and he impressed this upon me. It was sort of his legacy that I wanted to carry out."

• • •

George Kennan was checking his mailbox at Branford College at Yale, where he had gone to teach for a semester, when an agitated undergraduate said to him, "Mr. Kennan, the President of the United States wants to talk to you." Kennedy was calling to offer Kennan the ambassadorship to Poland or Yugoslavia. Kennan was delighted; he took Yugoslavia, whose independence from the Kremlin he had been among the first to predict.

Kennan had great hopes for the young President. Kennedy had won over the sensitive former diplomat a year earlier by writing to praise him for an article in *Foreign Affairs* that Kennan had written to rebut Acheson's attack on the Reith Lectures. The article "disposed of the extreme rigidity of Mr. Acheson's position with great effectiveness," Senator Kennedy told Kennan, "and without the kind of ad hominem irrelevance in which Mr. Acheson unfortunately indulged last year."

Kennedy was in most respects a conventional Cold Warrior, but he was sensitive to the need to improve relations with the Soviets. Unlike Dulles—and even Acheson—he wanted to hear out the Soviet watchers, to tap into some of the expertise that had been ignored for the last decade. He told Kennan that he did not want to be in the position of Truman, "entirely dependent," on his Secretary of State for advice. Kennan was charmed by Kennedy's solicitude. There was "a certain old-fashioned gallantry about him," Kennan later recalled, a "Lindberghian boyishness."

•   •   •

The day after he was elected President, Kennedy called Chip Bohlen and said that he had been sent a congratulatory telegram by Nikita Khrushchev. How should he reply? Taken aback, Bohlen told him to be courteous and avoid substance.

The phone calls kept coming. Kennedy wanted Bohlen's advice almost constantly, about Khrushchev, the Soviets, Laos, even routine questions of diplomatic protocol. The two became social friends; Kennedy enjoyed Bohlen's wit and easy charm. Unlike Dulles, Kennedy immediately recognized that Bohlen was a gifted diplomat, the best the Foreign Service had to offer. To Bohlen's great credit, he did not forget that he was a Foreign Service officer first and the President's friend second. Bohlen disapproved of Kennedy's ad hoc conduct of foreign affairs and his impatience with normal State Department channels; he believed Kennedy's disregard for the bureaucracy hurt morale. When Kennedy asked him, "What's the matter with that State Department of yours, Chip?" Bohlen answered, "You are, sir."

Bohlen had been rescued from Manila after Dulles's death by the new Secretary of State, Christian Herter (a fellow St. Paul's boy). Herter installed Bohlen as his special assistant for Soviet affairs (he could not make him Assistant Secretary or Counselor because he could not be sure of Senate confirmation). Bohlen stayed on as the department's Soviet expert under Rusk, with the promise that he would become ambassador to either England or France.

Less than a month after his inauguration—on February 11—JFK summoned his Soviet experts to the White House for a strategy session. There were four: Bohlen, Kennan, Llewellyn Thompson (who had replaced Bohlen as ambassador in Moscow), and Averell Harriman. After nearly a decade in the wilderness, they were again being heard.

All of them urged Kennedy to take steps to remedy the deep chill that had again settled over Soviet-U.S. relations after the Russians had downed a U-2 spy plane over Soviet soil on the eve of a summit meeting between Eisenhower and Khrushchev. The summit had collapsed. Bohlen, backed by the others, urged Kennedy to seek another. Tensions were building in Laos, where the Soviets were backing a "war of national liberation," and in Berlin, coveted more than ever by the Kremlin. There was much to discuss. Kennedy worried openly that he would be attacked by the right wing in Congress if he appeared too conciliatory. But he was curious to meet his Soviet counterpart face-to-face, and he agreed to seek a summit with Khrushchev.

Kennedy's openness and energy, his eagerness to solicit the views of the old Soviet hands, "delighted" Bohlen, his wife, Avis, wrote Charlie Thayer a few days after the meeting at the White House. The heady whirl of early Camelot swept Avis away: "The atmosphere bubbles and sparkles like champagne," she wrote Charlie. "All these new young alive faces bristling with desire to get started." It brought her

> back again to the days—almost of the war—conferences, meetings all the time—dinner parties and receptions... *most* exciting. The only hitch is that most of them are so young and now suddenly overnight Chip has become one of the "older men," rather than the younger group. George Kennan was here for two days—looks 20 years younger and is so full of smiles and cheer and dying to get started. Chip and George and Averell etc. have seen the President a total of about seven hours.... This is just about twice as much time as Eisenhower gave to Tommy and Chip combined in 8 years!

• • •

Averell Harriman was hugely relieved to be back in the inner council, advising a President. He had recovered from the shock of losing to Nelson Rockefeller in New York by going back to his peculiar source of regeneration, to Russia. Characteristically he had wasted little time. On January 9, 1959, only a week after turning over the governor's mansion to the Republicans, he had written Dean Acheson that he planned to tour the Soviet Union. "I don't see any reason why I can't plunge into battle just to keep trim," he wrote his old friend. He even wanted to go on to Red China, a totally closed society in the late fifties. Harriman retained Acheson as his lawyer to obtain permission from the State Department. Ever the cheap multimillionaire, he had admonished Acheson: "Please keep your price reasonable because I have a lot of expenses these days." The anti-Communist zealots hired by Dulles objected; Walter Robertson, the head of Far Eastern Affairs, told Acheson that Formosa and the other "free" Asian countries might think that Harriman was being sent by the U.S. to negotiate a secret peace with the Chinese Communists. Acheson was sarcastic. "You don't mean to say that you believe people abroad would think you fellows are sending a Democrat to negotiate for you?" But he failed to get Harriman's visa.

Harriman went to Russia ostensibly as a writer for *Life* magazine (he took as his ghostwriter and translator Bohlen's brother-in-law, Charlie Thayer, who after his purge from the Foreign Service had become a free-lance writer). Slightly stooped, weary-looking, and as usual indefatigable, Harriman traveled eighteen thousand miles within the U.S.S.R. He was regarded as a visiting dignitary and remembered as a war ally; common people cheered him everywhere, in factories, in train stations, in the streets. Indeed, he drew bigger and more enthusiastic crowds in Russia than he had campaigning in New York.

At the end of his journey, Harriman was granted long audiences with Khrushchev, who bluffed and blustered and threatened. Walking in the garden of his dacha, the Soviet leader warned Harriman, "We are determined to liquidate your rights in West Berlin. Your generals talk of tanks and guns defending your Berlin position. Your tanks will burn and the rockets will fly." But when Harriman said that he did not believe that the Soviets wanted to provoke war, Khrushchev calmed down. "We don't want war over Berlin," he said.

Though not a terribly subtle man himself, Harriman was able to understand what others in the frightened West failed to see. When Khrushchev fulminated "We will bury you!" he meant that Communism would outlast capitalism, not bomb it. Harriman was fascinated to hear Khrushchev run down Stalin as a brutal aggressor. He was reminded that Soviet Communism was not static, that it could evolve. When Khrushchev spoke repeatedly of the need for an arms-control agreement, Harriman believed he was sincere. Most of all, he was again convinced that the West could deal with the Soviets, provided the negotiations were handled by men like himself.

The Soviet leaders clearly believed that they could deal with him. He was a true capitalist; men like Khrushchev felt they could understand him, that he represented the real America. At a dinner, Khrushchev turned to Harriman and declared, "Do you suppose we consider it a free election when the voters of New York State have a choice only between a Harriman and a Rockefeller?"

When Khrushchev toured the U.S. in September of 1959, Harriman invited him to his house at 16 East 81st Street in New York, to sit in his library beneath his favorite Picasso and talk to some titans of finance and industry. About thirty were present, CEOs of large corporations, foundation heads, investment bankers. Offered a drink by Harriman, Khrushchev demanded some Russian vodka. The former governor gave him a glass of New York State brandy. "You rule America," Khrushchev pronounced to the congregation of capitalists. "You are the ruling circle. I don't believe any other view."

The first question came from John McCloy ("as a matter of official precedence," dryly noted an interloper at the gathering, John Kenneth Galbraith). It was not really a question but a statement. McCloy tried to persuade the Soviet leader that Wall Street was totally without influence in Washington. "Judge for yourself," he said "Almost all the bills proposed by Wall Street are automatically rejected by the Senate." Khrushchev stared disbelievingly at him and muttered with heavy sarcasm, "It appears that I have before me America's poor relations."*

In the fall of 1960, Harriman had called Khrushchev beseeching him to be equally tough on both presidential candidates, lest he help the Republicans by seeming to favor the Democrats. Harriman was delighted when Khrushchev wired him after the election to say the slate had been wiped clean, that the bitterness of the Dulles era would be forgotten.

Harriman had only one reservation about the forthcoming summit between Kennedy and the Soviet leader. He was worried that the green young American President would be shocked by the Russian's bluster and bravado, his threats that "the tanks will roll and the rockets will fly," and overreact by shouting back. Harriman wanted a private audience with the President to tutor him, to impart some of his collected wisdom on the handling of Soviet dictators.

Kennedy, however, was not listening. In truth, he had a low opinion of Harriman.

It is somewhat curious, in retrospect, that Harriman's name was missing altogether from the list of potential Secretaries of State. But though he would later revise his opinion, Kennedy at the time thought Harriman too old, too deaf, and too political. "Never has anyone gone so far with so little," Lord Beaverbrook had told JFK in 1958. A meeting with Harriman in November 1960, after the election, went badly: Kennedy asked a long, complicated question about foreign policy and Harriman answered, "Yes." A second meeting in December was worse. The President had made a point and Harriman, thinking he had heard his aide Jack Bingham speak, growled, "Don't be silly, Jack." On the way out Kennedy said to another Harriman aide, Mike Forrestal, "Do you think that you can get Averell to wear a hearing aid?"

---

*Harriman carefully cultivated his relationship with Khrushchev, whose peasant roots and ideology were diametrically opposed to his, but whose blunt manner was oddly compatible. Khrushchev became so fond of Harriman that in 1963 he half seriously suggested that Harriman come work for *him*, and that in exchange, he would send someone to work for Kennedy.

Nor did Harriman get any help from his old comrades. Lovett had been notably silent about his childhood friend when counseling Kennedy. McCloy would later say that Harriman's Truman-era colleagues had grown dissatisfied with Averell's politicking and increasing dovishness.

Harriman for his part had been cool to JFK, at least initially. John Kenneth Galbraith recalls hours spent walking up and down the beach at Sands Point in the summer of 1959 trying to persuade Harriman to back Kennedy for President, and hearing Harriman object to the fact that JFK "saw" Joe McCarthy. Harriman was finally persuaded largely by his perception that Kennedy would win. He even seconded Kennedy at the Democratic Convention, but he was disappointed because he believed the family never knew how hard he campaigned for JFK that fall (through a dozen states). He later told friends that his chances of a good job in the Administration had been torpedoed by old Joe Kennedy.

Arthur Schlesinger had mentioned Harriman to Kennedy on December 1. "He's too old hat," scoffed the President-elect. After some gentle pushing, Schlesinger and Galbraith managed to get Harriman the title of "Roving Ambassador." The President considered the appointment to be "decorative," Schlesinger recalled.

But Dean Rusk told Harriman that he planned to stay in Washington, and that he wanted Harriman to act as his emissary to Foreign Ministers' meetings and other such (dreary) international gatherings. Without complaint, Harriman, then nearly seventy, packed his bag and went off to do what he did best: meet with other sovereigns.

CHAPTER 21

*Khrushchev and McCloy
swimming at Sochi,
U.S.S.R.*

TWILIGHT
STRUGGLES

Reunion at the Brink

I n the long shadows of an early summer's evening in June of 1961,
Kennedy's young lieutenants briskly filed into the White House
for a meeting of the National Security Council. "The long twilight
struggle" had flared on two fronts, in Laos and Berlin. An air of crisis
pervaded; the new President was pressed to give meaning to the ex-
pansive rhetoric of his inaugural address, his promise to "pay any
price, bear any burden" to "assure the survival and success of liberty."

Two elderly gentlemen moved at a more stately pace in the damp
heat of summer. Both were tall, taller than the earnest young men
who had preceded them, and only slightly bowed in their late sixties,
their sixth decade of friendship. Reporters standing outside heard Averell

Harriman say, "It seems like old times, Dean," as he put his arm around Dean Acheson's shoulder and stepped by the marine guards into the inner sanctum of the West Wing.

Kennedy inherited his global commitments from the foreign policy Establishment he revered, so it is not surprising that in attempting to meet them he turned to Acheson and Harriman for advice. The two old men were not merely advisers in these early crises, however. In both Berlin and Laos, the dominating players were not the best and brightest of Kennedy's "new generation," but the aging war-horses of Harry Truman's old one. Yet Acheson and Harriman returned to power by different routes, and not as allies but as rivals: Acheson by invitation, as a hawk backing military force in Berlin; Harriman by insinuation, urging peaceful diplomacy for Laos.

•   •   •

On the eve of his inaugural, at a meeting set up by the ubiquitous Clark Clifford, Kennedy discussed with Eisenhower the "crisis points" of the world. The outgoing President warned his successor that Southeast Asia was tottering, and that Laos was the "key." If the Communists took Laos, Eisenhower added, they would bring "unbelievable pressure" on Thailand, Cambodia, and South Vietnam.

The Eisenhower Administration had already poured money into Laos, some $300 million, or about $150 for every inhabitant, twice the annual per capita income. The investment was a poor one; Laotian generals stole most of the money. Meanwhile, the Communist Pathet Lao were taking over the countryside. Because Dulles believed neutralism to be immoral, the U.S. had wrecked attempts to create a nonaligned regime. The CIA had backed a coup against a neutralist government under Prince Souvanna Phouma and replaced him with a politician named Phoui Sananikone. The agency then dredged up from France a Laotian military officer named Phoumi Nosavan. Phoumi overthrew Phoui, which, as George Ball points out, "could have been either a significant event or a typographical error." Phoumi was in turn overthrown by a young paratrooper named Kong Le. The Defense Department and the CIA continued to back Phoumi. Squinty-eyed, with a big affable smile, Phoumi was a dubious ally; he had refused to go to the capital for his swearing in because a soothsayer foresaw his violent death.

In early February, as the New Frontiersmen were still moving into their offices, Phoumi's army, with CIA support, set out to conquer Kong Le's men. Kong Le, who had sided with the Communist Pathet

Lao, held fast, however, and Phoumi's men broke and ran on the Plain of Jars.

To the Administration, this "Kung Fu movie," as Ball described it, was a serious crisis. It loomed as the first test of flexible response, of the capacity to fight small brush-fire wars. Walt Rostow, a former MIT professor who had been attacked by the McCarthyites in the early fifties as a Communist sympathizer, showed he was quite the opposite by recommending the air and sea lift of twenty-five thousand U.S. combat troops into the Mekong Delta. At the first meeting on the crisis, Defense Secretary McNamara suggested arming half a dozen AT-6s (old World War II fighters) with hundred-pound bombs and dropping them on the Communists. The Joint Chiefs were more realistic about Asian land wars: they wanted to go in with 250,000 men.

The President, however, was dubious. He had little desire to get tied up in a war in Laos. He hoped that the British would revive an earlier plan for an International Control Commission (ICC) to peacefully settle the dispute. At his urging, talks were scheduled in Geneva for May.

•   •   •

In early April, Averell Harriman was on an airplane bound for a CENTO meeting in Turkey when Dean Rusk told him to go on to Laos to prepare for the Geneva talks. Harriman dutifully went to the American PX in Ankara, bought an ill-fitting summer suit, and embarked on an eleven-day trip through southeast Asia. It was like the old wartime missions, except that he was almost twenty years older: he slept four nights in an airplane and visited seven different capitals. Landing in Vientiane, he found Laos in chaos, on the verge of falling to the Communists. General Lyman Lemnitzer, the chairman of the Joint Chiefs of Staff, was already there. Lemnitzer persuaded Harriman to join him in signing a cable calling for a small-scale intervention of U.S. troops.

The hawkish impulse was Harriman's last, provoked by his admiration for Lemnitzer and the panicked atmosphere of Vientiane. But Harriman was not an orthodox Cold Warrior bent on proving his toughness. From then on, he was to favor diplomacy over force of arms in Southeast Asia. His search for a political solution in Laos began almost immediately, on a side trip to New Delhi.

On his own, without State Department authorization, he sought out Souvanna Phouma, the neutralist Laotian prince who had been driven from the country by the CIA-backed coup during the Eisenhower Administration. French-educated, dandified, and opinionated, Souvanna was nonetheless a gentleman and a patriot. Harriman, who made up his mind quickly about people, sensed almost immediately that he could deal with Souvanna. The arrogant prince seemed to be the answer, the way to avoid fighting a brutal little war in Laos. Souvanna convinced Harriman that he did not want Laos to go Communist but rather to be a neutral country.

Harriman returned to Washington invoking Souvanna's name as the solution. The State Department was skeptical; still traumatized by the Dulles era, the careerists were suspicious of the Laotian prince, who had once traveled to Moscow and Peking. Rusk was no help. Harriman convinced Souvanna that he should come to Washington in late April to make his case in person, but the Secretary of State snubbed him. He said he had a speaking engagement in Georgia.

Harriman was further convinced that the Soviets wanted a peaceful settlement in Laos, that they did not wish to involve themselves in an Asian war. Finally, late in April, Harriman was granted an audience with President Kennedy to make his case. To his delight, he found the President entirely receptive. That night at a farewell party for John Kenneth Galbraith, who was off to India as ambassador, guests noticed that the normally dour Harriman was ebullient. Arthur Schlesinger recalls that he even outtalked Galbraith.

Harriman's reward was to be made chief negotiator at the ICC talks on Laos that began in Geneva in mid-May. When Kennedy stopped off to consult with de Gaulle en route to the Vienna summit with Khrushchev in late May, Harriman rushed to Paris, hoping to catch a few minutes with the President. For several hours, Harriman stood about in the hallway of the American Embassy, pacing nervously. He finally had to grab Kennedy by the elbow as he whisked out the door. "Mr. President," he asked, "I have just one question: Do you want a settlement on Laos or not?" Kennedy brusquely answered that he did. This was all the instruction Harriman needed—though he was to receive, and generally disregard, a great deal more from the Department of State.

At a formal dinner that night Harriman maneuvered himself close enough to Kennedy's chair to offer some advice about his upcoming meeting with Khrushchev. Don't take the Russian's bluster and bluff too seriously, said the veteran of many such situations. Joke with him; don't try to debate him.

• • •

Kennedy ignored Harriman's advice. Khrushchev huffed and puffed and carried on, vowed that the tanks would roll and the rockets would fly. The young President responded by becoming stiff and combative. As he left the Soviet leader, he said to him, "It will be a cold winter." Kennedy felt he had been bullied; he was determined to show his resolve. Shortly afterward, the opportunity arose in Berlin.

Ever since Stalin's humiliation during the Berlin blockade of 1948, the Western occupied zones of Berlin had been for the Russians "a bone stuck in the throat," as Khrushchev put it. (The Russian leader liked physical metaphors; he told Harriman that Berlin was a "bunion on your toes, which I can step on any time." Then he ground his foot for emphasis.) In 1958 Khrushchev had threatened to make Berlin a "free city," i.e., under Soviet control, but backed off. Now he threatened anew. He was afraid that West Germany would build its own Bomb, and he was embarrassed by the stream of refugees from East Berlin to West. He was further offended by the contrast between the gleaming, bustling West and the drab, run-down East. In Vienna, he delivered an ultimatum to Kennedy: he wanted the West out of Berlin.

To Dean Acheson, Berlin was a crucible, "the hardest test of Western will and determination since June 1950, when the Communists attacked Korea," he wrote his friend John Cowles, the owner of the Minneapolis *Star* and *Tribune*. "One sure way to lose the Cold War is to lose Germany; and one sure way to lose Germany is to convince the Germans that we are prepared to sacrifice German interests for an accord with Russia."

To John Kennedy, Acheson was the preeminent authority on Germany, the statesman with the most experience at dealing with Russians on the explosive issue of Berlin. Back in March, Kennedy had asked him to study the problem of Berlin and to propose a strategy for dealing with the Soviet threat. Inexorably, both because of a vacuum of leadership at State and because of his own force of will, the former Secretary began to assume inordinate power for a private lawyer already past retirement age.

Acheson was delighted to be back in the swing. Miss Evans, his loyal secretary of three decades, wrote Marshall Shulman, an old Acheson aide on April 6 that "DA is buoyed up by it all and looks better and younger than I have seen him in years."

When the British Prime Minister, Harold Macmillan, came to

Washington in early April, Acheson was invited to hold forth on Berlin. His recital was "rather bloodcurdling," Arthur Schlesinger later recalled. "Skipping over possibilities of diplomatic or economic response, Acheson crisply offered a formidable catalogue of military countermeasures, concluding tentatively in favor of sending a division down the *Autobahn*."

In the wake of Khrushchev's ultimatum to Kennedy in Vienna, Acheson delivered a report to the President on June 28 that was even more hawkish. In this test of wills, argued Acheson, any effort to negotiate would be a mistake. The Administration should instead declare a national emergency and fully mobilize its armed forces. A declaration of national emergency carried with it drastic steps: upping the defense budget by $5 billion, standby wage-and-price controls, and a tax increase. This should be enough to deter Khrushchev, Acheson concluded. Even so, the U.S. had to be prepared for the possibility of nuclear war.

Acheson, despite his disdain for Dulles, was calling for brinksmanship. His outlook was revealed by a chilling talk he had given to Columbia Journalism School students in 1959. The U.S., Acheson said, must be prepared to "raise tensions to the point where people no longer act coolly, they no longer act on the basis of cool calculation, but they act on the basis of fear. . . . So the Russians will say, 'We may get a strike when we're not expecting it.' This is the only thing to do. This is what you call the delicate balance of terror." As Paul Nitze later acknowledged, "Brinksmanship may have been discredited, but that was our policy."

At a meeting of the National Security Council on June 29, the day after he submitted his report, Acheson was the dominating force, cowing Cabinet members with his forceful declarations, leavened only by self-deprecating wit. He offered himself up as an "elderly unemployed person" to serve as a smoke screen for a military buildup, as one who would be willing to attend "interminable meetings" with the Soviets "where we can converse indefinitely without negotiating at all."

Among those listening to Acheson's bravura performance in the Cabinet Room that evening was Averell Harriman, there to brief the NSC on Laos. Despite his affectionate pat on his old friend's shoulder as the two had walked into the meeting on that warm June evening, Harriman was appalled by Acheson's hawkishness. Though he said nothing at the meeting, afterward he grumbled to Arthur Schlesinger:

"How long is our policy to be dominated by that frustrated and rigid man? He is leading us down the road to war." Harriman believed that the U.S. should explore diplomatic avenues with the Soviets before sending a column of tanks down the autobahn.

Harriman's voice did not carry in that charged atmosphere; Acheson's did. At the daily meetings of the Berlin Task Force in the Crisis Room on the seventh floor of the State Department, Acheson held sway. The task force was nominally headed by a former staffer of Acheson's, Foy Kohler; it included another formidable hawk, a man who had also once worked under Acheson, Paul Nitze. Abram Chayes, the State Department legal adviser who sat in on the meetings, recalls that "Dean was riding high. He had the feeling that he was in control." When Chayes, a dove, tried to come up with a less bellicose alternative than mobilization and declaration of national emergency, Acheson was cutting: "Abe, you'll see. You can try but you will find that it just won't write."

Acheson was in control partly because Dean Rusk was not. The Secretary was keeping his own counsel; already he had earned the nickname "the Buddha" for sitting silently through NSC meetings with an inscrutable half smile affixed on his bland face. "The Secretary never gives me anything to chew on, you never know what he is thinking," complained Kennedy to his aides. The White House was furious when Rusk's department took six weeks to produce any paper on Berlin, and then only a cut-and-paste job on the position papers used by the Republicans during earlier Berlin crises. Acheson, forceful and bold, filled the void. When Felix Frankfurter asked him who was "at the helm of the Ship of State?" Acheson was scornful: "Often no one," though "Adlai has a control wheel in New York," and "there are several around the White House which are not locked up at night, so that Caroline and some of the other children around there often play with them. . . . Then of course Dean Rusk has one in the State Department, but he hasn't learned how to work it very well."

Gradually, however, other voices began to be heard. Schlesinger, Abe Chayes, and Henry Kissinger, who was commuting from Harvard to act as a consultant to Mac Bundy, conspired to rebut Acheson's "declaration of war." On July 7, Schlesinger tapped out a persuasive memo warning the President not to see the issue as "are you chicken or not?" (Kissinger, at least, was careful to keep his lines open to Acheson. He wrote him on July 18, "The discussion at dinner the other day [with Administration officials about Berlin] showed such an appalling absence of subtlety and lack of understanding of intangibles on the part of almost everyone that only your presence prevented a real disaster.")

Kennedy himself had doubts about Acheson's hard line. He respected Acheson, he wanted his advice, but he found him too hawkish, too willing to take dangerous risks. Bobby Kennedy recalled that his brother also "found him irritating."

Acheson's caustic remarks began to grate on Kennedy. When the President had taken him aside in the Rose Garden and told him of the plan for the Bay of Pigs invasion, Acheson had been cutting. "You don't have to call in Price Waterhouse to discover that fifteen hundred Cubans aren't as good as twenty-five thousand Cubans," he had snorted. Then, after Kennedy seemed shaken by Khrushchev in Vienna, Acheson told a group of retired Foreign Service officers that observing Kennedy was like watching a gifted young performer with a boomerang knock himself out. Kennedy was more than irritated when this remark came back to him. Mac Bundy called Lucius Battle, Acheson's former special assistant who had risen to become a senior State Department official, to see if he couldn't persuade Acheson to show some discretion.

To Battle, it was almost as if Acheson was looking for trouble, like a child seeking attention. One evening after dinner that summer, Acheson seemed to be hanging about the Battles' house, looking for someone to talk to. Battle asked him if he wanted a nightcap. He did. He protested weakly to Battle that he thought his speech to the retired Foreign Service officers was off the record. "Oh, come on," said Battle. On August 18, Acheson wrote the President to apologize. "I am most distressed. I continually err in regarding my humor as less mordant and more amusing than the facts warrant."

Gradually, Kennedy's other senior advisers turned against Acheson on Berlin. Both McNamara and Bundy saw in Acheson's brinksmanship too great a risk of nuclear war. At an NSC meeting on July 13, Rusk spoke out against declaring a state of emergency. It "would have a dangerous sound of mobilization," said Rusk. Acheson cut in: "We must do what is sound and necessary in itself, and not act for the sake of appearances. If we leave the call of reserves to the end, we would not affect Khrushchev's judgment of the shape of the crisis any more than we could do so by dropping bombs after he had forced the issue to the limit." Rusk went on to express concern that a declaration of emergency would jeopardize the Administration's foreign aid bill in

Congress. Only one member of the NSC, Vice-President Lyndon Johnson, now completely sided with Acheson. On July 19, McGeorge Bundy wrote the President, "I believe there is general agreement that a national emergency is not now necessary, but a hard wing of the Kohler (Berlin Task Force) group led by Acheson and Nitze disagrees."

Acheson was distressed to see his support ebb. He wrote Harry Truman on July 14, "I find to my surprise a weakness in decision at the top—all but Bob McNamara, who impresses me as first class. The decisions are incredibly hard, but they don't, like bourbon, improve with aging." He expressed disdain for the Administration's concern with "image" and compared the President to a shortstop who wanted to make sure he "looked good" fielding a ball and hence muffed it. Concluded Acheson: "We ought to be acting now to bring home to Khrushchev that we are in deadly earnest about Berlin, which is only a symbol for our world position."

When President Kennedy addressed the nation on July 25, his speech was not the call to arms Acheson had urged. Though he did announce that he would bring up certain reserve and National Guard units and vowed that the U.S. would not quit Berlin, there was to be no national mobilization. He called on the Soviets to negotiate. "We do not want military considerations to dominate the thinking of either East or West. . . . In the thermonuclear age, any misjudgment on either side could rain more devastation in several hours than has been wrought in all the wars of human history."

Even so, Khrushchev regarded Kennedy's speech as "a preliminary declaration of war." At least that is the message he conveyed to his weekend houseguest, John J. McCloy.

McCloy, dressed in oversized bathing trunks lent to him by the Soviet dictator, was splashing about the Black Sea in late July in the cause of slowing the arms race. As Kennedy's special assistant for disarmament, he had come to the Soviet Union to try to establish a broad statement of disarmament principles. Khrushchev had graciously invited McCloy to spend two days at his dacha in Sochi, on the Black Sea. The Russian leader and the Wall Street lawyer played tennis together; McCloy, his River Club game still sharp, lobbed the ball gently to his less practiced and more portly opponent.

Off the court, Khrushchev ranted about Kennedy's speech. The Soviets were not backing down, he said; they wanted the U.S. out of Berlin. And if the Americans had any thought of shooting their way back in, they better remember that the Soviets had more men and

more tanks and far shorter lines of supply. McCloy, taken aback by
Khrushchev's extreme bluster, reported the tirade to Washington, where
it was received with alarm.

Acheson dismissed McCloy's alarums. He wrote Felix Frankfurter
on August 3:

> McCloy has caused quite a flurry. He repaired to the Black Sea with
> quite a harem, his wife, Ellen, daughter, Ellen, and Sharmane Douglas
> and had a weekend of talks in which Khrushchev said nothing that he
> has not said at least a dozen times. In the last talk he made extravagant
> and quite untrue statements about Kennedy's radio address, which McCloy
> had not seen. I should have thought the way to treat this quite unpleasant
> discussion was with "intelligent neglect," in Brandeis' words which you
> so often quote. Instead of this, he appears as a sort of modern Paul Revere,
> flapping his way through the sky to warn us that the Russians are coming,
> and give everyone the idea that we are in quite a dither about something,
> though God knows what!

Acheson had retreated to Martha's Vineyard "in a rather depressed
condition," he wrote Frankfurter. On the way he had stopped off to
commiserate in Maryland with Nitze and in Locust Valley with Bob
Lovett. Acheson was still adamant about the proper course: On August
4, he wrote Anthony Eden, "I'm strongly convinced that we must be
very tough and not let Mr. K set the pace. We must take great risks
to avoid greater ones."

The next move, however, was Khrushchev's. On August 13, a few
minutes after midnight, the Berlin Wall began to rise up between the
Eastern zone and the West. The East Germans laid barbed wire,
imposed roadblocks, tore up streets. The world felt itself sliding to the
brink. Kennedy himself privately put the odds on Armageddon at one
in five. In Washington, worried bureaucrats began stocking their
cellars with toilet paper and peanut butter; by late summer there were
macabre discussions at Georgetown dinner parties of fallout patterns
in metropolitan Washington. Paul Nitze invited the Soviet Ambassador, Mikhail Menshikov, to the Metropolitan Club for lunch to tell
him how much of the U.S.S.R. would be devastated by a nuclear
attack.

George Kennan returned from his embassy in Belgrade at once. He
told Schlesinger, "I'm expendable. I have no further official career
and I am going to do everything I possibly can to prevent war." On
August 15, he met with the President for forty-five minutes. His advice
was to stay cool, to use caution when dealing with the temperamental
Khrushchev. Kennan believed that the wall was an act to head off

confrontation, not cause it; that by stopping the flow of refugees and sealing off East Berlin Khrushchev hoped to bandage an open wound. Chip Bohlen gave Kennedy the same advice.

The President listened. But he also felt the need for some gesture; he could not simply sit back and do nothing. His answer was to dust off another old giant of the Cold War, General Lucius Clay, the old warrior who had wanted to ram an armored column down the autobahn in 1948, and send him to Berlin. Accompanied by the Vice-President, General Clay would welcome a battle group of fifteen hundred soldiers who would roll down the autobahn from West Germany. Just as Harry Truman had done in July of 1948, Kennedy sent Chip Bohlen along as a diplomatic hedge on Clay's warlike instincts.

The soldier, the diplomat, and the Vice-President left Andrews Air Force Base at 9 P.M. on a muggy evening in late August. On the flight, Clay regaled Lyndon Johnson with war stories of how he alone had felt that Berlin could be held against the Soviets in 1948, of how he alone had persuaded Truman to gear up the airlift. If only he had been allowed to smash through that armored column, Clay declared, then there would have been no Korean War. Bohlen just listened. He interjected only when Clay vowed that if he were the President right now, he'd tear down that wall. Bohlen mildly observed that such an act would be a good way to start World War III.

In Berlin, Clay and Johnson greeted the troops; the Vice-President seemed to be running for mayor, hugging women, kissing babies, patting dogs. Over the next two months, Clay could not resist a little brinksmanship; when East German police trained water hoses on American troops, Clay brought up tanks and bayonet-ready assault troops to face down the Soviets. At Checkpoint Charlie, a vital crossing point between East and West, U.S. and Russian soldiers played small, tense games of chicken. But the crisis gradually subsided. Kennan had been right: the wall had served to defuse the Berlin crisis, not bring it to war.

In August, after he returned from Martha's Vineyard, Acheson was asked by Mac Bundy if he supported General Clay's demands for vigorous action. Acheson said that it was too late. The time for bold steps had come and gone before the Soviets put up the wall.

Acheson was glum. He wrote Truman in late September that he believed Washington was about to hand Berlin to Russia. He saw appeasement everywhere. "I believe that this autumn we are heading for a most humiliating defeat over Berlin," he wrote his old boss. "I am now going to—in the current jargon—'phase out' for a while. To work for this crowd is strangely depressing. Nothing seems to get decided."

•   •   •

While Acheson was "phasing out," Harriman was trying to scramble back in. Laos was his ticket; he and Kennedy were "fully in the same mood," he later recalled, about the need to avoid an armed confrontation over the tortured little country. At Vienna, Khrushchev had shown no interest in confronting Kennedy over Laos; afterward, the President had called Harriman and said to him, "Governor, do you understand what I want?" Harriman replied that he did. Kennedy went on: "I want to have a negotiated settlement. I do not want to become militarily involved."

Bored by all the time he seemed to be spending at staff meetings in Geneva, the site of the settlement talks on Laos, Harriman began cutting the size of the U.S. delegation. After one of his aides, a young Foreign Service officer named William Sullivan, had cut the staff by one-third, Harriman grunted, "That's not good enough. I want it cut by half." Sullivan warned him that he could not do that without powerful resistance from the State Department bureaucracy. "The hell I can't," said Harriman. "Get rid of them."

Harriman admired young Sullivan, who was tough and bright and who had written thoughtful papers a year earlier recommending improved relations with the People's Republic of China and neutrality for Laos. Harriman wanted to make him his chief of staff. The problem was that Sullivan, then forty years old, was too junior. Harriman's answer had been simple: he ordered everyone senior to Sullivan to return to Washington.

Sullivan admired Harriman because he was remarkably free of cant. The State Department had become ossified in the fifties, distrusting Communists of any kind, not distinguishing between them, and making little effort to learn more. Harriman, on the other hand, saw the Communists as "human beings, not automatons," Sullivan later recalled. During the negotiations, Harriman came to know G. M. Pushkin, the Soviet Vice Foreign Minister, a squat, walleyed man with a quick sense of humor. From Pushkin, Harriman learned a lesson that would stay with him: that the U.S. and the Soviets have a parallel interest in Southeast Asia, to keep peace and control the Chinese. Harriman perceived that the Soviets and the Chinese had different interests and would soon fall out as allies. (He called Mao a "margarine

Communist" and didn't consider him much of a threat; his father's experience trying to build a railroad through China had convinced him that the Chinese had little interest in the outside world.) Harriman wired the State Department about the growing Sino-Soviet split, "but they didn't believe us," Sullivan recalled. "They thought we were dupes."

Harriman's method of dealing with State Department and CIA hawks was to ignore them. A CIA operative recalled making an impassioned plea to Harriman for more weapons and support for the anti-Communist forces: "Harriman turned to us, smiled, and asked politely what we had been talking about, showing us that his hearing aid had been turned off." He told Sullivan that he had received only two or three negotiating instructions in all of World War II, and he did not intend to become a puppet now. Instructions from Washington began to pile up, but Harriman hardly glanced at them. He knew that the State Department bureaucracy did not speak for the President, and that only his instructions mattered.

When Harriman wanted to open talks with the Red Chinese, whom the U.S. did not recognize, the State Department objected. Harriman went ahead anyway and began meeting with the Chinese representatives over chi, or tea, which actually meant vodka. Harriman was disgusted with the bureaucracy. He told Schlesinger that the State Department had become so brainwashed by the right-wingers under Dulles that it needed what the Chinese called "thought correction." (In November, Mac Bundy wrote JFK, "Averell has strong views on the people who have been shaping our policy in Southeast Asia. He will not volunteer these views in his talk with you, but he will probably respond with alacrity to any questions you might wish to ask him about his judgment of the people involved. P.S., today is his 70th birthday.")

At the end of August, Harriman had come back to Washington and asked the President if he could deal directly with Prince Souvanna Phouma, rather than be forced to truck with the CIA's client Phoumi. Kennedy approved. He reiterated that he wanted nothing better than "to get out of Laos, if we can."

The negotiations were slow and arduous. The Pathet Lao and neighboring North Vietnamese repeatedly broke their word and the Royal Laotian Army provided little leverage. (An American adviser, describing improved morale in the ranks, duly reported that before, when the troops were attacked by the Pathet Lao, they dropped their arms and ran. Now they took their weapons with them.) "How's it going?" a reporter asked Harriman. "Just about as badly as expected," he replied. Asked whether he was optimistic or pessimistic he replied, "Neither. I'm determined."

He was. He worked from nine until midnight; lunches were working lunches and dinners working dinners, recalled an aide, Chester Cooper. He personally chased Prince Sihanouk of Cambodia to Rome and tracked him down in a hotel to force him to sign an accord. Aides described his negotiating style as "water torture." He would make the same point over and over, letting it drip down until his adversaries gave in. He would use scorn judiciously. When the North Vietnamese, the most devious of the lot, spoke, Harriman would ostentatiously read *The New York Times*. When a North Vietnamese representative began calling the U.S. a warmonger, Harriman "accidentally" hit the "talk" button on his microphone and said to an aide, "Did that little bastard say we started World War II?"

Harriman finally succeeded in getting what he called "a good bad deal." After fourteen months and millions of words, the major powers and bordering countries signed an accord in July of 1962 guaranteeing Laos's neutrality. The North Vietnamese ignored the pact and continued to support the Pathet Lao, but a shaky neutralist regime under Souvanna was installed and preserved. The President's wish had been fulfilled: Laos was no longer a "crisis point."

Harriman's performance earned the admiration of the Kennedys. Bobby Kennedy, in particular, was drawn to the old diplomat. Both shared an impatience with bureaucratic foot dragging, a strong commitment to civil rights, an inner toughness and outward bluntness, and a willingness to change. Harriman's deafness, once considered a serious liability, became a source of bemusement. The Kennedys laughed about the time Harriman and Kennedy had begun to talk at once during a meeting in the Cabinet Room; the President had tried to override Harriman, but Averell just kept right on talking, slouched over in his chair, his eyes half closed. The President gave up and the others in the room began chuckling. "Did I say something funny?" asked Harriman. "No, Governor," Kennedy said with a smile, and the room broke up. Mac Bundy began calling Harriman "the Crocodile." ("He just lies up there on the riverbank, his eyes half closed, looking sleepy. Then, *whap*, he bites.") The nickname caught on: Bobby Kennedy gave Harriman a gold crocodile, and Harriman's staff gave him a silver one "from your victims."

The Kennedys decided to make use of Harriman's toughness and iconoclasm. In November of 1961, he was appointed Assistant Secretary of State for Far Eastern Affairs, a job that would allow him to shake the department out of its Dullesian rigidity toward Asian Communism.

Harriman, a Europeanist at heart, had wanted to be Assistant Secretary for European Affairs. He was sitting in his office in Geneva with Paul Nitze when Dean Rusk called to offer him Far East. Nitze, who already knew about Harriman's new post, watched Averell strain to hear what Rusk was saying over a scratchy transatlantic connection. "Yes, sir; yes, sir," said Harriman. "Whatever the President wants." He hung up and turned to Nitze. "What did he offer me?" "Far East," replied Nitze. "Damn," said Harriman. "I was hoping it was Europe."

•   •   •

The selection of Chip Bohlen to become ambassador to France was, for Washington, occasion for a whirl of parties. Almost every night during the first two weeks of October 1962, a bright Indian summer in the capital, dinners or dances feted the Bohlens. On the evening of October 15, McGeorge Bundy had just finished greeting guests at his party for the Bohlens when he was called away to the phone. At the other end of the secure line was Ray Cline, a deputy director of the CIA. He had chilling news: U-2 reconnaissance photographs showed a ballistic missile installation under construction in the woods near San Cristóbal, Cuba.

Bundy, sensitive to leaks at Georgetown cocktail parties, coolly told no one. Nor did he call the President. "I decided," he explained to Kennedy later, "that a quiet evening and a good night of sleep were the best preparation you could have in light of what you would face in the days ahead."

Around Washington, others who needed to know were quietly informed by the CIA that evening. At a formal banquet for the German Foreign Minister in the State Department's eighth-floor dining room, Dean Rusk was slipped a note by a waiter. When he returned from the phone, he calmly resumed his discussion of NATO, but at the first opportunity, he signaled Paul Nitze, an Assistant Secretary of Defense, to join him for a private conversation. Out on the terrace overlooking the Lincoln Memorial, dimly lit in the autumn night, Rusk told Nitze about the CIA photographs. When Defense Secretary Robert McNamara returned home from an evening with the Robert Kennedys at Hickory Hill, analysts were waiting to show him the evidence.

President Kennedy was still in his pajamas when Bundy came into his bedroom in the morning. "There is now hard photographic evidence," the adviser said, "that the Russians have offensive missiles in Cuba." Kennedy knew he was up against it. He had made it explicitly clear that Soviet missiles would not be tolerated in Cuba; the Soviets had made it equally clear that they would not put them there. Now he was being played as a weak dupe.

Ticking off a list of fourteen names, Kennedy ordered Bundy to convene an emergency meeting of an ad hoc group of advisers. They were to become the regulars of an Executive Committee, or ExCom, that for the next 12 days would manage the most dangerous superpower face-off of the nuclear age. When Bundy and Kennedy had finished calling top aides in the Administration, Kennedy decided there was one more man he wanted to consult, a Republican lawyer in private practice on Wall Street.

John McCloy, the only outsider called by Kennedy that day, was direct and sharp. The missiles could not remain in Cuba. The Soviets were testing Kennedy, and he had to respond, quickly and firmly. If need be, an air strike should be launched and the island invaded by American troops.

McCloy was preparing to leave on a private business trip to Germany, and Kennedy did not ask him to change his plans. But he told him to stay in touch. He might need advice, Kennedy said, experienced judgments from those who had been through such crises before and could be depended on to ask the right questions. As it turned out, only two other outsiders, in addition to McCloy, would be included in the critical deliberations: Dean Acheson and Robert Lovett.

Acheson was shown the photographs by Dean Rusk. He predictably and immediately took the side of action. The U.S., he argued, could not afford to sit back until the missiles became operative. Once the weapons "were pointing at our hearts and ready to shoot," it would be difficult to do anything about them. Thus Acheson said he opposed any course that would result in a protracted showdown.

Acheson, who joined the ExCom after it had already deliberated for a day, found the President's advisers divided. Defense Secretary Robert McNamara, breaking with his Joint Chiefs of Staff and his deputy Nitze, argued that "a missile is a missile"—those in Cuba were no more threatening than the long-range rockets based in Russia, and thus did not alter the power balance. Nonsense, snorted Acheson. "Missiles located ninety miles from our coast," he said, were for the Soviets "a much surer bet than long-range ones." They would be able to attack almost any city in the U.S., presenting a grave and clear threat to American security. The President's primary obligation was to protect American security, and that, he unequivocally stated, meant "taking the missiles out." In addition, the U.S. had to uphold the Monroe Doctrine, forbidding outside meddling in the Western Hemisphere; the President could not afford to vacillate when faced with such a blatant assault on national resolve. "Something should be done quickly," he said.

Despite his forceful views, Acheson did not consider himself the strongest of hawks. The way he saw the argument shaping up that Wednesday, there was a dangerous coalition forming between the diplomatic doves like George Ball and cautious pragmatists like Bob McNamara in favor of doing nothing at all. Pitted against them were military hawks who wanted to use the crisis as a pretext for invading Cuba. Korea had soured Acheson on the military; "when you get soldiers talking about policy," he later explained, "they want to go further and further in a military way... until their proposals are apt to be at least as dangerous as the original danger." Acheson's solution, as he saw it, was a middle ground: a surgical air strike, aimed only at the missiles. Some of the Russian technicians would no doubt be killed, but the general population would be spared.

Acheson was impatient with the circular debates swirling around the table. The formless nature of the meetings bothered him; there was no set structure, and ExCom members, from the President on down, seemed to come and go with the same randomness as the sporadic deliveries of coffee and sandwiches. Acheson continued to be disappointed by Dean Rusk. He felt the reticent Secretary—who kept his own counsel, sidestepped any responsibility for guiding discussion, and even skipped some critical sessions—was letting down the office of Secretary of State as well as the President. Acheson was disturbed that Rusk's rightful role was being assumed by the Attorney General, Bobby Kennedy. With reluctance but without hesitation, Acheson moved to fill what he saw as a void and to act as a counterpoint to the President's brother.

When the President had to step out on that first Wednesday to attend to official chores, RFK assumed control of the meeting. He had been bothered by the idea of a surprise attack—"I know how Tojo felt when he was planning Pearl Harbor," he had scribbled on a note to his brother the day before—and Acheson's forceful arguments provoked a strong reaction. The issue was above all a *moral* one, Bobby now proclaimed. America's traditions would not permit the launching of a surprise raid. He insisted: "My brother is not going to be the Tojo of the 1960s."

Despite his brashness, Bobby Kennedy, at thirty-six, was a dominating and persuasive advocate. But Acheson, at age sixty-nine, regarded RFK as an impetuous youth, "moved by emotional or intuitive responses more than by trained lawyer's analysis." By betraying moral anguish and engaging in sloppy thinking, cardinal sins in the Achesonian creed, Bobby drew the old statesman's scorn. Pearl Harbor was an utterly specious analogy, Acheson declared. The situations were in no way comparable: the U.S. had been warning other nations to keep their hands off the Western Hemisphere for 139 years. Acheson mocked RFK's example of Pearl Harbor with an analogy of his own: "Was it necessary to employ the early nineteenth-century method of having a man with a red flag walk before a steam engine to warn people and cattle to stay out of the way?"

Acheson was more deferential at a private meeting with the President the next day. For more than an hour the two men talked; Acheson reiterated his arguments and the President listened attentively. Unlike his prickly brother, the President was courteous and thoughtful with Acheson. More importantly, he was President, a distinction that Acheson had deeply understood ever since the day, some fifteen years earlier, when he had pored over maps of the eastern Mediterranean with Harry Truman. Kennedy rose from his rocking chair and stared out the French doors into the Rose Garden. "I guess I better earn my salary this week," he said. "I'm afraid you have to," answered Acheson. "I wish I could help more."

During those uncertain first days of deliberation, the air strike advocated by Acheson, with sporadic support from McGeorge Bundy, became known as the "fast track." The opposite approach—a quiet series of diplomatic moves designed to avoid a showdown—was meanwhile dubbed the "Bohlen plan."

Chip Bohlen cared little about Cuba. On a flight from Key West in April of 1961, Kennedy had tried to draw Bohlen out on the Cuba problem. The diplomat protested. He knew nothing about Latin America, had never set foot in Cuba, and did not have anything worthwhile to contribute on the subject. "All right, all right," the President said, dropping the subject. Bohlen later lamented: "If I had had my wits about me, I would have been in a position to have at least tried to convince the President to call off the plans for the disastrous Bay of Pigs invasion."

When Bohlen came to pay his official farewell call to the White House before departing for Paris, Kennedy had the surveillance photographs spread out on his desk. "Look at these," he said. France was forgotten for the next half hour. Kennedy described the ExCom and asked Bohlen to become a member.

Bohlen's job was to assess the likely Soviet response to any American action. The most dangerous of all things, he told the ExCom that first day, would be the killing of Soviet civilians. The Kremlin would be forced to respond, perhaps in a spasm of nuclear fury. Thus he strongly opposed a surprise air attack. The problem should be first approached by diplomatic means, perhaps a letter to Khrushchev.

At a final farewell dinner for the Bohlens that night at Joe Alsop's, the President, who was among the guests, pulled Bohlen out onto the porch to discuss the crisis. He was, as usual, irritated at the State Department. "Chip, what's wrong with that Goddamned department of yours? I can never get a quick answer." Bohlen, accustomed to bureaucratic compromise and diplomatic nuance, tried to explain that foreign policy making was not conducive to "quick ready-made solutions." As the Bohlens were saying their goodbyes to the Alsops and other guests, the President whispered to Avis, who had just finished packing her household and three children for Paris, "I wouldn't be too sure you are leaving. I think I may ask you to stay." Avis had no idea what he was talking about; as a good Foreign Service wife, she did not ask, or even question, her husband.

Kennedy, in fact, had asked Bohlen to stay on with the ExCom. Bohlen, however, argued to Rusk that it would be unwise for him to delay his departure, that it would arouse suspicion and give the Soviets warning that the U.S. had discovered the missiles. Rusk agreed. Kennedy, nonetheless, was irked and told an aide to page Bohlen at the airport and instruct him that he was "urgently desired" at the White House. Bohlen argued with the aide, Kenneth O'Donnell, insisting that he was scheduled to give a speech in New York in a couple of hours. Slightly incredulous that Bohlen was worried about a speaking engagment when Armageddon beckoned, O'Donnell insisted that Bohlen come to the White House at once. Bohlen asked to speak directly to the President. He told JFK that his plane to New York was leaving in fifteen minutes, and that he could not possibly cancel his speaking engagement without setting off speculation in the press. Frustrated, the President said, "Go on. I guess we'll have to do without you."

Bohlen left his advice in the form of a handwritten memo. He suggested that a private communication be sent to Khrushchev to allow him to back down and warned that an air strike "will inevitably lead to war."

Bohlen's motives in carrying on with his diplomatic duties and forsaking the ExCom are a source of controversy. Preserving secrecy was vital; even the President was maintaining his campaign schedule on behalf of congressional candidates, and members of the ExCom were sneaking into the White House through underground tunnels. Joe Alsop later argued that Bohlen's willingness to give up his seat at the most dramatic crisis of the age demonstrated extraordinary self-lessness and devotion to duty as a professional member of the Foreign Service. Bobby Kennedy, on the other hand, took a harsh view: "Chip Bohlen ran out on us, which always shocked me. That wasn't nec-essary. He could always have postponed it. But he decided to leave this country in a crisis." RFK is unfair; Bohlen was hardly a shirker. On the long voyage to France, Avis later told her children, Chip was exceedingly jumpy and taut, fretful that he was missing the challenge of his career. But he truly believed that he was doing his duty by conducting business as usual. It is likely as well that he knew his own limitations, felt that he had spoken his piece, and trusted his friend Llewellyn (Tommy) Thompson, his successor as ambassador to Mos-cow, to counsel the President on Soviet moves. His judgment on the last was correct; Thompson proved a very able adviser.

•   •   •

The President reached Bob Lovett by phone in New York and ordered him, "Come down at once." In Washington he was briefed by Bundy. On a small table near Bundy's desk Lovett noticed a pho-tograph of Henry Stimson. "All during the conversation," Lovett re-called, "the old Colonel seemed to be staring me straight in the face." Lovett invoked their mutual icon: "Mac, I think the best service we can perform for the President is to try to approach this as Colonel Stimson would." Bundy agreed; Stimson would be their "bench mark."

Lovett found Kennedy fuming after a session with Soviet Foreign Minister Andrei Gromyko. "All during his denial that the Russians had placed any missiles in Cuba," Kennedy said. "I had the pictures in the center drawer of my desk and it was an enormous temptation to show them to him." The President asked Lovett's advice. The former Defense Secretary proposed the same approach his protégé McNamara had been urging: a blockade, or "quarantine," of ships headed for Cuba, followed by a gradual increase of pressure as necessary.

An air strike may not be so clean-cut and simple as others claimed, Lovett warned. Though an advocate of air power since his days in the Yale Unit, he knew that quick, unsustained bombing runs were not terribly effective. Bombing needed to be relentless; a "surgical strike" against a small concealed target might not take out the missiles. A blockade, however, was a show of force that gave the Soviets a chance to back down. "We would look ridiculous," he believed, "if we grabbed a sledgehammer to kill a fly."

The President would have to resist pressure from the "bleeding hearts" to lift the blockade before it became effective, Lovett warned, but at least he would not be committed to uncontrollable combat. Bobby Kennedy came in from the Rose Garden and asked a few pointed questions, but it was clear to Lovett that both brothers agreed with his assessment about the "desirability of taking a relatively mild and not very bloodthirsty step first." As Lovett put it: "We can always increase the tempo of combat, but it is very hard to reduce it once the battle is joined."

Kennedy graciously asked Lovett to stay for a private dinner, but at age sixty-seven Lovett's lifelong hypochondria had hardly abated. He did not feel well enough, he replied; he was too tired.

Lovett, with his instinct for the center, had found it. By Friday, most members of the ExCom were leaning toward the blockade. Acheson, however, was a vocal holdout. As he had during the Berlin crisis, he argued that the U.S. was faced with a test of wills. The U.S. had to show it was willing to use force, to strike first and hard.

Again, Bobby Kennedy was his nemesis. During the Berlin crisis, when Acheson was so forcefully pressing a hard line, Robert Kennedy had reflected that he never wanted to be on the opposite side of an argument with Acheson. Now, however, he led the opposition. "For one hundred and seventy-five years," the younger Kennedy said, the United States "had not been [the type] of country" that starts wars; "a sneak attack," he said, "is not in our traditions."

Kennedy now held sway, and Acheson recognized that he had lost. When the ExCom began discussing detailed contingency plans for the blockade, the old statesman excused himself. He had given his advice, his course had been rejected, and he felt that it was improper for a man not in government to participate in formulating the details of a secret military operation. So he went off to his farm in Maryland for the weekend.

Acheson had just settled into a quiet Saturday evening in Sandy Spring when Rusk called him again. Kennedy had in fact chosen the blockade option and would announce it in a speech Monday night, Rusk said. He wanted Acheson to undertake a diplomatic mission: enlisting the support of Charles de Gaulle. Bohlen, traveling to France by boat, was still at sea, and Acheson himself had told Kennedy how important it was that a distinguished emissary be sent to critical European allies. In reply, Acheson quoted the adage of Oliver Wendell Holmes, that the U.S. was the least exclusive club in the world but it had the highest dues. "I guess if I belong to that club, I better do what I'm asked to do," he said. "You don't mind that your advice is not being followed?" asked Rusk. "Of course not," replied Acheson. "I'm not the President."

The passport office in Washington opened specially for one patron that Sunday: Acheson's secretary, Barbara Evans, was there to renew his lapsed passport. The banks were not as accommodating; top State Department officials chipped in to raise sixty dollars in pocket money for the departing emissary. When his plane stopped for refueling at Greenham Common air base in England, Acheson was met by his old friend David K. E. Bruce. In one pocket the distinguished ambassador had a bottle of Scotch, which Acheson gladly shared while waiting to resume his journey. In the other he had a revolver. "Why?" asked Acheson. "The department told me to carry it when I met you," said Bruce.

De Gaulle agreed to receive Acheson at the Elysée on Monday evening. Along with Cecil Lyon, the chargé d'affaires, and Sherman Kent, a CIA analyst, they wandered through the basement corridors and passageways of the palace to avoid the public entrance. Acheson was elated by the occasion, which seemed to remind him of an Alexandre Dumas novel. "Porthos, is your rapier loose in its scabbard?" he exclaimed to his companions.

"Your President has done me a great honor by sending so distinguished an emissary," said de Gaulle with elaborate politeness. Acheson, for once at a loss for words, responded with a deep bow. After reading the President's letter and speech, Le Grand Charles asked Acheson: Am I being consulted or informed? Informed Acheson answered, offering to show the photographs Sherman Kent carried with him. "Not now," said de Gaulle, waving them away. "These will only be evidence. I accept what you tell me as fact, without any proof of any sort needed."

Suppose, de Gaulle asked, the Soviets do not respond or try to break the blockade? What would the U.S. do then? Acheson, worried about the same possibility, was unsure of the answer. But he thought it unwise to let de Gaulle know this. "We will immediately tighten the blockade to include tankers," he said. "This will bring Cuba to a

standstill. If we have to go further, why of course we'll go further."
Replied de Gaulle: "That's very good."

Only after giving France's approval did de Gaulle succumb to curiosity and ask to peek at the photos. Studying them with a magnifying
glass brought out the old soldier in him. *"Incroyable,"* he exclaimed
at hearing they were taken from sixty-five thousand feet. As Acheson
rose to leave, de Gaulle told him, "It would be a pleasure to me if
these things were all done through you."

While Acheson was crossing the Atlantic, Lovett was flying back
to Washington from New York. He had left the capital on Saturday
afternoon, and on Sunday morning the President asked him to come
back and help draft the announcement of the quarantine. After lunch
at Hickory Hill, Lovett and Robert Kennedy went to the Oval Room
where the ExCom was working.

Midway through the session, the President motioned Lovett to join
him on the second-floor balcony overlooking the South Lawn and the
Washington Monument. Whatever the outcome, the President said,
the crisis was likely to involve tough negotiating, perhaps at the U.N.
Did Lovett think that Adlai Stevenson could handle it? Lovett had
been among those who jumped on Stevenson at the previous day's
ExCom meeting for being too soft, for proposing that America's missiles in Turkey and its base in Guantanamo, Cuba, be placed on the
bargaining table. No, Lovett said, Stevenson was not the man for the
job. Instead, he suggested, the President call in John McCloy. It was
a recommendation that Robert Kennedy had already made.

Lovett called McCloy's secretary at home that Sunday to help in
tracking him down in Frankfurt. "How soon can you get home?" he
was asked. McCloy responded that he was planning to go hunting
partridges in Portugal. "No, we mean right away" was the reply. "Well,"
said McCloy, "the plane has already gone." An Air Force plane was
promptly dispatched to fetch him.

Averell Harriman felt left out. Although he was then Assistant
Secretary of State for Far Eastern Affairs, he rightly thought of himself
as one of the nation's foremost Soviet experts, a man who had cultivated a relationship with Khrushchev, as he had with Stalin. Yet his
advice was not sought.

His ultimate humiliation came that Sunday, the day before Kennedy's speech. Still hoping to deflect speculation in the press about
Cuba, the White House used Harriman as a decoy. While members
of the ExCom were sneaking through bomb shelters and tunnels to

enter the White House unnoticed, Harriman's limousine was driven right up to the front of the West Wing. A few journalists were thrown off the scent, speculating about problems developing in the Far East. Harriman, who was brought to a private anteroom in the White House and left there, was miffed. "How long do I have to sit here?" he grumbled.

As Kennedy prepared to go on television, the Strategic Air Command, custodian of the nation's nuclear bombers, was put on Defcon 2; the only higher state of alert is Defcon 1, which means war. The planes began circling in the air, fully loaded, in what was the biggest alert in SAC history. The 1st Armored Division left Fort Hood, Texas, for deployment on the East Coast.

Kennedy's seventeen-minute address announcing the "quarantine" was calm and steady. The blame for the situation and the responsibility for resolving it were put squarely on Khrushchev. "He has an opportunity now," the President said, "to move the world back from the abyss of destruction."

It is hard to overestimate the sense of dread provoked by the sudden revelation of the world's first full-fledged nuclear showdown. In Los Angeles, out of the range of the missiles, housewives thronged the supermarkets. "One lady's working four shopping carts at once," said a manager. "Another lady bought twelve packages of detergent. What's she going to do, wash up after the bomb?" In Miami, a local judge took his two children and began driving to Missouri. In a small Nebraska town, an air-raid siren went off by mistake, sending citizens scurrying for shelter. Nor was fear confined to the ordinary public. When George Ball awoke that morning from a fitful sleep on the cot in his office, he looked up to find his boss, Dean Rusk, standing there. "We have won a considerable victory," said Rusk. "You and I are still alive."

During the edgy four days that followed, Harriman began to worry that the U.S. was forcing Moscow into a confrontation. He knew Khrushchev and understood his insecurities as well as his bluster. But the White House still showed no signs of wanting to hear the advice of the experienced diplomat. Harriman called his friend Arthur Schlesinger. Khrushchev was sending desperate signals that he wanted a way out, said the former ambassador. He was not behaving like a man who wanted war. "If we do nothing but get tougher and tougher," Harriman added, "we will force them into countermeasures. We must give Khrushchev an out."

Schlesinger asked whether Harriman had made these points to the

State Department. "They never ask my advice about anything outside the Far East," Harriman lamented.

Acheson, on the other hand, had arrived from Paris as ardent as ever for firm action. In a meeting with Kennedy that Thursday, held as the first ships were being stopped by the American Navy, Acheson pointed out that the missiles still remained in Cuba and work was progressing on them. Time was running out, he said. The blockade would do nothing to stop the deployment. An air strike, he emphasized once again, was the only method of eliminating them.

On the following night, a rambling and plaintive personal missive from Khrushchev came rattling off the telegraph wire at the State Department. It was hard to know what to make of the confused message. Rusk phoned Acheson and asked him to come by. As they waited for the rest of the translation to be transmitted, the two men sat drinking Scotch in Rusk's seventh-floor office. Acheson agreed with the assessment that Khrushchev must have written the letter himself. He imitated the pudgy chairman pacing back and forth in the Kremlin, dictating the letter and waving his stubby finger. He must have been, said Acheson, "either tight or scared."

The optimism prompted by Khrushchev's message worried Acheson. "So long as we had the thumbscrew on Khrushchev," he recalled thinking, "we should have given it another turn every day." His pessimism was, in fact, justified. The next day a more formal, harsher message arrived from Moscow, making demands that the White House would not meet.

Robert Kennedy suggested the ploy that broke the crisis: a response was sent accepting most of the points in Khrushchev's letter of Friday night and ignoring the formal message that had arrived on Saturday. Acheson called it "a gamble to the point of recklessness." Later, in assessing the strategy's success, he called it "homage to plain dumb luck."

But in his letter to President Kennedy at the end of that week, Acheson was very much the loyal public servant. "May I congratulate you on your leadership, firmness and judgment over the past tough week," he wrote. "We have not had these qualities at the helm in this country at all times. It is good to have them again. Only a few people know better than me how hard these decisions are to make, and how broad the gap is between the advisers and the decider." Responded Kennedy: "It is a comforting feeling to have a distinguished captain of other battles in other years available for present duty."

All that remained was working out the final agreement for verifying the removal of the missiles. When he arrived at the U.N., McCloy found that Stevenson was no longer nearly so soft as the Kennedys feared. In fact, McCloy noted, Stevenson was a "hopping mad hawk" after exposing the Soviet Ambassador Valerian Zorin's blatant lies in the Security Council session. Nevertheless, the White House wanted McCloy, not Stevenson, to take charge of the final negotiations.

As McCloy's counterpart, Khrushchev designated Deputy Foreign Minister Vasily Kuznetsov, a cultivated and gentle diplomat who spoke English fluently and had studied at Carnegie Institute of Technology in Pennsylvania. McCloy was a tough bargainer; he even resisted giving a pledge that the U.S. would not invade Cuba until he was ordered to do so by the White House.

One of the final sessions was held at McCloy's home in Stamford, Connecticut. Kuznetsov seemed worried that the house might be bugged and suggested they walk outside. Sitting on a wood-rail fence, they continued their conversation. "Well, Mr. McCloy," said Kuznetsov when they had finished. "We will honor this agreement. But never will we be caught like this again."

It was the prospect of such an unrestrained arms race that led President Kennedy to end his final message to Khrushchev with a plea for the resumption of nuclear test ban talks in Geneva. Begun in 1958, they had dragged to a halt after the Soviets shot down an American U-2 plane in 1960. After an informal moratorium, both sides had resumed testing in 1961, the Russians exploding a hundred-megaton bomb in the atmosphere. Scientists were beginning to pick up radiation in mothers' milk as the clouds circled the globe.

Kennedy wanted to salvage some reason from the superpowers' brush with madness. "Perhaps now, as we step back from danger, we can together make real progress in this vital field," the American President wrote his Soviet counterpart. He called for both countries to undertake "the great effort for a nuclear test ban."

• • •

Khrushchev agreed to resume the test ban talks in Moscow in July 1963. Kennedy's first choice to lead the U.S. delegation was McCloy, who during his stint as his disarmament adviser in 1961 had done considerable groundwork for an agreement. But when Kennedy asked McCloy to be chief U.S. negotiator, he begged off. His private interests again predominated; he was deeply involved in handling international negotiations for the world's major oil companies.

As an alternative, Rusk suggested Harriman, though with little enthusiasm. Despite Harriman's unsurpassed record at dealing with the Soviets, the Secretary considered him too much of an independent operator, too great a foe of the department's bureaucracy. Kennedy, however, was all for Harriman; his work on the Laos accords had won Kennedy's respect. Kennedy quickly approved Harriman's appointment, knowing that Rusk and his department might have second thoughts. Indeed, the next day State expressed reservations, too late.

Kennedy pleased Harriman at the outset by giving him wide latitude in his formal negotiating instructions. Noted Atomic Energy Commission chairman Glenn Seaborg: "The document was broadly couched, as was befitting an emissary of Harriman's experience and judgment."

When Harriman arrived at the Moscow airport on July 15, the press was out in force. "How long do you think you'll be there?" a reporter asked. Harriman figured that if he said the negotiations would be long and complex, the Soviets would feel compelled to make them so. "Well now," he answered, "if Chairman Khrushchev is as interested in having a test ban treaty as President Kennedy and Prime Minister Macmillan are, we ought to be out of here in two weeks."

Harriman had deliberately brought a small delegation noted more for its diplomatic skills than its technical expertise. "The expert is out to point out all the difficulties and dangers," he explained. At a stop in Britain on the way, he had secured from Macmillan a pledge that the British delegate, the shallow and ill-prepared Lord Hailsham, would take a back seat. The Soviets, indicating they meant business, designated Andrei Gromyko as their negotiator.

Khrushchev himself took an active interest in the proceedings, sitting through the entire first day's session at a massive Gothic meeting hall at the Kremlin. "Why don't we have a test ban?" he jovially announced at the outset. "Why don't we sign it now and let the experts work out the details?" Harriman took a blank pad of paper and shoved it toward the relaxed Soviet leader. "Here, Mr. Khrushchev, you sign first and I'll sign underneath."

Despite Khrushchev's jocularity, it quickly became clear to Harriman that the Soviets would not go along with a total ban on nuclear testing. The sticking point was verification; the Soviets were loath to permit on-site inspections. Atmospheric tests were easy to detect, but underground testing could be fairly well hidden.

Grudgingly accepting Soviet intransigence, Harriman reluctantly recommended giving up the quest for a total test ban, and the President agreed to try for a narrower ban, limited to aboveground testing. Years later, in retrospect, Harriman concluded that the U.S. should have pressed harder for a complete ban. "When you stop to think what the advantages were to us of stopping all testing in the early 1960s when we were still ahead of the Soviets," he lamented, "it's really appalling to realize what an opportunity we missed."

Harriman had a condition of his own: the right of any country to withdraw from the treaty if a country that had not signed (such as China or France) built its own bombs and began testing them. The Soviets were uneasy with this; their murky relationship with the Chinese made them reluctant to include a provision that seemed aimed primarily at Peking.

The Soviets tried to slide around this condition with candor that was not exactly disarming. The Leninist view of treaties, they maintained, always permitted them to be abrogated if they threatened the self-interest of the Soviet state. Gromyko held out for a right of withdrawal that vaguely referred to "extraordinary circumstances."

Harriman was aware that without a specific clause referring to an explosion by a country such as China, the Senate would never ratify the treaty. "If we don't have a right of withdrawal, we can't have an agreement," he said, picking up his papers and preparing to walk out. Lord Hailsham was alarmed. He sent a telegraph to Macmillan saying that Harriman's tough stance was threatening to wreck the talks, and the Prime Minister transmitted these concerns to Washington through Britain's ambassador, David Ormsby-Gore. When Kennedy heard what was happening, he broke into a smile. "Agree you should sit tight," he wired his negotiator. Harriman reflected: "I think his opinion of me rose." The Soviets backed down; the agreement was signed two days earlier than the two weeks Harriman had predicted.

Rather than wait for an exchange of cables, Harriman simply picked up a phone and with everyone listening called Kennedy directly (he later explained that he had not bothered to return to the privacy of the U.S. Embassy because "I knew they'd be listening whether we called from one place or the other").

It was still early morning when McGeorge Bundy, in the White House situation room, answered the person-to-person call from Moscow. Kennedy was brought on the line. "Great! Good luck!" he exclaimed. Just then, another call came through from Harold Macmillan in London. The British Prime Minister, not knowing a deal had been struck, began by apologetically explaining his concerns over Harriman's reported intransigence. Kennedy grinned and broke in, "Don't worry. It's been worked out."

As soon as he had hung up, Harriman walked back to the conference table and asked, "Where are the copies of the treaty we are supposed to initial?" he asked. The leather-bound documents were placed on the table, the mineral water was removed, and the photographers were invited in. Hailsham, in the manner of an English peer whose signature is simply his last name, penned just a single elaborate letter next to Harriman's WAH and Gromyko's Russian AG. Harriman had no respect for Hailsham, but he marveled at his lordly signature. "Did you see his 'H'?" he asked. "It was very beautiful."

The Kremlin courtyard, closed to all but secret police in Stalin's day, was opened to the crowds that evening. Shaking hands and pinching cheeks like a congressman, Khrushchev introduced "Gospodin Garriman" to the crowd. "We've just signed the test-ban treaty," he shouted. "I'm going to take him to dinner. Do you think he deserves it?" The crowd roared.

The outpouring was emotional for Harriman, a giddy triumph after three years of toiling stoically in obscurity. "Mr. Harriman showed himself to be worthy of the recommendation that you gave him in your letter," Khrushchev wrote Kennedy. "Furthermore, we never doubted this." Kennedy called the accomplishment "a shaft of light cut into the darkness."

Even Harriman's neighbors joined in the adulation. On the night he arrived home, they paraded down N Street outside his home holding candles and singing, "For He's a Jolly Good Fellow" and an old campaign song, adapted from George M. Cohan, "H-A-double-R-I-M-A-N spells Harriman." Harriman, in his shirt sleeves, came out on the steps to watch the celebration and mumble some words of thanks. A girl with a small baby in her arms held up her child to Harriman and thanked him for helping "make it possible for him to look ahead to a full and happy life."

•   •   •

Like an ambitious young careerist, Harriman, who turned seventy in 1961, slowly worked his way up through the State Department ranks. In March of 1963, he won his second promotion, from Assistant Secretary for Far Eastern Affairs to Under Secretary for Political Affairs. He advanced by fighting the bureaucracy, a cause Kennedy endorsed, not by ingratiating himself with Rusk. As Under Secretary, he formed a committee to root out and kill useless committees. As Assistant Secretary, he tried to rid Far Eastern Affairs of Dulles holdovers and bring about a less rigid stance toward Red China. FE is "a wasteland," he told Schlesinger; all the China experts had been exiled. (John Stewart Service was stamping passports in Liverpool, John Paton Davies was making furniture in Peru, and John Carter Vincent was gardening in Cambridge, Massachusetts.) By 1960, there were only two officials who could even speak Chinese in the State Department. Significantly, there were no experts on Vietnamese culture and history at all.

"Young blood," Harriman would grumble, "we need young blood." His own top advisers in 1963 were young men: Bill Sullivan, forty-two, his chief aide on the Laos negotiations; Roger Hilsman, forty-three, his successor at FE; and Michael Forrestal, thirty-five, a National Security staffer. The son of James Forrestal, Mike had been virtually adopted by Harriman after his father's suicide in 1949; in 1962, Kennedy had half joked that Forrestal's job on the White House staff was to be "my ambassador to that sovereign state known as Averell Harriman."

Though increasingly deaf, Harriman looked remarkably fit. When a young aide told Marie Harriman that her husband looked "terrific," she snorted, "You'd look terrific too if you did nothing but play polo until you were forty years old." Nevertheless, when Harriman, on a diplomatic trip to Buenos Aires, attended a reunion of the Argentine National Polo Team he had beaten in 1928, the old Argentine gentlemen were all leaning on canes or hunched over in chairs. Harriman, who had turned a double play in a State Department softball game against the Japanese Embassy that summer, felt sorry for the Argentines; they had never stopped playing polo.

Harriman busied himself with a wide range of chores in the Kennedy years, hacking at the bureaucracy, patiently negotiating over Laos, winning a quick test ban treaty. But increasingly he was preoccupied with America's involvement in Vietnam.

• • •

In later years, Harriman would erect an elaborate mythology about his early views on Vietnam, a faith that would be propagated by his aides and admirers. Harriman liked to say that he had heard Franklin Roosevelt warn against U.S. involvement in Vietnam back in 1944, and that he had heartily concurred at the time and thereafter. His followers like to point out that Harriman firmly opposed aiding France's effort in Vietnam, that he had tried to stop the French from diverting Marshall Plan funds to their war in Indochina. He had failed only because the Secretary of State, Dean Acheson, had interposed himself and permitted the transfer to preserve France as a NATO ally. Harriman later described Acheson's rationale as "a tragic theory."

In fact, Harriman had become a hawk on Vietnam by 1954, the year the French were finally defeated by the Vietminh. When Acheson, Harriman, Nitze, Kennan, and several other veterans of the Truman years gathered to discuss their experiences at a seminar at Princeton in May 1954, Harriman was the most ardent advocate of intervention, even more hawkish than Acheson. "I want to go on the record here," Harriman stated, "that I think we ought to take steps to get troops—American as well as many others—into Indochina and the Red River Delta before this thing begins to go." When others pointed out the difficulty of fighting land wars in Asia, Harriman responded, "I would hate to see us have any thought of abandoning the whole of Southeast Asia just because it's a difficult thing to do."

By the early 1960s Harriman had settled into an uneasy ambivalence about the U.S. involvement in Vietnam. He was wary of military involvement, but he could not abide the thought of simply abandoning the country to the Communists. This conflict would gnaw at him for years. It set him off on a long, groping quest for a negotiated peace that would climax, and ultimately founder, in his last diplomatic mission for the United States, as chief negotiator at the Paris Peace Talks in 1968.

Harriman's liberal allies from the Democratic Advisory Council of the 1950s, Chester Bowles and John Kenneth Galbraith, were also searching for a peaceful solution during the Kennedy years. Their model was Laos: they wanted to make Vietnam a neutral region. In April of 1962, Galbraith suggested this path to the President in a memo. He warned, "We have a growing military commitment. This could expand step by step into a major, long-drawn-out indecisive military involvement." Back from India for consultations, Ambassador Galbraith was staying with the Harrimans in Georgetown. He tried to enlist Harriman as an ally to lobby the President.

Harriman, along with Michael Forrestal, met with the President on April 6. He told Kennedy, in his somewhat laconic style, that while he agreed with some conclusions of the Galbraith memo, he had difficulty with others. It was important that the "overt association of [the] U.S. with military operations in Vietnam be reduced to an absolute minimum," Harriman stated. But he said it was not time yet to seek peace talks. South Vietnam's President Diem "is a losing horse in the long run," Harriman added, but he did not think that "we should work against him." U.S. policy should be to support the government of South Vietnam, but not Diem personally. The President observed guardedly that he wanted to be ready "to seize on any favorable moment to reduce our involvement," but he recognized that "the moment might yet be some time away." In a wary conversation laced with hedging and frequent "buts," neither the young President nor the old statesman seemed very happy with the choices. At any rate, Galbraith's plan was quickly shot down by the Joint Chiefs of Staff; they chastised the ambassador to India for even questioning the U.S. commitment to containing Communism in Southeast Asia.

Harriman did not have strong convictions about the American role in Vietnam. He preferred a low-profile approach for the U.S. After the Laos accords in July 1962 he told Cy Sulzberger that the U.S. should now retreat from the "front lines" in Southeast Asia and let others visibly share the burden. He added that the CIA had gotten the U.S. into "terrible messes" in Laos and Indochina and that the Truman Administration should have recognized Red China in 1949.

While wrapping up the Laos accords, Harriman had made an attempt to approach the North Vietnamese secretly about a settlement of their war with the South. His initiative was the first in a myriad jumble of diplomatic moves by Washington over the next decade. The meeting itself, in Geneva in June 1962, was an early taste of the ultimate frustration.

Harriman and Bill Sullivan had to sneak down a back alley and in through a kitchen door to a secret meeting place in order to see the North Vietnamese Foreign Minister, Ung Van Khiem. (The Americans did not want the South Vietnamese delegation, quartered in a hotel across the street, to know.) A small, squat man in a bulky Soviet suit that was so long it covered his chubby hands when he stood, Ung was brutal and contemptuous. He refused to concede that the North had anything at all to do with the fighting in South Vietnam. Harriman was "marvelously patient with this insulting little thug," Sullivan later recalled. He methodically probed every possibility, searching for some basis of dialogue. When Ung remained hostile and intransigent, Harriman at last stood up, towered over Ung, and dryly told him that he was in for "a long, tough war."

Harriman's preference for diplomacy was partly rooted in his disdain for the military. His skirmishes with General Clay in Germany and his all-out war with MacArthur in Korea had left him leery of gold-braided egos. He was impatient even with Maxwell Taylor, the "good general" embraced by the Kennedys and Establishment figures such as Acheson and McCloy. When Taylor recommended sending eight thousand combat troops to Vietnam in 1961, Harriman had bluntly told him, "You were wrong about wanting to send the 82nd Airborne into Rome and you've been wrong about everything since." From his State Department perch as Assistant Secretary for Far Eastern Affairs, Harriman had adamantly opposed the military's early use of napalm and defoliants in Vietnam. He was angry at Dean Rusk for ceding Vietnam policy making to the Pentagon. When Harriman would complain about napalm, Rusk would say, "No, I think I'll leave it to the Pentagon."

Harriman's successor in FE when he moved up to Under Secretary in March of 1963 was Roger Hilsman, an old Burma hand who had fought in World War II as a jungle commando. Mac Bundy called Hilsman "the confident guerrilla"; he was a brash proponent of unconventional warfare, of "counterinsurgency," and he proceeded to impose his views on anyone who would listen. He immensely irritated the Pentagon with his second-guessing; the generals did not appreciate it when, at meetings on Vietnam, Major Hilsman corrected their geography.

Counterinsurgency, known in the jargon of the time as CI, was in vogue among some of Kennedy's young lieutenants, particularly activists such as Walt Rostow, who believed that the U.S. had to play a greater role in the Third World. Rostow envisioned, his colleagues joked, "a TV in every thatched hut." The purpose of CI was in fact appealing: to win the hearts and minds of the peasants with land reform, honest elections, and generous amnesties, to field special forces that could instruct the locals how to harvest crops and deliver babies as well as how to fight guerrilla warfare. The President was sufficiently impressed to establish, with much fanfare, the Green Berets, an elite special forces unit trained in counterinsurgency.

George Ball later recalled that Harriman was "taken in" by Hilsman and his counterinsurgency ideas. According to Bill Sullivan, however, Harriman "never completely bought" counterinsurgency. He saw it mostly as an alternative to the conventional blunt tactics favored by the military ("grab 'em by the balls and their hearts and minds will follow" went the Pentagon saying). He believed that counterinsurgency would buy time for the diplomats to work out a Laos-type solution.

Whatever the merits of CI, it was never really tried in Vietnam. Hilsman had ambitious plans for a network of "strategic hamlets" to fence out the Viet Cong, but Diem handed the program over to his nefarious brother Ngo Dinh Nhu, who had little use for notions like land reform or honest elections. Brother Nhu was principally interested in crushing dissent.

In May of 1963, on the 2,587th birthday of Buddha, government troops opened fire into a crowd of monks, or *bonzes*, in Hue City, killing nine. President Diem refused to apologize; he did not want to lose face. The Buddhists, foes of the ruling Catholic family, began dousing themselves with gasoline and sitting in the lotus position while they burned to death. Madam Nhu, Diem's sister-in-law, exclaimed, "Let them burn and we shall clap our hands!" She called the self-immolations "*bonze* barbecues."

In Washington, at meetings of a special CI Committee that Harriman chaired, a debate raged that summer over what should be done with Diem and his unsavory relatives. CIA Director John McCone argued that Diem was "a son of a bitch, but he's our son of a bitch." Harriman, however, believed that Diem was in the thrall of his opium-addict brother Nhu, whom he suspected of cooperating with the Communists based on some suspicious CIA intercepts. He was appalled by the regime's brutality and the intensity of the Buddhist dissent (he failed to understand, Richard Helms of the CIA later grumbled, that for the Buddhists "self-immolation was just another way to heaven"). By August, according to Hilsman, Harriman "preferred a coup to Nhu."

On August 21, Nhu ordered his special forces to attack the Buddhist pagodas, which they did with machine guns and tear gas. The CIA reported that dissident generals in Diem's army feared they would be assassinated by Nhu's men. Harriman, Hilsman, and Michael Forrestal decided they needed to act quickly. On the afternoon of August 24, they drafted a telegram to the new U.S. ambassador to South Vietnam, Henry Cabot Lodge, authorizing U.S. support for a coup against the Diem regime.

It was a hot, sultry Saturday in Washington and most officials had fled the capital. Harriman and Hilsman tracked down George Ball, Acting Secretary of State during Rusk's vacation, on the ninth green of the Chevy Chase Club golf course. Ball, an Atlanticist and Stevensonian liberal, found the Nhus "noxious" and had no appetite for U.S. engagement in Vietnam. He had warned JFK in late 1961 that on its present course the U.S. would have 300,000 troops in Vietnam in five years. "George, you're crazy as hell, that just isn't going to happen," replied the President (actually, Ball underestimated the eventual number of troops by 200,000). Now, as he read the Harriman/Hilsman telegram, Ball was perfectly willing to go along, though he insisted that the message be cleared with the President. Reached in Hyannis Port, Kennedy seemed agreeable, but he worried that if the coup occurred, the U.S. might not find Diem's successor any better than Diem himself. Finally, he gave his authorization, on condition that the Secretaries of State and Defense also concurred. Dean Rusk went along, though he later said that he had agreed because he believed Kennedy had agreed. Bob McNamara, climbing Grand Teton Mountain in Wyoming, could not be reached. Nor could McCone at the CIA or General Taylor of the JCS or Bundy of the National Security Staff, though their deputies did sign on.

When the principals returned to Washington on Monday and learned of the telegram, they were outraged. The confusion that followed "illustrated the danger of doing business on the weekend," Mac Bundy later remarked. According to Bobby Kennedy, "the government split in two" over the telegram. Harriman was almost abusive to "Fritz" Nolting, the outgoing U.S. ambassador to Saigon and a Diem supporter. He said there was no reason to listen to Nolting now because his advice had been so bad in the past. He even refused to ride in the same limousine with Nolting, whom he described as "captivated" by Diem. Harriman was just as rough on the military brass, particularly Marine Corps General Victor "Brute" Krulak, the Joint Staff's officer in charge of counterinsurgency. (Some White House staffers later cranked out a parody of the minutes of one meeting: ". . . Governor Harriman stated that he had disagreed for 20 years with General Krulak and disagreed today, reluctantly, more than ever. He was sorry to say that he felt General Krulak was a fool and had always thought so. . . .")

President Kennedy was appalled at the infighting. "My God, my government is coming apart," he told a friend, journalist Charles Bartlett. The President was angry with Harriman for provoking the furor and then exacerbating it, and he told him so. Robert Kennedy later recalled that Harriman "seemed to age ten years that fall." RFK was so worried about his friend Averell that he spoke to his brother about inviting him into the Oval Office and stroking him a little, "rehabilitating him."

Meanwhile, the Administration vacillated. The telegram authorizing the coup was remanded, then revived. The dissident generals in Saigon froze, but they can hardly be blamed for uncertainty. Conflicting signals traveled over several different channels of communication between Washington and Saigon—a CIA channel, a State Department channel, Ambassador Lodge's private channel to the White House, channels the White House was not even aware of. Harriman, with his acute instinct for bureaucratic warfare, sniffed out a back channel between General Taylor and the head of the military mission in Saigon, General Paul Harkins, thereby regaining some of Kennedy's respect ("Harriman really is a shrewd old SOB"). Kennedy finally sent a mission to Saigon to report on what was happening; General Krulak of the marines declared that the war was going well, and Joseph Mendenhall of the State Department reported that the regime was collapsing. "You did go to the same country, didn't you?" asked Kennedy.

The President was unsure of what to believe, or do, about the war in Vietnam. With sixteen thousand U.S. military "advisers" already engaged, Kennedy saw clearly the risk of being drawn deeper in. "It's like taking a drink," he told an aide. "The effect wears off and you have to take another." Yet he feared the political fallout of withdrawing. According to Kenneth O'Donnell, he said, "If I tried to pull out completely now from Vietnam, we would have another Joe McCarthy Red Scare on our hands. But I can do it after I'm elected." Kennedy's true intentions are unknowable. But in the atmosphere of 1963, quitting Vietnam outright was almost unthinkable. A State Department official named Paul Kattenburg, head of the Interdepartmental Working Group on Vietnam, had the temerity to suggest that the U.S. consider withdrawing during an angry National Security Council meeting about Diem on August 31. Shocked silence fell over the Cabinet Room. "We will not pull out until the war is won," said Dean Rusk. "We're winning the war," said Bob McNamara. Kattenburg attended no more high-level meetings. He ended his career as a functionary in Guyana, not far from Devil's Island.

Beset by conflicting advice, frustrated, unsure, Kennedy finally did authorize a coup, or rather agreed with Ambassador Lodge's request "not to thwart" one. The Diem regime had become more extreme, raiding schools, locking up high-school and even elementary-school children. The generals finally revolted on October 31, but the coup was messy. Diem's body was found riddled with bullets and stab wounds.

John Kennedy was himself shot to death three weeks later. Bill Sullivan found Averell Harriman that afternoon sitting on the edge of his chair, in front of a television set, holding his head in his hands.

• • •

Lyndon Johnson had opposed the coup against Diem. Publicly, he had called Diem "the Winston Churchill of Southeast Asia." To journalist Stanley Karnow, he remarked, "Shit, man, he's the only boy we got out there." Johnson was suspicious of Harriman. He believed that Harriman had sent the first telegram authorizing a coup at 6 P.M. on a Saturday in August not out of a sense of urgency but out of desire to deceive. Equally suspect, Harriman was Robert Kennedy's friend. LBJ told aides that he would not trust Harriman "to take out my garbage."

Harriman was glum about Johnson's ascendancy. He read with foreboding a memo sent to State Department officials from the new President: ". . . and before you go to bed at night I want you to do one thing for me: ask yourself this one question . . . *what have I done for Vietnam today?*" Harriman was sure that LBJ was under the sway of hawks like Walt Rostow, who held the job first distinguished by George Kennan, director of Policy Planning at State. Harriman referred to Rostow as "the Air Marshal" for his advocacy of bombing the North (after reading a Rostow memo calling for air strikes, Harriman stated, "I never want to see another memo from that man"). It came as no surprise when LBJ appointed a committee to explore the question of bombing North Vietnam.

At the State Department, the doubters about the war were driven underground. Hilsman resigned a few hours before he was fired; LBJ was angry at Hilsman because he had seen him insult General Lyman Lemnitzer at a dinner party at the Harrimans'. As Hilsman walked out the door of the State Department, Harriman said to him, "If I were your age I'd resign too, but I'm not." Marie Harriman told Hilsman that if her husband was out of public office he would die.

He was instead "exiled to Africa," as he later put it, banished from Vietnam and assigned to deal with African affairs. He even lost his title in 1965 and became again a "roving ambassador," the job from which he had so assiduously worked his way up over the past four years. His friends began to worry about him, reading in his mournful face a sense of rejection and depression. The downcast expression masked resolution. On the street one day in early 1964 Harriman encountered Hilsman. "Johnson's going to escalate and it's not going to work," he told Hilsman. "He'll have to negotiate and he'll do it through the Russians. I'm the only one he can send."

CHAPTER 22

McNamara, Harriman, Johnson, Rusk at the White House

LBJ'S ESTABLISHMENT

"I told the President
he was wholly right"

Lyndon Johnson had learned the lessons of the Cold War too well. He had been conditioned by the hyperbole used by Acheson and others to persuade Congress to pay for the overseas commitments of the Truman Administration. As a congressman in the late forties, he had voted for the Marshall Plan, he explained, to "keep Stalin from overrunning the world." He subscribed to all the maxims that Acheson had made "clearer than the truth" and John Foster Dulles had hardened into dogma.

He knew the Lesson of Munich. Appeasement equaled weakness to Johnson; he would be "no Chamberlain umbrella man." It was a question of manhood; according to Johnson, "If you let a bully come in your front yard, he'll be on your porch the next day and the day after that he'll rape your wife in your own bed." He believed the domino theory. When President Kennedy sent LBJ to Vietnam, the Vice-President declared, "The basic decision in Southeast Asia is here.

We must decide whether to help these countries to the best of our ability or throw in the towel in the area and pull our defenses back to San Francisco." He remembered the Loss of China. Upon taking over the White House, LBJ told Ambassador Lodge, "I am not going to be the President who saw Southeast Asia go the way China went." He feared the Ghost of McCarthy. When the new left began protesting against the Vietnam War in the mid sixties, LBJ told George Ball, "Look, George, it's not those punks in the street that worry me, it's the right wing. That's the real beast if it ever gets unleashed."

Along with these fixed principles, Johnson brought to foreign policy the sophistication and subtlety of a Texas state legislator at a lobbyists' barbecue. Warned by the State Department before leaving on a tour of Southeast Asia not to shake hands with the Thais, who recoil from physical contact, Johnson exploded, "Dammit, I always shake hands and they love it!" When he took office, he thought he could buy off the North Vietnamese with a water project for the Mekong Delta, "bigger than the whole TVA." He was scornful when the State Department said pork barrel would not work as a tool of diplomacy. Why the hell not? Johnson demanded. It worked in Congress, didn't it? It worked with George Meany, didn't it? Why wouldn't it work with old Uncle Ho?

Johnson's attitude toward the foreign policy Establishment was "tremendously ambivalent," recalled Walt Rostow, who undertook to "explain" the Establishment to him. He was both possessive and deeply insecure. He bragged about his Rhodes Scholars and Harvard men as "my intellectuals" and exclaimed, "Goddamn it, I made it without their advantages and now they're working for me!" Yet he was afraid the "eastern lawyers" would trick him. "If something works out, Joe Alsop will write that it was Bundy that brilliant Harvard dean who did it," Johnson whined, "and if it falls flat he'll say it was the fault of that dumb ignorant crude baboon of a President." He solemnly told Hugh Sidey of *Time*, "I don't believe I'll ever get credit for anything I do in foreign affairs, no matter how successful it is, because I didn't go to Harvard."

In front of Sidey and other journalists, Johnson would mock Dean Acheson, raising his chin and affecting an imperious air. Dean Rusk recalled watching an "uproarious pantomime" of LBJ imitating Acheson testifying before a congressional committee. Johnson hated effeteness; he called where Acheson often vacationed, "that female island," and denounced professional diplomats like Chip Bohlen as "cookie pushers." He delighted in trying to overwhelm the

Socially Registered with his earthiness, sticking his face in theirs, cracking scatological jokes, summoning them to his bathroom to converse while he grunted on the toilet.

Yet he badly wanted their loyalty and respect. He craved consensus in his advisers and devotion among his followers. He wanted to be admired by Dean Acheson as much as he wanted to be loved by poor blacks. He wanted the Establishment's imprimatur, and he wanted the world to know that he had it.

During his 1964 campaign, Johnson told McGeorge Bundy, his National Security Adviser who was "one of them," to round up the usual Establishment luminaries and demonstrate that they were on his team. With his usual efficiency, Bundy set about putting together the President's Consultants on Foreign Affairs (Peace Panel).

In August, Bundy wrote a memo entitled "Backing from the Establishment." Bundy ridiculed journalists for using the term "Establishment" yet apparently did not hesitate to use it himself. "I think the key to these people is McCloy," he wrote to LBJ. "He is for us, but he is under very heavy pressure from Eisenhower and others to keep quiet. I have told him that is no posture for a man trained by Stimson." Bundy wrote McCloy a long letter on September 3 beseeching him to rally behind his President in the name of a bipartisan foreign policy. On September 4, McCloy wrote back resisting the whole affair as a political setup, and adding that Bob Lovett was also "most allergic." But Bundy brought McCloy around with a second long missive on September 7, and both McCloy and Lovett, as well as Acheson and a dozen other foreign policy elders from the private sector and academe, signed on. The announcement of the President's "Peace Panel" made page one of *The New York Times* on September 10, which was the main objective. Later that month, Bundy wrote Johnson, "In an effort to get a good story out of your meeting with this group tomorrow... the object would be to get a headline on Johnson, bipartisanship, peace, together with a picture of you meeting these men."

In his memoranda over the next year, Bundy began referring to Acheson, McCloy, Lovett, and other old statesmen brought in to counsel the President from time to time as "the Wise Men." The term was not altogether reverent. When C. Douglas Dillon, for instance, was unable to attend a meeting on January 28, 1966, Bundy headlined a memo to the President "Another Wise Man Bites the Dust." The committee appointed in the summer as a campaign ploy was considered too unwieldy to actually advise the President; when LBJ really wanted to hear what the Wise Men had to say, he summoned them in small groups or alone.

Johnson had begun calling on Dean Acheson, the acknowledged Chief Wise Man, immediately after taking office. On December 6, two weeks after Kennedy's assassination, Bundy wrote Johnson a memo:

> Re your lunch with Acheson: He is a determined believer in the "hard line." He sees Germany as the center of our policy and believes in paying no attention to General de Gaulle. . . . Acheson believes in action even during an election year (he remembers what Truman accomplished in '48) and he has little patience for less-developed countries, the UN, Adlai Stevenson, George Kennan, etc. He got on well with President Kennedy, although the President seldom took his advice but found him deeply stimulating. . . . After you have seen him, you may want to see Averell Harriman, who is at the opposite pole, if only to hold the liberals in line.

Over the next five years, LBJ repeatedly called on Acheson, whose law office was a short walk across Lafayette Park from the White House. He enlisted the old statesman to mediate a Greek-Turkish dispute over Cyprus, handle the troublesome de Gaulle on NATO problems, make peace with the Germans, and counsel him on the Vietnam War. The frequency of these missions is indicated by a note LBJ wrote Acheson on September 20, 1965: "I haven't seen you for much too long, and feel in need of a good talk. . ." LBJ had not seen Acheson for all of two months.

Johnson's other favorite was McCloy. "He called McCloy at the slightest provocation," recalls former CIA director Richard Helms. Among other assignments, Johnson put McCloy on the Warren Commission to investigate Kennedy's assassination, enlisted him to resolve a monetary crisis with Europe, and used him as an informal ambassador to Egypt and Iran (McCloy, as the chief representative of the world's oil companies, had better access to Middle Eastern leaders than the State Department). From time to time, Johnson did feel compelled to remind himself that McCloy was only a Wall Street lawyer and banker, while he was President. When George Ball suggested sending McCloy to reason with de Gaulle when the French were rebelling against NATO, Johnson retorted that "de Gaulle might well conclude that there was no government operating in the United States, just bankers from New York." According to the meeting notes, Johnson continued, "De Gaulle certainly was not going to succumb to a bunch of errand boys. He might react the way President Johnson would if de Gaulle started sending French bankers over here as his personal emissary."

To the Wise Men, however, Johnson was fawning. Even as a senator, he had begun stroking Acheson, writing him on September 11, 1957, "There is no keener intellect on the American scene than yours." A few months later the Texas senator told Acheson he was "the most respected adviser I have." Acheson could not resist twitting Johnson for claiming him as a camp follower. When a reporter called him in 1960 to ask about his role as Johnson's "foreign policy adviser," Acheson replied, "Lyndon Johnson? Six months ago I had a drink with him at Kay Graham's."

LBJ became even more effusive after he took over the White House. He showered Acheson with autographed pictures ("To Dean Acheson, a master logician and dedicated patriot"; "To Dean Acheson, a man of peace"; "To Dean Acheson, an American I admire most"). Acheson was wise to Johnson's glad-handing style; he knew, for instance, that LBJ handed out plastic busts of himself to world leaders in three sizes (small, medium, and large), depending on their stature. Writing a friend in December of 1963 Acheson made light of "my budding reputation as an 'elder statesman,' a sort of Barney Baruch, junior grade." He was wary of advisory panels of Wise Men; he told Dean Rusk they were "just a bunch of S.O.B.s from out of town." Yet he could not help but be a little flattered; more importantly, he longed to reassert his voice in policy making, even in the role of éminence grise. His daughter Mary recalls that when LBJ called on Acheson he would be "a little bit puffed up to be asked," but then "disillusioned" when he saw that his power was illusory after all.

Writing Anthony Eden in 1965, Acheson compared Johnson to the other Presidents he had served: "It is very hard to move from a majority leader of a small body—a purely manipulative job—to a position of world leadership. . . . It takes all of our Presidents a good deal of time to learn about foreign affairs." While FDR "never got a real grasp," Truman "caught hold pretty quick, perhaps in 18 months . . . Ike never learned much of anything. Kennedy was just catching on in 1963. LBJ tends to concentrate where the most noise is coming from."

Increasingly, the noise was coming from Vietnam. Kennedy's question to George Ball on the evening he authorized a coup against Diem—How can we be sure Diem's successors won't be worse than Diem?—had been prophetic. When Diem was finally murdered in November, Vietnam stumbled along, through coup after coup, seven changes of government in less than a year, until power rested with the likes of Prime Minister Nguyen Cao Ky. Flamboyant and corrupt, Colonel Ky fancied jump suits, purple scarves, and pearl-handled revolvers. He arrived at his first high-level conference with U.S. officials dressed in a white jacket, tight black pants, and red socks, looking like, one diplomat remarked, "a saxophone player in a second-rate night club."

Johnson watched the turmoil in Saigon with growing impatience. "I'm fed up with this coup shit," he declared. He wanted a strong ambassador in Vietnam, a proconsul who would restore order and bring the locals to heel. In an election year, he wanted someone who could neutralize the Republicans, keep them from making Vietnam a campaign issue. The obvious choice was Jack McCloy.

McCloy knew little about Johnson at the outset. He thought of him as a backbencher on foreign affairs in Congress and doubted that LBJ had learned much by kissing foreign babies on his occasional overseas forays as Vice-President. McCloy was dubious about Vietnam as well. He feared a ground war in Asia and saw Vietnam as a distraction from Europe. He had complained to Dean Rusk that Europe was, after all, "the Big Leagues." Nor did McCloy have any desire to re-enter government; he was extremely busy representing oil companies as a Wall Street lawyer.

Saying no, however, proved difficult. In the early summer of 1964, Johnson summoned McCloy into a little sitting room off the Oval Office, where he liked to do his serious arm twisting, and just about tore McCloy's arm off. He told McCloy that he had looked over all the candidates for the job, "the most important job he had to offer in the U.S. government," and he had decided that McCloy was the "finest proconsul ever." Embarrassed, McCloy pictured himself in a toga with a laurel wreath on his bald head. He politely said no, he wanted to stay on Wall Street. What is more, he had a very strong feeling that a heightened presence for the U.S. in Vietnam was the wrong step, that Vietnam was about the last place the U.S. should become involved. Johnson rode right over his objections. "We're organizing for victory over there, McCloy, and I want *you*. You are the only one now who is going to lead us to victory." He would not take no for an answer. McCloy, however, would not say yes. Johnson put his hand on top of McCloy's head and breathed close to him. He was not asking him to do it, he was urging him, directing him, *ordering* him. Still McCloy begged off. Johnson said it was a matter of patriotism; he said that McCloy must be *afraid*. McCloy protested that he had been through two world wars and served in and out of government for three decades. Johnson called him "yellow."

At this point, even McCloy, normally the calmest of men, became upset. He backed out of Johnson's sitting room, overwhelmed by being subjected to LBJ's Full Texan. He was repelled by Johnson, wanted nothing to do with him or his job. The post went to General Maxwell Taylor, a good soldier.

• • •

Dean Acheson shared McCloy's doubts about Vietnam. He had always regarded Asia as a nuisance, a distraction from Europe, a right-wing obsession, a dangerous spawning ground for General Mac-Arthur's apocalyptic dreams. He was not happy when his son-in-law Bill Bundy was chosen in early 1964 as Roger Hilsman's replacement as Assistant Secretary for Far Eastern Affairs. He had seen the job ruin too many other careers. Acheson himself preferred to think about Vietnam as little as possible.

Yet Vietnam was becoming harder and harder to ignore. In the summer and fall of 1964 and on into 1965 the U.S. faced provocations (real and imagined) in the Gulf of Tonkin, Bienhoa, and Pleiku. The demand for retaliation grew. In the late winter and early spring of 1965, the great escalation began, first with air strikes (Operation Flaming Dart, Operation Rolling Thunder), then with ground troops, though at first just marines to protect the American air bases.

In April 1965, six weeks after the first marines had stepped ashore at Danang, George Ball gave Dean Acheson a call. The two knew each other well from foreign policy debates in the Democratic Advisory Council during the fifties and from the Berlin and Cuban missile crises in the Kennedy Administration. Acheson and Ball represented opposing wings of the foreign policy Establishment, yet they were friends who respected each other. What is more, they were both Atlanticists. Ball was counting on his similarities with Acheson overcoming their differences when he asked, "Can I come talk to you?"

As Under Secretary of State, Ball had become a kind of in-house dove in the Administration, a designated "devil's advocate" who wrote memos that were duly read and rejected at the time and which now seem as prescient as George Kennan's best thinking in the 1940s. "Once on the tiger's back, we cannot be sure of picking the place to dismount," he had warned in the autumn of 1964. Watching with anxiety as the U.S. plunged into military engagement, he had gone to Johnson on April 20 to plead for the opportunity to offer a political alternative. The President gave him twenty-four hours to "pull a rabbit out of a hat." Ball hastily drafted a memo suggesting a cease-fire, general amnesty for the Viet Cong, and a coalition government. Johnson was not persuaded, but he was at least interested; for all his hawkish bluster, he too could sense the terrible cost of war. "I desperately needed at least one high-level confrere on my side," Ball wrote in his memoirs. "How could the President be expected to adopt the heresies of an Under Secretary against the contrary views of his whole top command? . . . I decided to seek help outside." He went to Acheson.

Together with Lloyd Cutler, another powerful Washington lawyer, Acheson reworked Ball's memo into a thirty-five-page plan for a political solution: a bombing pause and a general amnesty leading to local elections with VC participation, coupled with the withdrawal of all foreign troops. The plan required no negotiations (Acheson did not believe in them) but rather the unilateral action of the South Vietnamese government. With the carrot came a stick: if the Communists did not cooperate, the U.S. would resume bombing and insert ground troops.

The plan was presented on May 7 and was discussed by LBJ, Rusk, McNamara, Ball, and Acheson on May 16. Judging from the meeting notes, all the principals were willing to give it a try, though the discussion dwelled more on what Congress and *The New York Times* might say about ending a week-long bombing pause then in effect than on any long-range plans for peace. Moreover, the Acheson-Ball plan needed to be sold to the South Vietnamese government. This quickly proved impossible; in Saigon, Ambassador Taylor was resolutely opposed even to suggesting it. The plan was stillborn. It is perhaps an indication of the seriousness with which the proposal was taken that Robert McNamara, who can recall many details about the 1965 escalation, has no memory at all of the Acheson-Ball peace plan.

• • •

The spring of 1965 was a nostalgic time for Acheson. He christened a nuclear submarine for the Navy, the *George C. Marshall*; made a speech at the Truman Library about his old "Boss"; and went to his fiftieth reunion at Yale. Chronic stomach troubles that had plagued him for years had grown worse, however. He was stoical about his ailment; he wrote his old classmate Archie MacLeish that his "battered and shabby frame" could not spoil the fun of a Yale reunion, even though his doctor had gently advised him that "a well-adjusted man" would be reduced to a "psychological wreck" by "acute and perpetual trots." In truth, his growing infirmity depressed him, according to his daughter Mary; it slowed him down, affected his mood, made him less buoyant. His determined stoicism made him more rigid, more impatient with weakness in others.

Lyndon Johnson was likewise suffering from bouts of depression that early summer, over the war in Vietnam. The Pentagon wanted to go in all the way, with at least 200,000 ground troops; the Bundy brothers preferred a more gradual, but firm escalation, starting off with 85,000 troops. Johnson sensed that he would put as many as 600,0000 men in Vietnam before the war was over, and he felt trapped. He could not just cut out without arousing the right wing, and he could not escalate without getting caught in an Asian land war. Either way, he would drain off the political capital he needed to win his real cause, his Great Society social programs, up for congressional vote during the summer. He began to have nightmares about "that bitch of a war." He badly needed to be told he was doing the right thing; as always, he craved approval. So he called on the Wise Men, the architects of containment, the men who had bequeathed him this terrible burden.

They were assembled at the State Department on July 8, almost a score of them, mostly veterans of the Wall Street–Washington revolving door, like Lovett and McCloy. Hosted by the Secretaries of Defense and State, they perched their aging frames on the antiques of the formal eighth-floor meeting rooms overlooking the Potomac, and deliberated for most of a day on the hard questions before the President.

McCloy had deep qualms about the war. He spoke at length about how "impressed" he was with the "toughness of the situation." He doubted that merely "blunting the monsoon offensive" would bring Hanoi into a "negotiating mood." He predicted that the situation would remain "critical" for a long time. Yet after carefully laying out his doubts, he proclaimed that there was really no choice. America's credibility depended on her meeting her obligations and honoring her commitments. To Rusk and McNamara, he was adamant: "You've got to do it," he said. "You've got to go in."

Bob Lovett's doubts about the war were, if anything, greater than McCloy's. As he slouched uncomfortably in a Queen Anne chair, he frankly told McNamara and Rusk that he suspected that the government was painting too rosy a picture of the situation.

Years later, Lovett would remark that "getting into Vietnam was one of the stupidest things we ever did. We didn't know what the hell we were doing there." Yet like McCloy, he believed that once committed, the U.S. had to stick it out. He also recalled from his days of trying to bomb Japan and Germany into submission that no force should be spared. Once engaged in Vietnam, he held, the U.S. had to go in all the way.

Thus his ultimate conclusion was no different from McCloy's: the U.S. must send in ground troops, and enough to do the job. He cautioned only that it was not useful to speak in terms of "victory." What was really involved was preventing the expansion of Communism by force; in a sense, avoiding defeat.

Listening to these old sages, men he had admired all his life, Bill Bundy, the Assistant Secretary for Far Eastern Affairs who had line duty for Vietnam at the State Department, was impressed by their resolution and firmness. In his report to the President, he stated that most of the Wise Men assembled "felt that there should be no question of making whatever combat force increases were required. Several members of the group thought that our actions had perhaps been too restrained, and had been misconstrued by Hanoi that we were less than wholly determined."

To Bundy, it seemed that the Wise Men endorsed all the Cold War verities that underpinned U.S. engagement. He concluded in his report to Johnson that the group subscribed to the domino theory, that they believed if Vietnam fell Thailand would fall, and Japan and India would be in jeopardy; that if the U.S. backed out, Europe would lose faith in U.S. commitments; that Vietnam was a crucial test of U.S. willingness to stand up to "wars of national liberation"; that withdrawal was an "unacceptable" alternative.

At the end of the day, Johnson asked to hear from a few of the Wise Men directly. He chose a small group that included Lovett, McCloy, and Acheson to come to the White House for a drink and a chat at six-thirty that evening. Fortified with a cocktail, the elder statesmen were arrayed around the long mahogany table in the Cabinet Room to hear out the President's dilemma firsthand and to impart their wisdom.

Johnson came in, shook hands, and immediately launched off on a long tirade about the war. The effect on Acheson was not to make him share his own doubts about Vietnam, but to provoke him to tell the President to stop whining. Acheson described his reaction—and that of his colleagues—in a letter to Harry Truman.

> We were all disturbed by a long complaint about how mean everything and everybody was to him—Fate, the Press, the Congress, the Intellectuals

and so on. For a long time he fought the problem of Vietnam (every course of action was wrong; he had no support from anyone at home or abroad; it interfered with all his programs, etc., etc.). . . . I got to thinking about you and General Marshall and how we never wasted time "fighting the problem" or endlessly reconsidering decisions, or feeling sorry for ourselves.

Acheson fidgeted impatiently as he listened to Johnson wallow in self-pity. Finally, he could stand it no longer. "I blew my top and told him he was wholly right on Vietnam," Acheson wrote HST, "that he had no choice except to press on, that explanations were not as important as successful action."

Acheson's scolding emboldened the others. "With this lead my colleagues came thundering in like the charge of the Scots Greys at Waterloo," Acheson exulted to the former President. "They were fine; old Bob Lovett, usually cautious, was all out. . . . I think . . . we scored," he concluded.

They did. On July 10, Johnson wrote Acheson, "I am particularly strengthened by your support of our work in Vietnam, and I continue to feel that anything men of your standing can say to the country will be of great help." At a National Security staff meeting the next day, McGeorge Bundy smiled tightly and commented on Acheson's performance: "The mustache was voluble."

• • •

It is somewhat difficult to reconcile the Acheson-Ball Peace Plan, delivered only two months earlier, with Acheson's rousing war cry at the July 8 meeting of the Wise Men. Acheson's private letters to friends at the time show more ambivalence than he revealed to the President. Two days before the meeting, he took a hard line in a letter to Desmond Donnelly, a British member of Parliament: "Hanoi does not want a settlement and won't have one until convinced that they cannot win the war and will suffer from continuing it. We are not looking for a face-saving surrender." The next day, however, he expressed strong practical concerns to Erik Boheman, former Swedish ambassador to the U.S. and an old friend: "The Vietnamese problem is delicate, often infuriating, very hard and puzzling for the soldiers and others on the spot, but not basically obscure. By that I mean what needs to be done is not obscure. How to do it with the human material available in the God-awful terrain and against foreign-directed and supplied obstacles is very hard indeed." Significantly, Acheson added, "If we take over the war, we defeat our purpose and merely take the place of the French." Acheson had severe doubts about the ability of the South Vietnamese to sustain the fight themselves. These concerns were reinforced by a conversation he had with Henry Cabot Lodge, who was returning to Saigon for a second tour as U.S. ambassador. "He sees many problems of method because of the characteristics of our little brown brothers," Acheson wrote Lloyd Cutler.

Acheson's advice to Lyndon Johnson came at a crucial juncture of the Vietnam War. It was the moment that "America committed to land war on the mainland of Asia," Bill Bundy later wrote. "No more critical decision was made." It is hard to escape the conclusion that Acheson served his President poorly by telling him, in effect, to keep a stiff upper lip.

Bundy later wrote in his private unpublished memoir of the war that he left the White House after the Wise Men meeting on July 8 with a "slightly queasy feeling" that the group had been briefed too quickly and superficially, that there had been no real time to deliberate, and that "quickie" consultations were a bad idea. He did not share these reservations in his report to Johnson, however. LBJ had no reason to doubt the sincerity and conviction of the elder statesmen. Indeed, as Bundy himself later wrote: "The President probably expected that *most* of the Panel would be *generally* in favor of a firm policy. What he found was that *almost all* were *solidly* of this view, and this must have had a distinct impact on his personal and private deliberations." Bundy continued:

> There can be no doubt that a large strand in the President's make-up [was] that he should not fall short of the standards set by those who had played leading parts in World War II and throughout the period of American successes in the Cold War. Now a fair sample of these men, of the American "Genro," if you will, had advised him to see this one through.

Dean Acheson, Bob Lovett, and John McCloy, like the ancient Japanese *genro*, the wise elders who conducted affairs of state, had a historical perspective. Throughout the 1940s they had seen the folly of engaging in Asian land wars and had resisted. They had among themselves distinguished between interests that were vital, such as Western Europe, and those that were not, such as Formosa. Even in 1965, they harbored serious doubts about committing U.S. troops to the defense of the government of South Vietnam. Why did they fail to convey those doubts to the President?

Acheson, in particular, was betrayed by instincts that had served him well in other times. His penchant for action, his impatience with self-doubt, possibly exacerbated by age and bad health, interfered with his pragmatism. The example of Korea had weakened his long-standing inhibition against involvements in Asia. If it had been necessary to fight in Korea to save NATO, how was Vietnam any different? "Vietnam really rang his Korea bell," Bill Bundy later recalled. What is more, Acheson was not well informed; "quickie consultations" deprived him of the facts he needed to fully engage his lawyerly acuity.

Finally, and perhaps most importantly, American men were dying in the field in July 1965. It was awfully hard not to rally behind them and their embattled leader in Washington. The situation on the ground had markedly deteriorated between April, when Ball approached Acheson about his peace plan, and July, when Johnson asked his support for sending in more troops. The effect on Acheson was not likely to make him sound retreat.

Johnson was no better served by the "next generation" of foreign policy advisers, many of whom had learned their lessons, in some cases almost literally, at their elders' knees. Robert McNamara, the handpicked choice of Bob Lovett, came to office with almost no grounding in foreign affairs. He was, however, given on-the-job tutoring in the school of global power politics by Dean Acheson, who saw him frequently from 1961 on. "I looked to him as a God," McNamara recalled of his relationship with Acheson during those years. "I was tremendously sensitive to his thoughts. He was the wisest foreign policy adviser I worked with during seven years in government."

McGeorge Bundy, the true heir to Acheson, mirrored many of his views. The critical issue in Vietnam, the National Security Adviser believed, was "the confidence of America's allies and America's self-confidence." This was precisely the reason that Acheson intervened in Korea—not to rescue the South Koreans, but to convince America's allies that the U.S. stood firm against aggression. Bundy was, like the older generation, deeply affected by the lesson of Munich, that weakness in the face of aggression invites more aggression. His Harvard lecture on Munich in Government 180, "The U.S. in World Politics"—a course taken over by Henry Kissinger when Bundy left for Washington—was an annual event in Cambridge in the 1950s. Students would flock to hear Bundy tell, with verve and emotion, of the Nazi tanks rolling in, of the price of appeasement.

Bundy devoutly believed that it was America's duty to oppose aggression in its role of world leader. Writing in response to Archibald

MacLeish, Acheson's classmate and Bundy's fellow Bonesman who had publicly questioned the morality of the war, Bundy declared in July of 1965 that during "that terrible spring of 1940," America had accepted the "responsibility of holding and using power."

Dean Rusk was not only heir to the Acheson-Truman days, he was a veteran of them. He had been with Acheson during Korea, had urged him to stand up to MacArthur's defeatism. No matter how badly the war seemed to be going in Vietnam, Rusk would stoically say, "We were in tougher spots in Korea." He retained from those years less the pragmatism of his mentors than their clichés. Without self-consciousness, he used terms like the "Free World" and the "Communist Menace," not just in speeches but in private conversation. Seared by the Chinese pouring over the Yalu, he feared that Peking would come crashing in on behalf of the North Vietnamese, even though the Chinese and North Vietnamese people had been enemies for a thousand years, and even though the Chinese were at the time totally wrapped up in their Cultural Revolution. The lessons of the past for Rusk were too literal: if China intervened in Korea, it would in Vietnam; Vietnamese aggression was no different than Soviet or Nazi aggression; appeasement in Vietnam was like appeasement at Munich.

In retrospect, it seems that these second-generation members of the foreign policy Establishment were the victims of a strange process of acculturation, by which the propagandists began believing themselves. They had been "clearer than the truth" so many times with congressmen and journalists that they had began to take literally their own overstatements about the global threat of Communism, and more particularly the American commitment to resisting aggression wherever it occurred. In his private memoir, William Bundy, trying in an honest way to sort out the roots of involvement, wrote:

> President Johnson and the men in his policy circle would not have thought of themselves as ideologues in the world outside America's borders. But this core of common belief they did have, less perhaps than American leaders in the '50s but very much more than sophisticated intellectual opinion in the '70s. No account of the mental map of those who made decisions in mid-1965 would be complete without noting this point. Aggression and its dynamics, far more than communism as such, were the focus. But the communist element did contribute to the sense of threat and unfolding consequences that guided their actions, mine included.

This mind-set was by no means confined to the best and the brightest in 1965. In that same year, *New York Times* reporter David Halberstam, later the author of the best-selling chronicle of American hubris in Vietnam, declared, "Vietnam is a strategic country in a key area. It is perhaps one of only five or six nations that is truly vital to U.S. interests." In August of 1964, Neil Sheehan, the reporter who later broke the Pentagon Papers story, had written a *Times* story headlined "Much Is at Stake in Southeast Asia." It reported: "The fall of Southeast Asia or its denial to the West over the next decade because of the repercussions of an American defeat in Vietnam would amount to strategic disaster."

In *The Best and the Brightest,* Halberstam vividly portrays the hubris of Kennedy's and Johnson's lieutenants as they blindly, arrogantly, plunged into the quagmire. Yet the self-portrait of one of Halberstam's chief villains—William Bundy—offers a rather different, if no less tragic, view.

In February of 1965, as the U.S. began bombing the North, Bundy wrote that there was among Johnson's advisers "a sense of disaster avoided or postponed and there was the lift of action. But on the whole it was a period when no move seemed right, and the outcome remained wholly murky." In June, when the critical decision to send in large numbers of troops was being made, Bundy described himself "in a small state of personal crisis. Agreeing with his [George Ball's] view on the difficulties, I still could not accept the idea of American withdrawal." This ambivalence led to his recommendation of the gradual escalation, a compromise "middle way." Torn by conflicting instincts, unsure of the outcome, Bundy, of Groton and Yale and the Establishment, was left in exactly the same spot as Lyndon Johnson of San Marcos State Teachers College: trapped, not wanting to do too much or too little, but just enough to get by.

How the image of Bundy, groping and unsure, contrasts with Dean Acheson's own self-description in *Present at the Creation,* clear-eyed and exhilarated through crisis and war! The confidence, the sense of destiny and self-assurance that had so marked the men who had rebuilt the postwar world, were slowly stripped away by the corrosive acid of Vietnam. In the end, all that was left was a sense of duty.

In his class-day oration to the other Yale seniors in 1939, on the eve of World War II, William Bundy had earnestly declared, "If we are to consider ourselves as a group and a class of special significance, we must get right down to earth and perform special services, for it is only on that basis that the idea of class can be tolerated in a democracy."

Bundy shouldered the burden of his class at terrible cost. With growing anguish, his wife, Mary—Dean Acheson's daughter—watched her husband's career and life be consumed by the war. He, stoic, got ulcers. She, uncomplaining, got shingles. One night, when her husband returned home quietly ravaged by the daily ordeal, she gently asked him, "Should you go on?" Drained and miserable, yet feeling that he should see through what he had begun, he simply answered, "I've got to go on." While others were bailing out (some, like his brother Mac, with a shove from LBJ), Bill Bundy grimly hung on, a last exhausted link to a vanishing age.

•   •   •

Averell Harriman tried hard to become interested in the problems of Africa. Alarmed that the Soviet presence in Zanzibar threatened Tanganyika, he suggested to his State Department superiors that more attention be paid to this festering trouble spot. George Ball, Harriman's boss as Under Secretary, wrote back that "God watched over every little sparrow that fell," and that the U.S. "could not compete with Him." Harriman, Ball recalled, did not think the response was funny.

He was, as always, restless to work his way back into the inner circle. When Rusk instructed State Department officials to remain nonpartisan during the 1964 elections, Harriman responded by advising Johnson's staff that if the Secretary refused to act as department spokesman, then he was available. Harriman did not feel "that the department should be a eunuch incapable of defending itself," a Johnson aide, Douglass Cater, reported to the President. The offer was declined. Still, he continued to raise his hand like an eager schoolboy, even sending Johnson clippings about his speeches and travels. "Harriman is a good soldier," another Johnson aide, Jack Valenti, told the President.

Russia had always been Harriman's best card, and in the summer of 1965, he played it. It had become his *idée fixe*, almost an obsession, that Russia was the key that would free the U.S. from the bondage of Vietnam. Laos was his model: He envisioned, in a memo to Mac Bundy in April 1965, an agreement between the superpowers to honor a "neutral and independent" South Vietnam. A diplomatic solution was preferable to a military one, he told Bundy; any further escalation would provoke antiwar dissent in the U.S. He followed up by fishing for, and receiving, an invitation from the Kremlin to visit the Soviet Union in July.

Preoccupied with the escalating war, the Administration considered Harriman's trip a long shot at best. Johnson's aides doubted that Harriman would even be received by the Soviet leaders, much less make any progress toward a peaceful solution.

On July 10, two days after Acheson and the other Wise Men had met with Johnson at the White House, Harriman left for the Soviet Union. He was greeted at the Kremlin by Aleksei Kosygin, at the time Leonid Brezhnev's coequal as Soviet ruler. Harriman had first met Kosygin in 1942 and had renewed his acquaintance with him in 1959. He found him more serious and sober than Khrushchev, less blustery, but just as unyielding.

The Russian leader began on a hopeful note. The Soviets wanted an end to the Vietnam War. It interfered with U.S.-Soviet relations. Worse, Kosygin was worried that North Vietnam would become a Chinese puppet and further Peking's expansionism in Southeast Asia. He repeatedly said to Harriman, "Don't you realize that this war only helps the Chinese?" Kosygin gave Harriman more encouragement when he stated somewhat mysteriously, "In all confidence, I can only report that our Vietnamese comrades do not rule out a political settlement. That is all I can say, but this, it seems to me, is very important."

Then came the bad news. The Soviets were not eager to help persuade Hanoi to come to the peace table. They were loath to be seen by other Communist countries as collaborators with the U.S. They were unwilling, in other words, to play the role of mediator that Harriman envisioned for them.

Reading Harriman's cables, McGeorge Bundy shrugged off the exchange as "rather routine" in a report to the President. "While there has been more noise than substance in Harriman's visit, I think it has been worthwhile," the National Security Adviser concluded after he had debriefed Harriman upon his return from Moscow. Harriman had stopped in on other foreign leaders in Europe and reassured them that the U.S. was pursuing diplomatic alternatives. The trip had at least received some good press, Bundy noted. "And if such travels obviously give Harriman himself an unusual amount of personal pleasure, what is the harm in that?"

Harriman began to lobby almost shamelessly for a role to play in the Vietnam War. "I do feel I am more experienced and can be of more value to you than at any time since I have been working on international affairs," he wrote President Johnson in August. "I am still surprised when I think back to the time when President Roosevelt sent me on those extraordinarily responsible political and military missions during the war." FDR could afford to, Harriman pointedly explained, because he had "complete confidence in my personal loyalty to him."

Harriman also continued to push for a rational diplomatic approach to the war. The U.S. should have "realistic" negotiating goals, he wrote Walt Rostow at Policy Planning in August, i.e., a neutral South Vietnam instead of a client state.

No one in the Administration paid much attention, with one important exception. In the fall of 1965, Robert McNamara was beginning his long, bitter journey of disillusionment with the war. Slowly realizing that all his statistics about U.S. strength and firepower had marginal relevance to a jungle guerrilla war against a fanatic enemy, he began to cast about for a political solution. After chatting with Harriman at various Washington functions and Georgetown dinner parties, he later recalled, he became aware that the old Cold Warrior was on the same path, only farther along.

Before Christmas, McNamara visited Johnson alone at the LBJ ranch in Texas and urged a bombing pause as a peace feeler. Johnson was at first reluctant, but then embraced the idea of a "peace offensive," a giant public relations campaign to convince the North Vietnamese (and, perhaps more importantly, other nations around the world) that the U.S. was not a warmonger. McNamara suggested that Johnson appoint Harriman as his peace ambassador, to visit other countries and enlist their help in persuading Hanoi to come to the bargaining table.

Harriman got the call from Johnson that very week. "Averell, have you got your bag packed?" the President asked. "It's always packed," the aging diplomat answered. "Where do you want me to go?"

Johnson told him to "talk to some of your Eastern European friends and see what they'll do." Harriman asked him which ones. Johnson replied that was up to him, but that there was a plane warming up for him at Andrews Air Force Base. When Harriman called Rusk at the State Department, the Secretary had almost nothing to say. He was suspicious of back channels to the President in general and of Harriman in particular. McNamara, on the other hand, was warm and encouraging. The Defense Secretary told him to spread the word: the U.S. wanted peace negotiations.

Harriman ended up traveling for seventeen days, not just to Eastern

Europe but to India, Pakistan, Egypt, Iran, Thailand, Japan, Australia, Laos, South Vietnam, and the Philippines. He dutifully lobbied dour Communists in dreary ministries, foreign princes in their palaces, even the Shah on his Peacock Throne. He received effusive expressions of sympathy and support and little real help.

Still, Harriman at last felt that he had a foothold in Johnson's war council. He was determined to keep it, to show the President that he could be just as assured of his personal loyalty as FDR had been. He proved his fealty by behaving like a stern uncle to the wayward liberals of the party, especially Robert Kennedy, whom, as Harriman well knew, Johnson greatly feared. In early February, he acted as emissary to a group of liberal senators, including RFK, who opposed the resumption of the bombing after Johnson's New Year's peace offensive. Assembling the dissident senators at his home in Georgetown, Harriman argued that the North Vietnamese would only come to the bargaining table under the duress of force. "Harriman is first rate in placating a good number of liberals," Jack Valenti wrote the President in March. He added that "Bundy tells me [Harriman] spoke like a Dutch uncle to RFK." Harriman publicly denounced a speech by Bobby Kennedy suggesting that the Viet Cong's National Liberation Front be brought into a coalition government in South Vietnam. That night, Johnson personally called Harriman to thank him.

Harriman was equally convinced of the success of his efforts, and told LBJ as much, though the worth of this judgment is revealed by his suggestion that Eugene McCarthy be recruited to front for the war effort in the Senate cloakroom. "I had the impression that he could be persuaded to take a leadership role in supporting the President's policies," Harriman wrote the President, who was soon to discover precisely the opposite.

Harriman's scoldings began to disturb his old liberal friends, who were becoming more outspoken against the war. At a party at Senator John Sherman Cooper's in Georgetown, Harriman bluntly said to Arthur Schlesinger, "People like you are causing the death of GIs." Schlesinger concluded that Harriman had truly become a hawk, until a year later when the two talked at a meeting at the Truman Library. Harriman summoned Schlesinger to his suite at the Muehlebach Hotel in Kansas City at three in the afternoon, poured himself a drink (highly unusual behavior), and unburdened himself. To Schlesinger's relief, he said that he was still very much against the war, that he was working for a political solution, but that he was doing it from within. To maintain his credibility, he had had to publicly mouth the Administration line. Harriman explained himself to John Kenneth Galbraith the same way: "Inside influence depends on outside loyalty."

In later years, Harriman would grumble about "the old Cold Warriors who saw Vietnam as a Munich or Berlin." Yet in 1965, the Associated Press quoted him as declaring, "The Communists in Southeast Asia have to get it in their minds that South Vietnam is not a ripe plum that will fall to them. We cannot appease them. It would be like letting Hitler march into the Rhineland in the 1930s." In February of 1966, he complained to Cy Sulzberger that he was "bewildered" by RFK's "foolish" statements on the war, that he was irked at Walter Lippmann and *The New York Times* for their dovishness, and angry that press photographers refused to take pictures of Viet Cong atrocities. Even privately he was taking a tough line. In a memo to his personal files in May of 1966, he denounced RFK for "sounding like the worst of Arthur Schlesinger and Dick Goodwin on the subject of Communism—that it is quite different than it used to be and inferred we didn't have to worry so much." Could it be that Harriman still really believed in the Cold War verities in 1966? Or was he perhaps practicing the time-honored bureaucratic practice of writing rear-covering memoranda to files?

In truth, Harriman did not fit easily into "hawk" versus "dove" distinctions, at least as they came to be popularly understood. He did indeed favor a political solution and was from the first highly skeptical of trying to win the war by force of arms. But he abhorred the idea of simply withdrawing from Vietnam. "Cut and run" was his term for withdrawal, and he spat out the words with distaste. Harriman's dovishness should not be confused with the "Out Now" sentiments chanted by the antiwar movement. He emphatically differed with the isolationism implicit in the stands of liberals like George McGovern who argued that the U.S. had no business messing about with the destinies of other countries. The U.S. had to play an active role in opposing aggression, Harriman continued to believe, not just in Europe but in the Third World. After two decades, America's duties as defined by the Truman Doctrine were at the core of his world view, though not with the military emphasis others had attached to it. Though the sweeping commitments of the Truman Doctrine are blamed for U.S. involvement in Vietnam, Harriman argued in one oral history interview, it says "nothing about sending in troops." He distinguished between economic and military aid to allies—necessary and plausible steps, in his view—and unilateral military intervention.

During the early days of the Cold War, Harriman's views on dealing with the Soviets seemed, at times, hard to categorize. In his private counsel to Roosevelt and Truman, and in his public pronouncements, he was the foremost advocate of firmness. Yet he always believed in a businesslike and pragmatic approach to problems, in sitting down and bargaining with an adversary rather than letting rigidity and dogma lead to fruitless showdowns. That is why he urged sending Harry Hopkins to Moscow in 1945, why he favored a summit with Stalin, and why he even supported a postwar American loan to the Soviets. Those who were more ideological and less subtle saw this as waffling; yet for the man who had learned to deal firmly and pragmatically with Wall Street competitors and Trotsky's mining concession committee, there was no internal contradiction in this businesslike approach. Likewise, on Vietnam, Harriman deeply believed that the U.S. must stand firm for its interests. He disdained those who doubted the rightness of America's cause or were eager to retreat "to the movies and drink Coke." But it was important to have a sense of balance about goals, to be pragmatic in pursuing them. Ideological fervor would lead only to a deepening military morass. Like his father, he knew the value of sitting down and dealing with an adversary on a personal basis, of bargaining and negotiating and trying to find a solution to a difficult situation.

Convincing Lyndon Johnson that he was the diplomat who could best step in and settle the Vietnam War was exceedingly difficult. In his desire to become involved, Harriman not only had to bury his own doubts about the feasibility of military involvement; he also had to hide his own personal feelings toward Johnson, whom he heartily disliked. In confessing these sentiments to Sulzberger in early 1966, Harriman added that he did like Lady Bird, especially for her efforts to "beautify America," even if he hated the word "beautify."

The Texas politician and the ex-polo player were hardly easy company. Harriman tried to be a good sport when he was subjected to various initiation rituals at the LBJ ranch, such as driving ninety miles an hour in a Cadillac down dirt roads. One can picture them careening along side by side, Johnson in a loose-fitting cowboy shirt, drinking beer and telling off-color stories, Harriman buttoned up in a tie and jacket, dour-faced and silent. "I am sorry I disappointed you by not being surprised when you took to the water in your car," Harriman wrote the President after a trip to the ranch in November 1966. "By that time, I had become immune to your overcoming every obstacle." Harriman gamely responded to Johnson's patronage with flattery; when LBJ sent him a plastic bust of his head, Harriman wrote him, "It means a lot to have your bust, which now parallels FDR's in our library." Though Harriman did not much like LBJ, he was actually unperturbed by Johnson's crudeness, according to friends. LBJ was no more crass than Khrushchev, after all, and Harriman could get on with the Soviet dictator. The old diplomat also frowned on members of his own family disparaging the President. He would hush Marie when she sarcastically referred to LBJ as "der Fuehrer."

Johnson, for his part, was wary of Harriman. He felt he could not ignore him, that Harriman was a force both within the liberal wing of the party and the old foreign policy Establishment. But he was never convinced of his loyalty. To aides, he said the same thing about Harriman that he said about J. Edgar Hoover: "I'd rather have him inside the tent pissing out than outside the tent pissing in." He was highly suspicious of Harriman's ties to the Kennedys; he referred to RFK in his presence as "your friend Bobby." Harriman's Dutch uncle role backfired; Johnson began holding Harriman accountable for Kennedy's statements, which grew increasingly antagonistic to the Administration as Kennedy's dovishness grew. The day Harriman returned from a round-the-world peace trip for Johnson—during which he established a record of sorts by breakfasting in India, lunching in Pakistan, and supping in Italy—he attended his seventy-fifth birthday party thrown by the Kennedys at Hickory Hill. The papers gushed about the costume ball (Bob McNamara went as a silver bullet; RFK went as Harriman, dressed in a long leather trench coat he wore on his missions to Moscow) and marveled that the onetime polo-playing playboy was still dancing at 2 A.M. When Johnson saw Harriman, he ignored the fact that his envoy had just finished a grueling 27,570-mile trip to seventeen countries on behalf of peace and instead muttered darkly, "I understand you were at Hickory Hill again."

It became increasingly difficult for Harriman to keep a foot in both camps. He gave parties for Luci and Lynda Bird Johnson before their weddings, followed each time by a buffet dinner to which he invited the Kennedys and their friends. The first wedding parties, in August of 1966, seemed to go off smoothly, but by the time of the second round, in December of 1967, there was almost no overlap in the guest lists. Harriman lost far more points with Johnson for holding the Kennedy "after" party than he gained by hosting the prenuptial lunch.

In the summer of 1966, Johnson did grant Harriman his wish and put him in charge of all diplomatic efforts to secure an end to the war. But little real power came with the job. Harriman was given no more specific mandate than to look for diplomatic alternatives, recalled

Chester Cooper, Harriman's chief aide. Nothing was in writing, and it was not even clear that Johnson had consulted with Rusk and McNamara before creating the "Peace Shop," as Harriman's office was somewhat mockingly known. Cooper suspected that Johnson was engaging in some protective camouflage, so that he could say he had "given peace a chance." Harriman was not invited to the "Tuesday lunches," Johnson's inner council on the Vietnam War, and his initiatives were not taken very seriously. "He was a lonely guy sitting over there at State crunching out proposed negotiating papers," recalls Morton Halperin, Deputy Assistant Secretary of Defense in ISA, the Pentagon's "little State Department." "They were sent to me at the Pentagon. I just filed them in a filing cabinet and that's as far as they got."

Harriman continued to enjoy the support of the Secretary of Defense. McNamara urged Harriman to go to Moscow in May of 1966 and enlist Soviet aid in a settlement; he indicated to Harriman that he saw no value in further military escalation. A year later, as his agony grew, he told Harriman outright that it was "impossible to win militarily," that the U.S. must seek a negotiated settlement. Harriman said that the Soviets could not "deliver" Hanoi, but that they could be helpful if the U.S. agreed to stop bombing the North. The former governor and Democratic stalwart also raised political considerations, an increasingly important factor in his views on the war. He told McNamara that the Democratic Party would be "split in a way I've never seen it" if the war continued. By September 1967, McNamara was completely unguarded with Harriman. "Our record is appalling," he flatly stated. If the U.S. did not extricate itself from the war, he feared that the "country will tear itself apart."

By September of 1967 McNamara was in full dissent within the Administration. His wife was sick with bleeding ulcers and he appeared to be nearing collapse; in April of 1968 he would become president of the World Bank. Johnson's inner circle grew tighter and more hawkish. Both Rusk and Walt Rostow, who had replaced Mac Bundy as National Security Adviser, were skeptical of diplomatic solutions. * Rostow was an indefatigable optimist about the military situation; Rusk was merely stoic.

---

*Bundy had gradually fallen out of favor with LBJ, in part because he urged the President to level with the public about the extent of the escalation. In February of 1966, Bundy left the White House and became president of the Ford Foundation. John McCloy, the chairman of the Foundation's board, gave him the job.

• • •

All along, Harriman continued to push the Russian card. "The only real chance is Russia," he had told LBJ in October of 1966. Seven months later he would again urge, "I believe we can get with careful handling Soviet cooperation to end the conflict in Vietnam." Johnson, Rusk, and Rostow were not much interested; neither, it appears, were the Russians. Harriman knew from his conversation with Kosygin in 1965 that the Soviets were not eager to help pull the U.S. out of its quagmire, despite their desire for stability in the region. Still he had faith in his own powers of persuasion. "He was not unrealistic about Moscow's role in any peace negotiations," Cooper recalled. "But he may have overestimated his ability to get Russia to exert maximum leverage." The Soviets undoubtedly knew how little leverage Harriman himself had at the White House. The veteran Soviet ambassador to Washington, Anatoly Dobrynin, was close to Harriman, recalled Cooper, and he also "knew who sat where at dinner" in the Washington pecking order.

Though the Soviets took a low profile, an odd assortment of statesmen, politicians, journalists, and plain charlatans surfaced as go-betweens in a frustrating three-year search for peace. It was a halting diplomatic minuet that was marked by mixed signals, missed chances, bureaucratic infighting, false hopes, and a total lack of success. At one time or another the disparate cast included the Italian ambassador to Saigon, a Canadian diplomat, a Polish diplomat, two newspapermen associated with a California think tank, a pair of French intellectuals, Indira Gandhi, Anthony Eden, Harold Wilson, and Henry Kissinger. The initiatives, with code names like Sunflower and Marigold, all seemed hopeful and all failed. A Polish initiative (Marigold), for instance, seemed to have negotiations in the offing in Warsaw in late 1966. North Vietnam sent word first, however, that the U.S. had to pause in its bombing. Harriman pleaded for the pause, with the backing of McNamara. But Rostow suspected a trap and persuaded LBJ not to order the bombing pause. The talks collapsed—if they were ever destined to go anywhere. A Communist defector later said the whole operation was a sham.

In his memoirs, Johnson cites 17 peace initiatives either undertaken or explored by the Administration as proof of the great effort he made to find a peaceful settlement. Yet Johnson himself remained skeptical. "If I were Ho, I wouldn't negotiate," he would say.

In the end, Johnson's judgment was probably shrewd. Hanoi was probably never interested in any negotiated settlement except for one that would guarantee it victory. Diplomacy was merely a tool to get a united Vietnam under Hanoi's control. If anything, the North Vietnamese may have regarded U.S. peace initiatives in this period as signs of weakness, of indications that the U.S. was unwilling to sustain a war.

Harriman himself did not doubt Hanoi's toughness. Indeed, he had been the very first U.S. negotiator exposed to North Vietnamese intransigence, back in 1962 at his unpleasant meeting with the brutish North Vietnamese Foreign Minister Ung Van Khiem. Unlike many liberal intellectuals, he never thought a peaceful settlement was there for the asking. "I don't agree with you that these people are dying to negotiate," he told an aide. "They are dying to accept an honorable defeat on our part." Even if the Communists did sign an agreement, he doubted they would keep it for long; Laos had taught him that. "These fellows don't live up to an agreement for even one day," he growled.

At times, recalled Chester Cooper, Harriman seemed to accept that a negotiated settlement was only another term for a "decent interval," a way of buying face-saving time before Hanoi accomplished its ultimate war aim of total domination of the South. Yet the idea of just abandoning South Vietnam to the Communists appalled him. He had to believe that if only the Russians would lend a hand and apply some pressure on their comrades in Hanoi, then the North would agree to some sort of neutral coalition government in the South. It was admittedly a long shot. But he felt that he was the only man who could possibly pull off such a deal. Not unlike the North Vietnamese, Harriman was dogged, patient, and single-minded. He was willing to labor away without recognition or success, waiting for his chance.

•   •   •

The father of containment, George Kennan, was noticeably absent from the Administration's deliberations on Vietnam. With his usual foresight, he had warned against engagement in Vietnam as far back as 1948, and his views had only grown stronger since then. But he preferred to silently harbor them in the anonymity of academe.

Kennan's enthusiastic return to government under President Kennedy in 1961 had quickly soured. He was in many ways the ideal ambassador to Yugoslavia, a diplomat who had been among the first to foresee and encourage splits in the Soviet bloc, an envoy who could understand and get on with Tito. But as usual, he was baffled and frustrated by politics at home.

Congress had gone on record in 1959 with a Captive Nations Resolution pledging the U.S. to seek the "liberation" of all Communist countries, including Yugoslavia. Before leaving for Belgrade, Kennan won McGeorge Bundy's assurance that the new Administration would not observe Captive Nations Week as called for by the resolution, but the National Security Adviser's decision was reversed under congressional pressure. Kennan's discouragement turned to horror when Congress cut Yugoslavia out of the foreign aid bill. The final insult came when Wilbur Mills, the all-powerful chairman of the House Ways and Means Committee, decided to strip Yugoslavia of its "most favored nation" trading status, a basic staple of international comity.

Kennan immediately flew back to Washington and, like Alice falling down the rabbit hole, descended on Capitol Hill. Trying and failing to conceal his distaste, he dutifully lobbied congressmen. Informed that Yugoslavia was not a member of the Warsaw Pact, one Midwestern representative regarded him suspiciously and commented, "Aw, go on." Another legislator told him, "Well, Mr. Ambassador, you may be right, but I still can't see why we have to go on giving aid to a lot of damn Communists." Chairman Mills flatly rebuffed Kennan's entreaties. "So far as I can tell, he is a law unto himself in such matters," Kennan wrote his sister Jeannette. "[Mills] cares nothing for our opinions or those of anybody who knows anything about it, and is at liberty to create as much havoc as he likes in our foreign affairs, without being called to account or even obliged to offer any explanation. That," Kennan gloomily concluded, "is the way our system works."

Disgusted, Kennan resigned and once again retreated to Princeton. So world-weary was he that he told Robert Oppenheimer, his employer at the Institute for Advanced Study, that he did not even want to teach students and thereby risk getting caught up in the "chitchat" of world events. He wanted to be left alone, to research and write.

Knowing his opposition to the Vietnam War, peace activists tried to lure him into appearing at demonstrations and teach-ins. But Kennan, who loathed the rabble, begged off. "My views are known," he wrote William Sloane Coffin in August of 1965. "Now that they have been stated, and overwhelmingly rejected by influential American opinion, I can do no more, it seems to me, than to fall silent." He informed the activist Yale chaplain that he was in the midst of a "period of withdrawal and historical writing."

Kennan broke silence only when summoned by the Senate Foreign Relations Committee to testify in February of 1966. Congress at the time was faithfully funding the war, but a few doves were beginning to emerge, led by Foreign Relations Chairman William Fulbright (Johnson, borrowing a pun from Truman, called him "Halfbright"). Fulbright held the televised hearings with the hope of stirring dissent among opinion makers and influential citizens. His star witness was Kennan.

"An unusual hush fell over the pre-lunch drinkers at the Metropolitan Club," reported *The New York Times*, as Kennan's image flickered onto the television screen above the bar. The regulars at this Establishment oasis still had respect for Kennan. Yet Kennan's voice at these hearings carried far beyond the Metropolitan Club or the circulation of *Foreign Affairs*. Identified as the author of the Containment Doctrine, he reached into middle-class homes with his reasoned arguments against the war. His language was moderate; about the strongest pejorative he used to describe Administration policy was "unfortunate." But he made clear why he felt the war was wrong—because Vietnam was not a sufficiently vital interest to warrant several hundred thousand American combat troops—and what to do about it: "liquidate the involvement just as soon as this can be done."

Chain-smoking under the Klieg lights, Secretary of State Rusk offered the Administration's rebuttal, inveighing against the "steady extension of Communist power through force and threat." The message was familiar, but the domino theory was beginning to have a tinny ring to many Americans, not just to student protesters in the streets but to their parents at home watching these two old disciples of General Marshall debate on the evening news.

Rusk called Kennan after the hearing and strongly remonstrated against his former colleague's willingness to help out the antiwar movement. He told him that his dissent was "too late" and that the North Vietnamese were refusing to negotiate. Kennan related this unpleasant conversation in a letter to Llewellyn Thompson and reasserted his opinion that "we should detach ourselves" from the "parochial ambitions of General Ky and his associates." Yet Kennan was hardly sanguine about the alternatives. "I have a feeling of miserable unhappiness about this whole situation. I see a series of catastrophic possibilities and no favorable ones," he wrote Emmet John Hughes, a former Eisenhower adviser, in May. He said it was "shocking to see the President and Secretary of State doing all in their power to stimulate the most violent sort of American patriotic emotionalism."

Kennan was realistic about the war. The hope that the North Vietnamese would eventually give up was "chimerical," he wrote Arthur Schlesinger. He actually agreed with Dean Acheson that the North

Vietnamese were not likely to negotiate a peaceful settlement. But rather than try to bomb the North into submission, as Acheson "with his usual penchant for unconditional surrender" proposed to do, Kennan favored just letting the war "simmer down."

• • •

Bob Lovett hated advisory committees. He had refused to serve on any for JFK, joking that "a committee is a group of individuals who, as individuals, can do nothing, but who, as a committee, can meet formally and decide that nothing can be done." (Ever mindful of Congress, Lovett added that he exempted from this definition the committees of the House and Senate.)

Kennedy had been perfectly happy to use Lovett as a private adviser and exempt him from sitting on formal panels. The two men shared such an easy, informal relationship that the President did not hesitate to just call him on the phone.

Lovett did not get on nearly so well with Lyndon Johnson. The coarse Texan was too much of showman, too heavy-handed and overbearing for the polite banker, who had long since cut his own small-town Texas roots. Under pressure from Mac Bundy, Lovett did agree to serve on the President's Panel of foreign policy advisers, but he was happy to avoid its occasional meetings, usually pleading ill health or business commitments. He sent Jack McCloy a picture of the two of them sitting at a White House meeting of the "Elder Statesmen" at which everyone looks distracted or sleepy. "Bored of Advisers" read the inscription.

Lovett was almost as wary of the Vietnam War as he was of committees. But he continued to believe that once committed to South Vietnam, the U.S. had to honor its commitment. Though unhappy about the war, he approached it from the point of view of production and military capacity, just as did his protégé McNamara. Lovett differed from the Defense Secretary, however, in one critical respect: he thought the idea of a limited war was absurd. "If we stay in, we must stay in with a hell of a lot of firepower," he told *Fortune* magazine in October 1965. "You cannot skimp on power, you cannot fight half a war. And no quartermaster was ever hanged for ordering too much of what was needed."

Asked by LBJ in January of 1966 whether the U.S. should resume bombing the North after the Christmas pause, Lovett was all-out. Ducking a meeting of Johnson's senior foreign policy advisers, he gave his views to McGeorge Bundy by phone. "Lovett wishes we never got into Vietnam because he has such a painful memory of Korea," Bundy reported to the President. "He says he was a charter member of the Never Again Club. But now that we are in he would go a long way. He was against the pause in the first place, and he would favor a prompt and fairly massive air action in the North. He thinks we simply have to give adequate support to the massive forces we have placed in Vietnam."

•   •   •

The drafter of NSC-68 was, ironically, a dove on Vietnam. Paul Nitze did not believe that Vietnam was a vital interest, and he had a healthy and abiding aversion to Asian land wars. He had told Walt Rostow that his idea of sending twenty-five thousand men into Laos was "asinine" and had vehemently argued against the Taylor-Rostow recommendation of sending at least eight thousand combat troops to Vietnam in 1961. He doubted that the U.S. commitment could be limited (it was like being "a little bit pregnant," he argued), and after a trip to South Vietnam in late 1964 came home convinced that the war could become an "American Dien Bien Phu." Because of his experience with the Strategic Bombing Survey in World War II, he had little faith in the efficacy of bombing.

In early 1965 he warned McNamara that winning would require the commitment of at least 700,000 troops. "Are you recommending that we withdraw?" McNamara asked. "I guess that is what I'm recommending," Nitze answered. "Certainly not that we reinforce it with two hundred thousand men." McNamara asked him, "Well, if you were to withdraw from Vietnam, do you think that the Communists would test us somewhere else?" Nitze answered that he did. "Can you predict where they would test us?" He could not. "Under those circumstances, I take it that you can't be at all certain that the difficulty of stopping them there won't be any greater than the difficulty of stopping them in South Vietnam?" Nitze answered that he could not. "Well, Paul," McNamara said, shrugging, "you really don't offer me an alternative."

Nitze had been trapped by his own Cold War logic. Others began to notice that Nitze's opposition to the war became increasingly muted, that he seemed to waffle, denouncing the war in one conversation, grudgingly supporting it in another. "I could never figure out where he stood," remarked Leslie Gelb, the head of the Policy Planning Staff at Defense.

Nitze was acquiescent when Lyndon Johnson sought his advice in

July of 1965, the time of the first great escalation. Nitze, by then Secretary of the Navy, had been summoned to the White House with the other service Secretaries and the Joint Chiefs to give their opinions on the necessary number of reinforcements. The record shows that Nitze, who now had the interests of the Marine Corps to look after, expressed no qualms about escalation. Asked by the President, "Would you send in more force than Westmoreland requests?" he answered, "Yes, sir. It depends on how quickly." LBJ cut in, "Two hundred thousand instead of one hundred thousand?" Nitze: "We would need another one hundred thousand in January."

• • •

Chip Bohlen was quite content to have as little as possible to do with the Vietnam War. He spent the middle years of the decade doing what he did best, serving as a senior career diplomat in a sensitive post, as ambassador to France.

"Moscow was his habitat as a specialist, but Paris was the city of his dreams," wrote Harrison Salisbury. Bohlen's love of France dated from the Grand Tours of his childhood, during which he had been instructed by his Francophile mother to admire everything about the country, even the cows. He had returned to Paris again and again over the years, often as a respite from Moscow's gloom.

French-American relations were in crisis during Bohlen's tour of duty. Chafing under U.S. dominance, de Gaulle was acting up and asserting his independence, thereby jeopardizing the Western Alliance. He refused to participate in a multilateral nuclear force, vetoed Great Britain's entry in the Common Market, and then in the winter of 1966 delivered the real blow: he walked out of the military command of NATO and demanded that U.S. forces be withdrawn from France.

Bohlen was characteristically low-key in his approach to Le Grand Charles. He advised Johnson not to overreact to the French leader, to preserve America's long-term relationship with its historic ally by riding out the squalls of the moment. To the French, NATO did not mean much, he told Johnson; Paris still regarded itself tied to the U.S. by a mutual security pact.

Personally, Bohlen got on well with de Gaulle, shooting with him at his weekend retreat and conversing with him easily and fluently. Somewhat indiscreetly, however, Bohlen enjoyed mocking de Gaulle's grand manner at dinner parties in Paris society, where anti-Gaullism ran high. His cutting remarks made their way back to the proud general and further exacerbated tensions between Washington and Paris.

The diplomatic rough spots did little to interfere with Bohlen's great pleasure in the City of Light. The embassy was run smoothly by his old St. Paul's and Harvard roommate Cecil Lyon, his deputy chief of mission. There was plenty of time for diversion: he relished finding small, unknown, and superb restaurants, and he happily argued into the night with the French, who enjoyed passionate debate as much as he did. He gambled at Monte Carlo and tried to hide his losses from Avis. Short on funds as usual, he had to borrow Cecil Lyon's silk hat, which was much too small for him, when he went to call on de Gaulle. (Indeed, he had been able to accept the ambassadorship only after Kennedy dipped into a special presidential fund to augment his entertainment allowance.) But the American dollar went far in Paris in the mid-1960s, and the Bohlens entertained often and well—two or three formal dinners a month and innumerable small parties. They held off on large splashy affairs, like dress balls, Bohlen recalled, only because the Vietnam War was raging, and ostentatious celebration would have been unseemly.

Bohlen had growing doubts about the Vietnam War. On the eve of the Geneva conference in 1954 that split Vietnam into North and South, he had been fairly hawkish, advising Dulles not to concede too much to the Communists.* But he correctly foresaw that the North Vietnamese would never give up and sue for peace. The notion that the North Vietnamese could be bombed to the conference table, he wrote Tommy Thompson in 1966, "is a very fallacious argument since it seems to me that all Communist history shows that they will never yield to external pressure of this kind."

Bohlen did not volunteer this opinion to Johnson until he was asked. "What would you do about Vietnam if you were in charge of the country?" the President finally queried him in 1967. Bohlen replied that the bombing was "the worst thing the United States had done." It had forced the Soviets to render greater assistance to the North Vietnamese and alienated public opinion in Europe—all without having any effect on Hanoi. "None of these arguments were new," recorded Bohlen. Johnson had heard them before; he stopped asking Bohlen's advice.

---

*His cable is a classic example of his most opaque prose: "As a matter of speculative deduction, it is probable that Soviet influence on Chinese action is in direct ratio to the risk to the entire Communist bloc of a given course of action and if, for example, it was plainly evident to the Soviet Government (and to the Chinese) that the risk of a major conflict over Indochina was real, then I believe Soviet influence on China could and might be determinant. On the other hand..."

• • •

Like Lovett, McCloy was called upon by LBJ in 1966 to give his opinion on whether the U.S. should resume bombing the North after the Christmas pause. Like Lovett, McCloy said yes. The pause "hasn't been conducive to bringing about talks," he said at a meeting with Johnson at the White House. "We've been too excited, too panicky—an indication of weakness to the enemy."

Though McCloy had always doubted American involvement in Vietnam and came to oppose it, he hated to see the U.S. appear "weak." Even as late as 1972, McCloy grumbled to Louis Auchincloss at a dinner at the Century Club that U.S. troops were about to "scat out" of Vietnam. Auchincloss remarked that McCloy must still be a hawk at heart, or otherwise he would have used the term "withdraw." McCloy nodded, and glumly admitted that Auchincloss was right.

The antiwar movement that began welling up in the mid-sixties also distressed McCloy. The demonstrators seemed to McCloy damnably disloyal; what is more, the anti-elitist passion of the young was an affront to his very way of doing business, his conception of how government *ought* to be run. The effect was to make him appear more hawkish than he really felt. At a meeting on Vietnam at the Council on Foreign Relations in New York in 1967, a member, Cass Canfield, worried aloud that the war was alienating the public, particularly the young. McCloy seemed irked at the suggestion, and growled that the British had experienced dissent during the Boer War too without just giving up.

McCloy was much happier dealing with Europe. Along with Acheson, he was called in by Johnson to keep the Western Alliance from splitting apart when de Gaulle exited from NATO. McCloy agreed to help out with NATO's financial woes—U.S. dollars and British pounds were draining into Germany, where the troops were actually stationed, causing a currency crisis. Both Britain and the U.S. Congress were threatening to withdraw the troops. After two months of negotiations, McCloy was able to work out a complex deal that preserved the alliance he had so carefully nurtured through its infancy.

• • •

Acheson was deeply worried that NATO was being allowed to wither while the Vietnam War mushroomed. In 1965 he had written an article in *Foreign Affairs* "to prod LBJ into some consciousness that Europe exists and that some action is needed from the United States," he wrote Desmond Donnelly, a British MP. Acheson even faulted

Mac Bundy; in a later letter he told Donnelly that he did not regret Bundy's departure as National Security Adviser because he was "anti-German and believes we can make a deal with de Gaulle."

Acheson was furious at de Gaulle's defection from NATO. "What a tiresome creature that man is," he wrote Anthony Eden. At President Johnson's request, Acheson came over to the White House in March of 1966 to help salvage NATO and tame Le Grand Charles. After a few months, he was almost as exasperated by Johnson as he was by de Gaulle. He wrote Eden:

> In acting as chief of staff for the France-NATO crisis, I have found myself in the middle of a whole series of intra-U.S. Government vendettas—Defense v. State, White House v. State, JCS v. McNamara, Semitic-Gaullists v. European integrationists, and LBJ turn-the-other-cheekism v. DA let-the-chips-fall-where-they-mayism. This finally led to a press leak campaign, conducted out of the White House, directed against George Ball, Jack McCloy and me as anti-de Gaulle extremists. This all blew up at a White House meeting when, at some crack of LBJ's, I lost my temper and told him what I thought of his conduct and that I was not prepared to stand for any more of it. Rusk and McNamara dove for cover while Ball and I slugged it out with Mr. Big. . . . It was exhilarating and did something to clear the air.

Ball, for one, was delighted with Acheson's forthrightness and willingness to stand up to Johnson. "I shall miss your urbanity and disillusion when the cocktail hour rolls around," he wrote him after the old statesman had returned to his law firm in June. Yet Acheson's cyncism was not just an air he feigned. He wrote Harry Truman that the experience was "most disillusioning" about both Johnson and Dean Rusk. He regretted that he had ever recommended Rusk as Secretary of State. "He had been a good assistant to me, loyal and capable, but as number one he is no good at all. LBJ is not much better. . . . He creates distrust by being too smart. He is never quite candid. He is both mean and generous, but the meanness far too often predominates."

Acheson failed to persuade Johnson to pressure de Gaulle back into NATO. "So Europe is forgotten," Acheson lamented, "and a good deal that you, General Marshall, and I did is unravelling fast." Acheson was growing ever gloomier. "I am so depressed about the world that I do not trust my pen," he wrote Donnelly. "Who added the *sapiens* to *homo*? He ought to get his tail back—and be kicked."

Acheson was unable to persuade Johnson to take a hard line against de Gaulle, he believed, because the President was too distracted by the Vietnam War. But then everyone in Washington was preoccupied with the war by the summer of 1966. It had become all-consuming. Acheson could no longer shrug off Vietnam as an irritating nuisance, a noisy sideshow. Like the country at large, he had to face up to America's involvement in Southeast Asia, and decide whether to support it—or not.

CHAPTER 23

Harriman and Acheson

JUDGMENT DAYS

Last Supper
of the Wise Men

I n the fall of 1967, Lyndon Johnson badly needed reassurance. Brought home by television, the war was dragging on, stirring bitter dissent and strident, even cruel attacks on the President ("Hey, hey, LBJ, how many kids did you kill today?"). Johnson's Defense Secretary, Robert McNamara, the most self-confident man in his Cabinet, was visibly in torment. To his aides, Johnson worried that McNamara was on the verge of cracking up; he wondered aloud whether he was about to follow the example of James Forrestal.

Johnson felt martyred. He ranted against "gutless" bureaucrats who leaked "defeatist" information to "simpleton" reporters. "It's gotten so," he complained, "that you can't screw your wife without it being spread around by traitors." Like Lincoln, Johnson began to see himself a War Leader, waging an unpopular but noble struggle.

As he had at the time of escalation in 1965, the President turned to his Senior Advisory Group, the Wise Old Men (or WOMS, as they were called by White House staffers). There were eleven who responded to Johnson's summons in early November: Dean Acheson, the chief elder; Clark Clifford, LBJ's closest private adviser and a resolute backer of the war; Supreme Court Justice Abe Fortas, another LBJ crony and Clifford's fellow hawk; McGeorge Bundy, the former National Security Adviser who had graduated to Wise Men status; Maxwell Taylor, the Kennedys' favorite general and former ambassador to Saigon; Omar Bradley, the chairman of the JCS during the Korean War; Robert Murphy, General Lucius Clay's political adviser in Berlin and a high State Department official under Dulles; Henry Cabot Lodge, former ambassador to Vietnam; Arthur Dean, Dulles's law partner and U.S. armistice negotiator in Korea; Douglas Dillon, Kennedy's Treasury Secretary and a leader of the New York Establishment; and George Ball, the in-house dove who had resigned as Under Secretary of State the year before. One elder statesman who had never left government was also included: Averell Harriman.

It was a formidable assemblage, a rich blend of Wall Street and Washington, soldiers and diplomats, men who had shaped and preserved a bipartisan foreign policy consensus for two decades. Some had always been members of the Establishment (four of the twelve had graduated from Groton), others had picked up their credentials along the way. But all shared a familiarity with power and a conviction that the U.S. must fulfill its rightful role as world leader.

There were, however, two noticeable absentees from this august gathering. John McCloy had dropped out of the Senior Advisory Group altogether by November of 1967, while Robert Lovett, though still listed as a member, failed to attend.

Asked about their views on the war almost twenty years later, both Lovett and McCloy take on almost identical expressions: quizzical, pained, slightly vacant, as if they were troubled by some vague and undefined illness. It is revealing, though perhaps not surprising, that both men have little recollection of their roles in the Vietnam War. They can remember what they did in 1947 in precise detail, but Vietnam remains a void in their consciousness. About all they can recall is that they were against the war. Indeed, both adamantly insist that they opposed U.S. involvement from the first. The written record, however, shows that when asked by the President if they backed a certain step, such as sending in more troops or stepping up the bombing, they invariably said yes.

By the autumn of 1967, McCloy and Lovett had decided to have nothing further to do with Vietnam. Though both men were busy, neither was diverted by pressing demands on his time. While McCloy dropped out of consultations on Vietnam, he continued to report to the President on his conversations with Middle Eastern potentates whom he had visited on behalf of his Big Oil clients. McCloy's calendar for November 1 and 2, the dates of the Wise Men meeting, shows nothing but routine appointments. Lovett was suffering from his usual aliments and preoccupied with Union Pacific Railroad matters. But he had always found time to serve his Presidents before, and he could later recall no reason why he declined this particular call to duty.

Perhaps almost unconsciously, both men apparently decided that since they could no longer support the war, they would absent themselves from Johnson's war councils. They had no advice to offer on how the war might be won, and to advise him to simply get out was unthinkable. So they chose to remain silent. *

In retrospect, the quiet defections of Lovett and McCloy should have warned Johnson and his aides that support was slipping even within the Eastern Establishment. But at the November meeting of the Wise Men, this telltale warning was overshadowed by an outpouring of support from those who did heed the President's call.

Assembling for cocktails at seven-thirty in an eighth-floor diplomatic reception room at the State Department on November 1, 1967, the Wise Men were briefed by General Earle Wheeler, the chairman of the Joint Chiefs of Staff. The report from the field was buoyantly upbeat: all the statistics, the captured documents and body counts, showed that the U.S. was winning the war. The only problem, explained Secretary of State Dean Rusk, who was acting as host that evening, was that the public did not know it.

The Wise Men accepted the Administration line. Most spoke out in favor of the war effort. Acheson dryly remarked that the bulk of student dissent stemmed from an understandable desire to avoid combat. "There was hardly a word spoken that could not be given directly to the press," Walt Rostow exulted in a memo he wrote to the President after the meeting that night. "You may wish to have a full leadership meeting of this kind, introduced by yourself, after which you could put the whole thing on television."

---

*William Bundy, however, recalls that Lovett did make one telling suggestion to him over dinner that December: appoint an ombudsman to watch over what was being said to the press about the war effort, and blow the whistle if the briefings got out of line. According to Bundy, Lovett was thinking of Rostow's propensity for exaggeration.

Johnson met with the Wise Men the next morning in the Cabinet Room. "I have a peculiar confidence in you as patriots and that is why I picked you," he began. He wanted to know if he was on the right course in Vietnam, and if not, how to change it. The lack of public support and the negative press, he added, troubled him.

Acheson was the first called upon by the President. General Wheeler's briefing had encouraged the old statesman. "I got the impression that this is a matter we can and will win," he said. He had one caveat: He did not believe the bombing would bring Hanoi to the negotiating table. "We must understand that we are not going to have negotiations," he told the President. "When these fellows decide they can't defeat the South, then they will give up. This is the way it was in Korea. This is the way the Communists operate."

He was resolute: "We certainly should not get out of Vietnam." Then, as Johnson listened intently, he began to reminisce about another dark moment for an earlier President, the Chinese surprise attack in Korea in 1950. Acheson recalled that the military had become defeatist, but that Dean Rusk and George Kennan had come to his office and urged him to implore General Marshall to buck up the military. "We want less goddamn analysis and more fighting spirit," he quoted himself as saying. Together, they had persuaded Truman to hold fast, and a humiliating defeat had been averted.

Acheson's recollection of Korea was particularly vivid. He was, at that very moment, writing about the Korean War in his memoirs, poring over his memoranda of conversations, reaching back into his memory, and reliving that most intense crisis of his life. "The more I watch this war the more parallels I see to Korea and the more I admire my Chief," he wrote John Cowles (the "Chief" to Acheson was and would always be Truman, not his successor of the moment).

When he had finished recollecting Korea, Acheson made a suggestion to President Johnson out of another chapter of his memoirs. He told how his Citizens' Committee for the Marshall Plan had organized groups of leading citizens in every city with a population over 150,000 to talk up European recovery and create popular understanding and support. Such a committee was needed now, said Acheson: influential men to carry forth the word.

Johnson next called on the second generation. Mac Bundy said he agreed with nearly everything Acheson had said. Like Acheson, he was strongly influenced by Bob McNamara's disenchantment with the bombing, and he downplayed the significance of air strikes against the North. He further shared Acheson's view that negotiations were a false hope, even though, he acknowledged, the Administration could not admit this publicly. The real focus, he said, should be on strengthening the South. "Getting out of Vietnam is as impossible as it is undesirable," he declared. What was needed was more public support. The Administration should emphasize, he concluded in that memorable phrase, "the light at the end of the tunnel."

As he listened through the morning and at lunch, Johnson heard only determination to press on with the war. General Bradley, for instance, said that what was needed was more patriotic slogans. He had been to Vietnam and he could report that troop morale was high; the men got ice cream three times a week, and of all the soldiers he talked to, he heard negative remarks from "only two colored soldiers from Detroit who were more interested in the riots in Detroit than Vietnam." Clark Clifford declared that during Korea everyone had complained about "Truman's War," but just as that war had been right and necessary, so was this one. Johnson, cradling his four-month-old grandson, Patrick Lyndon Nugent, in his lap, basked in the warming talk of such esteemed men. There was, he concluded as the meeting broke up after lunch, "a sense of clarity and calmness in the group."

The serenity was briefly interrupted as the elder statesmen filed out of the Cabinet Room. George Ball had said very little during the meeting, but he was unable to contain himself. Deeply discouraged by the war he had opposed for so long, disappointed in his colleagues from the Establishment for not seeing its folly, he burst out at Dean Acheson and the distinguished men around him: "I've been watching you across the table. You're like a flock of buzzards sitting on a fence, sending the young men off to be killed. You ought to be ashamed of yourselves." The old men just stared back at him, stunned.

This dissonant note was ignored and soon forgotten by Johnson's advisers. They set about implementing the public relations campaign suggested by the Wise Men. The U.S. ambassador to Vietnam, Ellsworth Bunker, and the commander of U.S. forces, General William Westmoreland, made a speaking tour envisioning "the light at the end of the tunnel." Westmoreland declared: "I am absolutely certain that whereas in 1965 the enemy was winning, today he is certainly losing." The U.S. had reached the "crossover point": it was killing more of the enemy than the North Vietnamese could replace. On the peace front, Lyndon Johnson took off to Rome for a private audience with the Pope, to whom he gave a plastic bust of himself. Meanwhile, thousands of Viet Cong were slipping silently into the cities of South Vietnam as the lunar New Year known as Tet approached.

• • •

Eyes heavy, jaws slack, Averell Harriman had sat quietly through the Wise Men meeting. He made no comment about the war at all, opening his mouth only to agree glumly with Acheson that the Senate Foreign Relations Committee was no good at all, that it did not begin to compare with its heyday under Arthur Vandenberg.

Harriman was trying to stay low and on Johnson's right side. He continued to believe in a negotiated peace—unlike most of the other Wise Men—but he did not press his opinion publicly. His views were already well known to LBJ. "Harriman continues to believe that the best road to peace lies through the Communist capitals," Mac Bundy wrote the President that November, "and that he is the right man to travel that road."

Early in December, Harriman read with rising scorn some excerpts, printed in the Washington *Post*, of a TV interview of Acheson about the war in Vietnam. Acheson had been particularly prickly and querulous, dismissing a negotiated settlement as impossible and ridiculing his interrogators, a panel of college students, for fuzzy thinking. Repeatedly, Acheson likened the war in Vietnam to Korea, and insisted that the U.S. had no choice but to stick it out.

To Harriman, it was Acheson who was guilty of specious reasoning, not the students. He decided it was time to set straight his former rowing pupil.

Harriman was not so awed by Acheson as were most others, including the President. "To you he's the great Secretary of State," he would growl to his aide Dan Davidson. "But to me he's the freshman I taught to row at Yale." His relationship with Acheson was still tinged with rivalry and even resentment, yet he felt with Acheson a sense of shared history. "I rejoice that you are rapidly approaching the years of discretion," he had written Acheson in a teasing 73rd birthday note in April of 1966. "How kind of you to cheer me on this depressing anniversary," Acheson responded. He assured Harriman that he had no intention of becoming discreet.

In the early evening of December 12, 1967, Harriman took the short walk through Georgetown from his house on N Street to Acheson's house on P Street, where his old friend greeted him at the door and showed him to his front parlor. It was a cozy room of books and memorabilia, with a picture of Stimson and a Yale rowing cup and a comfortable settee by the front windows where the two old men could sit and talk.

Harriman did not hesitate to get to the point. He had long felt that Acheson was too rigid, too stuck in the past, and he told him so. He proceeded to lecture: Vietnam was entirely different from Korea, he said. Russia and China were no longer allies. In fact, the two countries were bitter enemies. Moscow wanted to end the war. The fighting in Vietnam was guerrilla, not conventional warfare. A war of attrition, so effective in Korea, was futile against the Viet Cong. It was impossible to stamp out the Communists militarily. The real problem was that Johnson was afraid to settle the war for fear of a right-wing reaction, and he was constantly pressured by the military and those two hawks, Clifford and Fortas, to widen the fighting.

Acheson listened to this litany without interrupting. To Harriman's surprise, he was almost agreeable. He said that he personally worried more about the left-wing nuts than the right-wing ones, but in any case, he was contemptuous of the opinions of Fortas and Clifford. What is more, he was highly suspicious of the military. This was one lesson from Korea that *was* applicable to Vietnam: don't believe the rosy predictions of the generals.

The two men talked into the evening, keeping Acheson's dinner guests waiting. Harriman implored Acheson to talk to the President, to level with him about his doubts about the war. Acheson protested that his influence had waned with Johnson, ever since he and Jack McCloy had "exploded" at the President over NATO. Forget that, said Harriman; go back to your old relationship: the President needs your advice to offset the military and the hawks. Acheson made no promises, but he seemed interested in trying to help.

Harriman was encouraged. "I found that he was not as rigid as I supposed," he wrote in a memo to file describing the conversation. Was his old rival a potential seatmate in this last long pull? Harriman decided to grease the oarlocks. Less than a week later, he wrote Acheson asking him to sign a photograph of the two of them together. "I haven't got an autographed picture of you, and I would particularly like you to autograph this one. It shows me trying to convince you of something I consider very important, and you're having none of it! I enjoyed our chat the other afternoon. Please ask Alice to forgive me for keeping you away from your other guests so long."

Back came the photograph from Acheson with an inscription: "To

Averell Harriman, whose friendship has strengthened and delighted me for more than half a century. Dean Acheson."

•   •   •

Acheson's doubts about the war were deeper than Harriman realized. His own feeling about the Wise Men meeting was hardly the "clarity and calmness" Johnson had divined. "The meeting was exhausting, interesting, full of agony and effort on the part of all of us except Our Hero, who was not impressed," Acheson wrote former British Prime Minister Anthony Eden (among friends, Acheson had taken to calling LBJ "Our Leader" or "Our Hero").

The lesson of Korea cut both ways to Acheson. Standing up to the Communists was not the only moral; standing up to the military was another. In his memoirs, he was writing about MacArthur, and facing up to his own equivocation while the megalomaniacal general plunged on to disaster. With Bob McNamara, whom he greatly admired and felt for, he had been having long conversations about the hawks at the Pentagon and their passion for indiscriminate escalation. McNamara had broken publicly with the advocates of bombing during congressional testimony in August; afterward, Acheson wrote Eden:

> Bob McNamara told me all about the situation a week ago. His report (to Congress) is the truth, but not the whole truth. Rather, a loyal lieutenant putting the best face on a poor situation. The fact is that the bombing of the North started as a morale builder for the South when things were very bad there. We have now run out of targets but the Republican hawks keep calling for more which produces useless casualties and encourages some Air Force fire-eaters to urge population bombing. LBJ has not HST's courage to say no to political pressures....

Vietnam was not all that worried Acheson. His well-ordered world was under serious assault in 1967—race riots in American ghettos, disarray in the Western Alliance—and Acheson held LBJ accountable. He confided to the former British Prime Minister:

> For the first time, I begin to think that LBJ may be in trouble. It is not Vietnam alone. The country would probably stay with him on that. But Vietnam plus the riots is very bad. It spells frustration and a sense of feebleness at home and abroad. Everyone pushes the USA around. Yellow men in Asia, black men at home, de Gaulle a ridiculous type in Europe, and Nasser threatens to have the Arab states seize what is regarded as

"our" oil properties. Americans aren't used to this, and LBJ is not a lovable type. He is the one to blame.

Increasingly, Acheson began to worry aloud to friends that Vietnam was a dangerous diversion from Europe, that the blundering, unsophisticated LBJ risked bringing down the whole delicate structure of the Pax Americana. "Our Leader ought to be more concerned with areas that count," he pronounced to guests at Sunday lunch at Harewood.

Acheson knew from talking to his son-in-law Bill Bundy that Johnson was becoming increasingly paranoid about leaks and dissent within his own Administration. The last real doubter, McNamara, was leaving the Pentagon in February to become president of the World Bank; a small, hawkish circle—principally Rusk and Rostow—now advised Johnson at the "Tuesday lunches." These war councils in the President's private dining room were closely held; line officers like Bundy were left to guess at Administration strategy. In self-defense, upperlevel officials at State and the Pentagon who were growing ever more doubtful about the war began holding their own strategy sessions on Vietnam. Calling themselves the "nongroup," they held "nonmeetings" over drinks every Thursday night. When Bundy contrasted this secretive and suspicious way of doing business with "the method of Acheson, Marshall, Lovett, and Harriman" during the Truman Administration, he was profoundly discouraged. The Tuesday lunch was "an abomination," he believed, and the "nongroup" hardly an adequate answer.

Acheson anxiously watched his son-in-law suffer. His daughter Mary confided to him that her husband was miserable, no longer a hawk on the war but unable to see any way out. She feared that Vietnam would ruin his career and tear apart his family. Acheson listened quietly, stoical about what must be borne, but sympathetic and disturbed. On Sunday evenings, when he and Alice stopped in at the Bundys' on their way home from Harewood, Acheson rarely discussed the war with Bill, preferring to let him rest, yet he could not help but see the physical and emotional toll. After Bundy returned from an LBJ around-the-world peace offensive at Christmastime, Acheson wrote Anthony Eden, "My poor son-in-law Bill Bundy came back on Christmas Eve from the flying circus—called by them the 'journey to nowhere.' In four and a half days he had spent five hours in bed. You and I lived in softer times, I am happy to say."

Angry demonstrators carrying Viet Cong flags in front of the White

House left Acheson taken aback at the virulence of the peace movement. "The anti-war demonstrations which we have just been through
are the worst yet," he wrote Eden on December 30. Yet the protesters
were no longer just longhairs in the streets. At lunch at the Metropolitan Club, Paul Nitze, now Deputy Secretary of Defense, told
Acheson about his own deepening opposition to the war. At cocktails
before dinner at Lucius Battle's, Stuart Symington, the onetime hawkish Secretary of the Air Force, berated Acheson about the war, insisting
that it was time to either flatten Hanoi or get out. The two old Cold
Warriors became so angrily engaged that they ignored their host's
repeated requests to come sit down for dinner. Many elegant dinner
parties were similarly disrupted that winter in Washington; the war
had divided not just the country, but the Establishment as well.

As Tet heralded in the Year of the Monkey in Vietnam, the Viet
Cong exploded in Saigon and the major cities of the South. A suicide
squad of VC penetrated the U.S. Embassy grounds. The U.S. retal-
iated massively with Operation Niagara, inflicting enormous casualties
on the Communists. As a military venture, the Tet offensive was a
defeat, but psychologically, it was a victory for the North Vietnamese.
"If this is a failure," stated Senator George Aiken of Vermont, "I hope
the Viet Cong never have a major success." The senator's incredulity
was shared by millions of Americans watching the carnage nightly on
the news, seeing U.S. marines torch huts with Zippo lighters and
hearing one commander calmly explain, "It became necessary to destroy the town in order to save it." The press turned on the war: "What
is the end that justifies this slaughter?" asked James Reston. "How will
we save Vietnam if we destroy it in battle?" Once reliable backers of
the war effort suddenly began to doubt—Walter Cronkite, *The Wall
Street Journal*, *Time*, and *Life*.

Acheson could not escape the clamor even in Antigua, where he
retreated in February for his annual winter holiday. As he wandered
down the beach one afternoon, he encountered author Linda Bird
Francke, who wore a peace symbol hanging from her neck. He examined it carefully. "What is that?" he asked. "The peace symbol,"
she replied. He allowed that he had mistaken it for the logo of a
Volkswagen. Even his old chums had become doves. John Cowles,
the publisher of the Minneapolis *Star* and *Tribune*, and Jay Gould,
scion of the robber baron, began to belabor the war over cocktails and
croquet.

The policies of the past were not easily forsaken by Acheson, who
had, after all, shaped many of them. "The constant cry of Mr.

Lippmann and others for 'new policies' is the result of an illusion. Policies do not wear out or become obsolete like models of automobiles merely by the passage of time," he wrote a friend in 1966.

Acheson was so scornful of the liberalism and change sweeping the 1960s that it is easy to think of him as a rigid old man, frozen in the myths of his own creation. Yet he was not dogmatic. He was a pragmatist, not an ideologue. Confronted with facts, he did not attempt to twist them to fit preconceived notions, or try to escape back into a dreamy world of bygone triumph. Even at age 74, he was able to face up to unpleasant reality. He was, what is more, a disciple of action. Crises made him alert, forceful, decisive; they drove him to act.

By the winter of 1968, Acheson was tired of being used. He was irked at being dusted off and displayed like a tarnished and nicked Cold War icon, manipulated by LBJ as well as by reporters like Reston and Joe Alsop, who would call him periodically for quotable wisdom. He felt that he was being not only used but taken; he suspected strongly that he was being asked to pronounce judgment on facts that were either false or incomplete. Acheson was a shrewd and meticulous lawyer; he would certainly never make an argument to the Supreme Court based on the quickie briefings he and other Wise Men had been served up on Vietnam. As one senior Defense Department official bluntly put it some years later, "Those briefings were a sham." They were designed less to inform the elder statesmen than to convince them.

Acheson sensed this, and rebelled against it. In February of 1968, he decided he would either learn all the facts about Vietnam or cease to lend his support to the war.

He was summoned to the White House on February 27. Exhausted from spending most of the night in the basement of the West Wing, where a scale model of the besieged marine base at Khe Sanh had been erected, Johnson vented and bellowed at Acheson. He was determined that the battle for Khe Sanh not repeat the terrible French defeat at Dien Bien Phu. "I don't want no damn Din Bin Phoos!" he roared. General Westmoreland had told the President that Tet had made the war "a whole new ball game." The Joint Chiefs wanted 200,000 troops. . . .

For forty-five minutes, Johnson ranted on. As usual, three television sets were blasting away, aides rushed in and out, the phones rang incessantly. Acheson just sat there. Westmoreland's phrase, "a whole new ball game," sounded eerily familiar to him; he recalled a cable from another panicked general in Korea: "We face an entirely different war..."

When it appeared to him that Johnson was more interested in delivering tirades than seeking advice, Acheson excused himself, walked out of the White House, and returned to his law office at the Union Trust Building across Lafayette Park.

The phone rang immediately; it was Walt Rostow asking why he had walked out. "You tell the President—and you tell him in precisely these words," Acheson said evenly, "that he can take Vietnam and stick it up his ass."

This message served to get LBJ's attention. The President came on the line and asked Acheson, as his President and commander in chief, to return. Though capable of lèse majesté to the individuals who occupied the office, Acheson was deeply loyal to the Presidency; he dutifully walked back across the street to the White House.

But he was still blunt: "With all due respect, Mr. President," he said, "the Joint Chiefs of Staff don't know what they're talking about." Johnson said this was a "shocking" statement. "Then maybe you should be shocked," said Acheson. He proceeded to refuse to say anything more until he had been fully briefed. He told Johnson that he wanted no more canned briefings—he wanted "full run of the shop"; he wanted to talk "to the engine-room people."

One by one, they began appearing at Acheson's house on P Street in the raw evenings of early March: Phil Habib, a tough-minded diplomat back from two years in Saigon; George Carver, a CIA analyst who had raw intelligence data that had not been first fed through Westmoreland's fact-massage parlor in Saigon; and General William DuPuy, former Army chief of operations in Saigon who had access to all combat field reports.

Like a senior litigator preparing for trial, Acheson grilled these men like law firm associates, testing their assumptions, pushing deeper and deeper into their files, demanding to see not just summaries but raw data about enemy troop strength and the battle reports of field commanders. Down the long and twisting tunnel he peered, looking vainly for a glimmer of light.

• • •

Another Washington lawyer was beginning to ask hard questions that February—the new Secretary of Defense, Clark Clifford.

He had long occupied a peculiar niche within the Establishment.

A Midwesterner, Clifford was not Grottie enough to claim membership by right, though in his own mind his comfortable upbringing in
St. Louis was every bit as respectable as Dean Acheson's in Middletown, Connecticut. He was Acheson's match in confidence and charm,
though perhaps slightly too suave and polished. Snobs thought they
could smell a touch of snake oil in Clifford's wavy silver-blond hair,
see a little too much sheen in his tailored double-breasted suits. As a
lawyer (the highest paid in Washington), he was known not for the
quality of his Supreme Court briefs, but for his connections in the
federal bureaucracy and on Capitol Hill.

Nonetheless, the real insiders, men like Acheson and Lovett, genuinely liked and respected Clifford. Though they had found him a
tad too expedient at times—about Palestine, for instance—they did
not doubt his basic integrity. Nor did they hesitate to make full use
of his political skills. As Truman's aide in the late forties, he served,
in effect, as an exalted salesman. Working closely and quietly with
Acheson, Forrestal, Lovett, and Harriman, he took their policies and
made them politically palatable. He became a megaphone that amplified—and sometimes oversimplified—the doctrine of containment.
Along the way he absorbed his own clichés. Years later, Clifford
recalled his mind-set:

> I, like the others, believed in two lessons: one, that neglect led to World
> War II, and two, that consistent resistance prevented World War III.
> That, if not in the conscious mind, was my unconscious thought process.
> So when the war in Vietnam became serious, the feeling was, oh, here
> we go again. We've got to stand up.

Like other Truman-era veterans, Clifford had initial doubts about
the war. Unlike most of them, however, he made those doubts clear
to the President. In the spring of 1965, as Johnson was deciding
whether to send in ground troops, Clifford wrote him that Vietnam
could become "a quagmire, without realistic hope of ultimate victory."
Then in July he had again warned, "I don't believe we can win in
South Vietnam. . . . I can't see anything but catastrophe ahead for our
nation."

Yet once Johnson had ignored this advice, Clifford became an
ardent hawk. Like Lovett, he felt that if the U.S. went to war, it had
to go all out. Along with his fellow member of Johnson's Kitchen
Cabinet, Supreme Court Justice Abe Fortas, Clifford resolutely urged
Johnson to drop more bombs, send in more troops. "The only way

to get out of Vietnam is to persuade Hanoi that we are too brave to be frightened and too strong to be defeated," he told Johnson in January of 1966, arguing in favor of ending a bombing pause.

When Defense Secretary Bob McNamara departed—literally in tears—at the end of February, Johnson looked to his small and dwindling circle of loyalists. Clifford seemed to be the perfect candidate, a Defense Secretary who would heed his commander in chief and vigorously prosecute the war. Johnson overestimated Clifford's fealty and underestimated his intelligence and independence of mind.

Before installing him at the Pentagon, Johnson charged Clifford with nothing less than a full-scale review of the war. This "A to Z" assessment was precipitated by General Westmoreland's request for another 200,000 troops. They were not all needed for Vietnam—at least right away—but rather to replenish the military's depleted ranks around the world. For political reasons, Johnson had resisted calling up the reserves; the Joint Chiefs, by a massive troop request, hoped to force his hand.

An hour after he was sworn in as Secretary of Defense on March 1, Clifford began his own education by having lunch in his private dining room with the Deputy Secretary, Paul Nitze.

The two old Truman veterans had seen each other often over the years around town and at the Metropolitan Club. Nitze knew that he could be forthright with Clifford. He told him that the war could not be won, that the bombing was a total failure, that the war was straining relations with the allies and shortchanging U.S. forces elsewhere. Significantly, while the U.S. was mired in Vietnam, the Soviets were beefing up their nuclear and conventional arsenals. The time had come to wind down the costly sideshow in Vietnam and return to the center stage, facing off the Soviets in Europe. In the short term, Nitze recommended that Westmoreland be given only token reinforcements and that the bombing of the North be halted.

Coming from the drafter of NSC-68, this message had a strong effect on Clifford. It heightened doubts that had been left by a tour of Southeast Asia over the past summer. Clifford had visited Thailand, the Philippines, Australia, and New Zealand—the dominoes that were supposed to topple next if South Vietnam fell—asking these countries to increase their token troop contributions (less than 20,000 men) to the American military presence in Vietnam. He came back empty-handed, "puzzled, troubled, concerned," wondering whether the domino theory was a meaningful metaphor after all. Fact had not squared with assumption; his lawyer's mind began to turn.

Around an oval oak table in the Secretary's dining room, Clifford gathered the Joint Chiefs and his top civilian aides and began asking some probing questions during that first week of March. How long would it take? One year? Five years? Ten years? How many more troops were enough to win: 200,000 more? 400,000? The chiefs could not answer. Clifford found himself thinking, "While I'm in this building, someone is going to want to round it off at a million." He asked the chiefs, "What is the plan for victory?" There was none. The generals' hope was to eventually wear out the enemy by attrition. Was there any sign that the Communists were getting worn down? Clifford asked. No, replied the generals.

As an old political operator, Clifford could hardly fail to be impressed by the peace campaign of Senator Eugene McCarthy of Minnesota. Begun as a quixotic gesture by a moody intellectual, McCarthy's challenge to LBJ for the Democratic nomination had swelled into a children's crusade. On March 12, McCarthy nearly beat LBJ in the New Hampshire primary, sending a deep shudder through the party ranks.

Clifford's political instincts were piqued not just by the roar of protest in the streets, but by the quiet discouragement of congressional hawks. Two Senate Armed Services Committee stalwarts—Henry Jackson of Washington and John Stennis of Mississippi—privately told Clifford that they had given up on the war; it was hopeless.

Insider Washington was restless, riled by leaks. The most serious came, ironically, from the ultimate bastion of secrecy, Skull and Bones. At a Bones reunion at Congressman William Moorhead's house in Georgetown on March 1, a Pentagon dove, Air Force Under Secretary Townsend Hoopes, told his clubmate, *New York Times* reporter Edward Dale, that the Administration was considering a massive troop increase. After some further digging, the *Times* broke the news: "Westmoreland Requests 206,000 More Men, Stirring Debate in Administration." When word of the story reached the Washington elite assembled at the Gridiron Club dinner on March 9, "it moved like wind through a field of wheat," recalled *Times* reporter Hedrick Smith. More bitterly, Walt Rostow remembered that "the story churned up the whole Eastern Establishment."

Meanwhile, Clifford's doubts about the war had intensified. "As time went on," he recalled, "my desire to get out of Vietnam went from opinion, to conviction, to passion. I was afraid that we were never going to get out. We were losing thousands of men and billions of dollars in an endless sinkhole. If I ever knew anything, I knew that: we had to get out."

By mid-March—only two weeks after he had taken the job as Defense Secretary—Clifford found himself unable to defend Administration policy on Capitol Hill. Asked to testify before the Foreign Relations Committee, he begged off, insisting that he was "still learning." It fell to Paul Nitze, his number two, to take his place. But Nitze refused. He coupled his refusal with a letter to the President offering to resign. Clifford managed to dissuade him from quitting, but Nitze was from then on cut out by the Johnson circle, never again invited to a Tuesday lunch.

Having convinced himself, Clifford began the arduous job of trying to persuade the President. This task was to require all of his wiles, as well as considerable courage. It would cost him his twenty-year friendship with Lyndon Johnson.

• • •

Clifford's transformation came as a tremendous relief, though not a total surprise, to Averell Harriman. Harriman had felt that Clifford, like Acheson, could be made to see reality once confronted by hard facts. After so many years as the only dove among the old Cold Warriors from the Truman days, Harriman could sense that his loneliness was coming to an end, that his old colleagues were slowly coming over to his side. He was encouraged when Jack McCloy sent him a copy of a speech he had given that winter in Chicago, chastising the Administration for losing sight of the "primacy of Europe" in its obsession with Vietnam. "I wish you could take a hand in settling Vietnam," Harriman wrote McCloy. "It is a frustrating business."

Harriman welcomed conversions from hawk to dove. But he was not seeking to foment public rebellion against the President, by any means. His correspondence with Bobby Kennedy, whose opposition to the war was becoming increasingly outspoken and whose political ambitions were rising, was highly cautionary. The old politician/statesman feared that if Kennedy became a renegade he would just polarize the Democratic Party and upset the delicate effort to prod Johnson toward a negotiated settlement of the war. "Vietnam is not easy," he had written Kennedy in February. "It is one of the toughest and most elusive situations we have ever been in. It is not difficult to be critical, but it is difficult to devise a route to an acceptable conclusion. I am all for stopping bombing *if* the other side will enter talks." He added a handwritten note: "We are going through a strange and tough experience in Vietnam. I am keen to discuss it with you. Ave."

But to Harriman, the real quarry was Acheson. He believed, correctly, that Johnson regarded Acheson as the embodiment of American foreign policy since World War II. If only Acheson could be made to see the error of the war, and to privately but firmly convey his change of heart to Johnson, then the President would surely be shaken—enough to begin a search for a political settlement. Once he really began thinking in terms of negotiated peace, Harriman hoped, the President would have to turn to his most experienced negotiator and authority on diplomatic initiatives toward Hanoi—Averell Harriman.

But first Acheson had to be convinced. Their discussion in December had left Harriman surprised and encouraged. During the winter, he had stopped by at P Street several times to stir his old schoolmate's doubts. "We are in a tough moment in Vietnam," he wrote Acheson right after Tet. "Keep an open mind."

When Acheson revealed to Harriman his blowup with the President at the end of February and his demand to learn the facts about the war, Harriman was naturally delighted. He knew as well the nature of Acheson's briefings, and that the old hawk's re-education was making him more dovish by the day. Here was the opening, the chance to swing his heaviest gun to bear on the President. On March 7—barely a week after Acheson's run-in with Johnson—Harriman called Acheson to badger him to return to the White House and express his newfound doubts about the war to LBJ. He sounded a little like big brother trying to goad little brother to jump off the high dive:

> HARRIMAN: Have you been called yet?
> ACHESON: No, I haven't.
> HARRIMAN: Aren't you going to offer?
> ACHESON: No, he's spoken two times about seeing me.
> HARRIMAN: You don't want to call Marvin Watson [the President's appointments secretary] to say you are available?
> ACHESON: No, I don't particularly want to shove myself. If he really wants me, he would remember it, don't you think?
> HARRIMAN: Well . . . I reluctantly say yes.
> ACHESON: If he thinks I'm an eager beaver it wouldn't be quite as effective. I want to wait a little while. If he doesn't do anything I'll talk to Dean Rusk about it.

Harriman and Acheson began discussing, cryptically, their contacts with some other pillars of the Establishment. The conversation, which

Harriman recorded and had transcribed for his files, has a faint whiff of conspiracy:

> HARRIMAN: All I can say is that a good deal of thought is going into things and that's all to the good.
>
> ACHESON: I saw John Lodge [former State Department official and Cabot's brother] today and he tells me he's working on a memo to the President.
>
> HARRIMAN: I have talked to your former law partner [Paul] Warnke [Assistant Secretary of Defense] and I'm going to see Paul Nitze, but I gather everyone is giving things a careful look. It may be that you'll get called.
>
> ACHESON: Cabot [Lodge] has an office somewhere near you. Have you seen him?
>
> HARRIMAN: Yes, we talked some weeks ago.

Acheson had not quite completed his tutorials. Phil Habib, one of the Saigon veterans who would make the evening trek to P Street to brief Acheson, recalled, "I sensed that he wanted to dig deeper." Habib showed Acheson his own evaluation of Tet, one that was a good deal more pessimistic than the Administration's claim that Tet had been a massive defeat for the North Vietnamese. Tet "was costly to the enemy and it did not succeed," Habib wrote, "but we paid a high price. . . . Old optimism is giving way to new doubts. . . . In many ways Tet is a new ball game in Vietnam. We were winning; steadily if not spectacularly. Now the other side has put in a lot of players and scored heavily against us. We did not win a 'victory' despite the losses inflicted on the enemy. The Tet offensive was a serious setback." Habib concluded that the situation was "far from hopeless," but that the U.S. would not be able to "recoup losses in the foreseeable future."

It was the battle reports from the field commanders that had the deepest impact on Acheson, his son, David, recalled. They conveyed to him an impression of suicidal determination by the enemy, and of confusion and low morale on the American side.

Acheson's study of the Vietnam War had paralleled his research of his own handling of the Korean War for his memoirs. Just as he was trying to decide what he should advise Lyndon Johnson to do about Vietnam, he was coming to grips with General Marshall's "strange quiescence" before MacArthur's mad plunge to the Yalu, and his own failure to warn the President before it was too late. The two strands of research intertwined: Acheson vowed not to make the same mistake twice.

• • •

The call from the White House came a few days after the conversation with Harriman. Could Acheson have lunch with the President on March 14?

He was kept waiting until 2 P.M. Finally the President appeared and launched into one of his soliloquies. Yes, the U.S. had taken a serious knock, but "Westy" and the Joint Chiefs were optimistic. If they could just get some patchwork replacements, they would be all right.

Acheson listened skeptically. "Mr. President," he finally cut in, "you are being led down the garden path." He told Johnson that he needed to hear more facts and less uninformed opinion. Personally, he did not believe much of what was reported by the military because it fluctuated so between optimism and pessimism. For instance, he gravely doubted Westy's estimate that he had killed or captured sixty thousand "Viet Minh" (Acheson still used the 1950's term) during Tet. Westmoreland reminded Acheson, he told Johnson, of Civil War General George McClellan, who had finally been relieved by Lincoln after nearly destroying the Union Army.

The real question, said Acheson, was whether the South Vietnamese could be made strong enough to fight their own war. If not, then Johnson would have to look for a "method of disengagement." Acheson doubted (and Harriman would have been sorry to hear this) that negotiations would be the answer. Hanoi was not interested in anything less than total control over South Vietnam. But Johnson had to learn this for himself—he had to stop talking to the generals and to Rostow and reach down farther into the ranks—as Acheson had done. Acheson even volunteered to supply him with names.

At that moment, Walt Rostow, the National Security Adviser, entered the room. Johnson asked Acheson to summarize his conclusions for Rostow. "Walt listened to me with the bored patience of a visitor listening to a ten-year-old playing the piano," Acheson recorded in a memo he wrote for his files.

"I have completed the second stage (High School) of my Vietnam education—a most remarkable one, from a rare and probably unsurpassed faculty—which has confused some of my early simple conclusions and shown the difficulties to be even greater than I thought," Acheson wrote a friend that evening. He was not quite ready to advise the President to disengage from Vietnam—his suggestion for now was a holding action while the President tried to learn more of the facts about the true state of the war. But Acheson's valedictory was not far off.

• • •

Lyndon Johnson saw even his old friends turning against him. On March 14, the same day Acheson told the President he was being "led down the garden path" by the military, he received an eight-page memorandum from Arthur Goldberg proposing a total bombing halt. Goldberg was an old ally; Johnson had made him U.S. ambassador to the U.N. To Johnson, Goldberg's defection from the war effort came as a personal betrayal.

"Let's get one thing clear!" he stormed at his advisers. "I'm telling you now that I am not going to stop the bombing! Now I don't want to hear any more about it. Goldberg has written me about the whole thing, and I've heard every argument, and I'm not going to stop it. Now is there anybody here who doesn't understand that?"

At the Tuesday lunches, Johnson watched Clark Clifford transform from stout warrior to brooding doubter. James Rowe, a Washington lawyer and Johnson's most trusted political adviser, bluntly told the President that he had nearly lost the New Hampshire primary to Eugene McCarthy on March 12 because he had become the war candidate, and the country no longer cared about winning the war. "Everybody wants to get out," Rowe bluntly told Johnson. "The only question is how."

Then, in the Ides of March, Johnson realized his worst dread: on March 16, Bobby Kennedy announced that he would challenge him for the Presidency.

Johnson could not sleep. His face was ashen, his eyes sunk and bleary. Folds of flesh hung down from his cheeks. Angry red sties began to pop out along his raw eyelids. He lashed out.

"We shall and we are going to win," he angrily declared to a meeting of businessmen on March 17. The next day he shrilly told a group of farmers, "The time has come when we ought to stand up and be counted, when we ought to support our leaders, our government, our men, and our allies until aggression is stopped, wherever it has oc-curred."

• • •

In his gruff avuncular way, Harriman admired Robert Kennedy. Under different circumstances, perhaps, he would have backed him for President. But Harriman still patiently hoped that if he showed his loyalty and steadiness to Johnson, he would be rewarded with responsibility.

RFK, who had given his son Douglas the middle name of "Har-

riman" in honor of Averell, called the old statesman after declaring
on television that he would challenge Johnson for the Democratic
nomination. The conversation was vintage Harriman:

KENNEDY: I'm running for President.
HARRIMAN: Next time tell the children to smile. Ethel looked great.
The kids looked bored.
KENNEDY: They were.
HARRIMAN: I don't expect to have a press conference soon, but if it
does come around I'm going to support the President.

Clifford watched Johnson's flailing with growing discouragement.
He felt that the President was just getting more hawkish, despite the
counsel of his closest friends. Briefly, he considered joining other
civilian doves at the Pentagon in a mass resignation. But listening to
Johnson rant at a Tuesday lunch on March 19, he had another idea.
As casually as possible, he suggested that perhaps the President would
like to reassemble the Wise Old Men, the group that had been so
calm and reassuring about the war back in November. Johnson, without hesitation, agreed.

Like all Clifford moves, this was a highly calculated one. He had
been checking around town, taking readings at the Metropolitan Club
and the Gridiron dinner, making a few phone calls to New York to
sample the mood at the Council on Foreign Relations and on Wall
Street. He knew exactly what Acheson was thinking because he had
made a point of going to see him privately at his home on P Street
and telling him of his own opposition to the war. "I told him of my
agony, in detail, so he might get the feel of it," Clifford later recalled.
In return, Acheson revealed his own doubts.

By now, Acheson's education was complete. His last required reading came not from Habib and the other government briefers, but from
an old newspaper friend, Wallace Carroll, a former *New York Times*
reporter who had become editor of the Winston-Salem (N.C.) *Journal
and Sentinel*. In mid-March, Carroll had sent Acheson a copy of a
full-page editorial he had written called "Vietnam Quo Vadis," outlining why in his view the U.S. had to withdraw from Vietnam. Late
on a Saturday night, March 23, Acheson called Carroll: "Wally, I've
been dragged through the bureaucracy and nothing makes sense. Why
is it that a guy from Winston-Salem can put all the facts together?"
He told Carroll that he had read Ambassador Bunker's and General
Westmoreland's cables, and then the field reports. He was convinced

that Tet was a disaster. "What really surprised me when we got into the whole question of Vietnam was that there was no political base on which to build," he said. The South Vietnamese were hopeless allies; it was time to begin an orderly disengagement. He told Carroll that he was going to the White House on Monday for a meeting on the war with other elder statesmen. Could he please send up twelve copies of the article? Wondering whether Acheson had ever heard of the Xerox machine, but eager to be of service, Carroll mailed the copies special delivery.

The next morning, Lucius Battle, Acheson's former assistant, ran into his ex-boss in the driveway at Johnson's Flower Center on Wisconsin Avenue above Georgetown. Though dressed in well-worn work clothes and clutching a flowerpot, the former Secretary of State, his mustache clipped, his bearing dignified and erect, still struck a magisterial pose. He stuck his head through Battle's open car window.

"I'm going to tell the President we have to get out of Vietnam," he said simply.

Battle was speechless. The creator of the Pax Americana, the old Cold Warrior who guarded America's commitments like a sacred trust, wanted out. To Battle, who knew well Acheson's pragmatism and ability to face hard reality, the decision was not altogether surprising. Nonetheless, he could not help but feel, as he watched the champion of the Western Alliance cradle his geraniums, that an era had passed.

It is not likely that Acheson himself sensed that he had crossed some great divide, that he had developed a sudden awareness of the limits of U.S. power and an appreciation of the forces of Third World nationalism. George Ball believes that Acheson approached Vietnam from a narrow, lawyerly point of view. "When the Supreme Court wants to make new law," said Ball, "they rarely come out and say so. They distinguish, rather than overrule, precedent. I think this is what he did on Vietnam." Recalled McGeorge Bundy: "Acheson was resistant to philosophical questions. He liked to quote Holmes that 'life is action.'" Said Clifford: "I don't think Acheson changed his philosophy about America's role in the world. Rather, he was always a realist."

If anything, Acheson felt he was acting to preserve the world order he had helped create, not change it. In a sense, Acheson was returning to basic principles. He was an Atlanticist. Europe, he had always believed, *was* the world; Vietnam was a diversion. A war without end was too high a price to pay for South Vietnam's freedom, especially since the South Vietnamese were so incapable of defending it themselves. A year later, at a party at Joe Alsop's, Acheson got into an argument with Walt Rostow about the strategic importance of Asia. Rostow insisted that Acheson must have believed at one time that America had to maintain a forceful presence in the region; why else intervene in Korea? "The only reason I told the President to fight in Korea," Acheson snapped back, "was to validate NATO." Bitterly, Rostow concluded that Acheson had decided that another year of war was "too much blood to spill for those little people just out of the trees."

Acheson was talking to Mac Bundy about Vietnam that March, and the younger man was in synch with the older. In Bundy's analytic mind, "the twin curves of patience and progress had intersected," i.e., the country was not willing to make the sacrifice necessary to win a prolonged war. In a carefully worded talk at Harvard in mid-March, the former National Security Adviser had begun to express publicly some of his concerns; the *Crimson* immediately blared, "Bundy Opposes Escalation." Actually, Bundy's doubts had been growing for some time. Despite his "light at the end of the tunnel" speech at the November Wise Men meeting, he had written Johnson a troubled letter ten days later questioning Westmoreland's "search and destroy" strategy and wondering if the time had not come to second-guess the military's conduct of the war. By March, Bundy was, in private at least, in full dissent; he wanted to find a way out of Vietnam.

·   ·   ·

Once more they were gathered, the Wise Old Men, the elder statesmen, or as some members of the press had begun less reverently describing them, "the Usual Suspects." The group that assembled at the State Department for briefings on the afternoon of Monday, March 25, was the same that had met with the President in November with two additions: Cyrus Vance, former Deputy Secretary of Defense and a sometimes troubleshooter for Johnson; and General Matthew Ridgway, the able soldier who had turned around U.S. forces in Korea after the disaster at the Yalu. Once again, McCloy and Lovett were absent. (McCloy, at least, was watching from the shadows; he had had lunch with Averell Harriman earlier that day.)

The Bundy brothers, greeting the Wise Men at the State Department, felt the need to prod them a little, to make them probe the substance of the briefings, to ask hard questions. At earlier such sessions, the elder statesmen had been "rushed down on the shuttle, without time to read," Bill Bundy recalled. "We fed them too well, and everyone would have one more drink than is useful for really hard thinking in the night." This time, the Bundy brothers, along with Under Secretary of State Nicholas Katzenbach, urged the Wise Men to read carefully the documents that had been assembled for them in a small library in the State Department that afternoon. In the evening, they were instructed to assemble on the eighth floor for dinner and a formal briefing.

It was possibly the most distinguished dinner party of the American Establishment ever held. The Cold War Knighthood, now bowed and balding but nonetheless formidable, sat down together to dine by candlelight and discuss the Vietnam War, the culmination of America's commitment to stopping aggression anywhere in the world. In quiet tones, they began to talk to one another about how that commitment might be curtailed.

Though they perhaps did not realize it, the Wise Men were meeting at the high-water mark of U.S. hegemony. Never again would America's global commitments extend so far. After this evening, the U.S. would begin to slowly and painfully pull back, to recognize the limits of its power. These men were about to play a critical role in reversing the momentum that they had done so much to generate over the last two decades. Though few were conscious of it, they were at one of history's turning points.

The moment was as significant for their role in America as it was for America's in the world. By dismantling their own creation, they were as well diminishing their own *raison d'être*. Never again would a President put such faith in the collective wisdom of the Establishment. For the Wise Men, this dinner was, in a sense, the last supper.

The President, who was not scheduled to meet formally with the group until the next morning, dropped by during the meal, shook hands all around, like a congressional candidate at a fund raiser, and left to go pick bombing targets in the White House Situation Room. After dinner, the group repaired to the State Department Operations Center on the seventh floor, where they were briefed by Habib of State, Carver of the CIA, and General DuPuy—Acheson's instructors for the past month.

Habib could tell which way the Wise Men were moving by their questions. "Do you think a military victory can be won?" asked Clark Clifford, who had come in his dual capacity as Defense Secretary and elder statesman. "Not under present circumstances," replied Habib. "What would you do?" Clifford asked. "Stop bombing and negotiate," he answered truthfully. Ambassador Goldberg was skeptical about

General DuPuy's claim that 80,000 of the enemy had been killed during Tet. He asked DePuy what the normal ratio of killed to wounded was. "Ten to one; three to one conservatively," he answered. Goldberg asked how many VC were in the field. "Two hundred thirty thousand," answered DuPuy. Goldberg did some quick arithmetic and determined that by conservative estimates they were now all in the hospital. "Then who the hell are we fighting?" he demanded.

A few, like Douglas Dillon, were deeply affected by the briefings. "In November, we were told that it would take us a year to win," he remembered. "Now it looked like five or ten, if that. I knew the country wouldn't stand for it." Others had come to the meeting with their minds already made up. "I could sense that the country was being torn up," recalled Vance. "We had to find a way out."

The meeting broke up toward 11 P.M. The old men looked somber as they filed out, George Ball recalled. "I was delighted," remembered Clifford; the questions and answers had been even more pessimistic and gloomy than he had dared hope.

"I smelled a rat," recalled Walt Rostow. "It was a put-up job." As Rostow, who had come to the dinner as Johnson's emissary and observer, listened to the downward drift of the discussion, he sensed the demise of an institution he had long yearned to join, and now felt bitterly disappointed in. "I thought to myself," he recalled, "that what began in the spring of 1940 when Henry Stimson came to Washington ended tonight. The American Establishment is dead."

• • •

Around a green baize table in the Operations Room of the State Department, the Wise Men convened again the next morning to discuss among themselves their conclusions. For many, the doubt of the prior evening had crystallized overnight into conviction: the U.S. must begin the process of disengagement from Vietnam.

"There must have been a mistake in the invitation list," Ball thought to himself. He could hardly believe what he was hearing from a group of such heretofore stalwart hawks. Neither, perhaps, could the new converts themselves. "There was a sense of shock," recalled Ball, "of people who had not expected to say what they were saying." Not everyone had made the switch. General Maxwell Taylor was appalled and "amazed" at the defection. "The same mouths that said a few months before to the President, 'You're on the right course, but do more,' were now saying that the policy was a failure," recalled Taylor. He could think of no explanation, except that "my Council on Foreign

Relations friends were living in the cloud of *The New York Times*."

The President finally heard the Wise Men in the Cabinet Room at 11 A.M. He had spent the morning getting bucked up by the generals. JCS Chairman Wheeler and General Creighton Abrams, who was slated to succeed Westmoreland as commander in Vietnam, had sought to minimize the damage of Tet. Now, the President summoned General Wheeler into the Cabinet Room and asked him to repeat his upbeat spiel to the Wise Men.

The U.S. was "back on the offensive," Wheeler reported. True, President Thieu had said that the South Vietnamese "could not take another Tet offensive," but Westmoreland had "turned this around."

Watching the dour faces around the table, Rostow concluded that the Wise Men "weren't listening." In fact, they were listening, just not believing. When Wheeler proclaimed that "this was the worst time to negotiate," Cabot Lodge leaned over to Acheson and whispered in his ear, "Yes, because we are in worse shape militarily than we have ever been."

At lunch, Johnson dismissed everyone but the Wise Men. He wanted to meet alone with them. Though government officials—Rusk, Rostow, CIA Director Helms, Paul Nitze, Goldberg, Katzenbach, Bill Bundy—had been present at all the earlier sessions, they were not invited to this one.

There was, however, one exception to the rule: Averell Harriman. Told that he was not invited to the luncheon meeting with the President, since he was a State Department official, he simply invited himself. No place had been set for him; when he arrived, the White House stewards had to add an extra one.

Harriman did not come to speak, but rather to watch and listen. While the Wise Men were facing up to the futility of military victory that he had recognized long before, Harriman was quietly pursuing his own separate agenda—persuading Johnson to bring Hanoi to the peace table.

The day before, a headline had appeared in *The New York Times*: "Harriman Head of Johnson Committee." The former governor had assembled a group of influential New York Democrats to back the President against the McCarthy and Kennedy challenges. Though Harriman was genuinely loyal to the President, he did not have LBJ's re-election foremost in mind when he organized the committee. He was, rather, picking up an old-fashioned political IOU.

Johnson went for the bait. As Harriman sat listening to the Wise Men hold forth in the Cabinet Room, the President slipped him a note. "Averell—thanks so much for your help," it read in Johnson's handwritten scrawl, "and most especially your aid in New York."

Harriman remained silent throughout the lunch. Afterward, however, he immediately wrote a note to LBJ. "From reports I gather New York, like Vietnam, is a bit soggy," he began gruffly. Then he got to the point: ever so gently, he reminded Johnson that he stood ready to negotiate with the North Vietnamese "when you think the time is right."

•   •   •

At the lunch with the President, Mac Bundy, the youngest Wise Man, reported on the group's earlier deliberations and summarized its views. There had been a "significant shift" since the last meeting of the Wise Men in November, he told the President. Acheson had best stated the new majority view at their meeting that morning when he had remarked, "We can no longer do the job we set out to do in the time we have left, and we must take steps to disengage."

Acheson, sitting erect at the President's right hand, spoke up. By late summer, he flatly declared, the U.S. had to begin the process of withdrawal.

Acheson's voice was firm, clear, and unemotional. His language was spare and to the point. He showed none of the rhetorical flourishes, none of the passion that he had flashed on a February morning twenty-one years before, when he had taken the White House floor to plead that unless the U.S. supported Greece and Turkey, the Communist infection would spread from one country to the next, like rotten "apples in a barrel."

Johnson went around the table soliciting comments, but the dominant force was Acheson. When Abe Fortas, who remained hawkish, protested that Bundy's summary did not accurately represent the group's view, Acheson cut him off. "It represents *my* view," he said.

At one point, General Wheeler, whom Johnson had asked in to take questions, took exception to Acheson's characterization of the Pentagon as "bent on military victory." Not so, said Wheeler. He realized that a "classic military victory" was not possible. Acheson regarded him coldly. "Then what in the name of God do we have five hundred thousand troops out there for?" he inquired. "Chasing girls?"

"*Can no longer do job we set out to do,*" Johnson jotted on a note pad, underlining vigorously for emphasis. "Adjust our course. *Move to disengage.*" His grandson, Lyn Nugent, came in and curled up on his lap, as he had during the Wise Men meeting the prior November. No one, however, not even a grandson whose middle name was Lyndon, could have comforted Johnson that afternoon.

One can imagine how he felt, surrounded by the Establishment he envied and resented, with Acheson leading the way, ripping up the roots of U.S. involvement, telling him, in effect, that the era of global containment was over. "They were intelligent, experienced men," Johnson wrote in his memoirs. "I had always regarded the majority of them as very steady and balanced. If they had been so deeply influenced by the reports of the Tet offensive, what must the average citizen be thinking?"

Johnson was not ready to capitulate quite yet, however. When the meeting broke up, he grabbed a few of the stragglers and began to rant. "Who the hell brainwashed those friends of yours?" he demanded of George Ball. He stopped General Taylor. "What did those damn briefers say to you?" Johnson went so far as to demand to hear the same briefings the Wise Men had received. Carver and DuPuy dutifully repeated theirs, but Habib, the most pessimistic briefer, left town. (Rostow let him go, figuring he had done enough damage.) "Tell me what you told them!" Johnson bellowed. They did; Johnson just shook his head. "I don't know why they've drawn that conclusion."

Clifford's exhilaration after the Wise Men meeting quickly dimmed. The President seemed just as bellicose as ever. He was scheduled to give a major address on the war on March 31, but as the speech moved through several drafts, Johnson continued to insist on unyielding rhetoric. There was no mention of negotiation or de-escalation. Reading over the latest version at a drafting session on March 28, Clifford could bear it no longer. "The President cannot give that speech!" he burst out, losing his customary poise. "It would be a disaster! This speech is about war. What the President needs is a speech about peace! The first sentence reads, 'I want to talk to you about the war in Vietnam.' It should read, 'I want to talk to you about *peace* in Vietnam.'"

Clifford anticipated resistance from his hawkish opposite at State, Dean Rusk. The two Secretaries had sparred increasingly over the past month, not with raised voices but with a perceptible edginess. Yet to his surprise, Rusk offered no opposition to Clifford's moderating suggestions.

Rusk's role in these critical weeks has long been obscure, but it was essential. Privately, this self-effacing veteran of the Truman era had as much impact on the President as the Wise Men.

After more than seven years as Secretary of State, the round-faced

Georgian remained inscrutable, a mystery to even his closest associates. Unable to know him, they came to regard him as a two-dimensional figure, a cardboard cutout of his idol, General Marshall. He
seemed locked in clichés: he feared—despite all evidence to the contrary—that the Chinese were about to pour over the Vietnamese border
at any moment, as they had over the Yalu in 1950. (Asked what the
stakes were in Southeast Asia he had replied ominously, "A billion
Chinese armed with nuclear weapons.") Recalling that the U.S. had
stood fast in Korea and fought back the Nazis and Japanese in World
War II, he was stoical. He was as well a tireless worker who sacrificed
his family life to his job, though on Saturday afternoons he could
sometimes be found in his office watching old war movies. (Rusk liked
to see John Wayne take on the Japs; it seemed to remind him of a
time when the enemy was seen clearly and the whole country was
behind the war effort.)

Though an adopted member of the Establishment, Rusk continued
to regard himself as an outsider. He was suspicious of the heavy East
Coast/Wall Street tilt of the Wise Men; back in 1965, he had urged
LBJ to include more southerners, westerners, and academics in the
group. He held himself aloof, he explained to Chip Bohlen, not just
because General Marshall had, but because "I'm a dour man from
Cherokee County, Georgia—such people just don't talk very much
about the things they feel most deeply." He considered it a "compliment" that he was the only Cabinet member that President Kennedy
called by his last name. "I was never part of the Hyannis Port, West
Palm Beach environment, was never pushed into Ethel Kennedy's
swimming pool, never played touch football," he wrote Bohlen in
1973. "None of this detracted from my deep commitment to the
President himself."

Rusk preferred to operate secretively, to confide only in the President, and no one else. Thus it is not surprising that Clifford did not
know that Rusk was, in a sense, ahead of him in pushing LBJ toward
a peace initiative.

Clifford believed that his only true ally in the inner circle was a
Johnson speech writer, Harry McPherson, who had become a committed dove and was trying almost desperately to sway the President.
What Clifford did not know was that on March 25—before the Wise
Men meeting—Rusk wrote Johnson, "My own mind is running very
close to that of Harry McPherson about a possible peace move." By
the time of Clifford's impassioned appeal on the twenty-eighth, Rusk

had already gone a long way toward persuading Johnson to declare a partial halt to the bombing of North Vietnam.

In fact, Rusk had suggested a partial halt as early as March 4—and in Clifford's presence. At the time, Clifford and the other doves in State and Defense had regarded Rusk's suggestion as a cynical gambit. They believed that Rusk was trying to con the American public with a bait-and-switch, aimed at rebuilding public support by halting bombing for a few months—during Vietnam's rainy season, when it was ineffective anyway—before once again escalating the conflict.

But Rusk was not a cynic. He hated the war and badly wanted to find a way to end it. He was skeptical about bringing the North Vietnamese to the bargaining table, but he believed, as he later put it, that "you've got to try everything." He recalled some long-shot diplomatic forays that produced results, specifically Kennan's secret mission to Malik to open peace talks on the Korean War in the spring of 1951.

Johnson trusted Rusk more than anyone. The Secretary was so slow, deliberate and cautious that Johnson could count on him to give careful, thoughtful advice. He accepted Rusk's argument that it was time to give diplomacy a chance with a partial bombing halt, as LBJ reasoned in his folksy way, "Even a blind hog sometimes finds the chestnut."

Johnson, in his terrific agony, had another, far more shocking announcement than a bombing halt in mind. By now he was devoting himself entirely to the war effort; the "Bitch War" of his nightmares had consumed all else, even his political ambition. He wanted to do something dramatic, to make a gesture that would show his absolute resolve to bringing the war to an honorable end. He decided to announce that he would not run for a second term in the White House.

The decision not to run again had actually been building for some time. Over the past year, he had told Lady Bird, Rusk, Rostow, and George Christian, his press secretary, that he did not want a second term, that he feared that he would end up like Woodrow Wilson, bedridden and too sick to govern. Now he saw a chance to couple his desire to leave office with a noble cause, the conclusion of a war that threatened to wreck his Presidency and tear apart his country.

"So tonight, in the hope that this action will lead to early talks, I am taking the first step to de-escalate the conflict," Johnson told the national television audience on the evening of March 31. "We are reducing—substantially reducing—the present level of hostilities. And we are doing it unilaterally, and at once." Then he delivered his shocker: "I have concluded that I should not permit the Presidency to become involved in the partisan divisions that are developing this political year. Accordingly, I shall not seek, and I will not accept, the nomination of my party for another term as your President."

Most Americans fastened on this last sentence of his speech. One, however, was more moved by an earlier line. After making a plea to the North Vietnamese to enter negotiations, he announced, "I am designating one of our most distinguished Americans, Ambassador Averell Harriman, as my personal representative for such talks."

•   •   •

Less than a week later, Hanoi accepted LBJ's invitation to talk. On April 3, the North Vietnamese announced that they were willing to meet with U.S. representatives to discuss peace negotiations.

For Harriman, the waiting was over; his patience and doggedness in pursuit of negotiations and Lyndon Johnson had been simultaneously rewarded. No longer would his peace plans be filed away unread. As Harriman knew he would, the President had despaired of a purely military victory and turned to diplomacy. And because of his experience and wisdom, not to mention patient scheming, Harriman was to be chief diplomat.

As the veteran of dozens of tedious and often fruitless negotiations, he was not the sort to be euphoric about the mere willingness to talk, however. He knew the severity of the task ahead. For one thing, the North Vietnamese had not agreed to negotiate a settlement but rather to discuss conditions for entering settlement talks. In essence, they had only agreed to talk about talking. Secondly, as Harriman well knew, Johnson would not give up much on the battlefield to get more promises from Hanoi.

Harriman's doubts were confirmed when he received his negotiating instructions. Flying by helicopter to Camp David on April 9 (the last time he had been to the President's Maryland retreat it was called Shangri-La and FDR was his host), Harriman was discouraged by his meeting with LBJ and his advisers. His instructions, recalled his aide Dan Davidson, "were basically, 'you stay there until they surrender on our terms.'" Only Clifford backed his argument for flexibility in dealing with the North Vietnamese. "There is no doubt that Clifford's initiative saved the instructions from mutilation," Harriman wrote in a memo to files. "The Secretary of State did not make any contribution."

The emnity between Harriman and Rusk was by now deep and irreversible. "Averell simply didn't believe that a second-rater like Rusk should get the job that was more rightfully his," a colleague of both men later said. "What is worse, he was indiscreet about it." Harriman would scoff among friends that Rusk was paralyzed by the past, frozen forever in December of 1950. Inevitably, his remarks got back to Rusk. The Secretary, who believed in orderly procedure and the chain of command, was naturally reluctant to have an independent sovereignty like Harriman floating about his department, doing as he pleased. Rusk sought whenever possible to keep him under tight rein.

Harriman's loyalty was to the President. "I will obey orders," Harriman told LBJ over the telephone on April 11. "I hope so," said Johnson. "I am a soldier," Harriman re-emphasized. "I will obey orders."

To make sure, Johnson decided to appoint another negotiator to accompany Harriman to the peace talks. He chose Cyrus Vance, a man of the Establishment who also had close ties to Johnson.

The President seemed to like the fact that Vance was a West Virginian, a country boy like him. In fact, Vance was the favorite nephew of John W. Davis, a West Virginian who was for several decades the most powerful lawyer on Wall Street. Vance had gone to Yale (where he had been a member of Acheson's secret society, Scroll and Key) and on to Wall Street. He had formed ties to Johnson by working as a Senate legislative counsel in the fifties, and LBJ had made him Deputy Secretary of Defense in 1964. A bad back, his children's tuition bills, and growing private disillusionment with the war forced him to leave the Pentagon in 1967, but he had continued to serve the President as a very effective troubleshooter during the Detroit riots. He was staying at the White House during the April 1968 riots in Washington when LBJ asked him to serve as Harriman's partner at the peace talks.

"I want to condition Harriman's mind to the fact that it is *joint* with Vance," Johnson told Rusk and Clifford. The President bluntly told Harriman that, while he was senior in age and experience, Vance was his coequal as a negotiator.

It was widely assumed that Vance was Johnson's "spy," sent to keep an eye on Harriman's dovishness and report back to Johnson when the old statesman strayed from the White House hard line. But if that was to be his role, recalled Vance, Johnson never told him.

It may be that Johnson simply assumed that Vance would be a restraining influence on Harriman; Vance, after all, had been a faithful, diligent Deputy Secretary of Defense. Johnson did not realize, however, what a dove Vance had become. Though Vance was never in any way disloyal to Johnson, he shortly became not just Harriman's partner, but his ally.

Harriman also had a strong moral supporter in Acheson. "We are not as young as we once were, but we still pack a wallop," Acheson wrote Harriman. "You must tell me what Our Leader is up to. I thought for a while that you had him on course, but I gather Bunker and Westy have fed him some raw meat. I don't envy you bargaining without a *goal*. Perhaps the Viet Minh will think you're being inscrutable, a well-known Western characteristic."

To one who had devoted his career to creating and restoring order, April 1968 was a very discouraging month. Acheson was aghast at the riots after Martin Luther King was shot in early April; black Washington was in flames and machine guns were mounted outside the White House, across from Acheson's office. "It is the kind of thing one reads about in Gibbon," he told a friend. To his daughter Jane he wrote:

> I just keep flowin' along, confident that we are going to hell in a hack. ... The last weekend was one to raise faith in the American Dream, with the whole damn town burning around us, Europe in a mess, and as big a mess in Washington as we have seen since the British burned it. Both they and the blacks botched the job. I had quite a birthday letter from LBJ—an extraordinary man, a real centaur—part man, part horse's ass.

Johnson had written Acheson an effusive greeting, telling him that his conduct in the Truman years was an example to him, since Acheson had so stoically endured "the calumnies, the outrages, and yes the viciousness" heaped on public servants who waged unpopular wars. "For my generation," wrote LBJ, "you have been the perfect public servant."

To Acheson, about the last honorable man left in town was Harriman. Though he had once teased him for his political ambition, he now had nothing but admiration for Harriman's patient duty in obscure government posts for the past seven years. In an article in the May *Foreign Service* journal, he honored his old friend's integrity by writing, "Ambassador Harriman has never been afraid of losing the Washington sweepstakes, the race of advisers."

The peace talks were scheduled to begin in Paris in May (Harriman had originally favored Warsaw, preferring proximity to the Soviets to luxury). As he left Washington for his last and most difficult diplomatic assignment in three decades of service to the Presidency, Harriman jotted a note to Acheson: "I'm off to Paris tomorrow. It is almost to the day 20 years ago that I arrived in Paris with the Marshall Plan, which was undertaken so largely at your initiative."

• • •

President Johnson dispatched Harriman on a skeptical note: "I'm glad we're going to talk, but I'm not overly hopeful," he declared at a Cabinet meeting on May 6. "Some of you think we want resolution of this in an election year. I want it resolved, but not because of the election."

Nonetheless, the Harriman and Vance delegation (code name: HARVAN) arrived in Paris the next day amidst great hoopla. Harriman's plane had to circle the airport several times just so it could land "live" on the evening news. The networks all sent their anchor men to Paris to broadcast from the site of the talks; expectations ran high, unreasonably so.

In fact, Hanoi had no intention of cutting a quick deal. Though the North Vietnamese had been badly bled by Tet, and needed time to regroup and recover, they accurately perceived that Tet had been a tremendous psychological victory, that it had sapped the will of the American people. Hoping to simply outlast the U.S., Hanoi adopted a strategy of "fighting and talking," lulling the U.S. with talk while advancing on the battlefield.

The opening bids of the two sides could hardly have been farther apart. The U.S. wanted North Vietnamese troops out of the South. Hanoi insisted on a total bombing halt before they would even begin to *consider* negotiations. Formally, the Paris Peace Talks were not real negotiations at all; they were described as "Official Conversations."

Reality quickly set in among the members of the American delegation. They moved from their rooms on the fifth floor of the Crillon Hotel to cheaper quarters on the first floor, and sent for their wives to join them for the long wait. It was not a gay sojourn. Paris was racked by *Les Evénements*; leftist students and *flics* (French police) battled in the streets. Harriman, the indefatigable world traveler, caught a severe case of the flu and—for the first time anyone would remember—was bedridden. He was nonetheless determined. "I'll stay in Paris as long as necessary," he had vowed to Nick Katzenbach, before leaving Washington. (Katzenbach could not resist asking, "Averell, would you feel the same way if the talks were in Rangoon?")

Almost immediately, and without asking Washington's permission, he opened secret, informal talks with the North Vietnamese at an out-of-the-way house in a Paris suburb. At the same time, he worked his Soviet connections: before leaving Washington, he had consulted with Ambassador Dobrynin (who was such a close personal friend that he was a regular guest at Harriman birthday parties and had vacationed with Harriman in Hobe Sound), and persuaded the Soviet envoy to assign V. A. Zorin, the Soviet ambassador to France, to closely monitor the talks. Harriman was, of course, hopeful that the Soviets would not just observe but participate.

In early June came an encouraging signal from the Kremlin. Chairman Kosygin wrote President Johnson that he believed—and that he had "grounds to do so"—that a complete bombing halt by the U.S. would bring a breakthrough and produce "prospects for peace." Johnson asked for further reassurance, but he got no answer. The Kremlin suddenly fell silent about the Vietnam War.

As he waited vainly for a move or sign from the Soviets, Harriman could not help but become somewhat discouraged. Though he saw himself as a realist about the Kremlin, he had long hoped that the Soviets could be persuaded—by him at least—to take a role in settling the war. At the same time, he knew that the Soviets were hardly eager to engage themselves in Southeast Asia, or help the Americans out of their quagmire. When the Soviets sent tanks to crush the Prague Spring in August, Harriman realized that the Kremlin was too preoccupied with its own problems to help him with his.

Though some, like Cyrus Vance, sensed Harriman's disappointment with the Russians, the old Crocodile showed no emotion. "We must be patient and tough," he told Cy Sulzberger. But American politics gave him a sense of urgency. A strongly partisan Democrat, he was eager to get a deal with the North to save Vice-President Hubert Humphrey's troubled candidacy and keep Richard Nixon, whom he could not abide, out of the White House.* He was convinced that if Nixon won, the war would drag on for four more years. "Averell was very sensitive to politics," recalled Vance. "He would say, 'It would be better if I went back to the States and worked for Hubert. That's the real answer.'"

Harriman could see that Humphrey was caught, unable to break away from Johnson and run as a peace candidate. With antiwar protest mounting, Harriman could also see that the Democratic Convention

---

*Robert F. Kennedy had been assassinated in June, on the night he won the California primary. Harriman was a pallbearer at the funeral.

in August would be a melee unless the hawk and dove wings of the party were reconciled. A breakthrough in Paris was badly needed.

In July, Arthur Goldberg and George Ball, a pair of eminent doves who were acting as emissaries for Humphrey, flew to Paris and met with HARVAN. (Harriman was discreet about this exercise; he refused to allow the young Foreign Service officer who served as his aide to pick up Ball and Goldberg at the airport.) The four men discussed what to do. Harriman and Vance already had in mind a proposal. The North Vietnamese had somewhat reduced the level of fighting in the South. Was this a gesture of good faith by Hanoi? Harriman proposed to treat it as such. In return, he suggested, the U.S. should impose a total bombing halt. In effect he was suggesting the same ploy that had worked during the Cuban missile crisis: ignore the harsh rhetoric and respond to the hopeful hints; assume the enemy wants peace and help him achieve it.

The first hurdle was not Hanoi, but Lyndon Johnson. And the timing was unfortunate. While HARVAN was concocting peace initiatives in Paris, Johnson had been in Honolulu promising his unyielding support to South Vietnamese President Thieu.

William Bundy, who passed through Paris on the way home from the Honolulu conference, was asked to make sure HARVAN's idea got a fair hearing in Washington. Back home, meeting alone with the President for the only time in his life, he discussed HARVAN's cable asking for a bombing halt. Johnson was in a surly, intransigent mood, angry at what he regarded as a liberal conspiracy against him and determined to eliminate political considerations from his conduct of the war. "I want you to know I'm not going to do it," he growled at Bundy. "Don't even say anything about it at the State Department."

The peace initiative was stillborn. In Paris, Harriman grew increasingly anxious about the election. He privately gave his blessings to a speech by Hubert Humphrey publicly calling for a total bombing halt—despite the President's refusal to back such a step. He even suggested to colleagues that Humphrey should resign as Vice-President, in order to disassociate himself from Johnson and his war policy.

The Crocodile was particularly snappish that summer. At a stag dinner for Arthur Goldberg and Bill Bundy, Harriman tore into the Administration hawks who, he believed, were sabotaging the chances for peace. He was irked at Ellsworth Bunker, the U.S. ambassador to Saigon, a fellow Yaleman whom Harriman had coached on the Yale freshman crew and whom he had helped coax into government back in 1950. After harshly criticizing Bunker, he turned his invective on one of Bunker's aides, Sam Berger, who had earlier been a loyal Harriman protégé. This was too much for Bundy. "Averell, you can't talk that way about Sam Berger," he protested, angrily rising from his chair. "If you continue I'm going to leave." Vance had to pull Bundy down by his coattails.

Harriman was troubled by a deeper conflict than his battles with LBJ and an old Eli. "He felt a great tension," recalled Vance. "We were a great power, but we were stuck. We couldn't cut and run, but we couldn't win." Harriman was aware of the concept of a "decent interval" (defined by young Foreign Service officers as the time between the departure of the last U.S. soldier and the rape of the first nun), but he preferred not to dwell on it. He wanted to believe that somehow a negotiated settlement could produce a viable, independent South Vietnam.

His hatred of Nixon helped push aside his fears of a bloodbath in Vietnam after the U.S. pulled out. Increasingly in his own mind he accepted the reality of a phased U.S. withdrawal that would ultimately leave Saigon to fend for itself. He had no real illusions about the ability of Thieu and Ky to sustain their government without U.S. combat troops. "You know how strongly I feel we should have an honorable peace," he told Nick Katzenbach. "But let me tell you one thing. Vietnam is nothing compared with Richard Nixon being elected President of the United States."

At a dinner party in October, Harriman unburdened himself to Cy Sulzberger. "He says Humphrey is doomed," Sulzberger recorded in his diary. "He won't fight, and he has crummy advisers. . . . Harriman now obviously detests the President and is quite dovish himself. But he admits he was a hawk two years ago. He hates Nixon. He claims Nixon won't appoint any of the distinguished men being talked of for Cabinet posts but will assemble the peers of Agnew."

The North Vietnamese were no more eager to see Nixon elected than Harriman was. Less than a month before the election, on October 11, they decided to give Humphrey's campaign a boost: they agreed to begin formal negotiations, with the NLF represented as well as Saigon, if the U.S. ceased all bombing. Belatedly but finally, the Soviets had stepped in to firmly encourage this concession by Hanoi. Against all his instincts, but under tremendous pressure from his advisers, Johnson agreed to Hanoi's conditions. Harriman had one last chance to pull off a miracle.

Then the South Vietnamese balked. Secretly encouraged by Nixon to hold out for a better deal from a Republican Administration, Thieu refused to sit down at the same table with the NLF. He called the North Vietnamese offer a "Communist trap." For weeks the talks hung in limbo while the different sides squabbled over the shape of the table. Should it be two-sided, with the U.S. and South Vietnam on one side and the NLF and North Vietnamese on the other? Three-sided, without a seat for the NLF? Four-sided? Round?

Harriman was the most patient of men, but he could see his time finally running out. "Averell was absolutely furious with Ky, the South Vietnamese Vice-President and coordinator of the delegation here," Sulzberger recorded. "Although he says 'you can never trust the Communists on anything,' he adds that they are behaving with dignity, unlike the 'cheap Ky.'" Sulzberger drew a deep guffaw from Harriman by suggesting that they solve the shape-of-the-table issue by using different-sized chairs, with a "baby's highchair" for Ky.

Through November and December on into January, the shape-of-the-table quarrel dragged on. "Averell is fed up," Sulzberger wrote on New Year's Day. "His dislike of President Johnson, Rusk, and Ambassador Bunker becomes more evident each day. I have a feeling Averell has almost more sympathy for Hanoi than the Saigon government at this stage."

The South Vietnamese finally agreed to sit down with the Communists (the NLF as well as the North Vietnamese) on January 16—four days before Richard Nixon's inauguration.

Weary and bitter, Harriman had already returned to Washington by then. His friends tried to cheer him with a huge party held simultaneously in three large houses in Georgetown. "This is the most distinguished gathering of the next four years," declared Paul Warnke, voicing the Washington Establishment view of the Nixon Administration as unwelcome interlopers.

The Republicans would hold the White House for eight more years, not four. Averell Harriman was seventy-eight years old. It is unlikely that he realized it, for he was as ageless as he was duty-bound, but his long service through peace and war had come to an end.

CHAPTER 24

Kennan and Harriman

LEGACY

"Never in
such good company"

B y the spring of 1970, the Establishment and its outposts were under siege. At Harvard, students were shouting "Ho! Ho! Ho Chi Minh! Ho Chi Minh is going to win!" In New Haven, Yippie leader Abbie Hoffman vowed to "burn Yale down." Old Blues anxiously and not unreasonably wondered whether their alma mater would still be standing for reunions in June.

The revolution seeped into the inner sanctum. When it was learned that David Rockefeller, chairman of the Council on Foreign Relations, had offered Bill Bundy the editorship of *Foreign Affairs* just before the 1970 Harvard-Yale game, many younger members bitterly protested. Word of the appointment came just before the sensational publication of the Pentagon Papers, the Defense Department's secret internal study of U.S. involvement in Vietnam, which documented

Bundy's role in escalating the war. The epithet "War Criminal" began to be heard even within the paneled chambers of the Harold Pratt House, the Council's mansion on Park Avenue.

The popular press saw cracks in the firmament; the cover line of a September 1971 *New York* magazine proclaimed "The Death Rattle of the Eastern Establishment." A year later David Halberstam traced the tragedy of Vietnam to the hubris of the ruling elite in his best-selling *The Best and the Brightest*. (Halberstam's cutting profile of Mac Bundy, published earlier in *Harper's Magazine*, "had points which could have been soberly put," Acheson wrote a friend, "but not by a smarty pants."

Acheson, the high priest of the old order, found himself in the unfamiliar and not entirely comfortable position of dissent. Although he continued to maneuver discreetly against the war, he did not relish life in the underground, and he began to squabble with his coconspirators, who he felt were becoming too vocal. "Clifford talks too much," he complained to Harriman at an embassy party; a Washington *Post* gossip columnist overheard and promptly printed the remark. Acheson had to apologize to Clifford, though he counseled him to follow Gambetta's maxim to would-be revolutionaries: "Think of it always, speak of it never; hostile ears are listening." Acheson also thought Harriman was becoming too outspoken, especially after he testified before Congress that "a timetable should be set for withdrawal of all U.S. troops."

The old rivalry between the former schoolmates, sublimated during the machinations that surrounded the March 1968 meeting of the Wise Men, surfaced again. Acheson "recalled sourly that Averell Harriman from 1965 to 1968 had been a complete hawk on Vietnam," Cy Sulzberger recorded in his diary, "although, he said, Averell simply does not remember this at all nowadays." Harriman was just as ungracious about Acheson's role. "You gave entirely too much credit to Acheson," he told Townsend Hoopes, whose *Limits of Intervention* described Acheson's role in the March revolt. "That was the only time in the entire war that he was right."

Scruffy, rude antiwar protestors offended Acheson. He wrote a friend that he preferred to use the word "juvenile" to "young" because it is "slightly pejorative." When his granddaughter Eldie, a student at Harvard Law School, expressed dismay that police were randomly locking up protesters at the May Day demonstrations in 1971, Acheson grumbled that the loss of civil liberties was "a small price to pay (since I was not a victim) for getting troublemakers off the streets for twenty-four hours."*

Acheson was not likely to remain on the outside with the picketers for long. Henry Kissinger, Nixon's National Security Adviser, admired the old statesman, and he was determined to make use of his wisdom and experience, even if President Nixon in past incarnations had been Acheson's mortal enemy. Kissinger himself had worked with Acheson for years; the two shared a realpolitik outlook on America's role in world affairs. (Kissinger also appreciated his elder's earthy bluntness. As a graduate student writing a research paper in 1953, he had posed a ponderous question about Acheson's reaction to a particularly "muscular" dispatch from General MacArthur in Korea. The paragon of old-world diplomacy arched an eyebrow and asked, "You mean before or after I peed in my pants?")

President Nixon both "revered and despised" the old foreign policy Establishment, Kissinger recorded. But like his predecessors, he could not resist calling on its tradition of service. When he finally came to know Acheson as a person rather than an effigy, he found his directness and acerbity refreshing.

"I am being drawn back without enthusiasm into Presidential consultation," Acheson wrote a friend. Though he loathed the very idea of Nixon, Acheson was immensely loyal to the office of the Presidency. Even at the age of seventy-six, he missed proximity to power. Indeed, he was so willing to forgive the past to serve in the present that his memoirs, published during Nixon's first year in office, make no mention of Senator Nixon's prominent role in the "attack of the primitives."

Acheson was hardly immune to flattery. "Nixon and Kissinger have been most considerate of me and some of my aging colleagues like McCloy and Nitze," Acheson wrote Anthony Eden. "They ask for, consider, and sometimes even follow our advice." He added that the White House had gone so far as to install a secure telephone line to his winter vacation home in Antigua, in the Caribbean. "My hopes for RMN are growing as I see more of him," Acheson wrote Bob Lovett. "I also find Henry Kissinger's funereal Germanic manner better

---

*Acheson's scorn for the rabble barely touched George Kennan's. Though he was the most consistent dove of all on Vietnam, Kennan declared, "I have no enthusiasm for street demonstrators. They tend to oversimplify issues, to get out of hand, to be taken over by the wrong people," he told *The New York Times.* Indeed, he regretted that police had not moved in faster to quell student uprisings. He was "sickened" over "the spectacle of angry, disorderly people, milling about, screaming obscenities, shouting other people down, brawling with the police. In the face of the provocation given, I find the charges of police brutality simply ludicrous."

suited to responsibility than to mere academic pronouncement. He is, I think, a better influence than either Mac Bundy or Walt Rostow." Nonetheless, Acheson did not hesitate to let Kissinger know when he was being "particularly ponderous," Kissinger recalled. "Can I put it this way?" Kissinger asked him once about a heavy bit of prose. "Certainly you can put it that way," Acheson replied, "but not if you want to get anywhere."

"Mr. Nixon and I have become friendly, an almost unbelievable possibility," Acheson confided to a friend in December of 1969. Flabbergasted by this transformation, Alice quizzed her husband one day when he floated home from a session with the President. "Did he flatter you?" she asked sternly. Acheson sheepishly admitted that he had allowed his vanity to be massaged by the attention.

The lovefest could not last. Though Acheson initially backed Nixon's "Vietnamization" of the war, he fell out when the President widened the war and stepped up the bombing. "I fear his judgment is very bad," Acheson wrote John Cowles after Nixon ordered the incursion into Cambodia in the spring of 1970. A year later, he wrote Anthony Eden, "The President seems rattled and prone to panicky stupidities." To Cowles he fumed, "The present Administration is the most incompetent and undirected group I have seen in charge since the closing years of the Wilson Administration."

Disgusted, Acheson began simply refusing to consult with the President on Vietnam, since his advice was clearly ignored. After his experience with LBJ, he declined to be used as an icon and prop for policies he did not support.

His pride, however, did not stop him from volunteering when the cause seemed just. In the spring of 1971, during the last year of his life, he heard the call again, to stand fast and defend an institution most dear to him, the Western Alliance.

Smarting from its quiescence in Vietnam, no longer willing to be used by Presidents as a passive instrument, Congress in the early seventies had begun to assert itself in foreign policy. The failure of intervention in Vietnam had stirred old isolationist yearnings; liberals and conservatives alike wanted to pull back America's commitments. In May, Senate Majority Leader Mike Mansfield, who embodied strands of both dovishness and isolationism, proposed to cut the U.S. troop commitment to NATO in half. Congressional leaders informed the White House that the measure had enough votes to pass.

With his creation in serious jeopardy, Acheson offered his services to Henry Kissinger. When Kissinger suggested that Acheson might talk to a few of his friends, the old Secretary responded, "It seems to me what we need is a little volley firing and not just a splattering of musketry." He proceeded to recruit a battery of former Secretaries of State and Defense, old High Commissioners for Germany, NATO commanders, and chairmen of the Joint Chiefs of Staff. Lovett and McCloy signed on; McCloy even flew to Germany to rally Chancellor Willy Brandt's support. The old warriors were gathered around Nixon in the Oval Office in an intimidating montage. To Kissinger, watching from the wings, "It was the final meeting of the Old Guard."

Acheson himself was outraged that Congress should dare to interfere with the foreign policy prerogative of the Executive. "You are the President," he instructed Nixon. "You tell them to go to hell." To the press, Acheson described the Mansfield amendment as "asinine" and "sheer nonsense." (Asked why the meeting had dragged on for several hours, Acheson responded, "We are all old and we are all eloquent.")

The assault of the elder statesmen shook the Capitol: the bring-the-boys-home initiative was defeated in the Senate by 61–36. Acheson wrote John Cowles:

> ... those of us who rallied to the President's side have been subjected to a degree of vilification unequaled since the McCarthy days. It has been great fun and resulted in a most satisfying victory. I got a charming note from RMN in which he said that I could now justly claim to have been present at the creation and the resurrection.

•   •   •

It was to be the dedicated warrior's last hurrah, his final defense of duty and honor in an age that seemed increasingly dominated by expediency. "I think the world not only seems to be going to hell in a hack," he wrote a friend, "but is actually going there."

His deteriorating health added to his gloom. He had been hospitalized for a while by a minor stroke, a bad case of the flu ruined a vacation in Antigua, and a thyroid condition left him with double vision. "Every croquet wicket is two," he complained to Anthony Eden. Far worse for a man whose life had been shaped by a sense of the power of words, reading became almost impossible at times.

Acheson sensed that his era was passing, and he did not much like what he saw was taking its place. "We are now in a period where there are mediocre men everywhere," he lamented to Cy Sulzberger.

"People have opinions but no knowledge, and leaders are made in the image of the masses. Democracy is only tolerable because no other system is."

Mediocre men. Throughout his life, he could never contain his scorn for mediocrity. And so, as his life grew to a close, he began to reminisce affectionately about a man who, though sometimes maddening or puzzling, was decidedly not mediocre. That September, Acheson sat down at Harewood and wrote to the childhood friend who had been a trusted companion, and an occasional rival, over life's long course.

They had met, Acheson recalled, "66 years ago this month," as schoolboys at Groton. "In most of those years that have passed we have joined in activities that sometimes have been pretty strenuous, first of all on the water, where we rowed, and later in government, where we struggled." There had been failure as well as success, dark days as well as moments of triumph, but they had gone through them together. "The first time I was ever fired I was in company with you," Acheson noted, referring to their dismissal as Yale crew coaches. "I have been fired since and so have you. I hope we can both say, 'never in such good company.'"

It was Averell Harriman's loyalty that Acheson valued above all. Theirs had been a time when a small group of men, whatever their disagreements, felt secure in trusting the fealty of their friends. In the new era, Henry Kissinger might maneuver to replace William Rogers as Secretary of State. But for all of his ambition and desire for the job, Harriman as National Security Adviser would never have done the same to Acheson, and indeed did just the opposite when the temptation presented itself. As Acheson concluded in his letter: "Your aid and steadfastness are one hundred percent reliable."

During the month that followed, Acheson's health and his spirits seemed to perk up a bit. He was able to get around more, to visit old haunts and see old friends. He seemed mellower somehow, as if he had reconciled himself to the disagreeable world he no longer had the power to change.

On a lovely, bright day in October of 1971, Acheson puttered about his garden at Harewood, readying it for winter. His old butler, Johnson, noticed that he seemed to be looking about, peering here and there, as if he were searching for something. Along about five, as the Indian-summer dusk settled over the Maryland countryside, Acheson went into his study. An hour later, Johnson found him there peacefully resting, dead of a stroke.

• • •

"Forty years in the Foreign Service is long enough," Chip Bohlen wrote in his memoirs. In 1969, he retired from the State Department. He was sixty-four years old, "with enough energy left to make a little money."

Bohlen was as usual strapped for funds, though not overly concerned about it. He still owned his cozy house on Dumbarton Street, full of books, Oriental rugs, and hunting scenes, "decorated in the Episcopal manner," as his son, Charlie, dryly put it. A Filipino couple looked after him and Avis; after he got a job as a consultant to Morgan Bank there was even money for a summer house on Martha's Vineyard.

Curiously, the product of St. Paul's and Porcellian was in his old age a Humphrey Democrat. He had a genuine sense of social injustice, and he would even say about socialism, "maybe that is the road we ought to go down." His children's friends enjoyed visiting Dumbarton Street because, while the old diplomat was formidable, he was also curious and open to debate. He disdained unkempt student radicals, however. Watching the tumultuous 1968 Democratic Convention, he had little sympathy for the protesters. "He thought their intellectual arguments were shallow," recalled his daughter Celestine. "And his instinctive reaction was why do they have to be so dirty and sloppy and foulmouthed?"

Though Bohlen was a dove, he was impatient with his children's argument that the war was immoral. He would quote Montesquieu: "'Twas not a crime, but a mistake." He continued to believe that the U.S. had a moral obligation to oppose aggression. Nor had Bohlen softened on the Soviets. In July of 1968, listening to chic liberals at a Georgetown dinner party extol the promise of the Prague spring, Bohlen cut in, "The Soviets will crush it." A month later, the tanks rolled.

If, in his last years, Bohlen deeply pondered his achievements and disappointments, he did not share his thoughts. To his children he seemed simply content with life. Bohlen did write his memoirs, but the exercise was torturous. He was both a poor writer and not terribly reflective; a New York Times reporter, Robert Phelps, had to rewrite the book, called Witness to History. Published in 1973, the memoir was pleasant and straightforward, but lacked the great sweep and rolling thunder of Acheson's Present at the Creation, which won a Pulitzer Prize in 1970. The titles reflected their authors; if Bohlen was far less history's shaper than Acheson, he was also more humble about it. ("If you had been as arrogant as Dean Acheson," wrote a friend, "you would have called your book, 'Sage Witness to History.'")

Still very much in love with Avis after almost forty years of marriage, he looked forward to a long and happy retirement in her company, traveling and visiting old friends. He was spoiled, and a little helpless without her. Once, when visiting Celestine at Radcliffe, he lost his wallet. "You better call the credit card companies," said Celestine. "We better call your mother," said Bohlen.

Sickness cheated him. He had quit smoking in the mid-sixties when he woke up blind in one eye from an arterial spasm (he took to chewing golf tees). He regained his sight, but his gut rebelled, first from diverticulitis, then, fatally, from cancer of the colon.

The last years were hard. In growing discomfort as his innards slowly rotted, he was increasingly infirm. For his last year, he had to endure the indignity of a colostomy, a plastic bag attached to his intestines hanging outside his stomach. For Bohlen, who had borne much in life but who loved good food and gay evenings, the illness was as disappointing as it was painful. "He would rather have died quicker and cleaner," recalled his son.

At the end, Bohlen even lost his love of argument. His old chum from St. Paul's and Harvard J. Randolph Harrison recalled trying to cheer him at his bedside with friendly debate. For more than fifty years Harrison had been able to cheerfully provoke his old school and club mate by taking a staunchly conservative line. But now, in the winter of 1973, Bohlen was just too sick.

•   •   •

George Kennan had not seen his old friend for years. Intellectually, they had grown apart. "Chip had become an Achesonian," Kennan recalled. In the late 1950s the two had argued "into the wee hours" over the Suez crisis during a weekend at Kennan's farm, but the debate had been their last. "He was always sensitive to hurting my feelings," Kennan recalled. "I think we just agreed not to argue." Unable to discourse, the two lost their bond and grew distant.

In the summer of 1973, Kennan heard that Bohlen was dying. After so many years, so much shared experience, he felt he had to see him one last time. He took the train from Princeton and arrived at Dumbarton Avenue to find Bohlen, whose charm and handsomeness he had envied so, a pale, emaciated specter. Bohlen bravely greeted him, "When I get over this . . ."

"I could see from his eyes that he knew he was going to die," recalled Kennan. "We avoided talking politics, and we really had nothing to say." Kennan quietly bade his dear partner farewell and left his bedside in tears. A few months later, on January 1, 1974, Bohlen passed away in his sleep.

•   •   •

Trim and erect, Kennan was strangely ageless. His head bald and smooth as a marble bust, his eyes clear blue and slightly sad, he sat alone in his book-strewn study at the edge of a forest in Princeton, writing history. He was as ever "the guest of one's own time and not a member of its household." The 1970s, with spreading shopping malls, discos and condos, Big Macs and Burger Kings, made him long even more for the age of Tolstoy.

From his remote perch, he watched American foreign policy erratically swing between extremes, from Kissinger's realpolitik to Carter's human rights crusade to Reagan's simplistic rhetoric of confrontation. Kennan yearned for those few years right after the war when a small band of able and selfless men controlled foreign policy relatively immune from the politicians. To the quintessentialy elitist Kennan, the spectacle of Congress blundering into the delicate arena of world affairs was abhorrent; equally discouraging was the gamesmanship of modern presidential advisers, leaking madly and trumping one another in a frenzy of self-promotion. Foreign policy, Kennan believed, had become political theater. By sacrificing realism to polemics, consistency to opportunism, America had forfeited its role as world leader. "For a country to be ruled this way," declared Kennan in an interview with historian Ronald Steel in the fall of 1984, "disqualifies it from active participation in the world."

Kennan was eighty years old in 1984, moody and disenchanted as ever, yet alert and penetrating. To see Russia once again caricatured by an American President as a voracious monster was, to him, a nightmare. The vision of the Soviets as an "Evil Empire" bent on destruction of the West was, he deeply regretted, the bastard child of his X-Article, always misperceived and long since disinherited, yet as resilient as a deep-rooted weed. "A great many people in an official position in this country don't seem to know that Stalin is dead," Kennan wearily remarked on more than one occasion. In his own view, the Soviets had become defensive and ossified, barely able to maintain their own empire, much less extend it. Certainly they were not about to invade Europe. Yet to Kennan's deep foreboding, the

U.S. seemed fixated on the military threat, caught in the "vast addiction" of the arms race. It was just this sort of paranoia and militarism that drew the Great Powers into World War I, Kennan wrote in a book published that fall, *The Fateful Alliance.*

As in 1914, the superpowers were once again steering blindly into harm's way, Kennan wrote, "this time for a catastrophe from which there can be no recovery." His pessimism at times was "almost total," he confessed gloomily. "I'm afraid that the cards are lined up for a war, a dreadful and final war."

In his morbid contemplations, he fastened on the greatest source of evil, not heedless politicians or clashing nationalism, but nuclear weapons themselves.

Ever since he had written his *cri de coeur* against the "Super bomb" in the fall of 1949, he had regarded nuclear weapons as the serpent in the garden. Though the Bomb might seem to offer ultimate security from attack, the mere existence of such lethal weapons is temptation too great in a world of dangerous passions. The Bomb is "a suicidal weapon," he argued, "devoid of rational application in warfare." By making triggers hair thin and warning times ever shorter, the arms race heightens jitters and the risk of terrible impulse. "The danger lies not in the possibility that someone else might have more missiles and warheads than we do, but in the very existence of these unconscionable quantities of highly poisonous explosives."

For Kennan, nuclear weapons became a last great crusade. The old geopolitical analyst, having pondered for a half century on the forces that drive nations apart and send them to war, chose as his last field of concentration the one force that could doom mankind.

He did not engage in this grim exploration as a theoretical exercise. Rather, he abandoned the obscurity and safety of academe to become a public figure once again, a controversial spokesman for arms control. He helped launch a public campaign calling on the West to adopt a policy of "no first use." Nuclear weapons will never be eliminated, he conceded, and some are necessary for deterrence. But the West should rely primarily on conventional forces; for NATO to threaten nuclear retaliation as its response to a conventional attack is to beckon annihilation. "If there is no first use of these weapons," he argued, "there will never be any use of them."

Kennan's allies in this ultimate cause were not dreamy ban-the-bomb types but former paladins of the Cold War, principally Robert McNamara and McGeorge Bundy. His case was made not just on the pages of *Foreign Affairs* but on op-ed pages of papers across the country

and before hot television lights in crowded press conferences. It provoked an immediate and sharp rebuttal by the Secretary of State,
Alexander Haig, who warned that a policy of "no first use" was "tan-
tamount to making Europe safe for conventional aggression."

Through most of his career Kennan was a loner who seemed almost
to prefer contrary and unpopular causes. His final one, like many of
those before it, was not likely to prevail, at least in the chilly clime
of the mid-1980s. Yet it ennobled the debate and forced policy makers
to question assumptions. The "no first use" doctrine certainly cannot
be dismissed, if for no other reason than history shows that Kennan's
warnings are ignored at risk.

It may seem curious to find Kennan, who had warned early and
often against engagement in Vietnam, joining forces with Bundy and
McNamara, a pair of former officials widely blamed for fulfilling his
prophecy. But Kennan bore no grudge. "I never questioned either one
about Vietnam," he recalled. "I thought Bundy was a staff man who
had his doubts about the war, and I sympathized with him. McNamara
I respected for changing."

In fact it is typical that Kennan was able to get along with men
whose policies he had once deplored, without showing a trace of
animus or even irony. Transcending his contrariness, as well as his
utter helplessness in bureaucratic struggles, was his deep sweetness of
nature. He never lost this gracious quality, not even in his relationship
with Dean Acheson, his prickly nemesis of the postwar years.

"Even George Kennan writes praising my treatment of him," Acheson told a friend in some amazement after *Present at the Creation*
was published. "I think you dealt with me fairly and generously in
your memoirs," Kennan had written. "There is nothing there to diminish in any way the feelings of respect and affection for you with
which I left our association in the Department 20 years ago and which
even our differences over Germany and Europe failed to dim."

At the very least, one would expect relations to be cool between
Kennan and Paul Nitze, the man who displaced him as Acheson's
chief planner. They could hardly have presented a greater contrast:
Nitze the smooth insider versus Kennan the insecure outsider, Nitze
the militarist versus Kennan the diplomacist, Nitze the doer versus
Kennan the thinker. Yet the two remained through all the years the
best of friends. Indeed, the toast that most deeply touched Kennan at
his eightieth birthday was delivered by Nitze. Raising his glass to his
gentle old foe, Nitze in his soft patrician voice praised Kennan as a
"teacher and an example for close to forty years." Smiling slightly,

Nitze remarked that "George has, no doubt, often doubted the aptness of his pupil. But the warmth of his and Annelise's friendship for Phyllis and me has never faltered." Rising to respond, Kennan graciously toasted Nitze as an example to him as well. Wrestling with self-doubt even as he entered his ninth decade, Kennan ruefully second-guessed his own long absence from government by praising Nitze's willingness to serve through each new Administration, regardless of disagreements over policy. "It may be best to soldier on," sighed Kennan, "and to do what one can to make the things you believe in come out right."

●   ●   ●

Friendship, no matter how enduring, could not paper over deep splits that cracked apart the foreign policy Establishment in the 1970s.

For two decades, the Establishment had held sway by sitting squarely astride the middle ground of "informed" public opinion. But by the seventies, the center no longer held; Vietnam had shattered the post–World War II consensus. Power swung to the extremes. The right was just as noisy as ever, but the left began to shout too. The sound heard abroad by U.S. allies was dissonance.

The old Establishment was not immune to the tugging and pulling. The split that had emerged between "soft" and "hard" wings in the Democratic Advisory Council back in the fifties, when the Achesonians had faced off against the Stevensonians, became more open and hostile. Vietnam forced nearly everyone, even the old guard, to choose sides between "hawk" and "dove." In the fifties, though they differed over method, the "hard" and "soft" camps did not quarrel over the fundamental assumption that the U.S. had a dominant world role to play. But now liberals had become quasi isolationists; they argued that the U.S. was badly overextended and had to pull back, that Communism was not monolithic and that its threat had been grossly overstated.

●   ●   ●

Vietnam had pushed Averell Harriman leftwards, made him reject many of the Cold War verities that he once believed and indeed helped propagate. He was not in full retreat; he never stopped believing in an active global role for the U.S. But by the 1970s he had come to accept the limits of intervention, and he was determined as ever to reduce tensions with the Soviets by negotiations and diplomacy.

He was delighted when his partner at the Paris Peace Talks, Cyrus Vance, was made Secretary of State by Jimmy Carter. Vance had just about the right world view for Harriman, a desire to deal with the Russians, a predilection for diplomacy over force, an appreciation for nuance and subtlety in foreign affairs. He had the right personal qualities: he was honorable, decent, and discreet. He was, as well, the right sort, a product of the inner sanctums of Yale and Wall Street. Harriman, of course, would be the first to deny that such things mattered any more, and in truth he was not a snob; but he could hardly avoid feeling a bond to someone so much of his world.

When Jimmy Carter won election in 1976 by running a populist campaign against insider Washington, his chief aide, Hamilton Jordan, vowed, "If, after the inauguration, you find a Cy Vance as Secretary of State and Zbigniew Brzezinski as head of National Security, then I would say we failed. And I'd quit."

The fact that Carter hired both men—and that Jordan did not quit— was held out at the time as evidence that the Eastern Establishment was alive, well, and still indispensable. But in fact the selection of Brzezinski and Vance showed precisely the opposite. Brzezinski and Vance were only superficially similar. True, they were both members of the Trilateral Commission, David Rockefeller's elite international meeting group, and regulars at the Council on Foreign Relations. But in fact, they couldn't have been more different, and their differences perfectly embodied how much the machinery of foreign policy making had evolved from the days of Lovett and Acheson, though not necessarily for the better.

To Brzezinski, Vance represented the "once dominant WASP elite" that was in its dotage. In his memoirs, Brzezinski scorned Vance's "gentlemanly approach to the world" and found it quaint that Vance was reluctant to authorize spying on foreign embassies. "Like Secretary Henry Stimson earlier, he seemed to feel that one should not read other people's mail," Brzezinski marveled. "All in all, in temperament and timing, Vance was no longer dominant either in the world or in America."

Brzezinski himself was not of the old Establishment ("it certainly was not easy for me to relate to it") but an exemplar of the new "Professional Elite," as I. M. Destler, Leslie Gelb, and Anthony Lake describe it in *Our Own Worst Enemy: The Unmaking of American Foreign Policy*. Like Kissinger, indeed like many of the new foreign policy activists who had arisen to challenge the Establishment in the sixties, he was both an academic and foreign born. Power did not come to him by birth or place; he had to grasp for it. His expertise and force derived not from experience in business or government—

or from anything he had accomplished—but from ideas. He was a polemicist; his stock-in-trade was the trenchant op-ed page piece, the well-considered quote. Politicians did not offend him; indeed he had actively sought out and cultivated Carter when the Georgia peanut farmer was still "Jimmy Who?" When Carter formed his government in January of 1977, Brzezinski maneuvered to insure that the real insider, the President's true counsel, was not the Secretary of State but the National Security Adviser; not Vance but himself.

Harriman, with his well-honed instincts for bureaucratic intrigue, saw immediately what Brzezinski was up to. "Ave was not too fond of Zbig to begin with," recalled William Sullivan, Harriman's protégé during the Laos negotations who had risen through the State Department ranks to become ambassador to Iran, "and he grew less fond when he realized what a dangerous type he was." Harriman remembered that when *he* was National Security Adviser to Truman he had sought to protect the Secretary of State. "If I had gotten in the way of the relationship between the President and the Secretary of State," he told friends, "I would have been fired, and properly so."

Harriman was able to observe Brzezinski close hand because the National Security Adviser was living in his home. The Harrimans, whose home had become a glorified boardinghouse for visiting dignitaries and out-of-town statesmen, had graciously offered to put up Brzezinski for a few weeks in January until he could move his family down from New York. The weeks turned into months, and Harriman found his houseguest increasingly arrogant and self-serving.

Harriman was equally disturbed that Vance let himself be trumped by Brzezinski. Privately, out at his estate in Middleburg, Virginia, where the Vances often came for the weekend, Harriman urged his old negotiating partner to stand up to his White House rival. Vance listened, but at first he refused to believe that Brzezinski's motives and actions were as base as everyone kept saying. Not until the Iran hostage crisis, when Vance discovered that Brzezinski had his own secret channel of communication with Iran, and Brzezinski just flat out lied and denied it to the President, did Vance fully appreciate with whom he was dealing. When Carter ignored Vance's warnings and took Brzezinski's advice to launch the hostage rescue mission that failed so ignominiously in the Iranian desert, Vance resigned from office, defeated and discouraged.

Harriman objected to Brzezinski's ideas as well as his methods. He felt the National Security Adviser was a belligerent hard liner toward the Soviets, and he frankly blamed his ethnic origins. "He thought

Zbig was basically a Pole who had never accepted the American ethos,"
recalled Sullivan. "He believed Zbig was perfectly willing to get the
U.S. into a confrontation with Russia for the sake of Poland."

All along, Harriman had never stopped working for better relations
between the U.S. and U.S.S.R. Though no longer in government,
he continued to serve as an occasional emissary to the Kremlin for
every President from Nixon to Reagan. He visited Moscow on diplomatic missions no less than a half dozen times after his eightieth
birthday: in 1971, 1974, 1975, 1976, 1978, and 1983.

At the time of his last trip he was ninety-one years old. The phenomenal robustness that had sustained him through those endless
plane flights to remote capitals had finally begun to fade (though
doctors had to *order* him to quit skiing when he turned eighty). He
was quite deaf, his vision was blurred, and he was becoming slightly
senile. His mental toughness was unbowed, however; to younger men,
he could still be the Crocodile, snapping off their foolish answers with
a curt dismissal. He was still a Washington presence, in part because
of the exertions of his politically active wife. In 1971, a year after
Marie's death, he had married Pamela Churchill Hayward, the beautiful young woman he had fallen in love with in wartime London
thirty years before.

Like Kennan, Harriman was disconsolate when Reagan began ful-
minating against the "Evil Empire." He felt it was his duty to assure
the Soviets that not all Americans had succumbed to such foolish
hyperbole. Besides, he had never met the new Soviet leader, Yuri
Andropov. He told friends that he wanted to take his measure.

One last time, Harriman accepted his standing invitation to visit
the Soviet Union. Well rested from a night in Armand Hammer's
suite at the International Hotel, he was completely alert as he sat down
one October morning in 1983 with Andropov at the familiar long
table in the Central Committee Headquarters in Moscow. He had
been there so many times that even the Soviet interpreter, Victor
Sukhoderev, knew him. From experience with Harriman's deafness,
Sukhoderev knew how to pitch his translation of Andropov's answers
so the old diplomat could hear.

The Soviet leader was gracious. "We remember well that you stood
with us when the Germans were firing at the gates of Moscow,"
Andropov said in greeting him. "You understand how important it is
that our two countries work together for peace."

They discussed the threat of war, the risk of miscalculation, the need for arms control. They agreed that both countries had to work to maintain normal relations, whatever the politics of the moment. When the conversation was over, the aging capitalist firmly shook the old Communist's hand and, with a gruff farewell, ended his years of personal diplomacy to the enigmatic nation he had first visited eighty-four years earlier as a boy.

That winter, Harriman was rolled by a wave on the Caribbean island of Barbados and broke his right leg. It is perhaps typical that Harriman was gamboling in the surf at the age of ninety-two, but the injury was nonetheless serious. His wife worried after the accident that "Averell was just tuning out." For the first time anyone could remember, he had no interest in the news, or current affairs, or even Russia. All he cared about was getting well. He brought to that task the same single-minded intensity he brought to other causes he had cared about. "Aren't you worried about Reagan?" the doctors would ask him. "I don't give a damn!" he would growl. "When am I going to walk again?"

His leg mended; he began worrying about Reagan and the Russians once more. "What do you think about U.S.-Soviet relations?" he would demand of visitors without any prefatory small talk. The Soviets did not forget him; on the fortieth anniversary of V-E Day in 1985, amidst speeches denouncing the U.S. as a warmonger, the News Agency Tass announced that Harriman had been awarded the Order of the Patriotic War, First Degree, for "his great personal commitment to the improvement and strengthening of Soviet-American cooperation."

Death could not be put off forever, but Harriman was not one to give in easily, even to mortality. For nearly a century he had bargained with formidable adversaries, from the Rector to Soviet dictators. As he approached the end of his time, he seemed locked in a prolonged negotiation with his Maker, seeking, no doubt, an honorable peace. In July of 1986, Harriman returned to Arden, where he died at the age of ninety-four.

· · ·

For John McCloy, the last years saw a slow ebbing of his peculiar mix of public and private power. The decline had less to do with McCloy, who remained fit and alert well into his eighties, than with the world changing around him.

When he resigned as chairman of the Chase in 1960 to return to the law, he did not leave Big Oil behind. He merely went from financing the petroleum industry's Middle Eastern empire to protecting it from the Justice Department.

Shortly after McCloy became the senior partner at Milbank, Tweed (renamed Milbank, Tweed, Hadley & McCloy), he was made general counsel to all the Seven Sisters. "My job was to keep them out of jail," he bluntly put it. As usual, McCloy seamlessly blended public and private concerns. After his chilly summit with Khrushchev in 1961, Kennedy summoned McCloy to the White House to discuss with him the threat of Soviet incursions in the Middle East. McCloy took the opportunity to plead for his clients on another matter altogether. The Arab oil-producing states were restless, he told the President. They had joined together to create a bargaining agent called OPEC. The organization was weak and divided for now, but it could become a real force to extract higher prices from the oil companies. That would hurt not just oil company profits, McCloy argued, but U.S. national security, which depended on a steady supply of cheap oil. To deal with the threat of OPEC, the oil companies would need to band together themselves. And to do that, they would need assurances from the Administration that the Justice Department would not sue them for breaking the antitrust laws.

"Then and there," McCloy recalled, JFK telephoned his brother, the Attorney General. McCloy was assured that if a crisis arose, and the oil companies needed to act as one, they would get a sympathetic hearing from the Department of Justice.

McCloy made sure his lines stayed open to the Justice Department. "I made it a point to call on each succeeding attorney general," McCloy recalled, "just for the idea of keeping the thing fresh in his mind, because any moment I was afraid we would have to do something."

The Arab countries had long been resentful of Western oil companies, which dictated prices and artificially held them low. But the Arab leaders were fundamentally conservative and could be reasoned with, stroked and cajoled by persuasive Westerners like John McCloy.

Not so Muammar Qaddafi. The hotheaded young revolutionary who had seized control of Libya in the late sixties did not hesitate to unilaterally jerk up oil prices. He got away with it because several of the independent oil companies had no other supplier. Qaddafi's boldness set off a chain reaction: all through the Middle East oil-producing states suddenly became profit hungry and began raising the price of oil.

The moment McCloy had warned about had arrived. In January

of 1971, representatives of the Seven Sisters—plus nineteen other oil companies that had retained McCloy's services—met in the old statesman's corner office on the forty-sixth floor of One Chase Manhattan Plaza. Outside in the anteroom, beneath the photographs inscribed to McCloy by every President since FDR, representatives of the State and Justice Departments sat reviewing drafts of the proposed cartel.

McCloy strongly urged the oil companies, many of whom had divergent interests, to band together to defy OPEC. He was blunt: "You either hang together, or hang separately."

McCloy succeeded in both hammering out a deal among the oil companies to "hang together" in bargaining with OPEC and at persuading the Attorney General John Mitchell not to sue them. It was, as historian Alan Brinkley has written, "a virtuoso display of private and public power exercised simultaneously."

But it did not last. The Arab countries had tasted independence and profits, and they wanted more—they wanted at least part ownership ("participation") in the oil concessions on their soil. A looming global oil shortage gave them leverage.

The 1973 Arab-Israeli war wrecked any power the oil companies had over OPEC. McCloy had seen the conflict coming, and anxiously warned the Administration not to ship arms to Israel for fear of provoking the Arabs. As he had done thirty years earlier on the questions of bombing Auschwitz and internment of Japanese-Americans, McCloy placed pragmatic considerations ahead of moral ones. "I kept jumping on him [National Security Adviser Kissinger] to say that it was an imperative of statesmanship to get the Middle East settled; that the Administration must not think in terms of the next New York election," McCloy recalled. Promising his clients that he would get a letter to Nixon, McCloy wrote to White House Chief of Staff Alexander Haig in October by special messenger warning against increased aid to Israel, arguing that the Soviets and Europeans would move into the Middle East if the U.S. was cut out. "Much more than our commercial interest in the area is now at hazard," McCloy beseeched the President. "The real stakes are both our economy and our security." The White House, in the throes of Watergate, did not even answer the letter for three days, and the arms shipments were made.

The Arabs did impose an oil embargo. The price of oil quadrupled in seven months. In the U.S., lines of cars circled gas stations all over the country, and the oil companies were widely, if unfairly, accused of conspiring with the Arabs to artificially create a shortage—especially when they announced large profits at the height of the energy crisis.

After years of comfortably aligning the national interest with his clients' interests, McCloy was appalled to see the oil companies so vilified. "It seems that it is only in the United States that an almost masochistic attack on the position of its own oil companies persists," he grumbled before a congressional investigation.

Authority itself seemed besieged in the mid-seventies. The President had been driven from office, foreign bribe scandals were breaking daily, talk of slush funds, and scandal in boardrooms as well as the White House reverberated throughout Washington. Under congressional pressure, the Justice Department revoked its promise to McCloy not to sue the oil companies for antitrust violations.

McCloy himself was not tarred. He managed to float above the furor, his integrity intact. When Gulf Oil was charged with making illegal contributions to Nixon, the directors turned to McCloy to conduct a public investigation. McCloy's report, fingering the oil company's highest officials for blame, was unblinking and impartial.

Yet McCloy's well-ordered world was in tatters. In Washington, Watergate and Vietnam had given a bad name to the private exercise of power. No longer could a small group of like-minded men sit down and quietly decide for the country; now, it seemed to McCloy, TV cameras and congressional committees followed decision makers everywhere, and thus froze them.

The broader rumblings of revolution around the world left McCloy perplexed. He favored Third World development, but had little feel for the nascent forces of nationalism. He was only slightly less obvious than his friends Acheson, Kennan, and Lovett, Europeanists all. They had never shown an interest in the Third World, and they were not about to develop one. "Point Four," Truman's famous call for aid to underdeveloped nations in his 1949 inaugural address, had been the creation of Truman's political advisers, not the State Department. Indeed, when a draft was shown to Lovett and Nitze, they "were neither enthusiastic nor impressed with its utility," dryly remarked Dean Acheson. Nor, for that matter, was Acheson, who regarded Point Four as political rhetoric, not a mandate to be carried out. Kennan was so disdainful of the underdeveloped world that he invariably used quotation marks around "Third World," as if he refused to accept its legitimacy.

In later years the Establishment's old guard (with the significant exception of Harriman) usually backed foreign regimes, no matter how repressive, against local insurgents. Horrifying their liberal friends, both Acheson and Kennan had little sympathy with black Africa, speaking out in favor of the white governments in Rhodesia and South Africa.

McCloy's own cause was the Shah of Iran. The two had dealt with each other for years; McCloy's law firm represented the Pahlevi family. To him, the Shah was a moderating force in OPEC, a man who could be reasoned with. When the U.S. at first refused to give the exiled Shah permission to enter the U.S. for medical treatment in 1979, McCloy was outraged. Along with David Rockefeller, his successor at Chase, and Kissinger, McCloy vigorously lobbied the Carter Administration to let the Shah in. "John is a very prolific letter writer," dryly remarked Secretary of State Vance. "The morning mail often contained something from him about the Shah."

Though Vance insists that the Old Boy lobbying did not affect him, the fatally ill deposed emperor was allowed to enter a U.S. hospital. Angry Iranian radicals promptly took over the U.S. Embassy in Iran, demanding that the U.S. expel the Shah. For the next 444 days, they held hostage fifty-two Americans.

McCloy was stunned, baffled, and chagrined. When a scruffy band of Islamic fundamentalists waving American-made rifles and shouting, "Death to America! Death to the Great Satan!" could paralyze the Administration and shame the U.S., it was increasingly apparent to him that his own day was over.

He had served dutifully as a Wise Man to every new Administration. Kissinger, for instance, recalls that when he returned from a round of arms talks in Geneva in 1975, the first person he called for advice was McCloy. The old arms controller came right over, missing his eightieth birthday party and never even mentioning it.

Yet McCloy could feel his influence waning in Washington. President Carter was an outsider who knew little of the old foreign policy Establishment and owed it nothing. When he invited McCloy to discuss disarmament, he herded him into the East Room along with fifty other people, like so many tourists. "It was a cattle show," McCloy sighed to *Time* columnist Hugh Sidey.

The Reagan Administration was more appreciative. Reagan put McCloy on his transition team; for his ninetieth birthday, McCloy was honored in a ceremony in the Rose Garden at the White House. The President, Vice-President, Secretary of State, and chairman of the Federal Reserve were among those present. "John McCloy's selfless heart has made a difference, an enduring difference, in the lives of millions," President Reagan declared. "Compared to me, what a spring chicken you are," said McCloy to Reagan.

The next night he was feted at the Council on Foreign Relations at a black-tie dinner attended by old Wall Street barons and various pillars of the Western Alliance, including former West German Chancellor Helmut Schmidt. David Rockefeller pronounced McCloy "the first Citizen of the Council on Foreign Relations," and presented him with a plaque to hang under his portrait—already prominently displayed on the council's dark paneled walls of the second-floor meeting room—that read: "Statesman, Patriot, Friend."

In an evening of encomiums, the praise at once most laudatory and humble came from Henry Kissinger: "John McCloy, I believe, heard the footsteps of God as he went through history," said Kissinger, quoting Bismarck, "and those of us who were not humble enough or whose ears were not sharp enough had the privilege of knowing that if we followed in his footsteps we were in the path of doing God's work."

McCloy listened, slightly embarrassed, his face downward, head slightly cocked, eyes glancing upward like a young boy anxious to please. His humility was characteristically sincere. "I know that many of the things said tonight were exaggerated," he said, "but they made me feel warm. My record has its pluses and minuses. I only hope that it has been credible, that people can say of me: he did his damnedest, the angels can do no more."

• • •

As he approached his tenth decade, McCloy, for years a most private man, began to compile his memoirs. He went about it in a characteristically informal way, dropping in on old friends and chuckling over familiar anecdotes while a tape recorder ran.

Inevitably, he found himself sitting with Bob Lovett out at Pleasance, Lovett's small estate in Locust Valley, swapping tales and reliving their days as the "Heavenly Twins" in Colonel Stimson's War Department. Lovett had missed McCloy's ninetieth birthday party. "My doctor won't even let me out on parole," he apologized to his old friend. He went on that "in the past sixty years of our friendship, one very special time stands out for me—our service together under Colonel Stimson in Washington. Strangely enough, that very unhappy period in the world stands out as one of the most exciting and happiest of my life." Now, as the two friends rambled on contentedly for almost six hours on a summer's day in 1984, they amused each other with various moments high and low, like Stimson's inability to work his squawk box and the time they conspired to spike Henry Morgenthau's plan to turn postwar Germany into a rural pasture. The conversation was light; neither man was the sort to go in for profound utterances about their lasting contributions to Western society. Yet there was running through the conversation an undercurrent of discouragement, sadness almost, about the way foreign affairs had been conducted in more modern times. Though neither man would ever be caught boasting unduly about his own achievements, when they measured the men who came after, they could not help but find most of them wanting. "I like to believe," McCloy wrote Lovett afterward, "that we had no axes to grind except to serve the country as well as we could."

Shy Bob Lovett, the most discreet and self-effacing of the Wise Men, had vanished from the public stage altogether by the 1970s. His "glass insides" were mostly shattered; part of his stomach and various internal organs had been removed; he was stricken by heart attacks and cancer both. Yet, like McCloy and Harriman and Kennan, he was indomitable, still going into his office on Wall Street at the age of eighty-nine.

His mind stayed lucid long after his battered frame had worn out. Greeting a pair of visitors whose total years fell well short of his, he put them at ease with the same grace and gentle charm that had melted congressional committee chairmen in the 1940s. After offering tea from a silver service, he sat back, rather uncomfortably, on an overstuffed chintz couch. (Occasionally, he would stagger to his feet and limp around on a walker; his buttocks, he matter-of-factly explained, had been replaced by steel plates, and he was unable to sit for long.) On the walls hung cheerful landscape paintings, including one by Alice Acheson. Behind him, through French doors, Adèle's garden flourished magnificently in the spring sunlight (he claimed not to be impressed with his dear wife's labors, insisting in his quirky way that he preferred darkened movie theaters).

He did not conceal his scorn for the current state of affairs. "I have a gut feeling that recent Secretaries of State are uncompromisingly mediocre," he allowed. In his day, Secretaries "were mostly damn good lawyers." Cy Vance, he added ruefully, was "too much of a lawyer—too cautious and compromising." He was displeased to see Congress assert itself in foreign affairs. "We now have 535 Secretaries of State," he said. "Everyone sounds out." Brzezinski, whom he referred to sardonically as "Zbiggy," drew his deepest scorn. "We shouldn't have a National Security Adviser like that who's not really an American," he protested, echoing Harriman's blunt nativism. "I can't imagine anyone negotiating with the Russians with his loathing and suspicion."

As Lovett passed his ninetieth birthday, he slowly faded and withered. He shrank to 89 pounds and complained with his undimmed humor that "my bones click." In January of 1986, Adèle, his companion of nearly seventy years, passed away. Each morning for the next three months, Lovett rose, painstakingly dressed himself in suit and necktie, and graciously answered the nearly three hundred letters of condolence that poured in. A few days after he had written his last remembrance of Adèle, he readied himself to join her.

On May 7, 1986, a half century after he first protested that he was not physically up to the rigors of government service, Robert Lovett died. In the bright light of a spring day, he was laid to rest in a laurel grove not far from his home, beside his mother, father, and wife. An editorial in the Washington *Post* recalled his service to the nation: "There is much by which to remember him and the people with whom he worked in those crucial years, but the greatest of their memorials is the long and durable peace among the countries that fought in the two world wars."

· · ·

Lovett's disenchantment with the new "Professional Elite" that supplanted his own Establishment could be dismissed as the maunderings of an elderly man whose time has passed. For years, after all, it was Lovett's Establishment that was blamed by revisionist historians for the Cold War, the arms race, Vietnam, and whatever else was dangerous and wrong about the postwar world. But as scholars and historians begin to examine the new foreign policy elite—polemical, leaky, self-interested, faction-ridden—they have begun to feel quite nostalgic about the old one.

The pendulum has swung partway back; the policies of Acheson and Lovett may have been flawed, but they were at least consistent; the men who made them may have been narrow-sighted, but they were good deal more selfless and disciplined than their modern counterparts. "There was a foreign policy consensus back then, and its disintegration during Vietnam is one of the great disasters of our history," states Kissinger. "You need an Establishment. Society needs it. You can't have all these constant assaults on national policy so that every time you change Presidents you end up changing direction."

By the mid-1980s, the tradition of a nonpartisan foreign policy elite, carrying on steadfastly through political whim and turmoil, had nearly vanished. The long line that began in Teddy Roosevelt's day at the turn of the century, that flourished in the postwar era and foundered so tragically during the Vietnam conflict, had very nearly come to an end. It had thrived for more than half a century, through Elihu Root and Colonel Stimson, through Acheson and Harriman, Lovett and McCloy, Bohlen and Kennan, and on down to the ill-starred brothers Bundy. But in the cynical seventies, its fading remnants, honorable men like Cyrus Vance, had been overwhelmed by a raw new order.

There was in 1985 but one true survivor, a single legacy from a lost age. Paul Nitze, Dean Acheson's brilliant protégé, never realized his ambition to become a Secretary of State or of Defense, perhaps because of a steely personality some found too reminiscent of his mentor's. Yet Nitze stayed on in public service through the eighties, pursuing power without at the same time sacrificing his integrity.

As an adviser and negotiator in the arcane but essential realm of arms control, Nitze became a master bureaucratic player, but so sports-manlike (or at least subtle) that he seemed a curious anachronism to younger, more brutally cutthroat colleagues. Like Kennan, he hardly seemed to age. Perpetually tan, his white hair thick and wavy, he was in astonishing physical condition. At one luncheon party out at his Maryland farm, he startled his guests by dropping to the floor and in his sixth decade, huffing out a few one-armed push-ups.

Throughout most of his career, Nitze has pushed the U.S. to build more and bigger defenses against the Soviets. Yet he remained willing to cut a deal with the Kremlin if it would truly enhance nuclear stability. Nitze's pragmatism has puzzled ideologues on both sides. Doves such as Jimmy Carter's arms control adviser, Paul Warnke, scorned him as a hawk, while Richard Perle, Reagan's hawkish As-sistant Secretary of Defense for International Security Policy, dismissed him as "an inveterate problem solver." Perle used the term pejoratively, to mean someone who solved problems for solution's sake, even if the problem was better left unsolved. But the description accurately cap-tures Nitze: he is an actor in the Achesonian tradition; he solves problems, regardless of political consequences.

Rarely was the triumph of ideology over pragmatism, of political posturing over serious statesmanship, so vividly demonstrated as during the weeks preceding the summit meeting between Reagan and Soviet leader Mikhail Gorbachev in November of 1985. While Reagan's aides squabbled with each other, leaking documents and nearly paralyzing White House decision making, Nitze quietly kept searching for a formula that the Soviets and Ronald Reagan could accept. Against the backdrop of incessant propagandizing and infighting, Nitze's self-less pursuit of real diplomacy seemed noble, if almost forlorn.

•   •   •

It is easy, of course, to put too much of a rosy glow on the postwar heyday of the old foreign policy Establishment. It was not always the "Periclean age" that McCloy imagined it to be. The bipartisan consensus collapsed over China and Korea, with unfortunate long-term effects on U.S. foreign policy. Acheson's battles with Congress were epic and destructive. To win congressional support, Truman's men consistently oversimplified and overstated the truth, and in so doing made anti-Communism dangerously rigid and U.S. commitments overly sweeping. With their penchant for action, Acheson and his cohorts sometimes failed to think first; their one visionary, George Kennan, was ignored after he came to be perceived as too soft and indecisive.

It can also be said, though perhaps with less justification, that they bore part of the responsibility for creating a world divided between East and West, overarmed and perpetually hovering at the brink. In theory, at least, the Grand Alliance of America, Britain, and the Soviet Union that won World War II might have held together to build an era of peaceful coexistence rather than Cold War. As tough and pragmatic men, Acheson, Harriman, and their cohorts were among the first to perceive—correctly—that Stalin was anything but a trustworthy ally. Even so, they would have been quite taken aback if they had realized in 1945 that for the next forty years—and perhaps for decades to come—the world would lurch from one crisis to another, driven on by a hair-trigger nuclear arms race. By overselling their cause and becoming fixated by some of their own rhetoric, they were doomed to watch as men less comfortable with subtleties and nuances shattered their vision of a stern yet stable modus vivendi between the U.S. and U.S.S.R.

All in all, it can be argued that by failing to anticipate the consequences of their words and actions, the men of the Establishment sowed the seeds of both the Vietnam tragedy and, ultimately, their own undoing.

Nonetheless, their victories were great. They did quite literally restore order from chaos, and, as Kissinger put it, "save the possibilities of freedom." They forced a reticent nation to face up to its global obligation, to act as magnanimous conqueror and rebuild friend and foe alike after World War II. They created an alliance that has securely preserved the West from aggression for onward of forty years. Compared to all earlier empires, the Pax Americana was extraordinarily generous and idealistic, indeed, sometimes overly so.

• • •

The leading role played by the U.S. after World War II was not inevitable. Had Congress dictated events, the U.S. might have turned inward to pursue isolationist normalcy and, in Harriman's phrase, "go to the movies and drink Cokes." In the wild mood swings between indifference to the world and anti-Communist paranoia that were to buffet America in the postwar years, the making of foreign policy required sure and steady hands.

It is difficult to overstate the enormity of the task that faced the small group of men who set out to salvage Europe and bond the West against the Soviet threat that did, in fact, emerge from the rubble of World War II. Indeed, from the perspective of four decades, the challenge seems so daunting that one wonders: Where did such discreet and anonymous men find such power and will?

The men most responsible for America's world role are, forty years later, half hidden in history's shadows. Even their collective identity is in eclipse. They were by and large private men, uncomfortable with celebrity and rarely in search of it. "There was a sense of selflessness, of not playing to the galleries," says Bill Bundy. They relished power, to be sure—Acheson once described his leaving office as akin to the end of a love affair. Yet they did not crave power merely to possess it.

Curiously, the small group of amateurs who revolved in and out of the State Department in the 1940s managed to get far more accomplished than the legions of full-time professionals who now inhabit the downtown think tanks and office warrens of Foggy Bottom, Capitol Hill, and the West Wing. Perhaps that is because the older generation was primarily concerned with serving their President and country, while the newer seems inordinately preoccupied with serving themselves. "My generation doesn't produce people in the selfless tradition of a McCloy," frankly admits Kissinger. "We're too nervous and ambitious." McCloy is almost bitter about the unwillingness of his successors on Wall Street to serve their country. Asked to name the next generation of lawyers and bankers wise in international affairs who might be called on to come to Washington, McCloy did not even pause to think. "You won't find one," he said. "Those lawyers don't exist anymore. They're all too busy making money."

McCloy's generation, it is true, did not have to worry much about material concerns. In an age of upper-class privilege, being "strapped" meant having to let go of the maid, or scale down a daughter's debutante ball. To be sure, all but Harriman and Lovett fretted from time to time about their finances, but a glimpse at the life-style of the poorest of them evokes little sympathy: George Kennan, after all, could afford a country house, albeit a ramshackle one, and to send his children to private schools (his son, inevitably, went to Groton).

The truth is that these men were not bound by mortal coils. They did not have to worry too much about the daily chore of child care, or about their wives' careers, or about paying the mortgage. They were relatively free to pursue what they really cared about: service to the country. In contrast to the careerists who now populate the official bureaucracy, or the grasping opportunists who value a sub-Cabinet post primarily as a springboard to a lucrative job with a government contractor, the amateurs of the old postwar Establishment actually seemed to enjoy their work. Public service was for them a demanding mistress, but a passionate one. Indeed, it seems to have been a sustaining life-force. In 1986, the year Harriman and Lovett died in their nineties, Kennan turned eighty-two and McCloy ninety-one.

These men owed no one. Free of political patrons, they served only the President. Even then, their loyalty was often more to the office than the man. They could afford the frankness born of intimacy; government in their time was virtually a club.

They did not need to grope for a sense of values. Though they mocked the Rector's pieties, they nonetheless lived by his ethics. Virtues that now seem almost quaint, such as placing loyalty over ambition, were to them commandments.

The leaders of the old Establishment were self-confident enough to be selfless. Not always personally secure—Kennan, certainly, was exceedingly fragile—but self-assured in a broader sense. Products of institutions that preached service to country, they came of age at a time when it was possible to believe sincerely that America had a duty to serve the world. They came to power during a time "when Washington was at its best," says George Ball, "and absorbed that yeasty atmosphere. It was an era when we weren't taking a parsimonious view, worrying about balancing the budget, but about how the hell we were going to save the world."

Acheson and Harriman, Lovett and McCloy, Bohlen and Kennan: they saw themselves, throughout their lives, not as public figures but as public servants. They rarely had to wonder about their place in society; they did not have to read the newspapers to know where they stood. Freed from the distraction of self, they were strangely liberated and empowered. They could bring their extraordinary energy, tempered by long exposure to the wider world, to the immense postwar task of rebuilding and making secure the shattered West.

There are, no doubt, diplomats and officials these days who are as brilliant as Acheson, as dogged as Harriman or McCloy, and as competent as Bohlen. There may even be some as prescient as Kennan and as honorable as Lovett. But there certainly does not now exist, and may never again, a breed of statesmen with the same synergism, the talent to work together in a way that transcends their contribution as individuals. Their triumphs and failures may be surpassed, but as a dying Acheson said to Harriman, "never in such good company."

For better or worse, they were positioned by the chance of history to have consequence far beyond their individual identities. Secure in their common outlook, empowered by the bonds of trust, they met the challenge of a demanding new age. In their sense of duty and shared wisdom, they found the force to shape the world.

ACKNOWLEDGMENTS

Our first debt is to our subjects. John McCloy, Robert Lovett, George Kennan, and Averell Harriman all graciously agreed to talk to us, often for many hours on end, about their lives and times. They also gave us wide access to their personal papers, scrapbooks, letters, and diaries. None of them asked for any measure of editorial control or even the right to see the manuscript before publication.

Their families were no less helpful, providing us with a rich store of recollections, letters, and photographs. Our thanks in particular to Pamela Harriman and to her husband's former assistant, Pie Friendly, for opening Harriman's personal files to us. Kathleen Harriman Mortimer provided us with family photographs as well as her recollections of the time she spent with her father in Moscow in the 1940s. Grace Kennan Warnecke contributed insight about her father and helped us sort through a lifetime of photographs. Her sister, Joan Kennan Pozen, allowed us access to her large collection of the letters her father wrote home as a young man and to the research and interviews she did on his early life. John McCloy II was similarly helpful in providing memories and photographs of his father. The late Adèle

Lovett was a charming hostess and raconteur; her thirty volumes of scrapbooks were an invaluable source of pictures and mementos. Alice (Mrs. Dean) Acheson shared with us vivid recollections of her late husband, her daily appointment calendars stretching back fifty years, and her family photographs. Two of Acheson's children, David Acheson and Mary (Mrs. William) Bundy, were especially kind with favors that ranged from giving us permission to see Dean Acheson's records as a Groton schoolboy to including us in a Christmas party for several generations of the Acheson family. William Bundy was a wise commentator on two generations of the old foreign policy Establishment—his father-in-law's and his own; he not only frankly and openly discussed the hard years of the Vietnam War with us but provided his unpublished memoir of the period. Chip Bohlen's children—Avis, Charles Jr., and Celestine—all took time to recall their father with affection and insight.

We are grateful as well to two men who play important supporting roles in our book, Paul Nitze and Clark Clifford. Both spent many hours offering insights into their own thinking as well as penetrating observations on the words and deeds of our principal subjects. Our thanks also go to Michael Forrestal, who taught us both about his father, James Forrestal, and about his surrogate father, Averell Harriman. In all, we owe a debt to nearly 100 people, listed in the bibliography and source notes, who shared with us their recollections, and who in many cases sat down with us on repeated occasions to relive their days in the company of the Wise Men.

The manuscript was carefully read, and in many instances corrected and improved, by Stephen Smith and Strobe Talbott. Our *Time* magazine colleagues who have worked with Smith and Talbott can attest to their extraordinary skill and judgment. Professor Bruce Kuniholm of Duke brought a serious scholar's scrutiny to our work, and Dan Davidson, who served as Averell Harriman's aide during the years that make up the climax of this book, gave us useful comments and corrections on the final chapters.

We owe special thanks to Ray Cave and Jason McManus, who as *Time's* managing editors allowed us to lead a double life as journalists and historians. *Time* is known as a benevolent employer; the fact that we could write this book while holding very busy jobs there is evidence that the reputation is well deserved. We also benefited greatly from the stimulation provided by many of our talented colleagues at the magazine who listened to our ideas and helped us refine them. Judith

Shapiro, the administrator of *Time*'s Nation section, was an invaluable help to us on occasions too numerous to recall.

A long list of librarians and archivists deserve our immense gratitude. We particularly want to thank the staffs of the Harry Truman Library (especially Dennis Bilger); the Lyndon Johnson Library (especially David Humphrey); the John Kennedy Library; the Seeley Mudd Library at Princeton; the Sterling Library at Yale; the Columbia Oral History Project; the Duke University Library; the New York Historical Society; the Council on Foreign Relations; the Library of Congress and the National Archives. Michael Tronick and Douglas Brown were very helpful at Groton, as were Julian McKee and Charles H. Clark at St. Paul's. Andrea Giles and Professor Ernest May of Harvard, who have been working with John McCloy on his own memoirs, generously aided us, as did the authors of a forthcoming biography of McCloy, Kai Bird and Max Holland. We are very grateful as well to Tom Schwartz for making available his Ph.D. thesis on McCloy's tour as German High Commissioner, and to Professor Charles Maier of Harvard for providing us with a valuable oral history of Governor Harriman.

At Simon and Schuster we received copious editing and warm encouragement from Alice Mayhew, who helped shape this project from the very start. She is the best in the business. Ann Godoff, Pat Miller, and Henry Ferris also provided expert support and thoughtful ideas. Our agent, Amanda Urban, did right by us, and then some, both as a friend and as a colleague.

Above all, we are grateful to our own families. Our parents, Irwin Isaacson and Evan and Anne Thomas, carefully read the manuscript and offered numerous useful suggestions, but these were mere fillips to decades of love, understanding, and tuition payments. We deeply regret that Betsy Isaacson, who encouraged this project with her unfailing cheer and wise counsel, did not live to see the final product. Louisa and Mary Thomas provided their father with just the right mixture of distraction and quiet. Our wives, Cathy and Oscie, put up with three years of their husbands' distracted mumblings to each other about the Cold War; through it all, they showed bemused patience and offered unflappable support.

NOTES

A Word About the Notes

Most of the notes below refer to passages ranging from one to five paragraphs in length or to a general theme that is developed in a particular section. Because we attempted to corroborate our information from as many sources as possible—and usually obtained similar or complementary information from a variety of interviews and sources—we have organized the notes in a way that presents all of the material that was used for each event, description, or piece of analysis.

By lumping together sources in this way, we hope to provide a more accurate description of how we triangulated information and derived our account of what occurred. For important quotations and facts that come from one specific source, we have tried to make clear either in the text or in the notes the precise citation for that piece of information.

Occasionally, of course, there were contradictions between the way different sources recounted an event. These conflicts are described either in the notes or the text.

All direct quotations come from memoirs, journals, primary source accounts, or notes made at the time. When people we interviewed recalled past conversations, these are used in quotes only if the person seemed confident of remembering the language that was used at the time.

Six Friends and the World They Made

ESTABLISHMENT STUDIES: Rovere, "Notes on the Establishment in America," 489–495 (reprinted in Rovere, *The American Establishment and Other Reports, Opinions, and Speculations,* 3–21); Hodgson, "The Establishment" (revised version in Hodgson, *America in Our Time,* 111–133); Halberstam, *The Best and the Brightest,* 4–9; Fritchey, "The Establishment," 46; Schlesinger, *A Thousand*

Days, 128; Lukas, "The Council on Foreign Relations," 34; Brzezinski, *Power and Principle,* 36–44; authors' interviews with Henry Kissinger, Clark Clifford, McGeorge Bundy, William Bundy, Paul Nitze, John McCloy, Robert Lovett, Arthur Schlesinger, Jr.

LEGACY OF THE POSTWAR ESTABLISHMENT: Destler, Gelb, and Lake, *Our Own Worst Enemy,* 91–126; Kissinger, *The White House Years,* 20–22, 59–60, 135, 257; Steel, "Acheson at the Creation," 206–216; Gaddis, "The Emerging Post-Revisionist Synthesis on the Origins of the Cold War," 171–183; Ignatius, "The Old Pro"; Kaplan, "The Eclipse of 'The Better Sort,'" 102–112; Auchincloss, *Honorable Men,* 240; Luce, "The American Century."

Chapter 1
World of Their Own

RELATIONSHIP OF HARRIMAN AND ACHESON AT GROTON: Harriman records in Groton School Archives, used with permission of Harriman; Acheson records in Groton School Archives, used with permission of David Acheson; authors' interviews with Averell Harriman, Alice Stanley Acheson; Groton yearbooks, 1904–1907; *Time,* "The Man from Middletown," 20–23.

ACHESON RECALLS HIS FRIENDSHIP WITH HARRIMAN: Letter from Acheson to Harriman, Sept. 15, 1971, Dean Acheson personal papers, Sterling Library, Yale University.

E. H. HARRIMAN'S CAREER: George Kennan [cousin of GFK], *E. H. Harriman*; Kouwenhoven, *Partners in Banking,* 155–158; Harriman folder in the partners' files of Brown Brothers Harriman & Co. papers in the New York Historical Society; Roland Harriman, *I Reminisce,* 10–19; Harriman and Abel, *Special Envoy,* 36–39; "Edward Henry Harriman," an unpublished memoir by Otto Kahn, in Harriman personal papers; Forbes, "New Business Star: Harriman II," *Forbes,* 45; Kahn, "Profiles: Plenipotentiary."

E. H. HARRIMAN'S BATTLES WITH ROOSEVELT: George Kennan, *E. H. Harriman,* Vol. II, 174–219, 242–261, 306–310; Harriman and Abel, *Special Envoy,* 43–45; Swaine, *The Cravath Firm,* Vol. II, 21–28; Phillips, *Felix Frankfurter Reminisces,* 46–49.

AVERELL HARRIMAN YOUTH AND PERSONALITY: Authors' interviews with Robert Lovett, Kathleen Harriman Mortimer, and family friends; Robert Lovett interview with Mark Chadwin, in Harriman private papers; Roland Harriman, *I Reminisce,* passim; Bland dissertation, "W. Averell Harriman: Businessman and Diplomat, 1891–1945," 1–28; Forbes, "New Business Star: Harriman II"; Murphy, "W. Averell Harriman," 57; Barcella, "The American Who Knows Stalin Best," 46.

E. H. HARRIMAN'S RELATIONS WITH AVERELL: Authors' interviews with Robert Lovett; Loving, "W. Averell Harriman Remembers Life with Father," 197–216; letters in Harriman private papers.

DESCRIPTION OF MARY HARRIMAN (SISTER OF WAH): Roland Harriman, *I Reminisce*, passim; Campbell, *Mary Williamson Harriman*; authors' interviews with Kathleen Harriman Mortimer; *The New York Times*, "Junior League Here Will Mark 60th Anniversary."

DESCRIPTION OF MARY HARRIMAN (MOTHER): Campbell, *Mary Williamson Harriman*; Kouwenhoven, *Partners in Banking*, 155; authors' interviews with Robert Lovett; Robert Lovett interview with Mark Chadwin, in Harriman private papers.

ARDEN HOMESTEAD: Roland Harriman, *I Reminisce*, 253–280; Kahn, "Profiles: Plenipotentiary"; Murphy, "W. Averell Harriman," 57; Harriman private papers; authors' interviews with Kathleen Harriman Mortimer and Robert Lovett; George Kennan, *E. H. Harriman*, Vol. II, 30–41.

HARRIMAN FAMILY TRIPS: Harriman and Abel, *Special Envoy*, 39–41; Roland Harriman, *I Reminisce*, 3, 6; Kahn, "Profiles: Plenipotentiary"; "Edward Henry Harriman," an unpublished memoir by John Muir, in Harriman private papers; George Kennan, *E. H. Harriman*, Vol. I, 185–212, Vol. II, 1–29; Kouwenhoven, *Partners in Banking*, 156; Harriman folder in the partners' files of Brown Brothers Harriman & Co. papers in the New York Historical Society; "The Harriman Alaska Expedition," C. Hart Merrimen, ed., in Harriman personal papers.

E. H. HARRIMAN CABLES PEABODY: Harriman and Abel, *Special Envoy*, 41; authors' interviews with Averell Harriman.

DESCRIPTIONS OF GROTON: Authors' interviews with alumni; Ashburn, *Fifty Years On*; Ashburn, *Peabody of Groton*; Nichols, *Forty Years More*; *Views from the Circle*; Canfield, *Up and Down and Around*; Biddle, "As I Remember Groton School."

HARRIMAN AT GROTON: Authors' interviews with Averell Harriman; Harriman records and letters in the Groton School Archives; Harriman letters to his father, in Harriman personal papers; Harriman and Abel, *Special Envoy*, 42–43; Roland Harriman, *I Reminisce*, 7–17; Bland dissertation, "W. Averell Harriman: Businessman and Diplomat, 1891–1945," 9–11.

EDWARD ACHESON'S DECISION TO SEND SON TO GROTON: Acheson, *Morning and Noon*, 22; Hamburger, "Profiles: Mr. Secretary," part II, 40.

ACHESON CHILDHOOD: Authors' interviews with Alice Stanley Acheson, David Acheson, Mary Acheson Bundy, personal friends on background; Acheson, *Morning and Noon*, 1–24; McLellan, *Dean Acheson: The State Department Years*, 1–14; Acheson, "Radiant Morn," Commencement Speech by Dean Acheson, Wesleyan University, June 1948; Baldwin, "Reminiscences of Middletown"; *Time*, "The Man from Middletown"; Hamburger, "Profiles: Mr. Secretary"; *Fortune*, "Secretary Acheson"; Smith, *American Secretaries of State and Their Diplomacy: Dean Acheson*, 1–4.

ACHESON AT GROTON: Acheson records in Groton School Archives; authors' interview with Alice Stanley Acheson; Acheson, *Morning and Noon*, 24; DGA, "The Snob in America," 262–265; Groton yearbooks and records; Hamburger, "Profiles: Mr. Secretary," Nov. 19, 1941.

ACHESON'S RAILWAY WORK: Acheson, *Morning and Noon*, 25–39.

ST. PAUL'S SCHOOL: Heckscher, *St. Paul's: The Life of a New England School*; Weil, *A Pretty Good Club*, 15–20; Stearns, *The Education of the Modern Boy*, 110–112.

BOHLEN CHILDHOOD: Authors' interviews with Bohlen's children, J. Randolph Harrison, Cecil Lyon, Paul Nitze, Eustis family members in New Orleans; Bohlen, *Witness to History*, 4; Wilmerding, "Charles Eustis Bohlen: Portrait of a Diplomat," unpublished term paper for Groton School, courtesy of Wilmerding; Heckscher, *St. Paul's*.

BOHLEN AT ST. PAUL'S: Authors' interviews with J. Randolph Harrison, Cecil Lyon, Bohlen's children, Paul Nitze; the *St. Paul's Record*; Bohlen files in St. Paul's archives, used with Bohlen family permission.

LOVETT AND HARRIMAN IN IDAHO: Robert Lovett interview with Mark Chadwin, in Harriman private papers; authors' interviews with Robert Lovett; Roland Harriman, *I Reminisce*, 169.

MEETING OF E. H. HARRIMAN AND R. S. LOVETT: Roland Harriman introduction of Robert Lovett at the Newcomen Society in 1949, Lovett folder in the partners' files of Brown Brothers Harriman & Co. papers in the New-York Historical Society; Kouwenhoven, *Partners in Banking*, 16–17; Roland Harriman, *I Reminisce*, 19–20; authors' interviews with Robert Lovett.

R. S. LOVETT/E. H. HARRIMAN RELATIONSHIP: George Kennan, *E. H. Harriman*, Vol. II, 318–320, 372–375; Kouwenhoven, *Partners in Banking*, 158; Harriman folder in the partners' files of Brown Brothers Harriman & Co. papers in the New York Historical Society; Robert Lovett interview with Mark Chadwin, in Harriman private papers; authors' interviews with Robert Lovett.

LOVETT FAMILY HISTORY: Fanton dissertation, "Robert A. Lovett: The War Years," 2–3; Margaret Case Harriman and John Bainbridge, "Profiles: The Thirteenth Labor of Hercules"; Kouvwenhoven, *Partners in Banking*, 158; authors' interviews with Robert Lovett.

LOVETT CHILDHOOD: Fanton dissertation, "Robert Lovett, The War Years," 2–4; Robert Lovett interview with Mark Chadwin, in Harriman private papers; authors' interviews with Robert Lovett; Margaret Case Harriman and John Bainbridge, "Profiles: The Thirteenth Labor of Hercules"; *The Dial* (Hill School yearbook), 1914.

LOVETT AT THE HILL SCHOOL: Authors' interviews with Robert Lovett, Larry Brownell (School Alumni Office); Fanton dissertation, "Robert A. Lovett: The War Years," 5; *The Dial* (Hill School yearbook), 1914; Chancellor, *The History of The Hill School*.

Chapter 2
Tap Days

McCLOY CHILDHOOD: Authors' interviews with John McCloy, John J. McCloy II (son), Benjamin Buttenwieser, Benjamin Shute, other friends on background; McCloy, "Return of the Native," speech to the Pennsylvania Club; *Time*, "Trouble for a Troubleshooter," 23–27; Schwartz dissertation, "From Occupation to Alliance: John J. McCloy and the Allied High Commission in the Federal Republic of Germany, 1949–1952"; letter of Joseph Reese to John McCloy, Sept. 20, 1946, and from McCloy to Reese, Sept. 27, 1946, the Penn Mutual Life Insurance Co., Philadelphia, both in McCloy's private papers; letter of Anna S. McCloy to the Equitable Life Assurance Society, New York City, Aug. 15, 1935; application of John S. McCloy for admission to the Association of the Bar of the City of New York, Bar Association records; John McCloy certificate of birth, Department of Public Health, Philadelphia; *The Peddie Chronicle*, Winter 1961, The Peddie School; McCloy interviews, "Conversations with Eric Sevareid: John J. McCloy," CBS Television (transcript), July 20, 1975.

McCLOY COLLEGE AND MILITARY SERVICE: Authors' interviews with John McCloy; *Time*, "Trouble for a Troubleshooter," 24; application of John S. McCloy for admission to the Association of the Bar of the City of New York, Bar Association records; Brinkley, "Minister Without Portfolio," 33; commission of John Snader

McCloy in the U.S. Army, recorded in Adjutant General's office, Mar. 12, 1918; Sevareid interview, July 20, 1975.

HARVARD LAW SCHOOL: Arthur Sullivan, *The Law at Harvard*; Morris Cohen, *A Dreamer's Journey*; Phillips, ed., *Felix Frankfurter Reminisces*.

KENNAN CHILDHOOD AND PERSONALITY: Authors' interviews with George F. Kennan, Jeannette Kennan Hotchkiss (sister), Frances Kennan Worobec (sister), Constance Kennan Bradt (sister), Kent Wheeler Kennan (half brother), Grace Kennan Warnecke (daughter), Joan Kennan Pozen (daughter); Kennan family interviews, used courtesy of Joan Pozen; unpublished letters of George Kennan to his father, courtesy of Joan Kennan Pozen; George F. Kennan, *Memoirs: 1925–1950*, 3–23; Wright dissertation, "George F. Kennan, Scholar-Diplomat," 2–9; Steel, *Imperialists and Other Heroes*, 38–57.

KENNAN GENEALOGY: Thomas Lathrop Kennan, *The Genealogy of the Kennan Family*; George Kennan letter to "My dear children," April 1961, courtesy Joan Kennan Pozen; George Kennan letter from Bad Nauheim, Germany, to his two daughters, February 1962, Kennan papers, Princeton; authors' interviews with George Kennan, Kent Kennan, Joan Pozen, Constance Bradt, Frances Worobec.

KENNAN MEETING WITH THE ELDER GEORGE KENNAN: Authors' interviews with Jeannette Hotchkiss and Frances Worobec; George Kennan, *Siberia and the Exile System*, abridged version, with an introduction by George F. Kennan.

KENNAN AT ST. JOHN'S: *The Trumpeter*, 1921, St. John's Military Academy yearbook; reports of Cadet G. F. Kennan, courtesy Joan Pozen; authors' interview with George F. Kennan; Joan Pozen interview with George F. Kennan.

KENNAN AT PRINCETON: Authors' interviews with George F. Kennan, Constance Bradt, Frances Worobec; Kennan letters and diaries at Seeley Mudd Library, Princeton, and personal letters home in the possession of Joan Pozen; Princeton's official reports of the standing of George Frost Kennan, courtesy Joan Pozen; Joan Pozen interview with George F. Kennan; George F. Kennan, *Memoirs: 1925–1950*, 9–17; Fitzgerald, *This Side of Paradise*.

DESCRIPTION OF YALE: Authors' interviews with Averell Harriman, Robert Lovett, David Acheson, and other alumni; Lewis, *One Man's Education*; *Yale College, 1871–1921* (New Haven: Yale, 1952); *Yale Record*, 1910–1918.

SKULL AND BONES AND SECRET SOCIETIES: Authors' interviews on background with former Bonesmen; Havemeyer, *Go to Your Room!*; "Secret Societies," *Yale Banner*, 1968; Owen Johnson, *Stover at Yale*.

HARRIMAN AT YALE: Authors' interviews with Averell Harriman, Pamela Churchill Harriman; *Yale Record*, 1913; *History of the Class of 1913*; Bland dissertation, "W. Averell Harriman: Businessman and Diplomat, 1891–1945," 12–18; Kahn, "Profiles: Plenipotentiary," May 10, 44–46; Harriman and Abel, *Special Envoy*, 34–36; Murphy, "W. Averell Harriman," 58–59; Kimball and Gill, *Cole*.

HARRIMAN'S WARTIME SHIPPING BUSINESS: Bland dissertation, "W. Averell Harriman: Businessman and Diplomat, 1891–1945," 23–29; Iden, "W. A. Harriman Seeks and Wins Front Rank in Marine Field," 121–127; Iden, "W. A. Harriman as Ship Operator," 175–181; Averell Harriman, "What Shipowners Are Up Against," 23–24; Harriman and Abel, *Special Envoy*, 6–7; Forbes, "New Business Star: Harriman II," 46; cited in Bland dissertation: "The application of Merchant Shipbuilding Corp. for settlement of accounts" and "W. A. Harriman & Co." general correspondence files, U.S. Shipping Board, Record Group 32, National Archives.

ACHESON AT YALE: Authors' interviews with David Acheson, others on background; *Yale Record*, 1915; McLellan, *Dean Acheson: The State Department Years*, 9–11; *Time*, "The Man from Middletown," 21–22; Hamburger, "Profiles: Mr. Secretary," Nov. 19, 40–41; Kimball and Gill, *Cole*.

ACHESON AT HARVARD LAW: Authors' interviews with David Acheson, Mary Acheson Bundy; Hamburger, "Profiles: Mr. Secretary," Nov. 12, 39; *Time*, "The Man from Middletown," 21–22; McLellan, *Dean Acheson: The State Department Years*, 11–14; letters to Felix Frankfurter, John Vincent, and George Day in *Among Friends: Personal Letters of Dean Acheson*, McLellan and Acheson, eds.

FRANKFURTER AT HARVARD LAW: Phillips, ed., *Felix Frankfurter Reminisces*; Lash, ed., *From the Diaries of Felix Frankfurter*; Frankfurter, *Of Law and Life and Other Things that Matter*, ed. by Kurland; Frankfurter, *Mr. Justice Brandeis*.

LOVETT AT YALE: Authors' interviews with Robert Lovett, Adèle Brown Lovett, Kate Jennings; *Yale Record*, 1918; Fanton dissertation, "Robert A. Lovett: The War Years," 6–8; Margaret Case Harriman and John Bainbridge, "Profiles: The Thirteenth Labor of Hercules," Nov. 13; *Time*, Sept. 8, 1941; *Time*, "The Bombers are Growing"; *Time*, "New Policy, New Broom."

YALE UNIT: Paine, *The First Yale Unit*; authors' interviews with Robert Lovett; Margaret Case Harriman and John Bainbridge, "Profiles: The Thirteenth Labor of Hercules," Nov. 13; *Time*, Sept. 8, 1941.

HARVARD: Aswell, ed., *Harvard 1926: The Life and Opinions of a College Class*; Samuel Eliot Morison, *Three Centuries of Harvard*; Amory, *The Proper Boston-*

ians; Canfield, *Up and Down and Around*; Steel, *Walter Lippmann and the American Century*, 10–32.

BOHLEN AT HARVARD: Authors' interviews with Cecil Lyon, Paul Nitze, J. Randolph Harrison, Celestine Bohlen; Wilmerding, "Charles Eustis Bohlen: Portrait of a Diplomat," unpublished term paper for Groton School; *Harvard Class Record*, 1927; Bohlen, *Witness to History*, 4.

Chapter 3
Joint Ventures

HARRIMAN'S SHIPPING BUSINESSES: Forbes, "New Business Star: Harriman II," 46; Bland dissertation, "W. Averell Harriman: Businessman and Diplomat, 1891–1945," 27–48; Kahn, "Profiles: Plenipotentiary," May 10; Iden, "W. A. Harriman as Ship Operator"; Averell Harriman, "What Shipowners Are Up Against."

HAMBURG-AMERICAN DEAL: Forbes, "New Business Star: Harriman II," 46; Bland dissertation, "W. Averell Harriman: Businessman and Diplomat, 1891–1945," p. 35; Iden, "W. A. Harriman Seeks and Wins Front Rank in Marine Field"; Iden, "W. A. Harriman as Ship Operator."

GERMAN-SOVIET VENTURES: Bland dissertation, "W. Averell Harriman: Businessman and Diplomat, 1891–1945," 50–61; *The New York Times*, Feb. 13, 1922; Larson dissertation, "Belief and Inference," 79; National Archives, Department of State Record Group 59, decimal file 861.51; Harriman and Abel, *Special Envoy*, 47–49.

SOVIET MANGANESE CONCESSION: Averell Harriman, *America and Russia in a Changing World*, 2–7; Harriman and Abel, *Special Envoy*, 47–52; Kahn, "Profiles: Plenipotentiary," May 10; Murphy, "W. Averell Harriman," 59–60; Harriman interview with authors; Bland dissertation, "W. Averell Harriman: Businessman and Diplomat, 1891–1945," 50–69; Larson dissertation, "Belief and Inference," 77–79; Averell Harriman, "In Darkest Russia"; Filene, *Americans and the Soviet Experiment*, 1917–1933, 109–119; National Archives, State Department Record Group 59, decimal file 861.637; Spurr, "Russian Manganese Concessions"; Litvinov, *Notes for a Journal*, 23; Brandon, "Very Much the Ambassador at Large."

HARRIMAN BECOMES A DEMOCRAT: Harriman and Abel, *Special Envoy*, 53–54; Bland dissertation, "W. Averell Harriman: Businessman and Diplomat, 1891–1945," 76–79; Brandon, "Very Much the Ambassador at Large"; Roosevelt, *The Autobiography of Eleanor Roosevelt*, 39–42.

HARRIMAN'S PERSONAL LIFE: Authors' interviews with Averell Harriman, Pamela Churchill Harriman, Kathleen Harriman Mortimer, Kitty Carlisle Hart, Robert Lovett, Adèle Brown Lovett, Kate Jennings, and other friends on background; Kahn, "Profiles: Plenipotentiary," May 10; Murphy, "W. Averell Harriman"; personal letters in Harriman private papers.

LOVETT'S EARLY CAREER: Authors' interviews with Robert Lovett; Fanton dissertation, "Robert A. Lovett: The War Years," 8–16; Lovett folder in the partners' files of Brown Brothers Harriman & Co. papers in the New York Historical Society; Roland Harriman, *I Reminisce*, 73–94; Margaret Case Harriman and John Bainbridge, "Profiles: The Thirteenth Labor of Hercules," Nov. 6 and 13; *Collier's*, "Averell Harriman"; Wooley, *In Retrospect: A Very Personal Memoir*.

LOVETT'S PERSONAL AND SOCIAL LIFE: Authors' interviews with Robert Lovett, Adèle Brown Lovett, Kate Jennings, and other Lovett friends on background; Margaret Case Harriman and John Bainbridge, "Profiles: The Thirteenth Labor of Hercules," Nov. 6 and 13; Fanton dissertation, "Robert A. Lovett: The War Years," 8–10; *Collier's*, "Averell Harriman."

MERGER OF BROWN BROTHERS AND HARRIMAN COMPANIES: Authors' interviews with Robert Lovett; Kouwenhoven, *Partners in Banking*, 7–20; Brown Brothers Harriman papers; Roland Harriman, *I Reminisce*, 73–94; Wooley, *In Retrospect: A Very Personal Memoir*; *New York Times*, Dec. 12, 1930; New York *World*, Dec. 12, 1930; *The Personality of a Bank*, by Brown Brothers Harriman & Co.; authors' interviews on background at Brown Brothers Harriman & Co.

HARRIMAN-LOVETT CORRESPONDENCE: Harriman and Lovett folders in the partners' files of Brown Brothers Harriman & Co. papers in the New York Historical Society; Harriman personal papers; scrapbooks of Adèle Lovett.

TODAY MAGAZINE: Letter from Lovett to Harriman, May 1, 1934, Lovett folder in the partners' files of Brown Brothers Harriman & Co. papers in the New York Historical Society; Moley, *After Seven Years*, 278–280.

UNION PACIFIC RAILROAD: Authors' interviews with Robert Lovett; letters from Lovett to Harriman, Feb. 1 and 6, 1934, Lovett folder in the partners' files of Brown Brothers Harriman & Co. papers in the New York Historical Society; Roland Harriman, *I Reminisce*; Union Pacific Annual Reports; *Fortune*, "Averell Was Quite a Businessman, Too"; Fanton dissertation, "Robert A. Lovett: The War Years," 16–20; Bland dissertation, "W. Averell Harriman: Businessman and Diplomat, 1891–1945," 85–88; Barcella, "The American Who Knows Stalin Best"; New York *World Tribune*, "Closeup: Mrs. Harriman"; Kahn, "Profiles: Plenipotentiary," May 10,; Margaret Case Harriman and John Bainbridge, "Profiles: The Thirteenth Labor of Hercules," Nov. 13.

HARRIMAN'S INVOLVEMENT WITH THE NEW DEAL: Bland dissertation, "W. Averell Harriman: Businessman and Diplomat, 1891–1945," 90–101; Schlesinger, *The Coming of the New Deal*; Averell Harriman, "Why the Little Fellow Needs the NRA," 19.

LOVETT ON THE NEW DEAL: Lovett letters to Harriman, Feb. 1 and 2, Mar. 16, 1934, June 26, 1940, others passim, Lovett folder, Brown Brothers Harriman partners' files; Lovett, "Gilt Edged Insecurity."

LOVETT-HARRIMAN CORRESPONDENCE ON EUROPEAN WAR: Harriman telegram to Lovett, Mar. 22, 1939, and Lovett telegram to Harriman, Mar. 22, 1939, Lovett folder, Brown Brothers Harriman partners' files.

Chapter 4
World Courts

McCLOY ON WALL STREET: Authors' interviews with John McCloy, John McCloy II (son), Ellen McCloy (daughter), Benjamin Buttenwieser, Robert Lovett, Benjamin Shute, other lawyers at Cravath, Swaine & Moore on background; Swaine, *The Cravath Firm*, Vol. II; *Time*, "Trouble for a Troubleshooter"; Schwartz dissertation, "From Occupation to Alliance," 10–21; application of John S. McCloy for admission to the Association of the Bar of the City of New York.

BLACK TOM: Swaine, *The Cravath Firm*, Vol. II, 636–644; authors' interviews with John McCloy, Benjamin Shute; Landau, *The Enemy Within*; Hall and Peaslee, *Three Wars with Germany*; *Harper's Magazine*, "The Black Tom Case"; *Time*, "Trouble for a Troubleshooter," 24.

ACHESON AND BRANDEIS: Authors' interviews with Alice Stanley Acheson, David Acheson, Philip Weiss, Gerhard Gesell; Acheson, *Morning and Noon*, 40–103; McLellan, *Dean Acheson: The State Department Years*, 15–29 (includes Frankfurter quotes); eulogy at the funeral of Louis Brandeis, by Dean Acheson, Washington, Oct. 7, 1941; Bickel, *The Unpublished Opinions of Mr. Justice Brandeis*; McLellan and Acheson, eds., *Among Friends: Personal Letters of Dean Acheson*, 36–41; *Fortune*, "Secretary Acheson," 166–168; Hamburger, "Profiles: Mr. Secretary," Nov. 12, and Nov. 19.

ACHESON AT COVINGTON & BURLING: Authors' interviews with Alice Stanley Acheson, David Acheson, Gerhard Gesell, attorneys at Covington & Burling on background; Acheson, *Morning and Noon*, 123–160; "U.S.-Norway Arbitration Award," *American Journal of International Law*, 1923, 287–298; McLellan, *Dean Acheson: The State Department Years*, 20–35; Acheson, *A Democrat Looks at His Party*; McLellan and Acheson (eds.), *Among Friends: Personal Letters of Dean Acheson*; Acheson personal papers and letters, Sterling Library.

ACHESON AT THE TREASURY DEPARTMENT: Acheson, *Morning and Noon*, 161–194; Schlesinger, *The Coming of the New Deal*, 212–216; Warburg, *The Money Muddle*, 145–148; Griffith Johnson, *The Treasury and Monetary Policy*, 26–28; McLellan, *Dean Acheson: The State Department Years*, 24–28; Tully, *F.D.R. My Boss*, 178; Seminar at Princeton with Dean Acheson, July 1953 (transcript in Acheson files, Truman Library, Independence, Mo.).

ACHESON'S PHILOSOPHY: Acheson, *Morning and Noon*, passim; Acheson, *A Democrat Looks at His Party*; Acheson, *Sketches from Life*; Acheson, *Present at the Creation*; McLellan and Acheson, eds., *Among Friends*, 20–35; authors' interviews with Alice Stanley Acheson, Gerhard Gesell, Arthur Schlesinger, Jr., Paul Nitze; Hamburger, "Profiles: Mr. Secretary," Nov. 12, and Nov. 19; *Fortune*, "Secretary Acheson"; McLellan, *Dean Acheson: The State Department Years*; Princeton Seminar with Acheson (transcript in Truman Library); Gaddis Smith, *American Secretaries of State and Their Diplomacy: Dean Acheson;* Gardner, *Architects of Illusion*, 202–231; Halberstam, *The Best and the Brightest*, 329–342; Steel, *Imperialists and Other Heroes*, 17–37; Speeches of Acheson at Sterling Library: "Notes on Judicial Self-Restraint," Maryland Bar Association, Atlantic City, July 4, 1936; "Some Social Factors in Legal Change," Law Club of Chicago, Jan. 22, 1937; "Cardozo and the Problems of Government," Bar and Officers of the U.S. Supreme Court, Nov. 26, 1938.

Chapter 5
A Pretty Good Club

KENNAN PREPARES FOR FOREIGN SERVICE: Kennan letters to family, courtesy of Joan Kennan Pozen; authors' interviews with George F. Kennan, Grace Kennan Warnecke, Joan Kennan Pozen, Jeannette Kennan Hotchkiss, Frances Kennan Worobec, Loy Henderson; Kennan letters to family in GFK papers, Princeton University; Wright dissertation, "George F. Kennan: Scholar-Diplomat," 11–14.

BOHLEN PREPARES FOR FOREIGN SERVICE: Bohlen, *Witness to History*, 4–8; authors' interviews with J. Randolph Harrison, Cecil Lyon, Mrs. William Eustis; Ruddy dissertation, "Charles C. Bohlen and the Soviet Union," 45–47; National Archives, State Department Record Group 59, C. E. Bohlen 123.

ASSESSMENTS OF BOHLEN AND KENNAN: Ruddy dissertation, "Charles E. Bohlen and the Soviet Union," 7; Harr, *The Professional Diplomat*, 317; Eisenhower, *The White House Years*, 212; Kissinger, *White House Years*, 135; authors' interview with Henry Kissinger.

DESCRIPTION OF FOREIGN SERVICE: Weil, *A Pretty Good Club*, 15–63; DeSantis, *The Diplomacy of Silence*, 11–44; Thayer, *Diplomat*; Heinrichs, *American Am-*

bassador: Joseph C. Grew and the Development of the U.S. Diplomatic Tradition, 1–103; Ilchman, *Professional Diplomacy in the U.S.*, 164–189; unpublished memoirs of Loy Henderson, Vol. II, 340–435 (courtesy of Loy Henderson).

BOHLEN IN PRAGUE: Bohlen, *Witness to History*, 8–9; Thayer, *Diplomat*, 132; National Archives, State Department Record Group 59 Bohlen; Thayer, "How Long Does It Take to Be a Soviet Expert?"; authors' interview with J. Randolph Harrison.

KENNAN IN HAMBURG: Unpublished Kennan letters, courtesy of Joan Pozen; authors' interviews with George F. Kennan, Loy Henderson; George F. Kennan, *Memoirs: 1925–1950*, 19–23; Wright dissertation, "George F. Kennan: Scholar-Diplomat," 14–16; National Archives, State Department Record Group 59 Kennan.

KENNAN AND ELEANOR HARD: Unpublished Kennan interview with Joan Kennan Pozen (courtesy of Mrs. Pozen); Kennan letters home, courtesy of Joan Pozen.

RUSSIAN TRAINING PROGRAM: Yergin, *Shattered Peace*, 17–40; Maddux, *Years of Estrangement*, 44–48; DeSantis, *Diplomacy of Silence*, 27–40; authors' interviews with Loy Henderson; unpublished memoirs of Loy Henderson, Vol. III, 454–462.

BOHLEN IN PARIS: Bohlen's letters home, Library of Congress, Bohlen Box 36; Bohlen, *Witness to History*, 9–12; authors' interviews with Randolph Harrison.

KENNAN IN BERLIN: Unpublished Kennan letters home; authors' interviews with George Kennan; National Archives, State Department Record Group 59: Kennan; George F. Kennan, *Memoirs: 1925–1950*, 31–37; Wright dissertation, "George F. Kennan: Scholar-Diplomat," 23–35; Kennan, "Memorandum on the Status of American Communists Residing in the U.S.S.R.," Department of State Files 861.012/31; Kennan, "The German Export Trade to Soviet Russia," Department of State Files 661.6211/39; "one firm and complete conviction," letter by Kennan to Walt Ferris, 1931, Kennan papers, Princeton University (cited in Wright dissertation).

KENNAN'S MARRIAGE TO ANNELISE SORENSEN: Unpublished Kennan letters, courtesy of Joan Pozen; George F. Kennan, *Memoirs: 1925–1950*, 37–40; authors' interview with Frances Kennan Worobec.

BOHLEN IN ESTONIA: Bohlen, *Witness to History*, 10–11; Thayer, "How Long Does It Take To Be a Soviet Expert?"; State Department Archives, 59:123 Bohlen; Bohlen letters, Library of Congress, Bohlen, Box 36; Grant, "The Russian Section, a Window on the Soviet Union," 107–115.

KENNAN IN LATVIA AND ESTONIA: Unpublished Kennan letters home; authors' interviews with George Kennan; George F. Kennan, *Memoirs: 1925–1950*, 26–31, 40–52; Wright dissertation, "George F. Kennan: Scholar-Diplomat," 35–37; National Archives, Kennan papers, Record Group, 59:123; Kennan, "Flashbacks," 52; Yergin, *Shattered Peace*, 20; "Formulation of Policy in the USSR," lecture by Kennan, 1947, Kennan papers, Princeton University.

KENNAN'S INTUITIVE APPROACH: Gellman, *Contending with Kennan*, 8; Rostow, "Searching for Kennan's Grand Design"; Gaddis, *Strategies of Containment*, 87.

RECOGNITION DEBATE: Maddux, *Years of Estrangement*, 1–43; Gaddis, *Russia: The Soviet Union and the United States*, 57–85; Browder, *The Origins of Soviet-American Diplomacy*, 3–74; authors' interviews with Loy Henderson, Elbridge Durbrow; unpublished memoirs of Loy Henderson, Vol. III, 479–529.

KENNAN'S VIEWS ON RECOGNITION: Authors' interviews with George Kennan, Loy Henderson, Elbridge Durbrow; unpublished Kennan letters home; George F. Kennan, *Memoirs: 1925–1950*, 49–58; Wright dissertation, "George F. Kennan: Scholar-Diplomat," 38–52; Kennan, "Gold and Foreign Currency Accounts of the Russian Government" (Dec. 1932), Department of State files 861.51/2539; Kennan, "Foreign Trade of Russia in 1932" (Aug. 1933), Department of State files 661.00/175; Kennan, "Notes on Russian Commercial Treaty Procedure" (April 1933), Department of State files 661.0031/30.

BOHLEN IN WASHINGTON, NOVEMBER 1933: Authors' interviews with Loy Henderson, George Kennan; Bohlen, *Witness to History*, 12; unpublished memoirs of Loy Henderson, Vol. III, 530–539.

KENNAN IN WASHINGTON, NOVEMBER 1933: Unpublished Kennan letters home; "Fair Day, Adieu!" an unpublished journal of 1933–1937 by Kennan, Kennan papers, Princeton University, 1–3 (referred to in text as Kennan's journal; a handwritten note says it was complete in 1938, but references in the text make it clear that it was not finished until sometime in 1939); authors' interviews with George Kennan, Loy Henderson, Frances Kennan Worobec, Jeannette Kennan Hotchkiss; Wright dissertation, "George F. Kennan: Scholar-Diplomat," 52–55; George F. Kennan, *Memoirs: 1925–1950*, 58; unpublished memoirs of Loy Henderson, Vol. III, 530–539.

BOHLEN'S VIEWS ON RECOGNITION: Bohlen, *Witness to History*, 12; Bohlen letters, Library of Congress, Box 36; Bohlen, *The Transformation of American Foreign Policy*, 16–17, 53–55; authors' interviews with Loy Henderson.

KENNAN'S JOURNEY TO MOSCOW: Kennan, "Fair Day, Adieu!" in Kennan papers, Princeton University, 3–5; authors' interviews with George Kennan; Kennan, "Flashbacks," 57.

KENNAN ORGANIZES EMBASSY: Kennan, "Fair Day, Adieu!" in Kennan papers, Princeton University, 6–12; authors' interviews with George Kennan; George F. Kennan, *Memoirs: 1925–1950*, 58–60; Thayer, *Bears in the Caviar*, 67–84 (Thayer, a great yarn spinner, is prone to exaggeration, and some of his tales have been toned down here after checking with other sources); Wright dissertation, "George F. Kennan: Scholar-Diplomat," 58–60.

THAYER JOINS STAFF: Thayer, *Bears in the Caviar*, 11–105; George F. Kennan, *Memoirs: 1925–1950*, 59.

BOHLEN'S ARRIVAL IN MOSCOW: Bohlen, *Witness to History*, 14–19; Thayer, *Bears in the Caviar*, 84–105; authors' interviews with Loy Henderson; Henderson's unpublished memoirs, Vol. III, 569.

SOCIAL LIFE IN THE EMBASSY: Authors' interviews with George Kennan, Loy Henderson, Elbridge Durbrow; Kennan, "Fair Day, Adieu!" in Kennan papers, Princeton University; Kennan, *Memoirs: 1925–1950*, 58–86; Bohlen, *Witness to History*, 14–36; Thayer, *Bears in the Caviar*, 67–153; Bohlen's unpublished letters, Library of Congress, Bohlen papers, Box 36; Henderson's unpublished memoirs, Vol. III, 570–650; Farnsworth, *William C. Bullitt and the Soviet Union*, 110–125; Wright dissertation, "George F. Kennan: Scholar-Diplomat," 56–60; Yergin, *Shattered Peace*, 22–33.

KENNAN'S INITIAL ATTITUDE TOWARD THE SOVIETS: Authors' interviews with George Kennan; "Fair Day, Adieu!" in Kennan papers, Princeton University; "The First Fifty Years," PBS television documentary, 1984; George F. Kennan, *Memoirs: 1925–1950*, 60–64.

BOHLEN'S INITIAL ATTITUDE TOWARD THE SOVIETS: Bohlen's unpublished letters in Bohlen personal papers, Library of Congress; authors' interviews with Loy Henderson; Bohlen, *Witness to History*, 26–27.

THE DACHA: Authors' interviews with George Kennan, Loy Henderson, Elbridge Durbrow, Grace Kennan Warnecke; Thayer, *Bears in the Caviar*, 130–143; Elbridge Durbrow's home movies (courtesy of Grace Kennan Warnecke); "The First Fifty Years: U.S.-Soviet Relations," PBS television documentary, 1984.

ASSESSMENTS OF KENNAN'S PERSONALITY: Authors' interviews with Loy Henderson, Elbridge Durbrow; Wright dissertation, "George F. Kennan, Scholar-Diplomat," 81; Bohlen, *Witness to History*, 17.

ASSESSMENTS OF BOHLEN'S PERSONALITY: Authors' interviews with George Kennan, Loy Henderson, Elbridge Durbrow; Henderson's unpublished memoirs, Vol. III 614; George F. Kennan, *Memoirs: 1925–1950*, 62–63.

KENNAN STUDIES PREREVOLUTIONARY DISPATCHES: Kennan, "Fair Day, Adieu!" in Kennan papers, Princeton University, 23–24; FRUS: The Soviet Union 1933–1939, 289–291.

KENNAN TRIP TO SOCHI: Kennan, "Fair Day, Adieu!" in Kennan papers, Princeton University, 42–43.

KENNAN'S DISILLUSIONMENT: George F. Kennan, Memoirs: 1925–1950, 70.

BOHLEN'S DISILLUSIONMENT: Bohlen's letters in Bohlen personal papers, Library of Congress; Bohlen, Witness to History, 27–36.

BULLITT'S DISILLUSIONMENT: Authors' interviews with George Kennan, Loy Henderson; Bohlen, Witness to History, 32–35; Farnsworth, William C. Bullitt, 124–154; FRUS: Soviet Union 1933–39, 224–225, 244–249; Bullitt, ed., For the President: Personal and Secret: Correspondence Between Franklin Roosevelt and William C. Bullitt, 160; Yergin, Shattered Peace, 25–26.

BOHLEN'S RETURN TO U.S.: Bohlen, Witness to History, 36–38.

KENNAN'S DISPATCHES: Kennan, "The War Problem of the Soviet Union," Kennan papers, Princeton University; Kennan, "Some Fundamentals of Russian-American Relations," Kennan papers, Princeton University (Kennan says in his Memoirs that he cannot find the memo, but it is in the library); George F. Kennan, Memoirs: 1925–1950, 70–74; Wright dissertation, "George F. Kennan: Scholar-Diplomat," 70–79.

KENNAN REPORT ON RADEK TRIAL: FRUS: Soviet Union 1933–39, 362–369; George F. Kennan, Memoirs: 1925–1950, 82–83; Kennan, "Fair Day, Adieu!" in Kennan papers, Princeton University, 66–70; Davies, Mission to Moscow, 32–46.

SEARCH FOR THE EMBASSY BUG: Thayer, Bears in the Caviar, 95–97; Kennan letter to Peter Bridges (who was writing a history of Spaso House), Sept. 30, 1963, in Kennan papers, Princeton University; George F. Kennan, Memoirs: 1925–1950, p. 189.

KENNAN'S TRANSFER: Davies letter to Kelley, Feb. 10, 1937, Davies papers, Library of Congress, cited in Wright dissertation, 104–105.

DESTRUCTION OF THE EASTERN EUROPEAN DIVISION: Authors' interviews with George Kennan, Loy Henderson; Bohlen, Witness to History, 39–40; George F. Kennan, Memoirs: 1925–1950, 83–85; Kennan, "Fair Day, Adieu!" in Kennan papers, Princeton University, 66–70; Henderson's unpublished memoirs, Vol. III, 802–803; Yergin, Shattered Peace, 34–35; Weil, A Pretty Good Club, 93.

KENNAN AND SOVIET-AMERICAN TRADE: Wright dissertation, "George F. Kennan: Scholar-Diplomat," 107–113; conversation between Kennan and O. C. Gruender of Milwaukee, Dec. 15, 1937, National Archives, State Department Record Group 59 Kennan.

KENNAN ON TREATMENT OF AMERICANS IN THE SOVIET UNION: Wright dissertation, "George F. Kennan: Scholar-Diplomat," 113–124; Kennan memoranda, Oct. 29, 1937, Dec. 23, 1937, Mar. 24, 1938, and Mar. 26, 1938, National Archives, State Department Record Group 59 Kennan; Kennan, "The Position of the American Ambassador in Moscow," Nov. 24, 1937; *FRUS: Soviet Union 1933–39*, 446–451; George F. Kennan, *Memoirs: 1925–1950*, 85–86.

KENNAN LECTURE AT FOREIGN SERVICE SCHOOL: Kennan, "Russia," May 20, 1938, in Kennan papers, Princeton University; Yergin, *Shattered Peace*, 37; Wright dissertation, "George F. Kennan: Scholar-Diplomat," 124–128.

KENNAN'S FULMINATIONS ON DEMOCRACY: Gellman, *Contending With Kennan*, 83–105; authors' interview with Joseph Alsop; examples of this attitude pervade most of Kennan's works, in particular: *American Diplomacy, Russia and the West Under Lenin and Stalin, Democracy and the Student Left, The Clouds of Danger*.

KENNAN'S 1930 REFLECTIONS: Wright dissertation, "George F. Kennan: Scholar-Diplomat," 24–26; Kennan letter to Volodia Kozhevnikoff, Oct. 20, 1930, in Kennan papers, Princeton University (cited in Wright).

KENNAN'S VIEWS ON AUSTRIAN AUTHORITARIANISM: Kennan, "Fair Day, Adieu!" in Kennan papers, Princeton University, 29–33.

KENNAN'S PROPOSED BOOK ON AMERICAN DEMOCRACY: "The Prerequisities" and "The Government," notes for a book "On the Problems of the United States," by Kennan, 1938, Kennan papers, Princeton University; Wright dissertation, "George F. Kennan: Scholar-Diplomat," 129–132.

KENNAN'S LATER VIEWS ON ELITISM AND AUTHORITARIANISM: Gellman, *Contending with Kennan*, 83–105; George F. Kennan, *Memoirs: 1925–1950*, 185; Urban, "A Conversation with George Kennan," 28–32.

BOHLEN'S RETURN TO MOSCOW: Bohlen, *Witness to History*, 42–46; Ruddy dissertation, "Charles E. Bohlen and the Soviet Union," 56; Henderson dispatch, Feb. 21, 1938, National Archives, State Department Record Group 59 Bohlen.

BOHLEN'S REPORT ON SUPREME SOVIET: Bohlen, *Witness to History*, 46–47; Ruddy dissertation, "Charles E. Bohlen and the Soviet Union," 56–58; *FRUS: Soviet Union 1933–39*, 509–513.

BOHLEN'S REACTION TO PURGES: Bohlen, *Witness to History*, 47–55; Bohlen interview, Columbia Oral History project, 14–15; authors' interviews with Loy Henderson.

BOHLEN'S ANALYSIS OF SOVIET CONDUCT: Bohlen, *The Transformation of American Foreign Policy*; "Creating Situations of Strength," speech by Bohlen, *Department of State Bulletin*, Aug. 4, 1952; "Key Characteristics of the Communist Threat," speech by Bohlen, *Department of State Bulletin*, Oct. 24, 1960; Bohlen interview, Columbia Oral History Project; Bohlen, *Witness to History*, 61–62; Ruddy dissertation, "Charles E. Bohlen and the Soviet Union," 12–42.

BOHLEN ON NAZI-SOVIET PACT: Bohlen, *Witness to History*, 56–87; Mosley, *On Borrowed Time: How World War II Began*, 229–377.

BOHLEN AND KENNAN IN BERLIN: Authors' interviews with George Kennan; Bohlen, *Witness to History*, 97–101; George F. Kennan, *Memoirs: 1925–1950*, 115–127; draft of a report on Soviet-German relations, 1940, by Kennan, in Kennan papers, Princeton University.

KENNAN'S ATTITUDE TOWARD THE NAZIS: Kennan, *From Prague After Munich*, 80–87; George F. Kennan, *Memoirs: 1925–1950*, 87–141.

Chapter 6
On Active Service

ACHESON'S VIEW ON ISOLATIONISM VERSUS IDEALISM: Acheson, *Present at the Creation*, 6.

ELIHU ROOT: Jessup, *Elihu Root*; Root, "A Requisite for the Success of Popular Diplomacy."

HENRY STIMSON: Stimson and Bundy, *On Active Service in Peace and War*; Elting, Morison, *Turmoil and Tradition*; Pringle, "Land of Woodley," 30–33; *Time*, "Secretary of War," 30–34.

McCLOY ENTERS GOVERNMENT: Authors' interviews with John McCloy; Stimson and Bundy, *On Active Service*, 342–343.

LOVETT ENTERS GOVERNMENT: Authors' interviews with Robert Lovett, Cass Canfield, Michael Forrestal; Fanton dissertation, "Robert A. Lovett: The War Years," 17–24; letter from Lovett to Harriman, June 26, 1940, Lovett folder, Brown Brothers Harriman partners' files, New York Historical Society; Cass Canfield interview, Columbia Oral History Project; Lovett report to Patterson, Nov. 22, 1940, Lovett papers, National Archives; Stimson diary, Dec. 20, 1940, in Stimson papers, Yale University; Rogow, *James Forrestal*; Albion and Connery, *Forrestal and the Navy*.

ACHESON ENTERS GOVERNMENT: Acheson, *Morning and Noon*, 216–227; authors' interviews with Alice Stanley Acheson; speech by Dean Acheson, Davenport College, Yale, in Acheson papers, Truman Library; speech by Dean Acheson, International Ladies Garment Workers Union, June 4, 1940, in Acheson papers, Truman Library; letter from McCloy to Acheson, Sept. 13, 1940, Acheson personal papers, Yale University.

HARRIMAN ENTERS GOVERNMENT: Harriman and Abel, *Special Envoy*, 3–20; authors' interviews with Averell Harriman, Kathleen Harriman Mortimer; Bland dissertation, "W. Averell Harriman: Businessman and Diplomat, 1891–1945," 102–111.

OVERVIEW OF ISOLATION DEBATE: Sherwood, *Roosevelt and Hopkins: An Intimate History*, 124–139; Chadwin, *The Hawks of World War II*.

PEARL HARBOR: Harriman and Abel, *Special Envoy*, 111–112; Acheson, *Present at the Creation*, 34–35; authors' interviews with John McCloy; McCloy interview for McCloy Oral History, 1983; authors' interviews with Robert Lovett, Adèle Brown Lovett; George F. Kennan, *Memoirs: 1925–1950*, 134–135; Bohlen, *Witness to History*, 112–113.

Chapter 7
Heavenly Twins

STIMSON'S STAFF: Authors' interviews with Robert Lovett, John McCloy, William Bundy, McGeorge Bundy; Stimson and Bundy, *On Active Service*, 340–344; Elting Morison, *Turmoil and Tradition*, 492–494; Harvey Bundy interview, Columbia Oral History Project; Assistant Secretary of War office files, Record Group 107, National Archives.

LOVETT AND McCLOY RELATIONSHIP WITH STIMSON: Authors' interviews with Robert Lovett, John McCloy, Adèle Brown Lovett; Margaret Case Harriman and John Bainbridge, "Profiles: The Thirteenth Labor of Hercules."

LOVETT, HARRIMAN, AND *NEWSWEEK*: Fanton dissertation, "Robert A. Lovett: The War Years," 177–178; letter from Harriman to Lovett, Apr. 20, 1943, Henry H. Arnold papers, Library of Congress.

McCLOY PERSONALITY AND STYLE: Lovett interview, Columbia Oral History Project; authors' interviews with Robert Lovett, John McCloy, James Rowe, Benjamin Shute, Cecil Lyon, Benjamin Buttenwieser, John McCloy II; McCloy interview, Columbia Oral History Project, April 1973; *Time*, "Trouble for a Troubleshooter," 23–27; Brinkley, "Minister Without Portfolio," 31–46; *Saturday Evening Post*, McCloy profile, 24.

LOVETT PERSONALITY AND STYLE: Authors' interviews with Robert Lovett, Adèle Brown Lovett, Robert S. Lovett II, John McCloy, Michael Forrestal, Kate Jennings; Lovett interview, Columbia Oral History Project; Fanton dissertation, "Robert A. Lovett: The War Years," 177–181; Margaret Case Harriman and John Bainbridge, "Profiles: The Thirteenth Labor of Hercules," Nov. 6, and Nov. 13; *Time*, "The Bombers are Growing"; Lovett profile, *The Saturday Evening Post*, Feb. 7, 1948; Bigart, "Pentagon Pitfalls."

McCLOY AND LEND-LEASE: Authors' interviews with John McCloy; *Time*, "The Bombers are Growing"; Stimson and Bundy, *On Active Service*, 360.

LOVETT AND CONGRESS: Authors' interviews with Robert Lovett, Senator Claude Pepper, former congressman Walter Judd; Bigart, "Pentagon Pitfalls."

LOVETT'S VISITS TO THE FRONT: Authors' interviews with Robert Lovett; Margaret Case Harriman and John Bainbridge, "Profiles: The Thirteenth Labor of Hercules," Nov. 6 and Nov. 13; Lovett profile, New York *Herald Tribune*, Jan. 3, 1951.

McCLOY'S VISITS TO THE FRONT: Authors' interviews with John McCloy; McCloy interview conducted by Eric Sevareid, CBS television, July 13, 1975; John McCloy Oral History, Defense Department Oral History Project.

McCLOY'S VIEWS ON JAPANESE INTERNMENT: Authors' interviews with John McCloy, Benjamin Shute, John McCloy Oral History, Defense Department Oral History Project; McCloy interview, conducted by Eric Sevareid; McCloy, "Repay U.S. Japanese?"; McCloy testimony, Commission on Wartime Relocation, Nov. 3, 1981.

HISTORY OF JAPANESE INTERNMENT: Irons, *Justice at War*; Commission on Wartime Relocation, *Personal Justice Denied*; Grodzins, *Americans Betrayed*; Stimson diaries, December 1941–February 1942, Yale University; *Time*, "Twenty Years After," 15–16.

AUSCHWITZ BOMBING DECISION: Authors' interviews with John McCloy; John McCloy Oral History, Defense Department Oral History Project; Mintz, "Why Didn't We Bomb Auschwitz?"; Wyman, *The Abandonment of the Jews*, 291–301; Chase, "The Decision Not to Bomb Auschwitz," private paper (courtesy of John McCloy); Assistant Secretary of War files, 1944, Record Group 107, folder on Jews, National Archives; Brinkley, "Minister Without Portfolio," 35–36.

SPOTTER PLANES: Authors' interviews with John McCloy; John McCloy Oral History, Defense Department Oral History Project; Arnold, *Global Mission*, 292–293.

PENTAGON CONSTRUCTION: Authors' interviews with John McCloy; McCloy interview, conducted by Eric Sevareid.

McCLOY AND CHURCHILL: John McCloy Oral History, Defense Department Oral History Project; McCloy interview, conducted by Eric Sevareid.

DARLAN AND De GAULLE: Stimson and Bundy, *On Active Service*, 557–561; McCloy interview, conducted by Eric Sevareid; McCloy interview, Columbia University Oral History Project; Brinkley, "Minister Without Portfolio," 34–35.

ROOSEVELT OFFERS HIGH COMMISSIONER'S JOB: Authors' interviews with John McCloy; McCloy interview, Columbia Oral History; John McCloy Oral History, Defense Department Oral History Project; McCloy interview, conducted by Eric Sevareid; Clay, *Decision in Germany*, 3–25.

AIR CORPS BUILDUP: Margaret Case Harriman and John Bainbridge, "Profiles: The Thirteenth Labor of Hercules," Aug. 6 and Aug. 13; *Time*, "The Bombers are Growing."

LOVETT MEETING WITH HOPKINS: Fanton dissertation, "Robert A. Lovett: The War Years," 41.

LOVETT'S PROCUREMENT METHODS: Margaret Case Harriman and John Bainbridge, "Profiles: The Thirteenth Labor of Hercules," Nov. 6; authors' interviews with Robert Lovett; Lovett Oral History, Columbia Oral History Project. Fanton dissertation, "Robert A. Lovett: The War Years," 42, 65, 150–152; Albion and Connery, *Forrestal and the Navy*, 105; Stimson diary, Apr. 9, 1941, Aug. 1, 1941, Yale University; Lovett memo to Hap Arnold, May 10, 1941, to Robert Patterson, Aug. 16, 1941, to Harry Hopkins, Mar. 28, 1942, to himself, Mar. 9, 1942, Assistant Secretary of War files, Record Group 107, National Archives; Herring, *Aid to Russia*, 2–48.

FORRESTAL'S PROCUREMENT METHODS: Authors' interviews with James Rowe, Marx Leva; Albion and Connery, *Forrestal and the Navy*, 64-108; Rogow, *James Forrestal*, 97-103.

LOVETT'S VISION OF AIR POWER: Authors' interviews with Robert Lovett; Henry Arnold papers, Library of Congress; Fanton dissertation, "Robert A. Lovett: The War Years," 134–172; Harriman and Abel, *Special Envoy*, 194; Lovett speech to University Club, Ira Eaker papers, Library of Congress; Holly, *Ideas and Weapons*, 159–172; Margaret Case Harriman and John Bainbridge, "Profiles:

The Thirteenth Labor of Hercules," Nov. 6 and Nov. 13; *Time*, "The Bombers are Growing"; Lovett memos to Stimson and Arnold, Lovett papers, National Archives.

U.S. STRATEGIC BOMBING SURVEY: Authors' interviews with Robert Lovett, George Ball, Paul Nitze; U.S. Strategic Bombing Survey, *Summary Report, European War*, and *The Effects of Strategic Bombing on the German War Economy*; Galbraith, *A Life in Our Times*, 192–227; Ball, *The Past Has Another Pattern*, 42–68, 406.

Chapter 8
Missions to Moscow

HARRIMAN AT THE ATLANTIC CONFERENCE: Harriman and Abel, *Special Envoy*, 75–76; Harriman private papers, Washington, D.C.; Feis, *Churchill Roosevelt Stalin*, 20–23; Sherwood, *Roosevelt and Hopkins*, 349–365.

HARRIMAN-BEAVERBROOK MISSION TO MOSCOW: Harriman and Abel, *Special Envoy*, 80–105; Herring, *Aid to Russia*, 15–17; Sherwood, *Roosevelt and Hopkins*, 391; Bland dissertation, "W. Averell Harriman: Businessman and Diplomat, 1891–1945," 130–142; Standley and Ageton, *Admiral Ambassador to Russia*, 63; Averell Harriman, *America and Russia in a Changing World*, 17–23; Averell Harriman, *Peace With Russia?* 13–14; Harriman memos to Harry Hopkins, Hopkins papers, Box 123, Roosevelt Library; Sherwood, *Roosevelt and Hopkins*, 387–389; Deane, *The Strange Alliance*, 88–89.

HARRIMAN'S FINANCIAL INTERESTS IN THE SOVIET UNION: Memo from J. D. Powell to Harriman, Sept. 20, 1943, and Harriman memo of July 11, 1941, Harriman personal papers, Washington, D.C.; Harriman and Abel, *Special Envoy*, 83; Brown Brothers Harriman partners' files, New-York Historical Society.

HARRIMAN'S RETURN TO LONDON: Harriman and Abel, *Special Envoy*, 123.

HARRIMAN AND THE SECOND-FRONT CONTROVERSY: Harriman and Abel, *Special Envoy*, 131, 138, 143–146; Herring, *Aid to Russia*, 61–65, 87–89; Deane, *Strange Alliance*, 17–44.

HARRIMAN AND LEND-LEASE SHIPMENT DELAYS: Harriman and Abel, *Special Envoy*, 140–142; Herring, *Aid to Russia*, 57–67; Hopkins memo, May 4, 1942, Hopkins papers, Roosevelt Library; Churchill, *Hinge of Fate*, 262–270.

HARRIMAN'S TRIP TO MOSCOW WITH CHURCHILL: Harriman and Abel, *Special Envoy*, 146–166; Churchill, *The Hinge of Fate*, 473–499; Harriman to Roosevelt,

FRUS, 1942, 618–620, 622; Sherwood, *Roosevelt and Hopkins*, 616–622; Bland dissertation, "W. Averell Harriman: Businessman and Diplomat, 1891–1945," 161–166.

KATYN FOREST MASSACRE: Harriman and Abel, *Special Envoy*, 199–201, 301, 349; George F. Kennan, *Memoirs: 1925–1950*, 200–203, 207; U.S. Select Congressional Committee on the Katyn Forest Massacre, *Report*.

HARRIMAN'S 1943 ANNOYANCE AT SOVIETS OVER POLAND: Harriman and Abel, *Special Envoy*, 206.

STANDLEY AND HIS RESIGNATION: Standley and Ageton, *Admiral Ambassador to Russia*, 92–98; Herring, *Aid to Russia*, 80–98, 106.

HARRIMAN OFFERED AMBASSADORSHIP: Harriman and Abel, *Special Envoy*, 218–220; Harriman to Roosevelt, July 5, 1943, *FRUS: Teheran*, 13–15; *The New York Times*, Oct. 3 and 22, 1943; Standley and Ageton, *Admiral Ambassador to Russia*, 489–490.

ACHESON AND UNRRA: Acheson, *Present at the Creation*, 65–80; Herring, *Aid to Russia*, 155.

HARRIMAN'S ARRIVAL AS AMBASSADOR: Harriman and Abel, *Special Envoy*, 239–240; notes and memos, Harriman personal papers, Washington, D.C.; Deane, *The Strange Alliance*, 3–5.

HARRIMAN'S AND KATHLEEN'S LIFE IN MOSCOW: Harriman and Abel, *Special Envoy*, passim; Kathleen Harriman letters to sister and mother, Harriman personal papers, Washington, D.C.; authors' interviews with Kathleen Harriman Mortimer.

MOSCOW FOREIGN MINISTERS CONFERENCE: Harriman and Abel, *Special Envoy*, 240–249; memos and cables, Harriman personal papers, Washington, D.C.; Harriman to Roosevelt, Nov. 5, 1943, *FRUS*, 1943, III, 589–593; Hull, *Memoirs*, Vol. II, 1278—1315.

HARRIMAN ON POLAND IN EARLY 1944: Harriman and Abel, *Special Envoy*, 262–315; memos and cables, Harriman personal papers, Washington, D.C.; Harriman cables, *FRUS*, 1944, III, 1223–1299; for an overview of the situation from the perspective of the London Poles, see Mikolajczyk, *The Rape of Poland*.

HARRIMAN'S NEGOTIATIONS FOR BOHLEN AND THEN KENNAN: Wright dissertation, "George F. Kennan: Scholar-Diplomat," 233–235; Ruddy dissertation, "Charles E. Bohlen and the Soviet Union," 96–102; Bland dissertation, "W. Averell Harriman: Businessman and Diplomat, 1891–1945," 203; "Memo on

Embassy Staff," by Harriman, Dec. 1, 1943, Harriman personal papers, Washington, D.C.; Harriman and Abel, *Special Envoy*, 229; Bohlen, *Witness to History*, 121–125, 133; George F. Kennan, *Memoirs: 1925–1950*, 180–181, 231; cables from Harriman to Hopkins, Harriman personal papers, Washington, D.C. (also in Hopkins papers, Roosevelt Library).

KENNAN IN PORTUGAL AND AT EUROPEAN ADVISORY COMMISSION: George F. Kennan, *Memoirs: 1925–1950*, 142–187.

KENNAN-BOHLEN ARGUMENT, MAY 1944: Authors' interviews with George Kennan; authors' off-the-record talk with a Kennan family member.

BOHLEN ON HARRIMAN: Letter from Bohlen to Charles Thayer, Dec. 10, 1958, Thayer papers, Truman Library.

KENNAN ON HARRIMAN: George F. Kennan, *Memoirs: 1925–1950*, 231–232; authors' interviews with George Kennan, Grace Kennan Warnecke, Kathleen Harriman Mortimer, Loy Henderson.

HARRIMAN ON KENNAN: Harriman Oral History Project, Kennedy Institute of Politics, Harvard University, 333.

KENNAN'S INITIAL VIEWS ON POLAND: George F. Kennan, *Memoirs: 1925–1950*, 206–210; authors' interviews with George Kennan.

HARRIMAN AND THE WARSAW UPRISING: Authors' interviews with Averell Harriman; Harriman and Abel, *Special Envoy*, 340–365; Bland dissertation, "W. Averell Harriman: Businessman and Diplomat, 1891–1945," 291–311; Harriman cables to Washington in August of 1944, *FRUS, 1944*, III, 1302–1389; Harriman Oral History Project, Kennedy Institute of Politics, Harvard University, 321–323; Mikolajczyk, *The Rape of Poland*, 75–85; Churchill, *Triumph and Tragedy*, 132–149; Harriman and McCloy, off-the-record discussion of the origins of the Cold War, in Harriman personal papers, Washington, D.C.

KENNAN AND THE WARSAW UPRISING: George F. Kennan, *Memoirs: 1925–1950*, 210–211; authors' interviews with Kennan.

HARRIMAN'S TOUGHENING STANCE ON LEND-LEASE IN EARLY 1944: Herring, *Aid to Russia*, 128–131; Harriman and Abel, *Special Envoy*, 290–310; Harriman cables to Washington, *FRUS, 1944*, IV, 1039–1055.

HARRIMAN AND MIKOYAN'S POSTWAR LOAN REQUEST: Herring, *Aid to Russia*, 150–154; Harriman cables to Washington, *FRUS, 1944*, IV, 1041–1055.

ACHESON AND POSTWAR LEND-LEASE CREDIT TALKS: Acheson, *Present at the*

Creation, 85; Harriman cables to Washington, *FRUS*, 1944, IV, 1114–1128; Herring, *Aid to Russia*, 157–159.

THE MULTILATERALIST OUTLOOK: Kuklick, *American Policy and the Division of Germany*, 1–18; Stimson and Bundy, *On Active Service*, 567; Hull, *Memoirs*, Vol. II, 81–85 and passim; authors' interviews with John McCloy, Robert Lovett.

THE MORGENTHAU PLAN, OVERVIEW: Kuklick, *American Policy and the Division of Germany*, 47–73; Morgenthau, *The Morgenthau Diary: Germany*, Vol. I, 415–859; Blum, ed., *From the Morgenthau Diaries: Years of War*, 1941–1945, 327–416, 451–464; Blum, *Roosevelt and Morgenthau*, 559–625.

McCLOY AND STIMSON MEETINGS ON THE MORGENTHAU PLAN: Authors' interviews with John McCloy, Robert Lovett; Stimson diaries, Aug. 21, 23, 26, Sept. 4, 7, 9, 11, 14, 16, 1944, Yale University; Stimson and Bundy, *On Active Service*, 568–583; Morgenthau, *The Morgenthau Diary: Germany*, Vol. I, 415, 425–430, 443, 452, 475; McCloy notes, in Stimson diaries, Sept. 20, 1944, Yale University.

HARRIMAN'S HARD LINE IN SEPTEMBER OF 1944: Harriman's cables to Washington, *FRUS*, 1944, IV, 992–998; Harriman and Abel, *Special Envoy*, 344–346.

KENNAN'S INFLUENCE ON HARRIMAN'S POSITION IN SEPTEMBER OF 1944: Authors' interviews with George Kennan, Averell Harriman; draft paper, by Kennan, Sept. 18, 1944, Kennan papers, Princeton University; Kennan memo to Harriman, Sept. 18, 1944, Kennan papers, Princeton University; Feis, *Churchill Roosevelt Stalin*, 433–436.

"RUSSIA—SEVEN YEARS LATER": George F. Kennan, *Memoirs: 1925–1950*, 225–230, 503–531; Wright dissertation, "George F. Kennan: Scholar-Diplomat," 264–277; personal memos, Harriman personal papers, Washington, D.C.

CHURCHILL'S SPHERES-OF-INFLUENCE DEAL: Bohlen, *Witness to History*, 162–164; Harriman and Abel, *Special Envoy*, 353–358; Churchill, *Triumph and Tragedy*, 216–231; Harriman cables to Roosevelt, Oct. 10, 11, 12, 1944, *FRUS*, 1944, IV, 1005–1015; Feis, *Churchill Roosevelt Stalin*, 449–454; George F. Kennan, *Memoirs: 1925–1950*, 222; Kuniholm, *The Origins of the Cold War in the Near East*, 100–125.

HARRIMAN IN WASHINGTON, NOVEMBER OF 1944: Harriman and Abel, *Special Envoy*, 364–370; transcript of Harriman background briefing, Harriman personal papers, Washington, D.C.; Henry Stimson diary, Oct. 23–24, in Stimson papers, Yale University; *New York Times*, Nov. 4, 1944.

MOLOTOV'S POSTWAR LOAN REQUEST: Harriman and Abel, *Special Envoy*, 384–

386; Harriman cables to Washington, *FRUS*, 1945, V, 942–947, and *FRUS, Yalta*, 313–323; Herring, *Aid to Russia*, 160–162; Blum, ed., *From the Morgenthau Diaries: Years of War, 1941–1945*, 304.

HARRIMAN AND BOHLEN AT YALTA: Harriman and Abel, *Special Envoy*, 318–417; Bohlen, *Witness to History*, 173–201; Bland dissertation, "W. Averell Harriman: Businessman and Diplomat, 1891–1945," 341–355; Harriman Oral History Project, Kennedy Institute of Politics, Harvard University, 341; Feis, *Churchill Roosevelt Stalin*, 489–559.

KENNAN-BOHLEN CORRESPONDENCE: Kennan letter, February 1945, Bohlen personal papers, Library of Congress; Bohlen letter, February 1945, Kennan papers, Princeton University; Bohlen, *Witness to History*, 175–177; authors' interviews with George Kennan.

HARRIMAN'S DISILLUSIONMENT OVER POLAND AFTER YALTA: Harriman cables to Washington, *FRUS*, 1945, V, 197, 817–824; unsent messages from Moscow, Harriman personal papers, Washington, D.C.; Harriman and Abel, *Special Envoy*, 421–431; Herring, *Aid to Russia*, 171–200; George F. Kennan, *Memoirs: 1925–1950*, 212; Sulzberger, *A Long Row of Candles*, 253–256; Harriman Oral History Project, Kennedy Institute of Politics, Harvard University, 326.

HARRIMAN'S WESTERN AID PLAN: Unsent messages from Moscow, Harriman personal papers, Washington, D.C.; Harriman cable to Washington, *FRUS*, 1945, V, 817–820; Herring, *Aid to Russia*, 200.

ROOSEVELT'S ATTITUDES BEFORE HIS DEATH: Feis, *Churchill Roosevelt Stalin*, 571–599; Harriman and Abel, *Special Envoy*, 439–440; Harriman, *America and Russia in a Changing World*, 38n; Harriman Oral History Project, Kennedy Institute of Politics, Harvard University, 304, 317.

HARRIMAN'S SUPPORT FOR A POSTWAR LOAN: Harriman cable to Washington, Apr. 11, 1945, *FRUS*, 1945, V, 996; Herring, *Aid to Russia*, 176.

Chapter 9
Words of One Syllable

TRUMAN TAKES OFFICE: Harry Truman, *Year of Decisions*, 1–27; Donovan, *Conflict and Crisis*, 3–14; Manchester, *The Glory and the Dream*, 351–374; *Time*, Apr. 23, 1945; Poen, ed., *Letters Home by Harry Truman*, 189; Ferrell, ed., *Off the Record: The Private Papers of Harry S. Truman*, 14–16; John McCloy's private diaries, courtesy of John McCloy; Leahy, *I Was There*, 347–348.

ACHESON ON TRUMAN'S ASCENSION: Authors' interviews with Lydia Kirk, Alice Stanley Acheson; Acheson, *Present at the Creation*, 103–104.

HARRIMAN LEARNS OF ROOSEVELT'S DEATH: Harriman and Abel, *Special Envoy*, 440; authors' interviews with Kathleen Harriman Mortimer, Elbridge Durbrow.

HARRIMAN'S MEETING WITH MOLOTOV: *FRUS*, 1945, V, 825–826; Harriman and Abel, *Special Envoy*, 440–441.

HARRIMAN'S REQUESTS TO RETURN HOME: *FRUS*, 1945, V, 212ff., 826; Harriman and Abel, *Special Envoy*, 441.

HARRIMAN'S MEETING WITH STALIN: *FRUS*, 1945, V, 826–828; *FRUS*, 1945, I, 289–290; Harriman and Abel, *Special Envoy*, 441–443.

TRUMAN PRESS CONFERENCE: *Public Papers of the Presidents: Harry Truman*, 1945, 11; *Time*, Apr. 30, 1945; Harry Truman, *Year of Decisions*, 49.

HARRIMAN'S FLIGHT TO WASHINGTON: Harriman and Meiklejohn notes, Harriman private papers, Washington, D.C.; authors' interviews with Kathleen Harriman Mortimer.

BOHLEN AND HOPKINS LEARN OF FDR'S DEATH: Bohlen, *Witness to History*, 209–212; Sherwood, *Roosevelt and Hopkins*, 880–882; Bohlen personal papers, Library of Congress.

BOHLEN AND STETTINIUS MEET TRUMAN: Harry Truman, *Year of Decisions*, 14–27; National Archives, notes of meetings, Bohlen papers, Record Group 59; Ferrell, ed., *Off the Record*, 18; Leahy, *I Was There*, 349.

HARRIMAN BRIEFS TOP OFFICIALS IN WASHINGTON: Authors' interviews with Averell Harriman, Kathleen Harriman Mortimer; Harriman and Abel, *Special Envoy*, 449–450; Stimson diary, Apr. 16, 1945, in Stimson papers, Yale University; Millis, ed., *The Forrestal Diaries*, 47; *FRUS*, 1945, V, 839–846.

DOMINO THEORY: Safire, *Safire's Political Dictionary*, 178.

HARRIMAN AND BOHLEN MEET WITH TRUMAN: Authors' interviews with Averell Harriman; *FRUS*, 1945, V, 231–234; Harriman and Abel, *Special Envoy*, 447–449; Harry Truman, *Year of Decisions*, 70–72; Donovan, *Conflict and Crisis*, 35–39; Byrnes, *Speaking Frankly*, 61; Stettinius memorandum, Apr. 22, 1945, cited in Yergin, *Shattered Peace*, 77.

COLD WAR ETYMOLOGY: Safire, *Safire's Political Dictionary*, 127–129.

TRUMAN MEETS WITH ADVISERS, APRIL 23: *FRUS, 1945,* V, 252–255; Harry Truman, *Year of Decisions,* 77–79; Harriman and Abel, *Special Envoy,* 451–453; Stimson diary, Apr. 23, 1945, in Stimson papers, Yale University; Stimson and Bundy, *On Active Service,* 608–611; Donovan, *Conflict and Crisis,* 40; Millis, ed., *Forrestal Diaries,* 48–51.

TRUMAN, HARRIMAN, BOHLEN, AND OTHERS MEET WITH MOLOTOV: *FRUS, 1945,* V, 256–259; Harry Truman, *Year of Decisions,* 79–82; Harriman and Abel, *Special Envoy,* 453–454; Bohlen, *Witness to History,* 213–214; Donovan, *Conflict and Crisis,* 41–42; Leahy, *I Was There,* 351–352. Bohlen's notes in *FRUS* and his autobiography do not mention the final exchange ("I've never been talked to . . ."), and in an interview with Robert Donovan he says he does not think the words were spoken. The exchange, however, is cited by both Truman and Harriman in their respective memoirs.

VIEWS ON TRUMAN'S NEW ATTITUDE: Donovan, *Conflict and Crisis,* 42–43; Leahy, *I Was There,* 352; Vandenberg, ed., *The Private Papers of Senator Vandenberg,* 176; Churchill, *Triumph and Tragedy,* 492; *Time,* Apr. 30, 1945; Larson dissertation, "Belief and Inference," 229.

MEETING AT THE ELBE: Weisberger, *Cold War, Cold Peace,* 9; *Time,* May 7, 1945.

HARRIMAN'S BRIEFINGS IN SAN FRANCISCO: Authors' interviews with Averell Harriman; Harriman and Abel, *Special Envoy,* 454–457; Bland dissertation, "W. Averell Harriman: Businessman and Diplomat, 1891–1945," 390–393; Larson dissertation, "Belief and Inference," 231, 253; Harriman interview, Dulles Oral History Project, Princeton University; *FRUS, 1945,* I, 389–398; Bohlen, *Witness to History,* 214–215; Steel, *Walter Lippmann and the American Century,* 419–420; Lippmann columns, Apr. 26 and May 12, 1945; *Time,* May 7, 1945; Stone, "Anti-Russian Undertow"; Gaddis, *The U.S. and the Origins of the Cold War,* 226–227.

ATTITUDES TOWARD ANGLO-AMERICAN ALLIANCE: Larsen dissertation, "Belief and Inference," 253; *The Nation,* May 25, 1945; Lippmann column, May 12, 1945; *New York Times,* June 1, 1945; Stimson and Bundy, *On Active Service,* 566.

V-E DAY IN WASHINGTON: Harry Truman, *Year of Decisions,* 205–208; *New York Times,* May 8–10, 1945; *Time,* May 14 and 21, 1945; Donovan, *Conflict and Crisis,* 51–52; Margaret Truman, *Harry S. Truman,* 241.

V-E DAY IN MOSCOW: George F. Kennan, *Memoirs: 1925–1950,* 239–244; *The New York Times,* May 8–10, 1945.

KENNAN AND THE POLISH BORDER DISPUTE: *FRUS, 1945,* V, 226–231, 276–278, 288–298; authors' interview with Elbridge Durbrow.

TRUMAN IS INFORMED OF THE BOMB: Stimson and Bundy, *On Active Service,* 635–643; Stimson diary, Mar. 13, 1944, in Stimson papers, Yale University; Truman, *Year of Decisions,* 85–87; Donovan, *Conflict and Crisis,* xii–xiv, 45–49; Giovannitti and Freed, *The Decision to Drop the Bomb,* 27–28, 49–52; Lieberman, *The Scorpion and the Tarantula,* 68–69; Hewlett and Anderson, *The New World,* 343; Sherwin, *A World Destroyed,* 162–164; Kurzman, *Day of The Bomb,* 212.

STIMSON AND McCLOY ON SPHERES OF INFLUENCE: Stimson diary, Apr. 16 and 26, May 8, 1945, in Stimson papers, Yale University; authors' interviews with John McCloy; McCloy diary entry for Apr. 30 and calendar notes, McCloy private papers; Stimson-McCloy telephone transcript, in Stimson papers, Yale University, cited in Yergin, *Shattered Peace,* 80.

BOHLEN ON SPHERES OF INFLUENCE: Policy Group document PG-14, Sept. 23, 1943, Box 119, Notter Records, National Archives; Mark, "Charles E. Bohlen and the Acceptable Limits of Soviet Hegemony in Eastern Europe."

HARRIMAN AND BOHLEN DISCUSSIONS ON THE FLIGHT HOME FROM SAN FRANCISCO, AND IDEA FOR HOPKINS MISSION: Harriman and Abel, *Special Envoy,* 459; Harriman itinerary, Harriman personal papers, Washington, D.C.; Bohlen, *Witness to History,* 215; Harry Truman, *Year of Decisions,* 110, 257–258; Sherwood, *Roosevelt and Hopkins,* 885–887; Ferrell, ed., *Off the Record,* 31; Harriman and McCloy, off-the-record discussion of the origins of the Cold War, in Harriman personal papers, Washington, D.C. For a different view of Hopkins' mission origins, see Alperovitz, *Atomic Diplomacy,* 68–71, 270–275. (Harriman in 1970 declared: "Alperovitz's thesis is so contemptible that I can hardly even discuss it." Harriman Oral History Project, Kennedy Institute of Politics, Harvard University, 456.)

STIMSON-McCLOY-HARRIMAN MAY 10 LUNCH: Stimson diary, May 10, 1945, in Stimson papers, Yale University; authors' interviews with John McCloy; McCloy diaries, May 9 and 10, 1945, McCloy private papers; Giovannitti and Freed, *The Decision to Drop the Bomb,* 57.

HARRIMAN-BOHLEN-McCLOY-FORRESTAL-GREW MAY 12 MEETING: Authors' interviews with John McCloy; McCloy's journal entry on May 12, courtesy of McCloy; Harriman Oral History Project, Kennedy Institute of Politics, Harvard University, 451; Grew, *Turbulent Era,* Vol. II, 1455–1457; Harriman and Abel, *Special Envoy,* 461; Millis, ed., *The Forrestal Diaries,* 55–57; Forrestal's unpublished diaries, May 12, 1945 (a fuller account of what appears in Millis).

HARRIMAN AND LEND-LEASE: Harriman and Abel, *Special Envoy*, 459–461; Bland dissertation, "W. Averell Harriman: Businessman and Diplomat, 1891–1945," 397–402; Larson dissertation, "Belief and Inference," 242–248; Sherwin, *A World Destroyed*, 176–178; Harry Truman, *Year of Decisions*, 227–229; Herring, *Aid to Russia*, 202–205.

TRUMAN AND DAVIES, MAY 13: Sherwin, *A World Destroyed*, 170–184; Joseph Davies journals, May 13, 1945, Library of Congress.

STIMSON AND McCLOY, MAY 13 AND 14: Stimson diary, May 13 and 14, in Stimson papers, Yale University; interviews with McCloy.

STIMSON, McCLOY, HARRIMAN, FORRESTAL, GREW, MAY 15: Stimson diary, May 15, in Stimson papers, Yale University; Millis, ed., *Forrestal Diaries*, 57; Hewlett and Anderson, *The New World*, 350; Sherwin, *A World Destroyed*, 190; Alperovitz, *Atomic Diplomacy*, 97–98.

HARRIMAN, BOHLEN, GREW, TRUMAN, MAY 15: *FRUS, Potsdam*, I, 12–14; Grew, *Turbulent Era*, 1462; authors' interviews with Averell Harriman.

STIMSON AND TRUMAN, MAY 16: Stimson diary, May 16, in Stimson papers, Yale University; Hewlett and Anderson, *The New World*, 351; Sherwin, *A World Destroyed*, 191.

GROWING PUBLIC FEARS, MAY 1945: *Time*, June 11, 1945; Larson dissertation, "Belief and Inference," 254–255.

GREW, HARRIMAN, BOHLEN, MAY 19: Grew, *Turbulent Era*, Vol. II, 1445–1446.

CONCLUDING PLANS FOR THE HOPKINS MISSION: Truman appointment sheet, May 19, in *Off the Record*, ed. by Ferrell, 31; Millis, ed., *Forrestal Diaries*, 58; Harriman Oral History Project, Kennedy Institute of Politics, Harvard University, 491; Sherwood, *Roosevelt and Hopkins*, 887; authors' interviews with Averell Harriman; see also source above on origins of the Hopkins mission.

THE HOPKINS MISSION: Authors' interviews with Averell Harriman, Kathleen Harriman Mortimer; Mortimer letters, Bohlen letter, and Harriman memos, Harriman personal papers, Washington, D.C.; Harriman and Abel, *Special Envoy*, 462–475; Bohlen, *Witness to History*, 218–223; Feis, *Between War and Peace: The Potsdam Conference*, 97–123; Sherwood, *Roosevelt and Hopkins*, 887–912; *FRUS, Potsdam*, I, 20–62; Harriman and McCloy, off-the-record discussion of the origins of the Cold War, in Harriman personal papers, Washington, D.C.; Ulam, *Expansion and Coexistence*, 385–386; Ruddy dissertation, "Charles E. Bohlen and the Soviet Union," 196–200; Bland dissertation, "W. Averell Harriman: Businessman and Diplomat, 1891–1945," 407–416. (Bohlen's notes in *FRUS* indicate that Hopkins pressed the issue of U.N. voting procedure, but Harriman's papers and book, and other documents, indicate that he took the lead.)

KENNAN AND HOPKINS: George F. Kennan, *Memoirs: 1925–1950*, 212–213, 247–251, 532–546; *FRUS, 1945*, V, 295–296; authors' interviews with George Kennan.

OPINION AFTER THE HOPKINS MISSION: Harriman letter to Truman, June 8, 1945, *FRUS, Potsdam*, I, 61–62; Bohlen letter, June 13, 1945, Harriman personal papers, Washington, D.C.; *Time*, June 18, 1945; Larson dissertation, "Belief and Inference," 268–272; Truman diary, June 7, 1945; Harriman Oral History Project, Kennedy Institute of Politics, Harvard University, 405. (Harriman says in retrospect: "If you've seen the telegrams, you'll find that Harry was far more optimistic about what he achieved in Moscow than I was." The cables do not bear him out.)

Chapter 10
Line Down the Middle

McCLOY'S REPORT ON HIS EUROPEAN TRIP: Authors' interviews with John McCloy; McCloy's private journals, April–May, 1945, courtesy of McCloy; Harry Truman, *Year of Decisions*, 101–105; Stimson diary, Apr. 19, 22, 23, 26, 1945, in Stimson papers, Yale University.

KENNAN'S VIEWS ON GERMANY, SPRING OF 1945: Authors' interviews with George Kennan; George F. Kennan, *Memoirs: 1925–1950*, 252–259; Wright dissertation, "George F. Kennan: Scholar-Diplomat," 295–309; Comments on PWC-141a, Kennan papers, Princeton University.

CHURCHILL's "IRON CURTAIN" TELEGRAM: *FRUS, 1945, Berlin*, I, 9; Safire, *Safire's Political Dictionary*, 339–340.

BACKGROUND ON REPARATIONS ISSUE: Kuklick, *American Policy and the Division of Germany*, 74–140; Gaddis, *The United States and the Origins of the Cold War*, 98–129, 220–243; *FRUS, 1945, Yalta*, 978–980; *FRUS, 1945*, III, 1176–1238; *FRUS, 1945, Berlin*, I, 435–548.

HARRIMAN AND KENNAN ON REPARATIONS: *FRUS, 1945*, III, 1176, 1191, 1195, 1200, 1204; Harriman Oral History Project, Kennedy Institute of Politics, Harvard Unviersity, 460; authors' interviews with George Kennan.

APPOINTMENT OF PAULEY: Harry Truman, *Year of Decisions*, 307–309; Donovan, *Conflict and Crisis*, 78; Mee, *Meeting at Potsdam*, 184.

LOVETT'S ROLE IN FORMULATING REPARATIONS POLICY: Fanton dissertation, "Robert A. Lovett: The War Years," 241–242.

KENNAN AND HARRIMAN ON PAULEY TALKS: *FRUS*, 1945, III, 1211–1213.

TRUMAN ON JUNE 17: Truman diary, in *Off the Record*, ed. by Ferrell, 47.

OPPENHEIMER ON JUNE 17: Sherwin, *A World Destroyed*, 304–305; Giovannitti and Freed, *The Decision to Drop the Bomb*, 121–123; Wyden, *Day One*, 170–171.

TIBBETS ON JUNE 17: Wyden, *Day One*, 198–199; Groves, *Now It Can Be Told*, 272–275.

STIMSON, McCLOY, GREW, MARSHALL MEETINGS OF MAY 29: Stimson diary, May 29, in Stimson papers, Yale University; Giovannitti and Freed, *The Decision to Drop the Bomb*, 96; McCloy notes, in Stimson papers, Yale University; Wyden, *Day One*, 159n.

BACKGROUND ON THE BOMB: Hewlett and Anderson, *The New World*, 350–372; Giovannitti and Freed, *The Decision to Drop the Bomb*, 69–187; Wyden, *Day One*, 129–247; Sherwin, *A World Destroyed*, 202–219.

McCLOY'S PROPOSALS OF JUNE 17 AND 18: McCloy has recounted this episode many times over the years, with occasional embellishments. The account here is drawn from McCloy's diaries for June 16, 17, and 18, his interviews with the authors, and the transcript of an interview, revised by McCloy, given to Fred Freed in 1965 for an NBC News "White Paper" on the topic. Excerpts are in Giovannitti and Freed, *The Decision to Drop the Bomb*, 135–138. The first record of McCloy's story is in Forrestal's diaries for Mar. 8, 1947 (see Millis, ed., *Forrestal Diaries*, 70–71). But Forrestal notes that he was not at any such meeting, even though the official minutes of the June 18 session list him as present (*FRUS*, 1945, *Berlin*, I, 903–910, 929–931). Nor do the minutes of that meeting contain any comments by McCloy, although they end by saying "certain other matters" were discussed (*FRUS*, 1945, *Berlin*, I, 889, footnote 2). McCloy's recollections that Stimson did not come to work that day are contradicted by McCloy's own diary (June 18, 1945, McCloy private papers). McCloy's diary also indicates that he was in Hastings-on-Hudson that Sunday for a family visit, although it is possible his meeting with Stimson took place when he returned that evening, as McCloy now recollects. See also: McCloy, *The Challenge to American Foreign Policy*, 40–42; Elting Morison, *Turmoil and Tradition*, 631; McCloy interview, conducted by Eric Sevareid, July 13, 1975, CBS television; Stimson and Bundy, *On Active Service*, 620.

WORK ON VERSIONS OF THE POTSDAM PROCLAMATION, LATE JUNE: Stimson

776 NOTES

diary, June 19, 26–30, July 2, 3, in Stimson papers, Yale University; Millis, ed., *Forrestal Diaries*, 71–72; Hewlett and Anderson, *The New World*, 364–370; Giovannitti and Freed, *The Decision to Drop the Bomb*, 140–149; FRUS, 1945, *Berlin*, I, 888–894.

HARRIMAN GOES TO POTSDAM: Harriman and Abel, *Special Envoy*, 481–484; FRUS, 1945, *Berlin*, I, 132, 144, 146, 722–723, 745; Harriman private papers, Washington, D.C.

BOHLEN GOES TO POTSDAM: Bohlen, *Witness to History*, 225–228; FRUS, 1945, *Berlin*, II, log of the President, 8–10.

BYRNES AND TRUMAN: Harry Truman, *Year of Decisions*, 22–23, 190–193, 317, and passim; Byrnes, *Speaking Frankly*, 67–72.

BYRNES'S RELATIONS WITH STIMSON, HARRIMAN AND OTHERS: Harriman and Abel, *Special Envoy*, 488; Harriman and McCloy, off-the-record discussion of the origins of the Cold War, Harriman personal papers, Washington, D.C.; Mee, *Meeting at Potsdam*, 4–7; Acheson, *Present at the Creation*, 111; Feis, *From Trust to Terror*, 18; Stimson diary, July 16–23, in Stimson papers, Yale University.

ATMOSPHERE AT POTSDAM: Bohlen, *Witness to History*, 228; Harriman and Abel, *Special Envoy*, 484–485; Stimson diary, July 16–23, 1945, in Stimson papers, Yale University; McCloy diaries, July 15–30, 1945; Feis, *From Trust to Terror*, passim; Mee, *Meeting at Potsdam*, passim.

STIMSON AND McCLOY PAPERS OF JULY 16: Authors' interviews with John McCloy; Stimson diary, July 16, in Stimson papers, Yale University; FRUS, 1945, *Berlin*, II, 631, 754–755, 1223–1224, 1265–1267, 1322–1333; McCloy diaries, July 16–20, 1945; Acheson, *Present at the Creation*, 113; Harriman and Abel, *Special Envoy*, 493.

ALAMOGORDO TEST RESULTS: FRUS, 1945, *Berlin*, II, 1360–1364; Hewlett and Anderson, *The New World*, 377–379; Lieberman, *The Scorpion and the Tarantula*, 98–99; Wyden, *Day One*, 210–213; Stimson diary, July 16–23, in Stimson papers, Yale University; McCloy diaries, July 16, 23–24.

STIMSON, McCLOY, AND HARRIMAN DISCUSS CONTROLLING THE BOMB: Stimson diary, July 19, and 23, 1945, in Stimson papers, Yale University; FRUS, 1945, *Berlin*, II, 1155–1157; authors' interviews with John McCloy; McCloy diaries, July 20, 1945; Stimson and Bundy, *On Active Service*, 638–641; Harriman and Abel, *Special Envoy*, 488; Averell Harriman, *America and Russia in a Changing World*, 73; Harvey Bundy interview, Columbia Oral History Project; Bland dissertation, "W. Averell Harriman: Businessman and Diplomat, 1891–1945," 427–428; Bohlen, *Witness to History*, 238.

INFORMING STALIN OF THE BOMB: Bohlen, *Witness to History*, 237; Harry Truman, *Year of Decisions*, 416; Byrnes, *Speaking Frankly*, 263; Leahy, *I Was There*, 429.

McCLOY'S VISITS TO BERLIN AND PAPERS ON GERMANY WITH STIMSON: Authors' interviews with John McCloy; McCloy diary, July 17, 25, and 26, 1945; *FRUS, 1945, Berlin*, II, 631, 754–757.

BYRNES'S PACKAGE DEAL ON REPARATIONS: *FRUS, 1945, Berlin*, II, 274–275, 471–476, 480–483, 503–505, 510, 565–601; Byrnes, *Speaking Frankly*, 85; Byrnes, *All in One Lifetime*, 302; Bohlen, *Witness to History*, 232–233.

McCLOY'S VIEWS ON REPARATIONS: McCloy diaries, July 23–30, 1945.

McCLOY LEAVES POTSDAM: Authors' interviews with John McCloy; *FRUS, 1945, Berlin*, II, 925–926; McCloy journals, July 24–31.

HARRIMAN LEAVES POTSDAM: Millis, ed., *The Forrestal Diaries*, 79; Bland dissertation, "W. Averell Harriman: Businessman and Diplomat, 1891–1945," 428–430.

BOHLEN LEAVES POTSDAM: Bohlen, *Witness to History*, 237–238.

STIMSON LEAVES POTSDAM: Stimson diary, July 25, in Stimson papers, Yale University; Wyden, *Day One*, 235–237; Hewlett and Anderson, *The New World*, 396.

STIMSON ON THE DECISION TO DROP THE BOMB: Stimson and Bundy, *On Active Service*, 629–632.

LOVETT'S ROLE IN ATOMIC-BOMB PLANNING: Fanton dissertation, "Robert A. Lovett: The War Years," 242–243; Lovett interview, Columbia University Oral History Project, 58 (cited by Fanton).

AMERICAN DESIRE FOR SOVIET ENTRY INTO THE JAPANESE WAR: Giovannitti and Freed, *The Decision to Drop the Bomb*, 205–208; Alperovitz, *Atomic Diplomacy*, 180–184; Stimson diary, July 23–24, in Stimson papers, Yale University; Stimson and Bundy, *On Active Service*, 637; Bohlen, *Witness to History*, 238; Harriman and Abel, *Special Envoy*, 489, 492; *FRUS, 1945, Berlin*, II, 1324; Byrnes, *All in One Lifetime*, 291; Sherwin, *A World Destroyed*, 244.

POTSDAM PROCLAMATION TO JAPAN: McCloy diaries, July 27, 1945, and notes with Aug. 30, 1945, entry; Harriman and Abel, *Special Envoy*, 492; Acheson, *Present at the Creation*, 113; Hewlett and Anderson, *The New World*, 395; Giovannitti and Freed, *The Decision to Drop the Bomb*, 226.

REVISIONIST THESIS ON MOTIVES FOR USING THE BOMB: Alperovitz, *Atomic Diplomacy*, passim; Sherwin, *A World Destroyed*, passim; Williams, *The Tragedy of American Diplomacy*, passim; Fleming, *The Cold War and Its Origins*, passim; Steel, *Imperialists and Other Heroes*, 79–89; Maddox, *The New Left and the Origins of the Cold War*, passim; Miles, "The Strange Myth of Half a Million Lives Saved"; Harry Truman, *Year of Decisions*, 419.

Chapter 11
The Blinding Dawn

BOMBING OF HIROSHIMA: Wyden, *Day One*, 243–247; Tibbets, "How to Drop an Atom Bomb"; Hewlett and Anderson, *The New World*, 416; Thomas and Morgan-Witts, *Enola Gay*, 289–324.

LOVETT AT PENTAGON: Authors' interviews with Robert Lovett; Wyden, *Day One*, 288; Groves, *Now It Can Be Told*, 328–330.

McCLOY IN ROME: Authors' interviews with John McCloy.

THE ATOMIC AGE: *New York Times*, Aug. 7, 1945; *Time*, Aug. 20, 1945.

HARRIMAN AND V-J DAY IN MOSCOW: Harriman and Abel, *Special Envoy*, 498–503; authors' interviews with Kathleen Harriman Mortimer; Mortimer letters and Harriman notes, Harriman personal papers, Washington, D.C.; Harriman Oral History Project, Kennedy Institute of Politics, Harvard University, 484. (Harriman had been very forceful in encouraging the Chinese Foreign Minister not to come to terms with Stalin regarding the concessions the Soviets would get for entering the war. "I had a lot of trouble getting Soong to stick to my tight interpretation," he later said. Harriman Oral History Project, Kennedy Institute of Politics, Harvard University, 453.)

STIMSON AND McCLOY WORK ON SEPTEMBER MEMO ON THE BOMB: Stimson diary, Aug. 12–Sept. 5, Sept. 8, 10, 12, 13; in Stimson papers, Yale University; Stimson and Bundy, *On Active Service*, 641–646; authors' interviews with John McCloy; Lieberman, *The Scorpion and the Tarantula*, 139–143; Hewlett and Anderson, *The New World*, 417–419.

McCLOY AND BYRNES: McCloy diaries and notes, Sept. 2, 1945, McCloy private papers.

SEPTEMBER 21 CABINET MEETING: Stimson diary, Sept. 21, Forrestal diaries, Sept. 21, and notes attached; Millis, ed., *The Forrestal Diaries*, 94–96; Harry Truman, *Year of Decisions*, 525–526; Lieberman, *The Scorpion and the Tarantula*, 144–149; Hewlett and Anderson, *The New World*, 420–421.

ACHESON UPON BECOMING UNDER SECRETARY: Authors' interviews with Mary Acheson Bundy, Alice Stanley Acheson, Barbara Evans (Acheson's secretary); Hamburger, "Mr. Secretary"; Acheson, *Present at the Creation*, 111–121; David Acheson, ed., *Among Friends*, 56–64; McLellan, *Dean Acheson*, 56–59; Larson dissertation, "Belief and Inference," 546–555; *The Nation*, Aug. 25, 1945; *Fortune*, "Secretary Acheson"; Reston, "The No. 1 No. 2 Man in Washington."

ACHESON ON CZECHOSLOVAKIA: *FRUS, 1945, IV*, 493–494.

ACHESON ADOPTS STIMSON'S VIEWS ON THE BOMB: Stimson diary, Sept. 13, 21, in Stimson papers, Yale University; Forrestal diaries, Sept. 21; Acheson, *Present at the Creation*, 124–125; Lieberman, *The Scorpion and the Tarantula*, 143–145; Hewlett and Anderson, *The New World*, 418–420; McCloy diaries, Aug. 30, 1945; authors' interviews with John McCloy.

ACHESON MEMO FOR TRUMAN: Acheson, *Present at the Creation*, 125; *FRUS, 1945, II*, 48–50; Lieberman, *The Scorpion and the Tarantula*, 151; Larson dissertation, "Belief and Inference," 557–559.

TRUMAN'S OCTOBER 3 MESSAGE: Acheson, *Present at the Creation*, 125, 743.

CONGRESSIONAL AND PUBLIC OPINION IN SEPTEMBER 1945: Gaddis, *The U.S. and the Origins of the Cold War*, 254–257.

KENNAN AND CONGRESSIONAL TOUR OF MOSCOW: Authors' interview with Senator Claude Pepper; George F. Kennan, *Memoirs: 1925–1950*, 276–277; *FRUS, 1945, V*, 881–884.

KENNAN MESSAGE ON ATOMIC CONTROL AND ESPIONAGE: *FRUS, 1945, V*, 884–886, see also 366; Hoyt Vandenberg (director of Central Intelligence) memo, June 27, 1946, Kennan papers, Princeton University.

MOLOTOV'S TOAST IN LONDON: Larson dissertation, "Belief and Inference," 459.

HARRIMAN'S TALK WITH BYRNES: Harriman and Abel, *Special Envoy*, 509–510; authors' interviews with Averell Harriman.

HARRIMAN'S PERSONAL OUTLOOK ABOUT STAYING ON AS AMBASSADOR: Authors' interviews with Averell Harriman, Kathleen Harriman Mortimer, Pamela Churchill Harriman, Louis Auchincloss, Patricia Alsop.

PAMELA CHURCHILL HARRIMAN: Authors' interview with Pamela Churchill Harriman; Bumiller, "Pamela Harriman," the Washington *Post* (includes quote about Harriman's looks); Foreman "Pamela Harriman's Role"; *Life* cover story on Pamela Churchill Harriman; Cholly Knickerbocker Observes, New York *Journal-American*, Sept. 13, 1949; *Sunday Mirror Magazine*, "New Triumphs of a Churchill"; *New York Times*, "Harriman and Mrs. Leland Hayward Will Marry," Sept. 18, 1971.

HARRIMAN-McCLOY TRIP THROUGH EUROPE, OCTOBER 1945: Authors' interviews with John McCloy; McCloy diary entries, Sept. 30, Oct. 7, 8, 1945, and cable to Washington, McCloy private papers; Harriman and Abel, *Special Envoy*, 510–511; Harriman and McCloy, off-the-record discussion of the origins of the Cold War, Harriman personal papers, Washington, D.C.

HARRIMAN AT STALIN'S DACHA: Harriman and Abel, *Special Envoy*, 511–516; *FRUS*, 1945, II, 562–576; Larson dissertation, "Belief and Inference," 466–469; Lippmann columns, Oct. 18 and Nov. 1, 1945.

McCLOY AND MacARTHUR: McCloy diary entries, Oct. 22–25, 1945, and teletype conference of McCloy, Bohlen, and Acheson, McCloy private papers.

McCLOY'S SPEECHES: Prepared text and transcript, speech to the annual dinner of the Academy of Political Science, New York City, Nov. 8, 1945, courtesy of McCloy; speech over NBC radio, Nov. 16, 1945, courtesy of McCloy; *Proceedings of the Academy of Political Science* (Vol. 21), Fall 1945.

McCLOY ASSESSMENTS: Interviews with Averell Harriman, Robert Lovett, and Harvey Bundy, Columbia Oral History Project; Kissinger, *White House Years*, 22–23; authors' interview with Henry Kissinger.

McCLOY LEAVES GOVERNMENT: Schwartz dissertation, "From Occupation to Alliance," 35–36; McCloy diaries, October-November 1945; authors' interviews with John McCloy, Benjamin Shute.

McCLOY AND THE COUNCIL ON FOREIGN RELATIONS: Record of meeting, Dec. 4, 1945; minutes from study groups and annual reports, archives of the Council on Foreign Relations, New York; Shepardson, *Early History of the Council on Foreign Relations*; Kraft, "School for Statesmen"; authors' interviews with John McCloy; McCloy diaries, August–November 1945.

LOVETT LEAVES GOVERNMENT: Authors' interviews with Robert Lovett, Adèle Brown Lovett; *Time* "New Policy, New Broom," 25; Fanton dissertation, "Robert A. Lovett: The War Years," 244–249; *New York Times*, Nov. 24, 1945; Stimson letter to Truman, Sept. 6, 1945, in Stimson papers, Yale University; Stimson diary, Sept. 21, 1945, in Stimson papers, Yale University.

ACHESON SPEECHES: McLellan, *Dean Acheson*, 66–68; Acheson, *Present at the Creation*, 130–131; *Department of State Bulletin*, Nov. 18, 1945.

BOHLEN'S POLICY ON SPHERES: National Archives, memo of Oct. 18, 1945, Bohlen papers, Record Group 59; Mark, "Charles E. Bohlen and the Acceptable Limits of Soviet Hegemony in Eastern Europe"; Larson dissertation, "Belief and Inference," 470; Byrnes, *Speaking Frankly*, 108; speech of Oct. 31, by Byrnes, *State Department Bulletin*, Nov. 4, 1945.

HARRIMAN AND LITVINOV: Harriman and Abel, *Special Envoy*, 518; FRUS, 1945, V, 921–922.

HARRIMAN'S VIEWS ON THE SOVIETS AND THE BOMB: *FRUS, 1945, V, 922–924*; Harriman and Abel, *Special Envoy*, 521; Bland dissertation, "W. Averell Harriman: Businessman and Diplomat, 1891–1945," 474.

PROPOSALS FOR ATOMIC CONTROL, NOVEMBER–DECEMBER 1945: Gaddis, *The U.S. and the Origins of the Cold War*, 271–272; Lieberman, *The Scorpion and the Tarantula*, 187–188; Larson dissertation, "Belief and Inference," 474–477; Hewlett and Anderson, *The New World*, 471–474.

ACHESON MOLLIFIES VANDENBERG ON PLAN: Acheson, *Present at the Creation*, 135; McLellan, *Dean Acheson*, 74; Gaddis, *The U.S. and the Origins of the Cold War*, 278–279; FRUS, 1945, II, 609–610; Hewlett and Anderson, *The New World*, 474–475.

MOSCOW CONFERENCE, DECEMBER 1945: Harriman and Abel, *Special Envoy*, 523–526; George F. Kennan, *Memoirs: 1925–1950*, 284–292; Bohlen, *Witness to History*, 249–253; Lieberman, *The Scorpion and the Tarantula*, 207–217; Larson dissertation, "Belief and Inference," 481–483.

ACHESON MOLLIFIES VANDENBERG ON MOSCOW CONFERENCE: Acheson, *Present at the Creation*, 135–136; McLellan, *Dean Acheson*, 75–76; Hewlett and Anderson, *The New World*, 474–475.

ACHESON AND TRUMAN'S SHOWDOWN WITH BYRNES ON THE WILLIAMSBURG: Authors' interviews with Clark Clifford; Larson dissertation, "Belief and Inference," 327–328; Acheson, *Present at the Creation*, 136; McLellan, *Dean Acheson*, 75–76; for the larger question of what Truman did or did not say to Byrnes, see Gaddis, *The U.S. and the Origins of the Cold War*, 285–290; Harry Truman, *Year of Decisions*, 250–252; Byrnes, *All in One Lifetime*, 342–343; Yergin, *Shattered Peace*, 158–162.

Chapter 12
Containment

HARRIMAN'S DEPARTURE FROM MOSCOW: Authors' interviews with Averell Harriman, George Kennan, Elbridge Durbrow; Harriman and Abel, *Special Envoy*, 531–535; Harriman's talk to embassy staff (Jan. 22, 1946), Harriman personal papers, Washington, D.C.; Harriman's radio interview with Quentin Reynolds (Mar. 3, 1946), Harriman personal papers, Washington, D.C.

STALIN'S FEBRUARY 9 SPEECH: *Vital Speeches*, Mar. 1, 1946.

REACTIONS TO STALIN'S SPEECH; Millis, ed., *The Forrestal Diaries*, 134–135; Gaddis, *The U.S. and the Origins of the Cold War*, 299–301; DeSantis, *The Diplomacy of Silence*, 173; Yergin, *Shattered Peace*, 166–167; *Time*, Feb. 18, 1946; *FRUS*, 1946, VI, 695n; Larson dissertation, "Belief and Inference," 337–339, 487.

NITZE'S TALKS WITH FORRESTAL AND ACHESON: Authors' interviews with Paul Nitze.

BOHLEN'S SUGGESTIONS OF FEBRUARY 1946: National Archives, memo of Feb. 14, Bohlen papers, Record Group 59; DeSantis, *The Diplomacy of Silence*, 173; Yergin, *Shattered Peace*, 165.

KENNAN'S LONG TELEGRAM: George F. Kennan, *Memoirs: 1925–1950*, 292–295, 545–559; *FRUS*, 1946, VI, 696–709; authors' interviews with George Kennan, Elbridge Durbrow, Loy Henderson; Wright dissertation, "George F. Kennan, Scholar-Diplomat," 393–410; Durbrow-Kennan letters, January 1946, Kennan papers, Princeton University. (Kennan, in his memoirs, exaggerates a bit in saying that the telegram was eight thousand words.)

REACTION TO THE LONG TELEGRAM: Authors' interviews with George Kennan, Averell Harriman, Elbridge Durbrow, Loy Henderson; George F. Kennan, *Memoirs: 1925–1950*, 294–295; Harriman and Abel, *Special Envoy*, 548; Millis, ed., *The Forrestal Diaries*, 135–140; Wright dissertation, "George F. Kennan: Scholar-Diplomat," 410; DeSantis, *The Diplomacy of Silence*, 172–179; National Archives, memos of Mar. 13 and 14, Bohlen papers, Record Group 59.

KENNAN AND FORRESTAL: Authors' interviews with George Kennan, Grace Kennan Warnecke, George Elsey, Michael Forrestal; Gardner, *Architects of Illusion*, 270–300; Rogow, *James Forrestal*, 200–203 and passim; Wright dissertation, "George F. Kennan: Scholar-Diplomat," 410–419.

ACHESON, LILIENTHAL, AND THE LONG TELEGRAM: Authors' interviews with

Loy Henderson; Lilienthal, *The Journals of David Lilienthal*, Vol. II, 25; Acheson, *Present at the Creation*, 151; Lieberman, *The Scorpion and the Tarantula*, 252.

THE ACHESON-LILIENTHAL REPORT: Hewlett and Anderson, *The New World*, 531–555; Lieberman, *The Scorpion and the Tarantula*, 233–259; Lilienthal, *The Journals of David Lilienthal*, Vol. II, 10–33; *New York Times*, Mar. 5, 8, 13, 18, 1946; Acheson, Lilienthal, McCloy, and others, "A Report on the International Control of Atomic Energy."

ACHESON'S ROLE IN ATOMIC CONTROL PLAN: Acheson, *Present at the Creation*, 151–156; Larson dissertation, "Belief and Inference," 561–567; Acheson interview (1955), Truman Library, postpresidential files; McLellan, *Dean Acheson*, 77–84; authors' interviews with Mary Acheson Bundy; Hamburger, "Profiles: Mr. Secretary," Nov. 19, 57–58.

McCLOY'S ROLE IN ATOMIC CONTROL PLAN: Authors' interviews with John McCloy; McCloy journal notes, Feb.–Mar. 1946, McCloy private papers; Acheson-McCloy letters, Acheson personal papers, Yale University; Forrestal letter to McCloy, Apr. 5, 1946, Forrestal papers, Princeton University; Hewlett and Anderson, *The New World* 548.

BRITISH LOAN NOT ORIGINALLY SEEN AS ANTI-SOVIET: Acheson, *Present at the Creation*, 132–133; McLellan, *Dean Acheson*, 92–94; FRUS, 1946, VI, 823–825; authors' interviews with Loy Henderson.

CHURCHILL'S "IRON CURTAIN" SPEECH: *Vital Speeches*, Mar. 15, 1946, 329–332.

REACTION TO CHURCHILL'S SPEECH: Gaddis, *The U.S. and the Origins of the Cold War*, 307–309; *New York Times*, Mar. 6 and 7, 1946; *Time*, Mar. 25, 1946; Larson dissertation, "Belief and Inference," 348–349; Yergin, *Shattered Peace*, 175–177; Margaret Truman, *Harry S. Truman*, 312.

ACHESON DINNER PARTY WITH BOHLEN, LIPPMANN, WALLACE: Blum, ed., *The Price of Vision* (Wallace diary, Mar. 5), 556–557; authors' interviews with Alice Acheson; Steel, *Walter Lippmann and the American Century*, 428–430; DeSantis, *The Diplomacy of Silence*, 176–177; Bohlen, *Witness to History*, 252. (Bohlen, in his memoirs, does not make it clear whether the remark from Mrs. Lippmann was at this dinner party, but Mrs. Acheson, consulting her date books for the time, says that all of the events occurred at the one party on Mar. 5.)

KENNAN'S CABLE ON LIPPMANN AND WALLACE: FRUS, 1946, VI, 721–723; authors' interviews with George Kennan.

HARRIMAN AND CHURCHILL: Harriman and Abel, *Special Envoy*, 548–549.

ACHESON AND CHURCHILL: Acheson, *Sketches from Life of Men I Have Known*, 62–63 and passim; authors' interviews with Alice Acheson.

ACHESON AND THE BRITISH LOAN DEBATE: McLellan, *Dean Acheson*, 92–95; Yergin, *Shattered Peace*, 178; Gardner, *Architects of Illusion*, 133.

OPINION POLL IN MARCH: American Institute of Public Opinion, Mar. 13, 1946, cited in Gaddis, *The U.S. and the Origins of the Cold War*, 315.

IRAN CRISIS, OVERVIEW: Kuniholm, *The Origins of the Cold War in the Near East*, 270–378; Gaddis, *The U.S. and the Origins of the Cold War*, 309–312; Larson dissertation, "Belief and Inference," 495–498; *New York Times*, Mar. 14–Apr. 30, 1946.

ACHESON INVOLVEMENT IN IRAN CRISIS: Acheson, *Present at the Creation*, 196–198; McLellan, *Dean Acheson*, 89–92; Kuniholm, *The Origins of the Cold War in the Near East*, 321–322 and passim.

HARRIMAN APPOINTMENT TO LONDON: Harriman and Abel, *Special Envoy*, 549–550; Harriman travel notes, Harriman personal papers; authors' interviews with Adèle Brown Lovett; Harriman and McCloy, off-the-record discussion of the origins of the Cold War, Harriman personal papers, Washington, D.C.

KENNAN TELEGRAM ON IRAN: Kennan papers, State Department files, National Archives, cited in DeSantis, *Diplomacy of Silence*, 177–178; Wright dissertation, "George F. Kennan: Scholar-Diplomat," 389.

ACHESON'S OUTLOOK: Acheson, "Random Harvest," *Department of State Bulletin*, June 16, 1946, 1045–1049; *Fortune*, "Secretary Acheson"; Hamburger, "Profiles: Mr. Secretary," Nov. 12.

McCLOY SPEECH AT AMHERST: *Amherst College Alumni News*, June 1946, cited in Schwartz dissertation, "From Occupation to Alliance," 21.

ACHESON'S WORLD ORDER: Reston, "The No. 1 No. 2 Man in Washington"; Acheson, "Random Harvest," *Department of State Bulletin*; *Fortune*, "Secretary Acheson"; Steel, "Acheson at the Creation," 206–216; Steel, *Imperialists and Other Heroes*, 17–37.

OVERVIEW OF TURKISH STRAITS CRISIS: Kuniholm, *The Origins of the Cold War in the Near East*, 359–374 and passim; Howard, *Turkey, the Straits and U.S. Policy*; Gaddis, *The U.S. and the Origins of the Cold War*, 335–337; Harry

Truman, *Years of Trial and Hope*, 95–98; authors' interviews with Loy Henderson.

ACHESON'S ROLE IN TURKISH STRAITS CRISIS: *FRUS*, 1946, VII, 830–848 (contains records of conversations); Acheson, *Present at the Creation*, 194–196; Larson dissertation, "Belief and Inference," 567–575; McLellan, *Dean Acheson*, 98–104; Millis, ed., *The Forrestal Diaries*, 192, 195–197; Jones, *The Fifteen Weeks*, 62; authors' interviews with Loy Henderson. (Acheson's recollection that Eisenhower was at the meeting is challenged by some historians; see Lyon, *Eisenhower: Portrait of a Hero*, 382, and Kuniholm, *The Origins of the Cold War in the Near East*, 362n.)

ACHESON'S RELATIONS WITH TRUMAN: Larson dissertation, "Belief and Inference," 326, 522; McLellan, *Dean Acheson*, 95–96; Acheson interview (1955), Truman Library, postpresidential files; Acheson, *Present at the Creation*, 149–150, 745; authors' interviews.

AMERICAN ATTITUDES, SUMMER OF 1946: *Life*, June 3 and 10, 1946; *Time*, Mar. 18, 1946; Manchester, *The Glory and the Dream*, 394–395.

KENNAN'S AMERICAN TOUR: Authors' interviews with George Kennan; Kennan's reports to State Department on his tour (August and September 1946), Kennan papers, Princeton University; speech to Representatives of National Organizations (June 1946), Kennan papers, Princeton University; George F. Kennan, *Memoirs: 1925–1950*, 298–304.

KENNAN'S WAR COLLEGE LECTURES AND MIXED OUTLOOK: "Russia," a lecture by Kennan (October 1946), Naval War College and elsewhere, Kennan papers, Princeton University; "Soviet-American Relations," lecture at the State Department (September 1946), Kennan papers, Princeton University (and in National Archives, Record Group 59); George F. Kennan, *Memoirs: 1925–1950*, 302–311; DeSantis, *The Diplomacy of Silence*, 189–190; authors' interviews with George Kennan.

KENNAN AND THE BOMB, 1946: Letter to Acheson, *FRUS*, 1946, I, 860–865; George F. Kennan, *Memoirs: 1925–1950*, 309–311; DeSantis, *The Diplomacy of Silence*, 189.

CLIFFORD-ELSEY REPORT: Authors' interviews with Clark Clifford, George Elsey, George Kennan; "Comments on the Document entitled 'American Relations to the Soviet Union,'" from Kennan to Elsey (Sept. 13) and from Kennan to Clifford (Sept. 16), Elsey papers, Truman Library; DeSantis, *The Diplomacy of Silence*, 190–191; Larson dissertation, "Belief and Inference," 363, 372–376; Krock, *Memoirs*, 422–482 (first publication of the secret report); Margaret Truman, *Harry S. Truman*, 347; Oral History interview with Clark Clifford (July 1971),

374–377, Truman Library; Oral History interview with George Elsey (July 1969), 261–267, Truman Library.

HARRIMAN'S RETURN: Harriman and Abel, *Special Envoy*, 553.

HARRIMAN AND FORRESTAL: Millis, ed., *The Forrestal Diaries*, 200; Forrestal letter to Harriman (Sept. 1946), in Harriman and Abel, *Special Envoy*, 552; authors' interviews with Michael Forrestal, Kathleen Harriman Mortimer.

KENNAN ON BUSINESSMEN: George F. Kennan, *Memoirs: 1925–1950*, 299; authors' interviews with George Kennan.

HARRIMAN'S LECTURE TO KENNAN'S CLASS: "Russia," transcript of a speech and discussion by Harriman at the National War College (Oct. 1946), Harriman personal papers, Washington, D.C.

OUTLOOK OF HARRIMAN AND KENNAN ON THE CAUSES OF THE COLD WAR: The dispute over who and what were responsible for the Cold War has kept two generations of historians gainfully employed, and the traditional, revisionist, and post-revisionist interpretations could fill a small library. In adition to the memos, speeches, and books already cited, a good source for Harriman's views is an off-the-record discussion he had in May 1967 with Arthur Schlesinger, Jr., John McCloy, and others (116-page transcript, Harriman personal papers, Washington, D.C.). Its themes are reflected in Schlesinger, "The Origins of the Cold War," 22–52. See also Averell Harriman, "Story of Our Relations with Russia," Harriman speech to the American Association of Advertising Agencies, April 1946, Harriman personal papers, Washington, D.C.; and Harriman Oral History Project, Kennedy Institute of Politics, Harvard University, 1969–1970. Kennan's views, in addition to the sources already cited, can be found in the chapter he wrote for Hammond, ed., *Witnesses to the Origins of the Cold War*, 27–33. The introduction to that book is one of many useful surveys of the traditional and revisionist literature. Another useful guide to the debate is Gaddis, "The Emerging Post-Revisionist Synthesis on the Origins of the Cold War." For the most recent description of Soviet tactics in imposing control over occupied countries, see Djilas, *Rise and Fall*.

KENNAN-FORRESTAL RELATIONSHIP: Authors' interviews with George Kennan, Michael Forrestal, John Ohly, Marx Leva, Patricia Alsop; Kennan letter to John Osborne (July 1962), Kennan papers, Princeton University; Kennan-Forrestal letters, Kennan papers and Forrestal papers, Princeton University; Forrestal appointment calender, Forrestal papers, Princeton University; George F. Kennan, *Memoirs: 1925–1950*, 354; Wright dissertation, "George F. Kennan: Scholar-Diplomat," 413–421; Gardner, *Architects of Illusion*, 270–300.

KENNAN COMMENTS ON WILLETT PAPER: "Dialectical Materialism and Russian

Objectives," by Edward Willett, in Kennan papers and Forrestal papers, Princeton University; comments on Willett paper, Kennan letter to Harry Hill (for Forrestal, October 1946), Kennan papers and Forrestal papers, Princeton University; Wright dissertation, "George F. Kennan: Scholar-Diplomat," 417–418.

KENNAN'S PAPER FOR FORRESTAL (LATER PUBLISHED AS THE X-ARTICLE): Kennan letter to Forrestal (October 30, 1946), Kennan papers, Princeton University; Wright dissertation, "George F. Kennan: Scholar-Diplomat," 418–419; "Psychological Background of Soviet Foreign Policy" (Jan. 1947), Kennan papers, Princeton University; Kennan (as "X"), "The Sources of Soviet Conduct."

PUBLICATION OF THE X-ARTICLE: Authors' interviews with George Kennan; Kennan-Armstrong letters, 1947, Kennan papers, Princeton University; George F. Kennan, Memoirs: 1925–1950, 354–355; "The Soviet Way of Thought and Its Effect on Soviet Foreign Policy," talk by Kennan, discussion meeting report, Jan. 7, 1947, archives of the Council on Foreign Relations, New York.

Chapter 13
Order from Chaos

WINTER OF '47: Donovan, Crisis and Conflict, 275–276; Mee, The Marshall Plan: The Launching of Pax Americana, 17–18; Kaiser, Cold Winter, Cold War, 9–37.

ACHESON AND THE BRITISH AIDE-MÉMOIRE: Jones, The Fifteen Weeks, 3–8; Acheson, Present at the Creation 217–219; FRUS: 1947, Vol. V, 23–29, 32–37; Larson dissertation, "Belief and Inference," Vol. I, 580–586; authors' interviews with Loy Henderson and Barbara Evans (Acheson's secretary).

ACHESON AND MARSHALL: Acheson, Present at the Creation, 140–144, 213–216; Acheson, Sketches from Life, 147–167; Lilienthal, Journals: The Atomic Energy Years, 159; Pogue, George C. Marshall, Vols. I–III.

ACHESON AND TRUMAN: Acheson, Present at the Creation, 184–185, 200; Acheson oral history seminar, July 2, 1952, Truman Library.

ACHESON AND THE TRUMAN DOCTRINE: Acheson, Present at the Creation, 108, 217–221; Jones, The Fifteen Weeks, 80–81, 131–135, 138–142, 152–154; Larson dissertation, "Belief and Inference," 587–601; Harry Truman, Year of Decisions, 105; Gaddis, The United States and the Origins of the Cold War, 344–345; State-War-Navy Coordinating Committee Subcommittee on Information Paper, "Information Program on United States Aid to Greece," submitted to Acheson, Mar. 4, 1947; drafts of Truman Doctrine speech, Jones papers, Truman Library; authors' interviews with Loy Henderson, Clark Clifford.

CRITICS OF THE TRUMAN DOCTRINE: George F. Kennan, *Memoirs: 1925–1950*, 314–317; Jones, *The Fifteen Weeks*, 154–155; Bohlen, *Witness to History*, 261; Lilienthal, *Journals: The Atomic Energy Years*, 159–160; Kennan to Bohlen, Mar. 20, 1947, Kennan papers, Princeton University; Elsey to Clifford, Mar. 8, 1947, Elsey papers, Truman Library; authors' interview with George Kennan.

TRUMAN'S SPEECH: Jones, *The Fifteen Weeks*, 168–170; *Time*, Mar. 24, 1947.

LEGACY OF THE TRUMAN DOCTRINE: Kuniholm, *The Origins of the Cold War in the Near East*, 410–425; Freeland, *The Truman Doctrine and the Origins of McCarthyism*, 319–360; Gelb and Betts, *The Irony of Vietnam: The System Worked*, 48–50, 201–203.

ANTI-COMMUNISM: Donovan, *Crisis and Conflict*, 292–298; Millis, ed., *Forrestal Diaries*, 243; Forrestal to Clifford, Jan. 31, 1947, Forrestal papers, Princeton University; Kennan lecture, Feb. 20, 1947, Kennan papers, Princeton University.

ACHESON AND VANDENBERG: Acheson, *Present at the Creation*, 223–224; Acheson, *Sketches from Life*, 123; Acheson to Vandenberg, Mar. 3, 1948, Acheson personal papers, Yale University; *Time*, May 12, 1947; authors' interview with Francis Wilcox (Vandenberg's chief aide).

CONGRESS AND LIPPMANN QUESTION ACHESON: Freeland, *The Truman Doctrine and the Origins of McCarthyism*, 109–112; Acheson, *Present at the Creation*, 225; Steel, *Walter Lippmann and the American Century*, 439–440; Bohlen, *The Transformation of American Foreign Policy*, 86.

OUTCOME IN GREECE: Yergin, *Shattered Peace*, 293–295; Djilas, *Conversatons with Stalin*, 141.

MOSCOW CONFERENCE: Bohlen, *Witness to History*, 262–263; 269; Yergin, *Shattered Peace*, 296–300; Price papers, include Bohlen oral history, 1953, Truman Library.

FORRESTAL AND THE MARSHALL PLAN: Millis, ed., *Forrestal Diaries*, 248–249, 251–252, 266–268; Forrestal to Clifford, Mar. 6, 1947, personal papers of Marx Leva (Forrestal's aide), Washington; Forrestal to Symington, Apr. 24, 1947, Forrestal papers, Princeton University.

KENNAN AND THE MARSHALL PLAN: George F. Kennan, *Memoirs: 1925–1950*, 325–353; Miscamble dissertation, "George Kennan, the Policy Planning Staff and American Foreign Policy," 1–75; Mee, *The Marshall Plan*, 88–89; *FRUS: 1947*, III, 223–230; Price papers, include Marshall, Bohlen, Kennan oral histories, 1952–1953, Truman Library (Marshall credits Kennan with most responsibility for creating Marshall Plan).

PRESS AND THE ESTABLISHMENT: Steel, *Walter Lippmann*, 440–442; *FRUS*: 1947, III, 242–243; Kennan to Acheson, May 23, 1947, Kennan papers, Princeton University; Price papers, include Reston oral history, Truman Library; authors' interview with Joseph Alsop.

ACHESON AND THE DELTA SPEECH: Acheson, *Present at the Creation*, 227–230; Leonard Miall Oral History, 1964, Truman Library.

VANDENBERG, TRUMAN, CLAYTON, AND THE MARSHALL PLAN: Jones, *The Fifteen Weeks*, 236; Acheson, *Present at the Creation*, 230–232; authors' interview with Clark Clifford.

BOHLEN AND THE MARSHALL PLAN: Bohlen, *Witness to History*, 263–264, 269; Price papers, include Marshall, Bohlen oral histories, 1952–1953, Truman Library.

ACHESON AND THE MARSHALL SPEECH: Acheson, *Present at the Creation*, 234; Mee, *The Marshall Plan*, 99–100 (Miall's recollection is that Acheson never actually mentioned the speech); Acheson's oral history seminar, July 2, 1953, Truman Library (Acheson recalls that he did).

MARSHALL'S HARVARD SPEECH: Jones, *The Fifteen Weeks*, 30; *New York Times*, June 6, 1947; *Time*, June 16, 1947; Mee, *The Marshall Plan*, 107; *FRUS*: 1947, III, 237–239.

DECISION TO INVITE SOVIETS: George F. Kennan, *Memoirs: 1925–1950*, 342; Bohlen, *The Transformation of American Foreign Policy*, 90–92; *FRUS*: 1947, I, 762–765, III, 327–328; Mee, *The Marshall Plan*, 124–137; Yergin, *Shattered Peace*, 310–317; authors' interview with Robert Lovett; Price papers, include Kennan, Bohlen, Harriman oral histories, 1952–1953, Truman Library.

LOVETT REPLACES ACHESON: Lovett to Acheson, Mar. 1, 1947, Apr. 5, 1947, Acheson to Jane Brown, May 3, 1947, Acheson personal papers, Yale University; Lovett Oral History, Truman Library; authors' interview with Robert Lovett.

Chapter 14
"Simple, Honest Men"

LOVETT ON WORLD SITUATION: Lovett to Eberstadt, June 13, 1947, Eberstadt personal papers, Princeton University; Yergin, *Shattered Peace*, 328; Forrestal diaries, July 26, 1947, Forrestal papers, Princeton University; Report of Discussion with Robert Lovett, May 12, 1947, Council on Foreign Relations archives; authors' interview with Robert Lovett.

LOVETT DEALS WITH EUROPE: *FRUS:* 1947, III, 335–337, 356–360, 372–375; Mee, *The Marshall Plan*, 177–182; authors' interviews with Lucius Battle, Jane Thompson.

KENNAN IN EUROPE: *FRUS:* 1947, III, 397–405; Mee, *The Marshall Plan*, 191–194; Lovett telcon with Senator H. Alexander Smith, Sept. 6, 1947, Lovett daily logs, New York Historical Society.

KENNAN AND THE X-ARTICLE: Kennan (as "X"), "The Sources of Soviet Conduct"; Lippmann, *The Cold War;* George F. Kennan *Memoirs: 1925–1950*, 356–360; Steel, *Walter Lippmann*, 444–445; Lovett telcon with Navy Secretary Sullivan, Dec. 3, 1947, Lovett daily logs, New York Historical Society.

LOBBYING CONGRESS ON INTERIM AID: Millis, ed., *Forrestal Diaries*, 296, 305; Yergin, *Shattered Peace*, 327–329; Bohlen, *Witness to History*, 270–271; Acheson, *Present at the Creation*, 235, 239; Lovett to Truman, Dec. 22, 1947, Truman papers, Truman Library; Price papers, include Francis Wilcox, Marshall oral histories, 1952–1953, Truman Library; Forrestal to Harriman, July 31, 1947, Forrestal papers, Princeton University; authors' interviews with Charles Burton Marshall, Kathleen Harriman Mortimer; Forrestal to Lovett, June 29, 1947, Forrestal papers, Princeton University; Forrestal telcon with Lovett, Nov. 19, 1947, Attorney General Clark telcon with Lovett, Oct. 28, 1947, Lovett daily logs, New York Historical Society; Mee, *The Marshall Plan*, 231–235.

McCLOY AS WORLD BANK PRESIDENT: Mason and Asher, *The World Bank Since Bretton Wood*, 48–61; Lockett, "High Commissioner for Germany"; McCloy, "The Lesson of the World Bank"; McCloy telcon with Lovett, Dec. 17, 1947, Lovett daily logs, New York Historical Society; authors' interviews with Robert Lovett and John McCloy; Ball, *The Past Has Another Pattern*, 77–79.

BOHLEN'S ROLE SELLING ERP: Bohlen to Thomas Stine, May 2, 1947, Bohlen personal papers, Library of Congress; authors' interviews with Robert Lovett, Cecil Lyon, Robert Reams, Patricia Alsop, Joseph Alsop, Jane Thompson, Charles Bohlen, Jr.; Wilmerding, "Charles Eustis Bohlen: Portrait of a Diplomat," unpublished term paper for Groton School.

LOVETT'S ROLE: Shepley telcon with Lovett, Mar. 29, 1948, Markel telcon with Lovett, Mar. 11, 1948, Krock telcon with Lovett, Nov. 17, 1948, Forrestal telcon with Lovett, Oct. 6, 1947, Acheson telcon with Lovett, Jan. 19, 1948, Bohlen telcon with Lovett, Mar. 1, 1948, Lovett daily logs, New York Historical

Society; authors' interview with Paul Nitze; Price papers, include Marshall oral history, 1952–1953, Truman Library.

KENNAN'S DOUBTS: Kennan to Charles Thayer, July 31, 1947, Kennan papers, Princeton University; authors' interviews with Patricia Alsop, George Kennan; Rostow, "Searching for Kennan's Grand Design"; Gaddis, *Strategies of Containment*, 87; National War College lecture, "Measures Short of War (Diplomatic)," Sept. 16, 1946, "Notes on the Marshall Plan," Dec. 15, 1947, "Comments on the General Trend of U.S. Foreign Policy," Aug. 20, 1948, in Kennan papers, Princeton University; George F. Kennan, *Memoirs: 1925–1950*, 364–365, 377–381, 405; *FRUS: 1947*, I, 770–777; *FRUS: 1948*, I, 510–529. The most insightful review of Kennan's thoughts, private and public, is in Gellman, *Contending with Kennan: Towards a Philosophy of American Power*.

Chapter 15
Crisis

CZECH CRISIS: Jean Edward Smith, ed., *The Papers of General Lucius D. Clay: Germany 1945–49*, Vol. II, 568–569; Millis, ed., *The Forrestal Diaries*, 382–399; Yergin, *Shattered Peace*, 343–360; Donovan, *Conflict and Crisis*, 357–361; Steel, *Walter Lippmann*, 451; *Time*, Mar. 15, Mar. 22, 1948.

HARRIMAN AND ERP: Vandenberg, ed., *The Private Papers of Senator Vandenberg*, 393; Kahn, "Profiles: Plenipotentiary"; White, *Fire in the Ashes*, 60; White, *In Search of History*, 281–282; Price papers, include Bissell oral history, 1952; Averell Harriman, "The Marshall Plan: Self Help and Mutual Aid"; Katz, "After 20 Years," authors' interview with Milton Katz; Barnet, *The Alliance*, 115, 120; Mee, *The Marshall Plan*, 251–252; Lovett Oral History, Truman Library; Harriman Oral History Project, 1971, Kennedy Institute of Politics, Harvard University.

FORRESTAL UNDER PRESSURE: Forrestal to Kenneth Reynolds, Mar. 17, 1948, Forrestal to William R. Matthews Mar. 3, 1949, Senator Tydings to Forrestal, Feb. 17, 1948, Forrestal papers, Princeton University; Millis, ed., *Forrestal Diaries*, 536–537; Ferrell, ed., *Off the Record: The Private Papers of Harry S. Truman*, 134; Donovan, *Tumultuous Years*, 53; authors' interview with Clark Clifford.

NATO: Kennan to Lippmann (unsent), Apr. 6, 1948, Kennan papers, Princeton University; George F. Kennan, *Memoirs: 1925–1950*, 360–361, 406–414; *FRUS: 1948*, III, 6–8, 40–42; Achilles Oral History, 1973, Hickerson Oral History, 1973, Truman Library; authors' interviews with Theodore Achilles and John Hickerson; Lawrence Kaplan, *The United States and NATO*, passim.

KENNAN AND MILITARY INTERVENTION: *FRUS: 1947*, V, 468–469; *FRUS: 1948*, III, 848–849; Gaddis, "Containment: A Reassesment"; Mark, "The Question of Containment"; "George Kennan on Containment Reconsidered" (letter from Kennan), *Foreign Affairs*, April 1978; Donovan, *Conflict and Crisis*, 366–367; authors' interview with Paul Nitze.

KENNAN-BOHLEN PEACE PLAN: Bohlen, *Witness to History*, 276–277; George F. Kennan, *Memoirs: 1925–1950*, 346–347; Eben Ayers diary, May 11, 1948, Truman Library.

KENNAN AND LOVETT RELATIONSHIP: Lash, ed., *From the Diaries of Felix Frankfurter*, 326; authors' interviews with Robert Lovett, George Kennan, John McCloy, John Hickerson, Theodore Achilles, and Robert Reams.

LOVETT AND VANDENBERG RESOLUTION: *FRUS: 1948*, III, 82–84, 92–96, 104–108; Vandenberg, ed., *The Private Papers of Senator Vandenberg*, 404; Yergin, *Shattered Peace*, 362; Lovett Oral History, Columbia University; authors' interviews with Francis Wilcox and Robert Lovett.

PALESTINE: Kurzman, *Genesis 1948*, 212–216; Donovan, *Conflict and Crisis*, 369–387; *FRUS: 1948*, V, part 2, 1005–1007; authors' interviews with Robert Lovett and Clark Clifford.

THE GERMAN QUESTION: Authors' interviews with Joseph Alsop, George Kennan; Mastny, "Stalin and the Militarization of the Cold War"; Bohlen, *Witness to History*, 274; *FRUS: 1948*, II, 71–73; Yergin, *Shattered Peace*, 366–369; Barnet, *The Alliance*, 40.

LOVETT AND CLAY: George F. Kennan, *Memoirs: 1925–1950*, 421; authors' interviews with George Kennan and Robert Lovett; Yergin, *Shattered Peace*, 373–375; Forrestal telcon with Lovett, June 26, 1948, Lovett daily logs, New York Historical Society; Jean Edward Smith, ed., *The Papers of General Lucius D. Clay*, Vol. I, xxx–xxxii, Vol. II, 696–697; Clay, *Decision in Germany*, 358–380; *FRUS: 1948*, II, 917–921.

McCLOY AND FORRESTAL: Authors' interviews with John McCloy, John Ohly (Forrestal aide); Forrestal diary, June 26, 1948, Forrestal papers, Princeton University; table on nuclear weapons 1947–1949 in National Resources Defense Council, *Nuclear Weapons Data Book*, 15.

BERLIN AIRLIFT: *FRUS: 1948*, II, 928–929; Millis, ed., *Forrestal Diaries*, 454–455; Rearden, *History of the Office of the Secretary of Defense: The Formative Years, 1947–1950*, 288–295; Jean Edward Smith, ed., *The Papers of General Lucius D. Clay*, Vol. II, 711–712, 736–737; Forrestal telcon with Lovett, June

30, 1948, Lovett daily logs, New York Historical Society; authors' interviews with John McCloy and Robert Lovett.

BLOCKADE DIPLOMACY AND WAR SCARE: Bohlen, *Witness to History*, 279–282; Millis, ed., *Forrestal Diaries*, 480–488; Rearden, *History of the Office of the Secretary of Defense: The Formative Years*, 295–297; Yergin, *Shattered Peace*, 392.

LOVETT AND 1948 ELECTIONS: Hoopes, *The Devil and John Foster Dulles*, 71–73; Pruessen, *John Foster Dulles: The Road to Power*, 383–388; Acheson telcon with Lovett, June 29, 1948, Lovett telcon with Clifford, Nov. 2, 1948, Lovett appointment book, Aug. 16, 20, Sept. 10, 11, 13, 22, 27, 1948, Lovett daily logs, New York Historical Society; authors' interviews with Robert Lovett, Clark Clifford, McGeorge Bundy.

ACHESON BECOMES SECRETARY OF STATE: Acheson, *Present at the Creation*, 239, 249–250; authors' interviews with Gerhard Gesell, James Rowe (friend of Acheson), Alice Stanley Acheson, Clark Clifford; *Time*, Feb. 28, 1949; Clifford telcon with Acheson, Dec. 8, 1948, Acheson personal papers, Yale University; Sidney Souers to Truman, Jan. 16, 1949, Souers papers, Truman Library.

ACHESON'S CHARACTER AND RELATIONSHIP WITH TRUMAN: Donovan, *Tumultuous Years*, 33–36; Acheson, *Sketches from Life*, 2–3, 15–16; Truman to Acheson, undated (probably October 1952), Acheson personal papers, Yale University; authors' interviews with Alice Stanley Acheson, Gerhard Gesell, Barbara Evans, William Bundy, Mary Acheson Bundy, Walter Judd, Lydia Kirk (Acheson friend). The limerick is in the Miscellaneous file, Acheson personal papers, Yale University.

ANTI-COMMUNISM AND ACHESON CONFIRMATION: Donovan, *Tumultuous Years*, 27–33, 37–39; Vandenberg, ed., *The Private Papers of Senator Vandenberg*, 469; authors' interview with Francis Wilcox; *Time* magazine file, Feb. 15, 1949, Frank McNaughton private papers, Truman Library.

DEATH OF FORRESTAL: Authors' interviews with Michael Forrestal, Robert Lovett, John McCloy, John Ohly and Marx Leva (Forrestal aides), Felix Larkin (Defense Department counsel); Millis, ed., *Forrestal Diaries*, 543–555; Rogow, *Victim of Duty*, 25–60.

"PLAN A": Yergin, *Shattered Peace*, 488; Kennan to Acheson, Jan. 3, 1949, Kennan papers, Princeton University; *FRUS: 1948*, II, 1287–1297, 1325–1338; *FRUS: 1949*, III, 102–105; authors' interview with George Kennan; Miscamble dissertation, "George Kennan, the Policy Planning Staff and American Foreign Policy," 143–145, 171; George F. Kennan, *Memoirs: 1925–1950*, 415–448;

authors' interview with Paul Nitze; Bohlen to Kennan, Oct. 25, 1948, Records of Charles Bohlen, National Archives; Bohlen, *Witness to History*, 282–284, 288; Sulzberger, *A Long Row of Candles*, 987; authors' interview with Barbara Evans.

CHINA: Acheson oral history seminar, July 22–23, 1953, Truman Library; Donovan, *Tumultuous Years*, 66–88; Nancy Bernkopf Tucker, *Patterns in the Dust: Chinese-American Relations and the Recognition Controversy, 1949–1950*; authors' interview with Walter Judd; David Acheson, *Among Friends*, 68; Council on Foreign Relations, *The United States and World Affairs, 1947–1948*; Cohen, "Acheson, His Advisers, and China, 1949–1950," in Berg and Heinrichs, eds., *Uncertain Years: Chinese-American Relations, 1947–1950*; FRUS: 1949, IX, 346–350, 356–364; Kennan draft of Acheson speech, Jan. 12, 1950, Kennan papers, Princeton University; Acheson, *Present at the Creation*, 355–358.

VIETNAM: Karnow, *Vietnam*, 160–177; Donovan, *Tumultuous Years*, 139–147; McLellan, *Dean Acheson*, 260–265; authors' interviews with William Bundy, Lucius Battle.

Chapter 16
"A Different World"

SOVIET BOMB: Donovan, *Tumultuous Years*, 98–100; Manchester, *The Glory and the Dream*, 488–489, 499; authors' interviews with George Kennan, Paul Nitze.

NITZE BACKGROUND: Authors' interview with Paul Nitze; Nitze oral histories for Truman Library, 1975, and Air Force Oral History Project, 1977, courtesy of Nitze private papers, Arlington, Va.; interview with John Kenneth Galbraith; Herken, "The Great Foreign Policy Fight."

SUPER BOMB DECISION: Authors' interviews with Paul Nitze, Robert Tufts (Policy Planning staffer); Lilienthal, *Journals: The Atomic Energy Years 1945–50*, 477, 480–482; FRUS: 1949, I 569–585; Schilling, "The H-Bomb Decision"; Miscamble dissertation, "George Kennan, the Policy Planning Staff and American Foreign Policy," 195; Acheson, *Present at the Creation*, 346–347; Arneson, "The H-Bomb Decision."

KENNAN, NITZE, AND ACHESON: FRUS: 1950, I, 22–44; Kennan to Bohlen, Nov. 17, 1949, Kennan papers, Princeton University; National Archives, Bohlen to Lovett, Dec. 19, 1949, Records of Charles E. Bohlen, National Archives; Acheson's remarks to National War College, Dec. 21, 1949, Acheson papers, Truman Library; Kennan to Acheson, Dec. 21, 1949, Acheson personal papers, Yale University; authors' interview with Paul Nitze; Acheson, *Present at the Creation*, 374.

ACHESON AND HISS: Authors' interviews with Alice Stanley Acheson, Lucius Battle, Paul Nitze; Acheson, *Present at the Creation*, 359–370, 381; Donovan, *Tumultuous Years*, 135–136; Lovett to Acheson, Mar. 11, 1949, Acheson to Lovett, Mar. 28, 1950, Lovett to Acheson, Apr. 14, 1950, Acheson to Lovett, Apr. 19, 1950, John Crocker to Acheson, Apr. 1, 1950, Jake Podoloff to Acheson, Jan. 30, 1950, Boylston Adams Tompkins to Acheson, Feb. 1950, Clark Clifford to Acheson, Mar. 21, 1950, Truman to Acheson, Mar. 31, 1950, Acheson personal papers, Yale University; Bohlen, *Witness to History*, 302; Acheson oral history seminar, July 22–23, 1953, Truman Library.

NSC-68; Authors' interviews with George Kennan, Paul Nitze, Robert Tufts, Henry Kissinger; *FRUS: 1950*, I, 127–138, 142–143, 145–147, 160–167, 196–200, 203–206, 221–225, 235–296; Rearden, *History of the Office of the Secretary of Defense: The Formative Years*, 526; Wells, "Sounding the Tocsin: NSC-68 and the Soviet Threat"; Gaddis and Nitze, "NSC-68 and the Soviet Threat Reconsidered"; Schilling, Hammond, and Snyder, "NSC-68: Prologue to Rearmament," in *Strategy, Politics, and Defense Budgets*; Nitze to Bohlen, Nov. 29, 1949, Records of Charles E. Bohlen, National Archives; Bohlen to Avis Bohlen, Jan. 26, 1950, Bohlen personal papers, Library of Congress; Acheson, *Present at the Creation*, 373–374, 378–379; Gaddis, *Strategies of Containment*, 98–126; Charles Murphy Oral History, Truman Library; Arneson, "The H-Bomb Decision"; Acheson oral history seminar, July 22–23, Oct. 10–11, 1953, Truman Library.

Chapter 17
War

WAR BREAKS OUT: Acheson, *Present at the Creation*, 402–415; Harry Truman, *Years of Trial and Hope*, 332; Goulden, *Korea: The Untold Story of the War*, xv, 3, 31, 41; Talbott, trans., *Khrushchev Remembers*, 367–370; Paige, *Korea Decision*, 110; authors' interview with Walt Rostow; George F. Kennan, *Memoirs: 1925–1950*, 484–487; Donovan, *Tumultuous Years*, 192–218; *FRUS: Korea 1950*, 156–61; authors' interview with Joseph Alsop.

HARRIMAN, KENNAN, BOHLEN ROLES: Lovett interview with Mark Chadwin, in Harriman private papers, Washington, D.C.; Harriman to Truman, May 20, 1950, Truman papers, Truman Library; Acheson, *Present at the Creation*, 410–411; Bohlen, *Witness to History*, 291–293, 303; Bohlen to Avis Bohlen, July 11, 1950, Bohlen personal papers, Library of Congress; George F. Kennan, *Memoirs: 1925–1950*, 486–500; Paige, *Korea Decision*, 147; Kennan to Acheson, June 30, 1950, Kennan papers, Princeton University; *FRUS: Korea 1950*, 258–259; *FRUS: 1950*, I, 342–344, 361–367.

McCLOY AND GERMAN REARMAMENT: Schwartz dissertation, "From Occupation to Alliance"; "The German Factor in U.S. Security Policy, 1946–1949," by Wolfgang Krieger, paper for the National Securities Studies Group, Harvard University, March 1984; Brinkley, "Minister Without Portfolio"; authors' interview with John McCloy; Acheson, *Sketches from Life*, 167–180.

HARRIMAN, JOHNSON, AND MacARTHUR: Donovan, *Tumultuous Years*, 261–267; Lovett interview with Mark Chadwin, Harriman private papers, Washington, D.C.; Kahn, "Profiles: Plenipotentiary"; Acheson oral history seminar, Oct. 10–11, 1953, Truman Library; authors' interview with Dan Davidson (Harriman aide); Ayers diary, July 3, Aug. 26, 1950, Truman Library; Harriman Oral History, 1971, Truman Library; Harriman Oral History, 1969–1970, Kennedy Institute of Politics, Harvard University; Harriman report to Truman, August 1950, Harriman private papers, Washington, D.C.; Goulden, *Korea*, 157; Manchester, *American Caesar: Douglas MacArthur, 1880–1964*, 493–517, 561–571; James, *The Years of MacArthur*, Vol. III: *Triumph and Disaster, 1945–1964*, 221–235; Acheson, *Present at the Creation*, 423–424; Harriman to Truman, July 1, 1950, Harriman private papers, Washington, D.C.; authors' interview with Patricia Alsop; Ferrell, ed., *Off the Record*, 189.

LOVETT TO DEFENSE: Lovett Oral History, 1971, Truman Library; authors' interviews with Felix Larkin, Adèle Brown Lovett.

DECISION TO CROSS THE 38TH PARALLEL: *FRUS: Korea*, 1950, 386–387, 449–454, 469–473, 486–487, 502–510, 574–576, 671–679, 705–707; Herken, "The Great Foreign Policy Fight"; Acheson to Nitze, July 12, 1950, Acheson papers, Truman Library; authors' interviews with George Kennan, Paul Nitze, Dean Rusk; Warren I. Cohen, *Dean Rusk*, 1–77; Viorst, "Incidentally, Who Is Dean Rusk?"; George F. Kennan, *Memoirs: 1925–1950*, 491–497, 500; George F. Kennan, *Memoirs: 1950–1963*, 23–24; Acheson, *Present at the Creation*, 429–430, 445, 451–452; Acheson to James Webb, August 1950, Acheson papers, Truman Library; Acheson to William Taylor, May 31, 1960, Acheson personal papers, Yale University.

INCHON TO WAKE: Manchester, *American Caesar*, 681–684, 689, 704; Acheson, *Present at the Creation*, 447–453, 456–457; Ridgway, *The Korean War*, 36–37; Acheson oral history seminar, Feb. 13–14, 1954, Truman Library; authors' interviews with C. B. Marshall, Lucius Battle; *FRUS: Korea* 1950, 793–794; Harriman Oral History, 1971, Truman Library.

Chapter 18
Nadir

FAILURE TO CONTROL MacARTHUR: Schnabel, *United States Army in the Korean War: Policy and Direction, The First Year*, 215–331; Acheson, *Present at the Creation*, 461–468; authors' interviews with Robert Lovett, Felix Larkin, C. B.

Marshall, Marshall Shulman (Acheson aide); Acheson oral history seminar, Feb. 13–14, Mar. 14, 1954, Truman Library; *FRUS: Korea 1950*, 1204–1208; Acheson to Forrest Pogue, Oct. 23, 1967, Acheson to Mathew Ridgway, Oct. 17, 1967, Acheson to Nitze, Nov. 1, 1967, Acheson to Richard Neustadt, May 9, 1960, Lovett to Acheson, Oct. 16, 1950, Acheson personal papers, Yale University; authors' interview with Forrest Pogue; Donovan, *Tumultuous Years*, 271, 295–303; Neustadt, *Presidential Power: The Politics of Leadership*, 123–151.

CHINESE ATTACK: *FRUS: Korea 1950*, 1242–1248, 1312–1313, 1323–1334, 1345–1347; Acheson, *Present at the Creation*, 472–479; Lovett and Acheson memoranda of conversation, Dec. 2, 3, 1950, Acheson-Marshall telcon, Dec. 4, 1950, Kennan notes on meeting with Marshall, Lovett, Rusk, Dec. 4, 1950, Acheson papers, Truman Library; Ferrell, ed., *Off the Record*, 202, 204; authors' interviews with Alice Stanley Acheson, Dean Rusk, George Kennan, Robert Lovett; Sulzberger, *A Long Row of Candles*, 595; Bohlen, *Witness to History*, 294; Kennan to Bohlen, Dec. 5, 1950, Kennan papers, Princeton University; George F. Kennan, *Memoirs: 1950–1963*, 26–35.

ACHESON BESIEGED: McLellan, *Dean Acheson*, 228; authors' interviews with Alice Stanley Acheson, Barbara Evans, Patricia Alsop, Townsend Hoopes, Dan Davidson, Lydia Kirk; Harriman Oral History Project, 1971, Kennedy Institute of Politics, Harvard University; Acheson, *Sketches from Life*, 134; Lovett to Acheson, December 1950, Jan. 21, 1951; Harriman to Truman, Nov. 17, 1950, Truman papers, Truman Library; Swift quote sent to Acheson is undated, Harriman private papers, Washington, D.C.; Sulzberger, *A Long Row of Candles*, 692–693.

MacARTHUR FIRED: *FRUS: Korea 1950*, 1615–1616, 1630–1633; Acheson, *Present at the Creation*, 512–528; Manchester, *American Caesar*, 616–677; Donovan, *Tumultuous Years*, 340–362; Goulden, *Korea*, 476–547; James, *The Years of MacArthur*, Vol. III: *Triumph and Disaster, 1945–1964*, 584–640; Harry Truman, *Years of Trial and Hope*, 507; authors' interviews with William Bundy, Robert Lovett.

PEACE FEELERS: George F. Kennan, *Memoirs: 1950–1963*, 35–37; Acheson, *Present at the Creation*, 532–533; Eugene Rostow to Acheson, February 1968, Acheson personal papers, Yale University.

KENNAN IN MOSCOW: George F. Kennan, *Memoirs: 1950–1963*, 12–13, 62–63, 105–167; Salisbury, *A Journey for Our Times*, 403–417; authors' interviews with John McCloy, Grace Kennan Warnecke, Harrison Salisbury.

LOVETT AS SECRETARY OF DEFENSE: Author's interviews with Robert Lovett, Townsend Hoopes; *New York Herald Tribune*, Dec. 28, 1952; *New York Times*, Oct. 29, 1952.

ACHESON'S LAST DAYS IN OFFICE: Kahn, *The China Hands: America's Foreign Service Officers and What Befell Them*, 191–193, 214, 234, 250–255; Acheson, *Present at the Creation*, 710–713; Acheson to Mrs. J. C. Vincent, Mar. 17, 1967, Acheson personal papers, Yale University; George F. Kennan, *Memoirs: 1950–1963*, 201–212, 214–218; authors' interview with Alice Stanley Acheson; Acheson ditty is in Miscellaneous file, Acheson personal papers, Yale University.

Chapter 19
Exile

ENTER DULLES: Hoopes, *The Devil and John Foster Dulles*, 3–145, 169; Dulles papers, McCloy oral history, 1965, Princeton University; Ambrose, *Eisenhower: The Presidency*, 20–22; for revisionist views, see Guhin, *John Foster Dulles: A Statesman and His Times*, and Pruessen, *John Foster Dulles: The Road to Power*.

HARRIMAN, ACHESON, AND DULLES: Sulzberger, *A Long Row of Candles*, 748, 777; Hoopes, *The Devil and John Foster Dulles*, 131–132; Dulles papers, Harriman oral history, 1965, Princeton University; Ferrell, ed., *Off the Record*, 261; authors' interviews with Arthur Schlesinger, Jr., Lucius Battle, C. B. Marshall; Acheson to Truman, Apr. 14, 1953, Acheson to Battle, Aug. 6, 1953, Acheson personal papers, Yale University.

KENNAN FIRED: Hoopes, *The Devil and John Foster Dulles*, 3–9, 147, 155–158; authors' interview with Grace Kennan Warnecke; Kennan to Jeannette Kennan, Jan. 26, 1953, private papers courtesy of Joan Kennan Pozen; George F. Kennan, *Memoirs: 1950–1963*, 168–189.

BOHLEN CONFIRMATION: Bohlen, *Witness to History*, 309–336; memo of Dulles telcon with Judd, Mar. 6, 1953, memo of Dulles telcon with Bohlen, Mar. 16, 1953, memo of Dulles conversation with Eisenhower, Mar. 16, 1953, memo of Dulles conversation with Bohlen, Mar. 30, 1953, Dulles papers, Princeton University; Dulles papers, Bohlen oral history, 1964, Princeton University; authors' interviews with Cecil Lyon, Avis Bohlen (daughter); Kennan to Jeannette Kennan, Mar. 20, 1953, private papers courtesy of Joan Kennan Pozen; Bohlen to Avis Bohlen, July 1, 1946, Felix Frankfurter to Avis Bohlen, Apr. 4, 1953, Bohlen personal papers, Library of Congress; Rosenau, "The Nomination of Charles Bohlen."

NITZE FIRED: Authors' interview with Paul Nitze; Acheson to Truman, Apr. 14, 1953, Acheson to Marshall Shulman, Oct. 14, 1953, Acheson personal papers, Yale University.

McCLOY AND DULLES: McCloy Oral History, 1973, Columbia University; authors' interview with John McCloy; Hoopes, *The Devil and John Foster Dulles*,

135–136; Dulles papers, Joseph Alsop Oral History, 1965, Lucius Clay oral history, 1965, Princeton University.

McCLOY TO WALL STREET: Brinkley, "Minister Without Portfolio"; authors' interviews with John McCloy, William Jackson (McCloy's law partner); McCloy, *The Challenge to American Foreign Policy*; "McCloy of the Chase," *Fortune*, June 1953; Dulles papers, McCloy oral history, 1965, Princeton University; Eveland, *Ropes of Sand: America's Failure in the Middle East*, 141–143.

LOVETT AND THE CIA: Schlesinger, *Robert Kennedy and His Times*, 454–458.

BOHLEN IN MOSCOW: Bohlen, *Witness to History*, 337–458; Salisbury, *A Journey for Our Times*, 454–456; Dulles papers, Bohlen oral history, 1964, Princeton University; authors' interviews with Cecil Lyon, Jane Thompson, Townsend Hoopes; Dulles telcon with Sherman Adams, Apr. 18, 1956, in Dulles Papers, Princeton University; Jacob Beam to Bohlen, July 23, 1973, Bohlen to Avis Bohlen, June 22, 1955, June 21, 1957, Bohlen personal papers, Library of Congress; Avis Bohlen to Charles Thayer, Apr. 16, 1958, Thayer papers, Truman Library.

KENNAN AT OXFORD: Kennan to Charles Thayer, Sept. 4, 1953, Avis Bohlen to Thayer, Apr. 16, 1958, Thayer papers, Truman Library; Kennan to Jeannette Kennan, Mar. 14, 1954, private papers courtesy of Joan Kennan Pozen; George F. Kennan, *Memoirs: 1950–1963*, 77–80, 229–266.

ACHESON IN EXILE: Authors' interviews with Grace Kennan Warnecke, Gerhard Gesell, Maxwell Taylor, Paul Nitze, John Kenneth Galbraith, Arthur Schlesinger, Jr.; Acheson to Kennan, Mar. 13, 1958, Kennan to Acheson, Mar. 20, 1958, Acheson to David Acheson, Aug. 3, 1956, Acheson to Lovett, Jan. 16, 1956, Lovett to Acheson, Feb. 3, 1959, Acheson to N. G. Annan, Nov. 13, 1958, Acheson to Joseph Alsop, Apr. 14, 1959, Acheson to John Dickey, Mar. 18, 1959, Acheson to Charles B. Gary, June 20, 1957, Acheson to Henry Kissinger, Feb. 16, 1960, and Kissinger letter folder generally, Acheson to Maxwell Taylor, July 27, 1959, Acheson to Eugene Rostow, Aug. 14, 1958, Acheson personal papers, Yale University.

HARRIMAN THE POLITICIAN: Authors' interviews with John Kenneth Galbraith, Paul Nitze, Robert Lovett, John McCloy, William Bundy, Pamela Churchill Harriman, Jonathan Bingham and Richard Wade (Harriman aides in Albany); Acheson to Truman, Nov. 23, 1955, Acheson letters, Yale University; Harriman Oral History, 1978, Columbia University; Sulzberger, *A Long Row of Candles*, 687; *New York Post*, Mar. 21, 1957; White, *America in Search of Itself*, 81–82.

Chapter 20
Passing the Torch

ACHESON AND KENNEDY: Acheson Oral History, 1964, Chester Bowles Oral History, 1965, 1970, Kennedy Library; Jacqueline Kennedy to Acheson, March 1958, Acheson to Mrs. Kennedy, March 1958, Acheson to Truman, Apr. 14, 1960, June 27, 1960, Nov. 22, 1960, Acheson to Louis Halle, Oct. 10, 1960, Acheson personal papers, Yale University; McLellan and Acheson, eds., *Among Friends*, 197; authors' interviews with Clark Clifford, Arthur Schlesinger, Jr., John Kenneth Galbraith, Theodore Sorensen.

LOVETT AND KENNEDY: Lovett Oral History, 1964, Kennedy Library; Robert F. Kennedy Oral Histories, 1964-1965, Kennedy Library; authors' interviews with Robert Lovett, Robert McNamara, Dean Rusk, Arthur Schlesinger, Jr.; Schlesinger, *A Thousand Days*, 126–128.

NITZE AND McGEORGE BUNDY: Authors' interviews with Paul Nitze, McGeorge Bundy, Arthur Schlesinger, Jr.; Nitze Oral History, 1964, Kennedy Library; Halberstam, *The Best and the Brightest*, 44–63.

McCLOY, KENNAN, BOHLEN, AND KENNEDY: Authors' interviews with John McCloy, John J. McCloy II (son); George F. Kennan, *Memoirs: 1950–1963*, 267–268; Kennan Oral History, 1965, Bohlen Oral History, 1965, Kennedy Library; Bohlen, *Witness to History*, 474–479; Avis Bohlen to Charles Thayer, Feb. 22, 1961, Thayer papers, Truman Library.

HARRIMAN AND KENNEDY: Harriman to Acheson, Jan. 9, 1959, Acheson personal papers, Yale University; Sulzberger, *Seven Continents and 40 Years*, 285; Harriman, *America and Russia in a Changing World*, 62; Harriman Oral History, 1969, Columbia University; Harriman Oral History, 1964, Kennedy Library; Galbraith, *Economics, Peace, and Laughter*, 257–267; *The Current Digest of the Soviet Press*, Nov. 11, 1959; Schlesinger, *A Thousand Days*, 144; Schlesinger, *Robert Kennedy and His Times*, 224; authors' interviews with Arthur Schlesinger, Jr., Michael Forrestal, John Kenneth Galbraith, Jonathan Bingham (Harriman aide), John McCloy, Robert Lovett, Pamela Churchill Harriman.

Chapter 21
Twilight Struggles

HARRIMAN AND ACHESON AT NSC: Authors' interview with Hugh Sidey.

HARRIMAN AND LAOS: Ball, *The Past Has Another Pattern*, 360–362; Halberstam, *The Best and the Brightest*, 86–89; Rust, *Kennedy in Vietnam: American Vietnam*

Policy, 1960–1963, 28–33, 41; Schlesinger, *A Thousand Days,* 313–315; Harriman Oral History, 1969, Columbia University; authors' interviews with Arthur Schlesinger, Jr., John Kenneth Galbraith, Michael Forrestal, William Sullivan, Abram Chayes.

ACHESON AND BERLIN: Authors' interviews with Arthur Schlesinger, Jr., Abram Chayes, McGeorge Bundy, Paul Nitze, Lucius Battle; Acheson to John Cowles, Aug. 5, 1963, Barbara Evans to Marshall Shulman, Apr. 6, 1961, Acheson personal papers, Yale University; Schlesinger, *A Thousand Days,* 354; Acheson speech, "The Role of the Press in International Affairs," to Columbia Journalism School, Apr. 3, 1959, Columbia Oral History program; Minutes of NSC Meeting, June 29, 1961, Kennedy Library; Schlesinger, *Robert Kennedy and His Times,* 427; Acheson to Frankfurter, Aug. 15, 1961, Kissinger to Acheson, July 18, 1961, Acheson to John F. Kennedy, Aug. 18, 1961, Acheson personal papers, Yale University; Robert Kennedy Oral Histories, 1964-1965, Kennedy Library; Minutes of NSC Meeting, July 13, 1961, McGeorge Bundy memo to President Kennedy, July 19, 1961, Kennedy Library; Acheson to Truman, July 14, 1961, Acheson to Anthony Eden, Aug. 4, 1961, Acheson to Frankfurter, Aug. 3, 1961, Acheson to Truman, Sept. 21, 1961, Acheson personal papers, Yale University.

McCLOY, KENNAN, BOHLEN, AND BERLIN: Authors' interviews with John McCloy, George Reedy (LBJ aide on trip to Berlin); Acheson to Frankfurter, Aug. 3, 1961, Acheson personal papers, Yale University; Barnet, *The Alliance,* 226–227; Schlesinger, *A Thousand Days,* 369; Bohlen, *Witness to History,* 484.

HARRIMAN AT GENEVA: Harriman Oral History, 1969, Columbia University; Harriman Oral History, 1964, Kennedy Library; authors' interviews with William Sullivan, Michael Forrestal, Chester Cooper, Paul Nitze; Sullivan Oral History, 1970, Kennedy Library; Cooper Oral History, 1966, Kennedy Library; Schlesinger, *A Thousand Days,* 384; Rust, *Kennedy in Vietnam,* 71; McGeorge Bundy memo to President Kennedy, Nov. 15, 1961, Bundy notes of White House meeting on Laos, Aug. 29, 1961, Kennedy Library; Cooper, *The Lost Crusade: America in Vietnam,* 182–191; Hilsman, *To Move a Nation: The Politics of Foreign Policy in the Administration of John F. Kennedy,* 138, 142–55.

OVERVIEW OF CUBAN MISSILE CRISIS: Abel, *The Missile Crisis*; Detzer, *The Brink*; Kennedy, *Thirteen Days*; Alsop and Bartlett, "In Time of Crisis"; Schlesinger, *Robert Kennedy and His Times,* 499–532; Schlesinger, *A Thousand Days,* 794–819; Sorensen, *Kennedy,* 667–718; Minutes of ExCom meetings, Kennedy Library.

McCLOY INVOLVEMENT IN MISSILE CRISIS: Authors' interviews with John McCloy, Andrea Giles, Robert Lovett; McCloy interview with Eric Sevareid, Part II, CBS

News, July 20, 1975; Wershba, "U.S. Adviser in U.N." (McCloy's later recollections that the President personally telephoned him in Germany appear to
be embellished; it was actually his own secretary who tracked him down.)

ACHESON INVOLVEMENT IN MISSILE CRISIS: Acheson Oral History, Kennedy
Library; Acheson, "Dean Acheson's Version of Robert Kennedy's Version of the
Cuban Missile Crisis"; authors' interviews with Cecil Lyon.

BOHLEN'S INVOLVEMENT IN MISSILE CRISIS: Bohlen, *Witness to History*, 474–
498; Bohlen Oral History, Kennedy Library; Robert Kennedy Oral Histories,
Kennedy Library; authors' interviews with Joseph Alsop, Avis Bohlen. (Bohlen
was told of the missile and attended the Alsop dinner on Oct. 17, not the following
day as he mistakenly recounts in *Witness to History*. Abel, in *The Missile Crisis*,
has the chronology correct.)

LOVETT'S INVOLVEMENT IN THE MISSILE CRISIS: Lovett Oral History, Kennedy
Library; authors' interviews with Robert Lovett.

HARRIMAN INVOLVEMENT IN MISSILE CRISIS: Schlesinger, *A Thousand Days*,
821–822; Abel, *The Missile Crisis*, 102.

HARRIMAN AND THE LIMITED TEST BAN: Seaborg, *Kennedy, Khrushchev and the
Test Ban*, 201–262; Schlesinger, *A Thousand Days*, 893–909; Ted Sorensen
Oral History, Kennedy Library; Harriman-Kennedy cables, reprinted in Seaborg;
Senate Foreign Relations Committee, August 1963, *Nuclear Test Ban Treaty
Hearings*; Sorensen, *Kennedy*, 734–745.

HARRIMAN AT FE AND EARLY VIEWS ON VIETNAM: Authors' interviews with Arthur Schlesinger, Jr., William Sullivan, Michael Forrestal, Roger Hilsman, Dan
Davidson, John Kenneth Galbraith; Sullivan, *Obbligato: Notes on a Foreign
Service Career*, 176–179, 189–190; Sullivan Oral History, 1970, Kennedy Library; Acheson oral history seminar, Truman Library; Galbraith, *Ambassador's
Journal*, 342; memo of Harriman meeting with President Kennedy, Apr. 6,
1962, Kennedy Library; Sulzberger, *Seven Continents and 40 Years*, 355; Harriman Oral History, 1964, Kennedy Library; Harriman Oral History, 1969,
Columbia.

HARRIMAN AND THE COUP AGAINST DIEM: Authors' interviews with Michael
Forrestal, George Ball, Richard Helms, Roger Hilsman, William Sullivan; Rust,
Kennedy in Vietnam, 94–182; Ball, *The Past Has Another Pattern*, 370–376;
Karnow, *Vietnam*, 277–311; Schlesinger, *A Thousand Days*, 906; Halberstam,
Best and the Brightest, 253–299; Robert Kennedy Oral Histories, Kennedy Li-
brary.

Chapter 22
LBJ's Establishment

LBJ AND THE WAR: Karnow, *Vietnam,* 319–321; authors' interviews with George Ball, McGeorge Bundy, Walt Rostow, Dean Rusk.

LBJ AND THE ESTABLISHMENT: Ball, *The Past Has Another Pattern,* 317–318; Karnow, *Vietnam,* 322; Halberstam, *The Best and the Brightest,* 435; Mc-Pherson, *A Political Education,* 322; Dean Rusk Oral History, 1981, Duke University; authors' interviews with Hugh Sidey, George Ball, McGeorge Bundy, William Bundy, Walt Rostow; McGeorge Bundy to President Johnson, Aug. 24, Sept. 22, 1964, Jan. 28, 1965, Bundy to John J. McCloy, Sept. 3, 7, 1964, McCloy to Bundy, Sept. 4, LBJ Library.

LBJ, ACHESON, AND McCLOY: McGeorge Bundy to President Johnson, Dec. 6, 1963, Johnson to Acheson, Sept. 20, 1965, Sept. 11, 1957, Feb. 24, 1958, LBJ Library; authors' interviews with Richard Helms, William Bundy, Mary Acheson Bundy; Rusk Oral History, 1981, Duke University; Acheson to John Fisher, Dec. 16, 1963, Acheson to Anthony Eden, undated (probably 1965), Acheson personal papers, Yale University.

McCLOY TURNS DOWN SAIGON: Authors' interview with John McCloy; McCloy Oral History, 1969, LBJ Library; Rusk memorandum of conversation with McCloy, June 20, 1964, LBJ Library.

ACHESON-BALL PEACE PLAN: Ball, *The Past Has Another Pattern,* 394; authors' interviews with George Ball, Lloyd Cutler, Thomas Ehrlich; Jack Valenti notes on meeting between Dean Acheson, George Ball, Robert McNamara, Dean Rusk, Lyndon Johnson, May 16, 1965, LBJ Library; William Bundy's private memoir on Vietnam, Chapter 24, 6–8, courtesy William Bundy.

1965 WISE MEN MEETING: McLellan and Acheson, eds., *Among Friends,* 269; William Bundy's notes on Meeting of President's Foreign Policy Advisers, July 8, 1965, LBJ Library; Acheson to Truman, July 10, 1965, Acheson personal papers, Yale University; Johnson to Acheson, July 10, 1965, LBJ Library; "The Establishment," by Godfrey Hodgson, in Tucker and Watts, eds., *Beyond Containment: U.S. Foreign Policy in Transition,* 145; Acheson to Desmond Donnelly, July 6, 1965, Acheson to Erik Boheman, July 7, 1965, Acheson to Lloyd Cutler, Aug. 25, 1965, Acheson personal papers, Yale University; Bundy Vietnam memoir, Chapter 26, 1, 27:12–21; authors' interviews with William Bundy, Robert Lovett, John McCloy.

"NEXT GENERATION": Bundy Vietnam memoir, 28:33, 22B:40; authors' interviews with William Bundy, McGeorge Bundy, Mary Acheson Bundy, Robert McNamara, Dean Rusk; Hoopes, *The Limits of Intervention*, 16–20.

HARRIMAN TO MOSCOW: Authors' interviews with George Ball, William Bundy; Douglass Cater to President Johnson, July 15, 1964, Jack Valenti to Johnson, Feb. 11, 1965, LBJ Library; Bundy Vietnam memoir, 27:13, 28:5; Averell Harriman, "My Moscow-Belgrade 'Vacation'"; Sulzberger, *An Age of Mediocrity*, 228; Harriman notes on meeting with Kosygin, July 28, 1965, Harriman personal papers, Washington, D.C.; McGeorge Bundy to President Johnson, July 15, Aug. 3, 1965, Harriman to Johnson, Aug. 17, 1965, LBJ Library; Harriman to Walt Rostow, Aug. 20, 1965, Harriman personal papers, Washington, D.C.

HARRIMAN COURTS JOHNSON: Authors' interviews with Robert McNamara, Chester Cooper, Dan Davidson, John Kenneth Galbraith, Arthur Schlesinger, Jr., Kathleen Harriman Mortimer; Harriman Oral History, 1969, LBJ Library; Harriman, *America and Russia in a Changing World*, 115–123; Harriman to McGeorge Bundy, Feb. 4, 1966, Harriman personal papers, Washington, D.C.; Valenti to President Johnson, Mar. 1, 1966, Harriman to President Johnson, Nov. 14, 1966, LBJ Library; Sidey, "Ave—Durable Servant of Four Presidents"; McPherson, "Capital Social Set Wonders About a Split in Partying."

HARRIMAN VIEWS ON VIETNAM: Authors' interviews with Arthur Schlesinger, Jr., John Kenneth Galbraith, Chester Cooper, Michael Forrestal, George Ball, Walt Rostow, William Bundy; Sulzberger, *An Age of Mediocrity*, 228; Harriman memo to files, May 16, 1966, Harriman personal papers, Washington, D.C.

HARRIMAN RUNS "PEACE SHOP": Authors' interviews with Chester Cooper, Morton Halperin; Harriman memos of conversation with McNamara, May 30, 1966, July 1, 1967, Sept. 19, 1967, Harriman to President Johnson, Oct. 3, 1966, May 27, 1967, Harriman personal papers, Washington, D.C.; Goodman, *The Lost Peace: America's Search for a Negotiated Settlement of the Vietnam War*, 1–6, 12–60; Cooper, *The Lost Crusade*, 284–368; Johnson, *The Vantage Point: Perspectives of the Presidency, 1963–1969*, 250, 579–589.

KENNAN IN YUGOSLAVIA AND ON VIETNAM: George F. Kennan, *Memoirs, 1950–1963*, 266–318; Kennan to Jeannette Kennan, Dec. 16, 1962, Kennan private papers courtesy of Joan Kennan Pozen; Kennan to Robert Oppenheimer, Nov. 16, 1972, Kennan to William Sloane Coffin, Aug. 27, 1965, Kennan to Llewellyn Thompson, Apr. 5, 1966, Kennan to Emmet John Hughes, May 31, 1966, Kennan to Arthur Schlesinger, Jr., Oct. 17, 1967, Kennan papers, Princeton University; *New York Times*, Feb. 11, 1966.

LOVETT AND VIETNAM: Authors' interviews with Robert Lovett, John McCloy;

Lovett Oral History, 1964, Kennedy Library; Burch, "The Guns, Butter, and Then-some Economy"; McGeorge Bundy to President Johnson, Jan. 26, 1966, LBJ Library.

NITZE AND VIETNAM: Authors' interviews with Paul Nitze, Leslie Gelb; Brandon, *Anatomy of an Error: The Inside Story of the Asian War on the Potomac, 1954–1969*, 169; Berman, *Planning a Tragedy: The Americanization of the War in Vietnam*, 113.

BOHLEN IN PARIS AND ON VIETNAM: Salisbury, *A Journey for Our Times*, 454; Bohlen, *Witness to History*, 499–525; authors' interviews with Cecil Lyon, Celestine Bohlen, and Charles Bohlen, Jr.

McCLOY AND VIETNAM: Notes on meeting of foreign policy advisers on resumption of bombing, Jan. 28, 1966, LBJ Library; authors' interviews with McCloy, Louis Auchincloss, Cass Canfield; Johnson, *The Vantage Point*, 306–311; McCloy Oral History, 1969, LBJ Library.

ACHESON AND NATO: Acheson to Desmond Donnelly, Dec. 9, 1965, Mar. 1, 1967, Acheson to Eden, May 17, June 29, 1966, George Ball to Acheson, July 15, 1966, Acheson to Truman, Oct. 3, 1966, Acheson personal papers, Yale University.

Chapter 23
Judgment Days

LBJ SUMMONS THE WISE MEN: Hoopes, *Limits of Intervention*, 113; Karnow, *Vietnam*, 513; Rostow to President Johnson, Oct. 24, 1967, LBJ Library; authors' interviews with Robert Lovett, John McCloy, and Andrea Giles (McCloy's assistant).

NOVEMBER 1967 MEETING OF THE WISE MEN: Rostow to President Johnson, Nov. 2, 1967, Jim Jones notes on meeting of foreign policy advisers, Nov. 2, 1967, LBJ Library; authors' interviews with Clark Clifford, McGeorge Bundy, Maxwell Taylor, George Ball; Ball, *The Past Has Another Pattern*, 407 (Ball incorrectly remembers that McCloy was present); Acheson to John Cowles, Aug. 21, 1967, Acheson personal papers, Yale University.

HARRIMAN CULTIVATES ACHESON: McGeorge Bundy to President Johnson, Nov. 10, 1967, LBJ Library; Harriman memo to files, Dec. 12, 1967, Harriman to Acheson, Dec. 18, 1967, Harriman private papers, Washington, D.C.; authors' interview with Dan Davidson.

ACHESON'S DOUBTS DEEPEN: Acheson to Anthony Eden, Aug. 27, Dec. 1, Dec.

30, 1967, Acheson to John Cowles, Aug. 7, 1967, Acheson to Matthew Ridgway, Oct. 17, 1967, Acheson personal papers, Yale University; authors' interviews with Harry McPherson, William Bundy, Mary Acheson Bundy, Nicholas Katzenbach, Lucius Battle, Linda Bird Francke, Townsend Hoopes, Leslie Gelb.

ACHESON FEBRUARY MEETING WITH LBJ: Acheson to John Cowles, Feb. 27, 1968, Acheson personal papers, Yale; Hoopes, *Limits of Intervention*, 204–205; authors' interviews with C. B. Marshall, Walt Rostow (Acheson told the "stick it..." story to Marshall at the time; Rostow says he has no recollection of it), Phil Habib.

CLIFFORD BECOMES DEFENSE SECRETARY: Authors' interviews with Clark Clifford, Paul Nitze, Morton Halperin, Walt Rostow, Townsend Hoopes; Clifford to President Johnson, July 25, 1965, memo of meeting of foreign policy advisers, Jan. 28, 1966, LBJ Library; Schandler, *The Unmaking of a President: Lyndon Johnson and Vietnam*, 92–218; Clifford, "A Vietnam Reappraisal: The Personal History of One Man's View and How It Evolved."

HARRIMAN AND RFK, ACHESON: Harriman to McCloy, undated (February 1968), Harriman to Robert Kennedy, Feb. 1, 1968, Harriman telcon with Robert Kennedy, Mar. 20, 1968, Harriman to Acheson, Feb. 5, 1968, Harriman telcon with Acheson, Mar. 7, 1968, Harriman private papers, Washington, D.C.

ACHESON MARCH MEETING WITH LBJ: Authors' interviews with Phil Habib, David Acheson; Habib memo "Observations on Vietnam," Feb. 26, 1968, Harriman private papers, Washington, D.C.; Acheson memo of meeting with President Johnson, Mar. 14, 1968, Acheson to John Cowles, Mar. 14, 1968, Acheson personal papers, Yale University.

JOHNSON BESIEGED: Kalb and Abel, *Roots of Involvement: The United States in Asia, 1784–1971*, 218–256; Brandon, *Anatomy of an Error*, 118–140; authors' interview with Clark Clifford.

ACHESON TURNS AGAINST THE WAR: Authors' interviews with Wallace Carroll, Lucius Battle, George Ball, McGeorge Bundy, Clark Clifford, Walt Rostow; McGeorge Bundy to President Johnson, Nov. 10, 1967, LBJ Library; Jay Gould to Acheson, Apr. 1, 1967, Acheson personal papers, Yale University.

MARCH 1968 MEETING OF THE WISE MEN: Authors' interviews with William Bundy, Nicholas Katzenbach, Phil Habib, Arthur Goldberg, Douglas Dillon, Cyrus Vance, Clark Clifford, Walt Rostow, Maxwell Taylor, Peter Swiers (Harriman aide); William Bundy Oral History, 1969, LBJ Library; "The Establishment," by Hodgson; Henry Cabot Lodge to Harriman, Mar. 27, 1968; *New York Times*, Mar. 25, 1968; Harriman appointment calendar, Mar. 25, 1968, Johnson handwritten note to Harriman, Mar. 26, 1968, Harriman to Johnson, Mar. 26,

1968, Harriman private papers, Washington, D.C.; McGeorge Bundy's notes on Wise Men meeting, Mar. 26, 1968, Johnson's handwritten notes in meeting file for Mar. 26, 1968, LBJ Library; Johnson, *The Vantage Point*, 418; Tom Johnson to President Johnson, Mar. 27, 1968, LBJ Library.

RUSK AND CLIFFORD: Authors' interviews with Dean Rusk, Clark Clifford, William Bundy, Nicholas Katzenbach, Walt Rostow, George Christian; Rusk to President Johnson, July 2, 1965, LBJ Library; Rusk to Bohlen, June 27, 1973, Bohlen personal papers, Library of Congress; Hoopes, "LBJ's Account of March 1968,"; Mar. 31, 1968, speech file, LBJ Library; Johnson, *The Vantage Point*, 427–437; Schandler, *The Unmaking of a President*, 266–289.

HARRIMAN TO PARIS: Authors' interviews with Dan Davidson, Peter Swiers, Chester Cooper, William Bundy, Cyrus Vance; Harriman memo to file, Apr. 9, 1968, Harriman telcon with President Johnson, Apr. 11, Harriman personal papers, Washington, D.C.; notes on meeting between Lyndon Johnson, Dean Rusk, Clark Clifford, Apr. 8, 1968, LBJ Library; Acheson to Harriman, Apr. 19, 1968, Acheson to Jane Brown, Apr. 13, 1968, Johnson to Acheson, Apr. 11, 1968, Harriman to Acheson, May 8, 1968, Acheson personal papers, Yale University.

HARVAN IN PARIS: Authors' interviews with Dan Davidson, Peter Swiers, William Bundy, Cyrus Vance, George Ball, Leslie Gelb, Nicholas Katzenbach; notes on President Johnson's meeting with foreign policy advisers, May 6, 1968; Harriman Oral History, 1969, Vance Oral History, 1969–70, LBJ Library; Karnow, *Vietnam*, 566; Brandon, *Anatomy of an Error*, 146–147; Sulzberger, *An Age of Mediocrity*, 463–464, 490–493; Goodman, *The Lost Peace*, 60–73; Solberg, *Hubert Humphrey*, 380–390; Harriman Oral History, 1969, Columbia.

Chapter 24
Legacy

ACHESON THE DISSENTER: Schulzinger, *The Wise Men of Foreign Affairs: The History of the Council on Foreign Relations*, 209–211; authors' interview with Townsend Hoopes; Sulzberger, *An Age of Mediocrity*, 660; Acheson to Jay Gould, July 24, 1969, June 7, 1969, Acheson to Anthony Eden, July 7, 1969, Acheson to Clifford, June 24, 1969, Acheson to John Cowles, Mar. 27, 1971, Acheson personal papers, Yale University; *New York Times*, June 2, 1958, Nov. 10, 1969 (Kennan).

LAST BATTLE: Kissinger, *The White House Years*, 939–949; Acheson to Jay Gould, Mar. 21, 1969, Dec. 3, 1970, Acheson to Anthony Eden, Jan. 19, 1970, Acheson to Lovett, Oct. 30, 1969, Acheson to Lincoln MacVeigh, Dec.

2, 1969, Acheson to Cowles, May 21, 1971, Richard Nixon to Acheson, May 20, 1971, Acheson personal papers, Yale University.

LAST DAYS: Authors' interview with Mary Acheson Bundy; Sulzberger, *An Age of Mediocrity*, 657; Acheson to Anthony Eden, Jan. 19, 1970, Acheson to Harriman, Sept. 15, 1971, Acheson personal papers, Yale University.

DEATH OF BOHLEN: Bohlen, *Witness to History*, 535; authors' interviews with Charles Bohlen, Jr., Avis Bohlen, Celestine Bohlen, J. Randolph Harrison, George Kennan.

KENNAN AND THE BOMB: Authors' interview with George Kennan; Steel, "The Statesman of Survival"; Gellman, *Contending with Kennan*, 139–157; Acheson to Jay Gould, Oct. 28, 1969, Kennan to Acheson, Oct. 21, 1969, Acheson personal papers, Yale University; Nitze's toast courtesy of Paul Nitze.

HARRIMAN IN RETIREMENT: Authors' interviews with Pamela Churchill Harriman, Peter Swiers, Leslie Gelb, William Sullivan; Brzezinski, *Power and Principle*; Vance, *Hard Choices*; Destler, *Our Own Worst Enemy: The Unmaking of American Foreign Policy*, 91–126.

McCLOY, OIL, AND THE SHAH: Authors' interviews with William Jackson (McCloy's law partner), James Akins and John Irwin (State Department officials), William Bundy, Hugh Sidey, Henry Kissinger; Brinkley, "Minister without Portfolio"; Sampson, *The Seven Sisters: The Great Oil Companies and the World They Made*, 208–282; Smith, "Why Carter Admitted the Shah"; tributes to McCloy at White House courtesy of Alessandra Stanley, *Time*; at Council on Foreign Relations by authors.

THIRD WORLD VIEWS: Authors' interview with William Bundy; Acheson, *Present at the Creation*, 265; Gellman, *Contending with Kennan*, 54–55.

LOVETT IN RETIREMENT: Authors' interviews with Lovett, McCloy; Lovett to McCloy, February 27, 1985; McCloy to Lovett, September 4, 1985, McCloy files, Milbank Tweed.

NITZE'S LATER CAREER: Authors' interviews with Paul Nitze; Talbott, *Deadly Gambits*, 52–55, 116–152; Kaplan, *The Wizards of Armageddon*, 380–381.

LEGACY: Authors' interviews with Robert Lovett, John McCloy, George Kennan, Henry Kissinger, William Bundy, George Ball.

SOURCES

Interviews

Alice Stanley (Mrs. Dean) Acheson
David Acheson
Theodore Achilles
James Akins
Joseph Alsop
Patricia (Mrs. Stewart) Alsop
Louis Auchincloss
George Ball
Lucius Battle
Jonathan Bingham
Avis Bohlen (daughter)
Celestine Bohlen
Charles Bohlen, Jr.
Constance Kennan Bradt
Larry Brownell
McGeorge Bundy
Mary Acheson (Mrs. William) Bundy
William Bundy
Benjamin Buttenwieser
Cass Canfield
Wallace Carroll
Abram Chayes
George Christian
Clark Clifford
Chester Cooper
Lloyd Cutler
Dan Davidson
C. Douglas Dillon
Peter Duchin
Elbridge Durbrow

Thomas Ehrlich
George Elsey
Mrs. William Eustis
Barbara Evans
Michael Forrestal
Linda Bird Francke
John Kenneth Galbraith
Leslie Gelb
Gerhard Gesell
Arthur Goldberg
Philip Habib
Morton Halperin
Averell Harriman
Pamela Churchill (Mrs. Averell)
   Harriman
J. Randolph Harrison
Kitty Carlisle (Mrs. Moss) Hart
Richard Helms
Loy Henderson
John Hickerson
Roger Hilsman
Richard Holbrooke
Townsend Hoopes
Jeannette Kennan Hotchkiss
John Irwin
William Jackson
Kate (Mrs. Brewster) Jennings
Walter Judd
Milton Katz
Nicholas Katzenbach
George F. Kennan
Kent Wheeler Kennan

Lydia (Mrs. Alan) Kirk
Henry Kissinger
Felix Larkin
Marx Leva
Henry Cabot Lodge
Adèle Brown (Mrs. Robert) Lovett
Robert Lovett
Robert S. Lovett II
Cecil Lyon
Ellen McCloy (daughter)
John J. McCloy
John J. McCloy II
Robert McNamara
Harry McPherson
Charles Burton Marshall
Ernest R. May
Kathleen Harriman (Mrs. Stanley)
   Mortimer
Paul Nitze
John Ohly
Claude Pepper
Forrest Pogue

Joan Kennan (Mrs. Walter) Pozen
Robert Reams
George Reedy
James Rowe
Dean Rusk
Arthur Schlesinger, Jr.
Marshall Shulman
Benjamin Shute
Hugh Sidey
Theodore Sorensen
William Sullivan
Peter Swiers
Maxwell Taylor
Jane (Mrs. Llewellyn) Thompson
Robert Tufts
Jack Valenti
Cyrus Vance
Richard Wade
Grace Kennan Warnecke
Philip Weiss
Francis Wilcox
Frances Kennan Worobec

Archives

   Alice Acheson personal papers, Acheson home, Washington, D.C. Includes daily appointment calendars for 1920–1960.
   Dean Acheson papers, Truman Library, Independence, Mo. Includes official letters and papers from his years at the State Department.
   Dean Acheson personal papers, Sterling Library, Yale University. Includes personal letters and papers.
   Henry H. Arnold papers, Library of Congress, Washington, D.C.
   Eben Ayers diary, Truman Library, Independence, Mo.
   Charles E. Bohlen personal papers, Library of Congress, Washington, D.C. Includes letters, papers, and material collected for his memoirs.
   Brown Brothers Harriman partners' files, New York Historical Society, New York City. Includes office files, clippings and correspondence of Averell Harriman, Roland Harriman, and Robert Lovett. Also includes Lovett's appointment calendar and daily diary from the 1940s.
   William Bundy's unpublished memoir of the Vietnam War. Courtesy of William Bundy, Princeton, N.J.
   Council of Foreign Relations archives, New York City. Includes transcripts of meetings, speeches, and study groups.
   John Foster Dulles papers, Seeley Mudd Library, Princeton University. In-

cludes correspondence and records of conversations with Bohlen, Kennan, Lovett, and McCloy.

Ferdinand Eberstadt personal papers, Seeley Mudd Library, Princeton University. Includes correspondence with Forrestal and Lovett.

George Elsey papers, Truman Library, Independence, Mo. Includes "Comments on the document entitled 'American Relations to the Soviet Union,'" by Kennan.

James Forrestal papers, Seeley Mudd Library, Princeton University. Includes letters, papers, and the unedited version of his diary.

Groton School Archives, records of Averell Harriman and Dean Acheson, used by permission of families.

Averell Harriman personal papers, Harriman home, Washington, D.C. Includes his letters, financial records, newspaper clippings, official memoranda, and research done for his book *Special Envoy*. In 1986, the papers were in the process of being transferred to the Library of Congress.

Loy Henderson private papers, Henderson home, Washington, D.C. Includes unpublished six-volume memoirs of his Foreign Service career and personal letters.

Harry Hopkins papers, Roosevelt Library, Hyde Park, N.Y. Includes Harriman and Kennan memos to Hopkins.

Lyndon Johnson papers, Johnson Library, Austin, Tex. Includes correspondence with Acheson, McCloy, Lovett, Harriman, Kennan, and Bohlen, notes of meetings and discussions with Johnson's foreign policy advisers (the Wise Men).

Joseph Jones papers, Truman Library, Independence, Mo. Includes speech drafts and materials for drafting Truman Doctrine.

George F. Kennan papers, Seeley Mudd Library, Princeton University. Includes personal letters, unpublished journals, drafts of articles and book notes, lectures at the National War College and elsewhere.

George F. Kennan personal papers, privately collected by Joan Kennan Pozen, Washington, D.C. Includes letters home as a child, school and college report cards, other letters, photographs, scrapbook clippings, and Joan Pozen's interviews with family members.

John F. Kennedy papers, Kennedy Library, Boston, Mass. Includes minutes of NSC meetings, minutes of ExCom in Cuban missile crisis, and correspondence with Acheson, Lovett, Harriman, Kennan, Bohlen, and McCloy.

Marx Leva personal papers, Washington, D.C. Includes correspondence with Forrestal.

Robert Lovett Assistant Secretary of War office files, Record Group 107, National Archives, Washington, D.C.

Robert Lovett private scrapbooks, Lovett home, Locust Valley, N.Y. Includes clippings and photographs.

John McCloy Assistant Secretary of War office files, Record Group 107, National Archives, Washington, D.C.

John McCloy private papers, Amherst College. Includes sporadic journals, letters, speeches, newspaper clippings and memoranda. (During research for this book, papers were at McCloy's law office, his home, and at the Council on Foreign Relations. In 1986, most were in the process of being transferred to Amherst College.)

Frank McNaughton private papers, Truman Library, Independence, Mo. Includes McNaughton's files as a *Time* correspondent covering Lovett and Acheson at State Department.

National Archives, Record Group 59, State Department files, Washington, D.C. Includes official papers of Kennan, Harriman, Bohlen, Acheson, and others organized by topic and name.

Paul Nitze personal papers, Arlington, Va. Includes oral histories and correspondence.

Harry B. Price papers, Truman Library, Independence, Mo. Oral histories of men involved in the making of the Marshall Plan, including Kennan, Bohlen, Marshall, and Harriman.

Sidney Souers papers. Truman Library, Independence, Mo. Includes National Security Council memos.

Henry L. Stimson papers, Sterling Library, Yale University. Includes his voluminous diary (available on microfilm), letters, and other papers.

Henry L. Stimson "safe files," Record Group 107, National Archives, Washington, D.C. The sensitive material relating to the bomb and other projects that was once kept in Stimson's office safe.

Charles Thayer papers, Truman Library, Independence, Mo. Includes correspondence with Bohlen and Kennan.

Harry Truman papers, Truman Library, Independence, Mo. Includes correspondence with Acheson, Harriman, Lovett, Forrestal, and McCloy.

Oral Histories

Dean Acheson oral history seminars on his State Department years with aides, including Averell Harriman and Paul Nitze, Princeton University, 1952–1953. Microfilm available at the Truman Library, Independence, Mo.

Dean Acheson Oral History, 1964, Kennedy Library, Boston, Mass.

Theodore Achilles Oral History, 1973, Truman Library, Independence, Mo.

Joseph Alsop Oral History, 1965, John Foster Dulles papers, Seeley Mudd Library, Princeton University.

Charles Bohlen Oral History, 1960, Columbia Oral History Project, Columbia University.

Charles Bohlen interview, 1953, Truman Library, Independence, Mo.

Charles Bohlen Oral History, 1964, John Foster Dulles papers, Seeley Mudd Library, Princeton University.

Charles Bohlen Oral History, 1964, Kennedy Library, Boston, Mass.

Chester Bowles Oral History, 1965, Kennedy Library, Boston, Mass.

Harvey Bundy interview, 1957, Columbia Oral History Project, Low Library, Columbia University.

William Bundy Oral History, 1969, Johnson Library, Austin, Texas.

Cass Canfield interview, Columbia Oral History Project, Columbia University.

Lucius Clay Oral History, 1965, John Foster Dulles papers, Seeley Mudd Library, Princeton, University.

Chester Cooper Oral History, 1966, Kennedy Library, Boston, Mass.

Averell Harriman interview, 1965, Dulles Oral History Project, Princeton University Library.

Averell Harriman Oral Histories, 1969, 1978, Columbia Oral History Project, Columbia University.

Averell Harriman Oral History, 1964, Kennedy Library, Boston, Mass.

Averell Harriman Oral History, 1969, Johnson Library, Austin, Texas.

Averell Harriman Oral History, 1971, Truman Library, Independence, Mo.

Averell Harriman Oral History Project, Kennedy Institute of Politics, Harvard University, 1969–1970, conducted by Professors Francis Bator, Ernest May, Charles Maier, and Richard Neustadt. Transcript courtesy of Professor Maier.

Averell Harriman and John McCloy, off-the-record discussion of the origins of the Cold War, 1967, conducted by Arthur Schlesinger, Jr. Transcript from Harriman personal papers, Washington, D.C.

John Hickerson Oral History, 1973, Truman Library, Independence, Mo.

George Kennan Oral History, 1965, Kennedy Library, Boston, Mass.

Kennan family interviews, 1972, conducted by Joan Kennan Pozen with George Kennan and his sisters, Pozen private papers, Washington, D.C.

Robert Kennedy Oral Histories, 1964–1965, Kennedy Library, Boston, Mass.

Robert Lovett interview by Mark Chadwin, 1968, Harriman private papers, Washington, D.C.

Robert Lovett Oral History, 1964, Kennedy Library, Boston, Mass.

Robert Lovett Oral History, 1971, Truman Library, Independence, Mo.

Robert Lovett Oral History, 1975, Columbia Oral History Project, Columbia University.

John McCloy interviews, 1975, CBS News, conducted by Eric Sevareid. Transcript courtesy of CBS News.

John McCloy interviews, "The Decision to Drop the Bomb," NBC News White Paper, 1964, conducted by Len Giovannitti and Fred Freed. Transcript courtesy of John McCloy.

John McCloy Oral History, 1969, Johnson Library, Austin, Tex.

John McCloy Oral History, 1973, Columbia Oral History project, Columbia University.

John McCloy Oral History, 1983, Defense Department Oral History Project. Transcript courtesy of John McCloy.

John McCloy testimony, Commission on Wartime Relocation, 1981, U.S. Congress, Government Printing Office, Washington, D.C.

Marshall Plan Oral History Project, Low Library, Columbia University.
Leonard Miall Oral History, 1964, Truman Library, Independence, Mo.
Charles Murphy Oral History, 1964, Truman Library, Independence, Mo.
Paul Nitze interviews for the Air Force Oral History Project, 1977, 1981, and the Truman Library, 1975 (not released to public), Nitze private papers, Arlington, Va.
Paul Nitze Oral History, 1971, Kennedy Library, Boston, Mass.
Public Broadcasting Service, "The First Fifty Years: U.S.-Soviet Relations, 1934–1984," television documentary, 1984.
Dean Rusk Oral History, 1981, Duke University, Durham, N.C.
Ted Sorensen Oral History, Kennedy Library, Boston, Mass.
William Sullivan Oral History, 1970, Kennedy Library, Boston, Mass.
Cyrus Vance Oral History, 1969–1970, Johnson Library, Austin, Texas.

Books

Abel, Elie. *The Missile Crisis*. Philadelphia: Lippincott, 1966.
Acheson, Dean. *A Democrat Looks at His Party*. New York: Harper & Brothers, 1955.
———. *Morning and Noon*. Boston: Houghton Mifflin, 1965.
———. *Present at the Creation*. New York: W. W. Norton, 1969.
———. *Sketches from Life of Men I Have Known*. New York: Harper & Brothers, 1961.
———. *Strengthening the Forces of Freedom*. Washington: Government Printing Office, 1950.
———. *This Vast External Realm*. New York: W. W. Norton, 1973.
Albion, Robert, and Robert Connery. *Forrestal and the Navy*. New York: Columbia, 1962.
Alperovitz, Gar. *Atomic Diplomacy*. New York: Simon & Schuster, 1965, and revised version, New York: Viking Penguin, 1985.
Ambrose, Stephen. *Eisenhower: The Presidency*. New York: Simon & Schuster, 1984.
———. *Rise to Globalism*. London: Penguin Press, 1971.
Amory, Cleveland. *The Proper Bostonians*. New York: E. P. Dutton, 1947.
Armstrong, Hamilton Fish. *Fifty Years of Foreign Affairs*. New York: Praeger, 1972.
Arnold, Henry H. *Global Mission*. London: Hutchinson, 1951.
Ashburn, Frank. *Fifty Years On*. New York: privately printed for Groton School, 1934.
———. *Peabody of Groton*. New York: Coward-McCann, 1944.
Aswell, Edward. *Harvard 1926: The Life and Opinions of a College Class*. Cambridge: Harvard University Press, 1951.
Ball, George. *The Past Has Another Pattern*. New York: W. W. Norton, 1982.

Barnet, Richard. *The Alliance: America-Europe-Japan—Makers of the Postwar World*. New York: Simon & Schuster, 1983.

———. *Roots of War: Men and Institutions Behind U.S. Foreign Policy*. Baltimore: Penguin, 1973.

Baruch, Bernard. *The Public Years*. New York: Holt, Rinehart and Winston, 1960.

Berman, Larry. *Planning a Tragedy: The Americanization of the War in Vietnam*. New York: W. W. Norton, 1982.

Bickel, Alexander. *The Unpublished Opinions of Mr. Justice Brandeis*. Cambridge: Harvard University Press, 1957.

Blum, John. *Roosevelt and Morgenthau*. Boston: Houghton Mifflin, 1970.

Blum, John, ed. *From the Morgenthau Diaries: Years of War, 1941–1945*. Boston: Houghton Mifflin, 1967.

———. *The Price of Vision: The Diary of Henry A. Wallace*. Boston: Houghton Mifflin, 1973.

———. *Public Philosopher: Selected Letters of Walter Lippmann*. New York: Ticknor & Fields, 1985.

Bohlen, Charles. *The Transformation of American Foreign Policy*. New York: W. W. Norton, 1969.

———. *Witness to History*. New York: W. W. Norton, 1973.

Brandon, Henry. *Anatomy of an Error: The Inside Story of the Asian War on the Potomac, 1954–1969*. Boston: Gambit, 1969.

Browder, Robert. *The Origins of Soviet-American Diplomacy*. Princeton: Princeton University, 1953.

Brown Brothers Harriman & Co. *The Personality of a Bank*. New York: privately published.

Brzezinski, Zbigniew. *Power and Principle*. New York: Farrar, Straus & Giroux, 1983.

Bullitt, Orville, ed. *For the President: Personal and Secret: Correspondence between Franklin D. Roosevelt and William C. Bullitt*, with an introduction by George Kennan. Boston: Houghton Mifflin, 1972.

Bundy, McGeorge, ed. *The Pattern of Responsibility* (speeches and statements of Acheson). Cambridge: Riverside Press, 1951.

Byrnes, James. *All in One Lifetime*. New York: Harper & Brothers, 1958.

———. *Speaking Frankly*. New York: Harper & Brothers, 1947.

Campbell, Persia. *Mary Williamson Harriman*. New York: Columbia, 1960.

Canfield, Cass. *Up and Down and Around*. New York: Harper & Row, 1971.

Chadwin, Mark. *The Hawks of World War II*. Chapel Hill: University of North Carolina, 1968.

Chancellor, Paul. *The History of The Hill School*. Pottstown, Pa.: Hill School, 1976.

Churchill, Winston. *Hinge of Fate*. Boston: Houghton Mifflin, 1948.

———. *Triumph and Tragedy*. Boston: Houghton Mifflin, 1950.

Clay, Lucius. *Decision in Germany*. New York: Doubleday, 1950.

Cochran, Bert. *Harry Truman and the Crisis Presidency*. New York: Funk & Wagnalls, 1973.

Cohen, Morris. *A Dreamer's Journey*. Boston: Little, Brown, 1949.

Cohen, Warren I. *Dean Rusk*. Totowa, N.J.: Cooper Square Publishers, 1980.

Cooper, Chester. *The Lost Crusade: America in Vietnam*. New York: Dodd, Mead, 1970.

Council on Foreign Relations. *The United States and World Affairs, 1947–48*. New York: Harper and Brothers, 1948.

Daniels, Jonathan. *The Man of Independence*. Philadelphia: J. B. Lippincott, 1950.

Davies, Joseph. *Mission to Moscow*. New York: Simon and Schuster, 1941.

Davis, Lynn Etheridge. *The Cold War Begins*. Princeton: Princeton University Press, 1974.

Davison, W. Phillips. *The Berlin Blockade*. Princeton: Princeton University Press, 1958.

Deane, John R. *The Strange Alliance*. New York: Viking, 1947.

DeSantis, Hugh. *The Diplomacy of Silence*. Chicago: University of Chicago, 1979.

Destler, I. M., Leslie Gelb, and Anthony Lake. *Our Own Worst Enemy*. New York: Simon and Schuster, 1984.

Detzer, David. *The Brink*. New York: Thomas Crowell, 1979.

Djilas, Milovan. *Conversations with Stalin*. London: Pelican Books, 1969.

———. *Rise and Fall*. New York: Harcourt Brace Jovanovich, 1985.

Donovan, Robert. *Conflict and Crisis: The Presidency of Harry S. Truman*. New York: W. W. Norton, 1977.

———. *Tumultuous Years*. New York: W. W. Norton, 1982.

Druks, Herbert. *Harry S. Truman and the Russians 1945–53*. New York: Robert Speller & Sons, 1966.

Eisenhower, Dwight. *The White House Years*. New York: Doubleday, 1963.

Eveland, Wilbur Crane. *Ropes of Sand: America's Failure in the Middle East*. New York: W. W. Norton, 1980.

Farnsworth, Beatrice. *William C. Bullitt and the Soviet Union*. Bloomington: Indiana University, 1967.

Feis, Herbert. *The Atomic Bomb and the End of World War II*. Princeton: Princeton University Press, 1966.

———. *Between War and Peace: The Potsdam Conference*. Princeton: Princeton University Press, 1960.

———. *Churchill Roosevelt Stalin*. Princeton: Princeton University Press, 1957.

———. *From Trust to Terror*. New York: W. W. Norton, 1970.

Ferrell, Robert, ed. *Off the Record: The Private Papers of Harry S. Truman*. New York: Harper & Row, 1980.

Filene, Peter. *Americans and the Soviet Experiment, 1917–1933*. Cambridge: Harvard University Press, 1967.

Fitzgerald, F. Scott. *This Side of Paradise*. New York: Scribner's, 1920.

Fleming, D. F. *The Cold War and Its Origins 1917–1960*, 2 vols. New York: Doubleday, 1961.

Frankfurter, Felix. *Mr. Justice Brandeis*. New Haven: Yale University Press, 1932.

————. *Of Law and Life and Other Things That Matter*, ed. by Philip Kurland. Cambridge: Harvard University Press, 1965.

Freeland, Richard. *The Truman Doctrine and the Origins of McCarthyism*. New York: Knopf, 1972.

FRUS: See U.S. Department of State, *Foreign Relations of the United States*.

Gaddis, John Lewis. *Russia, the Soviet Union and the United States*. New York: Wiley, 1978.

————. *Strategies of Containment*. New York: Oxford University Press, 1982.

————. *The U.S. and the Origins of the Cold War*. New York: Columbia, 1972.

Galbraith, John Kenneth. *Ambassador's Journal*. Boston: Houghton Mifflin, 1969.

————. *Economics, Peace, and Laughter*. Boston: Houghton Mifflin, 1971.

————. *A Life in Our Times*. New York: W. W. Norton, 1982.

Gardner, Lloyd. *Architects of Illusion*. Chicago: Quadrangle, 1970.

Gelb, Leslie, and Richard K. Betts. *The Irony of Vietnam: The System Worked*. Washington, D.C.: Brookings Institution, 1979.

Gellman, Barton. *Contending with Kennan: Towards a Philosophy of American Power*. New York: Praeger, 1985.

Giovannitti, Len, and Fred Freed. *The Decision to Drop the Bomb*. New York: Coward-McCann, 1965.

Goodman, Allen. *The Lost Peace: America's Search for a Negotiated Settlement of the Vietnam War*. Stanford: Hoover Institution Press, 1978.

Goulden, Joseph C. *Korea: The Untold Story of the War*. New York: Quadrangle, 1982.

Grew, Joseph. *Turbulent Era*, 2 vols. Boston: Houghton Mifflin, 1952.

Grodzins, Morton. *Americans Betrayed*. Chicago: University of Chicago, 1947.

Groves, Leslie. *Now It Can Be Told*. New York: Harper & Row, 1962.

Guhin, Michael A. *John Foster Dulles: A Statesman and His Times*. New York: Columbia University Press, 1972.

Halberstam, David. *The Best and the Brightest*. New York: Random House, 1972.

Hall, Reginald, and Amos Peaslee. *Three Wars with Germany*. New York: G. P. Putnam's, 1944.

Halle, Louis. *The Cold War as History*. New York: Harper & Row, 1967.

Hammond, Thomas, ed. *Witnesses to the Origins of the Cold War*. Seattle: University of Washington, 1982.

Harr, John Ensor. *The Professional Diplomat*. Princeton: Princeton University, 1969.

Harriman, Averell. *America and Russia in a Changing World*. New York: Doubleday, 1971.

———. *Peace with Russia?* New York: Simon and Schuster, 1959.

Harriman, Averell, and Elie Abel. *Special Envoy*. New York: Random House, 1975.

Harriman, Roland. *I Reminisce*. New York: Doubleday, 1975.

Havemeyer, Loomis. *Go To Your Room!* New Haven: Yale University Press, 1960.

Heckscher, August. *St. Paul's: The Life of a New England School*. New York: Scribner's, 1980.

Heinrichs, Waldo, Jr. *American Ambassador: Joseph C. Grew and the Development of the U.S. Diplomatic Tradition*. Boston: Little, Brown, 1966.

Herring, George. *Aid to Russia 1941–46*. New York: Columbia University Press, 1973.

Hewlett, Richard, and Oscar Anderson, Jr. *The New World*. University Park: Pennsylvania State Press, 1962.

Hilsman, Roger. *To Move a Nation: The Politics of Foreign Policy in the Administration of John F. Kennedy*. New York: Doubleday, 1967.

Hodgson, Godfrey. *America in Our Time*. Garden City, N.Y.: Doubleday, 1976.

Holly, J. B. *Ideas and Weapons*. New Haven: Yale, 1953.

Hoopes, Townsend. *The Devil and John Foster Dulles*. Boston: Little, Brown, 1973.

———. *The Limits of Intervention*. New York: David McKay, 1969.

Howard, Harry. *Turkey, the Straits and U.S. Policy*. Baltimore: Johns Hopkins, 1974.

Hull, Cordell. *Memoirs*. New York: Macmillan, 1948.

Ilchman, Warren. *Professional Diplomacy in the U.S.* Chicago: University of Chicago, 1961.

Irons, Peter. *Justice at War*. New York: Oxford, 1983.

James, D. Clayton. *The Years of MacArthur*, Vol. III, *Triumph and Disaster, 1945–1964*. Boston: Houghton Mifflin, 1985.

Jessup, Philip. *Elihu Root*. New York: Dodd Mead, 1938.

Johnson, Griffith, Jr. *The Treasury and Monetary Policy*. Cambridge: Harvard University Press, 1939.

Johnson, Lyndon B. *The Vantage Point: Perspectives of the Presidency, 1963–1969*. New York: Holt, Rinehart and Winston, 1971.

Johnson, Owen. *Stover at Yale*. New York: Collier Books, 1968 (first published in 1911).

Jones, Joseph. *The Fifteen Weeks*. New York: Harcourt, Brace & World, 1964.

Kahn, E. J. *The China Hands: America's Foreign Service Officers and What Befell Them*. New York: Viking, 1972.

Kaiser, Robert. *Cold Winter, Cold War*. New York: Stein and Day, 1974.

Kalb, Marvin, and Elie Abel. *Roots of Involvement: The United States in*

Asia, 1784–1971. New York: W. W. Norton, 1971.

Kaplan, Fred. *The Wizards of Armageddon.* New York: Simon and Schuster, 1983.

Kaplan, Lawrence. *The United States and NATO.* Lexington: University of Kentucky Press, 1984.

Karnow, Stanley. *Vietnam.* New York: Viking, 1983.

Kennan, George. *E. H. Harriman,* 2 vols. Boston: Houghton Mifflin, 1922.

―――. *Siberia and the Exile System,* with an introduction by George F. Kennan. Chicago: University of Chicago Press, 1958; originally published in 1891.

Kennan, George F. *American Diplomacy: 1900–1950.* New York: New American Library, 1951.

―――. *The Cloud of Danger: Current Realities of American Foreign Policy.* Boston: Little, Brown, 1977.

―――. *The Decline of Bismarck's European Order.* Princeton: Princeton University Press, 1979.

―――. *Democracy and the Student Left.* Boston: Little, Brown, 1968.

―――. *The Fateful Alliance: France, Russia and the Coming of the First World War.* New York: Pantheon Books, 1984.

―――. *From Prague After Munich.* Princeton: Princeton University Press, 1968.

―――. *The Marquis de Custine and His Russia in 1839.* Princeton: Princeton University Press, 1971.

―――. *Memoirs, 1925–1950.* Boston: Little, Brown, 1967.

―――. *Memoirs, 1950–1963.* Boston: Little, Brown, 1972.

―――. *The Nuclear Delusion: Soviet-American Relations in the Atomic Age.* New York: Pantheon Books, 1982.

―――. *On Dealing with the Communist World.* New York: Harper & Row, 1964.

―――. *Realities of American Foreign Policy.* Princeton: Princeton University Press, 1954.

―――. *Russia, the Atom and the West.* New York: Harper & Brothers, 1957.

―――. *Russia and the West Under Lenin and Stalin.* Boston: Little, Brown, 1960.

―――. *Soviet-American Relations, 1917–1920,* Vol. I, *Russia Leaves the War.* Princeton: Princeton University Press, 1954.

―――. *Soviet-American Relations, 1917–1920,* Vol. II, *The Decision to Intervene.* Princeton: Princeton University Press, 1958.

―――. *Soviet Foreign Policy, 1917–1941.* Princeton: Van Nostrand, 1960.

Kennan, George F., et al. *Encounters with Kennan: The Great Debate.* London: Frank Cass, 1979. Includes interviews and articles by others.

Kennan, Thomas Lathrop. *The Genealogy of the Kennan Family.* Milwaukee: privately printed, 1907.

Kennedy, Robert. *Thirteen Days.* New York: Norton, 1969.

Kimball, Robert, and Brendan Gill. *Cole*. New York: Holt, Rinehart & Winston, 1971.

Kissinger, Henry. *The White House Years*. Boston: Little, Brown, 1979.

Kolko, Gabriel. *The Roots of American Foreign Policy*. Boston: Beacon Press, 1969.

Kolko, Joyce, and Gabriel Kolko. *The Limits of Power: The World and United States Foreign Policy 1945–54*. New York: Harper & Row, 1972.

Kouwenhoven, John. *Partners in Banking*. New York: Doubleday, 1968.

Krock, Arthur. *Memoirs: Sixty Years on the Firing Line*. New York: Funk & Wagnalls, 1968.

Kuklick, Bruce. *American Policy and the Division of Germany*. Ithaca, N.Y.: Cornell, 1972.

Kuniholm, Bruce. *The Origins of the Cold War in the Near East: Great Power Conflict and Diplomacy in Iran, Turkey, and Greece*. Princeton: Princeton University Press, 1980.

Kurzman, Dan. *Day of the Bomb*. New York: McGraw-Hill, 1985.

———. *Genesis 1948*. New York: World, 1978.

LaFeber, Walter. *America, Russia and the Cold War*. New York: John Wiley & Son, 1976.

Landau, Henry. *The Enemy Within*. New York: G. P. Putnam's, 1937.

Lash, Joseph, ed. *From the Diaries of Felix Frankfurter*. New York: W.W. Norton, 1975.

Leahy, William. *I Was There*. New York: McGraw-Hill, 1950.

Lewis, Wilmarth. *One Man's Education*. New York: Knopf, 1967.

Lieberman, Joseph. *The Scorpion and the Tarantula*. Boston: Houghton Mifflin, 1970.

Lilienthal, David. *Journals: The Atomic Energy Years 1945–50*. New York: Harper & Row, 1965.

Lippmann, Walter. *The Cold War*. New York: Harper & Brothers, 1947.

Litvinov, Maxim. *Notes for a Journal*. New York: William Morrow, 1955.

Lyon, Peter. *Eisenhower: Portrait of a Hero*. Boston: Little, Brown, 1974.

Maddox, Robert. *The New Left and the Origins of the Cold War*. Princeton: Princeton University Press, 1973.

Maddux, Thomas. *Years of Estrangement*. Tallahassee: University of Florida, 1980.

Manchester, William. *American Caesar: Douglas MacArthur, 1880–1964*. Boston: Little, Brown, 1978.

———. *The Glory and the Dream*. Boston: Little, Brown, 1974.

McCloy, John. *The Atlantic Alliance: Its Origin and Future*. New York: Columbia University Press, 1969.

———. *The Challenge to American Foreign Policy*. Cambridge: Harvard University Press, 1953.

McLellan, David S. *Dean Acheson: The State Department Years*. New York: Dodd, Mead, 1976.

McLellan, David S., and David Acheson, eds. *Among Friends: Personal Letters of Dean Acheson*. New York: Dodd, Mead, 1980.

McPherson, Harry. *A Political Education*. Boston: Atlantic-Little, Brown, 1971.

Mason, Edward S., and Robert Asher. *The World Bank Since Bretton Woods*. Washington: The Brookings Institution, 1973.

May, Ernest. *Lessons of the Past*. New York: Oxford University Press, 1973.

Medvedev, Roy. *Let History Judge: The Origins and Consequences of Stalinism*. New York: Knopf, 1972.

Mee, Charles. *The Marshall Plan: The Launching of Pax Americana*. New York: Simon and Schuster, 1984.

———. *Meeting at Potsdam*. New York: M. Evans, 1975.

Mikolajczyk, Stanislaw. *The Rape of Poland*. New York: Whittlesey, 1948.

Millis, Walter, ed. *The Forrestal Diaries*. New York: Viking, 1951.

Moley, Raymond. *After Seven Years*. New York: Harper & Brothers, 1939.

Morgenthau, Henry. *The Morgenthau Diary: Germany*. Washington: Senate Judiciary Committee, 1967.

Morison, Elting. *Turmoil and Tradition*. Boston: Houghton Mifflin, 1960.

Morison, Samuel Eliot. *Three Centuries of Harvard*. Cambridge: Harvard University Press, 1936.

Mosley, Leonard. *On Borrowed Time: How World War II Began*. New York: Random House, 1969.

National Resources Defense Council. *Nuclear Weapons Data Book*. Cambridge, Mass.: Ballinger, 1984.

Neustadt, Richard. *Presidential Power: The Politics of Leadership*. New York: John Wiley & Sons, 1960.

Nichols, Alcosta. *Forty Years More*. New York: privately printed for Groton School, 1974.

Paige, Glenn D. *Korea Decision*. New York: The Free Press, 1968.

Paine, Ralph. *The First Yale Unit*, 2 vols. Cambridge: Riverside Press, 1925.

Phillips, Harlan, ed. *Felix Frankfurter Reminisces*. New York: Reynal, 1960.

Poen, Monte, ed. *Letters Home by Harry Truman*. New York: G. P. Putnam's, 1984.

———. *Strictly Personal and Confidential: The Letters Harry Truman Never Mailed*. Boston: Little, Brown, 1982.

Pogue, Forrest C. *Education of a General*. New York: Viking, 1963.

———. *George C. Marshall: Ordeal and Hope*. New York: Viking, 1966.

———. *George C. Marshall: Organizer of Victory*. New York: Viking, 1974.

Pruessen, Ronald W. *John Foster Dulles: The Road to Power*. New York: The Free Press, 1982.

Rearden, Steven L. *History of the Office of the Secretary of Defense: The Formative Years, 1947–50*. Washington: Historical Office of the Secretary of Defense, 1984.

Ridgway, Matthew. *The Korean War*. New York: Doubleday, 1967.

Rogow, Arnold. *James Forrestal*. New York: Macmillan, 1963.

———. *Victim of Duty*. London: Rupert Hart-Davis, 1966.

Roosevelt, Eleanor. *The Autobiography of Eleanor Roosevelt*. New York: Harper & Brothers, 1961.

Rovere, Richard. *The American Establishment and Other Reports, Opinions, and Speculations*. New York: Harcourt, Brace & World, 1962.

Rust, William J. *Kennedy in Vietnam: American Vietnam Policy, 1960–1963*. New York: Scribner's 1985.

Safire, William. *Safire's Political Dictionary*. New York: Random House, 1978.

Salisbury, Harrison. *A Journey for Our Times*. New York: Harper & Row, 1983.

Sampson, Anthony. *The Seven Sisters: The Great Oil Companies and the World They Made*. New York: Viking, 1975.

Schandler, Herbert. *The Unmaking of a President: Lyndon Johnson and Vietnam*. Princeton: Princeton University Press, 1977.

Schlesinger, Arthur, Jr. *The Coming of the New Deal*. Boston: Houghton Mifflin, 1958.

———. *Robert Kennedy and His Times*. Boston: Houghton Mifflin, 1978.

———. *A Thousand Days*. Boston: Houghton Mifflin, 1965.

Schnabel, James F. *United States Army in the Korean War: Policy and Direction, the First Year*. Washington: Government Printing Office, 1973.

Schulzinger, Robert D. *The Wise Men of Foreign Affairs: The History of the Council on Foreign Relations*. New York: Columbia University Press, 1984.

Seaborg, Glenn. *Kennedy, Khrushchev, and the Test Ban*, with a foreword by Averell Harriman. Berkeley: University of California Press, 1981.

Senate Foreign Relations Committee. *Nuclear Test Ban Treaty Hearings*. Washington: Government Printing Office, 1963.

Shepardson, Whitney. *Early History of the Council on Foreign Relations*. Stamford, Conn.: Overbrook Press, 1960.

Sherwin, Martin. *A World Destroyed*. New York: Knopf, 1975.

Sherwood, Robert. *Roosevelt and Hopkins: An Intimate History*. New York: Harper & Brothers, 1948.

Shulman, Marshall. *Stalin's Foreign Policy Reappraised*. Cambridge: Harvard University Press, 1963.

Smith, Gaddis. *American Secretaries of State and Their Diplomacy: Dean Acheson*. New York: Cooper Square Publishers, 1972.

Smith, Jean Edward, ed. *The Papers of General Lucius D. Clay: Germany 1945–49*. Bloomington: Indiana University Press, 1974.

Solberg, Carl. *Hubert Humphrey*. New York: W. W. Norton, 1984.

Sorensen, Theodore. *Kennedy*. Boston: Houghton Mifflin, 1965.

Standley, William, and Arthur Ageton. *Admiral Ambassador to Russia*. Chicago: Regnery, 1955.

Stearns, Alfred E. *The Education of the Modern Boy*. Boston: Little, Brown, 1928.

Steel, Ronald. *Imperialists and Other Heroes*. New York: Random House, 1971.

—. *Walter Lippmann and the American Century*. Boston: Little, Brown, 1980.

Stettinius, Edward. *Roosevelt and the Russians*. Garden City, N.Y.: Doubleday, 1949.

Stimson, Henry, and McGeorge Bundy. *On Active Service in Peace and War*. New York: Harper, 1947.

Sullivan, Arthur. *The Law at Harvard*. Cambridge: Harvard University Press, 1967.

Sullivan, William. *Obbligato: Notes on a Foreign Service Career*. New York: W. W. Norton, 1984.

Sulzberger, C. L. *An Age of Mediocrity*. New York: Macmillan, 1973.

—. *A Long Row of Candles: Memoirs and Diaries, 1934–1954*. New York: Macmillan, 1969.

—. *Seven Continents and 40 Years*. New York: Quadrangle, 1977.

Swaine, Robert. *The Cravath Firm*. New York: privately printed for Cravath, Swaine and Moore law firm, 1948.

Talbott, Strobe. *Deadly Gambits*. New York: Knopf, 1984.

Talbott, Strobe, trans. *Khrushchev Remembers*. Boston: Little, Brown, 1970.

Thayer, Charles. *Bears in the Caviar*. Philadelphia: J. B. Lippincott, 1950.

—. *Diplomat*. New York: Harper, 1959.

Thomas, Gordon, and Max Morgan-Witts. *Enola Gay*. New York: Pocket Books, 1978.

Truman, Harry. *Letters Home*, Monte Poen, ed. New York: G. P. Putnam's, 1984.

—. *Year of Decisions*. New York: Doubleday, 1955.

—. *Years of Trial and Hope*. New York: Doubleday, 1956.

Truman, Margaret. *Harry S. Truman*. New York: William Morrow, 1973.

Tucker, Nancy Bernkopf. *Patterns in the Dust: Chinese-American Relations and the Recognition Controversy, 1949–1950*. New York: Columbia University Press, 1983.

Tucker, Robert, and William Watts, eds. *Beyond Containment: U.S. Foreign Policy in Transition*. Washington: Potomac Associates, 1973.

Tully, Grace. *F.D.R. My Boss*. New York: Scribner's, 1949.

Ulam, Adam. *Expansion and Coexistence*. New York: Praeger, 1968.

U.S. Commission on Wartime Relocation. *Personal Justice Denied*. Washington: Government Printing Office, 1983.

U.S. Department of State. *Foreign Relations of the United States (FRUS)*. Series of volumes that include declassified cables and papers from each year or major international conference, usually published twenty years later. Washington: Government Printing Office.

U.S. Department of State. *State Department Policy Planning Staff Papers.* New York: Garland Publishing, 1983.

U.S. Select Congressional Committee on the Katyn Forest Massacre. *Report.* Washington: Government Printing Office, 1952.

U.S. Strategic Bombing Survey. *The Effects of Strategic Bombing on the German War Economy.* Washington: Government Printing Office, 1945.

Vance, Cyrus. *Hard Choices.* New York: Simon and Schuster, 1983.

Vandenberg, Arthur, Jr., ed. *The Private Papers of Senator Vandenberg.* Boston: Houghton Mifflin, 1972.

Views from the Circle (a collection of Groton graduates). Groton: privately printed, 1960.

Warburg, James. *The Money Muddle.* New York: Knopf, 1934.

Weil, Martin. *A Pretty Good Club.* New York: W. W. Norton, 1978.

Weisberger, Bernard. *Cold War, Cold Peace.* New York: American Heritage, 1985.

White, Theodore H. *America in Search of Itself.* New York: Harper & Row, 1982.

———. *Fire in the Ashes.* New York: William Sloane Associates, 1953.

———. *In Search of History.* New York: Harper & Row, 1982.

Williams, William Appleman. *The Tragedy of American Diplomacy.* New York: Dell, 1962.

Wooley, Knight. *In Retrospect: A Very Personal Memoir.* New York: privately printed.

Wyden, Peter. *Day One.* New York: Simon and Schuster, 1984.

Wyman, David. *The Abandonment of the Jews.* New York: Pantheon, 1984.

Yergin, Daniel. *Shattered Peace: The Origins of the Cold War and the National Security State.* Boston: Houghton Mifflin, 1977.

Articles

Acheson, Dean. "Dean Acheson's Version of Robert Kennedy's Version of the Cuban Missile Crisis." *Esquire* (February 1969).

———. "Radiant Morn." *Saturday Evening Post* (Dec. 15, 1962).

———. "Random Harvest." *Department of State Bulletin* (June 16, 1946).

———. "The Snob in America." *The Grotonian* (June 1911).

———. "The Illusion of Disengagement." *Foreign Affairs* (April 1958).

Acheson, Dean, David Lilienthal, John McCloy, and others. "A Report on the International Control of Atomic Energy." Washington: Government Printing Office, March 17, 1946.

Alsop, Stewart, and Charles Bartlett. "In Time of Crisis." *The Saturday Evening Post* (Dec. 8, 1962).

American Journal of International Law. "U.S.–Norway Arbitration Award" (1923).

Arneson, R. Gordon. "The H-Bomb Decision." *Foreign Service Journal* (May 1969).

Baldwin, Ray. "Reminiscences of Middletown." Middlesex County Historical Society: privately printed, 1969.

Barcella, Ernest. "The American Who Knows Stalin Best," a profile of Harriman. *Collier's* (May 3, 1952).

Berger, Marilyn. "An Appeal for Thought," an interview with Kennan. *New York Times Magazine* (May 7, 1978).

Biddle, George. "As I Remember Groton School." *Harper's Magazine* (August 1939).

Bigart, Homer. "Pentagon Pitfalls," profile of Lovett. New York *Herald Tribune* (December 23, 1952).

Bohlen, Charles. "American Aid in Restoring the European Community." *Department of State Bulletin* (January 18, 1948).

———. "The American Course in Foreign Affairs." *Department of State Bulletin* (February 6, 1949).

———. "Creating Situations of Strength." *Department of State Bulletin* (August 4, 1952.

———. "The North Atlantic Pact." *Department of State Bulletin* (April 3, 1949).

Brandon, Henry. "Very Much the Ambassador at Large," a profile of Harriman. *New York Times Magazine* (Mar. 5, 1967).

Brinkley, Alan. "Minister Without Portfolio—The Most Influential Private Citizen in America: The Life and Times of John McCloy." *Harper's Magazine* (February 1983).

Bumiller, Elisabeth. "Pamela Harriman." Washington *Post* (June 12, 1983).

Burch, Gilbert. "The Guns, Butter, and Then-some Economy." *Fortune* (October 1965).

Chase, Edward. "The Decision Not to Bomb Auschwitz," private paper (courtesy of John McCloy).

Clifford, Clark. "A Vietnam Reappraisal: The Personal History of One Man's View and How It Evolved." *Foreign Affairs* (July 1969).

Cohen, Warren. "Acheson, His Advisers, and China, 1949–50," in Berg and Heinrichs, eds., *Uncertain Years: Chinese-American Relations, 1947–50*. New York: Columbia University Press, 1980.

Collier's. "Averell Harriman." June 30, 1950.

Elson, Robert. "The New Strategy in Foreign Policy." *Fortune* (December 1947).

Forbes, B. C. "New Business Star: Harriman II." *Forbes* (Oct. 30, 1920).

Foreman, Laura. "Pamela Harriman's Role." *The New York Times* (Mar. 2, 1977).

Fortune. "Averell Was Quite a Businessman Too." May 8, 1978.

———. "Secretary Acheson." April 1949.

Fritchey, Clayton. "The Establishment." New York *Post* (Apr. 29, 1966).

Gaddis, John Lewis. "Containment: A Reassessment." *Foreign Affairs* (July 1977).

———. "The Emerging Post-Revisionist Synthesis on the Origins of the Cold War." *Diplomatic History* (Summer 1983).

Gaddis, John Lewis, and Paul Nitze. "NSC-68 and the Soviet Threat Reconsidered." *International Security* (Spring 1980).

Galbraith, John Kenneth. Review of George Kennan's *Memoirs: 1950–1963.* *New York Times Book Review* (Oct. 8, 1972).

Gati, Charles. "What Containment Meant." *Foreign Policy* (Summer 1972).

Grant, Natalie. "The Russian Section, a Window on the Soviet Union." *Diplomatic History* (Spring 1978).

Halle, Louis. "George F. Kennan and the Common Mind." *Virginia Quarterly Review* (Winter 1969).

Hamburger, Philip. "Profiles: Mr. Secretary," a profile of Acheson. *The New Yorker* (Nov. 12 and 19, 1949).

Harper's Magazine. "The Black Tom Case." December 1939.

Harriman, Averell. "In Darkest Russia." *The Eavesdropper*, Yale class book (December 1927).

———. "The Marshall Plan: Self Help and Mutual Aid." *Foreign Service Journal* (June 1967).

———. "My Moscow-Belgrade 'Vacation.'" *Life* (Aug. 27, 1965).

———. "Story of Our Relations with Russia." Supplement to the *Congressional Record* (Aug. 27, 1951).

———. "What Shipowners Are Up Against." *The Nation's Business* (April 1921).

———. "Why the Little Fellow Needs the NRA." *Today* (May 18, 1935).

Harriman, Margaret Case, and John Bainbridge. "Profiles: The Thirteenth Labor of Hercules," a profile of Lovett. *The New Yorker* (Nov. 6 and 13, 1943).

Herken, Gregg. "The Great Foreign Policy Fight." *American Heritage* (April/May 1986).

Hodgson, Godfrey. "The Establishment." *Foreign Policy* (Spring 1973).

Hoopes, Townsend. "LBJ's Account of March 1968." *The New Republic* (Mar. 14, 1970).

Iden, V. G. "W. A. Harriman Seeks and Wins Front Rank in Marine Field." *Marine Review* (March 1921).

———. "W. A. Harriman as Ship Operator." *Marine Review* (April 1921).

Ignatius, David. "The Old Pro," a profile of Paul Nitze. *The Wall Street Journal* (Aug. 1, 1985).

Kahn, E. J. Jr. "Profiles: Plenipotentiary," a profile of Harriman. *The New Yorker* (May 3, May 10, 1952).

Kaplan, H. J. "The Eclipse of 'The Better Sort.'" *The National Interest* (Fall 1985).

Kateb, George. "George F. Kennan: The Heart of a Diplomat." *Commentary* (January 1968).

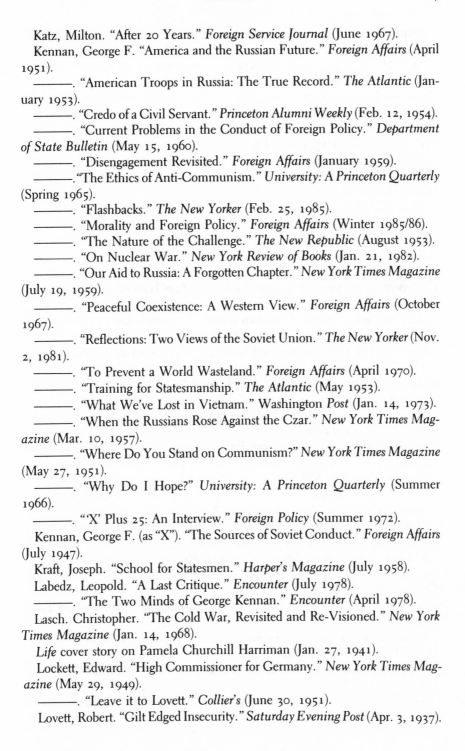

Katz, Milton. "After 20 Years." *Foreign Service Journal* (June 1967).

Kennan, George F. "America and the Russian Future." *Foreign Affairs* (April 1951).

———. "American Troops in Russia: The True Record." *The Atlantic* (January 1953).

———. "Credo of a Civil Servant." *Princeton Alumni Weekly* (Feb. 12, 1954).

———. "Current Problems in the Conduct of Foreign Policy." *Department of State Bulletin* (May 15, 1960).

———. "Disengagement Revisited." *Foreign Affairs* (January 1959).

———. "The Ethics of Anti-Communism." *University: A Princeton Quarterly* (Spring 1965).

———. "Flashbacks." *The New Yorker* (Feb. 25, 1985).

———. "Morality and Foreign Policy." *Foreign Affairs* (Winter 1985/86).

———. "The Nature of the Challenge." *The New Republic* (August 1953).

———. "On Nuclear War." *New York Review of Books* (Jan. 21, 1982).

———. "Our Aid to Russia: A Forgotten Chapter." *New York Times Magazine* (July 19, 1959).

———. "Peaceful Coexistence: A Western View." *Foreign Affairs* (October 1967).

———. "Reflections: Two Views of the Soviet Union." *The New Yorker* (Nov. 2, 1981).

———. "To Prevent a World Wasteland." *Foreign Affairs* (April 1970).

———. "Training for Statesmanship." *The Atlantic* (May 1953).

———. "What We've Lost in Vietnam." Washington *Post* (Jan. 14, 1973).

———. "When the Russians Rose Against the Czar." *New York Times Magazine* (Mar. 10, 1957).

———. "Where Do You Stand on Communism?" *New York Times Magazine* (May 27, 1951).

———. "Why Do I Hope?" *University: A Princeton Quarterly* (Summer 1966).

———. "'X' Plus 25: An Interview." *Foreign Policy* (Summer 1972).

Kennan, George F. (as "X"). "The Sources of Soviet Conduct." *Foreign Affairs* (July 1947).

Kraft, Joseph. "School for Statesmen." *Harper's Magazine* (July 1958).

Labedz, Leopold. "A Last Critique." *Encounter* (July 1978).

———. "The Two Minds of George Kennan." *Encounter* (April 1978).

Lasch. Christopher. "The Cold War, Revisited and Re-Visioned." *New York Times Magazine* (Jan. 14, 1968).

Life cover story on Pamela Churchill Harriman (Jan. 27, 1941).

Lockett, Edward. "High Commissioner for Germany." *New York Times Magazine* (May 29, 1949).

———. "Leave it to Lovett." *Collier's* (June 30, 1951).

Lovett, Robert. "Gilt Edged Insecurity." *Saturday Evening Post* (Apr. 3, 1937).

Loving, Rush, Jr. "W. Averell Harriman Remembers Life with Father." *Fortune* (May 8, 1978).

Luce, Henry. "The American Century," *Life* (Feb. 17, 1941).

Lukas, J. Anthony. "The Council on Foreign Relations." *New York Times Magazine* (Nov. 21, 1971).

Luttwak, Edward. "The Strange Case of George F. Kennan: From Containment to Isolationism." *Commentary* (November 1977).

McCloy, John. "The Lesson of the World Bank." *Foreign Affairs* (July 1949).

———. *Proceeding of the Academy of Political Science* (Vol. 21, Fall 1945).

———. "Repay U.S. Japanese?" *The New York Times*, Op-Ed Page (Apr. 10, 1983).

———. "Return of the Native." Pennsylvania Club, Philadelphia, March 1948.

McPherson, Myra. "Capital Social Set Wonders About a Split in Partying." *New York Times*, March 24, 1968.

Maier, Charles. "Revisionism and the Interpretation of Cold War Origins," in *Perspectives in American History IV* (Cambridge: Harvard University Press, 1970).

Mark, Eduard. "Charles E. Bohlen and the Acceptable Limits of Soviet Hegemony in Eastern Europe." *Diplomatic History* (Spring 1979).

———. "The Question of Containment: A Reply to John Lewis Gaddis." *Foreign Affairs* (January 1978).

Mastny, Vojtech. "Stalin and the Militarization of the Cold War." *International Security* (Winter 1984–5).

Miles, Rufus. "The Strange Myth of Half a Million American Lives Saved." *International Security* (Fall, 1985).

Mintz, Morton. "Why Didn't We Bomb Auschwitz?" Washington *Post* (Apr. 17, 1983).

Murphy, Charles J. V. "W. Averell Harriman." *Life* (Dec. 30, 1946).

The New York Times. "Junior League Here Will Mark 60th Anniversary." Mar. 18, 1961.

New York *World Tribune.* "Closeup: Mrs. Harriman." Aug. 3, 1956.

Nitze, Paul, and John Lewis Gaddis. "NSC-68 and the Soviet Threat Reconsidered." *International Security* (Spring 1980).

Pringle, Henry. "Laird of Woodley," a profile of Stimson. *The New Yorker* (Oct. 4, 1930).

Reston, James. "The No. 1 No. 2 Man in Washington." *The New York Times Magazine* (Aug. 25, 1946).

Root, Elihu. "A Requisite for the Success of Popular Diplomacy." *Foreign Affairs* (Vol. 1, No. 1) Autumn 1922.

Rosenau, James. "The Nomination of Charles Bohlen." *Case Studies in Practical Politics* (1958).

Rostow, Eugene. "Searching for Kennan's Grand Design." *Yale Law Journal* (June 1978).

Rovere, Richard. "Notes on the Establishment in America." *The American Scholar* (Autumn 1961).

Saturday Evening Post. McCloy profile. Nov. 1, 1947.

Schilling, Warner. "The H-Bomb Decision." *Political Science Quarterly* (March 1961).

Schilling, Warner, Paul Hammond, and Glenn Snyder. "NSC-68: Prologue to Rearmament," in *Strategy, Politics, and Defense Budgets.* New York: Columbia University Press, 1962.

Schlesinger, Arthur, Jr. "The Origins of the Cold War." *Foreign Affairs* (October 1967).

Seabury, Paul. "George Kennan vs. Mr. 'X': The Great Container Springs a Leak." *The New Republic* (Dec. 16, 1981).

Seabury, Paul, and Patrick Glynn. "Kennan: The Historian as Fatalist." *The National Interest* (Winter, 1985–1986).

Sidey, Hugh. "Ave—Durable Servant of Four Presidents." *Life* (Dec. 2, 1966).

Sigal, Leon. "Kennan's Cuts." *Foreign Policy* (Fall 1981).

Smith, Terence. "Why Carter Admitted the Shah." *New York Times Magazine* (May 17, 1981).

Spurr, Josiah. "Russian Manganese Concessions." *Foreign Affairs* (April 1927).

Steel, Ronald. "Acheson at the Creation." *Esquire* (Dec. 1983).

———. "Russia, the West, and the Rest." *New York Review of Books* (July 14, 1977).

Stone, I. F. "Anti-Russian Undertow." *The Nation* (May 12, 1945).

Sunday Mirror Magazine. "New Triumphs of a Churchill." May 13, 1956.

Taft, John. "Grey Eminences." *The New Republic* (Mar. 17, 1979).

Thayer, Mary. "How Long Does it Take to Be a Soviet Expert?" Washington *Post* (June 1, 1960).

Tibbets, Paul. "How to Drop an Atom Bomb." *Saturday Evening Post* (June 8, 1946).

Time. "The Bomb," cover story written by James Agee. Aug. 20, 1945. 1941.

———. "The Man from Middletown," cover story on Acheson, Feb. 28, 1949.

———. "The Bombers are Growing," cover story on Lovett. Feb. 9, 1942.

———. "New Policy, New Broom," cover story on Lovett. Mar. 29, 1948.

———. "Secretary of War," cover story of Stimson, Aug. 23, 1941.

———. "Trouble for a Troubleshooter," cover story on McCloy. June 20, 1949.

———. "Twenty Years After." Aug 11, 1961.

Ullman, Richard. "The 'Realities' of George F. Kennan." *Foreign Policy* (Fall 1977).

Urban, George. "A Conversation with George Kennan." *Encounter* (September 1976).

U.S. Strategic Bombing Survey, Summary Report. "European War and the Effects of Strategic Bombing on the German War Economy." (Washington: Government Printing Office, 1945.)

Viorst, Milton. "Incidentally, Who Is Dean Rusk?" *Esquire* (April 1968).

Wells, Samuel F. "Sounding the Tocsin: NSC-68 and the Soviet Threat." *International Security* (Spring 1968).

Wershba, Joseph. "U.S. Adviser in U.N." New York *Post* (Oct. 24, 1962).

Dissertations and Academic Papers

Bland, Larry. "W. Averell Harriman: Businessman and Diplomat, 1891–1945." Ph.D. thesis, University of Wisconsin, 1972.

Fanton, Jonathan. "Robert A. Lovett: The War Years." Ph.D. thesis, Yale University, 1978.

Krieger, Wolfgang. "The German Factor in U.S. Security Policy, 1946–1949." Paper for the National Security Studies Group, Harvard University, June 1985.

Larson, Deborah Welch. "Belief and Inference: The Origin of American Leaders' Cold War Ideology." Ph.D. thesis, Stanford University, 1982.

Miscamble, Wilson Douglas. "George Kennan, the Policy Planning Staff and American Foreign Policy." Ph.D. thesis, University of Notre Dame, 1980.

Ruddy, Thomas Michael. "Charles E. Bohlen and the Soviet Union." Ph.D. thesis, Kent State University, 1973.

Schwartz, Thomas Alan. "From Occupation to Alliance: John J. McCloy and the Allied High Commission in the Federal Republic of Germany, 1949–1952." Ph.D. thesis, Harvard University, June 1985.

Wilmerding, J. C. "Charles Eustis Bohlen: Portrait of a Diplomat." Unpublished history paper by a nephew of Bohlen's, Groton School, 1983.

Wright, C. Ben. "George F. Kennan: Scholar-Diplomat." Ph.D. thesis, University of Wisconsin, 1972.

PHOTO CREDITS

PICTURE SECTION

1 Courtesy Harriman Estate Office
2 Courtesy Mrs. Dean Acheson
3 Courtesy Mrs. Dean Acheson
4 Courtesy Robert A. Lovett
5 Courtesy St. Paul's School
6 Library of Congress
7 Harris & Ewing, Courtesy Grace Kennan Warnecke
8 Courtesy Mrs. Dean Acheson
9 Courtesy Robert A. Lovett
10 Courtesy Robert A. Lovett
11 Wm. J. Fallon, Amherst College Archives
12 Courtesy Harriman Estate Office
13 Courtesy Robert A. Lovett
14 *Time* magazine
15 *Time* magazine
16 Wide World
17 U.S. Signal Corps
18 Culver Pictures
19 Courtesy Robert A. Lovett
20 AP/Wide World
21 Courtesy Robert A. Lovett
22 Library of Congress
23 Walter Sanders/*Life* magazine © 1948 Time Inc.
24 Courtesy Robert A. Lovett
25 Courtesy Robert A. Lovett
26 George Skadding/*Life* magazine © 1948 Time Inc.
27 *Time* magazine
28 *Time* magazine
29 Public Relations Division, HICOG/Amherst College Archives
30 *Time* magazine
31 Robert Kelley/*Time* magazine
32 AP/Wide World/Amherst College Archives

33 Courtesy Harriman Estate Office
34 *Time* magazine
35 Air Force Photo, Courtesy Grace Kennan Warnecke
36 George Skadding/*Life* magazine © 1953 Time Inc.
37 Keystone
38 Philippe Halsman/*Life* magazine © 1956 Time Inc.
39 Lisa Larsen/*Life* magazine © 1951 Time Inc.
40 Wide World
41 Keystone
42 James Kavallines/*New York Herald Tribune*
43 UPI/Bettmann
44 John J. McCloy
45 Francis Miller/*Life* magazine © 1968 Time Inc.
46 Eddy van der Veen/*Time* magazine
47 Courtesy Mrs. Dean Acheson
48 Neil Selkirk

ILLUSTRATIONS IN TEXT

page 20   Bob Henriques/*Life* magazine © 1958 Time Inc.
page 21   © Karsh, Ottawa
page 22   © Karsh, Ottawa
page 23   Tommy Weber/*Time* magazine
page 24   Alfred Eisenstadt/*Time* magazine
page 25   Lemaire/Library of Congress
page 39   Courtesy Harriman Estate Office
page 65   Courtesy Robert A. Lovett
page 210   U.S. Signal Corps
page 314   Harris & Ewing/*Time* magazine
page 347   Bob Motter, courtesy Grace Kennan Warnecke
page 419   Thomas McAvoy/*Life* magazine © 1947 Time Inc.
page 535   Mark Kauffman/*Life* magazine © 1952 Time Inc.
page 589   Stan Wayman/*Life* magazine © 1960 Time Inc.
page 605   Courtesy John J. McCloy II
page 642   White House Photo
page 676   Courtesy Mary Acheson Bundy
page 714   Courtesy Grace Kennan Warnecke © 1981

INDEX